Introduction to Global Politics

Introduction to Global Politics is a major new textbook which introduces students to the key changes in current global politics in order to help them make sense of major trends that are shaping our world. The emphasis on change in global politics helps students recognize that genuinely new developments require citizens to change their beliefs and that new problems may appear even as old ones disappear. This text is designed to encourage students to think ahead in new, open-minded ways, even as they come to understand the historical roots of the present.

KEY FEATURES of *Introduction to Global Politics*

- Explains global politics using an historical approach which allows students to understand continuity as well as change
- Examines and assesses several types of theory so that students become aware of what theory is and why it is necessary for understanding global politics. The text applies and illustrates the main theories of international relations – realism, liberalism, and constructivism – throughout the text
- Integrates theoretical and substantive issues to help students understand abstract ideas by showing them how these ideas work in real life. Each topical chapter includes historical background, theoretical lenses through which to view the history, and commentary about how this history links with today's events
- Introduces students to all key aspects of global politics including the development of the nation-state, power, international law, war, foreign policy, security, terrorism, international organization, international political economy, the global South, the environment, and globalization
- Introduces students to the use of levels of analysis, an important conceptual tool that reappears throughout the text as an aid to understanding and explaining change and continuity in global politics
- Comprehensive global coverage – as well as US and European examples, extensive discussion of Asia, the Middle East, and the developing world. This makes the text equally useful for comparative politics courses

Richard W. Mansbach is Professor of Political Science at Iowa State University, USA. A former editor of *International Studies Quarterly*, Marshall Scholar, and three-time Fulbright Scholar.

Kirsten L. Rafferty is Assistant Professor of Government and International Studies at Berry College (Mount Berry, GA), USA.

Introduction to Global Politics

RICHARD W. MANSBACH

and

KIRSTEN L. RAFFERTY

Routledge
Taylor & Francis Group

LONDON AND NEW YORK

First published 2008
by Routledge
270 Madison Avenue, New York, NY 10016

Simultaneously published in the UK
by Routledge
2 Park Square, Milton Park, Abingdon, Oxon OX14 4RN

Routledge is an imprint of the Taylor & Francis Group, an informa business

© 2008 Richard W. Mansbach and Kirsten L. Rafferty

Typeset in Garamond and Gill
by Keystroke, 28 High Street, Tettenhall, Wolverhampton
Printed and bound in Spain
by Grafas SA, Barcelona

Library of Congress Cataloging in Publication Data
A catalog record for this book has been requested

British Library Cataloguing in Publication Data
A catalogue record for this book is available from the British Library

ISBN10: 0–415–77383–0 (pbk)
ISBN10: 0–203–94611–1 (ebk)

ISBN13: 978–0–415–77383–6 (pbk)
ISBN13: 978–0–203–94611–4 (ebk)

Rhoda Mansbach, for forty years
and
James and Patricia Rafferty

Contents

CONTENTS

CONTENTS

CONTENTS

List of Illustrations

Figures

Maps

Tables

Preface

In recent years, we have all witnessed a variety of remarkable events. Consider what the following headlines have in common and what they tell us about our rapidly changing world:

- September 12, 2001, *"US Attacked; Hijacked Jets Destroy Twin Towers and Hit Pentagon in Day of Terror"* and

- April 11, 2003, *"US Pilots Hitting Iraqi Positions Near Syria Border."*

These two events demonstrate that distance no longer limits how or with whom wars are fought, that sovereign frontiers may no longer pose barriers to an attack, and that conflict does not occur just between states.

- February 24, 2005, *"Drug Companies Cut Costs With Foreign Clinical Trials"*
- March 23, 2005, *"In India's Outsourcing Boom, GE Played a Starring Role."*

Giant transnational corporations like Microsoft, Royal Dutch/Shell Group, Toshiba, and their subsidiaries invest vast amounts around the globe and shift operations to countries with low labor and other costs of production, limiting the amount of control states exercise over activities like trade and providing corporations with the resources to compete with states for power and influence in global politics.

- January 23, 1998, *"Asia Market Turmoil Continues to Worsen; Stocks, Currencies Fall; Panic Selling Hits Rupiah {Indonesian Currency}"*
- April 20, 2002, *"Argentina Orders Banks to Close: Government Fears Economic Collapse as Cash Outflow Rises."*

The combined power of global financial networks and new technologies allow investors to withdraw funds instantaneously from any market in the world and convert currency on a large scale. These developments make states increasingly vulnerable to economic collapse and increasingly ineffectual in preventing it.

- May 3, 2005, *"Polio Virus Crosses Ocean, Spreads to Populous Indonesia"*
- June 7, 2005, *"An Avian Flu Pandemic Could Kill Millions."*

Global diseases, like AIDS, SARS, avian flu, and polio, may spread quickly to distant parts of the world, aided by cheap and convenient methods of travel. These diseases pose significant security, political, economic, and social challenges, particularly for the lesser developed countries that lack resources to provide additional health care and social services, such as vaccinations and medications or care for orphans.

Each story reflects a major event or trend in world affairs, but how do they "fit" into the larger scheme of global politics? How are they related to one another, and what do they tell us about the world since the Cold War ended? What's new about these events? What's old? What are their implications, and why should we care about them? These are the questions we address in this book because we believe the key theme in contemporary global politics is:

- The importance of recognizing *both* continuity and change and, consequently, the value of history to understanding the present and the future.

Among the most important changes in global politics are:

- The declining role of territory as new technologies, international economic markets, and cultural identities take prominence.
- The declining capacity of states to protect or meet the needs of citizens.

Introduction to Global Politics introduces students to key changes in current global politics in order to help them make sense of major trends that are shaping our world. Some current transformations portend new dangers, even as others promise a brighter, more peaceful, and more prosperous future. *And all these changes, both dangerous and promising, are related to one another*, thereby producing a world that in some respects could only have been imagined by science fiction writers – one in which territory and borders no longer matter, and corporations compete with states to achieve their objectives.

As noted, however, a study of global politics is a study of continuity as well as change. Thus, many events that initially appear new or unexpected actually have roots deep in history, such as the terrorist attacks on New York and Washington in 2001. Even the economic collapse of Asian economies in the late 1990s cannot be properly understood without consideration of the economic experiences and the long-term economic policies of the countries involved.

Second, the study of contemporary global politics reveals the diminished importance of controlling territory. Countries can fight wars thousands of miles away from their own territory, but they cannot necessarily defend their own territory against contemporary military threats, like missile strikes. Territory remains important, of course, but every day, new events challenge the historical preoccupation with extending and defending every square inch.

Third, studying global politics today reveals how porous the borders of nation-states have become and how easily persons, ideas, and things can be moved across them. Firms can trade goods and services with the click of a computer mouse, without ever leaving home. Currencies like the US dollar or European euro are no longer valuable only within one country's political boundaries, but are used all over the world. People are more mobile than ever before. As a consequence, states have less and less control over much of what goes on within their borders, and institutions and groups other than sovereign states are becoming more influential in the conduct of global politics. In sum, we are living in a period that challenges our preconception of states as the dominant actors in global politics.

Approach

The text entails the following assumptions.

A historical approach best allows students to understand continuity as well as change.
The best way to recognize patterns of change and continuity is by looking back – in other words, by looking at history. Often, policymakers in the field of global politics are unfamiliar with earlier ideas and events – to the detriment of the policies they make. They may see contemporary global politics as completely new, and different from the international politics practiced by states in the past. Practitioners and students also have an unfortunate propensity to react to events like the brutal destruction of New York's World Trade Towers without recognizing the event's histori-cal roots and its relations to more general and long-term processes like Western–Islamic relations.

In addition to helping us see the roots of events in today's world, acquaintance with past events *introduces us to consequences of change in the past.* We are currently in the midst of great change, but so were people in

1648, 1789, 1918, 1945, and 1990. The Peace of Westphalia in 1648, for example, marked the onset of an era of territorial states. The French Revolution in 1789 ushered in modern nationalism and the marriage of nation and state. In 1918, with the end of World War I, America emerged as a superpower; communism triumphed in Russia; and colonial empires eroded at an accelerating pace. In 1945, the end of World War II coincided with the use of weapons of mass destruction and the first indications of a coming confrontation with the Soviet Union. Finally, the world that emerged in 1990, with the end of the Cold War, signaled the disappearance of the Soviet Union and communism and revealed the new significance of many issues that we shall treat in subsequent chapters, such as ethnic and nationalist conflict, the strengthening of nonstate actors including global terrorist networks, and international human rights law.

An emphasis on change in global politics helps students recognize that genuinely new developments require citizens to change their beliefs and that new problems may appear even as old ones disappear.

This text views change as constant and, on that assumption, aims to sharpen and revise the ways students look at the world and the policies which global actors pursue. The earliest political thinkers, such as the Greek historian Thucydides (*c.*460–400 BC) and the Italian political philosopher Niccolò Machiavelli (1469–1527), tell us much about the politics of the eras in which they lived, and some of their ideas remain germane today. For example, Thucydides' depiction of how Athenian democracy eroded in the course of war finds echoes in today's concern that we should be careful lest we surrender our democratic freedoms in our effort to combat global terrorism. And, Machiavelli's self-interested prince seems uncomfortably similar to many of today's leaders, especially in authoritarian countries. Some of their other ideas, however, are less and less relevant to the issues we confront at present. For instance, many recent global institutions like the World Trade Organization would disappear if each state acted according to Machiavelli's advice that leaders should only keep their word when it is in their interest to do so.

Because the world around us continually changes, students must always be prepared to understand and deal with new issues and new actors and to set aside old ways of viewing the world. When we fail to do this and assume that the present and future will be just like the past, policy failures will likely result. Much of what politicians believe they understand about global politics is based upon how states, especially the United States and Soviet Union, acted during the Cold War. In many instances, these understandings drive them to expect that the great powers are and will continue to be the dominant actors in global politics. They articulate policies like deterrence or preemption that great powers have historically used in pursuit of their national interests. Indeed, this single-minded focus on states as the only actors appears to have been a key reason why President George W. Bush and his national security advisor, Condoleezza Rice, later to become secretary of state, were taken by surprise by the September 11th terrorist attacks. By overlooking new actors or issues, such as Al Qaeda and the threat of global terrorism, politicians are likely to adopt poor policies that are ineffective or even destabilizing.

Introduction to Global Politics is designed to force students to think ahead in new, open-minded ways, even as they come to understand the historical roots of the present.

An organization that weaves theoretical and substantive issues together helps students understand abstract ideas by showing them how these ideas work in real life.
The text links abstract theory and substantive global politics as closely as possible. Each topical chapter – whether dealing with war, human rights, or globalization – includes historical background, theoretical lenses through which to view the history, and commentary about how this history links with today's events. In this way, each chapter combines the historical material with the contemporary and the abstract with the concrete.

An in-depth historical section consisting of several narrative chapters, as well as historical background in other chapters, illustrates how specific issues evolve and how existing policies and ideas about them must be constantly revisited.

Organization of the text

The text opens with a chapter that presents the theme of change and continuity and the importance of history in global politics. It also introduces students to the use of levels of analysis, an important conceptual tool that reappears throughout the text as an aid to understanding and explaining change and continuity. It then analyzes several key theoretical perspectives that enable students to understand the substantive material that follows, and these perspectives reappear throughout. It explains the role of theory in understanding global politics, examines several types of theory, and assesses the role of theory and method so that students become aware of what theory is and why it is necessary for understanding global politics. In doing so, the chapter describes a range of assumptions and approaches to understanding global politics.

Since one must understand both history and change in order to understand the abstract issues of global politics, Part I of the text contains a series of historical chapters arranged chronologically that describe the evolution of global politics from Europe's Middle Ages, Confucian China, and the founding of Islam to the present day. These chapters permit readers to see how history and change play out in real life. The historical narratives are comprehensive – telling their stories from beginning to end, while examining how they continue to affect global politics years, even centuries, later. Taken together, they tell the story of how the contemporary global system evolved. Chapter 2 focuses on the birth of the modern state and two alternative, nonstate systems that emerged in the Islamic and Chinese worlds. This chapter compares the evolution of these systems and examines historical clashes between them and the West that erupted as each attempted to strengthen and expand. The consequences of these collisions loom large today. Chapter 3 examines the world wars, arguably the most important events in the twentieth century, focusing on explanations of the sources and consequences of each. Chapter 4 tells the story of the Cold War, including its causes and consequences. It considers the evolution of the epic collision between East and West that set the stage for the current era. The final narrative chapter focuses on four great issues in contemporary global politics: the challenge from China, the conflict between Israel and Palestine, the War on Terrorism, and the Iraq imbroglio. Each issue is placed in its historic context to highlight continuity and change within the issue as well as across global politics.

The body of the text consists of six parts, each reflecting a distinctive group of issues and ideas in contemporary global politics. Part I, The Past as Prologue to the Present, includes the historical narratives described above. This section provides students with the historical knowledge necessary to appreciate and apply the theories and ideas that appear later in the text. Part II, Living Dangerously in a Dangerous World, includes chapters on power and war in global politics and the technological innovations, including weapons of mass destruction, and normative changes that have ushered in a new era of total war. Part III, Actors and Institutions, considers foreign policy-making in a state context as well as the distribution and redistribution of authority in international and nongovernmental organizations. The section considers the intergovernmental organizations like the UN and regional organizations, as well as private humanitarian and advocacy groups. Part IV, Global Issues, deals with issues that challenge the global system as a whole:

international political economy, the problems that afflict less-developed countries in the global South, the variety of challenges to human security, and the threats to the global environment. Part V, Peoples and Cultures in Global Politics, focuses on peoples rather than states alone and on how questions of identity shape behavior. The chapter in this section treats issues of religion, ethnicity, nationality, civilizations, and changing rules and norms of behavior.

Part VI, And Tomorrow?, the final chapter in the text, deals with globalization, perhaps the most important feature of contemporary global politics. It examines the major features of globalization and assesses arguments in favor and against this phenomenon. The chapter then reviews 14 critical trends identified in the book and looks ahead and examines several plausible future scenarios – a globalized world, a world of liberal institutions, a world in chaos, and a realist world. As the text suggests, elements of each scenario can already be "dimly seen."

Pedagogical features

Introduction to Global Politics offers the following features to facilitate the instructor's task, and to engage students and help them understand key ideas and events in the world.

- *Student activities*   Each chapter concludes with a list of activities that students can undertake individually or in groups, inside or outside the classroom. These include suggested discussion and essay questions dealing with main themes and events in the chapter, as well as map exercises that encourage them to apply key concepts and theories to reality, to make connections among events, and to analyze the sources and consequences of events.

- *Figures, maps, and tables*   The text uses a rich mix of visual materials, including maps, photographs, cartoons, graphs, and reproductions of paintings. Such resources bring history and concepts to life, making it easier to understand and apply concepts and trends in global politics.

- *Cultural materials*   Each chapter ends with a list of films and/or novels, as well as other materials in the humanities, including poetry, that are relevant to the chapter content. Each list also includes a thought question or activity for students, based on one of the listed works. Instructors may also use these resources for specialized short courses in topics like war and film or literature and global politics.

- *Definitions of key terms*   The text also provides definitions of key terms in the margin of pages where they first appear and a complete glossary at the end of the book. This format reinforces students' knowledge and understanding of key elements of the field.

- *Boxed features* The text incorporates several boxed features, as described below.

  - *"Did you know?"* boxes offer snapshots of information to enliven events, cases, individuals, and issues discussed in the text. Their purpose is to deepen understanding of relevant points. For instance, a box on US foreign aid compares how much assistance the US *actually* gives to how much the American people *think* it gives.

  - *"Theory in the real world"* boxes are intended to illustrate the ways that theoretical approaches underlie and bring about the real policy choices leaders make. For example, one box illustrates how both liberal and realist arguments can be seen in President Bush's justification for war in Iraq in 2003.

  - *"Controversy"* boxes describe events, ideas, and norms that have generated disagreement among political leaders, scholars, or publics. These boxes portray the debates on global warming and preemptive war, for example. They alert you to the absence of consensus about the meaning of events, ideas, and ethics in global politics.

  - *"Key documents"* boxes present excerpts from documents central to the material in the text. Having access to these documents will enable you to immerse yourselves in the events being described and expands understanding of brief citations or allusions in the text. Such documents include historical speeches, agreements, and statements, such as the treaties of Westphalia and Versailles, Woodrow Wilson's Fourteen Points, and the United Nations Charter.

- *Further reading* Each chapter concludes with a list of key scholarly books and articles that will provide additional treatment of the theories and histories covered therein. Students will find this list particularly helpful for developing and researching papers and other assignments.

Supplements

- *Instructors' guide and test bank* This supplement contains brief summaries of each chapter and tips about key themes instructors may wish to pursue. It will also provide multiple choice questions and answers, as well as essay topics, chapter by chapter.
- *Interactive website* This site offers faculty and students numerous supplements to the textbook. For instance, there will be suggested activities, sample questions, study aids, and topics for self-testing, as

well as links ro instructor materials, including an instructor's manual
and lecture slides.
We expect that this text will excite students and tempt them to learn
more about global politics and the world around them.

Richard W. Mansbach

Kirsten L. Rafferty

1 An introduction to global politics

Change and continuity

September 11, 2001: On a clear September morning, a passenger jet was seen cruising, at a very low altitude, along the New York skyline. At precisely 8:46 a.m. (eastern daylight time), as onlookers watched from the streets below and from neighboring high-rises, American Airlines Flight 11 crashed into the north tower of the World Trade Center; the plane and tower burst into flames. Astonished observers and the media began to speculate as to the cause of this spectacular "accident." At 9:03 a.m., their worst fears were confirmed as a second plane, United Airlines Flight 175, crashed into the south tower of the World Trade Center in a ball of flames. By 9:30 a.m. President George W. Bush announced that the United States apparently had been the victim of a terrorist attack. Minutes later he halted all US air traffic for the first time in history. However, the danger was not over. At 9:37 a.m., another plane, American Airlines Flight 77, crashed into the Pentagon in the outskirts of Washington, DC. The public wondered: would the attacks end? Then, at 9:59 a.m. the unthinkable happened. The south tower of the World Trade Center collapsed. Only five minutes later, a portion of the Pentagon collapsed, while in Pennsylvania a fourth jet, United Airlines Flight 93, crashed into a field. It is believed the plane was on its way to Camp David, the US Congress, or the White House. At 10:28 a.m., the north tower of the World Trade Center also collapsed. It was later discovered that the passenger jets had been hijacked by 19 Muslim militants, most of whom were Saudi citizens who had been visiting the US on expired student visas.

Today, as 9/11 reminds us, **global politics** impinges on our lives more than ever. Everything from the air we breathe to the clothes we wear and the taxes we pay has a global dimension. Global news with vivid pictures of riots and wars is accessible on satellite television and online 24 hours a day. In fact, demonstrators around the world are often instructed to wait until a CNN correspondent appears before beginning. Beyond dramatic events like 9/11, we are reminded of how embedded we

global politics the political interactions among sovereign states, as well as nonstate actors.

Figure 1.1 World Trade Center, New York, 9/11/01

© PA Photos

are in the world around us when we turn on our Sony TV (that may have been manufactured in the United States or in Singapore), drive to work in a Honda or Volkswagen (or an "American" car that actually has parts from many countries), buy toys or shoes made in China, or sip a glass of Molson from Canada.

For centuries the United States enjoyed the protection of two great oceans and generally friendly neighbors and a high degree of economic self-sufficiency. Today, all that has changed. America's homeland is vulnerable to a variety of threats from fanatical terrorists to pandemic influenza. The United States must also confront the possibility that "**rogue states**" like North Korea and Iran will acquire nuclear weapons in violation of the Nuclear Nonproliferation Treaty. America's economy is hostage to the willingness of countries like China and Japan to keep purchasing US securities that provide the wherewithal to pay for America's burgeoning trade and budget deficits, and the effort of American corporations to compete in a globalized economy in which people around the world are increasingly **interdependent** leads to the outsourcing of US jobs to other countries and the reduction in benefits for workers at home. In fact, many of the most important issues in global politics such as environmental deterioration and the spread of diseases constitute **collective dilemmas**, that is, problems that no single state or group of states can solve on its own and that, therefore, require cooperation for solutions to be found.

The terrorist attacks in New York and Washington were an entirely different kind of threat that most decision-makers believed to be remote. They were not initiated by another **state** at war with the US like Japan's attack on Pear Harbor in December 1941. Rather they were planned and conducted by a highly coordinated network of Islamic militants. It took only 19 hijackers to cause nearly 3,000 deaths – the most deadly terrorist incident in history.

The world, then, is a dangerous place that, in some respects, is becoming more dangerous every day *owing to the speed with which change is taking place*. Rapid change is dangerous because leaders are unable to grasp the implications of what is happening and, therefore, are likely to misunderstand the sources and consequences of the perils they face and so fashion inappropriate policies to deal with them. Expectations are violated; old friendships wither; new foes emerge; and new dangers appear. Rapid change is also dangerous because there is less time for leaders to respond constructively in the face of impending catastrophe. Thus, many observers regard global warming as having reached a critical juncture. Nevertheless, leaders have done little to limit the release of "greenhouse gases" that produce global warming or to change the energy-intensive habits of citizens. If those who believe that global warming poses imminent environmental deterioration and weather changes are correct, the failure of statesmen to take account of it and change course means a future of melted icecaps, flooded coast lines, and even submerged island states.

rogue states countries that are said to flout the norms, rules, and practices followed by most other states.

interdependence a relationship in which two or more actors are sensitive and vulnerable to each other's behavior and in which actions taken by one affect the other.

collective dilemmas problems that require the cooperation of actors for solution and that no one actor can resolve on its own.

state a political entity that is sovereign and has a government that is said to enjoy exclusive control over a defined territory and population.

Threats and opportunities

Just as global politics consists of change and continuity, so it combines destructive factors and trends that threaten our well-being and perhaps even our survival with opportunities to avoid or cope with the threats that we can ignore only at our peril. Some of the challenges that we must address are:

- *Environmental deterioration* including global warming, the thinning of the protective ozone layer of the atmosphere accompanied by rising rates of skin cancer; destruction of the world's rain forests (the world's "lungs") and denuding of other forested areas; rapid urbanization owing to peasant flight to megacities in countries like China and India with accompanying pollution and urban poverty; the spread of deserts into formerly fertile regions of Asia, Africa, and Latin America; the elimination of species of plants and animals and reduction in biodiversity; and the accumulation of radioactive debris and nuclear waste.
- *Overpopulation* in poor countries that contributes to famine, diseases like AIDS, land hunger, political unrest, and large-scale migration to rich countries with aging and shrinking populations.
- *Resource depletion* as energy demands outstrip known reserves of petroleum and natural gas and as growing populations and economic development places ever greater stress on finite sources of fresh water and fertile land.
- Proliferating *religious and ethnic extremism* accompanied by *suicidal terrorism* directed against innocent civilians in order to create mayhem and cause maximum death and damage.
- The *spread of nuclear, chemical, and biological weapons* (weapons of mass destruction) to countries divided by profound political differences such as Pakistan and India and to apparently "irrational" regimes such as those in Iran and North Korea, and the growing prospect of terrorists acquiring such weapons.
- The *collapse of states* and the spread of chaos in selected regions.
- The rapid *global spread of pathogens* that threaten humans, livestock, and plant life and the threat of new pandemics such as the avian influenza.
- The *spread of trade disputes* which divide rich and poor countries and that threaten to end the liberal economic regime responsible for ever higher living standards around the world since World War II.
- *Growing disparities in wealth* between "winners" and "losers" in the course of globalization.
- The *growing resistance of the United States to working with international organizations* or to participate in multilateral ventures to respond to global problems.

Happily, there is another side to the story. Global politics has always consisted of both conflict *and* cooperation. Some global trends promise to enlarge human capacities and help us cope with, insulate ourselves from, and perhaps even avoid some of the worst dangers we face. Among the sources of optimism are:

- The *growing accumulation of human knowledge*, an "information revolution," and *the accessibility of new knowledge* owing to the spread of electronic technologies.
- *Growing economic productivity globally* owing to the introduction, spread, and improvement of computer-based technologies, the spread of giant **transnational corporations** (TNCs), and the mobility of global capital.
- The *development of renewable energy sources* derived from the sun, wind, and biomass.
- *Rapid economic development*, especially in China and India, that augers an overall reduction in global poverty.
- The *spread of democracy and democratic institutions* beyond North America, Western Europe, Australia, and New Zealand.
- The *continued authority of global institutions* such as the World Trade Organization and the World Health Organization that coordinate national policies and enforce global norms and practices.
- The *proliferation and networking of nongovernmental organizations* that lobby for global cooperation in dealing with global dangers, provide technical information and humanitarian aid, and foster links among peoples in different societies.
- The *regulation of key issues by informal groupings of nongovernmental groups, international institutions, and government bureaucracies* – known as **international regimes** – that foster interstate cooperation (see chapter 6, pp. 257–9).
- A *decline in interstate warfare*.
- The *proliferation of international law protecting the individual*, codifying human rights, and spreading norms of racial and gender equality.

Since knowing the past is critical to understanding the present, this chapter continues with a brief discussion of the role of history in global politics and its relationship to change. It then examines the several perspectives known as **levels of analysis** that we can use to explain events. Thus, we can think about global politics in terms of the individual, states, or the international system as a whole. Each perspective provides certain advantages and has certain costs. Our consideration of levels of analysis provokes us to think theoretically, and we turn to the question of what "theory" is and why it is necessary to make sense of the world around

transnational corporations (TNCs) economic enterprises with operations in two or more countries.

international regime a set of rules, norms, and decision-making procedures that govern actors' behavior in an international issue-area.

levels of analysis an analytical tool that simplifies theorizing by categorizing key factors in global politics at the level of the whole global system or of some of its constituent parts (individual, state).

us. We then examine several major controversies concerning how to theorize about and study global politics and analyze four key theoretical approaches to global politics: realism/neorealism, liberalism/neoliberalism, constructivism, and Marxism.

History and global politics: change and continuity

Global politics reflects both change and continuity. By change we mean *the transformation of key structures and processes that has a major impact on the nature of global politics.* Where there is significant and rapid change, there are discontinuities between past and present with features of the present not recognizable in the past. For example, the shift from the medieval European order of overlapping rights, privileges, and ownership based on a feudal agrarian economy to a world of **sovereign** states enjoying exclusive legal authority over internal affairs constituted a major transformation in global politics. So, too, was the shift in security and military strategy that was brought about by the introduction of nuclear weapons after World War II. More recently, the end of the Cold War produced a dramatically different world: the United States emerged as the world's only superpower; Russia, China, and the countries of Eastern Europe joined the global economic system; **globalization** linked the fates of people around the world as never before; and suicidal fanaticism produced an unprecedented security problem. None of these developments was predicted, and, therefore, there was little planning to deal with them.

The other side of change is continuity *which refers to the gradual evolution of structures or processes such that the present retains key features of the past.* Although global politics is constantly changing – with new events and new actors (countries and other groups whose behavior is relevant to global politics) emerging all the time – there is nonetheless much to be learned from the past experiences of states and other global actors. For example, terrorism is not new, even though certain features of contemporary terrorism are novel. In fact, few events – however unexpected – come from out of the blue. Much that seems novel actually has roots in the past, and familiarity with history makes the present more understandable, helps us to plan for the future, and allows us to avoid making the same mistakes over again. Although some aspects of every event are unique, history provides important analogies and vital experience.

An acquaintance with history is necessary for identifying change and continuity. Some political scientists delve far into the past in order to identify patterns. For example, George Modelski and William R.

sovereignty the status of states as legal equals under international law, according to which they are supreme internally and subject to no higher external authority.

globalization those processes that knit people everywhere together, thereby producing worldwide interdependence and featuring the rapid and large-scale movement of persons, things, and ideas across sovereign borders.

Thompson have proposed what they call *long-cycle theory*. They argue that history indicates that there are repeated cycles of large-scale war and global leadership that last about 100 years.[1] Each cycle consists of several stages, beginning with a global war that gives rise to a new dominant world leader or hegemon; thereafter the hegemon's authority is undermined and challengers to the hegemon appear; overextension and the high costs of hegemonic leadership cause the hegemon's decline; and a new war ensues from which a new hegemon emerges. In previous cycles, Portugal, the Netherlands, and Great Britain served as hegemons, and today the United States plays that role.[2] Given the length of the current cycle, however, the US should begin to decline and competitors like China or Russia should emerge. Modelski and Thompson believe that periods of hegemonic dominance are relatively peaceful compared to periods of relative equality between a hegemon and a challenger. Long-cycle theory followed on *power-transition theory*, according to which a hegemon will be challenged by another great power at the point where the latter becomes roughly as powerful as the hegemon.[3]

Change is part of the natural rhythm of our lives, but when it accelerates to the point where we are "strangers in a strange land,"[4] as many people all over the world felt in the aftermath of September 11th, people become fearful, anxious, mistrustful, and disoriented. Sometimes, as in this case, change is genuinely threatening and really does imperil the safety and well-being of individuals and society. Suicide bombers, who look forward to martyrdom and paradise, are particularly menacing, as threats of retaliation cannot prevent them from acting. However, at other times change is frightening, but does not have the same disastrous consequence. For instance, for over 300 years the territorial state has been the fulcrum of global politics. Thus the field became known as **international politics** or international relations because it focused exclusively on relations among (*inter*) sovereign states.[5] Such a focus is called "**state-centric.**" But some observers point to the gradual proliferation of important actors other than states such as giant transnational corporations like IBM and ExxonMobil, international organizations like the United Nations and the World Bank, and nongovernmental groups like Greenpeace and Al Qaeda as evidence that sovereign states no longer enjoy unchallenged primacy – and control – in global politics (a term that allows us to speak of a wider galaxy of actors than states alone). In the state-centric world, governments make most authoritative decisions, but in the expanded world of global politics, authoritative decisions are also made by numerous domestic, **transnational**, and international institutions and groups, both formal and informal, creating a complex universe of what is termed global

international politics the political interactions among states.

state-centric a perspective or model of global politics in which states are the source of all important activities.

transnational crossing national frontiers and involving social groups and nongovernmental actors.

governance authoritative demands, goals, directives, and policies of any actor, whether a government or not.

unilateralism a policy of behaving without consulting or cooperating with other actors.
multilateralism a policy of working with other states to achieve policy goals.

governance in which the governments of nation-states represent only one type of global authority.

Also, rapid economic change creates fears of future poverty and social dislocation. Workers in US industries like textiles will almost certainly lose their jobs in coming years owing to the growth of similar industries in Asia and South America, where production costs are lower than in America. The American economy will have to restructure and former textile workers will have to seek training and employment in other sectors. Likewise, rapid political change, such as the collapse of the Soviet Empire in the late 1980s and early 1990s, raises anxiety about reduced status, loss of freedom, or even threats of war and violence.

But whether or not we fear changes matters less than how we react to them. Dramatic change can lead to either conflict or cooperation among global actors. Some leaders genuinely learn from novel events, while others ignore them and keep on in the same old ways. When change encourages misperception and suspicion of others, political leaders may act on their own, as President Bush did with the 2003 Iraq War. Such **unilateralism**, which seemed to break with America's previous policy of **multilateralism** based on broad consultation and coordination with allies and friends, however well intentioned, sometimes frightens those who do not understand its motives and eats away at international cooperation. For example, in economics, a country may unilaterally impose tariffs on imported goods to reduce foreign competition and preserve jobs at home, and in military security, it may build new missiles to prevent an enemy missile attack. Unfortunately, citizens and leaders in other countries may view those tariffs as an assault on their workers and may interpret the missiles as a way of making their military forces obsolete. Other changes, in contrast, may enhance global cooperation. For example, international institutions such as the United Nations, the World Trade Organization, and the International Criminal Court encourage regional or global economic and political integration and work toward enforcing global peace. And the growing role of nongovernmental organizations such as the environmental advocate Greenpeace or the humanitarian group Amnesty International promote other kinds of global cooperation. Such institutions, some believe, may ultimately replace states as key actors in global politics.

As the preceding paragraphs illustrate, the world is changing in complex ways, and knowledge of history does not tell us how change takes place. Is change a random or stochastic process – a product of mere chance – or is it determined by the past? Is history linear and progressive, or does it take the form of long cycles? Such questions remain unanswered. However, political, economic, social, and cultural systems are becoming more interconnected as people, things, and ideas move freely across state frontiers. This process, known as globalization, erodes state borders, challenges the control states exercise over their populations, reduces the importance of territory, creates dangerous new forms of violence, and encourages globe-girdling economic and cultural forces.

Yet, not everything is new. War, for example, has been central to global politics for millennia. If we understood its causes, we would eliminate them to prevent the horrifying levels of death and destruction that accompany armed conflict. Instead, even as wars among states grow less frequent, wars involving terrorists, ethnic minorities, and other groups become more frequent, with the potential to become even more deadly. Notwithstanding numerous efforts to explain war, we still quote from ancient philosophers and writers like Thucydides, a Greek historian from the fifth century BC, to understand and explain them. Thucydides sought to identify the causes and consequences of war "for eternity." His great work, *The History of the Peloponnesian War*, told the story of a great war that pitted Athens and its allies against Sparta and its allies, culminating in the destruction of Athens, the birthplace of democracy. His claim that the relative power of the city-states provided an important explanation of why war erupted tells us that we should pay careful attention to rapid changes in power, for example, China's rapid increase in military and economic capabilities. However, rapid change in the distribution of power is only one possible cause of war. Even today, we still cannot explain the outbreak of war with certainty. The Greek city-states of Thucydides' world gave way over the centuries to larger, more powerful, and more dangerous political communities, territorial states, which dominated global politics for over three centuries and which continue to play a major role in today's world.

As a consequence of the complex relationship between change and continuity, global politics is simultaneously the most challenging and exciting subject you may encounter. Even political scientists do not agree on the nature and consequences of the changes underway in the **global system**. Thus, as this text introduces you to change and continuity in the global system and to the various theoretical interpretations of issues and events, we invite you to question and critique what you read here.

One can view global politics from any of several perspectives or levels of analysis. The core question here is whether the most powerful explanation for key events is to be found in the characteristics of individuals, states, or the global system as a whole.

Figure 1.2
Thucydides (c.460–400 BC)

global system the sum of the interactions of the actors in global politics and the consequences of that interaction.

Levels of analysis

As we observe events and trends in global politics, it quickly becomes clear that many complexly related factors are at work on the individual, state/organization, and global levels. Individuals, of course, make up states and other collective actors, and those actors, including states, in turn, make up the global system. Events on the global level often cascade down to affect states and individuals, and vice versa: Individuals and collectives can act in ways that have an impact on the global level. We refer to each of these sectors – individuals, collective actors, and the global system – as a different level of analysis. These levels, which are used to differentiate parts and wholes, are another tool political scientists use in developing theory to simplify a complex world. Each level plays an important role in global politics. As you will see below, each provides a different perspective on why actors take certain actions and not others. To achieve an accurate, detailed understanding of any event requires an awareness of the constraints actors face at each level. However, researchers seeking to explain or predict an event or to prescribe policy may focus only on the level that provides the greatest insight into the issue at hand.

The individual

At the individual level of analysis, researchers look at the characteristics of individuals, such as personality traits, ways of reaching decisions, and beliefs. For example, research focused on individuals might ask whether leaders make rational decisions, how their personal foibles affect policy, whether they allow their biases to affect their decisions and attitudes, and whether human beings in general are programmed to fight one another. Such questions reflect the individual level of analysis.

Many theorists have assumed that leaders are rational. This is perhaps an understandable (and some would argue necessary) simplification of reality on the part of theorists. Assuming **rationality**, however, is a heroic assumption which can only be tested by looking at real decision-makers within states. In its strongest version, rationality means that leaders choose the *best* of *all* alternatives in making policy based on comparing costs and benefits. This assumption lies behind a variety of theoretical efforts ranging from realism and neorealism to expected utility theory and mathematical modeling. However, the assumption is a dubious one, as leaders have limited time and information. At best, decision-makers with limited time choose the best of all *available* or *known* alternatives, a procedure called "satisficing" that yields what is called "bounded rationality." In Charles Lindblom's felicitous phrase, they seem to be

rationality acting to promote one's interests by adopting means that are conducive to achieving desired and feasible ends.

"muddling through"[6] step by step. At worst, decision-makers are driven by neuroses, compulsions, passions, and personal whims that seem far removed from rationality and, sometimes, even from reality.

Furthermore, the capacity for rational ends-means rationality diminishes as decision-makers interact with one another in cabinet meetings, bureaucracies, and governments. Political scientist Robert Jervis cites five reasons for this.[7]

- There is a need to form governing coalitions, often including individuals with divergent views.
- Disagreement may be so deep as to prevent a decision being made.
- Inconsistencies grow as different factions come to power over time.
- Majorities shift among competitors for power with different preferences.
- Divergent and inconsistent bureaucratic interests and perspectives influence decisions.

The state

On the state level of analysis, researchers focus on governments, decision-making groups, or agencies that determine the foreign policies of states and other actors, and on the societies on whose behalf those groups or agencies work. Examples of such actors include states like the United States, but also agencies like the US State Department and the United Nations Security Council. Among the key factors studied at this level are political systems, ideology, wealth and military power, territory and population, social identities such as religion and ethnicity, and government organization. Typical questions raised at this level of analysis include whether democracies are more peaceful than non-democracies, whether powerful states act differently than weak ones, whether ethnic or religious diversity lead to greater civil conflict, and whether leaders enter conflicts with other states in order to overcome domestic unpopularity.

Because there are several types of actors, it is useful to distinguish among groups *within* states and other actors, like corporations, and those actors as a whole. Thus, political parties and interest groups are to be found within states and constitute a different level of analysis than does the state itself of which they are a part. Indeed, there are subgroups even within political parties and interest groups.

In addition, states and other actors also may be parts of larger groupings like alliances or regions that can be regarded as constituting a discrete level of analysis. During the Cold War, for example, observers spoke of the "Free World" or First World, consisting of the United States and its allies, the Soviet Bloc or Second World that included the

Soviet Union and its allies, and the nonaligned bloc or Third World that included countries like India that were not members of the other groupings. Depending on the researcher's or policymaker's purpose, countries may be grouped by geography (Asian, European, Middle Eastern, African, and so forth), religion (Muslim, Christian, Hindu, and so forth), or ideology. Theorists create such groupings because they want to point out selected similarities and differences among countries.

The global system

At the global level of analysis, researchers focus on structure and distributions of power, wealth, nationality, and other key features of the world *as a whole*. In other words, it focuses on the global system, that is, the interactions of all actors on the global stage. The global level is the ultimate "whole" of which actors and individuals are "parts." Observers who use this level of analysis are preoccupied with patterns of events and behavior across the entire world. They believe that other levels, while useful, cannot tell the whole story about what is happening because these other levels cannot account for what are called **emergent properties**, attributes of global politics that emerge only because of the interaction of actors and/or individuals. To use a simple example, consider the Cold War. Many observers expected the Cold War to explode into World War III. After all, Washington and Moscow feared and mistrusted one another, had different ideologies and political systems, and were armed to the teeth (all state-level traits conducive to war). Yet, despite numerous conflicts, the two superpowers never resorted to war (though they came close on several occasions). Many argue that peace between them was an emergent property of the interaction of two states armed with nuclear weapons. Peace was less a consequence of the policies or intentions of the superpowers (the state-level explanation) and more a product of the possibility of nuclear retaliation and annihilation that nuclear weapons promised (a system trait). Thus, the logic of nuclear weapons imposes the same constraints on all states, regardless of their ideologies, political systems, or armaments. Consequently, and to the surprise of many, the very weapons that many feared would begin World War III may actually have prevented it.

Most scholars work at one or another of the levels of analysis. However, a few transcend levels as does political scientist Peter Gourevitch when he shows how "domestic structure may be a consequence" of "international systems," for example, how "political development is shaped by war and trade."[8] Another example of this is political scientist Robert

emergent properties
characteristics of a group that are the unforeseen consequence of interaction among its members.

Putnam's analysis of how national policies are shaped at the same time by interactions within a state and among states at the system level. Thus, "central decision-makers strive to reconcile domestic and international imperatives simultaneously."[9]

In this section, we have discussed how we can enrich our understanding of global politics by seeking clues at several levels of analysis – individuals, collective actors and their parts, and the global system as a whole. Each level offers different insights into global politics, and it is not surprising that different theoretical approaches also tend to emphasize different levels. You also will encounter these three levels of analysis in later chapters, as they are valuable for examining complex issues. Since the same facts, theories, and levels of analysis are available to everyone, why is there so much disagreement about events in global politics? The most important reasons, as we shall see, is that analysts use different theories to make sense of events.

Making sense of a complex world: theory and global politics

This section explains how theory helps us to make sense of both change and continuity in global politics. It explains what theory is, why it is used to make sense of politics, and how several types of theories and approaches have developed to give meaning to the welter of events in today's world. Scholars and practitioners use theory to seek patterns in past and present events because identifying patterns allows them to generalize about the world around them. Even when confronted with the same facts, different observers will tell different stories owing to their psychological predispositions, life conditions, personal experiences, and beliefs. For such reasons, you do *not* have to, nor should you, agree with everything you read in this book (as long as you can make a persuasive counter-argument). Instead, we hope to provoke you into thinking seriously about the world in which you live and to provide you with information and ideas that will assist you in constructing reasoned and reasonable arguments either in favor of or opposed to the claims that the book makes.

What is theory and why do we need it?

In what follows, we address the problem of how to explain and understand global politics. In a word, no one can look at *everything* in global politics – or in any field – at once without becoming completely confused. Instead, by focusing on *only* the most important factors and looking for patterns, the student of world affairs can gain clarity. But how can we do this? The effort to identify patterns in global politics entails theorizing. Theorizing fits individual events and cases into larger patterns, allowing us to generalize about global politics. Indeed, when theorists look at individual events, they should always ask, in the words of two international relations specialists: "Of what is this an instance?"[10] Theory thus simplifies the messy complexity of reality by pointing to only those factors that theorists believe are important.

This section begins by defining theory. It then explains two kinds of theory – empirical and normative – and the three purposes of theory – prediction, explanation, and prescription. The section concludes by considering how theory is constructed and tested in global politics research.

theory an abstract, simplified, and general proposition that answers "why" and "how" questions.

Theory consists of abstract, simplified, and general propositions that answer "why" and "how" questions such as "*why* do wars begin?" or "*how* do collective identities shape our behavior?" Most theory involves an effort to explain and/or predict actors' behavior in global politics. Theory is built on assumptions – initial claims that must be accepted without further investigation – that lead theorists to point to particular features of global politics. For example, as we noted earlier, many analysts construct theories based on the assumption that people are rational.

empirical theory (positivism) theories built on knowledge derived from experiment and experience.

There are two kinds of theory: empirical and normative. **Empirical theory** deals with what *is*. It is based on facts that can be observed either directly or indirectly through history books, memoirs, and documents. We use empirical theory to answer questions about how actors behave and what the consequences of their actions are. Examples of empirical propositions would be: "Suicide bombers are used by groups that are weaker than their adversaries" and "suicide bombings cause society to lose faith in the government's ability to provide security." These statements are empirical because researchers can collect and organize facts (**data**) about which groups conduct suicide bombings and on the political consequences of their bombings. Moreover, other researchers can evaluate these theories by collecting their own data. In other words, these propositions are testable. But those who study global politics are also interested in evaluating whether what actors do or cause to happen is right or wrong, and whether they *should* or *ought* to act as they do. Answers to such questions constitute **normative theory**, which explains what is right and wrong or moral and immoral. Such theory tends to take the form of a claim, rather than a proposition, and it cannot be tested because it is based on beliefs, logic, and values. An example of a normative claim would be that the use of suicide bombers as an instrument of policy is immoral. There is no way to test the accuracy or the morality of this proposition. There are those who believe that using suicide bombers to

data factual information.

normative theory theory concerning what is right and wrong.

kill innocents is never right and there are those who believe it is justified, at least in some circumstances. Numbers and statistics will rarely sway people to change deeply held opinions on such matters.

In addition, theory serves three primary purposes: prediction, explanation, and prescription. **Predictive theory** is empirical, forecasting what will happen under a specific set of circumstances. Much theory in global politics predicts. In other words, its main purpose is to generalize from the specific *without* making a leap of imagination. For example, some scholars have observed that states with democratic governments tend not to use war to settle disputes with other democracies, but, instead, use peaceful methods of dispute resolution like negotiation, mediation, and diplomatic pressure. In their theory, these researchers predict that democracies will not go to war with one another.

predictive theory theory based on induction that predicts what will happen under specified conditions.

Explanatory theory identifies causes of events and answers the difficult "why" questions. It, too, is always empirical: it involves leaps of imagination, often triggered by observations of reality. One notable example is the theory of gravity. According to legend, Sir Isaac Newton's theory of gravity was inspired by his observing an apple fall from a tree. His leap of imagination was that the force that brought the apple to the ground (gravity) might be the same force that kept the moon in its orbit around the earth. As in the case of gravity, for the most part, explanatory theory asserts general propositions, and those who apply the theory can use those propositions to explain specific instances. For example, Newton's general ideas about gravity could be applied to the Sun and other planets, as well as to the moon. In global politics, Stephen Walt wanted to explain the formation of military alliances. The basis of his theory was that states will enter alliances to balance against a common threat (the prevailing theory at the time was that states would balance against a stronger power, even if it did not seem to pose an imminent threat). He then applied his theory to alliances among states in the Middle East.[11] Others have applied it to other regions of the world as well.

explanatory theory theory that explains why things happen as they do.

Although good explanatory theories may permit good predictions, predictive theory need not explain. For example, the ancient Greeks developed theories which could explain the movement of the tides and its connection to what we call gravity quite well, but with this knowledge they did not spend much time developing theories to predict the exact times that high and low tide would take place. As you might imagine, the Greeks were not great sailors. By contrast, the Babylonians assumed that tides were dependent on the decisions of the gods – an explanatory theory that was false – but, by careful observation of tidal changes, they developed predictive theories that they could use to calculate high and low tides with great accuracy.

Insurance companies also rely on predictive theory that does not explain. Their theory is based on statistical inference: they infer from particular facts the probability or likelihood of a general proposition. Without this process, they could not stay in business. For example, by looking at the records of many individual automobile drivers, they infer general propositions, such as that accidents are more likely to occur in large cities, drivers below the age of 18 are more likely than their elders to get into accidents, and drivers who commute long distances are more likely to have accidents than those who only go short distances to get to work. Similarly, in global politics, some scholars look at large numbers of wars to infer whether the existence of alliances, arms races, or non-democratic states is connected to the outbreak of war.

Keep in mind, however, that moving from specific cases to general propositions can *never prove* general claims. Thus, just because a researcher finds a strong correlation (the statistical degree to which two or more factors are related and change together) between arms races and war, this does not mean that arms races and war *always* occur together. This is so because it is always possible that additional cases will violate the generalizations. Nor does it prove that arms races *cause* war because both factors may result from other factors of which we are unaware. In reality, theorists continuously move back and forth between specific observations and more abstract and general propositions.

Did you know?

Explaining why something happens involves identifying a "cause" and a "result." Usually theorists distinguish between two types of causes: *necessary* and *sufficient*. If some factor *must* take place for a particular result to occur, then that factor is a **necessary cause**. Although the presence of that factor does not assure the result, the presence of the result necessarily means that the causal factor was present. For example, if wars erupted *only* following arms races, then arms races are a necessary cause of war. Although arms races may occur without war ensuing, wars never occur without arms race preceding them. On the other hand, if the presence of some factor always guarantees a particular result, that factor is called a **sufficient cause**. If arms races are a sufficient cause of war, then, their occurrence assures that war will ensue.

---

necessary cause a factor that must be present for a particular result to follow but whose presence does not necessitate that result.

sufficient cause a factor that when present always assures that a particular result will follow.

prescriptive theory theory about correct policies to use to reach a desired objective.

Theory is also used for the purpose of prescription. **Prescriptive theory** recommends the adoption of particular policies to realize objectives. It combines both empirical and normative elements and recommends the adoption of particular policies to realize objectives.

Here *ought* and *should* are used to indicate the correct course of action *if one wishes to achieve a particular end*. Here is an example of a prescriptive proposition: "If the United States wishes to prevent the loss of jobs in its domestic textile industry to other countries, it should raise tariff barriers to imported textiles." This statement is empirical because it proposes that low tariffs (a form of tax) on imported textiles *are* correlated with a loss of American jobs in the textile industry. Data can be collected to evaluate the accuracy of the proposed relationship. The statement is also normative because it argues that the government *should* raise tariffs if it wants to reduce job losses. In sum, each kind of theory has its own uses: empirical theory may be used for explanation, prediction, or prescription (what to do to achieve desired outcomes), whereas normative theory tends to be employed only for prescription.

It is important to remember that theory is a tool researchers use to understand the complex reality of global politics because it simplifies reality and points to the relatively few factors that it regards as most important. Moreover, researchers use certain rules and procedures to build good theory and evaluate its accuracy. These rules and procedures are known as **methodology**. People sometimes confuse theory with methodology. In practice, however, the two are quite different. Theory attempts to answer questions of whether things will happen and why they do so, but methodology describes the rules and procedures used to evaluate and test a theoretical proposition. What methodology would a researcher use to arrive at this theory about the textile industry and the tariff barriers? How would she or he determine that imposing the tariff would achieve the desired result (saving jobs)? One methodology might involve the use of statistical inference to make predictions. Researchers who adopt this methodology use *quantitative* measures to achieve precision and clarity just as we use thermometers that tell exact temperature and barometers that tell exact air pressure. They might measure annual textile tariffs and unemployment rates in the textile industry over a period of decades and then use statistical methods to evaluate the relationship between these two variables. An alternative methodology might employ *qualitative* measures like detailed historical case studies to bring precise detail to the theory. Using this approach, we might examine two or three specific instances of a tariff increase in great detail to find out not only *whether* the proposed relationship exists, but also *why* it exists. Researchers must be very careful to explain their methodology in order to allow other researchers to evaluate their findings. A theory gains credibility as more researchers also test it.

This section has introduced the concept of theory as a tool that observers of global politics use to simplify the world in order to explain

methodology the rules and procedures by which research is conducted.

and predict events and to prescribe policies. Scholars as well as politicians need theory to eliminate some of the complexity of global politics. Once they understand the patterns or regularities that actors exhibit, they can better understand and manage global politics to reduce conflict and increase cooperation. However, as we will see in the next section, theorists have different world views, and these differences in turn shape their theories of global politics. Theorists do not always agree on the salient issues and problems in global politics, or the causes of or solutions to these problems.

The great debates: an introduction to different world views

We now turn to some of the key approaches that theorists have used to understand global politics and look at how these approaches have evolved over time. In discussing the evolution of theory in global politics, observers have found it useful to organize the discipline's history into three phases, each of which featured a debate about theory. The first phase featured a debate between two theoretical approaches: realism and liberalism. This debate centered on issues such as the relevant actors and issues in global politics and whether cooperation among actors was to be considered the exception or the norm in their relations. For instance, were states the only actors worth considering and, if not, which other actors were significant? Also, were states preoccupied by military security above all other matters, or could other issues, like trade, sometimes be more important? Were actors, by their very nature, prone to conflict or cooperation? The second phase involved a debate regarding how to theorize and conduct research. This debate involved, for instance, questions about whether theories should be based upon specific observations or deduced from general principles and whether the research methods natural scientists use could be adopted by political scientists. Finally, the third phase, known as the "Third Debate," involved more fundamental questions about research and theorizing. For example, is it really possible for researchers to observe political activity objectively? This debate gave rise to a third major school of thought, constructivism, which has come to rival realism and liberalism. Some of those who participated in the "Third Debate" were former Marxists, and we will briefly examine the Marxist perspective on global politics as well.

Each of these theoretical approaches developed in particular historical contexts. Although theories of power politics have existed for many centuries in many cultures, realism (a later version of power politics) arose in reaction to the alleged idealism and utopianism that dominated Western thinking in the years between World Wars I and II. The dominance of realism was then assured by the tensions of the Cold War. Liberalism emerged with the Enlightenment in the seventeenth century and the growing belief in the power of natural science and rationality to improve the human condition and foster individual liberty. It flourished in the aftermath of the American and French revolutions in the eighteenth century and the promise of nineteenth-century industrialization to improve the general standard of living. It then regained new life as a reaction to the senseless slaughter of World War I and again with the end of the Cold War. Marxism was a reaction to the dark side of the industrial revolution, especially the appalling living conditions of the new urban working class, and it gained advocates following the 1917 Bolshevik Revolution in Russia and the Great Depression of the 1930s, events that seemed to many to auger the imminent collapse of capitalism. Finally, the Third Debate erupted after the Cold War as a result of growing skepticism on the part of some observers about the ability of social science to deal effectively with mounting global woes such as economic and social inequality, environmental degradation, and endemic violence.

In the following sections, we will review each of these debates in turn to see how scholars build on one another's work and how theoretical issues and research tools have changed over time. What you should keep in mind is that even now *none of these debates is settled*.

realism an approach to global politics derived from the tradition of power politics and belief that behavior is determined by the search for and distribution of power.

Realism versus liberalism

The first of the three phases pitted **realists** against **liberals** (called idealists and utopians by realists). The realist, or power-politics, tradition can be traced back to ancient China and India, as well as to classical Western thinkers such as the Greek historian Thucydides, the Florentine political philosopher Niccolò Machiavelli (1469–1527), and the seventeenth-century English political theorist Thomas Hobbes (1588–1679). These individuals were not realists themselves, but they inform realist thought. What they had in common was a belief that the central elements of global politics were *power* and *security*. According to Machiavelli, rulers must always be preoccupied with power, even during peacetime; those who neglect military matters of power and security will surely lose power.[12] "I put for a general inclination of all mankind," wrote Hobbes, "a perpetual and restless desire of power after power that ceases only in death."[13]

Global politics, then, is for realists a struggle for power in which leaders must remain alert to the efforts of other states to acquire additional power that might endanger the security and survival of their own state. In the face of such efforts, according to realists, states will try to balance one

liberalism an optimistic approach to global politics based on the perfectibility of humankind, free trade, and democracy; focuses on individuals rather than states.

Figure 1.3 Niccolò Machiavelli (1469–1527)

Figure 1.4 The balance of power, as depicted by Honoré Daumier

Robert D. Farber University Archives & Special Collections Department, Brandeis University

balance of power policy of states aimed to prevent any other state(s) from gaining a preponderance of power in relation to its rivals.

great power in the eighteenth century, the name for a European state that could not be conquered even by the combined might of other European states. Today, the term is applied to a country that is regarded as among the most powerful in the global system.

unitary-actor approach the assumption that actors' internal attributes or differences among such attributes have little impact on foreign-policy behavior.

another's power either by forming alliances or increasing their armaments. Power, in other words, produces countervailing power, resulting in a **balance of power** (see chapter 2, pp. 68–71). In addition to focusing on global politics as a struggle for power, realists view states as the only important actors in global politics, a view sometimes labeled state-centric. Indeed, realists tend to look mainly at only a few leading states, usually called the **great powers**. Because they regard the distribution of power in global politics as critical and believe that states inevitably act according to the relative power they possess, realists think that factors internal to states such as type of government or features of society have little impact on foreign policy. For them the state is a **unitary actor**.[14]

Although realists agree about the centrality of power in global politics, they disagree about *why* the search for power is so central. Traditional realists see it arising in the hearts and minds of people owing to psychological needs, human nature, or original sin. In other words, they focus attention on the individual level of analysis. According to political scientist Hans J. Morgenthau, the most famous of America's realists, the source is "human nature," which "has not changed since the classical philosophies of China, India, and Greece."[15] Or, in the words of one of America's founding fathers, Alexander Hamilton (1757–1804), men are "ambitious, vindictive, and rapacious."[16]

The state of nature that Hobbes called "the war of every man against every man" lacked any central authority. Hobbes's three premises are that men are equal, that they must interact under conditions of anarchy, and that they are motivated by competition, fear, and glory.[17] Thus, Hobbes wrote, "kings and persons of sovereign authority because of their independency, are in continual jealousies and in the state and posture of gladiators, having their weapons pointing and their eyes fixed on one another." A world like this one had no place for "notions of right or wrong, justice and injustice."[18] This Hobbesian world is anarchic, the condition in which there is no authority above the actors in global politics. Hobbes's world features acute competition for power involving finite resources like territory. In such situations, the gain made by one actor is equivalent to the loss by another and is called a **zero-sum game** because if we add the winner's gains and the loser's losses the total equals zero.

The modern debate between the realists and liberals began in 1939, shortly before the Nazi invasion of Poland, with the publication of *The Twenty Years' Crisis, 1919–1939* by British historian E. H. Carr (1892–1982). Carr wrote his book "with the deliberate aim of counteracting the glaring and dangerous defect of nearly all thinking, both academic and popular about international politics in English-speaking countries from 1919 to 1939 – the almost total neglect of the factor of power."[19] With this purpose in mind, he distinguished between "utopia and reality," which he defined as "two methods of approach – the inclination to ignore what was and what is in contemplation of what should be, and the inclination to deduce what should be from what was and what is."[20] Following World War I, Carr argued, utopian liberals sought to prevent another war from erupting by drafting international treaties, implementing laws and free trade, and mobilizing public opinion. They believed, he continued, that ethics should and could dominate politics and that "the 'good' which consists in self-interest should be subordinated to the 'good' which consists in loyalty and self-sacrifice for an end higher than self-interest."[21] Unfortunately, Carr countered, in the absence of higher authority, there is no natural harmony of interests in global politics, only national interests that repeatedly clash.

Figure 1.5 Frontispiece of *Leviathan* by Thomas Hobbes

zero-sum game a situation of pure conflict in which the gain of one side is equal to the loss of the other.

Did you know?

A story grew that Hobbes's mother was so terrorized by rumors of the Spanish Armada's approach to England that she gave birth to her second son Thomas prematurely on April 5, 1588. In his words, "she brought forth twins – myself and fear."

idealism/utopianism a term coined by realists to deride other scholars of global politics who believe in the importance of international law, treaties, morality, and international institutions.

Following the war, a new generation of scholars, many of whom like Morgenthau had fled Europe during the conflict, placed the blame for World War II squarely on **utopianism** and **idealism**, whose advocates, they believed, had disapproved of the use of power. American and British leaders, argued realists, had tried to maintain peace in the 1920s and 1930s through morality, law, public opinion, disarmament agreements, and treaties – all of which ignored the realities of power. The problem, realists believed, was epitomized in the 1928 Kellogg-Briand Treaty (or Pact of Paris), which had outlawed war. Its Article I stated: "The High Contracting Parties solemnly declare in the names of their respective peoples that they condemn recourse to war for the solution of international controversies, and renounce it, as an instrument of national policy in their relations with one another."[22] Realists argued, however, that Japan and Germany, both signatories, made a mockery of international law and public opinion: Japan invaded China in the 1930s and Hitler violated one treaty after another on the road to war.

Realism has dominated the way in which most governments have approached global politics since the 1940s. For much of that time, US policy has been based on the importance of "negotiating from positions of strength," which has meant increasing or maintaining America's military and economic power and leadership in global politics, and avoiding commitments that would limit foreign-policy flexibility. For example, in 2000, Condoleezza Rice, future national security adviser and secretary of state to George W. Bush, made a classic realist-versus-liberal argument. She denounced the foreign policy of President Bill Clinton for its "attachment to largely symbolic agreements and its pursuit of, at best, illusory 'norms.'"[23] "Power matters," she argued, and a Republican administration would "proceed from the firm ground of the national interest, not from the interests of an illusory international community."[24]

The realist view focuses on power and especially the desire of leaders to acquire and wield power over others, thereby serving their country's national interest. Thus, a realist might explain America's invasion of Iraq that began on March 20, 2003 in terms of a US determination to exert influence over unfriendly governments in the Middle East and remove from power Iraq's President Saddam Hussein (1937–2006) who for many years had sought to become the leader of the region's Arab states, enlarge his country's territory at the expense of neighboring Iran, and gain control over neighboring Kuwait, thereby giving him great leverage over oil-rich Saudi Arabia.

anarchy the absence of a higher authority above sovereign states.

Following Hobbes, many contemporary realists contend that the drive for power grows out of the fact of **anarchy**. For later realists, or **neorealists** (also sometimes called *structural realists*), like political scientist Kenneth N. Waltz, all activity in global politics flows from the fact that structural conditions, especially anarchy, constrain actors from taking certain actions and permit them to take others. In other words, unlike traditional realists such as Carr and Morgenthau, neorealists focused attention on the level of the global system. Like Hobbes, Waltz reasoned deductively from his initial assumption that global politics is anarchic.[25] **Structure** simply refers to any set of relatively fixed constraints. Under anarchy, say the neorealists, actors are unable and unwilling to trust one another. Thus, as in older realism, actors seek power but mainly for survival rather than out of desire. They can depend only on themselves (self-help) for security, and in arming themselves for protection they frighten other actors, who then prepare for the worst, fearing that they will become the victims of aggression. This situation is called a **security dilemma**. Because of the existence of the security dilemma, actors will attempt to gain more relative to others in every transaction so they cannot be exploited by others at some point further down the road. This is known as seeking **relative gains**.

A neorealist explanation of the 2003 American invasion of Iraq would focus on the changing regional and global distribution of power. Iraq, it was believed, was on the verge of acquiring weapons of mass destruction that would threaten America's regional ally, Israel, provide Iraq with regional dominance, and perhaps even pose a threat to the United States itself. American intervention, then, was necessary to prevent a dramatic and unfavorable shift in the balance of power.

In contrast to realism, liberalism emerged between the seventeenth and nineteenth centuries in France, Britain, and the United States. Among the key figures in the development of a liberal perspective were pre-revolutionary French philosophers like Voltaire (François Marie Arouet) (1694–1778), who fought intolerance and superstition, and Denis Diderot (1713–84), who believed in the value of knowledge and social reform. Another liberal was the German philosopher Immanuel Kant (1724–1804), who advocated science and reason, favored global citizenship, and claimed that democracies were more peaceful than autocracies. British liberals of the eighteenth and nineteenth centuries included names such as the political philosopher John Locke (1632–1704), who argued that people had inalienable rights; the physician John Bright (1811–89) and the reformer Richard Cobden (1804–65), who both argued fervently for free trade; John Stuart Mill (1806–73), who believed that education could end warfare; and Adam Smith (1723–90), author of *The Wealth of Nations*, father of capitalism, advocate of free trade, and opponent of slavery. Thus, some liberals like

neorealism (structural realism) the school of realism that holds that the structural properties of global politics, especially anarchy and the distribution of power among states, cause conflict and war.

structure any set of relatively fixed constraints on global actors.

security dilemma a situation in which one actor's effort to increase its security makes other states less secure with the unintended consequence of greater insecurity for all.

relative gains efforts to gain more relative to others so as not to be exploited by others at some future point.

Figure 1.6 Capitalism at its best

© Original artist,
www.cartoonstock.com

"Have a good day, sweetie. Mommy has to go to the office now and attempt
to drive a stake through the heart of her competitors."

Mill stressed the individual level of analysis, while others such as Kant
and Smith emphasized the state level of analysis.

Classical liberals believed that history was moving toward improving
the lives of individuals, that such improvement was in everyone's interest,
and that it ought to be everyone's objective. Like Adam Smith, they
believed that the process would move faster if governments stayed out
of politics and economics. The free market was like an "invisible hand,"
they argued, that would transform the economic self-interest of greedy
individuals into a general good and reflect a natural harmony of interests
among people. Liberals argued, too, that global politics should be
transformed into the equivalent of their domestic societies – this was
their domestic analogy – free of violence, and characterized by orderliness,
security, prosperity, and well-being.

Most American liberals supported a particular form of liberalism –
noninterventionist liberalism – in which *by example alone* the virtues of
liberalism, especially its contribution to human freedom, would spread to
the four corners of the world. Americans, these liberals asserted, were not
obliged to right the wrongs of the world. Rather, they should be a shining
new example and build a new world that others would copy. America, in
their view, would be, like Biblical Jerusalem, "a city on the hill." This
idea was first applied to America by John Winthrop (1588–1649), an
early settler and a leader of the Massachusetts Bay Company and of the
colony it established. In a sermon that Winthrop gave in 1630, entitled

noninterventionist liberalism
the school of liberalism that
holds that history will bring
improvement in society without
help from external actors.

"A Model of Christian Charity," he declared: "For we must consider that we shall be as a city on the hill. The eyes of all people are upon us." This theme has been found in American thinking since, especially in the nineteenth century and in the 1920s and 1930s, which are described as eras of isolation. According to noninterventionist liberals, with the help of the American example the entire world would become more like America.

A second variety of liberalism, however, called **interventionist liberalism**, evolved as an alternative. Example alone was not sufficient to diffuse liberal ideas; instead, it was necessary for liberal states to intervene in other countries, sometimes by force, to spread these ideas. Those who held this view were often inspired by deep religious and ethical convictions. They contended that history sometimes needs a shove in the form of intervention from abroad and that it is the obligation of actors to right wrongs wherever they occur. The zealous effort of French revolutionaries and the armies of Napoléon after 1789 to extend "liberty, equality, and fraternity" across Europe was an early example of such liberalism, as were the efforts of four-time British Prime Minister William E. Gladstone (1809–98) to export human rights and individual choice to countries like Turkey's Ottoman Empire. Indeed, interventionist liberals like Gladstone and later Americans of this stripe had a deep commitment to encouraging human rights and bringing an end to atrocities by other governments both against their populations as well as other countries.

America's leading interventionist liberal was President Woodrow Wilson (1856–1924). Like many other interventionist liberals, he too was deeply ethical and religious. In 1917, Wilson justified US entry into World War I in order "to make the world safe for democracy." It was to be a "war to end all wars." Influenced by Kant, Wilson believed that peace would result from abandoning old power politics and balance-of-power practices and constructing an international organization that would be dominated by democratic and therefore peace-loving states. He articulated these principles, now known as Wilson's Fourteen Points, in a joint session to Congress on January 8, 1918. The most important of these points was the principle of **national self-determination**, which stipulated that every people who believed they were a distinct nation should have its own territorial state.

In some respects, American President George W. Bush is, like Wilson, a deeply religious interventionist liberal.[26] Thus, Bush claimed that among the most important reasons for invading Iraq in 2003 was the transformation of that country into a democracy in which Iraqis would enjoy freedom and human rights. Many observers failed to recognize this aspect of Bush's thinking because he was widely regarded as a conservative

interventionist liberalism a version of classical liberalism that sees it as a duty to intervene overseas to bring freedom, democracy, and other liberal virtues to people everywhere.

national self-determination the right of a nation to have their own territory and govern themselves.

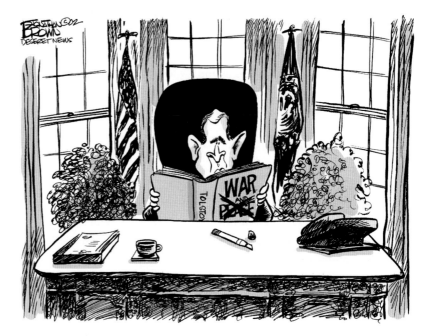

Figure 1.7 George Bush and the path to peace

© Original artist,
www.cartoonstock.com

variable-sum (non-zero-sum) game a situation in which the total gain for one party is *not* identical to the losses of the other; both can gain, both can lose, or one can gain or lose more or less than the other.

absolute gains efforts to ensure everyone gains something from cooperation.

justice fairness, honesty, and impartiality in dealing with individual citizens including according them equal treatment, upholding their rights, affording them what is legally theirs or theirs on the basis of merit.

neoliberalism the school of liberals that believes in the critical role of international organizations in improving the prospects for order and peace.

on most political issues. In fact, intervention in the name of liberty is one of the defining traits of Bush's supporters, who are known as neoconservatives or "neocons."

Despite the confusion of the terms liberal and conservative in the context of the Bush Administration, the liberal view of global politics remains very different from the realist perspective. In particular, liberals believe that in some areas of political life, like trade, all participants can profit or all can lose (this is called a **variable-sum game**). For example, all participants in a free trade relationship gain: more higher-quality products to choose from at cheaper prices. This is a variable-sum game in which all win. In these situations, liberals argue that actors are more concerned about their **absolute gains** (everybody gaining something) than about relative gains, or what they get compared to others. A variable-sum game encourages cooperation in order to maximize gains and minimize losses. By contrast, a zero-sum game is one of almost pure conflict because only one actor can win, while the other necessarily loses.

Unlike realists, liberals focus on individuals or humanity as a whole as key actors in global politics rather than states as a whole as key actors in global politics. In addition, power and prudence are less important in the liberal vision than **justice**.

As in the case of realism, liberalism has also evolved. Today, there is a variant of liberalism called **neoliberalism** or neoliberal institutionalism. Like neorealists, neoliberals theorize at the system level and assume that actors are both unitary and rational in the sense of judging alternatives on the basis of their costs and benefits. They emphasize that individuals everywhere depend on one another for survival and well-being and that they are linked by shared fates; that is, they are interdependent. Interdependence, in turn, produces cooperation.

According to neoliberals, states are not the only relevant political actors, and many actors are transnational rather than national or international, meaning that they are groups or organizations that exist across state boundaries. States, they believe, must share authority, especially in non-security issues, with **nonstate actors** ranging from transnational interest groups like the World Chamber of Commerce to international organizations like the World Trade Organization. Global actors, in their view, are increasingly interdependent; that is, actors' actions affect one another, and they depend on one another to achieve their objectives and assure their well-being and security. Interdependence, liberals believe, encourages actors to coordinate activities and cooperate in order to achieve their goals (see chapter 6, pp. 257–9).

Neoliberals are strong supporters of international organizations. Such organizations, they believe, help states coordinate their activities by allowing for repeated interactions during which trust among actors can grow, publicize and formalize collective rules and norms of behavior, and reduce **transaction costs** such as the cost of obtaining information. In these ways, international institutions promote order and achieve goals that no single state could achieve on its own. In particular, such institutions facilitate communication among states and provide crucial information that is needed to deal with complex technical issues. In the neoliberal vision, international organizations, along with governments and nongovernmental groups, may form international regimes that, though informal, enjoy considerable authority. Such regimes can provide guidelines, norms, and rules that are acceptable to states and allow the orderly management of particular issues. To these kinds of organizations we owe the efficient management of, for example, international trade, weather forecasting, air traffic control, and the eradication of certain diseases even in the absence of **supranational** authorities. Thus, neoliberals, like neorealists, focus on the level of the global system.

In sum, realists are pessimists who believe that war and other features of global politics are natural, inevitable, and irremediable. Liberals, by contrast, are optimists who believe that war and poverty can be eliminated and conditions globally can be improved. Realists think people are irredeemably aggressive and selfish, while liberals see them as cooperative and perfectible. Realists oppose any role for public opinion, which they regard as fickle and unwise, in foreign policy-making, and

nonstate actors actors whose members are individuals or groups other than sovereign states.

transaction costs the costs involved in any transaction other than the price paid such as time spent or information about others involved in the transaction.

supranational above the authority of national governments.

see the purpose of foreign policy as improving *state* security, while liberals want to democratize global politics and believe that foreign policy should benefit *individuals*. Realists also deplore anything that limits state sovereignty, while liberals applaud international institutions and seek to limit state sovereignty. For their part, constructivists regard sovereignty as a human invention that will condition the practices of actors only until political elites become committed to organizing global politics in different ways.

paradigm an example that serves as a pattern or model for something, especially one that forms the basis of research and theory.

Before leaving this debate, we need to point out that these perspectives are *tendencies* of politicians and theorists. They are not complete theories but, instead, are guidelines, sometimes called **paradigms**,[27] that direct attention to certain factors. Realism, for example, focuses attention and policy toward war, national power, and military capabilities, whereas liberalism turns attention and policy toward poverty, education, economic development, and human rights – all related to the welfare of people rather than states. Finally, both schools freely mix empirical with normative claims. Thus, they assert that the world *does* operate in a particular way (empirical), but when it does not do so it *ought to* (normative). Notice the contradiction here; the second claim denies at least part of the first by acknowledging that sometimes the world *does not* operate as expected. To see a contemporary example of the realist–liberal debate, refer to the *Theory in the Real World* box.

Theory in the real world

The concept of "liberalism" has been used in a variety of ways. We are using the concept as it was developed by Europe's classical liberals. In contemporary politics, classical liberals would appear to be "conservative" owing to their emphasis on individualism and individual liberty. The following illustrates some of these similarities and differences.

Classical liberalism	Contemporary conservatism	Contemporary liberalism
Maximize individual freedom	Maximize individual freedom	Maximize social welfare to enhance individual freedom for the deprived
Minimize role of government	Decrease role of government	Increase role of government
Free trade	Free trade	Managed trade

Traditionalism versus science

A second debate, which erupted in the 1960s, concerns methodology, that is, *how to conduct research* about global politics.[28] Traditional scholars studied history, philosophy, international law, and national and international institutions in order to understand the world. Their analysis often took the form of case studies, in which they carefully examined specific wars and policies to understand why these wars broke out or policies were chosen. Often, they immersed themselves in foreign cultures, learning local languages and local history in order to deepen their understanding of particular countries and regions. Finally, traditionalists routinely mixed their discussions of facts, or empirical evidence, with their views of what is right and wrong, making normative claims.

However, following World War II, the study of global politics came to involve scholars who were part of the **behavioral revolution**. Such scholars tried to emulate the research methods of natural scientists, such as physicists and chemists. These behavioralists, also called behavioral scientists, argued that instead of studying law, history, and institutions, political scientists should study how people *actually* behave. To do so, however, they believed that empirical and normative theory (facts and values) should be strictly separated and that combining them led to confusion because neither could be used to prove the other. Mixing empirical and normative claims also ran the risk, in their view, of turning scholarship into moral fervor. Traditionalists strongly disagreed with this, contending that, unlike natural scientists, all observers of global politics, whether they used traditional or behavioral methods, pursue a normative agenda. Although natural scientists do not study the orbits of planets with the objective of changing them, social scientists actually want to understand the world in order to change or reform it.

Although behavioralists, like traditionalists, conduct case studies, the behavioralists insist on identifying the **patterned behaviors** or regularities in the cases they study and, in turn, generalizing from them. Like natural scientists, behavioralists argue that research requires the gradual accumulation of facts and, with such accumulation, growing recognition of their broader meaning. You will recognize these ideas from our earlier discussion of predictive theories. Only by identifying patterns and regularities, behavioralists assert, is it possible to formulate general theories that can predict and explain other cases.

Using the methods of the natural sciences, such theorists begin by positing a **hypothesis** which is a tentative prediction or explanation that often takes the conditional form "if x, then y." The theorist then seeks to test the hypothesized prediction or explanation. For example, a theorist

behavioral revolution a shift in political science from the study of institutions, laws, history, and single case studies and toward the observation of human behavior or its artifacts with an eye toward uncovering general propositions.

patterned behavior behavior that is repeated over and over again and seen to be orderly and predictable.

hypothesis a tentative prediction or explanation that a theorist intends to test.

might believe that arms races produce wars and hypothesize "if arms races take place, wars will follow." Thereafter, the theorists might collect as many cases of war as possible and then examine those cases to discover whether in fact arms races did precede them. Since the theorist is trying to discern patterns, she may wish to look at many cases that constitute her data.

In their effort to deal with large amounts of data and be precise, social scientists turned to **quantification** and the use of statistics, a branch of mathematics that involves the collection, analysis, interpretation, and presentation of large amounts of quantitative data. Such analysis allows them to determine whether the co-appearance of the factors (called variables) they are examining (arms races and wars) constitute a genuine pattern or merely occur by chance. Numbers, they argue, are more precise than words, which can have many meanings. By contrast, an algebraic equation can have one meaning and one meaning only. The growing availability and sophistication of computers made it possible to collect, store, and analyze vast amounts of information and innumerable cases, thus expanding the scope of this kind of research.

Many issues in the traditionalist–behaviorist controversy remain with us today. Some of the most important include:

- *Complexity vs. uniformity* Traditionalists argue that human behavior is too complex to be understood in the way that nature is, and that scientific methods, therefore, cannot be applied to political science. Humans often behave in unpredictable ways, so their behavior exhibits far less regularity than that of other animals. By contrast, scientists claim that human beings, like all animals, are part of nature and, in principle, can be studied like any other natural phenomenon. Complexity, they contend, is in the mind of the observer and what appears to be complex at first blush becomes less so as more is learned.

- *Trees versus forests* Traditionalists contend that it is vital to understand the elements, or trees, of global politics in depth. They claim one cannot really understand China, a tree, for instance, unless one knows its culture, history, and language and thus is a China specialist. If one only speaks the language of statistics, which studies the forest, one is doomed to see China through the prism of one's own eyes and will never see the world as do the Chinese. Thus, to understand global politics, scholars must be trained as specialists on one or a few countries rather than as generalists who uncover broad patterns in global politics. Unfortunately, answer the scientists, the traditional approach leads to overemphasis on the specific and unique at the expense of the general. Traditionalists focus on individual trees in the forest and, as a result,

quantification the use of numbers and statistics to describe and explain political behavior.

overemphasize how each tree differs from the others. By contrast, the scientists, who study many instances or cases historically or around the world, can observe what is common among them and identify regularities.

- *Whole versus parts* According to traditionalists, scientists make a serious mistake by isolating what they believe to be important factors. In other words, traditionalists say, scientists tend to look at, say, alliances, ideologies, or military strategies in many cases but without clear understanding of the full context in which they operate. Only by viewing a factor in context, as it interacts with other factors, can scholars generate valid theories. Thus, any outcome or event can *only* be understood as the result of interaction among all of these factors. Nonsense, respond the scientists, who declare that for accuracy they must emulate the laboratory practices of natural scientists. Only by isolating individual factors, they say, can a researcher understand its impact without having to worry that other factors are instead producing an outcome.

- *Subjective versus objective* Traditionalists claim that by focusing on only those aspects of global politics that can be easily quantified and measured, scientists often ignore the subjective, or non-observable, side of global politics, especially the role of ideas, emotions, culture, identity, and beliefs. This dispute leads to a more general criticism of scientists by traditionalists to the effect that, by studying only what they can observe and quantify, scientists ignore the most important aspects of global politics. Scientists deny both claims, arguing that although the tools for studying subjective factors are less reliable than those for studying objective factors, those tools are improving, and scientists use them frequently to incorporate both subjective and objective factors in their analyses.

By the 1970s, it appeared as though the scientists had won the day. Behavioral scholars dominated research about global politics at many universities and were awarded most of the research funds provided by the US government. Traditional scholarship did not disappear, however, and opposition to behavioralism remained strong in government circles and at many universities, especially in Europe. And, as time passed, tolerance between advocates of both approaches grew.

Postpositivism, constructivism, and the "Third Debate"

A third major theoretical perspective called **constructivism** emerged in the 1980s out of dissatisfaction with realism and liberalism and the dominant influence of scientific methodology in global politics.

constructivism an approach to global politics that assumes that political structures and behavior are shaped by shared ideas and that actors' identities and interests are the result of those ideas.

postpositivists those who reject empiricism on the grounds that there are no objective facts and that reality is subject to interpretation.

foundationalists those who believe truth can be determined through empirical testing.

anti-foundationalists those who claim that there are no neutral, value-free tests to determine the truth of a proposition.

Constructivism was part of a larger movement of theorists who were dissatisfied with existing theories and especially with the rigid empiricism demanded by behavioralists and their de-emphasis of norms and values. Thus, in the late 1980s and early 1990s, a diverse group of scholars launched a new debate by asserting that the study of global politics had lost its soul and that empirical theory had failed to fulfill its promise. This group also believed that theorists of global politics had lost interest in solving the real problems of people and that a return to normative thinking was necessary.

Many of these critics call themselves **postpositivists** and **reflexivists** because they rejected empiricism – which they called positivism – and used reflection and reason instead. So began what political scientist Yosef Lapid called the "Third Debate,"[29] which was characterized primarily by a dispute over whether there is an objective reality that can be observed and serve as the basis of theories of global politics. Thus, a distinction emerged between those called **foundationalists** who believed that truth is accessible through empirical tests and self-styled **anti-foundationalists** who argued that there were no neutral, value-free tests for truth. Describing themselves as "exiles" and "dissidents" from the mainstream of global politics, anti-foundationalists argued that "truth" was inaccessible because all knowledge claims were really efforts on the part of those claiming to know the truth to acquire and maintain power over others. "Ambiguity, uncertainty, and the ceaseless questioning of identity," declared postmodernists Richard K. Ashley and R. B. J. Walker, "these are resources of the exiles . . . of those who would live and move in these paradoxical marginal spaces and times and who, in order to do so, must struggle to resist knowledgeable practices of power that would impose upon them a certain identity, a set of limitations on what can be done, an order of 'truth.'"[30]

Some of the extreme postpositivists, including those who refer to themselves as postmodernists, argued that we can never *know anything* with certainty because language is not objective and reflects only the version of reality of the speaker. Because language is socially determined, or constructed, words and concepts have no value outside of the social context in which they are defined and employed. There can be no objective reality, as every theorist's view of the world will be colored by the language she uses. Thus, the postpositivists abandoned the empiricists' demand for facts-through-observation in the belief that only insight and imagination could produce genuine theory and that the concepts needed to build theory can only be defined by the theorists and practitioners employing them. Given the subjectivity of language, at best positivists could look at what they believed to be tangible measures of abstract concepts they could not see. And, by limiting understanding to the observation of facts, positivists left no place for norms or values in their thinking.[31] For example, theorists cannot see religious values, but such values may nonetheless influence the decisions actors make. Positivists can only attempt to measure this concept by observing indicators like attendance at religious services and public statements of such values. Yet even this approach is problematic, as someone who possesses religious values may not attend services or publicly proclaim their values. Because such difficulties exist in observing abstract concepts, positivists tend to give them insufficient attention in their theorizing.

The problem with postpositivism, the positivists countered, was that, if truth is not knowable empirically or if everyone's interpretation is equally "truthful," then nobody's opinion can be better than anybody else's. Under those conditions, it becomes impossible to know what policies to follow, and theory has no prescriptive value. In addition, postpositivists do not have an alternative framework for explaining global politics. Finally, even if truth remains elusive, an enhanced ability to predict and explain are useful and, therefore, valuable.

Second, say the postpositivists, language and the ideas it expresses are themselves forms of power that reinforce social and political hierarchies. Positivists, they argued, ignore the normative implications of such hierarchies in which individuals and groups were marginalized. "Theory," in the words of political scientist Robert Cox, "is always *for* someone, and *for* some purpose."[32]

This "third" debate became heated during the 1990s because many empiricists came to loathe postpositivism as much as postpositivists hated empiricism. Political scientists Peter Katzenstein, Robert Keohane, and Stephen Krasner even argued that many postpositivists simply were not social scientists, declaring that "postmodernism falls clearly outside of the social science enterprise, and in international relations research it risks becoming self-referential and disengaged from the world, protests to the contrary notwithstanding."[33] The extreme reflexivists, claimed empiricists, were not engaged in making sense of the real world. Instead, they were playing language games, with double entendres and other clever word-play in which all interpretations of global politics were equally valid. Since extreme reflexivists regard all perceptions and preferences as equally valid, they are also called **relativists**. This means that they believe that there are no truths and that what is right or wrong varies from person to person or from society to society. One cannot, for example, claim that democracy is preferable to authoritarianism, that capitalism is superior to communism, or even that peace is better than war because there are no neutral bases for making such claims.

relativists those who believe that there are no clear truths and that what is right or wrong varies from person to person or from society to society.

Constructivism emerged as an effort to narrow the gap between empiricists and postpositivists. Constructivists claimed that people act in the world in accordance with their perceptions of that world, and that the "real," or objective, world shapes those perceptions. These perceptions, they continued, arise from people's identities that, constructivists argued, were shaped by experience and changing social norms. For example, those who think of themselves as "the poor" or "the powerless" perceive the world very differently from those who identify themselves as "the rich" or "the powerful." Once people know "who they are," they can understand their interests and forge policies to pursue those interests.[34]

However, unlike realists and liberals who assume that identities and interests are "givens" that remain largely unchanged, constructivists view identity formation as a crucial and dynamic process. For constructivists, interests are not inherent or predetermined, but rather are learned through experience and socialization. Where realists and liberals assume that actors are selfish individuals rationally maximizing their gains, constructivists view actors as social in the sense that their ideas and norms evolve in a social context. As a result, identities change over time in the course of interaction and evolving beliefs and norms and, as a result, so do interests. Constructivists ask such questions as how do norms evolve (for example, repugnance toward slavery, ethnic cleansing, or nuclear weapons), how do actors acquire their identity, and how do those identities produce actors' understanding of their interests. For example, how did the United States come to see itself as the "leader of the Free World" after World War II, and what policies serve the interests of the "leader of the Free World"? Since the Soviet Union defined its identity as "leader of the international communist movement," it necessarily defined its interests, and therefore its policies, differently than the United States. Constructivists argue that collective ideas and norms play a key role in producing identities and interests. For example, the members of the North Atlantic Treaty Organization (NATO) believe in democracy, and that belief plays a major role in how they define the alliance and its objectives.[35] Similarly, the evolution of norms opposed to apartheid (racial segregation) in South Africa played a key role in mobilizing countries around the world to oppose that system which ended in 1994. More recently, a normative consensus has grown concerning the desirability of United Nations humanitarian intervention in countries like Sierra Leone that have been overwhelmed by civil violence despite the older normative belief that sovereignty should preclude such intervention without the permission of the government in question. Table 1.1 summarizes the distinctions between positivism, postpositivism, and constructivism.

Table 1.1 Reality in the third debate

Positivists *(Empiricists)*	There is an *objective reality* that can be measured. Even factors that cannot be observed directly, like emotions and beliefs, can be measured indirectly through behaviors, statements, and so forth.
Constructivists	*Identity* shapes perceptions of "reality." One's view of reality depends upon one's identity, e.g., as poor/ wealthy, American/Russian, Christian/Muslim, or male/female.
Postpositivists	*Language* shapes perceptions of "reality." There is no universal truth to be uncovered in global politics.

The agent–structure problem

Since constructivists believe that how people identify themselves shapes how they act, their position concerning what theorists today call the **agent–structure problem**[36] is more compatible with the liberal belief that actors (leaders and states, for example) or "agents" shape global politics than with the neorealist belief that structural factors such as anarchy, the distribution of military capabilities across the global system, the global economic market, or culture force individuals to act as they do. For constructivists, agents have a capacity to act freely within the constraints of structure, and their perceptions of their environment, including structures, and their interaction with one another influence their behavior, which in turn shapes, or constitutes, structure (see Key document: The constitutive effects of ideas). Their beliefs and actions alter structure that in turn constrains them in new ways, a cycle that can be traced historically.

If, for example, actors view the global system as composed of states, they will turn to states to address the pressing problems of global politics. The fact that they turn to states will reinforce the dominant role of states in global politics. In contrast, if they view other entities – international organizations like the United Nations, for instance – as also important in global politics and they turn to these entities to manage global problems, their actions can actually make such entities more important. Constructivists remain empiricists but, unlike many empiricists, they focus largely on subjective factors like norms, ideas, and values.

Constructivists, some of whom believe that their approach is halfway between the structural determinism of neorealism and the belief of liberals that the world is infinitely malleable, argue that there are occasions when events profoundly affect the beliefs and norms of individuals and groups. On these occasions – major wars for example – leaders and other elites

agent–structure problem a controversy about whether individuals and groups play the major role in explaining global politics or whether features of global structure determine the behavior of actors.

may begin to see the world differently and, as they interact, produce a consensus around new norms and new ways of behaving. For example, after the widespread devastation of the Thirty Years' War (1618–48), leaders gradually revised the views of war, and a consensus evolved around the need to limit warfare and downplay religion and ideology as factors that intensified violence.

Key document   The constitutive effects of ideas

In a seminal book, constructivist Alexander Wendt examines the differences between causal and constitutive theorizing. One important concept for understanding the latter is *constitutive effects*. Wendt explains:

> To understand the difference that ideas and social structures make in international politics we need to recognize the existence of *constitutive effects*. Ideas or social structures have constitutive effects when they create phenomena – properties, powers, dispositions, meanings, etc. – that are conceptually or logically dependent on those ideas or structures, that exist only "in virtue of" them. The causal powers of the master do not exist apart from his relation to the slave; terrorism does not exist apart from a national security discourse that defines "terrorism." These effects . . . are not causal because they violate the requirements of independent existence and temporal asymmetry. Ordinary language bears this out: we do not say that slaves "cause" masters, or that a security discourse "causes" terrorism. On the other hand, it is clear that the master–slave relation and security discourse are relevant to the construction of masters or terrorism, since without them there would not *be* masters or terrorism. Constitutive theories seek to "account for" these effects, even if not to "explain" them.[37]

To some extent, the agent–structure issue overlaps with levels of analysis. Those who emphasize the dominance of structure tend to focus on the system level where critical structural factors like the global distribution of power and anarchy are located. By contrast, theorists who burrow into the state and individual levels of analysis are implicitly suggesting that the actions and beliefs of leaders and governments have an impact on key outcomes.

Constructivists might explain America's invasion of Iraq as a collision between two incompatible identities and the resulting clash of conflicting interests. America's *constructed identity* was that of a democratic society and global superpower with the responsibility to protect friendly governments from the ambitions of an authoritarian regime whose leader, Saddam Hussein, was flirting with those identified as militant Muslims such as Al Qaeda's leader, Osama bin Laden.

Feminist international relations

Many feminist thinkers were attracted to postpositivism because of its emphasis on the role of language and identity in creating power relations: because gender relations are almost always unequal, gender is "a primary way of signifying relationships of power." Gendered language reinforces such relationships. That is, for the most part, feminist theorists agree with political scientist J. Ann Tickner that people assign "a more positive value to [stereotypically] masculine characteristics" like power and rationality and a more negative value to stereotypically feminine characteristics like weakness and emotion. Thus, those who exhibit masculine traits wield more power than those who exhibit female traits. Those women who tend to succeed as national leaders – for example, Margaret Thatcher in Great Britain, Indira Gandhi in India, and Golda Meir in Israel – also tend to exhibit the same traits as their male counterparts. Such gender relations affect every aspect of human experience, including global politics.[38] In Tickner's view, "feminists cannot be anything but skeptical of universal truth claims and explanations associated with a body of knowledge from which women have frequently been excluded as knowers and subjects."[39]

Major theoretical approaches like realism and liberalism, argue feminist theorists, focus on "issues that grow out of men's experiences"[40] and, presumably, would be altered if account were taken of women's experiences. Women were largely absent from most accounts of international relations (IR) and international history. Thus, feminist theorist Cynthia Enloe was moved to ask rhetorically "where are the women?"[41] And Christine Sylvester posed the issue as follows:

> IR theory does not spin any official stories about such people or evoke "womanly" characteristics. . . . Feminists, however, find evocations of "women" in IR as the Chiquita Bananas of international political economy, the Pocohantas's of diplomatic practice, the women companions for men on military bases, and the Beautiful Souls wailing the tears of unheralded social conscience at the walls of war. Moreover, "men" are in IR too, dressed as states, statesmen, soldiers, decision makers, terrorists, despots and other characters with more powerful social positions than "women."[42]

How does the world look from a feminist perspective? Feminist theory, it is argued, views the world from the perspective of the disadvantaged and takes greater account of economic inequality, ecological dangers, and human rights in defining security than conventional (male) international relations theory, which emphasizes military issues.[43] Some feminists argue that they must abandon strict positivism because of "the contamination of its knowledge by the social biases against women."[44] Knowledge is not value-free, and feminist theory is skeptical about claims of "objective" truth and the meanings attached to such "truth."

Having examined the three principal schools of theory in global politics, we must now turn to a fourth perspective, Marxism. Marxism, which never acquired a major following in the United States, influenced generations of scholars and politicians, especially in the former Soviet Union, Eastern Europe, China, the developing world, and even Western Europe. Marxism, a revolutionary perspective that emphasizes change, still has numerous adherents despite the collapse of world communism with the demise of the Soviet Union.

Marxism

For a time, especially in the 1930s and 1940s, Marxist analysis of global politics was widely applied to global politics. Karl Marx (1818–83), the most influential social scientist of his era, himself had little to say about global politics as we understand it, but his followers sought to apply his ideas, as well as those of Bolshevik leader Vladimir Ilyich Ulyanov Lenin (1870–1924) and Leon Trotsky (1879–1940), to interpreting world affairs. Since Marxist theory focuses on economic forces, we will reserve some of this discussion for chapter 11 (pp. 511–14), which deals with international political economy, but an introduction is in order here. Inasmuch as Marx focused on the relationships of owners and workers in states, he tended to stress the state level of analysis, though contemporary Marxists, as we will see later, stress factors at the global system level, notably relations between rich countries that they call the "core" and poor countries that they call the "periphery."

Marx believed that it was necessary to combine an understanding of economics, political science, history, and philosophy in order to understand world affairs. Economic forces, however, in his view, were the locomotive that pulled the rest. In his view, the essential economic needs of people for goods such as food and shelter shaped all the features of society, including politics, art, literature, religion, and law. His basic idea, known as *dialectical materialism*, was that politics in general and historical change depended on the relationship between the means of production

"I'm using my website to spread Marxist propaganda. I'm a dot commie."

Figure 1.8 High-tech Marxism

© Original artist,
www.cartoonstock.com

(how goods are produced) and their relationship to those who were responsible for producing goods such as peasants and workers. Marx traced the history of how various modes of production had changed, thereby changing the relationship between owners and producers, until the onset of industrial capitalism. Like earlier economic systems such as feudalism, Marx predicted that **capitalism** and capitalist society, too, would be transformed into a "higher" stage, that of **communism**, by a revolution of the workers or proletariat to overthrow the rule of the owners or bourgeoisie.

Workers and owners each constituted a **class**, and Marx believed that conflict among classes was the way in which history evolved. All history, he believed, revolved around class struggle that pitted those who were exploited against those who were exploiting. Workers, he believed, were becoming ever more desperate and were being "pauperized" owing to capitalist efforts to cut costs by laying off workers and keeping their wages low. Unemployment, boom-and-bust economic cycles, overproduction, and under-consumption were producing a crisis for capitalism, especially in the most highly developed countries of Europe and North America where he expected revolution to erupt first. And, by the mid-nineteenth century when he was writing, Marx concluded that the time was fast approaching when the oppressed class (the proletariat) would rise up, initially in the most industrialized states, and overthrow its oppressors

capitalism an economic system based on the private ownership of property and the means of production and a free market for exchanging goods and services that allows competition.

communism a social system without states or classes featuring common ownership of property in which each member contributes according to capabilities and gains according to need.

class a social stratum sharing economic and political characteristics.

(the capitalists), thereby finally freeing the world from exploitation and class conflict.

Just as sovereign states and individuals are regarded by realists and liberals respectively as the key actors in global politics, for Marx and his followers the key actors were economic classes. "The history of all hitherto existing society," wrote Marx and his collaborator Friedrich Engels (1820–95) at the beginning of the *Communist Manifesto*, "is the history of class struggles."[45] Even political leaders were merely minor players whose actions were determined by economic forces and class conflict. Far from being the main actor in global politics, the state was regarded as an instrument in the hands of the dominant class to maintain its power, and it made no difference, as liberals insisted, whether or not it was democratic. In Engels's memorable phrase, "the state is nothing but a machine for the oppression of one class by another and indeed in the democratic republic no less than in the monarchy."[46] The state, Engels argued, becomes "the state of the most powerful, economically ruling class, which by its means becomes also the politically ruling class, and so acquires new means of holding down and exploiting the oppressed class."[47] However, following the revolution and the onset of a classless society, the state, Marx and Engels believed, would no longer have a function. It would then simply wither away.

As we shall see in chapter 10, Lenin revised much of Marx's original thinking, and contemporary Marxists continue to adapt Marxism to changing global conditions. Despite such revisions, all Marxists look to economic factors to explain and predict global politics. Thus, in explaining the American intervention in Iraq, Marxists might argue that its purpose was to increase the profits of military industries or provide America's capitalists with the means to exploit Iraq's oil resources as well as the oil resources of other countries in the Middle East.

Table 1.2 summarizes the key differences among realists, liberals, constructivists, and Marxists and illustrates how the four theoretical approaches speak to one another.

In this section, we have reviewed three major debates about how to look at global politics – the first between realists and liberals, the second between traditionalists and scientists, and the third between positivists (empiricists) and postpositivists. In addition to focusing on realism and liberalism, we have also examined constructivism and Marxism, each of which has a strong following among international relations theorists. The first debate focused on the relative importance of power and anarchy in global politics. The second and third largely involved the question of how to study the subject, especially the relative importance of empirical and normative analysis. None of these disputes has been solved, but each

Table 1.2 Realists, liberals, constructivists, and Marxists compared

	Realists	Liberals	Constructivists	Marxists
Level of Analysis	Traditional realists favor the individual level (human nature); neorealists focus on the global system.	Some liberals focus on the individual and some on the state level of analysis. Thus, John Stuart Mill stressed the individual level in advocating educating citizens, and Immanuel Kant emphasized the state level in advocating republic governments. Neoliberals stress the global system level.	Individual level in transmission of ideas and identities and in the key role of "agents" on altering "structure."	Traditional Marxists focus on the state level in emphasizing dominant economic system. Contemporary or neo-Marxists stress the relations of rich and poor countries and thus the global system level of analysis.
World view	Pessimistic: wars can be managed but not eliminated and the impediments to global cooperation are impossible to overcome owing to the problem of trust in a condition of anarchy. Policies should enhance power. Key actors are states.	Optimistic: wars are human inventions that can be prevented by reforms such as education, free trade, economic betterment, welfare, and democracy. Policies should enhance justice. Key actors are individuals or humanity as a whole.	Indeterminate: changing ideas produce new identities and interests. Whether or not conflict and violence are intensified or reduced depends upon the ideas that take root and attract widespread support and whether or not resulting identities and interests are compatible or not.	Optimistic: history is evolving as a reflection of changing economic forces that are creating the conditions for a world revolution by the proletariat. Wars are the result of class conflict. They can be eliminated by the end of capitalism and the introduction of a classless society. Policies should enhance equality. Key actors are economic classes.
Human nature	Aggressive and selfish with no natural harmony of interests among people. Human nature cannot be improved, and imperfect human beings cannot be perfect.	Benign; human beings are perfectible, and there exists a harmony of interests among people.	Malleable; human beings change behavior as a reflection of the changing norms that govern society.	Benign; human beings are perfectible, but only under socialism, following the elimination of classes. As long as capitalism remains, greed and selfishness dominate behavior.
Change	Key features of global politics are permanent and immutable; evils like poverty and war cannot be eliminated.	Key features of global politics are mutable and history is moving in a positive direction. Interventionist liberals think that history needs a push, while non-interventionist liberals think that their own societies can provide a model for others.	Key features of global politics are mutable though change is impeded by material factors. However, the evolution of ideas and resulting change in identities and interests can modify material factors that constitute global structure.	Key features of global politics are mutable and history is moving in a positive direction. Marx and Engels believed that history was evolving toward socialism; Lenin believed that history had to be pushed by a "vanguard of the proletarian" – the communist party.

continued

Table 1.2 (continued)

	Realists	Liberals	Constructivists	Marxists
Cooperation	Individuals and collective actors are naturally competitive; this propensity is assured by the anarchic nature of global politics.	Individuals and states can cooperate to overcome collective problems such as global pollution, poverty, and aggression.	Indeterminate. It depends on which ideas become dominant and on how universal the consensus is regarding those ideas.	Socialists and capitalist states cannot cooperate. Lenin and Stalin believed that war between socialist and capitalist countries was "inevitable"; after 1956, Soviet leaders argued that "peaceful co-existence" was possible.
Public opinion	Elitist; diplomacy should be conducted in secrecy by professional diplomats and politicians who, only in those conditions, can discuss differences freely and make deals to minimize conflict. Democracy is not a virtue in carrying out foreign affairs; public opinion is ill-informed, fickle, and short-sighted.	Favor public diplomacy ("open covenants openly arrived at" in Woodrow Wilson's words) and applaud public opinion as an obstacle to war.	Public opinion crucial in forming intersubjective consensus regarding norms and ideas, creating a collective identity, and formulating interests.	Public opinion reflects class perceptions and interests; it will mirror the dominant economic class in society.
National interest	Leaders serve the interests of their state by maintaining and improving its security rather than serving the interests of individuals or some vague global interests. Focus is mainly on a few states, the great powers. International institutions are suspect as they may pursue interests other than those of their state or attempt to wrest authority from states.	States exist to serve the interests of individuals. States should be limited in their ability to interfere in the lives of people. Free trade and human rights are key regardless of state interests.	The national interest is based on national identity; it is "what states make of it."	States serve the interests of the dominant economic class in society and define the national interest accordingly. Bourgeois states define the national interest in terms of economic imperialism and dominance over the "periphery" of poor states.
International institutions and organizations	States must be independent, autonomous, and free to act without limits on sovereignty. United Nations, international treaties, or other entanglements may limit such autonomy.	Support international organizations and institutions like the UN and the World Trade Organization (WTO) as encouraging peace and providing ways to overcome collective dilemmas.	Indeterminate as it depends upon dominant ideas and identities.	Support transnational institutions created by socialist societies.

Table 1.2 (continued)

	Realists	Liberals	Constructivists	Marxists
Society	Tend to ignore the role of *society* as opposed to government and its bureaucracies and see the relationship as one in which government operates in foreign affairs with little interference from social groups.	Focus on society and the relations among people rather than on state bureaucracies. Emphasis on the interdependence of actors and insistence that states cooperate to overcome global dilemmas like environmental pollution.	Intense focus on society as the source of ideas and identities created by interactions among individuals and/or social groups.	Focus on society, notably relations among classes – especially workers and capitalists – rather than on government.
Relative versus absolute gain	Actors do and should seek *relative* rather than *absolute* gain. *Some* states always profit more than others. Moreover, states that do not seek relative gains risk allowing others to gain resources that may provide them with a strategic advantage at some point in the future.	There are areas in political life, like trade, in which all participants can profit or all can lose *(variable-sum games)* and that there are few areas of political life in which the gain made by one actor is equivalent to the loss by another *(zero-sum game)*. Actors are more concerned about their *absolute gains* than about *relative gains.*	Indeterminate.	Focus on relative gains of socialists compared to capitalists.
Security	Military and economic security as the principal issues of global politics; support for large defense budgets and opposition to free trade that, they fear, will make countries less independent.	Human security consists of far more than military security. It includes protection from ill-treatment, starvation, homelessness, disease, poverty, and other conditions that may endanger or threaten the lives and well-being of citizens.	Indeterminate.	Human security consists of far more than military security. It involves economic equality and the fulfillment of basic material needs.

has helped us look at global politics from a variety of perspectives. Each argument points to different factors that we might study. But, surely, you may say, since the same facts, theories, and even levels of analysis are available to everyone, why is there so much disagreement about events in global politics? This is the question we turn to now.

Many theories, many meanings

People commonly differ in their interpretations of events in global politics. Sometimes, it even seems as though people are looking at entirely different worlds when they discuss the same events. Why is this so? First, different theories and frameworks point to different factors as the most important and, necessarily, ignore factors that others might regard as essential. Realists, for example, tend to focus on power; Marxists emphasize class and economic conditions; liberals pay attention to normative factors and institutions. It is as though different photographers were moving their cameras, and zooming in on whatever each regards to be the most important features in a scene. Or, like great impressionist painters such as Claude Monet and Auguste Renoir, each paints a world that only he can see.

Another set of reasons why people view the same events through different lenses has to do with differences in background, wealth, education, culture, age, and personal experience. Since individuals interpret what they see in terms of its impact on them, the meaning they assign to political events or trends will inevitably be unique to their circumstances. Whether or not people are Muslim affects how they interpret events in the Middle East and in other trouble spots such as Chechnya, Afghanistan, Kashmir, Indonesia, and Nigeria, where fellow Muslims are involved. Whether people are poor or rich or black or white also shapes the meaning they attach to events as well as their political preferences.

Regardless of theoretical orientation, age also affects one's view of events, as each generation draws analogies from their youth in interpreting the present. Elderly survivors of World War II may interpret America's invasion of Iraq in 2003 or North Korea's development of nuclear weapons quite differently from those who grew up during the Vietnam War of the 1960s and 1970s. The former may recall how the appeasement of Hitler seemed merely to whet his aggressive appetite and, thus, may conclude that the United States had to get rid of Saddam Hussein because he, too, was an aggressive dictator. Similarly, the older generation might believe that the US should take tough measures to force North Korea's paranoid dictator, Kim Jong Il (1942–), to end his country's nuclear program. In contrast, those whose political views formed during the Vietnam War may recall that US military forces became entrapped in Vietnam with no clear exit strategy and ultimately had to pull out without achieving victory. As a consequence, they may believe that the US should not have invaded Iraq but should have continued to use diplomatic and economic pressure to deal with the threat posed by Saddam Hussein. They might also emphasize a non-military solution to North Korean nuclear proliferation. Of course, not all people from the same generation will agree, as their views are also shaped by other factors listed above. However, the general principle here is that members of the same generation share the same formative events which then, to some degree, shape their views of later events.

The result of all these differences is that we live in a world of many stories, each told by people with different perspectives, both theoretical and personal. None of these stories is completely true, but most contain some elements of truth. At the same time, very few of these stories are completely wrong. As students, the more you familiarize yourselves with these different stories and see the world through the eyes of others, the more you will understand global politics. However, doing so requires great tolerance of others who hold views different from your own.

As the preceding suggests, theorists find little to agree on in global politics. They disagree on the relevant actors and issues, the dominant patterns in global politics, and even the best way to conduct research. This book tries to present a variety of positions on major theoretical and substantive issues and looks at key questions from various points of view. No single perspective tells all; all perspectives have something to contribute. Indeed, you should leave this chapter with a better understanding of the range of perspectives on global politics and why they exist. You do not have to agree with every perspective, or even any single perspective. However, you should be able to use the language and tools of the discipline to explain different perspectives and to formulate and articulate your own view of the world.

Conclusion

This chapter has examined why it is beneficial to examine global politics from different perspectives or levels of analysis (individual, state, and global system) and how each perspective enables the observer to see different aspects of events. Such different perspectives help us make sense of the world around us, that is, develop theories that describe, predict, and explain what is happening. Empirical theory, as we have seen, involves simplifying reality and identifying patterns of behavior by focusing on what matters most. Normative theory helps us distinguish what is ethical from what is not.

We reviewed several "great debates" over theory and method and examined several competing bodies of theory – realism/neorealism, liberalism/neoliberalism, constructivism, and Marxism. Each has different assumptions, and each contributes something to our understanding of global politics. In later chapters we will be applying both levels of analysis and the several theories we have reviewed in examining global issues.

In the next chapter, we will review the way in which the territorial state and the state system evolved in Europe. We will also examine the evolution of two other, quite different political systems that featured political communities that were not territorial states, that collided with Europe's states, and that continue to have an impact on the way Asians and Muslims look at global politics.

Student activities

Discussion and essay questions

Comprehension questions

1 What is the significance of change in global politics? Of continuity? Provide examples of each.
2 What are levels of analysis? How do different levels lend different insights into global events?
3 What is theory, and why is it important?
4 What are the key types of theory that help us understand global politics? How do they differ?

Analysis questions

5 In what ways have global politics changed in your lifetime? In what parts of the world have these changes occurred? Have these changes been a source of fear? Why or why not?
6 Is the state in decline in contemporary global politics? Why or why not?
7 What is the difference between empirical and normative theory? Provide examples of empirical and normative statements.
8 Write a dialogue between two people, one of whom approved of America's invasion of Iraq in 2003 and the other of whom opposed it. Explain which theoretical approach is most consistent with each position and why.
9 Compare realism, liberalism, constructivism, and Marxism. Which do you think holds more promise as a general explanation of contemporary global politics and why?

Map analysis

Take this opportunity to familiarize yourself with a world political map. Begin by dividing the map into geopolitical regions: North America;

South America; Europe; Central Asia; South, Southeast Asia, and the Pacific; and Africa. Which states are the largest? Which states do you think are the most influential? Select one of these states and research its role in the region. Were your expectations confirmed? Why or why not?

Cultural materials

Films provide many insights into change and continuity in seminal events in global politics. The critically acclaimed Chinese film *To Live* (1994) follows one family through China's tumultuous history between the late 1940s and the early 1970s. *Vukovar* (1994, Serbia-Croatia/Italy) tells the story of two newlyweds, one Serb and the other Croat, who are torn apart when the Bosnian civil war (1992–95) engulfs the town after which the film was named. On a much lighter note, the German film *Goodbye Lenin!* (2003) recounts the escapades of a young man who tries to hide the fall of communism from his mother – one of the few East Germans who still believes in the virtues of Communism – after she awakens from a coma. What contemporary films provide insight into ongoing change in global politics?

Science fiction offers an excellent means for assessing alternative world futures.[48] George Orwell's *1984* and Orson Scott Card's Ender Series provide two very different examples. Orwell's *1984*, written during the Cold War in 1949, portrays a totalitarian future in which the world is divided into three warring super-states. The government of one, Oceana, uses foreign war to prevent domestic revolt. Card's *Ender's Game* depicts a 100-years war in which insectoid aliens try to wipe out human life. Earth's government prepares for its defense by breeding child geniuses and training them as soldiers.

Many films and television series also contain parallels to global politics. The *Star Trek* franchise, for example, has created a future in which a twenty-first century nuclear war gives rise to a world government that eradicates poverty and disease and pursues space exploration. As founders of the United Federation of Planets, an entity akin to the United Nations, humans advocate peace and cooperation in interplanetary relations despite continuing conflict with other species such as Romulans, Cardassians, and Borg.

Read one of the books or view one of the television shows mentioned above and answer the following questions. How is the world portrayed *empirically* differently from our own? How is it *normatively* different? What assumptions about global/interplanetary politics drive the characters? What messages do you think the author is trying to communicate about our world?

Further reading

Bull, Hedley, *The Anarchical Society: A Study of Order in World Politics* (New York: Columbia University Press, 1977). Classic treatment of the global system as an international society in which interstate relations are regulated by international law, balance of power, and the use of force.

Carr, E. H., *The Twenty Years' Crisis, 1919–1939* (New York: Harper & Row, 1964). Classic analysis of pre-World War II utopians and realists.

Doyle, Michael W., *Ways of War and Peace* (New York: Norton, 1997). Detailed analysis of three intellectual traditions: realism, liberalism, and socialism.

Keohane, Robert O., *Power and Governance in a Partially Globalized World* (New York: Routledge, 2002). Collection of essays by the leading scholar of neoliberal institutionalism.

Keohane, Robert O. and Joseph S. Nye, Jr., *Power and Interdependence: World Politics in Transition*, 2nd ed. (Glenview, Il: Scott, Foresman/Little Brown, 1989). An alternative to realism that examines the relationship between politics and economics.

Morgenthau, Hans J., *Politics Among Nations: The Struggle for Power and Peace*, 7th ed., rev. by Kenneth W. Thompson and W. David Clinton (New York: McGraw-Hill, 2006). Updated edition of a realist classic that examines how nations define their interests in terms of power.

Waltz, Kenneth N., *Man, the State and War* (New York: Columbia University Press, 1959). Classic examination of the causes of war from three levels of analysis.

Waltz, Kenneth N., *Theory of International Politics* (New York: McGraw-Hill, 1979). Seminal work of the neorealist approach.

Wendt, Alexander, *Social Theory of International Politics* (Cambridge: Cambridge University Press, 1999). A constructivist critique of realism.

Part I
The Past as Prologue to the Present

2 The evolution of the interstate system and alternative political systems

Following the American Revolution, the Thirteen Colonies were loosely bound by the Articles of Confederation (1781) under which each "retains its sovereignty, freedom, and independence," established "a firm league of friendship with each other, for their common defense, the security of their liberties, and their mutual and general welfare." In addition, taxes "shall be laid and levied by the authority and direction of the legislatures of the several States."[1] Under these circumstances, the former colonies were prey to disunion and foreign dangers, and were hobbled by an inability to take united and decisive action. As a result, the Constitutional Convention convened on May 25, 1787 at the State House (now Independence Hall) in Philadelphia where it proceeded to ignore the requirement for unanimity in amending the Articles of Confederation and instead drafted a constitution, filled with compromises, over which later generations argued and fought, that established the sovereign state of the United States. As befit the representative of a sovereign state, the new government, like older European governments, was given **authority** to establish tariffs, levy taxes, borrow and coin money, raise an army and navy, and conduct foreign affairs with other sovereign states. "A firm Union," wrote Alexander Hamilton in Federalist Paper No. 9, "will be of the utmost moment to the peace and liberty of the States, as a barrier against domestic faction and insurrection."[2]

authority the idea of legitimate power or the right to exercise influence over others.

The United States was created relatively late in the evolution of the interstate system that has dominated global politics for over three centuries. That system, consisting of territorial states with fixed boundaries governed by central governments, was invented in Europe and spread around the globe by Europeans as they explored and conquered much of the rest of the world. Prior to the invention of the territorial state,

Figure 2.1   The signing of the Constitution of the United States in 1787 by Howard Chandler Christy, 1940
Christy, Howard Chandler (1873–1952), 1940 © Hall of Representatives, Washington DC, USA/The Bridgeman Art Library

empire a political unit having an extensive territory or comprising a number of territories or nations and ruled by a single supreme authority.

tribe a sociopolitical community consisting of a number of families, clans, or other groups who share a common ancestry.

nationalism the belief that a nation should be recognized as such, should enjoy equal rights with other nations, and should have political autonomy or independence.

global politics had been dominated by a wide variety of political forms such as **empires, tribes,** and cities. And, as we shall see in subsequent chapters, the dominance of territorial states is eroding and, although states remain the most important actors in global politics, they are beginning to share pride of place with other actors such as globe-girdling corporations, ethnic and religious communities, and nongovernmental organizations.

This chapter tells the story of how states first emerged in Europe and formed an interstate system that came to dominate global affairs. It describes the birth and evolution of the territorial state, and discusses how these political leviathans were transformed from the personal property of kings into communities owned by their citizens. It describes the rise of **nationalism,** especially during and after the French Revolution, and how state and nation became linked in communities that attracted the passions and highest loyalties of citizens who were willing to die in their name.

After describing the emergence and evolution of the state in Europe, we examine the evolution of two international systems that did *not* feature territorial states – imperial China and medieval Islam. Long before the territorial state emerged in Europe, China developed an imperial polity that was significantly different than the Western state. This polity, anchored in culture and language, provided the Han Chinese with a unifying identity even during eras in which they were divided into separate political communities governed by warlords who were constantly at one another's throats. Indeed, China is home to the oldest continuous historical tradition and one of the world's richest civilizations. Chinese ideas about global politics took their own shape, influenced greatly by Confucianism and differing from Western ideas as these evolved in Europe. This divergence continues to contribute to misunderstanding between the West and China even today as China becomes one of the world's great powers and is viewed by some Americans as a potential global rival.

Still another political form combining tribal traditions and religious convictions was born in Arabia. Like a whirlwind, Islam, lacking any concept of a territorial community with limited boundaries, swept out of the desert and overran the Byzantine and Persian empires. Thereafter, an Islamic empire, known as the Caliphate, built one of history's most sophisticated civilizations. In many ways, the Caliphate was analogous to the Catholic Church in Europe, especially during the Middle Ages. Like Islam, Europe was governed by a supranational **theocracy**, and the struggle of secular princes to liberate themselves from Roman tutelage was long and often bloody.

theocracy a system of government by religious leaders and based on religious dogma.

For militant Muslims, there is no place in Islam for notions of sovereign equality, nonintervention, or a society of states with exclusive jurisdictions.[3] As Islam originally evolved, government was subordinate to religion, and there were no acceptable limits to the expansion of the Islamic "community." We shall examine how these two traditions – one based on the territorial state and the other on a community of believers – collided and, in later chapters, how these colliding visions have re-emerged in contemporary global politics with the militant followers of Osama bin Laden seeking to restore the ancient Caliphate.

Indeed, just as Islam was at the outset hostile to the idea of territorial limitations, today, Islamic militants challenge not just the West but the supremacy of territorial states in general, including states' exclusive sovereign right to use force legitimately. It was Al Qaeda's rejection of and contempt for the basic norms on which **international politics** – or interstate relations – is based that explains the willingness of most states to align themselves against the threat of non-territorial terrorists. Thus, former US Secretary of State George P. Shultz, recognizing that "the state system has been eroding," defined the challenge posed by Al Qaeda as that of "an extensive, internationally connected ideological movement

international politics political interaction among sovereign states.

dedicated to the destruction of our international system of cooperation and progress." According to Shultz, the world's response must be to "shore up the state system. The world has worked for three centuries with the sovereign state as the basic operating entity, presumably accountable to its citizens and responsible for their well-being."[4]

The sovereign state, then, is an invention that only arrived relatively recently on the historical stage. Its capacity to mobilize resources and populations enabled Europeans to spread their institutions across the globe and allowed the state to play a dominant role in global politics for three centuries. However, as we shall see in chapter 15, human identities with and loyalties to a wide variety of other communities have always existed and are again rivaling those associated with the nation-state.

sovereignty the legal basis of the interstate system by which states are the supreme authorities within their boundaries and are legal equals of one another.

Realists and neorealists have been slow to grasp the changing role of nation-states in global politics. Little has changed, they argue, because there have always existed actors other than states and the principle of state **sovereignty** has always been honored in the breach. For this reason, political scientist Stephen Krasner refers to sovereignty as "organized hypocrisy."[5]

global governance the existence of order and authoritative decision-making in the absence of formal government.

Liberals, many of whom see the state as an obstacle to peace and favor **global governance**, or even global government, sometimes overstate the degree to which the state is in decline. They regard states as obstacles to human rights and free trade. Constructivists look for evolutionary change in the organization of global politics based on gradual shifts in people's norms away from the narrow nationalism of the past toward greater concern with **transnational** issues that threaten human well-being everywhere.

transnational relations direct interactions or transactions involving nongovernmental actors or social group.

All three groups of theorists are partly correct. States, as realists recognize, never were the only players in global politics, and major states, at least, remain key players today. Still, as liberals observe, people are interacting and organizing across state boundaries and are forming complex webs of cross-border alliances (international regimes), and there has been a genuine proliferation of international and nongovernmental groups (ranging from terrorists to giant corporations and banks) that are having ever greater impact on states and on global outcomes. Indeed, "global cities" have emerged so that, as sociologist Saskia Sassen argues, concentrations of capital and skills in cities like New York, Tokyo, and London make them global centers linked to one another through a financial "chain of production" yet largely disconnected from their own hinterlands.[6] Finally, constructivists correctly recognize that more and more people are demanding creative solutions to problems that have defied states' efforts, and they are contemplating new forms of transnational collaboration that break out of the narrow confines of state sovereignty.

Let us examine the emergence of the territorial state in Europe. Key steps in this process took place in Europe's Middle Ages (*c.*350–1450), Italy's city-states after about 1300, the large monarchical states of eighteenth-century Western Europe, and the nation-states of Europe after the French Revolution.

The emergence of the European interstate system

The state as we know it features a clearly defined territory and population and exclusive authority over that territory and population. However, for a state to come into existence, it must be "recognized" by other states as enjoying authority, and such recognition is often based on political considerations. Thus, the State of Israel which was proclaimed at midnight on May 14, 1948 might well not have survived had it not been recognized on that same day by the United States, in the person of President Harry S Truman. Taking their lead from Truman's action, other states followed suit in recognizing the legal independence of the new Jewish state.

The territorial state itself was a novel form of political community when it emerged in Europe. Prior to the state's appearance, Europe was dominated by the papacy, then a secular as well as religious power, city-states, and a large Germanic empire called the Holy Roman Empire. The pope and his entourage resembled a medieval king, with a court. He ruled the Papal State, had vassals who owed him allegiance and paid tribute, and made war. For its part, the Holy Roman Empire had originally been part of the empire of the Franks (a Germanic tribe) under Charlemagne (742–814). In 800, Charlemagne had received from the pope the title of Emperor (*Imperator Augustus*). In 962 Otto the Great reclaimed the imperial title, an event marking the establishment of the Holy Roman Empire. The empire did not consist of territorial states. Instead, it was comprised of a bewildering variety of small political entities called imperial counties, free lordships, ecclesiastical territories, free imperial cities, free imperial villages, and principalities that were themselves subdivided into electorates, duchies, palatine counties, margraviats, landgraviats, and princely counties. As states emerged, this welter of actors gradually disappeared.

Because of the importance of territory and sovereignty to the definition of the state, political scientists refer to the modern state as the "sovereign" or "territorial state." This terminology implicitly suggests that states could have taken on some other form in their evolution. Indeed, the modern state is a product of a particular historical experience. Partly because the state was a European invention, the last three centuries can be thought of as the European epoch of global politics. Later, we shall see how non-European political forms, customs, and political ideas are challenging the European epoch and how regions such as Asia and the Middle East are moving to the forefront of global politics. However, the central importance of the state in global politics is such that we first examine the state in its original European context.

How did the sovereign state emerge, and how has it evolved? What has been its role in global politics? To answer these questions, we go back in time. Scholars generally begin this story with Europe's medieval world. We divide the subsequent history into four broad stages that focus on Europe's Middle Ages, Italy's city-states, Europe's religious wars, and the French Revolution.

The transition from Europe's Middle Ages

The territorial state evolved out of Europe's Middle Ages as European princes sought independence from the two great institutions that saw themselves as heirs to the ancient Roman Empire, the papacy and the Holy Roman Empire. Map 2.1 shows their boundaries as well as those of subordinate political entities in Europe around 1100. As the two struggled for political supremacy, local princes played each against the other, and, as both grew weaker, princes gained ever more autonomy. As this process quickened, Europe's medieval **feudal system** began to crumble.

The struggle between the papacy and empire climaxed in the late eleventh and early twelfth centuries with a conflict over the investiture (appointment) of high church officials. These officials enjoyed both secular and religious authority and whoever controlled their appointment enjoyed significant political authority. The dispute, which pitted Pope Gregory VII (1020–85) against Emperor Henry IV (1050–1106), came down to the question of who should rule the church. In the end, the papal position triumphed, but both church and empire were sorely weakened.

Europe's feudal system was based on a hierarchy of relationships with the pope and the Holy Roman emperor at the top, nobles below them, and peasants, who were legally bound to the land, at the bottom. Each class owed economic and military obligations to those above it, in return for which they were supposed to receive military protection. The system was one of local economies, with production and commerce limited to local areas. During much of the Middle Ages, lords' manors and

feudal system the legal, political, and social system of medieval Europe, in which vassals held land from lords in exchange for military service.

Map 2.1 Europe, 1100

Church-run abbeys were the centers of regional economic and cultural activities, and those at higher levels of the hierarchy shared ownership of property. However distinct were the regions of Europe, inhabitants were bound by an overarching common identity as Christians.

Theory in the real world

Although in theory the feudal system was hierarchical, with a feudal superior, whether called a king, prince, duke, or count, as lord over his subordinates or *vassals*, in practice relationships were more complex. Vassals were supposed to provide service to the lord in return for military protection, but often failed to do so. In addition, one lord could have his own vassals, but also be vassal to another lord. Vassals could also pledge fealty to more than one lord.

War was in the hands of a class of warriors called knights, who owed military service to higher lords in return for local authority over peasants and their lands. Many controlled their local communities by means of a wooden or stone tower or castle that protected them from attack. Today, knights are recalled as heroic warriors, especially when defending the lords to whom they owed allegiance and to whom they rendered military service. They might also be viewed as criminals, but at the time, it was difficult to distinguish between common crime and legitimate war. Knights spent much of their time attacking one another, robbing peasants, and taxing merchants. Knightly violence was so endemic in Europe that it strangled trade, impoverished peasants, and weakened the kingdoms that knights were sworn to protect.

Europe's medieval system evolved slowly under the influence of social and economic change. In Flanders and northern Italy, self-governing towns emerged as urbanization quickened. With commerce, the need for money grew, and, despite the Church's prohibition of usury, banks began to appear. By the end of the thirteenth century, northern Italy, especially Florence, had become Europe's banking center and the Medici family its leading bankers (chapter 11, p. 502). Northern Europe saw the emergence of the Hanseatic League to foster trade (chapter 11, p. 502). Table 2.1 reveals how the European economy shifted from the Mediterranean region, northward between 1050 and 1500. In 1050, ten of Europe's largest cities were in Spain, led by Cordoba which was the capital of Islamic Spain, and only five were in Northern Europe. In contrast, by 1500, nine were in Northern Europe and ten were in Italy, reflecting both the commercial explosion that accompanied the Italian Renaissance and the shift in European political power from Spain to France.

Europe's economic growth was also fostered by technological change in the late Middle Ages. Europeans' took advantage of gunpowder which was invented in China during the ninth century, and European trade and naval power were aided by the astrolabe that had entered Europe from Islamic Spain in the early twelfth century, and the compass which apparently was first used in China around 1100. These inventions, as well as improvements in ships and clocks that aided navigation, were instrumental in the later European voyages of discovery and colonization. The combination of economic and technological progress was vital in transforming Europe from a backwater into the center of global political and military power.[7]

The emergence of a new class of urban merchants and long-distance traders in southern England, Holland, Belgium, and Italy increased demands for security and for freedom from the exactions of local knights. For their part, kings and princes sought to accumulate wealth in order

Table 2.1 The 20 largest cities in Europe, 1050 and 1500

1050		1500	
Cordoba	450,000	Paris	225,000
Palermo	350,000	Naples	125,000
Seville	90,000	Milan	100,000
Salerno	50,000	Venice	100,000
Venice	45,000	Granada	70,000
Regensberg	40,000	Prague	70,000
Toledo	37,000	Lisbon	65,000
Rome	35,000	Tours	60,000
Barbastro	35,000	Genoa	58,000
Cartagena	33,000	Ghent	55,000
Naples	30,000	Florence	55,000
Mainz	30,000	Palermo	55,000
Merida	30,000	Rome	55,000
Almeria	27,000	Bordeaux	50,000
Granada	26,000	Lyons	50,000
Speyer	25,000	Orleans	50,000
Palma	25,000	London	50,000
Laon	25,000	Bologna	50,000
London	25,000	Verona	50,000

to create armies that could resist the papacy and Holy Roman Empire and could tame local nobles, thereby permitting the formation of large territorial kingdoms. Thus, economic changes fostered the rise of a new commercial class that could provide kings with the fiscal means to create their own armies. Such armies provided kings with the means to assert their political independence of both the papacy and the Holy Roman Empire. And, as we shall see in the next section, Italy was the harbinger of the emerging era of independent and ferociously competitive actors.

The European state had serious rivals, and its triumph was gradual and tentative. As sociologist Charles Tilly argues, "as seen from 1600 or so, the development of the state was very contingent; many aspiring states crumpled and fell along the way."[8] A few princes wrested exclusive control of dynastic domains, which they then expanded at the expense of neighbors, and in doing so seduced the loyalties of and joined forces with an emerging urban commercial class. People did not immediately surrender their identities as villagers, Christians, or subjects of the Holy Roman Empire, but those identities became less central to their lives as the state increased its extractive and regulatory capacities.

In the end, territorial states, as political scientist Hendrik Spruyt argues, "arose because of a particular conjuncture of social and political interests in Europe"[9] during and after the Middle Ages and weathered the challenge of other political forms such as the papacy, the Holy Roman Empire, and Italian city-states – because its territorial logic mobilized societies more effectively, constructed professional bureaucracies, and organized relations among units more efficiently than did its rivals.[10] Unlike medieval political and economic activities, which were essentially local, the new territorial states extended their reach by allying with newly prosperous merchants and commercial interests and pacifying the king's adversaries and competitors.

Machiavelli's world: Italy's city-states

city-state the independent political entity consisting of a city and its outskirts that dominated global politics in ancient Greece and Renaissance Italy.

Small **city-states**, not unlike those of ancient Greece, first appeared in Italy in the tenth century, and it was in these cities that Europe's Renaissance, or rebirth, emerged between the fourteenth to the sixteenth centuries. Each city-state (see Map 2.2) had its own ruler, for example, the pope in Rome and the doge in Venice, and unceasing rivalry characterized the relations among these rulers. In the resulting condition of constant insecurity, there emerged in Florence a brilliant political philosopher and statesman, Niccolò Machiavelli (1469–1527). Machiavelli, whose most famous book was *The Prince*, introduced the idea that in order to ensure the survival of the state and its citizens, rulers must follow a political morality different than that of private persons. For example, acts that would be considered generous when undertaken by private citizens would be a wasteful expenditure of resources when undertaken by rulers. Where individuals would be seen as heroic in risking their lives to save another, Machiavelli's prince would be regarded as endangering the very survival of those he was supposed to protect. Interests rather than conventional morality were, for Machiavelli, at the heart of statecraft. These cynical but prudent ideas became very popular among statesmen in following centuries. Machiavelli remains as relevant today as he was in fifteenth-century Europe because realists argue that it remains impossible for actors to trust one another in global politics, and most leaders still place personal and national interests above the interests of the global community as a whole.

However, city-states ultimately lost out to larger, territorial states as the dominant form of political organization. Atlantic and Baltic trade routes enriched larger states to the north of Italy: Portugal, France, England, and the Netherlands. These used wealth to accumulate military power, which they then used to amass more wealth. Small city-states ruled by families of political upstarts and newly enriched traders simply could not compete militarily or economically with their larger rivals. Indeed, interstate politics in Renaissance Italy stood somewhere between what we

Map 2.2 Italy, 1494

think of as gangster politics and the politics of large territorial states. The dramatic shift in power northward to states like France and Spain became abundantly clear when a French army under King Charles VIII (1470–98) descended on Italy in 1494. In the words of contemporary historian Francesco Guicciardini: "[H]is passage into Italy gave rise to changes in dominions, subversion of kingdoms, desolation of countries, destruction of cities and the cruelest massacres, but also new fashions, new customs, new and bloody ways of waging warfare, and diseases which had been unknown up to that time."[11]

On the road to sovereignty

The evolution of the state accelerated during Europe's wars of religion, which took place following the Protestant Reformation and the Catholic Counter Reformation of the sixteenth and seventeenth centuries. The Peace of Augsburg (1555) was the first legal effort to establish a peaceful coexistence between Catholics and Protestants (in this case, Lutherans) (see Key document: Peace of Augsburg). The document granted princes new powers under the principle of *cuius regio, eius religio* ("he who governs the territory decides its religion"). Thus, the prince alone, as a sovereign, could determine his subjects' religion. This was a major step toward the independence of such principalities from the papacy and the Holy Roman Empire (both of which had demanded the continued dominance of Catholicism). The Peace of Augsburg did not end religious controversy, however, as Protestantism continued to spread, and the Catholic order of Jesuits tried to reconvert Lutherans to Catholicism.

Key document   Peace of Augsburg, Article 15

Article 15. In order to bring peace to the Holy Roman Empire of the Germanic Nation between the Roman Imperial Majesty and the Electors, Princes and Estates, let neither his Imperial Majesty nor the Electors, Princes, etc., do any violence or harm to any estate of the empire on the account of the Augsburg Confession, but let them enjoy their religious belief, liturgy and ceremonies as well as their estates and other rights and privileges in peace; and complete religious peace shall be obtained only by Christian means of amity, or under threat of punishment of the Imperial ban.[12]

It was in this atmosphere, after the Peace of Augsburg, that the political theorists Jean Bodin (1530–96) and Thomas Hobbes contemplated the idea of sovereignty. For them, sovereignty was an aspiration rather than a description of the world they knew. Bodin, a lawyer, lived in sixteenth-century France during an era of religious war between Protestant Huguenots and Catholic loyalists, both supported by outside powers. The king, a member of the Valois dynasty, enjoyed little independent authority or power, a condition that Bodin thought had to be changed if France was to be united. In his *Six Books of the Republic* (1576), Bodin defined sovereignty as the "power to make the laws" and argued that a sovereign state should enjoy "supreme power over citizens and subjects unrestrained by laws."

Living in England a century after Bodin, Hobbes described an even more authoritarian solution to the problem of civil war, which in England pitted royalist supporters of the Stuart King Charles I (1600–49) against parliamentary supporters of Oliver Cromwell (1599–1658). In *The Leviathan* (1651), Hobbes argued that absolutist government, whether monarchical or not, was necessary to maintain peace and security in a world in which everyone was constantly at or on the verge of war with everyone else. In order to escape that natural state, Hobbes imagined that the people would sign a social contract with the sovereign, or ruler, in which they surrendered political authority to the sovereign in return for security.

A critical moment for the application of these ideas and the development of the sovereign state arrived with a series of conflicts that began in 1618 and lasted 30 years, thus earning the name Thirty Years' War. Its initial stage centered on religious animosity unleashed by the Protestant Reformation, but, as it continued, it pitted Sweden, France, and several German princes against the Habsburg rulers of Austria and the Holy Roman Empire. The war was fought mainly in the territories of the Holy Roman Empire (Germany, Austria, Hungary, Bohemia, and Belgium) and featured unrestrained violence and widespread atrocities against civilians (see the Key document: The destruction of Magdeburg). This brutal war played an important role in the development of international law *between* rather than *above* states, which was a giant step toward recognizing the independence and equality of these territorial entities.

Key document   The destruction of Magdeburg

During the Thirty Years' War, there were few restraints in combatants' behavior, and civilians were the main victims of soldiers' brutality, as in the destruction by imperial troops of the fortified German city of Magdeburg on May 20, 1631, described in the following eyewitness account by the town's mayor, Otto von Guericke:

So then General Pappenheim collected a number of his people on the ramparts by the New Town, and brought them from there into the streets of the city. Von Falckenberg was shot, and fires were kindled in different quarters; then indeed it was all over with the city. . . . Nevertheless some of the soldiers and citizens did try to make a stand here and there, but the imperial troops kept bringing on more and more forces – cavalry, too – to help them, and finally they got the Krockenthor open and let in the whole imperial army and the forces of the Catholic League – Hungarians, Croats, Poles, Walloons, Italians, Spaniards, French, North and South Germans.

Thus it came about that the city and all its inhabitants fell into the hands of the enemy. . . . Then was there naught but beating and burning, plundering, torture, and murder. . . . When a marauding party entered a house, if its master had anything to give he might thereby purchase respite and protection for himself and his family till the next man, who also wanted something, should come along. It was only when everything had been brought forth and there was nothing left to give that the real trouble commenced. Then, what with blows and threats of shooting, stabbing, and hanging, the poor people were so terrified that if they had had anything left they would have brought it forth if it had been buried in the earth or hidden away in a thousand castles. In this frenzied rage, the great and splendid city that had stood like a fair princess in the land was now, in its hour of direst need and unutterable distress and woe, given over to the flames, and thousands of innocent men, women, and children, in the midst of a horrible din of heartrending shrieks and cries, were tortured and put to death in so cruel and shameful a manner that no words would suffice to describe, nor no tears to bewail it. . . .

Thus in a single day this noble and famous city, the pride of the whole country, went up in fire and smoke; and the remnant of its citizens, with their wives and children, were taken prisoners and driven away by the enemy with a noise of weeping and wailing that could be heard from afar, while the cinders and ashes from the town were carried by the wind to Wanzleben, Egeln, and still more distant places.[13]

During the Thirty Years' War, Protestant rulers within the Holy Roman Empire and beyond (France, Sweden, Denmark, England, and Holland) battled the Holy Roman Emperor and the ruling Hapsburg family, the Catholic princes of Germany, and in the end, Spain. The religious character of the war faded after 1635, and the war ended with the Peace of Westphalia in 1648. The peace treaty recognized that a united Catholic empire was an unrealizable dream and that the two religions had to coexist (see Map 2.3). German lands lay in ruins, and the population of the Holy Roman Empire had declined from about 21 million to 16 million during the war. Thus, the great princes of the time recognized that limits had to be placed on war, or they and their countries would become victims of mindless slaughter and destruction.

Their attempt to remedy this situation was embodied in a treaty between the Holy Roman Emperor and the King of France and their respective allies, a rambling document consisting of 128 articles of which only two – Articles 64 and 65 – introduced the contours of state sovereignty. By its terms, Calvinism, a Protestant denomination, was officially recognized, and the Peace of Augsburg, which the warring parties had failed to observe, was restored. The Peace of Westphalia recognized the authority of the German princes in the Holy Roman Empire.[14] Each gained the right to govern his own territory and make independent decisions about war and peace. In this way, Europe's states acquired sovereignty. A hierarchy of authority within the state, in which government acts as the authoritative surrogate for subjects or citizens, and exclusive control of territory became the defining attributes of the state after Westphalia.

According to Article 1 of the 1933 Montevideo Convention, a state "as a person of international law should possess the following qualifications: (a) a permanent population; (b) a defined territory; (c) government; and

Map 2.3 Central Europe, 1648

(d) capacity to enter into relations with the other states."[15] Sovereignty involves two principal and related conditions: a state's authority over everything within its territorial borders (an internal hierarchy of authority) and the legal equality of states regardless of size or power (the absence of hierarchy). The first of these, the **internal face of sovereignty**, means that no legal superior exists above states. The rulers of a sovereign state enjoy a monopoly of the means of coercion over citizens and are vested with

internal face of sovereignty
the complete legal authority that states enjoy over the subjects within their territorial boundaries.

external face of sovereignty
the legal equality of sovereign states.

power a psychological relationship between actors in which one influences another to behave differently than it would have if left to its own devices.

autonomy the capacity to behave independently.

dynastic sovereignty sovereignty that is vested in a monarch and the monarch's heirs.

sole authority to make, uphold, and interpret laws. The second condition, the **external face of sovereignty**, is derived logically from the first. Since each sovereign is the absolute authority within its boundaries, all sovereigns are *legally* equal and may not intervene in one another's domestic or internal affairs. Sovereignty confers various rights on states such as access to international courts, the right to defend their independence, and a degree of respect from other states that are not available to non-sovereign groups. But, at root, sovereignty, both internal and external, is a legal principle and should not be confused with **power** or **autonomy**.

From dynastic to popular sovereignty

Even after its establishment, the sovereign state continued to evolve (as it continues to do today). During the eighteenth century, **dynastic sovereignty** reigned. States were governed by conservative, absolutist monarchs who had more in common with one another than with their subjects and who sought to increase their personal power and assure the future of their dynasties. There was no conception of a national interest other than the interest of kings and their heirs.

The model state of the age was France under the "Sun King," Louis XIV (1638–1715). Aided by the great cleric-statesmen, Cardinals Richelieu (1585–1642) and Mazarin (1602–61), the king ensured the external security of his realm with a large professional army, the administrative and technical skills of a prosperous middle class, and a series of fortifications along France's frontiers. France was a great power in an age when that label meant a state that could not be conquered even by a combination of other major states and when states appointed ambassadors (as opposed to lesser diplomats) only at the courts of the great powers.[16] Louis reinforced the internal side of French sovereignty by centralizing authority at his court in Versailles and forcing French nobles to reside there. In this and other ways, the king made the formerly rebellious nobility dependent on him and his corps of administrators. The king kept his realm together by recruiting to government service members of France's middle class, who depended on and were loyal to the monarch. The web of administrators successfully tamed independent nobles, guilds, and recalcitrant cities throughout France.

In contrast to the Thirty Years' War, eighteenth-century wars were relatively mild affairs in terms of objectives though not in terms of the intensity of combat. Kings fought for limited aims, especially of a territorial nature, but without the intense passion that had accompanied the earlier religious wars. They sought to increase their wealth and stature but wanted to avoid any threat to their thrones, and they recognized that they had a common interest in respecting the principle of sovereignty. Europe was managed by a small group of great powers – England, France, Russia, Prussia, and Austria – sufficiently equal in power, so that none alone could dominate the others. Although they were highly competitive, all were governed by dynastic monarchs who respected one another's legitimacy. None was powerful enough to dominate the rest, and each respected the others' right to survive. Monarchs and noble families were bound together by blood and marriage; a common language (French); common norms, manners, and customs; and, most important, common fear of the disastrous consequences that unlimited war threatened for themselves, their dynasties, and their states. The way wars were waged reflected these principles.

Eighteenth-century tactics called for long lines of soldiers armed with inaccurate muskets and cannon to confront each other and keep shooting until one side fled or surrendered. Such tactics did not permit large-scale offensive movements and were designed to limit harm to civilians. Moreover, the logistics of this form of warfare limited movement, as baggage trains had to carry supplies for soldiers and fodder for the horses and mules necessary to move these supplies. Also, since taxes were low, revenue to fight wars was limited. An excellent description of warfare at the time was left by Prussia's Frederick the Great (1712–86). According to historian R. R. Palmer, for Frederick battle "was a methodical affair" in which "armies were arrayed according to pattern, almost as regularly as chessmen at the beginning of a game: on each wing cavalry, artillery fairly evenly distributed along the rear, infantry battalions drawn up in two parallel solid lines, one a few hundred yards behind the other, and each line, or at least the first, composed of three ranks, each rank firing at a single command while the other two reloaded." As a result, the wars of the age were wars of maneuver; "war became increasingly a war of position, the war of complex maneuver and subtle accumulation of small gains." After all, "Frederick was a dynast [hereditary monarch], not a revolutionary or an adventurer."[17]

The period is frequently cited as a model by realists because global politics was controlled by a small group of great powers, foreign affairs remained in the hands of professional diplomats, ideology was largely absent, and rulers regarded their domains as members of a European society of states. And the central and unifying norm of the epoch was the **balance of power**, an idea deeply rooted in the eighteenth-century mind and reflecting the principles of the science of mechanics that were in vogue. Some scholars, members of the "English School," also point to the period to criticize realism for its emphases on state egoism and constant conflict and its failure to recognize the existence of a "society of states."[18]

balance of power policy of states aimed to prevent any other state(s) from gaining a preponderance of power in relation to its rivals.

Balance of power, a basic element of realism, is found in many eras of global politics, including the Greek and Italian city-states, and ancient India. In eighteenth- and nineteenth-century Europe, balance-of-power thinking pervaded the politics of all the great powers. They believed that the only way to limit the power of aggressive states was to confront them with equal or greater power. This aim is reflected in a treaty between England and Spain that permitted the French king's grandson to become king of Spain but forbade the union of the two kingdoms. A union of France and Spain was seen as a "great danger which threatened the liberty and safety of all Europe," a danger which could be avoided "by an equal balance of power (which is the best and most solid foundation of a mutual friendship)."[19]

Realists believe that the balance of power was conducive to peace in the eighteenth century. However, they differ about what balance of power actually meant. Political scientist Ernst Haas catalogued eight meanings of the term: any distribution of power among states, an exact equilibrium of power, hegemony, a situation of stability (or peace), *realpolitik* (the use of power to accomplish one's objectives), a universal law or outcome, and a policy prescription.[20]

What is clear is that leaders of the time believed that, if the survival of any great power was threatened, others should join it in alliance and raise armies of sufficient size to frustrate the aggressor(s). Such alliances were temporary, based on expediency, and were expected to dissolve once they had achieved their objectives. A great power had no "permanent friends or enemies" and was expected to join former adversaries in new alliances if new threats to the status quo arose. No great power wished to destroy or permanently alienate an enemy, and all were usually willing to offer generous terms of settlement to bring wars to an end.

The balance was the keystone to a European society in which the boundaries among states were softened by the loyalties and identities of a ruling class. According to one observer, the balance was the product of the "common interest" of Europe's dynastic rulers in "the maintenance of order and the preservation of liberty,"[21] and Europe's statesmen came to see it as an essential aspect of Europe's laws and customs. French political philosopher Jean-Jacques Rousseau (1712–78) believed that the balance reflected a European civilization "united by an identity of religion, of moral standard, of international law."[22] Henry Lord Brougham (1778–1868), a nineteenth-century British political leader, compared the balance to a scientific discovery "as much unknown to Athens or Rome"[23] as the breakthroughs of Johannes Kepler (1571–1630) and his laws of planetary motion, or Sir Isaac Newton (1642–1727) and his law of universal gravitation.

The balance of power was evident in the dynastic wars of the period. Thus, during the War of the Spanish Succession (1701–14) caused by the effort of France's King Louis XIV to place his grandson on the Spanish throne, Austria, Britain, and the Netherlands joined together to thwart his ambitions. Some years later, in the War of the Austrian Succession (1740–48), England and Austria allied against Prussia and allies of Prussia's King Frederick the Great to reverse Frederick's seizure of Silesia following the death of Charles VI (1685–1740), Holy Roman Emperor and King of Austria. Although the war ended in a stalemate, Prussia retained Silesia, setting the stage for the Seven Years' War (1756–63) in which Austria, Sweden, France, Russia, and Saxony aligned themselves against Prussia and England. Only the sudden death of Russia's Empress Elizabeth (1709–62) saved Prussia. England, for its part, took advantage of the conflict to establish its supremacy in North America, where the war was called the French and Indian War.

Still, the balance of power had something odd about it. It featured respect for the sovereign independence and rights of great powers, but it had no such respect for smaller states, whose sovereignty was routinely violated. Poland, for example, one of the smaller states, was partitioned on three separate occasions (1772, 1793, and 1795) among Prussia, Russia, and Austria, three large states, as part of their effort to maintain their own security and assuage their pride.

Great Britain used the concept in a particularly subtle way. Britain, an island power with interest in acquiring lands outside Europe, was prepared to intervene on the continent when it thought the balance was in peril, as it did to oppose the ambitions of France's Louis XIV and Napoléon Bonaparte (1769–1821). British statesmen called their country a balancer, that is, a country that would join a war to prevent major shifts in the distribution of power. But British balancing was not limited to Europe. Thus, it was in the cause of the balance that British leaders influenced the United States to issue the Monroe Doctrine. The doctrine was announced by President James Monroe to Congress on December 2, 1822. It stated that European powers could not colonize the American continents or interfere in independent republics there. This policy reflected British and US concern about European meddling in the western hemisphere, especially any Spanish effort to regain control over former colonies in Latin America.

Monroe articulated this doctrine because he saw an opportunity for a distinctive US role in the Americas, but that role could only be enforced by a country with the power to do so, meaning Britain and its navy. However, Britain's true aim was not to assist the United States but to rein in France, which dominated Spain. British Foreign Secretary George

Canning (1770–1827) encouraged America's policy as a way to limit Spanish power and, by indirection, French efforts to expand. Declared Canning in 1826:

> But then, Sir, the balance of power! The entry of the French army into Spain disturbed that balance, and we ought to have gone to war to restore it! I have already said, that when the French army entered Spain, we might, if we chose, have resisted or resented that measure by war. But were there no other means than war for restoring the balance of power? . . . I resolved that if France had Spain it should not be Spain with the Indies. *I called the New World into existence to redress the balance of the old.*[24]

In other words, Canning's real goal was to keep France from upsetting the existing European balance.

Eventually, by the late nineteenth century, nationalism and democracy largely destroyed or rendered ineffective the personal and family bonds among aristocratic leaders and diplomats that maintained the commitment to balance and the flexibility vital for it to work. Some leaders and scholars still advocate the importance of maintaining a balance of power among states and have suggested, for example, that the combined opposition of France, Germany, and Russia to the 2003 Anglo-American invasion of Iraq represents a weak effort to balance power.[25] Although the concept of balance of power continues to influence realist theories, it has become less and less applicable to today's world for several reasons.

1 Balance-of-power theorists assume that there exists a state system[26] of equivalent units and not a system consisting of different kinds of actors such as states, terrorist groups, and corporations.

2 There has to be a relatively equal distribution of power among a sufficient number of major actors to permit any of them to be stopped. Currently, the world is dominated by one superpower, and it is difficult to imagine what coalition of adversaries could "balance" American military power.

3 It must be possible to estimate precisely the distribution of military power. In the eighteenth century, this was a relatively easy task that could be accomplished by counting population, amount of territory, and numbers of muskets and cannon. Today, such estimates are extremely difficult to make because of the various types of warfare that might be waged (conventional, nuclear, guerrilla, and terrorism among others) and because weapons are so different from one another. Questions such as how many tanks or planes are equivalent to one

nuclear weapon or one submarine are impossible to answer because each weapon has a different purpose.

4 Actors must be ideologically compatible in order to join each other in flexible alliances. During the era of dynastic war, as historian Edward Vose Gulick observes, "Europe was an in-group of states which excluded non-European countries and which displayed a high degree of homogeneity within itself."[27] Today, governments and people are divided by religion, economic beliefs, and other ideological factors.

5 For the balance to be maintained, diplomacy must be shielded from aroused publics and conducted by dispassionate professional diplomats who can negotiate with one another flexibly and make concessions when necessary. They understood how the balance worked, were alert to threats to it, and were willing to bargain with one another. Today's democratic leaders are under constant pressure from public opinion and are responsive to the most recent polls.

Thus, the utility of the balance of power declined as the idea of monarchical absolutism yielded to popular control of states. The idea that the state belonged to its people rather than to its ruler evolved slowly. Key steps in the process included England's Glorious Revolution of 1688 in which the Stuart King James II (1633–1701) was exiled, and the new king, William III (1650–1702), agreed to the Declaration of Rights which guaranteed constitutional government, and the American Revolution (1775–83). However, the most important single event in this process was the French Revolution (1789–99). The revolution was triggered by a combination of factors: French defeat in the Seven Years' War and the evident incompetence of the country's rulers; the example of the American Revolution in which Frenchmen like the Marquis de Lafayette (1757–1834) played a key role and brought home a belief in republican government; and the financial bankruptcy of the French monarchy. Before the revolution, sovereignty was embodied in the monarch, who justified his authority through a combination of religion and dynastic descent. After the revolution, authority had to be justified by the support of the people or the nation and became known as national or **popular sovereignty**.

Nation is an ambiguous concept that refers to a group of people united by ties such as shared history, religion, blood or kinship, language, and so forth; and nationalism refers to the passionate desire on the part of such people to defend and glorify their nation. However, a nation should *not* be confused with a state – a legal political entity, as described at the beginning of this section. In the case of eighteenth-century France, the people began to experience national feelings as though they were part of a

Did you know?

Eighteenth-century diplomats could be persuaded to see virtue in each other's positions when provided with a nice fat bribe. The French statesman, Charles Maurice de Talleyrand (1754–1838), reflected the ideals of his age. Talleyrand died the wealthiest man in Europe owing to the bribes he received but thought himself an honest man because he never accepted a sou unless he could keep his end of a bargain.

popular sovereignty
sovereignty invested in the entire people of a state.

great family whose ancestors could be traced back to ancient history. And, after the revolution erupted in 1789, "family" symbols of many kinds were adopted by "citizens" who had formerly been "subjects." A song, called *La marseillaise* in honor of troops from the city of Marseilles who had taken part in the revolution, was written by Claude Joseph Rouget de Lisle (1760–1836) and became the country's national anthem in 1792. Around the same time, the older flag, or *fleur de lis*, of the country's Bourbon dynasty was replaced by a modern French flag, or *tricoleur* (referring to the three colors of the French flag – red, white, and blue).

Even styles of dress and usage of words changed to reflect France's new nationalism. For example, during the revolution the term *sans-culottes* ("without knee breeches") was applied to laborers and other members of the lower classes who wore long trousers rather than the knee breeches worn by aristocrats. As for language, the French word for "state" was largely replaced by "fatherland" or "nation." The wedding of nation and state created a more powerful actor than had existed before because popular passions of the people were now placed at the service of the state's bureaucracies, including its military forces. Along with the emergence of the national sovereign state following the French Revolution came international or interstate politics as we have understood it for three centuries.

The French Revolution and the spread of nationalism changed the world forever. The revolution transformed the essential nature of states, and nationalism spread across Europe on the bayonets of Napoléon. As whole peoples became involved in war, and the capacity to wage war increased with industrialization, the size and intensity of wars grew dramatically.

The French Revolution infused greater passion into warfare as citizens fought for their country, and it brought an end to the mild political climate of the eighteenth century. The revolution and the execution of King Louis XVI (1754–93) and Queen Marie Antoinette (1755–93) marked the transition from dynastic to **national warfare**. The fact that the revolution had transferred sovereignty from the monarch to his subjects meant that they had a stake in their country's fate. One result was to inject warfare with new energy in which eager volunteers sought to defend *their* fatherland and export its ideals regardless of personal risk. The high morale in the French army contrasted with the tepid commitment of the soldiers in the armies of France's dynastic adversaries. Another result of this fervent nationalism was that it became costly for one country to occupy another, as local publics mobilized against occupying forces. In the long run, nationalism also became linked with ideologies such as fascism and liberalism. And, like nationalism after 1789, such

national wars wars fought with enthusiasm by citizens with a strong national attachment to their state.

"It's alright for you lot, you're
only aristos - I'm an accountant."

Figure 2.2 Heads up!

© Original artist,
www.cartoonstock.com

ideologies produced a greater willingness on the part of followers to fight
to the death, making it more difficult for diplomats to limit the extent or
purpose of wars. Rulers increasingly made decisions about foreign policy
to increase their popularity at home rather than to balance potential foes.

After 1789, a series of wars ensued by the French, who sought to spread
their new ideology beyond their borders. During these wars, known as the
French Revolutionary Wars (1792–1800), the French instituted a version
of conscription called the *levée en masse* (see Key document: The levée en
masse). The *levée* was proclaimed on August 23, 1793, and it raised an
army of 800,000 – larger than that of France's adversaries – in less than a
year. It took advantage of and encouraged mass enthusiasm to involve as
many people as possible in the war effort. The *levée* provided the basis for
the large armies that later fought for Napoléon, and it foreshadowed the
mobilization of entire populations during the world wars of the twentieth
century.

Key document   The levée en masse

The following extract from the original proclamation of the levée en masse illustrates the degree to which French society was mobilized for war after 1792.

1 From this moment . . . , all Frenchmen are in permanent requisition for the service of the armies. The young men shall go to battle; the married men shall forge arms and transport provisions; the women shall make tents and clothing and shall serve in the hospitals; the children shall turn old linen into lint; the aged shall betake themselves to the public places in order to arouse the courage of the warriors and preach the hatred of kings and the unity of the Republic.

2 The national buildings shall be converted into barracks, the public places into workshops for arms, the soil of the cellars shall be washed in order to extract there from the saltpeter.

[. . .]

5 The Committee of Public Safety is . . . authorized to form all the establishments, factories, workshops, and mills which shall be deemed necessary for the carrying on of these works, as well as to put in requisition, within the entire extent of the Republic, the artists and workingmen who can contribute to their success.

6 The representatives of the people sent out for the execution of the present law . . . are invested with the unlimited powers assigned to the representatives of the people to the armies.[28]

France's revolutionary wars spread domestic ideological strife into global politics as Europe's other great powers fought to prevent revolution from infecting their populations. The first of these wars began when France declared war on Hapsburg Austria on April 20, 1792, but the French army withdrew at the first sight of enemy outposts. The Austrians advanced into France, where the French held their ground, and the revolutionaries began to believe that the old world of autocracy was giving way to a new world of democracy and freedom. "From today and from this place," rhapsodized the pro-revolutionary German poet Johann Wolfgang von Goethe (1749–1832), "there begins a new epoch in the history of the world."

In its battles, France's national army made a variety of innovations. Less fearful of desertion and more willing to exploit civilians than its predecessors, the armies of the revolution depended less on supply trains and more on living off the land. This enhanced their speed and range. Also, armies were split into independent divisions, enhancing their flexibility. Gradually, they began to employ artillery and marksmen in the rear ("fire") and bayonet charges in the front ("shock"), and shock tactics replaced the wars of maneuver waged by dynastic armies. All in all, the era of revolutionary nationalism had a major impact both on the manner of waging war and the tone of global politics.

As the revolution took hold at home, France sought to export its ideas to the dynastic states of Europe by propaganda and war. French revolutionaries and then Napoléon Bonaparte set out to spread an ideology based on "liberty, fraternity, and equality" as expressed in a revolutionary manifesto of August 1789 entitled the *Declaration of the Rights of Man and of the Citizen*. France's 1791 constitution included a series of inalienable individual rights including equality before the law, freedom from arbitrary arrest and punishment, and freedom of speech, religion, and the press. The declaration also introduced democracy to France and denied the divine right of kings to rule. The revolution thus erected ideological barriers between states, and France came to be seen as a mortal threat to the remaining dynasties in Europe. Under Napoléon, France conquered all of Europe except Great Britain and Russia. In the end, nationalism, which had empowered France and French armies, was turned against Napoléon by his dynastic enemies to bring about his defeat.

France's declaration was influenced by America's young democracy, and some of its ideas are found in America's Declaration of Independence and Constitution. Only six months before the Declaration of Independence was signed in 1776, Thomas Paine (1737–1809) published a pamphlet called *Common Sense*, which stirred the imagination of American colonists by advocating an end to British rule and the adoption of republican institutions that many Frenchmen living under an absolutist monarchy found attractive. As a result of his views, Paine became very popular among French revolutionaries. In 1792, Paine came to the defense of the French Revolution in his treatise *Rights of Man*, which was a reply to British statesman Edmund Burke's (1729–97) denunciation of the revolution.

Burke, one of history's most articulate philosophical conservatives and a supporter of the American Revolution, was horrified by the excesses of the French Reign of Terror (1793–94) – a period that began because France's revolutionaries feared that their country would be betrayed to foreign enemies by aristocrats and other traitors at home. Burke rebuked France for wiping away all the country's old traditions, customs, and laws in a blood bath that featured "Madame Guillotine," who stood "grim and gaunt, with long thin arms stretched out towards the sky, the last glimmer of waning night striking the triangular knife."[29]

With the meteoric rise of Napoléon, a new, more frightening, and more destructive era in warfare began. Napoléon's popularity was a result of his military exploits. After putting down a royalist uprising in Paris (1795) with "a whiff of grapeshot" and conducting a series of brilliant campaigns in Italy (1796), he became the idol of French patriots. In 1798, he commanded an invasion of Egypt, but this victory was reversed the same year by a British fleet commanded by Napoléon's nemesis, Admiral Horatio Nelson (1758–1805), that cut French supply lines and forced Napoléon's retreat from Egypt.

In a coup d'état on November 9–10, 1799, Napoléon seized power in France and established a new regime called the Consulate, with him as first consul and virtual dictator. Napoléon became consul for life in 1802 and emperor of France in 1804. During this time, he continued to transform the revolutionary army, organizing it into a number of self-contained and powerful corps, each itself an army, consisting of three divisions, each with its own artillery and cavalry. With Europe at his feet in 1806, Napoléon formally abolished the Holy Roman Empire. He placed two brothers on the thrones of Holland and Westphalia, named his godson viceroy of Italy, enthroned his third brother as king of Naples, and then promoted him to king of Spain.

What Napoléon did not understand was the importance of controlling the seas. Thus, his fortunes began to shift after Lord Nelson's great naval triumph over the French at Trafalgar, off Cádiz, Spain, in October 1805.[30] From this point forward, Britain ruled the seas, but while the victory was a turning point in the Napoléonic Wars, Napoléon's defeat on land took several years more. How did this occur?

First, Napoléon's *Grande Armée* began to lose its revolutionary zeal as it incorporated more soldiers who were not French, but were subjects of conquered territories. The changing demographics of the French army contributed to Napoléon's loss of Spain in 1813, but his military supremacy ended only after his fateful decision to invade Russia. In June 1812, his *Grande Armée* of more than 500,000 from France and its subject states crossed into Russia. Despite a bloody victory at Borodino (1812) and the occupation of Moscow, Napoléon's war-weary army succumbed to a combination of Russia's scorched earth policy and the Russian winter. It was then destroyed in its retreat from Russia.

Still, Napoléon remained a symbol of French nationalism, and the power of nationalism sustained him again. After being defeated decisively in the Battle of Nations near Leipzig in October 1813, he was exiled to the Mediterranean island of Elba from which he escaped even while his enemies were negotiating a final European peace in Vienna. In March 1815 he landed in France and rallied his nationalist supporters. On June 18 Napoléon met his final defeat at the hands of a British–Prussian army in the Battle of Waterloo. Thereafter he was exiled to a remote island in the south Atlantic, St Helena, where he died in 1821.

Following Napoléon's defeat, a glittering assemblage of conservative statesmen – Klemens von Metternich (1773–1859) for Austria, Tsar Alexander I (1777–1825) for Russia, Prince Karl August von Hardenberg

(1750–1822) for Prussia, Viscount Castlereagh (1769–1822) for Britain, and Talleyrand for France – gathered at the Congress of Vienna in 1814–15 where they concluded the Treaty of Paris to restore the old order in Europe.[31] The congress limited France to its 1792 borders, restored the monarchy under Louis XVIII (1755–1824), and, consonant with the balance of power, allowed France to rejoin the great powers. Elsewhere, Russia was ceded territories in Poland and Finland; Austria was rewarded with Italian territory while ceding some lands to Prussia; the Netherlands once more became independent; and Britain gained additional French overseas territories.

The Congress of Vienna not only redrew the map of Europe but tried to prevent the re-emergence of another "superpower" like France under Bonaparte. To this end, it created the Concert of Europe "in the name of Europe which forms but a single whole."[32] The concert, an informal organization of Europe's great powers, required the summoning of ad hoc international conferences when it appeared that Europe's stability was menaced either by the aggression of one of their number or by domestic revolution. Recognition that domestic events could endanger global peace and allowance for intervention in domestic affairs in revolutionary conditions marked a major break with the older balance of power. Four major conferences were held between 1815 and 1822, and others in 1856, 1871, 1878, and 1884. The concert was an effort to re-establish the pre-Napoléonic pattern of global politics, including international consultation to avoid major disruptions, limited objectives, and shifting defensive alliances. What it could not do was do away with enthusiasm for nationalism and popular sovereignty that had been unleashed after 1789. Although the statesmen at Vienna tried to turn the clock back, they could not do so. The revolution and Napoléon's destructive warfare had unleashed new forces in global politics.

The modern nation-state emerged from the French Revolution and the Napoléonic Wars. The genie of nationalism could not be put back in the bottle, and the nineteenth century saw its spread and intensification, which, along with industrialization, made possible ever larger wars. Along with nationalism, new ideologies like socialism and racism justified Europe's colonial expansion and swept aside the conservative consensus of the previous century. The industrial revolution in Europe was accompanied by rapid urbanization and the growth of an urban working class that was attracted to new political doctrines, especially Marxian socialism. Moreover, growing citizen awareness of politics and citizens' desire to have a voice in running the state fostered the spread of democratic beliefs.

Increasingly, nineteenth-century Europe saw nationalism and democracy as natural partners, both of which challenged dynastic rule. "What had been a sovereigns' club," declares British political scientist Adam Watson, "would become a family of independent nations."[33] The democratic impulse was strongest in Western Europe, especially Britain and France, while to the east, in Russia, Prussia, and Austria, it ran up against a wall of authoritarian resistance on the part of conservative governments that feared that democracy and nationalism would spell their doom. Europe was fast dividing into liberal and conservative states.

Finally, popular democratic and national aspirations erupted in Europe in 1848 in a series of revolutions against monarchical despotism that began in Sicily and then spread like wildfire elsewhere. In Austria, the Hapsburg monarch successfully resisted the revolutionary tide, and Austrian armies crushed the national movements in its Italian (Lombardy) and Czech (Bohemia) provinces. And in Hungary, Austrian dominance was maintained and national aspirations brutally ended with the aid of a Russian army.

Nationalists and democrats throughout Europe looked to France, whose revolution had inspired "liberty, equality, and fraternity" and from where these norms had been forcibly extended across Europe. There, another Bonaparte, Louis-Napoléon (1808–73), nephew of Napoléon Bonaparte, was elected president in 1848 following the overthrow of King Louis Philippe (1773–1850). France declared the Second Republic (the First Republic had lasted from 1792 until 1804 when Bonaparte declared himself emperor), universal suffrage was established, and Louis-Napoléon was elected president. Five years later, emulating his famous uncle, he declared himself Emperor Napoléon III, thereby beginning France's Second Empire.[34]

Napoléon III, who stirred up and then became captive of French nationalism, was instrumental in securing the unification of Italy, which had been the site of unsuccessful nationalist revolutions in 1830 and 1848. In 1859, France, in alliance with Count Camillo Benso di Cavour (1810–61), Prime Minister of Piedmont-Sardinia, liberated much of northern Italy from Austrian occupation. In the south, the revolutionary Giuseppe Garibaldi (1807–82) and his volunteer "Red Shirts" seized Sicily and Naples in 1860 and advanced northward. Their union with the Piedmontese opened the way for the final unification of Italy under King Victor Emmanuel II (1820–78) in 1861. These events marked the demise of the Concert of Europe system.

However, a greater threat to European stability lay in the growing determination of German nationalists to unify their country which potentially would be the greatest power on the continent. In Prussia in the spring of 1849, the liberals who had been elected to the Frankfurt National Assembly drafted a constitution to create a federal union of the German states with a constitutional monarch and an elected legislature. However, Prussia's King Frederick William IV (1795–1861) contemptuously rejected the assembly's offer to elect him "Emperor of the Germans" because he believed that the only legitimate crown was one that was inherited. Throughout Europe, concessions that had been made by rulers under the threat of insurrection such as universal suffrage, liberty of the press and of assembly were cancelled, and monarchical despotism was restored in Prussia and Austria.

For the time being, the dream of a unified Germany was shattered. However, that dream would be realized some decades later under the leadership of Otto von Bismarck (1815–98) who was appointed Prussian prime minister in 1862. In a prescient speech to Prussia's parliament on September 30, 1862, Bismarck, a practitioner of *realpolitik*, warned that German unification would not be accomplished by resolutions of elected assemblies. Rather, "the great questions of the day will not be settled by speeches and majority decisions . . . but by blood and iron."[35] As we shall see in chapter 3, Germany's wars of unification would alter the complexion of Europe and set in train events that ultimately exploded in war in 1914.

Europe's territorial states were never the only political actors in global politics and a host of international, transnational, and subnational polities – "sovereignty-free actors" – have joined states as actors in what political scientist James N. Rosenau calls the "multi-centric" world that he contrasts to the "**state-centric**" world of past centuries.[36]

state-centric a model of global politics in which nation-states are the source of all important activities.

Long before the birth of Europe's states, much of East Asia was ruled by the Chinese Empire. Despite periods of fragmentation, the people of China retained a strong cultural affinity, and, for centuries, China's rulers believed that their empire was the center of the political and cultural universe. By the nineteenth century, however, European states had penetrated and weakened China, and the Chinese Empire ended in 1911. China's subsequent rulers, however, including the communists who came to power in 1949, continued to govern according to the principles of the sage-philosopher Confucius and sought to restore China to the greatness it had known in earlier centuries.

China: the Confucian empire

"The monumental Chinese achievement in the field of statecraft," writes Watson, "is usually held to be the more or less effective political unity that has assured domestic peace and order for most of Chinese history."[37] The distinctive Chinese political community and its outlook on foreign affairs were formed long before Thucydides recorded the Peloponnesian War in the fifth century BC.

Imperial China

empire a political unit having an extensive territory or comprising a number of territories or nations and ruled by a single supreme authority.

For much of its history China's political system, unlike Europe's state system, was a hierarchical **empire**. Unlike states, empires do not have fixed territorial boundaries and usually contain several national groups ruled by a single emperor. Foreign rulers who sent gifts or "tribute" to China's emperor might receive gifts and military protection in return. Such rulers accepted subordination in return for protection and trade and acknowledged "China's superiority by bowing down before the emperor, who held Heaven's Mandate (right to rule) to govern China and whose magnificent benevolence and compassion naturally attracted outsiders to come and also be transformed by civilization."[38] Key document: Letter from Emperor Qian Long illustrates how China's rulers viewed themselves as the center of world civilization.

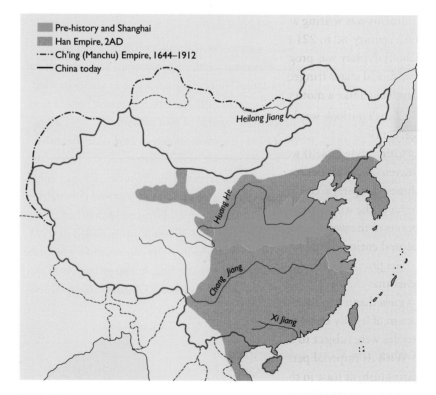

Map 2.4 Historical borders of China in four periods

Key document   Letter from Emperor Qian Long to King George III regarding a British request for trade privileges (1793)[39]

You, O King, live beyond the confines of many seas, nevertheless, impelled by your humble desire to partake of the benefits of our civilization, you have dispatched a mission respectfully bearing your memorial. . . .

Swaying the wide world, I have but one aim in view, namely, to maintain a perfect governance and to fulfill the duties of the State. . . . Our dynasty's majestic virtue has penetrated unto every country under Heaven, and Kings of all nations have offered their costly tribute by land and sea. As your Ambassador can see for himself, we possess all things. I set no value on objects strange or ingenious, and have no use for your country's manufactures. . . . It behooves you, O King, to respect my sentiments and to display even greater devotion and loyalty in future. . . . You, O King, from afar have yearned after the blessings of our civilization. . . . I do not forget the lonely remoteness of your island, cut off from the world by intervening wastes of sea, nor do I overlook your excusable ignorance of the usages of our Celestial Empire. . . .

China's philosophy of government that, in one observer's words, "largely determined the Chinese view of life, and therefore also the Chinese approach to foreign affairs" was strongly influenced by Confucius (551–479 BC) and that system "was already well established in its broad outlines in the first century of the Chou period (1027–221 BC)."[40] Confucius was writing at a turbulent time, China's "Warring States era" (fifth century BC to 221 BC), during which the "central authority of the [Chou] dynasty was progressively sapped, and the realm split into fifteen rival feudal states fringed and patched with many minor fiefs, so that the map looked like a motley of papal Italy familiar to Machiavelli."[41]

China's outlook was built on the conviction – reinforced by its age, continuity, and geographic isolation – that the Middle Kingdom (as China styled itself) was the center of the world and that the Son of Heaven (as the emperor was called) was ruler of the universe. And the Chinese Empire, according to historian John Fairbank, "remained the center of the world known to it, only vaguely aware of the other ancient centers of the west," never losing "its sense of all-embracing unity and cultural entity."[42]

The practical consequence of this egoistic view of the world was a belief that the political universe was centrally and hierarchically organized – a view diametrically opposite Europe's view of a horizontally organized system of legally equal sovereign states with no superior – and that all peoples were subject to the Son of Heaven.

With its imperial perspective, China's view of world affairs did not distinguish, at least in theory, between foreign and domestic politics and had no conception of a world of independent states. All peoples,

Did you know?

China in sixth century BC was home to one of the world's most studied military strategists, Sun Tzu, whose idea that all war is "based on deception" and who lauded the "divine art of subtlety and secrecy" greatly influenced China's communist leader Mao Zedong and his strategy of guerrilla warfare.

the Chinese believed, were under the rule of Heaven, and the emperor was responsible for governing them all, whether Chinese or not. All the emperor's subjects – whether Chinese or "barbarian" (non-Chinese) – should be treated similarly, in accord with Confucian norms. The Chinese conceived of the world as a series of concentric circles with the Middle Kingdom at the center. The next circle consisted of non-Chinese tribal groups that were permitted to govern themselves. Beyond this were the vassal polities that paid tribute to the Son of Heaven, such as Korea, Vietnam, and Cambodia, and still further out were countries like Portugal that had trade relations with China. Such vassal polities were expected to provide symbolic tribute to the emperor and their representatives had to perform the kowtow (ritual bow) when coming before the Son of Heaven. Today, the distinction between "Inner" and "Outer" Mongolia dates back to the fact that each was placed in a different circle in its relations with the Middle Kingdom.

The quality of rulership, Confucius taught, depended on adherence to traditional moral principles. Thus, China's outlook on world politics was infused with a strong normative element, as preoccupied with what ought to be as with what was. "Adherence to the correct teachings," writes Fairbank, "would be manifested in virtuous conduct and would enhance one's authority and influence."[43] In other words, moral behavior (Confucian principles) had the practical result of increasing imperial power. If an emperor ruled virtuously, the natural harmony of Heaven would prevail, not conflict as Western realists insist. Right, one might say, makes might. By contrast, a ruler's lack of virtue and his loss of the Mandate of Heaven reflected errors in policy. In the event of conflict, moral suasion and patience rather than coercion were, Confucians believed, the way to maintain order.

China's sense of superiority and its rulers' effort to isolate the empire from outsiders clashed with European, American, and Japanese expansionism, and China's ability to resist foreign penetration crumbled in the nineteenth century. The "foreigners" sought economic opportunities, and European and American missionaries were sent to convert the Chinese to Christianity. Britain took the lead in the 1830s, shipping large amounts of opium grown in British India to China in return for tea and other Chinese goods and spreading opium addiction among the Chinese. China tried to outlaw opium in 1836, and its efforts to halt British opium triggered war in late 1839, leading to China's humiliating defeat. The 1842 Treaty of Nanking ceded Hong Kong to Britain and effectively opened the country to British trade, causing a dramatic increase in opium imports. It also abridged China's sovereign rights. Thus, foreigners accused of a crime enjoyed **extraterritorial**

extraterritorial relating to persons exempt from the legal jurisdiction of the country in which they reside.

rights such as being subject to the laws of their country rather than China's. Americans and Europeans also enjoyed virtual control over the areas in which their legations and consulates were located.

A second opium war erupted in 1856, resulting in the virtual legalization of opium in China, the right of foreigners to hold property and spread Christianity throughout the country, and foreign control of the country's trade. By the end of the century, Germany occupied the Shantung Peninsula and Russia controlled Manchuria and the city of Port Arthur. In 1899, the United States, without a territorial sphere of its own in China, sent notes to the major powers asking them to declare that they would uphold China's territorial integrity and follow an open door policy in which all would enjoy equal trading rights in China.

The beginning of the end for China's last imperial dynasty, the Qing (also called the Manchus) began with its defeat in the Sino-Japanese War (1895), which marked a giant step in Japan's effort to build itself an Asian empire. Encouraged by China's imperial government, anti-foreign agitation by a secret society called the Boxers or "The Righteous and Harmonious Fists" climaxed in 1900 with the Boxer Rebellion. Violence against foreigners in Beijing led to the dispatch of an international force of Europeans, Americans, and Japanese that suppressed the Boxers and forced China's government to pay a huge indemnity and submit to other demands that limited China's sovereignty. After the overthrow of the Qing (1911–12), Sun Yatsen (1866–1925) became provisional president of the Republic of China but soon ceded power to the dictatorial general Yuan Shikai (1859–1916) whose death triggered the country's descent into an era of disorder and conflict among local warlords.

As we shall see in chapter 5, China did not forget the humiliating era of "unequal treaties" to which it was subjected, and the effort to rectify the situation dominated Chinese politics for over a century. Despite the end of the Chinese Empire, traditional ideas remained strong. Communist leader Mao Zedong (1983–1976), for instance, publicly likened himself to China's emperors, and the series of disasters that struck China in 1976, including the deaths of Mao, his long-time associate Zhou Enlai (1898–1976), and General Zhu De (1886–1976), and a deadly earthquake that leveled the city of Tangshan and killed some 250,000 people seemed to auger the withdrawal of Heaven's Mandate and readied the country for dramatic change.

Chinese history and culture, especially Confucianism, continue to exert influence in China and elsewhere in East Asia. The next section examines this influence in what observers have described as "Asian values" and how these contrast with "Western values" in questions of economic development.

Asian versus Western values

Confucianism and the values it celebrates have played a pivotal role in the evolution of East Asia's economies. This section reviews the differences between Asian and Western approaches to capitalism. These differences were evident in the tensions between the two approaches that surfaced during Asia's 1997–98 economic crisis (chapter 11, pp. 540–3). The economic crisis highlighted the tension between two different political and economic paths and philosophies and showed the importance of cultural differences in global politics, an issue examined in chapter 14.

Western values

The globalization of the world economy reflects the West's liberal traditions of unfettered capitalism, individual self-realization, limited government, and political democracy. The idea of individual prosperity growing out of entrepreneurial behavior in a free market has Western roots. And Western individualism flourished along with a profound belief in private property.

These economic beliefs received a strong boost in the West in the 1980s under the influence of US President Ronald Reagan (1911–2004) and British Prime Minister Margaret Thatcher (1925–). After a generation of growing government influence in economic life, Reagan and Thatcher demanded that economic policies return to the older liberal philosophy associated with Adam Smith and encourage, above all, individual freedom and initiative rather than social welfare. Proclaiming "the rolling back" of the state, Western politicians and economists of the 1980s embraced the idea that, if left alone, markets would solve most economic problems. State intervention, they argued, distorted markets and reduced individual initiative. Thus, during that decade the US and British governments sought to reduce government regulation of economic and social affairs and state intervention in and control of the economy.

Western leaders insisted that individual freedom had been eroded in previous decades owing to the proliferation of government bureaucracies responding to the demands of interest group politics. In this, they were influenced by American economist Milton Friedman (1912–2006) who argued that: "Equality before God – personal equality – is important precisely because people are not identical. Their different values, their different tastes, their different capacities will lead them to want to lead very different lives."[44] In other words, only individuals can know what they want. When elected politicians, in the name of the public good, try to reshape the social world through state intervention in the economy and the redistribution of resources, the result, Friedman claimed, is coercive government. Any government attempt to regulate the lives of individuals is an attack on their freedom, a denial of their right to be the ultimate judges of their own ends.

Western liberal tradition assumes that the less a government interferes in people's lives, the greater their opportunities for freedom. Government regulation is an attack on people's freedom, a denial of their right to be the ultimate judges of their own ends. The only legitimate way to order or organize human and material resources is through voluntary exchange, and the only justifiable political institutions are those that guarantee individual autonomy and freedom. The market, in this tradition, is the only institution that can provide a secure basis on which business and family life can prosper. The market, the argument continues, does away with the need for central authority, because buyers and sellers, consumers and producers, and savers and investors realize their own economic interests.

Western politicians insist that democracy and economic development are inseparable, and some Western observers suggested that Asia's economic crisis was a result of Asians' refusal to institute genuine democracy. According to Western liberal tradition, the free market is necessary for liberal democracy, and liberal democracy, in turn, is vital if citizens are to make informed economic decisions. To many Asians, this view reflects Western conceit. "In recent years," writes political scientist Samuel Huntington, "Westerners have reassured themselves and irritated others by expounding the notion that the culture of the West is and ought to be the culture of the world." Westerners, he continues, believe "not only that the West has led the world to modern society, but that as people in other civilizations modernize they also westernize, abandoning their traditional values, institutions, and customs and adopting those that prevail in the West." These views, Huntington argues are "misguided, arrogant, false, and dangerous."[45]

Asian values

Asia is hardly a monolithic region, and Asian cultures are diverse. Nevertheless, many Asians see their values as different from those of the West. Some, especially in East Asia, have claimed that Western values, however useful in Europe and America, are unsuited to Asian conditions and violate Asian traditions. Western social values such as deregulation, weak unions, and a minimalist welfare state are, Asians argue, fundamentally incompatible with their own practices and traditional social values.[46]

For their part, Asians had pursued an alternative path to economic growth featuring a high degree of state involvement in economic decisions. As first Japan and then Asia's newly industrializing countries, especially South Korea and Taiwan, and finally the little tigers of Southeast Asia clawed their way from poverty to prosperity, Asian politicians began to speak of the superiority of "Asian values." As articulated by regional leaders like Singapore's long-time Prime Minister Lee Kwan Yew (1923–), the Asian path to economic growth combined political authoritarianism with "managed" or state capitalism.

For many Asians, Western emphasis on individual liberty and the free market is alien,[47] and Lee Kwan Yew declared that "I do not believe that democracy necessarily leads to development. I believe that what a country needs to develop is discipline more than democracy."[48] While Westerners seek to maximize individual freedom and prosperity, many Asians, especially in China and Korea, remain loyal to social values like equality of outcome that are associated with the teaching of Confucius. "Asian values," in the words of one commentator "are different in kind, not in degree. They are self-reliant, yet somehow communitarian rather than individualistic; built on personal relationships and mutual obligation, . . . respectful of authority and hierarchy; and state interventionist, even into the private space of individuals. The word that summed up this – in part self-contradictory – spirit was Confucianism."[49] Asian leaders like Lee Kuan emphasize "the Confucian precepts of work, frugality, and hierarchy" that they believe, "underlie the dramatic economic growth achieved in East Asia by Japan in the 1970s and 1980s, the four 'tigers' (Korea, Taiwan, Hong Kong, and Singapore) in the 1980s and mid-1990s, and the three aspiring tigers (Thailand, Indonesia, and Malaysia) until the middle of 1997."[50]

Controversy

The degree to which Asian and Western values differ is hotly debated. Surveys conducted by Japan's Dentsu Institute for Human Studies in Japan, China, South Korea, Thailand, Singapore, and India (1998) and in Britain, France, Germany, Sweden, and the US (1997) indicated that Asian and Western values were more similar than many observers had thought and that Asians themselves differed significantly when asked about the relative importance of "financial wealth," "acquiring high-quality goods," "family relationships," "success in work," "mental relaxation," "leisure activity," "living for the present," "striving to achieve personal goals," and "having good relationships with others." On only two of the nine dimensions of value measured were Asians and Westerners significantly different.[51]

In both China and South Korea, Confucian norms remain influential, and foreign observers called the ethical system behind South Korea's dramatic economic growth New Confucianism or Confucian capitalism. Some of the assumptions of Confucian capitalism are:

- Individuals are not isolated, but are part of a complex system of human relations. Harmony and cooperation among people are more important than individual success. Therefore, obligation to the community is superior to individual rights and personal privacy.
- Confucianism is "family-centered," and social life cannot be separated from family relations. Organizations and groups are expected to run like families and reflect collective values. Confucianism is based on the "Five Relationships": father and son, husband and wife, king and minister, elder and younger brother, and friend and friend. The essential characteristic of these relationships except the last is *hierarchy*. Thus, the state is superior to its citizens whose duty is to serve the state, as sons are bound to serve their fathers.
- Like the father of a family who controls every aspect of family life, the state should play a leading role in economic development and public welfare.

The "chummy" relationship among Asian governments, politicians, banks, and businesses in which political influence or family ties provided preferential access to public funds and bank loans was dubbed in the West "crony capitalism." Western liberals regard crony capitalism as corrupt because it allows enterprises to prosper owing to political connections rather than economic performance. However, what Westerners sarcastically call "crony capitalism" is regarded as legitimate by Asians because it reflects Confucian obligations among family members and friends. In a Confucian society, the obligation of friends to one another is profoundly important – the glue that holds society together – just as hierarchical relations between superior and inferior in political and economic affairs are analogous to relations between father and children. In addition, Asian leaders praised their export-driven model of capitalism, which, it seemed, was surpassing Western "casino capitalism"[52] based on competition and free markets.

Asia's 1997–98 financial crisis was a challenge to Asian values as Western observers were quick to point out. Combined with a dramatic upswing in the US economy in the 1990s, the crisis seemed to deny the superiority of Asian values and placed its advocates on the defensive. When the economic storm struck, Asians were traumatized to discover that their governments would have to ignore the customary practices of citizens. They were angered by having to accept "reforms" that ran counter to political, economic, and cultural norms that had governed behavior for many generations.

An entirely different, nonstate community based on religion evolved in the Middle East, the Muslim Caliphate, and for several centuries it appeared destined to dominate global politics. Islam clashed with Christian Europe shortly after its birth, and the conflict between Islam and the West is a critical issue in contemporary global politics. In the end, the state was imposed on the Islamic world as Europe expanded its influence around the world, but, as we were grimly reminded on September 11, 2001, the contest between Islam and the West has never ceased. Let us now examine the emergence and evolution of the Islamic community.

Islam's founding and expansion: a nonstate alternative

In what follows, we trace Islam from its birth in Arabia in the seventh century to the present, focusing on the development of the Caliphate, a nonstate political community that extended across the Islamic community of believers, and Islam's recurrent conflicts with the West. As we chronicle Islam, we focus on clashes between Islam and the West as Islam made inroads into Europe and as Europeans attempted to reclaim Jerusalem. However, our examination also reveals historical divisions among Muslims, particularly between the Sunni and Shia sects, and between Arab and Turkish Muslims.

The Caliphate

All religions have their fundamentalists, and many have gone through bloody epochs. Europe in the sixteenth and seventeenth centuries was home to endless wars between Catholics and Protestants; Spain in 1492 was the scene of "ethnic cleansing" of Muslims and Jews. Hindus and Muslims in the Indian subcontinent have almost ceaselessly experienced or been on the verge of communal violence. Similarly, Islam's spread between the eighth and fourteenth centuries occurred by war and conquest. Islam was, in political scientist Adda Bozeman's colorful expression, an "empire-in-motion" and "the greatest of all caravans."[53] Relations among Muslims, particularly the Sunni and Shia sects, also have been prone to violence as each sought to advance its own interpretation of Islam. Yet, as in the other religions mentioned above, the vast majority of Muslims are peaceable, and Muslims in a variety of societies, for example the Tajiks, Uzbeks, Tatars, and others along Russia's southern border, harbor few religious passions.

Islam enjoys a long and illustrious past during which the religion spread worldwide out of Arabia, and a great and highly cultured empire, the **Caliphate**, took form.[54] The saga began in the seventh century in

Caliphate Muslim empire from 661 to 1258.

the city of Mecca, when Muhammad (571–632), a member of an Arab tribe called the *Quaraish*, launched a third great religious movement that worshipped a single god. Muslims believe Muhammad is the third and final prophet of God, or Allah (the Arabic name for God), after Moses and Jesus, and that he was visited by the Archangel Gabriel, who revealed Allah's word to him and instructed him to preach what came to be known as Islam. Muhammad recited these revelations to his companions, who compiled them in a text called the **Koran**. Muhammad's preaching on **monotheism** and social and economic justice stirred opposition in Mecca, whose inhabitants were predominantly **polytheistic** and tribal. Forced to flee from his own tribal leaders, Muhammad traveled to Medina. His flight from Mecca to Medina, known as the Hegira, marks the beginning of Islam. In practice, the new religion had much in common with its predecessors, Judaism and Christianity. In fact, all three regard themselves as the "children of Abraham," whom they believe to be a major prophet and the first monotheist.

> **Koran** the book composed of sacred writings accepted by Muslims as revelations made to Muhammad by Allah through the angel Gabriel.
>
> **monotheism** belief in a single god.
>
> **polytheism** worship of or belief in several gods.

At the time of Islam's birth, the dominant powers in the region were the Byzantine and Persian or Sassinid empires. The warriors of Islam conquered these empires between 632 and 637. The Islamic movement spread rapidly beyond Arabia on Arabic fervor and horses until it reached Spain in the west and India in the east. Egypt was Islamized by 641 and was conquered in the following years. The forces of Islam completed the conquest of North Africa, reaching modern Morocco in 669. In 710 they crossed the Strait of Gibraltar, into Spain, occupying the entire Iberian Peninsula in the following eight years. Islam's advance into western Europe was finally halted in 732 by the Frankish leader Charles Martel in the Battle of Poitiers, near modern-day Tours, France.

The eighth to the eleventh centuries witnessed the flowering of Islamic civilization. In 750, the Ummayad dynasty in Damascus, which had been established in 661, was overthrown and replaced by the Abbassid dynasty in Baghdad. Islamic culture flourished and reached its apogee under Abbassid Caliph Harun al-Rashid (786–809). The dynasty survived until the Mongols sacked Baghdad in 1258. During this period, Baghdad became a center of trade between Europe, Asia, and Africa. In fact, Europe owes much to Islam's preservation of classical Greek drama, philosophy, and science. "Arab scholars," as one historian observes, "were studying Aristotle when Charlemagne and his lords were reportedly learning to write their names. Scientists in Cordova, with their seventeen great libraries . . . enjoyed luxurious baths at a time when washing the body was considered a dangerous custom at the University of Oxford."[55]

> **Did you know?**
>
> *Jihad*, which is a duty of every Muslim, has two meanings. One is relatively benign, referring to the struggle of Muslims to resist passion and vice. The other, which is proclaimed by militant Muslims, refers to holy war against non-Muslims and the forcible spread of Islam.

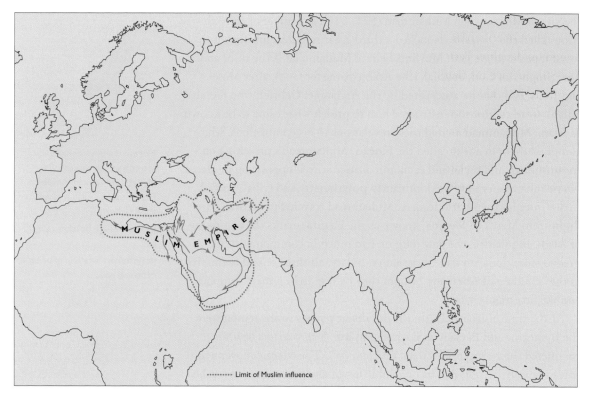

Map 2.5 Expansion of Islam by 1500

Cracks in the Islamic community

Islamic expansion was accompanied by repeated political turmoil, especially following the death of the prophet, and the question of who should succeed him would bedevil Muslims up to the present. When Muhammad died, a caliph (successor) was chosen to rule, but, since the caliph lacked prophetic authority, he enjoyed secular power but not authority in religious doctrine. The first caliph was Abu Bakr (573–634). He and his three successors were known as the "rightly guided," or orthodox, caliphs (*Rashidun*). They ruled according to the Koran and the practices of Muhammad. Thereafter, Islam divided into two hostile factions, Sunni and Shia, a division that divides today's Islamic world much as it did then. In addition, the single Caliphate began dividing into rival dynasties by the end of the eighth century.

The Sunni–Shia split began when Ali ibn Abi Ṭalib (599–661), Muhammad's son-in-law and heir, assumed the Caliphate after the murder of his predecessor, Uthman (574–656). Civil war ensued with the defeat of Ali at the hands of Uthman's cousin and governor of Damascus, Mu'awiya Ummayad (602–80) at the Battle of Suffin. Shortly afterwards Ali was murdered. Shias believe that Ali was the last legitimate caliph and that the Caliphate should pass down only to direct descendants of Muhammad through his daughter Fatima and Ali, her husband. Ali's son, Hussein (626–80), pursued his claim to the Caliphate, but the Ummayad rulers slaughtered him and his followers at the Battle of Karbala (680), a city in modern Iraq that remains even today the holiest of all sites for Shia Muslims. Muhammad's family line ended in 873, but Shias believe that this last descendent had not died but was "hidden" and would ultimately return. Some centuries later, while still awaiting the last **Imam**'s (religious leader) reappearance, the Shia established a council of 12 religious scholars or **ulema** who selected a supreme Imam. In recent decades, the late Ayatollah Khomeini enjoyed that status in Iran.

imam an Islamic religious leader.

ulema the community of Islamic legal scholars.

The dominant faction of Islam was known as Sunni. Sunnis did not demand that the caliph be a direct descendent of Muhammad and were prepared to follow Arabic tribal customs in government. Political leadership, in their view, was in the hands of the Muslim community at large. Since the first four caliphs, the religious and political authorities in Islam have never again united under one institution although some contemporary Islamic militants seek to restore the ancient Caliphate.

Islam and Christendom: the crusades

Clashes between Muslims and western Europeans continued, especially during Europe's crusades (1095–1271) to regain the Holy Land for Christianity. Islam still posed a threat to Europe when Pope Urban II declared in 1095 that Muslims had conquered Jerusalem and that they forbade Christian pilgrims to come to the city to pray. Pope Urban wanted the Christians to retake Jerusalem from the Muslims. "This royal city . . . situated at the center of the earth, is now held captive by the enemies of Christ and is subjected, by those who do not know God, to the worship of the heathen. She seeks, therefore, and desires to be liberated and ceases not to implore you to come to her aid. . . ." People shouted, "It is the will of God!"[56] He then summoned Christian Europe to free Jerusalem by force on what is called the First Crusade (1095–97). Many of the knights who went off to wage the crusade died of hunger, thirst, or disease, but they did conquer Jerusalem in a bloody slaughter and established a Christian military presence in what was called the Latin Kingdom of Jerusalem that lasted for about 200 years.

Two additional crusades were launched in the twelfth century. The Second Crusade was initiated in response to the Muslim capture of Edessa in modern-day Turkey, and it included a king of France and a Holy Roman emperor. However, the expedition was decimated and ended in

"Run for your lives!
It's the coming of Christianity!"

failure, although the European outposts in the region were able to survive.
In 1187, Jerusalem was regained by a Muslim army commanded by Prince
Saladin (1138–93), then ruler of Egypt.

That event triggered the Third Crusade, the most famous of these
expeditions, which was jointly commanded by the greatest princes in
Christendom: Richard I "the Lion Hearted" of England (1157–99), Philip
II Augustus of France (1165–1223), and Frederick Barbarossa (1122–90),
the Holy Roman Emperor (who died before reaching the Holy Land). The
three were political rivals, and the crusade accomplished little except the
founding of a number of Christian cities along the Mediterranean coast.
Although additional crusades were launched in the following century, the
Third Crusade was the last serious effort to wrest the Holy Land from
Muslim control. The consequences of these expeditions are still with us, to
be seen in the many crusader ruins and churches in the Middle East and in

Did you know?

Saladin or Salah al-Din
was an ethnic Kurd who
was born in Tikrit in
modern Iraq, the same
city in which Saddam
Hussein was born.

the uproar that George W. Bush caused among Muslims after the terrorist attack of 9/11 in his reference to an American "crusade" against terrorism.

The Ottoman Empire – Islam versus the West

With the end of the crusades, the story of Islam turns to the Turks. Describing Turkey's Ottoman Empire, political scientist Michael Barnett notes that it was far from being a territorial state in the European tradition. Instead: "Until the late nineteenth century, inhabitants of the Fertile Crescent existed within a variety of overlapping authorities and political structures. The Ottoman Empire, Islam, and local tribal and village structures all contested for and held sway over various features of peoples' lives." It was "great power intrusions," notably Russian, British, and French, that primarily set forces in motion in Turkey, stirring up the desire to emulate the Western states. Nevertheless, in Turkey, as elsewhere where Islam held sway, "while the great powers established a new geopolitical map, the political loyalties of the inhabitants enveloped these boundaries and challenged the very legitimacy of that map."[57]

Turkish nomads first settled in Asia Minor to escape the Mongols. They converted to Islam in the eighth and ninth centuries. The Seljuks, a Turkish people, settled in the Caliphate and were employed as mercenary warriors, especially against other Turkish groups, and finally, seized power from the Arab rulers of Baghdad. As Seljuk power waned, a number of small Turkish states emerged in the frontier lands between the Byzantine and Islamic empires. Led by a Muslim warrior named Osman (1258–1324), one group, the Ottomans, began to raid Christian Byzantine towns in 1299. The Ottomans[58] were a small Turkish tribe that arose in Anatolia after 1071 and were granted a small territory within the Islamic Empire. In 1301, the Ottomans seized power from the Seljuks, and ruled the new empire until its final dismemberment in 1922.

The Ottoman Empire, now the home of the Caliphate, expanded vigorously. First, Osman successfully defeated the redoubtable Byzantine Empire (the eastern half of the old Roman Empire and the home of eastern Christianity) in 1302. This defeat brought the clash between Islam and Christianity back to center stage. Between 1362 and 1389, the Ottomans penetrated further into Christian lands in the Balkans. This climaxed in their triumph over the Serbs in Kosovo, a battle that became a central myth in later Serbian nationalism. Then, after a period of weakness in the early fifteenth century, a new era of Ottoman expansion began, climaxing in the conquest of Constantinople (today, Istanbul), the capital of Byzantium, in 1452. And in the first decades of the sixteenth century intense conflict between Sunnis and Shiites

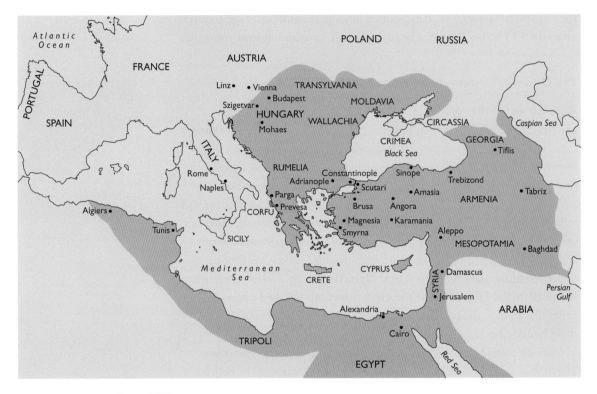

Map 2.6 The Ottoman Empire, 1580

produced Ottoman expansion into eastern Anatolia, northern Iraq, Syria, Egypt, and Arabia.

It was then that the Ottomans' greatest ruler, Sultan Suleyman "The Magnificent" (1520–66), came to power. Under Suleyman, the conquests of Syria and Serbia were completed, the island of Rhodes was taken, the Mediterranean and Aegean seas became Ottoman lakes, and incursions into Hungary began, which led to the temporary capture of Buda and Pest (today, the united capital city of that country). The Ottomans even laid siege to Vienna. Between 1541 and 1543, they seized Hungary and Slovenia from the Catholic Hapsburg dynasty. In 1524 they penetrated into Iran, then into southern Iraq in 1533, leading to Ottoman dominance of the Persian Gulf.

Although expansion continued – Cyprus, Azerbaijan, and the Caucasus as far as the Caspian Sea – and the struggle with Shiites in Iran persisted, the tide began to ebb with the defeat of the Ottoman fleet at the hands of a European fleet in the decisive Battle of Lepanto in 1571. Indecisive and episodic war with the Hapsburgs and Iranians also continued, and rebellion in the empire was endemic. Increasingly, the Ottomans were forced to grant trade concessions to European countries like England

and Holland. European interference in Ottoman provinces grew, and in 1649 Louis XIV of France declared his country to be the protector of the Christian Maronite community in Lebanon. Finally, the limits of Ottoman expansion were reached. Defeat followed defeat with Austria (1663–64) and Russia (1677–81), a new siege of Vienna was broken (1683), and Ottoman forces fled in disarray. The Ottomans continued to fight various European alliances until defeats led to the Treaty of Karlowitz (1699), which began the Ottoman withdrawal from Europe.

Thereafter, European primacy over the Ottoman Turks became ever more evident. Wars with Russia under Tsar Peter the Great (1672–1725) and his heirs over the next 100 years and with Venice, Austria, and the other European great powers further weakened the empire and gave rise to a Russian Empire ruled by the Romanov dynasty. Egypt fell in the grip of its own civil war, and the Ottomans were expelled from Iran. Greece was finally liberated in 1830 with the help of many Europeans including the great English romantic poet Lord Byron (1788–1824), who died in the effort. Owing to a new Russian war in 1829 the Ottoman Empire, now the "sick man of Europe," withdrew from many of its Balkan conquests, including Serbia. The Crimean War (1853–56) ended with vague Turkish promises to Russia to respect rights of non-Muslims, including Orthodox Christians, in Ottoman territories. Finally, beginning with the Treaty of San Stefano with Russia (1876) and the Congress of Berlin (1878), a series of events led to growing Austro-Russian competition with the Ottomans in the Balkans and, finally, the onset of World War I.

The last Ottoman sultan reigned between 1918 and 1922. The Sultanate was abolished on November 1, 1922, and the office of Caliph was terminated two years later. The Turkish Republic was declared on October 29, 1923, and Mustafa Kemal (Atatürk) (1881–1938) became the new country's first president. As a result, that part of the empire located in the Middle East was divided up among the victors of World War I, and most of the states in the region that exist today emerged.

Today, militant Muslims like Osama bin Laden have declared war on the interstate system that emerged in Europe. They recall Islam's glorious past and nostalgically call for the restoration of the Caliphate. Such militants are one of many factors that are eroding the power and independence of sovereign states and transforming the interstate system that was born in Europe over three centuries ago. States will not disappear for the foreseeable future, but they must confront a variety of challenges and must work with a growing variety of nonstate institutions.

Did you know?

Lepanto was the last naval engagement to feature oared galleys. Among the casualties at Lepanto was Miguel de Cervantes, Spanish author of *Don Quixote*.

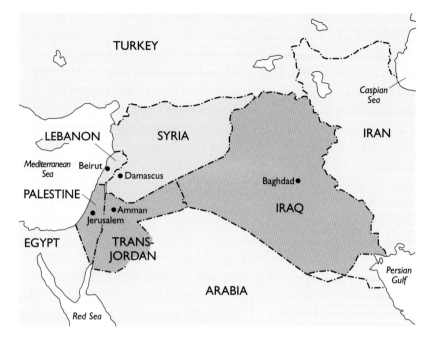

Map 2.7 The Middle East, 1920s

Conclusion

In this chapter, we have seen how the territorial state evolved in Europe out of the medieval feudal system to become the central actor in global politics for some three centuries. However, the territorial state, which was globalized as Europe conquered much of the rest of the world, was historically contingent. It was never the only form of political community in world politics and, as we shall see in later chapters, it must increasingly share pride of place with other political forms and identities. Indeed, this chapter has examined two prominent nonstate forms of political community – the Chinese Empire and the Islamic community – that were dominant at different historical moments. Both collided with expanding Western states and, though defeated, memories of them continue to exert influence today over the imagination of many Asians and Muslims.

Europe's state system, however, was the scene of two great twentieth-century cataclysms. And, the two world wars persuaded many people, especially liberals, that the state system was no longer viable and that the continued independence and autonomy of states would mean perpetual warfare much as realists admit. Thus, following both wars, there was a proliferation of international and nongovernmental institutions that sought to limit state sovereignty. In the next chapter, we examine the key events that led to the Great War (World War I) in 1914 and to World War II in 1939. World War I began the process of decolonization during which the peoples of Asia, the Middle East, and Africa finally achieved political independence. It also witnessed the collapse of four mighty empires – Russian, German, Ottoman, and Austro-Hungarian – and produced the Bolshevik Revolution in Russia, thereby creating tensions that later detonated the Cold War. World War II accelerated the process of decolonization until virtually no areas of the world remained under colonial rule. As we shall also see in the next chapter, the world wars set the stage for the rest of the twentieth century.

Student activities

Discussion and essay questions

Comprehension questions

1 What is the "territorial state" and how did it come to be?
2 Historically, how did Islam's Caliphate and the Chinese Empire differ from sovereign states as a form of political organization?
3 What is the difference between Sunni and the Shia Muslims?
4 Describe the evolution of relations between Islam and the West before the twentieth century.
5 What is the difference between "Western" and "Asian" values?

Analysis questions

6 Why does sovereignty matter?
7 How did the arrival of popular sovereignty change the world?
8 In your view, did history make today's clash between Islam and the West inevitable?
9 In what ways might Muslims, Confucians, and Westerners perceive the world differently, and might this matter?

Map analysis

Refer to maps 2.1 and 2.3. Compare them to a current map of Europe. How have political boundaries and divisions changed over time? Do any political entities on these maps still exist today?

Cultural materials

Islam does not permit the depiction of people in art or architecture, instead often using geometric patterns to represent the spiritual, not physical, qualities of people and objects. Circles and repeating patterns represent the infinite nature of Allah. Such patterns are evident in two of Islam's greatest architectural achievements – the Alhambra, a palace that was built in Granada, Spain, between 1338 and 1390, and the Taj Majal, a mausoleum in Agra, India, that was built between 1630 and 1648 by the Mughal Emperor Shah Jehan to honor his deceased wife, Mumtaz Majal. The Taj has a black and white chessboard marble floor, four tall minarets at the corners of the mausoleum, and a grand dome in the middle.

Another trait of Islamic architecture is a focus on interior space. Traditional Islamic homes and buildings are designed with high, windowless exterior walls and an interior courtyard. The exterior walls ensure privacy and protect inhabitants from severe climate. In contrast to the plain façade, the inside of these buildings may be ornate. This style is called architecture of the veil.[59]

Think about your own culture as it is depicted in art and architecture. For example, consider how the use of space reflects culture. Pick a home, school, office building, or place of worship. Which spaces in each type of building are considered public? Which are private? How does their design or decoration provide insight into culture? Also consider what the artwork used to decorate these spaces tells you about culture.

Further reading

Armstrong, Karen, *Islam: A Short History* (New York: Random House, 2002). Accessible introduction to the origins and evolution of Islam.

Bozeman, Adda, *Politics and Culture in International History: From the Ancient Near East to the Opening of the Modern Age*, 2nd ed. (New Brunswick, NJ: Transaction Publishers, 1994). Classic treatment of the historical evolution of different political communities.

Hall, Rodney Bruce, *National Collective Identity: Social Constructs and International Systems* (New York: Columbia University Press, 1999). Constructivist analysis of the evolution of Europe's state system.

Jackson, Robert H., *Quasi-States: Sovereignty, International Relations and the Third World* (Cambridge: Cambridge University Press, 1990). Thematic analysis of the value of state sovereignty in an age of eroding state capacity.

Krasner, Stephen D., *Sovereignty: Organized Hypocrisy* (Princeton, NJ: Princeton University Press, 1999). Brilliant realist argument that state sovereignty was always incomplete and that sovereignty remains as powerful today as in the past.

Spruyt, Hendrik, *The Sovereign State and Its Competitors* (Princeton, NJ:

Princeton University Press, 1994). Story of how the territorial state in Europe triumphed over rival forms of political organization.

Strayer, Joseph, *On the Medieval Origins of the Modern State* (Princeton, NJ: Princeton University Press, 1970). How the territorial state emerged from the Middle Ages.

Thomson, Janice E., *Mercenaries, Pirates, and Sovereigns* (Princeton, NJ: Princeton University Press, 1994). Fascinating argument that states did not achieve a monopoly of the means of coercion until quite late in their development.

Tilly, Charles, *The Formation of National States in Western Europe* (Princeton, NJ: Princeton University Press, 1975). How modern states emerged in Europe as centers of military and political power.

Van Creveld, Martin, *The Rise and Decline of the State* (Cambridge: Cambridge University Press, 1999). Riveting analysis of the factors producing the territorial state and of those leading to its erosion.

3 The world wars

On June 28, 1914, the heir to the throne of Austria-Hungary was assassinated during an official visit to the Bosnian city of Sarajevo. At 2 p.m. on Thursday, July 30, 1914, Tsar Nicholas II (1868–1918), Russia's ruler, met with his foreign minister, Sergei Sazonov (1860–1927), to discuss the crisis that was engulfing Europe following the assassination. The tsar, under pressure from his generals to mobilize Russia's armies to meet the possibility of war, balked, declaring that he did not want the moral responsibility for "the thousands and thousands of men who will be sent to their deaths."[1] The foreign minister insisted, arguing that it was vital "to do everything necessary to meet war fully armed and under conditions most favorable to us." Nicholas finally gave way, and Sazonov telephoned the army's chief of staff with this message: "Now you can smash your telephone [so that the tsar could not change his mind again]. Give your orders, General!"[2] Although the tsar's decision made war inevitable, in his diary he wrote, "After lunch I received Sazonov and Tatischev. I went for a walk by myself. The weather was hot . . . had a delightful bathe in the sea."[3]

This chapter focuses on the world wars: World War I (1914–18), then called the Great War,[4] the events of the war, and its consequences, including World War II (1939–45). Studying these wars will allow you to step back and see in action many of the issues of war and peace that we will discuss in later chapters, including the relationship between politics and war. Analyzing the causes of the world wars also demonstrates efforts to build theory and explain war by reference to levels of analysis. These events are important in another respect as well: They began the modern era of global politics, including many of the problems that we face today.

The chapter opens by examining the events leading up to World War I, particularly those that so escalated fear and hostility in Europe that war seemed unavoidable. The chapter then analyzes the many sources of the war according to their levels of analysis and considers how political

Figure 3.1 The Battle of the Somme by Richard Caton Woodville II
Woodville, Richard Caton II (1856–1927) © Private Collection/The Bridgeman Art Library

scientists have used this case to generalize about war. It then describes how World War I permanently altered global politics and ushered in the modern world. It reviews the sequence of events during what has been called the "twenty years' crisis"[5] following World War I that led to the next world war: the harsh treatment of Germany in the Versailles Treaty, the failure of the League of Nations, and the policy of appeasement practiced by the West in the series of crises in the 1930s. The chapter closes by assessing the sources of World War II.

Events leading to the Great War

The Great War began as a local collision between Serbia and Austria-Hungary. As described above, it was triggered by the assassination in Sarajevo of Archduke Franz Ferdinand (1863–1914), heir to the Hapsburg throne of Austria-Hungary, by a young Serbian nationalist named Gavrilo Princip (1894–1918). The local conflict spread because the members of two major alliances upheld their commitments: Great Britain, France, and Russia (the **Triple Entente**), and Germany and Austria-Hungary

Triple Entente the alliance between France, Great Britain, and Russia that entered the war against Germany and Austria-Hungary in 1914.

Triple Alliance the alliance between Germany, Austria-Hungary, and Italy (which declined to honor its commitment) that entered World War I.

Social Darwinism the theory that nations and races are subject to the same laws of natural selection as Charles Darwin had perceived in plants and animals in nature.

Did you know?

The term "survival of the fittest" was not coined by Charles Darwin, but by Herbert Spencer (1820–1903), the leading spokesman for the Social Darwinists.

distribution of power the distribution among actors in global politics of the capacity to compel one another to carry out their preferences.

(the **Triple Alliance**). Although Italy was also a member of the Triple Alliance, it failed to meet its obligations. *These alliances were unique in that, unlike the shifting balance-of-power alliances of the previous century, they were permanent, even in peacetime.*

There were both long- and short-term sources of World War I. For example, throughout the nineteenth century, the world had undergone profound change. Industrialization and nationalism expanded the capacity to fight large wars. The century also featured growing racism associated with the popularity of a set of ideas known as **Social Darwinism**. That concept – a distortion of Charles Darwin's theory of natural selection – was (mis)applied to states and people. Social Darwinists argued that a process of competition and struggle among human beings determined who survived. These views were associated with unfettered capitalism and were used to justify war as the means of survival of nation-states. The idea was also used to justify imperialism by those who claimed that some races are superior to others. Later, the Nazis eagerly seized upon similar ideas. Thus, claiming that the war started because of the assassination of an archduke would be trivial. Furthermore, because these events are largely *unique* to a single war, they tell us little about the sources of war more generally. In this section, we will take a broader view, exploring the many intersecting events that led to war. We begin by examining the long-term events on the road to war including the growth in German power and ambition, the formation of peacetime alliances that split Europe into two armed camps, the aggressive behavior of Germany's emperor, Europe's colonial rivalries, arms races at sea and on land, ethnic and social turmoil in Austria-Hungary and Russia, and nationalism run amok.

German unification and Europe's diplomatic revolution

The years between the turn of the century until 1914 gave rise to a series of dangerous trends and events that exacerbated tensions among Europe's major countries that eventually exploded in 1914. For realists, the most important trend was a shift in the **distribution of power** in Europe that resulted from the unification of Germany following three wars – Schleswig-Holstein (1864), Austro-German (1866), and Franco-Prussian (1870). United Germany was governed by an emperor (*Kaiser*). The emperor appointed a chancellor, who was responsible to the monarch and was responsible for overseeing the various government ministers. The architect and manager of German unification before and after the wars of unification was the powerful and brilliant "Iron Chancellor," Prince Otto von Bismarck (1815–98).

North Sea

Baltic Sea

DENMARK

Copenhagen

SCHLESWIG

GRAND
DUCHY OF
OLDENBURG

GRAND DUCHY OF
MECKLENBURG-
SCHWERIN

HOLSTEIN
(to Austria
in 1865)

Lübeck

Danzig

Hamburg

LAUENBURG

Stettin

NETHERLANDS

Bremen

KINGDOM OF
HANOVER
(to 1866)

GRAND DUCHY OF
MECKLENBURG-
STRELITZ

PRINCIPALITY OF
SCHAUMBURG-
LIPPE

DUCHY OF
ANHALT

Berlin

LIMBOURG

PRINCIPALITY OF
LIPPE-DETMOLD

DUCHY OF
BRUNSWICK

Posen

BELGIUM

Cologne

PRINCIPALITY
OF WALDECK

ELECTOR
OF HESSE
(to 1866)

THURINGIAN STATES

RUSSIAN
EMPIRE

Leipzig

DUCHY OF
NASSAU
(to 1866)

K. OF SAXONY
Dresden

Breslau

Frankfurt

GRAND DUCHY
OF HESSE

Prague

Königgrätz

BAVARIA

GRAND DUCHY OF BADEN

Nuremburg

Bohemia

Moravia

Cracow

LUXEMBOURG

FRANCE

Stuttgart

KINGDOM OF
WÜRTTEMBERG

KINGDOM
OF
BAVARIA

AUSTRIAN EMPIRE

Brünn

Nikolsburg

Munich

Vienna

Pozsony

LIECHTENSTEIN

Buda • • Pest

| | Prussia in 1865 | | Annexed by Prussia, 1866 | —— Border of the North German Confederation from 1867 |
| | Other German states | | Austrian possessions from 1866 | ······ The German Confederation in 1866 |

Map 3.1 The Unification of Germany, 1865–66

Bismarck was a skilled practitioner of power politics. Although
not a nationalist himself, he manipulated German nationalism for
his purposes and pursued a policy called **realpolitik**. Repeatedly he
invoked nationalist feelings to cow political opponents or ram spending
bills through Germany's parliament. As a result of Bismarck's efforts,
German unification brought a great increase in the country's territory
and population as well as economic expansion. For example, Germany
passed Britain in 1900 in the production of steel, vital to make railroads
and armaments, and outpaced the rest of the world in its chemical and
electrical industries. Overall, German per capita income quadrupled

realpolitik a policy premised on
material factors, especially
power, rather than on theoretical
or ethical considerations.

between 1860 and 1913, and the aggregate size of the German economy increased over six-fold.[6] Such growth fueled concern elsewhere in Europe about the possibility that Germany was becoming the greatest of the great powers in Europe and a competitor for overseas markets and opportunities for foreign investment. Still, as long as the political environment remained stable and tranquil, there was little hostility toward Germany.

Bismarck was at heart a conservative; and, having unified Germany, he harbored no additional territorial ambitions. Instead, he tried to preserve the status quo in Europe by enmeshing potential adversaries in a web of treaties constructed to maintain the isolation of France which had become Germany's implacable adversary owing to Germany's seizure of the two frontier provinces Alsace and Lorraine after the Franco-Prussian War.

Bismarck formed the Dual Alliance (1879), by which Germany and Austria-Hungary agreed to help each other in the event either was attacked. He also organized the Three Emperors League (1872, 1881), which promised solidarity among Europe's three conservative monarchs (Russia's tsar, Germany's kaiser, and Austria-Hungary's emperor). Bismarck's third key arrangement was the Reinsurance Treaty (1887), which promised that under certain circumstances, Russia and Germany would be benevolently neutral if either became involved in war. The parties were not bound to neutrality, however, if Germany attacked France or Russia attacked Austria. On the surface, the three agreements seemed to contradict each other because Russia and Austria were engaged in a fierce competition in the **Balkans** that could spark a war between the two. Bismarck did all he could to prevent this, declaring that the Balkans were "not worth the bones of a single Pomeranian grenadier."

In 1890, the mercurial young Kaiser Wilhelm II (1859–1941), only recently enthroned, dismissed Bismarck in what turned out to be a catastrophic decision. Wilhelm, like many of the kings and princes of the time, was closely linked by blood and personal friendship to other monarchs, notably his cousins George V of Britain (1865–1936) and Tsar Nicholas II of Russia, his uncle Edward VII of Britain (1841–1910), and his grandmother, Britain's Queen Victoria (1819–1901). Unlike the previous Kaiser, who had let Bismarck run matters, the new Kaiser wanted to make his own decisions. Moreover, he harbored great ambitions for a German Empire. In contrast to Bismarck, who had no interest in competing with Britain and France for overseas colonies and imperial booty, the Kaiser eagerly sought colonies in Africa, China, and the southern Pacific to increase German trade and prestige. In time, his "world politics" (*Weltpolitik*) amassed an overseas empire of over one million square miles and some 13 million inhabitants. The combination of growing German military and economic power alienated

Balkans a peninsula in southeastern Europe that includes Slovenia, Croatia, Bosnia and Herzegovina, Macedonia, Serbia and Montenegro, Albania, Greece, Romania, Bulgaria, and European Turkey.

and frightened other European countries and the result was a process in which adversaries started to gang up against Germany.

The Kaiser's ambitions alone would have stirred suspicion among other European powers, but they seemed even more dangerous owing to his provocative words and behavior. He loved to wear uniforms, strut in front of his soldiers, and in the words of one observer, "always negotiated with a pistol on the table." An example of the Kaiser's combustible diplomacy was the so-called Daily Telegraph Affair. This incident involved an interview with the Kaiser that was published in London's *Daily Telegraph* on October 8, 1908, in which he referred to the English as "mad as hares" and indicated that the Germans really disliked the British. In the same interview, he also insulted the Russians, French, and Japanese. He further infuriated Great Britain by his support of South Africa's Boers in the Boer War (1899–1902).

Neither the Kaiser nor Bismarck's successors as chancellor had the Iron Chancellor's subtlety or skill in manipulating the complex system of alliances and relationships with other countries. After Bismarck left, one of the Kaiser's first acts was to terminate the Reinsurance Treaty with Russia because, he claimed, it was incompatible with the Dual Alliance. Unfortunately, in doing so, the Kaiser alienated Russia, ended French isolation, and set in motion a diplomatic revolution in Europe.

In a stroke, the Kaiser brought an end to the delicate alliance system that Bismarck had maintained and new alliances formed to counter German power. On August 18, 1892, Russia and France concluded an agreement to aid one another in the event of hostilities with the members of the Triple Alliance, pledging that their military "forces shall engage to the full with such speed that *Germany will have to fight simultaneously on the East and on the West*."[7] In 1898, following a dangerous military confrontation at an isolated desert oasis called Fashoda in the Egyptian Sudan, British and French leaders negotiated an end to their colonial disputes, agreeing that Britain would control Egypt and the Suez Canal, while France would enjoy a privileged position in Morocco. Their agreement, the Entente Cordiale, was reached on April 8, 1904. In 1907 the Anglo-Russian Entente ended key colonial disputes between Russia and Britain in Persia, Afghanistan, China, and India. Germany was never mentioned in either agreement, but the Germans regarded the end of these colonial tensions as dangerous steps in a potential anti-German alliance. In fact, Germany rightly saw the Anglo-Russian Entente as the last link in the Triple Entente that encircled the Germans in 1914, completing the prewar alliance system (see Table 3.1). Germany was encircled, and mistrust between the two alliances became endemic. It

Table 3.1 Key European alliances prior to 1914

The Dual Alliance	1879	Germany, Austria-Hungary
Three Emperor's League	1881	Germany, Russia, Austria-Hungary
Austro-Serbian Alliance	1881	Austria, Serbia
The Triple Alliance	1882	Germany, Austria-Hungary, Italy
The Austro-German-Romanian Alliance	1883	Austria-Hungary, Germany, Romania
The Franco-Russian Alliance	1894	France, Russia
The Russo-Bulgarian Military Convention	1902	Russia, Bulgaria
The Entente Cordiale	1904	France, Britain
The Anglo-Russian Entente	1907	Britain, Russia
The Triple Entente	1907	France, Britain, Russia

was this historic sequence that encouraged theorists to examine the relationship between alliances and war (see chapter 8, pp. 380–1).

In summary, this diplomatic revolution formalized the division of Europe, as many countries in Europe came to dislike and fear German power and German intentions. Nowhere was this dislike more evident than in Great Britain.

Arms races, nationalism, the Balkan imbroglio

The onset of an Anglo-German naval arms race also enhanced Anglo-German hostility and suspicion and sparked the more general interest in the relationship between war and arms racing described in chapter 7. Although Britain viewed Germany's growth in industry, population, trade, and even colonies as tolerable, it viewed the growing German navy as a mortal threat. And British concern was well founded. Germany's naval expansion, which involved increasing the number of big-gun battleships, then regarded as the ultimate weapon in naval warfare, seemed to threaten Britain's dominance of the seas so essential for maintaining the British Empire. Even worse, Germany's naval expansion also challenged the security of the British Isles, which for centuries had depended on naval superiority as their protection from invasion.

German naval expansion was carried out by Grand Admiral Alfred von Tirpitz (1849–1930), who declared, "For Germany the most dangerous naval enemy at present is England. It is also the enemy against which we most urgently require a certain measure of naval force as a political power factor."[8] At Tirpitz's urging, the first German Navy Bill (1897) authorized construction of 19 battleships over a five-year period. Although the German fleet would not equal Britain's, Britain had a great empire and global responsibilities, whereas the German navy would be concentrated in the Baltic and North Sea where it posed an immediate risk to Great Britain itself and to the British home fleet.

The naval arms race was marked by growing hostility, bitterness, and suspicion. Before it ended, German naval construction had caused a virtual panic in Britain, which depended upon preponderant sea power for its security. Only so long as the British navy reigned supreme, was the country invulnerable to German armies. In addition, Britain imported much of its food and raw materials from overseas, and these imports would be vulnerable to Germany's growing fleet.

To meet what was seen as a deadly threat from Germany, Britain began construction of a new type of battleship featuring great improvements in speed, armaments, and armor – notably the number and quality of its big guns. The first of these, *HMS Dreadnought*, was commissioned in 1905 and was seaworthy within the year. Quickly, Germany began to construct its own dreadnoughts. *HMS Dreadnought* made all existing battleships obsolete. *Dreadnought* was an inherently dangerous weapon because it negated Britain's earlier superiority in older battleships and thus threatened to alter the naval balance between the two countries in Germany's favor.

The dreadnought competition greatly intensified British fears. On March 29, 1909, the British Foreign Secretary declared that

> the situation is grave . . . (and) is created by the German program [of building a battle fleet]. Whether the program is carried out quickly or slowly the fact of its existence makes a new situation. When that program is completed, Germany, a great country close to our own shore, will have a fleet of thirty-three Dreadnoughts. . . . It is true that there is not one of them in commission yet; but it is equally true that the whole program . . . when completed . . . will be the most powerful fleet that the world has yet seen. That imposes upon us the necessity, of which we are now at the beginning – except so far as we have Dreadnoughts already – of rebuilding the whole of our fleet.[9]

The Anglo-German naval rivalry was accompanied by an arms race on land that pitted France and Russia against Germany and Austria-Hungary. Both sides sought to conscript ever larger numbers of soldiers into their armed forces in order to be better prepared for the war they feared was approaching. This competition made Europe an armed camp.

The alliance system and the tensions generated by the arms races fueled **nationalism** all over Europe, which in turn intensified tensions and mutual suspicions. German nationalism focused on achieving a world

nationalism the belief that a nation should be recognized as such, should enjoy equal rights with other nations, and should have political autonomy or independence.

empire to match the country's growing economic and military might. In France, nationalism focused on regaining Alsace-Lorraine and reversing the verdict of the Franco-Prussian War. In Russia, nationalism focused on defending fellow Slavs in Serbia and elsewhere from Austria-Hungary's threats and in regaining the prestige that Russia had lost in its defeat at the hands of Japan in the 1905 Russo-Japanese War. Finally, in Austria-Hungary, nationalism on the part of the Slavic peoples who were dominated by their Austrian and Hungarian rulers took the form of violent efforts to achieve national independence.

After 1867, the polyglot Austro-Hungarian Empire became known as the Dual Monarchy because its new constitution gave the Hungarian and Austrian governments authority over their own regions and dominance over Slavic peoples such as the Czechs and Poles. In this respect, the ramshackle empire resembled the dynastic states of medieval Europe more than the nation-states that had evolved during the eighteenth and nineteenth centuries. Austria-Hungary's troubles lay in its national diversity (see Table 3.2) and especially in the fervent demands of the Slavic peoples in the Empire for independence from their Austrian and Hungarian oppressors. Moreover, Slavic agitation *within* Austria-Hungary was intensified by support for the Slavs from *outside*. Austria's southern neighbor, Serbia, viewed itself as the kernel of a future and much larger Slavic state.[10] In addition, Serbia and the Slavic inhabitants of Austria-Hungary enjoyed the sympathy of Russia, also a Slavic country, in which many people harbored dreams of a greater Slavic empire.

Table 3.2 National-ethnic distribution within Austria-Hungary in 1914 (%)

German	24
Hungarian	20
Czech (Slavic)	13
Polish (Slavic)	10
Ruthenian (Slavic)	6
Croatian (Slavic)	5
Serb (Slavic)	4
Slovak (Slavic)	4
Slovene (Slavic)	3
Italian	3

Clearly, many tensions plagued relations within and between Austria-Hungary and Russia stemming from security and territorial issues. The central question was which of these two great empires would control the Balkans, with Russia acting as protector of the Slavs within and outside Austria-Hungary, and which would fill the power vacuum that was growing in the Balkans as Ottoman Turkey, derisively referred to as the "sick man of Europe", retreated from the region.

Crisis diplomacy

The years before 1914 were punctuated by repeated international crises, often pitting Germany against Britain, France, and Russia. These crises tested the solidarity of the alliance system, revealed Kaiser Wilhelm's harsh negotiating style, and reflected the waves of nationalism and ethnic conflict that were sweeping across Europe. At least four of these incidents merit brief attention: the First Moroccan Crisis (1905–06), the Bosnian Crisis (1908–09), the Second Moroccan Crisis (1911), and the Balkan Wars (1912–13).

The First Moroccan Crisis began after Britain promised to support French claims to that country. Germany was incensed by growing French influence in Morocco, which violated an earlier treaty and excluded Germany from a strategic position in North Africa. Thus, in March 1905, Kaiser Wilhelm II sailed to Morocco, where he declared Morocco's sultan to be an independent sovereign and where he offered German protection against French influence. The Germans also called for a conference to discuss Morocco's future. At the conference, held in 1906, Germany tried to split its adversaries but instead found itself virtually isolated. Only Austria-Hungary supported Germany, while Britain, the United States, and Russia supported France. As a result, France achieved greater influence in Morocco than it had previously enjoyed, and France and Germany were more alienated from each other than ever.

Five years later a second crisis over Morocco erupted between France and Germany. The crisis was triggered after France dispatched troops to the city of Fez, ostensibly to restore order. Claiming that France's action violated the 1906 agreement that had ended the First Moroccan Crisis, Germany sent a warship to the Moroccan port of Agadir. Again, Britain backed France, and again Germany was forced to back down. The episode further poisoned Franco-German relations and reaffirmed Franco-British unity in the face of German belligerence.

Another major crisis exploded in 1908, this time in the Balkans, and brought Europe to the brink of war. The crisis centered on the fate of Bosnia-Herzegovina, formerly an Ottoman province in the Balkans, which had fallen under Austro-Hungarian control in 1878. In 1908, while Europe's attention was focused on other events including revolution in Turkey and the defeat of Russia in the 1904–05 Russo-Japanese War, Austria-Hungary decided to annex Bosnia-Herzegovina and make it part of the empire.

The crisis opened with a meeting between the Austrian and Russian foreign ministers on September 19, 1908. A trade of sorts was in the wind: Russia would ignore the Austrian annexation in return for which the Austrians would support Russia's effort to secure free passage for

Russian warships past Constantinople and through the Dardanelles from the Black Sea into the Mediterranean. However, a misunderstanding over timing poisoned Austro-Russian relations. The Austrians declared the annexation of Bosnia-Herzegovina on October 3rd before the Russians were able to gain the consent of the other European powers for their side of the deal. Given its military weakness so soon after defeat in Asia, Russia had no choice but to swallow its anger and allow Austria to proceed with the annexation, but the residue of bitterness between the two countries enhanced Russian willingness to settle scores in 1914.

The fate of the Balkans continued to bedevil European politics when in 1912 the Ottoman Turks decided to reverse their declining fortunes and attack Serbia. Two wars ensued (the Balkan Wars) over the fate of the region. In alliance with Bulgaria, Montenegro, and Greece, Serbia attacked Turkey. An armistice was reached in December, but Greece continued the war with Turkey. Hostilities resumed in January, after the Turks rejected the terms demanded by Serbia and its allies. Serbia, Greece, and Montenegro now ganged up against Bulgaria; Turkey and Rumania joined the fray later. A final treaty brought an end to hostilities in November 1913. The outcome was inconclusive, but almost everyone in the Balkans harbored grudges against one another and sought revenge for real and imagined wrongs.

The final descent to war

The combustible combination of nationalism, ethnicity, and territorial rivalry in the Balkans sparked the final crisis that brought on war – the assassination of Archduke Franz Ferdinand and his duchess during a state visit to Bosnia. Bosnia, inhabited largely by Slavs, had been the site of numerous plots against Austria-Hungary's Hapsburg rulers, especially after the 1908 annexation. Austria-Hungary placed the blame for the assassination squarely on Serbia, which had for years been agitating for the independence of Austria-Hungary's Slavic subjects, and saw the crisis as an opportunity to deal with Serbia once and for all. Thereafter, when Russia decided to support Serbia and Germany declared for Austria-Hungary, the alliance system transformed a Balkan conflict into a continental conflagration.

Before reacting to the assassination, Austro-Hungarian officials wanted to make certain that they would have the assistance of their powerful ally, Germany, especially if Russia were to side with its fellow Slavs in Serbia. A German commitment, they believed, would deter Russia from entering the conflict. At a high-level conference held in Berlin, the Austro-Hungarian representative concluded that the German

Kaiser had agreed to the proposed Austro-Hungarian actions against
Serbia, and the Kaiser and his chancellor reported this information to
the Emperor Franz Joseph in a telegram to Austria-Hungary's foreign
minister (see Key document: The blank check). Some historians argue
that at least some of Germany's leaders, far from merely hoping to deter
Russia, actually hoped that war would begin so that Germany could
defeat Russia before Russia's growing military power made it a mortal
threat to Germany.[11] The Kaiser's agreement to follow Austria-Hungary
is often cited when holding Germany responsible for World War I.

Key document   The blank check,[12] July 6, 1914

After the assassination in Sarajevo, Count Leopold von Berchtold (1862–1942), the Austro-
Hungarian foreign minister, drew up a letter for the Emperor Franz [Francis] Joseph to sign and
send to Wilhelm II, to try and convince him of Serbia's responsibility for the deaths. On July 6th,
Wilhelm and his Imperial Chancellor Theobald von Bethmann-Hollweg (1856–1921)
telegrammed Berchtold that Austria-Hungary could rely on Germany for support in whatever
action was necessary to deal with Serbia – in effect offering Austria-Hungary a "blank check."

*Telegram from the Imperial Chancellor, von Bethmann-Hollweg, to the German Ambassador at Vienna.
Tschirschky, July 6, 1914*

Confidential. For Your Excellency's personal information and guidance

The Austro-Hungarian Ambassador yesterday delivered to the Emperor a confidential personal letter from
the Emperor Francis Joseph, which depicts the present situation from the Austro-Hungarian point of view, and
describes the measures which Vienna has in view. . . .

His Majesty (Wilhelm II) desires to say that he is not blind to the danger which threatens Austria-Hungary
and thus the Triple Alliance as a result of the Russian and Serbian Pan-Slavic agitation. . . .

Finally, as far as concerns Serbia, His Majesty, of course, cannot interfere in the dispute now going on
between Austria-Hungary and that country, as it is a matter not within his competence. The Emperor Francis
Joseph may, however, rest assured that His Majesty will faithfully stand by Austria-Hungary, as is required by
the obligations of his alliance and of his ancient friendship.

Berlin, July 6, 1914
BETHMANN-HOLLWEG

With German support, the Austrians made the first move. Three weeks
after the assassination, claiming to have evidence of Serbian complicity
in the plot to kill the archduke, the Austrian government issued an
ultimatum to Serbia. In the ultimatum, which Austria-Hungary's leaders
had framed so that Serbia would find it unacceptable, the Austrians

demanded that Serbia agree virtually to surrender its sovereignty by permitting Austria-Hungary to run the investigation of the assassination plot in Serbia. The ultimatum and the list of demands that it contained were designed to end once and for all the Serbian menace to the empire's unity (see Key document: The Austro-Hungarian ultimatum). By forcing Serbia to reject the ultimatum, Austria-Hungary's leaders believed they would have the excuse they needed for war. In fact, Serbia responded by accepting most of Austria's demands. Nevertheless, on July 25th, Austria-Hungary mobilized its army, and three days later declared war on Serbia.

Key document   The Austro-Hungarian ultimatum to Serbia,[13] Vienna, July 22, 1914

The history of recent years, and in particular the painful events of the 28th of June last, have shown the existence of a subversive movement with the object of detaching a part of the territories of Austria-Hungary from the Monarchy.

The movement, which had its birth under the eye of the Serbian Government, has gone so far as to make itself manifest on both sides of the Serbian frontier in the shape of acts of terrorism and a series of outrages and murders. . . .

[T]he Royal Serbian Government has done nothing to repress these movements. It has permitted the criminal machinations of various societies and associations directed against the Monarchy, and has tolerated unrestrained language on the part of the press, the glorification of the perpetrators of outrages, and the participation of officers and functionaries in subversive agitation.

It has . . . permitted all manifestations of a nature to incite the Serbian population to hatred of the Monarchy and contempt of its institutions.

This culpable tolerance of the Royal Serbian Government had not ceased at the moment when the events of the 28th of June last proved its fatal consequences to the whole world.

It results from the depositions and confessions of the criminal perpetrators of the outrage of the 28th of June that the Sarajevo assassinations were planned in Belgrade; that the arms and explosives with which the murderers were provided had been given to them by Serbian officers and functionaries belonging to the Narodna Odbrana; and finally, that the passage into Bosnia of the criminals and their arms was organized and effected by the chiefs of the Serbian frontier service.

The above-mentioned results of the magisterial investigation do not permit the Austro-Hungarian Government to pursue any longer the attitude of expectant forbearance which they have maintained for years in face of the machinations hatched in Belgrade, and thence propagated in the territories of the Monarchy. The results, on the contrary, impose on them the duty of putting an end to the intrigues which form a perpetual menace to the tranquility of the Monarchy.

To achieve this end the Imperial and Royal Government see themselves compelled to demand from the Royal Serbian Government a formal assurance that they condemn this dangerous propaganda against the Monarchy; in other words the whole series of tendencies, the ultimate aim of which is to detach from the

Monarchy territories belonging to it and that they undertake to suppress by every means this criminal and terrorist propaganda.

In order to give a formal character to this undertaking the Royal Serbian Government shall publish on the front page of their "Official Journal" of the 13–26 of July the following declaration:

"The Royal Government of Serbia condemn the propaganda directed against Austria-Hungary – i.e., the general tendency of which the final aim is to detach from the Austro-Hungarian Monarchy territories belonging to it, and they sincerely deplore the fatal consequences of these criminal proceedings.

The Royal Government regret that Serbian officers and functionaries participated in the above-mentioned propaganda. . . .

The Royal Government, who disapprove and repudiate all idea of interfering or attempting to interfere with the destinies of the inhabitants of any part whatsoever of Austria-Hungary, consider it their duty formally to warn officers and functionaries, and the whole population of the Kingdom, that henceforward they will proceed with the utmost rigor against persons who may be guilty of such machinations, which they will use all their efforts to anticipate and suppress."

This declaration shall simultaneously be communicated to the Royal army as an order of the day by His Majesty the King and shall be published in the "Official Bulletin" of the army.

The Royal Serbian Government shall further undertake:

(1) To suppress any publication which incites to hatred and contempt of the Austro-Hungarian Monarchy and the general tendency of which is directed against its territorial integrity;

(2) To dissolve immediately the society styled "Narodna Odbrana," to confiscate all its means of propaganda, and to proceed in the same manner against other societies and their branches in Serbia which engage in propaganda against the Austro-Hungarian Monarchy. . . . ;

(3) To eliminate without delay from public instruction in Serbia, both as regards the teaching body and also as regards the methods of instruction, everything that serves, or might serve, to foment the propaganda against Austria-Hungary;

(4) To remove from the military service, and from the administration in general, all officers and functionaries guilty of propaganda against the Austro-Hungarian Monarchy whose names and deeds the Austro-Hungarian Government reserve to themselves the right of communicating to the Royal Government;

(5) To accept the collaboration in Serbia of representatives of the Austro-Hungarian Government for the suppression of the subversive movement directed against the territorial integrity of the Monarchy;

(6) To take judicial proceedings against accessories to the plot of the 28th of June who are on Serbian territory; delegates of the Austro-Hungarian Government will take part in the investigation relating thereto;

(7) To proceed without delay to the arrest of Major Voija Tankositch and of the individual named Milan Ciganovitch, a Serbian State employee, who have been compromised by the results of the magisterial inquiry at Sarajevo;

(8) To prevent by effective measures the cooperation of the Serbian authorities in the illicit traffic in arms and explosives across the frontier, to dismiss and punish severely the officials of the frontier service at Shabatz

Loznica guilty of having assisted the perpetrators of the Sarajevo crime by facilitating their passage across the frontier;

(9) To furnish the Imperial and Royal Government with explanations regarding the unjustifiable utterances of high Serbian officials, both in Serbia and abroad, who, notwithstanding their official position, have not hesitated since the crime of the 28th of June to express themselves in interviews in terms of hostility to the Austro-Hungarian Government; and, finally,

(10) To notify the Imperial and Royal Government without delay of the execution of the measures comprised under the preceding heads.

The Austro-Hungarian Government expect the reply of the Royal Government at the latest by 5 o'clock on Saturday evening the 25th of July.

Russia did decide to come to the defense of Serbia. In a memorandum to the Russian Foreign Ministry in St. Petersburg, Russian Foreign Minister Sazanov explained why:

> The assassination of the Austrian Archduke, Franz Ferdinand, and his wife in Sarajevo has created an international crisis. Austria will probably use this as a pretext to retaliate against Serbia, an action that could quickly involve the entire Continent. . . . His Majesty, Nicholas II, has already decided to allow the Foreign Ministry the greatest latitude possible in determining Imperial policy, but the Tsar and I have already concluded the following:
> • Public opinion will insist upon war if that is only alternative to national humiliation.
> • Mobilization against Imperial Russia shall be considered an act of war.
> • Involvement of Imperial Russia in a general conflict on the European continent, especially a two-front war involving Germany, would not be in its best interests.[14]

Fulfilling its promise to back Austria-Hungary if war ensued, Germany declared war on Russia on August 1st and then on Russia's ally, France. The last major power to join the contest was Great Britain, even though it had no formal legal commitment to its two partners in the Triple Entente. However, Britain had a serious moral obligation, especially to France with which it had made secret but informal military arrangements, including the agreement that in the event of war, Britain would defend France's coast along the Atlantic Ocean in return for which the French navy would defend the Mediterranean on its southern coast. The trigger for British entry in the war was the German invasion of neutral Belgium. Thus, what had begun as a limited war in the Balkans, owing to the alliance system, had spread across all of Europe.

In 1915, Italy joined the Triple Entente, thereby betraying its earlier obligations as a member of the Triple Alliance in return for territorial promises made in the secret Treaty of London. And, in 1917, the United States, which had been neutral but also tilted in favor of Britain, joined the war owing to Germany's resumption of unrestricted submarine attacks on both enemy and neutral vessels that were helping to supply its adversaries. Millions of soldiers joined the war with enthusiasm, including a young Adolf Hitler (1889–1945) who won several awards for bravery, but that enthusiasm quickly turned to despair.

Figure 3.2 Adolf Hitler
Photo by Heinrich Hoffmann, courtesy of Dr. Herz and Prof. Dr. Loiperdinger

Explaining the outbreak of World War I

How do scholars explain the outbreak of World War I? Moreover, why do they wish to do so? In answer to the second question, political scientists examine cases like that of World War I in order to generalize about war and identify similarities it may have with other wars. Levels of analysis, introduced in chapter 1, are a tool they use to untangle the general and unique causes of wars and other events. As we untangle the causes of World War I in the following discussion, we will employ the individual, state, and global levels to make such generalizations as well.

Individual-level explanations

First, on the individual level, we can theorize that the war broke out because of *anachronistic leaders*. Leaders were out of step with the times and, thus, failed to resist the march to war. Following this individual-level explanation, it can be argued that leaders such as the emperors Franz Joseph (1830–1916), Wilhelm II, and Nicholas II were the products of an earlier era of dynastic states. They did not understand the forces of nationalism, public opinion, industrialization, and technology or know how to cope with them. Moreover, they were hereditary rulers who had not been selected for merit or intelligence, and they were dedicated to preserving their personal rule and their dynasties as much as preserving their nation-states or international peace. At best, however, this is only a partial explanation, because other more "modern" leaders behaved much in the same way. For example, neither the French nor British leaders, selected by democratic elections, did much better. In addition, the argument requires us to assume that such leaders *could control events*; that is, we overlook structural factors like distribution of power. Other individual-level explanations point the finger of blame at the characteristics of particular leaders: Kaiser Wilhelm's ambition and belligerence, General Helmuth von Moltke's (1848–1916) fear of Russia, and Tsar Nicholas's weakness and vacillation.

State-level explanations

Another explanation, at the state level of analysis, might be called the *aggressive state* argument. Specifically, some historians claim that Germany started the war to prevent Russia from becoming too powerful and that this was the reason German leaders gave Austria-Hungary the "blank check" to do what it wished to Serbia. In fact, there were two wars: one declared by Austria-Hungary against Serbia was intended as a localized conflict; the other, a general war "deliberately started" by Germany "to keep from being overtaken by Russia."[15] In other words, though Germany was Europe's most powerful country in 1914, it feared that in a few years Russia would surpass it. Then, Russia would pose a mortal threat to German security, and it would be too late for Germany to defeat Russia. Thus, Germany was willing to fight in 1914 to prevent Russia from getting too powerful. Indeed, German Chancellor Bethmann-Hollweg, one author of the infamous "blank check" telegram, admitted that Germany had fought a **preventive war**, but he then shifted the blame to others: "Yes, My God, in a certain sense it was a preventive war. But when war was hanging above us, when it had to come in two years even more dangerously and more inescapably, and when the generals said now it is still possible without defeat, but not in two years time."[16] Others point to German colonial ambitions, its desire to become a world power, and its intensifying nationalism after 1890 as creating a climate in which hostility intensified.

preventive war a war launched by one actor in order to prevent another actor from growing strong enough in the future to pose a threat.

Using these arguments to justify their actions, the victors forced Germany to admit to its responsibility for starting the war in Article 231 of the Versailles Treaty, which read: "The Allied and Associated Governments affirm and Germany accepts the responsibility of Germany and her allies for causing all the loss and damage to which the Allied and Associated Governments and their nationals have been subjected as a consequence of the *war imposed upon them by the aggression of Germany and her allies*" (emphasis added). In other words, the actions and rhetoric of Germany's government in the decades before the war and its belligerent policies, so the argument goes, produced a climate of fear and suspicion which gave birth to war. The allies used Article 231 to justify their demand that Germany pay them reparations for the costs of the war.

Another explanation, also at the state level, is that *weak states* caused the war. This argument focuses in particular on Austria-Hungary and Russia, and their domestic affairs. After all, those were the two countries whose actions triggered war. In the case of Austria-Hungary, this explanation focuses on the national and ethnic troubles within the empire, especially Slav discontent. This claim implies that societies composed of different groups of people or nations are more likely to go to war than societies in which most people are like one another. Although not as ethnically diverse as Austria-Hungary, Russia was weakened by the social discontent of its people. Opposition to the government grew after Russia's defeat at the hands of Japan, and the subsequent 1905 Revolution proved a foretaste of the 1917 Bolshevik Revolution. What is important is that both versions of this argument suggest that interstate war is the product of domestic turmoil. As we will see in chapter 8 (p. 356), one version of this argument claims that political leaders start wars overseas to divert public attention from difficulties at home.

As a Marxist, Russian Bolshevik leader Vladimir Lenin (1870–1924) explained the war by focusing on economic and class factors inside states – again emphasizing the state level. In his essay "Imperialism, the Last Stage of Capitalism," written during the war, Lenin argued that as the strains within capitalist societies grew, these societies sought to ease social tension by overseas **imperialism** and the acquisition of colonies that could provide raw materials, cheap labor, outlets for surplus capital investment, and markets for exports. This explanation emphasized that social peace at home could be bought for a time by exploiting foreign laborers. Lenin theorized that, in time, however, war would erupt out of intensified competition among capitalist societies for colonies in a world in which there was no further room to expand. Imperial latecomers like Germany, the United States, and Japan became aggressive when they found how little the British and French had left for them.

imperialism the political control of one state by another.

Though intriguing, the imperialist explanation suffers from the fact that the 1914 war exploded in the Balkans not in the colonial areas of Africa or Asia or between the colonial powers. Furthermore, Russia and Austria-Hungary, the two initial adversaries, were relatively uninterested in overseas expansion. Thus, Lenin's argument ignores the fact that colonial competition had been most intense among countries that became allies before 1914 (Britain, France, and Russia) and that their colonial rivalries had been settled before the war. Countering Lenin's theory, one observer declared that the "war arose, immediately, out of the rivalries of two of the landlocked, contiguous, and semi-feudal, as opposed to the oceanic, capitalist and highly developed empires."[17]

A state-level variation of the Marxist theme was the belief that World War I took place because of the efforts of the international arms industry to sell more and more of its products. Firms such as Krupp in Germany, Schneider-Creusot in France, Vickers in Britain, and Skoda in Austria-Hungary were "merchants of death," willing to sell arms to everyone.

Nationalism, too, receives a lot of attention in state-level analyses of the sources of war, particularly as a background factor in creating a hostile atmosphere. After the French Revolution of 1789, when nationalism became a political force, leaders could no longer barter territory and populations. Instead, citizens, who had formerly been subjects, became intensely and passionately involved in foreign relations in defense of their "people." In the case of World War I, Slavic nationalism threatened Austria-Hungary; Russian nationalism placed pressure on the tsar to aid Serbia; French nationalism demanded the return of the "lost provinces" of Alsace-Lorraine; and nationalism everywhere rallied people behind their leaders when war finally came.

Global system-level explanations

A popular explanation at the global level of analysis that had been used by Thucydides many centuries earlier (chapter 1, p. 9) is that the war was a result of the *changing distribution of power* in Europe. This argument asserts that growing German industrial and military power produced a security dilemma (see chapter 1, p. 23) by creating fear in Britain, France, and Russia that led to *arms racing* and *alliances* that divided Europe into two armed camps. Anglo-French-Russian fear then led to the encirclement of Germany and, in turn, to growing fear in Berlin that Germany had to strike then or weaken over time.

A particularly provocative system-level explanation is called system-overload theory. It contends that in 1914, major adversaries found that their expectations about the world no longer held true and that past customs and unspoken rules of behavior were being violated. Increasingly, they no longer knew what to expect and were overwhelmed by panic. In this atmosphere, decision-makers could not cope, and after the assassination of the archduke, the decision-making systems suffered a "nervous breakdown."

A related system-level argument focuses more narrowly on rapid *technological change*, the inability of statesmen and generals to understand its implications, and the war plans of generals that put a premium on striking first. Those who make this argument cite as evidence the role of mobilization in the race to war and the consequent removal of authority from the politicians to the generals. They also argue that when generals do not recognize the effects of technological change, they prepare for the wrong kind of war, as they did when they planned to take the offensive in 1914 (see chapter 6, pp. 286–7, for first strike in the nuclear era).

3: THE WORLD WARS

In summary, World War I, like all wars, had *many* causes, and these must be sought at all levels of analysis. Leaders in 1914 were remarkably incompetent and did little to call a halt to events. German policy and rhetoric after 1890 frightened its neighbors, and German leaders did irresponsibly cede the initiative to Austria-Hungary during the crisis following the archduke's assassination. Slavic discontent within Austria-Hungary did threaten to pull the empire apart and was exacerbated by Serb interference. The Russian government did sense it could not afford to back down in the face of threats to a fellow Slav state, especially in light of discontent at home. Colonial rivalries had created tensions among Europe's great powers, and arms sales did foster militarism. Arms races and alliances did produce mutual suspicions and divided Europe into armed camps. War plans did pressure governments to act impetuously and gave them little time to examine possible alternatives to war. During the crisis, the bureaucracies did function poorly, and leaders felt overwhelmed by events. Intense and widespread nationalism did encourage national rivalry and make it difficult for leaders to back down when push came to shove. To some extent, all of the causes cited above played a role in the descent to war. Moreover, influences at the individual, state, and global levels likely all played a part – interrelated in complex ways that we are still trying to untangle. In the next section, we examine the war's aftermath and how the settlement in turn created the conditions for later conflicts.

The Peace of Versailles and its consequences

World War I ended in mutual exhaustion. Germany had been defeated on the battlefield, though no allied troops were present on German soil, and German civilians were starving as a result of the British blockade of German ports. Finally, as huge numbers of fresh American troops poured into France, German leaders, having run out of replacements, recognized the inevitable. The armistice was signed on the "eleventh hour of the eleventh day of the eleventh month," or 11/11/11, in a railroad car near the French city of Compiègne, and the guns fell silent on the Western front. Twenty-two years later Hitler took his revenge by forcing the French to surrender in exactly the same rail car in Compiègne.

The Paris Peace Conference, held at the Palace of Versailles, opened on January 12, 1919, and was attended by the political leaders of 32 countries representing three-quarters of the world's population.

At the conference,[18] the victorious war leaders – America's Woodrow Wilson (1856–1924), David Lloyd George of Britain (1863–1945), Georges Clemenceau of France (1841–1929), and Vittorio Orlando of

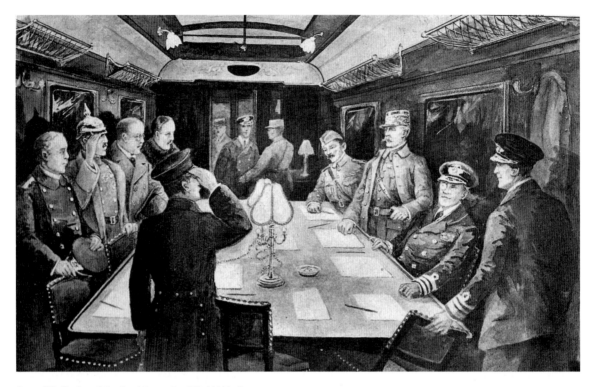

Figure 3.3 Signing of the Armistice ending World War I
© Roger-Viollet

Italy (1860–1952) – thrashed out their differences and literally remade the world. Each had his own objectives, however. Britain sought to recreate a workable balance of power and safeguard its empire. France sought to dismember Germany and create security for itself in Europe. Italy sought the territories it had been promised during the war. And Wilson sought a liberal world that reflected his Fourteen Points. In the end, Wilson conceded his principles one after the other in order to get the last of them, a league of nations, and Germany and the other defeated powers were forced to sign treaties that provided a very different peace than they had anticipated. The Versailles arrangements and continued upheaval in Europe created a new world and changed the maps of Europe and the Middle East. In addition to signing the Versailles Treaty with Germany, the victors and the defeated Central Powers signed four other treaties during the meetings: the treaties of St. Germain (with Austria), Trianon (with Hungary), Neuilly (with Bulgaria), and Sevres (with Turkey).

Figure 3.4 The victorious leaders at Versailles. From left to right: David Lloyd George (Great Britain), Vittorio Orlando (Italy), Georges Clemenceau (France), Woodrow Wilson (US)
Courtesy of the National Archives (Records of the Office of the Chief Signal Officer, 1860 – 1982) photo no. 111-SC-55456

Woodrow Wilson and the Fourteen Points

The man of the hour was US President Wilson, who was greeted as a hero and fêted in the major capitals of Europe. Not only had American entry into the war tilted the balance, but Wilson was the author of the Fourteen Points on the basis of which Germany surrendered. Wilson, a religious liberal interventionist, represented his Fourteen Points as "the general principles of the settlement" in a speech before a joint session of Congress on January 8, 1918 (see Key document: President Woodrow Wilson's Fourteen Points). Overall, Wilson sought a forgiving and generous peace with America's defeated enemies. Unfortunately, this was *not* what America's allies wanted; instead, they wished to impose a harsh peace on Germany that would prevent any revival of German military power that might again endanger their security. Wilson's idealism was not welcomed by allied leaders. Indeed, his Fourteen Points so irritated French President Clemenceau that he is said to have ridiculed the proposal by observing that "God Almighty only had Ten Commandments!"

Key document   President Woodrow Wilson's Fourteen Points[19]

It will be our wish and purpose that the processes of peace, when they are begun, shall be absolutely open and that they shall involve and permit henceforth no secret understandings of any kind. The day of conquest and aggrandizement is gone by; so is also the day of secret covenants entered into in the interest of particular governments and likely at some unlooked-for moment to upset the peace of the world. It is this happy fact, now clear to the view of every public man whose thoughts do not still linger in an age that is dead and gone, which makes it possible for every nation whose purposes are consistent with justice and the peace of the world to avow now or at any other time the objects it has in view.

We entered this war because violations of right had occurred which touched us to the quick and made the life of our own people impossible unless they were corrected and the world secure once for all against their recurrence. What we demand in this war, therefore, is nothing peculiar to ourselves. It is that the world be made fit and safe to live in; and particularly that it be made safe for every peace-loving nation which, like our own, wishes to live its own life, determine its own institutions, be assured of justice and fair dealing by the other peoples of the world as against force and selfish aggression. All the peoples of the world are in effect partners in this interest, and for our own part we see very clearly that unless justice be done to others it will not be done to us. The program of the world's peace, therefore, is our program; and that program, the only possible program, as we see it, is this:

I   Open covenants of peace, openly arrived at, after which there shall be no private international understandings of any kind but diplomacy shall proceed always frankly and in the public view.

II   Absolute freedom of navigation upon the seas, outside territorial waters, alike in peace and in war, except as the seas may be closed in whole or in part by international action for the enforcement of international covenants.

III   The removal, so far as possible, of all economic barriers and the establishment of an equality of trade conditions among all the nations consenting to the peace and associating themselves for its maintenance.

IV   Adequate guarantees given and taken that national armaments will be reduced to the lowest point consistent with domestic safety.

V   A free, open-minded, and absolutely impartial adjustment of all colonial claims, based upon a strict observance of the principle that in determining all such questions of sovereignty the interests of the populations concerned must have equal weight with the equitable claims of the government whose title is to be determined.

VI   The evacuation of all Russian territory and such a settlement of all questions affecting Russia as will secure the best and freest cooperation of the other nations of the world in obtaining for her an unhampered and unembarrassed opportunity for the independent determination of her own political development and national policy. . . .

VII Belgium . . . must be evacuated and restored, without any attempt to limit the sovereignty which she enjoys in common with all other free nations.

VIII All French territory should be freed and the invaded portions restored, and the wrong done to France by Prussia in 1871 in the matter of Alsace-Lorraine, which has unsettled the peace of the world for nearly fifty years, should be righted, in order that peace may once more be made secure in the interest of all.

IX A readjustment of the frontiers of Italy should be effected along clearly recognizable lines of nationality.

X The peoples of Austria-Hungary, whose place among the nations we wish to see safeguarded and assured, should be accorded the freest opportunity to autonomous development.

XI Rumania, Serbia, and Montenegro should be evacuated; occupied territories restored; Serbia accorded free and secure access to the sea; and the relations of the several Balkan states to one another determined by friendly counsel along historically established lines of allegiance and nationality. . . .

XII The Turkish portion of the present Ottoman Empire should be assured a secure sovereignty, but the other nationalities which are now under Turkish rule should be assured an undoubted security of life and an absolutely unmolested opportunity of autonomous development, and the Dardanelles should be permanently opened as a free passage to the ships and commerce of all nations under international guarantees.

XIII An independent Polish state should be erected which should include the territories inhabited by indisputably Polish populations, which should be assured a free and secure access to the sea, and whose political and economic independence and territorial integrity should be guaranteed by international covenant.

XIV A general association of nations must be formed under specific covenants for the purpose of affording mutual guarantees of political independence and territorial integrity to great and small states alike.

A number of the Fourteen Points proved highly contentious, later poisoning the peace that was concluded. To begin, the first point declared that diplomacy in the future should be public, leading to "open covenants," and this angered the British, French, and, most especially, the Italians, who during the war had concluded a number of secret treaties that contained egregious territorial promises. The Italians even walked out of the peace conference over the issue, angry that they were being deprived of promised territories along the Dalmatian Coast of the Adriatic Sea. In fact, the rise of **fascism** in Italy under Mussolini in 1922 owed much to Italian dissatisfaction over this issue. But the British and French, too, objected to Wilson's position, which negated secret agreements between them and complicated their efforts to divvy up Ottoman territories in the Middle East.

Freedom of the seas, the second point, was anathema to Britain, whose leaders perceived the demand as a danger to the British Empire. Disarmament, the fourth point, was also fiercely debated. The French

fascism an anti-democratic political philosophy that advocates rule by a nationalist dictator aided by a mass party enforcing obedience by using violence.

especially were concerned lest they find themselves again vulnerable to Germany. In the end, the Germans were profoundly disillusioned because *only they* were disarmed.

However, it was points VIII through XIII that proved the stickiest both during the peace talks and in the long run. Each in its own way represented Wilson's deep belief in national self-determination. In the next section, we will examine the principle of national self-determination as applied in the peace agreements more closely, to see how such a simple-sounding idea came to create such devastation.

Versailles and the principle of national self-determination

collective security the principle under which the invasion of *any* country would automatically bring forward the combined might of *all* countries.

Mandates of the League of Nations colonial territories taken from the defeated states of World War I and entrusted by the League of Nations to the victors that were to prepare them for independence.

In addition to alienating Germany, Italy, and Japan,[20] Versailles had other major consequences, some of which still influence global politics. The treaty created the League of Nations, the predecessor of today's UN and the organization that gave voice to the idea of **collective security**. Another consequence was to strip the Ottomans of their territories in the Middle East. The Ottoman Empire was divided into several artificial political entities, including Iraq, Syria, and Palestine, each of which consisted of peoples of different ethnic, religious, and tribal groups. These were turned over to Britain and France as **Mandates of the League of Nations** – that is, regions that were entrusted to Western states that were to help prepare them for later independence. The conference also established Yugoslavia, another artificial nation-state, from remnants of the Austro-Hungarian Empire. In the case of Iraq, the same cleavages still threaten to tear the country apart; in the case of Yugoslavia, they have already done so. Still another consequence was to violate promises made to *both* the Arabs and the Jews during World War I, a failure partly but directly responsible for conflict between Israel and the Palestinians today. In addition, the disaster in Europe, the postwar feebleness of the European powers, Wilson's rhetoric of self-determination, and the price paid in the war by Europe's colonies all combined to set in motion the forces of decolonization (see chapter 12, pp. 559–76).

In the end, the principle of national self-determination was the most important and durable outcome of the peace conference. Then, as now, national self-determination is a poorly understood concept. The first problem was a practical one: how to define a *nation*, an issue that still defies agreement (see chapter 15, pp. 712–15). Is a nation a community that exists only in people's imaginations? Is it a group of people who share a language, religion, history, myth system, or race? Is a nation defined by the presence of only some of these, or does it have to have all of them? The meaning of self-determination was also obscure. Did it mean an

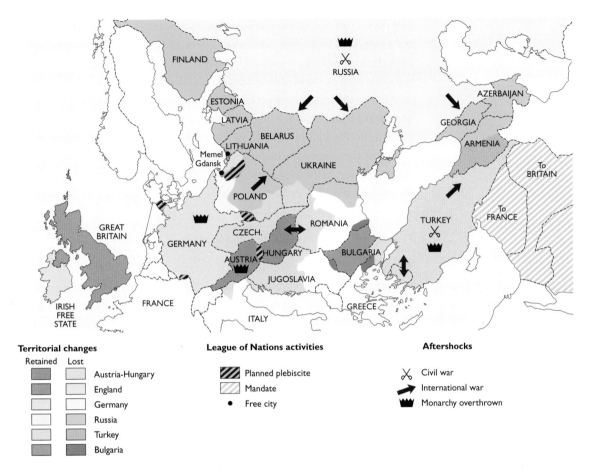

Map 3.2 Europe in the aftermath of World War I

independent sovereign state, greater autonomy within an existing state, or some other arrangement?

A second problem had to do with *how* to split up multinational empires, especially Austria-Hungary and Ottoman Turkey, because in these places, ethnic groups lived together, especially in multinational cities like Vienna, Warsaw, Jerusalem, and Prague. The way these difficult issues were addressed at that time contributed to today's **ethnic cleansing** and helped create the problems of ethnic and religious hostility in the division of Cyprus, the conflicts in Bosnia and Kosovo, the reconstruction of Iraq, and the Arab–Israeli and related Palestinian dilemmas.

National self-determination is a noble-sounding principle, but it has repeatedly been used to smash states along religious, tribal, and ethnic lines, with the result being chaos, violence, and state failure. In recent years, the Soviet Union, Yugoslavia, Czechoslovakia, and Iraq, as well as other states have been torn apart by groups claiming self-determination.

ethnic cleansing a euphemism for the murder or expulsion from a territory of people from a particular ethnic background.

Self-determination questions have come up in other contexts as well. For example, should African-Americans or Hispanics in North America have their own separate nations? What of self-conscious nations without territory such as the Kurds in Iraq, Syria, Turkey, and Iran?

Among the immediate problems created by the Versailles settlement, none was greater than the anger it created among Germans who regarded it as vindictive and unfair and, in consequence, their determination to throw off the shackles it had imposed on them. As we shall see, this determination helped lead to the rise of Hitler and the Nazis and, in the end, to World War II.

The Versailles Treaty and the humiliation of Germany

The harsh peace that was imposed on Germany at Versailles fundamentally altered global politics. More than any other single factor, the Versailles Treaty was responsible for Hitler's rise to power. Germany lost its military and merchant fleets, and its army was limited to 100,000. Germany was also required to disarm the Rhineland along its border with France. In addition, Germany had to turn over its coal mines in the Saar region to France until a referendum could be held 15 years later. Germany also surrendered all its overseas colonies, including islands in the Pacific that Japan would use for bases in the next world war. Finally, Germany was required to make reparations for the costs of the war.

German resentment at the Versailles Treaty was fueled by a belief that Germany had not *really* been defeated. German armies remained intact, and German soil had not been invaded. Extreme nationalists fostered a myth that Germany had been "stabbed in the back" by socialists and Jews. The Kaiser's abdication in November 1918 and flight to Holland and the delivery of the country into the hands of a weak civilian government headed by socialists forced to sue for peace fostered the legend that socialist politicians in the new Weimar Republic had betrayed their country. Hitler's subsequent rise to power was a consequence of his **anti-Semitism** and anti-communism and of his repeated demand that the terms of the Versailles Treaty be overthrown.

anti-Semitism irrational dislike, prejudice, or hatred of the Jews.

Recognizing that the Versailles Treaty was neither sufficiently moderate nor sufficiently harsh to keep the peace but, instead, would certainly provoke German efforts to overthrow it and that the result would be another war, France's Marshal Ferdinand Foch (1859–1921), commander of allied armies on the Western Front in 1918, lamented: "This is not a treaty, it is an armistice for twenty years."[21]

The following section turns to the League, the first major international organization established to maintain peace and security. It describes the

League's institutions and history, and the road that led, in the end, to its abject failure.

The League of Nations

Unlike the Concert of Europe, which had been the product of a realist vision of global politics, the League of Nations was a liberal effort to bring an end to war by doing away with the balance of power and creating a supranational international organization. The League never achieved these goals. Its efforts to maintain peace during the 1920s seemed to bode well for its future, but, even in those early years, disagreements among leading members about its purposes and the absence of major states were causes for concern. It proved unable to surmount major challenges to the existing global order in the 1930s and became largely irrelevant for resolving key issues leading up to World War II. What follows describes the League's origins, organization, and history and evaluates the reasons for its failure.

Origins and controversies

The League of Nations was part of the Versailles Treaty, and the League Covenant was incorporated as the first 26 articles of that treaty. It was originally the last point of Wilson's Fourteen Point plan, and Wilson, as we saw, fought doggedly for its inclusion in the peace treaty. During World War I, influential groups in Britain, the United States, and France had called for a permanent international organization to maintain peace. Among the most persuasive advocates for such an institution was Lord James Bryce (1838–1922), a leader of the British Liberal Party, who, like Wilson, believed that the balance of power, instead of preventing war, was a cause of conflict and had to be replaced by something better.

Woodrow Wilson sought to base the League on the lofty principle of collective security under which the invasion of *any* country would automatically bring forward the combined might of *all* countries. The idea of collective security assumed that all the members of the organization shared a common interest in global peace and stability and that, therefore, it was in the national interest of each state to aid any victim of **aggression**, even if this required violating other treaties or alliances. In meeting aggression promptly, states would be serving the collective good of humankind. This assumption was succinctly summarized by the League representative of Haiti, on the occasion of Italy's invasion of Ethiopia (1935–36) when he declared that: "Great or small, strong or weak, near or far, white or colored, let us never forget that one day we may be somebody's Ethiopia."[22] In effect, collective security

aggression the initiation of actions that violate the rights and interests of other actors.

autonomy the capacity to make independent decisions.

required states to surrender their **autonomy** in questions of war and peace to the League. Wilson, like philosophers Kant and Rousseau (see chapter 9, pp. 404–6), believed that most potential aggressors or "bad states" would be ruled by autocrats and that peace would ensue only when the true sentiments of mankind were respected.

Collective security was supposed to prevent aggression by the certainty that League members would combine their might to punish aggressors. Like the flexible balance-of-power alliances that collective security was expected to replace, League members were to have no permanent friends or enemies; and like balance of power and the later idea of credible deterrence, collective security sought to prevent aggression by the threat of war. Realists never had much hope for collective security because it required actors to entrust their security to others. Their pessimism was reinforced by a distribution of power between World Wars I and II such that any of a number of dissatisfied great powers – Japan, the USSR, Germany, or Italy – individually had the military capability to resist the League's collective sanctions.

Theory in the real world

The global debate both before and after the 2003 American invasion of Iraq reflected renewed interest in some of the norms of collective security, especially the belief of some opponents of the invasion that war is illegal and illegitimate unless it is approved by an international organization. Realists argue that such claims are insincere, as nothing in the UN Charter requires this and, in any event, many states that opposed the war had historically shown no inclination to follow such a norm. Finally, even opponents to the Iraq war make no claim that members are obligated to aid victims of aggression. In contrast to realists, constructivists might argue that the Iraq debate and the widespread demand that countries use force only after Security Council approval reflect the evolution of norms in the direction advocated by Wilson and fellow liberals.

The League Covenant (see Key document: Selections) was the work of a special committee of the 1919 Paris Peace Conference. It described the major institutions of the new organization and their responsibilities, as well as the rights and responsibilities of members. The Covenant established three permanent organs – the Assembly, the Council, and the Secretariat. It also linked the existing International Labor Organization (ILO) and, in 1921, the Permanent Court of International Justice to the new organization.

The Assembly acted as a regular diplomatic conference in which each member enjoyed a single vote regardless of size or power. In this sense, it reflected the principle of sovereign equality among states. The Assembly was empowered to deal "with any matter within the sphere of action of the League or affecting the peace of the world." Like the Assembly, the League Council could deal with all matters affecting world peace, and neither body was superior to the other. Although provision was made for permanent as well as elected members on the Council, permanent members enjoyed no special status. Decisions of both the Assembly and the Council required *unanimous votes*, a provision which gave every member, large or small, a veto over League decisions. This rule reflected the powerful influence in global politics of ideas like sovereignty, equality, and self-determination, but made it nearly impossible for the League to reach decisions on consequential issues.

Figure 3.5 The League of Nations Assembly
F.H. Julien /Library and Archives Canada /C-016765

The Covenant, like the later UN Charter, laid out a series of alternatives in the event of a threat to the peace. Among its less dramatic options were **arbitration**, judicial settlement, and investigation. If the Council became involved it was obligated to investigate and issue a report. The Covenant then specified members' collective obligations in the event war continued. An aggressor would "be deemed to have committed an act of war against all other Members of the League" and be subject to "severance of all trade or financial relations" by other states.

arbitration the process of resolving disputes by referring them to a third party, either agreed on by them or provided by law, that is empowered to make a judgment.

Key document   Selections from the League of Nations Covenant[23]

ARTICLE 10

The Members of the League undertake to respect and preserve as against external aggression the territorial integrity and existing political independence of all Members of the League. In case of any such aggression or in case of any threat or danger of such aggression the Council shall advise upon the means by which this obligation shall be fulfilled.

ARTICLE 11

Any war or threat of war, whether immediately affecting any of the Members of the League or not, is hereby declared a matter of concern to the whole League, and the League shall take any action that may be deemed wise and effectual to safeguard the peace of nations. . . .

ARTICLE 12

The Members of the League agree that, if there should arise between them any dispute likely to lead to a rupture they will submit the matter either to arbitration or judicial settlement or to enquiry by the Council, and they agree in no case to resort to war until three months after the award by the arbitrators or the judicial decision, or the report by the Council. . . .

ARTICLE 14

The Council shall formulate and submit to the Members of the League for adoption plans for the establishment of a Permanent Court of International Justice. The Court shall be competent to hear and determine any dispute of an international character which the parties thereto submit to it. . . .

ARTICLE 15

If there should arise between Members of the League any dispute likely to lead to a rupture, which is not submitted to arbitration or judicial settlement in accordance with Article 13, the Members of the League agree that they will submit the matter to the Council. Any party to the dispute may effect such submission by giving notice of the existence of the dispute to the Secretary General, who will make all necessary arrangements for a full investigation and consideration thereof. . . .

The Council shall endeavor to effect a settlement of the dispute. . . . If the dispute is not thus settled, the Council either unanimously or by a majority vote shall make and publish a report containing a statement of the facts of the dispute and the recommendations. . . .

ARTICLE 16

Should any Member of the League resort to war in disregard of its covenants under Articles 12, 13 or 15, it shall *ipso facto* be deemed to have committed an act of war against all other Members of the League, which hereby undertake immediately to subject it to the severance of all trade or financial relations, the prohibition of all intercourse between their nationals and the nationals of the covenant-breaking State, and the prevention of all financial, commercial or personal intercourse between the nationals of the covenant-breaking State and the nationals of any other State, whether a Member of the League or not.

It shall be the duty of the Council in such case to recommend to the several Governments concerned what effective military, naval or air force the Members of the League shall severally contribute to the armed forces to be used to protect the covenants of the League.

And, according to Article 16, if necessary, the Council could recommend the use of military force on the part of members to bring an end to aggression. In sum, aggression would be met by collective sanctions and, if necessary, by collective force. However, unlike Wilson's original conception of collective security, the obligations outlined in the Covenant were voluntary and limited.

The United States never joined the League, and its absence, along with the absence of at least one other great power throughout the League's history was a key source of the League's ineffectiveness. The Soviet Union did not join the League until 1934 and was expelled in 1939; Germany joined in 1926 but left in 1933 when Hitler came to power; Japan left the League in 1933; and Italy left in 1937.

America's refusal to join the League of Nations illustrates the links between global and domestic politics. By the US Constitution, the President may sign an international treaty on behalf of his country, but the Senate must ratify that treaty by at least a two-thirds majority. By 1919, the United States was weary of war and overseas involvement and beginning to look inward, as reflected in the policy of **isolationism** begun the following year. In addition, many senators and many Americans

isolationism a policy aimed at avoiding overseas political and military involvement.

generally were wary of the implications for American sovereignty of the commitment under Article 10 of the Covenant to aid all victims of aggression. Still, Wilson might have had his League had he been prepared to compromise with his opponents, but he was not and instead chose to fight by taking his case to the country.

The fight over the League began when Wilson returned from Europe in February 1919. Senate opposition was led by Henry Cabot Lodge (1850–1924) of Massachusetts, who was the Republican majority leader and chairperson of the Foreign Relations Committee in the Senate. Lodge announced his opposition to the mutual guarantee contained in Article 10 of the League Covenant only a few days after Wilson's return, but the debate was suspended by the adjournment of the 65th Congress and Wilson's return to Paris. The 66th Congress was deeply divided when it opened in May 1919, and Wilson might have won the day had he been willing to divide the difference. Those who supported US membership in the League were called internationalists. They were mainly Democrats. A plurality of senators, both Republican and Democratic, took a middle position, seeking to add mild reservations[24] to the treaty in order to safeguard American sovereignty. A small group of Republicans, including Lodge, demanded major changes in the treaty and were called "strong reservationists," but only about 15 senators were genuine "irreconcilables."

In the end, Wilson adamantly refused to compromise. The Versailles Treaty, including the League Covenant, was officially submitted to the Senate for ratification on July 10, 1919, setting the stage for one of the great dramas in American foreign policy history. Throughout the summer, Lodge conducted hearings on the treaty, and beginning in September Wilson set out on an 8,000-mile journey around the country, delivering 40 speeches in 22 cities in support of the League. On September 25th in Pueblo, Colorado the president collapsed and was rushed home to Washington, where he suffered an incapacitating stroke.

A month later the Senate considered Lodge's reservations to the treaty, which included exemption from the commitment under Article 10 to aid victims of aggression. Basically what united the treaty's opponents was their belief that only the Congress could authorize the use of force by the United States and could therefore override League decisions to use force, a position later held by congressional opponents of the Vietnam War. Despite British and French willingness to accept American reservations to the treaty, Wilson refused, and in May 1920 the Senate defeated the effort to ratify the Versailles Treaty and the League Covenant.

Key document   Wilson's appeal for support of the League of Nations

Why, my fellow citizens, this is one of the great charters of human liberty, and the man who picks flaws in it . . . forgets the magnitude of the thing, forgets the majesty of the thing, forgets that the counsels of more than twenty nations combined and were rendered unanimous in the adoption of this great instrument. . . .

I do not believe, if you have not read it yourself and have only listened to certain speeches that I have read, that you know anything that is in it. Why, my fellow citizens, the heart of the Covenant is that there shall be no war. . . .

The bulk of it is concerned with arrangements under which all the members of the League . . . that they never will go to war without first having done one or other of two things – either submitted the question at issue to arbitration, in which case they agree absolutely to abide by the verdict, or, if they do not care to submit it to arbitration, submitted it to discussion by the council of the League of Nations. . . . All that you are told about in this Covenant, so far as I can learn, is that there is an Article X. I will repeat Article X to you; I think I can repeat it verbatim, the heart of it at any rate. Every member of the League promises to respect and preserve as against external aggression . . . the territorial integrity and existing political independence of every other member of the League; and if it is necessary to enforce this promise – I mean, for the nations to act in concert with arms in their hands to enforce it – then the council of the League shall advise what action is necessary. Some gentlemen who doubt the meaning of English words have thought that advice did not mean advice, but I do not know anything else that it does mean, and I have studied English most of my life and speak it with reasonable correctness.

The point is this: The council cannot give that advice without the vote of the United States. . . .

I tell you, my fellow citizens, I can predict with absolute certainty that within another generation there will be another world war if the nations of the world do not concert the method by which to prevent it.

But I did not come here this morning, I remind myself, so much to expound the treaty as to talk about these interesting things that we hear about that are called "reservations". A reservation is an assent with a big but. We agree – but. Now, I want to call your attention to some of these buts. . . .

Now – every lawyer will follow me in this – if you take a contract and change the words, even though you do not change the sense, you have to get the other parties to accept those words. Is not that true? Therefore, every reservation will have to be taken back to all the signatories of this treaty. . . .

[W]e cannot rewrite this treaty. We must take it or leave it, and gentlemen, after all the rest of the world has signed it, will find it very difficult to make any other kind of treaty. As I took the liberty of saying the other night, it is a case of "put up or shut up." . . . The world cannot deal with nations who say, "We won't play!" The world cannot have anything to do with an arrangement in which every nation says, "We will take care of ourselves."[25]

Thus, the United States never joined the League and Congress turned down President Warren G. Harding's (1865–1923) compromise effort to join the World Court as a non-member of the League. Although the League became something quite different from what Wilson had envisioned, it nevertheless thrived in its early years, and the 1920s created optimism that the great experiment might yet work.

The League's record in securing peace

The 1920s were fortunate years for the League of Nations, largely because leaders and peoples remembered the carnage of World War I so well that the prospect of another war appalled them. In addition, the 1920s was an era of prosperity, and satisfaction with the state of things was generally high. Few wanted to end prosperity or stoke the fires of war again.

During much of the 1920s, German foreign policy was directed by Gustav Stresemann (1878–1929) who, though strongly nationalist, believed that Germany could advance its aims by cooperating with its former enemies. An agreement was reached in 1924 to reduce German reparations in return for large American loans. The symbol of Stresemann's policy of accommodation was the 1925 Treaty of Locarno signed by Germany, France, Britain, and Italy that guaranteed Germany's western boundaries (though not its eastern ones), including the permanent demilitarization of the Rhineland designed to protect France from attack, in return for which French troops would leave the Rhineland, which they did in 1930.

During the 1920s, the League had several notable successes, particularly in the economic and social realms. Among its successful activities were providing aid to refugees and reducing the global traffic in opium. It also afforded some members with economic relief and fostered cooperation in health, labor, and other functional areas. Finally, it set up the system of mandates under which administrators of former German and Turkish colonies were encouraged to ready those areas for political independence.

The League also had several early collective security successes. These included settling a Swedish–Finnish dispute over the Aaland Islands in the Baltic Sea (1920–21), preventing conflict over the boundaries of Albania (1921), dividing the region of Upper Silesia (1922), and avoiding a conflict between Greece and Bulgaria (1925). Despite these accomplishments, however, League weaknesses were already becoming apparent. For example, the League was unable to act at all when the Poles seized Vilnius from Lithuania in 1920 and when the French occupied the industrial Ruhr in 1923 in an effort to force Germany to pay the reparations it owed. Germans responded with passive resistance secretly financed by the German government through money that it printed. The result was catastrophic inflation in Germany that wiped out people's savings.

It became clear that the League was largely powerless in disputes that involved large states. Thus, in 1923 the murder of an Italian diplomat in Greece led Italy's fascist dictator Benito Mussolini (1883–1945) to bombard and then occupy the Greek island of Corfu. Instead of acting decisively, the League left the matter in the hands of a "conference of ambassadors," and under British and French pressure, the Greeks actually had to pay Italy an indemnity before Italian troops would leave the island.

Unfortunately, the moderation of the 1920s evaporated as political and economic conditions worsened in the 1930s. The Great Depression (see chapter 11, pp. 514–19) became worldwide in the early 1930s and with it spread a willingness to seek desperate solutions to economic woes. In this atmosphere, accumulated dissatisfaction led to authoritarian solutions in countries that had never accepted the outcome of World War I – fascism in Italy, Nazism in Germany, and militarism in Japan.

Evidence that the League could not deal with the aggression of major states grew when, in 1931, Japanese troops, without authorization from their government, invaded and occupied China's industrial province of Manchuria. Their excuse for the invasion was an incident that their own officers had staged, the blowing up of a section of the South Manchuria Railway. Under pressure from militarists at home, the Japanese government set up a puppet state in Manchuria called Manchukuo and placed on its throne Henry Pu Yi who had been the last emperor of China as a child, and whose life was depicted in the 1987 film *The Last Emperor*.

The League reacted anemically to Japan's aggression, which was an unwelcome distraction from the world's growing economic and social distress. The major European powers were unprepared to antagonize Japan, and the League carried out its obligations to the extent of sending a commission to "study" the problem. Japan vetoed an initial attempt by the Council to impose a ceasefire, and by the time the League commission reached the scene in spring 1932, Japan had already established Manchukuo, had attacked the Chinese city of Shanghai, and had seized China's province of Jehol as a buffer zone. It took a year before the League adopted its commission's report. Known as the Lytton Report, it supported China's claims against Japan but implied that Japan had been provoked. Its recommendations – that China and Japan sign trade and nonaggression treaties and set up a joint "special administration" over Manchuria – were "well-intentioned daydreaming."[26] In the end, the League merely scolded Japan with no other effect than to provoke Japan to abandon the organization.

The United States, as a Pacific power, was probably best situated to pressure Japan. But America was not in the League, and US foreign policy was in the grip of isolationism. What realists would later denounce as idealism and utopianism was perhaps reflected in the efforts of America's Secretary of State Henry L. Stimson (1867–1950) to deal with the issue. Frustrated by Japanese stalling, in 1932 he declared that the US would not recognize any territorial changes resulting from Japan's invasion. This act had no impact on Japanese militarists, who by this time largely controlled their country's foreign affairs. Even Stimson understood that his only weapons were, as he put it, "spears of straws and swords of ice."[27]

Other examples of League paralysis followed. Germany's withdrawal from the League and from the League-sponsored World Disarmament Conference in 1933 following the installation of Hitler as German chancellor was a major blow, indicating that the Nazis were not prepared to cooperate with League efforts to strengthen peace. League failure to stop the Chaco War (1932–35) between Bolivia and Paraguay over a largely uninhabited region of South America further eroded confidence in the organization.

However, the League's next great challenge was Mussolini's invasion of Ethiopia in 1935. The two key factors in Mussolini's decision were his desire to carve out an empire for Italy like that already ruled by Britain and France and to avenge Italy's military disaster in the 1896 Battle of Adowa – an earlier Italian effort to build an empire. On December 5, 1934, a skirmish took place at a small Italian base in Ethiopia, and Mussolini used this as a pretext to demand compensation. On January 3, 1935, Ethiopia's Emperor Haile Selassie (1892–1975) appealed to the League for protection against Italian aggression, but unknown to him, a few days later the British and French foreign ministers secretly agreed to let Mussolini have Ethiopia because they hoped that Italy would join them in opposing German ambitions and power. A full-scale Italian invasion of the country began in February and saw the use of poison gas and strategic bombing against Ethiopian civilians. In the words of historian Piers Brendon: "The gas scorched earth and contaminated water. It ravaged villages, poisoned livestock and corroded Ethiopia's will to resist."[28]

In accordance with Article 16 of the Covenant, the League declared Italy an aggressor and authorized the imposition of economic sanctions against it, but strategic materials and oil were excluded from the embargo list. Moreover, the attempt to invoke economic sanctions failed because major states carried out their obligations half-heartedly. Britain, whose control of the Suez Canal gave it a stranglehold on the movement of Italian supplies to Ethiopia, was unwilling to undertake any action that would precipitate a sudden break with Italy, which it saw as a potential balance-of-power ally against Germany in Europe. Winston Churchill (1874–1965) described the British predicament when he wrote of then Prime Minister Stanley Baldwin (1867–1947): "The Prime Minister had declared that sanctions meant war; secondly, he was resolved that there must be no war; and thirdly, he decided upon sanctions."[29] The same unwillingness on the part of leading states to equate global opposition with national interest continued to haunt the League just, as we will see in chapter 9, as it haunts the UN today.

Following the Ethiopian fiasco, the League proved helpless in the face of a series of conflicts and aggressive acts by Hitler and others, including the Spanish Civil War (1936–39), Germany's 1936 remilitarization of the Rhineland, Japan's renewed invasion of China in 1937, Hitler's 1938 occupation of Austria and his threat to attack Czechoslovakia later that year. All these events, as we shall shortly see, were dominated by Europe's leading states with the League relegated to insignificance. The League's last memorable action was expelling the Soviet Union from the organization in December 1939 following the Soviet attack on Finland. This act, coming a few months *after* Germany's invasion of Poland (September 1, 1939) and the beginning of World War II, was peculiarly futile in that it seemed to ignore the real danger to Europe's security. By 1940, only a few employees remained at the League headquarters in Geneva, and the organization was officially disbanded in 1946.

The League of Nations proved a noble but failed experiment in international organization. Of 37 disputes between 1920 and 1937, only 14 were referred to the League, and only six of these were settled by League efforts.[30] A number of factors at different levels of analysis account for League failure.

At the *global system* level, one source of League failure was the **multipolar** distribution of power that enabled major states like Japan to resist collective action. Another was the global economic collapse of the early 1930s, which made democratic governments and publics look inward, attend to economic issues, refuse to spend what was necessary to strengthen themselves militarily, and ignore uncomfortable and potentially costly overseas security problems.

multipolar a system in which there are several major powers with roughly equal power.

At the *actor level*, perhaps the most important source of League failure was the widespread belief on the part of leading states that collective action was not in their national interest. Thus, the major dissatisfied states – Japan, Germany, and Italy – repeatedly violated the League Covenant, and their major opponents, Britain, France, and the United States (outside the League) saw their national interests as incompatible with the use of vigorous measures to halt aggression, especially outside Europe. In addition, the League itself was, as we have seen, hamstrung by institutional weaknesses like the requirement for unanimity in the Assembly or Council. Even League decisions were only recommendations.

Finally, at the *individual level*, the experiences and memories of individual political leaders of the time were an important source of the policies of their states. Two leading examples of this were Hitler and Neville Chamberlain (1869–1940), who served as British Prime Minister between 1937 and 1940. Hitler had been a hero in World War I, winning medals for bravery and for a time blinded by a gas attack. He attributed Germany's defeat to treason by Jews and socialists, and he was determined to reverse the "shameful" verdict of the Treaty of Versailles. Much of this is related in *Mein Kampf* (see an excerpt in the Key document in chapter 10).

For Chamberlain, who had fought on the winning side in World War I, the thought of renewed carnage was inconceivable. Chamberlain was, writes one historian, "so deeply, so desperately, anxious to avoid war that he could not conceive of its being inevitable."[31] Hitler intuitively knew how to take advantage of Chamberlain's longing for peace, as well as the widespread Western feeling that the Versailles Treaty had been too harsh toward Germany. The result, as we shall see, was Chamberlain's policy of **appeasement**.

Although the failure of the League brought the world closer to World War II, the story of the origins of that war is still not complete. The global failure to cope effectively with economic collapse also played a key role in Hitler's rise and the onset of world war. The next section examines the triumph of the Nazis in Germany and that country's decision to rearm.

appeasement a policy of concessions that aims to satisfy another actor's grievances and thereby keep the peace.

Hitler comes to power

Hitler's popularity and his rise to power could not have taken place without the Great Depression and the resulting alienation of many Germans from their democratic system. Germany was especially hard hit by the Depression and the drying up of American loans. By 1932, unemployment in Germany reached six million, about one-quarter of all German workers. Between 1929 and 1932, German foreign trade declined by two-thirds and industrial production by half. In March 1930, Germany's governing coalition collapsed as a result of the burgeoning costs of aiding the unemployed. This marked the beginning of Germany's slide toward authoritarian government as the country's president, the aged World War I military hero Field Marshal Paul von Hindenburg (1847–1934), invoked emergency powers under Article 48 of the Weimar Constitution to appoint a new chancellor and cabinet. For the next two years, the chancellor, Heinrich Brüning (1885–1970), called the "hunger chancellor" by his opponents, governed without a majority in the Reichstag, Germany's parliament.

In September 1930, Brüning decided to hold parliamentary elections with disastrous results. Public dissatisfaction with the government's economic performance combined with sheer desperation to produce a dramatic increase in votes for the anti-democratic Communists and Nazis to almost one-third of the German electorate. In the 1928 elections, the Communists had won 54 seats in the 608-seat Reichstag and the Nazis 12; in the 1930 elections, the Communists took 77 seats and the Nazis 107. Thus, in two years Hitler's Nazis were transformed from a marginal political party to the second largest in the Reichstag. As conditions worsened, more and more Germans flocked to the Nazis. In March 1932, the Nazis won 230 seats which, along with the 89 seats won by the Communists, meant that a majority of Germans were in favor of extremists who sought to end German **democracy**. Following Hitler's appointment as chancellor in January 1933, the Nazis increased their total to 288 Reichstag seats in the March 1933 elections.[32] Between 1929 and 1932, membership in the Nazi Party soared from 170,000 to 1,378,000. In addition, large numbers of unemployed Germans joined the communist and Nazi paramilitary storm troopers that roamed the streets of German cities, brawling with one another and terrorizing citizens.

With Hitler's ascent to power, Germany began massive and rapid rearmament which entailed enormous public spending and created sufficient employment to end the Depression in the country by 1936. Hitler was planning to take Germany to war and demanded that the country become economically self-sufficient. To this end, Nazi Germany tried to maximize exports and minimize imports. In 1936, Germany began an ambitious Four-Year Plan intended to increase self-sufficiency by imposing state control upon essential economic sectors and encouraging the development of synthetic substitutes for vital raw materials. Owing largely to rearmament and public works, Germany's 1939 gross national product was over 50 percent above its 1929 level, and Germany had created a military machine that would threaten world domination.

Had the West stood up to Hitler, would things have turned out differently? As we now see, however, Western leaders did not do so.

democracy a political system based on the right of all persons to participate in government, often by electing representatives of the people.

Did you know?

Hitler was the first politician to make extensive use of airplanes in campaigning for office and was a persuasive speaker and propagandist. Nowhere is Nazi propaganda more skillfully revealed than in the 1934 film by Leni Riefenstal (1902–2003) called *Triumph of the Will*, which depicts the Nuremberg Rally.

Appeasement and the onset of World War II

As governments and publics preoccupied by economic woes at home turned inward they had little interest in taking bold foreign policy actions, or in spending money to increase their military power or oppose aggression overseas. This was clearest in Britain. Throughout the 1930s, Britain continued to respond to the economic crisis with austerity, including cuts to the country's military budget that left the country sorely unprepared for war. For much of the Depression (1931–37), Chancellor of the Exchequer Neville Chamberlain fought to keep Britain's budget balanced and to limit the country's military spending. In 1937, Chamberlain became Britain's prime minister and had to lead the country through successive crises in relations with Hitler. Aware of his country's military weakness for which he was partly responsible and desperate to delay war until Britain's defenses were rebuilt, Chamberlain was the author of a policy of appeasement.

Appeasement in Europe

The policy of appeasement was a deliberate policy on the part of Britain intended to satisfy German grievances in order to avoid war. To this day, it remains a topic of intense debate. Critics of appeasement contend that it whetted the appetite of the dictators in Germany, Italy, and Japan, giving them confidence and making them more aggressive. At least four factors contributed to convincing British leaders, especially Chamberlain, of the need for such a policy:

- Widespread revulsion among British elites at the prospect of another world war.
- Britain's lack of military preparedness, especially its inadequate air force.
- A widespread belief that Germany had been treated too harshly by the Versailles Treaty and had legitimate grievances that should be satisfied.
- Widespread public opposition in Britain to rearmament and a strong desire to work through the League of Nations.

Again and again, Hitler justified his actions between 1933 and 1939 by invoking Wilson's own principle of national self-determination, demanding that territories in other countries such as Austria and Czechoslovakia with communities of German speakers be returned to the Third Reich. After becoming Germany's chancellor, Hitler set out to destroy the Versailles Treaty. Within months, Germany left the League of Nations and began rearming. In 1934 Germany and Poland agreed to a nonaggression pact (that Hitler never intended to keep) that effectively nullified France's alliance with Poland. Also in 1934, following the assassination of Austria's Chancellor Englebert Dolfuss (1892–1934) by local Nazis, Germany appeared on the verge of occupying that country. To prevent this, Mussolini sent four army divisions to the Brenner Pass where they could sweep into Austria in the event of German aggression. This was followed by a 1935 meeting among British, French, and Italian leaders at the Italian resort of Stresa where they agreed to oppose "by all practical means any unilateral repudiation of treaties which may endanger the peace of Europe." Unfortunately, this "Stresa front" collapsed quickly under the weight of Italy's invasion of Ethiopia.

The year 1935 saw dramatic gains by Hitler. In January, a plebiscite in the Saar led to that region's reunification with Germany. Next, in March

1935, Hitler violated the Versailles Treaty's limitations on the German army by announcing general conscription in Germany, as well as programs for building an air force and a navy. In June, Germany and Britain reached an agreement limiting Germany to a navy one-third the size of Britain's. This agreement was a gross violation of the armament clauses of the Versailles Treaty because it effectively permitted the Germans to rebuild their fleet.

During 1936, Hitler's provocative foreign policy escalated. First, he concluded an alliance with Italy (which had been alienated from Britain and France during the Ethiopian adventure) and, shortly after, an alliance with Japan. On March 7, 1936, Hitler embarked on the military reoccupation of the Rhineland (prohibited under the Versailles and the Locarno treaties), despite the opposition of his own generals. His action was a bluff, however, as the German army was not ready to fight Britain and France. Indeed, it has been argued that Germany's military leaders might have overthrown Hitler had he met Western resistance. The West, however, backed down – an example of the policy of appeasement, due in part to military weakness and in part to public opposition to war.

In July 1936, the Spanish Civil War erupted between the supporters of Spain's Republic and the fascist supporters of General Francisco Franco (1892–1975). Hitler intervened to extend Nazi influence and the Spanish Civil War was soon transformed into a symbolic confrontation of left- and right-wing forces in Europe. Franco was supported by German and Italian military units and the Republic was aided to a lesser degree by the Soviet Union and by volunteers from the US and many European countries. For their part, Britain, France, and the US refused to get involved. Their policy of nonintervention combined with German and Italian help to Franco, assured the latter's triumph in 1939.

The next crisis occurred over Austria. In January 1938 Austrian police learned of a Nazi plot to seize power in Vienna. At a meeting between Hitler and Austrian Chancellor Kurt von Schuschnigg (1897–1977) the following month, Hitler employed threats of military intervention to force Schuschnigg to agree to admit Austrian Nazis to his government and allow Germany to control Austria's foreign policy. On returning to Vienna, Schuschnigg tried to call a referendum on the agreement, sending Hitler into a rage. Schuschnigg was then forced to resign. On March 12, in violation of the Versailles Treaty's prohibition of German–Austrian unification or *Anschluss*, Hitler invaded his homeland in the name of the German *Volk* (people) and annexed it to the Third Reich.

Later that year, Hitler began a campaign against Czechoslovakia, claiming that that country was abusing ethnic Germans in the fortified border region of the Sudetenland. Hitler demanded that Prague hand over the region, site of the country's most formidable defenses, or face war. Chamberlain and French Prime Minister Edouard Daladier (1884–1970) desperately sought to appease Hitler. After an initial visit to Germany, Chamberlain returned home to announce that his visit meant "peace in our time." Shortly thereafter, with Hitler still threatening to attack Czechoslovakia, Chamberlain and Daladier were back in Germany, where they visited Hitler at his mountain home outside Munich. There, along with Italy's Mussolini, they agreed to force Czechoslovakia to cede the Sudetenland.

After the event, Chamberlain justified his action by claiming that Britain was unprepared for war and could have done nothing to save Czechoslovakia. "You have only to look at the map," he wrote in his diary,

> to see that nothing France or we could do could possibly save Czechoslovakia from being overrun by the Germans, if they wanted to do it. The Austrian frontier is practically open; the great Skoda munitions works are within easy bombing distance of German aerodromes, the railways all pass through German territory, Russia is 100 miles away. Therefore we could not help Czechoslovakia – she would simply be a pretext for going to war with Germany. That we could not think of unless we had a reasonable prospect for being able to beat her to her knees in reasonable time, and of that I see no sign.[33]

Appeasement reached its zenith in the 1938 Munich agreement. This agreement convinced Hitler that the British and French would not stand up to him and that he could get away with occupying the rest of Czechoslovakia, which he did in March 1939,[34] and conquering Poland (despite unilateral British and French guarantees to that country). The Munich agreement also persuaded Soviet dictator Josef Stalin (1879–1953) that the British and French were not serious about forming an alliance against Hitler. As a result, on August 23, 1939, Stalin concluded a nonaggression pact with Hitler that divided Poland between them and freed Hitler to invade that country a week later. With Germany's invasion of Poland on September 1, World War II began in Europe.

On the road to Pearl Harbor

The road that ended in Japan's surprise attack on the American fleet at Pearl Harbor on December 7, 1941, an act that brought the world war to Asia, began in China. Following their 1931 seizure of Manchuria, the Japanese army continued to expand into China. Within Japan, which had

Did you know?

Theodor Seuss Geisel (1904–91), popularly known as Dr. Seuss, was the chief editorial cartoonist and author of over 400 editorial cartoons for the New York newspaper *PM* between 1941 and 1943, many of which satirized Hitler and Mussolini.

Figure 3.6 Signing the Nazi-Soviet non aggression pact, August 23, 1939
Courtesy of the National Archives, (National Archives Collection of Foreign Records Seized, 1675–1983) photo no. 242-JRPE-44

been hard hit by the Depression, military extremists waged a campaign of assassination and terror against government officials and prominent supporters of democracy. By 1937, they had largely succeeded in gaining power. At the same time, Japan embarked on a major expansion of its armed forces.

Then, on July 7, 1937 at the 800-year old Marco Polo Bridge across the Yongding River at the town of Wanping on the road to Beijing, Japanese units were fired upon. The conflict escalated quickly across the plains of north China, beginning a full-scale war between Japan and China that did not end until 1945. Despite hideous Japanese atrocities, including the "rape of Nanking" in December 1937, Japan was unable to conquer China. For its part, the US grew increasingly concerned about Japanese imperialism in Asia, and began to send aid to China, evading America's Neutrality Act by arguing that China and Japan were not technically at war. In a speech in Chicago on October 5, 1937 known as the "Quarantine Speech" which clearly referred to Japan, President Franklin D. Roosevelt (1882–1945) declared:

> The political situation in the world, which of late has been growing progressively worse, is such as to cause grave concern and anxiety to all the peoples and nations who wish to live in peace and amity with their neighbors. . . . Without a declaration of war and without warning or justification of any kind, civilians, including vast numbers of women and children, are being ruthlessly murdered with bombs from the air.
> . . . Innocent peoples, innocent nations are being cruelly sacrificed to a greed for power and supremacy which is devoid of all sense of justice and humane considerations. . . . It seems to be unfortunately true that the epidemic of world lawlessness is spreading. And mark this well: When an epidemic of physical disease starts to spread, the community approves and joins in a quarantine of the patients in order to protect the health of the community against the spread of the disease.[35]

The United States had already taken tentative steps to aid Great Britain in its war against Germany. Despite strong isolationist sentiment, following the invasion of Poland Congress agreed to allow Britain and France to purchase arms on a cash-and-carry basis. Perceiving a growing threat from Japan, in July 1940 the United States placed an embargo on the export of high-quality scrap metal and aviation fuel to Japan – vital resources necessary for Tokyo to continue waging war in China. Then, following Japan's invasion of French Indochina in September 1940, the US embargoed the export of all scrap metal and steel to Japan.

In the same month, the United States agreed to give Britain 50 destroyers needed to protect British convoys against German submarines in return for leasing several British air and naval bases in the western hemisphere. In March 1941, the US passed the Lend-Lease Act under which large amounts of supplies were sent to Britain (and later the Soviet Union) on credit. And, in August, Roosevelt met with Churchill, who had become British prime minister in May 1940, off the Newfoundland coast where the two leaders issued the Atlantic Charter, articulating their common ideals of freedom and national self-determination. Then, in August, the US Congress enacted conscription into law by the margin of a single vote.

Japanese–American negotiations about the war in China began in the spring of 1941 and continued with little success throughout the year. Forty meetings were held between US Secretary of State Cordell Hull (1877–1955) and Japan's ambassador between March and December.

Fearing an imminent Japanese attack on the Dutch East Indies (Indonesia) in an effort to secure critical raw materials, the US embargoed the export of oil to Japan in September. This confronted Japanese leaders with the stark choice of ending their war in China or going to war with the United States.

After the failure of one last effort to reach an agreement, the Japanese government, now led by General Hideki Tojo (1884–1948), decided on war. Although US intelligence had learned that war was imminent, the shock of Japan's surprise attack on Pearl Harbor on Sunday, December 7, 1941 and the destruction of America's battleships at anchor was devastating. Eighteen American ships were sunk at Pearl Harbor, and 2,403 Americans died and 1,178 were wounded. Declaring December 7th as "a day which will live in infamy," the following day Roosevelt asked Congress to declare war on Japan. Germany and Italy declared war on the US three days later, making the new war a global one.

World War II called forth an enormous effort on the part of the Grand Alliance – the United States, the USSR, and Britain. Battles such as Dunkirk, the Battle of Britain, El Alamein, Stalingrad, Kursk, Anzio, Guadalcanal, and Iwo Jima became legends. New weapons of fearsome power, especially the two atom bombs dropped on Japan in 1945, changed global politics for ever. As a result of the war, Germany and Japan were reduced to rubble, and only two great powers remained – the United States and the Soviet Union. And within two years of the end of the war, these two great allies had become foes in a new conflict pitting two ways of life – capitalism and communism – against one another.

Explaining the outbreak of World War II

Untangling the causes of World War II allows political scientists to generalize further about war and to identify the similarities it may have with other wars. In the following section, we review some of the causes of World War II by level of analysis.

Individual-level explanations

An individual-level explanation for World War II might focus on Hitler's ambitions and his racist ideology. According to this thesis, Hitler's ambitions exceeded those of the German populace and the German political and military elites. The Germans certainly wished to revise the terms of Versailles to restore Germany to its pre-1914 status, but it was Hitler who fancied European hegemony and global domination. Hitler was "dedicated to the acquisition of power for his own gratification and to the destruction of a people whose existence was an offence to him and whose annihilation would be his crowning triumph. Both the grandiose barbarism of his political vision and the moral emptiness of his character make it impossible to compare him in any meaningful way with any other German leader."[36] This thesis, though, offers only a partial explanation of the war. As we shall see, other levels of analysis offer additional explanations for World War II and suggest that a war would have occurred, even without Hitler.

State-level explanations

An alternative explanation, at the state level of analysis, is that significant challenges within European states contributed to the outbreak of World War II. For instance, economic collapse led to the rise of the Nazi regime within Germany, driving voters to Hitler. In Great Britain, appeasement was thought a realistic strategy, given scarce economic resources.

Furthermore, social and economic cleavages in Britain and France made it politically difficult for these states to deal firmly with Germany. In Britain, there was significant popular opposition to rearmament; trade unions opposed the industrial conscription that it would entail while the middle class wished greater spending on social programs. Those political elites that favored rearmament were fragmented and could not unite to oppose Chamberlain's appeasement policy. France was plagued by a chronically unstable Third Republic (with 35 cabinet changes between 1918 and 1940) and a hopelessly divided society. Political factions argued endlessly over whether Hitler posed a serious threat and, if so, how France should manage it. On the ideological left, Communists pushed for an alliance with the USSR, while the Socialists insisted France use the League of Nations to restrain Hitler. The political right wanted to ally with Germany (arguing "better Hitler than Blum" [France's Socialist leader]) to balance the threat posed by the Soviet Union.[37]

Global system-level explanations

At the global level, explanations for the war focus on the Versailles Treaty system, the balance of power in Europe, the failure of collective security, and the spread of extremist ideologies. First, as noted above, the Versailles Treaty placed all of the blame for World War I on Germany, thus fueling German anger but not preventing German rearmament. A second, realist, explanation considers Europe's balance of power. The absence of a major power capable of balancing a rising Germany encouraged aggressive German policies. Either the United States or the USSR might have played such a role, but both were unwilling to become involved until late in the game. Third, the failure of collective security and the League also ensured Hitler would not be deterred. Finally, the emergence and growth of communism and fascism in Europe fueled conflicts between states.

Conclusion

This chapter has examined the events leading up to two world wars and has analyzed the sources of war according to their level of analysis. We have seen that both world wars can be attributed to numerous, reinforcing, causes at each level of analysis. Several prominent theoretical explanations exist for each war, but no single explanation is sufficient.

Some of the key factors contributing to World War I were German unification and the change it brought to the global balance of power, Europe's diplomatic revolution that abolished Otto von Bismarck's intricate system of alliances and established in its place rigid blocs, arms races on land and sea, the spread of fierce nationalism, and intense competition for colonies culminating in military crises. Our understanding of the outbreak of the war is furthered by considering key individuals – such as Kaiser Wilhelm and Tsar Nicolas – who were unable and unwilling to cope with these grand transformations in global and domestic politics.

A similar complex web of factors led to the outbreak of World War II, including the terms of World War I, leading many analysts to view World War II as a mere continuation of the first. In particular, the Versailles Treaty system alienated Germany, Italy, and the Japanese and fueled a desire on their part to recoup power and status, as well as territories and peoples. The League of Nations, which was intended to prevent another war by means of collective security, failed because key states did not participate and member states chose to purse their own national interests over the global collective interest. Additionally, European leaders erroneously thought that Hitler could be appeased if he were allowed to expand into neighboring Austria and Czechoslovakia. Hitler himself provides a partial explanation for war, as his plans for conquest were fueled by his racism and fascist ideology.

This examination of the world wars has also introduced the idea that they permanently altered global politics by creating many of the conditions that continue to fuel conflicts in global politics today. This is particularly true of World War I. The Versailles Treaty system's application of national self-determination planted the seeds of several of today's most intractable ethnic conflicts, particularly in the Balkans and Central Asia.

World War II also produced significant changes as we shall see in chapter 4 where we turn to the next great twentieth-century struggle, the Cold War. That conflict, which pitted the capitalist, democratic United States against the communist Soviet Union, never erupted into a hot war. However, the chronic hostility between the two superpowers and their allies affected all aspects of global politics until the Cold War's end in 1989.

Student activities

Discussion and essay questions

Comprehension questions

1 What was the revolution in diplomacy and how did it contribute to the outbreak of World War I?
2 Who were the key leaders in Europe in 1914 and 1939, and what role did each play in the outbreak of war?
3 What were the most important consequences of World War I?
4 What were the causes of World War II?

Analysis questions

5 Which level(s) of analysis provide(s) the best explanation for the outbreak of World War I? World War II? Why?
6 What is meant by the claim that World War II was a continuation of World War I?
7 Based upon your reading of chapter 1, how would realists and liberals differ in their interpretations of the causes of the world wars?

Map analysis

Using a blank map, identify the areas surrendered by Germany after World War I and the new states that emerged from the dissolution of the Russian, Austro-Hungarian, and Ottoman empires. How would you expect these changes to alter European and global politics?

Cultural materials

The world wars have been the theme of a number of critically acclaimed films. Among the best of those depicting the futility of World War I were the 1931 version of *All Quiet on the Western Front* that could not be shown in Germany because of Nazi demonstrations against it, and the 1937 French classic, *The Grand Illusion*, directed by Jean Renoir, the son of the French impressionist painter, Auguste Renoir. The bloody and tragic struggle of ANZAC troops at Gallipoli is depicted in the 1981 film *Gallipoli*, starring the young Mel Gibson. The 1957 film *Paths of Glory* deals with the French mutinies of 1917. The classic 1951 Hollywood film, *The African Queen*, starring Humphrey Bogart and Katharine Hepburn, uses the war in East Africa as its background. British military activity in the Middle East sought to protect the Suez Canal and drive the Ottoman Turks out of the region. The most memorable of these campaigns was directed by the British adventurer T. E. Lawrence, known as Lawrence of Arabia. Starting in Mecca, Lawrence successfully instigated the "Arab Revolt" against the Turks. He chronicled his adventurers in an exaggerated way in *Seven Pillars of Wisdom*, which he published in 1927. This revolt helped trigger the collapse of Turkey's Middle Eastern empire and create the map of the region that we know today. Lawrence's exploits were reproduced in David Lean's 1962 film *Lawrence of Arabia*.

Although many films were made about World War II during and immediately after that war, two recent releases are especially noteworthy: *Saving Private Ryan* (1999) starring Tom Hanks and *Enemy at the Gates* (2001) starring Jude Law. Watch one of these films and consider what the film tells the viewer about world wars I and II. Who were the dominant actors? What interests did they pursue and how did they do so? What general lessons, if any, can the film teach about great power war?

Further reading

Brendon, Piers, *The Dark Valley: A Panorama of the 1930s* (New York: Random House, 2000). Gripping account of the major events of the decade such as the Depression and the rise of the Nazis in Germany, the Fascists in Italy, and the militarists in Japan.

Carr, E. H. *The Twenty Years' Crisis: 1919–1939* (New York: Palgrave, 2001). This classic volume written before World War II is one of the foundation texts of the realist school.

Fromkin, David, *Europe's Last Summer: Who Started the Great War in 1914?* (New York: Vintage Books, 2005). Provocative analysis of the onset of World War I that lays much of the blame on German leaders.

Fussell, Paul, *The Great War and Modern Memory* (New York: Oxford University Press, 1975). Classic account of the impact of the Great War on the generation of authors and artists who witnessed it and on Western culture more generally.

Keegan, John, *The Second World War* (New York: Penguin Books, 1990). Highly readable but comprehensive single-volume history of World War II.

Keegan, John, *The First World War* (New York: Vintage, 1998). The best single-volume account of the war by one of the world's leading military historians.

Kershaw, Ian, *Hitler: 1889–1936 Hubris* (New York: W.W. Norton, 1998). Comprehensive analysis of Hitler's rise to power.

Macmillan, Margaret, *Paris 1919: Six Months That Changed the World* (New York: Random House, 2002). Engrossing history of the Versailles Conference and its consequences by the granddaughter of Britain's wartime prime minister.

Tuchman, Barbara W., *The Guns of August* (New York: Macmillan, 1962). A classic and accessible account of the onset of World War I.

4 | The Cold War

On May 1, 1960 an American U-2 spy plane piloted by CIA employee Francis Gary Powers was shot down over Soviet air space. For almost five years, these planes, flying at over 70,000 feet, had been photographing the Soviet Union's most secret installations. Believing the pilot to be dead, the Americans claimed that the plane had gone off course from Iran while investigating weather conditions. The story was almost immediately shown to be false when Soviet Premier Nikita S. Khrushchev (1894–1971) produced the pilot with photographs of the crash site near the city of Smolensk, thousands of miles from where the Americans claimed it was supposed to be. Furiously, Khrushchev demanded that US President Dwight D. Eisenhower (1890–1969) apologize, and, when Eisenhower refused, Khrushchev canceled a summit meeting with Eisenhower that was due to be held in Paris. As this incident illustrated, intelligence gathering was a major activity during the Cold War, and both sides developed sophisticated technological means to help them do so.

The **Cold War**[1] which followed close upon the end of World War II was the great struggle of the second half of the twentieth century that shaped today's world. With the defeat of Germany, Italy, and Japan, the Cold War dominated global politics. In this conflict, the United States and its allies, including supporters of the economic and political systems known as **capitalism** and **democracy**, engaged in ideological warfare against the Soviet Union and its allies, advocates of an alternative, and incompatible, economic and political system known as **communism**. Numerous events during this era also seemed to indicate that conflict was the norm in global politics, and realism held sway in analyses of global politics at that time.

The theme of continuity and change is visible in the Cold War. In significant ways, this era marked a break with the past. It ushered in the nuclear age, and featured the (related) absence of major power war. In fact, the Cold War is described by historian John Lewis Gaddis as the "long

Cold War the period of hostility short of open warfare between the United States and its allies and the USSR and its allies that erupted after World War II and lasted until 1989.

capitalism an economic system based on the private ownership of property and the means of production and a free market for exchanging goods and services that allows competition.

democracy a political system based on the right of all persons to participate in government, often by electing representatives of the people.

communism a social system without states or classes featuring common ownership of property in which each member contributes according to capabilities and gains according to need.

Figure 4.1 American U-2 spy plane. The U-2 made its first flight in August 1955. On October 14, 1962, the U-2 photographed the Soviet military installing offensive missiles in Cuba.
US Air Force photo

peace" because of the remarkable absence of such wars in contrast to earlier eras.[2] In other ways, however, the period reveals continuity, with the ongoing emphasis on the role of major powers in driving global politics and the ever-present possibility of conflict. And the events of this period have shaped the world we live in today. We shall see through the remainder of the text that our understanding of Cold War politics has profoundly affected the manner in which we – laypersons, scholars, and policymakers – understand and react to contemporary global issues.

The chapter begins by examining the roots of Soviet–Western suspicion after World War I and during World War II. It then tells how the Cold War began in Europe, especially in regard to disagreements over Germany and Eastern Europe. It examines how American views of the USSR changed as agreements reached at the Yalta and Potsdam summits were violated. Mutual mistrust led each side to reevaluate the other's motives. The chapter then shows how we can explain the onset of cold war using different levels of analysis and different theoretical lenses. The Cold War deepened as the United States adopted the Truman Doctrine and Marshall Plan, and instituted the strategy of containment to halt Soviet expansionism. The military side of the conflict grew with the Soviet explosion of an atomic bomb, the US adoption of NSC-68 which advocated American rearmament, the communist overthrow of China's pro-Western government, and the Korean War. At home, rabid anti-communism took the form of McCarthyism, just as anti-capitalism led to purges in the USSR. The chapter then examines the Vietnam War and its immense consequences for American society.

The Cold War began to change with the 1962 Cuban missile crisis. Thereafter, mutual fear of nuclear war produced a set of tacit norms and rules governing US–Soviet behavior. However, Soviet–American détente in the 1970s abruptly ended with the 1979 Soviet invasion of Afghanistan. Surprisingly, the final stages of the Cold War witnessed an increase in Soviet–American tension during the first Reagan administration. The chapter shows how a process begun after Mikhail Gorbachev became General Secretary of the Communist Party in 1985 culminated in the ending of the Cold War, and it examines several alternative explanations for this epic development. The chapter concludes by looking briefly at Russia's evolution since the Cold War's end.

détente periods of lessened tension between the United States and Soviet Union during the Cold War.

Background to the Cold War

Soviet–Western mistrust dated back to the communist overthrow of the Tsarist (imperial) government of Russia in February 1917 and the subsequent overthrow of Russia's provisional government by Lenin's Bolsheviks in October 1917. The young Soviet state was wary of Western intentions, especially after Western and Japanese intervention in North Russia and Siberia in summer 1918. American President Woodrow Wilson justified intervention as part of the effort to keep the Russians fighting the Germans and Austrians in World War I, but Western actions owed much to a profound dislike for communism. "The fact is," writes historian John Lewis Gaddis, "that a fundamental loathing for Bolshevism influenced all of Wilson's actions with regard to Russia and the actions of his Allied counterparts." This antipathy was mutual for "the Bolsheviks made no secret of their fundamental loathing for the West."[3]

In fact, the United States did not recognize the Communist government until 1933, by which time Soviet fear of Hitler had become acute. Suspicions between the USSR, on the one hand, and Britain and France, on the other, grew in the late 1930s when it appeared that each side was hoping the Nazis would attack the other. These suspicions produced the 1939 Soviet–Nazi Nonaggression Treaty, signed just days before the Nazis invaded Poland from the west, thereby starting World War II.

Thrown together by Hitler's invasion of the Soviet Union in June 1941 and US entry into the war in December 1941, the two allies continued to harbor suspicions of one another. The Soviet Union, which was suffering enormous casualties, suspected that the Americans and British were trying to let Moscow fight the war for them, a suspicion heightened by repeated delays in the Western invasion of continental Europe prior to the landings in Normandy on D-Day (June 6, 1944). For their part, the Americans and British were concerned about Soviet political motives as the Red Army moved westward after 1942. With the defeat of the Nazis, the glue that had held the alliance together disappeared.

Iron Curtain a metaphor Winston Churchill coined in 1946 to describe the line separating the area in Europe under Soviet control from the free countries in Western Europe.

On March 5, 1946, in a speech at Westminster College, in Fulton, Missouri, British leader Winston S. Churchill coined the term **iron curtain** to describe the abyss between East and West (see Key document: "Iron curtain speech"). In his speech, Churchill blamed the Soviet Union and its desire for ideological and political–military expansion for the emerging East–West conflict. Drawing on the lessons of World War II and the allies' appeasement of Germany, he argued that another war could be avoided, but only if Britain and the United States acted quickly to demonstrate their military strength and pose a united front against the Soviet Union.

The next section examines the origins of the Cold War in Europe. It shows how both sides acted in ways that violated postwar expectations and seemed to pose a threat to each other's security.

Key document "Iron curtain speech", Winston S. Churchill, March 5, 1946[4]

The United States stands at this time at the pinnacle of world power. It is a solemn moment for the American democracy. For with this primacy in power is also joined an awe-inspiring accountability to the future. . . . Opportunity is here now, clear and shining, for both our countries. To reject it or ignore it or fritter it away will bring upon us all the long reproaches of the aftertime.

I have a strong admiration and regard for the valiant Russian people and for my wartime comrade, Marshal Stalin. There is deep sympathy and goodwill in Britain – and I doubt not here also – toward the peoples of all the Russias and a resolve to persevere through many differences and rebuffs in establishing lasting friendships.

It is my duty, however, to place before you certain facts about the present position in Europe.

From Stettin in the Baltic to Trieste in the Adriatic an iron curtain has descended across the Continent. Behind that line lie all the capitals of the ancient states of Central and Eastern Europe. Warsaw, Berlin, Prague, Vienna, Budapest, Belgrade, Bucharest and Sofia; all these famous cities and the populations around them lie in what I must call the Soviet sphere, and all are subject, in one form or another, not only to Soviet influence but to a very high and in some cases increasing measure of control from Moscow. . . .

In a great number of countries, far from the Russian frontiers and throughout the world, Communist fifth columns are established and work in complete unity and absolute obedience to the directions they receive from the Communist center. Except in the British Commonwealth and in the United States where Communism is in its infancy, the Communist parties or fifth columns constitute a growing challenge and peril to Christian civilization.

Origins of the Cold War in postwar Europe

Although the alliance of Great Britain, the United States, and the Soviet Union triumphed in the end, suspicion between West and East grew as each side came to fear that the other would be a threat to its security once World War II ended. The United States and the Soviet Union found themselves in a bipolar world, a situation in which they were the only powers still in a position to influence global politics in a significant way, and each was the only power that could harm the other. The former great powers – Britain, France, Germany, and Japan – were devastated. Britain, for example, had lost about one-third of its wealth and lacked food and coal to feed and heat itself, its troops in Europe, or the Germans for whom British occupation forces were responsible. France suffered not only great material damage, but devastating psychological harm owing to its collapse in 1940 and subsequent occupation by Germany. Defeated Germany, Italy, and Japan were in ruins. Germany was divided and occupied by the victors, and Japan was occupied by American armed forces. Europe's "winners" and "losers" were all heavily in debt, and all, in varying degrees, needed US assistance to meet basic demands.

Politically, too, Europe was in shambles. The British, French, and Dutch empires were unraveling. In France and Italy, government instability was exacerbated by powerful Communist parties which enjoyed popular support partly because of their reputation for having fought the Nazi occupiers during the war and partly because of their countries' ruinous economic conditions. By contrast, following World War II the United States was economically vigorous and politically stable, accounting for 45 percent of world manufactures and enjoying large trade surpluses and huge gold reserves.[5] American military might was at a peak. Its armies occupied Western Europe and Japan, its navy was the world's largest, and it had a monopoly on a new, revolutionary weapon, the atom bomb. The Soviet Union had borne the brunt of the war against Germany, suffering more than 20 million dead and the destruction of over two decades of socialist construction. Nevertheless, 175 Soviet divisions remained in the heart of Europe, a fact that became more and more important as US forces in Europe were demobilized. Politically, Joseph Stalin's ruthless regime had survived the Nazi onslaught, and no one dared oppose the aging and increasingly paranoid tyrant. The Soviet Union, as one of the victors and with armies occupying Central Europe, expected to share in the spoils of war,

Thus, global leadership was suddenly handed over to the Soviet Union and the United States, neither of which had much experience in global politics. In short order, the United States found itself possessing what

Norwegian historian Geir Lundestad called an "empire by invitation."[6] It did not take long for misunderstandings over Soviet–Western postwar arrangements for Germany and Eastern Europe, agreed on at the Yalta and Potsdam conferences of 1945, to poison East–West relations.

The breakdown of Soviet–American cooperation

The US–Soviet–British alliance had won the war, and it seemed reasonable to believe their cooperation would continue. US President Franklin D. Roosevelt (1882–1945) had envisioned such agreement in his postwar plans. He expected the United States to remain active in world affairs and not return to the isolationist policies of the 1920s and 1930s, and he hoped that the wartime allies would remain peacetime collaborators, especially in the new UN Security Council.

Disillusioned by the failure of the League of Nations to avert World War II (see chapter 3, pp. 135–38), Roosevelt and Secretary of State Cordell Hull abandoned the unilateralism of much of America's past and sought to keep the peace by cooperation among the great powers, described by Roosevelt as "the Four Policemen" (the United States, Soviet Union, Great Britain, and China).[7] Although **spheres of influence** (areas of dominant influence for specific countries) and power politics were nowhere made explicit, they were implicit in the proposal. This idea was even more explicit in Churchill's October 1944 proposal to Stalin. "The moment was apt for business," recalled Churchill, "so I said [to Stalin], 'Let us settle about our affairs in the Balkans. Your armies are in Romania and Bulgaria. We have interests, missions, and agents there. Don't let us get at cross-purposes in small ways. So far as Britain and Russia are concerned, how would it do for you to have ninety percent predominance in Romania, for us to have ninety percent of the say in Greece, and go fifty-fifty about Yugoslavia?'"[8] The spirit of the time was reflected in a letter from American diplomat George F. Kennan (1904–2005) to fellow diplomat Charles E. Bohlen (1904–74) in which Kennan asked: "Why could we not make a decent and definite compromise with it [the USSR] – divide Europe frankly into spheres of influence – keep ourselves out of the Russian sphere and keep the Russians out of ours?"[9]

Several summit meetings were held to iron out the differences among the major powers, the most important of which were held at Yalta in the Soviet Crimea in February 1945 and Potsdam, near Berlin, in July–August 1945. Both shaped the postwar settlement in Europe and fed the misunderstanding that was beginning to characterize Soviet–Western relations. One set of Yalta agreements dealt with representation and

sphere of influence
a geographic region dominated by one major actor.

voting arrangements for the proposed UN organization. The Soviet Union demanded that all of its republics be seated in the UN General Assembly. Washington objected, and a bargain was struck whereby the USSR was given three seats in the General Assembly and the United States could have the same number if it wished. A second agreement provided for veto power for the five permanent members of the Security Council (the United States, the USSR, Britain, France, and China), ensuring that they would have to cooperate if the Council were to function.

The disposition of defeated Germany was a critical issue at Yalta. Agreement was reached on creating four occupation zones in Germany (American, Soviet, British, and French), with France acquiring a zone only after much wrangling. This was a key compromise because it assured continued US involvement in European affairs and ratified the division of Germany among the victors that would remain until the end of the Cold War. Agreements were also reached on German war reparations and on establishing a coalition government including communists and noncommunists in Poland. The most controversial decision at Yalta was the "Declaration on Liberated Europe," which pledged the participants to foster free elections and guarantee basic freedoms in all liberated countries. When the Declaration was not honored by Stalin, it became a powerful rationale for US suspicions about Soviet intentions. One impetus for American willingness to strike these deals at Yalta was to get a Soviet commitment to enter the war against Japan three months after the war in Europe came to an end.

Controversy

At the Yalta Conference in February 1945, President Franklin D. Roosevelt agreed to the reorganization of the Polish government "on a broader democratic basis with the inclusion of democratic leaders from Poland itself and from Poles abroad" that would be "pledged to the holding of free and unfettered elections as soon as possible on the basis of universal suffrage and secret ballot."[10] The Soviet Union failed to honor this agreement, imposing a satellite government in Poland in part because for Stalin it "was a question of strategic security not only because Poland was a bordering country but because throughout history Poland had been the corridor for attack on Russia."[11] Some of Roosevelt's critics argue that the president was duped and, in effect, gave the Soviet Union control over Poland. By contrast, Roosevelt's defenders argue that he got the best deal that was possible but that the United States had little political leverage in Poland because that country was already occupied by the Red Army. In January 1945, Roosevelt himself pointed out to a group of US senators that "the occupying forces had the power in the areas where their arms were present and each knew that the others could not force things to an issue. The Russians had the power in Eastern Europe." Shortly after Yalta, he made the same point: "Obviously the Russians are going to do things their own way in the area they occupy."[12] In his appreciation of power, Roosevelt was clearly more of a realist than many observers realized.

Figure 4.2 Churchill, Roosevelt, and Stalin at the Yalta Conference, February 1945
Courtesy of the National Archives (Records of the Office of the Chief Signal Officer, 1860–1982) photo no. 111-SC-260486

Further discussions were held on the future of Europe at the Potsdam Conference, a few months after Germany's surrender. By then the atmosphere had begun to change. At Potsdam, the United States was represented by Harry S Truman (1884–1972) who had become president after Roosevelt's death on April 12, 1945 at Warm Springs, Georgia and who was more suspicious of Stalin's intentions than his predecessor. Churchill, too, was replaced in the middle of the conference following the election in Britain of Labour Party leader Clement Attlee (1883–1967).

Even though the question of Poland and its borders was to be a principal topic at Potsdam, the USSR announced it had already reached agreement with the Communist government in Poland on that country's new boundaries. The new boundary with Germany followed the Oder and West Neisse rivers from the Baltic Sea to Czechoslovakia, involving the surrender of East Prussia by Germany to Poland (and expulsion of German inhabitants) in compensation for the Soviet annexation of territories in eastern Poland. The Soviet fait accompli, while increasing Soviet security, reduced the prospects for fruitful bargaining, and disagreement was papered over in a statement indicating that the boundary question "shall await the peace settlement."[13]

Expectations still remained high that the Soviet Union would be prepared to negotiate honestly over the future of Germany and Eastern Europe. The hope was that what were called the **Yalta Axioms** would

Yalta Axioms the belief of US leaders before the Cold War that it was possible to bargain with the Soviet Union and that the USSR was much like other states that designed foreign policies based on power.

Figure 4.3 "Big Three" and Foreign Ministers at Postdam, July 1945
US Army, courtesy of the Harry S Truman Library

continue to govern US–Soviet relations.[14] One of these reflected the realist perspective that the Soviet Union was like other states and thus driven fundamentally by power considerations. This axiom implied that the USSR would seek to advance its interests but would also recognize that its power had limits. Rational calculation would, therefore, restrain Soviet behavior. The United States hoped to use rewards such as economic aid and international control of atomic energy as inducements to obtain Soviet compliance with the Yalta Declaration on Liberated Europe and the agreement on how to treat defeated Germany. Despite its defeat Germany remained the key to European security. Its strategic geographic position, highly trained population, and economic potential made it the focus of both Western and Soviet concern.

Ministerial meetings late in 1945 and early in 1946 were disappointing, and Anglo-American fears of the Soviet Union seemed to be realized when the Soviet Union refused to cooperate in administering conquered Germany. Although the four victors had divided Germany into administrative zones, they had agreed to treat the country as a single economic unit. This made sense because Germany's eastern sector was primarily agricultural and the western region mainly industrial. The victors had also agreed that reparations would be paid, especially to the Soviet Union, which had suffered so greatly at the hands of the Nazis. The USSR was to receive all the industrial equipment in the Soviet zone, plus one-quarter of such equipment from the Western zones on condition that no reparations be taken from current German production until the country had accumulated sufficient foreign-exchange reserves to buy necessary imports to feed, clothe, and house its inhabitants. Otherwise, the United States, Britain, and France would be forced to subsidize their former enemy.

In fact, the Soviet Union quickly removed capital equipment from its own zone without informing its allies of what was being taken. It also refused to permit shipment of agricultural goods to the Western zones. The US commander in Germany, General Lucius Clay (1897–1978), responded by suspending reparations from the Western zones to the USSR. Stalin's objectives in Germany were to obtain as much in reparations as possible to finance Soviet reconstruction and eliminate any prospect of a German revival that might again imperil Soviet interests. However, the immediate result was a rapid cooling of East–West relations, and the division of Germany.

The United States and Great Britain were determined that their zones should become economically self-sufficient, so that they would not have to underwrite the German economy and so that Germany could contribute to the overall economic recovery of Europe. To hasten the economic revival of the Western zones, US Secretary of State James Byrnes (1879–1972) proposed in July 1946 that they be unified. France initially refused because it feared a rejuvenated Germany. Nevertheless, the British and American zones were unified in January 1947, and "Bizonia" came into existence, and by the spring France had merged its zone as well. The result was to solidify the division of Germany and eliminate Western influence from the Soviet zone, which became the German Democratic Republic. The Western zones were later united and became the Federal Republic of Germany.

Eastern Europe was the second major source of growing East–West friction. Free and democratic elections were not held, as promised at Yalta; the USSR annexed the independent Baltic republics of Lithuania, Estonia, and Latvia; and Moscow installed or aided new Communist governments in Eastern Europe – Bulgaria, Romania, Poland, East Germany, Albania, Yugoslavia, and, finally, in February 1948, Czechoslovakia. These events profoundly affected American public opinion, especially in communities like Chicago, New York, and Buffalo with their large Eastern European populations. The Czech coup and the murder of the country's foreign minister, Jan Masaryk (1886–1948), son of the country's founder, were the final steps in communizing Eastern Europe, all of which now found itself in the shadow of Soviet power.

Outside Europe, too, events were taking place that threatened East–West cooperation. Soviet interference in Iran continued until the end of 1946. Under UN pressure, Soviet troops were finally withdrawn from that country in May, but a Soviet-supported separatist regime remained in Azerbaijan until December. In addition, Moscow began to demand the cession of the Turkish provinces of Kars and Ardahan and a revision of the Montreux Convention governing Soviet passage through the Dardanelles. On the other hand, the sudden halt of US lend-lease aid to the Soviet Union and Truman's abrupt dismissal of Secretary of Commerce (and former Vice President) Henry Wallace (1888–1965) after Wallace had argued publicly for a conciliatory policy toward the USSR were perceived as insensitive to Soviet interests.

Spiraling mistrust

Soviet actions eroded belief in the Yalta Axioms and triggered growing American acceptance of what historian Daniel Yergin calls the **Riga Axioms**.[15] Unlike the Yalta Axioms, the Riga Axioms assumed that the Soviet Union was driven by Marxist–Leninist ideology rather than power. According to these axioms, the Soviet Union's totalitarian structure, combined with its ideological fervor, was the ultimate source of its policies at home and abroad. In Yergin's words, according to the Riga Axioms, "doctrine and ideology and a spirit of innate aggressiveness shaped Soviet policy. . . . The USSR was committed to world revolution and unlimited expansion."[16] Or, as a constructivist might put it, the messianic communist identity that had taken root in the Soviet Union after the 1917 Bolshevik Revolution had created a set of interests in spreading Marxism–Leninism that were inimical to Western capitalism and Western preference for the global status quo.

Riga Axioms the belief that Soviet policy was driven by ideology rather than power.

Changing US–Soviet perceptions of each other at the time are revealed in several documents. Nothing conveys more clearly the perception of the USSR that was emerging in official Washington early in 1946 than the so-called Long Telegram sent by Kennan, then a counselor in the US embassy in Moscow and already an influential policy advisor, in response to an urgent request by the State Department for clarification of Soviet conduct. The Long Telegram was sent to Washington shortly after Stalin had declared that a clash between the USSR and the West was inevitable and that the West was seeking to encircle the Soviet Union.

Kennan's view of the Soviet Union was almost entirely negative, with mistrust and basic incompatibility between the two superpowers dominating his analysis. Kennan began by assessing Soviet intentions towards the United States. "We have here," he wrote, "a political force committed fanatically to the belief that, with the US there can be no permanent modus vivendi [practical compromise], that it is desirable and necessary that the internal harmony of our society be disrupted, our traditional way of life be destroyed, the international authority of our state be broken, if Soviet power is to be secure." Kennan then explained the role of ideology in Soviet behavior and how it warped the Soviet view of reality: "It [the USSR] is seemingly inaccessible to considerations of reality in its basic reactions. For it, the vast fund of objective fact about human society is not, as with us, the measure against which outlook is constantly being tested and reformed, but a grab bag from which individual items are selected arbitrarily and tendentiously to bolster an outlook already preconceived."[17] Kennan's prognosis of the Soviet menace was gloomy indeed:

> Efforts will be made . . . to disrupt national self-confidence, to hamstring measures of national defense, to increase social and industrial unrest, to stimulate all forms of disunity. . . . Where individual governments stand in [the] path of Soviet purposes pressure will be brought for their removal from office. . . . In foreign countries Communists will . . . work toward destruction of all forms of personal independence, economic, political, or moral.[18]

Although Kennan offered several general suggestions about what could be done to combat the Soviet threat in the Long Telegram, he had no specific prescription for US foreign policy. That was to await publication of his "Mr. X" essay in the influential journal *Foreign Affairs* a year later.

From documents released later, we know that the Soviet Union at the time held a similar view of American intentions. The Soviet ambassador to the United States, Nikolai Novikov (1903–1989), sent a secret report to Soviet foreign minister Vyacheslav Molotov (1890–1986) in September 1946 outlining "the imperialist tendencies of American monopolistic capital" which is "striving for world supremacy."[19] American policy, Novikov argued, was particularly dangerous because its leadership had changed, and the United States was embarked on a course of action to achieve "global dominance." "The ascendance to power of President Truman, a politically unstable person but with certain conservative tendencies, and the subsequent appointment of [James] Byrnes as Secretary of State meant a strengthening of the influence of US foreign policy of the most reactionary circles of the Democratic party." The United States had instituted a military draft, increased defense expenditures, and based military forces around the world, actions that Novikov believed had the single purpose of using military power to achieve "world domination." No longer was the United States interested in cooperating with the USSR. Instead, US policy towards other countries was "directed at limiting or dislodging the influence of the Soviet Union from neighboring countries" and securing "positions for the penetration of American capital into their economies."[20]

Novikov's views are a **mirror image** of those in Kennan's Long Telegram. Soviet leaders saw the United States as driven by capitalist imperatives and bent on world domination. American leaders saw the Soviet Union as driven by Marxist–Leninist imperatives and bent on world revolution. Each side demonized the other as expansionist while assigning benevolent motives to itself, and the private images of policy advisors like Kennan and Novikov were reflected in public utterances by their respective leaders.

mirror image the propensity of groups and individuals to hold similar views of each other; we see in others what they see in us.

Interpreting the beginning of the Cold War

Causes for the onset of the Cold War can be found at all levels of analysis. At the individual level, we might focus on the anti-communism of Western leaders like Winston Churchill and Harry Truman. Churchill, for example, had vigorously denounced Bolshevism following the 1917 Revolution and had dispatched British naval units to Archangel and Murmansk to aid the "Whites" (anti-communists) against the "Reds" (Bolsheviks). Truman, as we noted, was considerably more suspicious of Soviet motives than Roosevelt had been and, as we shall see, initiated policies to limit Soviet influence.

Stalin, too, played a major role in the onset of the Cold War. Stalin has been described as inordinately suspicious, even paranoid by the end of World War II, seeing enemies all around him, at home and abroad. Whether because he feared the West or harbored expansionist dreams, Stalin ordered the communization of Eastern Europe, refused to cooperate with the West in postwar Germany, was responsible for the Korean War, and generally acted in ways that were bound to produce concern in the West.

At the state level, perhaps the most pervasive interpretation of the onset of the Cold War is that it was caused by a clash between two diametrically opposed and competing economic, social, and political systems. The Cold War was, from this perspective, a clash between Soviet communism and American capitalism and between Soviet totalitarianism and American democracy. We have seen how both Kennan and Novikov cited domestic development to explain the deterioration of US–Soviet relations. Those seeking explanations at this level might look at the efforts of the Communist Party of the Soviet Union (CPSU) to strengthen its hold on the USSR by raising the specter of a foreign threat. In the United States, with the 1948 elections on the horizon, the competition between the Republican and Democratic parties for votes, especially in regions with large blocs of voters with Eastern European roots, could explain the "toughening" of American foreign policy toward the Soviet Union. An alternative explanation might focus on the influence of defense industries in both countries.

Finally, at the level of the global system, theorists would focus on the bipolar distribution of military power. This neorealist explanation emphasizes that postwar **bipolarity** meant that the only major security threat to each superpower was the other superpower, thereby creating a **security dilemma**. Poised along the Iron Curtain, the Red Army appeared an imminent threat to Western Europe. In turn, the United States, as the sole possessor of nuclear weapons, would have seemed highly threatening to the Soviet Union. From the Soviet perspective, securing Eastern Europe and Germany was vital to preventing attack from the West and so, for reasons of geography and power, Soviet leaders had acted like their predecessors, the tsars. As early as 1835, the French political philosopher, Alexis de Tocqueville (1805–59), had predicted that the two great powers would collide because of their growing power and vastly different cultures:

> There are, at the present time, two great nations in the world which seem to tend towards the same end, although they started from different points: I allude to the Russians and the Americans. Both of them have grown up unnoticed; and whilst the attention of mankind was directed elsewhere, they have suddenly assumed a most prominent place amongst the nations. . . .
>
> All other nations seem to have nearly reached their natural limits, and only to be charged with the maintenance of their power; but these are still in the act of growth; all the others are stopped, or continue to advance with extreme difficulty. . . . The Anglo-American relies upon personal interest to accomplish his ends, and gives free scope to the unguided exertions and common-sense of the citizens; the Russian centers all the authority of society in a single arm; the principal instrument of the former is freedom; of the latter servitude. Their starting-point is different, and their courses are not the same; yet each of them seems to be marked out by the will of Heaven to sway the destinies of half the globe.[21]

Realists, liberals, constructivists, and Marxists would analyze the sources of the Cold War rather differently. As noted above, realists, especially neorealists, would stress the existence of a **power vacuum** in Central Europe and East Asia that had been created by the defeat of Germany and Japan and the weakness of other European and Asian

bipolarity a political system with two centers of power.

security dilemma the inability of actors under conditions of anarchy to trust each other; the fear of aggression created in one actor by the growth of military power in another.

power vacuum an area not under the control of any strong country and that strong states may wish to control to prevent others from doing so.

countries. The United States and USSR each recognized that only the other could threaten its security, and the steps each took to increase that security, although in their national interests, frightened the other. Thus, both were trapped in a security dilemma. Neither wanted the other to enjoy a preponderance of power, and each sought to prevent this by arming and forging alliances, thereby maintaining a balance of power. In addition, realists might put forward a geopolitical explanation of the Cold War as a consequence of traditional Russian expansionism in search of warm water ports and defensible boundaries.

Liberals would focus on Soviet authoritarianism as a key source of conflict. Soviet leaders could cement their authority at home by focusing public attention on an imagined threat from abroad, and their abuse of human rights at home, as well as in occupied Eastern Europe, alienated public opinion in the United States. The absence of Soviet–American interdependence meant that there were few impediments to Soviet–American competition.

Constructivists would focus on the contrasting identities of the two superpowers that gave rise to conflicting interests. They would point out how, after 1917, a consensus emerged among Soviet leaders and citizens about the USSR's identity as the vanguard of a world Marxist revolution, and they would also focus on the emergence of an American identity as leader of "the free world." The USSR saw itself as the leader of the communist world, just as the United States identified itself as the leader of the capitalist world. Competing world views produced incompatible beliefs about how societies ought to be organized politically and economically. The West viewed capitalism as the basic principle for organizing society, and the East advocated **socialism**. The United States viewed itself as a democracy in which individual freedom and entrepreneurial activity were encouraged; the USSR, as a socialist society, sought to encourage economic equality, collective responsibility, and centralized economic planning. Each regarded the other's version of democracy as a sham that gave power to the few at the expense of the many.

Marxists viewed the policies of the United States and its allies as part of a transnational capitalist effort to strangle socialism in general and the Soviet state in particular, and to spread capitalism and free trade globally, make non-Western countries economic dependencies of the most developed Western states, and obtain new markets for exports and new sources of key raw materials. "Capitalist encirclement" and "Western imperialism" summarized the Marxist belief that economic and class imperatives shaped Western policies after World War II and that giant corporations and banks, protected by Western governments that they controlled, were the engines driving capitalist expansion.

socialism a political and economic system involving government ownership and administration of the means of production and distribution of goods.

Even with the availability of ever more Soviet and American documents, we may never achieve consensus over the causes of the Cold War. Once begun, however, as we shall see in the next section, the conflict spread and deepened.

The Cold War spreads and deepens

The Cold War entered a new and more dangerous stage early in 1947. By enunciating the Truman Doctrine, the United States threw down the gauntlet and officially adopted a confrontational approach toward the Soviet Union.

Containment

Early in 1947, Great Britain informed the United States that it could no longer provide financial assistance to Turkey or Greece, where a communist-led insurgency threatened the country's stability. Fearing that additional countries were in danger as well, President Truman (1945–53) on March 12 requested $400 million from a skeptical Congress for economic and military assistance for Turkey and Greece. Truman placed the situation in the context of broader changes that he saw taking place in global politics. Truman's speech, known as the Truman Doctrine, marked America's first major Cold War commitment, as it espoused assisting "free people" anywhere who were threatened by totalitarian governments that restricted political, economic, social, and cultural life. Although the United States had "made frequent protests against coercion and intimidation, in violation of the Yalta agreement, in Poland, Romania, and Bulgaria," those protests had proved insufficient. The United States must now be willing, Truman declared, "to help free peoples to maintain their free institutions and their national integrity against aggressive movements that seek to impose upon them totalitarian regimes." The sweeping language of the speech and the worldwide commitment to assist any state threatened by **totalitarianism** gained it the status of a "doctrine" and a lasting policy for the United States. Yet Truman's speech was more than that: it was a virtual declaration of Cold War. The issue was beginning to overshadow everything else on the global agenda.

Truman's speech became the basis for many later American commitments to resisting communist expansionism beyond Europe (see Key document: President Truman's address). The speech was also the basis of the **containment** policy that was adopted by the United States during much of the Cold War. Following Truman's declaration, George Kennan, author of the Long Telegram, published an article under the pseudonym

totalitarianism a form of authoritarianism exercising control over society, even the minute details of individual lives, often by means of technology and a single mass political party.

containment a US foreign policy that sought to prevent the spread of communism by applying diplomatic and economic pressure on the USSR.

"Mr. X" in the influential journal *Foreign Affairs* in which he outlined a policy of putting pressure on the Soviet Union by "the application of counter-force at a series of constantly changing geographical and political points" aimed at producing a change in both the USSR's internal structure and its international conduct. This policy was based on "patient firmness" in countering communist expansion, initially by use of economic and ideological tools, but in time, as reinterpreted by American officials, coming to rely increasingly on alliances and bases around the world and on military force.[22] Thereafter, the United States embarked on a global strategy to confront what it believed to be a Soviet policy of expansionism. Notwithstanding changes in nuance and tactics, containment remained the basis of American foreign policy for four decades.

Key document   President Truman's address to Congress[23]

Mr. President, Mr. Speaker, Members of the Congress of the United States: The gravity of the situation which confronts the world today necessitates my appearance before a joint session of the Congress. The foreign policy and the national security of this country are involved.

One aspect of the present situation, which I wish to present to you at this time for your consideration and decision, concerns Greece and Turkey. The United States has received from the Greek government an urgent appeal for financial and economic assistance. . . .

The very existence of the Greek state is today threatened by the terrorist activities of several thousand armed men, led by communists, who defy the government's authority at a number of points, particularly along the northern boundaries. . . .

Meanwhile, the Greek government is unable to cope with the situation. The Greek army is small and poorly equipped. It needs supplies and equipment if it is to restore the authority of the government throughout Greek territory. Greece must have assistance if it is to become a self-supporting and self-respecting democracy.

The United States must supply that assistance. We have already extended to Greece certain types of relief and economic aid, but these are inadequate. . . . Greece's neighbor, Turkey, also deserves our attention. . . .

One of the primary objectives of the foreign policy of the United States is the creation of conditions in which we and other nations will be able to work out a way of life free from coercion. . . .

We shall not realize our objectives, however, unless we are willing to help free peoples to maintain their free institutions and their national integrity against aggressive movements that seek to impose upon them totalitarian regimes. This is no more than a frank recognition that totalitarian regimes imposed on free peoples, by direct or indirect aggression, undermine the foundations of international peace and hence the security of the United States. . . .

At the present moment in world history nearly every nation must choose between alternative ways of life. The choice is too often not a free one. One way of life is based upon the will of the majority, and is distinguished by free institutions, representative government, free elections, guarantees of individual liberty, freedom of speech and religion, and freedom from political oppression.

The second way of life is based upon the will of a minority forcibly imposed upon the majority. It relies upon terror and oppression, a controlled press and radio, fixed elections and the suppression of personal freedoms.

I believe that it must be the policy of the United States to support free peoples who are resisting attempted subjugation by armed minorities or by outside pressures.

I believe that we must assist free peoples to work out their own destinies in their own way.

I believe that our help should be primarily through economic and financial aid which is essential to economic stability and orderly political processes. It would be an unspeakable tragedy if these countries, which have struggled so long against overwhelming odds, should lose that victory for which they sacrificed so much. Collapse of free institutions and loss of independence would be disastrous not only for them but for the world. Discouragement and possibly failure would quickly be the lot of neighboring peoples striving to maintain their freedom and independence. . . .

If we falter in our leadership, we may endanger the peace of the world – and we shall surely endanger the welfare of our own nation.

In ensuing years in carrying out containment, the United States concluded numerous alliances culminating in a global alliance network. Washington entered the Inter-American Treaty of Mutual Assistance (Rio Treaty) with 21 western hemisphere countries in 1947; the North Atlantic Treaty Organization (NATO) with 12 (later 15) European states in 1949; the ANZUS Treaty with Australia and New Zealand in 1951; the Baghdad Pact with Turkey, Pakistan, Iraq, Iran, and Britain in 1954 (renamed the Central Treaty Organization [CENTO] in 1959 after Iraq left the alliance); and the Southeast Asia Treaty Organization (SEATO) with countries within and outside the region in 1954. Bilateral pacts were completed with the Philippines, Japan, South Korea, and Taiwan early in the 1950s. The United States also undertook economic and military assistance programs worldwide that linked US security to that of recipients, and a vigorous campaign began at home and abroad to warn against the danger posed by the USSR.

However, American officials realized that the Cold War could not be won simply by military force. Poverty and despair made people amenable to communism, and it was necessary to rectify these conditions if Communist parties in countries such as France and Italy were to be kept from power. In June 1947, in a speech at Harvard University, US Secretary of State George C. Marshall (1880–1959) announced the Marshall Plan – a massive effort to help rebuild Western Europe by providing economic assistance and, if possible, attract some of the countries of Eastern Europe from the Soviet embrace. (The chill in East–West relations and the threat of Stalinist coercion prevented this from happening.)[24] The accompanying American requirement that Europe establish common institutions to administer Marshall aid was a first step along the road to Europe's economic and political integration (see chapter 9, pp. 432–4).

Two years later, the United States and its European friends established the North Atlantic Treaty Organization in order to meet what they perceived as a growing Soviet threat to Europe. NATO and the nascent European community both served to reintegrate recently defeated Germany (or at least its western areas; the eastern areas were under Soviet occupation) into Europe and the West. For their part, the Soviet Union established a counter alliance in 1955 called the Warsaw Pact which was dissolved at the end of the Cold War. NATO continues to exist today, although its purposes have changed dramatically since the end of the Cold War (see chapter 9, pp. 441–2). NATO was forged as at first a political and later a military shield behind which the United States would reconstruct the countries of Western Europe that had been ravaged by World War II. In return, the countries of Western Europe would accept America's political leadership. This arrangement survived until the worst of the Cold War had passed and Europe had been restored to prosperity and vigor.

From the beginning of the Cold War, a series of crises confronted Western Europe. These usually involved probes in which the two sides sought to find out what they could get away with without causing war, often involving unilateral actions that one side viewed as justified or harmless but that provoked the other side to retaliate. Several of these crises involved Soviet efforts to impede Western access to Berlin, the former and present capital of Germany.[25] Like Germany as a whole, the city had been divided among the victors of World War II – the Soviet Union, the United States, Great Britain, and France – and was located deep within the Soviet zone (see Map 4.1) with Western access guaranteed. In May 1948, however, the Soviet Union, anticipating the West's establishment of a new state from their zones in Germany, blockaded Western road, water, and rail access to Berlin. Soviet anger had been sparked by a unilateral Western currency reform in its zones that had been implemented because of Soviet refusal to treat Germany as a single economic unit. In response to the blockade, late in July, the Western powers began a massive airlift to the beleaguered city to loosen the Soviet stranglehold there. By one estimate, US and British aircraft transported "over 1.5 million tons of food, fuel, and other goods into Berlin (the highest load in one day exceeded 12,000 tons)"[26] during the ten months to the end of the blockade in May 1949. The peaceful conclusion to the Berlin blockade was an important learning experience

Map 4.1 Divided Germany

for both sides in how West and East could confront each other in a crisis and, with some imagination, avoid direct resort to arms.

Other dangerous crises involving Berlin took place in the late 1950s and early 1960s, especially in August 1961, when the Soviet Union constructed what came to be known as the Berlin Wall, dividing Berlin in two. The Wall was built to curtail the flight of people from the East to the West – an embarrassment to the Soviet Union and the East German communists – and it stood as a symbol of the abyss separating East and West until it was torn down on November 9, 1989.

Militarizing the Cold War

To this point, the Cold War had been largely waged in Europe and had remained mainly a political and ideological context. Events now took place that raised the stakes involved and that began to militarize the East–West contest. On August 29, 1949, the Soviet Union conducted its first successful test of an atom bomb, shocking the West which had believed that the USSR was still far from acquiring nuclear weapons. This achievement had been aided by espionage conducted by Soviet spies such as Klaus Fuchs (1911–88), German-born head of the physics department of the British nuclear research centre at Harwell and British-born physicist Alan Nunn May (1911–2003), both of whom had worked on the wartime Manhattan Project that developed the US atom bomb. The Truman administration commissioned a classified report to be written by Paul Nitze (1907–2004),[27] then head of the State Department's Policy Planning Bureau, and issued by the National Security Council[28] on April 14, 1950.

NSC-68

The report, called NSC-68, marked a dramatic shift in American policy toward militarizing the Cold War. Unlike Kennan's Long Telegram, which greatly influenced Nitze, NSC-68 stressed the USSR's growing military capabilities and called for massive enlargement and improvement in American military capabilities to meet the Soviet threat. What was necessary was "a build-up of military strength by the United States and its allies to a point at which the combined strength will be superior . . . to the forces that can be brought to bear by the Soviet Union and its satellites."[29] Thus, NSC-68 marked a shift from Kennan's belief that the Soviet threat was largely political and ideological and that containment should rest mainly on political and economic means to a more aggressive form of containment based on military power. Where Kennan doubted that the Soviet threat could "be effectively met entirely by military means,"[30] NSC-68 saw growing Soviet military power and its willingness to use it as part of a systematic global strategy to destroy the West. Without this, containment would be a "bluff." Where Kennan's version of containment was largely passive, awaiting changes in Soviet domestic society, NSC-68 advocated an active version of containment to encourage such changes and advised against any return to **isolationism**.[31]

isolationism a policy aimed at avoiding overseas political and military involvement.

In a bipolar world, according to NSC-68, the United States and Soviet Union were engaged in a **zero-sum** conflict in which cooperation was impossible. Thus, "the Soviet Union, unlike previous aspirants to

zero-sum a relationship of pure conflict in which a gain for one actor is equal to the loss for another.

hegemony," was moved "by a new fanatic faith," that leads it to try to "impose its absolute authority over the rest of the world."[32] Using a realist perspective, NSC-68 declared that Soviet leaders regarded the United States as the principal threat to their ambitions and so had to be destroyed. The report predicted that the USSR would stockpile hundreds of atom bombs by 1954 and that a surprise nuclear attack on the United States would then become possible, even as the Red Army continued to threaten Western Europe. "Only if we had overwhelming atomic superiority and obtained command of the air," the report continued "might the USSR be deterred from employing its atomic weapons as we progressed toward the attainment of our objectives."[33] President Truman did not immediately sign NSC-68, but, when North Korean forces swept across the 38th parallel into South Korea on June 25, 1950 and seemed to validate the report, Truman added his signature.

Key document   NSC-68[34]

Two complex sets of factors have now basically altered this historic distribution of power. First, the defeat of Germany and Japan and the decline of the British and French Empires have interacted with the development of the United States and the Soviet Union in such a way that power increasingly gravitated to these two centers. Second, the Soviet Union, unlike previous aspirants to hegemony, is animated by a new fanatic faith, antithetical to our own, and seeks to impose its absolute authority over the rest of the world. Conflict has, therefore, become endemic and is waged, on the part of the Soviet Union, by violent or non-violent methods in accordance with the dictates of expediency. With the development of increasingly terrifying weapons of mass destruction, every individual faces the ever-present possibility of annihilation should the conflict enter the phase of total war.

The design, therefore, calls for the complete subversion or forcible destruction of the machinery of government and structure of society in the countries of the non-Soviet world and their replacement by an apparatus and structure subservient to and controlled from the Kremlin. To that end Soviet efforts are now directed toward the domination of the Eurasian land mass. The United States, as the principal center of power in the non-Soviet world and the bulwark of opposition to Soviet expansion, is the principal enemy whose integrity and vitality must be subverted or destroyed by one means or another if the Kremlin is to achieve its fundamental design.

. . . [T]he Soviet Union is seeking to create overwhelming military force, in order to back up infiltration with intimidation. In the only terms in which it understands strength, it is seeking to demonstrate to the free world that force and the will to use it are on the side of the Kremlin, that those who lack it are decadent and doomed. . . . The possession of atomic weapons at each of the opposite poles of power, and the inability (for different reasons) of either side to place any trust in the other, puts a premium on a surprise attack against us. It equally puts a premium on a more violent and ruthless prosecution of its design by cold war, especially if the Kremlin is sufficiently objective to realize the improbability of our prosecuting a preventive war.

The "loss of China"

The Cold War spread beyond Europe to Asia when a Communist government under Mao Zedong took power in China in 1949, thereby uniting the country under a single government for the first time since the overthrow of China's Manchu dynasty in 1911. China's turn toward communism was the result of a drawn-out civil war between Communist forces and the Nationalist Government. This conflict reinforced Western fears that communism was inherently expansionist and that Communist countries would employ military means to spread the ideology. It also hardened Western resolve to contain the spread of communism.

Despite the efforts of Sun Yatsen, provisional president of China's new republic and founder of its most powerful political party, the Nationalist Party or Kuomintang (KMT), to unify the country, China increasingly became an arena of conflict among quarreling warlords. Seeking allies to assist him, Sun recruited a young officer named Chiang Kai-shek (1887–1975) as his military aide. Sun also accepted assistance from the Communist International (Comintern) beginning in 1921, and Chiang was sent to study in the Soviet Union in 1923. After Sun's death in 1925, Chiang became leader of the Nationalists and succeeded in expanding their control over large areas of China. Chiang also continued cooperating with China's Communist Party (CCP) until 1927 when he turned ferociously upon his former allies, arresting and murdering hundreds of them in Shanghai, thereby starting a civil war that lasted over two decades. Shortly thereafter Chiang became the recognized leader of China's government. Those communists who survived fled the cities into the countryside.

Chiang's forces pursued the communists, but, after four unsuccessful military operations aimed at destroying the communists in China's western Jiangxi Province, in 1933 Chiang succeeded in encircling his communist enemies. Facing the possibility of annihilation, the communists broke out of the trap in October 1934 and began the legendary year-long "Long March" under the leadership of Mao Zedong, crossing 6,000 miles of mountains and marshes until reaching northern Shaanxi Province, deep in the heart of China, in October 1935. Only 10 percent of Mao's original force remained.

Following Japan's 1937 invasion of China, the Nationalists and Communists were forced into an uneasy alliance. In fact, their cooperation during World War II was virtually non-existent, each side weighing its moves with an eye to gaining territorial and other advantages over its domestic foe when their civil war resumed. As early as 1940, the Nationalists were using their best troops to fight the Communists, and

Chiang's refusal to risk his forces against the Japanese infuriated his American advisors, notably General Joseph W. Stilwell who referred to Chiang derogatorily in his letters as "the peanut." It was, then, hardly surprising that with the end of World War II civil war again engulfed China.

Mao Zedong made guerrilla tactics famous during China's civil war. Mao argued that guerrilla forces should befriend local populations and blend in among them. "The people are like water and the army is like fish." In this way Mao used China's rural areas to cut off and surround the Nationalists, who controlled most of China's cities. Mao called his strategy **people's war** and described it as beginning with ambushes and skirmishes and ending in conventional battle as enemy forces became weaker.

people's war Mao Zedong's theory of peasant guerrilla warfare.

With Japan's surrender, the USSR, which had entered the Pacific war only days earlier, seized control of Manchuria and provided the Communists with large amounts of Japanese arms. However, Stalin did little to encourage Mao to seize power. Between December 1945 and January 1947, General George Marshall sought unsuccessfully to foster a ceasefire between the Nationalists and Communists. A series of campaigns followed in which the Nationalist armies, weakened by corruption and confined to the cities, began to collapse, culminating in Chiang's flight to the island of Taiwan (called Formosa by the Japanese) and the establishment of the People's Republic of China on October 1, 1949. On Taiwan, Chiang established a virtual dictatorship, continued to call himself the legitimate ruler of the Republic of China, and until his death repeatedly threatened to reconquer the mainland. Sino-American hostility escalated when Mao turned to the USSR for economic aid and diplomatic support in his efforts to take China's seat in the UN.

What was called the "loss" of China was realized, finally, in 1971, when the United Nations expelled the Nationalist delegation and accepted a Communist delegation as legitimate representatives of China. The island, which both Mao and Chiang agreed was part of China, remains a bone of contention to this day (see chapter 5, p. 204).

McCarthyism at home

The loss of China intensified a climate of fear and hysteria about alleged communist infiltration of American institutions that was called McCarthyism after Senator Joseph McCarthy (1908–57) of Wisconsin. Confrontations with the Soviet Union such as the 1948 Berlin blockade and the Soviet Union's 1949 explosion of an atomic bomb, years before Americans had expected it to acquire this technology,[35] had produced growing concern about the "Red Menace." In addition, sensational allegations of espionage by Soviet agents such as American Alger Hiss (1904–96), president of the Carnegie Endowment for International Peace, and physicist Klaus Fuchs (1911–88) were exploited by demagogic politicians, notably McCarthy. On February 9, 1950, McCarthy declared that he had in his hand "a list of 205, a list of names that were made known to the Secretary of State as being members of the Communist Party and who nevertheless are still working and shaping policy in the State Department."[36]

A similar process unfolded in the USSR. Stalin believed himself to be surrounded by traitors and spies. Purges were conducted against Soviet citizens, including World War II veterans, who had had any contact with Westerners, and the number of prisoners held in the Soviet "Gulag Archipelago" (the network of Soviet forced-labor camps around the country) grew dramatically.[37]

The victory of Mao Zedong in China provided McCarthy and other "red baiters" with additional fodder. Who, they wanted to know, had "lost China"? The answer, they claimed, lay in treason by the State Department: foreign service officers and China specialists such as John Carter Vincent (1900–72), John Stewart Service (1909–99), John Paton Davies, Jr. (1908–99), and Owen Lattimore (1900–89)[38] whose only crime had been to predict correctly that Mao's forces would triumph over the corrupt Nationalists. Such individuals, they reasoned, must have worked to undermine America's wartime ally, Chiang Kai-shek. Lattimore, who had given the Chinese Communists "credit for having a more nearly democratic structure than the Kuomintang, despite their doctrinaire base" and were not, he argued, "mere tools of the Kremlin,"[39] was a special target. "Perhaps not every schoolchild," writes historian Robert P. Newman, "could identify Lattimore as the architect of American policy in the Far East, but by the end of March 1950 every scoundrel in the country, and some abroad, knew that Lattimore had been targeted as another Hiss. Would-be informants came crawling out of the woodwork, drawn to McCarthy as moths to light, each peddling a new version of Lattimore's evil deeds."[40] Lattimore and the others were disgraced and hounded out of the State Department, which was largely deprived of China experts for years afterwards.

The Korean War

The Cold War in Asia became a hot war and the wave of anti-communist hysteria in the United States intensified when communist North Korea invaded South Korea on June 25, 1950. Like Berlin, divided Korea was an anomaly – it was in neither the Western nor the Eastern camp. In a January 1950 speech, US Secretary of State Dean Acheson (1893–1971) declared that South Korea was outside the US defense perimeter in East Asia. This speech, which indicated that the United States would not get involved in a war on the Asian mainland or interfere in China's civil war, may also have suggested to Stalin that North Korean aggression would be left unanswered.

In fact, on hearing of the North Korean attack, President Truman reversed the position outlined earlier by Acheson and dispatched to South Korea US troops based in Japan as occupation forces. American intervention was authorized by the United Nations and, although most allied forces were American and South Korean, the Korean War was waged in the name of the UN. In ordering US intervention, President Truman explicitly recalled the failure of the policy of appeasement that the British and French had pursued with Hitler, as well as with the Japanese and Italians, in the 1930s. Truman believed that this strategy had made the allies look weak and had provoked additional Nazi aggression. Thus, to justify his position on South Korea, Truman wrote:

> In my generation, this was not the first occasion when the strong had attacked the weak. I recalled some earlier instances: Manchuria, Ethiopia, Austria. I remembered how each time the democracies had failed to act it had encouraged the aggressors to keep going ahead. Communism was acting in Korea just as Hitler, Mussolini, and the Japanese had acted ten, fifteen, and twenty years earlier. I felt certain that if South Korea was allowed to fall Communist leaders would be emboldened to override nations closer to our own shores.[41]

American leaders believed that the communists had invaded South Korea to probe America's willingness to resist communist expansionism and that the invasion was also a prelude to possible Soviet aggression in Europe. In fact, Stalin was behind the invasion. "In the Soviet archives," writes historian Paul Lashmar,

> are a number of documents, including this telegram, sent to Stalin by his ambassador in North Korea, General Shtykov, two days after the start of the war, which conclusively show that the North attacked the South with Stalin's full knowledge: "The troops went to their start position by 24,00 hrs on 24 June. Military activities began at 4–40 local time. . . . The attack by the People's Army took the enemy completely by surprise."[42]

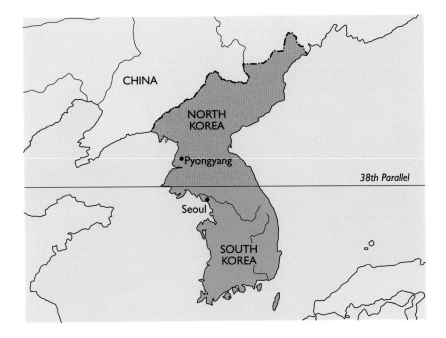

CHINA

NORTH
KOREA

•Pyongyang

38th Parallel

Seoul

SOUTH
KOREA

Map 4.2 Korea and the
38th Parallel

With the Korean invasion, American leaders feared that if the United
States allowed one country to "fall" to communism, then others would
follow until communist forces reached Western Europe, and this could not
be allowed to happen. Despite American involvement, the bloody struggle
continued for three more years, enlarged by the intervention at Stalin's
urging of 200,000 Chinese "volunteers" in October 1950, as UN forces
under American General Douglas MacArthur (1880–1964) seemed on
the verge of uniting the entire Korean peninsula.[43]

The Korean War ended in a ceasefire in 1953, but a treaty officially
ending the war has *never* been signed, and Korea remains today one of the
most dangerous flashpoints in the world.

Although the Korean War's military outcome was inconclusive, its
political impact was profound. The war, thousands of miles from Europe,
confirmed that the Cold War was global. For Americans, the Korean War
ended what political scientist Robert Jervis called "the incoherence which
characterized US foreign and defense efforts in the period 1946–1950"[44]
and propelled the United States in the direction of fully implementing
the containment doctrine.

The Korean War militarized the Cold War in both Europe and Asia and
transformed a regional struggle into a global one. Also, Mao's triumph in
China and the Korean invasion had important domestic consequences for
the United States. For example, in 1952, General Dwight D. Eisenhower
(1890–1969), hero of D-Day in World War II and the first commander of
NATO, was overwhelmingly elected President of the United States partly

Figure 4.4 North Korean and Chinese representatives signing the truce agreement with the United Nations command in Panmunjon, July 27, 1953 Courtesy of the National Archives (General Records of the Department of the Navy, 1804–1958) photo no. 80-G-625728

because of dissatisfaction with Truman's failure to either end or win the war in Korea. Apparently threatening to use nuclear weapons in Korea, Eisenhower swiftly concluded a ceasefire with China and North Korea, though not a permanent peace. Also, the events in Asia brought about a dramatic increase in American military spending and transformed NATO from a political into a military alliance, with a large number of American troops based in Europe, especially West Germany, a permanent headquarters and staff in Brussels, Belgium, and a Supreme Allied Commander Europe (SACEUR) who has always been an American officer. By 1953, US defense expenditures had soared to over 13 percent of gross national product (GNP) and remained above 8 percent during much of the 1960s.[45] These expenditures began to decrease in the 1970s, only to rise again in the 1980s as the Reagan defense buildup began (see in the next section). Estimates of defense spending by the Soviet Union range from 10 to 20 percent of GNP (and even higher) throughout the Cold War. These expenditures fueled both a conventional and a nuclear arms race.

The Asian dimension of the Cold War again became inflamed during the Vietnam War, in which the United States sought to resist the unification of that country under a communist government led by Ho Chi Minh.

The Vietnam War

Vietnam was made a French protectorate in 1883 and was integrated into France's colonial empire in Indochina (which also encompassed Laos and Cambodia) in 1887. The most important figure in Vietnam's effort to achieve independence was Ho Chi Minh (1890–1969) whose vision for his country combined nationalism and communism. During the 1919 Versailles Peace Conference, Ho tried to persuade US President Woodrow Wilson that the Vietnamese should enjoy national self-determination and that French colonialism should be brought to an end, but his proposal fell on deaf ears.

During World War II, French Indochina was occupied by Japan. Following Japan's defeat, France sought to reoccupy Indochina, and Ho warned the French that: "You can kill 10 of my men for every one I kill of yours, yet even at those odds, you will lose and I will win." Towards the end of the first war in Indochina, the United States, convinced that the struggle in Indochina was an example of communist expansion rather than anti-colonialism, was underwriting about 75 percent of the war's costs, and Secretary of State John Foster Dulles (1888–1959) was determined to hold the line against communist expansionism. Dulles and other American leaders viewed events in Vietnam as part of the larger Cold War, believed that the Soviet Union and Maoist China were behind Ho Chi Minh, and feared that American failure to contain communism in Vietnam would be seen by America's foes as a sign of weakness and an indication that the United States would not uphold its commitments elsewhere.

At a press conference held shortly before the climactic French 1954 defeat at Dienbienphu in northern Vietnam, President Dwight D. Eisenhower set forth the assumption on which later US involvement in Vietnam would be based when he declared: "You have broader considerations that might follow what you might call the 'falling domino' principle. You have a row of dominoes set up, you knock over the first one, and what will happen to the last one is that it will go over very quickly. So you have a beginning of a disintegration that would have the most profound consequences." The "domino theory" shaped the way American leaders evaluated the impending French defeat at Dienbienphu and the prospective victory of the communist forces in Indochina. In fact, for a time, the United States contemplated intervening to prevent the imminent French defeat.

Following the French defeat in 1954, a conference was held in Geneva, Switzerland, that produced an agreement, temporarily partitioning Vietnam, with a communist regime in the north and the anti-communist Ngo Dinh Diem (1901–63) as first president of South Vietnam. The agreement also stipulated that internationally supervised elections be held throughout Vietnam in July 1956 to determine the country's future. At American urging, Diem refused to hold the elections, and a second Indochinese conflict began in 1959. The north began to support violence to overthrow the government in the south in Saigon (renamed Ho Chi Minh City after the war) and unite Vietnam under communist rule. Thus began the second Vietnam War which lasted until 1975.

Under presidents Eisenhower and Kennedy, the United States provided South Vietnam with advisors, supplies, and training, but after Diem's overthrow and death in a 1963 military coup, US involvement grew. In the 1964 Gulf of Tonkin Resolution, the Congress gave President Lyndon B. Johnson (1908–73) permission "to take all necessary measures to repel any armed attack against the forces of the United States and to prevent further aggression." Some 27,000 American troops were in Vietnam at the time, but additional troops began to arrive in March 1965 and, at its peak, America's military presence in South Vietnam exceeded 500,000. Commanded by General William Westmorland (1914–2005) in the crucial years between 1964 and 1968, America's conscript soldiers suffered increasing casualties confronting a foe they little understood in a war in trackless jungles in which there were no front lines and in which they could not tell the difference between innocent civilians and enemy combatants.

Throughout this period, Ho followed Mao's example in fighting a "people's war." Guerrilla tactics were a feature of this conflict. Guerrillas and their supplies were sent south along the Ho Chi Minh Trail (Map 4.3) that ran through Laos and Cambodia. With its troops far more poorly armed than those of the United States, Vietcong guerrillas tried to avoid pitched battles, so they favored ambushes and hit-and-run tactics that aimed to produce American casualties and erode political support for the war back home. Like Mao's guerrillas, Ho's forces paid special attention to building safe base camps that sometimes involved complex systems of underground tunnels.

America's strategy of using large-scale conventional air and ground forces with enormous firepower played into enemy hands because it led to the deaths of large numbers of civilians and destruction of their villages. As a result, the sympathies of Vietnamese civilians became more and more pro-Vietcong. Ho understood that his goal could only be won on the political front. To this end, on January 30, 1968, the first day of Tet, the Vietnamese festival of the lunar New Year, the Vietcong launched a surprise offensive against American and South Vietnamese forces in which provincial capitals throughout the country were seized. In a bold stroke, the Vietcong struck Saigon, and invaded the US embassy. After bitter

Did you know?

During the the Vietnam War, more US Ambassadors were killed worldwide in accidents and terrorism than generals in Vietnam.

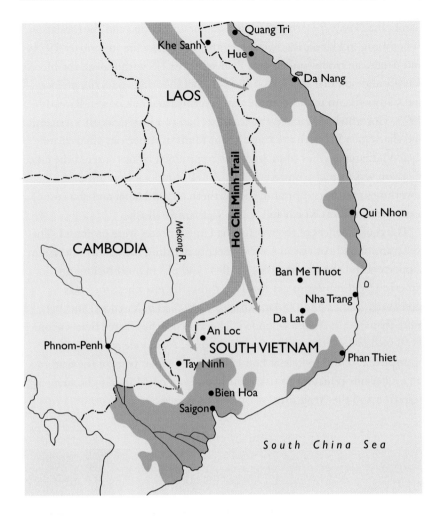

Map 4.3 The Ho Chi Minh Trail

fighting, US forces repelled the Tet Offensive, inflicting terrible losses on the enemy.

Notwithstanding his military defeat, Ho's strategy persuaded many Americans that his forces could strike when and where they wished and that the United States could not win the war at acceptable cost. The Tet Offensive was a media disaster for the White House and for Johnson's presidency, and American public opinion rapidly turned against the war, with conservatives frustrated by US failure to use all its might to win the war and liberals regarding American intervention as immoral. Johnson declined to run for office in 1968, and Richard M. Nixon (1913–94), claiming he had a "secret plan" to end the war, was elected president and gradually reduced the American presence while "Vietnamizing" the war by increasing the role of South Vietnamese forces. Finally, after lengthy negotiations conducted by Secretary of State Henry Kissinger (1923–), punctuated by American military efforts such as the "secret bombing" of

Cambodia (1969–73), the 1970 invasion of Cambodia, and the escalation of bombing in Hanoi, the two sides agreed to a ceasefire in January 1973, and American troops pulled out. Even after the US withdrawal, the bloody war ground on until 1975, engulfing the neighboring countries of Laos and Cambodia, in which communist governments took power. By early 1975, Ho, who had ignored the ceasefire, had conquered South Vietnam, and the war ended with the tumultuous flight of American officials and their Vietnamese allies from Saigon as communist troops entered the city. Vietnam was formally united on July 2, 1976 under a Communist government with its capital in the northern city of Hanoi and at a cost of some three million North and South Vietnamese deaths.

The consequences of the war for the United States were profound. The war transformed American politics, deeply dividing the country between supporters and opponents of the conflict, and placing inhibitions on American willingness to get involved militarily elsewhere for years afterwards. About 58,000 American soldiers died in Vietnam, and more than 300,000 were wounded. The war cost the United States about $130 billion and triggered inflation at home. As morale at the front plummeted, so did morale at home. During the final years of the war, troops became reluctant to risk their lives, even refusing to fight, and desertion and the "**fragging**" of officers increased.

fragging the practice of some US soldiers in Vietnam who threw grenades into the tents of gung-ho officers.

Figure 4.5 General Nguyen Ngoc Loan (shooting Vietcong) © PA Photos

At home, an antiwar movement mushroomed after the Tet Offensive. Teach-ins against the war became common at universities. As antiwar sentiment mounted, so did violence, leading to the police killing of four students at Kent State University in Ohio and two at Jackson State College in Mississippi. Racial hostility also increased owing to the disproportionate number of African-Americans who could not get deferments from military conscription. In 1967, the group Vietnam Veterans Against the War was formed. The Key document: John Kerry's 1971 testimony reflects this group's disillusionment with the war.

Key document   John Kerry's 1971 testimony about vietnam

On April 22, 1971, a young Vietnam veteran named John Kerry (1943–) testified against the war before the Senate Committee on Foreign Relations. Kerry later became a senator from Massachusetts (1985) and Democratic candidate for president (2004). In his testimony he described how many veterans became disillusioned.

We found that not only was it a civil war, an effort by a people who had for years been seeking their liberation from any colonial influence whatsoever, but also we found that the Vietnamese whom we had enthusiastically molded after our own image were hard put to take up the fight against the threat we were supposedly saving them from.

We found most people didn't even know the difference between communism and democracy. They only wanted to work in rice paddies without helicopters strafing them and bombs with napalm burning their villages and tearing their country apart. They wanted everything to do with the war, particularly with this foreign presence of the United States of America, to leave them alone in peace, and they practiced the art of survival by siding with whichever military force was present at a particular time, be it Vietcong, North Vietnamese, or American.

We found also that all too often American men were dying in those rice paddies for want of support from their allies. We saw first hand how money from American taxes was used for a corrupt dictatorial regime. We saw that many people in this country had a one-sided idea of who was kept free by our flag, as blacks provided the highest percentage of casualties. . . .

We rationalized destroying villages in order to save them. We saw America lose her sense of morality as she accepted very coolly a My Lai and refused to give up the image of American soldiers who hand out chocolate bars and chewing gum. . . .

We watched the US falsification of body counts, in fact the glorification of body counts. We listened while month after month we were told the back of the enemy was about to break. . . . [W]e watched while men charged up hills because a general said that hill has to be taken, and after losing one platoon or two platoons they marched away to leave the hill for the reoccupation by the North Vietnamese because we watched pride allow the most unimportant of battles to be blown into extravaganzas, because we couldn't lose, and we couldn't retreat, and because it didn't matter how many American bodies were lost to prove that point.[46]

The reasons for American intervention remain confused to this day. They included ending Chinese support for wars of national liberation, such as the one in Vietnam; fear that communist powers would invade other countries in Southeast Asia; and fear that if America showed weakness, the Soviet Union and its allies would be emboldened to act aggressively elsewhere.

The Cold War winds down

At its zenith, the Cold War encompassed events across the entire world, as illustrated in Map 4.4. In Europe, NATO faced off against the Soviet alliance system, the Warsaw Pact. Around the rest of the world, countries that considered themselves to be nonaligned members of the Third World and, therefore, members of neither the Western (First World) or Soviet (Second World) blocs repeatedly became arenas for conflict between Americans and Soviets and between their proxies. For example, when the Congo (formerly the Belgian Congo) gained independence in 1960, it became an arena of Cold War conflict until the ascent of American-supported Joseph Mobutu (1930–97), who remained in power until well after its end. Similar struggles took place throughout Africa, Asia, and Latin America, and in countries such as Somalia and Angola civil war

Map 4.4 The Cold War, 1945–1960

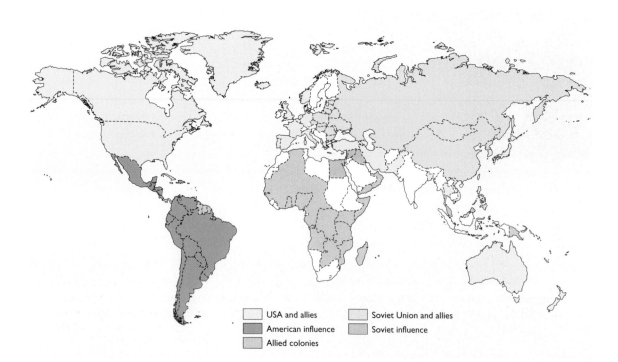

	USA and allies		Soviet Union and allies
	American influence		Soviet influence
	Allied colonies		

raged long after the end of the Cold War with weapons that had been supplied to local supporters by both sides at the height of the East–West conflict.

Moreover, the conflict raged in every arena of human activity. Each side sought to prove that it was superior in terms of its economics, art, literature, music, sports, technology, and so forth. Indeed, the space race became a feature of the Cold War when the Soviet Union became the first country to launch an intercontinental ballistic missile (ICBM) (August 1957), the first to launch a space satellite (Sputnik) (1957), and the first to put a man into space (April 1961).[47] The United States placed the second man in space only a month later.

Fortunately, the Cold War never led to a nuclear exchange between the Soviet Union and the United States. Such an exchange appeared imminent on several occasions, especially during the Cuban missile crisis in the autumn of 1962, when the Soviet Union secretly installed nuclear missiles on the island of Cuba. The Soviet action violated US expectations that neither superpower would meddle in the other's neighborhood. Thus, despite rhetoric about "rolling back" communism in Eastern Europe, the United States had remained largely passive when East Berliners rioted against Soviet rule in 1953, when Hungarians staged an unsuccessful revolution against Soviet occupation in 1956, and following the Soviet

Figure 4.6 Aerial reconnaissance photo of the San Cristobal missile site in Cuba, October 1962
The Dino A. Brugioni Collection, National Security Archive, Washington, DC

1968 invasion of Czechoslovakia. By contrast, in 1962 the USSR was deeply involved in an adventure only 90 miles from US shores.

Soviet leader Nikita S. Khrushchev (1894–1971) appears to have ordered the missiles to Cuba because he wished to compensate for the US strategic nuclear advantage in having military bases along the Soviet periphery in Europe, Asia, and the Middle East. Khrushchev also feared that the United States would seek again to overthrow Cuba's communist president, Fidel Castro (1926–), as it had in 1960 when it provided covert support for an invasion of anti-communist Cuban exiles at the Bay of Pigs. The ensuing crisis lasted 13 tense days[48] during which President John F. Kennedy imposed a naval blockade around Cuba and threatened war with the Soviet Union to force the removal of Soviet missiles (see chapter 8, pp. 368–9). Although as part of the final settlement of the crisis the United States pledged not to invade Cuba and at a later date removed its obsolete missiles from Turkey, the Soviet retreat from Cuba was partly responsible for Khrushchev's 1964 ouster as head of the Communist Party of the Soviet Union (CPSU). Soviet leaders clearly had in mind Khrushchev's Cuban adventure at that time when they accused him of "hair-brained schemes" and replaced him with Leonid Brezhnev (1906–82).

Many observers believe that war did not occur because both sides possessed enough nuclear weapons that any war between them ultimately would lead to mutual suicide. There had been earlier temporary thaws in the Cold War. For example, after Stalin's death in 1953, there began a brief period during which Soviet–American relations were warmed by the "spirit of Geneva" (named after a 1955 summit conference in that city). In 1956, Khrushchev denounced Stalin, and "peaceful coexistence" became the official Soviet policy toward the West. However, the Cuban missile crisis marked a fundamental change in superpower relations as both sides became more careful about the use of nuclear weapons and, as we shall see in chapter 8 (pp. 381–87), both sides began to approach arms control more seriously as a way of reducing the risks of nuclear war.[49] Later crises that threatened superpower **escalation** provided additional impetus for the superpowers to develop procedures to avoid conflict. Among these were the US bombing of the North Vietnamese port of Haiphong in May 1972 that damaged Soviet vessels in the harbor and US–Soviet confrontation during the 1973 Yom Kippur War (see chapter 5, p. 216).

The period after 1962 was widely known as the era of détente because it entailed a progressive reduction in tension. Among the most important of the developments during this period was intensification of serious arms control negotiations, after which most nuclear tests were banned, military tests in space were outlawed (1963), nuclear weapons proliferation was banned (1968), the number and type of Soviet and American

escalation an upward spiral in the level of conflict or violence.

intercontinental ballistic missiles (ICBMs) were limited (1972, 1979), and intermediate-range nuclear forces (INF) were eliminated (1987). In addition, both sides agreed to confidence-building measures, or actions to increase trust (see chapter 8, pp. 382–3). Among the most important of these was the Helsinki Conference of 1975 in which 35 countries in Europe as well as the Soviet Union, Canada, and the United States signed an agreement that legalized Europe's post-World War II territorial boundaries and promised progress in human rights.

In addition, a split arose between China's Communists and the Soviet Union in the 1960s. After the war, Mao soon became dissatisfied with the paltry amount of aid received from the USSR. Further complicating this relationship, after Stalin's death in 1953, the two Communist states became engaged in an ideological dispute over interpretations of Marxism. Mao defended Stalinism and opposed US–Soviet détente. China publicly accused the USSR of betraying Marxism and, in 1964, China became a nuclear power and, thus, a possible alternative leader of the world communist movement. China and the USSR were further divided by territorial disputes. The Sino-Soviet split culminated in March 1969, when Chinese and Soviet forces clashed along their common border in the Xinjian region of China. The Chinese–Soviet schism lasted until the late 1980s. Its effect was to weaken global communism and provide an opportunity for the United States, as Mao came to regard the USSR as a greater threat to Chinese security than the United States.

Thus, although the superpowers continued their rivalry after the 1962 missile crisis, mutual fear of nuclear war and the defection of China from the Soviet bloc encouraged the evolution of a series of unspoken rules that reduced the risks of conflict. Gradually, these rules allowed the expectations of the two adversaries to converge around the status quo.[50] Among these were:

- Avoid direct military confrontation by using proxies or substitutes such as the Vietnamese, Syrians, and Israelis, who were involved in their own regional conflicts. Direct military confrontation was too dangerous, although conflicts involved superpower proxies such as US-backed Somalia against Soviet-backed Ethiopia.
- Design weapons systems that could survive an enemy attack and deploy surveillance systems, especially satellites, to make "surprise attacks" unlikely.
- Avoid tampering directly within the adversary's sphere of influence, as when the United States refused to get directly involved in Hungary's effort to throw off communism in 1956, or when the Soviet Union remained passive during the 1965 US intervention in the Dominican Republic, its 1983 invasion of the Caribbean island of Grenada, and

stayed out of the Vietnam War. Churchill's Iron Curtain became a line of demarcation between the two adversaries.

- Engage in non-military contests involving propaganda, espionage, subversion, overt and covert economic, political, and military assistance and other techniques of "informal penetration,"[51] and engage in economic and technological competition or struggles for prestige.
- Improve communication between Washington and Moscow, as in the establishment of a direct link called the Hotline in 1963.

However, Soviet–American détente was short-lived. In the mid- and late 1970s, relations were poisoned by a new Soviet arms buildup and by growing Soviet involvement in the Horn of Africa and southern Africa. The USSR was angered by President Jimmy Carter's (1924–) human rights policy and intrusive American efforts to force the Soviet Union to ease barriers to Jewish emigration from the USSR. Then, on December 24, 1979 Soviet troops flooded across its border with Afghanistan and occupied the country, bringing an abrupt end to US–Soviet détente. As early as July 1979, President Carter had authorized covert assistance to the enemies of Afghanistan's pro-Soviet government and, according to the president's National Security Advisor Zbigniew Brzezinski, had sought to increase the probability of a Soviet invasion in order to draw "the Russians into the Afghan trap."[52] The following year, Carter embargoed grain exports to the USSR (even though American farmers stood to lose a lucrative market), and the United States boycotted the 1980 Olympic Games in Moscow. In addition, a US arms buildup began in the last year of the Carter administration and was accelerated by President Ronald Reagan (1911–2004).

With the 1980 election of President Reagan US–Soviet relations deteriorated, especially during Reagan's first term (1980–84), and there began a period some call the second Cold War. The Reagan administration's initial strategy was to refocus American policy on the Soviet threat. It set out to "win" the arms race by taking advantage of America's economic and technological superiority and by directly challenging the USSR in regional conflicts by supporting anti-Soviet proxies. Secretary of State Alexander Haig (1924–) acknowledged a tougher line in 1981 when he described Soviet power as the "central strategic phenomenon of the post-World War II era" and added that the "threat of Soviet military intervention colors attempts to achieve international civility."[53] President Reagan's antipathy toward the Soviet Union was evident in his "evil empire" speech, which he delivered on June 8, 1982 to the British House of Commons. Echoing Churchill's iron curtain speech, he declared that: "From Stettin on the Baltic to Varna on the Black Sea, the regimes planted by totalitarianism have had more than thirty years to establish their legitimacy. But none – not one regime – has yet been able to risk free elections. Regimes planted by bayonets do not take root." And he asked rhetorically whether freedom must "wither in a quiet, deadening accommodation with totalitarian evil?"[54] A year later, Reagan described the contest between the United States and USSR as a "struggle between right and wrong, good and evil."[55] Among those who influenced Reagan was Paul Wolfowitz (1943–) who served as Director of Policy Planning in the State Department and then as Assistant Secretary for East Asian and Pacific Affairs. Already a lead **neoconservative**, Wolfowitz would later become Undersecretary of Defense (and later President of the World Bank) under President George W. Bush and be a key advocate of America's 2003 invasion of Iraq.

The heart of the tough US policy was a massive arms buildup. A $180-billion nuclear modernization program was begun in which new land-based and sea-based missiles and long-range bombers were added to America's arsenal. New intermediate-range nuclear missiles (INF) were subsequently deployed in Western Europe to counter similar Soviet weapons. In 1983 Reagan also proposed a comprehensive antiballistic missile system called the Strategic Defense Initiative (SDI) (nicknamed "Star Wars" by its critics) to protect the American homeland from nuclear attack.

At first, the Soviet Union responded in kind, continuing to deploy mobile intermediate-range missiles, building new long-range missiles, and modernizing its nuclear submarine fleet. It also continued to assist pro-communist militants in Afghanistan, Angola, Kampuchea (Cambodia), and Ethiopia. Finally, it abruptly broke off arms-reduction talks after American INF deployments began in Western Europe in November 1983.

Nevertheless, even as Moscow continued to command an immense military establishment and to underwrite numerous foreign-policy ventures, cracks began to appear in the country's social and economic fabric that required dramatic remedy. Economically, the Soviet Union was becoming a second-rate power. The centrally planned economic system established in the 1920s and 1930s that was dominated by defense and heavy industry and by collectivized agriculture remained largely unchanged and had begun to atrophy.

Soviet GNP continued to rise through the 1970s, but overall economic performance was uneven. By the mid-1970s, the system began to run down. The Soviet leaders who followed Khrushchev – Leonid Brezhnev (1964–82), Yuri Andropov (1982–84), and Konstantin Chernenko (1984–85) – all elderly and in poor health, were unable to end the economic stagnation. Corruption, alcoholism, poor service, and cynicism

neoconservative sometimes shortened to "neocon," neoconservative refers to those who advocate US intervention overseas to further democracy and individual freedom.

became widespread. Agriculture remained a great problem, and, by the 1980s, the USSR had come to depend on Western grain imports to make up shortfalls at home. Finally, as the Soviet economy became more complex, "muscle power" – the key to earlier economic growth – became less important, and access to high technology became critical. The Soviet economy was afflicted by technological obsolescence, low productivity, and scarcity of consumer goods, and GNP growth virtually halted in the early 1980s. In short, the Soviet economy was no longer able to support large-scale defense spending or adventures around the world.

The end of the Cold War

On March 11, 1985, a critical step took place in bringing an end to the Cold War, when Mikhail Sergeyevich Gorbachev (1931–) assumed the reins of power of both the Communist Party of the Soviet Union and the Soviet government. Gorbachev recognized that defense spending was eating up much of the Soviet budget, that the Soviet Union was on the verge of economic collapse, and that it had fallen light years behind the United States in critical areas of technology. Indeed, concerns about the level of Soviet technology and the absence of openness in the country were dramatically heightened on April 26, 1986, when a nuclear meltdown at the Chernobyl power plant near the city of Kiev sent radioactive debris over the western USSR, Eastern Europe, and Scandinavia. This was the worst nuclear accident in history and led to the evacuation of hundreds of thousands from areas that remain contaminated to this day.

The Gorbachev reforms and the resolution of key issues

Gorbachev recognized that, unless matters changed, the Soviet Union would gradually become a minor factor in world affairs and would grow more and more impoverished. For these reasons, he decided to reform the USSR. He announced the two most important of these reforms at the 27th Congress of the Communist Party of the Soviet Union in 1986. They were **perestroika** – Gorbachev's program of economic, political, and social restructuring – and **glasnost** – a policy of openness in public discussion that would enhance the legitimacy of Soviet institutions and reform the Communist Party.

perestroika policy of economic restructuring initiated by Soviet leader Mikhail Gorbachev.

glasnost policy of openness initiated by Soviet leader Mikhail Gorbachev.

Domestic pressures were the incentive for Gorbachev to seek an end to the Cold War. Overseas adventures and unproductive investments in defense could not continue if domestic reform were to succeed. Gorbachev

Figure 4.7 Presidents Gorbachev and Reagan signing an arms control agreement
Courtesy of the National Archives (Collection RR-WHPO: White House Photographic Collection, 01/20/1981–01/20/1989) photo no. NLS-WHPO-A-C44071

therefore set out to move Soviet thinking away from belief in the need for nuclear "superiority" toward acceptance of "sufficiency." He would reduce Soviet force levels, adopt a new nonprovocative conventional-force posture, and scale back Soviet global commitments. All these steps meant greater flexibility to address the crisis at home.

By the second term of the Reagan administration (1984–88), the stage was set for reordering superpower relations. A new attitude developed in Washington for several reasons. The US arms buildup was producing alarming budget deficits at home, and continued increases in military spending were no longer assured of congressional or public support. In addition, the country's mood favored more cooperation with the USSR, especially in arms control. President Reagan himself concluded that it was possible to end the Cold War and saw himself a man of peace. Accommodative moves by both sides followed. New negotiations on intermediate and strategic nuclear weapons began early in 1985, and the first summit meeting since 1979 between Soviet and American leaders was held in November. Additional summits followed.

Major arms control agreements were reached, and genuine efforts were made to address old regional differences. Soviet troops withdrew from Afghanistan; civil war ended in Angola so that Cuban troops could leave that country. However, the most dramatic example of Soviet–US cooperation followed Iraq's invasion of Kuwait in August 1990. Presidents Gorbachev and George H. W. Bush hastily arranged a meeting in Helsinki, Finland, and jointly condemned Saddam Hussein's aggression. The two then cooperated in passing UN resolutions demonstrating the global community's resolve to reverse the aggression.

Since the Cold War had begun in Eastern Europe and Germany, it was fitting that the revolutionary changes that finally brought an end to the conflict should also take place in the same countries. Poland led the way. By the end of 1989, a noncommunist government had come to power in that country. When it was clear that the USSR would not intervene as it had in the past, the challenge to communist power quickly spread. Within the year, Czechoslovakia, Hungary, East Germany, and other Eastern European countries had abandoned communist rule and held democratic elections, thereby fulfilling the promise of Yalta over four decades later.

Internationally, the key to ending the Cold War lay in Germany. Germany's division had kindled the Cold War, and ending that division was a prerequisite for ending it. Political fissures in East Germany, long regarded as the keystone in the Soviet empire, became apparent in spring 1989 when many East Germans took advantage as barriers were dismantled between Austria and Hungary to travel to Hungary as "tourists" and then flee to West Germany. By August, a trickle had become a deluge of 5,000 emigrants a week. Unlike 1961, when the USSR had prodded East Germany to build the Berlin Wall to halt a similar exodus, Soviet leaders did nothing to stop this massive flight. Simultaneously, mass demonstrations broke out in East German cities, notably Leipzig. On November 9, 1989, the Berlin Wall was opened.

German reunification, which had seemed unthinkable until then, became suddenly possible, and in November 1989 West German Chancellor Helmut Kohl (1930–) presented a plan for reunification. In summer 1990, Gorbachev agreed to a reunified Germany that would remain within NATO, and in October 1990 the two Germanys were officially reunited.

At the Malta Summit (December 1989) and the Washington Summit (June 1990), the Cold War was formally brought to a close with commitments between the two superpowers for future cooperation. Two agreements reached in late 1990 clarified the new relationship. The first was a treaty drastically reducing and limiting conventional weapons in Europe, and the second was a nonaggression pact between NATO and the Warsaw Treaty Organization that included a formal declaration that the two sides were no longer adversaries.

By his reforms, Gorbachev unintentionally had started a process that brought about the collapse of the Soviet Communist Party and the totalitarian Soviet state, and that ended the Cold War. It was hard for observers to believe their own eyes as democratic movements led to the replacement of Communist regimes with democratic ones throughout the Eastern bloc. After decades of debate about the future of Germany, that country was rapidly reunited, and the Warsaw Pact disappeared.

Figure 4.8 Boris Yeltsin directing opposition against the coup to overthrow Gorbachev in 1991 © PA Photos

Within the Soviet Union, multiparty elections were held, and nascent capitalism, including the concept of owning private property, was introduced, accompanied by a great wave of fraudulent economic practices, organized crime, and deterioration of medical and educational facilities. Ethnic conflict, popular unrest, growing autonomy of several non-Russian regions of the Soviet Union, and rapid decline of Soviet influence overseas were some of the results of the Soviet Union's dramatic changes, which produced resistance to Gorbachev's policies on the part of conservative politicians and generals. This resistance climaxed in an effort to overthrow Gorbachev on August 19, 1991. In the end, he was briefly restored to his positions as leader of the Communist Party and Soviet government, with the help of Boris Yeltsin (1931–2007), who had become Russia's first elected president in June 1991. In August Yeltsin suspended all activities of the Communist Party in Russia, and within a week Gorbachev called upon the party's central committee to dissolve itself. With the demise of Soviet communism, Yeltsin became the paramount leader, and Gorbachev faded from the scene. Still, as a result of his bold policies, Gorbachev was awarded the 1990 Nobel Prize for Peace.

Shortly thereafter nationalism reigned supreme as one Soviet republic after another declared its independence: Lithuania, Estonia, Latvia, Moldova, Belorus, Ukraine, Georgia, Armenia, Azerbaijan, Kazakhstan, Uzbekistan, Tajikistan, Turkmenistan, and Kyrgyzistan. In December 1991, most of these joined Russia in a loose grouping called

Map 4.5 Commonwealth of Independent States

the Commonwealth of Independent States (CIS) that two years later became an economic common market.

The end of the Cold War was an optimistic moment in global politics. The end of the Cold War and the collapse of the Soviet Union and its Communist Party brought down the curtain on an era of global politics that had begun at the onset of the twentieth century. The end of the Cold War altered, or in some cases removed, the rationale for many American foreign policies, including global security arrangements like NATO, budget decisions about military spending, and human rights policies. Even though the Cold War drew to a close well over a decade ago, American foreign policy continues to lack the coherence and consensus that existed during that epic struggle. In fact, no single issue dominated America's foreign-policy agenda until the emergence of the shadowy and frightening threat of militant Islam accompanied by its threat of new and more dangerous versions of global terrorism. Unfortunately, the ending of the Cold War did not bring an end to global violence. War remains one of the most critical, if not *the* most critical, topics in global politics.

Explaining the end of the Cold War

As with the onset of the Cold War, a variety of explanations at different levels of analysis have been offered for its end.

At the individual level, the end of the Cold War owes much to the belief of Mikhail Gorbachev that the only way the Soviet society and economy could be rejuvenated was by cooperating with the West, obtaining Western technology, reducing defense spending, and joining the global economy from which the Soviet-dominated "Second World" had isolated itself. In addition, President Ronald Reagan increasingly began to see himself a man of peace, and a dramatic shift took place in his attitude toward the Soviet Union. At the state level, the end of the Cold War owed much to growing Soviet economic weakness, technological backwardness, and social malaise. Finally, at the level of the global system, the dramatic growth in American power combined with an equally dramatic reduction in Soviet power can also explain the Cold War's end.

From the same perspective, neorealists argue that the Cold War's end was brought about by the increase in American military power and growth in American overseas activity, that, combined with the Soviet decline, marked the Reagan years and produced a unipolar system in which the United States was dominant. Liberals would point to the triumph of democracy in Eastern Europe and the Soviet Union and to antiwar and pro-arms control sentiment of growing segments of the American public as explanations for the end of the Cold War.

From the constructivist perspective, the end of the Cold War can be viewed as the consequence of the growing desire of Soviet citizens for democracy and a higher standard of living that set in train the evolution of a new set of beliefs and norms favoring democracy and free enterprise and a decline in Soviet self-identity as leader of the global communist revolution. Thus, Russians no longer believed they had an interest in spreading Marxism–Leninism or in propping up Marxist regimes in Eastern Europe or elsewhere.

Russia after the Cold War

The dissolution of the Soviet Union proved traumatic for many Russians who had been raised to believe in communism and the historic mission of the USSR. Nevertheless, Russia, by far the largest independent state to emerge from the former Soviet Union, remains a major factor in global politics. It is the largest country in the world in terms of territory, retains an enormous arsenal of nuclear weapons – second in size only to America's – and is a key player in the global energy market. Thus, Russia has the world's largest reserves of natural gas, the second largest coal reserves, and the eighth largest oil reserves. It is currently the world's largest exporter of natural gas and the second largest exporter of oil.[56]

The Cold War over, it seemed that an era of Russo-American harmony was at hand. Briefly, it appeared that Russia would fall prey to political extremists, especially right-wing nationalism, but this concern has waned. In addition, Russia faced apparently insurmountable economic woes. Following the introduction of free market reforms in October 1991, real incomes plummeted by 50 percent in six months, and production fell by 24 percent in 1992 alone, and an additional 29 percent the following year. In 1992, hyperinflation of more than 2,000 percent gripped Russia, and the country's public health and social security systems rapidly eroded. Following Yeltsin's call for new parliamentary elections, his political foes tried to seize power. The result was crushed in October 1993 when Yeltsin declared a state of emergency and summoned army units to Moscow to shell Russia's parliament building. One result of the problems facing Russia and other former East bloc members has been widespread nostalgia for communism.

Reform in Russia has been so slow that one elderly lady remarked, "The Russian won't budge until the roasted rooster pecks him in the rear."[57] Integrating Russia into the global economy meant educating Russians in the basics of capitalism and transforming state-owned enterprises into private companies. This process was accompanied by vast corruption and mushrooming crime, both of which continue to afflict the country to such an extent that the Russian system is called "gangster capitalism." Economic reform also posed a dilemma for Russia's leaders because it brought with it unemployment, rising prices and taxes, and declining production. Nevertheless, there was gradual improvement until Russia fell victim to fallout from Asia's 1998 economic crisis, resulting in a collapsing stock market, an imploding ruble, and skyrocketing interest rates. Indeed, between December 1991 and December 2001, the ruble lost 99 percent of its value against the US dollar.[58]

Since 1998, foreign investment in Russia has grown, and high oil prices have helped bring about a sustained economic recovery. In 2002, the European Union and the United States declared Russia a market economy, and the process is well underway to bring Russia into the World Trade Organization, thereby integrating the country into the global economic system. Serious economic problems remain, however. Poor infrastructure, red tape, complex rules, corrupt officials, burgeoning economic inequality, ethnic conflict, and the continuing economic dominance of a few "oligarchs" (tycoons) continue to deter investors, as do growing political centralization and fears about the future of democracy in Russia under President Vladimir V. Putin (1952–).

Overall, then, there are causes for optimism and pessimism about Russia. According to two observers:

> Some see the sudden spurt of growth over the last four years as an indicator of more improvements to come. . . . They emphasize the country's advanced human capital, its reformed tax system, and its mostly open economy. Others see bureaucratic regulations and political interventions . . . as serious barriers that will stymie Russia's growth. In politics, optimists anticipate increased democratic competition and the emergence of a more vigorous civil society. Pessimists predict an accelerating slide toward an authoritarian regime that will be managed by security service professionals under the fig leaf of formal democratic procedures.[59]

Their own view is relatively optimistic. Russia, they argue has made great strides from being a "communist dictatorship to a multiparty democracy" and has become "a normal, middle-income capitalist economy."[60]

In foreign affairs, Russia, despite grumbling, has permitted several of its former satellites to join NATO (Bulgaria, the Czech Republic, East Germany, Estonia, Hungary, Latvia, Lithuania, Poland, Romania, and Slovakia) and the European Union. Although Russia still tries to bully some of its neighbors like Georgia, it has cooperated with America's War on Terrorism, participating with the United States, China, Japan, North Korea, and South Korea in negotiations over North Korea's nuclear aspirations. And it has joined the West in proposing a compromise solution to the problem of Iran's efforts to obtain nuclear weapons that would move Iran's enrichment of uranium to Russia.[61]

Conclusion

This chapter has reviewed several explanations for how the Cold War emerged and has traced the evolution of the conflict that dominated global politics during the second half of the twentieth century. It has described how American foreign policy toward the Soviet Union evolved in light of previous experiences, especially the appeasement of Nazi Germany in the 1930s and the surprise attack on US forces at Pearl Harbor in December 1941. It has traced how the Cold War began in Europe and then spread outward to become a global contest, and it shows how the initial political confrontation was militarized following the Korean War.

The chapter also examines alternative explanations for the end of the Cold War ranging from a shift in the global balance of power to the emergence of new thinking in the Soviet Union under the leadership

of Mikhail Gorbachev. The end of the Cold War and the collapse of
the Soviet Union left the United States alone atop the global hierarchy,
without major adversaries in what has been called a "unipolar moment."
In the next chapter we will review some of the most important challenges
to global peace and order in contemporary global politics, challenges that
in some cases are as dangerous as was the Cold War.

Student activities

Discussion and essay questions

Comprehension questions

1 What was the Truman Doctrine and why was it important?
2 What role did the Vietnam War have in the Cold War?
3 What is the doctrine of containment? How did it evolve during the
   Cold War?

Analysis questions

4 What do you think was the main source(s) of the Cold War? If you
   name multiple sources, were they equally important? Why or why not?
5 Why did the Cold War not become World War III?

Map analysis

Using Map 4.4, list the countries that were members of NATO and the
Warsaw Pact during the Cold War. Go to the NATO homepage on the
internet (www.nato.int). How has NATO's membership changed since
the Cold War ended in 1989? What implications does this change in
membership have for US and European military security?

Cultural materials

1 There are a variety of Cold War novels and films, especially the novels
   of author John Le Carré, such as *The Spy Who Came in from the Cold*,
   and the films based on these novels starring Michael Caine. James
   Michener's *The Bridges of Toko-Ri* (remade as a film starring William
   Holden) is an excellent fictional work about the Korean War, as are the
   book and film *M.A.S.H.*, which was turned into a popular television
   program starring Alan Alda. In 2000 the film *Thirteen Days* starring

Kevin Costner graphically retold the story of the 1962 Cuban missile crisis. And a variety of excellent films about the Vietnam War have appeared, including *The Deer Hunter* (1978) starring Robert De Niro, *Full Metal Jacket* (1987), *Apocalypse Now* (1979) starring Marlon Brando, and *Platoon* (1986) starring Tom Berenger. Watch one of these films or read one of these books and consider what the film/book tells the viewer/reader about the relevant era in global politics. Who were the dominant actors? What interests did they pursue and how did they do so? What lessons, if any, can the film/book teach us about the contemporary world?

2 In 1952, playwright Arthur Miller wrote *The Crucible* in which the 1692 Salem witch trials are used as a substitute for the McCarthy "witch trials." Do you think the Salem witch trials are a suitable metaphor for McCarthyism?

Further reading

Gaddis, John Lewis, *The Long Peace: Inquiries into the History of the Cold War*, new ed. (New York: Oxford University Press, 1989). Classic analysis of how the United States and the USSR managed to avoid war with each other during four decades of tension.

Gaddis, John Lewis, *We Now Know: Rethinking Cold War History* (Oxford: Oxford University Press, 1997). With new material from newly opened Soviet, Eastern European, and Chinese archives, Gaddis evaluates the strategic dynamics of the Cold War.

Gaddis, John Lewis, *The Cold War: A New History* (New York: Penguin Press, 2005). Accessible but comprehensive description and analysis of the major events in the Cold War from beginning to end.

Judge, Edward H. and John W. Langdon, eds., *The Cold War: A History Through Documents* (Upper Saddle River, NJ: Prentice-Hall, 1999). Collection of over 130 edited documents (speeches, treaties, statements, and articles) that depict the rise and end of the Cold War from 1945 through 1991.

Lafeber, Walter, *America, Russia, and the Cold War, 1945–2002, Updated* (New York: McGraw-Hill, 2002). Highly readable account of the Cold War from beginning to end.

5 Great issues in contemporary global politics

The story of 9/11 as told by a New York fireman:

> The south tower of the World Trade Center has just collapsed.
> I am helping my friends at Ladder Company 16, and the firefighters
> have commandeered a crowded 67th Street crosstown bus. We go
> without stopping from Lexington Avenue to the staging center on
> Amsterdam. . . .
>
> At Amsterdam we board another bus. . . . We walk down West
> Street and report to the chief in command. . . . His predecessor chief
> earlier in the day is already missing, along with the command center
> itself, which is somewhere beneath mountains of cracked concrete
> and bent steel caused by the second collapse, of the north tower. . . .
>
> I walk through the World Financial Center. . . . It seems the
> building has been abandoned for decades, as there are inches of dust
> on the floors. . . .
>
> Outside, because of the pervasive gray dusting, I cannot read the
> street signs as I make my way back. There is a lone fire company down
> a narrow street wetting down a smoldering pile. The mountains of
> debris in every direction are 50 and 60 feet high, and it is only now
> that I realize the silence I notice is the silence of thousands of people
> buried around me.[1]

On September 11, 2001, the world suddenly changed – not just
for Americans, but also for people around the world. Until that day,
Americans believed they were insulated from the violence that afflicts
so many parts of the world. The terrorist attacks on New York and
Washington triggered America's War on Terrorism, one of the great issues
in contemporary global politics. In this chapter, we examine four key
issues to evaluate how the world has changed and how it has remained the
same. We begin with changing Chinese–US relations, which some believe
may soon dominate global politics.[2] We then turn to three flashpoints in

Figure 5.1 A high-angle view of the area known as Ground Zero showing the rubble and debris of the collapsed World Trade Center buildings located in New York City, New York (NY), following the 9/11 terrorists attacks
Courtesy of the US Department of Defence/Aaron Peterson

the clash between Islam and the West: the Israeli–Palestinian conflict, Afghanistan and the War on Terrorism, and the war in Iraq.

The challenge from China

Chinese–US relations have historically fluctuated between partnership and competition, but have always been tinged with mistrust. Debates have raged in the West, and particularly the United States, over whether to treat China as a strategic partner or competitor. Those who argue for partnership, especially liberals, say that China is a rising economic superpower preoccupied with economic growth. They believe China is becoming integrated into the global economic system and, barring internal political turmoil, will likely remain peaceful. Thus, establishing

Boston, MA
American Airlines Flight 11
and United Airlines Flight 175
depart from Logan Airport

Somerset County, PA
10:00 a.m.
United Airlines Flight 93
crashes 80 miles southeast
of Pittsburgh

Newark, NJ
United Airlines
Flight 93 departs
Newark International

New York City, NY
8:45 a.m.
American Airlines Flight 11
crashes into the north tower
of the World Trade Center

9:03 a.m.
United Airlines Flight 175
flies into south tower of WTC

Washington, DC
American Airlines Flight 77
departs Dulles International

Arlington, VA
9:40 a.m.
American Airlines Flight 77
crashes into the Pentagon

Figure 5.2 September 11, 2001: Timeline of Terrorism
Found at www.infoplease.com/ipa/A0884881.html; reproduced by permission of Pearson Education, Inc.

a strong partnership makes economic sense. Those, especially realists, who see China as a competitor counter that this Asian giant cannot remain peaceful at its current rate of economic and military growth. Ultimately, it will try to dominate Asia.[3] In China's view, although the West has long tried to block its economic and political ascendance, the country must work with the capitalist powers to achieve prosperity and occupy its rightful position as a world power. The following sections examine the evolution of mutual mistrust, as well as the decision to cooperate.

The previous chapter showed how this complex relationship began in World War II, when the United States and China were allies and the US supported Chiang Kai-shek, and how relations then soured with the communist triumph in China's civil war and the subsequent Korean War.

From hostility to engagement

one China policy the policy of the Chinese government that there is only one China and Taiwan is part of it.

China's civil war ended with two governments – one in Beijing, China (the People's Republic of China or PRC), and one in Taipei, Taiwan – each claiming to be China's legitimate ruler. The PRC's **one China policy** stipulated that Taiwan was a "breakaway province."

Map 5.1 China

The **Sino-Soviet split** marked the beginning of a period of American engagement with China, as it became clear that the two countries had a common adversary in the USSR. For Mao Zedong (1893–1976), it was better to "ally with the enemy far away . . . in order to fight the enemy who is at the gate,"[4] and for the United States it was an opportunity to play the USSR and China against each other. A turning point came in 1971 when, in April, China took a first step toward normalizing relations and invited a US table tennis team to China. US President Richard M. Nixon reciprocated in June by revoking a 21-year-old trade embargo against China. In July, Henry Kissinger, then Assistant to the President for National Security Affairs, secretly flew to Beijing to arrange a meeting between Nixon and Chinese Premier Zhou Enlai. By October, the United States ceased opposing the PRC's entry into the UN. In February 1972, Nixon and Zhou met and agreed to cooperate against the Soviet Union, and full diplomatic relations were established on January 1, 1979. By the terms of the bargain, the United States would end diplomatic relations with Taiwan and support the PRC's one China policy. For its part, China renounced the use of force in seeking to bring Taiwan back into the fold.

Sino-Soviet split the ideological split between China and the USSR that resulted in closer Sino-American ties.

Strategic partners or strategic rivals?

Since then, analysts have repeatedly wondered whether the two countries can be partners. Although they have become increasingly interdependent, they remain wary of each other. Their most serious disagreements involve Taiwan, military modernization and buildup, North Korea, human rights, and access to scarce energy resources, and occasional crises have threatened the relationship. During the 1999 Kosovo War, a US bomber hit the Chinese embassy in Belgrade, Serbia with five 2,000-pound satellite-guided bombs. Washington claimed that the incident was accidental; the Chinese believed it was intentional. Another US–Chinese crisis was touched off by a 2001 mid-air collision between a Chinese jet fighter and a US EP-3 spy plane that had to land on China's Hainan Island. Beijing was infuriated by the event and demanded that the United States cease its surveillance of the PRC. The crisis was defused when Washington expressed its formal "regret," and China repatriated the US crew. Overall, the US–China relationship, as Secretary of State Condoleezza Rice observed, is "good" but "complex."[5]

American efforts to pressure China on issues such as human rights, the sale of missile technology to Iran and Pakistan, and its occupation of Tibet by threatening to reduce economic ties were largely fruitless, and led President Bill Clinton (1946–) in 1997 to advocate a policy of "constructive engagement" toward China by promoting economic and political ties. "The emergence of a China as a power that is stable, open and nonaggressive . . . rather than a China turned inward and confrontational," declared Clinton, "is deeply in the interests of the American people" and is "our best hope to secure our own interest and values and to advance China's."[6] "Constructive engagement" has remained the US policy toward China ever since.

Taiwan

From time to time, China anticipates that Taiwan might declare independence – usually in the context of Taiwanese elections. At these times, Taiwan reemerges as a source of Sino-American tension. Relations reached a crisis point in 1995–96 as Taiwan was about to conduct its first democratic presidential election. The incumbent, Lee Teng-hui, was the first native islander to become president, and China viewed his efforts to strengthen diplomatic relations with other countries as a threat to the one China policy. In 1995, China unsuccessfully urged the United States to deny Lee's request for a visitor's visa, claiming that he was engaged in separatist activities. Then, in an effort to influence the 1996 election against Lee, China test fired missiles across the Taiwan Straits to frighten Taiwanese voters. The United States sent warships to the area, and China's leaders interpreted this as US support for Taiwanese independence, souring US–Chinese relations for some time.

Since then, China has rattled sabers in each Taiwanese election to influence the vote against pro-independence candidates. In 2000, China threatened military action if Taiwan declared independence, and in 2005, China passed a law authorizing military action if Taiwan took concrete steps toward formal independence. In the event that pro-independence forces "cause the fact of Taiwan's secession from China, or that major incidents entailing Taiwan's secession from China should occur, or that possibilities for a peaceful reunification should be completely exhausted, . . . [China] shall employ nonpeaceful means and other necessary measures to protect China's sovereignty and territorial integrity."[7]

Military buildup

To realists, China's recent military modernization – termed "peaceful rise" by the PRC – forecasts greater US–Chinese competition. China has the third largest military budget in the world, and since the 1990s, its military buildup has included modernizing its long-range ballistic missile force, developing cruise missiles, and deploying hundreds of short-range mobile ballistic missiles opposite Taiwan – all of which worries US military planners who are committed to defend the island. In 1996, US military planners "dismissed the threat of a Chinese attack against Taiwan as a 100-mile infantry swim," but, by 2005, US leaders were concerned that China posed a real threat to Taiwan with the possibility of war in the near future.[8] A 2005 US Defense Department report declared: "China's military modernization could provide China with a force capable of prosecuting a range of military operations in Asia – well beyond Taiwan – potentially posing a credible threat to modern militaries operating in the region."[9]

In the event of a conflict, the United States would not necessarily have a decisive advantage. China has slimmed down its huge army and emphasized training for high-tech warfare. It has a modern navy that includes 55 attack submarines, Russian-made nuclear subs that can fire missiles while submerged, and 40 amphibious lift vessels capable of carrying tanks and troops.[10] China has also enhanced its strategic deterrent force with submarine-launched long-range missiles that can survive an initial nuclear strike, and it has developed land-based ICBMs able to strike anywhere in the United States.[11] As a result, the United States is pursuing a "hedging strategy" toward China to be on the safe side, reinforcing American forces in the Pacific and strengthening relations with Japan.[12]

North Korea

Washington and Beijing have tried to cooperate to end North Korea's nuclear weapons program. Neither country wants an unstable nuclear North Korea, but beyond that their goals differ. China is apprehensive about the collapse of North Korea's regime because it fears a US-dominated Korea, is concerned about turmoil on its border, and feels obliged to help a fellow communist country. In contrast, Washington fears a nuclear North Korea because it might spark a nuclear arms race in East Asia involving Japan and South Korea and because North Korea might provide nuclear weapons to terrorists or other American foes. Both countries hope that China's economic and political support, which helps keep North Korea's economy from imploding, will give China enough leverage to end North Korea's nuclear program. Yet, China, increasingly with the support of South Korea, also hopes that the foodstuffs and energy supplies it provides will encourage North Korea to follow its example of economic and social reform.

China has exercised less influence on North Korea than the United States had hoped. Since 2003 China has hosted several rounds of multilateral talks involving the parties concerned with North Korean nuclear proliferation but has been unwilling to exert significant pressure, perhaps fearing that too much pressure would destabilize North Korea's regime, risking a refugee crisis on China's border.

Human rights

The United States has been active in promoting human rights in China – accusing Beijing of violating civil and political rights, particularly of ethnic minorities and political activists. Such violations are often recalled in the violent images of the 1989 Tiananmen Square protest (see chapter 12, p. 589).

More recently, China has been criticized for repressing the Falun Gong movement. Falun Gong's millions of followers constitute a secular, spiritual, nonpolitical movement that employs Buddhist and Taoist exercises and meditation to promote spiritual and physical well-being, but the Chinese government opposes it as a potential source of political opposition. It argues that Falun Gong is a cult that harms its followers by advocating natural cures over professional medical care. China even blamed Falun Gong for hampering efforts to stop the spread of SARS (severe acute respiratory syndrome) in 2003. China has outlawed Falun Gong and has arrested and tortured thousands of followers.

In past years, the United States linked trade with China to improvements in that country's human rights record. However, in 1994,

Figure 5.3 Bill versus China
© Chappatte in "Die
Weltwoche",
www.globecartoon.com

President Clinton severed the linkage between China's human rights
policies and US–Chinese trade, admitting what was already evident, that
US political and economic interests outweighed human rights concerns.

Energy

China and the United States have become strategic competitors over
scarce energy resources. In 2003, China overtook Japan as the world's
largest oil consumer after the United States. China consumes about six
million barrels of oil a day, and the United States 20 million, and China's
thirst for oil is expected to equal America's by 2020.

Anticipation of future needs has left China scrambling to diversify its
oil supply and circumvent US influence over the major oil-exporting
nations and the sea lanes from the Middle East.[13] Thus, China has
acquired drilling and refining rights in about 30 countries, including
Sudan and Iran, countries where US companies have not been allowed
to invest, as well as Brazil and Venezuela in America's backyard. In Iran,
China has provided technology that can be used to make nuclear weapons
in exchange for oil.

In June 2005, the China National Offshore Oil Corporation (Cnooc),
largely owned by the Chinese government, offered $18.5 billion for
Unocal, a major US oil company. Members of the US Congress called on
the government to reject Cnooc's bid on national security grounds. These
protectionist voices fear that China may keep Unocal's Asian reserves

for itself and increase its ties to major oil producers in Africa and Latin America, to the detriment of US influence. At the last minute, Chevron made a successful bid to acquire Unocol, thus heading off US–Chinese conflict over this issue.[14] However, as we shall see in chapter 12 (p. 590), growing economic competition is becoming a critical issue in US–Chinese relations.

We now turn to the Middle East and one of the most durable and explosive issues in global politics, the conflict over Palestine.

Israel and Palestine

Among the key issues dividing the United States and the Muslim world are America's support of Israel, the continuing conflict between Israel and Palestine, and Israel's occupation of areas won from its enemies in the 1967 Six Day War. Like so many other Western–Islamic flashpoints, this one dates back millennia, to biblical times, when Palestine was the home of the Jewish people. In AD 70, however, Roman conquerors brought the biblical Jewish state to an end and destroyed Jerusalem, making Judea a Roman province.

Thus began a process that became known as the Jewish Diaspora, or "dispersion" of the Jews out of Palestine. Many settled in Babylon, and some fled to Egypt. All retained their religion, identity, customs, and their religious book, the Torah. And the memory of Jerusalem and the hope of returning to Palestine were harbored by Jews around the world.

In this section, we examine the development of the modern conflict between Israel and the Palestinians, focusing on Jewish, Arab, and Palestinian nationalism and their conflicting claims to the same small territory. We also consider how successive wars produced insecurity and hostility and how international organizations have intervened to try to reverse the conflict spiral.

Palestine: after World War I

In the late nineteenth century, with Palestine governed by the Ottoman Empire, Theodore Herzl (1860–1904) launched a movement among Jews in Europe called *Zionism*. Fueled by anti-Semitism in Europe, Zionism advocated the return of the Jewish people to their ancient homeland with the aim of founding a new Jewish state. Following Herzl's death, Chaim Weizmann (1874–1952), later the first president of the new Israel, tried to gain Western support for a Jewish state. In 1906 Weizmann met British Foreign Secretary Arthur James Balfour (1848–1930), and the two became good friends. Then, in 1917, Balfour publicly committed

Figure 5.4 President Harry S Truman and Chaim Weizmann on the occasion of the founding of Israel
Courtesy of the Harry S Truman Library

his country to help establish a Jewish state in Palestine. The Balfour Declaration, made in a letter to Lord Rothschild (head of the Zionist Federation in Britain), owed much to British sympathy for Zionism but was also an effort to encourage continued Jewish participation in the fight against the Ottoman Turks during World War I. The British understood the potential problem of maintaining good relations with Arab Palestinians while endorsing a Jewish state by including assurances in the Balfour Declaration that "civil and religious rights" of others in Palestine would be protected. Britain was also aiding the Arab Revolt against the Turks and promising future statehood to Arab leaders elsewhere in the Middle East.

Key document Balfour Declaration 1917[15]

November 2nd, 1917

Dear Lord Rothschild,

I have much pleasure in conveying to you, on behalf of His Majesty's Government, the following declaration of sympathy with Jewish Zionist aspirations which has been submitted to, and approved by, the Cabinet.

His Majesty's Government view with favour the establishment in Palestine of a national home for the Jewish people, and will use their best endeavors to facilitate the achievement of this object, it being clearly understood that nothing shall be done which may prejudice the civil and religious rights of existing non-Jewish communities in Palestine, or the rights and political status enjoyed by Jews in any other country. . . .

Yours sincerely,

Arthur James Balfour

With the collapse of the Ottoman Empire after World War I, Britain was granted a League of Nations Mandate over Palestine. The mandate covered Palestine (what is Israel and Gaza today) and Transjordan (modern Jordan and the West Bank). The terms of the League mandate confirmed the Balfour Declaration. The preamble declared that

the Mandatory should be responsible for putting into effect the declaration originally made on November 2nd, 1917, by the Government of His Britannic Majesty, and adopted by the said Powers, in favor of the establishment in Palestine of a national home for the Jewish people, it being clearly understood that nothing should be done which might prejudice the civil and religious rights of existing non-Jewish communities in Palestine, or the rights and political status enjoyed by Jews in any other country.

Article 4 of the mandate recognized an "appropriate Jewish agency" in matters regarding "the establishment of the Jewish national home," and the Jewish Agency that was established became the government of Israel when that country became independent. Finally, Article 6 explicitly authorized British authorities to "facilitate Jewish immigration" in cooperation with the Jewish Agency.

The immigration of European Jews ensued. By 1922, about 84,000 Jews lived in Palestine along with 643,000 Muslim and Christian Arabs. During the years of the Palestine Mandate (1922–47), large-scale Jewish immigration from abroad, mainly from Eastern Europe, took place. The inflow swelled in the 1930s as Nazi persecution of Europe's Jews intensified. The British sought to limit this influx, and in 1939 promised to create an Arab state within a decade and limit Jewish immigration to 75,000 for five years, followed by the cessation of such immigration. The Arabs rejected the proposal. Simultaneously, Arabs from

Egypt, Transjordan, and Syria flowed into Palestine, which produced tensions over land, water, and other scarce resources. Overall, the Jewish population in Palestine swelled by 470,000 between World Wars I and II, and the non-Jewish population grew by 588,000. In 1921 and 1929, Arab riots erupted in protest to Jewish immigration, and both sides organized militias. Larger Arab attacks against Jewish settlements took place starting in 1936 in what was called the Arab Revolt.

Circumstances changed dramatically after World War II, as news of the European *Holocaust*, Hitler's murder of six million Jews in an effort to wipe out the entire Jewish race, became known. Sympathy for the survivors was understandably high. The British, however, fearful of antagonizing the Arabs and losing Arab oil, refused to allow Jewish immigration into Palestine and interned some 50,000 Jewish refugees on Cyprus. Nevertheless, some 70,000 managed to gain entry into Palestine between 1945 and 1948.

Confronted by British and Arab hostility, the Jewish independence movement split. Those who followed leaders like David Ben-Gurion (1886–1973), Israel's first prime minister, tried to use diplomacy to gain independence, while others like Menachem Begin (1913–92), one of the founders of Israel's Likud Party and later also the country's prime minister (1977–82), turned to violence. Begin directed a number of major terrorist operations including the bombing on July 22, 1946 of Jerusalem's King David Hotel, the site of the British military command, in which 91 people died.

Israel: the founding

Fed up with an insoluble conflict, Britain announced in 1947 that it would surrender its mandate in Palestine. After tumultuous debate the UN General Assembly adopted Resolution 181 on November 29, 1947 under which Palestine would be partitioned into Jewish and Arab states. Although the Jewish population agreed to partition, the Arab Palestinians rejected it. There then began what Israelis call the War of Independence, as Arab armies from Egypt, Iraq, Syria, Transjordan, and Lebanon sought to drive the Jewish community from Palestine. On May 14, 1948, after bitter and bloody fighting and the flight of thousands of Palestinians from their homes, Israel declared its victory, and in turn, its independence. The new State of Israel was about 50 percent larger than called for in the UN partition plan. Israel now covered all of the Palestinian Mandate west of the Jordan River, except the Gaza Strip and West Bank territories, which were to be administered by Egypt and Jordan until their final status could be determined.

The Suez War

Following the War of Independence, Israel was beset by terrorist attacks launched from neighboring countries. Arab infiltrators murdered Jewish farmers and attacked economic targets. Israelis retaliated against targets on the Egyptian side of the border. Arabs also organized an economic boycott, blacklisting non-Arab enterprises that did business with Israel, and Israeli shipping was prevented from entering the Gulf of Aqaba or the Suez Canal.

These conditions set the stage for Israeli participation, along with Britain and France, in the invasion of Egypt in the 1956 Suez War. This war is significant for stoking mutual Israeli and Arab insecurities, as well as Western–Arab tensions resulting from the intervention of outside parties. Egyptian President Gamal Abdel Nasser (1918–70) was a key player. Nasser was an ardent Arab nationalist and an advocate of creating a pan-Arab state throughout the Middle East. Thus, in 1958 he brought about a union with Syria called the United Arab Republic, which, however, survived only three years. Western suspicion of Nasser grew after he negotiated an agreement to purchase Soviet arms from Czechoslovakia at the same time that he sought Western support for construction of the Aswan Dam as a source of hydroelectric power.

Learning of the Czech arms deal, the United States withdrew its offer of aid for constructing the Aswan Dam. At the same time, in accordance with a 1954 agreement, Britain was removing its troops from the Suez Canal zone in Egypt. The Suez Canal, a vital link between the Mediterranean and the Red Sea, had for almost a century linked British possessions in Asia to Europe. In July 1956, Nasser nationalized the waterway.

Fearing that Nasser posed a threat to oil supplies and was trying to oust the European colonial powers from the Middle East and North Africa, and seeking his overthrow, British and French leaders persuaded the Israelis to invade Egypt's Sinai Peninsula while they prepared to intervene in Egypt to "restore order." On October 29, 1956 Israeli forces seized the Gaza Strip and the Egyptian islands that blockaded the Gulf of Aqaba, and quickly reached the Suez Canal. An Anglo-French ultimatum to Egypt and Israel to cease fighting was issued only *after* the Israelis had reached the canal, and British and French troops began to invade Egypt on November 5.

However, the allies had made a critical error in failing to inform Washington in advance of the operation. Secretary of State John Foster Dulles, furious at not having been consulted, took steps to force the invaders out by terminating US loans, thereby threatening their financial collapse. With the United States and USSR united against the invasion, on November 7, the UN General Assembly overwhelmingly demanded that the invaders leave Egypt, and the first large UN peacekeeping mission was established – the UN Emergency Force (UNEF) (see chapter 9, p. 419) – though not permitted by Israel on its side of the ceasefire line. By the end of 1956, Anglo-French forces had departed, and by March 1957 Israel had withdrawn from the Sinai (except for the Gaza Strip). The war made President Nasser a hero throughout the Arab world and hastened the exit of the European colonial powers from the Middle East.

The Six Day War and its consequences

The 1967 Six Day War changed the face of the Middle East and continues to cast a shadow over the region. In particular, the war stimulated the growth of Palestinian nationalism. Following the Suez conflict, Arab leaders continued to refuse to recognize Israel's right to exist. Attacks from Syria's Golan Heights against Israeli settlements in Galilee were especially troublesome, and Arab rhetoric grew increasingly belligerent. In April 1967, Israeli aircraft shot down six Soviet-supplied Syrian jets. A month later, Egyptian troops began to mass on Israel's border; Syrian formations gathered on the Golan Heights; and Jordan entered into a defense treaty with Egypt. On May 16, the Egyptians ordered UNEF out of the Sinai. A week later Egypt again began to blockade Aqaba. This was an act of war.

Israel was in a perilous situation. It, too, had mobilized its military forces, but as a small country, surrounded by enemies and dependent on a citizen army whose soldiers were essential to its civilian economy, Israel saw few alternatives. Thus, on June 5th, Israel launched a **preemptive war**. A massive Israeli air strike destroyed the Egyptian air force on the ground. When Jordan launched its ground attack on the same day, as many as 350,000 Palestinian Arabs fled the West Bank and crossed the river into Jordan.

preemptive war a war initiated to gain the advantage over an adversary that is itself about to strike.

In less than a week, Israeli forces were at the gates of Cairo, Damascus, and Amman, and a ceasefire was declared. In that brief time, Israel tripled its territory. In addition to the Golan Heights, it had captured the Sinai Peninsula, the Gaza Strip, the West Bank, and that part of the city of Jerusalem that had previously been in Jordanian hands. Israel declared united Jerusalem its "eternal" capital.

In November 1967, the United Nations adopted Resolution 242 (see Key document: UN Security Council Resolution 242), which established a framework for peace. By its terms, Israel would withdraw

Territories conquered and occupied by Israel as of 10 June 1967

Map 5.2 The Near East after the 1967 June War

from territories occupied in the war in exchange for peace with its neighbors. Although both sides accepted this framework, they interpreted its meaning differently. For example, did the phrase "withdrawal from territories" mean *all* territories or *only some*? In addition, Israel argued that peace had to precede withdrawal from the conquered territories, whereas the Palestinians sought Israeli withdrawal first and only then an end to hostilities. Along with the land-for-peace formula, Resolution 242 called for the right of all nations to live in security and for a just settlement of the problem of Palestinians who had fled their homes. These issues still remain at the heart of the Israeli–Palestinian problem.

Resolution 242 accelerated Palestinian nationalism and fostered the growth of the Palestine Liberation Organization (PLO),[16] which had been founded in Cairo in 1964 by Yasser Arafat (1929–2004). In Israel, any semblance of political consensus was shattered. The political right, centering on the Likud Party, sought a restoration of biblical Israel, which would entail annexation of the West Bank and Gaza. The political left, notably Israel's Labor Party, was prepared to exchange the lands captured in 1967 for peace.

Key document   UN Security Council Resolution 242 (November 22, 1967)

The Security Council

Affirms that the fulfillment of Charter principles requires the establishment of a just and lasting peace in the Middle East which should include the application of both the following principles:

Withdrawal of Israeli armed forces from territories occupied in the recent conflict;

Termination of all claims or states of belligerency and respect for and acknowledgement of the sovereignty, territorial integrity and political independence of every State in the area and their right to live in peace within secure and recognized boundaries free from threats or acts of force; . . .

From crisis to crisis: the Yom Kippur War, Lebanon, and Camp David

During the period after 1967, Arab–Israeli relations resembled a fever chart, improving and then worsening until the cycle went around again. Continued Israeli occupation and Palestinian resistance created mutual suspicion and fear and, inevitably, attack and counterattack, including yet another war between Israel and its Arab neighbors, and an Israeli incursion into Lebanon to ensure Israel's security. The most important development was the emergence of a Palestinian effort to acquire statehood and end Israel's occupation. Thereafter, Arab states surrendered their authority to speak for Palestinians when a summit conference sponsored by the Arab League declared the PLO to be "the sole legitimate representative of the Palestinian people."

War again erupted in 1973, the so-called Yom Kippur War, pitting Egypt and Syria against Israel. The 1973 war broke out after the two sides failed to agree on UN Resolution 242. For at least two years before the war erupted, Egyptian President Anwar Sadat (1918–81), backed by the Soviet Union, had threatened to resort to force if Israel did not return Arab territories. Recognizing that Israel had become a permanent presence in the region, Sadat abandoned Nasser's unrealistic goal of decisive victory over Israel and focused on regaining control of territories lost in 1967. On October 6, the holiest day of the Jewish year, Yom Kippur (Day of Atonement), Egypt and Syria launched a surprise attack against Israel and moved rapidly to recover their lost territories. Unprepared for the attack, the Israeli army was outnumbered and suffered high casualties.

As Israel struggled to regain the initiative, the war became a full-scale Cold War crisis. The USSR and then the United States sent massive amounts of supplies to their respective friends. Israeli forces invaded Syria and crossed the Suez Canal, encircling Egypt's Third Army. The Soviet leadership saw this as a challenge to its interests and threatened to intervene. Soviet pilots began to fly Egyptian aircraft, and both superpowers prepared for possible war, including a nuclear exchange. Fortunately, US Secretary of State Henry Kissinger undertook direct negotiations with Soviet leaders in Moscow, and a ceasefire was declared on October 25. As a result of the fighting, both Israel and Egypt lost the equivalent of a full year's **gross national product**. Israel no longer seemed invincible and became more dependent on the United States, while Egypt and Syria became dependent on the USSR. An even more important consequence was the doubling of oil prices by the Organization of Petroleum Exporting Countries (OPEC), which sought to change American policies toward the Middle East by declaring an oil embargo against the US in 1973 (chapter 14, pp. 661–3). This was an unusual reversal of fortune for the United States whose economic power allowed it to use economic sanctions frequently to coerce adversaries like Cuba and North Korea.

gross national product (GNP) the total value of all goods and services produced by a country in one year.

In January 1974, an agreement was reached by which Israel partially withdrew from the Suez Canal and a UN buffer force was inserted between the opposing armies. Israeli forces also withdrew from Syrian territory except for the Golan Heights. A year later another agreement widened the Sinai buffer zone. Thereafter, Sadat became disillusioned with the USSR as a partner, expelled Soviet advisors from Egypt, and sought improved ties with the West and Israel. On November 19, 1977, he became the first Arab leader to visit Israel where, in Jerusalem, he met with Israel's Prime Minister Menachem Begin (1913–92) and spoke before the Israeli parliament (the Knesset).

The next year, Sadat met with Begin and President Jimmy Carter (1924–) at Camp David, Maryland, and reached the Camp David

Accords. As a result, Sadat and Begin shared the 1978 Nobel Peace Prize. The leaders reaffirmed Resolution 242 and agreed to a three-stage process of negotiations on the status of Palestine. The tangible outcome was an Egyptian–Israeli deal to conclude a treaty of peace and return the Sinai Peninsula to Egypt. In effect, Egypt and Israel concluded a separate peace that, despite periodic strains, still survives. Other Arab leaders were infuriated by the arrangement. In September 1981, Sadat turned his army on his Muslim foes at home, and in the following month he was assassinated by a group called Islamic Jihad, which later joined forces with Al Qaeda. Sadat was succeeded by his vice president, Hosni Mubarak (1981–), who continued Sadat's policies.

Despite the warming political climate in the Middle East resulting from the Camp David Accords, the situation soon deteriorated. In 1982, Israel launched "Operation Peace for Galilee" into southern Lebanon to increase the security of northern Israel and destroy the PLO infrastructure in Lebanon. In addition, Israel's bitterest enemy, Syria, had acquired virtual dominance in Lebanon. During the 1982 invasion, the PLO was expelled from Lebanon, and Israel's Christian allies staged bloody attacks on Palestinian refugee camps, for which then Israeli Defense Minister Ariel Sharon (1928–)was blamed. In 1985, most Israeli troops withdrew

Figure 5.5 Anwar Sadat, Menachem Begin, and Jimmy Carter at Camp David. At Carter's invitation, Sadat and Begin met at Camp David in September 1978. These discussions were oftentimes heated and nearly broke down on several occasions, but an agreement was finally reached. Courtesy of the Jimmy Carter Library

"I GUESS THAT'S WHY IT'S CALLED THE PRESIDENT'S RETREAT!"

Figure 5.6 The Camp David
Retreat
www.geoffhook.com

from Lebanon, but Israeli units remained in a "security zone" north of
Israel's border.

The 1982 Israeli invasion also resulted in the establishment of an
Iranian-supported Shia terrorist group called Hezbollah or "Party of
God." Hezbollah is dedicated to liberating Jerusalem and destroying
Israel, and it advocates establishing Islamic rule in Lebanon. Hezbollah
has also actively participated in Lebanon's political system since 1992
and has become a major political force in the country. Among its actions
were bloody suicide truck bombings of the American embassy and US
Marine barracks in Beirut in October 1983. In 1985 Hezbollah operatives
skyjacked TWA Flight 847 during which a US Navy diver was murdered,
and the group was responsible for kidnapping Americans and other
Westerners in Lebanon in the 1980s and attacking the Israeli embassy in
Argentina in 1992 and the Israeli cultural center in Buenos Aires in 1994.
Hezbollah's continued attacks against Israeli soldiers in Lebanon finally
forced Israel to reconsider the costs of its Lebanese security zone, and it
withdrew in 2000. The United States and France seek the group's
disarmament to enhance the independence of Lebanon.

Following the assassination of Syria's leading opponent in Lebanon
in February 2005, Lebanon's former prime minister, Rafik al-Hariri, an
action many blamed on Syria, world pressure mounted for an end to Syrian
dominance of Lebanon and the withdrawal of its military and security

forces from that country. Within months the Syrians were out, and a UN-sponsored investigation of Hariri's murder implicated high Syrian officials. Then, in July 2006, Hezbollah triggered a new round of violence with Israel by kidnapping two Israeli soldiers. With US approval, Israel's then set out to destroy Hezbollah, largely through airpower, but the effort proved unsuccessful. The group and its leader Sheikh Hassan Nasrallah emerged from the conflict with enormous popularity not only among Shia Muslims but the Muslim world as a whole because of its ability to resist Israeli military power.[17] Hezbollah is now an influential player in Lebanese and regional politics, especially as Lebanon's central government remains weak and divided.

Oslo and the intifadas

From the 1980s, the Israel–Palestinian conflict became the main focus of attention in the Middle East. On December 9, 1987, an Israeli truck driver accidentally killed four pedestrians in the Gaza Strip. Palestinians soon took to the streets throwing stones and violently protesting Israel's occupation of Gaza and the West Bank. The first intifada ("throwing off," as a dog throws off fleas) had begun, featuring mass demonstrations and stone throwing by young Palestinians. No group was in charge of the intifada, though the PLO as well as militant Islamic groups such as Islamic Jihad and Hamas quickly became involved.

At root, the PLO was a nationalist group seeking an independent Palestinian state, whereas the Islamic militants wanted a region-wide Islamic state that would include present-day Israel. As time passed, violence grew, and the militant groups became more popular among Palestinians living in densely populated and impoverished conditions. Israel responded with arrests, economic sanctions, and the expansion of Jewish settlements in the West Bank and Gaza. These settlements were special targets of militant Palestinians, and as Palestinian violence increased, so did the violence of Israeli retaliation.

Confronted by continuing violence, the parties agreed to attend a formal international conference in Madrid in 1991, while, at the same time, meeting secretly in Oslo, Norway. These talks, conducted out of the glare of media attention, climaxed in the 1993 Oslo Accords. This agreement established Palestinian self-rule under a Palestinian National Authority led by Arafat in the Gaza Strip and the town of Jericho in the West Bank. Two years later under Oslo 2 most of the remaining West Bank towns were added to self-governing Palestine. The outlines of a future Palestinian state were evident, but the problem lay in how to achieve this objective. Sadly, progress was halted in 1995

Figure 5.7 Palestinian Intifada
Courtesy of Musa Al-shaer

after an Israeli extremist who objected to the turnover of any part of biblical Judea and Samaria (the West Bank) to the Palestinians murdered Israeli Prime Minister and 1994 Nobel Peace laureate Itzhak Rabin (1922–95).

Both sides were hamstrung by their own extremists – Palestinian terrorists and Israeli settlement advocates – who tried to prevent any agreement between the two sides. To break the deadlock, the Clinton administration sponsored another round of Palestinian–Israeli negotiations at Camp David in 2000. But time ran out for the Clinton administration with the November presidential election when Arafat refused to accept a virtually completed agreement. Thereafter, Israelis elected a hard-line Likud Party government led by Sharon to replace the conciliatory Labor Party government of Ehud Barak (1942–). Following this failure to achieve agreement, a second intifada erupted. Sharon himself triggered renewed violence by visiting the Al Aqsa mosque in Jerusalem, an action that provoked the Palestinians who believed the mosque should be off limits to Israelis.

The second intifada was more violent than the first. Between September 2000 and September 2005, over 3,200 Palestinians were killed by Israeli security forces, and almost 1,000 Israeli civilians and soldiers in Israel proper and in Israeli settlements were killed by the Palestinians.[18] It featured bloody and fanatical Palestinian suicide attacks against Israeli civilians, followed by Israeli economic reprisals, large-scale ground incursions in and reoccupation of Palestinian towns, and targeted assassinations of Palestinian militants through helicopter and missile strikes.

Yet another effort to end the Israeli–Palestinian conflict was proposed by US President George W. Bush (1946–)in collaboration with Russia, the UN, and members of the European Union. The proposal, or "road map" to peace, was made public on April 30, 2003. It entailed a series of steps that each side would take toward settling their differences. For instance, in the early stages, Palestinians would "undertake an unconditional cessation of violence," including suicide bombings, and initiate political reforms such as conducting free elections, writing a democratic constitution, and reorganizing security services. Israel would end curfews and stop demolishing Palestinian houses, withdraw its forces from Palestinian towns that it had reoccupied during the second intifada, and "freeze" the building of settlements in Gaza and the West Bank. The second stage was supposed to run from June to December 2003, after Palestinian elections, and create an independent Palestinian state with "a leadership acting decisively against terror and willing and able to build a practicing democracy." This state would be committed to respect Israel's security. A final stage aimed to settle border questions, the Jerusalem question, and the refugee and settlement issues.

As of 2007, little progress had been made even in the first stage. During much of 2004, violence intensified as the Palestinian Authority failed to rein in militant groups like Hamas, while Israel isolated Arafat and stepped up military reprisals and assassinations of militant leaders including Hamas founder Sheik Ahmed Yassin (1937–2004). Despairing of reaching a settlement with the Palestinians, Israel began construction of a wall along its border that would enclose additional Palestinian territory in order to prevent terrorists from infiltrating its cities and protect some of its key West Bank settlements.

As always, domestic politics on both sides played a key role. In Israel, Prime Minister Sharon's effort to promote Israel's withdrawal from the Gaza Strip met with bitter opposition from militant Jewish settlers and from militants in his own political party. Among the Palestinians, a change in leadership occurred: The death of Yasser Arafat in November 2004 accelerated a struggle between Palestinian moderates and extremists, and between an older and younger generation of leaders. In January 2005 elections, Mahmoud Abbas (1935–), a pragmatist who was a key figure in the Oslo Accords, was elected President of the Palestinian Authority. Even as extremists on both sides continued trying to sabotage peace efforts, Israel unilaterally withdrew from the Gaza Strip in August 2005, forcing Israeli settlers there to leave their homes.

Then, in January 2006 the domestic politics of both Israel and Palestine were dramatically muddled by two unexpected events: Ariel Sharon's incapacitating stroke and the victory of Hamas in elections to the Palestinian Assembly. In Israel, Deputy Prime Minister Ehud Olmert (1945–) became acting prime minister, even as Hamas, hitherto a terrorist organization, began to form a Palestinian government with Ismail Haniya (1963–) as its prime minister. Once again, fate had intervened to throw Israeli–Palestinian relations into disarray.

Feuding between Hamas and the PLO intensified, punctuated by violence. And Israel and the West refused to have anything to do with Hamas until it accepted Israel's right to exist and prior agreements reached with the Palestinian Authority. All foreign funding to the Hamas-controlled government ceased, and living conditions for Palestinians in Gaza rapidly declined. Then, in June 2006 several Israeli soldiers were killed and one was kidnapped by Hamas militants, triggering Israeli air and ground raids in Gaza.

As we saw earlier, matters grew worse the following month when Hezbollah launched rockets against northern Israel and kidnapped two Israeli soldiers, and Israel retaliated with a massive artillery and bombing campaign against Lebanon. Hezbollah intensified its rocket attacks against Israeli civilians, and Israeli troops entered Lebanon in an unsuccessful effort to push Hezbollah out of southern Lebanon. An uneasy ceasefire was declared on August 14, 2006, following UN Security Council Resolution 1701 that called for an end to hostilities, the withdrawal of Israeli forces, the disarmament of Hezbollah, and the emplacement of a UN peacekeeping force of up to 15,000 troops in southern Lebanon.[19] The Islamic regime in Iran, as Hezbollah's major source of arms and financing, appeared to emerge from the conflict with greater prestige and made it clear that it would not accept UN demands that it disarm.[20] And in June 2007 chaos engulfed Gaza as virtual civil war erupted between Hamas and PLO supporters.

Impediments to peace

In addition to conflicts over the status of the West Bank and Gaza Strip, other issues stand in the way of a Palestine–Israeli settlement. One is the status of Jerusalem, a city holy to three great religions. Before 1967, the city was split between Israel, which controlled West Jerusalem, and Jordan, which controlled East Jerusalem. Israelis regarded the 1967 unification of the city as the most important outcome of the Six Day War. However, both sides regard the city as their capital and want control of its holy sites, notably the remains of the great Temple (Beit ha-Midkash) built by King Solomon – known as the Wailing or Western Wall – and the great mosque of Al Aqsa, an important site in Islam that contains the Dome of the Rock from which the prophet Muhammad is said to have ascended to heaven. Moreover, many Palestinians continue to live in East Jerusalem, as well as in the city's suburbs.

Another issue involves the distribution of the region's scarce resources, especially water. Existing water resources are barely adequate to meet the demand posed by rapid Palestinian population growth and the need for irrigation in the arid region. International institutions like the World Bank are trying to help solve this problem.[21] Israel controls much of the water of the Jordan River and began to regulate West Bank ground water after 1967. Available water in the Middle East and North Africa (MNA) was declining in 1999 and is expected to fall below the scarcity level in the near future as the region's population grows. Inadequate water promises growing regional tension.

One of the most durable consequences of the Middle Eastern wars was the flight of large numbers of Arab Palestinians from their homes. Between 600,000 and 760,000 Arab Palestinians fled to neighboring Arab countries after the 1948 War of Independence.[22] This number grew dramatically during later wars. As a result, the issue of the "right of return" of Palestinian refugees to Israel proper is a festering problem that remains unresolved. Some observers see the plight of Palestinian refugees as analogous to the plight of Jewish refugees after World War II.

The treatment afforded Palestinian refugees varied within Arab countries. Refugees fared best in Lebanon, where they were given citizenship, but many were confined to squalid refugee camps in southern Lebanon. Palestinians also fled to Syria, the Gaza Strip, and the Persian Gulf States of Kuwait, Bahrein, Qatar, Oman, and the United Arab Emirates.[23] These countries treated the refugees more harshly, ghettoizing them in camps. The UN provides significant assistance to refugees in the camps through its Relief and Rehabilitation Administration (UNRRA), and Resolution 242 referred to the need for a "just settlement of the refugee problem."

Controversy

One of the most controversial issues in Israeli–Palestinian relations involves the Palestinians who fled their homes in 1948. The Israeli version is that Arab leaders like Jerusalem's Grand Mufti, Haj Muhammed Amin al-Husseini, called on the Palestinians to flee and, had the Arabs accepted the UN plan for partition, there would have been no refugees. The Arab version is that the Israelis drove the Palestinian refugees from their homes. There is probably some truth to both stories.

The heart of the problem is in deciding what "just settlement" means. Palestinians demand the right to return to the property they left behind when they fled or to be reimbursed for it. Israelis see no moral obligation to return property abandoned during the wars that, in their view, were a result of Arab aggression. Few countries, except under duress, have ever had such an obligation, and Israelis fear that the return of large numbers of Palestinian refugees, whose numbers have grown dramatically owing to a high birthrate, would drown Israel's Jewish population.

In sum, several factors stand in the way of a lasting solution to the Israeli–Palestinian conflict:

- *The number and variety of issues reinforce mutual hostility* The various issues are intertwined, making it difficult to solve one without also solving the others. Even worse, compromise on some issues is complicated by the fact they are highly symbolic. Disagreement over Jerusalem, for example, reflects a fundamental clash, and compromise is difficult because there is no easy way "to split the difference" or divide matters of symbolic importance.

- *Non-Middle Eastern countries provide belligerents with foreign allies and make regional hostilities part of larger global tensions* During the Cold War, Soviet–US hostility was reflected in Soviet support for Egypt, Syria, and Iraq versus US support for Israel and Saudi Arabia. Today, complicating factors include European–American differences, the War on Terrorism, and outsiders' problems in balancing their views on the Palestine question against their need for Middle Eastern oil and their fear of inciting hatred in the Muslim world.

- *Both the Palestinians and Israelis have fragile political systems and are confronted by powerful extremists* Under Arafat, the Palestinian Authority was corrupt, authoritarian, and inept and was divided among factions. As a result, in early 2006, Palestinians gave Hamas a massive electoral victory and a mandate to form a government that must work with Mahmoud Abbas. Israel is the only democracy in the region, but because it has a large number of political parties in its parliament and because of the great abyss that separates left and right, leaders are often unable to form a majority coalition that is willing to make hard decisions such as dividing Jerusalem or disbanding Jewish settlements in the West Bank. This may change with the formation of a new centrist political party, Kadima, by Ariel Sharon who announced in November 2005 that he was leaving the ultraconservative Likud Party. However, Sharon's stroke in January 2006 and the subsequent conflict in Lebanon clouded the future of the new party and the peace process more generally. Outside the government are Israeli extremists like Yigal Amir, who regarded it as his religious duty to assassinate Prime

Minister Rabin. Thus, neither government commands the authority to take the needed steps to peace, and both fear civil war if they do so.

- *The small size of the areas at stake exacerbates security problems for both sides* The issue of size is most evident in the case of the Golan Heights. Whoever controls the heights controls the land below in Israel and Syria. Additionally, Muslims and Jews live close to one another in Jerusalem and elsewhere. As a result, every inch of land becomes a security concern.

- *Israel and Israelis are perceived as Western interlopers in a non-Western part of the world* Arabs regularly identify Israelis as heirs of the Christian "Crusaders." Moreover, Israel is an economically developed and largely secular society with sophisticated technology, advanced science, democracy, and Westernized customs and perceptions. By contrast, Arab societies, like other less-developed regions, feature poverty, illiteracy, rapid population growth, and traditional customs and ideas. In some respects, the boundary between Israel and Palestine symbolizes the confrontation of the developed and less-developed worlds.

- *The length of time that the problem has festered and the presence of inflexible leaders and groups make the players more rigid* Only time will tell whether and for how long the cycle of violence will persist. In the end, lasting peace in the region may not prove possible until one or several major power(s) physically intervene(s) to separate the foes. The plight of the Palestinians continues to serve as an excuse for Islamic terrorism, the issue to which we now turn.

Afghanistan, 9/11, and the War on Terrorism

There are over one billion Muslims in the world today, with large Islamic communities in the Middle East, South Asia, Central Asia, Southeast Asia, North Africa, and sub-Saharan Africa. There are also growing communities in Europe and the United States. Most Muslims live in the less developed world, and many are victims of rapid population growth, poverty, and joblessness. Confronted by the challenges of modernization, secularism, and globalization, Muslim political consciousness and activism have intensified in recent decades, and Islam is increasingly divided between moderate reformers and militant fundamentalists.

Conflict in many countries such as Afghanistan, Pakistan, Egypt, Algeria, and Indonesia have deepened Islamic identities, encouraged militant transnational Islamic loyalties, and incited Muslims to fight in foreign lands.[24] For example, Muslim veterans of the war against the Soviet Union in Afghanistan, calling themselves the *Harkat-ul Ansar*,

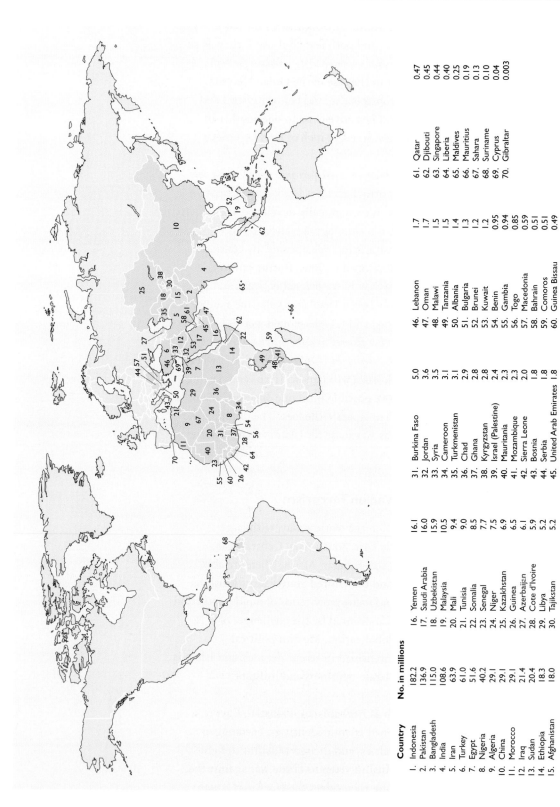

Country	No. in millions
1. Indonesia	182.2
2. Pakistan	136.9
3. Bangladesh	115.0
4. India	108.6
5. Iran	63.9
6. Turkey	61.0
7. Egypt	51.6
8. Nigeria	40.2
9. Algeria	29.1
10. China	29.1
11. Morocco	29.1
12. Iraq	21.4
13. Sudan	20.4
14. Ethiopia	18.3
15. Afghanistan	18.0

16. Yemen	16.1
17. Saudi Arabia	16.0
18. Uzbekistan	15.9
19. Malaysia	10.5
20. Mali	9.4
21. Tunisia	9.0
22. Somalia	8.5
23. Senegal	7.7
24. Niger	7.5
25. Kazakhstan	6.9
26. Guinea	6.5
27. Cote d'Ivoire	6.1
28. Cote d'Ivoire	5.9
29. Libya	5.2
30. Tajikstan	5.2

31. Burkina Faso	5.0
32. Jordan	3.6
33. Syria	3.5
34. Cameroon	3.1
35. Turkmenistan	3.1
36. Chad	2.9
37. Ghana	2.8
38. Kyrgyzstan	2.8
39. Israel (Palestine)	2.4
40. Mauritania	2.3
41. Mozambique	2.3
42. Sierra Leone	2.0
43. Bosnia	1.8
44. Serbia	1.8
45. United Arab Emirates	1.8

46. Lebanon	1.7
47. Oman	1.7
48. Malawi	1.5
49. Tanzania	1.5
50. Albania	1.4
51. Bulgaria	1.3
52. Brunei	1.2
53. Kuwait	1.2
54. Benin	0.95
55. Gambia	0.94
56. Togo	0.85
57. Macedonia	0.59
58. Bahrain	0.51
59. Comoros	0.51
60. Guinea Bissau	0.49

61. Qatar	0.47
62. Djibouti	0.45
63. Singapore	0.44
64. Liberia	0.40
65. Maldives	0.25
66. Mauritius	0.19
67. Sahara	0.13
68. Suriname	0.10
69. Cyprus	0.04
70. Gibraltar	0.003

Map 5.3 Countries with Muslim populations of 10 percent or more (1996)

have infiltrated Indian-occupied Kashmir, fought Indian troops and police, and kidnapped and murdered Western hostages.

Growing Islamic militancy and religious fervor have prompted some observers to view the conflict between the West and Islam as a clash of competing civilizations (see chapter 15, pp. 731–6). Militant Muslims, including Osama bin Laden's Al Qaeda terrorists, claim to act on behalf of a universal Islamic community. For them, the enemy is variously the United States, Israel, Christianity, globalization, or the secular West. Militants argue that, in journalist Judith Miller's words, "rule is a prerogative not of the people, but of God, who appointed the prophet, who, in turn, prescribed the general precepts of governance in God's own words, the Koran."[25]

The growth of militant Islam came to the attention of Americans in 1978–79 when supporters of the Ayatollah (holy man) Ruhollah Khomeini (1900–89), the spiritual leader of Iran's Shia Muslims, overthrew the country's long-time American friend, Shah Muhammad Reza Pahlavi (1919–80), setting off an Islamic revolution in Iran. Khomeini then declared the establishment of the Islamic Republic of Iran to be governed by the country's leading Shia mullahs (religious clerics) organized as a Council of Guardians and sworn to govern according to the teachings of the Koran. Americans were aghast when Iranian students overran the US embassy in Teheran in November 1979 in violation of international law, and held the entire staff hostage. Despite an unsuccessful military raid by US forces in 1980, some 44 US hostages were held for 444 days until January 1981.

Since then, Western observers have increasingly viewed strident Islam, as Miller puts it, in "images of car bombs, murder, and young, bearded holy warriors bent on historic revenge."[26] Terrorist bombings in areas as diverse as Bali in Indonesia, Nairobi in Kenya, Istanbul in Turkey, Madrid in Spain, and London have reinforced this perception. Also, in an era of globalization, many Islamic ideas seem to challenge the ideology of modernity. Indeed, some Western officials have gone so far as to speak of a "Green Menace" (green being the color of Islam) in terms once reserved for "Red" communists.

The wave of militancy sweeping the Muslim world owes much to events in Afghanistan during the last decades of the Cold War, especially the Soviet invasion of 1979 and the long and successful resistance by Islamic fighters, including many non-Afghans. Many Muslims, including Arabs like Osama bin Laden, were transformed into militants, and trained to fight in the Afghan resistance to Soviet occupation of that country, and were aided and armed by the United States. After the Soviet withdrawal from Afghanistan, these fighters directed their efforts toward overturning

Figure 5.8 American hostage and militant Iranian students © PA Photos

secular governments and opposing Western influence elsewhere. Those efforts ultimately led to Al Qaeda's bloody attacks on New York's World Trade Center and the Pentagon in Washington, DC. In turn, the United States invaded Afghanistan, overthrew the fundamentalist Taliban rulers of that country, and tried to capture Osama bin Laden and his lieutenants. In examining these events, this section focuses on the rising tensions between Islam and the West, as well as on conflicts between Islamic and secular forces in the Muslim world.

The Afghan background

Afghanistan has a turbulent history dominated by the absence of authoritative rule at the center, and powerful and disputatious tribal groups. These features help explain why the Soviet invasion failed, even as earlier British incursions had failed.

Taking advantage of Afghan weakness when civil war engulfed the country between 1819 and 1826, Great Britain invaded Afghanistan, partly out of fear of Russia's aggressive intents toward neighboring

British India. This First Anglo-Afghan War (1839–42) climaxed with the slaughter of a British army at the hands of the Afghans. British fears of Russia persisted, however, and the British reentered the country in 1878, igniting the Second Anglo-Afghan War. Two years later, British forces again withdrew from Afghanistan and its fearful terrain of deserts and mountains, though retaining control of key areas along the frontier. In the following years, the Russians seized a slice of territory on Afghanistan's northern border. In response, the British severed what is today's Pakistan from Afghanistan and made it part of their Indian Empire. British–Russian tensions in the region were eased by the 1907 Anglo-Russian Convention of St. Petersburg which recognized Afghanistan as a buffer region, an agreement that was the final step in the formation of the Triple Entente. Nevertheless, in 1919, new British fears led to the Third Anglo-Afghan War, which ended in yet another British defeat.

Notwithstanding persistent political instability, Afghanistan stayed out of the world's headlines until Prince Mohammad Daoud became Prime Minister in 1953 and established close ties with the Soviet Union.

The Soviet invasion and Islamic resistance

The birth of the Islamic guerrilla movement in Afghanistan dates from a bloody 1978 communist coup. Angered by the new regime's efforts to secularize and centralize the country, conservative Islamic warriors took up arms. The regime's incompetence triggered a Soviet invasion of the country in December 1979, and the USSR installed "their man," Babrak Karmal (1929–96), who became a hated figure for many Afghans. With US help, resistance grew against the regime, and Soviet occupation ended in Moscow's defeat and withdrawal in 1989.

In 1992, the country again descended into warring tribal strife. In 1996, however, a new Islamic force, the Taliban, consisting of deeply religious graduates from traditional Islamic seminary schools called **madrasas**, seized control of the country, declaring Afghanistan to be an Islamic state. Afghans initially welcomed the Taliban because it had ended violence and corruption, but its enforcement of a ferocious brand of fundamentalism alienated it from many traditional tribal Afghans. Religious police destroyed televisions with axes, banned music, made men wear beards, forced women to remain at home, required them to wear the *chador* (the traditional long black robe of Islamic women), and imposed a brand of Islam similar to that of the ultraconservative Wahhabi movement, which views the Koran and Hadith (Muhammad's statements) as the only legitimate sources of law for Muslims.

madrasas Muslim religious schools.

Al Qaeda, Islamic terrorism, and the War on Terrorism

Under the Taliban, Afghanistan became a sanctuary and training area for Islamic militants who came from regions as disparate as Chechnya in the Russian Caucasus, Palestine, Western Europe, Saudi Arabia, Indonesia, Kashmir, Kosovo, and Xinjiang in China. Most important of these were Osama bin Laden (1957–) and his shadowy organization of stateless Muslim terrorists who moved their base from Sudan to Afghanistan in 1996. There, in 1998 and 1999, he was targeted by the Clinton administration and the CIA, and a number of efforts were made to kill or capture him, including notably a cruise missile strike on a terrorist training camp in August 1998 following the bombing of US embassies in East Africa.

Bin Laden, a wealthy Yemeni-born militant, espoused a form of militant and aggressive Sunni Islam that interprets the Muslim duty called **jihad** to mean holy war against infidels and the forcible imposition of Islam on non-Muslims (see Key document: Excerpts from Osama bin Laden). He was involved in the bombings of the World Trade Center in 1993 and the Khobar Towers housing American servicemen in Saudi Arabia in 1996. He was also instrumental in the 1998 bombings of US embassies in Kenya and Tanzania and the 2000 attack on the destroyer *USS Cole* in Yemen. Bin Laden supported the causes of Islamic militants around the world, and Al Qaeda training camps in Afghanistan attracted many foreign Muslims. He also decried US support of Israel, Russia's war in Chechnya, and Serbia's war against Bosnia's Muslims. However, bin Laden's special cause was the expulsion of Western, especially American, economic, political, and military influence from Saudi Arabia.

On September 11, 2001 the world was horrified by the skyjacking of four commercial aircraft at airports in Boston, Newark, and Washington, DC by members of Al Qaeda who then crashed two of the planes into New York's World Trade Center and one into the Pentagon.[28] Over 3,000 people died in the suicide attacks that day.

The event was the single most horrendous act of terrorism in history and transformed US foreign policy over night. President George W. Bush declared a War on Terrorism and demanded that the Taliban turn over bin Laden. The refusal of the Taliban and its leader, "One-Eyed" Omar, to do so triggered the October 2001 American invasion of Afghanistan that, in alliance with a coalition of tribal and ethnic forces called the Northern Alliance, overthrew the Taliban. In June 2002, Hamid Karzai (1957–) was selected to head a coalition government consisting of Pashtuns, Tajiks, Hazaras, and Turkmen representing the major ethnic groups in the country. In late 2004 Karzai was elected president of Afghanistan. Efforts

jihad a holy war undertaken as a sacred duty by Muslims.

Key document   Excerpts from Osama bin Laden's 1996 "Declaration of War against the Americans Occupying the Land of the Two Holy Places"[27]

It should not be hidden from you that the people of Islam had suffered from aggression, iniquity and injustice imposed on them by the Zionist-Crusaders alliance and their collaborators; to the extent that the Muslim's blood became the cheapest and their wealth as loot in the hands of the enemies. Their blood was spilled in Palestine and Iraq. . . . Massacres in Tajikistan, Burma, Kashmir, Assam, Philippines, Fatani, Ogadin, Somalia, Erithria, Chechnya and in Bosnia-Herzegovina took place, massacres that send shivers in the body and shake the conscience. All of this and the world watch and hear, and not only didn't respond to these atrocities, but also with a clear conspiracy between the USA and its allies and under the cover of the iniquitous United Nations, the dispossessed people were even prevented from obtaining arms to defend themselves.

The people of Islam awakened and realized that they are the main target for the aggression of the Zionist-Crusaders alliance. . . .

The latest and the greatest of these aggressions, incurred by the Muslims since the death of the Prophet . . . is the occupation of the land of the two Holy Places [Saudi Arabia] . . . by the armies of the American Crusaders and their allies. . . .

Today your brothers and sons . . . have started their Jihad in the cause of Allah, to expel the occupying enemy from of the country of the two Holy places. And there is no doubt you would like to carry out this mission too, in order to re-establish the greatness of this Umma [Islamic Community] and to liberate its' occupied sanctities. . . .

It is now clear that those who claim that the blood of the American soldiers (the enemy occupying the land of the Muslims) should be protected are merely repeating what is imposed on them by the regime; fearing the aggression and interested in saving themselves. It is a duty now on every tribe in the Arab Peninsula to fight, Jihad, in the cause of Allah and to cleanse the land from those occupiers. . . .

My Muslim Brothers of The World:

Your brothers in Palestine and in the land of the two Holy Places are calling upon your help and asking you to take part in fighting against the enemy – your enemy and their enemy – the Americans and the Israelis. They are asking you to do whatever you can, with one's own means and ability, to expel the enemy, humiliated and defeated, out of the sanctities of Islam.

Table 5.1   Suspected al-Qaeda terrorists acts

1993	February	Bombing of World Trade Center (WTC); 6 killed.
	October	Killing of US soldiers in Somalia.
1996	June	Truck bombing at Khobar Towers barracks in Dhahran, Saudi Arabia; killed 19 Americans.
1998	August	Bombing of US embassies in Kenya and Tanzania; 224 killed, including 12 Americans.
1999	December	Plot to bomb millennium celebrations in Seattle foiled when customs agents arrest an Algerian smuggling explosives into the US.
2000	October	Bombing of the *USS Cole* in port in Yemen; 17 US sailors killed.
2001	September	Destruction of World Trade Center; attack on Pentagon. Total dead 2,992.
	December	Man tried to detonate shoe bomb on flight from Paris to Miami.
2002	April	Explosion at historic synagogue in Tunisia left 21 dead, including 14 German tourists.
	May	Car exploded outside hotel in Karachi, Pakistan; killed 14, including 11 French citizens.
	June	Bomb exploded outside American consulate in Karachi, Pakistan; killed 12.
	October	Boat crashed into oil tanker off Yemeni coast; killed 1.
	October	Nightclub bombings in Bali, Indonesia; killed 202, mostly Australian citizens.
	November	Suicide attack on a hotel in Mombasa, Kenya; killed 16.
2003	May	Suicide bombers killed 34, including 8 Americans, at housing compounds for Westerners in Riyadh, Saudi Arabia.
	May	4 bombs killed 33 people targeting Jewish, Spanish, and Belgian sites in Casablanca, Morocco.
	August	Suicide car bomb killed 12, injured 150 at Marriott Hotel in Jakarta, Indonesia.
	November	Explosions rocked a Riyadh, Saudi Arabia housing compound; killed 17.
	November	Suicide car bombers simultaneously attacked 2 synagogues in Istanbul, Turkey; killed 25 and injured hundreds.
	November	Truck bombs detonated at London bank and British consulate in Istanbul, Turkey; killed 26.
2004	March	10 bombs on 4 trains exploded almost simultaneously during the morning rush hour in Madrid, Spain; killed 202 and injured more than 1,400.
	May	Terrorists attacked Saudi oil company offices in Khobar, Saudi Arabia; killed 22.
	June	Terrorists kidnapped and executed American Paul Johnson, Jr., in Riyadh, Saudi Arabia.
	September	Car bomb outside the Australian embassy in Jakarta, Indonesia; killed 9.
	December	Terrorists entered the US consulate in Jeddah, Saudi Arabia; killed 9 (including 4 attackers).
2005	July	Bombs exploded on 3 trains and a bus in London, England; killed 52.
	October	22 killed by 3 suicide bombs in Bali, Indonesia.
	November	57 killed at 3 American hotels in Amman, Jordan.

Adapted from "Terrorist Acts Suspected of or Inspired by al-Qaeda," www.infoplease.com/ipa/A0884893.html, as it appeared on March 29, 2007, © 2007 Pearson Education, Inc. Reproduced by permission of Pearson Education, Inc. publishing as InfoPlease. All rights reserved

to find bin Laden were unsuccessful, and tribal conflicts in the country persisted.

America's War on Terrorism was waged both overseas and at home.[29] American CIA, FBI, and special operations forces have pursued Muslim militants in such diverse settings as the remote tribal areas along Pakistan's border with Afghanistan, the island of Mindanao in the Philippines, Djibouti and Somalia in East Africa, and Yemen. Indeed, Washington justified the US invasion of Iraq in March 2003 by calling it the new "front line in the war on terror," implying a link – never confirmed – between Saddam Hussein and Al Qaeda.

At home, America's anti-terrorist campaign led to dramatic new security measures, including the creation of a Department of Homeland Security and the passage of the Patriot Act. Lengthy security checks at US and foreign airports became common after 9/11, and the United States required that foreign visitors be fingerprinted and photographed by their own countries before getting entry visas. Washington also required that foreign airports and seaports put in place new forms of high-tech security used in America. Such requirements reflected an effort to extend US rules to other countries, which is called asserting "extraterritorial jurisdiction."

The Patriot Act, passed in October 2001, included a series of measures meant to enhance American security against terrorists. Some of these measures, however, seemed to circumscribe individual privacy and other rights. The law authorized enhanced surveillance procedures. It made it easier for police officials to search suspects or seize evidence and facilitated cooperation with foreign law enforcement agencies. The Patriot Act also provided stiffer penalties for terrorists or those assisting terrorists, and it sought to integrate the work of state and federal authorities, including the FBI and CIA. Finally, the law tried to encourage citizens to report suspicious activities or individuals to law enforcement agencies and to upgrade immigration and visa procedures.

Of special concern to civil rights advocates was the internment of about 1,000 mainly Muslim immigrants by the Justice Department. About 600 "enemy combatants" taken prisoner in Afghanistan and elsewhere were held at the US naval base at Guantánamo Bay in Cuba without the rights available either to accused criminals in the United States or to prisoners of war. The International Committee of the Red Cross vigorously protested their status, but the Bush administration argued that infringement of some individual rights was necessary in light of the severity of the threat.

The War on Terrorism continues and will probably last for many years. Although most Muslims, whatever their political and religious preferences, are peaceable, incidents such as the 2005 terrorist bombings in London, which have been linked to Muslim citizens in the UK, threaten to increase domestic strife and create greater Muslim–Western hostility. A crucial piece of this is the situation in Iraq, the newest flashpoint in Islamic–Western tensions and a critical test of the effectiveness and wisdom of US foreign policy.

The Iraq dimension

Two wars in little more than a decade have led to the virtual collapse of authority in Iraq and a vicious insurgency against occupying US troops and the Iraq government. The following section traces the evolution of the Iraq issue through an extraordinary series of events, beginning with the country's birth after World War I.

The birth of modern Iraq

The story of modern Iraq is relatively recent. The British constructed the country in 1920 out of three former provinces of the Ottoman Empire which had ruled them since 1534. The British objective was to secure in a single British-controlled country the major oil resources of the region. However, the inhabitants of the three provinces of Mosul, Baghdād, and Al Başrah had little in common, resulting in an artificial entity held together mainly by authoritarian leaders.

Today, Iraq's population is about 75 percent Arab and 20 percent Kurdish, while about 60 percent of the Arab population is Shia and 35 percent Sunni.[30] One source of conflict follows from the fact that the minority Sunnis formed a political and economic elite in Saddam Hussein's regime. A passage by historian Margaret MacMillan about the founding of modern Iraq from the ashes of the Ottoman Empire has an eerie ring, as US forces in Iraq try desperately to pacify the country:

> In 1919 there was no *Iraqi people*; history, religion, geography pulled the people apart, not together. Basra looked south, toward India and the Gulf; Baghdad had strong links with Persia; and Mosul had closer ties with Turkey and Syria. Putting together the three Ottoman provinces and expecting to create a nation was, in European terms, like hoping to have Bosnian Muslims, Croats, and Serbs make one country. As in the Balkans, the clash of empires and civilizations had left deep fissures. . . . There was no *Iraqi nationalism*, only Arab.[31]

The British went ahead in the belief that their rule of Iraq would continue well into the future. Faisal I (1885–1933), the Arab leader who along with T. E. Lawrence (1888–1935) (known as Lawrence of Arabia) led the Arab revolt against the Ottomans in World War I, was made king, and Britain granted Iraq its independence in 1932. Faisal remained in power because he had the support of the Iraqi army and the British and because he was willing to grant Iraq's religious and ethnic groups considerable autonomy. Increasingly, however, political and economic influence fell into the hands of an international oil consortium. Faisal died in 1933 and was replaced by his son Ghazi, who was in turn succeeded by his infant son, King Faisal II in 1939.

During World War II, a group of anti-British Iraqi nationalists who enjoyed warm relations with Nazi Germany staged a coup. British troops landed in May 1941 and restored a pro-Western government. Thus, during the early years of the Cold War, Iraq under Faisal II remained a close ally of the West and was an original signatory of the 1955 Baghdad Treaty, an anti-Soviet grouping that included Turkey and Britain.

Matters changed suddenly when a 1958 military coup d'état abolished Iraq's monarchy and proclaimed a republic. The new government was close to Egypt's President Nasser and, with Nasser, sought to expel Western influence from the Middle East and foster Arab unity and nationalism. In 1963 officers associated with the Baath Party overthrew this regime, and turmoil ensued until a 1968 coup brought to power the Baath Party governing through a newly established Revolutionary Command Council with Saddam Hussein as vice chair. Saddam became Iraq's president in 1979.

The Baath Party was nationalist, secular, and socialist. As a nationalist party, it sought Arab unity and an end to foreign influence and, consistent with this policy, it opposed the partition of Palestine. In foreign policy, the Baathist government was hostile toward the West and sought closer ties to the USSR, which sided with the Arabs in their conflict with Israel. In 1972, Iraq signed a Treaty of Friendship and Cooperation with the USSR.

Because the Baath Party was secular, Iraq was not governed by Islamic law. In practical terms, this meant that Iraqi women were better educated and enjoyed more rights than women in other Islamic states. Finally, because the Baath Party was socialist, Iraq's government took an active role in the economy, particularly in the oil sector, which it nationalized in the 1970s. These traits defined the Iraqi regime through Saddam Hussein's reign.

Saddam Hussein and the Iran–Iraq War

Between 1981 and 1988, Iraq and Iran fought one of the bloodiest wars of the late twentieth century. The war reflected historical animosity between Arabs and Persians (Iraqis and Iranians, respectively) and between Sunni and Shia Muslims. In particular, Saddam Hussein's Sunni regime feared that Iranian Shia fundamentalism would infect Iraq. But the war was also a product of regional politics. Saddam sought to make Iraq a dominant regional power. Iran was Iraq's main competitor and posed a threat to

Iraq's regime. Saddam also sought additional oil and territory, especially control of the 110-mile long Shatt al Arab tidal river that flows from the Tigris and Euphrates into the Persian Gulf with its adjacent tidal marshes. Thus, in 1981 Saddam Hussein invaded Iran, which had been weakened by its Islamic Revolution and subsequent turmoil.

Saddam's decision to invade Iran reflected poor judgment and overweening personal ambition. The war lasted eight years and was fought like World War I, with trenches, massed attacks, and mustard and nerve gas. Civilians on both sides were victims of missile attacks, air bombardment, and artillery. Initially, Iraqi advantages in tanks and other modern weapons produced a series of victories, but in 1982 the tide turned as Iran sent masses of armed child "martyrs" against Iraqi positions and used human wave tactics. Thereafter, the war became one of attrition, as it did on the Western Front between 1914 and 1918. As many as a million people died in the war. Iraq suffered about 375,000 casualties, a figure proportionally equivalent to over five million US casualties.

Each side sought to destroy the other's capacity to export oil. This aspect of the conflict was especially dangerous, owing to the heavy dependence of both Europe and the United States on Persian Gulf oil. Commercial vessels, especially oil tankers, on both sides, as well as those sailing under neutral flags, were victimized. When a US-flagged oil tanker, the *Sea Isle City*, was struck by the Iranians in October 1987, US forces retaliated by destroying two Iranian oil platforms in the Gulf. Soon, the Soviet Union and then the United States stepped up efforts to end the war, "tilting" toward Iraq from fear that an Iranian-style Islamic republic might come to power in Iraq. Finally, in August 1988 both countries, exhausted, accepted UN Security Council Resolution 598, which demanded that they agree to a ceasefire. In the end, none of the issues was resolved, and the front was virtually the same as it had been eight years before.

The Persian Gulf War

Hardly had the Iran–Iraq War ended when Saddam Hussein turned his attention to Kuwait, a small oil-rich country that had been founded in 1756 as an autonomous sheikdom. Kuwait, like Iraq, was administered by Britain after World War I, becoming independent in 1961. Within a month of independence Iraq invaded the new country, claiming ownership of Kuwait as a former province of the Ottoman Empire. British forces repelled the invasion and, in 1963, Iraq recognized Kuwait's independence.

After the Iraq–Iran War, Kuwait, along with other Arab states, loaned Iraq vast sums to assist in the latter's reconstruction, and by 1990 Iraq owed Kuwait $10 billion. However, Kuwait hampered Iraq's ability to repay its loans by pumping more oil than was permitted by OPEC (chapter 14, p. 661). This action drove down oil prices and, consequently, Iraq's oil revenue. Iraq demanded that Kuwait forgive its share of the debt and help repay what Iraq owed other Arab states. The Iraqis also accused the Kuwaitis of "slant drilling" oil along their common desert border; that is, employing equipment that enabled Kuwaitis to steal Iraqi oil from Kuwait's side of the border. Finally, Baghdad accused the Kuwaitis of ingratitude in light of the fact that Iraq had represented *all* Arabs in its struggle with Iran.

Iraqi pressure on Kuwait continued into the summer as Iraq sent military units to the border. Nevertheless, Saddam assured Egypt's president that he would not invade Kuwait, and he provided a similar assurance to America's ambassador in Baghdad, April Glaspie. Ambassador Glaspie responded: "I have direct instruction from the President [George H. W. Bush] to seek better relations with Iraq."[32] Based on this conversation, a controversy erupted following Iraq's invasion of Kuwait as to whether the ambassador had clearly communicated Washington's opposition to an invasion.

On August 2, 1990, Hussein sent an army of 150,000 troops and 2,000 tanks into Kuwait, conquering the country in a matter of hours. The UN Security Council rapidly passed resolutions condemning the invasion and ordering Iraq out of Kuwait, and then authorized sanctions against Baghdad. President George H. W. Bush applauded Russian–US cooperation in the Security Council as additional evidence of how the world had changed since the end of the Cold War. Invoking Woodrow Wilson's idea of collective security, British Prime Minister Margaret Thatcher declared: "Iraq's invasion of Kuwait defies every principle for which the United Nations stands. If we let it succeed, no small country can ever feel safe again. The law of the jungle would take over from the rule of law."[33] "Iraq," declared Bush, "will not be permitted to annex Kuwait. And that's not a threat. It's not a boast. It's just the way it's going to be."[34]

The Persian Gulf War began shortly after that. On August 7, US forces began to deploy in Saudi Arabia,[35] initially to deter a further Iraqi thrust toward the Saudi oil fields, in a defensive effort dubbed Operation Desert Shield. The following day Saddam announced the annexation of Kuwait. At the end of November, another Security Council Resolution gave Iraq until January 15, 1991 to withdraw or face the members' "use of all necessary means" to expel it from Kuwait. This was the first occasion since the 1950 Korean War that the Security Council had invoked Articles 39 and 40 in Chapter VII of the Charter authorizing the use of military force. Saddam tried to deter a military response by taking Western hostages and hinting at Iraq's possible use of chemical weapons and missiles. Nevertheless, the US Congress voted to support the war. The votes were, however, close: 250 to 183 in the House and 52 to 47 in the Senate.

With UN approval, the United States, which ultimately sent 400,000 troops, formed a diverse military coalition that provided an additional 200,000 troops. The main contributors were Britain, France, and Saudi Arabia, with additional contingents from Kuwait, Syria, Egypt, Morocco, Niger, Senegal, Pakistan, Bangladesh, Oman, Qatar, Bahrain, and the United Arab Emirates. Others such as Canada, New Zealand, Argentina, Australia, South Korea, and several European countries contributed in other ways, and German and Japanese financial assistance eased America's fiscal burden. Israel posed a particularly delicate problem for the United States because Saddam threatened and then carried out Scud-missile attacks against that country. However, had Israel joined the war, Arab members would have withdrawn from the coalition. Among Arab states, Iraq enjoyed little support except from Jordan, Yemen, and the PLO.

Two days after the UN deadline, Operation Desert Storm began with a massive air assault against Iraq. The campaign featured a variety of high-tech weapons including Tomahawk cruise missiles and F-117 stealth bombers. This was the first large-scale use of precision, or "smart," weapons.

The land offensive began on February 24, 1991, and Iraqi resistance swiftly collapsed. So rapidly did coalition forces sweep northward that some Iraqi soldiers were buried alive in their entrenchments by US and British tanks equipped with bulldozer blades to breech the mounds of earth behind which Iraqi troops were hiding. Iraqi forces put up little fight, but in an act of malicious and massive eco-terrorism, they set fire to Kuwaiti oil wells as they fled. The war was won in 100 hours. On February 28, the Bush administration declared a ceasefire because it sensed that further slaughter of Iraqi troops would have a disastrous public-relations effect and feared that a total collapse of Iraq would trigger a conflict among Turkey, Syria, the Kurds, Iran, and perhaps others to divide up the spoils and fill the resulting power vacuum. That decision later proved a source of great controversy in the United States.

Despite Saddam's rout in what he called the "mother of all battles," he had survived, and his regime brutally put down a rebellion by the Shia population in southern Iraq and then launched an equally brutal campaign against dissident Kurds in the north. Thereafter, in accordance

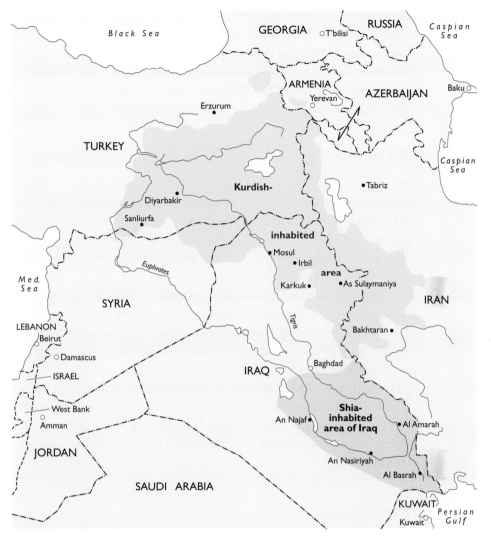

Map 5.4 Iraqi ethnic groups

with the ceasefire that ended the Persian Gulf War, US and British aircraft enforced "no-fly zones" to protect Iraq's Shia and Kurdish populations.[36] Low-level combat between Anglo-American aircraft and Iraqi air defense units continued until the next war. UN sanctions against Iraq also were maintained after the war and progressively worsened conditions for ordinary Iraqis as their government misused funding made available by oil sales.

Under the agreement ending the war, Iraq had to meet several conditions to end sanctions, including admission of liability for damages, destruction of biological and chemical weapons and the missiles to deliver them, abandonment of nuclear weapons development programs, and acceptance of international inspectors to assure Iraqi compliance.

Between 1991 and 1998, a UN Special Commission on Iraq (UNSCOM) made progress in dismantling and monitoring Iraq's weapons of mass destruction (WMD) and long-range missile programs, but it was unable to verify Iraq's claim that it had destroyed all its WMD. Iraq's refusal to cooperate fully with UNSCOM prompted US–British air strikes in December 1998.

The Iraq War

Between 1991 and 2003, the United States and Iraq continued to engage in hostile behavior and rhetoric toward each other. After September 11, 2001 Anglo-American air operations in the "no-fly zone" intensified both to pressure Saddam Hussein to readmit UN arms inspectors and suppress Iraqi air defenses in anticipation of the Anglo-American invasion of Iraq called "Operation Iraqi Freedom."

The descent to another war with Iraq began in 2002. In his January State of the Union, President George W. Bush identified Iraq as part of an "axis of evil," along with Iran and North Korea, and vowed that the US would "not permit the world's most dangerous regimes to threaten us with the world's most destructive weapons."

Nevertheless, Saddam Hussein resisted pressure to readmit UN weapons inspectors to Iraq. He did, however, continue to negotiate with UN Secretary General Kofi Annan and Hans Blix, who had been named to head the UN Monitoring, Verification and Inspection Commission (UNMOVIC).

Did you know?

President Bush got the idea for the phrase "axis of evil" by combining President Ronald Reagan's description of the Soviet Union as the "evil empire" with the term axis as used in World War II. "Axis" was publicized in a speech in Milan's cathedral by Italian dictator Benito Mussolini on November 1, 1936 to describe relations between Germany and Italy. Since an axis in mathematics describes a straight line around which a geometric figure can rotate, the term suggested that the two countries wanted Europe to revolve around the line connecting Berlin and Rome, their capital cities.[37]

On September 12, 2002, a year and a day after 9/11, President Bush went before the UN to demand that the organization enforce its own resolutions against Iraq. If not, Bush declared, the United States would act on its own. Many of America's European allies, especially the German and French governments, as well as Russia and China, took strong exception to US threats of war against Iraq. On October 11 US pressure on the UN and Iraq increased when the Congress authorized war against Iraq if necessary. A month later the UN Security Council unanimously approved a resolution demanding that Iraq permit new WMD inspections, but the Council divided over whether this resolution was sufficient to authorize US military action, with Washington claiming that it was. Within days Saddam Hussein accepted the resolution. Blix and his inspectors arrived in Baghdad and began their work, and Iraq denied that it harbored WMD.

Despite apparent Iraqi cooperation with the UN, President Bush approved the deployment of US troops to the Persian Gulf region, and US, British, and Australian troops prepared for the operation. In his 2003 State of the Union, Bush again declared that the United States was prepared to attack Iraq with or without UN approval, and the following month Secretary of State Colin Powell (1937–) presented US intelligence findings to the Security Council, some of which later turned out to be faulty. The "coalition of the willing" – the United States, Britain, and Spain – then proposed a resolution declaring that Iraq had "failed to take the final opportunity afforded to it in Resolution 1441" (see Key document: Security Council Resolution 1441) and that the time had come to authorize the use of military force.[38] Governments that opposed war, notably France, Russia, and China (all permanent members of the Security Council with the right to veto Council resolutions), argued for more time to allow inspectors to complete their job. Claiming that Resolution 1441 did not authorize the use of force but only threatened "serious consequences," France, Russia, and Germany asked that inspections be extended to ensure that "the military option should only be a last resort," and that there is "a real chance to the peaceful settlement of this crisis."[39] A lack of support for the US-backed draft meant that the coalition would have to go it alone.

After ordering the UN inspectors out of the country, the United States opened its war against Iraq on March 19, 2003 with a sudden cruise missile attack on Baghdad. Described as a **decapitation attack**, the initial air strike targeted Saddam Hussein and other Iraqi leaders in Baghdad. Precision-guided weapons played an even larger role in this conflict than they had in the 1991 war. American and British forces, mainly in Kuwait, moved northward into Iraq, facing little resistance in their march toward Baghdad. By April 4, Baghdad International Airport was in coalition hands, and the following day US troops entered Baghdad. Within a few days, Baghdad fell, and British troops occupied Basra, the country's second largest city.

decapitation attack an attack that aims to kill an enemy's leaders.

Key document   Security Council Resolution 1441 (December 20, 2002)[40]

The Security Council

. . . Recognizing the threat Iraq's noncompliance with Council resolutions and proliferation of weapons of mass destruction and long-range missiles poses to international peace and security. . . .

Deploring the fact that Iraq has not provided an accurate, full, final, and complete disclosure . . . of all aspects of its programs to develop weapons of mass destruction and ballistic missiles with a range greater than one hundred and fifty kilometers, and of all holdings of such weapons, their components and production facilities and locations. . . .

Deploring further that Iraq repeatedly obstructed immediate, unconditional, and unrestricted access to sites designated by the United Nations Special Commission (UNSCOM) and the International Atomic Energy Agency (IAEA), failed to cooperate fully and unconditionally with UNSCOM and IAEA inspectors. . . .

Deploring the absence, since December 1998, in Iraq of international monitoring, inspection, and verification, as required by relevant resolutions, of weapons of mass destruction and ballistic missiles, in spite of the Council's repeated demands that Iraq provide immediate, unconditional, and unrestricted access to the United Nations Monitoring, Verification and Inspection Commission (UNMOVIC), . . . and the IAEA; and regretting the consequent prolonging of the crisis in the region and the suffering of the Iraqi people. . . .

Deploring also that the Government of Iraq has failed to comply with its commitments . . . with regard to terrorism, . . . to end repression of its civilian population and to provide access to international humanitarian organizations to all those in need of assistance in Iraq, and . . . to return or cooperate in accounting for Kuwaiti and third country nationals wrongfully detained by Iraq, or to return Kuwaiti property wrongfully seized by Iraq. . . .

Determined to ensure full and immediate compliance by Iraq without conditions or restrictions with its obligations under resolution 687 (1991) and other relevant resolutions and recalling that the resolutions of the Council constitute the governing standard of Iraqi compliance. . .

Determined to secure full compliance with its decisions,

Acting under Chapter VII of the Charter of the United Nations,

1   Decides that Iraq has been and remains in material breach of its obligations under relevant resolutions . . . ;

2   Decides . . . to afford Iraq . . . a final opportunity to comply with its
    disarmament obligations . . . ;

3   Decides that . . . the Government of Iraq shall provide to UNMOVIC, the
    IAEA, and the Council, not later than 30 days from the date of this
    resolution, a currently accurate, full, and complete declaration of all
    aspects of its programs to develop chemical, biological, and nuclear
    weapons . . . ;

13 Recalls . . . that the Council has repeatedly warned Iraq that it will face
    serious consequences as a result of its continued violations of its
    obligations. . . .

On April 14, the Pentagon announced that large-scale fighting had
ended, and on May 1 President Bush declared victory. In July, Saddam
Hussein's two sons were killed, and in December Saddam himself
was captured without a fight and later put on trial for crimes against
humanity and executed in December 2006. Despite these
accomplishments, the conflict continued. In fact, the real war had only
just begun. An insurrection against US and British occupation forces
spread, beginning in 2003, killing more Americans after the "victory"
than before.[41] Sunni Muslims who had been favored by Saddam and
militant jihadists from outside Iraq waged guerrilla-style war against
American and British forces. They also attacked Iraqis who supported the
US-backed coalition and foreign civilians who had come to Iraq to
participate in its reconstruction. Using roadside bombs, car bombs and
suicide bombings, terrorists also targeted Shia Muslims and Kurds, in an
effort to trigger communal violence and foster anti-American feeling as a
result of spiraling insecurity.

While advocating democracy for Iraq, the United States first tried to
prevent the majority Shia community from taking over the government
in a manner that would threaten the Sunni and Kurdish minorities. An
American plan for elections based on a complex system of caucuses was
rejected by Shia Grand Ayatollah Ali al-Sistani who demanded a system
of direct voting that would reflect the Shia majority. The United
States agreed, and elections for a Transitional National Assembly were
held on January 30, 2005. Most Iraqi Sunnis boycotted the election,
and a Shia alliance won a bare majority of 140 seats, while Kurds won
75 seats, leaving them the second most powerful group in the National
Assembly. In April 2005, the Assembly elected a Kurd as president and
a Shia as prime minister. The executives worked well into May to select a
35-member cabinet to represent Iraq's main domestic groups, and they
appointed a committee to prepare a new constitution that was approved

Figure 5.9 The search for
Saddam's weapons
© Original artist,
www.cartoonstock.com

"I see weapons of mass destruction!"

in October 2005. Elections in December 2005, in which Iraq's Sunnis
did participate, produced another victory for the Shia alliance which won
128 of 275 seats in the new parliament with the Shia politician
Nouri al-Maliki (1950–) as prime minister. Subsequent events saw little
reduction in violence in Iraq either in attacks against US forces or among
Shias, Sunnis, and Kurds. By 2007, Iraq seemed on the verge of full-scale
civil war.[42]

Global opposition to US policies – especially the unilateral overthrow
of the Iraqi regime – remained strong as it became clear that the financial
costs of pacifying and reconstructing Iraq were vastly higher than
estimated and that no weapons of mass destruction could be found.
UN weapons inspectors concluded that such weapons had been largely
eliminated a decade earlier. Flawed US and British intelligence, combined
with a desire of US and British leaders to find a "smoking gun," was
largely to blame for the faulty belief that Iraq had WMD. As violence
continued in Iraq, the issue became as divisive in the United States as the
Vietnam War.[43]

Figure 5.10 Former President of Iraq, Saddam Hussein, makes a point during his initial interview by a special tribunal, where he is informed of his alleged crimes and his legal rights
Courtesy of US Department of Defence

Theory in the real world

The realist–liberal disagreement repeatedly crops up in global politics. President George W. Bush provided a number of reasons to explain why the United States was right to invade the country of Iraq in 2003. Prior to the war, his major justification was that Iraq had weapons of mass destruction that could alter the regional and perhaps even the global balance of power, posing a danger to many of America's friends. This was a classic realist argument based on national interest and the distribution of power. When such weapons were not found, the President's arguments for the invasion emphasized that Saddam Hussein was a dictator who brutalized his own citizens and that the United States was obligated to bring freedom and democracy to Iraq. These normative and interventionist liberal claims echoed those of an earlier American president, Woodrow Wilson.

Realists deplore the destruction of the old Iraqi regime and its armed forces for creating a power vacuum that has produced virtual civil war and invites meddling in Iraq on the part of Iran, Turkey, and other Iraqi neighbors fearful that one or the other may acquire preponderant influence there.[44] The transformation of Iraq into a virtual failed state has removed a key barrier to the extension of Iranian influence in the region. With the election as president of a hard-line anti-American, Mahmoud Ahmadinejad (1956–), who has refused to end Iran's enrichment of nuclear fuel, declared that Israel must be "wiped off the map" and described the Holocaust as a "myth," Iran has become increasingly assertive. In addition, a CIA National Intelligence Estimate completed in April 2006 concluded that the American intervention in Iraq fostered Islamic extremism and made the threat of terrorism worse than it had been.[45]

Although pleased by the effort to install democracy in Iraq, liberals deplore America's failure to form a larger multilateral coalition or get UN approval for its actions before intervening, as well as US violations of human rights such as abuses in the prison of Abu Ghraib. Constructivists dislike the fact that the war in Iraq has increased the numbers of Muslims around the world as well as in Iraq who identify themselves as *jihadists* and adversaries of the West and, therefore, see their interests as served by fighting Western influence.

And the future?

Was the decision to go to war against Iraq a wise one? Will the war ultimately have positive or negative results? Only the future can answer these questions. In the short term, the war against Iraq accomplished less than the United States had hoped. It did not improve Arab–Israeli relations, nor did it advance the War on Terrorism. Moreover, the hostility between the United States and much of the Muslim world has become an abyss. According to a report commissioned by the Bush administration and issued in October 2003 ("Changing Minds, Winning Peace"): "Hostility toward America has reached shocking levels" among Muslims, and "Arab and Muslim nations are a primary source of anger toward the United States, although such negative attitudes are paralleled in Europe and elsewhere."[46] Confronted with growing opposition at home and abroad, the administration accelerated its timetable for granting self-rule to Iraq. In all likelihood, violence and animosity will continue to mark US–Muslim relations in the future, and the struggle between Islamic moderates and extremists will persist for many years.

Conclusion

This chapter has examined some of the major issues in contemporary global politics. China's growing power poses one of these. The country has emerged from decades of self-imposed isolation to become a major player in global politics and economics. Change is the air: China has adopted capitalist methods, memories of Mao Zedong are fading, and he is no longer mentioned in Chinese schools texts.[47]

The three other issues involve Western relations with the Muslim world and are related. The first, the Israel–Palestine issue, has persisted for almost six decades, with roots going back further. From time to time, it has seemed tantalizingly close to resolution, only to deteriorate. The second issue centers on Islamic terrorism against the West, the contest among moderate and militant Muslims for dominance among Muslims worldwide, and the war in Afghanistan. American support for Israel is cited as one reason for Muslim animosity toward the United States, but the issue is more complex. The final issue, the war in Iraq, also has its roots in earlier events. The United States claims that the war is part of the struggle against global terrorism, but, in fact, the war has actually contributed to Muslim militancy.

Iraq has become increasingly anarchic with power divided among ethnic and religious competitors. Anarchy and power are, of course, two of the most important concepts in global politics, and in the next chapter we will examine these concepts and the different approaches to them in some detail.

Student activities

Discussion and essay questions

Comprehension questions

1 What are the sources of recurring tensions in US–China relations?
2 What are the major reasons behind contemporary American–Muslim tensions in world affairs?
3 What are the major divisions in Iraq, and how do they affect the conflict there?
4 Did 9/11 begin the conflict between Islam and the West? If not, describe the evolution of relations between the two.

Analysis questions

5 Do you expect greater conflict or cooperation in future US–China relations? Why?
6 What alternative futures can you imagine regarding the relationship between Islam and the West?
7 What would be a "just" solution to the Israeli–Palestine conflict?
8 Write a dialogue based on one of the following:

   a A lunchtime conversation between Iraqi and American leaders about relations between Iraq and the United States.
   b A breakfast meeting between US President George W. Bush and the head of the American Civil Liberties Union about the Patriot Act.
   c A dinner conversation between an Israeli and Palestinian leader over the future of Palestine.

Map analysis

On a blank map of the Middle East, identify the countries bordering Iraq. What are their relations with key Iraqi groups – Sunni, Shia, and Kurdish?

Cultural materials

Numerous films and books portray the great issues depicted in this chapter. *Divine Intervention* (2002), *Rana's Wedding* (2002), and *Gaza Strip* (2002) portray Palestinian life under Israeli occupation; *Alila* (2003) and *Yana's Friends* (1999) examine life in Tel Aviv and *A Time of Favor* (2000) depicts Jewish life in a West Bank settlement. Contemporary Iraq is also making its way onto film. *Turtles Can Fly* (2004) is about refugee children in Iraqi Kurdistan as they wait for the 2003 Iraq war to begin. A Turkish film with a very different tone, *The Valley of the Wolves Iraq* (2006), is extremely critical of US soldiers in Iraq as it depicts the deaths of innocent people and the treatment of prisoners in Abu Ghraib prison. View one or more of these films. What message is the film sending about "the great struggles"?

Further reading

Chan, Gerald, *Chinese Perspectives on International Relations* (New York: St. Martins Press, 1999). Analysis of Chinese approaches to international relations.

Goldstein, Avery, *Rising to the Challenge: China's Grand Strategy and International Security* (Palo Alto, CA: Stanford University Press, 2005). Analysis of China's increasing economic and military power.

Kamrava, Mehran, *The Modern Middle East: A Political History since the First World War* (Berkeley: University of California Press, 2005). Development of the modern Middle East with an emphasis on economic development, the Israeli–Palestinian conflict, and democratization.

Kepel, Gilles, *Jihad: The Trail of Political Islam* (Cambridge, MA: Harvard University Press, 2002). In-depth study of the development of political Islam.

Marsh, Christopher and June Teufel Dreyer, eds., *US–China Relations in the 21st Century* (Lanham, MD: Rowman and Littlefield, 2004). Analysis of key issues in contemporary US–China relations.

Meital, Yoram, *Peace in Tatters: Israel, Palestine, and the Middle East* (Boulder, CO: Lynne Rienner, 2005). The major developments in the Israeli–Palestinian peace process between 2000 and 2004.

Rashid, Ahmed, *Taliban: Militant Islam, Oil, and Fundamentalism in Central Asia* (New Haven, CT: Yale University Press, 2001). Analysis of the Taliban's rise and its impact on Afghanistan.

Woodward, Bob, *Plan of Attack* (New York: Simon and Schuster, 2004). Detailed examination of US decision-making leading up to the 2003 Iraq war.

Part II
Living Dangerously in a Dangerous World

6 Anarchy, power, and war

Between November 1944 and April 1945, in a desperate effort to cause panic and weaken the US war effort, Japan launched 9,300 giant bomb-laden paper balloons, known as Fugos, via the jet stream to kill Americans, start forest fires, and destroy buildings. This unusual case of the "balloon bombs" highlights several traits of power this chapter considers. Japan developed these bizarre weapons to gain an advantage over the militarily superior United States, and the United States was unable to provide an adequate defense. The US Air Force established a balloon early-warning line off the coast of Washington State, but failed to destroy the balloons. By the end of July 1945 some 230 of the balloons had been recovered, mainly in British Columbia, Washington, Oregon, California, and Montana, most of the remainder having been lost at sea. The Japanese effort failed, and the Fugos only briefly gained national attention in May 1945, when members of a Sunday school class picnic – five children and one chaperone – were killed outside of Bly, Oregon when they moved one and it exploded, causing the only casualties in the continental US during World War II. Fearing the very panic the Japanese hoped to provoke, US officials only reported the Japanese balloon bomb project publicly after this incident to warn people to avoid balloon debris.[1] Thus, actors are creative in their efforts to accumulate and use power, but rarely can they be assured of the effect their power will have on others.

This chapter begins with a focus on anarchy. Recall that anarchy – the absence of a central authority above sovereign states – describes the structure of the modern global system, as realists and some liberals view that system. However, each theoretical perspective has its own interpretation of the impact, meaning, and implications of anarchy.

Following the discussion of anarchy, the chapter considers how political scientists have defined two closely related concepts – **power** and **influence**. Actors sometimes fight wars to gain more power, but they also

power a psychological relationship between actors in which one influences another to behave differently than it would have if left to its own devices.

influence an actor's ability to cause another actor to behave differently than it would otherwise have.

use influence to sway others without going to war. Power is a critical and central concept, and we will examine what it is and how it is used in global politics. According to realists and neorealists, power is the defining attribute of the field of global politics and is *the* essential factor in explaining the way the world works. "We assume," writes realist Hans Morgenthau in a much-cited formulation, "that statesmen think and act in terms of interest defined as power."[2] And the "main signpost that helps political realism find its way through the landscape of international politics is the concept of interest defined in terms of power."[3] Whether or not one agrees with Morgenthau, it is indisputable that power has always been a central feature of global politics and has been a subject of analysis at least since Thucydides. And the concepts and theories that grew out of this history still influence our understanding of global politics today – sometimes appropriately and sometimes not. Thus, though formal interstate war is in decline, military force – a key element of power in global politics – remains an attractive instrument to actors. For these reasons, scholars of global politics have long tried to understand and explain power and the ways in which it can be used.

The chapter then turns to interstate war: a phenomenon in which relative military power is central. It considers anarchy and power as alternative explanations of the causes of war. Realists regard war as an inevitable institution in an anarchic system, although they offer suggestions about how to moderate its most pernicious effects. Liberals admit the impact of anarchy but argue that international institutions and the democratization of states can reduce its impact and even prevent its occurrence. Constructivists regard war as an "invention" and social institution. Historically, societies have regarded war as a legitimate institution, but normative change holds out the possibility that war might disappear. Finally, classical Marxists view war as the companion and consequence of capitalist rivalries and class conflict and believe that it will disappear once capitalism has been relegated to the "dustbin of history."

Let us now examine how the major theoretical perspectives approach anarchy and how each views its significance. Anarchy is a central feature of realist analyses of interstate conflict. Although the term is commonly understood as a state of disorder or chaos, this is not what political scientists mean when they describe the global system as anarchic. In fact, most political scientists agree that there is order to global politics in the sense that there are common expectations, and even commonly understood norms, of state behavior. Thus, a group of scholars collectively known as "the English School" has long argued that, despite the absence of world government, the supremacy of sovereign states, and the distribution of authority and power among states, there exists a genuine international society. International society, as political scientist Hedley Bull argues, exists "when a group of states, conscious of certain common interests and common values, form a society in the sense that they conceive themselves to be bound by a common set of rules in their relations with one another, and share in the working of common institutions."[4] Does such a society exist? Bull answers in the affirmative, arguing that "order is part of the historical record of international relations" and "there has always been present, throughout the history of the modern state system, an idea of international society."[5] Thus, **anarchy** does not necessitate disorder but only refers to *a situation in which there is no higher authority above sovereign states*. And as we shall see, there are many disagreements – both among realists and between realists and other theoretical traditions – over its significance.

anarchy the absence of a higher authority above sovereign states.

Realism and the condition of anarchy

All realists view anarchy as a fundamental trait of the international system, although for neorealists it is the single trait that most constrains states as they interact in the global arena. Anarchy for neorealists (as for neoliberals) is a given within which actors must survive. Actors are treated as analogous to economic firms that have to compete and survive in a free market, and power in global politics is regarded as analogous to money in economics. For neorealist theorists, anarchy logically produces a self-help system: states, having no higher power or authority to turn to in times of crisis, must provide for their own security. Such a system is predisposed to conflict and war, even when states share common interests. This does not mean that peace is but a distant dream. In fact, most states are at peace most of the time. However, the condition of the international system is such that states must always prepare for war. This state of anarchy is akin to a Hobbesian state of nature in which all men are equal and their very equality is the source of conflict (see Key document: Thomas Hobbes). In this environment, "*states recognize that . . . there is no overarching authority to prevent others from using violence, or the threat of violence, to destroy or enslave them.*"[6] Consequently, states are consumed with achieving power and security to protect themselves from such threats. Thus, says Kenneth Waltz, "With many sovereign states, with no system of law enforceable among them, with each state judging its grievances and ambitions according to the dictates of its own reason or desire – conflict, sometimes leading to war, is bound to occur."[7]

Key document   Thomas Hobbes, "Of the Natural Condition of Mankind, as Concerning Their Felicity, and Misery," _Leviathan_[8]

Nature hath made men so equall, in the faculties of the body, and mind; as that though there be found one man sometimes manifestly stronger in body, or of quicker mind than another; yet when all is reckoned together, the difference between man, and man, is not so considerable as that one man can thereupon claim to himselfe any benefit, to which another man may not pretend, as well as he. . . .

From this equality of ability, ariseth equality of hope in the attaining of our Ends. And therefore if any two men desire the same thing, which nevertheless they cannot both enjoy, they become enemies; and in the way to their End . . . endeavour to destroy, or subdue one another. . . .

And from this diffidence of one another, there is no way for any man to secure himselfe, so reasonable, as Anticipation; that is, by force, or wiles or to master the persons of all men he can, so long, till he see no other power great enough to endanger him; And this is no more than his own conservation requireth, and is generally allowed. . . .

So that in the nature of man, we find three principall causes of quarrel. First, Competition; Secondly, Diffidence; Thirdly, Glory.

The first maketh man invade for Gain; the second, for Safety, and the third, for Reputation. The first use Violence, to make themselves Masters of other men's persons, wives, children, and cattell; the second, to defend them; the third, for trifles, as a word, a smile, a different opinion, and any other signe of undervalue. . . .

Hereby it is manifest, that during the time men live without a common Power to keep them all in awe, they are in that condition which is called Warre; and such a warre, as is of every man, against every man. For WARRE, consisteth not in Battell onely, or the act of fighting; but in a tract of time, wherein the Will to contend by Battell is sufficiently known: and therefore the notion of _Time_, is to be considered in the nature of Warre; as it is in the nature of Weather. For as the nature of Foule weather, lyeth not in a showre or two of rain; but in an inclination thereto of many dayes together: So the nature of War, consisteth not in actual fighting; but in the known disposition thereto, during all the time there is no assurance to the contrary. All other time is PEACE.

This preoccupation with security leads states to increase their capabilities relative to others and to prevent others from increasing their relative capabilities. This pursuit of relative gains (see chapter 1, p. 23) hinders cooperation because today's friend may become tomorrow's foe, and modest gains made by that friend today may pose a threat in the future. Political scientist Joseph Grieco has labeled such behavior _defensive positionalism_. States, he argues, want to achieve and maintain "relative capabilities sufficient to remain secure and independent in the self-help context of international anarchy."[9] John Mearsheimer labels this view of anarchy _defensive realism_ because it assumes states are not inherently aggressive, but only wish to survive. He and other offensive realists, in contrast, argue that states do indeed seek to dominate. For them, anarchy forces states to maximize their power, for "even if a great power does not have the wherewithal to achieve hegemony (and that is usually the case), it will still act offensively to amass as much power as it can, because states are almost always better off with more rather than less power. In short, states do not become status quo powers until they completely dominate the system."[10]

We see that realists of all stripes view anarchy as a source of competition and conflict in global politics. Shortly we will examine in detail the security dilemma that anarchy produces. But first, we consider how other theorists view the relationship between anarchy and interstate conflict.

The neoliberal critique: cooperating under anarchy

Anarchy has held a far less central place in liberal theories than in realist theories, but an exception is to be found in neoliberalism. You may recall from chapter 1 that neoliberals share a number of assumptions with realists. In particular, they agree that states are the primary actors in global politics, that they are unitary-rational actors, and that they *exist in a condition of anarchy*. However, while neoliberals agree anarchy is significant for explaining state behavior, they view its implications differently than do realists. Up to a point, their understanding of the meaning of anarchy is the same: it describes an absence of an authority above states in global politics. Neoliberals, though, do not believe that conflict logically or necessarily follows from this condition. First, like neorealists, neoliberals view states as rational egoists, but rather than pursuing relative gains as neorealists contend, for neoliberals this means that they seek to maximize their own interests independent of the gains or losses of others.[11] Accordingly, in their dealings with others, states are most interested in achieving absolute gains to their well-being, without regard for the gains others may also achieve. States seek cooperation to achieve common interests but without a higher agency to enforce their agreements "cheating is both possible and profitable."[12] Thus, for neoliberals, the real obstacle to cooperating under anarchy is not relative gains-seeking behavior, but the tendency of actors to cheat so as to maximize their own gains.

Interdependence, institutions, and regimes

Moreover, as we noted in chapter 1, liberals of all stripes believe that anarchy is modified by **interdependence** among actors. Actors have

interdependence a relationship in which two or more actors are sensitive and vulnerable to each other's behavior and in which actions taken by one affect the other.

multiple channels of communication among governments and among societies, and they interact on numerous issues. As the world grows more complex, they increasingly depend on one another for security and economic well-being, and the actions of each will have a ripple effect that ultimately has an impact on others. Interdependence may be symmetrical, that is situations in which actors are equally dependent on each other, or asymmetrical, that is situations in which some actors depend more on others than others depend on them.

complex interdependence
an interdependent relationship among actors characterized by multiple channels of interaction, multiple issues, and the absence of military force.

Neoliberals refer to situations of mutual dependence as **complex interdependence**, a concept that neoliberal political scientists Robert O. Keohane and Joseph S. Nye argue "is clearly liberal rather than realist" and stands "in opposition to a realist ideal-typical view of world politics."[13] Thus, actors are *sensitive* to one another's behavior and may be *vulnerable* as well. Sensitivity is the speed with which changes in one part of the world affect other parts and the magnitude of those effects. Thus, if the US Federal Reserve were to raise interest rates at home, the effect would be global and almost instantaneously foreign funds would flow into the United States in search of higher rates of return. Vulnerability refers to the alternatives actors have in seeking to limit the effects of change. For example, the West is highly vulnerable to oil shortages because at present there are few adequate energy substitutes.

Neoliberals acknowledge that the realist perspective is useful under conditions where military security is at stake, but they claim that this perspective is less useful to understanding issues in which friendly actors are interacting or in which politics and economics mix, as in trade or investment. Military capability, they say, is largely irrelevant to such issues.

Cheating is much more easily controlled than competition over relative gains. So, unlike their neorealist counterparts, neoliberals see a way to achieve cooperation under anarchy: international institutions or international regimes (some scholars use these terms interchangeably). Keohane explains that institutions are "persistent and connected sets of rules (formal and informal) that prescribe behavioral roles, constrain activity, and shape expectations."[14] International regimes are a form of institution that exists within a particular issue-area of global politics. A regime is a set of principles, rules, norms, and decision-making procedures that regulate activity in a given issue of international relations. For regime theorists, *principles* are "beliefs of fact, causation, and rectitude"; *norms* are standards of behavior defining the rights and obligations of actors; *rules* allow and disallow specific actions; and *decision-making procedures* refer to the practices for making and implementing collective choices.[15]

An international institution, thus viewed, is much more than an international organization like NATO or the EU. Oran Young expresses the contrast between institutions and organizations most clearly: "organizations . . . are material entities possessing physical locations (or seats), offices, personnel, equipment, and budgets. . . . Organizations generally possess legal personality in the sense that they are authorized to enter into contracts, own property . . . and so forth."[16] International organizations may exist to administer international institutions, but others are free-standing entities.

For Keohane and other neoliberals, such institutions have multiple benefits. In regard to cheating, they make it possible to monitor and verify agreements, and they offer the possibility of punishment should a state renege on a promise. Additionally, institutions reduce the costs involved in negotiating and implementing agreements. They do so by providing access to more and better-quality information, including knowledge of other states' intentions, the strength of their preferences, their willingness to abide by agreements, and the extent of their capabilities. They further reduce uncertainty in global politics by linking cooperation across a range of related issues.[17]

The rise and decline of a regime: nuclear nonproliferation

One of the most dangerous trends in global politics today is the proliferation of weapons of mass destruction (WMD). When the Cold War ended few countries possessed nuclear weapons. At that time, the United States, the Soviet Union, Britain, France, and China were the nuclear powers. Although vertical proliferation – increasing armaments within a country – largely ended with the break-up of the Soviet Union, horizontal proliferation – spreading nuclear weapons to other actors – became a serious problem. India[18] and Pakistan, which are de facto nuclear powers, and Israel, which also has a nuclear capability, have never signed the Nuclear Nonproliferation Treaty (NPT). In recent decades, other countries have acquired nuclear weapons (North Korea) or are seeking to do so (Iran). A number have relinquished nuclear weapons: in 1991 South Africa voluntarily dismantled six completed bombs; in the 1990s Ukraine and Belarus returned to Russia the nuclear weapons they inherited when the Soviet Union collapsed.

Today's nuclear nonproliferation regime evolved out of efforts during the Cold War to limit horizontal proliferation. In 1963, US President John F. Kennedy predicted that, if left unchecked, 15 to 20 states could join the nuclear club within the decade (see Key document: President Kennedy's press conference). The nuclear nonproliferation regime is designed to regulate the spread of nuclear weapons to non-nuclear weapons states to prevent the massive proliferation President Kennedy predicted. The fundamental principle underlying this regime is that nuclear proliferation must be limited, because the more nuclear weapons states there are, the more likely it is that nuclear weapons will eventually be used. This principle, as well as the regime's norms, rules, and some decision-making procedures, are primarily (but not exclusively) found in the Nuclear Nonproliferation Treaty. The cornerstone of this regime, the NPT (see also chapter 8, p. 383), was signed in 1968 and entered into force in 1970. Today its membership is nearly universal, with only India, Pakistan, Israel, and North Korea – all de facto or presumed nuclear states – not participating. The NPT has four main provisions:

1 No nuclear power is to transfer nuclear weapons technology to non-nuclear states.
2 No non-nuclear-armed state is to develop nuclear weapons technology.
3 All non-nuclear states that use nuclear energy are to have safeguards and are to conclude a treaty with the International Atomic Energy Agency (IAEA) for inspecting nuclear facilities.

disarmament any effort to reduce the number of weapons in actors' arsenals.

4 Nuclear weapons states are to pursue negotiations to end the nuclear arms race and begin nuclear **disarmament**.

The NPT regime is widely criticized for having a dual standard. The United States, Russia, Britain, France, and China are recognized as nuclear weapons states because they had such weapons when the NPT was negotiated. They are supposed to make progress toward nuclear disarmament but have not done so,[19] even while others are prohibited from acquiring *any* nuclear weapons.

Figure 6.1 Nuclear hypocrisy
Steve Benson,
www.politicalcartoons.com

Key document   President Kennedy's press conference

In 1963, as efforts were underway to negotiate a nuclear test ban
treaty, US President John F. Kennedy discussed in a press conference
the dangers of nuclear proliferation – both vertical and horizontal.

Q Mr. President, after all of the years of failure in attempting to reach a
nuclear test ban agreement at Geneva, and in view of the current stalemate
at the Geneva Conference, do you still really have any hope of arriving at a
nuclear test ban agreement?

The President Well, my hopes are somewhat dimmed, but nevertheless,
I still hope. The fact of the matter is . . . what we are disagreeing about are
the number of inspections, but at least the principle of inspection is
accepted. Now, the reason why we keep moving and working on this
question, taking up a good deal of energy and effort, is because personally
I am haunted by the feeling that by 1970, unless we are successful, there
may be 10 nuclear powers instead of 4, and by 1975, 15 or 20.

With all the history of war, and the human race's history unfortunately
has been a good deal more war than peace, with nuclear weapons
distributed all through the world, and available, and the strong reluctance
of any people to accept defeat, I see the possibility in the 1970's of the
President of the United States having to face a world in which 15 or 20 or
25 nations may have these weapons. I regard that as the greatest possible
danger and hazard.

Now, I am not even talking about the contamination of the atmosphere
which would come when all of these nations begin testing, but as you
know, every test does affect generations which are still away from us. . . .
Now, the other point I want to make is that we test and test and test, and
you finally get weapons which are increasingly sophisticated. But the fact
of the matter is that somebody may test 10 or 15 times and get a weapon
which is not nearly as good as these megaton weapons, but nevertheless,
they are two or three times what the weapon was which destroyed
Hiroshima, or Nagasaki, and that was dreadful enough.

So I think that we have a good deal to gain if we get a test agreement,
and so we are going to keep at it. Now, Members of Congress, who may
object to that will have their chance to vote "aye" or "nay" if we are
successful in a treaty and we present it to the Senate. In the meantime, we
are going to stay at it.[20]

Additional norms and rules of the nuclear nonproliferation regime are articulated in a wide array of organizations, agreements, and less formal arrangements, including the International Atomic Energy Agency (IAEA), the Nuclear Suppliers Group (NSG), the Proliferation Security Initiative (PSI), and several Nuclear Weapons Free Zones (NWFZs).

The International Atomic Energy Agency is a central element in this regime. The IAEA was created in 1957 as part of the United Nations system to work with its member states, of which there are 142 today, and other partners to support safe, secure, and peaceful nuclear technologies. The IAEA does this primarily through **safeguards** agreements negotiated with member states. Member states declare to the IAEA all nuclear materials in their possession and all activities employing nuclear materials and regularly submit their activities and facilities to IAEA inspectors for review. This allows the IAEA to verify that non-nuclear weapons states are upholding their NPT obligation not to develop a nuclear weapons program. Since the early 1990s, and the discovery of a clandestine nuclear weapons program in Iraq following the Persian Gulf War, the IAEA also has attempted to uncover undeclared nuclear activities. Thus, the IAEA is a vital component of the nonproliferation regime for its efforts to monitor declared nuclear materials and ensure they are not diverted to nuclear weapons programs in non-nuclear weapons states and to uncover and stop undeclared activities.[21]

The Nuclear Suppliers Group is a third element in the nuclear nonproliferation regime. The NSG is an **export-control** group comprised of 30 countries that supply nuclear materials, equipment, and technology on the global market. This group meets regularly to establish guidelines for nuclear and nuclear-related exports in an effort to ensure that such materials and technologies are not sold or transferred to countries aspiring to develop nuclear weapons programs. Ultimately, however, participating governments implement the guidelines in accordance with their national laws and licensing requirements. There is no global authority to compel states to implement the export controls.

The Proliferation Security Initiative (PSI) is an informal arrangement – not a treaty or an organization – intended to stop the transfer of nuclear materials to terrorists and countries that are suspected of developing WMD programs. Participants patrol the seas, air, and land, searching vessels suspected of shipping WMD and related materials to potential proliferators. All interdictions must take place under existing international and national laws, which do not allow ships to be searched simply because they are suspected of transporting WMD. However, PSI partners have begun to expand their legal authority by negotiating bilateral boarding agreements that pre-approve boarding some ships or

safeguards measures intended to ensure the security of nuclear materials and technologies.

export controls rules limiting the export of goods, technology, and data, particularly that which is considered to have a dual-use or a military purpose.

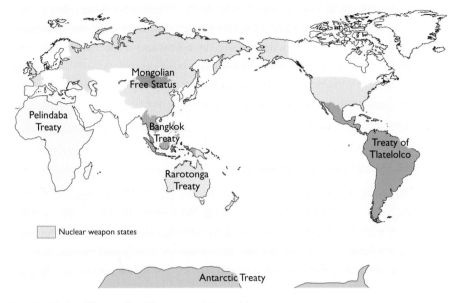

Map 6.1   Nuclear Weapons Free Zones around the world

grant approval to board more quickly. Since US President George W. Bush first announced the arrangement in May 2003, over 75 states have expressed support for the initiative or actively committed to it.[22]

Nuclear Weapons Free Zones constitute yet another element in the nuclear nonproliferation regime. These are regions in which it is illegal to "develop, manufacture, stockpile, acquire, possess, or control any nuclear explosive device."[23] Civilian nuclear programs – to generate energy – are allowed within NWFZs. Antarctica (Antarctic Treaty), the South Pacific (Treaty of Rarotonga), Latin America and the Caribbean (Treaty of Tlatelolco), and Southeast Asia (Bangkok Treaty) are all NWFZs (see Map 6.1). African states have negotiated a treaty creating a NWFZ (the Treaty of Pelindaba), but this agreement has yet to enter into force. These arrangements seek to prevent horizontal proliferation as well as achieve the complete disarmament of nuclear weapons states.

Each of these arrangements contributes to the nuclear nonproliferation regime by reinforcing the regime's underlying principle that steps should be taken to halt the spread of nuclear weapons and articulating norms and rules in support of this principle. However, there are several weak features to this regime, all of which follow from anarchy. In particular, without a global authority to coerce them, some states can refuse to participate as India, Pakistan, Israel, and North Korea have done. Others challenge the underlying principle that non-nuclear weapons states should not develop a nuclear weapons capability at the same time that they participate in one or more elements of the regime. Iran sits here today. North Korea also challenged this principle when it was still a party to the NPT. Finally, even those states that agree with the principle of nonproliferation may not uphold the norms and rules that have developed to stop it – often for domestic political reasons.

We now examine the dangers of horizontal proliferation to understand why nonproliferation has achieved the status of a principle in global politics.

Dangers of horizontal proliferation

Some scholars are not greatly concerned by horizontal proliferation. Neorealist Kenneth Waltz argues that "with more nuclear states the world will have a promising future" because he believes that the United States and Russia will retain immense superiority in WMD and that the spread of nuclear weapons will enhance deterrence and prevent war much as it did in the Cold War.[24] There are, however, several reasons why such optimism is probably misplaced.

1 The leaders of some of the nuclear aspirants are ruthless and may be risk-takers. North Korea's Kim Jong Il (1942–) has spent most of his life isolated from the world outside his country. Known as the "Dear Leader," he succeeded his father Kim Il Sung (the "Great Leader") (1912–94) in 1994 and, like his father, has been elevated to almost god-like status by those surrounding him. His ruthlessness is reflected in policies that simultaneously make North Korea's military expenditures the highest in the world in relation to the country's total wealth, while causing massive famine that killed millions of North Koreans.

   Iran is governed by highly conservative Shia mullahs who have supported international terrorism. In June 2005, the country elected as its president Mahmoud Ahmadinejad, a former mayor of Tehran.[25] In one speech, he declared that Israel should be "wiped off the map,"[26] and he has called the Holocaust a "myth," suggesting that it was invented to provide an excuse for creating Israel. Overall, leaders like Ahmadinejad have little respect for international norms that they believe serve Western interests.

2 The fact that more fingers would be on more triggers creates a higher probability of a nuclear accident. As more countries acquire WMD, there is a greater likelihood that an individual in a sensitive position might become irrational or that human mistakes and technical mishaps could lead to an accident or a fatal mistake in judgment.

3 Countries most eager to obtain WMD are involved in dangerous regional quarrels that threaten war. Pakistan and India remain at odds

over Kashmir; Iran has threatened Israel; and the Korean Peninsula remains one of the world's most dangerous places.

4   The acquisition of WMD by some countries increases incentives for others to obtain similar weapons. In Asia, for example, North Korea's WMD creates pressure on Japan to acquire such weapons, and acquisition of nuclear weapons by Iran's Shia leaders could produce pressure on Sunni Arab countries like Saudi Arabia to emulate them.

5   Recent nuclear states are armed with relatively primitive delivery systems that are vulnerable to an enemy's first strike. As we shall see, this is a dangerous situation in which incentives to attack first are high and strategic stability is low.

6   Finally, the proliferation of WMD to additional countries heightens the possibility that such weapons may find their way into the hands of terrorists like Osama bin Laden who would have few scruples against using them.

Let us now examine the two most vexing cases of nuclear proliferation: North Korea and Iran.

North Korea and Iran

The United States and Britain invaded Iraq in 2003 partly to prevent Saddam Hussein from acquiring WMD. In fact, the other two members of what George W. Bush had called the "axis of evil," North Korea and Iran, were much closer to acquiring usable nuclear weapons than Iraq.[27]

North Korea began constructing a nuclear reactor at Yongbyon in 1980 which became operational several years later. Inspections by the IAEA[28] in 1992 suggested that North Korea had diverted weapons-grade plutonium from the facility that could be used to manufacture nuclear weapons. In May 1994, North Korea began to remove spent fuel rods from Yongbyon but refused to allow the IAEA to inspect them in order to determine how long they had been in the reactor to find out whether some had been secretly removed earlier, possibly for diversion to WMD. When North Korea announced its intention to withdraw from the NPT, the United States agreed to resume negotiations with North Korea on a broad range of issues provided the North Koreans reversed that decision and allowed the IAEA to inspect the reactor. However, by mixing the old and new fuel rods it extracted from the reactor, North Korea made it impossible for IAEA inspectors to determine whether some had been clandestinely removed at an earlier date.

As it became evident in the early 1990s that North Korea was bent on acquiring nuclear weapons, US–North Korean negotiations were held to settle the problem. Often stormy, the negotiations involved threats of

Figure 6.2 The 5MW nuclear
reactor at the Yongbyon facility
Courtesy of DigitalGlobe

sanctions and even war. The sudden death of North Korea's long-time
leader Kim Il Sung in July 1994 slowed the pace of negotiations, even
as North Korea had amassed enough used nuclear fuel rods to make
several bombs. A US–North Korean deal (Framework Agreement) was
hammered out under which (1) North Korea would freeze its nuclear
program, would not refuel its Yongbyon reactor, and would allow
inspections of its used fuel rods; (2) the United States and North Korea
would establish diplomatic and economic relations; (3) North Korea
would open its nuclear installations to international inspection within
five years; (4) North Korea would replace its graphite nuclear reactor
(from which plutonium can be reprocessed relatively easily) with
light-water reactors provided by South Korea; (5) North Korea would
remain a party to the NPT; (6) the United States would provide enough
free coal and fuel to satisfy North Korea's interim energy needs; and
(7) North Korea would ultimately dismantle key plants involved in its
nuclear program.

The agreement, however, fell apart amid acrimony. Things seemed to
go well at the beginning with an easing of US economic sanctions against
North Korea and initial steps toward constructing a light-water reactor in
the North. However, in 2002 the United States learned that North Korea
was secretly trying to enrich uranium for making nuclear weapons, and in
October of that year the North Koreans admitted this, even though it
violated both the NPT and the 1994 agreement. The following month
US fuel shipments to North Korea were halted. For its part, North Korea

expelled IAEA inspectors and restarted its Yongbyon plutonium reactor, ostensibly to replace the fuel oil that the United States was not providing in order to generate electricity. Showing new flexibility, the Bush administration announced it had no plans to attack North Korea and joined new talks in April 2003. These so-called six-party talks involved the two Koreas, Russia, China, Japan, and the United States and aimed to persuade North Korea to give up its WMD program in return for economic and political benefits.[29]

American intelligence agencies estimated that by early 2005, North Korea had stockpiled about 13 nuclear bombs from uranium and plutonium,[30] as well as missiles, one of which it launched in the direction of Japan that year. On February 10, 2005, North Korea publicly declared that it had nuclear weapons that it needed to deter a US attack and was leaving the six-party talks. Nevertheless, a new round of talks was held and in September 2005 the negotiators announced an agreement in principle under which North Korea would give up its nuclear weapons, the United States and South Korea would affirm that they have no such weapons in Korea, the United States would publicly declare it will not attack the North, and the United States and Japan would begin to normalize diplomatic and economic relations with North Korea. A major stumbling block, however, remained concerning whether the United States and South Korea would construct light-water nuclear reactors in North Korea to provide for that country's energy needs. The US demands at a meeting in November 2005 that North Korea shut down its nuclear programs before it would consider making such a commitment, accomplished little.

The final proof emerged that nonproliferation efforts had failed when, on October 9, 2006, North Korea announced it had conducted its first test of a nuclear weapon. The blast was a fraction of that achieved over Hiroshima in 1945, but atmospheric tests confirmed that a nuclear warhead had been detonated. This test, however, does not mark the end of the regime's involvement in North Korea. Efforts continue to persuade North Korea to abandon its program. On October 14, the UN Security Council voted to impose weapons and financial sanctions on North Korea. In addition, Resolution 1718 demands that North Korea not conduct any more nuclear tests or launch ballistic missiles, that it rejoin the NPT, and that it abandon "all nuclear weapons and existing nuclear programmes in a complete, verifiable and irreversible manner."[31] In February 2007, a tentative agreement was reached under which North Korea would shut down its Yongbyon reactor, readmit IAEA inspectors, and provide information about all its nuclear programs in return for fuel supplies, direct talks with the US leading to normalizing diplomatic relations, and release of North Korean funds previously frozen in Macao bank.

North Korea's resistance to US counter-proliferation efforts seems to have emboldened Iran to take additional steps toward acquiring nuclear weapons as well. Iran apparently embarked on an effort to acquire WMD and ballistic missiles after its bloody conflict with Iraq (1981–88). Information surfaced in 2002 that Iran was using its pilot nuclear facilities at Natanz and Arak to make weapons-grade uranium. In 2003, IAEA inspectors acquired evidence of these efforts. In addition, Iran and North Korea have worked together on missile development, and US intelligence obtained computer files that suggested that Iran was designing a missile cone for a nuclear warhead.[32]

On behalf of the European Union, Britain, France, and Germany, with American approval, sought to dissuade Iran from its enrichment efforts in return for political and economic benefits, and in November 2004 Iran temporarily did so. In August 2005, Iran again began to convert uranium, though not enriching it, leading the three European countries to ask the IAEA to bring the matter to the UN Security Council. In January 2006, Iran once more began uranium enrichment in its centrifuges at Natanz, refusing a compromise offered by Russia to enrich Iranian uranium and then returning it to Iran for use in generating energy.

As these two brief cases illustrate, the nuclear nonproliferation regime is designed to prevent non-nuclear weapons states from violating the global norm against the proliferation of nuclear weapons and to uncover and reverse such violations when they occur. This is consistent with the neoliberal view of international institutions and regimes as efficient solutions to problems of collective action. It is an imperfect regime, but this is understandable – indeed, expected – in an anarchic global system. Constructivists, however, to whom we now turn, do regard anarchy as a problem that states have created for themselves in a "world of our making."[33]

The constructivist critique: "Anarchy Is What States Make of It"

Unlike neorealists and neoliberals, constructivists challenge the idea that anarchy is the dominant feature of global politics. In particular, they argue that a self-help international system does not logically follow from anarchy. Rather, a self-help system is an institution, defined as a "relatively stable set or 'structure' of identities and interests," constructed out of interactions among actors in anarchy. Constructivist Alexander Wendt argues "it is through reciprocal interaction . . . that we create and instantiate the relatively enduring social structures" that define our identities and interests.[34] In other words, security systems based upon self-help only evolve out of cycles of interaction in which each actor behaves in a manner that is threatening to others. This series of interactions creates an expectation (an institution) that the "other" cannot be trusted. According to Wendt, in the absence of preexisting social institutions, there is no reason to assume other actors will be threatening (see Key document: "Anarchy Is What States Make of It").

Hostility need not be a product of anarchy. So how to account for the emergence of this cycle of interactions that results in a self-help system? Some states, Wendt argues, may become predisposed to aggression either because of human nature, domestic politics, or as a result of some past wrong. By this theory, just one aggressive state forces all others to practice self-help power politics.

Key document   "Anarchy Is What States Make of It"[35]

In a seminal article, constructivist Alexander Wendt argued that realists were incorrect in claiming that anarchy – a key structural feature – makes hostility and conflict inevitable. Instead, using an imagined alien visit to Earth as an illustration, Wendt argued that interaction creates identities that define interests and that structure does not determine behavior.

> Would we assume, a priori, that we were about to be attacked if we are ever contacted by members of an alien civilization? I think not. We would be highly alert, of course, but whether we placed our military forces on alert or launched an attack would depend on how we interpreted the import of their first gesture for our security – if only to avoid making an immediate enemy out of what may be a dangerous adversary. The possibility of error, in other words, does not force us to act on the assumption that the aliens are threatening: action depends on the probabilities we assign, and these are in key part a function of what the aliens do; *prior to their gesture, we have no systematic basis for assigning probabilities*. If their first gesture is to appear with a thousand spaceships and destroy New York, we will define the situation as threatening and respond accordingly. But if they appear with one spaceship, saying what seems to be "we come in peace," we will feel "reassured" and will probably respond with a gesture intended to reassure them, even if this gesture is not necessarily interpreted by them as such.[36]

The debate over anarchy reflects differences over the relative importance and role of power in global politics. We will now examine power and influence and the competing versions of its impact on the way actors behave in an anarchic world.

The quest for power and influence

What is power, and how do we know it when we see it? Power has always been central to studies of conflict. Realists in particular use power to explain behavior in global politics, arguing that the field is defined by a struggle for power in which actors' interests are determined by how strong or weak they are relative to one another. Power is pervasive, then, and realists regard it as the "currency" of global politics in the sense that, like money, it is a means to achieve goals, a reserve or stockpile for future contingencies, and an asset in itself. They believe that all instruments of foreign policy, including diplomacy, trade, alliances, and treaties, should be judged by how they enhance national power.[37]

According to one scholar: "Power in international politics is like the weather. Everyone talks about it, but few understand it."[38] Most people think they know a powerful actor when they see one, but that does not mean that everyone agrees on what makes that actor powerful. It is tempting to conceptualize power as a tangible object or capability that permits an actor to do as it wishes. Thus political scientist Inis Claude defines power as "military capability – the elements which contribute directly or indirectly to the capacity to coerce, kill, and destroy."[39] However, this definition confuses capabilities that *might* contribute to power with power itself. If we fall prey to this confusion, then we cannot satisfactorily explain how a few thousand Iraqi insurgents can resist the US superpower. Thus, most analysts agree that power is a *relationship* in which one actor can cause another to do what it wishes. It is, as Kenneth Waltz puts it "the capacity to produce an intended effect."[40] Part of the reason why some observers regard power as a thing rather than a relationship is because the word is a noun and has no verb form. By contrast, influence can be used as a verb that links a sentence's subject (the influencer) with a direct object (that which is influenced) and so conveys the idea of a relationship.

Actors can use capabilities in different ways to increase their influence. Thus, political scientist Joseph Nye makes an important distinction between (1) "the direct or commanding method of exercising power" by use of coercion and rewards (**hard power**) and (2) influence by virtue of cultural attraction and ideology that shape others' preferences (**soft power**).[41] Unlike hard power, soft power arises from cultural and reputational factors that produce prestige, and Nye believes that America's soft power is more effective and durable than its hard power. With soft power, an actor's preferences are seen as legitimate. Soviet dictator Josef Stalin, when warned of the pope's influence in Eastern Europe, is reputed to have asked "The Pope? How many divisions has he got?" Stalin apparently believed that because the pope lacked hard power

hard power power based on the use of coercion and rewards.

soft power power based on culture and reputation and that is used to set the global agenda and shape the preferences of others.

he was unable to exercise influence. As the USSR would discover in later decades, especially after John Paul II (1920–2005), who was from Poland, became pope in 1978, papal influence among Eastern European Catholics was considerable. Indeed, John Paul played a major role in undermining Soviet influence in Eastern Europe and ultimately bringing about the end of communism.

Soft power is related to what is called **structural power**. Political economist Susan Strange described structural power as "the power to decide how things shall be done, the power to shape frameworks within which states relate to each other, relate to people, or relate to corporate enterprises,"[42] a definition similar to that of neo-Marxist Immanuel Wallerstein who wrote of the ability of a leading country to "impose its rules and its wishes (at the very least by effective veto power) in the economic, political, military, diplomatic and even cultural arenas."[43] Such power may flow from the reputational and cultural factors, including a dominant language like English and control of expertise and knowledge, encompassed by soft power, and allows a global leader to make the "rules of the game" and force others to follow those rules. Strange described four sources of structural power: (1) control over security from violence, (2) control of economic production, (3) control of systems of finance and credit, and (4) influence over knowledge and information.[44] Thus, in the nineteenth century, Great Britain exercised structural power that initiated and maintained a system of free trade and expanded and upheld a system of international law. Similarly, after World War II, the United States enjoyed unique structural power that allowed it to construct and maintain the Bretton-Woods system (chapter 11, p. 519) of international economic institutions, including the World Bank (IBRD), the International Monetary Fund (IMF), and the General Agreement on Tariffs and Trade (GATT).

The idea of soft power is also implicit in the postpositivist view that language or "discourse" is a source of power because it imposes specific interpretations and meanings upon political life. In turn, those who control the "meaning" of events and institutions in global politics are able to influence others to think as they do, while ignoring other interpretations and those who hold them. Postpositivists, writes political scientist Jennifer Sterling-Folker, do not regard meaning-making as "an individual or a random activity." Instead, it "precedes from society and culture" and involves the "subjugation" of some individuals and groups by others.[45]

Hard power assumes two forms – coercion, or "sticks," and rewards, or "carrots." Coercive power is "the ability to move others by the threat or infliction of deprivations," and reward power is "the ability to do so

structural power the power to determine how things will be done.

deterrence a strategy aimed at preventing an adversary from acting in a certain way by threatening to retaliate with military force.

compellence the threat or use of force to make an adversary alter its behavior.

appeasement a policy of concessions that aims to satisfy another actor's grievances and thereby keep the peace.

capabilities resources available to actors that can be used to influence other actors.

through promises or grants of benefits."[46] Sometimes hard power is called *situational power* because its use involves manipulating negative and positive incentives that worsen or improve an adversary's situation. Coercion involves making an adversary modify its behavior to avoid or end punishment and other disincentives, whereas reward involves the use of positive incentives contingent on the target's doing as the influencer wishes. Threats and promises are like debts that must be paid if actors are to keep their reputations, and they should be distinguished from coercion and rewards. As we shall see in chapter 8 (pp. 336–7), threats are the bases of **deterrence** and **compellence** strategies.

Promises and rewards are the bases of **appeasement**, a strategy of achieving agreement or maintaining peace by making concessions to satisfy another actor's justified grievances. As we saw in chapter 3 (pp. 139–42), appeasement gained an infamous reputation in the 1930s in Western efforts to satisfy Hitler, with disastrous results, and came to mean giving in to the demands of those making threats. However, the strategy was used frequently and with great success by diplomats in the eighteenth century to influence one another peacefully.

One way to infer power is to observe actors' relative capabilities. **Capabilities** are an actor's *means of achieving power*. Determining which capabilities enhance power can be complicated, as many sources of power exist. Some capabilities are tangible, and thus relatively easy to measure, while others like morale and leadership are intangible and can only be estimated. Tangible capabilities include:

- *Military capability* How large an army does an actor have? How many weapons? What kinds of weapons and of what quality? In short, the greater the military capability of an actor on all of these dimensions, the greater its power tends to be. However, it is rare for a country to rank high on all dimensions of military capability. For example, as an actor acquires more technologically advanced weaponry, it may reduce its army's size.
- *Economic resources* How large is the actor's gross national product? Is the actor industrialized? What is its level of technological development? Does it have a diversified economy?
- *Natural resources* Does the actor have access to resources to support its military and economic capabilities?
- *Population* How large is an actor's population? A large population can contribute to a larger military and labor force, but it is important to consider a population's age, health, and education. Are there enough people of the right age to fight or work? Do they have the skills to use modern military technology? Is the population united behind its government, or do cleavages threaten internal unity?

- *Geography*   How large a territory does an actor control? Does it have access to the sea? Does its terrain provide natural defenses like mountains and rivers? Do the terrain, climate, and geography permit agriculture or other industry?

The Composite Index of National Capabilities (CINC) provides an example of how political scientists use such tangible capabilities to analyze state power. This composite, part of the Correlates of War (COW) dataset,[47] is made up of six tangible indicators of power: military personnel, military expenditures, iron and steel production, energy consumption, total population, and urban population. Figure 6.3 illustrates relative US and Russian power, using CINC scores, since the outbreak of World War II.

Tangible capabilities tell only part of the story, however. Consider the following relationships:

China versus Japan   China has a larger population and a larger economic market than Japan, but Japan has a higher level of technology. China's GDP is about twice Japan's. China also has a larger army than Japan and has nuclear weapons, but many of Japan's advanced technologies could be converted to military applications (including nuclear weapons). Finally, Japan has a military alliance with the United States. Which is more powerful, China or Japan?

Vietnam versus the United States   The United States had military, economic, and resource preponderance, but failed to win its war against communist North Vietnam. After 20 years of involvement, the United States withdrew the last of its troops in 1973, and North Vietnam achieved its goal of unifying the entire country under its leadership. Which country was more powerful?

The answers to such questions are elusive for several reasons. Most important, specific capabilities do not produce generalized power because they are only suitable for particular situations. Japan's technology is critical to China's effort to modernize, while China's market is a vital destination for Japan's exports. In this sense, each has leverage over the other. Finally, US military superiority in Vietnam was insufficient to achieve victory because the real struggle was for what President Lyndon Johnson called "the hearts and minds" of the Vietnamese people. Compared to North Vietnam's combination of ideology, nationalism, and guerrilla tactics, America's military prowess was poorly suited to this task.

A second reason why an actor's advantage in tangible resources is not sufficient to judge its relative power is the role of intangible resources

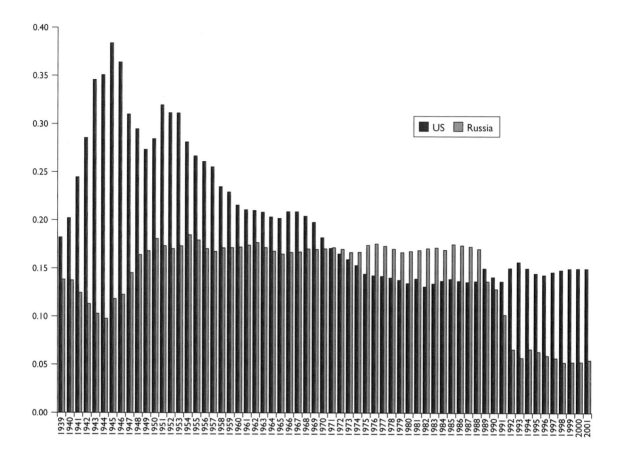

Figure 6.3 US and Soviet power compared

resolve the willingness to use force.

which determine how effectively an actor can utilize its tangible capabilities. The most important of these intangible factors are:

- ***Resolve*** Economic, military, and other tangible resources have little value if a government lacks the will to use them. Is an actor determined to use resources to realize its foreign-policy goals? In the case of Vietnam, Americans wearied of the prolonged struggle before their foes did and were less willing to accept high casualties than were the Vietnamese.
- *Leadership and skill* Are leaders able to rally citizens in support of policies? Can they effectively mobilize resources to pursue their policy? US policy in the Vietnam War, for example, was undermined by President Johnson's inability to mobilize public support for his policy between 1965 and 1968.
- *Intelligence* Do decision-makers understand the interests and capabilities of potential foes? Do they have reliable information about adversaries' intentions and capabilities? The absence of such information has been a key impediment to US efforts to fight global terrorism.

- *Diplomacy* How effectively do a country's diplomats represent its interests abroad? Effective diplomats can communicate their country's interests, gauge others' interests, anticipate others' actions, and negotiate compromises.

Did you know?

Former CIA Director, Ray S. Cline, developed a mathematical equation for power:

$$Pp = (C + E + M) \times (S + W)$$

In this formula, each element is given a numerical value and combined this way: Potential power is composed of Critical mass (population, land, and position) plus Economic, and Military capabilities times Strategic purpose (goals and objectives) and Will. In Cline's analysis of the Cold War, the United States received a numerical score of 35 and the USSR a score of 67.5.[48]

A number of conclusions about power flow from what we have said.

1 Many elements of power cannot be measured before an actor uses its capabilities. For example, when analysts refer to "US power" or the "power of Iraqi insurgents," they are really describing their expectations about how well these actors can mobilize and use the resources available to them. In other words, they are referring to **potential power** rather than **actual power**.

2 Power is perceptual. What matters most is how much power others *think* an actor has, rather than how much it *really* has. Sometimes, an actor can manipulate others into thinking it has more power than it really has, for example, by bluffing them into thinking it will use capabilities that it has no intention of using or does not even have.

3 Power is relative in the sense that "more" or "less" power *always* implies a comparison with the power of other actors. Thus, South Africa and Nigeria are superpowers in relation to other African countries, as is China in relation to its Asian neighbors.

4 Capabilities that are of use in one context may be of little value in another. Thus, the quality of US military forces promises great power in the event of war, but it does not afford any advantage where trade is at stake. Indeed, employing the wrong capabilities may actually harm one's interests. For example, if the United States threatened military action in the event of a trade dispute with Europe – say, because Europeans refused to import America's genetically modified foods – this would be counter-productive, alienating the Europeans.

potential power the capabilities that an actor might use to create a power relationship.

actual power the power an actor is able to realize in practice; actual power can only be measured by observing the changed behavior of others.

5 An actor's relative power can only be inferred by observing whether the target has altered its behavior, in what direction, and to what extent as a result of the actor's effort. In other words, relative power only becomes visible *after* it has been exerted.[49] A powerful actor can alter the behavior of those it seeks to influence, whereas a weak one cannot. Analysis that is simple in theory, however, is complex in practice. For example, it is difficult to determine what caused the change in the target's behavior. Perhaps, the target had intended to change its policies on its own. We speak of the *chameleon effect* (named after the small lizard that changes colors to blend with its surroundings) when a target changes policies because it wants to rather than because of the power of the influencer. We speak of the *satellite effect* when actors behave in tandem, and observers misinterpret the direction of the influence. Thus, during the Cold War, when the USSR and Ukraine voted the same way in the UN, an ill-informed observer might erroneously have concluded that the Ukraine was exerting power over the Soviet Union rather than the reverse.

6 Sometimes a power relationship remains almost invisible and can only be inferred. Deterrence reflects the puzzle. Deterrence aims to prevent an adversary from pursuing aggressive goals by threatening military force in retaliation if it does so. The problem is that when deterrence is successful, the adversary will *not have acted*. During the Cold War, the USSR did not attack the US, but we cannot know whether it ever intended to do so or not. Paradoxically, it is easier for us to know when deterrence has failed, because then the adversary will have visibly defied the threat.

To this point, we have considered what power is and some of the problems in measuring it. We have also examined the capabilities that give rise to power. But how do actors use their capabilities?

As you have seen in this section, power is a central concept for analyzing global politics, especially for realists who try to discern the relationship between power and war. Realists regard war as the most important fact of global politics. Historically, states have repeatedly resorted to war to get what they want, and the threat of war has served as a principal instrument for exercising influence. But are wars necessary to achieve objectives? How do wars happen? Can they be prevented? Such questions have long fascinated scholars and practitioners alike.

In what follows, we will review a variety of efforts to determine the causes of war. Many of these efforts are the work of those described in chapter 1 (pp. 29–31) as scholars who were part of the behavioral revolution and sought to emulate the research methods of natural scientists. What follows provides a taste of such scholarship. These scholars realized that identifying causes of war that cannot be altered (such as human nature) are of little use to policy-makers. If the factors that trigger war cannot be changed, then policies cannot be fashioned to prevent its outbreak. We might as well shrug our shoulders, conclude that sooner or later we will find ourselves in another war, and turn our energy to more rewarding research problems. In fact, as we shall see, there are many kinds of wars and many possible causes.

Explaining war between states has long been a central objective of international relations scholars, as war is one phenomenon that most cultures and peoples have in common. As one prominent war scholar observes: "Genesis records two thousand years of history from biblical creation to the time [of] . . . the first war. Never again would two thousand years pass – or even two hundred – without war."[50] However, war is a concept that in popular discourse refers to a diverse group of activities. For instance, conflicts defined as wars vary widely in their *scope* – from internal conflicts among subnational groups to conflicts between neighboring states, to world wars. They also vary in *intensity* – from a few hundred deaths to tens of thousands, even millions, of deaths. And they vary in their *duration* – from, as in the Six Day War (June 5–10, 1967), a few short days (or hours in the event of a nuclear exchange) to decades, as in the Hundred Years' (1337–1453) or Thirty Years' wars (1618–48).

The first step in analyzing complex international events like war is to define and categorize the phenomena being studied. In practice, this means distinguishing between interstate and intrastate wars: those waged *between* and *within* states. Because international relations scholars have long focused on interstate relations, there is a substantial body of theory explaining war between states. Only in recent decades, with an upsurge in civil wars, have scholars begun to focus on intrastate wars as well. One widely accepted definition of interstate war among behavioral scholars is "a military conflict waged between (or among) national entities, at least one of which is a *state*, which results in at least 1,000 battle deaths of military personnel."[51] This definition is arbitrary, as any must necessarily be, but it allows for the systematic collection and analysis of war data by scholars who share an identical definition of the phenomenon that they are studying. Recent research has expanded a typology of war to include, in addition to interstate war, extra-state wars between a state and a nonstate actor outside its borders and intrastate wars between or among two groups within a state's borders.[52]

In this section we introduce the factors that political scientists believe contribute to the outbreak of interstate war. As we saw in chapter 1, political scientists find it helpful to separate the sources of war according to the level of analysis at which they operate. Although explanations from each level increase our understanding of war, no single explanation is adequate.

The global system and war

Neorealists, especially, emphasize the global system in explaining the outbreak of war. For neorealists, the global system, a set of interacting and interdependent units[53] is greater than the sum of its parts, and it influences these parts. In other words, the global system predisposes behavior like conflict and war among actors.

For neorealists, three elements differentiate global systems: (1) ordering principles, (2) character of the units, and (3) the distribution of power. First, systems can also be classified according to their *ordering principle*, that is, the way in which the units are related to one another. Anarchy for neorealists (as for neoliberals) is a given within which actors must survive. Actors are treated as analogous to economic firms that have to compete and survive in a free market, and power in global politics is regarded as analogous to money in economics. Such a system is decentralized. An alternative ordering principle might be centralized and hierarchical – as in world government or **empire**. Historical examples of hierarchical worlds include ancient Rome and imperial China. The influential neorealist Kenneth Waltz compares domestic and international systems by describing the former as "centralized and hierarchic" in contrast to "international-political systems" that are "decentralized and anarchic." Under anarchy, actors "stand in relation of coordination" and "each is the equal of all the others." "None is entitled to command; none is required to obey."[54]

Second, systems can be classified by their *units* or parts. The principal units can be states, empires, or some other type of actor. One can even envision a system in which corporations, ethnic groups, or religious groups are the principal actors. According to Waltz, under anarchy, states "remain like units"[55] because all confront the same challenge to their survival and must act in the same way or risk survival. Although Waltz admits that states are not the only actors in global politics nor need they remain the most important, he remains skeptical about the possibility that other actors like transnational corporations will emerge to challenge them.

Finally, systems are classified according to the distribution of capabilities among the units, a feature called system **polarity**. Because the first two elements change slowly, neorealists emphasize the importance of changes in the distribution of capabilities among actors. A system's

empire a political unit having an extensive territory or comprising a number of territories or nations and ruled by a single supreme authority.

polarity the number of power centers in a global system.

Unipolar global system	One major power	=	The US
Bipolar global system	Two major powers	=	The US and USSR
Multipolar global system	Three or more major powers	=	Britain, France, Austria, Prussia, and Russia

Figure 6.4 The distribution of power

distribution of power may be unipolar, bipolar, or multipolar. In a **unipolar** system, as depicted in Figure 6.4, there is one dominant actor called a **hegemon** that is so powerful that no other actor or coalition can challenge its dominance. A **bipolar** system is characterized by two dominant actors or blocs, and a **multipolar** system has three or more dominant actors or blocs.

Taken together, the elements of a system impose **structure**, or a set of opportunities and constraints on the behavior of actors within the system. Here are several examples of how the elements of a system affect the actors within it:

- if states are the dominant units in a global system (in terms of their number and/or legitimacy), other actors, such as international organizations and transnational corporations, will have little influence;
- if a system has a hierarchical structure, great powers may limit the autonomy of lesser units, just as the US government limits the 50 American states; or
- if a system is unipolar, the dominant actor will face few constraints on its behavior and can determine rules in the system, but may severely restrict the autonomy of other actors.

Let us now examine three related system-level properties that are associated with war: the security dilemma, arms races, and the balance of power.

unipolarity an international political system dominated by one center of power.

hegemon an actor that is able to dominate the global political system.

bipolarity a political system with two centers of power.

multipolarity a political system having three or more dominant centers of power.

structure any set of relatively fixed constraints on global actors.

Controversy

Theorists disagree about whether a unipolar, bipolar, or multipolar system is more stable and peaceful. Advocates of bipolarity believe that in a bipolar world the two principal actors can easily monitor each other's power and intentions, thereby removing much of the uncertainty in global politics that is associated with the outbreak of war. War, they believe, is more likely in a unipolar world because one or more actors will try to challenge the hegemon. A multipolar world, in some views, produces dangerous uncertainty because there are so many major actors. "It is to a great extent," wrote Waltz during the Cold War, "that the world since the war has enjoyed a stability seldom known where three or more powers have sought to cooperate with each other or have competed for existence."[56] Two superpowers "supreme in their power have to use force less often" and are "able to moderate each other's use of violence and to absorb possibly destabilizing changes that emanate from uses of violence that they do not or cannot control."[57]

Others argue that multipolarity moderates hostility because actors have common as well as clashing interests that produce shifting alliances in which there are no permanent enemies.[58] Finally, some theorists believe that global politics is most peaceful when there is a single dominant power that is strong enough to enforce peace.

Security dilemmas and arms races

security dilemma a situation in which one actor's effort to increase its security makes other states less secure with the unintended consequence of greater insecurity for all.

Many theorists attribute wars to a **security dilemma** that arises from anarchy in which, as Waltz suggests, "Wars occur because there is nothing to prevent them."[59] In an anarchic world, actors have to provide for their own security. This is a *self-help* world in which actors cannot trust one another to cooperate because each knows that the others are also looking out for their own best interests. For English political philosopher Thomas Hobbes (1588–1679), anarchy pits all against all and produces a situation in which life is "solitary, poor, nasty, brutish, and short." "Hereby it is manifest that, during the time men live without a common power to keep them all in awe, they are in that condition called war, and such a war as is of every man against every man."[60] Under these conditions, actors prepare for the worst case, but doing so actually makes everyone less secure. This problem is known as the security dilemma.

The security dilemma occurs when one actor unilaterally seeks to improve its security, perhaps by enlarging its military forces. However, others may see this action as hostile, thereby increasing their insecurity. Since the worst case would be to permit any actor to gain a decisive military advantage, they may also enlarge their military forces. The outcome is greater tension and higher defense expenditures for *all* actors even though all are acting defensively to protect themselves. The result is an **arms race**, an escalating spiral of fear and insecurity that is destabilizing and can produce war. The Anglo-German naval arms race

arms race an action–reaction process in which increases in armaments by one state is reciprocated by an increase in armaments by the other.

before World War I (see chapter 3, p. 106) is often cited as an example of an unfolding security dilemma, and the Theory in the Real World provides a contemporary illustration of a missile defense system.

Theory in the real world

During his campaign and first year in office, President George W. Bush advocated developing a national missile defense to protect the US from a nuclear weapon launched by a rogue state like North Korea. American officials argued that a missile defense was necessary in a world in which Americans could never be certain of adversaries' intentions. However, many opposed missile defense, pointing out that such a program would escalate into an arms race. They argued that in response, other actors would develop their own anti-missile systems as well as adding additional missiles capable of overwhelming US defenses.

Furthermore, the argument goes, despite US assurances that its missile defense program does not seek to reduce the capability of Russia or China to retaliate in case of a US nuclear attack, both countries will feel less secure once a US missile defense system is deployed. Why? If the United States were "invulnerable" to retaliation, it might become more reckless – more willing to go to the brink of war to get its way because it has less to fear from nuclear war. It does not matter whether or not the United States actually intends to start a war. What matters is that Chinese and Russian leaders *believe* war to be possible in the future and so deploy additional missiles to overwhelm any US missile defense system. Of course, they may have no intention of *using* their missiles against the United States, but they may wish to have them to deter an American attack. Nevertheless, the US might not assume that Russia's and China's intentions were peaceful, and might then expand its missile defense system. The result is an arms race and growing tension, with a corresponding increase in the likelihood that a nuclear exchange might actually occur – even though no one wished such an outcome.

The logic of the security dilemma – actors that are interdependent and hostile but are unable to trust each other – is similar to that of French philosopher Jean-Jacques Rousseau's stag–hare parable. Rousseau (1712–78), who also influenced realist thought, illustrated the problem of creating trust among actors in an anarchic setting in a story about the state of nature, an imaginary world before society existed. He imagined five hungry men who met in order to cooperate in trapping a stag that would be sufficient to feed *all* of them. Rousseau then imagined that a hare, enough to feed only one of them, appears. What, he asks, will the men do? His answer was that each must try to capture the hare because he knows that all the others may do the same out of self-interest.[61] Thus, rather than cooperating, the men become competitors – perhaps even sabotaging each other – which is precisely what a realist says that all humans and nations will do when faced with a similar choice between relying on the possibility of cooperation or the certainty of acting alone.

Rousseau is suggesting that cooperation is impossible because of the absence of trust. Neorealists like Waltz who accept that argument believe that states seek only enough power to ensure their security. They are *defensive realists*. By contrast, other realists like John Mearsheimer who believe that states try to accumulate as much power as they possibly can are called offensive realists. *Offensive realists*, argues Mearsheimer, believe that "the international system creates powerful incentives for states to look for opportunities to gain power at the expense of rivals, and to take advantage of those situations when the benefits outweigh the costs. A state's ultimate goal is to be the hegemon in the system."[62]

The problem of building trust under anarchy is also reflected in the *prisoner's dilemma* game. In classic form, this dilemma involves the arrest of two robbery suspects. The police have insufficient evidence to convict them of the crime, but they can be convicted of a lesser crime. The police place the suspects in separate cells, where they cannot communicate, and offer each the same deal. If both confess, each will receive a sentence of eight years in prison. If neither confesses, both will receive one-year prison sentences. However, if one confesses and the other does not, the former will be released without jail time, while the latter will receive a ten-year jail sentence.

The matrix in Figure 6.5 illustrates the logic of the dilemma. Each cell shows the prison time that corresponds to each strategy. If both Prisoners 1 and 2 refuse to talk, both receive a one-year sentence. If both squeal, they get eight-year sentences. If only Prisoner 1 squeals, he will go free but Prisoner 2 will go to jail for ten years. Each player has two strategies:

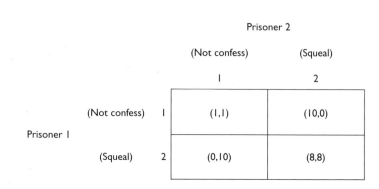

Figure 6.5 Prisoner's dilemma matrix

to cooperate (not confess) or to defect (squeal). Defection (squealing) is the dominant strategy because both want to avoid the worst case of ten years in prison. Were the two able to communicate in a way that created trust, neither would confess, and both would be better off. As in the stag–hare parable, neither is prepared to trust the other lest she receive a ten-year sentence, known as the "sucker" payoff.

The dilemma arises because the best solution for both, known as the socially optimal outcome, would be not to confess (1,1). However, since both players fear becoming the "sucker," neither will cooperate. A similar situation exists in disarmament negotiations when each actor, in the absence of clear proof that the other is disarming, has a powerful incentive to keep some of its arms hidden in order to prevent the worst possible outcome, one in which it had disarmed but its adversary had not.

In fact, research suggests that if prisoner's dilemma games are repeated, cooperation tends to develop. If one player takes a risk and does not confess, the other player may rethink its position, and trust begins to develop. In time, players reciprocate each other's trust, thereby overcoming the dilemma. A single prisoner's dilemma game, like Rousseau's stag–hare parable, is an end-of-the-world or one-shot event which does not permit **reciprocity**. By suggesting that reciprocity is indispensable in creating common interest in not cheating, we acknowledge that global politics involves continuing interaction in which each actor's behavior conditions others' expectations for the future.[63] Thus, the "shadow of the future" may dampen the degree to which security dilemmas produce war.

reciprocity strategy by which one actor behaves toward others as they have behaved toward it.

It is also worth noting that some constructivists believe that the security dilemma has been weakened in the modern era by emerging norms respecting the right of the sovereign state to exist. According to constructivist Alexander Wendt, the international system has gone through a qualitative structural change in which the "kill or be killed logic of the Hobbesian state of nature has been replaced by the live and let live logic of the Lockean" culture.[64] Sovereignty is no longer just "a property of individual states, but also an *institution* shared by many states" and formalized in international law.[65]

Having considered how anarchy can lead to war even when actors pursue defensive policies, we turn to the distribution of power and its role as a source of war.

Equality versus preponderance of power

Rapid, threatening change in the distribution of capabilities among actors is often cited as a cause of war. Thucydides, for example, writes in his

History that what made the Peloponnesian "war inevitable was the growth of Athenian power and the fear which this caused in Sparta."[66] Theorists differ, however, about whether rough equality of power among major actors or a preponderance of power in the hands of one of them is more conducive to peace.

According to balance-of-power theory, peace is most likely when power is distributed so that no single actor can dominate others. Actors must constantly monitor others' capabilities and form alliances to counterbalance those that are becoming too powerful. In this theory, then, power creates countervailing power, regardless of actors' intentions.[67] Actors can balance in one of two ways. The first, internal balancing, involves actors' increasing their own capabilities perhaps by increasing military budgets or developing new weapons. In these ways, actors maximize their freedom of action. They are not bound by pledges

Figure 6.6 European Equilibrium
Robert D. Farber University
Archives & Special Collections
Department, Brandeis University

to or depend on others for their security. However, internal balancing cannot be accomplished quickly and is inadequate when facing an imminent threat. In the second balancing strategy, external balancing, actors restore a favorable balance of power by entering **alliances** with one another to counter an aggressive foe. Balance-of-power alliances must be fluid arrangements that change as old threats fade and new ones emerge, and there must be no permanent friends or enemies or ideological barriers to limit alliance flexibility. Although alliances allow for rapid response, they impose significant costs on actors, committing them to certain courses of action, limiting their autonomy, and leaving them dependent on others for security.

alliance a formal agreement to cooperate to achieve joint security.

There are numerous refinements of the balance-of-power arguments. Some argue that polarity is likely to affect "the efficiency of the balancing process." For instance, political scientists Thomas Christensen and Jack Snyder argue that multipolarity causes two alliance dilemmas that may increase the likelihood of conflict. In multipolarity, where alliance partners are roughly equal in their capabilities, there is a significant degree of security interdependence within alliances. Great powers that perceive a defensive advantage in such a world may engage in "buck-passing" by turning the responsibility to balance against a rising power over to another state or coalition, whereas great powers that perceive an offensive advantage will turn to "chain-ganging," allying with a reckless state with which its own security is intertwined.[68] Thus, in the 1930s France engaged in "buck-passing" by leaving key decisions as to how to respond to Hitler in British hands, and in 1914 Germany engaged in "chain-ganging" when it gave its "blank check" to Austria-Hungary.

Others argue that states will modify their balancing behavior when they do not fear for their survival. According to the theory of "soft balancing" second-tier powers, like China, France, Germany, India, and Russia, that do not have the capability to challenge a dominant power like the United States will form diplomatic coalitions with the implicit threat of "upgrading" their alliances.[69] For instance, in the months leading up to the 2003 war in Iraq, a coalition led by France, Germany, and Russia strongly opposed US efforts for an invasion. In the UN Security Council, these states threatened to veto any resolution calling for the use of force, either implicitly or explicitly, issuing a statement in February 2003 that "We will not let a proposed resolution pass that would authorize the use of force."[70]

Balance-of-power advocates believe that relative equality in power among major actors reduces the likelihood of war because equality increases uncertainty about a war's outcome and such uncertainty induces caution. Would the United States have initiated war against Iraq in 2003 if American leaders believed they had a 50–50 chance of losing?

Other theorists believe that, in contrast to the balance-of-power theory, global politics is most stable when a single actor is preponderant, that is, sufficiently powerful so that other actors cannot challenge its leadership. A hegemon fears no one and has no reason to go to war, and weak countries do not dare start a war. Some theorists who hold this view note regular cycles of preponderance and war throughout history. Thus, political scientist A. F. K. Organski proposed a *power transition theory*, according to which hegemons develop extensive global commitments and shape the global order to reflect their interest in maintaining hegemony.[71] In turn others accept the hegemon's leadership because they do not have the power to challenge it and benefit from global services that the hegemon provides – especially security and economic leadership. However, it is expensive for a hegemon to maintain its dominance. As the hegemon gradually loses power, others grow relatively stronger, and, when their power approximates that of the declining hegemon, *hegemonic war* will ensue, as a challenger seeks to overtake the hegemon and the hegemon seeks to preserve its status.

Controversy   The nuclear balance

In the nuclear era, the nuclear balance of power has also become a useful analytical concept. Many analysts agree that international politics fundamentally changed once nuclear weapons came on the scene. However, the impact of nuclear weapons has varied, depending upon the nuclear balance of power. Initially, the United States held a nuclear monopoly, only broken when the Soviet Union tested its own atomic weapon in 1949. The US maintained nuclear primacy – meaning that it had the capability to destroy all of an adversary's forces in a **first strike** – until the 1960s when the Soviet Union achieved a rough nuclear parity. Some analysts argue that this nuclear balance has since collapsed and that, today, the United States has regained nuclear primacy. Such assertions are controversial on two counts. First, does the US really have nuclear primacy? Is its nuclear arsenal so strong, and are those of other nuclear powers so weak, that the US is capable of initiating a successful first strike – that is, one that will destroy the adversary's ability to retaliate? Second, what are the implications for global politics if the US does, indeed, have nuclear primacy?

In regard to the first question, political scientists Keir Lieber and Daryl Press argue that the US has achieved nuclear dominance by improving its own

first-strike capability
the ability to launch an attack and successfully destroy an enemy's capability to retaliate.

nuclear forces as Russia's forces decline and China's are slow to modernize. Since the end of the Cold War, Lieber and Press argue, the US has replaced the missiles on its submarines with Trident II D-5 missiles, which have larger-yield warheads. The US Air Force has placed nuclear-armed cruise missiles (which are not visible to Russian and Chinese radars) on its B-52 bombers and it has improved the B-2 stealth bomber so it can fly at even lower altitudes to evade enemy radar. It has also improved the accuracy and yield of its remaining Intercontinental Ballistic Missiles (ICBMs). Yet as the US has been improving its nuclear arsenal and nuclear delivery systems, Russia's "strategic nuclear arsenal has sharply deteriorated." Lieber and Press cite substantial cuts in the number of weapons and delivery systems; delivery systems that have exceeded their expected service lives, and an early warning system that is "a mess," with "a gaping hole in . . . coverage that lies to the east of the country, toward the Pacific Ocean" (where US strategic nuclear submarines [SSBNs] are based). They further argue that China's nuclear arsenal is even more vulnerable. China does not have an early warning system and its ICBMs are not ready to launch on warning (before incoming nuclear warheads strike China).[72] Not so, say critics like Peter Flory, a US Assistant Secretary of Defense, and Pavel Podvig, a political scientist and expert on Russia's strategic forces. Flory counters that the US also is decreasing the numbers of its operational nuclear forces, removing from strategic service four ballistic missile submarines and retiring all Peacekeeper missiles. Similarly, Podvig responds that Russia is decommissioning weapons and launchers it no longer needs and is developing new generations of mobile ICBMs, which would likely survive a first strike.[73] As this debate illustrates, comparing nuclear force levels is no easy task.

Political scientists are also at odds over the implications of nuclear primacy. "Hawks" believe that US nuclear primacy will deter conflict. Potential adversaries, like Russia and China, will think twice before making nuclear threats. "Doves" counter that Washington might be emboldened to act more aggressively in its foreign relations if the US enjoys nuclear primacy, particularly given US dominance in conventional military and economic terms. Finally, "owls" fear that US primacy will produce crisis instability: that other nuclear powers will adopt strategic policies, like giving control over nuclear forces to low-level commanders, which make an accidental nuclear war more likely.[74]

In the same vein, George Modelski proposes a *long-cycle theory* of world leadership in which unipolarity is most stable.[75] Modelski views modern history as a series of long cycles, each of which consists of four phases. In the first phase (world power), a new dominant world power that has emerged after a world war consolidates and maintains its preponderant position, largely through naval power (and today air power). However, the costs of global leadership bring about the power's eventual decline in a second phase (delegitimation). In the third phase (deconcentration), emerging rivals challenge the declining hegemon and conflict grows. This is followed by a fourth phase (global great power war) which leads to a new cycle of hegemony. Modelski observes these cycles beginning in the sixteenth century, when the Italian/Indian Ocean Wars (1494–1516) created Portuguese hegemony. Modelski then relies on the long cycles to explain the rise of successive hegemons – the Netherlands, Britain, and the United States.

Still another systemic explanation of war focuses on the ease of offensive war relative to defensive war. Offense dominance may be a result of technological developments that make conquest easier than defense as was the case with the uniting of tanks and aircraft in Germany's strategy of *Blitzkrieg* in World War II (see chapter 7, pp. 304–5). According to theories of the offense–defense balance, war is more likely when the offense enjoys advantages over the defense. Political scientist Stephen Van Evera theorizes that offense dominance is more likely to lead to war than defensive dominance because attacking first affords significant advantages.[76] The offense–defense balance also contributes indirectly to war by fueling other processes associated with an increased likelihood for conflict. For instance, Robert Jervis theorizes that offense dominance gives rise to security dilemmas.[77]

Thus there are several persuasive system-level explanations for war. For a more complete picture, however, we must consider characteristics of states that political scientists believe contribute to or inhibit the outbreak of war.

Conclusion

This chapter has examined two of the most important and controversial theoretical concepts in the study of global politics — anarchy and power. We have seen how realists, liberals, and constructivists view anarchy from very different perspectives and reach very different conclusions about its impact on the world around us. From a realist perspective, anarchy leads to the gloomy conclusion that competition and conflict are inherent in global politics and probably cannot be modified. For liberals, the pernicious effects of anarchy can be modified by international regimes, institutions, and organizations. Finally, constructivists argue that leaders and actors have the capability to determine whether anarchy produces conflict or not.

Power, the second crucial concept discussed in this chapter, is seen by realists as the currency of global politics and the factor that defines the discipline. Power is necessary to survive. However, as we have seen power is an elusive concept – difficult to define and to measure. There are, moreover, different types of power. Actors need capabilities to amass power, but capabilities are rarely useful in all situations. They may be useful in some contexts but not in others. Moreover, power is not a generalizable quality. Instead, it is relevant in relationships between specific actors and is a relational concept.

War, a topic central to global politics, especially realist analyses, is our subject in the next chapter as well. There, we will examine the evolution of warfare, including military technology, from the era of dynastic European states to present-day irregular warfare and terrorism.

Student activities

Discussion questions

Comprehension questions

1 What is power and how can you measure it?
2 Compare and contrast the realist, liberal, and constructivist versions of anarchy and its consequences.
3 What is the "security dilemma," and how can we escape it?

Analysis questions

4 Evaluate the relative power of the United States and Al Qaeda. Which actor has more power and why? Use the Internet to research this question.
5 Does anarchy, in your view, condemn us to perpetual conflict and violence?
6 Does power always result in influence? Why or why not?
7 Evaluate the strength of the nuclear nonproliferation regime. What are the greatest weaknesses of this regime? What are its strengths?
8 Do you think that today's global politics constitutes an "international society"? What evidence supports this view, and what evidence denies it?
9 Is "prisoner's dilemma" an accurate reflection of global politics? How might repeated interactions among states and other actors modify the assumptions of the prisoner's dilemma game?

Map analysis

Refer to Map 6.1, Nuclear Weapons Free Zones around the world. Which regions do not have a NWFZ? Why do you think NWFZs have not taken hold there?

Select one NWFZ for further study. Use the Internet to find out why member states have opted to outlaw nuclear weapons in their region. Has participation in an NWFZ created any particular foreign-policy problems for member states? What additional insights does your research provide into the nuclear nonproliferation regime?

Cultural materials

The space race that took place during the Cold War was a competition between the United States and Soviet Union to explore and exploit space and the moon to increase the power and prestige of each state. The space race had a profound effect on both American and Soviet society. Each country advertised its successes in space, for example, on its postage stamps. In what ways does society commemorate such accomplishments today?

Further reading

Baldwin, David A., ed., *Neo-realism and Neo-liberalism* (New York: Columbia University Press, 1993). A comparison of neorealist and neoliberal ideas on power and anarchy.

Bull, Hedley, *The Anarchical Society: A Study of Order in World Politics* (New York: Columbia University Press, 1977). International society according to the "English school."

Keohane, Robert O., *After Hegemony: Cooperation and Discord in the World Political Economy* (Princeton, NJ: Princeton University Press, 1984). A neoliberal view of how political institutions can survive without a dominant hegemon.

Keohane, Robert O. and Joseph S. Nye, *Power and Interdependence: World Politics in Transition*, 3rd ed. (New York: Addison-Wesley Longman, 2001). The seminal work on international regimes.

Krasner, Stephen D., ed., *International Regimes* (Ithaca, NY: Cornell University Press, 1983). A classic, edited volume on regimes.

Mearsheimer, John J., *The Tragedy of Great Power Politics* (New York: W.W. Norton, 2001). The bible of aggressive realism.

Morgenthau, Hans J., *Power Among Nations*, 7th ed., rev. by Kenneth T.

Thompson and W. David Clinton (New York: McGraw-Hill, 2006). A seminal work on the role of power in global politics.

Nye, Joseph S., Jr., *Soft Power: The Means to Success in World Politics* (New York: Public Affairs, 2004). Analysis of culture and ideals as sources of power.

Waltz, Kenneth N., *Theory of International Politics* (Reading, MA: Addison-Wesley, 1979). Neorealist view of the dominant role of anarchy and power distribution.

Wendt, Alexander, "Anarchy Is What States Make of It: The Social Construction of Power Politics," *International Organization* 46:2 (Spring 1992), 391–425. The constructivist version of anarchy.

7 The changing nature of war

At 8:15 on the morning of August 6, 1945, a single B-29 bomber, the *Enola Gay*, piloted by Paul W. Tibbets dropped a nuclear bomb, known as "Little Boy," on the Japanese city of Hiroshima. Hiroshima had been selected as the target because it had not been previously bombed, thereby making it easier for American observers to judge the effects of the atom bomb. The atomic explosion cut a blast of light across Hiroshima's sky "from east to west, from the city toward the hills. It seemed a sheet of sun."[1] It is estimated that 140,000 of Hiroshima's 350,000 inhabitants were killed in the atomic blast and as a result of radiation. Five square miles were devastated, and more than 60 percent of the city's buildings were destroyed.[2] Although nuclear weapons have not been used in combat since World War II, wars today are just as violent. In Rwanda, where a brutal civil war erupted between two dominant ethnic groups, Hutus and Tutsis, in April 1994, an estimated 800,000 people were killed. For four days, the attacking Hutus killed thousands, smashing heads with stones and decapitating and slicing open bodies with machetes. Maimed victims hid among the corpses, pretending to be dead, as they watched family members die.

The atomic bombing of Hiroshima and, three days later, Nagasaki ended World War II and marked a giant step toward the possibility of total war. Movement toward total war can occur in two related ways: (1) increases in destructive power and (2) the breakdown of norms protecting innocent civilians in wartime. Both characterized the destructive Thirty Years' War. During the two centuries after 1648, European leaders sought to limit warfare in ways that would reduce civilian casualties and material damage, both of which threatened their states' wealth and stability. And, in ensuing centuries, international law evolved to protect civilians in wartime.

Europeans began to regard warfare as an instrument of statecraft, and, as we shall see, the spokesperson for this perspective and eloquent

Figure 7.1 1940s – atomic burst. At the time this photo was taken, smoke billowed 20,000 feet above Hiroshima while smoke from the burst of the first atomic bomb had spread over 10,000 feet on the target at the base of the rising column. August 5, 1945. Two planes of the 509th Composite Group, part of the 313th Wing of the twentieth Air Force, participated in this mission; one to carry the bomb, and the other to act as escort.
US Air Force photo

absolute war war in which adversaries use every available means to defeat one another.

opponent of **absolute war** was a Prussian military thinker and general named Karl Maria von Clausewitz (1780–1831). Clausewitz, who was a realist at heart, witnessed the explosion in the size and intensity of warfare brought about by the French Revolution and Napoléon Bonaparte, and he feared that this trend threatened to sever the link between politics and violence. Factors at all three levels of analysis pressed the level of violence upward. Highly nationalistic leaders came to power; states became militarized and fell under the sway of uncompromising ideologies like nationalism, Marxism, and, later, fascism, and, at the system level, **industrialization** and advances in military technology made possible previously unimagined levels of violence.

industrialization a process in which production and manufacturing are mechanized, bringing with it a complex of political, social, and economic changes.

This chapter traces the breakdown of efforts to limit violence and protect civilians during wartime. The destructive power of weaponry and the vulnerability of civilians increased significantly in the nineteenth century and then in the two world wars of the twentieth. However, the introduction of nuclear weapons and the spread of biological and chemical weapons were especially dramatic steps on the path to total war. Such **weapons of mass destruction** (WMD) are inherently indiscriminate and therefore pose an unprecedented threat to civilians. Although both the United States and Soviet Union engaged in a continual effort to develop new and better weapons, they did not let this competition run out of control, and both worked to prevent additional countries from acquiring WMD.

weapons of mass destruction (WMD) nuclear, biological, or chemical weapons that can kill large numbers of people indiscriminately.

Recent decades have seen still more fearful developments on the road to total war. Among these, we will first consider irregular, or unconventional, war, beginning with **guerrilla wars** in which subnational groups, often fighting a much stronger national army (in terms of military capability), employ tactics very different from those in interstate wars like World Wars I and II. We then consider conflicts in **failed states**. In such states, national armies tend to degenerate into the personal militias of powerful warlords and conflict becomes endemic. As we shall see, these irregular conflicts are much more complex than the interstate wars that dominated the nineteenth and twentieth centuries. They tend to take a particularly high toll among civilians and may spark humanitarian crises, as in Rwanda in 1994 or Darfur, Sudan in 2006, and they may spill over into neighboring states. Another frightening development is the proliferation of global terrorism. Terrorism is a strategy that rejects the norms and rules that previously governed warfare and protected civilians. Indeed, it is a strategy that explicitly targets innocent civilians. The prospect of terrorists armed with WMD is, as we shall see, of particular concern.

guerrilla warfare use of hit-and-run tactics including ambush and surprise raids.

failed state a state that has collapsed and cannot provide for its citizens' basic needs.

Let us begin by examining Clausewitz's ideas on war, ideas that reflected the views of European statesmen that wars had to be carefully managed and controlled. Clausewitz was inspired to express his fears for the future in a classic work of military strategy that is still widely used today. In his book, he laid out a series of key ideas about the relationship between war and politics to which we shall now turn.

War as an extension of politics

Clausewitz argued that war was a *political* instrument, like diplomacy or foreign aid. For this reason, he can be regarded as a traditional realist (as defined in chapter 1). In this, he echoed Thucydides who had shown over two millennia earlier in his *History* how dreadful the consequences of unlimited war could be.

Clausewitz feared that unless politicians controlled war it would degenerate into a "fight" with no clear objectives except the destruction of the enemy. Clausewitz had a great deal of military experience. He served in the Prussian army until captured in 1806, later helped reorganize it, served in the Russian army (1812–14), and finally fought at Waterloo. Clausewitz cautioned that war was being transformed into a fight among whole peoples without limits and without clear political objectives. In his three-volume masterpiece, *On War (Vom Krieg)*, published after his death, he explained the relationship between war and politics.

> **Key document   Karl Maria von Clausewitz, "What Is War?"[3]**
>
> Now, if we reflect that War has its root in a political object, then, naturally this original motive which called it into existence should also continue the first and highest consideration in its conduct. . . . Policy, therefore, is interwoven with the whole action of War, and must exercise a continuous influence upon it. . . . We see, therefore, that War is not merely a political act, but also a real political instrument, a continuation of political commerce, a carrying out of the same by other means. . . . [T]he political view is the object. War is the means, and the means must always include the object in our conception.

Clausewitz believed that the rise of nationalism and the use of large conscript armies could produce absolute war. These would be wars to the death rather than wars waged for specific and limited political objectives. He particularly feared leaving war to the generals because their idea of "victory" – the destruction of enemy armies – contradicted the aim of politicians, who viewed victory as the attainment of the political objectives for which they had started the war. Such ends might range from limited to large, and, Clausewitz asserted, wars should be fought only at the level necessary to achieve them. "If the aim of the military action," he wrote, "is an equivalent for the political objective, that action will in general diminish as the political objective diminishes," and this explains why "there may be Wars of all degrees of importance and energy, from a War of extermination down to the mere use of an army of observation."[4] Generals, he argued, should not be allowed to make decisions regarding when to start or end wars or how to fight them because they would use *all* the means at their disposal to destroy the enemy's capacity to fight, even though that might convert a limited conflict into an unlimited one.

In this way, Clausewitz foresaw World War I, in which generals dictated to political leaders the timing of military mobilization and pressed politicians to take the offensive and strike first. In effect, the insistence of the military commanders on adhering to preexisting war plans like the Schlieffen Plan and mobilization schedules took decision-making out of the hands of civilian leaders and limited the time such leaders had to negotiate with one another to prevent the war's outbreak. The generals also pressured statesmen to uphold alliance commitments, thereby spreading the war across Europe. Clausewitz's thinking is evident in Robert F. Kennedy's (1925–68) recollection of the 1962 Cuban missile crisis: "I thought, as I listened, of the many times that I had heard the military take positions which, if wrong, had the advantage that no one would be around at the end to know."[5]

Wars, Clausewitz argued, should be "political acts," "intended to compel our opponent to fulfill our will."[6] They were not mere slugfests animated by hatred and fanaticism in which the "victor" was the gladiator who remained alive at the end. Instead, Clausewitz argued, force should be only a *means* – a "real political instrument," as was diplomacy in a politician's arsenal. Wars should be a continuation of politics by other

bargaining an interactive process involving threats and promises between two or more parties with common and conflicting interests seeking to reach an agreement.

means, or instruments of forceful **bargaining**, and not ends in themselves. Since wars should only be initiated to achieve the political aims of civilian leaders, it was logical, he contended, that, if the "original reasons were forgotten, means and ends would become confused." In that case, he believed, the use of violence would become irrational. For war to be usable, it must, he believed, be limited. Unfortunately, several developments, especially industrialization, enlarged warfare precisely in the direction that Clausewitz feared.

On the road to total war: the world wars

Beginning in the nineteenth century, as an accompaniment to the industrial age, a great expansion of war and a rapid evolution of military technology took place, climaxing with the development of weapons of mass destruction in the twentieth century. The combination of nationalism and developing technology in that epoch transformed Clausewitz's fears into a reality far more dangerous than even he imagined.

The industrialization that marked the nineteenth and early twentieth centuries had a great impact on all social institutions, including warfare. The reasons were threefold. First, industrialization made the home front, where weapons and supplies were manufactured, as important to the war effort as the armies in the field; it also made economic installations and civilians who worked in factories legitimate targets of enemy attack. The wars that followed involved submarines that were used to try and starve civilians, strategic bombing of urban centers, and weapons of ever greater destructive power. Second, industrialization dramatically increased the production and standardization of armaments and other supplies necessary to deploy large armies all year round, sustain increased firepower, and adopt strategies of **attrition**. Finally, industrialization concentrated large numbers of people in cities, where they came under the spell of new ideologies such as nationalism and socialism. Greater public involvement in politics forced rulers to find ideological goals to justify war. However, fueled by these ideological goals, wars became more difficult to end or limit through compromise.

attrition the gradual erosion of an enemy's army by constant attack.

The impact of industrialization and public involvement in war and peace was first evident in the American Civil War (1861–65), in which railroads and the telegraph and the mass production of industrialization were available to hundreds of thousands of fighting men, especially in the North. Clausewitz's fear of unlimited war was realized when General William T. Sherman (1820–91) conducted his march through Georgia from November 16 to December 21, 1864, laying waste to the region from "Atlanta to the sea." Sherman is said to have coined the phrase "War is Hell" in an 1880 speech in Ohio.

Although America's Civil War was dismissed by Prussian General Helmuth von Moltke as "two armed mobs chasing each other around the country, from which nothing could be learned,"[7] in many ways, it was a preview of World War I. Although much of World War I took place in France and Belgium, it was also fought in Central Europe, the Middle East, South Asia, East Asia, and Africa. It was the first truly modern war and the first total war in the sense that it was waged by huge armies of conscripted citizens, equipped with modern weapons and sustained by modern industry. For the first time, whole societies were mobilized in the struggle for victory. Casualties were higher than in any previous conflict, "Sucking up lives at the rate of 5,000, and sometimes 50,000 a day" on the Western front, "the known dead per capita of population were 1 to 28 for France, 1 to 32 for Germany, 1 to 57 for England and 1 to 107 for Russia."[8] In the five-month Battle of the Somme (July–November 1916), Britain and France paid a price of 600,000 casualties in return for 125 square miles of mud. At the Battle of Verdun, from February to December of that same year, the combatants suffered 1.2 million casualties. During the conflict, a total of over ten million were killed, and another 20 million were wounded. To sustain a war of this magnitude required both the fruits of industrialization and the fervor of xenophobic nationalism.

World War II, in many ways a continuation of the previous world war, was even more global, reaching Asia and Europe, as well as North Africa and the South Pacific. World War II began with Germany's invasion of Poland on September 1, 1939, pitting Britain and France against Nazi Germany and fascist Italy. Following the conquest of Poland and a period of deceptive calm (called the "phony war"), Germany conquered Norway and Denmark and then invaded France, forcing France to surrender in May 1940 and Britain to evacuate its army hurriedly from Dunkirk in France. The Germans then sought to bring Britain to its knees in the aerial Battle of Britain (1940) and the intense bombing of British cities called the Blitz, in both of which British deployment of radar was decisive in compensating for British inferiority in numbers of aircraft and pilots. Germany and Italy also sought to destroy Britain's links to its colonial possessions in Asia by extending the war to North Africa, attempting to seize the vital British-controlled Suez Canal in Egypt, and using submarines in the Battle of the Atlantic in an effort to starve the British.

The failure of these efforts and Hitler's abiding hatred of Bolshevism and the Soviet Union led Hitler to abandon plans to invade the British Isles and to turn east. On June 22, 1941, Hitler invaded the Soviet Union, despite the nonaggression treaty signed by Germany and the Soviet Union less than two years earlier. By the time the Germans surrendered in May 1945, some 20 million Soviet citizens had died.

The war again expanded following the surprise Japanese attack on the United States at Pearl Harbor (December 7, 1941). The Pearl Harbor attack followed a period of growing US–Japanese tension caused by Japan's invasion of Manchuria in 1931 and China in 1937 and America's effort to contain Japan by applying economic sanctions. Japan's attack on Pearl Harbor was accompanied by its conquest of much of Southeast Asia, including the British naval base at Singapore and the US-owned Philippines.

The Pacific campaign, regarded as secondary to the war against Germany, was fought largely by the Americans and British. General Douglas MacArthur (1880–1964) commanded army troops moving northward through New Guinea and the Philippines, and Admiral

Chester W. Nimitz (1885–1966) commanded naval and marine forces moving westward in an island-hopping campaign. The latter included some of the bloodiest battles of the war in terms of casualties as a ratio of troop strength – Guadalcanal, Iwo Jima, and Okinawa – in which Japanese soldiers fought to the death and Japanese *kamikaze* pilots engaged in suicide missions against American warships. This was a new tactic that terrified adversaries and foreshadowed the "suicide bombings" of today. When making their final attack Japanese suicide pilots were told to remember that:

- Crashing bodily into a target is not easy. It causes the enemy great damage. Therefore the enemy will exert every means to avoid a hit.
- Suddenly, you may become confused. You are liable to make an error. But hold on to the unshakeable conviction to the last moment that you will sink the enemy ship.
- Remember when diving into the enemy to shout at the top of your lungs: "Hissatsu!" ("Sink without fail!") At that moment, all the cherry blossoms at Yasukuni shrine in Tokyo will smile brightly at you.[9]

Until the Anglo-American landings in Normandy, France, on D-Day, June 6, 1944, the war in Europe against Germany was conducted mainly by the Soviet Union. Confronted by overwhelming military forces on two fronts, Germany finally surrendered less than a year later. The war in Asia lasted until August 1945, when Japan surrendered shortly after the atomic bomb attacks on Nagasaki and Hiroshima, and the Soviet Union's declaration of war against Tokyo.[10]

Although war has been a brutal and murderous activity since ancient times, we have seen that it has repeatedly grown in size and destructiveness. Civilians were the major victims of war in Europe's religious conflicts. The efforts of kings to limit war following the Thirty Years' Wars worked up to a point but then, despite the ideas of Clausewitz, gave way to its rapid growth after the French Revolution and Napoléon. Additional efforts to control or limit war proved fruitless in the face of nineteenth-century industrialization and technological development that made it an ever more terrifying prospect from the American Civil War through World War II. We now turn to a systematic discussion of the relationship between technology and war.

Technology and interstate wars

As the previous section on the changing nature of war suggests, military technology is a key factor in the conduct of war. But adversaries rarely understand the implications of changing technology. Often, leaders study the last war to prepare for the next one. The failure to recognize that warfare has changed and to adapt to those changes is especially prevalent among winners of previous wars. By contrast, losers are more likely to learn from their past errors. Sometimes modest technological innovations have a profound impact, such as the introduction of stirrups in China and later into Europe which enabled mounted warriors to use hand-held weapons, especially bows and arrows, without falling off their horses.

Technology and the conduct of World War I

Among the most important results of the industrial revolution were the development of railways and steamships, both critical for fighting World War I. So, too, was the invention of the Bessemer process in 1850 for making steel. Another major military advance was made possible by the canning of food – introduced by a French chef in 1795 who sought to win a prize offered by Napoléon for a way to prevent military food supplies from spoiling. Canned food made it possible to feed large armies in distant places and to campaign even in winter when fresh food was unavailable.

Virtually all of Europe's statesmen and generals failed to appreciate the extent to which technological innovations had tipped the strategic balance away from offensive to defensive dominance. And interstate war is most likely, argues political scientist Robert Jervis, when the offense has the advantage and when it is not possible to distinguish between offensive and defensive postures, conditions that existed in 1914.[11]

Some technological advances in warfare had already been introduced in the nineteenth and twentieth centuries, but their implications for war and politics were not appreciated by the generals and statesmen in 1914. For example, in 1873 Joseph Glidden (1813–1906) from DeKalb, Illinois received a patent for "barbed wire" (also called "the devil's rope" and "concertina wire"), a simple device that later became a deadly barrier to frontal infantry and cavalry assaults. In World War I, during the hours of darkness, "wiring parties" inserted wiring posts in front of their trenches and then attached reels of barbed wire. After many bloody episodes, instead of charging the enemy, attacking forces began to fire artillery across the field of battle to punch holes in the wire.

Another technological advance that dramatically enhanced the defense was the machine gun that could be used with deadly effect against masses of infantry and cavalry advancing across open ground. It was invented in 1884 by the American Hiram Maxim and could fire over 500 rounds a minute.[12] The machine gun itself was made possible by the invention of smokeless gun power, which was probably invented by a Prussian artillery captain around 1864. However, it was not until 1885 that a

French inventor successfully made smokeless powder that could be used in guns. The British were among the first to adopt the machine gun, using it extensively in colonial conflicts in the late nineteenth and early twentieth centuries. Also, the 1905 Russo-Japanese War witnessed the extensive and destructive impact of the weapon against advancing infantry and cavalry.

Other technological developments that altered the tactical nature of warfare in ways disadvantageous to an offensive strategy were breech-loaded and rifled guns, which stabilized bullets by spinning them in flight. Although developed earlier, this innovation was widely deployed in the nineteenth century, dramatically increasing the range, accuracy, speed, and quality of firearms, especially the French artillery. Few military leaders in 1914 recognized how effective artillery could be used against masses of infantry and cavalry moving across no man's land or to smash troops, massing behind the lines in preparation for an attack. The best known artillery piece was manufactured by the German firm of Krupp. It was nicknamed "Big Bertha" or "Fat Bertha" in honor of Gustav Krupp's beautiful wife. "Big Bertha" could fire a 2,200-pound shell at a range of nine to 15 miles. This 43-ton howitzer (a cannon with a bore diameter greater than 30 mm that fires shells in a curved trajectory) had a crew of 200, had to be moved by tractors, and took over six hours to reassemble.

The implications of the new military innovations were there to see if Europe's leaders had looked at the right conflicts, for example, the American Civil War and the Russo-Japanese War. In the American Civil War, Union armies commanded by General Ulysses S. Grant (1822–85) forged a victorious strategy against the Confederacy out of huge mass armies, and engaged in a war of attrition that depended on massed artillery, trenches, and industrialization and resupply by railroad.

Instead, Europe's statesmen and generals looked to the successful experience of the three wars of German unification (1863, 1866, and 1870) where few of the military innovations described above had played a major role. These wars had ended quickly, in single battles, won by the side that had struck first. As a result, the main lesson that leaders drew was that taking the offensive right away was necessary for survival. Ignoring the enormous increases in firepower, French strategists,[13] for example, concluded that the secret of getting soldiers across open ground even in the presence of machine guns and artillery lay in the moral dimension of war, specifically in the resolve of the troops. Railroads, military strategists believed, were critical in enabling them to mobilize and move huge armies to a particular point where they could launch an immediate offensive to smash through the enemy front. However, in World War I, railroads would prove even more important for transporting the fruits of industrialization, especially the vast numbers of artillery shells and other ordnance necessary for modern armies.

Nowhere was the single-minded preference of Europe's generals for offensive operations more clearly revealed than in the military plans prepared in advance by all the major states. The best known, Germany's Schlieffen Plan, named for Count Alfred von Schlieffen (1833–1913), Chief of Germany's Great General Staff between 1891 and 1905, had been repeatedly revised prior to 1914. Like other European war plans made before 1914, the Schlieffen Plan was based on the primacy of the offensive, the key to which was military mobilization, which was viewed by statesmen and generals in 1914 in somewhat the same way strategists in the nuclear era thought about a nuclear first strike (see p. 286). Military mobilization encompassed calling up troops from around the country, gathering them together at mobilization centers where they received arms and supplies, and transporting them and their logistical support to the front. In other words, winning required a country to invest significant time and expense so that it could strike its adversary before the latter could launch its own offensive. German leaders endowed mobilization with particular importance because they foresaw a two-front war against France and Russia and concluded that the only way they could triumph was by striking rapidly against France in the west and, after defeating the French Army, wheeling eastward to confront Russia which, as the least advanced of the European powers, would, they expected, take longest to mobilize and prepare for war.

The importance generals attached to mobilizing and striking first as the key to survival and victory meant that there was little time for diplomacy or negotiation to prevent war from breaking out. If mobilization timetables were ignored or if enemies were permitted to mobilize first, the generals argued, then they would not take responsibility for the consequences. *This belief effectively shifted the decision about whether and when to go to war from political leaders to the generals.* Political leaders had little time to consider matters, as they were being pressured by their generals to go to war quickly or be held responsible for their countries' defeat. In this respect, the plans forced leaders to reverse completely the relationship between war and politics and between politicians and generals that Clausewitz had advocated about a century earlier. For the Germans in 1914, according to the Schlieffen Plan, this meant attacking Belgium and France before Russia could mobilize.

During the war, other innovations further transformed the nature of warfare. Among the most important were the airplane and the tank, both of which evolved in the years after the war to become the bases for Nazi tactics 20 years later. The airplane had only been invented 11 years before the war, and until the war's final stages was mainly used for scouting and engaging in aerial combat with enemy planes. However, the gigantic German dirigibles called *Zeppelins* repeatedly bombed Britain. By 1918, planes had also begun to strafe and bomb enemy positions.

The tank was first used by the British on September 15, 1916. Initially, it had little impact on the war because the early models tended to break down frequently. Mud fouled their treads; drivers could not see where they were going; and they were intolerably hot inside and so noisy that they announced the beginning of attacks clearly to the enemy. However, tanks were improved so that in November 1917, the British massed some 400 of them in the Battle of Cambrai, which finally enabled the Allies to break through Germany's strongest defensive fortifications known as the Hindenburg line.

World War I was also the setting for the first large-scale use of submarines in combat. This weapon, which continues to play a key role in military strategy in the nuclear age, proved invaluable to the Germans in the Great War as a means of disrupting Britain's supply routes, even while the British surface fleet enforced a blockade on Germany. On September 5, 1914, a German U-boat (*Unterseeboot*) fired the first wartime torpedo, sinking a British light cruiser in Scottish waters. A little over two weeks later another German U-boat sunk three British cruisers in just over one hour off the Dutch coast. In October, U-boats claimed their first merchant vessel.

Under international law of the time, naval vessels were supposed to take the crews of enemy ships aboard before sinking them. Initially, Germany tried to follow this custom, but in time it proved impossible owing to the small size of submarines and the danger to submarines in surfacing to take aboard enemy sailors. As both sides sought to starve each other by preventing supplies from getting through, the toll taken by submarines in ships and lives, including civilians, grew dramatically. In February 1915, Germany declared all the waters off the British coast a war zone in which all ships, including neutral ones, would be sunk without warning. While making tactical sense, the decision was politically sensitive, especially after the German sinking of the British liner *Lusitania* in May 1915 with the loss of 1,200 civilians, including 128 Americans. In September, fearing the anger of still neutral America, Germany agreed to cease unrestricted submarine warfare but resumed it again in February 1917 in a desperate gamble to bring Britain to its knees quickly. This decision, followed by the sinking of other US ships and the publication of a German effort to bring Mexico into the war against

Did you know?

The tank was so named in a British effort to keep their innovation a secret from the Germans. Initially, these weapons were shipped to France in crates marked tanks so that they appeared to be the large tank-like bathtubs that were in use near the front.

the United States,[14] finally brought an enraged America into the war on April 6, 1917.[15]

World War I also saw the first use of poison gas in warfare, and gas became a much feared weapon – one of indiscriminate terror and, in time, a weapon of mass destruction. Heavier than air, gas could be delivered with devastating effect upon soldiers in their trenches. The Germans first used poison gas in the second Battle of Ypres on April 22, 1915. Thought initially to be a smokescreen, the attack sent surviving French and Algerian defenders into panic. The British first used poison gas in September 1915 at Loos. Unlike the Germans, who had used shells to deliver gas, the British released it from opened canisters, so that depending on the wind, the gas might shift back upon the British themselves. Many gas victims were blinded, and the injuries it caused were intensely painful. The possibility of a poison gas attack meant that soldiers had to put on crude gas masks; and, if these proved ineffective, an attack could leave a victim in agony for days and weeks before he finally succumbed to his injuries. Chlorine and mustard gas were the most widely used, and 85,000 soldiers died, with over one million injured in gas attacks. Overall, the combination of modern technology and the resulting war of trench warfare and attrition produced unprecedented casualties.

Technology and the conduct of World War II

Having lost World War I, Germany turned its imagination to the next war, as did Japan, which had been embittered by the refusal of the Western allies to meet its demands in Asia. The Germans were impressed by the role tanks had played in the final stages of the war in France and by the ideas of French reformers like the young Colonel Charles de Gaulle (1890–1970) who advocated wars of mobility, featuring tanks and airplanes.[16] German planners were struck by the potential of aerial bombardment and submarine warfare, both of which had been introduced during World War I. As a result, they developed a strategy called *Blitzkrieg* (Lightening War) that combined mechanized and armored warfare with tactical air support and psychological warfare. They first tested part of this strategy during the Spanish Civil War (1936–39), especially in an infamous air attack on the Basque town of Guernica (see Theory in the real world on the bombing of Guernica).

Theory in the real world

At 4:30 p.m. – the busiest time of the day – on April 26, 1937, without provocation, German bombers of the Condor Legion attacked Guernica, in Spain, in order to test the tactics of the new *Luftwaffe* (air force) and its new *Blitzkrieg* strategy. For over three hours, the squadron rained bombs and gun fire on the helpless town. Over a third of Guernica's residents were killed or wounded. One survivor recalled that the "air was alive with the cries of the wounded. I saw a man crawling down the street, dragging his broken legs. . . . Pieces of people and animals were lying everywhere. In the wreckage there was a young woman. I could not take my eyes off her. Bones stuck through her dress. Her head twisted right around her neck. She lay, mouth open, her tongue hanging out."[17] Guernica is remembered today, partly owing to the passionate antiwar painting by the Spanish artist Pablo Picasso (1881–1973) that hangs today in the Prado Museum in Madrid, Spain.

Blitzkrieg depended on concentrating large numbers of tanks and mechanized vehicles in a small area, then punching through enemy defenses and wheeling behind his defending armies, severing supply routes and surrounding pockets of resistance in the process. The armored *panzers* (tanks) were closely supported by aircraft, the most notorious of which was the dive-bombing *Stuka*. In the invasion of France, this aircraft was used to bomb and strafe refugees, partly to "herd" them in ways that would clog roads and bridges and impede the movement of French army units. Moreover, in order to cause maximum fear among civilians, the *Stuka* was equipped with sirens called "Jericho Trumpets."

In contrast to Germany, France assumed that coming wars would resemble World War I – that is, wars of attrition dominated by static defenses in which both sides try to wear each other down. Looking to the past, France built a line of fortifications along its frontier with Germany from Belgium to the Swiss Alps. The Maginot Line, as it was called, was named after former minister of war, André Maginot (1877–1932). This strategy proved ineffective, however, because in invading France in 1940, the Germans avoided the Maginot Line entirely and swept through Luxembourg and the Ardennes Forest.

For its part, Japan was impressed by the claim of US General Billy Mitchell (1879–1936) that even the largest battleships were vulnerable to airpower. After World War I, Mitchell, a leading US airman of that war, tried to get the US Navy to pay more attention to the vulnerability of naval ships to airpower. To make his case, he conducted bombing tests in 1921 and 1923 that sank several battleships, including the German battleship *Ostfriesland* and the old US battleship *Alabama*, but Navy officials were not persuaded to explore these new ideas about warfare. Japanese officials were, however, and they used the time to build aircraft carriers, six of which were involved in their attacks on Pearl Harbor and the Philippines. In addition, they developed land-based Japanese aircraft, which they later used to sink the British battleship *Prince of Wales* only three days after the attack on Pearl Harbor. Only after the United States lost its battleships at Pearl Harbor did it emulate Japan and rely increasingly on naval aircraft in its island-hopping campaign.

Controversy

Between February 13 and 15, 1945, British and American bombers destroyed the German city of Dresden. Since then controversy has raged over the necessity and utility for the raid on a city that many claim had no military value. By 1945 the city housed numerous refugees fleeing from the East from where Russian forces were rapidly advancing as well as large numbers of German casualties. The allies' purpose in bombing Dresden was to disrupt German communications and transportation to the eastern front. Another possible purpose was to illustrate Western military power to the advancing Soviet army. Two waves of British bombers dropping high explosives and incendiaries attacked during the night and early morning, followed by American heavy bombers the following day. Much of the old city was burned down, with temperatures reaching 1,500°C (2,700°F) in a firestorm in the city's center. Between 25,000 and 35,000 Germans died in the raids, and the Nazis cited the attack in propaganda, urging Germans to resist to the end. The American novelist Kurt Vonnegut (1922–2007) was one of seven US prisoners of war who survived the bombing in a meatpacking cellar called Slaughterhouse Five, and he witnessed the effects of the bombing. Vonnegut's 1969 novel, *Slaughterhouse Five*, was based on this experience.

Large-scale strategic bombing was a central feature of World War II and was a major step toward Clausewitz's much feared absolute war. German attacks on London and Rotterdam indiscriminately targeted civilians. The allies did the same with greater effect. In one case, 1,300 British and American bombers attacked the German city of Dresden on February 13–15, 1945, and 334 American B-29s raided Tokyo on March 9–10. Both times incendiary bombs were used that created fire storms, sucking oxygen from the air and asphyxiating thousands of victims. In Tokyo, the fire storm destroyed about 16 square miles of the city and killed over 100,000 people. The atom bomb attacks on Hiroshima and Nagasaki in 1945 brought total warfare yet closer to reality (see the official bombing order from July 1945 in Key document: The order to bomb Hiroshima and Nagasaki). However, German atrocities against foes, and especially the murder of millions of European Jews in the Holocaust, constituted an unprecedented erosion of the protections previously accorded civilians in wartime.

Key document   The order to bomb Hiroshima and Nagasaki

TOP SECRET[18]

DECLASSIFIED

25 July 1945

TO: General Carl Spaatz

Commanding General

United States Army Strategic Air Forces

1   The 509 Composite Group, twentieth Air Force will deliver its first special bomb as soon as weather will permit visual bombing after about 3 August 1945 on one of the targets: Hiroshima, Kokura, Niigata and Nagasaki. To carry military and civilian scientific personnel from the War Department to observe and record the effects of the explosion of the bomb, additional aircraft will accompany the airplane carrying the bomb. The observing planes will stay several miles distant from the point of impact of the bomb.

2   Additional bombs will be delivered on the above targets as soon as made ready by the project staff. Further instructions will be issued concerning targets other than those listed above.

3   Discussion of any and all information concerning the use of the weapon against Japan is reserved to the Secretary of War and the President of the United States. No communiqués on the subject or releases of information will be issued by Commanders in the field without specific prior authority. Any news stories will be sent to the War Department for specific clearance. . . .

(Sgd) THOS. T. HANDY

THOS. T. HANDY

General, G.S.C.

Acting Chief of Staff

copy for General Groves

TOP SECRET

Technology and the Cold War standoff

Along with the sheer explosive power of nuclear weapons came new technologies to deliver them. For example, the 1940s and 1950s saw significant improvements in aircraft. Propeller-driven B-29s that could deliver a single atom bomb were replaced first by the turboprop B-36, and then by the all-jet B-52 with their larger payloads. The B-52 was used in Vietnam and still remains in use today. Also, beginning in the 1960s, both the Soviet Union and the US introduced **intercontinental ballistic missiles** (ICBMs), which allowed each to attack the other in minutes. Along with this development came the miniaturization of nuclear weapons so that each bomber or missile could deliver payloads measured in megatons (millions of tons of TNT) rather than kilotons (thousands of tons of TNT) as had been the case with the atom bombs of 1945. These technologies heightened the threat to noncombatants, making them the principal victims of nuclear war, and they also did away with the **hard shell of impermeability**[19] that armies and frontiers used to afford to states.

In tandem with these technological advances came new efforts to manage and limit wars, particularly because the Cold War was dominated by fear that the two superpowers would end in mutual annihilation. Moreover, nuclear war, according to some scientists, would have four related environmental consequences – "obscuring smoke in the troposphere, obscuring dust in the stratosphere, the fallout of radioactive debris, and the partial destruction of the ozone layer" – that combined would cause a period of darkness and cold on earth, a **nuclear winter**.[20] These conditions would destroy agriculture in the northern hemisphere and make water unavailable owing to freezing and contamination. Such concerns produced intense debate about the morality of war.

Still, world leaders sought ways to defend their countries against missiles. Proposed technologies included space satellites to give warning of attacks, an **antiballistic missile** system proposed by the United States in 1967, and President Ronald Reagan's Strategic Defense Initiative (SDI) in 1983, popularly known as "Star Wars" because it was based on satellite-based sensors and weapons. In 2001, President George W. Bush approved a more limited system of ground-based antiballistic missiles that can, it is claimed, destroy a small number of enemy missiles, especially those launched by "rogue states" like North Korea. This new system is currently being deployed, but many observers fear that the technology will not work and that, in any event, an enemy can overwhelm the system merely by building additional missiles or using alternative delivery systems.

intercontinental ballistic missile (ICBM) ballistic missile with a range of 3,000 to 8,000 nautical miles.

hard shell of impermeability the capacity, now largely gone, of states to defend their frontiers by military means.

nuclear winter a period of cold and darkness following a nuclear war, caused by the blocking of the sun's rays by high-altitude dust clouds.

antiballistic missile (ABM) missile designed to destroy incoming enemy missiles.

In recent years, concern has grown about chemical and biological weapons that are relatively inexpensive and potentially available to terrorists and "rogue" states. Chemical weapons, which employ toxic chemical compounds, can be grouped into several types of agents: *nerve agents* (e.g., sarin gas) prevent nerve messages from being transmitted throughout the body; *blood agents* (e.g., hydrogen cyanide) prevent the transfer of oxygen to tissue; *choking agents* (e.g., chlorine) irritate the respiratory tract; and *blistering agents* (e.g., mustard gas) cause painful burns and blisters. Biological weapons deliberately inflict disease by means of microorganisms, like viruses and bacteria, and naturally occurring toxins like venom. Some biological and chemical weapons are designed to kill, sometimes very quickly, while others only to incapacitate. These weapons are frightening, however, because they are relatively cheap to make and easy to disperse — and cannot discriminate between combatants and civilians or between friend and foe.

Following World War I, the use of chemicals was banned by the 1925 Geneva Protocol. And in 2002 most countries signed the Chemical Weapons Convention, which banned production and use of all chemical weapons, and the destruction of existing stocks of such weapons by 2005. Nevertheless, a number of countries are believed to have acquired such weapons, including Iran. Iran and Iraq used gas warfare in their 1981–88 war, and Iraq used gas against its Kurdish citizens in 1989. Also, the 1972 Biological Weapons Convention outlawed the development, production, or use of biological weapons. However, several incidents hold out the prospect that terrorists may acquire chemical or biological weapons. In March 1995, a Japanese Buddhist sect, Aum Shinrikyo, released sarin gas in a Tokyo subway station killing 12 people and sickening thousands more; and, in recent years, unknown terrorists have tried to spread anthrax in the United States through the US Mail.

One of the most notable of America's efforts to cope with the threat of unlimited war and the huge number of civilian casualties it would cause is the use of modern microelectronic technologies in warfare with the goal of making warfare more effective and less bloody.

The era of smart weapons

Taking advantage of the great strides in microelectronic technologies, the United States is pioneering a new form of high-tech "smart" warfare that aims to reduce the need for weapons of mass destruction and that promises to reduce American and enemy casualties, especially among civilians. Smart weapons are so accurate and lethal that they render conventional enemy aircraft and tanks virtually useless, but it remains unclear whether

Figure 7.2 Brainy bombs
© Original artist,
www.cartoonstock.com

"The smart bombs are getting too smart!"

such warfare can be used effectively against the major threats in global politics. This weapons advantage also has serious drawbacks. For example, countries that cannot compete at the high-tech level may conclude that, since it is futile to use conventional weapons against American forces, they must acquire weapons of mass destruction to deter American action in the first place. Also, some observers believe that even the most high-tech weapons will prove ineffective in fighting terrorism or guerrilla warfare. This leads some to ask if this is the right strategy for the United States, or whether Washington should be developing a leaner, more flexible military establishment that relies more heavily on Special Forces than on technology.

Starting in the Persian Gulf War of 1991, the United States began to unveil a new generation of "smart," or precision-guided, weapons that can hit targets with unprecedented accuracy. New microelectronic technologies allow US commanders to keep track of entire battlefields and communicate with and coordinate forces on the ground, at sea, and in the air. Improved versions of these systems were used in Kosovo (1999) and Afghanistan (2001–02). In 2003, US forces swept across the Iraqi desert, while much of the US arsenal consisted of precision weapons ranging from small armed Predator drones (small remote-controlled planes with television cameras and sometimes armed with missiles) to Tomahawk cruise missiles (unmanned aircraft that are self-contained bombs) and laser-guided munitions dropped by bombers (including stealth aircraft that cannot be seen by radar) and fired by naval vessels far from their targets.

These new technologies amount to what some call a "revolution in military affairs" (RMA)[21] that is bringing about a dramatic improvement in communication, coordination, planning, and intelligence that will include a Pentagon Internet or "Internet in the sky" that would provide comprehensive information to soldiers in the field.[22] This new military Internet will coordinate military operations and provide US commanders with instantaneous intelligence about their enemies' movements in battle. Smart weapons promise to reduce US and enemy casualties because, unlike the artillery, gravity bombs, and nuclear weapons of previous eras, they can hit military targets with minimal harm to surrounding areas and innocent civilians. Advocates of such warfare argue that soldiers will not have to slog it out in mud, jungle, or desert or fight it out house to house, and that civilians will be relatively safe in warfare.

These improvements are part of a new "American Way of War" that emphasizes speed, precision, and stealth. At the heart of this strategy, according to the American military thinker Steven Metz, "is a vast improvement in the quality and quantity of information made available to military commanders by improvements in computers and other devices for collecting, analyzing, storing, and transmitting data"[23] in order to manage the battlefield. The goal is to create a "system of systems" linking sensors in space, on the ground, in the air, and at sea in order to provide unprecedented information for purposes of command, control, and coordination in battle.[24] The near future may see innovations that dwarf today's weapons – robots for combat and intelligence as well as nanotechnology (technology for microscopic devices) and soldiers equipped to be "part human, part-machine cyborg."[25]

One key element in the "American Way of War" – the unwillingness to put soldiers at risk and the effort to reduce casualties – is rooted in a perception that citizens are less willing to die for their country than was the case in earlier American wars. In addition, Western norms are increasingly incompatible with large-scale collateral damage to adversaries (see Theory in the real world). Defending against – and then retaliating for – terrorist assaults on homeland targets is one thing; fighting in foreign wars without a powerfully convincing "national interest" at stake is quite another. High-tech war is one possible answer to limiting the destructiveness of war and reducing casualties and collateral damage.

In this, its use is in traditions of limiting violence by the Church in the Middle Ages, the kings of the eighteenth century, and liberals in the nineteenth and twentieth centuries.

Theory in the real world

On May 1, 2003, George W. Bush announced from the aircraft carrier USS *Abraham Lincoln* that major combat operations in Iraq had ended. His description of the conduct of the conflict exemplifies the "American Way of War":

> In the images of falling statues, we have witnessed the arrival of a new era. For hundreds of years of war, culminating in the nuclear age, military technology was designed and deployed to inflict casualties on an ever-growing scale. In defeating Nazi Germany and Imperial Japan, Allied forces destroyed entire cities, while enemy leaders who started the conflict were safe until the final days. Military power was used to end a regime by breaking a nation.
>
> Today, we have the greater power to free a nation by breaking a dangerous and aggressive regime. With new tactics and precision weapons, we can achieve military objectives without directing violence against civilians. No device of man can remove the tragedy from war; yet it is a great moral advance when the guilty have far more to fear from war than the innocent.[26]

Thus, high-tech war has benefits, but questions exist about its overall effectiveness. For example, in 2003, US technology pounded Iraq's army, but some of its main military units survived only to fight on in the postwar period of irregular warfare. In the War against Terrorism launched in Afghanistan by the United States after September 11, 2001, high-tech warfare proved of little value in managing a bewildering array of rival ethnicities, religious factions, criminal networks, and warlord bands. The Taliban and Al Qaeda were put to flight easily, but the search for Osama bin Laden and most of the Al Qaeda leadership came up short because of difficult terrain and dependence on unreliable Afghan and Pakistani proxies.

High-tech systems themselves, like computers, are vulnerable to high-tech retaliation in the form of cyberwar (computers attacking computers).[27] Concerns about the exposure of US computer systems to cyberattack led the Clinton administration to plan for a comprehensive

Figure 7.3 Smart bombs/
simple bombs
© Original artist,
www.cartoonstock.com

computer monitoring system. "Instead of using explosives to kill and
destroy, the warrior of the future" may be armed "with a laptop computer
from a motel room," and thus, "[h]acking, virus-writing, and crashing
data information systems – as well as defending against enemy hackers
and virus writers – may become core military skills, as important as the
ability to shoot."[28] Future war "may see attacks via computer viruses,
worms, logic bombs, and trojan horses rather than bullets, bombs, and
missiles."[29]

An important relationship has always existed between technology and
warfare, and this relationship has become more threatening with the
introduction of weapons of mass destruction. Such weapons partly explain
how some countries became great powers, but the relationship between
power and weaponry is more complex still. As we shall see in the
following sections, many of today's most deadly conflicts rely on
unconventional, and sometimes primitive, weapons and tactics.

Irregular wars

The end of the Cold War marked a profound shift in the nature of war:
a substantial increase in the number of civil wars. In recent decades, the
world has seen a proliferation of ethnic, nationalist, and religious conflicts
among subnational groups. As shown in Table 7.1, *intrastate*, or civil, wars
are now more prevalent in global politics than *interstate* wars. A number
of factors contribute to this change including the breakup of large

Table 7.1   Numbers of wars between 1820 and 1997

Decade	International wars	Civil wars	Total wars
1820–29	8	7	15
1830–39	5	11	16
1840–49	12	9	21
1850–59	14	8	22
1860–69	13	14	27
1870–79	14	9	23
1880–89	15	3	18
1890–99	20	9	29
1900–09	10	7	17
1910–19	14	11	25
1920–29	8	12	20
1930–39	11	8	19
1940–49	8	9	17
1950–59	9	20	29
1960–69	9	16	25
1970–79	10	26	36
1980–89	4	19	23
1990–97	1	24	25

multi-ethnic federations, notably the Soviet Union and Yugoslavia, and the loss of generous foreign aid packages that allowed frail, but friendly, regimes to maintain control over rebellious factions through the Cold War. As we shall see, the developing world has been the site of much of the world's bloodiest violence in recent years. Although there have been few conventional wars in this region, for the most part the developing world has been the scene of intermittent irregular or unconventional warfare.

Such warfare is very different from the conventional wars in the developed world that characterized much of the three centuries of warfare after the 1648 Peace of Westphalia. Europe's dynastic states, conscious of the devastation of the religious wars of the sixteenth and seventeenth centuries, followed policies in which civilians were largely left alone by warring armies as long *as they did not themselves take up arms*. Thus, a distinction arose between legitimate warfare and crime. When civilians took up arms they were regarded by states as rebels and criminals and, therefore, subject to execution. The distinction between war and crime does not exist in most of the conflicts that afflict the developing world, and, though the term guerrilla (meaning "little war" in Spanish) was first used by Spanish irregulars who rose up against Napoléon's occupation of their country, guerrilla warfare has been a feature of conflict in the less-developed countries (LDCs).

In recent years, the collapse of states in the developing world has produced regional and global instability and bred warriors whose use of new and more deadly forms of violence is inspired by religion, nationalism, and greed. These conflicts have witnessed a proliferation of civil strife in which the distinction between civilians and soldiers has blurred. Often combatants fight on behalf of nonstate groups, including bands of domestic insurgents, foreign terrorists, revolutionaries, and even criminals. As a rule, combatants in the LDCs lack the organizational skills, high technology, and material resources needed to wage conventional war and, instead, utilize forms of violence suited to the poor and weak.

We begin this exploration of unconventional violence observing the evolution and tactics of guerrilla warfare. We then consider the role of collapsing states in the spread of violence.

Guerrillas, anti-colonial struggles, and revolutionaries

Unconventional warfare has existed in much of history. How has guerrilla warfare been used in the past, and how has it evolved? In this section, we shall show how such warfare has served the interests of those seeking to topple governments in the developing world, especially in the hands of Chinese, Latin American, and Vietnamese revolutionaries.

In 500 BC, Chinese general Sun Tzu wrote a military treatise, *The Art of War*, in which he argued that it was best to avoid conventional battles and instead use deception whenever possible. In his view, "the skillful leader subdues the enemy's troops without any fighting; he captures their cities without laying siege to them; he overthrows their kingdom without any lengthy operations in the field."[30] In general, Sun Tzu regarded unconventional warfare as the strategy for the weak when fighting the strong, with whom they cannot compete in conventional warfare.

According to the Old Testament, Joshua used guerrilla tactics against his enemies. So did American Minutemen during the Revolutionary War, French snipers (*francs-tireurs*) in the Franco-Prussian War, Philippine insurgents against US forces after the Spanish–American War, Boer raiders in the Boer War, and the partisan resistance against the Nazis in World War II. All these cases involved the weak in conflict against the strong.

Guerrilla strategists drew inspiration from the tactics pioneered by Mao Zedong during China's civil war (chapter 4, pp. 173–5), especially his wedding of guerrilla tactics to political warfare. Mao had a powerful influence on Ho Chi Minh and his Vietnamese revolutionaries (chapter 4, pp. 179–82). Mao's ideas also influenced Latin American revolutionaries, especially Fidel Castro (1926–) and Che (Ernesto) Guevara (1928–67) in their successful campaign in overthrowing Cuban dictator Fulgencio Batista (1901–73) and installing a communist regime in 1959. Che, who was Argentine, served as a minister in Castro's government before emerging in 1966 as a guerrilla leader in Bolivia, where he was captured and executed a year later. Che wrote two books on guerrilla warfare in which he recommended its use to America's opponents in the developing world. His ideas were widely read throughout the less-developed regions of the world where they inspired the use of unconventional warfare by revolutionaries.

Guerrilla tactics proved especially effective when used by anti-colonial movements in Africa and Asia. They played a key role in the Algerian Revolution (1954–62), as well as the independence struggles of Angola, Mozambique, Zimbabwe, and Namibia. They were also employed effectively by the African National Congress in its struggle to overthrow the white supremacist (*apartheid*) regime in South Africa.

Nevertheless, state institutions never completely took root in some LDCs and, in recent decades, some of these war-torn countries have collapsed or threaten to do so. We now turn our attention to a number of cases of such states and to the violence that has afflicted them.

Machetes and failed states

Recent decades have witnessed an upsurge in violence within and across states owing to national, tribal, and ethnic conflicts, largely in the world's postcolonial and impoverished regions. There, Europeans imposed states and borders that the inhabitants never fully accepted. When the colonial governments withdrew, the governments that followed were unable to provide minimal services to citizens (see chapter 12). When combined with poverty, overpopulation, and environmental stress, state institutions in these countries collapsed, resulting in what are called failed states. And failed or failing states such as Afghanistan, Iraq, and Somalia are "havens" for terrorists.[31]

The governments of such states are deemed illegitimate by their citizens, are unable to exercise authority over the state's territory, cannot provide security or essential services to citizens, and usually confront armed opponents. Some observers believe that the United Nations or the West should administer failed states until they can manage their own affairs. Critics argue that this would be a new form of colonialism.

A recent analysis associated 12 conditions with state weakness.[32] They are:

1 *Demographic pressures* in which population outstrips resources like food.

2   *Refugees and internally displaced persons* who have grievances against the government such as many Sunni Arabs in Iraq.

3   *Vengeance-seeking groups* with grievances based on the belief that they are unfairly treated.

4   *Chronic and sustained flight* from the country by highly trained and educated citizens.

5   *Uneven economic and social development* in which some groups have fewer economic and educational opportunities than others.

6   *Sharp and severe economic decline* reflected in high unemployment and corruption.

7   *The loss of legitimacy by the state* in which citizens no longer regard it as authoritative and view it as serving only the interests of a corrupt minority.

8   *The absence or collapse of public services* such as education and health care.

9   *The rule of law and human rights* are applied unevenly.

10 *The security apparatus has fractured into "states within the state"* and take the form of militias favoring particular groups or leaders rather than providing security for the general population.

11 *The risk of fractionalized elites is high* as in Iraq where Shia, Sunni, and Kurdish leaders vie for power.

12 *The intervention of other states and external actors* in the country's domestic affairs.

Based on these indicators, as of 2006 there were 20 failed states, an additional 20 that were in danger of failing, and 20 more that were borderline, including such major countries as Russia and China.[33] Six of ten weakest states are in Africa – Sudan, the Democratic Republic of the Congo, Ivory Coast, Zimbabwe, Chad, and Somalia – and the others are Iraq, Haiti, Pakistan, and Afghanistan.

We will examine several cases of failed states in Africa, including those of Somalia, Liberia, Rwanda, and the Democratic Republic of the Congo, where governments have collapsed and armies have become personal militias for tribal groups, warlords, and local thugs. Each of these cases has had a critical impact on contemporary global politics:

- In Somalia, the death of 18 US soldiers (portrayed in the film *Black Hawk Down*) drove the Clinton administration to avoid other humanitarian interventions;

- Liberia became the archetype of limitless and endless violence for nonpolitical reasons;

- Rwanda became a prototype of ethnic **genocide**; and

- Congo became the model for **transnational war**, involving soldiers from several states in the region.

genocide the extermination of an ethnic, racial, or cultural group.

transnational war war involving unofficial militias and violent groups that flows across state frontiers.

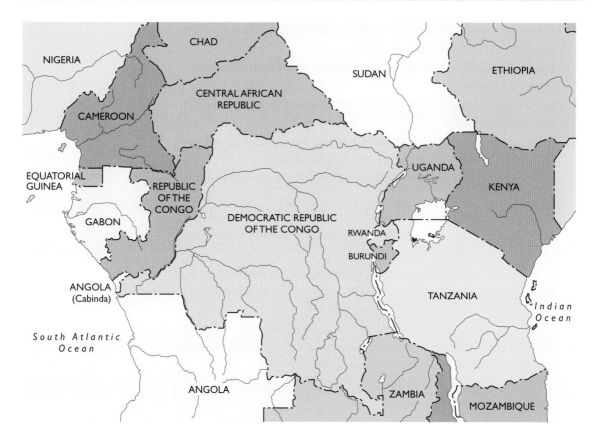

Map 7.1 Central Africa

In such cases, the distinction between legitimate war and crime has vanished, and civilians are the leading victims of humanitarian disasters that uproot millions. In the violence that engulfed such countries, political ends are scarcely visible. Instead, combatants, not unlike soldiers in the Thirty Years' War, seek personal power, loot, or vengeance against opponents.

In *Somalia*, after the 1991 overthrow of dictator Mohamed Siad Barré (1919–95), civil war broke out among rival clan chiefs. During the next two years, some 50,000 were killed and as many as 300,000 died in an accompanying famine. In late 1992, US forces landed in Somalia to lead a UN-sponsored effort to restore order and permit the movement of relief supplies. However, on October 3, 1993, 18 American soldiers were killed in Somalia's capital, Mogadishu, and US forces abruptly left the country. Recently, the clan militias, despite American aid, were defeated by an Islamist movement that is confronting a weak provisional government that is being propped up by Ethiopia.[34] Somalia still has no functioning central government and is a haven for Islamic terrorists and criminals. Whoever "wins" power in Somalia will find little worth winning as the country, like the Horn of Africa more generally, is the site of explosive overpopulation, a devastated environment that has only 5 percent of its original habitat, and a vast quantity of arms – three cows will buy a Russian AK-47 and five cows will purchase a US M-16.[35]

Between December 1989 and 1996, the West African country of *Liberia*, which had been founded by freed American slaves in 1816, was engulfed in civil war. What began with the overthrow of the government of President Samuel K. Doe (1951–90), rapidly deteriorated into a violent war among warlords and their personal militias. The militias drafted children as young as 8 years of age and caused thousands of civilian deaths as they destroyed the country's capital, Monrovia, and ravaged its economy. The war cost 150,000 lives and displaced over one million Liberians.

A peace agreement was brokered in August 1996 by a monitoring group of the Economic Community of West African States (ECOWAS) with UN help under which a military contingent authorized by the ECOWAS was to oversee the return of normalcy in Liberia. The next year saw the election of Charles Taylor (1948–) as the country's president. Taylor, who in 1985 had escaped from a prison in Massachusetts where he had been charged with embezzlement, had sparked the war in the first place, and he had helped to trigger civil war in neighboring countries Sierra Leone, Guinea, and the Ivory Coast in search of booty, especially diamonds. Confronted by economic sanctions, global pressure, and the prospect of renewed civil strife, Taylor stepped down and went into exile in Nigeria in August 2003. He was subsequently arrested in 2006 as he tried to cross into Cameroon and was put on trial in Freetown, Sierra Leone before the UN Special Court for Sierra Leone.

Taylor's interference in Sierra Leone, spearheaded by a 1991 invasion, was aimed at securing control over that country's diamond mines. Even as government forces tried to repel the invaders, a brutal anti-government group called the Revolutionary United Front (RUF) led by Foday Sankoh (1937–2003) emerged, aided by Taylor, aiming to gain control of the country's diamonds for itself. Civil strife continued in the following years, displacing more than one-third of the country's population, and marked by frequent changes in the government in Freetown, the country's capital. After the governing military junta was overthrown in 1997, a Nigerian peacekeeping force entered the country. During the next two years, RUF rebels terrorized the country, kidnapping children and forcing them to be soldiers, raping women, and hacking off the limbs of men, women, and even children. Despite a series of ceasefires, the killing continued until November 2000. In 2004, a UN-sponsored international tribunal was convened to prosecute the killers.

Africa's bloodiest conflict began with the attempted genocide of ethnic Tutsis in *Rwanda* in 1994 by ethnic Hutus. For centuries, Tutsi kings in

Rwanda and neighboring Burundi had imposed a feudal system in which Hutus were serfs. Both the German and Belgian colonial rulers in the region had maintained Tutsi domination. However, beginning in Rwanda in 1959, three years before the country's independence, tribal violence broke out when a series of elections led to Hutu-dominated governments. Thereafter, periodic spasms of tribal violence continued in both Rwanda and Burundi. In 1990 the Tutsi-dominated Rwandan Patriotic Front (RPF) began an effort to overthrow the Hutu government from bases in Uganda.

Thereafter, a conspiracy of Hutu military leaders evolved to exterminate the Tutsis, and the massacre began in April 1994 after a plane carrying the presidents of Rwanda and Burundi was shot down near Kigali, Rwanda's capital. In the murderous weeks that followed, between one-half and one million Tutsis were killed, often by machete-wielding Hutu neighbors, many of whom were forced against their will by militants to participate in atrocities. After the US experience in Somalia, the United States and other members of the global community, although aware of the genocide that was taking place, were unwilling to intervene.

Figure 7.4 Remains of genocide victims at Nyamata church, Rwanda
Richard Horsey

Simultaneously, the Tutsi-dominated RPF invaded the country, seized the capital Kigali, and set up a new government. RPF forces then chased the Hutu militias out of Rwanda. Recalling these events ten years later, a member of the International Rescue Committee wrote of how he "went to Goma, Zaire, in July 1994, just days after over 1 million refugees fled there from Rwanda. . . . The repugnant nature of everything that happened there: murder, torture, a government killing its people, genocide – overwhelmed me and many others."[36] Bill Clinton later called the failure to intervene in Rwanda the greatest regret of his presidency. "All over the world," he declared, "there were people like me sitting in offices, day after day, who did not fully appreciate the depth and the speed with which you were being engulfed in this unimaginable terror."[37]

By the middle of July, over a million Hutus had fled to squalid refugee camps in eastern Congo (then Zaire). There, Hutu militias took control of the camps and staged raids into Rwanda, making it impossible for civilians to return home. In autumn 1996, Tutsi-led Rwandan forces invaded several of the camps, forcing many refugees home or deeper into Congo and routing the Hutu militias that, with many refugees, fled further and further westward into jungles. The struggle became linked to politics in Congo, which had been disintegrating politically and economically since the early 1990s and where dissatisfaction with long-time dictator Mobutu Sese Seko (1930–97) had grown.

Congolese Tutsis, aided by the Rwandan government, clashed with elements of the Congolese army that tried to force them from the country. By late October, anti-Mobutu forces had formed under the command of Mobutu's long-time foe, Laurent-Désiré Kabila (1939–2001). Kabila's rebels, aided by Uganda, Rwanda, Burundi, Angola, and Zambia, all angered by Mobutu's support of rebels in their countries, began to move against him. All were seeking political influence in Congo as well as a share of Congo's resources, especially diamonds, timber, and tantalum (coltan) – a metal vital in making cell phones. Most of eastern Congo fell into rebel hands quickly. The Congolese government in the capital of Kinshasa, long unable to exercise authority over its own forces or over the country's huge hinterland, was no longer able to exercise sovereignty. By spring 1997, all the country's major cities had fallen to Kabila's forces. On May 16, Mobutu fled, and Kabila declared himself president.

Kabila himself then lost popularity owing to his authoritarian style of rule. He alienated his Rwandan and Ugandan allies by turning against them and Congo's Tutsis as he sought to shore up his waning support among the Congolese. In mid-1998, the Tutsis, aided by Rwanda and Uganda, moved against Kabila in a replay of what had happened two years earlier. Kabila, in turn, was aided by Angola, Zimbabwe, Namibia,

Chad, and Sudan. Like Germany in the Thirty Years' War, Congo became a carcass on which other states fed, and the initial conflict had become a genuine transnational war. Between 1998 and 2006, about four million died – over 1,000 each day, many of whom were children – as a result of the war and accompanying hunger and disease, making the conflict perhaps the most deadly since 1945.[38] Kabila was assassinated in January 2001 and replaced by his son Joseph who began negotiations with the various rebel groups, and in July the multiple parties agreed to form a government together. Elections were held in August 2006, and a runoff in October resulted in Joseph Kabila's reelection. However, the loser, Vice-President Jean-Pierre Bemba, disputed the outcome, and it did not end the regional divisions between the country's east and west.[39]

State failure and violence, especially in Africa, have had tragic consequences, giving rise to savage violence against civilians. The next section examines the possibility of similar violence in larger and more critical states.

Others at risk of state failure

Civil violence also threatens the integrity of several larger and more resource-rich states, including Colombia ("in danger"), Nigeria ("in danger"), and Indonesia ("in danger") (see Map 7.1), and this section briefly describes the prospect for state failure in those states. Also, the disintegration of Yugoslavia (see chapter 15, pp. 723–31) showed that Europe was not immune to the disease, and events in Haiti, where President Jean-Bertrand Aristide (1953–) was overthrown in 2004, reflect similar problems.[40]

Colombia has suffered from endemic violence since the late 1940s. The violence increased dramatically in the 1960s as leftist guerrilla groups, inspired by the Cuban revolution, took up arms. By the late 1990s, however, the guerrillas were ceded control of large areas in the country's southeastern region that still remain largely in their hands. At the same time, on the other side of Colombia's political spectrum, paramilitary right-wing groups used terror against leftists and innocent civilians. These guerrilla groups fund themselves by kidnapping and selling protection to cocaine producers. The rising violence and the failure of the state to cope with it threaten Colombia's existence and reflect the difficulty governments have in dealing with irregular forms of warfare.

Nigeria, with Africa's largest population and oil reserves, faces a variety of bitter identity cleavages and also finds its future in jeopardy. Some of its cleavages result from the imposition of boundaries by the country's former colonial master. As a result of those boundaries, the country consists of four main tribal groups concentrated in different regions of the country: Hausa (north), Fulani (north), Ibo (east), and Yoruba (west). Each is fragmented by clan, lineage, and village affiliations. Religion forms a second cleavage, with Hausa and Fulani largely Muslim, Ibo Catholic, and Yoruba Muslim and Anglican. Civil war erupted in 1967 after the Ibo, angered by mistreatment at the hands of the dominant Hausa, declared their region the independent Republic of Biafra. By January 1970, the Ibo had lost, but their anger and resentment remain. In recent years, religion has become a potent source of division owing to a resurgence of Islam in the country's north with the result that large areas were placed under Koranic law (*sharia*). Thus, tribal, religious, and regional strains threaten to erupt into large-scale violence and menace the country's very survival.

Centrifugal forces are visible in a number of regions of heavily populated and oil-rich *Indonesia*. Since 1989, for example, Aceh, a Muslim oil-producing region in northern Sumatra, has sought independence in a violent struggle. A number of peace agreements have been made and broken in recent years between the Acehnese and Indonesia's leaders, and the army imposed martial law on the region in May 2003. However, as a result of cooperation between the Indonesian army and the Acehnese following the devastating tsunami of December 2004, prospects for peace there have greatly improved.

Map 7.2 Indonesia

Figure 7.5 After the tsunami
in Aceh, 2004
Courtesy of International Aid

Elsewhere, in Irian Jaya (now Papua) on the western half of the island
of New Guinea, the Dutch retained control until 1962 when the area
was placed under UN authority for six years after which a referendum was
to be held in which Papuans would choose either independence or
integration into Indonesia. Unwilling to wait, Indonesia immediately
seized control, and, after a rigged 1969 election, West Irian was formally
annexed by Indonesia. Since the 1960s, the Free Papua Movement has
been fighting for independence, and the region was granted significant
domestic autonomy in January 2002. Papua New Guinea, across the
border on the eastern half of the island, had been a German and British
colony and gained full independence in 1975.

Also in Indonesia, the Molucca Islands (see Map 7.2), especially
Ambon, have witnessed repeated violent clashes between Muslims
and Christians, many of whom remained pro-Dutch after Indonesia's
independence. In April 1950, a separatist Republic of South Molucca
was declared at Ambon that was crushed within months triggering the
exodus of thousands of Ambonese soldiers to the Netherlands. A peace

Figure 7.6 After the October 2002 Bali bombing
Photo courtesy of Australian Federal Police

agreement between the factions was signed in 2002, but trouble has not ended.

Ethnic violence has also wracked Kalimantan, the Indonesian region of Borneo which it shares with Malaysia with which Indonesia had a border conflict between 1962 and 1966. There, indigenous Dayaks, sometimes resorting to their traditional practice of headhunting, seek to expel the minority Muslim Madurese, who migrated to Kalimantan because of the Indonesian government's policy of moving people from densely populated to less-populated regions.

Finally, Indonesia was forced out of East Timor, which it had seized in 1975 when Portugal gave up its colony. In the ensuing years, the Indonesian army sought to suppress the Timorese independence movement called Fretilin during which as many as 200,000 Timorese were killed. In August 1999 in a UN-supervised referendum, the East Timorese voted for independence. In the interim, Indonesian authorities engaged in a fruitless effort to crush armed insurrection by East Timorese secessionists, and were faced with strong international pressure. Following the vote, Indonesian military units and Timorese militias opposed to independence violently attacked the East Timorese. The violence ended only after the intervention of a UN force that administered the country until it became officially independent in May 2002.

Islamic terrorism arrived in Indonesia in October 2002, when the bombing of a nightclub on the resort island of Bali frequented by Western tourists cost almost 200 lives. A second bombing struck Bali in late 2005. The perpetrators were affiliated with *Jemaah Islamiyah*, a militant Islamic movement linked to Al Qaeda. In sum, Indonesia is threatened with violence and state failure owing to religious, regional, and national differences.

In sum, several major countries around the world face potential state failure owing to endemic violence and civil war. Intrastate or civil wars are different than interstate wars in a number of ways. As we shall see in the next section, they have different causes, pose different problems, and are especially difficult to resolve.

Intrastate war

A number of factors have contributed to the spread of civil strife in global politics since the end of the Cold War, including the breakup of large multi-ethnic federations, notably the Soviet Union and Yugoslavia, and the loss of generous foreign aid packages that had allowed frail, but friendly, regimes to maintain control over rebellious factions.

The goals, conduct, and course of these intrastate wars are significantly different from the interstate wars that dominated recent centuries. Intrastate wars pose a challenge to the conventional wisdom regarding war because they are so varied in terms of their causes and their conduct. Some are fought by rebels seeking control of a government, booty, and territory; others are fought by ethnic minorities seeking independence; still others, like the civil war in Rwanda, seem devoid of any material objective other than mass murder. In terms of their conduct, intrastate wars tend to be unconventional wars that rely on guerrilla warfare, in stark contrast to interstate wars.

Did you know?

Since 1992, all forms of war have become less frequent and less violent. The number of armed conflicts has fallen by more than 40 percent and the number of "very deadly" wars has fallen by 80 percent. From 1950 to 2002, the average number of people killed per conflict has fallen from 38,000 to just over 600.[41]

What is distinctive about these intrastate wars and what makes them so violent? We begin by considering what political scientists mean by a civil war. J. David Singer and Melvin Small emphasize the kinds of political entities involved. They argue that whereas an interstate war is a military conflict "in which at least one sufficiently active participant on each side is a qualified nation member of the interstate system,"[42] a civil war is an *internal* conflict. (In both cases, they require at least 1,000 battle deaths each year for the conflict to be categorized as a war.) Some analyses exclude mass killings, such as those that occurred in Rwanda, specifying that government forces and identifiable rebel forces must participate and suffer at least 5 percent of the casualties.[43] Such civil wars may be ethnic or non-ethnic in nature. Non-ethnic civil wars involve disputes over control of the state, namely its institutions and territory. They are *militarized contests for political power*. Ethnic civil wars, in contrast, are waged among groups that see themselves as distinct ethnic, national, or religious communities. Their identities and goals are incompatible with those of the group in control of the state. Indeed, they want more than control of the state; they want to redefine or divide it.

Sources of intrastate war

Understanding the causes of intrastate wars is imperative in order to manage and contain them. Such wars have profound effects: they destroy national economies, leaving civilian populations impoverished; they can spill over into neighboring states and become a regional problem, particularly when transnational ethnic communities are involved; and participants often contribute to and profit from transnational criminal networks. We now consider the dominant explanations for intrastate wars – ethnic and non-ethnic – by levels of analysis. Bear in mind that, in general, intrastate wars are very complex, and, thus, several of the following factors must be considered to explain the outbreak of any particular war. As in efforts to uncover the causes of interstate wars, most of the research on the causes of intrastate wars is empirical in nature, reflecting the efforts of the field's "scientists" to discern patterned behavior in global politics.

The fallout of interstate conflict: the global level of analysis

At the level of the global system, some conflicts begin as a result of interstate conflict. According to political scientists Raymond Taras and Rajat Ganguly, a conflict between a state containing a minority transnational ethnic group and an **irredentist** neighbor (for example,

irredentism a claim to territory based on historical ties to the land or an ethnic or cultural affinity with its population.

Serbia in 1914) may create an ethnic conflict within the state. The irredentist state's claims to its ethnic kin may create expectations among that group that it will gain independence from the status quo state, producing antagonism between the ethnic group and its government. Also, if pressure is too great from the irredentist state, the status quo state may begin to repress the minority ethnic group, reducing its civil and political liberties, and/or strengthen efforts to assimilate it into the majority population. Finally, under such repression, the ethnic group may try to break free from the status quo state, either to join the irredentist state or to form a new independent state.[44] Interstate conflict can be an important contributing factor to the outbreak of intrastate conflict in regions like Africa and Central Asia where there are significant transnational ethnic groups.

Internal conflict may also be a product of rivalries that lead external powers to side with different factions that become their proxies in countries in which they are competing. During the Cold War, for example, the United States and USSR competed with each other in many less-developed countries, each backing its own faction. Angola, the Democratic Republic of the Congo, and Nigeria are only a few of the countries in which such competition took place.

State-level explanations

There are also several possible sources for intrastate wars at the state level. The dominant explanations emphasize deep, historical animosities, conflicts over scarce resources, redressing past and present injustices, and security dilemmas arising from conditions of domestic anarchy. We examine each of these explanations in turn.

Ethnic hatred There is controversy over the extent to which ethnic hatred is a genuine cause of intrastate wars, even those that appear to be identity wars. Some of the earliest explanations for ethnic warfare emphasized ancient, or primordial, animosities. According to this explanation, some groups have deep grievances that reach far back into history. The only way to achieve peace is by the presence of a strong central authority, and when such an authority disappears, conflict reignites. This is one explanation offered for recurring conflict in the Balkans. Serb nationalists, for instance, trace the conflict between Serbs and Kosovar Albanians (chapter 15, pp. 706–7) back to the 1389 Battle of Kosovo Pojle in which the Serbs were defeated by the Ottoman Turks. Serb nationalism has long sought to "avenge Kosovo," even though it is probably true that both Serbs and Albanians fought side by side in this battle.

This explanation is controversial and inherently unsatisfying. After all, if ancient hostility is the primary factor in contemporary identity conflicts, then the long periods of peace among such groups is difficult to explain. In addition, if we accept the explanation, it follows that it will be virtually impossible to prevent future conflict, and the future looks bleak for the Balkans, Iraq, Afghanistan, and other regions that have religious and ethnic minorities. In fact, many ethnic and national groups live together peacefully and resolve disputes without war. The Czechs and Slovaks, for example, opted for a peaceful "Velvet Divorce" that was finalized on January 1, 1993. Thus, political scientist Paul Collier concludes that ethnic strife is really a "myth," and that "conflicts in ethnically diverse countries can be ethnically patterned without being ethnically caused."[45] We now examine the rival explanations.

Economic explanations   Collier argues that historical grievances are an excuse for rebel leaders and that economic incentives and opportunities provide more persuasive explanations for civil wars.[46] In fact, studies suggest that there is a higher incidence of civil war in low-income countries with weak governing structures that depend heavily on natural resources for their export earnings. Thus, one rational-choice economic explanation is loot seeking – civil war for private gain. Valuable natural resources like petroleum (Iraq), diamonds (Sierra Leone), or timber (Cambodia) offer incentives for conflict because they provide rebels with the means to fund and equip their groups and, if they succeed, to survive as an independent state. But the mere presence of natural resources is not sufficient for conflict. War is more likely to erupt if rebels have labor to take advantage of the resource and if the government is too weak to defend its natural resources.

A variant of the loot-seeking argument focuses on the gain from war itself. Leaders, on both sides of the conflict, create infrastructure in government and society to wage war and invest heavily in weapons and training of soldiers. They profit personally from these investments and, thus, have little incentive to stop fighting.

Justice seeking   Alternatively, civil wars may be a product of groups seeking revenge and justice for past and present wrongs. Such wars are likely to break out when there is significant social fragmentation, with large numbers of unemployed and uneducated young men, political repression, or social fragmentation. According to the *theory of relative deprivation*, people rebel when they receive less than they think they deserve and, thus, seek to right economic or political wrongs. Such groups believe that they are deprived of national wealth that is given to other groups or that they are being denied a voice in the political system. But it is not just recognizing deprivation that causes war. Rather, the incentives to rebel include the group's perception that the deprivation is unfair, that others receive what they are denied, and that the state is unwilling to remedy the situation. This theory also explains why both relatively privileged and deprived groups may mobilize. The former, like the Tamils in Sri Lanka and the Sikhs in India, mobilize to protect their advantaged position, while the latter, for example, India's Dalits or "untouchables", mobilize to end discrimination.[47]

Minorities in Nigeria mobilize over such distributional issues. There are about 40 distinct ethnic minorities in the oil-rich Niger Delta region, all of which have seen little political or economic gain from Nigeria's oil riches, despite the fact that the region accounts for 75 percent of Nigeria's export earnings (and oil accounts for over 90 percent of Nigeria's national revenue).[48] Rather, they remain impoverished while oil wealth flows to dominant ethnic groups in other parts of the country. The government has responded to their demands for improved economic and political status with violent repression. Thus, observers speak of the "resource curse" and the "curse of oil" because the great wealth it brings produces corruption on the part of leaders who skim off profits for themselves and their cronies, inflation, indifference to other economic sectors, environmental damage, inequality, resentment, and, in the end, strife.

In an effort to combat the "curse of oil," the World Bank agreed to provide funding for an oil pipeline in Chad on the condition that the government put aside its profits in special funds to improve citizens' lives. Unfortunately, Chad went back on the agreement,[49] but the idea of establishing a fund beyond a government's control to prevent waste and misuse – and conflict – is a promising one.

Security dilemmas As we saw in chapter 6 (pp. 280–3), a security dilemma exists when one actor's efforts to enhance its security threaten others and produces the unintended consequence of greater insecurity for all. Although realists regard security dilemmas as a source of interstate conflict in anarchic global systems, they can also be sources of conflict within states whenever governing structures disintegrate creating a condition of domestic anarchy in which each group's efforts to defend itself appear threatening to others. The dilemma is intensified by the inability to distinguish adequately between offensive and defensive weapons and the tendency of each party's rhetoric to signal offensive intentions. Domestic security dilemmas can be particularly severe because they are likely to be coupled with predatory goals, given the resource or economic dimension to many civil conflicts.[50]

Individual-level explanations

It is necessary to tread carefully in the realm of individual-level explanations of civil, and particularly ethnic, conflicts. As the previous pages suggest, civil conflicts, including those with an ethnic dimension, occur in a political, economic, and historical context in which factors from each dimension reinforce the incentive and opportunity for war. Yet, individual-level explanations provide insights about the passions of ordinary citizens in many of today's most violent intrastate conflicts such as the Rwanda genocide and ethnic cleansing in Bosnia and Kosovo.

Psychologists have tried to understand the complex relationship between individual identity and intergroup conflict. One such effort, *social identity theory*, emphasizes the role of psychological processes in explaining conflict among groups. Its central proposition is that individuals desire – indeed have a psychological need – to belong to groups that have positive and distinct identities. Each individual's social identity comes from belonging to a group (or groups) that has some value attached to it. Individuals in groups engage in social comparison with other groups to assess their group's and their individual position and status. Individuals whose group membership provides a negative or indistinct social identity will seek to change it. They may seek to be absorbed into a dominant group, redefine a previously negative characteristic of their group, create new dimensions for comparison, or engage in direct competition with the dominant group.[51] When the first three options are unavailable, as when there are historic injustices, resource inequalities, or privileged groups that are unwilling to allow change, direct conflict is likely.

Managing intrastate war

There are significant obstacles to managing intrastate conflicts because participants often must live together once the conflict ends. It is difficult to negotiate agreements that all parties can, literally, live with. Thus, most civil conflicts do not end in negotiation. Between 1940 and 1990, only 20 percent of civil wars (compared to 55 percent of interstate wars during that same period) ended by negotiation. Indeed, according to political scientist Barbara Walter, most internal wars "ended with the extermination, expulsion, or capitulation of the losing side."[52] Walter argues that there are inherent qualities to civil wars that make them particularly difficult to resolve. One difference from interstate wars is that the adversaries cannot keep their separate militias if they negotiate a peace. This poses an obstacle to settlement because there is no neutral police force or governing authority to enforce the peace agreement. As in the reliance of Iraq's Shia, Sunni, and Kurdish populations on their own armed militias, each group views its armed forces as its only "remaining means of protection" and the only way to keep the peace. Thus, settlement increases the vulnerability of at least one party; this vulnerability, Walter argues, makes it unlikely the party will abide by the agreement to disarm and increases its sensitivity to any treaty violations by other parties. So, what can be done to ease this dilemma?

Foreign intervention

External countries or institutions, especially international organizations, can intervene to provide diplomatic support, military security, and economic aid, but the role of these third parties is complicated. Most analysts agree that foreign intervention entails risk and under some circumstances may intensify, rather than resolve, an existing conflict. Analysts also disagree over the details of what kind of aid is best and how much is appropriate. We examine several alternative arguments in turn.

First, outside parties can intervene to guarantee the implementation of the agreement and protect both sides as they disarm. Third-party intervention may be necessary to end a civil war. Walter's statistical analysis of 41 civil wars finds that a credible third-party guarantee provides the best explanation of war termination and can overcome the problems discussed in the previous section. Walter emphasizes that this kind of intervention only succeeds when the third party has a self-interest in upholding the bargain, is willing and able to use force to punish anyone who violates the agreement, and is able to signal its willingness to do so, for example by stationing enough forces on the ground to deter violations.[53]

Successful third-party intervention requires that external forces remain until the mutual vulnerability of the parties is overcome, either by the installation of a new, neutral government, or by successful efforts to rebuild trust and ease security fears. Significantly, external actors do not have to be neutral parties and, in the case of a large power disparity between adversaries, third-party forces biased in favor of the minority can be beneficial.

Chaim Kaufmann, who studied intrastate conflicts with an ethnic dimension, also finds that foreign intervention can be decisive when it tips the balance of power among adversaries. Thus, Kaufmann believes that a third party must pick sides, much as did UN-sponsored Australian forces that intervened in East Timor in 1999. The Australians sided decisively with the East Timorese who were seeking independence from Indonesia against those who sought to remain part of Indonesia. Kaufmann goes farther than Walters in arguing that third parties are needed to separate warring ethnic groups and exchange populations into safe zones, and only then can they provide effective security guarantees.[54]

Third parties can also intervene by providing foreign aid. Sometimes such aid, in the form of donations of cash and weapons from **diasporas**, can fuel a conflict. However, aid that is carefully timed and distributed can be used to manage a conflict, particularly in the delicate early stages of peace implementation. For instance, after a peace is reached, there may remain large numbers of young men who have spent most of their lives fighting and who lack the skills or emotional stability to be integrated into a peaceful society. The domestic reforms necessary to ensure a peace are costly and governments recovering from civil war are cash-strapped. Foreign economic assistance can be used to train former soldiers to become economically productive members of society or to integrate them into a genuinely national army.

diaspora a community of people living outside their original homeland.

Power-sharing agreements

The division of political power among combatants provides another means to manage ethnic conflict. According to the power-sharing model, authority must be decentralized and shared among groups. Democratic institutions that provide combatants equal opportunity to participate in elections are insufficient, as it takes time for such institutions to take root and, in the meantime, it is easy for one group to co-opt governing institutions and exclude others from participating. The kinds of arrangements that are most successful at protecting all groups include **federalism** and **consociationalism**.

Under federalism, power is divided between a national-level government and provincial governments. Provinces may correspond to each of the country's ethnic or other groups as in Nigeria where the principal tribal groups dominate specific provinces. Under consociationalism, key government offices, including ministries and executive positions, are divided among all groups. Since 2003, Iraq has adopted both of these arrangements in its early stages of nation building. The Iraqi constitution of October 2005 created a federal system in which Kurds have an autonomous region in northern Iraq, Shiites have an autonomous region in the south, and Sunnis dominate central Iraq.

federalism a political system in which authority is divided between a central authority and constituent political units.

consociationalism a political system in which there is an explicit bargain that power be shared among distinct ethnic, religious, or linguistic groups.

Iraq's interim executive leaders also represented a consociational bargain. A Kurd, Jalal Talabani, was selected as Iraq's interim president; a Shiite, Ibrahim Jaafari, became the interim prime minister and was succeeded by another Shiite, Nouri al-Maliki; and a Sunni was named to fill one of Iraq's two vice-presidential slots. Such political bargains are designed to ensure all groups have a political voice and none feels permanently disenfranchised.

However, power-sharing arrangements may not be sufficient to resolve conflicts. Indeed, federal arrangements may actually create the conditions for later wars of secession. In Iraq, oil reserves located in the Kurdish and Shiite regions provide each group with an economic incentive to seek autonomy or even independence. Sunnis, with little oil, would naturally fight to keep Iraq intact. Additionally, sharing executive power requires a long-term commitment to cooperate. Peace is only sustained as long as all parties adhere to the bargain.

Physical separation

When opposing groups are intermixed in the same territory, as in Iraq's capital Baghdad, physically separating them can also limit conflicts, particularly ethnic wars. This strategy of territorial division removes some of the immediate causes of such wars, including ethnic cleansing. Of course, this solution may also entail the forcible transfer of populations, which is expensive and which does not eliminate hostility between groups, and in fact may intensify it. Thus, conflict between Greece and Turkey after World War I was brought to an end only after the massive movement of Greeks out of Turkey and Turks from Greece.

We now turn to another dangerous trend in irregular warfare: global terrorism. Ignoring legal and normative limits, modern terrorists seem willing to push violence as far as they can, including the use of WMD. Let us now examine the origins and evolution of this phenomenon.

Global terrorism

terrorism form of irregular warfare that aims to intimidate enemies and publicize grievances by attacking or threatening noncombatants.

The nightclub bombing in Bali (August 2003) like the destruction of New York's World Trade Towers (September 2001), the bombing of commuter trains in Madrid, Spain (March 2004), and the bombings in London's subway and buses (July 2005) are examples of the growing danger of **terrorism** to the security of civilians and governments. Terrorism involves the threat or use of violence against noncombatants either by states or militant groups. It is a weapon of the weak to influence the strong that aims to demoralize and intimidate adversaries. Weak or not, modern terrorists use modern technology. Al Qaeda, for example, makes extensive use of e-mail to maintain contact with terrorist cells around the world and satellite television to disseminate propaganda.

The terms "terrorist" and "terrorism" imply disapproval and are rarely used to describe friends. According to a widely cited aphorism, "one person's terrorist is another's freedom fighter," meaning that terrorism is in the eye of the beholder. To avoid this problem, we define terrorists by the *means* that are used rather than the *goals* or *causes* terrorists pursue. Terrorism – both state-supported and independent – has today evolved into a global danger, much of which, as we saw in the last chapter, involves religiously inspired violence, especially by Muslim militants.

Early terrorist activity

Terrorism dates back centuries and was often associated with religion. The Zealots, Jewish opponents of Rome's occupation of Palestine in the first century AD, killed Romans in daylight and in front of witnesses in order to frighten Roman authorities and other Jews who might collaborate with them. Terrorism was also practiced by the Assassins, or "hashish-eaters," eleventh-century militant Shia Muslims who murdered those who refused to adopt their version of Islam. A Hindu religious cult called the Thugees also used terrorism – ritually strangling their victims as sacrifices to Kali, the goddess of destruction. Until eliminated by the British in the nineteenth century, the Thugees committed as many as a million murders.

During the French Revolution, the state used terrorism against its actual, imagined, or potential enemies. "Terror," declared French revolutionary Maximilien Robespierre (1758–94) in 1794, "is nothing other than justice, prompt, severe, inflexible; it is therefore an emanation of virtue; it is not so much a special principle as it is a consequence of the general principle of democracy applied to our country's most urgent needs."[55] Ironically, in the end, Robespierre himself fell victim to the guillotine where he was executed without a trial.

In the nineteenth century, **anarchists** who opposed governments of any kind used terrorism widely. Although most anarchists pursed their cause peacefully, some advocated violence. Several world leaders fell victim to assassination, called "propaganda of the deed" by anarchists, between 1881 and 1901, including US President William H. McKinley (1843–1901), France's President Marie-François Sadi Carnot (1837–94), and Italy's King Umberto I (1844–1900). These assassinations influenced a Russian group called People's Will, which tried but failed to assassinate Tsar Alexander II in 1881. One of the group's members was Alexander Ulyanov (1866–87), Vladimir Ilich Lenin's older brother.

anarchist one who seeks to overturn all constituted forms and institutions of government.

Lenin (1870–1924), Russia's revolutionary leader, used terrorism himself after Russia's 1917 Bolshevik Revolution and was responsible for launching the Red Terror against his enemies in the summer of 1918. Directed by Felix Dzerzhinsky (1877–1926), founder of the Bolshevik secret police, the Cheka, terrorist methods were used against all social classes but especially against peasants who refused to surrender their grain to the Soviet government. But Lenin's use of state terror paled before the murderous acts of his successor Josef Stalin (1878–1953), who during the Soviet effort to collectivize farms and industrialize society killed millions of Soviet citizens. By 1934, the Gulag or system of prison camps for Soviet political prisoners held several million people accused of all sorts of trumped-up crimes. The Gulag, later made infamous in Alexander Solzhenitsyn's novel *The Gulag Archipelago*, consisted of labor camps that stretched across Siberia and the Soviet far north in which over a million died.

Many of those who were sent to the Gulag were victims of the Great Purge (1936–38), in which Stalin eliminated all his enemies – real and imagined. The purge featured public trials of Stalin's old comrades such as Nikolai Bukharin (1888–1938) and Lev Kamenev (1883–1936), and of any Bolshevik who had offended the dictator, even in a minor way. Victims included two-thirds of the officer corps of the Soviet Army, and nine-tenths of the members of communist republic and regional central committees. Unable to arrest his arch-foe Leon Trotsky (1879–1940), who had fled the Soviet Union, Stalin arranged for his assassination in Mexico City by a Stalinist agent, Ramón Mercader.

Other examples of state-sponsors of terrorism used against citizens or foreign enemies include Libya, under Colonel Muammar Qaddafi (1942–), who was responsible for the bombing of Pan Am Flight 103 over Lockerbie, Scotland, in 1988 with the loss of 270 lives. North Korea, Iraq, and Iran – the "axis of evil" in the words of President George W. Bush – have also used state-sponsored terrorism against enemies.

Concern about international terrorism grew in the 1960s and 1970s with the emergence of revolutionary left-wing groups in Europe. Typical was the Baader-Meinhof Gang, also known as the Red Army Faction, which assassinated businessmen and politicians to protest capitalism. Italy's Red Brigades, which engaged in kidnapping, bombing, and assassination of policemen and is remembered for the kidnapping and murder of Italy's former Prime Minister Aldo Moro in 1978, was similar.

Some European groups like Basque Fatherland and Liberty (ETA) in Spain and the Provisional Irish Republican Army in Northern Ireland have used terrorist tactics to seek national independence for their people.

More important was the proliferation of Palestinian terrorist groups after Israel's triumph in the Six Day War in 1967. Loosely organized under the rubric of the Palestine Liberation Organization (PLO), these groups used terrorism to force others to recognize the plight of Palestinians and to intimidate supporters of Israel. One group, the small Palestine Liberation Front (PLF), even hijacked the Italian cruise liner *Achille Lauro* in 1985, murdering an elderly Jewish-American who was confined to a wheelchair. Other groups resorted to skyjackings and murder. One of the most notorious of these groups was Black September, which took its name from the month it was violently expelled from Jordan in 1970. Black September was responsible for killing 11 Israeli athletes at the 1972 Olympics in Munich, Germany. The Lebanon-based Shia group Hezbollah, specialized in kidnapping Westerners and was responsible for murdering Jewish citizens outside the Middle East, for example in Argentina.

Today's terrorist threat

These groups, whether European or Middle Eastern, used violence more selectively than today's terrorist groups like Al Qaeda and Hamas. Their political objectives were generally clear, as they sought to air grievances, influence adversaries to change policies, provoke enemies to overreact, and, by doing so, produce new sympathizers to their cause. Implicit in their use of terror was that people could avoid being victims simply by switching sides. By contrast, today's religious and ethnic terrorists display a fanaticism that muddles their political message.[56] They are unconcerned by the numbers of lives they take and offer few incentives for potential victims to avoid their fate. Suicide bombings were pioneered by Sri Lanka's Liberation Tigers of Tamil Eelam (LTTE),[57] which used women (called "black birds") with explosives strapped to themselves to murder enemies. Palestinian suicide bombers, too, can conduct a war of attrition at low cost. However, such bombings pose serious moral questions, and defenders cannot easily deter those who want to become martyrs.

Key document   Excerpt from US State Department Country Reports on Terrorism[58]

In 2005, we saw indications of:

- An increasing AQ [Al Qaeda] emphasis on ideological and propaganda activity to help advance its cause. This led to cooperation with al-Qaida in

Iraq . . . and with AQ affiliates around the globe, as well as with a new generation of Sunni extremists;

- The proliferation of smaller, looser terrorist networks that are less capable but also less predictable;
- An increased capacity for acts of terror by local terrorists with foreign ties (demonstrated in the July 7 London bombings);
- An increase in suicide bombings. The July 7 London bombing was the first such attack in Europe (three of the four terrorists were second-generation British citizens of South Asian descent); we also noted a marked increase in suicide bombings in Afghanistan;
- The growth of strategically significant networks that support the flow of foreign terrorists in Iraq.

The number of victims claimed by terrorist attacks (see Figure 7.7) has soared in recent years. According to the US State Department, there were some 11,000 terrorist attacks in 2005, resulting in over 14,600 fatalities, with about 360 suicide bombings accounting for 3,000 deaths.[59] If terrorist groups acquire weapons of mass destruction – nuclear, biological, or chemical – they can smuggle them into the United States, Europe, and elsewhere, and use them to kill thousands or even millions.[60] Although it is hard to imagine what might justify such actions, the fanaticism and anger of many post-9/11 terrorists make such attacks plausible. If their objective is to do as much harm as possible, an attacker has no motive to warn the target or reveal its identity at all. In sum, five features distinguish these "new terrorists":

1 Their level of fanaticism and devotion to their cause is greater than their predecessors'.
2 Their willingness to kill large numbers of innocent people indiscriminately contrasts with their predecessors' violence against specific individuals of symbolic importance.
3 Many of the new terrorists are prepared to give up their own lives in suicidal attacks.
4 Many of the new terrorist groups are transnational and are linked globally to similar groups.
5 They make increasing use of modern technologies like the Internet, and it is widely feared that some seek to obtain weapons of mass destruction.

As you can see, terrorism is not a new phenomenon, yet some aspects of terrorist activity today are new. One of these is the use of modern technology against the very states that have pioneered its use in modern

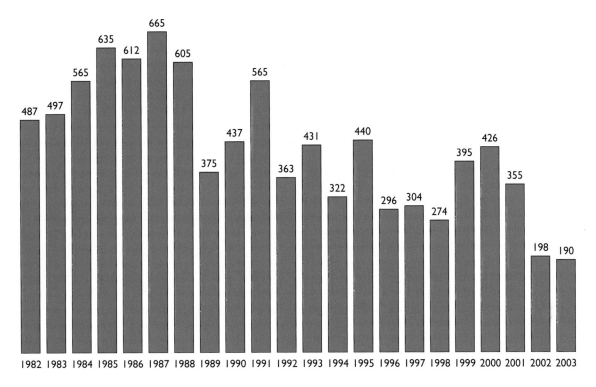

In past years, serious violence by Palestinians against other Palestinians in the occupied territories was included in the database of worldwide international terrorist incidents because Palestinians are considered stateless people. This resulted in such incidents being treated differently from intraethnic violence in other parts of the world. In 1989, as a result of further review of the nature of intra-Palestinian violence, such violence stopped being included in the US Government's statistical database on international terrorism. The figures shown above for the years 1984 through 1988 have been revised to exclude intra-Palestinian violence, thus making the database consistent.

Investigations into terrorist incidents sometimes yield evidence that necessitates a change in the information previously held true (such as whether the incident fits the definition of international terrorism, which group or state sponsor was responsible, or the number of victims killed or injured). As a result of these adjustments, the statistics given in this report may vary slightly from numbers cited in previous reports.

Figure 7.7 Total international terrorist attacks, 1982–2003
U.S. State Department

warfare. A second is its global range. A third is the growing destructiveness of modern terrorists and the absence of clear political motives on their part. Terrorists seek to avoid conventional wars with organized and uniformed armies in the field. All, to some extent, oppose the status quo, are fighting states, and accelerate the erosion of state authority. Finally, terrorists ignore existing global norms, especially those intended to protect innocent civilians.

Conclusion

In this chapter, we have seen how modern war and conflict have evolved over the course of the nineteenth and twentieth centuries to shape the modern world. In the nineteenth century, the West's greatest military strategist, Karl Maria von Clausewitz, wrote extensively on the relationship between war and politics. He feared that future wars would grow beyond the political aims for which they were fought. Clausewitz's fears were realized as industrialization and ideology caused wars to grow more and more global until they threatened the very survival of humankind. The two world wars saw a dramatic growth in the level of violence and the geographic spread of war, as well as erosion of norms protecting civilians.

We have also considered unconventional forms of conflict and violence that characterize the modern world, including guerrilla warfare, failed states, and terrorism. Irregular wars and failed states plague the developing world where they produce humanitarian crises, including genocide. Although terrorism dates back for centuries, it is changing as today's terrorists employ modern technology, have a global range, exhibit more ambiguous political motives, and achieve greater destructiveness. Finally, high-tech precision weapons and the tactics they involve are having a great impact on warfare, especially in reducing civilian casualties and collateral damage.

In the next chapter, we turn our consideration to foreign policy and state- and individual-level explanations of state behavior, especially as it relates to the outbreak of war.

Student activities

Discussion questions

Comprehension questions

1 Describe Clausewitz's view of war. Is it applicable to contemporary global politics?
2 What were the most important technological innovations in the two world wars?
3 How do irregular wars differ from conventional wars?
4 How are modern terrorists different from terrorists in earlier eras?
5 What makes today's weapons "smart" weapons?

Analysis questions

6 How have high-tech weapons affected warfare?

7 Do today's conflicts pose more of a threat to states or to individuals than conflicts in previous eras? Why or why not?

8 Do the innovations in war and technology described in this chapter fundamentally alter the conduct of world politics?

Map analysis

Locate as many current wars as you can on a map. You can find lists of current conflicts at GlobalSecurity.org and the International Crisis Group (www.crisisgroup.org). Indicate which conflicts are conventional interstate wars, which are guerrilla insurgencies, and which are products of failed states. What trends can you identify?

Cultural materials

1 General Sherman's 1864 march through Georgia and his scorched-earth tactics provided the background for the 1939 Hollywood extravaganza *Gone With the Wind*, regarded by many as the greatest film of all time, and it was celebrated in the Henry Clay Work (1832–84) song *Marching Through Georgia*:

Bring the good old bugle, boys! we'll sing another song –
Sing it with a spirit that will start the world along –
Sing it as we used to sing it fifty thousand strong,
     While we were marching through Georgia.

[Chorus] "Hurrah! Hurrah! we bring the Jubilee!
Hurrah! Hurrah! the flag that makes you free!"
So we sang the chorus from Atlanta to the sea,
     While we were marching through Georgia.[61]

Considering what you have read about the development of war and warfare in this chapter, do you think the devastation wrought against civilians by Sherman's march through Georgia was justified?

2 In Yemen, the government uses poetry to moderate Islamic extremism, one source of terrorism in the Islamic world. There is a long tradition in this country of the government sending poets to remote areas to communicate the government's message to villagers who are often skeptical of soldiers and government officials, but who respect poets.

One of the most recent in a long-line of poets is Amin al-Mashreqi. His poems attempt to weaken religious extremism by appealing to countrymen's sense of national pride. He writes:

O men of arms, why do you love injustice?
  You must live in law and order
Get up, wake up, or be forever regretful,
Don't be infamous among the nations.[62]

What is Mashreqi's message? What message would you convey to extremists to turn them away from terrorism?

Further reading

Chaliand, Gérard, ed., *The Art of War in World History: From Antiquity to the Nuclear Age* (Berkeley, CA: University of California Press, 1994). Comprehensive anthology on military strategy throughout history.

Clausewitz, Carl von, *On War* (New York: Penguin Classics, 1982). Classic statement of the relationship of war and politics with an excellent introduction by Anatol Rapoport.

Gray, Colin S., *Modern Strategy* (Oxford: Oxford University Press, 1999). Systematic analysis of strategic issues in the post-Cold War era ranging from outer space to cyberspace and from nuclear war to irregular violence.

Hoffman, Bruce, *Inside Terrorism* (New York: Columbia University Press, 1998). Readable and comprehensive analysis of terrorism and its tactics through the ages.

Joes, Anthony James, *Resisting Rebellion: The History and Politics of Counterinsurgency* (Lexington: University Press of Kentucky, 2004). Comprehensive account of guerrilla insurgencies with lessons for counterinsurgency operations.

Keegan, John, *A History of Warfare* (New York: Vintage Books, 1994). Extraordinary account of the origins and evolution of warfare from the battle of Megiddo (1469 BC) to the nuclear age.

O'Neill, Bard, *Insurgency and Terrorism: From Revolution to Apocalypse* (Herndon, VA: Potomac Books, 2005). Provides a policy-oriented analysis of modern insurgency movements and their tactics.

Pape, Robert, *Dying to Win: The Strategic Logic of Suicide Terrorism* (New York: Random House, 2005). Systematic and thoughtful analysis of suicide terrorism.

Van Creveld, Martin, *Technology and War: From 2000 BC to the Present* (New York: Free Press, 1991). A brilliant account of the impact of changing technology on the nature of war.

Part III
Actors and Institutions

8 Foreign policy and war

Sino-American relations, long characterized by mistrust, received a severe blow on May 7, 1999 when a US bomber taking part in NATO's Balkan air campaign set out to bomb the federal directorate for supply and procurement in Belgrade, but instead bombed the Chinese embassy. The building was targeted with "deadly accuracy": "two bombs struck one side . . . , shearing away its polished stone façade, devastating a rear entrance and tossing large chips of tiling, cooking-gas canisters and a utility pole 20 yards."[1] A third bomb hit the roof, spewing fire and smoke out of the front of the building. Predictably, the bombing sparked outrage across China, where angry protestors, with government support, mobbed US diplomatic missions, throwing rocks and paint, calling the Americans "Nazi murderers" and demanding "blood for blood."[2] American officials apologized, blaming the error on an outdated map.

Two aspects of this story are of special interest. First, it shows that foreign policies may not be implemented as intended by their architects, and it demonstrates some of the ways in which individual and bureaucratic errors produce unintended consequences. A *New York Times* investigation found no evidence that the bombing had been deliberate, but it did find a "bizarre chain of missteps" in American intelligence and military organizations.[3] Among these missteps, the investigation uncovered a scramble within NATO to find new targets as Serbia held out against the air assaults. Some officials argued that in the rush, many targets were not vetted as carefully as they should have been. Having only a street address to work with, officers of the CIA's Counter-Proliferation Division located their target using two tourist maps and a 1997 National Imagery and Mapping Agency map that had no street addresses. And, once they submitted the proposed location on a targeting form available on the military's secure intranet, there was no further scrutiny of the target.

The case also suggests that both internal and external factors shape the foreign policy process. There was genuine public anger in China toward the Chinese government for its perceived weak response to the bombing and considerable concern among China's leaders that if the demonstrations were not controlled they would lead to all sorts of undesirable pressure on President Jiang Zemin (1926–) and Prime Minister Zhu Rongji (1928–).[4] To satisfy their domestic audience, they demanded an official apology for what they called a "barbaric act," a full public accounting of how the bombing occurred, appropriate punishment of those responsible, and compensation. However, within several weeks, as China's leaders looked ahead to negotiations with the United States about China's admission to the World Trade Organization, they became willing to accept only enough of their demands "so that a skeptical public and leadership hardliners could be convinced that Beijing was justified in resuming more normal relations with Washington."[5]

This chapter examines the characteristics of states, groups, and individuals that shape foreign policy. Decision-makers must respond to external factors, but internal or domestic factors that constitute the state and individual levels of analysis also influence **foreign policy**. In fact, the contemporary state is at the nexus of global and domestic politics and is constantly buffeted by forces from within both arenas.

Chapter 6 portrayed global politics as a product of the structure of a world system of states. From this system-level perspective, all states are similarly constrained by the system's structure and can be expected to act the same way under similar circumstances. You may recall that realists believe that if there is an unfavorable change in the global balance of power, the "losers" may adapt by increasing their armaments or joining **alliances** to restore a favorable balance. This chapter, in contrast, focuses on the other levels of analysis, introducing the myriad of factors *within* states – their governments, societies, and leaders – that contribute to the development and implementation of foreign policy and that help explain why states in similar circumstances often adopt different policies.

The chapter begins with a discussion of foreign policy, considering the meaning of the concept as well as its purposes. It goes on to consider the various factors that shape policy concerning national security. The final sections of the chapter consider the policies available to states for providing security. In the case of interstate conflicts, it examines **deterrence, diplomacy,** alliance policy, and **arms control** and **disarmament**. Bear in mind throughout that, while the chapter emphasizes security policy, the factors it describes apply to other issues as well.

foreign policy the sum of an actor's goals and purposive actions in global politics.

alliance a formal agreement to cooperate to achieve joint security.

deterrence a strategy aimed at preventing an adversary from acting in a certain way by threatening to retaliate with military force.

diplomacy the art of conducting negotiations and managing relations among actors.

arms control any approach designed to regulate levels and types of arms in a manner that enhances strategic stability.

disarmament any effort to reduce the number of weapons in actors' arsenals.

What is foreign policy?

Traditionally, the idea of foreign policy refers to how a state will interact with other global actors, but this definition has limitations in today's complex world. Even now, there is no consensus on what "foreign policy" means. Some observers conceive of foreign policy as *a complex system of agencies and actions intended to alter the behavior of other states and allow their own state to adapt to the global environment*. By this account, foreign policy involves the conversion of inputs such as information about the actions of other states or public opinion into output such as diplomacy, alliance formation, or higher defense budgets. Others conceive of foreign policy as *decision-making*, that is, *how individuals in leadership and policy-making positions respond to factors and conditions outside the state*. In the words of political scientist Charles Hermann, "foreign policy consists of those discrete official actions of the authoritative decision makers of a nation's government, or their agents, which are intended by the decision makers to influence the behavior of international actors external to their own polity."[6]

These definitions raise a series of common issues about the analysis of foreign policy:

1 Who makes foreign policy?
2 What are the objectives of foreign policy?
3 What generates a foreign policy?
4 Who is targeted by foreign policy?
5 Is foreign policy different from domestic policy?

Despite differences in definition, observers have traditionally focused on states and bureaucracies as the key sources of foreign policy. These actors seek to further the **national interest**, a vague and much-debated concept that refers to the goals that a state or its leaders believe will collectively benefit their citizens but that is more than the sum of individual interests. Realists think of national interest in terms of power that assures state's survival, security, and well-being. Thus, Hans Morgenthau argued that the United States "has had two great interests in foreign policy," maintaining "its security and . . . its predominance in the Western Hemisphere" and maintaining "the European balance of power."[7] Statesmen, "as trustees of the national interest,"[8] are presumed by realists to be able to discern the national interest through rational analysis. Nevertheless, almost any goal can be considered a means to achieve the national interest. For example, President Richard Nixon cited the national interest to justify ordering a break-in into the office of Daniel Ellsberg's psychoanalyst's office in 1971 following Ellsberg's leaking of information about the Vietnam War.

national interest the idea that a state has a set of goals that will collectively benefit its citizens.

Realists conceive of foreign policy as generated by external factors, generally actions on the part of other states or characteristics of the structure of the global system. In their perspective, foreign policy is distinct from other kinds of public policy in that there is a clear division between the international and the domestic realms. Foreign policies are *explicitly* designed to **influence** other states and global actors while domestic policies are designed to influence or regulate domestic actors.

In reality, the answers to these questions are not so simple. First, states, bureaucracies, and individual leaders are all significant foreign policy actors, but so are societal groups, the general public, and nongovernmental and international organizations. Some of these nonstate actors play an important role in shaping foreign policy. Others have their own foreign policies. For example, the NGO Oxfam actively campaigns to end global poverty, pursue social justice, and control the arms export industry.[9]

Second, interest groups and bureaucracies have different views of the objectives of foreign policy, how policies affect their group, and what constitutes the national interest. As we shall see, numerous government bureaucracies, each with its own perspectives and interests, are involved in defining and implementing foreign policy. Foreign, defense, trade, energy, and even agriculture ministries all play a role in designing or advocating foreign policy, but they often pursue different goals and use different means to accomplish those goals. Societal groups, like labor or human rights organizations, pursue still different objectives. And sometimes politics makes a strange bedfellow. For example, the pro-Israeli tilt of the Bush administration is strongly supported by evangelical Christians in the United States because many believe that the ingathering of Jews in Israel is a prerequisite for the second coming as described in the Book of Revelation.[10] Third, foreign policy is actually generated by a multitude of external and internal factors, including the changing distribution of power, conflicts among social groups, or a need for natural resources. Fourth, policies are often intended to target *both* state and nonstate actors.

Foreign policy is crafted to balance internal and external factors, and only by examining domestic and external politics together can we paint a comprehensive picture of a country's foreign policy. As we shall see, some aggressive externally oriented policies, like war, are undertaken for domestic purposes such as unifying a divided public rather than for some external gain, while some domestic policies, such as repression of an ethnic minority, may be intended to influence a foreign audience. Thus, as US and foreign governments and their bureaucracies interact with one another

influence an actor's ability to cause another actor to behave differently than it would otherwise have.

at home and abroad, as well as with the nonstate actors, the distinction between foreign and domestic policies breaks down.

For these reasons, it is necessary to look both within and outside of states to identify the sources of foreign policy. According to this expanded view of the term, foreign policy *is the sum of an actor's goals and purposive actions in global politics* and is virtually inseparable from domestic policy. This sum total of goals and purposive actions can produce a policy of diplomacy and negotiation, isolation, alliances, nonalignment, and even war. In the next section, we consider factors at the domestic and individual levels of analysis that may produce a policy of war.

War and the domestic sources of foreign policy

As we saw in chapter 7, there are several persuasive system-level explanations for war: the distribution of power, security dilemmas, and **arms races**. If we only consider war through the system-level lens, it may seem as if the onset of war is an unstoppable process. But, in fact, war is one of many foreign policy options available to states, often pursued simply because other options are exhausted or are inadequate to protect a state's vital interests. Thus, for a more complete picture, we must consider characteristics of states that political scientists believe contribute to or inhibit the decision to go to war. Among these factors, the most prominent are regime type, economic systems, nationalism and public opinion, domestic politics, and decision-makers themselves.

arms race an action–reaction process in which an increase in armaments by one state is reciprocated by an increase in armaments by the other.

Those who study these factors are among the leading empiricists or positivists in the field of international relations and strongly believe that the growth in knowledge and understanding is a cumulative process. Much of their research utilizes statistical techniques and avoids overt normative analysis. In an exhaustive analysis of these scholars, political scientist John Vasquez shows that most of these scholars were influenced by realist theory by which he means that they assume that politics is a struggle for power, only nation-states have significant power, and, therefore, only nation-states matter.[11]

State characteristics and war

Unlike the neorealist emphasis on system-level factors, liberals look within states for causes of war. They focus on a state's form of government and economic system, the strength of nationalism, public opinion, and the actions of foreign policy bureaucracies. The result is a deeper, albeit more complex, explanation for war. Let us look at each of these factors in turn.

Regime type: the "democratic peace"

democratic peace theory
the theory that democracies do
not fight wars with one another.

Political theorists have long been interested in whether democracies are
more peaceful than other forms of governments. **Democratic peace
theory** posits that democracies are more peaceful, at least in relations
with one another. This claim is derived from the ideas of German
philosopher Immanuel Kant. In his philosophical sketch *Perpetual Peace*,
Kant argued that for reason to prevail people must enter civil society and
create the state "in which," according to neorealist Kenneth Waltz, "rights
are secured, and with them the possibility of moral behavior."[12] But only
one kind of state, Kant argued, can foster individual moral development
and international peace – one with legal equality of citizens and
representative institutions, especially an autonomous legislature (though
not necessarily based on democracy). Kant thought that republics like
these, unlike authoritarian states, produce cooperation because they act
in citizens' interests, and peace serves those interests. In war only
profiteers and the ruling aristocratic elite can benefit. Thus, Kant argued,
as more states became liberal republics, they would gradually form a
peace among themselves, which he called a "pacific union" or "pacific
federation." This system would not be a world government or world state,
but more like a nonaggression pact among democracies – a pact in which
they would agree to avoid violence in resolving their disputes.

Kant's ideas about democracy and peace were revived by political
scientist Michael Doyle[13] and were taken up by "scientific" scholars
(chapter 1, p. 29) enthused by the end of the Cold War and the apparent
triumph of liberal democracy over communism.[14] Democratic peace
theory gained additional popularity in the early 1990s with the
publication of political scientist Bruce M. Russett's *Grasping the Democratic
Peace*.[15] Although it does not appear that democracies are less willing to
fight wars than other regimes in general, it *does* appear that democracies
do not fight one another.

Democratic peace theory provides two explanations for peaceful
relations among democracies. The first rests on democratic norms.
According to this explanation, democracies are defined by their respect
for individual rights and liberties and nonviolent means of conflict
resolution. Democratic leaders expect that other democracies will abide
by the same norms, thus preventing a rash decision to go to war. The
second explanation rests on democratic institutions, claiming that conflict
among democracies is rare because domestic checks and balances among
the branches of government slow the decision to go to war and make the
process visible to outsiders.

Political scientists Paul Hensel, Gary Goertz, and Paul Diehl have
extended the democratic peace hypothesis to "rivalries," which can range

from isolated to enduring conflicts that "involve frequent and intense militarized competition between the same pair of states" over extended periods of time.[16] Their analysis indicates that, like wars, rivalries are less likely to occur between democratic states than in cases where at least one actor is not a democracy.

Despite the evidence in support of the proposition, democratic peace theory has remained the subject of intense debate. Research findings, for example, vary depending on how one defines a democracy.[17] Furthermore, political scientists Edward D. Mansfield and Jack Snyder show that, even though democracies do not fight one another, countries that are making the transition from dictatorship to democracy actually "become more aggressive and war-prone, not less, and they do fight wars with democratic states."[18] For this reason, countries like Russia that are becoming more democratic but have not completed the process may become more warlike than before. Theorists also debate whether democracy, rather than some other factor, is the reason for peaceful relations.[19] For example, democratic societies are usually wealthier than other states, suggesting that *wealth* rather than democracy may be the key factor in causing peace (more on this below).

Theory in the real world   The Bush doctrine

Democratic peace theory has a key place in the foreign policy of President George W. Bush. The Bush doctrine states that the US should act to spread democracy. According to the National Security Strategy of the United States (September 2002): "America will encourage the advancement of democracy and economic openness . . . because these are the best foundations for domestic stability and international order." The doctrine optimistically predicts that, once democratic institutions exist in Iraq, democracy will spread to neighboring countries that will in turn adopt peaceful policies. "No other system of government," declared President Bush, "has done more to protect minorities, to secure the rights of labor, to raise the status of women, or to channel human energy to the pursuits of peace. . . . When it comes to the desire for liberty and justice, there is no clash of civilizations. People everywhere are capable of freedom, and worthy of freedom."[20] However, since countries in transition to democracy may actually be more warlike than other regimes, efforts to spread democracy may actually lead to more wars.

Economic systems and war

Other explanations for war-prone foreign policies focus on state-level economic factors. Just as some scholars thought that democracy and peace are related, others have probed the relationship between capitalism and peace. Liberals and Marxists reach opposite conclusions about the relationship between capitalism and war. Liberals believe that free-market capitalism in which competition fosters wealth brings peace. Marxists, by contrast, believe that capitalism makes the capitalist class of owners wealthy at the expense of workers and that these gaps in wealth produce class conflict that will climax in revolution that will end capitalism (see chapter 11, pp. 511–3).

Liberal theory claims that free trade promotes economic efficiency and prosperity. It is only when there are barriers to trade that actors are likely to go to war to acquire raw materials. Liberals argue that economic interdependence produces peace. Free-market societies, they believe, are inherently opposed to war because it is bad for business, so that the expansion of free trade and finance creates interests within society that restrain warlike leaders. As states become economically dependent on one another, they come to recognize that *their* prosperity depends on the prosperity of others. In addition, war wastes economic resources and severs trade so that all participants end up as losers. Thus, the liberal British economist Sir Norman Angell (1872–1967), winner of the 1933 Nobel Peace Prize, argued that no country could win a war, at least not from an economic perspective, because war destroys the economic interdependence among peoples that was the source of their wealth. In his book *The Great Illusion*, published shortly before the outbreak of World War I, Angell argued

> that the commerce and industry of a people no longer depend upon the expansion of its political frontiers; that a nation's political and economic frontiers do not now necessarily coincide; that military power is socially and economically futile, and can have no relation to the prosperity of the people exercising it; that it is impossible for one nation to seize by force the wealth or trade of another – to enrich itself by subjugating, or imposing its will by force on another; that in short, war, even when victorious, can no longer achieve those aims for which people strive.[21]

In a modern version of this argument, David Bearce claims that economic interdependence and the creation of commercial institutions like free-trade areas, customs unions, common markets, and monetary unions produce peace in three ways. (1) They make war costly for society and for political leaders. (2) Economic institutions provide information about other states' capabilities and intentions thereby reducing misperceptions and unjustified fears that cause war. (3) Economic institutions build trust by regularly bringing high-level political leaders together.[22]

In contrast to liberal theory, Marxist analyses anticipate global conflict as capitalism spreads. Emphasizing the exploitative nature of capitalism, British economist John Hobson (1858–1940) developed an influential theory of **imperialism**. Hobson argued that imperialism was a product of the two dilemmas of capitalist society: overproduction and underconsumption.[23] Under capitalism, he claimed, business owners and industry profit by paying workers low wages, and impoverished workers are unable to purchase the goods and services produced by modern industry. However, rather than paying higher wages or investing their profits in domestic welfare programs, capitalists, argued Hobson, seek new foreign markets in which to sell their surplus goods and invest their profits. Their frantic search for new colonies and markets, he concluded, would cause Europe's states to collide. War could be averted only if capitalists paid their workers higher wages and improved their living standards. Lenin grafted Hobson's views onto Marxism, arguing that underconsumption and overproduction were root causes of imperialism and that, once the world was completely divided among the capitalist states, expansion could only come at someone else's expense, thereby leading to war.[24]

> **imperialism** the political control of one state by another.

Nationalism and public opinion

Nationalism and nationalist public opinion can also contribute to war, theorists argue, but their role is ambiguous. For example, are nationalist feelings actually a source of war or merely instruments used by governments to rally support for war? Liberals see public opinion as inherently peaceful, but nationalism and excessive patriotism, sometimes called *chauvinism* (after Nicholas Chauvin, a fanatical soldier under Napoléon), on the part of publics can intensify wars and make them difficult to end. Aggressive nationalists in Britain were called "jingoists," a term first used in connection with the followers of British Prime Minister Benjamin Disraeli (1804–81) who wanted Britain to ally with Turkey against Russia in 1877. The terms came from a song of the period:

> **nationalism** fervent attachment to a national or ethnic group.

We don't want to fight, but by Jingo, if we do,
We've got the ships, we've got the men,
We've got the money, too!

Figure 8.1 Vladimir Lenin
Library of Congress, Prints
and Photographs Division,
Photograph by Soyuzfoto.
[ca. 1920], LC-USZ62-101877

Surprisingly, there has been relatively little theorizing about the
impact of nationalism on war. Stephen Van Evera argues that nation-states
are *more likely* to become involved in wars when national groups pursue
the recovery of lost territories, believe that only they deserve statehood,
and oppress other nationalities in their countries.[25] A nationalist ideology,
he contends, requires that all fellow nationals be gathered in a single
national state, as when Hitler demanded that all Germans or *Volk*,
wherever they might live, be united under the banner of the Third Reich.
This ideology fuels conflict with other states in which members of the

nation live. Thus, Hitler's demands that Czechoslovakia surrender the Sudetenland, home to many ethnic Germans, triggered a major crisis in 1938 (chapter 3, p. 141).

Serbian nationalism after 1992 also illustrates the role of nationalism in foreign policy (see chapter 15, pp. 712–8). As Yugoslavia came apart, Serbian President Slobodan Milošević sought to extend Serbia's control over Serbs living in neighboring successor states, especially Croatia and Bosnia, while refusing to recognize other nations' similar claims to independence and statehood. Serbia also antagonized its neighbors by repressing national minorities in territories under its control, especially Croatians and Bosnian Muslims in Bosnia and Albanians in Kosovo. As this case shows, leaders may rouse nationalism to rally support for themselves, using national symbols, like flags and anthems, to stir up passions. Once passions are inflamed, wars become difficult to stop, or even to manage.

The impact of public opinion on foreign policy varies. In democracies, where public opinion matters most, the public rarely speaks with a single voice, even on national security issues, and it must compete with numerous domestic and foreign interest groups to have its preferences heard by decision-makers. At best, it is difficult to evaluate the extent to which the public influences leaders as opposed to being influenced by them. Elite-centric models regard public opinion as emotional and subjective, and thus a poor guide for foreign policy. They view the executive branch as having significant power in transmitting information on international issues and shaping public opinion. Other models find greater balance between public opinion and elite influence in the foreign policy process. The strongest of these alternatives maintain that public opinion sets the boundaries for acceptable, and thus politically feasible, policies. However, the weight of public opinion may also vary across the foreign policy process. One such study posits that in non-crisis situations the public is most attentive, and thus applies the most pressure, early in the policy-making process when leaders are selecting a policy. In crisis situations public attention builds slowly and becomes more influential as a policy is implemented.[26]

Yet another model of public opinion contends that, when a crisis appears, the public tends to rally around its leaders and their policies. For example, when diplomatic efforts to avoid war with Iraq failed in 2003, public support for the war in the United States grew rapidly, as did support for the president and congress. Polls in the months leading up to the war found that the percentage of Americans supporting war remained steady, between 52 and 59 percent. As diplomacy began to break down in March 2003, support increased to 64 percent in favor of war. Once the bombing campaign began, it increased further to 72 percent in favor. President Bush's personal rating jumped 13 percent during this time.[27]

Domestic politics: war as a diversion from domestic issues

Some theorists believe that domestic political conditions provide one of the causes of war. According to the "scapegoat hypothesis" also called the diversionary theory of war, political parties and governments sometimes provoke conflict overseas to divert the public's attention from problems at home. In other words, political leaders blame other countries for their own woes and in this way provide an "enemy" against which the public can unite and, in doing so, forget contentious domestic issues. Thus, in George Orwell's novel *1984*, the country of Oceania led by Big Brother heaps the blame for all of its problems on the other two countries with which it shares the world, Eurasia and Eastasia.

The evidence in support of the diversionary theory of war is mixed. So, when are leaders likely to employ force abroad to divert attention away from problems at home? One explanation hinges on the strength of domestic opposition. If political opposition is weak, there is less incentive to adopt a diversionary policy. One study has found that leaders of democratic states may use force to divert attention away from domestic economic conditions, but authoritarian states, in which opposition is tightly controlled, do not. This finding seems contrary to the democratic peace proposition, but the conditions that nullify the democratic peace are rare.[28] A second explanation turns to the availability of a meaningful external target for a diversionary war. The likelihood of conflict increases when there is a feasible target whose defeat will demonstrate the leader is competent, despite his inability to manage problems at home.[29]

It has been suggested that the Bush administration reflected the diversionary theory by creating an external threat to divert public attention from the Enron scandal at home. In his 2002 State of the Union Address, President Bush labeled Iran, Iraq, and North Korea an "axis of evil," because they sought to develop nuclear weapons. His speech came shortly after the Enron Corporation, an energy and commodities trading company that had contributed heavily to the president's 2000 election campaign, became one of the biggest bankruptcies in American history. A scandal ensued when it was discovered that Enron had used illegal accounting practices and that its managers had retired with huge fortunes while employees lost their jobs and the retirement savings they had invested in Enron stock. Some critics claimed that President Bush's speech was timed to divert American attention from this embarrassing scandal.

A group of theorists known as "neoclassical realists" similarly argue that domestic politics can affect the likelihood of war, although the affect is not a direct one. According to these theorists, systemic pressures are "translated" through the domestic political process. Thus, political scientist Randall Schweller argues that there are domestic political obstacles to adopting a balance-of-power strategy. In particular, a government may be unable or unwilling to balance a potential adversary if the domestic political costs and risks are too great as it might be if the United States entered an alliance with a former foe.[30] Imagine, for example, the public outcry if an American leader tried to ally with a country like Iran or North Korea in an effort to create a balance against some other potential foe like China.

Each of these theories contributes to our understanding of foreign policy decisions to go to war. For example, some wars of aggression such as Iraq's 1990 invasion of Kuwait had strong economic motives. Nationalism was a powerful force in triggering the three wars of German unification in the late nineteenth century and in the outbreak and duration of World Wars I and II. Nationalist yearnings of minorities in Austria-Hungary threatened to destroy that empire in the years before 1914, and its rulers decided to attack Serbia in that year after the assassination of the heir to the throne of Austria-Hungary partly to paper over internal divisions. And in 1914, Russia went to war in part to divert public opinion from domestic woes.

Decision-makers also play a key role in triggering foreign policies to go to war. In the next section, we examine the impact of how decisions are made by governments on the outbreak of war. Like the four theories we have just discussed, this approach focuses on the state level of global politics.

Decision-making, decision-makers, and war

Abstract collectivities like states do not make decisions about war and peace. Real people, with passions, ambitions, and physical and psychological limitations, make those decisions. Some decision-makers make decisions on the basis of preconceptions, do not search for alternatives, and only want information that confirms their preconceptions. By contrast, others use their experience to make decisions, actively seek alternatives, and want as much information as possible.[31] Some leaders are enthusiastic about challenges, optimistic, active, and flexible, whereas others are rigid, passive, and would prefer to avoid challenges.[32]

Thus, political scientists have tried to explain and predict the decisions that leaders make, to evaluate good and bad decision-making, and to determine when decision-making will lead to war. We will examine four models of foreign policy decision-making: the rational actor model (RAM), the cognitive model, the affective model, and prospect theory. Two additional models – government politics and organizational behavior – consider the limitations of group decision-making. None provides complete understanding of a particular decision, but each affords different insights and suggests how decision-making can lead to war through misperception or misunderstanding.

Realists, in particular, favor the *rational actor model (RAM)*. This model assumes that decision-makers want to minimize losses and maximize gains. It also assumes that they have a set of clearly defined preferences, which they can consistently rank in order from the most to the least desirable. According to this model, whenever a decision must be made, leaders begin by recognizing and defining the problem to be addressed. At this stage, they gather information about the issue, including other actors' definition of the problem and their intentions and capabilities. Decision-makers then determine their own goals and canvass all policy options, evaluating each according to its costs and probability of success. Finally, they select that option that will achieve their preferences at the least cost. In a much-cited passage that reflects an assumption that leaders are rational, Morgenthau declares: "We assume that statesmen think and act in terms of interest defined as power and the evidence of history bears that assumption out. That assumption allows us to retrace and anticipate . . . the steps a statesman – past, present, or future – has taken or will take on the political scene."[33]

In reality, decision-makers never have perfect information and, with limited time and information, are aware of relatively few alternatives in any situation. Instead, according to game theorists Donald R. Luce and Howard Raiffa, the rational decision-maker is one who when faced with two alternatives "will choose the one which yields the more preferred outcome."[34] According to **expected utility theory**, the most common application of this approach, leaders consider the consequences (utility) associated with each alternative course of action, including the risk entailed and the possibility of punishment and rewards. They then compare the costs and benefits of alternative outcomes and consider the probability of each occurring. Thus, two states in a dispute will compare the "expected utility" (expected benefits minus costs) of war, negotiation, and appeasement. They will go to war when they believe that the expected utility of war exceeds the expected utility of negotiations or appeasement.

expected utility theory an approach to decision-making predicated on the belief that leaders are rational and seek to maximize gains.

Rational actor models are valuable for simplifying reality and making logical assumptions, and many scholars incorporate rationality as a simplifying assumption even if they do not say so explicitly. However, as we saw in chapter 1 (p. 10), decision-makers are incapable of perfect rationality. At best, they are capable of limited or bounded rationality. Recognizing this, expected-utility (also called rational-choice) theorists have incorporated bounded rationality into their models of conflict and war, and these allow for incomplete information, miscalculations, and misperception.[35] Nevertheless, critics of this approach argue that it is impossible to determine accurately the utility (positive or negative) of a given outcome or the probability of that outcome. Instead, decision-makers are limited to describing outcomes in vague terms such as "good" and "bad" and can only guess at the probability of their occurring.

Other theorists employ cognitive and affective models of decision-making that do not assume rationality to provide an even more accurate account of how decisions are really made. A *cognitive approach* to decision-making involves assessing distortions in perception owing to ambiguities in real-life situations under conditions of stress. It assumes that decision-makers cannot assimilate and interpret all the information necessary to make rational decisions and that they see what they expect to see and expect others to see the world as they do. Worse, decision-makers are uncomfortable when information contradicts their expectations about the world around them, and they unconsciously interpret such information in ways that make it conform to their expectations, using shallow analogies and other "tricks" to reduce uncertainty.

Political scientist Ole R. Holsti's analysis of Secretary of State John Foster Dulles – a principal architect of US foreign policy in the 1950s – shows how cognitive processes may be assessed to understand foreign policy.[36] Holsti concluded that Dulles's personality and his experience with the Soviet Union predisposed him to see that country and everything it did negatively. Holsti concluded that Dulles had a closed belief system about the Soviet Union and that when Soviet leaders acted in ways that contradicted Dulles's negative views of the USSR he would paint their behavior in the most sinister light possible. Thus, whenever there was evidence that Moscow might be seeking a thaw in the Cold War – for example, when in 1955 it proposed to restore Austria's independence – Dulles explained it away as a ruse or as evidence that the USSR was growing weaker. Decision-makers like Dulles discount or misinterpret information about facts that contradict their values and beliefs.

Cognitive self-delusion helps explain why misperception is common in foreign policy. Political scientist Robert Jervis argues that decision-makers tend to emphasize the significance of information that they expect, while ignoring information they do not expect or wish to hear.[37] For example, President Richard Nixon ignored information that indicated American strategy in Vietnam was not working. Jervis also concluded that decision-makers assume that if their intentions are peaceful other leaders will recognize that fact. Yet, when decision-makers perceive others to be acting in a hostile way they tend to conclude that such hostility is intentional.

Cognitive errors also result when decision-makers reason from analogy, assuming that a current problem or situation is like a past situation or problem that decision-makers remember. For example, American leaders were prone to compare Saddam Hussein with Hitler and to conclude that appeasement would encourage Saddam to be aggressive as it did Hitler. Such reasoning is dangerous because rarely are two situations sufficiently similar to draw such analogies or schemas (simplified models), and false analogies are likely to produce the wrong "lessons" and inappropriate policies.[38] These cases involve cognitive errors caused by using heuristics (efficient rules of thumb or simplified shortcuts) to oversimplify complex situations.

Other theorists argue that leaders' personal emotions such as insecurity and hostility also distort perceptions and affect the quality of decision-making. Using an *affective model*, psychologists Irving Janis and Leon Mann examined the relationship between stress and decision-making.[39] They concluded that in the absence of stress leaders may be careless in seeking information or analyzing policy options. Moderate levels of stress, they believe, enhance decision-making by forcing leaders to search carefully for information and evaluate available options critically before reaching a decision. However, high stress levels, they concluded, can produce severe decision-making pathologies like procrastination or uncritical acceptance of all incoming information.

Finally, *prospect theory* offers an additional perspective that considers how "framing" of problems influences decision-making. The theory contends that people tend "to make decisions based upon the value that they attach to particular choices"[40] in respect to a given reference point and that they treat gains and losses from that reference point differently. Simply put, leaders do not want to lose what they already have. They are prepared to take risks when there is the "prospect" of making gains, but they will be very cautious when there is a "prospect" of losses. Because "losses subjectively hurt more than gains feel good . . . the sting of loss is more acute than is the enjoyment derived from an equal gain."[41]

None of these models assumes that physical or psychological factors *necessarily* produce decision-making pathologies that make bad decisions

in 1914 in letting their respective allies, Austria-Hungary and Russia, take the lead. (4) "The armed forces are the instruments of foreign policy, not its master," a rule that the generals in 1914 violated when they pressured their political leaders to mobilize as quickly as possible, thereby precluding serious negotiations to prevent war. (5) Governments should lead, not follow, public opinion, a maxim that afflicted British leaders in the 1930s who fell victims to the widespread pacifism in the country and refused to heed Winston Churchill's plea to stand up to the Nazis until it was almost too late.

Thus, diplomats must assess their country's objectives given its actual and potential power and gauge other states' objectives in light of their power. In doing this, they must avoid both overconfidence and under-confidence, lest they blunder into war. Overconfidence may produce unnecessarily aggressive policies, whereas under-confidence may whet an enemy's aggressive appetite.

Diplomats must also assess the extent to which their country's objectives are compatible with those of other countries and then decide whether to use persuasion, compromise, or the threat of force to pursue their country's ends. *Persuasion* involves convincing others to adopt the diplomat's expressed preferences, but alone is rarely sufficient if vital interests are at stake. *Compromise* involves making concessions to achieve a mutually satisfactory solution to a dispute. Successful compromises often link cooperation in one area (say, human rights) with cooperation in another (say, trade). This strategy is called **issue linkage**. Compromise is more likely than persuasion to bring diplomatic success if vital interests are involved. *Threats of force* are most credible when vital interests are at stake, but they can lead to a war that no one wishes if they are made frequently, as did Germany's Kaiser Wilhelm II in the decade before 1914.

Diplomats today enjoy less flexibility and authority than in the past owing to modern communications technology, which allows them to remain in almost constant touch with their superiors at home. In earlier centuries, communication between diplomats and leaders was slow and episodic, and diplomats were virtual proconsuls who had to make critical decisions on their own because timely guidance from home was unavailable. By contrast, contemporary diplomats receive instructions continually and have little room to act on their own. One consequence is that diplomacy is conducted today far more than in the past with an eye to the vagaries of domestic politics rather than in response to events in the country in which diplomats are stationed.

issue linkage a bargaining strategy in which an actor gains favorable concessions in one issue area, by making concessions in another.

Did you know?

Shuttle diplomacy refers to the use of a third-party mediator who "shuttles" back and forth between actors in conflict. Former US Secretary of State Henry Kissinger's shuttle diplomacy was credited with helping to bring Israel and Egypt to the negotiating table for the 1979 Camp David Accords.

defense the use of power to prevent an attack or minimize damage from an attack.

compellence the threat or use of force to make an adversary alter its behavior.

game an interaction among actors characterized by rules and strategies in which each actor's outcome depends partly on what other actors do and in which actors try to outwit one another.

preemptive war a war initiated to gain the advantage over an adversary that is itself about to strike.

preventive war a war launched by one actor in order to prevent another actor from growing strong enough in the future to pose a threat.

Foreign policies based on the use of force

We now examine three foreign policy strategies for managing conflict that require the threat or use of military force: **defense**, deterrence, and **compellence**. Each involves using force for a different end: defense to repel an attack, deterrence to dissuade another actor from attacking or taking unacceptable steps, and compellence to make it act differently or to undo an action already taken. Deterrence and compellence are examples of strategic interaction, situations in which no actor has complete control over events, and the outcome for any actor depends as much on what others do as on what it does. And as in strategic **games**[47] like chess and poker, much depends on each actor's expectations of what others are likely to do. Most conflict situations, then, involve bargaining among actors under conditions in which no actor enjoys complete control.[48]

Military force has many uses. We often think of it as a means to defend territory and interests from attack. In particular, according to political scientist Robert Art, *defense* refers to the ability to "ward off an attack and to minimize damage to oneself if attacked."[49] Defense may be passive or active. Passive defense employs civil defenses, bunkers, the hardening of weapons systems, and increasing weapons mobility, while active defense involves directing military force against a potential or an actual attacker and may include missile defense and **preemptive** and **preventive** war.[50] When used defensively, force is not directed against civilian populations, but may be deployed prior to or after an attack, or used in a defensive first strike. In a *preemptive* strike, a state anticipates an imminent attack and strikes first to gain the advantage, whereas in a *preventive* strike it anticipates an attack in the more distant future – perhaps even years away – and attacks first to prevent the perceived adversary from developing the capability to strike. In both cases, Art argues, "it is better to strike first than to be struck first." Preemption, defined as use of force when confronted by an imminent enemy attack, is legal under international law. However, as we shall see later (p. 389), the Bush administration has altered the meaning of the concept.

Deterrence and compellence were developed during the Cold War. Both strategies involve the use of force to bargain in ways that limit the actual level of violence in war and prevent it from getting out of hand, much in the way that Clausewitz theorized about war. We begin by examining deterrence, describing how the superpowers developed the strategy during the Cold War and considering its utility today. We then turn to compellence, also called coercive diplomacy, and the use of force to make an adversary alter its behavior.

Deterrence and survival

Deterrence aims to prevent an enemy from attacking in the first place. Because deterrence relies on threats, many actors view it as cheaper than defense *unless the threat need be carried out*. Deterrence is a strategic interaction that relies on threats, usually of military retaliation, that constitute commitments to use force in the event of aggression. Deterrence assumes that actors are rational enough to weigh the likely costs and benefits of any course of action. Its goal is to convince an adversary that the costs of attacking will exceed its benefits. To this end, deterrence uses military force passively, meaning that actors do not actually use force but rely on the *threat* of force to influence the adversary. While this strategy is not new, its significance grew during the Cold War when nuclear weapons threatened the survival of the principal adversaries.

Elements of deterrence

For an actor to persuade a challenger that the costs of aggression would be greater than the benefits, it must exercise the "three Cs" of deterrence: communication, capability, and credibility. First, the deterring actor must *communicate* to a challenger what actions are unacceptable and what punishment will ensue if it behaves aggressively. Second, the deterring actor must demonstrate that it has the *capability* to back up its threats. Thus, if an actor threatens to employ weapons it is known not to have, the threat would be worthless. Third, threats and commitments must be *credible* or believable. That is, the deterring actor must convince its adversary that the threatened punishment will actually be carried out if its threats are ignored. In fact, actors sometimes confront adversaries over relatively unimportant matters merely to enhance their "bargaining reputation" for "toughness," thereby enhancing their credibility in other situations. Thus, the major justification for America's intervention in Korea in 1950 was to prove that the US would not countenance communist expansion anywhere and would resist Soviet expansion in Western Europe just as it was resisting communist aggression in Korea. And, according to Assistant Secretary of Defense John T. McNaughton (1921–67), "70 percent" of America's reason for getting involved in Vietnam was to enhance other commitments.[51]

Credibility does not require certainty. If stakes are high, as in a nuclear confrontation, a threat can be credible as long as there is at least *some* probability, however modest, that it will be carried out. This is why few people willingly play "Russian Roulette" – a game played by placing a single round in a revolver, spinning the cylinder, aiming the revolver at one's own head, and pulling the trigger – even when the prize for winning is high. Russian Roulette, like nuclear confrontation, entails some probability of being killed. Thomas Schelling calls the possibility that matters could get out of hand leading to mutual disaster a "threat that leaves something to chance,"[52] and he suggests that all that is needed for a threat to be credible is to show that in a confrontation *"the final decision is not altogether under the threatener's control."*[53] Thus, no matter how careful actors are during a flaming crisis and however much they wish to avoid war, there is some chance that a collision will take place as it did in 1914.

Paradoxically, to make deterrence credible, an actor must make its enemy think it is sufficiently irrational to risk its own annihilation for the sake of preventing aggression.[54] However, *if deterrence fails, meaning that the adversary does not heed the deterrent warning*, an actor would probably not wish to carry out its threat because both would perish in the process. As political scientist Edward Rhodes declares: "This seeming paradox reflects the difference between what is rational to threaten and commit oneself to do in advance – *ex ante* – and what is rational to do if the threat fails – *ex post*. The *ex ante* self-denial of future rationality may be a means of credibly committing oneself to the execution of deterrent threats that would be irrational *ex post* to carry out."[55] When the specter of nuclear war looms, as it did in the 1962 Cuban missile crisis, it is preferable for an actor to persuade its enemy that it is not crazy after all. Instead, it becomes rational to step back from the brink of a nuclear abyss by behaving flexibly and preventing **escalation**. In short, deterrence only works when threats are credible, but too much credibility can be dangerous. How to balance the need for strength and risk-taking with an image of reasonableness and credibility is an unsolved puzzle of the nuclear age.

escalation an upward spiral in conflict and violence.

During the Cold War, deterrence assumed four forms, distinguished by the immediacy of the threat they were designed to prevent and the scope of the territory being protected. The first two, general and immediate deterrence, are distinguished by the imminence of the challenge. *General deterrence* does not try to deal with any *particular* threat, but instead is a broad effort to create an atmosphere in which others will not contemplate aggression. Two ways an actor may accomplish this are to alter the global balance of military power in its favor and develop new weapons. Neither is accomplished quickly, and general deterrence is a long-term strategy.

During the Cold War, the US pursued general deterrence by creating a global alliance structure that covered almost every geographic region: the North Atlantic Treaty Organization, the Southeast Asian Treaty Organization, the Central Treaty Organization, the Australia/New Zealand/US alliance (ANZUS), the US–Japan alliance in the Pacific, and the Rio Pact in the western hemisphere. This extended network of alliances communicated to the Soviet Union that the US had global interests and that the USSR and its allies could not wage aggression in any region unchallenged.

Immediate deterrence operates when an actor makes an explicit retaliatory threat in response to a specific challenge to its interests. Immediate deterrence operated during the 1962 Cuban missile crisis, when US officials (before learning of the existence of Soviet missiles in Cuba) informed Moscow that "it would be of the gravest consequence if the Soviet Union placed missiles in Cuba" and that "it shall be the policy of this nation to regard any nuclear missile launched from Cuba against any nation in the Western Hemisphere as an attack by the Soviet Union on the United States, requiring a full retaliatory response upon the Soviet Union."[56]

Both general and immediate deterrence can be either primary or extended. *Primary deterrence* involves preventing an enemy from attacking one's homeland, and *extended deterrence* involves preventing aggression against an ally. America's nuclear umbrella, which extended over allies in Europe, Asia, and the Pacific during the Cold War, involved extended deterrence. The US pledged to retaliate, even to use nuclear weapons, if the USSR or its allies attacked an American ally like West Germany or Japan. The Key document relating to NATO provides an example of Cold War deterrence policy.

Extended deterrence is more difficult to accomplish than primary deterrence, because a threat to retaliate after an attack on one's homeland is inherently more credible than a commitment to risk suicide on behalf of an ally. On the one hand, the guarantor must be tough and willing to take risks to convince an enemy that its commitment is credible. On the other hand, the guarantor must be prudent enough to reassure its allies that it will not trigger a war in which they will be embroiled against their will. Unfortunately, the appearance of prudence, though reassuring to allies, may also be taken as a lack of resolve. To overcome this dilemma, the US stationed troops in vulnerable locations, for example in the city of Berlin and right on the borders between East and West Germany and North and South Korea to serve as "tripwires." Such troops would be unable to defend themselves in the event of an enemy attack but were positioned so that the US would necessarily become involved if such an attack took place. This had the effect of dramatically increasing the credibility of US commitments to defend its European and Asian allies. During the Cold War, the United States relied primarily on a strategy of general extended deterrence to dissuade the USSR from attacking the US or its allies.

Key document   North Atlantic Military Committee MC 14/2 (Revised)

The US nuclear deterrence strategy was adopted by the NATO alliance. The following document contains NATO's 1957 strategic concept outlining how nuclear deterrence would operate. Note how the document refers not only to the capabilities underlying deterrence, but also to the allies' will to use those capabilities.

FINAL DECISION ON MC 14/2 (Revised)

A Report by the Military Committee on

OVERALL STRATEGIC CONCEPT FOR THE

DEFENSE OF THE NORTH ATLANTIC TREATY ORGANIZATION AREA[57]

Section IV

THE STRATEGIC CONCEPT

23 The overall defensive concept of the North Atlantic Treaty Organization is to promote the preservation of peace and to provide for the security of the North Atlantic Treaty area by confronting the potential aggressor with NATO forces that are so organized, disposed, trained and equipped that he will conclude that the chances of a favorable decision are too small to be acceptable, and that fatal risks would be involved if he launched or supported an armed attack.

24 Our chief objective is to prevent war by creating an effective deterrent to aggression. The principal elements of the deterrent are adequate nuclear and other ready forces and the manifest determination to retaliate against any aggressor with all the forces at our disposal, including nuclear weapons, which the defense of NATO would require.

25 In preparation for a general war, should one be forced upon us,

a   we must first ensure the ability to carry out an instant and devastating nuclear counter-offensive by all available means and develop the capability to absorb and survive the enemy's onslaught.

b   Concurrently and closely related to the attainment of this aim, we must develop our ability to use our land, sea and air forces for defense of the territories and sea areas of NATO as far forward as possible to maintain the integrity of the NATO area, counting on the use of nuclear weapons from the outset. We must have the ability to continue these operations in combination with the nuclear counter-offensive until the will and ability of the enemy to pursue general war has been destroyed.

strategic stability a condition in which leaders have few incentives to launch a military first strike.

vulnerability the degree to which an actor's nuclear retaliatory force can be destroyed by an enemy attack.

Two additional concepts at the heart of any deterrence relationship are **strategic stability** and **vulnerability**. Strategic stability refers to the incentives or disincentives actors have to attack an adversary first. If actors fear that their ability to retaliate is at risk, they may be tempted to use nuclear weapons first – "use them or lose them" – especially during crises when tempers are frayed and stress is high. Such a relationship is *unstable*.

This, as we saw, was the situation in 1914 when major powers felt they had to mobilize or lose the war. By contrast, if actors believe their retaliatory systems could survive an enemy first-strike attack, they feel less pressure to use those weapons quickly, and the relationship is *stable*.

It is a paradox of deterrence that stability, and therefore safety, actually increases if enemies lack the means to defend their civilian populations. As long as adversaries can destroy each other's population no matter which of them acts first, strategic stability will remain high. Although it appears to turn common sense on its head, effective civil-defense efforts or antiballistic missiles – missiles that shoot down other missiles – reduce stability (even though they may save lives in the event of war). The reason is that *such efforts reduce the deterrent effect of a threat to retaliate*. If the logic appears convoluted, imagine your thoughts on awakening to a news report that an enemy's citizens had moved into air-raid shelters during the night. You would probably conclude that the enemy was planning to attack and was making sure its citizens would survive the inevitable retaliation. In sum, the greater the vulnerability of both actors' retaliatory forces, the more likely they are to use nuclear weapons quickly to avoid their being destroyed first, and the lower the strategic stability. By contrast, the greater the vulnerability of population centers, the higher the strategic stability, as both populations are held hostage to their governments' good behavior; that is, each can wipe out the other so neither better start a war.

Nuclear deterrence in the Cold War

Although deterrence was the foundation of US military policy during the Cold War, the strategy was repeatedly refined to make the threat more credible in response to changing circumstances. Early in the nuclear era, the United States enjoyed a monopoly of nuclear weapons, while the USSR maintained conventional military superiority (manpower, tanks, and artillery), especially in Europe. With their monopoly of nuclear weapons, the US and its allies had two options to counter a Soviet attack. They could build up strong conventional forces to *repel* a conventional attack, or they could rely on their nuclear superiority to *deter* the enemy from attacking. Conventional forces are costly, requiring huge investments in large armies (including housing, food, and logistics). Nuclear weapons are relatively cheap because few weapons promise enormous destructive power.

Unwilling to sacrifice "butter" for "guns," the nuclear option was attractive to the US in the 1950s. In 1954, President Dwight D. Eisenhower (1890–1969) adopted a policy that relied on nuclear weapons to deter the USSR or its allies from aggression. The NATO

Figure 8.2 Dayton, Ohio – Mark 28 thermonuclear bomb on display at the National Museum of the US Air Force
US Air Force photo

allies maintained a minimal level of conventional forces near the Iron Curtain to mark a "line in the sand" or "tripwire" that Soviet forces dare not cross. If they did so, the US *might* escalate to the nuclear level right away. This strategy was called "massive retaliation." "It should not be stated in advance," wrote Secretary of State John Foster Dulles, "precisely what would be the scope of military action if new aggression occurred" because "the choice in this respect is ours and not his."[58]

Did you know?

The "guns–butter" metaphor was first used by Nazi leader Hermann Goering in a 1935 radio address to the German people in which he declared: "Some people in international life are very hard of hearing. They can only be made to listen if they have guns. We have no butter, comrades, but I ask you: would you rather have butter or guns? Shall we bring in lard, or iron ores? I tell you, being prepared makes us powerful. Butter only makes us fat!"[59]

However, two problems arose in regard to massive retaliation. The first was the possibility that the USSR might limit itself to low-level and very limited aggression that would seem insufficiently important to merit nuclear retaliation. Would an American threat to use nuclear weapons be credible, for example, in the event of Soviet harassment of Western efforts to resupply Berlin? In other words, massive retaliation seemed excessive when confronted by "salami tactics," that is, small demands (like thin slices of a salami) that collectively add up to something larger (the whole salami).[60]

Second, once the Soviet Union became a nuclear power in 1949 and gained a long-range delivery capability in 1957, it could retaliate if the United States used nuclear weapons first as it threatened to do according to the doctrine of massive retaliation. In addition, both superpowers had a dangerous **first-strike capability** because, during a crisis, each, fearing an enemy attack, might be tempted to attack first lest its retaliatory force be destroyed by the enemy's first strike. For strategic stability, the nuclear forces of each had to be able to survive the other's first strike and still be able to retaliate with a second strike that would destroy the enemy's population centers. Only then would neither superpower have an incentive to attack the other first. Thus, in an era of two or more nuclear powers, a **second-strike capability** was crucial for credible deterrence.

On October 4, 1957, the USSR launched the world's first successful artificial satellite into space. The satellite, called *Sputnik*, was a test version of an intercontinental ballistic missile (ICBM), and its successful launch meant that the USSR would soon be able to strike the US homeland. Prior to 1957, nuclear warheads could be delivered only by strategic bombers, warplanes designed to travel great distances and drop weapons on enemy territory. The United States had the more advanced

first-strike capability the ability to launch an attack and successfully destroy an enemy's capability to retaliate.

second-strike capability the capability to absorb an enemy first strike and deliver a counterblow to the enemy.

Figure 8.3a Replica of Little Boy, the atom bomb dropped on Hiroshima
Courtesy of the Nuclear Weapon Archive

Figure 8.3b Trinity Test bomb: the first atomic bomb was detonated at the Trinity test site, New Mexico, July 1945
Courtesy of Los Alamos National Laboratory, Photo taken by Jack Aeby

bombers and, because many were based in Europe, it also had a capacity to send bombers over Soviet territory quickly in the event of war. This gave the US a decisive first-strike advantage. However, *Sputnik* changed this. Suddenly, the United States was vulnerable to nuclear attack, and massive retaliation was no longer credible. If US territory were vulnerable to a nuclear strike, who would believe that Washington would escalate to the nuclear level right away in response to a Soviet provocation in Europe or Asia? US decision-makers feared that if they continued to rely on massive retaliation, they might invite a preemptive first strike from Moscow.

Therefore, after *Sputnik*'s launch, Albert Wohlstetter, an influential policy analyst at the RAND think-tank, argued that to keep the threat of nuclear retaliation credible, the United States needed a second-strike capability (see Key document: Excerpts from Albert Wohlstetter).[61] It had to acquire more weapons and also protect its existing weapons so that they could survive a Soviet first strike and retaliate against the USSR.

Key document   Excerpts from Albert Wohlstetter, "The Delicate Balance of Terror"[62]

Because of its crucial role in the Western strategy of defense, I should like to examine the stability of the thermonuclear balance which, it is generally supposed, would make aggression irrational or even insane. The balance, I believe, is in fact precarious. . . . Is deterrence a necessary consequence of both sides having a nuclear delivery capability, and is all-out war nearly obsolete? Is mutual extinction the only outcome of a general war? . . . To deter an attack means being able to strike back in spite of it. It means, in other words, a capability to strike second. In the last year or two there has been a growing awareness of the importance of the distinction between a "strike-first" and a "strike-second" capability, but little, if any, recognition of the implications of this distinction for the balance of terror theory. . . . Some of the complexities can be suggested by referring to the successive obstacles to be hurdled by any system providing a capability to strike second, that is, to strike back. Such deterrent systems must have (a) a stable, "steady-state" peacetime operation. . . . They must have also the ability (b) to survive enemy attacks, (c) to make and communicate the decision to retaliate, (d) to reach enemy territory with fuel enough to complete their mission, (e) to penetrate enemy active defenses, that is fighters and surface-to-air missiles, and (f) to destroy the target in spite of any passive civil defense.

The development of ballistic missiles in the late 1950s and 1960s raised new fears about vulnerability. The first generation of missiles on both sides sat above ground and because their liquid fuel was too volatile to be left onboard, the missile had to be fueled before launch. Such weapons made tempting targets for a first strike. A second generation of missiles was developed that used less volatile solid fuel and were based in underground concrete silos, making them difficult to destroy and easy to launch quickly. Even more revolutionary were submarine-launched missiles that were invulnerable owing to a combination of concealment and mobility. In time, American and Soviet nuclear-powered submarines with submarine-launched ballistic missiles (SLBMs) would spend months at a time lying silent and undetected under the polar icepack, ready to retaliate if war began.

Did you know?

It is estimated that 128,000 nuclear warheads were built worldwide between 1945 and 2002. All but 2 percent of these warheads were built by the US and the USSR.[63]

By the late 1960s, the strategic balance began to change toward relative "parity" or equivalence in US and Soviet force levels. Although the USSR depended more than the United States on land-based missiles, the two sides were roughly equal after taking account of the quantity and quality of strategic nuclear warheads and nuclear launchers. Moreover, once both had achieved a second-strike capability, any nuclear war would result in **mutual assured destruction** (MAD). Most observers viewed MAD as highly stable because mutual vulnerability meant that neither side had an incentive to start a nuclear war. Indeed, one group of scientists concluded that the environmental consequences of nuclear war might be the extinction of life itself. A combination of "obscuring smoke in the troposphere, obscuring dust in the stratosphere, the fallout of radioactive debris, and the partial destruction of the ozone layer," would, in their view, bring about a period of life-threatening darkness and cold on earth, a **nuclear winter**.

Thus, the United States and USSR began to seek ways to manage their arsenals and preserve this stable balance. One valuable foreign policy tool to this end was arms control, to which we will turn shortly. During the 1960s and 1970s, technological change also contributed to stability, especially the proliferation of space satellites that enabled first the US and then both superpowers to recognize a nuclear launch quickly and to verify arms-control agreements. However, technology sometimes stabilizes and sometimes destabilizes deterrence, depending mainly on two factors, *destructiveness* and *accuracy* of weapons. A combination of highly destructive and accurate nuclear weapons can dramatically reduce strategic stability because they enhance the possibility of a successful first-strike attack on an enemy's retaliatory force. During the 1980s, a number of new weapons such as America's highly accurate Minuteman III, and MIRVed (multiple independently targetable reentry vehicles) missiles threatened to destabilize MAD for this reason.

As American threats to use nuclear weapons first for purposes of extended deterrence grew less credible in the 1960s and 1970s, the US adopted a new security policy for NATO called *flexible response*. This was still a deterrence strategy, but the threat of retaliation was less clear than before. Now, American leaders threatened that if the United States or its allies were attacked, the West would respond in a "balanced and proportional way" short of nuclear war. But if an enemy continued to escalate a conflict, the US would *eventually* respond with nuclear weapons. Under this policy, the "line in the sand" was ambiguous. There was no clear tripwire that would automatically trigger a nuclear war. Given the vulnerability of US territory to a nuclear strike, officials believed that flexible response was more credible. To one degree or another, flexible response remained the foundation of US deterrence policy until the end of the Cold War.

mutual assured destruction (MAD) a nuclear deterrence strategy based on each state's ability to launch devastating nuclear retaliation even if an enemy attacks it first.

nuclear winter a period of cold and darkness following a nuclear war, caused by the blocking of the sun's rays by high-altitude dust clouds.

Nuclear deterrence today

When the Cold War ended, American officials did not immediately abandon nuclear deterrence, and it remains a central element of US security policy. However, deterrence seems poorly suited for dealing with some of the threats the United States now faces. First, threats have grown more diffuse, and it is not always clear who must be deterred.

Second, deterrence is a psychological as much as a political-military strategy that assumes rational decision-makers who evaluate costs and benefits and only act when they expect to reap net benefits. Today, concern focuses on aspiring nuclear powers, like North Korea and Iran, which may be more willing to take risks than were Cold War adversaries, including "gambling with the lives of their people, and the wealth of their nations."[64] The perception that "rogue states" are less rational means that the leaders of these states may not evaluate costs and benefits in the same way – and may value striking the US more than they value protecting their own populations against retaliation.

Third, the utility of deterrence has also been challenged with the emergence of shadowy terrorist networks like Al Qaeda. Not only does it appear that these actors are not rational in the sense described above, but, for the most part, they do not operate from a single territorial state and use suicidal fanatics who are virtually impossible to deter. With no territorial entity to retaliate against and with terrorist leaders dispersed and hidden, the United States cannot issue a credible retaliatory threat. Indeed, in the event of a terrorist attack using weapons of mass destruction, the victim may not even know the attacker's identity.

This section has introduced the concept of deterrence and has provided an overview of how deterrence operated during the Cold War and after. However, deterrence is only one strategy for using force. The next section examines how actors can use force to make adversaries reverse or alter their behavior.

Compellence and coercion

Unlike deterrence, which involves the passive use of force, compellence, also called coercive diplomacy, uses limited force to make an actor alter its behavior or undo a fait accompli (something already completed). Compellence is strategic interaction that involves calculating the amount of force to stop the opponent from engaging in undesirable behavior and, as in deterrence, requires that adversaries communicate their interests and intentions. If they fail to do so, war may erupt, and both parties may be worse off. We will focus on the factors that contribute to a successful compellence strategy. As we saw in chapter 4, the 1962 Cuban missile crisis demonstrates how actors can employ both deterrence and compellence and avoid mutual disaster.

Compellence is more complicated than announcing a threat or unleashing force and then waiting for an opponent to back down. Instead, it coerces an enemy, *not by the pain it causes, but by the prospect of still greater pain in the future in the event of non-compliance*. Successful compellence convinces an enemy of the following:[65]

1 there is an urgency about complying with the demand to alter its behavior;

2 the coercing actor is more highly motivated than the opponent; and

3 the consequences of staying the course will be escalation and still greater pain for the adversary.

This is bargaining pure and simple. If the enemy fails to comply, the coercing actor must decide whether to back down or intensify the use of force.

The 1999 NATO air strikes in Kosovo illustrate compellence in action. In this instance, NATO commenced air strikes against Serbian targets to compel the Serbian government to stop its policy of ethnic cleansing in Kosovo, gradually increasing the damage done to Serbia's infrastructure. The Serbs finally ceased fighting, in part because of the threat of still greater NATO escalation.

Coercive bargaining involving the use of force risks setting off a conflict spiral in which one actor responds to the violent acts of the other with its own use of violence. Such a hostile spiral resembles the game of *chicken* (see Figure 8.4). This is a game in which two cars speed toward each other, straddling the road's center line. The object is to see which driver will "chicken out" and swerve first. If both drivers swerve (outcome 1:1), both suffer loss of reputation. If only one swerves, there is a loser and a winner (outcomes 1:2 and 2:1). If neither swerves, both are big losers in the inevitable suicidal collision.

		Driver 2	
		(Swerve)	(Not swerve)
		1	2
(Swerve)	1	(−5,−5)	(−5,+5)
(Not swerve)	2	(+5,−5)	(−50,−50)

Driver 1

Figure 8.4 Chicken Matrix

Disaster occurs in chicken when both actors believe the other is bluffing, and neither swerves. In 1914, Europe's leaders tried to bully one another to make concessions to avoid collision. No one swerved, and all were losers in the resulting conflagration. Disaster can be avoided only when one player is persuaded that the other is irrationally prepared to risk suicide by not swerving. Otherwise, *mutual fear forces the players to cooperate and, thus, avoid the worst case.* The way one wins a game of chicken is by making the adversary believe that one is sufficiently irrational to risk mutual disaster. This game demonstrates the general problem of making credible commitments that serve the strategies of both deterrence and compellence. Like the adversaries in 1914, the United States and the USSR engaged in a chicken game during the 1962 Cuban missile crisis. Fortunately, the outcome was different because the Soviet Union "swerved"; "we were eyeball to eyeball," declared Secretary of State Dean Rusk (1909–94) as the crisis ended, "and the other guy just blinked."

A number of tactics are available to a hot-rodder (or a political leader) in a chicken game. For example, she might throw the steering wheel out the window, making it impossible to swerve. This makes the commitment not to chicken out, however irrational, quite credible. It forces the second hot-rodder to swerve because (s)he has what Thomas Schelling calls the "last clear chance" to avoid mutual suicide. "In strategy," writes Schelling, "when both parties abhor collision the advantage goes often to the one who arranges the status quo in his favor and leaves to the other the 'last clear chance' to stop or turn aside."[66] Figure 8.5 summarizes the differences between deterrence and compellence.

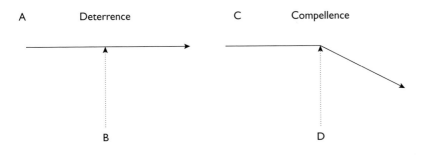

Actor B anticipates Actor A will engage in an undesirable behavior and threatens to retaliate if it does so.

Actor D employs threats and force to make Actor C change its behavior and cease action that is underway

Figure 8.5 Deterrence and compellence

Alliances

Another policy to manage insecurity is that of forming military alliances. In contrast to the relatively short-term balance-of-power alliances we discussed in chapter 7, some alliances like NATO are permanent international organizations. Such alliances are normally intended to aggregate military power against potential foes. Realists view alliances as useful tools for managing conflict, both to prevent war and fight it if necessary.

Alliances can serve both to deter enemies and to balance power. However, theorists differ in their understanding of what alliances balance against. One school argues that alliances form to balance against power *itself*. Today, for example, some observers believe that Russia and China are trying to balance American power with a grouping called the Shanghai Cooperation Organization, consisting of themselves plus Uzbekistan, Tajikistan, Kyrgyzstan, and Kazakhstan.[67]

However, political scientist Stephen Walt argues that another country's power itself is not inherently threatening. Instead of balancing against power itself, he contends, actors ally to counter specific threats and presumed aggressive intent or to halt aggression.[68] By contrast, actors will not balance against those they regard as non-threatening, however powerful they may be. Thus, the countries of Western Europe do not try to balance America's great power because they do not regard the United States as a threat to their security or survival. In Walt's view, then, when actors perceive a threat from another actor or bloc of actors, they ally to protect themselves from that threat. Actors have two options: to *ally against* or to *bandwagon with* the adversary. In the bandwagon option, actors may join the adversary to ensure that they do not become its victims or to gain the anticipated spoils of victory. Thus, in the late 1930s fascist Italy chose to bandwagon by joining Nazi Germany rather than entering an alliance with Britain and France to balance German power.

Power aggregation is not the only motive for alliances. Actors sometimes form alliances to express ideological or cultural solidarity. In 2004, seven former members of the Soviet bloc formally joined NATO: Bulgaria, Estonia, Latvia, Lithuania, Romania, Slovakia, and Slovenia. In this case, NATO's enlargement had less to do with fear of aggression than with the spread of democratic and free-market principles in Europe and with a commitment to political stability in the region. Thus, while realists focus on alliances as aggregates of power, liberals emphasize how shared experience, culture, and language, as well as close economic and personal ties, contribute to alliances like NATO and, even more, to bilateral relations between countries like the US and Britain.

But how effectively do alliances deter war? Some analysts believe that alliances, when considered purely in regard to their ability to aggregate military capabilities, may actually encourage war because they appear threatening to non-members. Even if actors build alliances for defensive purposes, they communicate that they are anticipating war. In doing so, they make outsiders less secure and may engender counter-alliances and arms races.[69] And, as in World War I, alliances may spread wars that do occur. Thus, liberals like President Woodrow Wilson concluded that balance-of-power alliances were causes of war and wanted to replace them with a collective security system (chapter 3, p. 127).

Figure 8.6 NATO headquarters and flags from the 26 member states
Courtesy of NATO

Arms control and disarmament

Actors also manage conflict through disarmament and arms control. Those who favor disarmament believe that weapons themselves cause war and that reducing the numbers of weapons and even eliminating them are necessary to prevent war. Those who advocate arms control believe that some types of weapons are more likely to provoke war than others and that the way to prevent war is not simply to eliminate weapons wholesale but to reinforce stability in deterrence relationships. Thus, arms control is a strategy to prevent arms races from driving security policy and often involves restricting or eliminating certain classes of weapons that may reduce strategic stability by provoking preemptive war. Arms control may also involve limiting research and development, as well as deployment, of new, qualitatively different but dangerous weapons. In a few cases, arms control may even involve increasing the number of weapons that are believed to stabilize strategic relations. Thus, in the 1960s, some American strategists, including Secretary of Defense Robert McNamara (1916–), sought to encourage the Soviet Union to acquire spy satellites that they believed would reduce Soviet fears of an American nuclear attack.

Realists tend to promote arms control rather than disarmament because they see arms as necessary to preserving security and deterrence, while they regard disarmament as dangerous and utopian in a hostile world. Thus, beginning in the late 1960s, realists promoted arms control agreements like the 1972 ban on antiballistic missiles. This ban, they believed, would preserve the stability of deterrence by assuring that each side could retaliate if attacked by the other, which, in turn, would keep the Cold War from turning hot. For their part, liberals favor disarmament because they believe that if weapons exist, sooner or later they will be used. Constructivists see both policies as useful in creating precedents that may promote a future consensus in favor of additional steps to reduce tension.

Arms control and disarmament can be achieved in a number of ways. First, actors can place numerical limits on weapons and delivery systems. The major bilateral arms control and disarmament agreements of the Cold War and post-Cold War eras (see Table 8.1) included such limits. The Strategic Arms Limitation Talks (SALT) I was an arms control agreement designed to prevent US and Soviet nuclear arsenals from growing significantly larger by limiting the number of strategic land-based and sea-based weapons to those already in existence or under construction. The 1972 Antiballistic Missile (ABM) Treaty limited the superpowers to two missile defense systems on their territories (later reduced to one). It also restricted the number of radars and interceptors for each site. Next, the Strategic Arms Reduction Talks (START) I (1991) reduced the number of missile launchers and warheads available to each party, as well as the throw-weight (lifting power) of their ballistic missiles. And START II (1993) placed an even lower cap on the strategic nuclear warheads each side could have. The Intermediate Range Nuclear Forces (INF) Treaty of 1987 eliminated *all* ground-based nuclear missiles with a range of 500–5,500 kilometers and was, therefore, an example of genuine disarmament. Finally, the Strategic Offensive Reduction Treaty

(SORT) of 2002 will limit strategic nuclear warheads to between 1,700 and 2,200 by December 31, 2012.

A second way arms control and disarmament can be achieved is for actors to restrict the development, testing, and deployment of weapons. For example, the multilateral 1967 Outer Space Treaty banned the deployment of nuclear weapons in space, and the 1996 Comprehensive Test Ban Treaty (CTBT) prohibited nuclear testing for peaceful or military purposes. The Biological Weapons Convention (1972), the Chemical Weapons Convention (1993), and the Ottawa Landmine Convention (1997) banned entire categories of weapons. According to the biological and chemical weapons treaties, states are not permitted to develop, produce, or in any way acquire or stockpile biological or chemical weapons.

Third, actors can limit the transfer of weapons among countries. The biological and conventional weapons conventions contain such restrictions, as does the 1968 Nuclear Nonproliferation Treaty (NPT), which bans the transfer of nuclear weapons or nuclear-weapons technology to non-nuclear powers. The NPT, which was extended in perpetuity in 1995, is the basis of the nuclear nonproliferation regime, the set of rules regulating nuclear weapons proliferation (see chapter 6, p. 259).

Even when actors agree that arms control and disarmament are necessary to preserve security, it remains difficult to negotiate agreements because actors wish to maintain sufficient arms as insurance against future conflict. Moreover, since actors cannot predict one another's future intentions, it is in their interest to maintain arms sufficient to counter future as well as present threats.

Agreements also face technical obstacles. First, weapons are not always easily comparable. How, for example, can one compare a relatively slow moving bomber that can carry many nuclear weapons to a missile that can achieve intercontinental range in a matter of minutes but may only have a single nuclear warhead? Weapons vary in terms of their quality, accuracy, mobility (and hence vulnerability to attack), and destructive power. Second, how can actors verify one another's compliance? Will they permit "on-site" inspection or rely on "national technical means" like satellite surveillance? Confidence-building measures are necessary to overcome problems like these. Table 8.1 illustrates that, as time passed, US–Soviet agreements became more substantial. Early agreements placed relatively few limits on weapons, but they had the broader goal of building trust between the superpowers, thereby increasing their confidence in each other and making possible more ambitious agreements later on.

This process gathered steam as the Cold War came to an end. For example, in 1991, President George H.W. Bush announced plans to

Table 8.1 Summary of key arms control and disarmament agreements

Treaty	Year signed	Parties (as of 2004)	Terms	Status in 2004
Nuclear weapons				
Nuclear Nonproliferation (NPT) Treaty	1968	188	Limited proliferation of nuclear weapons to the known nuclear powers as of January 1, 1967. Non-nuclear states pledged not to engage in nuclear weapons programs. Nuclear-weapons states pledged not to transfer nuclear weapons knowledge or materials, but to share peaceful nuclear energy technology with non-nuclear states.	Entered into force in 1970 and was extended indefinitely in 1995.
Outer Space Treaty	1967	97	Bans nuclear weapons in space and prohibits military activities on celestial bodies.	Entered into force 1967.
Strategic Arms Limitation Talks (SALT) I	1972	US USSR	Interim five-year agreement limited the number of land- and sea-based strategic offensive nuclear weapons to those already in existence or under construction.	Expired in 1997.
Antiballistic Missile (ABM) Treaty	1972	US USSR	Permanently limited the weapons and radars that could be used in a missile defense system. Signatories could only deploy two limited systems; restricted research and development and testing of new systems.	Abrogated in 2002.
Strategic Arms Limitation Talks (SALT) II	1979	US USSR	Set limits on the number and types of strategic missile launchers each state could have.	Never entered into force.
Intermediate Range Nuclear Forces (INF) Treaty	1987	US USSR	Superpowers agreed to eliminate all ground-launched ballistic and cruise missiles with a range of 500–5,500 kilometers. Reductions were completed by June 1, 1991.	Entered into force 1988.
Strategic Arms Reduction Talks (START) I	1991	US Russia Belarus* Ukraine* Kazakhstan*	1,600 deployed ICBMs, SLBMs, and heavy bombers for each side, carrying no more than 6,000 warheads; limited the throw-weight of ballistic missiles; 15-year agreement with the option to extend for successive five-year periods.	Entered into force 1994; all parties met the agreement's December 2001 implementation deadline.

Table 8.1 (continued)

Treaty	Year signed	Parties (as of 2004)	Terms	Status in 2004
Nuclear weapons				
Strategic Arms Reduction Talks (START) II	1993	US Russia	Cap of 3,000–3,500 strategic nuclear warheads for both sides.	Never entered into force; superseded by SORT.
Comprehensive Test Ban Treaty (CTBT)	1996	170	Prohibits any nuclear explosion for peaceful or weapons purposes.	Not ratified.
Strategic Offensive Reduction Treaty (SORT) or Moscow Treaty	2002	US Russia	Parties agreed to limit strategic nuclear warheads to between 1,700 and 2,200 by December 31, 2012.	Entered into force 2003.
Nuclear Weapons Free Zones (NWFZs)				
Treaty of Tlatelolco	1967	33	Creates an NWFZ in Latin America and the Caribbean	Entered into force 1968.
Treaty of Rarotonga	1985	13	Creates an NWFZ in the South Pacific	Entered into force 1986.
Treaty of Bangkok	1995	10	Creates an NWFZ in Southeast Asia	Entered into force 1997.
Treaty of Pelindaba	1996	0	Creates an NWFZ in Africa	Not yet in force; ten more signatories must ratify.
n/a	n/a	0	Central Asian NWFZ	Negotiated in 2002, no treaty signed.
Biological and chemical weapons				
Biological Weapons Convention (BWC)	1972	150	Bans the development, production, and stockpiling of biological agents; reaffirms the 1925 Geneva Protocol that bans the use of biological weapons; allows biodefense programs.	Entered into force 1975.
Chemical Weapons Convention (CWC)	1993	161	Bans the development, production, stockpiling, acquisition, transfer, and use of chemical weapons and requires their destruction within a specified period of time (depending on the weapon).	Entered into force 1997.

Table 8.1 (continued)

Treaty	Year signed	Parties (as of 2004)	Terms	Status in 2004
Conventional weapons				
Conventional Armed Forces in Europe (CFE) Treaty	1990	30	Set equal limit on the number of tanks, armored combat vehicles, heavy artillery, combat aircraft, and attack helicopters that NATO and the former Warsaw Pact could deploy between the Atlantic Ocean and the Ural Mountains; adapted in 1999 to replace the alliance limits with national arms ceilings.	Entered into force 1992.
Open Skies Treaty	1992	26	Allows each party to conduct short-notice, unarmed reconnaissance flights over the others' territories to collect data on military resources and activities.	Entered into force 2002.
Ottawa Landmine Convention	1997	141	Obligates states to give up anti-personnel landmines and to destroy their stockpiles.	Entered into force 1999.

* START I was negotiated and signed by the US and the USSR, but the USSR disintegrated in December 1991, leaving Belarus, Ukraine, and Kazakhstan as independent nuclear powers. The Lisbon Agreement (May 1992) made these new states parties to START I.

cut land- and sea-based short-range nuclear weapons by 2,000 and to remove from strategic alert all strategic bombers and Minuteman II missiles that were to be eliminated under START II. Soviet President Mikhail Gorbachev reciprocated with cuts of his own.[70] In 1991, the US initiated the Cooperative Threat Reduction (CTR) Program, under which it provides financial and technical assistance to Russia and the former Soviet republics to dismantle nuclear weapons and assure that remaining weapons are not stolen or sold. CTR money was used to destroy nuclear weapons in the post-Soviet states of Kazakhstan, Ukraine, and Belarus and continues to help Russia secure its nuclear stockpiles and dismantle old weapons.

Foreign policy and the proliferation of WMD

As we saw in chapter 6, the proliferation of weapons of mass destruction (WMD) is one of the most dangerous trends in contemporary global politics. The nuclear nonproliferation regime discussed there represents a multilateral effort to halt the spread of nuclear weapons. However, states also may act unilaterally to pursue nonproliferation, particularly by developing their defenses. Often, when states act unilaterally, they do so out of fear that the multilateral regime may fail and hostile, perhaps even "irrational" states may gain a WMD capability.

Since the late 1990s, defensive strategies including missile defense and preemptive war have gained equal if not greater prominence in American policy as an insurance policy in case deterrence fails (see Controversy on Saddam Hussein and WMD). With the passage of the 1999 Missile Defense Act, the United States intensified its efforts to research and deploy a workable missile defense system to protect US territory. Its missile defense efforts have since expanded to include the development of regional defenses, known as theater missile defenses, for Europe and Japan.

Controversy

Prior to the 2003 invasion of Iraq, US policymakers debated whether Iraq could be deterred from developing and using weapons of mass destruction. The heart of the debate centered on rationality. Those who argued that deterrence was sufficient believed Saddam Hussein was a rational calculator, while those who opposed deterrence saw him as "unstable" and "a risk taker."

One of those who argued that Iraq could have been deterred, journalist Patrick Cockburn, declared: "When [Hussein] did have lots of these weapons and missiles, he didn't dare use them, because it was always true that the counterattack would be greater than the attack."[71] Other proponents of this position argued that Saddam Hussein was a "survivor." According to one US government analyst, Hussein could be deterred because all dictators want to stay in power. "We know he did not use his anthrax, his sarin, his mustard or anything else during the previous Gulf War [1991] because George Bush [senior] told him it would be met with American violence."[72]

On the other side, analysts countered that Saddam Hussein was not rational because he only accepted information favoring policies he desired and discounted information that contradicted his preferences. Specifically, in the 1991 Persian Gulf War, he believed that his armed forces would defeat the US-led coalition – even when all evidence suggested otherwise. Still others argued that Saddam Hussein could not be deterred because he had "nothing to lose" by using WMD and that he may have been convinced that WMD were the only way to achieve victory over superior US power.[73] By the war's end, Saddam Hussein had not used WMD against American forces. Does this mean he was deterred? We may never know.

The idea of these "active" defenses (meaning the missile defense programs) was not entirely new. The US repeatedly looked into missile defenses during the Cold War and even briefly deployed a missile defense system in the 1970s. What is new is that by the early twenty-first century defensive strategies have become as prominent as deterrence in the US quest for security.

The most ambitious effort to construct an effective missile defense was contained in a 1983 proposal by President Ronald Reagan for a Strategic Defense Initiative (SDI), dubbed "Star Wars." The proposal was notable not only because of the revolutionary technology it required but because it was a giant step away from MAD. The president had been horrified to learn that this strategy for mutual survival depended on holding populations hostage. According to one source, the president "is alleged to have postponed his SIOP [Single Integrated Operations Plan – the list of enemy targets to be struck in the event of war] briefing for three years after assuming office," and that briefing "reportedly left him ashen-faced and speechless."[74] "Wouldn't it be better," Reagan asked, "to save lives than avenge them?" "What if free people could live secure in the knowledge that their security did not rest upon the threat of instant United States retaliation to deter a Soviet attack, that we could intercept and destroy strategic ballistic missiles before they reached our own soil or that of our allies?"[75]

There were several proposed SDI variants, but all depended on exotic new technologies like X-ray lasers. Billions of dollars later SDI seemed an expensive illusion, but the idea of an antiballistic missile (ABM) system did not go away. During the 1991 Persian Gulf War, the United States used Patriot missiles to intercept Soviet-supplied Scud missiles fired from Iraq toward Saudi Arabia, Kuwait, and Israel. Postwar analysis showed that the Patriot was unreliable and that, fortunately, the Scuds were ineffective.

During the 1990s, an advanced version of the Patriot missiles was developed and tested with few successes until 1999, and the United States collaborated with Israel to develop the Arrow missile system that was successfully tested in 1998. The Clinton administration authorized funding to develop a limited ABM system to protect the United States from an attack by North Korea or an accidental missile launch by China or Russia. After 2000, the Bush administration stepped up the pace of ABM development, seeking to deploy a system that would be effective against limited attacks by rogue states like North Korea or Iran. Realizing that going ahead with deployment of this system would violate the 1972 Antiballistic Missile (ABM) Treaty the United States notified Russia in December 2001 of its intent to withdraw from that treaty and did so in June 2002, so that it could develop and deploy a missile defense system. It remains an unanswered question whether the proposed system will work as planned.

Then, following the September 2001 terrorist attacks on New York and Washington, DC, the United States adopted a new policy of preemption. In a speech delivered at West Point in June 2002 (see Key document), President George W. Bush enlarged the meaning of preemption to allow the use of force without evidence of imminent attack. Bush was convinced that the threat of international terrorism was too great to have the luxury of waiting for clear evidence of an enemy's intent to attack before acting decisively. The new version of preemption would be an additional instrument of foreign policy. Condoleezza Rice, then the president's national security advisor, defended the new policy, arguing that: "There has never been a moral or legal requirement that a country wait to be attacked before it can address existential threats."[76] And in the first Bush–Kerry presidential debate on September 30, 2004, Senator John Kerry seemed to agree when he declared that "No president, through all of American history, has ever ceded, and nor would I, the right to preempt in any way necessary to protect the United States of America."[77]

Key document   President George W. Bush's 2002 graduation speech at West Point[78]

In a speech to graduating cadets at West Point, President Bush defined the new strategy of preemption that was employed against Iraq in 2003.

In defending the peace, we face a threat with no precedent. Enemies in the past needed great armies and great industrial capabilities to endanger the American people and our nation. The attacks of September the 11th required a few hundred thousand dollars in the hands of a few dozen evil and deluded men. . . .

The gravest danger to freedom lies at the perilous crossroads of radicalism and technology. When the spread of chemical and biological and nuclear weapons, along with ballistic missile technology – when that occurs, even weak states and small groups could attain a catastrophic power to strike great nations. . . .

For much of the last century, America's defense relied on the Cold War doctrines of deterrence and containment. . . . But new threats also require new thinking. Deterrence . . . means nothing against shadowy terrorist networks with no nation or citizens to defend. Containment is not possible when unbalanced dictators with weapons of mass destruction can deliver those weapons on missiles or secretly provide them to terrorist allies. . . .

Homeland defense and missile defense are part of stronger security, and they're essential priorities for America. Yet the war on terror will not be won on the defensive. We must take the battle to the enemy, disrupt his plans, and confront the worst threats before they emerge. . . .

Our security will require the best intelligence, to reveal threats hidden in caves and growing in laboratories. . . . And our security will require all Americans to be forward-looking and resolute, to be ready for preemptive action when necessary to defend our liberty and to defend our lives.

In sum, some states are turning to foreign policies like preemption and missile defense to provide additional insurance should weapons of mass destruction proliferate to new and hostile states.

Conclusion

This chapter has introduced the concept of foreign policy and the idea that states and other actors craft policies to influence actors beyond their borders. We have also examined theories about why some states pursue more warlike policies than others. Liberal theorists claim that democracies do not fight one another and that as more countries become democratic, there will be less war. Marxists believe that capitalist states collide in search of resources and markets. Nationalism and public opinion can promote war and be manipulated by governments to rally support. Wars also may be instigated by leaders to turn public attention away from problems at home and unify a country.

The process by which states make and implement policies may also trigger war. Assuming rationality is questionable, cognitive and affective models examine how individuals may make decisions on the basis of their biases and emotions. The bureaucratic and organizational models of decision-making help explain how intra-governmental dynamics influence the policy and sometimes contribute to war.

We have seen that actors pursue a variety of policies to assure their security. Sometimes they rely on the use or threat of force, as in deterrence and compellence. However, leaders also attempt to resolve conflicts without force by means of diplomacy, alliances, and arms control and disarmament agreements. In the next chapter we turn to interstate efforts to manage violence and disorder by resort to international law and organization.

Student activities

Discussion questions

Comprehension questions

1   What is foreign policy? Provide examples of different foreign policy orientations.
2   Are leaders rational and, if not, what are the key impediments to rational action?
3   What domestic factors may contribute to the outbreak of war?
4   What are the major policies available to a state to assure its security?

Analysis questions

5 What do explanations at the state and individual levels of analysis contribute to our understanding of war that we cannot get from the global level of analysis?

6 Given the policy options available to states, why do you think wars continue to break out?

7 What alternatives besides war did the Bush administration have in confronting Iraq in 2003?

Map analysis

Various research institutes provide data about ongoing wars. Visit the website http://www.globalsecurity.org/military/world/war/on the Internet to learn about current wars.

1 Mark these wars on a map, using a different color for interstate wars, intrastate wars, and mixed wars.

2 What do you learn about the nature of contemporary war? What kinds of war are dominant today? What regions are most unstable?

Cultural materials

Poetry has been written about warfare since biblical times. Using a reference such as *The Oxford Book of War Poetry* or a website such as http://www.warpoetry.co.uk/, compare and contrast the views toward war and nationalism of two poets such as Rudyard Kipling and Wilfrid Owen or the views of poets toward two wars such as World Wars I and II.

Further reading

Agnew, John, *Hegemony: The New Shape of Global Power* (Philadelphia, PA: Temple University Press, 2005). Examines US hegemony and its impact on others.

Fukuyama, Francis, *The End of History and the Last Man* (New York: Free Press, 1992). Classic statement of the triumph of liberal democracy with the end of the Cold War.

Janis, Irving, *Victims of Groupthink* (Boston, MA: Houghton Mifflin, 1972). Classic study of how small decision-making groups become dysfunctional.

Jervis, Robert, *Perception and Misperception in International Politics* (Princeton, NJ: Princeton University Press, 1976). Classic analysis of the sources and role of misperception in foreign policy.

Ray, James Lee, *Democracy and International Conflict: An Evaluation of the Democratic Peace Proposition* (Columbia, SC: University of South Carolina Press, 1995). A review of some of the vast "democratic peace" literature.

Russett, Bruce M. and John R. Oneal, *Triangulating Peace: Democracy, Interdependence, and International Organizations* (New York: Norton, 2001). Carefully argued analysis of how democracy, interdependence, and international organizations combine to increase the probability of peace.

Schelling, Thomas C., *The Strategy of Conflict* (Cambridge, MA: Harvard University, 1966). The classic statement of bargaining theory.

Stoessinger, John G., *Crusaders and Pragmatists* (New York: W.W. Norton, 1979). A simple but useful typology of foreign policy leaders.

Vasquez, John A., *The War Puzzle* (Cambridge: Cambridge University Press, 1993). Probably the best single volume on the causes of war.

Vasquez, John A., *The Power of Power Politics: From Classical Realism to Neotraditionalism* (Cambridge: Cambridge University Press, 1998). An impressive analysis of the theoretical beliefs of empiricists seeking the causes of war.

Wittkopf, Eugene R. and James M. McCormick, eds., *The Domestic Sources of American Foreign Policy: Insights and Evidence*, 4th ed. (Lanham, MD: Rowman & Littlefield, 2004). An excellent collection of articles on the impact of factors at the state and individual levels of analysis.

9 International law and organization and the quest for peace

25 October 1962: at the height of the Cuban missile crisis, with the United States and USSR poised on the brink of nuclear war, America's UN Ambassador Adlai E. Stevenson sought to convince the world that the Soviet Union was responsible for the crisis. Stevenson, twice an unsuccessful Democratic presidential candidate, was armed with 26 black and white aerial photographs to make his case. He had been sent to New York by President John F. Kennedy (1917–63) despite Kennedy's fear that Stevenson was too conciliatory to make a convincing presentation to the Security Council. Kennedy was wrong, as the ambassador gave the performance of his life. Turning to Soviet UN Ambassador Valerian Zorin (1902–86), Stevenson asked, "Do you, Ambassador Zorin, deny that the USSR has placed and is placing medium- and intermediate-range missiles and sites in Cuba? Yes or no – don't wait for the translation – yes or no?" Zorin angrily replied that he was not in an American courtroom. When Zorin declared that he would answer only after consulting with his government, Stevenson announced that he was "prepared to wait for [his] answer until hell freezes over."[1]

This chapter examines the role of **international law**, **international organizations** (IGOs) and **nongovernmental organizations** (NGOs) in global politics. International law consists of principles and rules derived from custom and treaties that states and other groups are obliged to observe in dealing with one another. An international organization is an institution that is created by sovereign states and established by, and given legal recognition in, a treaty. Such organizations can be universal in scope as is the United Nations or regional as is the European Union (EU). They may also be either multifunctional and pursue a variety of goals like the UN or be specialized like the World Health Organization (WHO) that seeks to improve health conditions globally. NGOs are organizations whose members are individuals who do not represent any government.

international law the body of legally binding rules that governs relations among states and other groups and that also increasingly provides rights for individuals in relation to states.

international organization (IGO) an organization established by and whose members are sovereign states.

nongovernmental organization (NGO) an organization whose members are individuals who do not represent the government of any state.

Figure 9.1 America's UN Ambassador Adlai Stevenson urges the UN Security Council to support a resolution to stop missiles and related materials from being delivered to Cuba in 1962 The Dino A. Brugioni Collection, National Security Archive, Washington, DC

Both have proliferated since the beginning of the twentieth century, and by 2004 there were about 7,300 IGOs and almost 51,000 NGOs.[2]

We open with a discussion of international law – its sources, origins, and evolution, with special attention to the concept of just war. We then turn to international organizations, focusing on the United Nations, its establishment, principal agencies, and, most important, the evolution of its efforts to keep peace. Consonant with the theme of continuity and change, the chapter shows that the United Nations retains many features of the failed League of Nations, while adapting to new circumstances and pioneering new approaches to maintaining peace. Change and continuity are evident in comparing the UN at its outset with the UN during the Cold War years and after and in the challenges the UN faces as new forms of conflict spread and its single most powerful member remains ambivalent about whether to work with the UN or on its own. At the end of the day, the UN's future is cloudy, and it remains unclear whether the organization will suffer the same ignominious end as did the League.

The chapter then examines the evolution of regional IGOs, especially the most successful of these, the European Union. The chapter concludes by examining NGOs and their growing role as sources of expertise and norms in global politics that have created a rudimentary global **civil society**.

civil society a complex global network of institutions that link individuals with common values from many countries who regularly communicate ideas and coordinate activities.

The "law of nations"

Historically, international law has reflected the absence of any central authority above states and the decentralization of force in global politics.

Much of international law, even today, deals with the rights and duties of sovereign states, and most of it was created by Europeans during the long epoch of European dominance of global politics. International law differs from domestic law in a number of ways. First, there is no authoritative legislature in global politics to make law. Instead, as we see in the next section, international law emerges from the customs of states and the treaties they sign with one another. Second, there is no executive that can enforce international law. Third, there is no independent judiciary with the authority to interpret such law. While some observers believe that the UN is evolving to become a legislator and enforcer of international law, states still bear the principal burden of enforcing and interpreting the law for themselves.

The dominant theoretical approaches disagree on the significance of international law. Realists tend to dismiss international law because of the absence of a means to enforce it and label legal enthusiasts "idealists" and "utopians." Liberals strongly support international law and would like to replace reliance on power with reliance on legal norms. Constructivists view the evolution of international law as a key reflection of changing global norms even though it is often violated.

Although international law cannot be enforced in the way that domestic law can, it does anchor and legitimate certain norms and expectations of behavior while creating a moral climate in which some forms of behavior are seen as wrong and unjust. Today, for example, norms have evolved against aggressive war. Increasingly, too, as we shall see, norms are evolving against the mistreatment of individuals by their governments. Despite the absence of an enforcement mechanism, most countries obey international law most of the time. They do so for a variety of reasons – because it helps accomplish their objectives, because they want other countries to reciprocate, and because they fear reprisals and would lose others' trust.

In addition, despite violations of international law, most countries are sensitive to legal issues and justify their actions in terms of international law. For example, at the height of the Cuban missile crisis, Soviet leader Nikita Khrushchev argued that President Kennedy was trying to compel the Soviet Union "to renounce the rights that every sovereign state enjoys, you are trying to legislate in questions of international law, and you are violating the universally accepted norms of that law."[3] In contrast, US officials like Nicholas Katzenbach (1922–), deputy attorney general, argued that "US military action could be justified in international law on the principle of self-defense."[4]

But where does international law originate and evolve? The next section addresses these questions.

Sources and evolution of international law

International law deals with a variety of subjects but, not surprisingly, over the centuries much of it has dealt with issues of war and peace. The sources of international law are described by the International Court of Justice (ICJ) in Article 38 of its statute. Thus, when the ICJ is asked to render advisory opinions about the meaning of international law, it draws from the following sources:

a   international conventions, whether general or particular, establishing rules expressly recognized by the contesting states;

b   international custom, as evidence of a general practice accepted as law;[5]

c   the general principles of law recognized by civilized nations;

d   . . . judicial decisions and the teachings of the most highly qualified publicists of the various nations, as subsidiary means for the determination of rules of law.[6]

Historically, because there is no global legislative body, custom has been the most important source of international law. Custom and the precedents it sets as a source of law date back to the Roman concept of *jus gentium* (law of nations). Customary law arises from established and repeated practice over lengthy periods of time that becomes widely, though not necessarily universally, accepted. For example, the International Court of Justice cited "customary rules" regarding the use of force in its 1986 ruling against the United States in a case involving the mining of Nicaragua's harbors. "In order to deduce the existence of customary rules, the Court deems it sufficient that the conduct of a State should, in general, be consistent with such rules, and that instances of State conduct inconsistent with a given rule should generally have been treated as breaches of that rule."[7] For its part, the International Committee of the Red Cross has identified 161 rules that have emerged through custom, including the principle of proportionality in attack in war, the obligation to protect medical personnel and journalists, and the prohibition of attacks on objects needed for civilian survival.[8]

Thus, international law has always been based on a set of practices that is constantly evolving. Such practices become habitual because people find that they are useful in a practical sense, enabling actors to cooperate tacitly and achieve desired objectives informally. Often, customs arise among actors through the practice of reciprocity; that is, actors treat others as they themselves are treated.

Like custom, treaties are agreements that actors enter into voluntarily and, like contracts, that impose obligations on signatories. However, if treaties are widely observed, they may come to be regarded as customary and thus place obligations on countries that have not signed them. Today, treaties have become more important sources of international law than custom, and many of the law-making treaties signed in recent decades, many drafted by the UN International Law Commission, have codified and formalized long-standing customs. After they are signed, such treaties have to be ratified by the signatories' legislatures that must also enact the laws necessary to implement them.

The Geneva Conventions, for example, consist of four law-making treaties. The first to protect the sick and wounded in wars was adopted in 1864 and revised in 1949; the second and third concerning the treatment of the wounded and of prisoners of war were adopted in 1929; and the fourth, which extended protections to civilians, was adopted in 1949. Several of these were adapted from the 1907 Hague Convention (see p. 406). Another important example is the 1982 Law of the Sea Convention (initially drafted in 1958) that deals with issues such as the sovereignty of coastal states beyond their land territory and the rights of such states over the seabed and subsoil.[9] Thus, a state enjoys sovereignty over the seas extending 12 nautical miles off its shores[10] though it must allow ships from other countries "innocent passage" in those waters. Resources beyond the 12-mile limit were defined as "the common heritage of mankind, the exploration and exploitation of which shall be carried out for the benefit of mankind as a whole, irrespective of the geographical location of States."[11] Although coastal states have sovereign rights over the continental shelf up to 200 nautical miles from shore, an International Seabed Authority was established with headquarters in Kingston, Jamaica to "organize and control activities on the deep ocean floor in areas beyond the areas of national jurisdiction."[12] Advanced countries argued that this limited the freedom of their companies to exploit seabed resources, and the United States did not sign the treaty until 1994.

Other law-making treaties include the arms control and disarmament agreements described in chapter 8, whether bilateral like the 1991 START accord or multilateral like the Nuclear Nonproliferation Treaty. As we shall see, there has also been a proliferation of multilateral law-making treaties in areas such as human rights (chapter 10) and the environment (chapter 14).

Sovereign states designed international law to benefit themselves, maintain the system that they dominated, and manage violence so that it would not threaten that system. Statehood requires control of a defined territory and population and the capacity to engage in relations, but existing states can decide whether to recognize new states as they arise. Sovereignty itself is a cornerstone of international law, entailing recognition that there is no higher authority above states, that states are supreme within their territorial boundaries, and that other states must not intervene in their internal affairs. Thus, the UN's founders at no time considered the UN a means of undermining sovereignty which is enshrined in Article 2, which states that the organization "is based on the principle of the sovereign equality of all its Members" (paragraph 1). "Nothing contained in the present Charter shall authorize the United Nations to intervene in matters which are essentially within the domestic jurisdiction of any state" (paragraph 2). Under Article 51 of the UN Charter, states retain "the inherent right of individual or collective self-defense if an armed attack occurs against a Member of the United Nations, until the Security Council has taken measures necessary to maintain international peace and security." Thus, the law that states promulgated for themselves emphasized their independence and equality – two of the key features of sovereignty – and their unique right to deal with one another.

Indeed, the emergence of the state system and international law are inseparable. Part of that process was a shift away from the medieval idea that rulers were constrained by a higher law to the idea that law exists *between* rather than *above* states. Previously, the only limit on sovereigns was believed to be **natural law**, or that imposed from above by God. By contrast, law between states is voluntary, requiring the consent of the participants. The belief that international law requires the consent of actors is called **legal positivism**.[13] As we shall see in the next chapter, the disagreement between those who believe in natural law and those who are legal positivists still persists.

Early scholars of international law were mainly churchmen like the sixteenth-century Spanish theologians Francisco de Vitoria (1480–1546) and Francisco Suárez (1548–1617), but the Dutch jurist Hugo Grotius (1583–1645) is usually referred to as the "father of international law." In the midst of the Thirty Years' War in 1625, Grotius published his most famous work, *On the Law of War and Peace*, which he wrote because of "a lack of restraint in relation to war, such as even barbarous races should be ashamed of." "I observed," he continued, "that men rush to arms for slight causes, or no cause at all, and that when arms have once been taken up there is no longer any respect for law, divine or human."[14] While asserting the continuing importance of natural law, Grotius argued that the customs of nations also had the force of law and, as in contract law, interstate agreements are binding. Violations of such agreements, he believed, caused war because they infringed on the rights of others.

Grotius believed that once a body of law had been established and codified, states would be able to form stable expectations of one another's obligations and would, as a result, be less likely to go to war because of misunderstanding and misperception. He also believed that international

natural law principles of law derived from nature, right reason, or God.

legal positivism a theory that international law is derived from voluntary agreements among states and that contends that states are bound only by the rules that they freely accept.

law could curb the sorts of abuses against civilians that were taking place during the Thirty Years' War. In sum, Grotius envisioned an international society of sovereign states that were bound together by a shared set of norms and laws and his work greatly influenced "English School" scholars who call themselves "Grotians".

Those who followed Grotius reinforced his idea that international law was law between rather than above states. The Dutch lawyer Cornelis van Bynkershoek (1673–1743) developed the idea that custom allowed observers to determine law with regard to such issues as the status of diplomats and the rights of neutral ships during wartime. The Swiss diplomat Emmerich de Vattel (1714–67) emphasized the equality and independence of states, the importance of treaties, and the illegality of intervention by one state in the affairs of another. Natural law, he believed, was applicable to individuals but not to states. A strong believer in the importance of balance of power, de Vattel played a major role in developing the idea that sovereign states are legally equal regardless of differences in power.

Thus, until very recently *states have been the sole subjects of international law and have enjoyed an exclusive role in creating and enforcing such law*. In recent decades, international organizations have also become sources and subjects of international law.

Just war

For centuries, scholars have argued about whether there could be "just wars," wars that were morally right and could, therefore, be thought of as legal. Pacifists like the Quakers deny there can be a just war. The sixth of the Ten Commandments, after all, declares quite clearly and without exception that "Thou shalt not kill."

Just war theory had its origins in ancient Greece and Rome. The Roman orator and philosopher Marcus Tullius Cicero (106–43 BC) argued that war had to be publicly declared and could only be waged for self-defense or retribution, in which case compensation had to be requested before the war could be initiated. However, to a large extent, just war theory had religious origins, especially in the thought of Christian theologians like St. Augustine (354–86) and St. Thomas Aquinas (1227–74).

Augustine argued that just war could be waged only in self-defense and to restore peace. "We do not seek peace in order to be at war," he wrote, "but we go to war that we may have peace," and a "just war" is "one that avenges wrongs, when a nation or state has to be punished, for refusing to make amends for the wrongs inflicted by its subjects,

Did you know?

The term international law was coined by the British utilitarian philosopher Jeremy Bentham (1748–1832) in his *Principles of International Law* (1786–89).

or to restore what it has seized unjustly."[15] Aquinas claimed that war had to be authorized by a legitimate ruler with a just cause such as self-defense, and it had to be waged against evil. "Belligerents," he declared "should have a rightful intention, so that they intend the advancement of good, or the avoidance of evil."[16]

Grotius was a pioneer in the effort to determine whether war is ever justified and, if so, under what conditions. He answered the first question in the affirmative but added that "war ought not to be undertaken except for the enforcement of rights."[17] This implies that war could be conducted for political ends, but even then its conduct must reflect the law as derived from a combination of natural law and contract theory. Moreover, the rule of law did not cease during wars. For Grotius, a war could be just only if it met certain criteria. A war was just if it had a just cause, such as when it was a response to aggression or to an insult to God. Grotius argued that a just war had to be declared by the proper authorities and had to have a moral intent. Finally, a just war, in his view, had to be waged in a just manner. In this, he meant that soldiers should not employ brutal practices and that the means that they used should be proportional to the goals being sought. Justice, in his view, also required that the war offer a reasonable prospect for achieving its goals. Otherwise, it would result in a waste of life and treasure.

In this way, Grotius distinguished between just reasons for war (*jus ad bellum*) and just conduct of war (*jus in bello*). One can think that a war is just while condemning the way it is fought, a position of great importance in the development of international law governing war crimes and crimes against humanity in contrast to laws that make it illegal to plan and carry out aggressive war.[18]

Did you know?

Hugo Grotius is still recalled in his native Holland for his daring escape from Loevestein Castle in 1621 after his arrest for religious heresy. While in prison, Grotius was allowed his books, which were brought to him and then taken away in a wooden chest that was about four feet long. With the aid of his wife, he squeezed himself into the chest and was carried out by his own guards. Grotius made his way to France, where he was received by Louis XIII and provided a small pension that helped support his family as he worked on *The Law of War and Peace* (1625).[19]

Let us examine Grotius's criteria for just war more closely. Grotius believed that the most important just cause for war is self-defense in resisting aggression. The right of self-defense has long been recognized as a legitimate reason for war, a right clearly stated in Article 51 of the UN Charter. However, defining aggression creates heroic problems, and almost all belligerents justify their actions by accusing their adversary of committing aggression (see Controversy on aggression in this chapter).

It is not even clear that a country that attacks first is the aggressor. After all, the key US justification for invading Iraq in 2003 was that Iraq was the actual aggressor because it was developing weapons of mass destruction and because it had repeatedly flouted UN resolutions calling for Iraq to comply with weapons inspections. Needless to say this contention is controversial. Had there existed evidence of an imminent Iraqi attack on the United States or against a third state, America's action would have been easier to justify.

In fact, wars have been started over what may seem trivial reasons. In April 1731, for example, Robert Jenkins, master of the ship *Rebecca*, had his ear cut off by Spanish seamen who then looted the ship. In 1738, Jenkins told his story to the House of Commons and showed his pickled ear. Britain then declared war on Spain in what came to be known as the War of Jenkins's Ear (1738–41). Although the war broke out in the context of intense colonial rivalry between Britain and Spain, it illustrates how a narrow legal pretext can serve to justify going to war.

Grotius's requirement that a war must be declared by proper authorities is also open to interpretation. Historically, this has been taken to mean that war must be declared by the sovereign, whether a king or a democratic legislature. However, what if war is declared by a tyrant who enjoys little public support or by a government that has been imposed on a country by another country? More recently, some observers claim that war is illegal unless it is approved by the UN Security Council. Thus, in 1991 the UN Security Council authorized the use of force to expel Iraq from Kuwait, but refused to do so in 2003. This prompted Secretary-General Kofi Annan to declare in 2004 that "From our point of view and the UN charter point of view, it [US and British invasion] was illegal."[20]

Grotius also believed that a just war requires good intentions and must not be undertaken for reasons of self-interest. But most leaders are able to persuade themselves and often their citizens that the national interest is the same as the general interest. Hitler, for example, argued that the Nazi invasion of Russia in 1941 was undertaken to defend the world from the threat of communism. President Bush has argued that America's invasion of Iraq was undertaken to spur the spread of democracy around the world.

Grotius's requirement that war only be initiated if it has a reasonable chance of achieving its goals raises a knotty ethical question: if the cause is sufficiently important, such as ridding the world of a genocidal murderer like Hitler, how can the effort of small countries like Greece or Norway to resist the Nazis, however futile, be regarded as unjust? Furthermore, how can we measure a "reasonable chance" of success?

Perhaps the least controversial of Grotius's requirements for a just war is that the ends be proportional to the means used. This contention assumes that minimizing the loss of blood and treasure in war is desirable in itself and that, as a matter of course, punishment should reflect the extent of an offense. On this principle, the proper response to the seizure of a vessel at sea by a foreign power could be the retaking of the ship or the seizure of a similar ship from the enemy. Retaliation should not be excessive, for example razing an enemy's city.

discrimination in warfare, distinguishing between legitimate and improper military targets.

proportionality in international law, the norm that a response to a wrong should not exceed the harm caused by the wrong.

As a rule, Grotius's injunction that just wars must be waged justly has been the basis for considerable international law regarding the laws of war. Two general principles are involved here: **discrimination** and **proportionality**. The first involves the question of what constitute legitimate targets in war, while the second concerns the amount of force that is permissible. Indiscriminate attacks on civilians and non-military targets are regarded as illegal. Thus, some argue that the use of nuclear weapons is illegal even in the absence of a specific ban on such weapons because they necessarily involve the deaths of innocent civilians and the destruction of protected sites such as hospitals and churches. The principle of discrimination, however, became increasingly difficult to apply in the twentieth century, as civilians became part of the war effort as workers in armaments factories. In addition, the spread of irregular warfare has made it increasingly difficult for soldiers to know who is and who is not a potential combatant. When women and children strap suicide bombs to their bodies, soldiers have no choice but to consider them as legitimate targets.

The principle of proportionality applies both to the waging of war and, as we have seen, to the definition of a just war. Soldiers must try to limit violence to that which is necessary to achieve an objective. Enemies who surrender should not be killed, nor should those who are wounded and no longer capable of fighting. This principle governed the US decision to cease attacking Iraqi soldiers who were fleeing Kuwait in 1991 during the Persian Gulf War. Colin Powell, then chairman of the Joint Chiefs of Staff, recalls that the decision was made to end attacks on the Iraqis who were fleeing northward along what came to be called the "highway of death" where, in his words, "people were just being slaughtered as our planes went up and down." As Powell explained: "You don't do unnecessary killing if it can be avoided. At some point you decide you've accomplished your objectives and you stop."[21] More recently, Israel's response in 2006 to the kidnapping of its soldiers by Hamas and Hezbollah by using massive airpower was described by UN officials as "disproportionate."

Those who violate these principles, whether or not they are obeying orders or whether or not they know the law, should, Grotius demanded, be held accountable for their actions. However, through much of history, leaders have evaded this responsibility and only since World War II have serious efforts been made to arrest and try those who are responsible for war crimes. A variety of modern authors have taken up the just war tradition, for example the US Conference of Catholic Bishops in 1993.

An interesting effort to assert a just war policy was made by political scientist Joseph S. Nye, Jr. in the mid-1980s, a time when debate over the morality of nuclear deterrence had reached a crescendo owing to renewed US–Soviet tension. Indeed, a May 1983 pastoral letter written by the American National Conference of Catholic Bishops to American Catholics accepted nuclear deterrence as a legitimate strategy *only* if countries rejected nuclear war as an acceptable outcome, foreswore the search for nuclear superiority, and viewed deterrence only as a step on the road to nuclear disarmament. In this spirit, then, Nye argued that nuclear deterrence was "conditionally moral" provided it met three conditions: the principle of proportionality must be followed; the means used had to have an upper limit; and policy should reflect "a prudent consideration of consequences in both the near term and the indefinite long term." Nye then outlined five "maxims of nuclear ethics":

1 Self-defense is a just but limited cause.
2 Never treat nuclear weapons as normal weapons.
3 Minimize harm to innocent people.
4 Reduce risks of nuclear war in the near term.
5 Reduce reliance on nuclear weapons over time.[22]

In practice, few national leaders have paid much attention to the just war tradition, and, despite the limits on warfare that were its objective, civilians have increasingly become the victims of warfare. The ratio of civilian to military deaths in wartime has reached new highs and shows little prospect of declining. However, international and nongovernmental organizations are increasingly involved in efforts to prevent the outbreak of violence and warfare and to bring an end to violence when it does erupt.

Types of international organizations

International organizations depend on states for their creation, purposes, and survival. Realists repeatedly make this point, arguing that IGOs can be no more than instruments of powerful states and can survive only so long as those states wish them to. By contrast, liberals believe that IGOs can become greater than the sum of their parts (members) and can and should behave independently of states. For their part, constructivists look for evolutionary change in the organization of global politics based on gradual shifts in people's norms away from the narrow nationalism of the past toward greater concern with transnational issues that threaten human well-being. Constructivists recognize that more and more people are demanding creative solutions to problems that have defied states' efforts and are ready to contemplate new forms of transnational collaboration that break out of the narrow confines of state sovereignty. Constructivists conclude that IGOs could evolve from being the tools of states into more independent institutions *provided that norms evolve in that direction*.

Thus, we can imagine three types of IGOs. The first fit the realist model and do no more than their leading member states ask of them. The second are organizations that can collaborate with states to achieve collective goals that would be difficult for states to coordinate on their own, like preventing the spread of disease. In the case of conflict, semi-autonomous IGOs might **mediate** or **arbitrate** disputes, suggest ways to reach agreement, provide forums for diplomats to meet, or separate adversaries, helping them end conflicts without "losing face." The third are IGOs that have acquired genuine autonomy and can pursue their own policies. IGOs can evolve from one to another of these and may exhibit features of all three at the same time.

What follows focuses on the UN and the EU. We begin by considering the ideas of early liberal thinkers about the possibility for creating an IGO to keep peace and then examine some pioneering institutional experiments.

Early ideas and efforts

The desire for an international organization to keep the peace has a long history and is associated with liberal thinkers, especially two eighteenth-century philosophers, Immanuel Kant and Jean-Jacques Rousseau. Both believed that such organizations could reduce interstate conflict. Like liberals generally, both extolled the power of **rationality** and thought that people would pursue their rational self-interest if they knew what it was. They assumed the perfectibility of people and states and the possibility that IGOs could overcome anarchy.

Kant, as we saw earlier, believed republics were a source of peace. Interstate relations, he believed, were analogous to those among individuals in an imaginary state of nature. States could escape anarchy

mediation intervention by a third party in a dispute in order to help adversaries reach an agreement.

arbitration process of resolving disputes by referring them to a third party, either agreed on by them or provided by law, that is empowered to make a judgment.

rationality acting to promote one's interest by adopting means that are conducive to achieving desired and feasible ends.

by improving internally to make "perpetual peace" possible and by uniting voluntarily in an IGO.

Kant, argue political scientists Bruce Russett and John Oneal, regarded IGOs as one of three related and reinforcing elements, along with democracy and economic interdependence, in establishing peace. They contend that Kant's assertion implies that "the more international organizations to which two states belong together, the less likely they will be to fight one another or even to threaten the use of military force."[23]

Rousseau's analysis parallels Kant's, though he reached a somewhat different conclusion. Like Kant, Rousseau saw the condition of states as analogous to that of individuals in a state of nature. He too argued for the need to escape from the state of nature into civil society. But where Kant had thought that the existence of "good" states – republics – and a *voluntary* confederation would be sufficient to ensure peace, Rousseau proposed something closer to a world state that "shall unite nations by bonds similar to those which already unite their individual members, and place the one no less than the other under the authority of the Law." This new institution "must be strong and firm enough to make it impossible for any member to withdraw at his own pleasure the moment he conceives his private interest to clash with that of the whole body."[24]

Both Kant and Rousseau recognized that international organizations had existed throughout history to mitigate conflict. One of the earliest, first recorded in 776 BC, was the Greek Olympic Games. Every four years, free-born Greek males came from all over the Greek world to compete at the sanctuary of the god Zeus located at Olympia. Many leading athletes were soldiers who traveled directly from battle to the games. During the games, war among Greek city-states ceased, and soldiers laid down their arms for seven days before, during, and after the festival, because fighting was disrespectful to the gods. And the winners' first obligation was to their gods, not their city-state.

Since then, other IGOs have tried to encourage cooperation. As we saw in Chapter 2, a loose organization called the Concert of Europe was formed after Napoléon's defeat in 1815. The Concert was not a full-fledged IGO but rather an informal mechanism for consultation that helped states cooperate while retaining their autonomy, and it was not equipped to deal with the powerful forces that propelled Europe to war in 1914.

Other ancestors of modern IGOs were the 1899 and 1907 conferences convened in The Hague, the Netherlands. The first, sponsored by Russia's tsar, whose ministers wanted a moratorium on weapons improvements because Russia could not keep up with its rivals,[25] drew representatives from 26 countries, and unsuccessfully tried to bring about

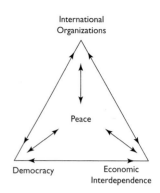

Figure 9.2 The Kantian triangle

international disarmament. It succeeded in banning aerial bombing, chemical warfare, and the use of hollow point (dumdum) bullets. It also established a Permanent Court of Arbitration, located in the Peace Palace in The Hague, to arbitrate disagreements among countries, and the United States eagerly set about negotiating treaties to specify the scope of issues the United States would submit to arbitration. The 1907 Hague Convention attracted 46 countries, including the United States, which advocated establishing an international court to make decisions based on international law. It also placed additional limits on warfare, including restrictions on submarines and armed merchant vessels.

These conferences were novel in that they aimed to remedy defects in the global system itself rather than resolve a particular war. Both led to agreements that provided important precedents for later changes in international law. The two Hague conventions, along with the Geneva Conventions, were expressions of the laws of war, and constructivists regard these precedents as important in changing our views of war and the need to manage violence.

As noted in chapter 3 (pp. 127–38), the League of Nations was the first effort at establishing a universal IGO to keep peace. For liberals, the idea of such an organization remained alive even during the dark days of World War II, and under the direction of Secretary of State Cordell Hull, US planning for the League's successor began even while war still raged. Intensive planning among the allies climaxed at the UN Conference on International Organization in San Francisco in April 1945. Although those who attended the San Francisco meeting made some changes to earlier ideas in deference to the smaller countries, the crux of the UN Charter was settled in bargaining among the Big Three (the United States, Britain, and the USSR). Since then the United Nations has become "an enormous body that, among other things, buys half the world's children's vaccines, protects 22 million refugees, is host to 7,500 meetings in Geneva alone and is the world's biggest purchaser of condoms."[26]

The United Nations

The United Nations is a great experiment in cooperating to achieve peace and security. Its founders tried to avoid the shortcomings of the League, while pursuing similar goals. Unlike the League, the UN has become a universal organization. Fifty-one states were charter members, and membership expanded dramatically, especially during decolonization in the 1960s and 1970s and, more recently, with the breakup of the USSR and Yugoslavia. By 2007 the UN had 192 members, the most recent of which are Switzerland, which in 2002 abandoned its steadfast refusal to join lest membership imperil its cherished neutrality, East Timor (Timor-Leste), and Montenegro. The Holy See (The Vatican), Palestine, and the EU are not members, but maintain permanent representation at the United Nations.

This section begins by examining early expectations for the United Nations and then describing the responsibilities of the UN's principal organs or agencies. As we shall see, these have evolved in response to transformations in global politics.

Early expectations

The UN's birth reflected recognition that a new international institution was needed to help states cooperate to attack the sources of war. In the words of Article 1 of the Charter, the UN's purpose was to "maintain international peace and security, and to that end: to take effective collective measures for the prevention and removal of threats to the peace, and for the suppression of acts of **aggression** or other breaches of the peace."[27] However, during the Cold War, superpower deadlock spurred the UN to develop novel **peacekeeping** techniques. The end of the Cold War again altered the global political landscape, as the United States and Russia began to cooperate on a variety of issues. Although initial hopes were high, expectations about the UN and its future were tempered as the extent of post-Cold War problems became apparent.

aggression the initiation of actions that violate the rights and interests of other actors.

peacekeeping the use of lightly armed military forces to separate warring parties, contain violence, and impose calm in situations of potential violence.

Controversy

One highly contested issue in global politics is defining aggression. There is consensus that aggression involves a premeditated attack by one actor on another. But there agreement ends. Which side is the aggressor if one side uses military force first based on evidence that the other is on the verge of using force against it? In June 1967, for example, Israel attacked neighboring Arab states after it had overwhelming evidence of an imminent Arab attack and with the knowledge that unless it attacked first it would lose the war. Was Israel the aggressor because it attacked first, or were its foes aggressors because they had mobilized military forces around Israel? Is it aggression if one actor takes steps that may endanger a foe sometime in the future even though it is not planning for an immediate conflict?

In 1981, Israel destroyed Iraq's French-built Osirak nuclear facility near Baghdad, claiming that Saddam Hussein was going to use it to produce nuclear weapons. Although the United States scolded Israel for the action, only two decades later the United States justified its attack on Iraq on the claim that the same Iraqi dictator was trying to acquire weapons of mass destruction. Was Israel an aggressor in 1981, the United States in 2003, or Saddam Hussein for trying to acquire WMD?

Finally, are there non-military forms of aggression that justify the use of violence? What of trade sanctions or embargos? What of spreading propaganda or inciting violence by foreign opponents of governments? Such acts intentionally aim to harm others, but if we accept such a broad definition of aggression, would there be any "innocent" members of the global community?

The Charter's framers sought to update the League Covenant. For example, the UN, more than the League, emphasizes global economic and social issues, reflecting a belief that conflict arises from poverty. To avoid the political divisions of 1919 that had prevented American entry in the League, US leaders adopted a policy of **bipartisanship** in which both Democrats and Republicans were widely consulted in planning the UN. Furthermore, the UN's founding was separated from the general peace settlement that ended World War II.

bipartisanship the effort to include and gain the approval of members of both political parties in the formation of foreign policy.

Although an effort was made to present the UN as a new organization, many of its features were adopted from the League, and most of its organs had League parallels.

UN organs

The UN major organs are the General Assembly, the Security Council, the Secretariat, the International Court of Justice, and the Economic and Social Council.[28] Despite differences in state power, the UN maintains the fiction of "sovereign equality" in the General Assembly, where all countries from the United States to Kiribati have a single vote. In ridding itself of the League requirement for unanimous voting, the UN made it easier for decisions to be made. The General Assembly has to approve the UN budget (Article 17) and receives regular reports from other UN organs, including the Security Council (Article 15). The Assembly can discuss any issue relating to maintaining peace (Article 12), but *not* if a matter is before the Security Council. General Assembly resolutions are *not* binding, and public debate in the Assembly often takes place only *after* member states have failed to resolve conflicts by quiet diplomacy. The purpose of such debate is less to solve problems than publicize

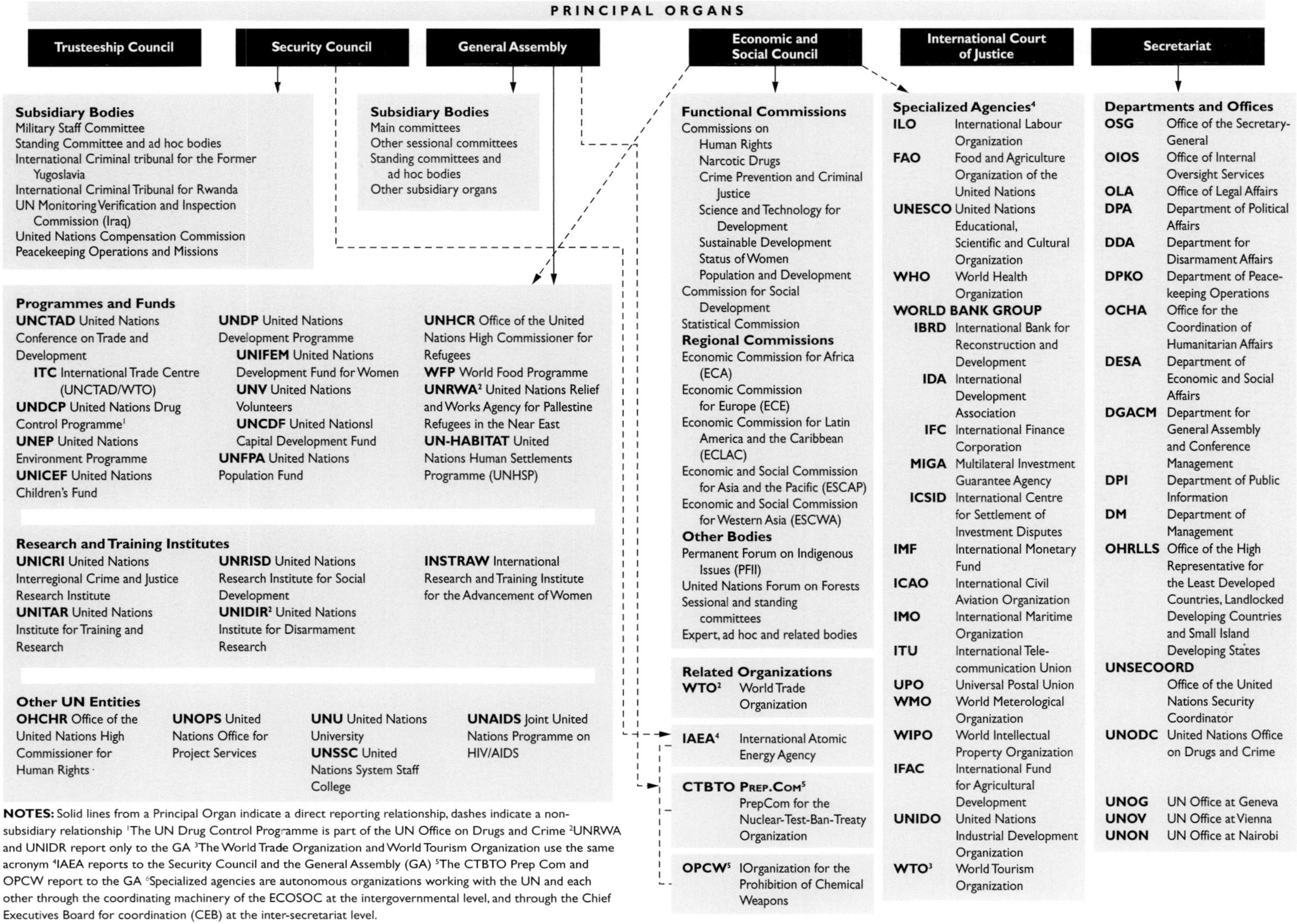

PRINCIPAL ORGANS

Principal Organs (top row)

Trusteeship Council | Security Council | General Assembly | Economic and Social Council | International Court of Justice | Secretariat

---

Trusteeship Council

Subsidiary Bodies
Military Staff Committee
Standing Committee and ad hoc bodies
International Criminal tribunal for the Former Yugoslavia
International Criminal Tribunal for Rwanda
UN Monitoring Verification and Inspection Commission (Iraq)
United Nations Compensation Commission
Peacekeeping Operations and Missions

General Assembly

Subsidiary Bodies
Main committees
Other sessional committees
Standing committees and ad hoc bodies
Other subsidiary organs

Programmes and Funds
UNCTAD United Nations Conference on Trade and Development
ITC International Trade Centre (UNCTAD/WTO)
UNDCP United Nations Drug Control Programme[1]
UNEP United Nations Environment Programme
UNICEF United Nations Children's Fund

UNDP United Nations Development Programme
UNIFEM United Nations Development Fund for Women
UNV United Nations Volunteers
UNCDF United Nations Capital Development Fund
UNFPA United Nations Population Fund

UNHCR Office of the United Nations High Commissioner for Refugees
WFP World Food Programme
UNRWA[2] United Nations Relief and Works Agency for Pallestine Refugees in the Near East
UN-HABITAT United Nations Human Settlements Programme (UNHSP)

Research and Training Institutes
UNICRI United Nations Interregional Crime and Justice Research Institute
UNITAR United Nations Institute for Training and Research

UNRISD United Nations Research Institute for Social Development
UNIDIR[2] United Nations Institute for Disarmament Research

INSTRAW International Research and Training Institute for the Advancement of Women

Other UN Entities
OHCHR Office of the United Nations High Commissioner for Human Rights

UNOPS United Nations Office for Project Services

UNU United Nations University
UNSSC United Nations System Staff College

UNAIDS Joint United Nations Programme on HIV/AIDS

Economic and Social Council

Functional Commissions
Commissions on
Human Rights
Narcotic Drugs
Crime Prevention and Criminal Justice
Science and Technology for Development
Sustainable Development
Status of Women
Population and Development
Commission for Social Development
Statistical Commission

Regional Commissions
Economic Commission for Africa (ECA)
Economic Commission for Europe (ECE)
Economic Commission for Latin America and the Caribbean (ECLAC)
Economic and Social Commission for Asia and the Pacific (ESCAP)
Economic and Social Commission for Western Asia (ESCWA)

Other Bodies
Permanent Forum on Indigenous Issues (PFII)
United Nations Forum on Forests
Sessional and standing committees
Expert, ad hoc and related bodies

Related Organizations
WTO[2] World Trade Organization

IAEA[4] International Atomic Energy Agency

CTBTO Prep.Com[5] PrepCom for the Nuclear-Test-Ban-Treaty Organization

OPCW[5] IOrganization for the Prohibition of Chemical Weapons

---

International Court of Justice

Specialized Agencies[4]
ILO International Labour Organization
FAO Food and Agriculture Organization of the United Nations
UNESCO United Nations Educational, Scientific and Cultural Organization
WHO World Health Organization

WORLD BANK GROUP
IBRD International Bank for Reconstruction and Development
IDA International Development Association
IFC International Finance Corporation
MIGA Multilateral Investment Guarantee Agency
ICSID International Centre for Settlement of Investment Disputes

IMF International Monetary Fund
ICAO International Civil Aviation Organization
IMO International Maritime Organization
ITU International Telecommunication Union
UPO Universal Postal Union
WMO World Meterological Organization
WIPO World Intellectual Property Organization
IFAC International Fund for Agricultural Development
UNIDO United Nations Industrial Development Organization
WTO[3] World Tourism Organization

Secretariat

Departments and Offices
OSG Office of the Secretary-General
OIOS Office of Internal Oversight Services
OLA Office of Legal Affairs
DPA Department of Political Affairs
DDA Department for Disarmament Affairs
DPKO Department of Peace-keeping Operations
OCHA Office for the Coordination of Humanitarian Affairs
DESA Department of Economic and Social Affairs
DGACM Department for General Assembly and Conference Management
DPI Department of Public Information
DM Department of Management
OHRLLS Office of the High Representative for the Least Developed Countries, Landlocked Developing Countries and Small Island Developing States
UNSECOORD Office of the United Nations Security Coordinator
UNODC United Nations Office on Drugs and Crime

UNOG UN Office at Geneva
UNOV UN Office at Vienna
UNON UN Office at Nairobi

NOTES: Solid lines from a Principal Organ indicate a direct reporting relationship; dashes indicate a non-subsidiary relationship. [1]The UN Drug Control Programme is part of the UN Office on Drugs and Crime. [2]UNRWA and UNIDR report only to the GA. [3]The World Trade Organization and World Tourism Organization use the same acronym. [4]IAEA reports to the Security Council and the General Assembly (GA). [5]The CTBTO Prep Com and OPCW report to the GA. [6]Specialized agencies are autonomous organizations working with the UN and each other through the coordinating machinery of the ECOSOC at the intergovernmental level, and through the Chief Executives Board for coordination (CEB) at the inter-secretariat level.

Figure 9.3 The United Nations system
Courtesy of the United Nations

grievances, embarrass foes, and rally allies. The debates make good theater but deepen disagreement and make it harder for participants to compromise.

In the UN's early years, the General Assembly consisted mainly of America's European and Latin American allies, and the organization as a whole served as a reliable tool of US foreign policy. But, as membership grew, the United States found itself less able to command voting majorities in the Assembly, as these coalesced around the less-developed countries (LDCs) which had strong interests in redistributing global wealth. During the last decades of the Cold War, the Soviet bloc and the LDCs found they had mutual interests in opposing the United States, and, for that reason, Washington tended to ignore the Assembly.

The UN Security Council enjoys "primary responsibility for the maintenance of international peace and security" and has authority to "investigate any dispute, or any situation which might lead to international friction or give rise to a dispute." In contrast to the League Council, the Security Council does not have to wait for a dispute to be brought to it before it acts, and the UN's founders believed that the Council would play a dominant role in keeping peace. Its key powers regarding peace and security are found in the Charter's Chapters Six ("Pacific Settlement of Disputes") and Seven ("Action with Respect to Threats to the Peace, Breaches of the Peace, and Acts of Aggression").

The Charter permits the Security Council to order a spectrum of actions ranging from inquiry and mediation to "complete or partial interruption of economic relations and of rail, sea, air, postal, telegraphic, radio, and other means of communication." In recent decades, the Council has imposed sanctions against countries such as South Africa, Iraq, Serbia, and Libya, but they are rarely imposed because they create hardships and political complications for countries that enforce them. Finally, if sanctions prove inadequate, the Council "may take such action by air, sea, or land forces as may be necessary to maintain or restore international peace and security." To this end, the UN Charter states that members "shall join in affording mutual assistance in carrying out the measures decided upon by the Security Council." Only twice has the Council authorized force to enforce the peace: in 1950 when North Korea invaded South Korea and in 1990 when Iraq invaded Kuwait.

The structure of the League and UN councils also differs. Like the League Council, the Security Council has permanent and temporary members, but with a difference in voting. Under the Charter, the "Big Five" (the United States, the USSR [now Russia], China, France, and Britain) were designated permanent members, and six (later ten) states were elected to rotate as nonpermanent members. Voting on most issues requires that the majority include *all* permanent members, giving each a **veto** (Article 27). The veto reflects recognition that an IGO cannot run roughshod over large states. Recalling League failures in the 1930s, the UN's architects realized that pivotal states must be supportive if collective action is to work.

veto the legal power of any of the permanent members of the UN Security Council to reject a Council resolution.

An important precedent was set when the Soviet representative's absence from the Council during a vote on the Korean War was counted as an abstention and implied neither consent nor disagreement. This interpretation allows permanent members to dissociate themselves from a Council resolution without being obstructionist. Permanent members that wish to show disapproval but do not want to alienate those that support a resolution can abstain from voting. During the era of US dominance in the UN, the USSR cast the most vetoes as its only defense against US voting majorities in the Council, mainly to prevent admission of new pro-American members. Declining US influence in the UN led the United States to cast its first veto in 1970. By 2003, the United States had cast 76 vetoes, a third of which blocked resolutions aimed against Israel.[29]

The Secretariat is the UN executive organ and is directed by a Secretary-General who manages the organization's bureaucracy and finances and oversees the operation of all agencies and personnel, from technicians and policemen to doctors and soldiers. With operations in New York as well as in Vienna, Geneva, and Nairobi, the Secretariat employs a large corps of over 52,000 international civil servants who have an astonishing range of responsibilities. By Article 100, UN employees must not receive instructions from outside the organization, though this policy is often breached.

The criteria for employment (Article 101) are to be "the highest standards of efficiency, competence, and integrity." These criteria are difficult to fulfill, however, owing to an additional requirement that employees be hired from all geographic regions, some of which have few trained personnel. On the plus side, the UN has been a kind of school for civil servants from LDCs, many of whom return home to serve their countries effectively. On the minus side, it has also meant that, while most of its employees are dedicated and honest, the UN has always been plagued by some incompetent officials who rarely return home and enjoy sinecures in New York, Geneva, or Vienna.

The Secretary-General, who is appointed by the General Assembly on the recommendation of the Security Council, is the world's leading civil servant. Between 1946 and 2006, the UN had only eight secretaries-general, the most recent being Ghana's Kofi Annan who after two terms (1996–2006) was replaced by Ban Ki-moon, formerly South

Korea's foreign minister. In large measure, their personalities and skills have determined their effectiveness. For example, Sweden's Dag Hammarskjold (1953–61) was an activist, Austria's Kurt Waldheim (1971–81) and Peru's Javier Pérez de Cuellar (1982–92) were accused of being anti-Western, and Egypt's Boutros Boutros-Ghali (1992–96) was a spokesperson for the interests of LDCs.

The Secretary-General's position is a difficult one because he must navigate between the conflicting interests and demands of member states. The safest path is to be passive, doing only what powerful states demand, as did the League's Secretary-General between 1919 and 1933. But that is also a formula for institutional failure. Like the UN itself, the Secretary-General has to walk a fine line between following the wishes of members, especially the most powerful, and taking initiatives to meet UN responsibilities. This is especially difficult when key members are divided and when UN actions are scrutinized for any trace of partiality. Boutros-Ghali was viewed by the Clinton administration as unwilling to reform the UN, and, as a result, the United States prevented his reelection to a second term. By contrast, Kofi Annan was able to maintain the confidence of most members, despite criticizing the American intervention in Iraq in 2003, until he was accused in 2004 of involvement in a scandel concerning Iraq's sale of oil while Saddam Hussein was in power. An independent inquiry found no evidence of Annan's involvement, but evidence that his son benefited from the scandal tainted the remainder of his term.

The International Court of Justice (ICJ), made up of 15 justices who reflect geographic and political diversity, is the successor to the League's Permanent Court of Justice. The ICJ can decide cases brought to it or provide advisory opinions when asked to do so. Few states have accepted the ICJ's compulsory jurisdiction, and most have decided, case by case, whether to allow the ICJ to render a binding decision. In 1984, for example, the United States refused to accept the ICJ's judgment in a case brought by Nicaragua's Sandinista government related to US support for the anti-communist contras.

The ICJ is valuable when the parties to a dispute want to resolve their differences, as did Singapore and Malaysia in 2003 when they found themselves in a territorial dispute over two small islands. However, it is rarely useful in highly politicized cases. For example, in an advisory opinion to the General Assembly during its 2003–04 session, the ICJ stirred up a hornet's nest by ruling that the "security fence" constructed by Israel for protection against terrorist attacks was illegal because it involved annexing Palestinian territory and it violated the human rights of about 56,000 Palestinians, by enclosing them in enclaves cut off from the rest of the West Bank.[30] Israel refused to accept the ICJ's decision, invoking its right of self-defense as guaranteed under Article 51, and both Israel and the United States denied the ICJ's jurisdiction in the matter.

The League had paid little attention to economic and social issues that national leaders regarded as "low politics" in contrast to the "high politics" of military security and war. Influenced by liberal thinking, the UN's founders recognized that conflict arises from many sources including poverty, hunger, and ignorance. To confront these issues, they established the Economic and Social Council (ECOSOC) with the task of reporting on global "economic, social, cultural, educational, health and related matters" about which it may make recommendations, and incorporated a group of **specialized agencies** that are responsible for particular functional tasks.[31]

specialized agencies IGOs with responsibility limited to a single, often narrow, area of human behavior.

Economic and social issues

ECOSOC is a large institution that accounts for 70 percent of the UN's budget and employees, and it consults with many of the nongovernmental groups that are registered with it. ECOSOC also oversees the specialized agencies (see Table 9.1) whose tasks range from improving food security (Food and Agriculture Organization) and promoting peaceful uses of atomic energy (International Atomic Energy Agency) to promoting cooperation in telecommunications (International Telecommunication Union). The most important of these are the World Bank Group and the International Monetary Fund that we will examine in chapter 11.

Several of these predate the UN. For example, the Universal Postal Union was established in 1874; the International Labor Organization is the only surviving major institution established by the 1919 Treaty of Versailles;[32] and the World Health Organization is a successor to the League's Health Organization. The nineteenth century and the early decades of the twentieth witnessed the emergence of such specialized agencies intended to meet peoples' needs for economic and social welfare. Proponents of such arrangements thought that the absence of interstate cooperation to deal with such problems caused war. They also believed that such organizations could prosper because they were nonpolitical and did not threaten state authority. Among these were the Central Rhine Commission (1804) and the European Commission for the Control of the Danube (1856) to facilitate navigation. Such organizations, the antecedents of the UN specialized agencies, were based on the idea of **functionalism**. This idea, developed by British social commentator Leonard Woolf (1880–1969) and Rumanian political economist David Mitrany (1888–1975), was that states were economically and socially

functionalism a theory that conflict can be reduced if actors cooperate in technical and nonpolitical areas and that such cooperation will then become habitual and spread to other areas.

Table 9.1 The UN specialized agencies

Specialized agency	Acronym	Year created	Description
Food and Agriculture Organization	FAO	1945	Aids states in improving the production, sale, and distribution of agricultural products.
International Civil Aviation Organization	ICAO	1974	Draws up rules for civil aviation and promotes aircraft safety.
International Fund for Agricultural Development	IFAD	1977	Seeks to reduce rural poverty and improve nutrition for the poor by promoting food production, social development, environmental sustainability, and good governance.
International Labor Organization	ILO	1919	Provides labor standards and promotes workers' rights and welfare.
International Maritime Organization	IMO	1948	Promotes interstate cooperation on shipping issues such as maritime safety, oceanic pollution from ships, and piracy.
International Telecommunication Union	ITU	1856	Seeks to improve global telecommunications, especially in poor countries.
UN Educational, Scientific and Cultural Organization	UNESCO	1946	Fosters cooperation in education, science, and culture, encourages the preservation of cultural treasures and maintains a World Heritage List that, by 2004, consisted of 788 sites ranging from Australia's Tasmanian Wilderness to the Acropolis in Athens and the Statue of Liberty in New York.
UN Industrial Development Organization	UNIDO	1966	Encourages technological transfer to and industrial development in less-developed countries.
Universal Postal Union	UPU	1874	Seeks to standardize and improve postal service globally but especially in poorer countries.
World Health Organization	WHO	1946	Seeks to prevent disease and encourage primary health care. WHO played a key role in limiting the spread of the deadly ebola virus in Africa in 1995 and in coping with the outbreak of severe acute respiratory syndrome in 2003.
World Intellectual Property Organization	WIPO	1967	Tries to protect the rights of authors, inventors, and others who create intellectual property from illegal theft and use.
World Meteorological Organization	WMO	1951	Coordinates the exchange of weather information and is involved in a variety of environmental issues including climate change and ozone depletion.

interdependent and that if they overcame their economic and social problems war would be less likely.

Functionalists believed that creating organizations to manage particular global problems would be like casting stones into a pond, each producing ever-widening ripples into new areas. Success would bring greater success, and new institutions would be built to meet other human needs. Global efforts to address one demand (like monitoring disease) would produce new demands (like stopping the spread of AIDS). Functionalists were convinced that states would more readily surrender nonpolitical technical and economic responsibilities than core sovereign responsibilities like military security. Such steps, they thought, would gradually erode state sovereignty until there emerged a complex network of international organizations to perform states' welfare functions while reducing the prospect of war. Convinced of the possibility of change in global politics, functionalists were optimistic liberals with much in common with contemporary neoliberals, especially their high hopes for the role of IGOs in improving the prospects for peace.

In practice, functional institutions like the UN's specialized agencies have done little to limit state sovereignty. And, although such organizations have facilitated interstate cooperation, the tasks they perform are rarely nonpolitical because they redistribute funding and welfare in ways that produce "winners" and "losers." For example, the UN Educational, Scientific and Cultural Organization (UNESCO), a specialized agency that is supposed to foster education and preservation of global cultural monuments, became a target of US wrath owing to its fiscal mismanagement, support for limiting press reporting in the developing world, and its anti-Israeli statements. Between 1984 and 2003, the United States withdrew from UNESCO, claiming that the agency had become too highly politicized.

Recognizing these flaws in functionalist thinking, other theorists, closer to the constructivist tradition, emerged in the 1950s advocating **neofunctionalism**. Led by political scientist Ernst Haas, neofunctionalists argued that expanding global cooperation should not be taken for granted. Instead, they saw the expansion of cooperation as the consequence of political pressure on the part of interest groups that see such cooperation as in their interest. Genuine progress, they believed, requires both *extending* **supranational** authority to new issues and *deepening* that authority. And if these processes go far enough, they may lead to a shift in loyalties from states to new political communities.[33]

A hypothetical case reflecting neofunctional thinking is that of business groups in several countries that seek to eliminate interstate trade barriers. To achieve this, they lobby governments to form a common market. Thereafter, corporations may organize across borders to take advantage of the new opportunities and lobby for additional steps like standardization of tax and welfare policies. Because so many economic and social policies are linked, creating a functional institution to foster cooperation on one issue may create pressures for cooperation on others. Unlike functionalism, neofunctionalism emphasizes the political nature of technical issues and describes a *political* process of change.

neofunctionalism a changed version of functionalist theory claiming that organizations established by interstate agreements create political pressures for additional agreements and greater authority for existing IGOs.

supranational transcending national authority.

Despite its attention to economic and social issues, the United Nations has been deeply involved since its establishment in trying to prevent wars or end them once they have begun. The next section examines the evolution of these efforts and their relative success.

The UN and the maintenance of peace

Although the UN record is mixed, it has enjoyed more success in maintaining peace than did the League. The UN has used many mechanisms in this effort, including nonbinding resolutions, fact-finding missions, observers, economic and military sanctions, peacekeeping forces, and, on a few occasions, military force.

UN missions are approved by the Security Council and planned by the UN's Department of Peacekeeping Operations. Between 1948 and 2005, there were 60 missions, most since 1988.[34] The first – the Special Committee on the Balkans (1947–52) – consisted of 36 observers who were sent to confirm that Greece, Albania, Bulgaria, and Yugoslavia were complying with recommendations during Greece's communist-led civil war. The largest mission to date has been the United Nations Protection Force (UNPROFOR) (1992–95) in Bosnia, which at top strength numbered almost 40,000 military and over 5,000 civilian personnel. The smallest consisted of only two representatives of the Secretary-General who were sent to observe events in the Dominican Republic following US intervention in that country in 1965.

Currently, 103 countries are providing peacekeeping personnel in 17 missions around the world (see Map 9.1) involving over 67,000 civilian and military peacekeepers.[35] This number is growing as a result of the dramatic enlargement of the UN Interim Force in Lebanon (UNIFIL) following the violence between Israel and Hezbollah during the summer of 2006. Some of these missions are very dangerous. Almost 2,000 UN soldiers have been killed, and in 2003, 22 UN employees, including UN envoy Sergio Vieira de Mello, were victims of a suicide bombing in Iraq.

Maintaining peace during the Cold War

The UN's founders hoped that the victorious World War II allies would continue cooperating to maintain peace. Yet even as the UN was being established, Cold War clouds were gathering, and, with both superpowers having a veto, the Security Council was paralyzed almost from the outset. Owing to differences between the superpowers, peace enforcement was impossible, and any effort to mobilize the UN against either would result

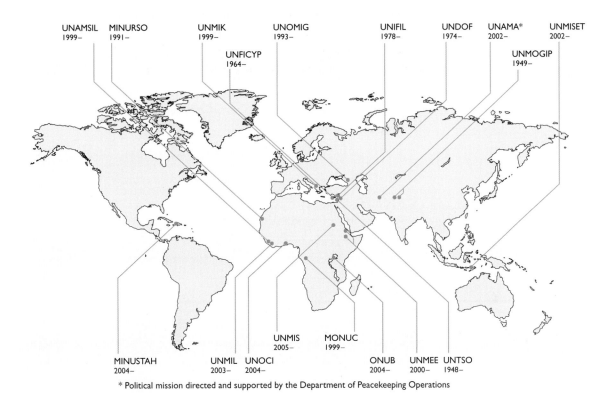

Map 9.1   Ongoing UN peacekeeping missions

in the institution's collapse. The Council came to resemble a debating club and, for many of the great events of the Cold War, it had to sit on the sidelines.

The Charter did not provide for peacekeeping as it evolved. Chapter Six of the Charter dealt with peaceful settlement of disputes, assuming that if conflicts could be postponed and the parties made to discuss their differences, wars triggered by national pride, ignorance, or emotion could be prevented. However, the techniques of peaceful settlement – "negotiation, enquiry, mediation, conciliation, arbitration, judicial settlement, resort to regional agencies or arrangements, or other peaceful means" (Article 33) – are useful *only* if adversaries want to avoid conflict. They are ineffective when hostility is deep-seated and adversaries are willing to go to war to achieve their ends.

Unlike Chapter Six, Chapter Seven sought to deal with overt aggression by means of **peace enforcement**. As initially conceived, the Security Council was to have primary responsibility in enforcing peace. Articles 39–42 of Chapter Seven empower the Council to require member states to take whatever action, including force, is needed to maintain or restore

peace enforcement
authorization under the provisions of chapter 7 of the UN Charter for member states to use military force to end aggression.

417

peace. Articles 43 and 45 sought to give the Council "teeth" by calling for agreements to provide the UN with a permanent military force that has never been established.

Key Document   Excerpts from Chapter Seven of the UN Charter

Action with respect to threats to the peace, breaches of the peace, and acts of aggression

Article 39
The Security Council shall determine the existence of any threat to the peace, breach of the peace, or act of aggression and shall make recommendations, or decide what measures shall be taken . . . to maintain or restore international peace and security . . .

Article 41
The Security Council may decide what measures not involving the use of armed force are to be employed to give effect to its decisions, and it may call upon the Members of the United Nations to apply such measures. These may include complete or partial interruption of economic relations and of rail, sea, air, postal, telegraphic, radio, and other means of communication, and the severance of diplomatic relations.

Article 42
Should the Security Council consider that measures provided for in Article 41 would be inadequate or have proved to be inadequate, it may take such action by air, sea, or land forces as may be necessary to maintain or restore international peace and security.

Under these circumstances, the UN role in maintaining peace evolved, shifting authority from the Council to the Assembly where, in the 1950s, the United States enjoyed paramount influence. Following China's intervention in Korea, the General Assembly acted to circumvent the veto in the Security Council by adopting the Uniting for Peace Resolution, which permits the Assembly to meet in emergency session if the Council is deadlocked. The Assembly itself could then recommend "collective measures in the case of a breach of the peace or act of aggression."[36]

Although the Security Council remained deadlocked, the UN developed an innovative process to allow it to act in cases in which the superpowers were *not* directly involved. A technique was needed that was more robust than Chapter Six but less provocative than Chapter Seven. Peacekeeping, drawing on elements from both, was this technique, a sort of "Chapter Six-and-a Half."

During the 1950s and 1960s, the Arab–Israeli conflict and postcolonial conflicts in Africa and Asia threatened to entangle the superpowers. Concern that Soviet or US involvement in local wars might lead to superpower confrontation convinced Secretary-General Hammarskjold (1905–61) that the UN had to act to prevent this. "Preventive action," he declared, "must, in the first place, aim at filling the vacuum so that it will not provoke action from any of the major parties, the initiative from which might be taken for preventive purposes but might in turn lead to a counter action from the other side."[37]

The first explicit peacekeeping mission took place in 1956 following the Anglo-French–Israeli effort to seize the Suez Canal from Egypt. A United Nations Emergency Force (UNEF) was sent to the Sinai Desert to separate Egyptian and Israeli forces. UNEF helped both sides to "save face" by creating a buffer zone between them. Egypt demanded that UNEF leave just before the outbreak of the 1967 Six Day War, but peacekeepers (UNEF II) returned after the October 1973 Yom Kippur War, remaining until the 1979 Egypt–Israeli peace treaty was concluded.

Following UNEF, peacekeeping became popular. Between 1960 and 1963, the Operation in the Congo (ONUC) oversaw the withdrawal of Belgian colonial forces, tried to maintain law and order, and maintained the independence and territorial integrity of the new country. The Congo operation was so complex that it almost proved too much for the UN. It illustrated how dangerous it was for the UN to get involved in civil wars and how difficult it was to remain impartial in such conflicts.

Another major mission began in Cyprus in 1964, where the UN Force in Cyprus (UNFICYP) was sent to prevent a resumption of fighting between the island's Greek majority and Turkish minority communities. Consisting of military contingents and civilian police units, the mission successfully interposed itself between the two communities. However, overcoming the underlying division proved elusive, and in 1974 Turkish forces invaded the island to protect the Turkish minority. Four decades after the mission began UNFICYP remains in Cyprus as evidence that the presence of a peacekeeping force does not solve underlying political differences between adversaries. Although resolution seemed imminent in 2004 based on a plan proposed by Secretary-General Annan, hopes were dashed when the Greek Cypriot community voted down the agreement.

During the Cold War, peacekeeping missions involved fact-finding, monitoring of borders, verification of agreements, supervision of

Figure 9.4a UN peacekeeping mission in Cyprus
UN/DPI Photo

Figure 9.4b UN peacekeeping mission in Cyprus: members of the Danish contingent in Ferret Scouts approach an observation post near Skouriotissa
United Nations/John Isaac

disarmament, demobilization of enemy forces, and maintenance of security in elections. However, as long as the Cold War persisted, operations remained limited in scope and objective. Key features of successful peacekeeping during the Cold War were:

- Adversaries must be states, not parties to a civil war.
- The physical line separating adversaries must be clear.
- Both sides in a conflict must consent to a UN presence, and UN forces should remain only so long as both wish them to.
- UN forces must be impartial, and personnel must be drawn from countries that are not deeply involved in the Cold War.
- The use of force should be minimal, and UN soldiers should be only lightly armed for self-defense.
- A mission should have a narrow mandate to prevent confrontations while foes seek solutions.

Peacekeeping was never intended to solve highly contentious issues. Instead, it was to facilitate a solution by delaying or limiting violence, thereby creating an atmosphere conducive to negotiation. Some have argued that perversely peacekeeping sometimes had a negative result: allowing disagreements to fester so that they became more difficult to resolve. However, the Cold War's end seemed to offer the possibility for more vigorous UN action in the service of peace.

Maintaining peace after the Cold War

The onset of US–Russian cooperation seemed to herald the dawn of a new era in UN peace enforcement. Following Iraq's 1990 invasion of Kuwait, the superpowers agreed to invoke peace enforcement for the first time since the Korean War. In ensuing years, the UN embarked on a series of ambitious, complex, and controversial missions involving **humanitarian intervention** and state building that stretched its capabilities and ignored features of earlier peacekeeping such as gaining the approval of warring parties in advance and not using soldiers from the superpowers. However, by the late 1990s, US disenchantment with the cost of UN operations and a growing American propensity to act outside the UN framework as it did in Iraq in 2003 created a new crisis for the organization.

The most formidable challenge facing the UN today is the violence and human suffering in the developing world. Repeatedly, civil strife and the collapse of central authority in LDCs have been accompanied by the rise of warlords and rogue militias that engage in ruthless savagery against civilian populations. Humanitarian concerns and the need to restore order have led the UN to intervene in the domestic affairs of such states despite the norm of sovereignty and with varying success to reconstruct state institutions. However, these new conflicts feature several traits that distinguish them from those that were the sites of successful first-generation peacekeeping operations:

- No clear line separates foes, which are not just states, but rebel groups, warlords, and ethnic communities engaged in unconventional warfare.
- Peacekeepers find it difficult to be impartial; they may identify aggressors and lay blame, particularly for gross human rights violations like ethnic cleansing in Bosnia.
- Frequently, parties do not consent to a UN presence because they have something to gain from conflict or view the UN as their adversary.
- Peacekeepers are more heavily armed because missions are more dangerous.
- Missions have broad mandates to solve conflicts by rebuilding governing institutions, ensuring respect for human rights, and delivering humanitarian aid.

In 1991, the small Asian country of Cambodia became a testing ground for humanitarian intervention. Cambodia was a victim of the Vietnam War and, after falling under the rule of the communist Khmer Rouge, had experienced a murderous campaign at the hands of its own

humanitarian intervention intervention by states or by an IGO into the domestic politics of another state to protect people from human rights abuses or other threats to their survival.

leaders, during which some 1.7 million Cambodians died. After the regime was ousted following a war with Vietnam in 1978, low-level violence continued between remnants of the Khmer Rouge and the Vietnamese-supported government. In 1991, when the parties agreed to end the conflict, political authority in Cambodia was divided between the UN Transitional Authority in Cambodia (UNTAC) and a council of Cambodians from the country's various political factions. UNTAC oversaw preparations for elections and began efforts to rebuild the shattered country until its mission ended in 1993. At its peak, the UN contingent consisted of 15,991 troops and more than 50,000 Cambodians to organize elections.

The most complex post-Cold War UN operation was the UN Protection Force (UNPROFOR) which operated in the former Yugoslavia between 1992 and 1995. Some 42 countries, including the United States, contributed troops to the mission. UNPROFOR originated as a temporary effort to protect areas in Croatia in the midst of Yugoslavia's collapse. When the conflict expanded into a civil war in Bosnia among

Figure 9.5 Bosnian women pray in 2001 at a memorial to "Srebrenica, July 1995"
© PA Photos

Serbs, Croatians, and Muslims, UNPROFOR imposed a no-fly zone in Bosnia. It also tried to assure the delivery of supplies to Sarajevo, which was under siege and artillery bombardment by Bosnian Serb forces in the surrounding hills. From the Serb perspective, UN efforts to protect Bosnian Muslims meant that the UNPROFOR was taking sides and was another enemy.

UNPROFOR was also charged with protecting other Bosnian Muslim towns similarly besieged. One unit, a battalion of lightly armed Dutch soldiers, was responsible for protecting the town of Srebrenica. In what became Europe's worst massacre since World War II, Bosnian Serb forces overran the city in June 1995, killing some 7,500 Bosnian Muslims in a UN "safe area." The Dutch battalion offered no resistance and allowed the Serbs to take away Muslims who had sought refuge at the UN base.

Such UN operations were far larger and more complex than those during the Cold War, and it is unlikely that such operations can be sustained in future without large-scale US involvement. Thus, the Bosnian conflict was brought to an end only after NATO intervention and the extensive participation of US forces. Even where Americans are not directly involved, the United Nations has to rely on the United States and other major countries for logistics, transport, and funding. The demands placed on UN personnel are so extensive that they threaten to overwhelm the organization's capacity. Whole armies and large-scale contingents of administrators, not small contingents of peacekeepers, are necessary where governments have collapsed, violence is endemic, and refugees number in the millions. Thus, growing burdens and the reluctance of leading members to provide necessary resources threaten the UN's continued effectiveness as an agent of peace and security. UN burdens are growing rapidly at a time when the United States is hesitant to entrust its interests to the organization. In the next section, we address the question of America's sometimes strained relations with the United Nations.

The UN and American unilateralism

American enthusiasm for the United Nations waned in the 1970s as it became apparent that the United States could no longer dominate the organization as it had earlier. Confronting vocal opposition to American policies toward Vietnam, South Africa, and the Middle East among many developing countries, combined with demands for greater US economic aid, political conservatives in the United States, like US opponents of the League in 1919, grew fearful that the United Nations threatened US sovereignty and national interest. American leaders were repeatedly angered by anti-Israeli rhetoric and majorities that challenged US policy in the Middle East and by what they regarded as the UN's careless fiscal practices. Increasingly, conservatives argued that the United States does not need the United Nations as much as the UN needs the United States and that the United States should not support UN actions that are not in America's national interest. Secretary-General Annan's deputy responded to this: "The prevailing practice of seeking to use the UN almost by stealth as a diplomatic tool while failing to stand up for it against its domestic critics is simply not sustainable. You will lose the UN one way or another."[38] The uneasy US–UN relationship became entangled in the organization's repeated financial crises, but its roots go deeper, to questions about America's role in the world and changing norms about the use of force.

The United Nations depends on members for funding. They are assessed on the basis of their capacity to pay as determined by national income, and the scale is regularly reviewed. Until recently, the maximum percentage paid by any single member was set at 25 percent, an amount paid only by the United States. However, under American pressure this ceiling was reduced to 22 percent in 2000. Under the new scale, Japan is assessed at 19.66 percent and Germany 9.84 percent.[39] By contrast, almost half the member states pay the minimum of 0.01 percent. Assessments pay for the organization's regular budget, which was $3.1 billion in 2004–05. UN peacekeeping is also funded by a system of assessments. Peacekeeping costs approved for 2005–06 are over $5 billion,[40] with the US paying 27 percent and the five leading donors paying over 70 percent. Overall expenditures by the UN and its agencies run to about $10 billion a year, or $1.70 per capita based on members' populations.

In the 1950s and 1960s, the Soviet Union was the UN's leading deadbeat, having fallen behind in paying its dues, but in recent decades the United States has earned this dubious distinction. As US criticism of the UN grew in the late 1970s, so did congressional reluctance to meet America's financial obligations to the UN. Matters worsened during the Reagan years (1980–88), when the United States refused to fund programs that aided the Palestine Liberation Organization or SWAPO (the armed independence movement in Namibia).

By the end of 1988, the United States still owed most of its regular and peacekeeping dues.[41] President George H.W. Bush persuaded Congress to reverse its policy and by 1992 had reduced the US debt to the UN. During the Clinton years (1992–2000), acrimonious domestic debate ensued over UN financing, producing several compromises that reduced but did not eliminate the US debt. As of December 31, 2004, members owed $357 million for the regular budget, of which the US debt was $241 million, 68 percent of the total.[42] Under the George W. Bush administration, the United States sought to cap the UN budget until the organization instituted far-reaching reforms desired by Washington. Although the United States did not prevent the UN from lifting the cap when bankruptcy seemed imminent, along with Japan and Australia it publicly "disassociated" itself from the decision.[43]

One way the United Nations has tried to cope with financial crisis is through agreements with corporations for joint development projects. In an unprecedented act of philanthropy, in September 1997 CNN founder Ted Turner announced that he would donate $1 billion over the next decade to UN programs "like refugees, cleaning up land mines, peacekeeping, [and] UNICEF."[44] And in January 1999, Secretary-General Annan proposed a "Global Compact" between the UN and business leaders that specifies the nature of cooperation in human rights, labor standards, and environmental practices. Today 1,500 firms, including business giants Citigroup, Nestlé, Nike, and Starbucks, participate.[45]

The debate over UN financing was symptomatic of larger issues concerning America's role in the world. Is it in the interest of the world's only superpower to limit its capacity to act as it wishes, or is the legitimacy conferred by acting within the constraints of the UN important enough to justify those constraints? These questions were sharply posed in the 2002–03 debate in the UN Security Council over whether to invade Iraq.

After Saddam Hussein's defeat in the Persian Gulf War of 1990–91, the Security Council passed several resolutions demanding that Iraq provide full disclosure of its effort to acquire weapons of mass destruction. On November 8, 2002, the Council unanimously passed Resolution 1441, offering Iraq "a final opportunity to comply with its disarmament obligations" or face "serious consequences." The resolution also demanded that UN weapons inspectors be given "immediate, unconditional, and unrestricted access" to all suspected sites in order to assure Iraq's compliance.[46] Although Iraq acceded to these demands, American officials remained dissatisfied with the description of its weapons programs that Iraq provided the following month. The subsequent reports by UN weapons inspectors in early 2003 found that Iraq had not fully disarmed but was cooperating with the inspectors. In their March report, UN inspectors indicated that they needed more time to finish their work.

By this time, the American military buildup in the Middle East was almost complete, and American and British leaders argued that Resolution 1441 gave them authority to invade Iraq. The other permanent members of the Council, notably France and Russia, disagreed, arguing that another resolution was necessary to authorize a war.[47] It was clear that France and probably Russia would veto such a resolution and that few of the Council's members would vote for it. Thus, on March 17, without waiting for international inspections of Iraq's alleged weapons of mass destruction to be completed, President George W. Bush declared that diplomacy was at an end. American willingness to move ahead without UN approval, combined with its efforts to force other countries into supporting its position, produced widespread resentment.

The 2003 invasion to topple Saddam Hussein posed a new challenge for the organization, and it triggered a debate over whether a country can legally resort to force without UN authorization. Historically, states have enjoyed a sovereign right to use force at their discretion, and the change in this norm is uneven across countries.

It is unclear whether superpower **unilateralism** portends the UN's demise or a new but different role for the organization. American willingness to act without UN approval is not new. Washington paid little attention to the United Nations during the Vietnam War, and in 1999 neither the United States nor its NATO allies obtained UN approval for intervention in Kosovo. However, if the world's only superpower ignores the United Nations, the organization's future is bleak.

unilateralism the practice of acting alone, without consulting friends and allies.

Events in Iraq notwithstanding, constructivists can point to the evolution of global norms in the direction of **multilateralism** and humanitarian intervention in which countries cooperate under UN auspices to end violence, even if this requires intervention in the internal affairs of sovereign states. Thus, in 2004, the UN threatened sanctions against Sudan if the government of that country failed to end the threatened **genocide** of black African Muslims at the hands of government-supported Arab gangs in the Darfur region of Sudan. The UN's effort to send peacekeepers to Sudan, however, was initially thwarted by Sudanese objections, but in November 2006 Sudan changed its position "in principle" to assist the small African Union contingent already there.[48]

multilateralism a policy of working with other states to achieve policy goals.

genocide the extermination of an ethnic, racial, or cultural group.

American unilateralism in Iraq was widely unpopular and created serious strains between America and its friends. As reflected in Table 9.2, favorable opinions of the United States among America's European friends declined precipitously following the 2003 invasion, and people in Western Europe, Russia, and elsewhere regard American actions in Iraq as a greater danger to world peace than Iran or North Korea. Many Europeans believed that in invading Iraq, the United States was overreacting to terrorism and thought that the Iraq war undermined the War on Terrorism and would only increase the threat.[49] Indeed, despite

Table 9.2 15-Nation global attitudes survey, June 2006

Favorable opinions of the United States

	1999–2000	2002	2003	2004	2005	2006
	%	%	%	%	%	%
Britain	83	75	70	58	55	56
France	62	63	43	37	43	39
Germany	78	61	45	38	41	37

Dangers to world peace

% saying 'great danger'	Iran	US in Iraq	North Korea	Israeli–Palestine conflict
	%	%	%	%
United States	46	31	34	43
Britain	34	41	19	45
France	31	36	16	35
Germany	51	40	23	51
Spain	38	56	21	52
Russia	20	45	10	41
Indonesia	7	31	4	33
Egypt	14	56	14	68
Pakistan	4	28	8	22
Nigeria	15	25	11	27
Japan	29	29	46	40
India	8	15	6	13
China	22	31	11	27

Britain's "special relationship" with the United States and its key role in America's "coalition of the willing" that invaded Iraq in 2003, in June 2006 two-thirds of Britons said their opinion of the US had worsened in recent years. This led a prominent British political scientist to declare that "there has probably never been a time when America was held in such low esteem on this side of the Atlantic."[50]

When small countries behave unilaterally, it is one thing; but when the United States does, it is another. If the UN's most powerful member persistently acts without regard to the organization, the UN is likely to become more and more irrelevant, as did the League of Nations. Unilateralism in Iraq provided the United States with a degree of flexibility that would have been unthinkable had the UN been involved. But the cost, especially in legitimacy, was high. Without UN support, many people around the world, including many Americans, claimed that the US had no right to do what it did in Iraq. This absence of legitimacy might have mattered less if the United States had won a quick victory and left behind a democratic regime in Iraq. However, though the initial victory was quick, political chaos ensued, accompanied by insurgent and terrorist violence.

With no apparent way of getting out of Iraq quickly, the Bush administration began to rethink its policy. Cajoled by American leaders, UN officials played a key role in returning legal sovereignty to Iraq at the end of June 2004 and in planning for Iraqi elections in January 2005.

The UN and the future

In recent years American dissatisfaction with the UN combined with revelations about inefficiency and, in some cases, corruption has produced calls for reforming the organization. For example, in 2005 the UN's reputation was tarnished by revelations of corruption in the Iraq oil-for-food program and allegations of sexual exploitation by UN peacekeepers. However, there is little agreement about what type of reform is needed. Liberals would like to increase the UN's authority, while US neoconservatives would like to limit that authority. For its part, the US Congress has pressed the UN to be more frugal and make its finances more transparent.

In November 2003, Secretary-General Kofi Annan set up a "high-level panel of eminent personalities" to look into the possibility of UN reform. Among the ideas considered was changing Security Council membership. One alternative involved adding six more permanent members, probably Germany, Japan, Brazil, India, Egypt, and either South Africa or Nigeria, and three additional members serving two-year terms. Another would add eight semi-permanent members for renewable four-year terms plus one additional member for a two-year term. Although the "Big Five" would retain their preeminence, other major countries such as Japan, Germany, and India would acquire greater status than before. The suggested changes in Council membership have been controversial and are unlikely to be adopted. For example, China opposes adding Japan, which it sees as a rival in Asia; Italy believes that if Germany is added, it should also be given a seat; and the United States has supported the addition of Japan but not Germany.

The panel identified six key challenges facing the UN in coming years: interstate conflict, internal violence, social and economic threats, weapons of mass destruction, terrorism, and crime. With these threats in mind, the panel also considered greater scope for UN humanitarian intervention and the preventive use of force (as the United States undertook against Iraq) but only after a "serious and sober assessment" of the threat by the Security Council.[51] In March 2005, the Secretary-General recommended that the General Assembly consider the panel's alternatives for Council membership. In addition, the Secretary-General proposed that the UN pressure rich countries to contribute 0.7 percent of the gross national income[52] as foreign aid and codify rules on using military force as recommended by his panel.[53]

The six challenges all require a stronger and more independent UN than presently exists. For instance, problems of internal violence, social malaise, economic decline, terrorism, and crime produce state failure. As such failures proliferate pressure will grow for the UN to intervene in situations that are so desperate that the organization will literally have to manage those countries. Running a country, however, is not an easy job as the UN discovered in Kosovo where efforts to hold local elections and foster local control face virulent Serb opposition and efforts to limit local control enflame Albanian nationalists in the region.[54]

The problem of powerful states pursuing narrow national interests rather than a larger collective good of peace plagues the UN as it did the League. Thus, the United States effectively killed Annan's reform program when US Ambassador John Bolton (1948–), a long-time UN critic, introduced over 750 amendments to the Secretary-General's reform proposal, including eliminating references to new foreign aid commitments and calling for progress toward nuclear disarmament and halting global warming.[55] Bolton threatened to block the UN's 2006–07

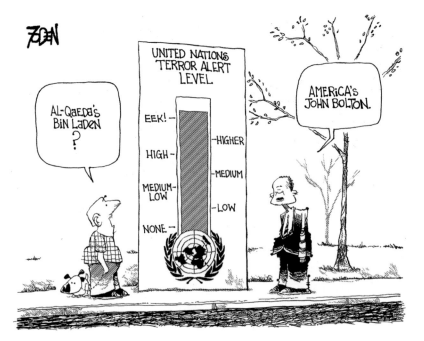

Figure 9.6 John Bolton and the UN
© Original artist,
www.cartoonstock.com

budget unless the reforms preferred by the United States were instituted. He also demanded that the Secretary-General repudiate "personally and publicly" Deputy UN Secretary-General Mark Malloch Brown who had criticized Bolton indirectly when he called for an end to "too much UN-bashing and stereotyping" by American officials.[56]

Unilateralism is not a US monopoly. American unilateralism in Iraq has been mirrored by Iranian and North Korean intransigence about their development of nuclear weapons (in both cases condemned in Security Council resolutions), China's refusal to loosen its hold on Tibet, Israeli unilateralism in occupied areas of Palestine, and Russian policy in Chechnya. However, the US attitude is crucial, and a large minority of Americans holds unfavorable views of the UN, again in sharp contrast to majorities in Britain, France, Germany, and even Russia who hold favorable views. Like those of an earlier generation, many Americans fear the UN as a threat to US sovereignty. Some also believe that the US financial contribution to the organization is too high, that the UN bureaucracy is corrupt, and that the UN has become a vehicle for anti-American rhetoric.

In sum, none of the roles available to IGOs described at the beginning of this chapter alone can do justice to the UN. On the one hand, the policies of dominant states like the United States prevent the UN from pursuing the genuinely independent role advocated by liberals. On the other, the UN is more than an instrument of leading states, as realists claim. Instead, as constructivists believe, norms are evolving to the effect that the UN should play a greater role in maintaining peace than in the past. Whether this will happen or whether the UN will suffer the same fate as the League of Nations remains to be seen.

We now turn to regional IGOs, some of which have become major actors in global politics. The EU is the most complex and advanced of these institutions, and we examine its evolution and Europe's **political integration** since World War II. We then examine several other regional organizations in Africa, the Americas, Asia, and Europe.

political integration
a voluntary process of joining together to create a new political community.

Regional international organizations

The regional distribution of IGOs varies significantly, with Europe the principal site of such organizations. Its evolution, one of the world's most promising experiments in interstate organization, reflects the functionalist and neofunctionalist ideas that we looked at earlier.

The European Union

The most far-reaching experiment in regional organization today is the EU. Even Stephen Krasner, a realist who believes that the sovereign state remains as dominant today as in the past, admits that the EU is something different. "The European Union," he writes, "offers another example of an alternative bundle of characteristics: it has territory, recognition, control, national authority, extranational authority, and supranational authority." He continues: "There is no commonly accepted term for the European Union. Is it a state, a commonwealth, a dominion, a confederation of states, a federation of states?" Krasner concludes that the EU is unique and that it "is not a model other parts of the world can imitate."[57]

Labels aside, the key question is: To what extent is the EU more than the sum of its member states? Liberals argue that over time European governments have surrendered bits and pieces of their sovereignty to the EU. In fact, the EU is a complex hybrid polity in which authority is shared among EU bureaucrats, historic nation-states, large provincial regions, and even cities. States are penetrated by European influences through law, regulations, bureaucratic contacts, political exchange, and the appointment of national politicians to community positions. In turn, the domestic politics of member states affect the community as a whole. In Europe, declare three authors, "the state has become too big for the little things and too small for the big things."[58]

Let us examine the origins of Europe's efforts to integrate. The story begins at the end of World War II, when Europe's leaders and publics concluded that, after three major wars in under a century, the time had come to build an edifice to prevent a fourth.

From the end of World War II to the Schuman Plan

Europe was in shambles in 1945. Germany was divided and occupied, and the United States sought to revive Europe's economy as part of an effort to restart global peacetime economic activity, renew Europe as a market for American goods, and reduce the attraction of communism to Europeans. The first step was creating an environment in which reconstruction could take place. To this end, the United States adopted a two-prong strategy. The first, providing Europe with the means to rebuild, began with the Marshall Plan. The second, to strengthen European security, culminated in the 1949 formation of the North Atlantic Treaty Organization (NATO). Both prongs sought a united Western Europe as a counterweight to the USSR.

The Marshall Plan offered economic assistance, *subject to European coordination of the relief effort* (see chapter 4, p. 168). This was a first step on the long road toward European unity. In 1948, the Organization for European Economic Cooperation (OEEC)[59] was established to coordinate Marshall aid. Until the European Economic Community was established, the OEEC played an important role in encouraging trade and providing Europe with currency convertibility.

Marshall Plan aid was offered to all of Europe, including the countries of Eastern Europe, but Stalin pressured them to reject it because he feared it would increase US influence in the Soviet bloc. Moreover, despite the OEEC, Europe's aid request was little more than a list of individual country requests rather than a serious effort at broad cooperation. Nevertheless, the division of Germany and the key role of West Germany on the Cold War's front line assured continued US interest in European integration. A European entity, it was thought, would make the new Germany part of something larger than itself, thereby assuaging the fears of other Europeans about a resurgence of German nationalism while allowing the Germans to contribute to Europe's reconstruction and security.

The key to Western Europe's industrial potential was the Ruhr Basin, site of Europe's largest coal and steel production. Placing this region under international control would force France and West Germany, enemies for much of the previous century, to cooperate. Despite French suspicions, the first big step toward European integration was largely the work of a far-sighted French economist and former League of Nations official, Jean Monnet (1888–1979). "There will be no peace in Europe," Monnet declared in 1943, "if States re-establish themselves on the basis of national sovereignty, with all that this implies by way of prestige policies and economic protectionism. If the countries of Europe once more protect themselves against each other, it will once more be necessary to build up vast armies."[60] On May 9, 1950, French Foreign Minister Robert Schuman (1886–1963), in a speech prepared by Monnet, proposed the integration of the French and German coal and steel industries under a supranational institution called the High Authority. Joined by Italy, Belgium, the Netherlands, and Luxembourg, the Schuman Plan became the basis for the 1951 European Coal and Steel Community (ECSC).

Theory in the real world

Europe has become what political scientist Karl W. Deutsch in the 1950s described as a "pluralistic security community" – a group of independent sovereign states among which war is unthinkable.[61] In the decades after Deutsch wrote, Europe achieved the three conditions that he believed were necessary for such a community: (1) "Compatibility of major political values," (2) "Capacity of the governments ... of the participating countries to respond to one another's messages, needs, and actions quickly, adequately, and without resort to violence," and (3) "Mutual predictability of the relevant aspects of one another's economic, political, and social behavior."[62]

The continuing process of European integration

The ECSC sparked enthusiasm for additional European integration. Although a proposal for an integrated European army died in 1954, West German rearmament was accomplished with the country's 1955 admission to NATO. That year the foreign ministers of the six ECSC members met in Messina, Sicily to examine other ways to advance European integration. However, the prospect of integration was given a dramatic push by the 1956 Suez War in the Middle East which persuaded French leaders that France could no longer act alone. According to one version, West German Chancellor Konrad Adenauer (1876–1967) said to French Premier Guy Mollet (1905–75) that: "France and England will never be powers comparable to the United States. . . . There remains to them only one way of playing a decisive role in the world: that is to unite Europe. . . . We have no time to waste; Europe will be your revenge."[63] The result was the 1957 Treaty of Rome that created the European Atomic Energy Community (EURATOM) to pool resources for the peaceful use of atomic energy and the European Economic Community (EEC) or Common Market. The Common Market involved eliminating all tariffs on trade among members and creating a common external tariff. It also entailed common policies in agriculture and transportation and the free movement of people among member states. The Common Agriculture Policy (CAP), which was enacted to provide Europe's politically powerful farmers with a guaranteed income by maintaining price supports, became a European institution, an obstacle to free trade in agriculture, and a drain on Europe's financial resources (see chapter 13, p. 611). Community decisions, made by a Council of Ministers but carried out by a High Commission responsible to the community as a whole, required only a majority, as members renounced their right to block decisions unilaterally.

Britain initially refused to join, fearing the loss of sovereign independence, and, instead, sponsored a loose free-trade group called the European Free Trade Association. Although Britain changed its view in 1961, its efforts to join the Common Market were twice vetoed by France's President Charles de Gaulle (1890–1970), and Britain, Ireland, and Denmark only became members in 1973.

The next step was the 1967 Merger Treaty under which the institutions of the ECSC, EEC, and EURATOM were merged into the European Community (EC). By 1968, all tariffs among members had been eliminated, and the following year agreement was reached on a scheme for regular financing of the EC budget based on member contributions. In 1979, the first direct elections were held for a European Parliament. Thereafter, Greece (1981), Portugal (1986), and Spain (1986) joined the EC. The EC's enlargement led to the creation of the European Regional Development Fund under which wealthier members provided development aid to poorer members.

The signing of the Single European Act (SEA) in 1986 was a giant step toward the surrender of sovereignty by EC members. It involved some 300 rules for removing impediments to the formation of a single internal economic market and required members to harmonize policies and standards in areas such as tax, health, safety, labor, and environmental policy.

The 1992 Maastricht Treaty was an even bigger step, formally creating the European Union. Europe was given a new structure that consisted of "three pillars" (Figure 9.7). The European Community remained the EU's core but with the addition of a second pillar involving cooperation in Common Foreign and Security Policy (CFSP) and a third in Justice and Home Affairs (JHA). Progress in these last two has been slow. The CFSP tries to foster foreign policy dialogue to forge a common European position on global issues. Although some common positions have been

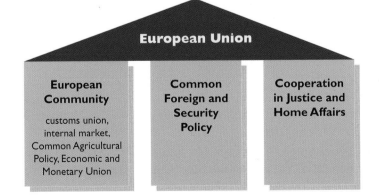

Figure 9.7 The three pillars of the European Union
http://www.dadalos-europe.org/int/grundkurs2/etappe_4.htm

adopted, Europeans remained divided on questions such as how to deal with the break-up of Yugoslavia in 1991 and 1992. Efforts to establish a common policy on European defense outside of NATO have also foundered despite the formation of a Common Security and Defense Policy in the 1997 Amsterdam Treaty and a commitment to build an all-European rapid-reaction force to deal with sudden crises without US assistance. Standing above and coordinating the activities of the three pillars is the European Council where national leaders meet and bargain. Administration is in the hands of the European Commission with commissioners in charge of specific administrative departments.

The Maastricht Treaty also began a process of transforming the EU into a single Economic and Monetary Union by linking members' national currencies and committing members to the creation of a single European currency. The year 2000 saw the introduction of the new "euro zone" with the replacement of national currencies by a single currency called the euro and the establishment of a European Central Bank responsible for monetary policy for the EU as a whole. Although Britain, Sweden, and Denmark opted out from the controversial decision, the countries that joined the euro zone accepted stringent requirements (called the Stability and Growth Pact), including limits on domestic inflation, budget deficits, and long-term interest rates. By 2004, the euro had become a powerful currency and a rival to the US dollar in international transactions.

Another major development was the EU's eastward expansion. In 2004, ten more states were admitted to the EU: Poland, Hungary, Slovenia, Slovakia, the Czech Republic, Lithuania, Latvia, Estonia, Malta, and Cyprus. In 2007, Romania and Bulgaria joined, and preliminary negotiations have begun regarding Turkey's possible admission. Since expansion, the EU, with a population that exceeds that of the United States by almost 75 million and a larger gross domestic product (GDP) (see figures 9.8 and 9.9),[64] has become a major force to reckon with in global politics.

Expansion has, however, complicated efforts to harmonize members' foreign policies. Several new members, notably Poland, supported American intervention in Iraq despite German and French opposition. This prompted US Defense Secretary Donald Rumsfeld in February 2003 to compare what he called the "old Europe" unfavorably with the "new Europe." An irritated French President Jacques Chirac (1932–) responded undiplomatically: "These countries have been not very well behaved and rather reckless of the danger of aligning themselves too rapidly with the American position." "They missed a good opportunity to keep quiet."[65]

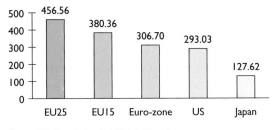

Figure 9.8 Population in 2003 (millions)

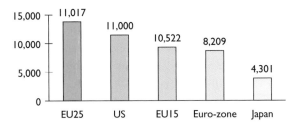

Figure 9.9 Gross Domestic Product (GDP) in 2003 (USD billions)

Nevertheless, Europe has taken tentative steps to coordinate foreign policies. It now has the equivalent of a foreign minister. EU policemen began serving in Bosnia in 2003, and EU soldiers were deployed some months later in Macedonia to reduce the risk of civil strife there. The EU has undertaken several peacekeeping missions, one in Aceh in Indonesia and another along the border between Ukraine and Transdniestria, a region that seceded from Moldova. In addition, the EU has endorsed the NATO mission in Afghanistan and is solidly behind the effort of Germany, Britain, and France to dissuade Iran from enriching nuclear materials that could be used for nuclear weapons.[66]

Despite the advances toward integrating Europe, Monnet's goal of a "United States of Europe" remains elusive. In some respects the EU has become greater than the sum of its parts, an institution that represents the interests of Europeans rather than those of states. However, states still retain considerable sovereign independence. Thus, in an effort to form a more perfect union, the EU began the process of drawing up a constitution for Europe as a whole.

A European constitution

The EU embarked on its most ambitious project to date when, at a December 2001 summit in Laeken, Belgium, European leaders adopted a declaration of principles as the basis for a continental constitution. As a result of the Laeken Declaration, the European Council established a Convention on the Future of Europe to draft a constitution that was completed by July 2003.

The proposed constitution combined the treaties of Rome and Maastricht but added several new features. For example, it committed members to aid one another in the event of a terrorist attack and proposed a European arrest warrant to facilitate law enforcement. The constitution described the EU as a "legal personality," a claim giving it equal juridical status with sovereign states. Three principles governed the constitution: conferral, subsidiarity, and proportionality. By the *principle of conferral*, those areas of policy not explicitly granted to the EU by members would remain under state authority. This is similar to the clause in the US Constitution that reserves to states all powers not explicitly granted to the Federal Government. By the *principle of subsidiarity*, the EU could act only when members agreed that their individual actions were inadequate to achieve the goals sought. Finally, the *principle of proportionality* decreed that EU actions should go no further than necessary to achieve its goals.

On June 18, 2004, EU members approved the draft European Constitutional Treaty, but it still had to be ratified by all 25 members individually. However, Europeans who feared the loss of national sovereignty disliked several features of the draft. Their chief target was the substitution of qualified majority voting for unanimity in some decisions. They objected, too, to a clause that made EU legislation superior to national laws, even though this had been the case for decades.

The draft was subject to furious controversy during much of 2005. Initially, several members approved the constitution, but, on May 29, 2005, French voters decisively rejected the proposed constitution in a referendum, and a week later Dutch voters did the same. Most voters had not actually read the document but were disenchanted by a variety of factors ranging from high unemployment, fear that the EU would impose neoliberal economic policies, concern about foreign immigration, and opposition to proposed Turkish entry in the EU. Although the proposed EU constitution may be revised and brought back for consideration in a few years, for the time being progress toward European integration has halted.

In sum, the EU is a novel regional organization in which members have surrendered some of their sovereignty. However, Europe's unique history creates doubts as to whether the EU is a model for regional integration elsewhere. To date, no other regional IGO has come close to achieving the EU's level of integration. Nevertheless, as we shall see, significant IGOs have been established on every continent.

Other regional organizations

Regional IGOs exist in all the world's geographic areas, and virtually every country is a member of at least one such organization. The first prominent African regional organization was the Organization of African Unity (OAU), founded in 1963, but it was so ineffective that in 2002, it was succeeded by the African Union (AU).[67] With a Pan-African parliament, a commission, a court of justice, and a development bank, the AU seeks to emulate the EU. The AU's first peacekeeping mission was to Burundi in 2003 to supervise a ceasefire agreement between warring Hutus and Tutsis. In 2004, it sent peacekeepers to protect civilians in the conflict in Darfur. In recent years, the AU has been partly eclipsed by the Economic Community of West African States (ECOWAS), consisting of 15 West African countries and dominated by its largest member, Nigeria.[68] Founded in 1975 to promote economic development, ECOWAS has also become involved in peacekeeping in a turbulent region, sending peacekeepers to Liberia, the Ivory Coast, Burundi, and, most recently, Darfur.

Politically, the most important IGO in the Americas is the Organization of American States (OAS).[69] Founded in 1948, the OAS

Figure 9.10 North American Free Lunch Agreement
© Original artist,
www.cartoonstock.com

includes all 35 countries in the western hemisphere, though communist Cuba has been excluded since 1962. Occasionally, the OAS has tried to balance the influence of the "Colossus of the North," while at other times it has supported US policy – for example, in the 1962 Cuban missile crisis. However, the most important regional economic group in the Americas is the North American Free Trade Agreement (NAFTA). The project began with the 1989 US–Canada Free Trade Agreement (FTA), which became NAFTA when Mexico joined in 1992. NAFTA, which went into effect in 1994, created a free-trade area and a mechanism for deciding trade disputes among members.[70] By 2003 virtually all tariffs among the three countries had been eliminated. Hailed by business sectors for stimulating trade, generating jobs, and reducing prices, it was opposed by US labor unions that feared the loss of jobs to poorly paid Mexicans and by environmentalists who believed that firms would move to Mexico to avoid US environmental requirements. Both groups remain suspicious of NAFTA.[71]

NAFTA has benefited Mexico and Canada. Mexico's northern region along the US border has become a manufacturing and assembly center for all of North America. American and Mexican firms have set up a variety of joint ventures there, and Mexico's share of the US import market jumped from 6.9 percent in 1993 to 11.6 percent in 2002. Canada sends over half of what it produces to its giant southern neighbor and almost 87 percent of its exports to its NAFTA partners.[72] Although US firms and jobs have moved south of the Río Grande, the US economy has also benefited from NAFTA. American agricultural exports to Mexico virtually doubled between 1994 and 2000. Prices of goods from Canada and Mexico have tumbled in the United States, and jobs have been created as well as lost. Politically, NAFTA reflects North American interdependence and has encouraged Mexico to pursue greater democratization and confront the troubling issues of narcotics and illegal immigration.

The most ambitious, but as yet unrealized, free-trade project in the Americas is the Free Trade Area of the Americas (FTAA).[73] The idea was first broached at a summit of 34 regional leaders in Miami in late 1994. There, states agreed to launch a continental free-trade area with authority to resolve regional trade disputes. At a 1998 meeting in Costa Rica, participants agreed to general principles for the free-trade area. Since then, the project has lost much of its momentum owing to differences over the scope and speed of negotiations between the United States and several Latin American states, especially Brazil and Venezuela under its flamboyant anti-American president, Hugo Chávez (1954–).

Asia also hosts several ambitious regional IGOs. The most successful is the Association of Southeast Asian Nations (ASEAN), founded in

1967. ASEAN conducts regular meetings to discuss regional issues and has proposed a Treaty of Amity and Cooperation with other states in the region that has been signed by China, India, Japan, and Pakistan. At their 2003 summit ASEAN's members agreed to speed up economic integration, with a free-trade area in place by 2020.

A more ambitious but less successful effort is the Asia–Pacific Economic Cooperation (APEC)[74] forum. With US backing, the leaders of 15 Pacific Rim countries gathered in Seattle in 1993 and called for the elimination of impediments to trade and investment among them. At APEC's 2004 meeting, President Bush sought to promote US foreign policy objectives such as efforts pressing Iran to end its nuclear weapons program. However, the meeting showed that initial enthusiasm for a free-trade zone among Pacific Rim countries had waned, especially with American efforts to conclude bilateral trade agreements with several APEC states.[75] Were APEC to become a free-trade area, it would be the largest in the world.

The EU is not Europe's only important regional organization. The North Atlantic Treaty Organization[76] remains the world's most powerful military alliance. Established in 1949 to provide security for Western Europe, NATO became an unprecedented peacetime alliance with a permanent secretariat and a military headquarters that represented the US commitment to deter Soviet aggression. The alliance's core was Article 5 of the treaty by which the United States affirmed that it would regard an attack on its allies as an attack on itself. Because the USSR never invaded Western Europe, Article 5 was first invoked on September 12, 2001 to provide assistance to the United States the day after terrorists attacked New York and Washington.[77]

Since the Cold War's end, NATO has grappled with how to remain relevant. One way it has done so is by expanding eastward to Russia's borders to spread stability and democracy across Central and Eastern Europe. In 1990, the former East Germany became part of NATO, and in 1999 the Czech Republic, Poland, and Hungary were admitted. Five years later Bulgaria, Estonia, Latvia, Lithuania, Rumania, Slovakia, and Slovenia were added. To ease Russian fears of NATO expansion a NATO–Russia Council was created for joint decision-making on issues such as terrorism, nuclear proliferation, crisis management, and arms control.

Today, NATO's main role is assuring stability along Europe's frontiers, a role it played during the 1999 Kosovo crisis. In fact, the Kosovo conflict was the first in which alliance forces were deeply engaged. More controversial are US efforts to persuade NATO to meet crises beyond Europe. In August 2003, in its first mission outside the

European–Atlantic region, NATO took over command of the International Security Assistance Force[78] to pacify Afghanistan. US forces in Europe have already been reduced since the Cold War and will be reduced further as part of America's shift away from heavily armed forces meant to defend Europe against a Soviet invasion to more mobile forces to deal with crises elsewhere in the world.

Another important European organization is the Organization for Security and Cooperation in Europe (OSCE).[79] The OSCE, originally called the Conference on Security and Cooperation in Europe (CSCE), evolved as a forum for reducing East–West tensions during the Cold War. It is recalled for the discussions it hosted in Helsinki, Finland between 1973 and 1975 that led to a US–Soviet agreement to recognize Europe's frontiers, including the boundary between West and East Germany. In 1990, the CSCE's members signed the Charter of Paris for a New Europe that officially recognized the Cold War's end, and in 1994 the organization changed its name to the OSCE. The OSCE is the world's largest regional security group with tasks including promoting confidence-building measures among adversaries, pressing for human rights, managing potential crises, and encouraging democratization. In 2004, its observers in Ukraine helped convince the world that that country's presidential election was rigged and that new elections should be held.

International organizations and peace

Do international organizations contribute to peace? The answer seems to be that they do, a finding to cheer liberals and confute realists. In a pioneering analysis, Russett and Oneal identified six ways in which IGOs help maintain peace: (1) coercing aggressive states, (2) mediating among those in conflict, (3) providing information to reduce uncertainty and avoid misunderstandings, (4) solving problems in ways that help states see their interests in new ways, (5) promoting shared norms, and (6) "building a shared sense of values and identity among peoples."[80]

Russett and Oneal conclude that IGOs were most beneficial before World War I and less so in the period between the two world wars, "but have been an important force for peace in the years after 1945." The UN, they argue, "is a far more influential organization" than was the League of Nations, and, overall, today's IGOs "are more complex and effective than were their predecessors."[81]

Having examined the changing role of IGOs in global politics, we turn to the role of NGOs. These groups are having an impact in a variety of ways, especially in linking people from different societies and, as functionalists would predict, in performing tasks that governments, especially in the developing world, cannot perform for themselves.

Nongovernmental organizations

One of the salient features of global politics in the early twenty-first century is the proliferation in nongovernmental organizations (NGOs) that link people transnationally in many realms of human activity. According to British political scientist Peter Willetts, "many NGOs . . . have their membership measured in millions, whereas 37 countries in the UN have populations of less than one million."[82] The UN officially recognizes about 1,400 NGOs, and many play a growing role as sources of information and expertise and as lobbyists at UN-sponsored international conferences like the 1993 World Conference on Human Rights in Vienna, Austria.

One of the earliest NGOs was the Red Cross. It owes it birth to Henry Dunant, a Swiss businessman. Dunant (1828–1910), who was traveling in northern Italy in June 1859 hoping to meet French Emperor Napoléon III from whom he sought assistance for a business deal, came upon the village of Castiglione where thousands of wounded soldiers lay following the French victory over Austria in the Battle of Solferino. There, Dunant assisted women from the village who were trying to help the wounded. Deeply moved by his experience, Dunant later published a book in which he asked: "Would it not be possible, in time of peace and quiet, to form relief societies for the purpose of having care given to the wounded in wartime by zealous, devoted and thoroughly qualified volunteers?"[83] Dunant's question persuaded several influential Swiss reformers to establish an International Committee for Relief to the Wounded, which later changed its name to the International Committee of the Red Cross (ICRC), later to become one of the best known NGOs in global politics.

Today, NGOs encompass a vast array of groups that deal with environmental, human rights, gender, humanitarian, and other transnational issues.[84] They are not-for-profit, voluntary citizens' groups, which, according to the UN, are "organized on a local, national or international level to address issues in support of the public good."[85] They are independent of governments and usually do not represent a particular political ideology, economic system, or religion. Until recently, most were limited to placing issues on the global agenda by publicizing them. Increasingly, however, they have become authoritative actors in their own right, with legitimacy derived from expertise, information, and innovative political techniques.

Equally important is NGOs' growing role in creating norms that states feel obliged to follow. For this reason, NGOs figure importantly in the ideas of constructivists who focus on the evolution of norms in global politics.[86] Working together across national borders, NGOs have formed effective networks of experts and advocates, called **epistemic communities**. Such experts and advocates frequently meet with one another at international conferences, and, as constructivists point out, the information and ideas that they disseminate play an important role in changing norms that may redefine states' interests.

epistemic communities
communities of experts and advocates who share information about an issue and maintain contact with one other.

It was an epistemic community in Britain that led to opposition to the Atlantic slave trade in the early nineteenth century. This community consisted mainly of Quakers and Evangelical Christians led by British abolitionist William Wilberforce (1759–1833). By spreading information about the conditions in which African slaves were shipped across the Atlantic Ocean and protesting the practice, Wilberforce and his followers changed the way British politicians and public opinion thought about the slave trade.

In recent years, other epistemic communities have also spurred changes in global norms. For example, the stream of information from environmental groups has convinced most governments that global warming is a growing threat, and, in consequence, many countries have concluded that their interests demand action on their part to slow that process. Other epistemic communities specializing in issues such as human rights, banning landmines, and economic development have had a similar impact.

NGOS are, according to liberal theorists, creating a global civic society in which like-minded individuals from many countries regularly communicate ideas and coordinate activities to promote democracy, environmental protection, racial and religious tolerance, and similar norms. The idea of civic politics is that NGOs participate in global governance and can contribute to global change.[87] In such a society, citizens in many countries voluntarily organize NGOs and network across national frontiers to find solutions to common problems. As more NGOs are established beyond the control of governments and become strong independent institutions, civic society deepens.

Citizens' political awareness and engagement are vital to a healthy democracy. Thus, the proliferation of these voluntary institutions, it is believed, fosters democracy in the countries in which they are located and creates the conditions for the spread of democracy globally. For these reasons, some governments, notably Russia's, are trying to curb NGO independence in their countries.

Conclusion

International law and organization continue to reflect both change
and continuity. The role of state sovereignty remains central; however,
international law has evolved beyond being a "law of nations" and, as
we shall see in the next chapter, is becoming a law of "persons" as well.
In no area is this more evident than in human rights in which new
protections for individuals are challenging the prerogatives of sovereignty,
especially the prohibition against external noninterference in domestic
affairs and the absolute authority of the state over its citizens.

Student activities

Discussion and essay questions

Comprehension questions

1 Describe the ideas of Kant and Rousseau regarding the role
   of international organization in global politics.
2 Compare and contrast UNEF with UNPROFOR. How are they
   different?
3 How can IGOs contribute to keeping peace?

Analysis questions

4 What is the difference between unilateralism and multilateralism in
   foreign policy; which is more likely to achieve America's national
   interests?
5 What is the likely future of the United Nations?
6 What is meant by global civic society? If such a society existed, how
   would global politics be different?

Map analysis

What does Map 9.1 tell you about which countries and regions are
currently trouble spots in global politics?

Cultural materials

Art can be used to make political statements. The UN exhibits many
such works. For example, in 1964 Marc Chagall presented a stained glass
window memorializing former Secretary General Dag Hammarskjold and

those who died with him in a plane crash in 1961. The window contains many symbols of peace and love, including motherhood and people struggling for peace. Try drawing a picture that you think would symbolize the UN and describe the symbolic elements in the picture.

Amnesty International uses various artistic media to promote its causes. Beginning in 1976, Amnesty International UK began to sponsor a regular "Secret Policeman's Ball" comedy event, with participants such as Sting, John Cleese, and other members of Monty Python's Flying Circus. Research an NGO in your community (including campus social, environmental, and political groups). How do they raise funds and awareness of their causes?

Further reading

Barnett, Michael and Martha Finnemore, *Rules for the World: International Organizations in Global Politics* (Ithaca, NY: Cornell University Press, 2004). Analysis of how international organizations as bureaucracies can make rules, exercise power, and act independently of members.

Dinan, Desmond, *Ever Closer Union: An Introduction to European Integration*, 3rd ed. (Boulder, CO: Lynne Rienner, 2005). Explores EU history, institutions, and policies.

Forsythe, David P., Roger A. Coate, and Thomas G. Weiss, *The United Nations and Changing World Politics*, 4th ed. (Boulder, CO: Westview Press, 2004). Comprehensive exploration of the UN's role in issues of peace, human rights, and development.

Goldsmith, Jack A. and Eric Posner, *The Limits of International Law* (Oxford: Oxford University Press, 2005). Controversial work that argues states only follow international law when it suits their national interest.

Keck, Margaret and Kathryn Sikkink, *Activists Beyond Borders: Advocacy Networks in International Politics* (Ithaca, NY: Cornell University Press, 1998). Fascinating analysis of how NGOs form transnational networks to advocate for social causes.

Khagam, Sanjeev, James Riker, and Kathryn Sikkink, eds., *Restructuring World Politics: Transnational Social Movements* (Minneapolis, MN: University of Minneapolis Press, 2002). Excellent stories of how transnational social movements are changing global politics and creating civil society.

Malone, David M., ed., *The UN Security Council: From the Cold War to the 21st Century* (Boulder, CO: Lynne Rienner, 2004). Comprehensive analysis of the Security Council's history and politics.

Scott, Shirley V., *International Law in World Politics: An Introduction* (Boulder, CO: Lynne Rienner, 2004). Thorough treatment of the development of international law in the areas of human rights, arms control, humanitarian law, and the environment.

Walzer, Michael, *Just and Unjust Wars: A Moral Argument with Historical Illustrations* (New York: Basic Books, 2000). Classic treatment of war and justice.

10 Human rights

The individual in global politics

The human rights group Amnesty International tells the story of an 11-year-old girl who fled with her family from the civil war in southern Sudan to a refugee camp outside Khartoum, the country's capital. On May 5, 1999, she became lost on her way home after visiting relatives in another camp and was taken to a police station. There, she was brutally raped by police officers. After taking her to a hospital, the police claimed that she had been found outdoors and was suffering from malaria. In the hospital, doctors discovered that she was a rape victim. Efforts to bring the police to justice have thus far been unsuccessful, and the child continues to suffer from the physical and psychological trauma of the assault.[1] Unfortunately, **human rights** are routinely violated around the world, and rape remains common as a way to terrorize women.

This chapter focuses our attention on normative theory (chapter 1, p. 14), on what is right and wrong, moral and immoral, and on how we "ought" to behave in global politics. Human rights abuses against women in Sudan are wrong and, as we shall see in this chapter, are recent manifestations of the long-term prejudice against women. Indeed, the Fourteenth Amendment to the US Constitution, which provided equal rights to newly freed African-American slaves, explicitly limited "the right to vote" to "male inhabitants," thereby explicitly excluding women – black and white – from those rights. Shocked by the insertion of "male" into the Constitution, the suffragette, Susan B. Anthony (1820–1906) exclaimed that "the only tenable ground of representation is universal suffrage, as it is only through universal suffrage that the principle of 'Equal Rights to All' can be realized."[2]

Even the Declaration of Independence, perhaps the clearest expression of human rights in US history, began by excluding women: "We hold these truths to be self-evident, that all men are created equal, that they are endowed by their Creator with certain unalienable Rights, that among these are Life, Liberty and the pursuit of Happiness." And since the Revolution, Americans have looked to their government as a guardian of the rights described in the Declaration and as guaranteed in the Bill of Rights of the Constitution. However, the Declaration is an idealized view of human rights that is rarely realized in most countries in the world today, including the US. When the Declaration was written in 1776, most governments treated their people as subjects from whom rulers had to extract resources and obedience. Except for a few liberal philosophers in England and France, few thinkers or politicians thought that people had rights apart from those granted them by their sovereigns. Even in the United States, enslaved blacks, like the girl in Sudan, were regarded as less than a complete human being, being counted in the Constitution as three-fifths of a person.

Are states required to treat their citizens humanely? After all, states are sovereign and, therefore, enjoy unlimited legal power over those living on their territory. Also, being sovereign, they have no legal superiors. And, under traditional international law, only sovereign states enjoyed rights, and only states were "juridical persons" with legal standing in each other's courts. The traditional view was that if a sovereign ruler or his representatives wished to exploit or abuse subjects, it was no one else's business, and no one had a right to intervene in the domestic affairs of another country.

Historically, governments have limited or violated the rights of individuals for many reasons – for example, to promote their ideology and induce fear. Dictators often forced citizens to accept official ideological, religious, and political views and persecuted those who did not do so. Many rulers continue to jail opponents arbitrarily, use torture to extract information from political prisoners, deny justice and equality to racial and ethnic groups, treat women as chattel, torture and kill opponents to still dissent, and in general abuse citizens.

Although Americans do not like to think that they violate human rights, abuses committed by US soldiers in Iraq have come to light. According to Amnesty International, the mistreatment of Iraqi prisoners at the Abu Ghraib prison near Baghdad in 2004 was part of an "iconography of torture, cruelty and degradation" that followed the September 11 terrorist attacks on New York and Washington and reflected a "well-trodden path of violating basic rights in the name of national security or 'military necessity.'"[3] And some US soldiers may be guilty of war crimes against Iraqi civilians.[4]

As in the past, some regimes are led by pathological leaders who commit incomprehensible atrocities. Hitler intentionally caused the genocide[5] of over six million Jews and the deaths of countless others – gypsies, gays, socialists, and Slavs – whom he regarded as inferior. Soviet tyrant Josef Stalin oversaw the deaths of millions by starvation, slave labor, and execution. Idi Amin (1928–2003) oversaw the murder of hundreds of thousands of Ugandans, especially those of the Acholi and Lango tribes, during his brutal dictatorship from 1971 until 1979. According to Welsh journalist and eyewitness Tony Trainor: "By 1974 his regime was murdering hundreds of thousands of its own people and Amin fed the heads of opponents to crocodiles and boasted of eating human flesh, keeping human heads in the freezer as his nation starved."[6] And Pol Pot (1925–98), leader of the communist Khmer Rouge in Cambodia, ordered the genocidal deaths of as many as two million – more than one in five – in an effort to remake Cambodian society.

However, as democracy spread during the eighteenth and nineteenth centuries, especially in the West, and with it the belief that law requires the consent of the governed, the ideas that governments should not treat subjects arbitrarily and that people had rights apart from those granted by rulers also spread. Today, liberals generally advocate greater reliance on **international law** to maintain peace and advance human rights. By contrast, realists declare that international law need only be obeyed when it serves states' interests, and that human rights must take a back seat to the demands of power and national interest. For their part, constructivists regard rights as social constructs that evolve as more and more people regard them as legitimate and morally justified. They emphasize that, even though states often violate international law and human rights are routinely abused, legal and normative precedents are being set and norms are evolving that, over time, will constrain the arbitrary behavior of states and limit their sovereign independence.

Human rights are a special category of "rights." But what are "rights"? Most theorists agree that **rights** are moral entitlements possessed by people by virtue of who they are or what they have done.[7] Rights are claims that others are duty-bound to respect. In other words, rights entail corresponding duties.[8] They establish a relationship between those who possess those rights and others such as governments against whom those rights are asserted. As such, rights can only exist in social organizations.

Norms against human rights violations are growing, and global politics has witnessed the proliferation of legal protections for individuals since World War II. Although international law has for much of the previous three centuries jealously protected the prerogatives of rulers and the sovereignty of their states, that is beginning to change. The savagery of warfare and especially the Holocaust in World War II persuaded people that those responsible for atrocities should be held accountable. Beginning with the trials of German and Japanese individuals for **war crimes** in the postwar Nuremberg and Tokyo trials and continuing with the elaboration of human rights law by the UN and other international organizations,

international law the body of legally binding rules that govern relations among states and that increasingly provide rights for individuals in relation to states.

rights privileges and prerogatives to which one has an established claim.

war crimes abuse of enemy soldiers or prisoners of war during wartime.

individuals – both perpetrators of abuses and their victims – are acquiring increasing status in international law. And the growing willingness of such organizations to authorize **humanitarian intervention** where there are gross abuses, and hold national leaders accountable for what they do to their own people, threatens to undermine the essential core of state sovereignty.

Thus, despite the guarantee of state sovereignty in the UN Charter, Secretary-General Kofi Annan, declared that: "As long as I am Secretary General," the UN "will always place human beings at the center of everything we do." Although "fundamental sovereignty, territorial integrity, and political independence of states" continue to be a "cornerstone of the international system," Annan continued, sovereignty cannot provide "excuses for the inexcusable."[9] Annan's view seems to place a higher value on the rights of individuals in global politics than on state sovereignty. As we shall see in the next section, this has not been the case during most of the history of global politics. International law evolved as the law of nations, not the law of individuals.

We begin this discussion of human rights in global politics by describing the Holocaust, an event so terrible that it provided an impetus to holding states and their leaders responsible for what they did to their citizens, as well as the citizens of other countries. We then examine the sources, universality, and codification of such rights since World War II, and the protections they provide individuals. Some of the controversy over human rights involves the status of women. Are women's rights also human rights? In what ways are women treated unequally? Among the most important concerns involving women are the various forms of violence practiced against them, as described in the incident that opened this chapter, and the question of whether women should enjoy reproductive independence. Finally, should we respect the role of women as defined by different cultures, or should women everywhere enjoy equality with men?

The Holocaust

During World War II, civilians experienced unprecedented atrocities and, as noted in chapter 7 (pp. 313–40), in recent decades new types of war and warfare have proliferated in which innocent civilians have become the principal victims. Despite the growing effort to hold perpetrators accountable for war crimes and **crimes against humanity** in the Nuremberg and Tokyo war crimes trials, **genocide** and **politicide** have become increasingly common in global politics in recent decades. As Table 10.1 shows, since 1945 the mass killing of innocent civilians has

humanitarian intervention intervention by states or by an IGO into the domestic politics of another state to protect people from human rights abuses or other threats to their survival.

crimes against humanity ill-treatment of civilians in wartime defined at the Nuremberg trials to include "murder, extermination, enslavement, deportation and other inhumane acts against any civilian population."

genocide the extermination of an ethnic, racial, or cultural group.

politicide mass killings in order to eradicate a group of people owing to their political or ideological beliefs.

Table 10.1 Genocides, politicides, and other mass murder since 1945.

Nation	Years of episodes since 1945	Cumulative civilian death toll	Major killers	Main divisions	Stage in 2002
AFRICA					
Burundi	1959–62 1972 1988 1993–95 1996–present	50,000 Hutus 150,000 Hutus 25,000 Hutus 50,000 Tutsis, 100,000 Hutu 2001: 5,000	Tutsi government Tutsi army Tutsi army Hutu rebels Tutsi army	Ethnic, political	Genocidal massacres
Sudan	1956–72 1983–present	2 million Nuer, Dinka, Christians, Nuba, southerners 2001: 10,000	Khartoum gov't NIF gov't, militias, rebels	Political, religious, racial, ethnic	Politicide, Genocide
Democratic Republic of the Congo	1945–60 1960–65 1977–79 1984 1994–97 1997–present	1,000s Africans 1,000s civil war 1,000s civil war 80,000 Hutus, Banyamulenge, 10,000 Hema, Lendu 2 million (civil war) 2001: 80,000	Colonial forces Rebels, army Rebels, army Kabila/Rwandan army, Ugandan, Rwandan armies, rebels, DRCongo and allied armies	Racial, colonial, economic Political, ethnic	Politicide, Genocidal massacres
Côte d'Ivoire	1998–present	100s Bambara, Senoufo, Bété, Burkinabe	Gov't police, rebels	Ethnic, national, Religious, political	Massacres
Algeria	1954–63 1991–present	160,000 OAS, Harkis, settlers 50,000 Berbers 2001: 5,000	French legions, OAS, rebels Islamic Armed Group (GIA)	Colonial Religious, political	Massacres
Liberia	1990–2000 2001–present	100,000 Krahn, Gio, Mano, etc. 2001: 1,000s	Doe gov't army, Taylor rebels Gov't, rebels	Political, ethnic	Politicide
Uganda	1972–79 1980–86 1994–present	300,000 Acholi, Lango, Karamoja 250,000 Baganda, Banyarwanda 1,000s LRA foes 2001: 100s	Amin gov't army, police Obote gov't army, police Lord's Resistance Army	Political, ethnic, religious	Massacres
Nigeria	1966–70 1972–2000 (sporadic) 2001–present	1 million Ibos Tiv, Hausa, Yoruba Ogoni, others 2001: 1,000s	Nigerian army Ethnic mobs Nigerian army, police	Political, ethnic, religious	Preparation
Zimbabwe	1982–84 1998–present	20,000 Ndebele, MDC, white farmers 2001: 100s	Gov't army 5th Brigade, ZANU-PF militias	Ethnic, political	Preparation

Table 10.1 (continued)

Nation	Years of episodes since 1945	Cumulative civilian death toll	Major killers	Main divisions	Stage in 2002
AFRICA (cont)					
Somalia	1988–present	100,000 Somalis, Isaaq clan 2001: 100s	Warlord/clan militias	Political, clan	Preparation
Sierra Leone	1991–present	100,000 (civil war) 2001: 1000s	Revolutionary United Front, other militias	Political, ethnic	Polarization
Rwanda	1959–63 1993 1994 1995–present	10,000s Tutsi 800,000 Tutsi 1,000s Hutus 2001: 100s	Hutu gov't Hutu Power gov't Interahamwe Rwandan gov't	Ethnic, political	
Congo-Brazzaville	1959–68 1997–2000	5,000 Gov't foes 1,000s (civil war)	Gov't army, police, rebels	Colonial Political, ethnic	Polarization
Central African Republic	1966–79 2001	2,000 Bokassa foes	Gov't army, police	Political, ethnic	Polarization
Ethiopia	1945–74 1974–79 1994–2000	150,000 Oromo, Eritreans, Somali 750,000 Class enemies, Oromo 10,000s (war with Eritrea)	Selassie monarchy Derg communists Army	National, religious, ethnic	Polarization
Eritrea	1960s–2000	10,000s Eritreans (independence war with Ethiopia)	Ethiopian armies, police	National, religious, ethnic	Organization
Equatorial Guinea	1975–79	50,000 Bubi, Nguema foes	Macias Nguema regime	Political, ethnic	Organization
Senegal – Casamance	1990–2001	1,000 Diola (civil war)	Senegalese army, rebels	Political, ethnic	Organization
Kenya	1952–60 1991–93	1,500 Kikuyu colonials 1,000s Nilotics	Colonial forces MauMau Kikuyu Ethnic militias	Ethnic, political	Organization
Angola	1961–62 1975–present	40,000 Kongo, 500,000 Umbundu, Ovimbundu 2001: 5,000	Colonial army Gov't, UNITA armies, allies	Colonial Political, ethnic	Organization
Chad	1965–96	10,000s southern Saras, civil war	Gov't army, Libyan army, rebels	Ethnic, racial, religious, political	Organization
Morocco – Western Sahara	1976–present	1,000s: Sahrawis	Moroccan army, Polisario rebels	Political, ethnic	Organization

Table 10.1 (continued)

Nation	Years of episodes since 1945	Cumulative civilian death toll	Major killers	Main divisions	Stage in 2002
AFRICA (cont)					
Mali	1990–93	1,000 Touaregs	Malian army, Touareg rebels	Ethnic, political	Organization
Mozambique	1975–94	1 million by MPLA, Renamo	Renamo, MPLA	Political, ethnic	Organization
Madagascar	1947–48	50,000 Malagasy nationalists	French colonial forces	National, racial, political, ethnic	Organization
South Africa	1987–96	1,000s Zulus, Xhosa, ANC	Gov't police, ethnic militias	Racial, political, ethnic	Organization
	1996–present	Boer farmers	ethnic militias		
Botswana	1990–present	100s Küng, Caprivi Namibians	Gov't police	Economic, political, ethnic	Organization
Egypt	sporadic	100s Copts	Muslim fundamentalists	Religious, political	Organization
AMERICAS					
Colombia	1948–58	150,000	Political parties	Political	Politicide
	1975–present	10,000s	Marxists, rightist death squads, drug cartels	Political, narcotics cartels	
		2001: 1,000s			
Venezuela	1945–70s,	1,000's Yanomami	Settlers, miners	Racial, ethnic	Polarization
Brazil	1945–64	300,000 Vargas foes, Indians	Gov't police, settler militias	Political, economic, racial, ethnic	Organization
	1964–65 sporadic massacres	1,000s: Kayapo, Yanomami, etc.	Settlers, miners		
Guatemala	1950s–80s	200,000 Mayans	Gov't army, death squads	Racial, ethnic, political	Organization
Cuba	1945–59	100s rebels	Rightist gov'ts	Political	Organization
	1959–present	75,000 "counter-revolutionaries"	Castro gov't		
Argentina	1976–80	20,000 leftists	Army, police	Racial, ethnic Political	Organization
Chile	1973–76	10,000s leftists	Army, police	Political	Organization
Nicaragua	1970–79	1,000s Sandinistas	Gov't army	Political	Organization
	1980–89	10,000s Contras	Sandinista army		
El Salvador	1980–92	10,000s leftists	Army, militias	Political	Organization
Paraguay	1945–62	1000s Indians	Army, settlers	Racial, ethnic	Organization
	1962–74	1000 Aché Indians	Settlers		
Mexico	1945–2001	10,000s Indians, gov't foes	Army, police	Ethnic, political	Organization
Chiapas		10,000s Mayans			

Table 10.1 (continued)

Nation	Years of episodes since 1945	Cumulative civilian death toll	Major killers	Main divisions	Stage in 2002
ASIA					
North Korea	1949–present	2 million+ 2001: 10,000s	Gov't, army, police	Political, class	Politicide
India	1947 1949–present (sporadic)	100,000s Muslims, Hindus 2001: 100s	RSS mobs Muslim mobs	National, religious, ethnic, political	Politicide, genocidal massacres
Kashmir	1947–present	2001: 1,000s	Rebels, police		
People's Republic of China	1949–77 1977–present	35 million "class enemies," religious minorities, Uighurs Muslims, Christians 2001: 1,000s	Maoist communist gov't, PRC army, Red Guards, police executions	Political, national, class, economic, ethnic, religious	Politicide
Sri Lanka	1983–present	1000s: Tamil and Sinhalese civilians 2001: 100s	Anti-Tamil mobs Tamil Tiger rebels	Ethnic, national, political, religious	Politicide, genocidal massacres
Burma (Myanmar)	1945–48 1948–62 1962–78 1979–present	1,000s rebels 15,000 rebels, govt 100,000 Shan, Muslims, Karen, Christians 2001: 100s	Burma Ind Move U Nu govt, rebels Burmese gov't SLORC gov't	Ethnic, political, religious	Politicide, genocidal massacres
Indonesia	1965 1966–present	500,000 communist 10,000s: Aceh 1,000s: Irian Jaya 1,000s: Moluccas 1,000s: Sulewesi 2001: high 1000s	Suharto gov't Suharto gov't and successors Laskar Jihad Laskar Jihad	Political, ethnic Religious, political Political, religious, ethnic, national	Politicide, genocidal massacres
Philippines	1972–present	1,000s pro-gov't officials, separatists, communists	Marxists, gov't Army, Moros, Abu Sayyef	Political, religious	Political massacres (by terrorists)
Nepal	1996–present	2,600 anti-Maoists 2001: 100s	Maoist rebels	Political	Political massacres
Afghanistan	1978–93 1993–96 1996–2001 1996–2001 2001–present	700,000 (civil war) 50,000+ 30,000 (civil war) 50,000+ Tajiks, Uzbeks, Hazara 10,000+ 2001: 10,000s	Soviets Mujahidin Warlords Taliban, Al Qaeda Northern Alliance Anti-Taliban	Political, national, religious, ethnic	Preparation
Uzbekistan Fergana Valley	1991–present	1,000s 2001: 100s	Muslim fundamentalists	Political, religious	Preparation

Table 10.1 (continued)

Nation	Years of episodes since 1945	Cumulative civilian death toll	Major killers	Main divisions	Stage in 2002
ASIA (cont)					
Pakistan	1947	61,000 Hindus	Muslim mobs	Political, national,	Preparation
East Pakistan:	1971	1.5 million Bengalis	West Pakistan army	ethnic, religious	
(now Bangladesh)		and Hindus	Army		
West Pakistan	1973–77	Sindhis			
	1978–present	2001: 100s			
Tibet	1959–1990s	1.6 million Tibetan Buddhists 2001: 100s	PRC communist Chinese gov't	National, political, religious, ethnic	Polarization
Azerbaijan	1988–94	10,000s Azeris and Armenians	Azeri and Armenian armies	Ethnic, political, religious national	Polarization
Cambodia	1945–66	5,000 king's foes	Royal gov't	Political, class,	Polarization
	1966–75	15,000 Vietnamese	Lon Nol gov't	ethnic, religious,	
	1968–75	360,000 pro-gov't	Khmer Rouge	national	
	1975–79	1.7–2.2 million class enemies, Cham Muslims, city people, Vietnamese, Eastern Zone	Khmer Rouge		
	1979–93	230,000 (civil war)	Samrin govt, KR		
	1993–present	1,000s gov't foes 2001: 100s	Hun Sen gov't		
French Vietnam	1945–53	10,000s leftists	French colonials	Political, class,	Organization
South Vietnam	1954–75	90,000 leftists	South Viet gov't	ethnic, national	
North Vietnam	1954–75	1 million class enemies, minorities	North Viet gov't		
People's Democratic Republic Vietnam	1975–present	10,000s boat people, reeducated	Vietnamese gov't		
Laos	1945–60	10,000s leftists	Royalists, French	Political, ethnic	Organization
	1960–75	100,000 anti-	Pathet Lao		
	1975–present	communists, Hmong 2001: 100s	People's Democratic Republic		
East Timor	1965–2000	200,000 Timorese	Indonesian army, militias	Political, ethnic, national, religious	Organization
EUROPE					
Russia – Chechnya	1943–57	50,000 Chechens	USSR army	Ethnic, national,	Politicide, massacres
	1994–present	2001: 1,000s	Russian Army	religious, political	
Yugoslavia: Kosovo	1998–2001	10,000 Albanian Kosovars, 100s Serbs	Yugoslav Army Kosovo Lib Army	Ethnic, religious, national, political	Polarization

Table 10.1 (continued)

Nation	Years of episodes since 1945	Cumulative civilian death toll	Major killers	Main divisions	Stage in 2002
EUROPE (cont)					
Yugoslavia		650,000 Serbs	Croatian Fascists	Political, ethnic,	Denial
Croatia	1941–45		(Ustashi)	national, religious	Polarization
Serbia, Bosnia	1941–45	100,000 Croats,	Serb Partisans		
(including		Muslims	(Chetniks)		
1941–45 relevant	1945–87	1 million Tito foes	Tito gov't		
to later conflicts)	1993–2001	1,000s dissidents	Milošević gov't		
Macedonia	1999–2001	100s Albanians, Macedonians	Albanian rebels, Macedonia gov't	Political, ethnic	Polarization
Bosnia	1992–98	200,000 Muslims, Croats, Serbs	Bosnian Serbs, Croats, Muslims	Ethnic, religious, national, political	Polarization (partition)
Georgia: Abkhasia	1993–present	100s Abkhasians 2001: under 100	Georgian army, separatist rebels	National, ethnic, political	Polarization
Northern Ireland	1964–present	3,000 Catholics, Protestants 2001: under 100	Irish Republic Army, Protestant extremists	Religious, class, political, national	Polarization
Croatia	1991–95	50,000 Serbs, Bosnian Muslims	Croat army, militias	Ethnic, national, religious, political	Organization
USSR (state no longer exists)	1945–53	15 million "class enemies"	Soviet police, army, NKVD	Political, national, ethnic, religious	Not applicable (state no
	1945–47	1 million repatriated Soviet nationals	NKVD, KGB secret police		longer exists)
	1954–91	6 million dissidents			
USSR national minorities, esp. in Crimea, Dagestan Ingushetia	1945–91	400,000 Karachai, Meshketians, Balkar Crimean Tatars, Ingushi	Red Army, Secret police		
MIDDLE EAST					
Israel–Palestine	1948–55, 1956, 1967, 1973, 1987–93	1,000s Israelis, 1,000s Palestinians 1,162 Palestinians 160 Israelis 2001: 240 Israelis	Irgun, Arab terrorists, Israeli army, police, Fatah, Hamas	National, religious, ethnic, political	Politicide, massacres
	2000–present	777 Palestinians			
Iraq	1961–present	190,000 Kurds, Shiites, Kuwaitis 2001: 1,000s	Iraqi army, presidential guard	Political, ethnic, national, religious	Denial Genocide Politicide
Turkey	1984–present	10,000s Kurds 2001: 100's	Turkish army	Ethnic, religious, national, political	Denial Preparation
Syria	1981–82	21,000 Kurds, Sunni Muslims	Syrian army, police	Political, religious, national	Polarization

Table 10.1 (continued)

Nation	Years of episodes since 1945	Cumulative civilian death toll	Major killers	Main divisions	Stage in 2002
MIDDLE EAST (cont)					
Iran	1953–78 1978–92	26,000 Shah foes 60,000 Kurds, monarchists, Bahai	Secret police, Iranian army, revolution guards	Religious, ethnic, political, national	Polarization
Cyprus	1963–67	2,000 Turks, Greek Cypriots	Greek Cypriots Turks	Political, religious, ethnic, national	Polarization (partition)
Lebanon	1974–91	55,000 Christians, Muslims, Druze	Religious militias Hezbollah, Phalangists	Religious, political	Polarization

Notes
The column entitled 'stage in 2002' ranks each situation according to its seriousness. The most serious rankings, "genocide, politicide and massacres" indicate that, as of 2002, mass killings were taking place. "Preparation" indicates that the situation was on the verge of mass killings. "Polarization" indicates that social and political cleavages were so serious that there was potential for mass killings. "Organization" means that hostile groups were being formed that might create dangerous polarization in societies.

occurred on almost every continent. There have been 28 cases of mass killings or potential mass killings in Africa, 18 in Asia, 11 in the Americas, nine in Europe, and seven in the Middle East.

The concept of genocide – the eradication of an entire people – dates back to World War II and the Nazi effort to murder all of Europe's Jewish people. Six million Jews died in the Holocaust. Before that, however, **anti-Semitism** had existed in Europe for centuries. Massacres and **pogroms** of Jews were common in medieval Europe, especially during the Crusades, and Jewish people were commonly required to live in ghettos and wear identifying marks. They were also widely forbidden to own land or enter into many professions and businesses. However, the term anti-Semitism was only coined in the late nineteenth century, an era characterized by the spread of racist theories and myths in Europe and the US. The French writer Joseph Arthur, Count of Gobineau (1816–82) was especially influential in spreading the ideas of Nordic supremacy and anti-Semitism with his treatise *On the Inequality of the Human Races*, and people such as the German opera composer Richard Wagner (1813–83) and US industrialist Henry Ford (1863–1947) were virulently anti-Semitic.

During the late nineteenth century, Austria, where Hitler was born and raised, was a hotbed of racist thinking, and Hitler made anti-Semitism the core of his brutal ideology. Dismayed by Germany's defeat in World War I, Hitler became active in Germany's right-wing anti-democratic movement in the 1920s. In *Mein Kampf* (*My Struggle*), Hitler clearly

anti-Semitism irrational dislike, prejudice, or hatred of Jews.

pogrom an organized campaign of persecution sanctioned by a government and directed against an ethnic group, especially against the Jewish population of tsarist Russia.

Did you know?

The term Holocaust, as used in the New Testament (Mark 12:33) meant "burnt offerings and sacrifices," and it came to mean "complete destruction by fire."

revealed his hatred of the Jews as well as other "non-Aryans," whom he held responsible for all of Germany's woes, especially the rise of communism and what he believed to be the "degeneracy" of modern society (see Key document: Excerpts from *Mein Kampf*).

Key document   Excerpts from Chapter 11, "Nation and Race," of Hitler's *Mein Kampf*

No more than Nature desires the mating of weaker with stronger individuals, even less does she desire the blending of a higher with a lower race, since, if she did, her whole work of higher breeding, over perhaps hundreds of thousands of years, might be ruined with one blow. . . .

If the Jews were alone in this world, they would stifle in filth and offal; they would try to get ahead of one another in hate-filled struggle and exterminate one another, in so far as the absolute absence of all sense of self-sacrifice, expressing itself in their cowardice, did not turn battle into comedy here too. . . .

With satanic joy in his face, the black-haired Jewish youth lurks in wait for the unsuspecting girl whom he defiles with his blood, thus stealing her from her people. With every means he tries to destroy the racial foundations of the people he has set out to subjugate. Just as he himself systematically ruins women and girls, he does not shrink back from pulling down the blood barriers for others, even on a large scale. It was and it is Jews who bring the Negroes into the Rhineland, always with the same secret thought and clear aim of ruining the hated white race by the necessarily resulting bastardization, throwing it down from its cultural and political height, and himself rising to be its master. . . .

The defeats on the battlefield in August, 1918, would have been child's play to bear. They stood in no proportion to the victories of our people. It was not they that caused our downfall; no, it was brought about by that power which prepared these defeats by systematically over many decades robbing our people of the political and moral instincts and forces which alone make nations capable and hence worthy of existence. . . .

No sooner did Hitler come to power in 1933 than the Nazis began to institute policies against the Jews that would culminate in the murder of millions of innocent people. Initially, Jews were dismissed from government and from schools. Then, by the 1935 Nuremberg Laws, German Jews were stripped of their citizenship, and Jews were forbidden to marry non-Jews. In 1938, additional laws were passed that made it illegal for Jews to become lawyers and for Jewish doctors to treat non-Jewish patients. The government also transferred Jewish businesses to non-Jewish Germans at prices well below their value.[10] Some of Germany's Jews emigrated, but most could not or did not, unable to comprehend what lay in store for them. Among the best known of Jewish émigrés were Albert Einstein (1879–1955), the greatest physicist of his time, who left Germany in 1933, and Sigmund Freud (1856–1939), the founder of modern psychology, who fled Vienna in 1938.

Nazi violence against the Jews began in earnest on the night of November 9, 1938, called *Kristallnacht* (Crystal Night), when the windows of Jewish-owned shops were shattered and many Jewish citizens were beaten or interned in concentration camps. With the onset of World War II and Germany's conquest of much of Europe, the Nazis began to contemplate a "final solution to the Jewish question." Accompanying the Nazi invasion of the Soviet Union in June 1941 were mobile groups called "action squads" that were organized specifically to kill Jews.

Key document   Excerpts from "Babi Yar"[11] by Yevgeni Yevtushenko

In only two days, 33,000 Ukrainian Jews were shot and buried in a ravine by the name of Babi Yar. That event is recalled in a moving poem by the Russian poet Yevgeni Yevtushenko.

No monument stands over Babi Yar.
A steep cliff only, like the rudest headstone.
I am afraid.
Today, I am as old
As the entire Jewish race itself.
I see myself an ancient Israelite.
I wander o'er the roads of ancient Egypt
And here, upon the cross, I perish, tortured
And even now, I bear the marks of nails. . .
I see myself a boy in Belostok
Blood spills, and runs upon the floors,
The chiefs of bar and pub rage unimpeded
And reek of vodka and of onion, half and half.
I'm thrown back by a boot, I have no strength left,
In vain I beg the rabble of pogrom,
To jeers of "Kill the Jews, and save our Russia!"

My mother's being beaten by a clerk. . . .
It seems to me that I am Anna Frank,
Transparent, as the thinnest branch in April,
And I'm in love, and have no need of phrases,
But only that we gaze into each other's eyes.
How little one can see, or even sense!
Leaves are forbidden, so is sky,
But much is still allowed – very gently
In darkened rooms each other to embrace.
– "They come!"
– "No, fear not – those are sounds
Of spring itself. She's coming soon.
Quickly, your lips!"
– "They break the door!" . . .
Wild grasses rustle over Babi Yar,
The trees look sternly, as if passing judgment.
Here, silently, all screams, and, hat in hand,
I feel my hair changing shade to gray.
And I myself, like one long soundless scream
Above the thousands of thousands interred,
I'm every old man executed here,
As I am every child murdered here. . . .

On January 20, 1942, at a secret conference convened by Reinhard Heydrich (1904–42), second in command of the *Schutzstaffel* (SS) (an elite unit that ran the network of German concentration camps), in Wannsee, a Berlin suburb, it was decided that the genocide of the Jews would begin. Gas chambers were built at several concentration camps in Poland including Sobibór, near Lublin; Treblinka, northeast of Warsaw; and Auschwitz in Upper Silesia. From all over Europe, Jews were shipped to these camps, where they were systematically murdered according to a program supervised by Adolf Eichmann (1906–62). In 1960, long after the war had ended, Israeli agents kidnapped Eichmann from Argentina and brought him to trial, where he was sentenced to death and executed for his crimes.

The Holocaust not only produced the term genocide but forced the world to confront the phenomenon head on. Although evidence had come to light of what the Nazis were doing, and tales of the death camps were widely circulated in the US, the USSR, and Britain during World War II, the discovery of the death camps, as well as Japanese war crimes, produced shock and horror. Thus, in 1948 the UN General Assembly passed the Genocide Convention, which made genocide a crime. Article 2 of the convention defined genocide as "acts committed with intent to destroy, in whole or in part, a national, ethnic, racial or religious group" by the following means:

(a) Killing members of the group;

(b) Causing serious bodily or mental harm to members of the group;

(c) Deliberately inflicting on the group conditions of life calculated to bring about its physical destruction in whole or in part;

(d) Imposing measures intended to prevent births within the group;

(e) Forcibly transferring children of the group to another group.[12]

President Truman submitted the Genocide Convention to the US Senate for ratification, but the Senate delayed approval until February 1986 owing to concern about its implications for US sovereignty.

The allies were determined to bring those responsible before the bar of justice. Although some have called the trials of German and Japanese war criminals "victors' justice" – punishment imposed by the war's winners on its losers – the trials marked a major step in holding individuals responsible for their acts and not permitting them to hide behind the protection of state sovereignty.

The evolution of international criminal tribunals

The idea for bringing individuals to trial for war crimes dates to the end of World War I. A provision of the Versailles Treaty called for the trial of the German Kaiser, but Wilhelm fled to Holland at the war's end, where he received political asylum and lived long enough to witness the German conquest of that country in World War II. The trials of other Germans for alleged crimes were prosecuted with little energy or success in German courts. Indeed, until 1945, only national courts could deal with alleged war criminals.

The trials of the Germans at Nuremberg after World War II were unprecedented because they were conducted before international tribunals. A special war-crimes court was established with jurists from the US, the USSR, Britain, and France. The accused were not permitted to use the traditional defense of "superior orders"; that is, they could not claim that they had been given orders by superiors to act as they had. Nor could they use the defense based "reason of state" – that is, that their actions, however regrettable, were in their country's national interests. The defendants were accused of three categories of crimes as defined by the Charter of the International Military Tribunal at Nuremberg: war crimes, crimes against humanity, and **crimes against**

crimes against peace planning, provoking, and waging an aggressive war.

Figure 10.1 Dachau concentration camp
Bundesarchiv Bild 152-27-04A

peace (see Key document: Article 6 of the International Military Tribunal at Nuremberg).

Key document   Article 6 of the International Military Tribunal at Nuremberg[13]

The following acts, or any of them, are crimes coming within the jurisdiction of the Tribunal for which there shall be individual responsibility:

(a) CRIMES AGAINST PEACE: namely, planning, preparation, initiation or waging of a war of aggression, or a war in violation of international treaties, agreements or assurances, or participation in a common plan or conspiracy for the accomplishment of any of the foregoing;

(b) WAR CRIMES: namely, violations of the laws or customs of war. Such violations shall include, but not be limited to, murder, ill-treatment or deportation to slave labor or for any other purpose of civilian population of or in occupied territory, murder or ill-treatment of prisoners of war or persons on the seas, killing of hostages, plunder of public or private property, wanton destruction of cities, towns or villages, or devastation not justified by military necessity;

(c) CRIMES AGAINST HUMANITY: namely, murder, extermination, enslavement, deportation, and other inhumane acts committed against any civilian population, before or during the war; or persecutions on political, racial or religious grounds in execution of or in connection with any crime within the jurisdiction of the Tribunal, whether or not in violation of the domestic law of the country where perpetrated.

These charges include two especially controversial aspects. First, the fact that the accused could be held accountable for crimes against humanity "whether or not in violation of the law of the country where perpetrated" meant that they could be prosecuted even where the Nazis had passed laws that permitted their acts. To some, this provision seemed to violate domestic sovereignty. The accused could also be tried for crimes against humanity that had been committed *before* the war began.

Even more controversial was the category of crimes against peace. Because going to war was regarded as a legitimate right of sovereign states, no such crime had existed before World War II. Although Germany had signed the 1928 Kellogg-Briand Pact (Pact of Paris) whose signatories condemned "recourse to war for the solution of international controversies" and renounced war "as an instrument of national policy in their relations with one another,"[14] most countries did not take it seriously. And, it had not been enforced against countries that had waged war after that date. Therefore, the law prohibiting crimes against peace and conspiracy to wage an aggressive war has an *ex post facto* (after the fact) flavor to it. In fact, no one was charged with crimes against peace without being charged with other crimes as well. The Nuremberg trials lasted almost a year. Of the 21 defendants, 11 were sentenced to death by hanging, three were acquitted, and seven went to prison. Of those sentenced to death, one, Hermann Goering (1893–1946), committed suicide just hours before he was scheduled to be executed.

The Defendants at Nuremberg. Front row, from left to right: Hermann Goering, Rudolf Hess, Joachim von Ribbentrop, Wilhelm Keitel, Ernst Kaltenbrunner, Alfred Rosenberg, Hans Frank, Wilhelm Frick, Julius Streicher, Walther Funk, Hjalmar Schacht. Back row from left to right: Karl Dönitz, Erich Raeder, Baldur von Schirach, Fritz Sauckel, Alfred Jodl, Franz von Papen, Arthur Seyss-Inquart, Albert Speer, Konstantin van Neurath, Hans Fritzsche.

Figure 10.2 The defendants at Nuremberg
Courtesy of the National Archives (National Archives Collection of World War II War Crimes Records, 1933–1950)
photo no. 238-NT-592

Accused Japanese war criminals were also made to stand trial between 1946 and 1948. Twenty-seven Japanese leaders were brought before the International Military Tribunal for the Far East in Tokyo. The court included justices from 11 allied nations that had fought Japan. According to the indictment, the defendants had promoted a scheme of conquest that

> contemplated and carried out . . . murdering, maiming and ill-treating prisoners of war (and) civilian internees . . . forcing them to labor under inhumane conditions . . . plundering public and private property, wantonly destroying cities, towns and villages beyond any justification of military necessity; (perpetrating) mass murder, rape, pillage, brigandage, torture and other barbaric cruelties upon the helpless civilian population of the over-run countries.[15]

Did you know?

Scientists in Unit 731 of the Imperial Japanese Army used human subjects, including allied prisoners of war, to test the value of diseases such as anthrax, cholera, typhoid, and plague for biological warfare, killing thousands in the process. When the war ended, the unit's commanders burned their records and destroyed their facilities. Later, at the recommendation of General Douglas MacArthur, a deal was reached with American authorities under which the scientists provided the results of their research in return for immunity from war crimes prosecution. Some of the scientists involved in Unit 731 went on to successful careers in politics, academe, and business after the war.

Seven of the accused were sentenced to death, including former Prime Minister Hideki Tojo and General Tomoyuki Yamashita (1885–1946) , who was in charge of Japan's occupation of British Malaysia and Singapore. The Yamashita case proved highly controversial because Yamashita was convicted of crimes committed by Japanese troops in the Philippines over whom he had little control. Japan's Emperor Hirohito (1901–89) was never brought to trial because the US believed that his cooperation was critical to America's postwar occupation of Japan and efforts to democratize and reform Japanese society.

The postwar trials established the principle that individuals are responsible for their acts in time of war. In this, the trials departed from the tradition of treating states as responsible for the actions of leaders. In recent decades, additional efforts have been made to reassert this principle.

Did you know?

Iva Toguri D'Aquino (1916–2006), better known as "Tokyo Rose" was tried and convicted for her acts in World War II. A first-generation Japanese-American who was raised in Los Angeles, she was visiting Japan when war broke out and was unable to return to the US. Under Japanese pressure, she renounced her American citizenship and broadcast radio propaganda to American troops in the Pacific. Convicted of treason, Mrs. D'Aquino was sentenced to ten years in prison. In 1977, she was granted a pardon by President Gerald Ford.

Figure 10.3 Hideki Tojo
Courtesy of the National Diet Library
Website

Cold War politics precluded the use of international criminal tribunals for the next several decades because the superpowers repeatedly clashed over the meaning of human rights. Yet, the precedent was revived, albeit employing national courts, during the Vietnam War, a brutal guerrilla conflict in which atrocities were committed by both sides. In 1969 US Lt. William Calley (1943–)was tried for the murder of Vietnamese civilians in the hamlet of My Lai. According to witnesses, Calley had ordered his company of soldiers to shoot everyone in the village. Calley was convicted and sentenced to life in prison in 1971, but President Richard Nixon ordered him to be placed under house arrest, where he served less than four years until his 1974 release. The Calley case created an uproar at the time. Some observers argued that Calley was being used to cover up the deeds of more senior officers and that, although US forces had committed many atrocities, he was being unfairly selected as a scapegoat.

A major step toward anchoring the principle of individual responsibility for war crimes was taken with the establishment of the International Criminal Tribunal for the former Yugoslavia (ICTY) in The Hague, the Netherlands, by a May 1993 resolution of the UN Security Council.[16] The ICTY was set up to deal with the atrocities that had been committed in the former Yugoslavia after 1991 and was the *first genuinely international tribunal* of its kind, the first to hold such trials since Nuremberg and Tokyo, and the first to invoke the Genocide Convention. The court was mandated to prosecute crimes against humanity, violations of the laws of war, and genocide committed in the several Yugoslav wars. The court, which is still operating, consists of 16 permanent judges selected by the UN General Assembly and an independent prosecutor.

Among the individuals indicted by the ICTY, the most important is Slobodan Milošević (1941–2006), former head of state of the Federal Republic of Yugoslavia. Milošević was charged with crimes committed in Kosovo, Croatia, and Bosnia that included ethnic cleansing and genocide. Regarding Kosovo, it is alleged that "forces of the FRY and Serbia acting at the direction, with the encouragement or with the support of the Accused, executed a campaign of terror and violence directed at Kosovo Albanian citizens." As regards Croatia, Milošević was said to have "participated in a 'joint criminal enterprise' between at least August 1 1991 and June 1992. The purpose of this enterprise was the forcible removal of the majority of the Croat and other non-Serb population from approximately one-third of the territory of the Republic of Croatia, an area he planned to become part of a new Serb-dominated state." Finally, in the case of Bosnia, Milošević was charged with

- Two counts of genocide and complicity in genocide.
- Ten counts of crimes against humanity involving persecution,

extermination, murder, imprisonment, torture, deportation and inhumane acts (forcible transfers).

- Eight counts of grave breaches of the Geneva Conventions of 1949 involving willful killing, unlawful confinement, torture, willfully causing great suffering, unlawful deportation or transfer, and extensive destruction and appropriation of property.
- Nine counts of violations of the laws or customs of war involving attacks on civilians, unlawful destruction, plunder of property and cruel treatment under Article 3 of the Statute.[17]

Milošević's trial began on February 12, 2002, with the prosecution completing its presentation two years later and the defense beginning to present its case at the end of August 2004. The court had made the point, clearly and forcefully, that individuals, including heads of state, must take responsibility for acts committed by themselves and their subordinates that violate international law. The proceedings were cut short by Milošević's death in 2006.

The UN authorized a second international tribunal following the 1994 genocide in Rwanda which had led to the murder of hundreds of thousands of Rwandan Tutsis. The new tribunal, the International Criminal Tribunal for Rwanda (ICTR),[18] was located in Arusha, Tanzania, and held its first trial in January 1997. Although the Arusha tribunal confronted a host of difficulties in getting underway, it managed to indict many of the Hutu leaders of the genocide. In 2002 the UN approved a Special Court for Sierra Leone, a country that suffered a ten-year civil war in which rebel forces supported by Liberia's President Charles Taylor used amputations and rape to gain control of Sierra Leone's diamond mines. This court, which began hearing cases in June 2004, combines both domestic and international law. In 2003, an agreement was reached to bring to trial Cambodia's surviving leaders of Khmer Rouge, and the trial began in August 2006.[19]

These UN-backed tribunals have been controversial, particularly in regards to their efficiency and funding. It took over two years to begin trying cases in the ICTY and ICTR, and many trials last for months. Progress also has been slowed by the failure of authorities in Republika Srpska (Serb area of the Republic of Bosnia and Herzegovina) and Serbia and Montenegro, as well as Rwanda, to act upon tribunal arrest warrants for Serbs and Tutsis. Furthermore, these ad hoc tribunals have operated at great expense, having accounted for over 10 percent of the UN's regular budget in 2000. In 2003, such concerns led the Security Council to call upon both courts to complete all trials by 2008 (at which time remaining cases will be turned over to domestic Yugoslav and Rwandan court systems).[20]

Largely in response to concerns about the efficiency and cost of ad hoc tribunals, representatives from 160 countries and some 250 nongovernmental organizations met in Rome, Italy, in 1998 to take the first step toward establishing a *permanent* international court to try individuals for war crimes, genocide, crimes of aggression,[21] and crimes against humanity. The meeting overwhelmingly approved establishing a new International Criminal Court (ICC), consisting of 18 judges elected by secret ballot and located in The Hague.[22] The ICC was born on July 1, 2002, after the treaty establishing it had been ratified by 60 states.

Unlike the tribunals set up to deal with crimes in Yugoslavia and Rwanda, the ICC is a permanent institution with global jurisdiction. Its establishment was a giant step in making individuals, including heads of state and other government officials, the subjects of international law. In fact, one difference between the ICC and the International Court of Justice is this focus on individuals. The ICC is not designed to replace national courts, but to exercise jurisdiction where states are unwilling or unable to prosecute individuals accused of "the most serious crimes of concern to the international community."[23] The ICC prosecutor can undertake independent investigations as well as accept cases put forward by member states or by the UN Security Council. Each case is tried by three judges, of whom two must agree for there to be a conviction.

The United States is a staunch opponent of the ICC. Many of the same arguments concerning sovereignty that divided the US Senate during the debate over the League of Nations (chapter 3, p. 131) were marshaled against US ratification of the ICC. Although President Bill Clinton signed the treaty establishing the ICC shortly before leaving office, he did not submit it to the Senate for ratification, and in May 2002 President George W. Bush announced that the US would not ratify the agreement. US opposition to the ICC was based on fear that politically motivated charges might be brought against American soldiers serving overseas, including those on UN peacekeeping missions. Thus, American soldiers who were accused in 2004 of mistreating Iraqi prisoners at the Abu Ghraib prison could be liable to prosecution before the ICC.

American opponents of the ICC demanded that the United States, as a permanent member of the UN Security Council, be able to veto ICC prosecutions of its citizens. Along with China, the US also opposed the court's authority to try citizens of countries that did not sign the agreement. In addition, the United States has, with great success, pressured countries to sign bilateral agreements under which they agree to exempt American soldiers from such prosecution. Unless the US changes its position toward the ICC, it is hard to imagine that the court will ever enjoy the legitimacy or resources necessary to succeed.

In April 2005, the ICC was handed its first major case by the Security Council when it was asked to investigate the massacre of black Sudanese by Arab militias called the janjaweed in the Darfur region of western Sudan. The Court was sent the names of 51 suspects by a UN commission of inquiry, along with voluminous evidence of atrocities.[24] The US abstained from voting on the resolution asking the ICC to investigate the Darfur case, thereby not preventing its passage. Acting US Ambassador to the UN, Anne W. Patterson, explained that the US remained opposed to the ICC but did not block the resolution because the resolution had explicitly granted Americans immunity from prosecution: "The United States continues to fundamentally object to the view that the ICC should be able to exercise jurisdiction over the nationals, including government officials, of states not party to the Rome Statute. . . . We decided not to oppose the resolution because of the need for the international community to work together in order to end the climate of impunity in Sudan."[25] Shortly thereafter, the ICC issued arrest warrants, its first, against the leaders of the Lord's Resistance Army, a group that has terrorized northern Uganda for two decades and kidnapped more than 20,000 children.[26]

One problem that is evident in cases such as those of Darfur and the Lord's Resistance Army is that once the ICC or any other international court initiates efforts to bring the perpetrators of crimes to justice, there is no longer any incentive for those perpetrators and their followers to cease their violence. In effect, peace becomes a hostage to justice. Should peace be sacrificed for justice, or should perpetrators be forgiven in order to facilitate a negotiated compromise that would bring peace?[27]

With or without US support, the prospect that heads of state could be hauled before a court of law for their role in human rights abuses and war crimes was reinforced by Spain's effort in 1998 to bring General Augusto Pinochet to justice for human rights abuses committed while he was Chile's dictator (1973–90). When Pinochet surrendered power, he received assurance that he would not be prosecuted in Chile for alleged crimes. However, in 1998, a Spanish judge sought Pinochet's extradition from Britain, where he was visiting for medical treatment. In 2000, the British government decided that Pinochet could legally be extradited to Spain but released him, claiming that his health was too poor to stand trial. The Pinochet precedent bodes ill for leaders who violate international law, suggesting that in the future they could be arrested and indicted for their actions when visiting other countries. This precedent is based upon the *doctrine of universal jurisdiction*, by which any court may exercise jurisdiction over crimes against humanity.

Controversy

In 1993, Belgium adopted a universal jurisdiction law that allowed victims of human rights abuses anywhere in the world to file complaints in that country. Under the law an unsuccessful effort was made to prosecute Israeli Prime Minister Ariel Sharon in 2002 for alleged crimes against humanity arising from the 1982 massacre of Palestinians by Lebanese Christian militias in the Sabra and Shatila refugee camps. The US, in particular, objected to the law for the same reason that it opposed the ICC, concern that its citizens might be prosecuted for frivolous reasons. Under intense US pressure, Belgium rescinded the law in 2003.

Just as national courts like Spain's are becoming available for holding leaders responsible for criminal acts, so US courts are being used by those seeking justice from leaders who have abused their human rights. Using an obscure eighteenth-century statute, individuals have found that they can seek civil damages against visiting leaders who have violated their civil rights. Thus, the 1789 Alien Tort Claims Act allows federal courts to try "any civil action by an alien for a tort only, committed in violation of the law of nations or a treaty of the United States,"[28] and in 1980 a Paraguyan citizen invoked the law successfully against a Paraguyan official who had killed his son (*Filartiga* v. *Pena-Irala*). Since then, several cases have been brought against visiting foreign officials. Among those who have been sued under this law are former Philippine President Ferdinand Marcos (1917–89), Bosnian-Serb leader Radovan Karadžić (1945–), and two Salvadoran generals, as well as officials from Haiti, Ethiopia, Rwanda, and Indonesia. In 2000, five Chinese democracy advocates even tried to sue former Chinese Prime Minister Li Peng (1928–) for his role in the 1989 Tiananmen Square massacre of student demonstrators in Beijing. And a suit was brought against Zimbabwe's President Robert Mugabe (1924–) during his visit to the UN in September 2000. In June 2004, the US Supreme Court upheld the Alien Torts Act (*José Francisco Sosa* v. *Humberto Alvaréz-Machain, et al.*) but warned courts not to use the law to impede the ability of congress and the president to conduct foreign policy.

In sum, the agreement of national courts to adjudicate cases of human rights violations committed against foreigners in other countries is a development that reflects the shift in international law from being a law of nations to becoming a law of people. We now turn our attention to the growing emphasis in international law on individuals and the evolution of human rights in global politics, an issue that directly challenges the prerogatives of sovereign states. In what follows, we examine the sources, content, and impact of human rights on global politics in recent decades. Few topics more vividly portray the speed and degree of change in global politics that is the theme of this book.

Individual rights under international law

Interest in human rights reflects growing recognition that individuals, as well as states, are subjects of international law. But what rights do individuals have, and what are the sources of these rights? Do states determine citizens' rights? Do individuals have intrinsic rights, even if states do not recognize them? When states and international organizations try to end other states' human rights abuses, does this violate sovereignty? In this section, we will examine each of these questions.

Sources of human rights

The idea of human rights is derived from the belief that God and nature confer dignity on all human beings. This tradition of **natural law** dates back to Greek Stoicism and Roman law, as well as to efforts during Europe's Middle Ages and Renaissance to limit rulers' arbitrary behavior. Natural law theorists like St. Thomas Aquinas argue that actual law should reflect law as it *ought* to be. Their approach was, therefore, normative rather than empirical (chapter 1, p. 14).

> **natural law** principles of law derived from nature, right reason, or God.

In practice, however, some states do not subscribe to human rights. Thus, the belief that such rights are universal cannot be based in **legal positivism**, which as we saw in the last chapter provides that states are only subject to rules they freely accept by signing a treaty or habitually acting in conformity with them. However, those who argue in favor of universal human rights claim that there are higher rules of international morality known as *jus cogens* ("compelling law"). According to what is called *normative hierarchy theory*, states must observe human rights that are international norms derived from *jus cogens*. Thus, by Article 53 of the 1969 Vienna Convention on the Law of Treaties, drawn up by the UN's International Law Commission: "A treaty is void if, at the time of its conclusion, it conflicts with a peremptory norm of general international law."[29] This convention, which has been ratified by most of the global community, would seem to accept the existence of those higher norms that constitute *jus cogens*.

> **legal positivism** a theory that international law is derived from voluntary agreements among states and that contends that states are bound only by the rules that they freely accept.

Certain precedents also allow us to argue that there is basis in custom for universal human rights. One of the most important of these in the West was the Magna Carta (Great Charter), issued by England's King John on June 15, 1215 under pressure from England's barons. The barons were in rebellion against the growing tax burden imposed by the king without their consent to support his wars in France and against the harsh methods he employed to collect those taxes.[30] In the Magna Carta, the king agreed to limit his arbitrary powers and follow existing customs. In this, he admitted that no one in England, including himself, was above the law of the land and that he and his government had to follow the laws that they made.[31]

Although the Magna Carta was issued in response to the specific grievances of England's barons, some of its clauses have evolved into general principles of US law and justice, and it granted a number of liberties that today are regarded as fundamental rights in most liberal democracies. For example, clause 20 of the Magna Carta that guarantees that "a free man shall be fined only in proportion to the degree of his offense" is the basis of the Bill of Rights' guarantee that "[e]xcessive bail shall not be required, nor excessive fines imposed, nor cruel and unusual punishments inflicted." Clauses 28, 30, and 31 of the Magna Carta are the bases of the US Fourth Amendment guarantee against "unreasonable searches and seizures." And when the Magna Carta declares that "no official shall place a man on trial upon his own unsupported statement," it is a foretaste of the Fifth Amendment right "to not commit self-incrimination."

Magna Carta's clause 39 which states that no one would be imprisoned "except by the lawful judgment of his equals or by the law of the land" is the basis for trial for jury as guaranteed by the Sixth Amendment of the Bill of Rights, as is the right of prisoners to know what offenses they are charged with, what evidence exists, and the right to confront and cross-examine the accuser. The same clause is also the basis for the concept of **due process**, under which the law must be enforced in accordance with established and well-known legal procedures, including safeguards for the protection of individual rights. In other words, accused criminals are guaranteed procedural fairness. Part of due process is the right of habeas corpus, the right of a prisoner to be brought to court to determine whether or not imprisonment is legal as determined by the facts and by the law. Thus, the Fifth Amendment of the Constitution states that no one "shall be . . . deprived of life, liberty, or property, without due process of law" by the federal government, and the Fourteenth Amendment requires that the states apply the same principle. In addition, by clause 40, King John promised not to "sell" or "deny or delay right or justice," thereby allowing all his subjects equal access to courts of law, another of the basic rights enjoyed by Americans.

Other precedents for universal human rights include the English Bill of Rights (1689), the American Declaration of Independence (1776), and the

due process in law, the administration of justice according to established rules based on the principle that no one can be deprived of life, liberty or property without suitable legal procedures and safeguards.

" I won't advise it, but you do have the right to remain silent. "

Figure 10.4 Humane interrogation
© Original artist,
www.cartoonstock.com

French Declaration of the Rights of Man (1789), all of which contain lists of basic rights. However, political philosophers such as David Hume (1711–76) and Jeremy Bentham (1748–1832) opposed basing individual rights on natural law and natural rights (calling them "nonsense on stilts"[32]), because such law lacked a factual basis. In addition, since ideas such as natural law and *jus cogens* have Western roots, they lack appeal in non-Western societies in Africa and Asia. And, as increasing numbers of non-Western states entered global society with the end of Europe's colonial empires, some were unwilling to accept rules that they had not made. Some non-Western leaders adopted a position toward human rights called **cultural relativism**, the claim that ethical beliefs are different in different cultures and that there are few, if any, universal principles of human rights.

cultural relativism the belief that ethical beliefs vary by culture and that there are few, if any, universal principles of human rights.

Controversy

Global terrorism has posed knotty problems for human rights analysts. In Afghanistan in 2001 some American citizens were captured while fighting for the Taliban *against* the US. On the one hand, such captives are not legitimate soldiers of sovereign states and therefore are not automatically protected by the laws of war. On the other hand, do those who have fought against the US and who were captured in a foreign country merit the constitutional protections of American citizens in the United States?

During the Afghanistan war, an American citizen, Yaser Esam Hamdi, was captured while fighting for the Taliban. Hamdi was labeled an "enemy combatant" by his captors and, they argued, he could be held until the war was over. Hamdi was imprisoned initially at Guantánamo Bay, Cuba until he was transferred to a naval brig at Charleston, South Carolina. Held incommunicado, at no time did he have access to an attorney.[33] Hamdi sued, claiming that as a US citizen he was entitled to habeas corpus and was being held in violation of the Fifth and Fourteenth Amendments. The government argued that Hamdi was not entitled to habeas corpus because he was captured in a combat zone on foreign soil and posed a grave threat to national security. On June 28, 2004, the US Supreme Court ruled in favor of Hamdi.

Writing for the plurality (two additional justices wrote a separate opinion), Justice Sandra Day O'Connor admitted that there were "weighty and sensitive governmental interests in ensuring that those who have in fact fought with the enemy during a war do not return to battle against the United States." However, she continued, "it is equally vital that our calculus not give short shrift to the values that this country holds dear" and that it is "during our most challenging and uncertain moments that our Nation's commitment to due process is most severely tested." In a dissenting opinion, Justice Clarence Thomas declared that Hamdi's "detention falls squarely within the Federal Government's war powers" and that the "plurality utterly fails to account for the Government's compelling interests."[34] Hamdi was released in October 2004, renounced his US citizenship, and was sent to Saudi Arabia, where he had agreed to remain for at least five years.

Although the idea of human rights originated in the West, other cultures have well-developed traditions that involve respect for the dignity of human beings. Often, rulers are obligated to give such respect in return for the obedience of those they rule. In this case, individuals do not have a fundamental entitlement to human rights. Traditions of such reciprocity exist in civilizations such as Islam, Confucian China, Africa, and Hindu India. Confucian rulers are obliged to serve the general interest of the people, but the Chinese language did not have a word for "rights" until the nineteenth century. If China's leaders did not abuse their people, it was *not* because people had inherent rights but because that was the way an enlightened Confucian ruler was expected to behave.

Does the absence of a "rights" tradition undermine the claim for universal human rights? Or is cultural relativism merely an excuse for repression? These are controversial questions. Some non-Western leaders argue that human rights should be interpreted differently in non-Western settings. They contend that the need for economic development in their countries may require limiting individual liberties.

Despite the claim of cultural relativists that human rights vary depending on cultural norms, most countries have accepted as legal obligations the growing body of human rights law that has been legislated by the UN since World War II. Let us examine the key advances in human rights law in recent decades and consider the degree to which it has been observed.

The elaboration of human rights

Human rights have been developed and expanded by means of international organizations and legal instruments. The UN Office of the High Commissioner for Human Rights (OHCHR) employs the principal UN human rights official – the High Commissioner.[35] The OHCHR accepts the idea of universal human rights, which it describes in its mission statement as "universal, indivisible, interdependent and interrelated." Lacking enforcement powers, the OHCHR depends on persuasion and observation to improve governments' human rights policies. In addition to the OHCHR, the UN has several committees to monitor compliance with human rights treaties.

There is also a UN Human Rights Council that is empowered to examine, monitor, and publicly report on human rights situations in specific countries or territories.[36] The Council replaced the cumbersome 53-member UN Human Rights Commission in 2006. The Commission had become an embarrassment because countries like Cuba and Sudan that regularly violated human rights were members. However, the reformed Council was a half-hearted compromise that fell short of the US desire to replace the old Commission with a much smaller body.[37]

The most important human rights document remains the 1948 Universal Declaration of Human Rights,[38] a comprehensive listing of civil, political, social, and economic rights. This document is not a binding treaty, but a declaration of aspirations adopted by the General Assembly that asserts "the inherent dignity and of the equal and inalienable rights of all members of the human family" as "the foundation of freedom, justice and peace in the world." In 1966, the Universal Declaration of Human Rights was reinforced by two multilateral treaties: the international covenants on civil and political rights and on economic, social and cultural rights. Collectively, the three documents are known as the International Bill of Human Rights.

One way to think about individual entitlements is to conceive of human rights as negative or positive in relationship to state actions.

negative rights the rights of individuals not to suffer from undue government interference in political, economic, and social independence and autonomy.

Negative rights are those that prevent a government from interfering with individual liberty and usually involve political and civil rights and liberties. Such rights as freedom from government regulation of speech, the press, or religion, so familiar in the US Bill of Rights, are examples of negative rights. In the West, negative rights are part of the tradition that dates back to the Magna Carta. The International Covenant on Civil and Political Rights consists largely of negative rights.

positive rights the rights of individuals to have their essential needs such as food and health seen to by government.

Positive rights, which are stipulated in the International Covenant on Economic, Social and Cultural Rights, refer to a government's obligations to provide for citizens' economic and social welfare — for example, education, employment, and health care. Socialists emphasize positive rights as prerequisites for negative rights and, in general, argue that individual liberty is meaningless without economic and social equality and security. They claim that the absence of such equality and security in the developing world constitutes what they call **structural violence** (see chapter 12, p. 580).

structural violence physical or psychological violence which is carried out, not by individuals, but by structures, for example the injustices of the worldwide trading system.

Positive rights in the West are a more recent development than negative rights, dating back to socialist proposals in the late nineteenth and early twentieth centuries and to President Franklin Roosevelt's New Deal of the 1930s. Thus, negative and positive rights are often referred to as first and second generation rights, respectively. American society still gives relatively less weight to positive than negative rights, but global norms, as reflected in the UN's Millennium Goals, are evolving toward giving both equal weight.

Other agreements supplement the three we have described, including the 1948 Genocide Convention mentioned earlier. In addition, in 1949, the four Geneva Conventions governing treatment of civilians and prisoners of war in wartime became law. In 1950, the European Convention on Human Rights was signed, and the following two years brought the Convention Relating to the Status of Refugees and the Convention on the Political Rights of Women. In ensuing years, other conventions were adopted to deal with a variety of human rights issues: the status of stateless persons (1954), abolition of slavery (1956), abolition of forced labor (1957), consent to marriage (1962), elimination of racial discrimination (1965), suppression of apartheid (1973), discrimination against women (1979), torture (1984), and the rights of the child (1989).

Since reliable enforcement mechanisms are lacking, human rights observance relies heavily on voluntary compliance by states or on the emergence of a genuine global policy consensus, as happened in the case of eliminating apartheid in South Africa. There are a variety of efforts to chart progress in human rights. For example, Freedom House, a US-based nonprofit organization, publishes an annual country-by-country evaluation of political and civil rights called the "comparative survey of freedom."[39] As of 2004, 88 countries (46 percent) with a population of almost 2.9 billion people were described as "free" (as based on a checklist of questions on political rights and civil liberties largely derived from the Universal Declaration of Human Rights), 54 (28 percent) as "partly free," and 49 (26 percent) countries with 2.4 billion people as "not free." As shown in Figure 10.5, the percentage of free countries has consistently grown in the past three decades. According to Freedom House, the highest percentage of free countries is in Western Europe (96 percent) and the lowest in North Africa and the Middle East (6 percent). Not surprisingly, freedom is closely related to wealth in global politics, and the absence of freedom and democracy is most common in poor countries.

Data from the World Values Survey suggest that democracy requires specific "social and cultural conditions" and "is not something that can be easily attained by simply adopting the right laws."[40] Surely, this is one reason for the difficulty in building democracy in Iraq after US intervention in that country in 2003.

Since 9/11, a debate has raged over whether Islam and freedom are compatible. Although the question remains unanswered, Freedom House found that only two Muslim-majority countries were free, 17 were partly free, and 28 or 60 percent remained not free. Only nine (19 percent) of Muslim-majority countries had democratic electoral systems. However, relatively fair elections have taken place recently in Iraq and Palestine, and Egypt has inched slowly toward a more open political system.

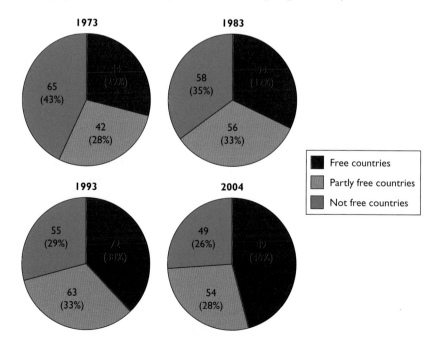

Figure 10.5 Global Trends in Freedom
Freedom House, www.freedom-house.org

Explanations of human rights abuse

What accounts for violations of human rights around the world? There is no simple answer, and several factors – economic, political, and social – probably explain why some states do not respect citizens' rights.

Among the economic factors associated with human rights abuses is a declining standard of living. Human rights abuses often occur when economic conditions deteriorate and people search for scapegoats. Political factors also play a role in explaining human rights abuses. As a rule, democratic governments have greater respect for human rights than do authoritarian regimes, though even democracies may violate citizens' rights, especially during wartime. Thus, the US violated the rights of Japanese-Americans during World War II and some Arab-Americans, as well as Iraqi and Afghan prisoners, as part of the War on Terrorism and the invasion of Iraq. Early in the American Civil War, President Abraham Lincoln authorized the suspension of habeas corpus out of concern for "public safety." The Constitution does not give this power to the president, and since only Congress is authorized to declare martial law, Lincoln's action was almost certainly unconstitutional. Nevertheless, democracies tend to have greater respect for individual rights than authoritarian governments, which often give a higher priority to state interests.

Social factors, too, are related to human rights abuses. For example, abuses tend to occur in societies that are cleaved along ethnic, racial, religious, or ideological lines, where social cohesion is fragile. By contrast, societies that are culturally homogeneous have fewer human rights violations.

Recent decades have seen the proliferation of NGOs seeking to protect and improve human rights globally.[41] Perhaps the best known is Amnesty International.

Amnesty International

Amnesty International (AI)[42] is a global organization of individuals concerned about human rights, especially the rights of political prisoners. AI was the brainchild of Peter Benenson (1922–2005), a British lawyer, who was deeply disturbed by the 1961 imprisonment of two Portuguese students who, in a Lisbon restaurant, had publicly drunk a toast to liberty in their country. In a letter to a British newspaper, *The Observer*, Benenson called for an international campaign to help "the forgotten prisoners." Forty years later, Benenson recalled what had inspired his idealistic action: "Open your newspaper – any day of the week – and you will find a report from somewhere in the world of someone being imprisoned, tortured or executed because his opinions or religion are unacceptable to his government. The newspaper reader feels a sickening sense of impotence. Yet if these feelings of disgust all over the world could be united into common action, something effective could be done."[43]

The Observer publicized Benenson's "Appeal for Amnesty 1961," in which he asked private citizens around the world to protest against the jailing of prisoners for political or religious beliefs. AI's first mission was undertaken in 1962 to Ghana, followed by a mission to Czechoslovakia on behalf of imprisoned Catholic Archbishop Josef Beran (1888–1969). From 1969, the organization became increasingly involved in drafting human rights legislation, such as the UN's 1975 Declaration against Torture, and it began to receive widespread recognition for its work. In 1974, Sean McBride (1904–88), chair of AI's International Executive Committee, was awarded a Nobel Peace Prize; AI itself was awarded a Nobel Peace Prize in 1977 for "having contributed to securing the ground for freedom, for justice, and thereby also for peace in the world."

Today, AI has over 1.5 million members in more than 150 countries headed by an International Executive Committee, with its own research council, and an International Secretariat in London, all funded by voluntary contributions. For more than four decades, AI has sought to free political and religious prisoners, assure fair trials for those arrested, eliminate torture, execution, and other harsh punishment of political prisoners, and bring those who abuse human rights to justice.

AI's principal weapons are publicity, education, and political pressure. AI staff interview victims, "adopt" prisoners whose cases AI publicizes, investigate the facts surrounding individual cases, and publish detailed reports. The group presses governments to approve human rights treaties and live up to them. AI accomplishes much of these activities by making sophisticated use of the Internet with its website at http://web.amnesty.org. In addition, AI organizes public demonstrations, sponsors letter-writing campaigns, or uses e-mail to inform others about human rights violations. The group also sponsors special entertainment events to publicize its activities and raise funds. Thus, it observed the fiftieth anniversary of the Universal Declaration of Human Rights in 1998 by collecting 13 million pledges to support the declaration and sponsoring a concert in Paris on Human Rights Day with performances by entertainers like Bruce Springsteen.

The power of publicity was illustrated by the case of Luis Basilio Rossi, a history professor at São Paulo University, Brazil, who was arrested by Brazil's military regime in February 1973. Rossi's wife managed to sneak a note to their neighbor's daughter describing what had happened, and her message was forwarded to London by one of AI's researchers in Brazil. AI quickly organized a letter-writing campaign to Brazilian officials. Some weeks later, when Rossi's wife was summoned to police headquarters, she was told: "Your husband must be a more important person than we thought because we've got all these letters from all over the world." In October, Rossi was released from prison.[44]

AI has campaigned for: the prosecution of Augusto Pinochet (1915–2006) for human rights abuses committed while he was Chile's military dictator between 1973 and 1990, establishment of the International Criminal Court, and abolition of the death penalty in the US, which, according to AI, reflects racial discrimination. In recent years, AI has lobbied to end the illegal diamond trade in failed states like Sierra Leone (2001), the global arms trade (2002), police abuse in southern Africa (2002), and political killings by Guatemala's armed forces (2002). It has also pressed Colombia to observe citizens' human rights in the midst of civil war (2002) and sought to prevent human rights abuses against Muslims since the September 11 terrorist attacks in the US (2002).[45] At present, AI is running global campaigns to end violence against women, eliminate the death penalty globally, outlaw the use of child soldiers, encourage humane treatment of employees of transnational corporations, support human rights advocates in Latin America, end the use of torture, obtain justice for the victims of genocide and ethnic cleansing, and protect the human rights of refugees and asylum seekers.[46]

In recent decades human rights law has rapidly extended into issues of gender. As we shall see, the status of women has become now a burning human rights concern, with the movement toward equal rights for men and women in much of the West clashing with opposition in Islamic and some Catholic societies.

Women's rights as human rights

Historically, women have systematically been treated as inferior to men in most societies. But is such treatment a violation of women's human rights? In an eloquent presentation to the Fourth World Conference on Women meeting in Beijing, China in 1995, first-lady Hillary Clinton (1947–) declared that the time had come for the world to hear "that it is no longer acceptable to discuss women's rights as separate from human rights." "It is a violation of human rights," she continued "when babies are denied food, or drowned, or suffocated, or their spines broken, simply because they are born girls. . . . It is a violation of human rights when women are doused with gasoline, set on fire and burned to death because their marriage dowries are deemed too small."[47]

International law now provides explicit protection for women. In 1946, the UN established a Commission on the Status of Women. In 1952 the Convention on the Political Rights of Women was adopted, and in 1957 the Convention on the Nationality of Married Women was added. The most important of such conventions was the 1979 Convention on the Elimination of All Forms of Discrimination against Women, which defined discrimination against women as "any distinction, exclusion or restriction made on the basis of sex which has the effect or purpose of impairing or nullifying the recognition, enjoyment or exercise by women, irrespective of their marital status, on a basis of equality of men and women, of human rights and fundamental freedoms in the political, economic, social, cultural, civil or any other field."[48] The Convention dealt with the legal status of women, guaranteeing them the right to vote, hold public office, and represent their countries internationally. It went on to outlaw discrimination against women in education, employment, and economic and social activities and directly addressed several highly sensitive issues, asserting that women should have rights equal to men in holding property, choice of spouse, and parenthood. Even more sensitive was the attention paid by the Convention to women's reproductive rights.

In 1983, UNESCO asked the Commission on the Status of Women to set up a procedure to review complaints of sex discrimination, and the Commission did so. A decade later the World Conference on Human Rights brought the status of women into the mainstream of human rights concerns, and the Vienna Declaration and Program of Action endorsed the appointment of a new Special Rapporteur on violence against women. Despite these advances, women are still not treated equally in much of the world. As we shall see shortly, violence toward women remains a major problem, and women's efforts to achieve equality are deeply enmeshed in questions of reproductive autonomy.

Gender (in)equality

Nowhere do women enjoy the same opportunities as do men. The UN has developed two measures of gender inequality. One, the gender empowerment measure (GEM), is based on economic participation and decision-making, political participation and decision-making, and power over economic resources. The other, the gender-related development index (GDI), combines lifespan, knowledge, and standard of living. As revealed in Table 10.2, women fared best on both measures in the West, especially in Scandinavia. The United States ranks eighth worldwide on the second index, but only fourteenth on the first.

Table 10.2 Ranking of the ten best and worst countries in gender equality

Rank	Gender-related development index (GDI) country	Gender empowerment measure (GEM) country
1	Norway	Norway
2	Sweden	Sweden
3	Australia	Denmark
4	Canada	Finland
5	Netherlands	Netherlands
6	Iceland	Iceland
7	Belgium	Belgium
8	United States	Australia
9	United Kingdom	Germany
10	Finland	Canada
168	Democratic Republic of the Congo	Democratic Republic of the Congo
169	Central African Republic	Central African Republic
170	Ethiopia	Ethiopia
171	Mozambique	Mozambique
172	Guinea-Bissau	Guinea-Bissau
173	Burundi	Burundi
174	Mali	Mali
175	Burkina Faso	Burkina Faso
176	Niger	Niger
177	Sierra Leone	Sierra Leone

UNDP, Human Development Report 2004 (New York: UN Development Programme, 2004)

Of the 177 countries examined, inequality was most pronounced in sub-Saharan Africa, also the world's poorest region. Examining individual measures, we find that the education gap is especially pronounced in Africa and the Middle East. Women in Islamic countries like Saudi Arabia account for only about 10 percent of earned income.[49] Even in the US, as shown in Figure 10.6, the wage gap between men and women in the same job did not significantly narrow until the 1990s and remains significant.

The data suggest that women suffer the greatest inequality in traditional societies where men control public life and women are relegated to the home and family. Women in traditional societies exercise little control over their own bodies, and the large numbers of women who remain pregnant throughout their fertile years become economically and politically dependent on men. In modern societies, by contrast, women have acquired greater autonomy and have assumed new roles as birth control became available.

Traditional societies that remain largely rural and agricultural value male children more than females because males work the fields, serve in

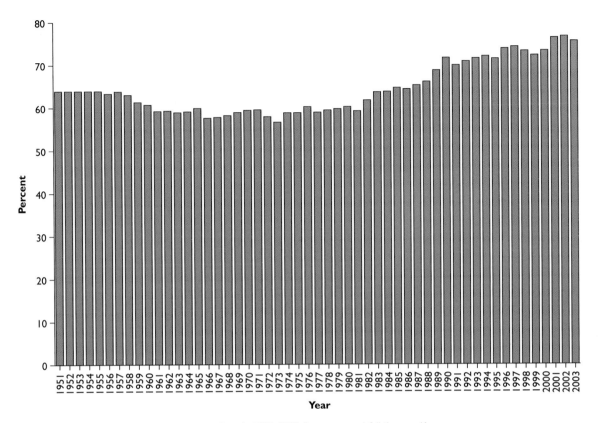

Figure 10.6 Women's earnings as a percentage of men's, 1951–2003 (for year-round, full-time work)
Reproduced by permission of National Committee on Pay Equity

the military, and provide financial security for their elders. By contrast, females are still widely considered burdensome dependents who must be fed and clothed until they are married. Such thinking has led to customs such as leaving new-born female infants outside to die; *suttee*, a former Hindu practice in India in which a widow immolated herself on her husband's funeral pyre; and selling women into sexual slavery and prostitution.

Violence against women – termed by one group "hidden gendercide"[50] – perpetuates gender inequality and reflects unequal power relations. Let us examine some of the forms that such violence takes, including domestic violence, female genital mutilation, honor killings, and rape.

Violence against women

Like inequality, violence against women exists in all societies, traditional and modern,[51] and is a major contributing factor to women's ill-health:[52]

- In Egypt 35 percent of women reported being beaten by their husband at some point in their marriage (UNICEF, 2000).
- In Bolivia 17 percent of all women aged 20 years and over have experienced physical violence in the previous 12 months (WHO, 2002).
- In Canada the costs of violence against the family amount to $1.6 billion per year, including medical care and lost productivity (UNICEF, 2000).
- In the United States a woman is battered, usually by her husband/ partner, every 15 seconds (UN Study on the World's Women, 2000).

Vigorous efforts have been made to reduce violence against women. The statute of the International Criminal Court stipulates that rape, sexual slavery, enforced prostitution, forced pregnancy, and enforced sterilization are war crimes, but this does not address the issue of domestic violence described in the statistics above.

Nor does it address the coercion and violence that occur because of the widespread preference for male children. Families in India and China use prenatal amniocentesis and ultrasound scanning to learn the gender of fetuses, thereafter aborting females.[53] "Of course," declared an Indian physician, "the women want only a boy. If we tell them it is a girl, they will feel very sorry; there will be a sadness in their face. . . . And the husband will be saying right away, 'O.K., you are going for an abortion.'"[54] Indeed, it is estimated that as many as 86.5 million females are "missing" from Asia's populations as a result of these practices. According to one study, when "one child is allowed to live while another is actively or passively killed,"[55] the result may endanger domestic and international peace and security. In fact, the "young surplus males" are becoming a source of belligerence and strife both at home and abroad.

One custom that stubbornly resists elimination is genital mutilation, which is still practiced in Africa and the Middle East where men demand that the women they marry be virgins who will not fall prey to sexual temptation afterwards. As many as 130 million women have undergone one or another version of genital mutilation, and some two million women become victims of the practice every year (see Map 10.1 and Key document: Female genital mutilation).

honor killings the murder of women for dishonoring the family or clan.

Another source of violence against women are so-called **honor killings**, in which women are murdered by members of their own family for an alleged offense that "dishonors" that family, such as sexual relationships outside marriage. According to Amnesty International, more than 5,000 honor killings occur in Pakistan, Afghanistan, Yemen, Lebanon, Egypt, Jordan, the West Bank, and Gaza every year,[56] with almost 500 such killings in Pakistan alone in 2002.[57]

Key document   Female genital mutilation: an insult on the dignity of women,[58] by Okumephuna Chinwe Celestine, a Nigerian journalist

I got the first experience of this when I was as young as eight years. Just behind my father's house in the village I heard a voice of a young girl shouting desperately for help inside a closed door. Out of curiosity and desire to render help I dashed out of my father's house and stole into the building where the save-my-soul cry was coming from.

I peeped through the keyhole. To the greatest surprise and shock of my life I saw for the first time in my life one of the evils women inflict upon themselves. This is also the greatest and most barbarous of my people's culture. . . .

It was later that I learnt that in my culture, Igbo culture of the South-Eastern Nigeria of West Africa, women are not supposed to enjoy sex as men. Sex is a prerogative that is supposed to be monopolized by men only. . . .

Reasons for that include custom and tradition, religious demand, protection of virginity, prevention of promiscuity, increasing sexual pleasure for the husband, family honor, aesthetic reasons, purification, enhancing fertility, giving a sense of belonging to a group and increasing matrimonial opportunities. . . .

Islamic attitudes toward women's sexual rights are controversial. Under Muslim law, accusations of improper sexual behavior against women require four witnesses, but if found guilty penalties are severe. In recent years, for instance, several of Nigeria's largely Muslim northern states adopted strict Islamic law, or *Sharia*, under which extramarital sex by women is punishable by death. The following are among the decisions that have been handed down under *Sharia* in that country:[59]

- *August 2000*: Amina Abdullahi was sentenced to 100 lashes for having premarital sex.
- *November 2000*: Attine Tanko was found guilty of having extramarital sex after the discovery that she was pregnant. Her boyfriend, the father of the child, was flogged 100 times and sentenced to jail time. The court ruled that after she weaned the baby she, too, would receive 100 lashes.
- *October 2001*: Convicted of adultery, Safiya Hussaini was sentenced to death by stoning, even though she alleged that she was raped by a neighbor. She was later acquitted because the law was not yet in effect when she became pregnant.
- *March 2002*: Amina Lawal Kurami was sentenced to death by stoning for bearing a child out of wedlock.

Fortunately, international protest has led Nigeria's courts to pardon or reverse the charges against those condemned to death under *Sharia* because of the potential harm to Nigeria's reputation.

Rape is one of the most brutal manifestations of male hostility toward women in wartime. From the Roman conquest of the Sabines in 290 BC to the Japanese enslavement of Korean, Chinese, Filipino, and Dutch "comfort women" in military brothels during World War II, rape has been used to affirm male domination of women. In recent decades, systematic rape was used to terrorize populations and produce ethnic cleansing in Bosnia, Kosovo, and Rwanda. More recently, rape has been used as a weapon against black African Muslims in the Darfur region of Sudan.

- In Rwanda between 250,000 and 500,000 women were raped during the 1994 genocide (International Red Cross report, 2002).[60]
- In Sierra Leone 94 percent of displaced households surveyed had experienced sexual assaults, including rape, torture, and sexual slavery (Physicians for Human Rights, 2002).
- In Iraq at least 400 women and girls as young as 8 were reported to have been raped in Baghdad during or after the war, since April 2003 (Human Rights Watch Survey, 2003).
- In South Africa 147 women are raped each day (South African Institute for Race Relations, 2003).
- In the US a woman is raped every 90 seconds (US Department of Justice, 2000).
- In Bosnia and Herzegovina 20,000–50,000 women were raped during five months of conflict in 1992 (IWTC, Women's GlobalNet #212, October 23, 2002).
- In some villages in Kosovo, 30–50 percent of women of child-bearing age were raped by Serbian forces (Amnesty International, 27 May 1999).

With the establishment of the International Criminal Court in 1998, the practice of rape in wartime was outlawed, and since then individuals have been brought to trial for rape in both the international criminal tribunals for the former Yugoslavia and for Rwanda. Still, judging from the statistics above, the crime of rape has not been eliminated in either war or non-war settings.

Ultimately, women cannot achieve equality with men until they take control of when and how they become pregnant. Reproductive issues, the topic we turn to next, are central to women's health and well-being and their possibility for economic advancement.

Reproductive independence

Women's status, especially their autonomy, health, and economic potential, is tied to contentious issues of reproduction. In the West, many women believe that questions of reproductive rights and birth control, including abortion, are equivalent to the issue of women's control over their own bodies and, therefore, their freedom. In the developing world, where maternal complications are among the leading causes of death among women aged between 15 and 44, the issue of reproductive rights is closely connected to health issues.

The 1994 UN Conference on Population and Development in Cairo, Egypt, was a major step toward recognizing women's reproductive rights as a serious issue. Birth control and abortion rights featured prominently at the conference. Declared Norway's Prime Minister Gro Harlem Brundtland (1939–), "Morality becomes hypocrisy if it means accepting mothers' suffering or dying in connection with unwanted pregnancies and illegal abortions and unwanted children."[61] The conference's final "Program of Action" proclaimed the right of women to make their own decisions about their families and recommended controlling population growth by improving the status of women's rights worldwide, especially by providing access to education and birth control.

The conference's decisions were vigorously challenged by Catholic and Islamic religious leaders. Shortly before the conference opened, a majority of the world's Catholic cardinals decried "cultural imperialism" in which "abortion on demand, sexual promiscuity and distorted notions of the family are proclaimed as human rights."[62] Muslim spokesmen also objected to some of the conference positions, even though many Muslims have long approved of birth-spacing and contraceptive use.

Women's rights received even stronger backing the next year at the UN-sponsored Fourth World Conference on Women, in Beijing, China. Some 50,000 people from over 180 countries attended the official meeting of the enormous nongovernmental organization forum trying to influence the official delegates. The resulting Beijing Declaration affirmed the rights of women to be universal human rights, stating that the "explicit recognition and reaffirmation of the right of all women to control all aspects of their health, in particular their own fertility, is basic to their empowerment."[63] Nevertheless, this right is still ignored in many parts of the world.

In the United States, domestic politics greatly affects women's reproductive rights. The abortion issue, in particular, has been highly controversial for years, with social liberals supporting a woman's rights to control her reproductive system and social conservatives opposed to abortion. In 1984 US President Ronald Reagan ended funding to international organizations that were alleged to promote abortion for birth control. The Clinton administration reversed this policy, which was again restored under President George W. Bush in 2001. Under this policy, foreign NGOs that receive funding for family planning services from the US Agency for International Development must withhold information from women about the possibility of legal abortion. Called the "Global Gag Rule" by opponents, the policy is contrary to the rights enjoyed by American women under US law.

In 2003, President Bush extended the policy to foreign NGOs that receive funding from the US Department of State. In addition, the president refused to release funds appropriated by Congress for the UN Population Fund (UNFPA), which is the world's largest provider of family planning. The president based his position on an unproven claim that UNFPA supported coerced abortion in China. The US also froze funding to the World Health Organization Human Reproduction Program. Finally, in 2004, the US stood alone at the regional planning meeting of the Economic Commission for Latin America and the Caribbean in opposing a declaration expanding access to reproductive health and the protection of women's reproductive rights.[64]

Respect for the rights of women varies globally as indicated in Map 10.1. Despite the controversies surrounding reproductive rights, great strides have been made toward gender equality in Europe and the US

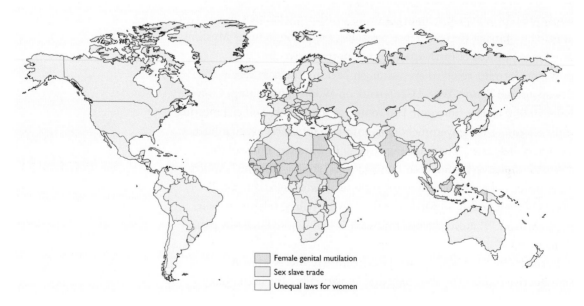

Female genital mutilation
Sex slave trade
Unequal laws for women

Map 10.1 Countries with significant gender inequality

in recent decades. Progress has been slower elsewhere, especially in Africa and the Middle East. Much of the reason for this difference is cultural and, as we shall see in the next section, opponents of gender equality argue that there should be greater respect for cultural differences.

Should women have equal rights . . . everywhere?

The claim that human rights are culture-bound appears frequently in the context of women's equality. For example, Muslims, whose practices toward women are widely criticized in the West, contend that they are victims of cultural bias. Muslims argue that instead of perpetuating inequality and repression, traditional Muslim customs toward women encourage modesty and family stability. In addition, such practices, they believe, provide women with protection. Furthermore, they note, women are treated differently in different Muslim societies, and Westerners tend to focus on extreme cases like Afghanistan's Taliban rather than more moderate Islamic regimes. Indeed, many Muslim women do not regard themselves as oppressed. A 2005 poll revealed that, although a majority of Muslim women want to be able to vote and serve in government, most regarded gender equality as an issue of Western women, while they saw other issues as more important.[65]

For the most part, arguments based on cultural relativism fall on deaf ears, especially among Western women. The Convention on the Elimination of All Forms of Discrimination against Women recognizes that cultural norms have an impact on human rights and are partly responsible for the inequalities that women face. Thus, in its preamble the convention declares the need for "a change in the traditional role of men as well as the role of women in society and in the family." Furthermore, Article 5 of the convention stresses the importance of modifying "the social and cultural patterns of conduct of men and women, with a view to achieving the elimination of prejudices and customary and all other practices which are based on the idea of the inferiority or the superiority of either of the sexes or on stereotyped roles for men and women." The 1995 Beijing Declaration also dismissed cultural relativism as a justification for gender inequality:

> The full realization of all human rights and fundamental freedoms of all women is essential for the empowerment of women. *While the significance of national and regional particularities and various historical, cultural and religious backgrounds must be borne in mind, it is the duty of States, regardless of their political, economic and cultural systems, to promote and protect all human rights and fundamental freedoms.*[66]

Theory in the real world

What do "human rights" mean in practice? What is their function in the modern world? UN declarations proclaiming the rights of women have had little real effect on their status in many countries. According to Michael Ignatieff, "rights are meaningful only if they confer entitlements and immunities on individuals; they are worth having only if they can be enforced against institutions such as the family, the state, and the church. . . . This remains true even when the rights in question are collective or group rights."[67] The authors of the Universal Declaration of Human Rights debated this very issue of the status of individuals versus collective groups like the state. In the first big argument over the content of the declaration, Charles Malik, a Lebanese diplomat and advocate of individual rights, asked: "When we speak of human rights . . . we are raising the fundamental question, what is man? . . . Is man merely a social being? Is he merely an animal?" Yugoslavia's delegate answered that "human liberty consists in 'perfect harmony between the individual and the community' and that the common interest, as embodied in the state, takes priority over individual claims."[68]

Iraqi women are asking similar questions today. Nearly one-third of Iraq's new parliamentarians are women, and while they agree that women must have a voice in Iraqi politics, they are divided on the role women should play – and the rights they should have – in Iraqi society and government. Should the new Iraqi constitution protect women's rights, or should it protect traditional community values, like Islamic law and the family? One group of women parliamentarians, the secularists, demands that women hold at least ten of 30-odd ministerial positions in the new Iraqi government and that they receive 40 percent of the party slates in future elections. These women also seek assurances that the new Iraqi constitution will respect women's rights. The other group, the traditionalists, wants assurances that Islamic law will be incorporated in Iraq's legal code and that traditional values, like the family, will be respected. These women argue that it is fair to grant women a smaller share of inheritances than men because in Iraqi society men are expected to support their poorer relatives.

They also advocate laws that would allow men to have multiple wives because women comprise a larger proportion of the Iraqi population than men and Iraqi culture disapproves of relationships outside of marriage. "We have different traditions [than the West]," says one member of this traditional group. "What is acceptable to you is not acceptable to us."[69]

Of course, it is one thing to legislate human rights protections and another to enforce them. For the most part, publicity and shame have been the most effective weapons against regimes that carry out human rights abuses. More robust approaches have had varying success. For example, President Jimmy Carter came to office in 1976 intent on raising the profile of human rights as a global issue. Although the Carter administration argued vigorously for human rights, its behavior reflected the practical necessity of compromising with unsavory reality. Thus, the Carter White House repeatedly was more willing to enforce its human rights policy on small countries like Guatemala than on large ones like Argentina, and on enemies like the Soviet Union than friends like Indonesia. Subsequent administrations played down human rights, while trying to use the issue to embarrass the USSR and China in public forums like the UN until the end of the Cold War. When, in June 1989, the administration of President George H. W. Bush confronted a dilemma following China's massacre of students demonstrating for democracy in Beijing's Tiananmen Square, it condemned China's brutality while trying not to alienate China's leaders or harming Sino-America's trade.

US efforts to influence China's authoritarian government to improve its human rights performance has had only modest success. Why? America must temper its efforts with its desire to maintain strong economic ties with China and work with China's leaders to combat global terrorism and persuade North Korea to end its nuclear weapons program. During the 1990s, US efforts to threaten China by restricting trade grew less and less credible as America's own exporters became more dependent on China's market. The dilemma sharpened during the 1990s as widespread reports circulated in the US about China's repression of ethnic Tibetans, export of goods made by prisoners, and organ transplants of executed prisoners. During the 1992 presidential campaign, candidate Bill Clinton charged President H. W. Bush with "coddling" China. However, following his election, President Clinton also tried to avoid any action that would endanger America's burgeoning trade with China, and in May 1994 he announced that trade and human rights issues would no longer be linked. "China," Clinton declared, "has an atomic arsenal and a vote and a veto in the UN Security Council. It is a major factor in Asian and global security. . . . China is also the world's fastest growing economy."[70] The outcome was one that realists approved and liberals deplored: in the case of China, economic and military power had trumped human rights idealism.

Conclusion

This chapter has examined how international law is undergoing a transformation from being the "law of nations" to becoming the "law of people." The transformation in law was sparked by the Holocaust in World War II, and the Nuremberg and Tokyo trials confirmed individual responsibility for human rights violations in wartime. These precedents have been followed by the establishment of a series of international courts, climaxing with the International Criminal Court. The chapter then traced the sources of human rights from natural to positivist law and how international institutions and nongovernmental organizations have emerged to advocate human rights, sponsor human rights legislation and end human rights abuses.

Among the most important issues in human rights today is the status of women. We have seen how violence plagues women in most societies and how cultures differ in the treatment of women. This took us to the knotty problem of whether human rights are universal or culture-bound. Should all cultures apply the same norms and rules, or should we respect differences in the way different societies regard human rights and treat their citizens?

The next chapter examines the growing importance of economics in global politics and the several theoretical approaches to the subject: mercantilism, liberalism, and Marxism. It considers the major international economic institutions – the World Bank, International Monetary Fund, and World Trade Organization – as well as the giant transnational corporations that play an ever greater role in determining our prosperity and well-being.

Student activities

Discussion and essay questions

Comprehension questions

1   What position would a legal positivist take with regard to universal human rights?
2   What are the key sources of international law?
3   How and why has international law changed in recent decades?
4   Describe the main types of violence against women. How has the global community tried to deal with this problem?

Analysis questions

5   Should national leaders be subject to indictment for violations of human rights when they are visiting other countries?
6   Are human rights universal, or are they limited by tradition and culture?
7   Do Islamic societies have the right to deny women the rights enjoyed by Western women? Should the West try to force Islamic countries to grant women these rights?
8   Evaluate the US position regarding the International Criminal Court. Should the US sign the Rome Statute?
9   Do countries have a responsibility to intervene in the domestic affairs of other countries in order to remedy human rights abuses? Explain your position.

Map exercise

Using Table 10.1, locate on a blank world map the major genocides and politicides that have taken place in global politics. What inferences can you draw from the locations of such conflicts?

Cultural materials

Among the many books written about the Holocaust, perhaps the most touching remains the diary of a 13-year-old German Jewish girl in Holland named Anne Frank. Anne and her family fled Germany in 1933 and settled in Holland. In 1942, two years after the German invasion of that country, Anne began to write her diary. Between July and August 1944, the Franks remained in hiding until they were betrayed and sent to the death camp at Auschwitz in Poland. Anne and her older sister, Margot, were then sent to the Bergen-Belsen concentration camp, where Anne died in March 1945. *The Diary of Anne Frank*, first published in 1947 and translated into English in 1952, is still widely read around the world. "In spite of everything," wrote Anne, "I still believe that people are really good at heart."

Another moving artistic memorial to the Holocaust was the 1993 film *Schindler's List* directed by Steven Spielberg. This Academy Award-winning film tells the true story of a German businessman named Oskar Schindler who saved Jewish refugees by disguising them as workers in a Polish factory.

Read *The Diary of Anne Frank* or view *Schindler's List* and reconsider the analysis questions, particularly numbers 5, 6, 7, and 9 above. Has your answer to any of these questions changed?

Further reading

Delaet, Debra, *The Global Struggle for Human Rights: Universal Principles in World Politics* (Belmont, CA: Wadsworth, 2006). Introduction to human rights in theory and practice, emphasizing the political nature of human rights issues.

Donnelly, Jack, *Universal Human Rights in Theory and Practice* (Ithaca, NY: Cornell University Press, 2002). A theory of universal human rights with implications for development and democracy, humanitarian intervention, and group rights.

Forsythe, David P., *Human Rights in International Relations* (Cambridge: Cambridge University Press, 2000). Examination of the processes and actors that create human rights norms.

Ishay, Micheline R., *The History of Human Rights: From Ancient Times to the Globalization Era* (Berkeley: University of California Press, 2004). Essential history of the development of human rights.

Maogoto, Jackson Nyamuya, *War Crimes and Realpolitik: International Justice from World War I to the 21st Century* (Boulder, CO: Lynne Rienner, 2004). Examination of the history and evolution of international criminal justice.

O'Byrne, Darren J., *Human Rights: An Introduction* (New York: Pearson, 2003). Case study approach to human rights that considers political prisoners, torture, slavery, genocide, and refugees.

Part IV
Global Issues

⊓ International political economy

Newmont Mining is the world's largest gold producer. Its Minahasa mine on Sulawesi Island dumped arsenic, mercury, and lead into Buyat Bay, contaminating the bay's fish and causing illness. Indonesia's environmental standards are lower than America's, and the company's system for disposing of tailings at Minahasa was banned in the United States under the Clean Water Act. The company denied charges that villagers' health problems were due to arsenic poisoning, claiming that their symptoms were due to poor nutrition and inadequate sanitation. In August 2004, a legal aid group brought suit against Newmont for millions in damages. Although the Minahasa mine ceased production, the company feared that local pressure could end production at its lucrative Sumbawa mine, and officials were concerned that Indonesia would then lose significant foreign investment.[1] In 2006, the company agreed to pay Indonesia $30 million in a "good-will agreement" to settle the lawsuit and escape more serious punishment.[2]

Transnational corporations (TNCs) like Newmont are key actors in the global economy, and, as we shall see, the question of whether or not they are a positive force elicits heated debate in **international political economy** (IPE). International political economy examines how economic and political forces influence each other. At its center are relationships among states, international organizations, TNCs, and the global market.

Interdependence and the globalization of markets have had a profound impact on economic affairs. Today's economic interdependence, however, is not unique and was as high or higher in the years before World War I. What is different is that since the end of the Cold War, markets have become global, and globalization has brought about an unprecedented integration of national economies, complicating countries' efforts to control their own economic fate. World trade in goods and services has soared – increasing from $6.45 trillion in 2000 to $9.12 trillion in 2004 – and interstate economic competition has grown more intense as greater

transnational corporations (TNCs) economic enterprises with operations in two or more countries.

international political economy (IPE) analysis of the relationship between economics and politics.

Figure 11.1 Security tape surrounds the Newmont Mining site in Sulawesi

© PA Photos

effort is expended in increasing productivity and efficiency. One example of this change, as we saw in chapter 5, is the economic competition flowing from China's rise as an export superpower, a destination for jobs and industries formerly located in Europe and North America, and a magnet for **foreign direct investment** (FDI).

Economic globalization reflects a revolution in economic practice caused by the proliferation of TNCs and massive flows of foreign direct investment for which they are responsible. FDI consists of corporate investments from overseas, including *greenfield investments* (investment in new production facilities or the expansion of existing facilities) that create

foreign direct investment (FDI) overseas investment in buildings, machinery, and equipment.

new production capacity, jobs, and new technology and *mergers and acquisitions* that involve the purchase of existing facilities. By contrast, **portfolio (indirect) investment** involves the purchase of stocks and bonds.

Corporate investment provides capital for countries' economic growth and jobs, and its impact grew dramatically starting in the 1980s with wider acceptance of free-market ideologies. In 2003 alone, FDI amounted to $560 billion, and there were 53 corporate mergers and acquisitions worth over $1 billion each. FDI from the US to other countries reached an all-time high of $252 billion in 2004, reflecting a desire of US-based TNCs to move operations overseas.[3] Most FDI flows into developed countries in North America, Europe, and East Asia where corporate sales and interstate trade are greatest and where corporations meet less resistance than in developing countries where fear of exploitation remains high. Currently, China, India, and the United States are the leading recipients of FDI.[4]

Since World War II trade barriers have fallen, and economic policies that include the privatization and deregulation of public industries and the free movement of capital have spread. Other changes in recent decades involve technological advances, which have increased financial flows geometrically. In the 1970s, for example, the value of foreign exchange transactions was about $18 billion a day, and by 2004 it had reached almost $1.9 trillion, increasing 57 percent since 2001.[5] Such huge flows often involve **speculation**, making financial markets volatile, and crises can unfold almost overnight.

The chapter begins by looking at the historical emergence of a global political economy. It then examines three principal theoretical approaches to IPE – **mercantilism**, **economic liberalism**, and **Marxism**. Thereafter, it turns to the major international institutions of the global economic system, and the ways they have evolved: the International Monetary Fund (IMF), the World Bank (also known as the International Bank for Reconstruction and Development), and the General Agreement on Tariffs and Trade (GATT) along with its successor the World Trade Organization (WTO). The chapter then examines the enormous and expanding role of TNCs in the global economy and concludes by discussing the future of the global economy.

The beginnings of a global economy

For much of history, there was no global financial or economic system. Trade was mainly local and limited to barter – the direct exchange of goods without money. When barter was inadequate owing to distance or

portfolio (indirect) investment foreign investment in a country's stocks and bonds.

speculation engaging in risky business transactions on the chance of a quick profit.

mercantilism belief that economic policy should increase state power by protecting infant industries, increasing imports, and restricting exports.

economic liberalism belief in free trade and the dominance of a free market.

Marxism a revolutionary doctrine based on the belief that history proceeds through class struggle.

the bulk of goods for trade, precious metals like gold and silver were used to make payment. Rome established a monetary system throughout its empire, and long after that empire collapsed its gold coins were in use and accepted everywhere. However, matters changed as Europe emerged from the Middle Ages.

Europe's medieval world evolved slowly under the influence of social and economic change. In Flanders, Belgium, and in northern Italy, self-governing city-states emerged as commerce flourished. Growing trade required money, and banks began to appear. By the end of the thirteenth century, Florence had become Europe's banking center with 80 banks, and, as money replaced barter, trade within Europe and between Europe and other lands expanded rapidly. Florentine bankers such as the Bardi and Peruzzi families established branches around Europe and became immensely rich, involved in trading grain, wool, and silk, as well as making loans and exchanging currency. The most important Florentine banking family was the Medici family, later to become the city's rulers. It was to Lorenzo the Magnificent (1449–92) that Machiavelli dedicated *The Prince*. At its height, the Medici's banking empire had nine branches outside Florence at which it made loans, kept deposits, and invested in commerce and industry. Its most important client was the pope for whom it collected tithes (10 percent of earnings) from across Europe and, under Cosimo de Medici (1389–1464), it actually managed papal finances. The Medicis also loaned money at high interest rates to Europe's rulers, especially when they wished to wage war. This was a risky proposition as the Peruzzi and Bardi families discovered when England's King Edward III (1327–77) could not repay his loans during the Hundred Years' War (1337–1453), and they were bankrupted.

As commerce spread northward from Italy, merchant groups from commercial cities along the Baltic Sea such as Hamburg and Lübeck formed the Hanseatic League, in the twelfth century. The league provided security for merchants, standardized weights and measures, and fostered trade among Russians, Scandinavians, Germans, Poles, and English. By the fourteenth century, some 60 cities were members of the league. Thereafter, the European voyages of discovery created new economic linkages with distant peoples and places, climaxing in the establishment of Europe's empires and the planting of European colonies on distant shores.

As territorial states emerged as the principal actors in global politics in the seventeenth and eighteenth centuries, they assumed the role of providing money and regulating trade. Along with the state, the first international monetary system developed. This was the **gold standard** under which gold and money were equivalent. Under this system, national

gold standard a monetary system in which the basic unit of currency is equal in value to and exchangeable for a specified amount of gold.

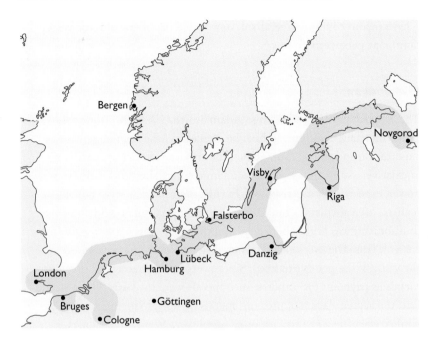

Map 11.1   The Hanseatic League, major cities, 1367

currencies were linked to gold that was kept in national treasuries. Imports were paid for with gold from countries that imported more than they exported.

As the global economy grew, several theoretical approaches evolved concerning the relationship between economics and politics, the most important of which were mercantilism, liberalism, and Marxism.

Theories of political economy

There are three dominant theoretical traditions in IPE – mercantilism, liberalism, and Marxism – each with distinctive analytic and normative elements. Mercantilism dominated economic thinking between the sixteenth and late eighteenth centuries. Although it was eclipsed by liberalism in the nineteenth century, a modern version of mercantilism still influences many countries where it takes the form of **protectionism** for home industries. The second perspective, economic liberalism or free-market **capitalism**, arose in the late eighteenth and early nineteenth centuries, spread by British and American advocates. Marxism developed in the nineteenth century as an alternative to liberalism, with socialists and communists advocating various Marxist approaches as alternatives to capitalism (a term coined by Karl Marx). However, three factors – the Cold War's end, the influence of free-market capitalists, and globalization

protectionism the practice of shielding a country's domestic industries from foreign competition by taxing imports.

capitalism an economic system based on private ownership of the means of production and a free market for exchanging goods and services.

– have made economic liberalism, now called neoliberalism, today's dominant perspective.

Mercantilism

The Scottish political economist Adam Smith (1723–90) coined the term "mercantile system," which he defined as "the encouragement of exportation and the discouragement of importation."[6] Mercantilism's normative assumption was that economic policy should advance state power, especially military power. In this, mercantilists were political realists. Mercantilists believed that the accumulation of gold and silver (bullionism) was highly beneficial and that there was little to gain from trade because the precious metals used to pay for imports balanced the value of the goods exported. Since every country accepted precious metals as payment for imports, such metals were the basis of wealth. In fact, the accumulation of precious metals by not producing any goods while increasing a country's money supply was highly inflationary.

The mercantilist era was one of warfare and colonial rivalry among Europe's powers. Spain's conquest of South and Central America in the sixteenth century and the country's access to precious metals made it the superpower of its age, and its New World colonies became part of a great imperial trade bloc. By 1600, Spain's American empire consisted of New Spain (the mainland north of the Isthmus of Panama, the West Indies, and Venezuela) and Peru (South America south of New Spain except for Brazil), each governed by one of the king's personal representatives or viceroys. Spanish mercantilism prohibited non-Spanish vessels from visiting Spanish colonies, banned foreign exports from its colonies, and required that exports to its colonies be re-exported through Spain. In addition, Spain's colonies were not permitted to manufacture a wide range of products, and until 1720 all colonial trade had to be re-exported through the city of Seville.

England's imperial ambitions brought it into conflict with Spain whose treasure ships were attacked by English privateers like Sir Francis Drake (1540–96), who in 1578 brought back Spanish treasure that earned his investors a profit of over 4,000 percent.[7] England's emergence as a naval power dates from the defeat of the Spanish Armada in 1588.

Mercantilism thrived in an era during which Europe's states, having emerged from feudalism, were centralizing their authority by building specialized bureaucracies and hiring mercenaries for their armies and navies. Like realists, mercantilists believed that the success of a state's economic policies could be judged not by the increase in *absolute* wealth, but by the increase in wealth *relative* to its rivals. States, according to mercantilists, should be self-sufficient in industries, especially those needed to wage war. To this end, leaders did not allow skilled labor to emigrate or capital goods (goods used to produce other goods) to be exported.

Mercantilists argued that **infant industries**, even if inefficient, should be nurtured and protected behind a protectionist wall even though this meant that prices for consumers would be higher and their choices fewer. Alexander Hamilton (1755–1804), America's first Secretary of the Treasury, delivered to Congress a "Report on Manufactures" (1791) in which he eloquently defended the need for such policies in the young republic: "It is well known," he argued, "that certain nations" help their manufacturers to export "particular commodities" and help "their own workmen to undersell and supplant all competitors, in the countries to which those commodities are sent." Hamilton concluded: "To be enabled to contend with success, it is evident, that the interference and aid of their own government are indispensable."[8] Hamilton, like other mercantilists, also encouraged exports to acquire precious metals and favored manufacturing over agriculture because its products could be more readily exported.

Under mercantilism, economics and politics became entwined in several ways. Mercantilists regarded **tariffs** on imports as a major source of government income to pay for arms and armies. To this end, Europe's monarchs constantly interfered in their countries' economies, regulating production of goods associated with security and establishing state monopolies, corporations, and trading companies. Mercantilists also supported imperial expansion and the establishment of overseas colonies to obtain larger markets for their products and exclusive access to critical raw materials. In addition, new manufacturing industries were granted overseas monopolies, while potential competitors were shut out of home and colonial markets by quotas, tariffs, and outright import bans.

Mercantilists also encouraged population growth to provide colonists with laborers. And they encouraged the building of merchant ships and navies, a policy beneficial to England's North American colonies because it facilitated the movement of settlers to the New World and aided trade between England and North America. During the late seventeenth century, King Louis XIV encouraged the growth of French shipping by providing public **subsidies** to shipbuilders and placing heavy duties on foreign ships entering French ports. The king's comptroller general of finance, Jean Baptiste Colbert (1619–83), placed high tariffs on foreign goods and rewarded French families for having large numbers of children. He also extended France's empire by colonizing Canada, Louisiana, and Haiti.

infant industries industries that have recently been established and are thought to have the potential to achieve comparative advantage if protected until they mature.

tariff a duty levied by a government on imported goods.

subsidies government financial contributions that benefit home industries by reducing production costs.

England's mercantilist policies played a key role in relations between the American colonies and the mother country. The 1651 Navigation Act required that goods shipped to and from English colonies or imported by England from its colonies use only English vessels manned by English crews. This law was directed principally against England's arch rival, Holland, and, later, also against France. Since England's North American colonists were regarded as English, the act benefited them at first. However, colonial unrest grew when in 1663 the Navigation Act was amended to require that colonial exports to Europe be sent to an English port before being re-exported elsewhere. The colonists also chafed under England's prohibition on the export of colonial products like tobacco and rice to countries other than England, as well as subsequent laws that prevented colonists from manufacturing products such as woolens, hats, and iron that might compete with English manufacturers.

Mercantilism began to give way to economic liberalism during the industrial revolution and Britain's conversion to free trade. The industrial revolution (*c.*1760–1830) transformed Britain from an agrarian to an industrial society. Industrialization and accompanying urbanization empowered a commercial middle class, greatly enlarged the numbers of urban workers, and advanced the spread of democracy, evidenced by Britain's 1832 Reform Act, which expanded the number of eligible British voters.

To provide cheap food for its growing urban population, Britain took a giant step away from mercantilism by revoking its Corn Laws. These had prevented the import of grain into Britain in order to protect the profits of large landowners who feared that imports would reduce prices. The laws had kept the price of bread high to the detriment of workers in Britain's expanding towns and cities, and industrialists feared that high bread prices would make them pay higher wages. Poor harvests in 1816 and 1839 pushed bread prices sky high, creating urban unrest, and producing opposition to the Corn Laws. In 1838, the liberal economist Richard Cobden (1806–65), along with the reformer John Bright (1811–89) and other advocates of laissez-faire economic principles, founded the Anti-Corn Law League. Economic depression between 1840 and 1842, followed by the 1845 failure of the Irish potato crop and the Irish famine, aided the cause of opponents of the Corn Laws, and the laws were repealed in 1846.

By 1860 Britain had become an advocate of free trade, and, for another half-century, Britain's hegemonic power was instrumental in maintaining an open trading system. Mercantalism, though, did not disappear. The United States, for example, maintained high tariff walls behind which its industries could flourish. Also, throughout the nineteenth and early twentieth centuries, the European powers maintained tariff walls around their overseas empires.

Today, an updated form of mercantalism – called neomercantilism – persists, even in the face of spreading globalization. Few countries wish to remain self-sufficient under conditions of globalization, an exception being "the hermit kingdom" of North Korea whose leaders propounded a Korean variant of self-sufficiency called *juche* (self-reliance). Today, economic nationalism often takes the form of **nontariff barriers** to trade, for example campaigns that urge citizens to buy home products, rules that require governments to purchase goods made by home industries, or rules that impose technical standards on imported manufactured products. Subsidies, tax breaks, and quotas are other ways governments protect home industries without imposing tariffs.

Occasionally, governments pressure each other to accept "voluntary" export restraints. Thus, in the 1980s the United States pressured Japan to limit the number of automobiles it exported to the US. Sometimes, countries impose complex regulations on foreign imports that require cumbersome and expensive inspection processes, justified for safety or health reasons. For example, as a result of a single case of mad cow disease (bovine spongiform encephalopathy, BSE) in the US in 2003 Japan required that every American cow slaughtered for export to Japan be individually inspected.[9]

Pockets of mercantalism exist in most countries. Fears that jobs will be lost through **outsourcing** to other countries where labor costs are low produce resistance to free trade, especially among labor unions. However, while protectionism may save the jobs of those in *inefficient* industries, other countries may retaliate with their own protectionist measures, thereby reducing exports and jobs in *efficient* industries. Mercantilism's opponents argued that, while protectionism aids particular groups, it harms society as a whole by increasing prices and reducing the range of goods available to consumers. Thus, the French economist Frédéric Bastiat (1801–50) published a satirical pamphlet entitled "The Petition." In it he ridiculed an imaginary group of candle makers who seek protection from "the ruinous competition of a rival who apparently works under conditions so far superior to our own for the production of light that he is *flooding* the *domestic market* with it at an incredibly low price; for the moment he appears, our sales cease, all the consumers turn to him, and a branch of French industry whose ramifications are innumerable is all at once reduced to complete stagnation." Their "rival" is the sun! And the candle makers want the government "to pass a law requiring the closing of all windows, dormers, skylights, inside and outside shutters, curtains, casements, bull's-eyes, deadlights, and blinds – in short, all openings,

nontariff barrier any policy that intentionally makes it more difficult or expensive for foreign competitors to do business in a country.

outsourcing subcontracting the purchase of labor or parts by a company with a source outside the company's home country.

holes, chinks, and fissures through which the light of the sun is wont to enter houses, to the detriment of the fair industries with which, we are proud to say, we have endowed the country, a country that cannot, without betraying ingratitude, abandon us today to so unequal a combat."[10]

Recent decades have witnessed growing reliance on economic liberalism and market capitalism. The next section examines the origins and major features of economic liberalism.

Economic liberalism

Unlike mercantilism, the underlying norm of economic liberalism is that economic policies serve to improve citizens' standard of living, not increase state power. In this, it is akin to political liberalism, much as mercantilism is related to realism.

As a coherent perspective, economic liberalism was pioneered by Adam Smith and the English economist David Ricardo (1772–1823). In *The Wealth of Nations* (1776), Smith argued that trade impediments impoverish rather than enrich. Precious metals, he believed, were less important than manufactured goods. Countries could achieve **economies of scale** by specializing in goods that they could produce most efficiently. Smith described how markets produce general welfare, arguing that competition among numerous self-interested individuals and enterprises benefit society as a whole because competition results in a wide choice of goods at low prices. An "invisible hand" transforms individual greed into social prosperity. However, individuals would only act this way if private property and the rights to buy and sell were assured. State interference

economies of scale reductions in unit cost owing to increased production.

Figure 11.2 Adam Smith, author of *The Wealth of the Nations*

Key document   The "Invisible Hand" from Adam Smith's *The Wealth of Nations*

As every individual . . . endeavors as much as he can both to employ his capital in the support of domestic industry, and so to direct that industry that its produce may be of the greatest value; every individual necessarily labors to render the annual revenue of the society as great as he can. He generally, indeed, neither intends to promote the public interest, nor knows how much he is promoting it. . . . [H]e intends only his own gain, and he is in this, as in many other cases, led by an invisible hand to promote an end which was no part of his intention. . . . By pursuing his own interest he frequently promotes that of the society more effectually than when he really intends to promote it.[11]

in economic life, Smith contended, should be limited to providing national defense and public goods such as roads and schools. Beyond this, government interference only distorted markets, thereby reducing social welfare.

To Smith's ideas, Ricardo added the insight that free trade was beneficial because in specializing, countries achieved a **comparative advantage**. Ricardo showed that, even if one country could produce all its goods more inexpensively than other countries, it would still be better off specializing in whichever good it could produce *most* efficiently relative to its trading partners.[12] A country might have a comparative advantage in producing a product even if it were absolutely less efficient than other countries in producing that product.

To illustrate the idea, imagine a lawyer who is opening a law office. At first, to save money the lawyer types all her own letters and documents, but, as new clients come, she realizes that to spend time with them requires a secretary. The secretary she hires actually types more slowly and makes more mistakes than the lawyer did; she is better at *both* jobs than the secretary and, therefore, has an *absolute advantage* over him in both law and typing. Nevertheless, it would be foolish for her to do all the work herself or split both jobs with her new secretary. By letting the secretary do the typing, the lawyer can see more clients, thereby focusing on her specialty. The secretary, though an inferior typist, still has a comparative advantage in typing over the lawyer. Thus, comparative advantage does *not* mean being able to do something better than anyone else. By doing her own typing, the lawyer would surrender the opportunity to earn a higher income by taking on more clients. This is called an **opportunity cost**, and, by comparing opportunity costs, one can determine in what one should specialize. In this case, the lawyer would save some money by doing her own typing but would sacrifice the opportunity of gaining much more money by accepting additional clients.

Now consider an economic example: China and the United States can both produce oranges and rice. If each devotes all available resources to oranges, the US could grow 100 tons of oranges and China could grow 200 tons. If both allocate all their resources to rice, each can produce 100 tons. Thus, China can grow oranges much less expensively than the US, and both can produce rice at the same price. China enjoys an *absolute* advantage in producing oranges, and both can grow rice equally efficiently.

Why should they trade with each other? The answer lies in opportunity costs. For the US, the opportunity cost of producing one ton of oranges is one ton of rice and vice versa. But for China the opportunity cost of producing one ton of rice is 1/2 ton of oranges, and the opportunity cost of one ton of oranges is two tons of rice. Since China has a lower opportunity

comparative advantage the ability to produce a good at lower cost, relative to other goods, compared to other countries.

opportunity cost the cost of something in terms of opportunity forgone.

cost of producing oranges, its *comparative advantage* lies in specializing in oranges and letting the US grow rice. Were China to use its limited resources to grow both, it would sacrifice the larger advantage it enjoys in growing oranges. In other words, China would incur opportunity costs – the costs of forgoing the benefits that would accrue from growing oranges. For its part, the US has a comparative advantage in growing rice. If both countries produce and consume their own oranges and rice, they will jointly produce a total of 150 tons of oranges and 100 tons of rice. But, if they trade oranges for rice at the price of one ton of oranges for 2/3 tons of rice, together they can produce 200 tons of oranges and 100 tons of rice, thereby providing more oranges at no increase in cost.

> **Key document   Excerpt from David Ricardo's *On the Principles of Political Economy and Taxation* (1817) concerning "Comparative Advantage"**
>
> Under a system of perfectly free commerce, each country naturally devotes its capital and labor to such employments as are most beneficial to each. This pursuit of individual advantage is admirably connected with the universal good of the whole. By stimulating industry, by regarding ingenuity, and by using most efficaciously the peculiar powers bestowed by nature, it distributes labor most effectively and most economically: while, by increasing the general mass of productions, it diffuses general benefit, and binds together by one common tie of interest and intercourse, the universal society of nations throughout the civilized world. It is this principle which determines that wine shall be made in France and Portugal, that corn shall be grown in America and Poland, and that hardware and other goods shall be manufactured in England.[13]

Economic liberals recognize that production cost is only one of many factors determining why people buy one company's goods rather than another's. Corporations can also improve sales by selling goods at lower prices than competitors, appealing to customers' tastes and preferences, and providing high-quality products. As a result, artificial barriers to free enterprise limit the range and quality of goods available to consumers.

Economic liberalism has evolved since Smith and Ricardo. Today's giant corporations are rivals in markets that have too few competitors to assure genuine competition based on comparative advantage. Global trade increasingly occurs within these corporations and their subsidiaries. Success is measured by the share of the global market a corporation gains

– as well as the profits it earns. Also, unlike manufacturers in earlier centuries, corporations can improve their comparative advantage by moving to countries with low labor costs or few regulations.

Today's neoliberal economists still favor free markets, the elimination of trade barriers, and minimal government interference in markets, but they see a greater role for international economic institutions than did classical economic liberals. They argue that the free movement of investment capital and labor will produce greater wealth for the world as a whole even though inefficient countries and industries may suffer. Economic efficiency, they believe, matters more than economic equality. With free markets, inequality may grow, but even the poorest become absolutely better off because of the overall growth in wealth. And concentrations of wealth provide needed capital investment for further economic growth.

Critics of economic liberalism view unregulated capitalism as a source of economic inequality and exploitation of the poor. In fact, many countries that have rapidly opened their markets to foreign exports have experienced rapidly increasing wage inequality.[14] Out of this critique emerged a third competing economic perspective: Marxism.

Marxism

Repelled by the injustices of the industrial revolution, Karl Marx (1818–83) and his associate, Friedrich Engels (1820–95), offered a revolutionary alternative to capitalism that conceived of global history as a struggle between economic classes rather than among states. In the 1848 *Communist Manifesto*, Marx and Engels warned that a "specter is haunting Europe – the specter of communism" and called on the world's workers to rise up against their capitalist oppressors. Marx's ideas were later modified by Vladimir Lenin (1870–1924), then transformed into a totalitarian ideology by Soviet dictator Josef Stalin (1879–1953), and adapted by Mao Zedong (1893–1976) to the peculiarities of rural China.

The evolution of Marxism

Marx and Engels were driven by humanitarian motives, and Europe's socialist parties later adopted many of their ideas as the bases for social reform. Marxist ideas also influenced the less-developed countries (LDCs) in the 1960s and 1970s, and although the Cold War's end made Marxism seem less relevant, a number of influential theorists continue to view problems of international political economy through Marxist lenses.

Key document   Excerpt from Friedrich Engels, *The Condition of the Working Class in England* (1845)

A pretty list of diseases engendered purely by the hateful greed of the manufacturers! Women made unfit for childbearing, children deformed, men enfeebled, limbs crushed, whole generations wrecked, afflicted with disease and infirmity, purely to fill the purses of the **bourgeoisie**. And when one reads of the barbarism of single cases, how children are seized naked in bed by the overseers, and driven with 39 blows and kicks to the factory, their clothing over their arms, how their sleepiness is driven off with blows, how they fall asleep over their work nevertheless, how one poor child sprang up, still asleep, at the call of the overseer, and mechanically went through the operations of its work after its machine was stopped; when one reads how children, too tired to go home, hid away in the wool in the drying-room to sleep there, and could only be driven out of the factory with straps; how many hundreds came home so tired every night, that they could eat no supper for weariness and want of appetite, that their parents found them kneeling by the bedside, where they had fallen asleep during their prayers. . . .[15]

bourgeoisie the middle class in society that supports the capitalist economic system.

dialectical materialism the Marxist belief that material factors constantly change owing to the tension between conflicting economic forces.

As we saw in chapter 2, Marx and Engels believed that history evolved as a result of changing modes of production that allowed some economic classes to dominate and exploit others. The historical process, Marx and Engels argued, was inevitable, evolving through the clash of opposing forces in a process called **dialectical materialism**. Economic conditions, according to Marx, determine politics, not the other way around. Each historical period featured a struggle between classes that climaxed in a violent revolution, overthrowing the dominant class. In Europe's Middle Ages, a feudal class dominated economic and political life that, Marx declared, was overthrown by a new capitalist class, which, in turn, would be overthrown by the working class as industrialization changed the way goods were produced. Revolution, Marx predicted, would first occur in advanced industrialized countries like England and Germany which had large numbers of impoverished workers. Once capitalism was overthrown and socialism established, he predicted, the historical cycle of revolutions would end, and the state would "wither away."

Under capitalism, capitalists owned the means of production, and workers owned nothing but their own labor which they sold to capitalists. Capitalists dominated the state and its coercive bureaucracies, enabling them to preserve their privileges. "Capital," Marx declared, "is dead labor, which, vampire-like, lives only by sucking living labor, and lives the more, the more labor it sucks."[16] Capitalists paid workers less than the value of their labor, keeping the difference between the cost of labor and the income derived from selling their products for themselves. Capital investment, Marx argued, would increase production but reduce wages and employment to increase profits, thereby impoverishing more and more workers. As capitalist greed impoverished more workers, economic crises would grow more frequent. In the end, the **proletariat** would rise up against its oppressors and destroy capitalism.

Following the revolution, a new system, **socialism**, would emerge in which workers would own the means of production and exchange and would be compensated justly, according to their contribution rather than according to the capitalist law of supply and demand. The wealth of society would be distributed "from each according to his ability, to each according to his work." After socialism, the world would enter the stage of **communism**, a classless society that distributed wealth "from each according to his ability, to each according to his needs."[17]

Marx's predictions of revolution remained unrealized by the time World War I began, and so in 1916, Lenin tried to explain why. Lenin argued that workers in the world's highly industrialized countries had been bought off by the fruits of overseas imperialism. Instead of becoming poorer as Marx had predicted, their poverty had been eased by profits brought home from Europe's colonial empires, earned by exploiting those whose countries had been colonized. Lenin argued that revolution would not happen spontaneously as Marx had thought. Instead, workers had to be led by a communist party, consisting of dedicated revolutionaries as the "vanguard of the proletariat." Lenin claimed that revolution had occurred in backward Russia first rather than in more highly developed countries because Russia was the "weakest link in the chain" of imperialism.

Once in power, the communist party would govern according to the principle of *democratic centralism*,[18] which meant that members could debate policies but, once a decision had been made, all were bound to obey it. Lenin used this principle to impose a dictatorship after seizing power in the Soviet Union, and he also concluded that the state would *not* wither away in the foreseeable future owing to the persistence of "class enemies." Lenin's successor, Stalin, used the same principles to justify his murderous purges and to foster **totalitarianism** in the USSR. He favored building "socialism in one country," a nationalist slogan that he used to justify the hardships suffered by Soviet citizens during the period of collectivization of agriculture and industrialization in the USSR in the late 1920s and 1930s.

Today, the only countries that call themselves Marxist are China, North Korea, Laos, Vietnam, and Cuba. Despite the end of communism as a political force, Marxian economics continues to exert influence in analyses of IPE, particularly studies of underdevelopment (see chapter 12, pp. 576–83).

proletariat the class of industrial workers who lack their own means of production and hence sell their labor to live.

socialism a political system in which the state controls the means of production and provides for citizens' basic needs.

communism a social system without states or classes featuring common ownership of property in which each member contributes according to capabilities and gains according to need.

totalitarianism a political system in which rulers control all aspects of society.

During the early twentieth century, the three IPE approaches continued to compete, but liberalism remained dominant. Although all countries retained some mercantilist practices and Marxism took hold in the USSR after 1917, free-market capitalism dominated the global economy until the disaster of the Great Depression. This event scarred a generation and threatened the survival of global capitalism.

The Great Depression

No economic event has had a more searing impact than the 1930s Great Depression. It traumatized a generation of Americans and contributed to the rise of Nazism in Germany and militarism in Japan. Beginning with the collapse of stock prices on Wall Street, the Depression spread across the United States and then across the oceans to Europe and Asia, destroying the global economic system and encouraging people to seek extreme political solutions. In this section, we will examine the causes, course, and consequences of the Depression.

The 1920s witnessed widespread prosperity, stock speculation, and an optimistic belief in ever higher living standards. "We in America today," declared President Herbert Hoover (1874–1964) on taking office in 1928, are "nearer to the final triumph over poverty than ever before in the history of any land."[19]

The Depression begins

Fueled by low interest rates, growing stock dividends and personal savings, speculation pushed stock prices well above their value as reflected by dividends or corporate earnings. People borrowed money to buy stocks and then put up these stocks as collateral to buy more (a practice called "buying on margin"). Thus, stockbrokers' loans jumped from about $5 million in 1928 to $850 million by September 1929. Fearing the "bubble" might burst, the US Federal Reserve tried to curb stock speculation by raising interest rates, thereby making it more expensive for people to borrow money. However, rising interest rates led businesses to reduce spending, production, and employment. Despite a decline in stock market prices in September, few Americans thought that the prosperity of the 1920s would end. Then, on October 24, "Black Thursday," a record number of shares changed hands. So heavy was the volume that morning that the ticker tape fell behind by an hour and a half, and many investors were in a panic to sell stock before prices fell further. Pandemonium reigned as crowds gathered outside stock exchanges, and police were dispatched to prevent violence. By early afternoon, stock exchanges in

Chicago and Buffalo had shut down, and 11 speculators had committed suicide.

A number of important bankers gathered at J. P. Morgan and Company to try and end the panic selling, and Thomas Lamont, a senior partner at Morgan, announced that: "There has been a little distress selling on the Stock Exchange . . . due to a technical condition of the market."[20] The company's floor broker and vice-president of the New York Stock Exchange Richard Whitney announced he was purchasing 10,000 shares of US Steel at 10 points above its price at that moment. The panic subsided, and stock prices stabilized on Friday and Saturday.

The worst seemed over until, on Monday October 28th, selling resumed and then, the following day, recalled as "Black Tuesday," the Dow Jones stock average dropped 13 percent. Still, false optimism remained, and John D. Rockefeller declared: "These are days when many are discouraged. In the 93 years of my life, depressions have come and gone."[21] Nevertheless, by 1932, US stocks were worth about one-fifth of their 1929 value; manufacturing had declined by over half; and unemployment had soared to over one-quarter of the workforce.[22]

The stock market crash was followed by the collapse of agricultural prices. Following World War I, America's agricultural sector largely missed out on the country's prosperity, suffering from overproduction, low prices, and excessive debt. The depression exacerbated these problems. As global agricultural markets contracted, grain prices fell, and a combination of overproduction and declining demand made it impossible for many farmers to free themselves from debt. When farmers could not repay debts, rural banks were forced to close their doors. Drought on the Great Plains added to farmers' woes, and many were forced to sell their farms and head westward to California as migrant workers. So many migrants left Oklahoma, the center of the "Dust Bowl," that migrants in general were labeled "Okies." The bumper crop of 1931 also proved disastrous for American farmers, with cotton falling to 6 cents a pound in September.[23]

In an effort to balance their budgets at a time of declining tax revenues, governments cut spending, thereby further reducing the demand for goods and causing economic contraction. Furthermore, at the time, countries were on the gold standard, forcing governments to maintain fixed exchange rates that made international trade easier by permitting currencies to be exchanged in terms of gold. To prevent the outflow of gold that would result if banks sold their currency in anticipation of its losing value, governments kept interest rates high. This made it difficult for businesses or consumers to borrow. And by raising interest rates and seeking to stop the outflow of gold, America's Federal Reserve reduced the

liquidity crisis a situation in which there is inadequate cash for the needs of consumers and businesses.

amount of money in the country available to buy goods, creating a **liquidity crisis**. Economic contraction reduced taxes further, thereby forcing governments to cut budgets still more, and individuals curbed personal spending. And, as the value of their assets — stocks and property — declined, panic-stricken people tried to take their money out of banks which ran out of cash, had to close their doors, and went under. In two days in June 1931 alone, 18 banks in Chicago collapsed.[24] By 1933, about 11,000 of America's 25,000 banks had failed, and a general decline in economic confidence led firms and individuals to hold the money they still had.

Governments and economists at the time believed that the depression would be self-correcting and opposed government intervention. According to widely held beliefs, weak businesses and banks deserved to go bankrupt and, when they did, resources would be freed up for successful enterprises. What took place, however, was a vicious cycle of higher unemployment and declining production and consumption, leading to **deflation**. Falling prices led investors to delay investing until prices had fallen lower, and consumers who had money to spend did not do so in anticipation of further price declines. Businesses let workers go because no one could buy their products, and, as unemployment grew, fewer people had money to spend.

deflation persistent decrease in consumer prices.

The Great Depression spreads

High levels of interdependence spread the depression across the Atlantic, quickly bringing down the unstable financial system that had yoked the economies of the US and Europe after World War I.

The United States had emerged from the war as the world's chief financier and the source of loans to Europe. When the US economy crashed, American investment and loans to Europe ceased, causing economic chaos across the Atlantic. The spreading economic disease became apparent with the collapse of the giant Austrian bank Creditanstalt in June 1930 in what was the largest bank failure in history. Creditanstalt had grown rapidly in previous years by taking over smaller institutions, but it had been weakened by holding several Austrian industries that had become virtually bankrupt and was surviving by virtue of short-term US, French, and British loans. When rumors circulated that the French were demanding immediate repayment of their loans, panic seized Europe's financial markets.

The world economic system was a house of cards. By the Versailles Treaty, Germany was obligated to pay war reparations to France and Britain. Reparations were used by France and Britain to repay the US for the funds they had borrowed during the war to purchase American arms. Americans then loaned the funds sent by the French and British to Germany to enable that country to pay its reparations bill. With the crash, US loans to Germany dried up; German payments to Britain and France ended; and the British and French could no longer repay their debts to the US. German efforts in 1931 to obtain a moratorium on reparations payments were supported by President Hoover, who was also willing to cancel much of France's war debt to the US. However, European delay doomed the effort to forgive German debts, and an effort to get the US Congress to declare a moratorium on Anglo-French debt repayment was defeated, thereby intensifying the financial crisis.

The countries that were most deeply in debt to the US – Germany and Britain – suffered most from the Great Depression. On September 20, 1931, Britain abandoned the gold standard, triggering panic in Europe as banks sought to sell British pounds because of the expected drop in their value. No longer would the Bank of England peg the value of its currency to gold and exchange gold for pounds at a set rate because doing so had kept the value of the pound relatively high in comparison to other currencies. This, in turn, increased British imports of relatively inexpensive foreign products and overpriced British goods abroad, thereby reducing British exports. The drop in the pound's value was costly to countries which owned British securities, especially the US and France. With no dominant great power or **hegemon** to make governments coordinate policy in the 1930s, countries tried to save themselves at one another's expense. Britain had played that role of hegemon before World War I and the US would do so after 1945, but in the 1930s, no single country could or tried to impose economic order.

In Germany, the unemployed swelled the ranks of the Nazis and intensified the search for scapegoats. Civil servants and the elderly saw their savings wiped out, and the middle class abandoned the Weimar Republic and began to endorse "extreme" solutions. Although Japan was less directly affected, it saw its export markets dry up, and unemployment grow in industries such as silk making. Without markets for its goods, the prospect of obtaining an Asian empire for raw materials and protected markets became more popular, and support for Japan's militarism grew.

As the economic crisis spread, governments tried to stabilize their economies by boosting tariffs and devaluing their currencies. These policies made imports more expensive and exports less expensive and more competitive. By boosting foreign demand for its products, a country could increase production and hire more workers, thereby improving economic conditions. However, higher tariffs and currency devaluation by one country also meant that the exports of other countries became less

hegemon a state that enjoys preponderant influence over others.

competitive and that production in those countries declined and unemployment rose. Thus, unilateral tariff increases and currency devaluations were called *beggar-thy-neighbor policies* (policies designed to improve one's own country's economic situation at the expense of that of others). Such policies triggered retaliation by others, leading to a downward spiral in trade that left all countries worse off than before.

In June 1930 the United States passed the highly protectionist Smoot-Hawley Tariff. The tariff's main purpose was to protect ailing US farmers from the competition of cheap agricultural imports and stem the decline in agricultural prices, but Congress added tariffs on industrial goods for political reasons. Other countries retaliated, resulting in a general contraction of global trade. For example, Canada, America's leading trading partner, responded by dramatically raising tariffs on US products.[25] Thus, between 1929 and 1932, the value of US exports to Europe fell from $1.3 billion to just $390 million, while European exports to the US dropped from $2.3 billion to $784 million. World trade plummeted by two-thirds.[26] As shown on Map 11.2, the depression's impact was felt all across Europe, and between 1929 and July 1932 global

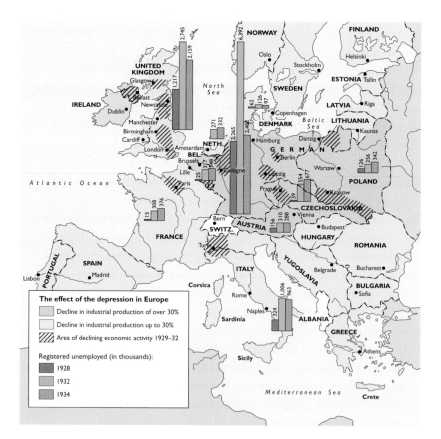

Map 11.2 The effect of the Depression in Europe

industrial production plummeted by 38 percent. Not until 1937 did global economic activity reach its 1929 level.[27]

Franklin D. Roosevelt, elected president in 1932, tried to end the depression at home with an avalanche of economic and social reforms that were collectively called the New Deal. Although the New Deal advanced the cause of social and economic justice, the Depression persisted until World War II when a combination of military conscription and wartime budget deficits ended high unemployment and raised US industrial production.

The experience of the Great Depression persuaded world leaders to establish economic institutions at the end of World War II to foster cooperation and discourage beggar-thy-neighbor policies. The next section examines the origins of these institutions – the IMF, the World Bank, and the GATT – and their evolving economic roles.

The Bretton Woods institutions

The first steps in building a new economic order were taken at the July 1944 UN Monetary and Financial Conference at Bretton Woods, New Hampshire. At Bretton Woods, the representatives of 44 governments agreed to establish the IMF to help states with short-term **balance-of-payments** problems and the World Bank to provide long-term capital for poor states. This arrangement represented a compromise between the ideas of British economist John Maynard Keynes (1883–1946), who led his country's delegation to Bretton Woods, and Harry Dexter White (1892–1948), the chief international economist at the US Treasury in 1942–44 who drafted a blueprint for the IMF. Keynes had sought a powerful independent institution to balance American economic power, whereas White sought an organization that would be an adjunct to US economic power.

balance of payments a tabulation of a country's debt and credit transactions with other countries.

The conference also wished to encourage tariff reduction to stimulate world trade, and the 1947 Havana Conference adopted the General Agreement on Tariffs and Trade (GATT) as the charter for a proposed International Trade Organization (ITO). Fearing that the ITO would undermine US sovereignty, however, Congress refused to approve its establishment. The GATT did remain as an international forum to promote tariff reduction and resolve trade disputes. The most important GATT norm was the **most-favored-nation (MFN) rule** that requires countries to treat one another equally in trade relations by according the same (lowest) tariff rates on imports from all countries. If one country reduces tariffs on the imports of another country, it has to extend those same reductions to other countries.

most-favored nation (MFN) rule requirement for countries to treat one another equally in trade relations.

The IMF, World Bank, and the GATT became the three pillars of the global economic system. And, as that system evolved, so did the role of these institutions. Today, they reflect the growing economic interdependence of actors in a globalizing world and play a key role in spreading and reinforcing neoliberal norms.

The International Monetary Fund

The IMF was established in reaction to the irresponsible monetary practices that contributed to the Great Depression and was designed to promote economic stability by regulating monetary policy and currency exchange rates – the price of a country's currency in terms of other countries' currencies. The IMF is an intergovernmental organization managed by a board of governors. Day-to-day work is handled by a managing director. The managing director is customarily nominated by the European Union, an arrangement that is balanced by the leading role of the US in selecting the World Bank president.

Stable exchange rates are important because trade and investment require payment in money. Countries have different currencies, and the currency of one country cannot be used to buy goods from another. Thus, it is necessary for importers to convert money into the currency of the countries from which they are purchasing goods. Currency is a commodity like wheat or iron, and its value varies according to supply and demand. If more people want dollars because they believe the dollar's value will rise, the demand for dollars increases, and the dollar's value relative to other currencies like the euro or the yen goes up. The result is a "strong dollar." But, if the demand for dollars declines, the dollar's relative value also declines, resulting in a "weak dollar." When the relative value of a country's currency is high, it can purchase imported goods inexpensively, and imports rise. Since a country's products are priced in its currency, a strong currency means that its exports are expensive for foreigners to buy, and exports decline. Thus, countries that want to increase exports may devalue their currency relative to other currencies.

For much of the nineteenth and early twentieth centuries, countries adhered to the gold standard, under which the value of all currencies were linked to fixed quantities of gold into which they could be converted. Since currency exchange rates were fixed, exchange rates were stable, thereby facilitating the settlement of trade transactions. After 1933, the US abandoned the gold standard in favor of a modified system in which gold coins were no longer used but gold still defined the value of the dollar at a fixed rate of $35 an ounce.

The IMF's main task was to restore a monetary system based on convertible currencies and **fixed exchange rates** and prevent competitive devaluations. However, fixed exchange rates make the system rigid. Under fixed exchange rates in which the value of world currencies was pegged to the US dollar, it was not possible for a country to devalue its currency, thereby increasing exports and reducing imports.[28] The IMF was responsible for maintaining stable exchange rates by providing short-term loans to help states manage temporary balance-of-payments deficits.[29]

The IMF's task grew more complicated and its role expanded with the collapse of part of the Bretton Woods system in the early 1970s. To combat domestic inflation and a spiraling balance-of-payments deficit during the Vietnam War, the Nixon administration decided that the United States could no longer afford to subsidize global trade by maintaining a strong dollar. On August 15, 1971, the US announced it would no longer maintain a system of fixed exchange rates and that dollars could no longer be converted into gold.

Several reasons account for this decision. First, as monetary interdependence deepened, it became difficult to coordinate so many states' policies. Transnational banks and corporations had learned how to take advantage of slight fluctuations in interest and currency rates, for example by buying "cheap" gold and selling dollars in the belief that the US dollar was overvalued, and these practices were beyond IMF control. Second, Europe and Japan had recovered the prosperity they had lost in World War II and wished to reduce their dependence on the US and pursue more independent policies. Washington had previously been willing to accept a trade deficit and an outflow of dollars to help allies recover from World War II by providing them with funds to purchase needed imports. By 1971, this was no longer necessary. Third, American spending to wage war in Vietnam and combat poverty at home had stimulated global inflation. US inflation meant that dollars were worth less, but, since adjustment was impossible with fixed exchange rates, that inflation was exported to its allies. Fourth, the Nixon administration wanted to stem the decline in the US trading position but could not do so as long as fixed exchange rates prevented the dollar's devaluation.

America's action began an era in which currencies were permitted to "float" in relation to one another, their value being determined by supply and demand. With few exceptions, **floating exchange rates** remain the norm today. With huge amounts of money racing around the world every day, maintaining monetary stability – vital for world trade – can be a serious problem.

IMF funds that are loaned to countries to bolster their currencies are provided by member states, each with a quota based on its economy's size

fixed exchange rate a system in which the value of one currency against other currencies is not permitted to vary.

floating exchange rate a system in which the value of a currency against other currencies is determined by supply and demand.

that is reviewed every five years. In addition, the IMF has a large gold reserve, over 103 million ounces that it can sell for additional funds. As of mid-2006, the IMF had available about $327 billion.[30] A country's quota determines its voting power in the organization. Thus, the world's richest countries dominate the IMF. The United States has 17.1 percent of the votes in the IMF in contrast to tiny Palau with 0.013 percent of a vote. The IMF's 11 richest members, mostly from North America and Western Europe, dominate the organization with almost 54 percent of the votes. A member's quota also determines how much it may borrow from the IMF in a financial crisis.

As guardian of the world's monetary system, the IMF monitors economic trends and advises members about monetary policies. It consults annually with members – "surveillance discussions" they are called – about their policies. The IMF also establishes standards for good financial practices that help countries avoid economic crises. Such crises occur owing to economic woes such as large and persistent budget deficits, high external debt burdens, weak or corrupt banking systems, overvalued currency, natural disasters, and domestic violence and wars. Such factors reduce exports and increase imports, thereby creating balance-of-payments deficits, loss of investor confidence, and panic selling of foreign-owned assets in the country (called "capital flight"). And speculators can undermine a country's economy overnight by massive sales of its currency, causing its value to collapse.

hard currency a currency that is generally accepted for payment of obligations.

In a crisis, the value of a country's currency drops precipitously in relation to other currencies, and the country loses **hard currency**, as people sell local currency for US dollars, European euros, Japanese yen, or gold. The outflow of hard currency and gold make it impossible for a country to pay its debts, most of which require repayment in hard currency, or to import essentials because sellers refuse payment in local currency. As local currency depreciates, people's savings and pensions may be wiped out. Economic activity comes to a standstill, causing massive unemployment, industrial closures, and widespread hardship.

austerity policies aimed at balancing the budget by reducing expenditures.

In such crises, the IMF can play a key role by lending the beleaguered country hard currency and arranging with foreign banks and other countries to reschedule its foreign debt, thereby ending financial panic. The country must pay a price for IMF loans, however, usually by agreeing to demands that its government introduce economic reforms, liberal trade and investment policies, higher interest rates to attract foreign investment, and budget **austerity** to reduce deficits, end inflation, and restore confidence in its currency. These policies reflect the "Washington Consensus," a set of neoliberal policies ranging from tax reform and lower public spending to free trade and privatization of public industries.[31] Although these policies are said to represent the thinking of the major international economic institutions about how to deal with economic crises, some have argued that no such consensus ever existed.[32]

The IMF is widely viewed as a surrogate for the wealthy countries that dominate it and as an advocate of those countries' free-market economic ideology. IMF aid has strings attached to it that entail a loss of national control over the economy. IMF conditions are stated in a Structural Adjustment Program that outlines the economic policies a country must follow to receive loans. Such programs reflect the IMF belief in economic liberalism and privatization. They often require currency devaluation to enhance exports and reduce imports, the balancing of government budgets (by raising taxes and reducing expenditures), lifting of government restrictions on imports, exports, and private investment, and ending state subsidies.

Once the IMF approves a country's reform program and makes loans to it, other countries and foreign banks are likely to reinvest in the country – a step critical to restoring economic health. Most IMF assistance is made through agreements called Stand-By Arrangements in which loans are extended at market-based interest rates. However, poor countries can obtain low-interest **concessional loans**. IMF loans peaked at almost $72 billion in 2004 but, with improved economic conditions, had dropped dramatically to about $19 billion by mid-2006.[33]

concessional loans loans at interest rates below market rates.

When South Korea was faced with a financial crisis in 1997–98, the IMF set strict conditions for lending funds. According to the IMF–Korean agreement, the rescue program's objective was to "narrow the external current account deficit to below 1 percent of GDP in 1998 and 1999, contain inflation at or below 5 percent, and – hoping for an early return of confidence – limit the deceleration in real GDP growth to about 3 percent in 1998, followed by a recovery toward potential in 1999."[34] The agreement also required South Korea to make institutional and structural reforms – such as freeing the country's central bank from political influence on the bank's lending decisions. South Korea also had to open its financial and equity markets to foreign investment, reduce restrictions on capital investment, review the way in which corporations were managed, and make it easier for Korean enterprises to shed workers.

Like others faced with IMF conditions, South Koreans regarded IMF conditions with resentment. To many, they appeared a denial of the country's sovereignty. The fact that South Korea – its government and electorate – had to accommodate its policies to the wishes of the IMF and foreign bankers seemed to mock the country's young democracy. Democracy notwithstanding, the country's economic fate was in the hands of foreigners, and its government was helpless in the face of foreign pressures.

The austerity policies imposed as IMF conditions produced added resentment. High interest rates and lower government spending meant an economic slowdown, accompanied by higher prices and spreading unemployment. Korean workers were furious at the ending of the system that had guaranteed them lifetime employment in return for loyalty to their employer. National boundaries afforded no protection against economic storms from overseas, and globalization had eroded the capacity of governments to control economic policy at home.

As in the Korean case, IMF reform programs may produce social and political unrest. Declines in government spending and the end of subsidies for staples may produce soaring unemployment, rising costs for basic goods, and reduced public services.[35] These conditions can create a powerful popular backlash against a government and the IMF, place strains on social and political institutions, and threaten political stability. As the "enforcer" of economic neoliberalism, the IMF advocates government nonintervention in economic life and greater reliance on the global market. It regards market stability as more important than a state's economic autonomy. Countries have little choice but to accept IMF conditionality – the conditions it attaches to loans – because private banks will no longer extend loans and, without IMF aid, default is the only (unpalatable) alternative.

Having examined the role of the IMF, we turn to the second institution conceived at Bretton Woods, the World Bank. The World Bank, which actually consists of several agencies, is a major source of development assistance for poor countries and increasingly has become an advocate of sustainable development.

The World Bank

The World Bank was originally established to fund post-World War II reconstruction but soon turned to the task of economic development. Like the IMF, the World Bank is an intergovernmental grouping of 184 states with a board of governors and executive board. The bank's president is by custom an American, and in 2005 President George W. Bush nominated Paul Wolfowitz, a neoconservative who, as Undersecretary of Defense, had vigorously promoted the 2003 invasion of Iraq. Accused of improper activities, Wolfowitz was forced to resign in 2007.

Funded by members' contributions and by borrowing on global capital markets, the bank makes lending decisions on market principles – loan rates and prospects for repayment. For years, the bank funded large, splashy infrastructural projects such as dams that critics argued provided little help to the very poor and ignored environmental consequences. In recent years, however, as we shall see in chapter 12, the bank has focused increasingly on the problems of the world's poorest countries and provides borrowers with low interest loans to stimulate sustainable economic development. This "mission creep" has been controversial, with critics claiming that it has expanded the World Bank's agenda until it has become unachievable.[36]

The World Trade Organization (WTO) is the third pillar of the global economic system. Like the IMF and World Bank, the WTO is responsible for a specific aspect of global economics, in this case world trade. In this role, it, too, promotes a neoliberal economic agenda, and many view it as the world's leading institutional exponent of globalization.

The General Agreement on Tariffs and Trade/World Trade Organization

Global prosperity depends on people's ability to sell their products to one another. At Bretton Woods, the GATT was negotiated to encourage a liberal trading order based on the most-favored-nation norm.[37] Keep in mind that the GATT was an agreement, or treaty, but unlike the IMF or World Bank, was not an international organization.

Over the years, a series of eight highly successful "negotiating rounds" occurred within the GATT framework to reduce obstacles to free trade. In the five decades following the GATT's establishment, world trade quintupled and average industrial tariffs fell to one-tenth their 1948 level. The early Dillon (1960–61) and Kennedy (1964–67) rounds reduced trade and nontariff barriers in key industrial sectors, and the Tokyo Round (1973–79) achieved deep tariff cuts and launched efforts to agree on controversial issues such as favorable trade treatment for poor countries.[38]

Theory in the real world

The Bretton Woods institutions were established by liberals who believed that eliminating tariffs and other trade restrictions would enhance global trade and produce greater overall wealth. This belief has been borne out by the experience of the global economy since World War II. Since the war, industrial tariffs have dropped to less than 5 percent in industrial countries, while global economic growth averaged 5 percent a year and world trade grew at an average of 8 percent a year between 1945 and 1980.

The Uruguay Round (1986–94) was more ambitious and complex than its predecessors, addressing vexing issues such as agricultural subsidies,

intellectual property property like books or computer software that reflects intellectual achievement and is protected by patents, copyrights, and trademarks.

trade in services (like insurance), rules for governing **intellectual property**, and establishment of the GATT's powerful successor, the World Trade Organization. In the end, agricultural subsidies were cut (though not as much as originally hoped), protection for intellectual property was expanded, rules for investment and trade in services were set, and tariffs were slashed by an average of one-third. But the Uruguay Round's most important accomplishment was establishment of the WTO on January 1, 1995. Since then, the WTO has become a symbol of economic globalization and a target for anti-globalization groups.

The WTO is intended to provide "the common institutional framework for the conduct of trade relations among its members." It is based on norms of non-discrimination in trade, reciprocity of access to markets, lower trade barriers, stability of trade relations, and elimination of unfair trade practices such as government export subsidies or dumping (selling below cost to capture a market). These norms and the rules governing members' trade relations are codified in a series of treaties. The GATT regulates trade in goods. The other treaties, as their names suggest – General Agreement on Trade in Services (GATS), Trade-Related Aspects of Intellectual Property Rights (TRIPS), and Dispute Settlement agreement – regulate trade in services, protect intellectual property rights, and create a dispute settlement mechanism to adjudicate trade conflicts that arise among WTO members.

Unlike the GATT, the WTO has teeth that help it enforce trade rules. It is empowered to resolve trade disputes promptly, and its decisions stand unless *all* members oppose them. GATT decisions, by contrast, could be blocked by the opposition of *any* member. Under the WTO agreement, each member agrees that its laws and practices must measure up to WTO rules and, in doing so, surrenders some control over its economic destiny.

The WTO Dispute Settlement Body is empowered to render mandatory decisions in trade disputes. If a country's policies are judged to violate trade rules, it must change those policies or the WTO may authorize countries harmed by those policies to impose retaliatory trade sanctions. American opponents of the WTO were concerned that this commitment would undermine US sovereignty and weaken US environmental and health regulations which by WTO regulations must be "least trade restrictive." The WTO can interpret such regulations as efforts to exclude exports of states with less stringent environmental or health standards.

Environmentalists argue that LDCs have lax standards and that these should be raised by banning imports from countries that do not provide environmental protection or worker safety. Environmentalists are suspicious of the WTO's dedication to environmental protection because of its decisions, including one in which the WTO declared illegal the US Marine Mammal Protection Act which banned tuna imports caught in nets that endanger dolphins. LDCs claim that environmental protests are ruses to keep out their imports and that the costs involved in improving environmental and safety standards would raise the prices of their products, making them uncompetitive. For poor countries, poverty reduction and economic growth are more important than environmental and safety concerns.

WTO rules limit states' unilateral efforts to protect their industries. The United States, for example, tries to stop foreign firms from selling goods in the US at prices below the cost of production. Such dumping is regarded as an unfair trade practice under Section 301 of the 1974 Trade Act. American firms frequently petition the government to use Section 301 against foreign competitors. Although WTO rules do not bar Section 301, they allow the WTO to determine whether it is being used as a genuine response to dumping or as a way to protect home industries.

Trade disputes are brought before the WTO's Dispute Settlement Body. The WTO first tries to settle disputes amicably. If consultations are held, they frequently produce efforts to have the dispute mediated. If they fail, the Dispute Settlement Body may establish a formal panel composed of independent experts, who are supposed to reach a decision within six months. Once a decision is reached, the loser may appeal to a standing WTO Appellate Body whose decision is final. Once a decision is reached, the panel indicates the steps a country must take to end its violation of WTO rules. If the country fails to comply, the state that brought the complaint may ask for compensation.

The WTO has reviewed a wide variety of complaints, though trade in agriculture has generated the most disputes.[39] Most have been brought by developed countries against one another or against LDCs, but the LDCs are also using the WTO to correct what they view as trade injustices by rich states. Between January 2005 and July 2006, 24 cases were brought to the WTO. Six were brought against the United States involving a range of trading partners and issues. Ecuador and Mexico, for example, brought complaints to the WTO about US anti-dumping duties on Ecuadoran shrimp and Mexican stainless steel. For its part, the US initiated four complaints in the same period about such matters as Turkish barriers to American rice exports and Chinese barriers to American automobile parts.[40]

The United States has frequently used the WTO, and, along with the EU and Japan, has been a frequent target of others' complaints. Let us examine a few celebrated cases to see the kind of disputes that lead countries to ask the WTO for relief. The first involves a complaint against the United States.

The steel case

In March 2002, President George W. Bush imposed tariffs of about 30 percent on a variety of imported steel products in order to protect the troubled US steel industry from cheap imports and provide political cover for Republican candidates in steel-producing states in upcoming congressional elections. The US tariff affected steel imports from the EU, Brazil, South Korea, and Japan. During the first year of the tariffs, EU steel exports to the US plummeted by 37 percent.

In July 2003, the WTO ruled against the United States, declaring that Washington had failed to show that its steel industry was endangered by foreign imports,[41] and the EU announced it was ready to impose some $2.2 billion in retaliatory duties on US exports – for example on Florida oranges – carefully selected to cause harm in states critical to President Bush's 2004 re-election. Following a US appeal, the WTO Appellate Body upheld the ruling, and the Bush administration grudgingly agreed to abide by it.[42]

Genetically modified crops

A second case illustrates the difficulty in distinguishing between efforts to maintain health and safety standards and policies designed to protect domestic industry. Since its inception, the WTO has grappled with the vexing issue of whether national environmental and safety regulations are imposed for legitimate ends or whether they serve as subtle but illegal barriers to free trade. Only a fine line separates the two. GATT rules allow countries to impose rules for safety and environmental protection as long as they "are not applied in a manner which would constitute a means of arbitrary or unjustifiable discrimination between countries where the same conditions prevail, or a disguised restriction on international trade."[43]

In May 2003, the United States complained to the WTO that a 1998 EU moratorium on the import of genetically modified (GM) food violated trade rules because there was no evidence that such foods were harmful. Under the moratorium, the EU refused to import GM foods until new regulations for labeling and tracing the origins of such foods were in place. Owing to pressures from American farmers and their congressional representatives, the US decided to pursue the matter in the WTO even though it threatened to worsen US–European relations already strained by America's war in Iraq.

Genetically modified food is common in the US and elsewhere because GM crops reduce the need for pesticides and herbicides while providing products with features that consumers find appealing. Most US soybeans and cotton and much of its corn are grown from genetically modified seeds. Many Europeans, however, denouncing what they call "Frankenfood" and claiming that it is potentially dangerous to health and biodiversity, have tried to keep it off the market and have US food exports clearly labeled if it contains more than 1 percent GM foods. American farmers and producers of GM seeds, like Monsanto, lobbied vigorously for action to pry open European markets, arguing that labeling is expensive and unfairly implies that there is something unsafe about the product.[44] In 2006, a WTO panel declared that the EU had illegally banned some GM products.[45]

Controversy

The introduction of genetically modified crops and animals has produced passionate debate over their relative merits and costs. Those who favor GM see it as a means of reducing the cost and enhancing the quality and quantity of food, thus increasing food security. Genetic modification, in their view, improves the quality of crops and enhances their resistance to disease and pests. Moreover, GM animals are more productive and healthier, and the environment benefits from decreased use of herbicides and pesticides and from conservation of water and soil. GM opponents fear its impact on human health – for example the possibility that GM products may trigger new allergies. They also fear that GM crops and animals may crowd out existing species, reducing biodiversity and increasing the possibility of disaster if disease afflicts surviving species.

Figure 11.3 Protest in Britain against the World Trade Organization's decision on genetically modified foods

Courtesy of FoE Europe

No global trade round has been completed since 1994. A new round was initiated at a WTO conference in Doha, Qatar in 2001. There, it was agreed that negotiations would focus on freeing trade in agriculture and services, both contentious issues in global trade, with an eye toward reaching agreement by 2005. However, as we shall see in chapter 13 (p. 612), agreement, which requires consensus in the WTO, has been elusive owing to acrimonious conflict over reducing agricultural subsidies in the developed world to enable LDCs to sell their products overseas. Efforts to reach agreement collapsed in July 2006 as the US and the EU failed to agree over agricultural subsidies and developing countries like Brazil refused to open their markets to developed countries' manufactured goods and services until Western markets were opened to their agricultural goods.

Although US Trade Representative Susan Schwab reaffirmed America's commitment to a successful outcome, legislation known as Presidential Trade Authority or "fast track" that gives the president authority to negotiate trade agreements to which congress cannot add amendments expired on June 30, 2007, thereby reducing the prospect for US approval of any deal.

This examination of the GATT and the WTO completes our review of the three institutional pillars of the global economic system. Will these pillars remaining standing, however, if the United States withdraws its support of them?

Hegemonic stability

hegemonic stability theory
the theory that global order results from the domination of a single great power and that for the order to be maintained this dominance must continue.

According to what is called **hegemonic stability theory**, the global economy and the institutions that sustain it require the support of a single powerful state or hegemon to prevent countries from pursuing selfish economic interests. By this theory, which is rooted in realism, only a hegemon can promote and enforce the rules of the global trade and monetary systems, and, in doing so, it benefits both itself and provides the world with a collective good. The economic order can survive only so long as a hegemon, like Britain in the nineteenth century or the United States today, finds that the system is in its interest and sustains it by providing leadership. When no hegemon is willing to provide financial resources during monetary crises or political support for international economic institutions, the rules that govern the economic order may be widely flouted. Then, as in the 1930s, states may follow their narrow economic self-interest by erecting trade barriers and carrying out destructive currency devaluations.

Hegemonic stability theory became prominent in the 1980s when it appeared that America was entering a period of economic and political decline and that Japan might overtake the US as an economic superpower. However, the end of the Cold War, Japan's anemic economic growth, and the surging US economy in recent decades silenced those who feared the end of American hegemony. More recently, America's growing willingness to go it alone, the growth in protectionist sentiment in the US, and the spate of trade disputes that have pitted the US against Europe and China have rekindled fears for the future of the liberal economic order.

Will the United States abandon the global economic order it helped construct or stay the course and support that order? Economic issues, more than other foreign policy questions, are embedded in domestic politics, and economic policies are routinely made in response to domestic interest groups rather than global economic needs. Were the US to surrender its leading role in fostering economic cooperation, international economic institutions would be hard pressed to maintain the open trading system that evolved after 1945.

The possibility of US withdrawal does not mean that the existing system is in imminent danger. Most countries recognize that their prosperity depends on cooperation with one another. However, the Great Depression showed that the stability and survival of the global economic system cannot be taken for granted. Bad times, as in the 1930s, place great strains on global economic cooperation and encourage economic nationalism.

No less important to the global economy than the major international economic organizations are the giant transnational corporations (TNCs) that have proliferated in recent decades. Let us now examine the role of these economic giants.

Transnational corporations: engines of global capitalism

TNCs are the engines of global capitalism, knitting peoples together in a vast system of economic exchange. Transnational economic enterprises have existed for centuries, and some enjoyed many of the perquisites of sovereignty. These companies were, as political scientist Janice Thomson puts it, "endowed with nearly all the powers of sovereignty."[46] The British East India or the "John Company" was, at its height, virtual ruler of India with an army of 150,000.[47] By its charter, the company could acquire territory, exercise legal jurisdiction, wage war, make treaties, and issue its own currency. Founded to obtain for Britain a share of the East Indian spice trade, its ships first arrived in India in 1608, and its penetration of India began after its navy defeated a Portuguese fleet in 1612 off India's northwest coast.

Thereafter, the company established posts along India's east and west coasts to trade in cotton and silk goods, indigo, saltpeter, and spices from South India, and founded English settlements in Calcutta, Bombay, and Madras. Its governing responsibilities grew after Robert Clive (1725–74) defeated the local ruler of Bengal in the 1757 Battle of Plassey, bringing an end to the independence of northern India's Mughal emperor. Thereafter, British influence gradually increased in India until, following a bloody rebellion of Britain's Indian troops in the 1858 Sepoy Mutiny, the company was dissolved, and London instituted direct rule.

The next section examines TNCs' role in the contemporary world, evaluating the extent and sources of their power and the nature of their goals.

The global reach of TNCs

The role of TNCs has expanded in recent decades, and their numbers grew from 7,000 in 1970 to over 50,000 in 1997. Although they may have a national center, they are transnational because they engage in direct foreign investment and conduct business in more than one country. Some have many subsidiaries: Ford, for example, has units in 96 countries.[48] TNCs are organized to pursue a coherent global strategy that permits their units to pool knowledge, technology, and financial resources. Of the world's 50 largest TNCs, 17 have American roots, 13 Japanese, and seven German.[49] However, the "nationality" of TNCs is at best blurred. Thus, only 65 percent of the content of a Ford Mustang is from the US or Canada, while Toyota's Sienna is assembled in Indiana of almost entirely US-made parts; General Motors imports Korean-made cars sold as Chevrolets; and 67 percent of Japanese cars sold in North America are made in North America.[50]

Most TNCs are located in the developed world while many of their foreign affiliates are in the developing world, and they have immense economic clout. The combined sales of the world's 200 largest TNCs account for over a quarter of global economic activity, and the value of their sales exceeds the combined gross national income of 182 of the world's countries. These corporations have sales valued at almost twice the income of the poorest four-fifths of the world's population ($7.1 trillion to $3.9 trillion), and one-third of all world trade is conducted among units within corporations.[51] Between 2005 and 2006, the profits of the world's leading 2,000 companies soared by 32 percent to $1.7 trillion, and combined they had total sales of $24 trillion, total assets of $88 trillion, with 35 million employees.[52] Indeed, 51 of the 100 largest economies in the world are corporations, and the leading 500 TNCs are responsible for almost 70 percent of global trade.[53] The value of Wal-Mart's 2004 sales *alone* was more than the gross national income of all but 17 countries or almost the equivalent of the gross national income of *all* of sub-Saharan Africa.

Size is only one measure of TNC impact. Others are foreign assets and number of employees. General Electric, with assets of over $229 billion, ranks first among TNCs, and Wal-Mart employs 1,400,000 people of whom 300,000 are non-American. Some companies are highly globalized such as the Canadian media giant Thompson, which employs 98 percent of its employees overseas.[54]

TNCs enjoy other strengths. They can shift investments to escape government regulation, high taxes, or labor unrest. They can ally with one another and invest in countries that provide a hospitable atmosphere, while disinvesting elsewhere. They can establish subsidiaries in countries with low wages and lax environmental standards, outsourcing jobs from some countries to others. Factors such as labor skills and costs, proximity to markets, and quality of transportation and communication systems make some countries attractive to TNCs. By lowering taxes, improving roads and ports, educating citizens, eliminating environmental rules, reducing corruption, and capping labor costs, countries such as China and Ireland have been especially successful in attracting TNCs.[55]

Corporate mergers have created concentrations of economic power in key sectors of the global economy, leading to concern that some may become global monopolies able to control the supply and price of the goods and services they provide. Fear of such corporate power was reflected in the 2004 decision of a European court against Microsoft for using unfair tactics to maintain monopolistic control over computer software. The court decided that Microsoft, by preinstalling its Windows Media Player in its Windows operating system (used in 90 percent of the world's personal computers), was giving itself an unfair advantage over competitors. Documents written by Microsoft officials such as a 1997 memo written by the company's general manager to its CEO William Gates III (1955–) suggested the corporation's intent to shut out potential rivals.[56] By its decision, the court upheld an earlier decision of the EU Commission requiring Microsoft to pay $613 million in fines. The Commission also demanded that Microsoft share information about its Windows operating system with rival software producers and sell its operating system without the preinstalled media player. Microsoft argues that its only sin is being too successful. Additional fines were levied against Microsoft in 2006 for its failure to obey Europe's 2004 antitrust ruling.

TNCs try to minimize national impediments to trade or investment and prevent politics from interrupting the smooth transaction of business.

Table 11.1 The world's fifty wealthiest entities ($billion)

1.	United States	10,110
2.	Japan	4,266
3.	Germany	1,870
4.	Great Britain	1,486
5.	France	1,343
6.	China	1,210
7.	Italy	1,098
8.	Canada	701
9.	Mexico	597
10.	Spain	594
11.	India	502
12.	Brazil	497
13.	South Korea	473
14.	Netherlands	386.8
15.	Australia	386.6
16.	Russia	308
17.	Switzerland	274
18.	Wal-Mart Stores	256
19.	Belgium	240
20.	BP	233
21.	ExxonMobil	223
22.	Sweden	222
23.	Austria	190
24.	General Motors	186
25.	Poland	177
26.	Turkey	174
27.	Norway	172
28.	Hong Kong	167
29.	Ford Motor	164
30.	Denmark	163
31.	DaimlerChrysler	157
32.	Argentina	154
33.	Indonesia	150
34.	Toyoto Motor	136
35.	General Electric	134.2
36.	Royal Dutch/ Shell Group	133.5
37.	Total	132
38.	Greece	124
39.	Thailand	122
40.	Finland	122
41.	South Africa	114
42.	Chevron Texaco	112.9
43.	Mitsubishi	112.8
44.	Iran	112.1
45.	Mitsui & Co.	112
46.	Portugal	109
47.	Venezuela	103
48.	Egypt	98
49.	Carrefour Group	96.9
50.	Allianz Worldwide	96.88

> **Did you know?**
>
> If Wal-Mart were a country, it would be China's eighth largest trading partner.[57]

Their goals are profits for shareholders, sales growth, and security and autonomy. Although governments have weapons they can use against TNCs, including taxation, capital controls, regulation, and, in extreme cases, nationalization, they rarely do so because they seek corporate investment, expertise, and technology, and, with the exception of companies that extract resources, TNCs can pick up and leave.

However, are these engines of capitalism benevolent or malevolent forces in global politics? Neoliberals see TNCs as wealth creators and sources of economic development. Others, notably Marxists, are suspicious because many corporations originate in wealthy states and enjoy the support of Western governments. Those who applaud globalization also laud the role of TNCs in spreading wealth and modernity. However, critics points out that there is also a down side. The following section examines some of the criticisms of corporate behavior.

Criticisms of TNCs

There are several criticisms of TNCS. One is that they expropriate local resources and export them for their own benefit so that poor countries lose control over their own assets. According to this argument, TNCs return a disproportionate share of profits to their home countries, plowing little back into host countries, and prefer to make products for export rather than products useful to poor peasants or residents of urban slums in host countries.

Another criticism is that TNCs create little local employment and reward executives for employing the fewest possible number of workers. Overall, the 200 largest TNCs accounting for 28 percent of world trade employ less than 1 percent of the world's workers.[58] And when TNCs do create jobs, argue critics, they hire few locals for senior positions and create privileged urban elites with little stake in helping local development.

Another criticism is that TNCs increase local demand for useless, unhealthy, and dangerous products like cigarettes and, like Newmont Mining, act in ways that harm the environment. One case involved the chemical giant Union Carbide that was implicated in an environmental disaster in Bhopal, India, in which thousands died. The plant, built in a densely populated neighborhood, produced the pesticide carbaryl and the organic compound methyl isocynate. On the night of December 2–3, 1984, water accidentally flowed into the methyl isocynate holding tank, causing a chain reaction in which heat combined with the chemicals to corrode the steel tank, allowing methyl isocynate to escape as a toxic gas. Chemical scrubbers for treating the gas were shut off for maintenance; the

Figure 11.4 Bhopal, India, December 2–3, 1984

Courtesy of Rai Hurai

refrigeration unit for maintaining the chemical at low temperatures was out of order; and the alarm system failed. With no warning, the gas settled over the shantytowns of Jaiprakesh and Chhola, killing sleeping residents and blinding and choking others who fled into the streets where they suffocated. Victims sued Union Carbide for $3 billion in damages, and in a 1989 settlement the company agreed to pay $470 million. In addition, Union Carbide's CEO, Warren Anderson, was indicted in Bhopal for culpable homicide and was declared a fugitive from justice by a local magistrate in 1992 for failing to appear in court.

Ultimately, the survivors received little from the settlement. Accused of negligence, the company claimed that an employee had willfully caused the disaster by sabotaging the tank from which the gas had escaped. In 2001 the Bhopal plant was acquired by the Dow Chemical Company. Although the Bhopal site remains contaminated by toxic chemicals, Dow contends that it has no further responsibility for the disaster because of the earlier settlement.

Thus, TNCs must walk a fine line as regards the environment. They want to keep costs down, but they do not want unfavorable publicity or the potential costs of legal action. Their dilemma is highlighted by the problems faced by oil companies in Nigeria, Africa's largest oil producer and the fifth largest source of US oil imports. Much of Nigeria's oil comes from the Niger Delta where ethnic Ogoni inhabitants claim they get few benefits from the oil that is pumped from their region and have frequently been victims of oil spills. Ogoni protesters have repeatedly interrupted Nigeria's oil exports.[59] Grievances have led to violence that caused numerous deaths in 2004. Local hostility has led to sabotage of oil installations, the kidnapping of company employees, and a major decline in Nigerian oil exports.[60] According to Amnesty International, the companies, though not the principal cause of violence in the Niger Delta, have a "responsibility to promote human rights within their sphere of influence."[61]

Another criticism is that TNCs meddle in local politics in ways ranging from outright bribery to illicit campaign contributions. After the discovery that Lockheed Corporation had bribed Japanese officials, the US enacted the 1977 Foreign Corrupt Practices Act, which forbids American companies from paying bribes to win foreign business. In 1997, the world's developed countries agreed to ban bribery by companies seeking contracts, and several major corporations signed an agreement to show "zero tolerance" against paying bribes.[62] Despite these efforts, many TNCs use middlemen or make small "facilitation" payments that they claim are not bribes to win business. Corporations argue that corruption is so prevalent in some countries that they cannot do business otherwise and that, since other firms continue to pay bribes, they cannot compete unless they "play the game."

In some cases companies have even been involved in efforts to overthrow governments. "I spent most of my time as a high-class muscle-man for big business, for Wall Street, and the bankers," admitted US Marine General Smedley D. Butler (1881–1940).

> Thus, I helped make Mexico . . . safe for American oil interests in 1914. I helped make Haiti and Cuba a decent place for the National City Bank boys to collect revenues. I helped in the raping of half a dozen Central American republics for the benefit of Wall Street. . . . I brought light to the Dominican Republic for American sugar interests in 1916. I helped make Honduras "right" for American fruit companies in 1903.[63]

The case of "big oil" illustrates the lengths to which governments have gone to help "their" companies. During the 1920s, the world's seven leading oil companies, known as the "seven sisters," formed an **oligopoly** over world oil production, refining, and distribution. Among the largest was the British-owned Anglo-Iranian Oil Company (later to become British Petroleum or BP) which was established after oil was discovered in Iran in 1908. Shortly before World War I the company arranged a deal with the British government whereby Britain would receive a steady oil supply in return for government investment in the company.

In April 1951, Mohammad Mossadegh (1880–1967) became Iran's premier and set out to end the foreign presence in his country. Negotiations had already begun between Iran and Anglo-Iranian over Iran's demand for higher royalties for oil. When these broke down, Iran's parliament moved to **nationalize** the company, then Britain's single largest overseas investment. Britain responded by banning Iranian oil and imposing a naval blockade. When Iran's Shah refused to grant Mossadegh emergency powers, he resigned but was reappointed after massive street protests. Mossadegh then moved rapidly to institute social reforms and drew closer to Iran's communist party. In October 1952, British and US intelligence officials began consultations about overthrowing Mossadegh. The operation climaxed in August 1953 as street battles swept Teheran, and Iranian soldiers arrested Mossadegh who was convicted of treason, spent three years in prison, and remained under house arrest until his death.[64] A year later Iran's new government and a consortium of oil companies reached an agreement to restore the flow of Iranian oil.

Iranians still cite Mossadegh's ouster as evidence of Western hostility, and the episode was used by militants to mobilize Iranians against the US

oligopoly the market condition that exists when there are so few sellers that each can affect the price of a product being sold.

nationalize to convert from private to government ownership and control.

after the 1979 Iranian revolution. In 2000, US Secretary of State
Madeleine Albright (1937–) declared that the US had erred in acting as it
did in 1953, admitting that "the coup was clearly a setback for Iran's
political development and it is easy to see now why many Iranians
continue to resent this intervention by America."[65]

Finally, TNCs have been accused of human rights abuses. Some firms
use "sweatshop" conditions in poor countries that would be illegal in rich
countries. Nike, the maker of sports equipment, was accused of using
child labor in unsafe conditions. In November, 1997, a leaked internal
audit of Nike revealed company abuses at its Vietnam facility, and
resulting publicity forced Nike to improve working conditions in its
plants. In May 1998, Nike agreed to end its use of child labor and to
introduce US occupational and health safety standards in its Asian
factories. Corporations defend such practices, arguing that if they adopt
US labor standards in the LDCs, they will increase costs and might have to
cease operating. The main casualties would be the LDCs, which would
lose investment and jobs. The criticisms have produced efforts to reform
TNCs, and a number of reforms have been instituted to curb their abuses.

Reforming TNCs

In 2003, UNESCO adopted a set of norms "on the responsibilities of
transnational corporations . . . with regard to human rights."[66] Also,
Secretary-General Annan tried to forge a closer relationship between
TNCs and the UN. In 1999 at the annual World Economic Forum in
Davos, Switzerland, Annan proposed a "Global Compact" between the
UN and TNCs consisting of nine (later ten) voluntary principles that
corporations agree to uphold. With the cooperation of the International
Chamber of Commerce, the Global Compact was launched at a meeting
attended by executives from 50 major corporations, followed by a June
2004 Global Compact Leaders Summit. The principles of the Global
Compact deal with human rights, labor, the environment, and
corruption:[67]

1 Protect international human rights.
2 Refuse to participate or condone human rights abuses.
3 Support freedom of association and recognize the right to collective
   bargaining.
4 Abolish compulsory labor.
5 Abolish child labor.
6 Eliminate discrimination in employment.
7 Implement an effective environmental program.
8 Undertake initiatives that demonstrate environmental responsibility.

9   Diffuse environmentally friendly technologies.
10   Promote anti-corruption initiatives.

Some TNCs have taken steps to fulfill the compact. For example, Mexico's largest steel corporation set up a cyber-based environmental management system; a Brazilian subsidiary of the British-American Tobacco Company started a program to end the use of child labor; and DaimlerChrysler began a project in Brazil to maintain the rainforest by encouraging the growing of natural fibers.[68]

Did you know?

William Gates III, the founder and CEO of Microsoft, is worth almost as much as the national income of Bangladesh.[69]

We have seen how global economic processes are being globalized. With this in mind, let us examine the changing relationship between states and economic markets that transcend national frontiers.

States and markets

Historically, the growth of Europe's territorial states helped create national markets.[70] Today, economic markets have expanded beyond the frontiers of territorial states, and for consumers, producers, and investors, national boundaries are inconveniences to be overcome. "On the one hand," argues political scientist Robert Gilpin, "the state is based on the concepts of territoriality, loyalty, and exclusivity," while "the market is based on the concepts of functional integration, contractual relationships, and expanding interdependence of buyers and sellers." Gilpin continues: "For the state, territorial boundaries are a necessary basis of national autonomy and political unity. For the market, the elimination of all political and other obstacles to the operation of the price mechanism is imperative."[71]

Today's states are ceding authority in the economic realm to other institutions such as TNCs and the WTO, thereby diluting their sovereign independence. As domestic economies become more vulnerable to events and decisions beyond their borders, leaders enjoy diminished control over national economies and are losing their ability to regulate the national economy in the public interest. Although states still control traditional means of coercion, these avail little when capital takes flight, currencies fluctuate, or trade deficits produce unemployment. Thus, for many people global markets have produced economic disadvantage and political turmoil.

Globalized markets are a fact of modern economic life that individual governments can only ignore if they are prepared to pay a high price.[72] It is impossible to insulate citizens from globalization's economic effects without their sacrificing its benefits. How can governments control economic policy on behalf of citizens if their economic fate is determined by currency speculators, banks, transnational corporations, investors, stock brokers and mutual funds, and buyers and sellers in other countries? This problem was vividly revealed during Asia's 1997–98 economic crisis.

The Asian contagion

In the 1970s and 1980s, the countries of Southeast and East Asia made dramatic economic strides. Emulating economic policies pioneered by Japan, governments encouraged exports and investment, helped corporations identify attractive economic niches, directed investment to selected industries, provided loans and subsidies, and protected national firms from foreign competition. The aggressive efforts of Asia's newly industrializing countries (NICs) to foster economic growth earned them the title "Asian tigers" and made them major players in global trade and finance. For example, South Korea, which had been devastated during the Korean War and had been among the world's poorest countries in the early 1960s, celebrated its entry into the elite "rich man's club" of the Organization for Economic Cooperation and Development in 1996. By 1998 its economy had become the world's eleventh largest.

The contagion unfolds

Asia had experienced low inflation and high employment owing to citizens' willingness to work long hours, save their earnings, and forgo large wage increases. Asia's governments worked closely with their private sector to select and assist industries with potential to compete successfully with Western competitors. Although specific policies varied, their governments financed the dramatic growth in their economies by a combination of overseas investment and borrowing from foreign banks.

Since US interest rates were lower than Asian rates during the 1990s, Asian banks found it cheaper to borrow US dollars and convert them into local currency than to borrow at home. The banks then invested much of this borrowed money in high-risk bond markets in Southeast Asia, Russia, and Latin America. Since they had to repay foreign loans in hard currency, they gambled that local currency would not decline in value relative to the US dollar and the Japanese yen. This gamble proved costly.

Although borrowing forced Asian banks into debt to foreign banks, high interest rates in Asia continued to attract foreign dollars. Many of these dollars were invested in local stock markets, sending stock prices higher, while others were invested in real estate that was used as collateral for the growing mountain of debt. Asia's financial crisis erupted on July 2, 1997, about a month after the failure of Thailand's largest finance company, when speculators began to dump Thai currency in expectation that its value would decline. As investors rushed to buy US dollars and get their money out of the country, the exchange value of the Thai baht went into free fall. When Thailand abandoned its effort to maintain (or peg) its currency's value at the rate of 25 to the dollar, the baht's value dropped by almost 20 percent in a matter of hours.

Foreign banks then discovered that financial institutions throughout Asia were facing solvency problems similar to Thailand's. Within days, speculators began to sell other Asian currencies, including those of Indonesia, Malaysia, and the Philippines, and investors dumped local stocks and bonds. Before it was over, local stock markets and currencies had collapsed, businesses had gone bankrupt, and unemployment had soared.

The contagion spreads

In the autumn of 1997, the crisis spread beyond Southeast Asia. In October, the financial tidal wave struck Hong Kong whose stock market dropped 40 percent. A wave of competitive currency devaluations took place in Southeast and East Asia, and threatened to spread to other **emerging markets**. In South Korea, foreign investors began to sell local investments, and Korean enterprises desperately tried to repay their foreign debts. This led to a growing demand for dollars and a slide in the value of Korean currency. South Korea's supply of dollars dwindled rapidly as foreign banks refused to lend their dwindling store of dollars. By December, South Korea had no remaining hard currency and was on the verge of default. The government then requested IMF assistance, admitting that the country could no longer pay its debts, and the IMF, World Bank, and the Asia Development Bank agreed to lend South Korea $58 billion.

As investors lost confidence in Asia's economies, their fears grew to encompass other emerging markets. Stock markets in Argentina, Brazil, and Mexico dropped precipitously, and even the New York Stock Exchange suffered its single largest price decline on October 27, losing 7

emerging market a financial market of a developing country.

percent of its value. The contagion spread to Russia, which defaulted on about $40 billion in debt in August 1998, and then Brazil. Russia had accumulated enormous debt after 1995 to pay its budget deficits and, as its debt mounted, the world price for oil – a key source of Russia's income – dropped. With the Russian ruble in free fall and the government's debt default, Russia's stock market lost three-quarters of its value in a matter of months.

Part of the problem facing emerging markets lay in their weakened competitive position following devaluations in China's and Japan's currencies and the rising value of the dollar to which their currencies were pegged. As a result, exports by Asia's tigers slowed, and Western investment began to shift from the NICs to China. Finally, the value of real estate plummeted, leaving banks with little collateral for bad loans.

As Asia's financial troubles multiplied, it became clear that banking systems had made many loans to politically influential clients, sometimes under pressure from governments, with little consideration for the risk involved. In Indonesia, for example, cronies and relatives of President Suharto (1921–) repeatedly received loans for questionable projects. In South Korea, the government nurtured gigantic but poorly managed business conglomerates, providing them with preferential credit, protecting them from foreign competition, promoting particular industries, discouraging labor unrest, and bailing them out when they were in financial trouble. These conglomerates enjoyed great political influence, building close ties with politicians whom they helped or even bribed. However, competition from China, with cheaper labor costs, eroded South Korea's competitive edge, and its large but indebted corporations took speculative routes to profits – real estate and stock market purchases. When the value of these investments plummeted in the 1990s, their collateral disappeared, and Korean banks were left with a pile of bad debts.[73]

A number of factors account for the rapid spread of the economic crisis. One was the high level of integration of global financial markets. A second was economic interdependence associated among trading partners. Thus, the devaluation of one country's currency reduced imports from its trading partners, leading to speculative attacks on their currencies and forcing the devaluation of their currencies as well. Indeed, some politicians argued that Western speculators rather than Asian economic policies were the major cause of the economic meltdown. "They can speculate with any currency," declared Malaysia's prime minister, "and their speculation is so designed that they can either revalue a currency or devalue a currency to any level. They hold this power, and they can literally make or break you by just by doing that."[74] A third factor was the dramatic increase in the size and speed of global capital movements, financial transactions, and even rumors made possible by new communications technologies. A fourth was the propensity of investors to view all emerging economies in much the same way and conclude that the problems confronting one also confronted the others.

A final factor lay in the weakness of local banking systems. Banks in much of the region were poorly supervised, subject to intense political pressure to make foolish loans, and hid little information about the loans they made. With growing economic uncertainty, a raft of foreign debt, the prospect of collapsing banking systems, overproduction, and diminishing exports, markets took fright, and the crisis erupted as stock prices crashed and currency values collapsed.

Asia's economic crisis showed that in a globalized world when financial instability shakes one country, it may spread outward like ripples in a pond. Resulting turmoil may be contagious as speculators take advantage of currency fluctuations and withdraw funds not only from the country at risk but from others facing similar problems. This contagion effect had been apparent some years earlier during Mexico's 1994 economic crisis – called the "Tequila Effect."[75] Writing of that crisis, Moises Naim described an economic world in which conventional geography played no role and in which the concept of "neighborhood" assumed a new meaning. Financial markets, he argued, "tend to cluster those countries perceived to be in the same 'neighborhood' and to treat them roughly along the same lines. This time, however, the neighborhood is no longer defined solely in terms of geography. The main defining criterion is the potential volatility of the countries; the contagion spread inside risk-clusters, or volatility neighborhoods."[76] And when a "volatility neighborhood" is extensive, as it was in 1997–98, the global economic system as a whole may be at risk.

Conclusion

This chapter has examined the evolution of the global economy. It reviewed competing economic perspectives and described the destructive consequences of the depression and the creation and evolution of the three principal international economic institutions that were intended to prevent a repetition of the errors made during the depression.

We saw how the world's leading economic powers, far from resisting economic globalization after World War II, viewed the process as in their interest and crafted policies to encourage and accelerate it. Under US leadership, the world economic system expanded until, with the end of the Cold War, it encompassed the former members of the Soviet bloc. With China's 2001 admission to the WTO and Russia's application to join that body, the system has become global. But will a global market governed by neoliberal principles persist, or might it erode as it did during the depression?

The next chapter examines the world's less-developed countries, known as the global South, from their colonization by Europe to the present day. Although the global South is a politically and economically diverse group of countries, they are becoming integrated in the global economy and, after decades of economic stagnation, are becoming significant factors in the global economy.

Student activities

Discussion and essay questions

Comprehension questions

1 Compare and contrast the assumptions of mercantilism, liberalism, and Marxism.
2 Compare and contrast the roles played by the IMF, World Bank, and WTO.
3 What are the pros and cons of TNCs?
4 How has the expansion of the global market affected the state?

Analysis questions

5 Write an imaginary discussion about the global economic system among Alexander Hamilton, Karl Marx, and Adam Smith.
6 Assess the effectiveness of IMF conditionality for achieving the IMF's declared goals.
7 Do you think the liberal economic order will persist? Why or why not?

Map analysis

Pick a major TNC such as IBM or General Electric. Using the company's annual report or an Internet source, find out in which countries they own facilities and locate these facilities and the company's headquarters on a world map. What can you infer about the company's global presence and influence from this map?

Cultural materials

A 1993 film, based on Michael Crichton's *Rising Sun*, reflected fears among Americans at the time that, with Japanese investments in the US.

Japanese political influence in the country was also growing. Indeed, Crichton paints a highly unflattering picture of Japanese business practices and customs. He refers to the Japanese as "the most racist people on the planet" and refers to pro-Japanese Americans as "Chrysanthemum Kissers." Do you think foreign investment leads to foreign political influence, or does such investment provide the host country with greater influence? Do you think that foreign investment in China today is reducing that country's independence?

Further reading

Eichengreen, Barry J., *Globalizing Capital: A History of the International Monetary System* (Princeton, NJ: Princeton University Press, 1996). Brief, readable history of the development of the international monetary system over 150 years.

Frynas, Jedrzej George and Scott Peg, eds., *Transnational Corporations and Human Rights* (New York: Palgrave Macmillan, 2003). Case studies of the impact of TNCs on human rights in a variety of settings.

Gilpin, Robert, *Global Political Economy: Understanding the International Economic Order* (Princeton, NJ: Princeton University Press, 2001). A survey of key theories and issues in international political economy.

Grieco, Joseph M. and G. John Ikenberry, *State Power and World Markets* (New York: W.W. Norton, 2002). Introductory text that places equal emphasis on politics and economics in the international political economy.

Haggard, Stephan and Robert Kaufman, eds., *The Politics of Economic Adjustment: International Constraints, Distributive Conflicts, and the State* (Princeton, NJ: Princeton University Press, 1992). Comparative analysis of the political aspects of economic crisis in developing countries.

Kindleberger, Charles P., *The World in Depression, 1929–1939* (Berkeley, CA: University of California Press, 1973). Still the best one-volume explanation of the depression, its causes, and its consequences.

Madeley, John, *Big Business, Poor Peoples: The Impact of Transnational Corporations on the World's Poor* (London: Zed Books, 1999). Provocative but balanced analysis of whether TNCs enrich or impoverish people in the developing world.

Schwartz, Herman M., *States versus Markets: The Emergency of a Global Economy*, 2nd ed. (New York: Palgrave, 2000). The development of the global capitalist economy from the nineteenth century with an emphasis on changing relations between states and markets.

12 The global South

In November 2006, China invited African leaders to Beijing, where President Hu Jintao (1942–) announced a broad aid package including $5 billion in new loans, debt relief, and technical assistance. China's interest in Africa has skyrocketed in recent years, and it has become Africa's third largest trading partner after the United States and France. China's trade with Africa has increased from $14.6 billion in 2000 to nearly $40 billion in 2005, with estimates that it could reach $100 billion by 2010. China has also invested heavily in infrastructure, including railroads in Nigeria and Angola, roadways in Rwanda, and Africa's largest hydroelectric dam in Ethiopia. China's interest in Africa is fueled by its appetite for fuel and raw materials. Angola and Sudan alone provide China with 25 percent of its oil imports.[1]

The impact of these changes is being felt throughout Africa as African countries sell raw materials to Chinese firms that then flood Africa's market with finished manufactured goods. In Kano, Nigeria, for example, numerous Chinese restaurants have appeared, a Chinese shoe factory employs over 2,000 workers, and Chinese products fill store shelves. Says the owner of a Kano textile factory who has had to cut his workforce from 335 to 24 workers: "Without a little protection, if the Chinese bring their finished cotton to Nigeria, you cannot compete with them. . . . The gap is so wide that if you just allow them to come in, you are killing Nigerian companies."[2] Critics of China's policy say it is little better than the unequal trade policies European colonizers followed earlier in Africa and that China's policies will seriously impede long-term development.

As we shall see, the plight of the world's less-developed and postcolonial countries that constitute the global South[3] is a critical issue in world politics. The colonial history of many of these poor countries has contributed to their contemporary political, economic, and social problems. The chapter opens by reviewing this history, beginning with how Europe's colonial empires were established. It then examines the process of **decolonization** that shaped a new generation of leaders in the

decolonization the process by which the major colonial powers granted independence to the majority of states in the Third World.

Figure 12.1 The presidents of Zimbabwe (Mugabe) and China (Jintao) at the Beijing Summit of the Forum on China–Africa Cooperation, November 2006

© PA Photos

global South. The section focuses on independence movements, and their long-lasting effects in Latin America, India, Indonesia, and Africa. The chapter then analyzes the debate over **nation building**, **modernization**, and **nonalignment** policies that postcolonial governments pursued, often unsuccessfully, to achieve political stability, economic development, and foreign policy independence.

You should look upon this chapter along with the two that follow as a single unit dealing with non-military threats to human survival and well-being. Thus, chapter 13 addresses a variety of human security issues such as poverty, disease, and crime; and chapter 14 examines the rapidly accelerating dangers to our global environment. Let us now examine the historical process of Europe's outward expansion.

nation building efforts to create a sense of belonging and cohesion among a disparate group of people in a common state.

modernization economic and political development in the Third World.

nonalignment policy of not entering into military alliances with members of the two blocs during the Cold War.

Europe's empires and the developing world

For centuries, Europe's contact with the world beyond its shores was episodic, limited to acquiring luxury goods like spices and silks from Asia, often through Arab merchants. Occasionally intrepid explorers like the Venetian Marco Polo (1254–1324) traveled the fabled Silk Road to China, inflaming the imagination of generations of Europeans who sought wealth and fame by finding a direct route to the East. Explorers like Christopher Columbus (1451–1506) (who sailed on behalf of Spain's King Ferdinand and Queen Isabella)[4] took advantage of new ship-building techniques and new navigation aids, mapmaking, and telling time to increase Europe's knowledge of the world across the seas and whet Europeans' appetite for riches from the East.

The conquerors

By the middle of the sixteenth century, European countries, starting with Portugal and Spain, began to erect empires built on trade that stretched across the known world. They were followed by the Dutch, then the British and French. These global powers would come into conflict wherever their commercial interests overlapped. Many used trading companies to build their empires where they established colonies and

Figure 12.2 Which way to the Indies?

© Original artist,
www.cartoonstock.com

"HERE WE COME; READY OR NOT!"

created military and economic institutions to protect them. In addition, their superior arms and organization, along with the diseases they brought from the Old World, proved devastating for indigenous peoples and their civilizations.

Explorers like Columbus gave Spain its claim to the New World, but Spain's empire was actually established in the early 1500s by a group of ambitious soldier-explorers called conquistadores who sought gold and silver and chased after the mythical fountain of youth. Among the most famous were Hernán Cortes (1485–1507), who with 500 soldiers laid waste to Mexico's Aztec Empire of Moctezuma II (c. 1466–1520), and Francisco Pizarro (1475–1541), who destroyed Peru's Inca Empire in 1532 and executed its ruler Atahualpa (c. 1502–33).

The Portuguese and Spaniards were followed a century later by the Dutch who had become the world's leading seafarers and first sailed around the Cape of Good Hope in 1595. Political and religious tolerance at home, representative government, and the growth of a capitalist spirit of commerce all helped Holland challenge Spain and Portugal for colonial supremacy. In 1602, the Dutch parliament established the Dutch East India Company which was awarded a tax-free trade monopoly with Asia and empowered to mint coins, establish colonies, and maintain its own armed forces. That company, like others established at the time, was a private commercial-military enterprise run by merchant adventurers who sought to exploit overseas riches. By 1669 it had an army of 10,000 and almost 200 ships. It was in the service of the Dutch East India Company in 1609 that explorer Henry Hudson (?–1611) aboard the *Half Moon* entered the Hudson River in New York.

Indonesia, including the Moluccas, the fabled "Spice Islands," became the center of Holland's trading empire with its capital at Batavia (now Jakarta) on the island of Java. Holland wrested control of the spice trade from Portugal and expelled the Portuguese from Malaya and Ceylon (Sri Lanka), and Dutch trading stations were established in India. A second company, the Dutch West India Company, established the Dutch presence in North America between 1624 and 1664 centered on the trading colony of Nieuw Amsterdam (later New York City) and Guiana in South America.

By the late the seventeenth century, the Dutch Empire had been eclipsed by the French and, more importantly, the British whose penetration of North America and India expelled the Dutch from those regions. During the eighteenth century, Great Britain also ended French influence in North America and India, and British expansion, more than any other single factor, produced European worldwide dominance.

The British, too, made use of private and semi-private companies to build their empire. The most prominent was the British East India Company (1600–1874). Managed by a governor and 24 directors selected by shareholders, the company ruled much of India for two centuries. The charter granted by Queen Elizabeth I in 1600 gave the company a trade monopoly in the East Indies as well as sovereign rights that allowed it to wage war, negotiate treaties, print money, and make and enforce laws. In 1689 the company established administrative districts in Bengal, Bombay, and Madras, beginning its rule of India. Led by Robert Clive (1725–74), the company became India's virtual ruler. Britain reduced the company's independence and took direct control of India after the Sepoy Rebellion (1857–59), a bloody uprising by Indian troops employed by the company.

By century's end, the British too had been driven out of North America, and Spain's control of Central and South America was ending. European **imperialism** and **colonialism** led to the destruction of indigenous peoples and culture in the New World and helped the slave trade from Africa to the Americas to thrive. The trade provided laborers for the plantation economies in the Caribbean, where the local population had been greatly reduced by European predation, and the American South involving the export of sugar, cotton, and tobacco. Eli Whitney's (1765–1825) invention of the cotton gin in 1793 increased the demand for slaves as cotton became the most important crop in the southern states and, between 1798 and 1808, about 200,000 slaves were brought to the United States. Merchants, especially British, built coastal forts in West Africa, purchased slaves from tribal chiefs, and transported and sold them in the Americas at great profit.

The movement to abolish the slave trade began in the late eighteenth century. In 1787, Granville Sharp (1752–1806) formed the Society for the Abolition of the Slave Trade which attracted support from among British Quakers. They were joined by a member of Parliament, William Wilberforce (1759–1833), who became the leading spokesperson for Britain's spreading abolitionist movement. In 1807, Britain made the purchase, transport, and sale of slaves illegal; in 1833, it was declared illegal throughout Britain's empire; and in 1834 Britain made it illegal to own slaves. The ban on the slave trade was enforced by the British Navy. Although the US, too, had banned the slave trade in 1819, slavery there was not abolished until the end of the Civil War in 1865. Constructivists cite the spread of opposition to the slave trade and slavery as reflecting the evolution of norms in global politics that began with the French Revolution, but a number of economic factors, including the need for free labor in industry, made this shift easier.

imperialism the political control of one state by another.

colonialism the political control of a dependent territory and its people by a foreign military power.

Despite the end of the slave trade, European imperialism gained a new lease on life in the nineteenth century. Several factors produced a scramble for territories in Asia and Africa that had not yet been colonized by Europeans. Among these were (1) industrialization in Europe and the need for new markets, (2) heightened nationalism in Europe, (3) the desire for naval bases and coaling stations, raw materials, and opportunities for capital investment, (4) a desire to "export" surplus population, (5) growing missionary zeal to spread Christianity, (6) a belief that imperial possessions brought prestige, and (7) a conviction in the superiority of European civilization, bordering on racism,[5] whose destiny and responsibility was to rule "lesser" races. This sense of destiny led the British poet Rudyard Kipling (1865–1936) to urge Americans and Europeans to "take up the White Man's burden" and France to pursue its "civilizing mission." The US, having spread from the Atlantic to the Pacific, joined the imperial race in the late nineteenth century, seizing Cuba, Puerto Rico, and the Philippines in the Spanish–American War (1898) and annexing Hawaii the same year. The ability to control tropical diseases such as malaria, yellow fever, and amoebic dysentery that had prevented European penetration of the tropics was also a factor in nineteenth-century imperialism, and superior European technology, along with the efficiency of Europe's state bureaucracies, facilitated Europe's conquests. By 1914 the world had been virtually parceled out among the Western imperialists.

Not all Europeans were equally dedicated to imperial expansion. The urge was strongest in countries with industrialists, militarists, patriots, or clergy who had a strong interest in imperialism. Thus, even though imperialism did not bring large economic and political benefits to Europeans as a whole, the policy did benefit specific individuals and groups. Europeans were excited by the exploits of intrepid explorers such as Paul Du Chaillu (1831–1903) in West Africa, Karl Peters (1856–1918) in East Africa, and the journalist Henry M. Stanley (1841–1904) who, after a journey of almost nine months in Central Africa in 1872 as a correspondent for the *New York Herald*, finally found the Scottish medical missionary David Livingstone (1813–73), in what is today Tanzania, whom he greeted with "Doctor Livingstone, I presume."

Imperial occupation of territory in the face of politically conscious and mobilized masses is now often a source of weakness rather than strength. Whereas Europe's imperial expansion was facilitated by the co-optation of small local elites, today, the spread of political consciousness greatly complicates efforts to occupy foreign territory for more than short periods. While in earlier centuries it took few Europeans to conquer and control India, Algeria, and Indochina, no number of highly armed European soldiers would suffice to retain imperial control by the late twentieth century. Russia's experience in Afghanistan, like America's in Vietnam, is a metaphor for the fate of unwanted imperial occupiers. These are practical lessons in the difficulty of controlling foreign territory when opposed by aroused and mobilized mass publics.

Latin America was one of the earliest regions to be conquered by European adventurers, and the imperial possessions in the region achieved their independence earlier than those of Asia and Africa.

Imperialism in the Americas

Latin America, as we have seen, was conquered by the Spaniards and Portuguese during the early stages of Europe's outward expansion. "America," as historian John Parry observed, "was not discovered by the Europeans; it was truly a meeting of two cultures who had not known each other previously."[6] The conquest of the Americas destroyed the sophisticated indigenous civilizations and reduced the indigenous Amerindian populations to servitude. The Amerindians were forcibly converted to Catholicism by the missionaries who accompanied the conquistadores and were made to mine the silver and gold that enriched the coffers of Spain. And to this day, in much of the region, descendants of the Amerindians remain poorer and politically less influential than descendants of the European conquerors.

Portugal's sixteenth-century trading empire included Brazil, East and West Africa, and the Malay Peninsula. However, the largest of Europe's early empires was Spain's, which at its peak included all of Central and South America (except Brazil), Mexico, much of North America including Florida, Texas, the lands along the Mississippi River, the American Southwest, and many Caribbean islands. Spain's empire extended to areas along Africa's west coast as well as Asia, including the Philippine Islands, named after Spain's King Philip II. To prevent the Spaniards and Portuguese from coming to blows, the pope divided the New World between them in the 1493 Treaty of Tordesillas. The Spanish divided their conquests into viceroyalties overseen by a Council of the Indies and gradually the colonial economies added chocolate, coffee, tobacco, and indigo to the products exported back to the Old World.

The Spanish and Portuguese conquests of Latin America and the Spanish penetration of North America, especially Florida and the Southwest, were eclipsed in the seventeenth and eighteenth centuries by the British and French colonization of the Atlantic coast and Canada. British–French rivalry in North America was an extension of their struggle for supremacy in Europe. It climaxed in the French and Indian

War (1754–63), an extension in America of the Seven Years' War in Europe (see chapter 2, p. 69). The war was waged over conflicting claims to "Ohio," a vast land stretching east from the Appalachians to the Mississippi and north from the Gulf of Mexico to the Great Lakes, and over competition for the fur trade and the rich fishing grounds off Newfoundland. The war resulted in the British conquest of Canada and the Ohio Valley and the growing self-confidence of Britain's North American colonies that bore much of the brunt of the conflict. Indeed, less than two decades later British rule south of Canada would come to an end with the Treaty of Paris that confirmed the mother country's decisive defeat in the American Revolution and its recognition of an independent United States.

The conquest and colonization of the Americas were, however, only the first wave of Europe's outward expansion. A second wave of imperialism followed later in Asia and then Africa. The next section reviews Europe's penetration and conquest of much of Asia. The two most important steps in this were Europe's growing economic and political control of China and the British conquest of India.

Imperialism in Asia

In Asia, France took Indochina, and Britain gained Burma, Malaya, and the port city of Singapore. However, the great prizes were China (see chapter 2, p. 80), Japan, and India.

Japan was opened to Western trade when a US naval squadron under Commodore Matthew Perry (1794–1858) sailed into Tokyo Bay in 1853 and forced Japan to sign a treaty under which two ports would be opened to US ships that could purchase such necessities as coal, food, and water.[7] Thereafter, Japan sought to emulate the West and began to penetrate China and Korea, first by defeating China in the Sino-Japanese War (1894–95) and then Russia in the Russo-Japanese War (1905). It then established a **protectorate** over Korea in 1905 and annexed that country in 1910.

protectorate a state or territory that is under the protection of a more powerful state.

Elsewhere in Asia, the most important imperial outpost was British India. As noted above, India was effectively conquered and governed by the British East Company until the Sepoy Rebellion. Thereafter, the company was disbanded, and the British government instituted direct rule with a secretary of state for India in the cabinet, a governor general or viceroy as British representative to the formally independent princely states of India, and Queen Victoria (1819–1901) assuming the title of Empress of India. Under the British Raj, the country was administered by British officials in the Indian Civil Service. Few Indians were admitted to

Figure 12.3 Disraeli presenting Queen Victoria with India

© Original artist,
www.cartoonstock.com

"NEW CROWNS FOR OLD ONES!"

(ALADDIN *adapted.*)

the civil service until the twentieth century. In India, as elsewhere, the British lived in exclusive settlements, seldom mixing with locals.

Much of Asia was already in European hands by the time the European powers turned their attention to Africa. It is to this last stage in the growth of Europe's colonial empires that we now turn.

Imperialism in Africa

In 1875 less than one-tenth of Africa had been colonized, yet 20 years
later only one-tenth remained independent (Ethiopia and Liberia). As in
the New World and Asia, Europe's governments set up companies to
explore, conquer, and conduct trade in Africa. In 1888, the British and
German East African companies were established. The next year the South
Africa Chartered Company of Cecil John Rhodes (1853–1902) was
founded to explore the valley of the Zambezi River in southern Africa.

Britain led the race in Africa. Starting from the Cape of Good Hope
in South Africa, British influence spread northward into Bechuanaland in
1885 (today, Botswana), Rhodesia in 1889 (today, Zimbabwe and
Zambia), and Nyasaland in 1893 (today, Malawi). As shown by Map 12.1,
British holdings in East Africa stretched the length of the continent
from South Africa northward, all the way to Egypt on the shores of the
Mediterranean, including Sudan, Uganda, Kenya, and Tanzania. In West
Africa, its colonies included Nigeria, seized by the Royal Niger Company
between 1886 and 1899, as well as Sierra Leone and Ghana (the former
Gold Coast). The British tended to use indirect rule to govern their
territories, that is, governing through indigenous African leaders within
the colonial administration.

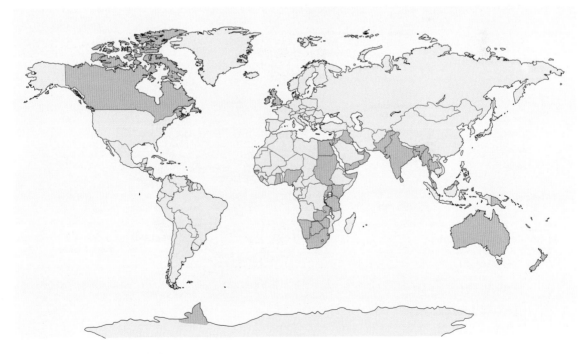

Map 12.1 The British Empire, 1914

Britain's closest competitor was France which unsuccessfully tried to establish a belt of colonies stretching from east to west across the continent that included the African kingdom of Dahomey (today, Benin) and a vast interior region of almost one million square miles called French Equatorial Africa founded in 1910 that consisted of Gabon, Middle Congo, and Ubangi-Chari-Chad (today, the Central African Republic and Chad). As shown on Map 12.2 , the French empire in Africa ultimately included three colonies in North Africa – Algeria, Morocco, and Tunisia

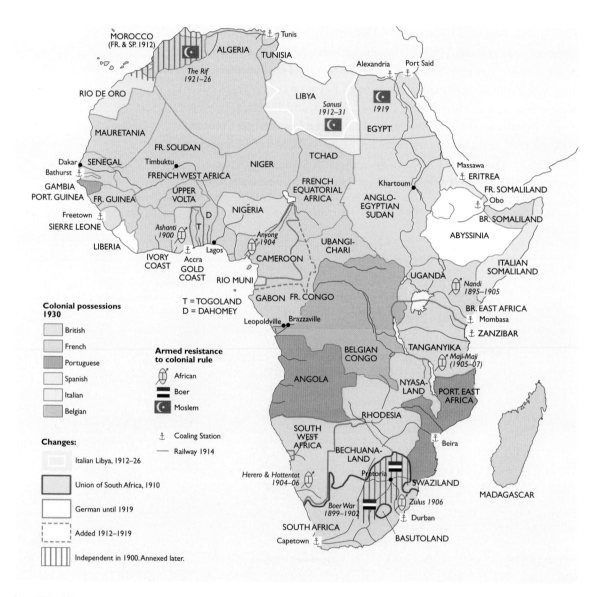

Map 12.2 Africa in the early twentieth century

– plus much of West Africa including what is today Senegal, Guinea, Chad, Niger, Mali, the Ivory Coast, Mauritania, and Cameroon, as well as part of Somalia and the island of Madagascar off Africa's east coast. Unlike the British, the French tended to impose direct rule on their colonies and made an effort to **assimilate** indigenous peoples, replacing local customs with French culture. Using a policy of **divide and rule** France sought to weaken pre-colonial political and social institutions in Africa.

assimilate to absorb a culturally distinct group into the dominant culture.

The boundaries of Africa's states were imposed by European administrators with little attention to ethnic and tribal groups. In some cases, colonial administrators divided such groups into different states and, in others, enclosed hostile groups within the same state.

divide and rule retaining control by keeping the opposition divided.

One of the most brutal colonial ventures took place in the vast region of Central Africa that is today the Democratic Republic of the Congo. That region was not explored by Europeans until 1867 when Stanley, after finding Livingstone, voyaged down the Lualaba (Upper Congo) River. Stanley's adventure impressed Léopold II, King of the Belgians, who decided to acquire the region for himself as a private citizen, hoping thereby to increase his country's prestige, wealth, and power. Léopold sent Stanley back to establish the Congo Free State to be governed by a company of which he was sole owner. This Stanley did with great energy, obtaining for the king a land of 900,000 square miles some 80 times the size of Belgium. Léopold's colony was harshly governed; resources were extracted with no concern for the Congolese who served as slave labor for Léopold's agents (see Key document: Selection from Joseph Conrad's *Heart of Darkness*).

Key document Selection from Joseph Conrad's *Heart of Darkness*[8]

The exploitation of the Congo in the late nineteenth century is brilliantly evoked in Joseph Conrad's novel *Heart of Darkness* (1899).

At last we turned a bend, a rocky cliff appeared, mounds of turned-up earth by the shore, houses on a hill, others, with iron roofs, amongst a waste of excavations, or hanging to the declivity. A continuous noise of the rapids above hovered over this scene of inhabited devastation. A lot of people, mostly black and naked, moved about like ants. A jetty projected into the river. . . .

A horn tooted to the right, and I saw the black people run. A heavy and dull detonation shook the ground, a puff of smoke came out of the cliff, and that was all. . . . They were building a railway. . . .

A slight clinking behind me made me turn my head. Six black men advanced in a file, toiling up the path. They walked erect and slow, balancing small baskets full of earth on their heads, and the clink kept time with their footsteps. Black rags were wound round their loins, and the short ends behind wagged to and fro like tails. I could see every rib, the joints of their limbs were like knots in a rope; each had an iron collar on his neck, and all were connected together with a chain whose bights swung between them, rhythmically clinking. . . .

They were dying slowly – it was very clear. They were not enemies, they were not criminals, and they were nothing earthly now, – nothing but black shadows of disease and starvation, lying confusedly in the greenish gloom. Brought from all the recesses of the coast in all the legality of time contracts, lost in uncongenial surroundings, fed on unfamiliar food, they sickened, became inefficient, and were then allowed to crawl away and rest.

Germany was an imperial latecomer. Otto von Bismarck (1815–98), who controlled the country's foreign affairs between 1862 and 1890, thought colonies were of little value. What mattered to him was Europe's balance of power, and he was delighted if his adversaries busied themselves in far-off colonial ventures. Bismarck, however, had to contend with other Germans who wished their country to build an empire equal to that of Britain and France. After Bismarck's ouster in 1890, German policy abruptly shifted, and the country joined the colonial scramble as part of a new world policy aimed at building world commerce and acquiring global power and prestige. By the time World War I erupted, Germany had colonies in the Pacific including Western Samoa, German New Guinea, a sphere of influence in China, and a number of African protectorates including Togo, the Cameroons, Rwanda, Burundi, Tanganyika, and Namibia.[9]

The last and least successful of Europe's imperial powers was Italy. Envious of France's North African holdings, Italy seized modern Eritrea in the late 1880s and in 1889 added the southern part of Somalia. The Italians also claimed a protectorate over Ethiopia (then, the kingdom of Abyssinia), but the invading Italian army was destroyed in 1896 in a humiliating defeat at Adowa at the hands of Emperor Menelik II's Amhara warriors.[10] This was the greatest defeat of a European army by non-Europeans since the beginning of Europe's colonial expansion centuries earlier, and some think it marked the beginning of the end of European imperialism. One of the last acts in Europe's conquest of Africa was Italy's 1911 seizure of Libya from the Ottoman Turks, finally giving Rome a tenuous foothold in North Africa, which it would lose in World War II.

Colonial rivalries in Africa inevitably produced friction among the competitors. To minimize these conflicts and compromise conflicting territorial claims, Bismarck, with French cooperation, convened a conference in Berlin in 1884–85. All the major European powers, as well as the US, were represented at the Berlin Conference, and the result was to minimize conflict in realist fashion by dividing most of Africa into **spheres of influence** in which countries that "effectively" occupied African territories would own them. In a patronizing statement of European superiority, Europeans were bound "to watch over the preservation of the native tribes, and to care for the improvement of the conditions of their moral and material well-being" and were to assist all undertakings "which aim at instructing the natives and bringing home to them the blessings of civilization."[11]

> **sphere of influence** a geographic region dominated by a major power.

By the beginning of the twentieth century the first steps toward self-rule had been taken in a few of Europe's colonies. However, the movement toward decolonization gathered steam with the exhaustion of the European powers in World War I and, even more, World War II. The next section deals with this dramatic movement that ended with the independence of a multitude of new states in Latin America, Asia, and Africa.

Decolonization

Like Europe's expansion, decolonization took place in two distinct stages. The first in the eighteenth and nineteenth centuries saw the independence of the Americas. The second, one of the most momentous developments of the twentieth century, culminated in the emergence of a host of new states in Asia and Africa.

In retrospect, the outstanding feature of decolonization in Asia and Africa was the speed with which it took place. However, the process of throwing off colonial rule in these regions remained muted until world war so weakened the European colonial powers that their resources proved inadequate to maintain their empires. Colonial troops were critical to the British and French war effort, and Woodrow Wilson's advocacy of national self-determination proved infectious, providing an ideological basis for aspiring nationalists in Asia and Africa. In 1931, the British Parliament enacted the Statute of Westminster by which Britain's so-called "White Dominions" (Canada, Australia, and New Zealand) were given independence within the British Commonwealth, but London still had no plans for dismantling its global empire.

Constructivist analysis is useful to understand this process. As the idea of national self-determination took root among European liberals, it spread among colonial subjects who were educated at European institutions such as Oxford, Cambridge, and the Sorbonne in Paris, or in European-run schools back home. Gradually, the idea that colonial subjects had a right to govern themselves and decide their own destiny gained wider acceptance among both rulers and ruled.

Latin America

Latin America, which had been among Europe's earliest conquests, was also one the first regions to achieve independence. The 1780s witnessed a series of bloody but unsuccessful rebellions involving hundreds of thousands of Amerindians in the Andean highlands of Peru and Bolivia that were brutally suppressed. Between 1791 and 1804, Haiti was the scene of a successful slave revolt against French rule led by Toussaint L'Ouverture (1743–1803). However, the collapse of the Portuguese and Spanish empires, when they occurred, was swift, taking place in the short span of two decades (1806–26).

In 1808, the Queen of Portugal and her son João fled to Brazil to escape Napoléon Bonaparte. A year after João returned to Portugal as king, his son Pedro declared the independence (1822) of the Empire of Brazil. Following the invasion of Spain in 1807 by Napoléon and his replacement of Spain's king with his brother Joseph Bonaparte, the Spanish people rose up against French occupation, beginning a guerrilla war in 1808 that lasted until 1814. Spain's weakness and preoccupation with Napoléon provided an opportunity for those of Spanish descent known as Creoles who chafed under Spanish rule.[12] On September 16, 1810, Father Miguel Hidalgo y Costilla (1753–1811), a Creole priest, called upon Mexicans to rise up against Spain. However, the violence and extremism of Hidalgo and his Amerindian followers alienated both Spaniards and Creoles, and in 1811 Hidalgo was captured and executed. These events precipitated a war that lasted until 1821 when Spain finally recognized Mexican independence in the Treaty of Córdoba.

Elsewhere in South America, the dominant figures in the wars of liberation were Simón Bolívar (1783–1830), a wealthy landowner, and José de San Martín (1778–1850), both of whom were influenced by the American and French revolutions and the philosophy of the eighteenth-century European Enlightenment with its emphasis on natural rights, science, and the liberating power of reason. Bolívar led the liberation movement that saw Venezuela declare independence in 1810. Although the end of the Napoléonic Wars enabled Spain to reconquer much of the region by 1816, Bolívar renewed the struggle which lasted an additional five years and in which he finally triumphed with the help of English and Irish mercenaries. In 1819 Colombia was liberated, then Peru (1821), Ecuador (1822), and, finally, following the 1824 battle of Ayacucho, Bolivia (1826). San Martín commanded the independence forces in Argentina (1816), crossed the Andes with Bernardo O'Higgins (1778–1842) to liberate Chile (1818), and finally linked up with Bolívar in Peru. Finally, in 1823 the United States issued the Monroe Doctrine to prevent any further effort by Spain to regain its lost American possessions.

Elsewhere, decolonization had to wait until the other European imperial powers, especially Britain and France, had grown weaker. The bloody struggle of World War I would serve this purpose. Let us now examine decolonization and its effects in India, Indonesia, and Africa.

India: from colony to great power

Among the first steps in decolonization was a movement toward self-government in India at the end of the nineteenth century in which Indians were appointed to advise the British viceroy and participate in legislative councils. Indians, some of whom were elected, were given further roles in central and provincial legislatures under the 1909 Government of India Act. These elected representatives became spokespersons for Indian self-government and critics of the British Raj and carried with them a growing sense of nationalism.

Gandhi and India's decolonization movement

In 1885, 73 Indian delegates, mainly Western-educated professionals and provincial leaders, met in Bombay to found the Indian National Congress, later the Indian Congress Party. At first, the Congress was little more than a debating club representing a narrow set of urban professionals who sent suggestions to the government. However, by 1900 it had come to represent Indians, mainly Hindus, from all the country's regions, though it had little appeal for the country's Muslim minority. Resenting their inferior status, many Muslims supported British rule, and in 1906 the All-India Muslim League was founded to enhance Muslims' political status in India.

In 1905 Indian nationalism was roused by the ill-considered partition of Bengal by the British Viceroy Sir George Curzon (1859–1925)[13] that seemed a British effort to divide and rule the country. Led by Congress, Indian nationalists began a successful boycott of British goods and agitated violently against the partition. Finally, during his 1911 visit to India, British King George V (1865–1936) announced a reversal of the partition and a shift of India's capital from Calcutta to a new city called New Delhi.

In December 1916, the Congress Party and the Muslim League met and agreed to seek self-government and constitutional reform, including separate Hindu and Muslim electorates. By the 1919 Government of India Act, more Indians were given the vote, legislative councils dominated by elected representatives were given greater authority, and selected ministers, especially those responsible for public welfare, were made responsible to elected legislators. Nevertheless, the movement toward Indian self-government remained glacial as key ministries remained in British hands.

The massacre of hundreds of Indians on April 13, 1919 in the city of Amritsar, the holy city of India's Sikhs, a religious minority founded in the sixteenth century, galvanized Indian nationalists. The massacre grew out of a general strike called by India's nationalist leader Mohandas K. (Mahatma) Gandhi (1869–1948) to protest British efforts to investigate "criminal conspiracies" involved in India's nationalist movement. When a huge crowd protested the deportation of two Indian nationalists from the Punjab and the ban on Gandhi's entry in the province, it was fired upon, and angry mobs then attacked and killed Europeans. Local authorities called in the army and prohibited all public meetings. When a large number of Sikhs gathered to protest, the British commander opened fire on the crowd without warning. Protests erupted throughout India, and several areas were placed under martial law. In December, the Congress Party met in Amritsar and called on Britain to grant India national self-determination, and some Sikhs abandoned the path of nonviolence, forming a terrorist group called the Babar Akalis that assassinated British soldiers until it was repressed in 1924.

These events energized India's nationalist movement and its two leaders, Gandhi and Jawaharlal Nehru (1889–1964). Born in Gujarat in Western India, Gandhi studied law in London and traveled to South Africa where he sought to improve the status of that country's Indian community, returning to India in 1915. It was in South Africa that Gandhi, influenced by the Russian author Leo Tolstoy's (1828–1910) *The Kingdom of God Is Within You* and the American philosopher Henry David Thoreau's (1817–62) idea of **civil disobedience**,[14] developed the strategy of nonviolent resistance to protest injustice. Termed *satyagraha* (combining the Hindu words for "truth" and "holding firm"), the strategy involved illegal but peaceful protest like work stoppages and hunger strikes in which protesters were arrested and sometimes imprisoned. Gandhi believed that such acts would in time soften the attitudes of the authorities.[15] By contrast, violent protest, he believed, only intensified anger and oppression, and, unlike Machiavelli, he argued that the ends could *not* justify the means. "The means," he declared, "may be likened to a seed, the end to a tree, and there is just the same inviolable connection between the means and the end as there is between the seed and the tree."[16] In addition to steadfastly opposing violence, he also tried to reconcile India's Hindus and Muslims. Gandhi thus became India's "conscience," and, when he was assassinated on January 30, 1948 by a Hindu fanatic, he was mourned by the entire country.

civil disobedience illegal acts designed to bring public attention to laws regarded as unjust.

Figure 12.4 Mohandas (Mahatma) Gandhi in the 1920s

Jawaharlal Nehru, the son of an Indian attorney, was educated at Cambridge University and returned to India in 1912 where a few years later he became a follower of Gandhi. During the 1920s, Nehru rose to the leadership of the Congress Party, advocating social reform in addition to political independence. With Gandhi's help, Nehru became leader of the Congress in 1929, and the following year tried to declare India's independence and was promptly arrested. However, the impact of the event was dramatic, as millions of Indians flocked to the Congress Party, and the British were forced to recognize it as an authentic voice of Indian nationalism. Unlike Gandhi, Nehru was an admirer of socialist principles, including the USSR's planned economy, and socialism became the basis of his policies later as prime minister of independent India.

In 1935, Britain passed the Government of India Act, providing for a gradual process toward Indian self-government within the British Empire and greater Indian participation in the country's civil service. Under this law, Britain's viceroy retained immense powers to intervene in the country's affairs, as well as control of the country's foreign, defense, and financial affairs. Overall, the act was a compromise between British politicians who wished to advance India's independence and diehards who bitterly opposed it. It was intended to assuage Indian moderates and weaken the appeal of the Congress Party, but achieved neither of these objectives.

From World War II to partition

World War II accelerated the decolonization movements in India and elsewhere. In areas occupied by Japan such as Dutch Indonesia, French Indochina, and British Burma, the mystique of European colonial rule was smashed, and postwar European efforts to regain control were doomed to failure in the face of growing independence movements. In India, the Congress Party opposed Britain's decision to bring India into the war. Led by Gandhi, a Quit India Movement against Britain was organized in 1942 whose followers demanded immediate independence, and launched a boycott of British goods and staged protests around the country. Gandhi, Nehru, and other Congress leaders were imprisoned until the end of the war. Nevertheless, millions of Indians fought for Britain during the war.

By 1945 Britain, much weakened and governed by Prime Minister Clement Attlee (1883–1967) and the socialist Labour Party, was willing to accept Indian independence. In 1946, at Gandhi's insistence, Nehru was selected as president of the Congress Party and future first leader of independent India. During the same year, elections swept Congress into control of India's Constituent Assembly and most of its provinces. Its

Did you know?

Mohandas Gandhi and his philosophy of nonviolent social protest greatly influenced US civil rights leader Martin Luther King, Jr. (1929–68). King became acquainted with Gandhi's ideas at seminary in a lecture given by Dr. Mordecai W. Johnson, president of Howard University, and became convinced that Gandhi's principle of the moral power of nonviolence could enhance the status of African-Americans.

most formidable political opponent was the All-India Muslim League, headed by Muhammad Al Jinnah (1876–1948) (known as the "father of Pakistan"), which demanded an independent Muslim state. As independence approached, Hindu–Muslim violence mounted. Finally, India's last viceroy, Lord Louis Mountbatten (1900–79), proposed the country's partition into two – India, a secular state with a Hindu majority, and Pakistan, a Muslim state. On August 15, 1947, India became independent with Nehru as prime minister, a position he held until his death in 1964. India's constitution was signed on January 26, 1949, and in 1952 the country conducted its first democratic national elections. Despite profound poverty, the injustices of a **caste** system, and widespread ethnic and religious tensions, India has remained a secular society and the world's most populous democracy.

caste a hereditary social class system of traditional Hindu society.

The partition triggered a massive population movement, with millions of Muslims moving to Pakistan and similar numbers of Hindus fleeing Pakistan to India. Law and order collapsed, and massive violence raged across the subcontinent. From this witches' brew emerged the conflict between India and Pakistan over Kashmir, one of the most dangerous flashpoints in global politics. At the time of partition, most of British India consisted of nine provinces directly ruled by London, but about 40 percent of the country consisted of princely states, governed by local rulers under British influence. The arrangement for partition allowed these rulers to choose whether to join India or Pakistan, their selection depending on the religion of the ruler and his subjects. A few, notably, Hyderabad (later forcibly incorporated into India) and Kashmir, had rulers whose religion differed from that of most subjects and were hotly contested.

The Kashmir dispute

Following attacks by Muslim tribal irregulars and under Indian political pressure, Kashmir's Maharajah Hari Singh (1895–1961)and its elected Muslim Prime Minister Sheikh Muhammad Abdullah (the "Lion of Kashmir") (1905–82) opted to join India even though a majority of the state's inhabitants were Muslim. Nehru then sent Indian troops to repel the attacks. The first of three Indian–Pakistani wars over Kashmir ensued, continuing until 1948 when the issue was taken to the UN Security Council.

By Resolution 91, the Security Council in 1951 imposed a ceasefire and demanded the removal of Indian and Pakistani troops, stating that "the final disposition of the State of Jammu and Kashmir will be made in accordance with the will of the people expressed through the democratic method of a free and impartial plebiscite conducted under the auspices of the United Nations."[17] Despite Pakistani demands that such a plebiscite be held, India has never permitted it, and neither country removed its troops from Kashmir. The ceasefire line, known as the Line of Control, still separates Pakistani and Indian-held areas of Kashmir (see Map 12.3). Not only did the Line of Control divide Kashmir's Muslim community, it also left India in control of the origin of the rivers of the Indus River basin on which much of Pakistan's agriculture depends.

The Kashmir situation deteriorated in 1962 when India and China clashed over the region of Aksai Chin, which still remains in China's hands. In addition, a small area known as the Trans-Karakoram, claimed by India, was ceded by Pakistan to China in 1963. Since then, Kashmir has been divided among Pakistan which controls the northwest region, India which holds the central and southern areas, and China which occupies a northeastern sector. Both India and Pakistan continue to claim the entire region.

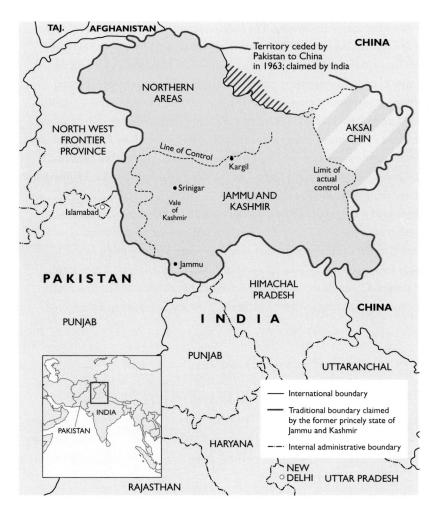

Map 12.3 The Kashmir region

Key document   Request for help from Kashmir's Maharajah Hari Singh to British Viceroy Lord Louis Mountbatten[18]

Dated: 26 October 1947

My dear Lord Mountbatten,

I have to inform your Excellency that a grave emergency has arisen in my State and request immediate assistance of your Government.

As your Excellency is aware the State of Jammu and Kashmir has not acceded to the Dominion of India or to Pakistan. Geographically my State is contiguous to both the Dominions. . . .

Though we have got a Standstill Agreement with the Pakistan Government that Government permitted steady and increasing strangulation of supplies like food, salt and petrol to my State.

Afridis, soldiers in plain clothes, and desperadoes with modern weapons have been allowed to infilter into the State. . . . The result has been that the limited number of troops at the disposal of the State had to be dispersed and thus had to face the enemy at the several points simultaneously, that it has become difficult to stop the wanton destruction of life and property and looting. The Mahora powerhouse which supplies the electric current to the whole of Srinagar has been burnt. The number of women who have been kidnapped and raped makes my heart bleed. The wild forces thus let loose on the State are marching on with the aim of capturing Srinagar, the summer Capital of my Government, as first step to over-running the whole State.

The mass infiltration of tribesmen drawn from distant areas of the North-West Frontier coming regularly in motor trucks using Mansehra–Muzaffarabad Road and fully armed with up-to-date weapons cannot possibly be done without the knowledge of the Provisional Government of the North-West Frontier Province and the Government of Pakistan. In spite of repeated requests made by my Government no attempt has been made to check these raiders or stop them from coming into my State. The Pakistan Radio even put out a story that a Provisional Government had been set up in Kashmir. . . .

With the conditions obtaining at present in my State and the great emergency of the situation as it exists, I have no option but to ask for help from the Indian Dominion. Naturally they cannot send the help asked for by me without my State acceding to the Dominion of India. I have accordingly decided to do so and I attach the Instrument of Accession for acceptance by your Government. The other alternative is to leave my State and my people to freebooters. On this basis no civilized Government can exist or be maintained. This alternative I will never allow to happen as long as I am Ruler of the State and I have life to defend my country. . . .

In haste and with kind regards,

The Palace, Jammu   Your sincerely,
26th October, 1947   Hari Singh

Two more wars between India and Pakistan followed in 1965 and 1971, with Indian victories in both. The second led to the division of East and West Pakistan and the emergence of a new country, Bangladesh, in place of the former East Pakistan. By the 1972 Simla Agreement, India and Pakistan pledged to settle their differences by peaceful means and abide by the Line of Control. However, in 1989 there began an insurgency in Indian-controlled Kashmir that still continues. Pakistan denies assisting the insurgents, but they enjoy sympathy from elements in the Pakistani army and sanctuary in Pakistan-controlled Kashmir. For its part, the Indian army uses brutal tactics against those sympathizing with the insurgency and has been charged with large-scale human rights violations.

In 1999, infiltration by Muslim militants and Pakistani regulars along the rugged Kargil ridges in the Himalayas triggered another conflict between India and Pakistan in which the Indian Army conducted a successful campaign featuring heavy artillery and air attacks in freezing temperatures at altitudes approaching 18,000 feet. The reason for Pakistan's infiltration, apparently planned by General (now President) Pervez Musharraf (1943–), was to attract world attention to the Kashmir issue. Pakistan's defeat produced a 2002 agreement to curb infiltration into Indian Kashmir. Although the Kargil War was limited, it triggered fears that it might escalate into a nuclear confrontation between India and Pakistan, and US President Clinton exerted pressure on Pakistan to back down.

South Asian politics were dramatically altered by the terrorist attacks of September 11, 2001 on New York and Washington. The US quickly sought warmer relations with Pakistan, which borders Afghanistan, and pressed Pakistan to reduce its support for Muslim insurgents in Kashmir. After a terrorist attack on India's Parliament in early 2002, tensions again rose, and there were renewed fears of another war and a nuclear exchange between India and Pakistan. Fortunately, diplomatic efforts reduced tension, and brought about a reduction in troops along their mutual border and a renewal of direct negotiations between the two countries that culminated in a November 2003 agreement for a ceasefire along their border and along the Line of Control. Additional steps, including confidence-building measures such as a bus service across the Line of Control, have created optimism for permanent peace between the two South Asian rivals.

Many Kashmiris seek independence for their region, but both India and Pakistan oppose this. India still regards the entire region as part of its country, and Pakistan still demands a UN plebiscite to determine the area's future. Although a future agreement may involve some adjustment to the Line of Control, it will probably involve the continued division of Kashmir, with greater autonomy for the Kashmiris.

Theory in the real world

Mahatma Gandhi was a **pacifist**, and he translated "nonviolence" from the Hindi word "*ahimsa*" (avoiding harm to others). "I object to violence," he declared, "because when it appears to do good, the good is only temporary; the evil it does is permanent."[19] "We are," he argued, "constantly being astonished these days at the amazing discoveries in the field of violence. But I maintain that far more undreamt of and seemingly impossible discoveries will be made in the field of nonviolence."[20] Nevertheless, though Gandhi's pacifism influenced followers of nonviolence elsewhere, it had little permanent impact on his own country. Since independence, India has fought several wars with Pakistan and China, has violently repressed the secessionist aspirations of ethnic minorities like the Nagas and Assamese, and has been the scene of repeated communal violence between Hindus and Muslims and violent abuse of "untouchables" or Dalits (those at the bottom of India's caste system).

pacifist one who refuses to support violence or war for any purpose.

Indonesia

Despite the costs of World War II, the Europeans sought – unsuccessfully – to reoccupy their former Asian colonies after Japan's defeat. Japan granted Indonesia, the fourth most populous country in the world and a major oil exporter consisting of almost 13,700 islands stretching 3,200 miles across the Indian and Pacific oceans, its independence in 1944 under a government led by Achmed Sukarno (1901–70) who had collaborated with his country's occupiers. Sukarno dreamt of a Greater Indonesia that would incorporate Portuguese Timor, British Malaya, and North Borneo. By the Jakarta Charter, Indonesia would be an Islamic state but one in which Muslim leaders would play a secondary role to a strong president. Shortly after Japan's surrender, Indonesia's leaders declared their country's independence, and British troops entered the country a month later. Dutch efforts to resume control were unsuccessful, and disorder spread, climaxing in bloody battles between British forces and armed Indonesians in Surabaya in East Java in late 1945.

An agreement between the Dutch and Indonesians for Indonesian autonomy while retaining a political link to the Netherlands was signed in May 1947. However, two months later the Dutch launched a "police action" against Indonesian nationalists in Sumatra and East Java which was halted in January 1948 when UN-sponsored negotiations left the Dutch temporarily in control of the areas they had seized. The Dutch resumed their efforts to suppress Indonesia's nationalists by force in December

1948, arresting and exiling Sukarno. This action produced an international backlash, and in January 1949 the UN Security Council demanded the restoration of Indonesia's nationalist government. The Dutch were no longer able to retain their colonial status, and finally on December 27, 1949, Indonesia became a sovereign country with its capital in Jakarta.

During the 1950s, Sukarno became increasingly authoritarian, imposing what he called "guided democracy." In 1963, he proclaimed himself president for life, and, much to America's annoyance, formed closed ties to communist China at the height of the Cold War. An attempted communist coup late in 1965, which led to the murder of several Indonesian generals, was savagely repressed by Indonesia's army and led to widespread and murderous attacks on the country's large ethnic Chinese minority. There followed a military coup in which General Mohammad Suharto seized power. Suharto followed a pro-American policy and, under what he called the "New Order," governed as a dictator until the 1997–98 Asian financial crisis (see chapter 12, pp. 540–3) and revelations of widespread corruption tainted him and members of his family. Confronted by widespread unrest, Suharto ceded power in May 1998 and was replaced as president by Vice-President Jusuf Habibie (1936–). Between 1998 and the present, Indonesia has evolved into a democracy. Habibie was succeeded in rapid succession by Abdurrahman Wahid (1940–) and Megawati Sukarnoputri (1947–) (ironically, Sukarno's daughter). Then, in 2004 Indonesian democracy was solidified by the electoral triumph of Susilo Bambang Yudhoyono (1949–).

Did you know?

Former Indonesian leader Mohammad Suharto is said to have stolen between $15 and $35 billion from his country during this 31 years in power. Others among the most corrupt former leaders were: Ferdinand Marcos: $5–10 billion (Philippines, 1972–86); Mobutu Sese Seko: $5 billion (Zaire, 1965–97); Sani Abacha: $2–5 billion (Nigeria, 1993–98); and Slobodan Milošević: $1 billion (Yugoslavia, 1989–2000).[21]

The size and geographic fragmentation of Indonesia exacerbates ethnic and religious differences and encourages secession by dissident groups. For example, although the country is largely Muslim, the island of Bali is Hindu. After independence from Holland in 1949, Indonesia was held together largely by the army, but the army's hold weakened after the Asian financial crisis.

Decolonization in Africa

In February 1960, British Prime Minister Harold Macmillan
(1894–1986) declared in a speech to South Africa's Parliament that ever
"since the break up of the Roman empire one of the constant facts of
political life in Europe has been the emergence of independent nations"
and that this desire had become worldwide. "Today," he continued, "the
same thing is happening in Africa. . . . The wind of change is blowing
through this continent, and whether we like it or not, this growth of
national consciousness is a political fact." Instead of resisting this tidal
wave, Macmillan argued that the West must come to terms with it
because, in his view, "the great issue in this second half of the twentieth
century is whether the uncommitted peoples of Asia and Africa will swing
to the East or to the West."[22] And, in December 1960, the UN General
Assembly approved the Declaration on Granting Independence to
Colonial Countries and Peoples that proclaimed "the necessity of bringing
to a speedy and unconditional end colonialism in all its forms and
manifestations."[23]

Decolonization in Africa had begun and, before it was over, numerous
new, often impoverished and unstable, countries would join the global
system (see Map 12.4). For the most part, the process was peaceful though
in some cases, such as the civil war which afflicted the former Belgian
Congo (today, the Democratic Republic of the Congo) from 1960 until
1964, independence proved traumatic. Britain and France, the major
colonial powers, realized that change was inevitable and, though the
French still hoped to make some of its colonies integral parts of their
country, both recognized that it was necessary to grant their colonies
greater autonomy. Increasingly, they transferred daily administration from
Europeans to Africans and transformed local advisory councils into elected
bodies with significant responsibilities. At the same time, nationalist
political parties were established and grew.

British Africa

Africa's leading colonial power, Britain, was the most successful of the
European countries in peacefully transferring sovereignty to its colonies,
and the British Empire was transformed into a voluntary association called
the British Commonwealth. The major exception to a peaceful transition
in British Africa was the Mau Mau insurgency in Kenya between 1952
and 1960 that ended in Kenya's independence in 1963 under the
leadership of Mau Mau leader Jomo Kenyatta (1889–1978) and his
Kikuyu tribe.

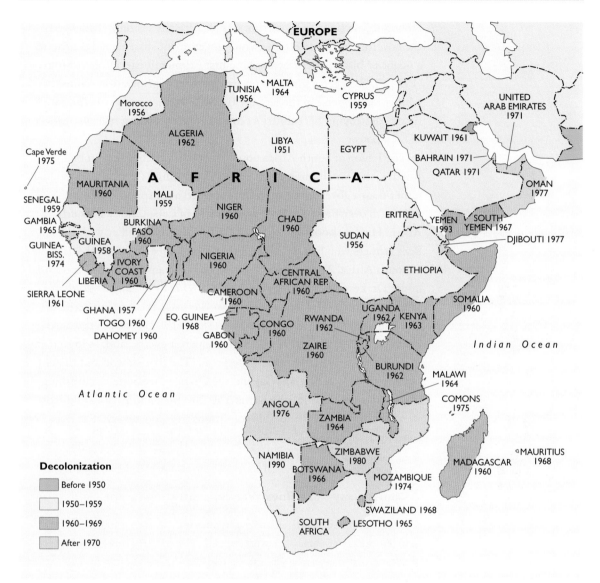

Map 12.4 Decolonization in Africa

The British faced a different problem in the case of Southern Rhodesia. In 1889 Cecil Rhodes was granted a charter to found the British South Africa Company, which ruled Zimbabwe and Zambia (collectively named Rhodesia, after Rhodes, in 1894) until 1923. Rhodesia split into Northern (Zambia) and Southern (Zimbabwe) Rhodesia in the 1960s, and Southern Rhodesia was governed by a white minority government. That government declared unilateral independence from Britain in 1965, but neither London nor the UN recognized the act. Instead, foreign economic sanctions and guerrilla war by Africans at home challenged the government. In 1980, the white government surrendered control to a majority black government whose first prime minister, Robert Mugabe (1924–), had been a guerrilla leader in the war of liberation against his white predecessors. In the late 1990s, Mugabe increasingly became a tyrant, destroying his country's economy and shredding its constitution to hold power.

The Union of South Africa posed an even more complex problem. Rhodes, still for all intents and purposes working as a private individual rather than a government official, supported a conspiracy by British settlers to overthrow the Boer government of Cape Colony in South Africa. His **freebooting** helped bring Britain into conflict with the Dutch Boer farmers who had established the Orange Free State and the Transvaal in South Africa. The unsuccessful raid on the Transvaal that he sponsored under Dr. Leander Starr Jameson (1853–1917) in January 1896 that sought to start a rebellion of British workers was the first in a series of events that climaxed in the Boer War (1899–1902). The Boers waged guerrilla warfare against the British, a superior enemy, and, as in so many irregular wars, atrocities were widespread. The British won and thereby came to control both Transvaal and the Orange Free State, establishing concentration camps in which over 150,000 Boer and African civilians were interned under deplorable conditions (see Controversy: The Boer War concentration camps).

freebooting pirating or looting.

Controversy   The Boer War concentration camps

Heated controversy erupted in Britain about the use of concentration camps to house Boer civilians. Ms. Emily Hobhouse (1860–1926), a British reformer and humanitarian, played a key role in publicizing and ending the horrible conditions in the British concentration camps. She arrived in South Africa late in 1900 and visited a number of the camps, including one at Bloemfontein. She later wrote of a second visit to that camp:

> The population had redoubled and had swallowed up the results of improvements that had been effected. Disease was on the increase and the sight of the people made the impression of utter misery. Illness and death had left their marks on the faces of the inhabitants. Many that I had left hale and hearty, of good appearance and physically fit, had undergone such a change that I could hardly recognize them.[24]

She then returned to Britain where she launched a publicity campaign against camp conditions. She met resistance from the British government, which was more interested in winning the war than in minimizing Boer casualties – whether soldier or civilian.

The significance of these events is that what began as an effort by greedy British adventurers seeking personal profit and power became an international conflict that led to the independence of South Africa, an illustration of how individuals can affect global politics as a whole. Moreover, that war showed that civilians were increasingly military targets and victims of warfare, a major change from the previous century.

In 1910, the British incorporated the Boer areas into the Union of South Africa, and the country was governed by a Boer (also called Afrikaner) government. South Africans participated on the British side in both world wars, and British economic relations with white South Africans were close. Problems in the country mounted after 1948 when the Afrikaner government introduced the racist policy of *apartheid*, the rigid, legally sanctioned separation of the races.

The struggle against apartheid from both within and outside the country continued until the early 1990s, when the apartheid laws were revoked. In 1994, South Africa elected its first majority government and black president, Nelson Mandela (1918–). Mandela was head of the African National Congress (ANC), which had led the resistance against the white government and thereafter became the dominant political force in South Africa. Under Mandela's successor, President Thabo Mbeki (1942–), South Africa has become Africa's most politically stable and powerful country and plays a key role in the continent's international organizations, especially the African Union and the South African Development Community.

French Africa

The French experience with decolonization proved more difficult than the British. In addition to Ho Chi Minh's guerrilla insurgency in Indochina (chapter 4, pp. 179–83), France confronted a massive insurrection in Algeria. In November 1954, Algeria's National Liberation Front (FLN), heartened by the success of the Indochinese insurgency, began a guerrilla war against French colonial authorities in their country. France responded with a massive military effort, and the Algerian war raged for eight years, becoming a nightmare for the French, with both sides employing terrorist tactics. France's Algerian dilemma was complicated by the presence of a large population of European settlers who violently opposed French abandonment of the country.

Theory in the real world

The West Indian psychoanalyst Frantz Fanon (1925–61), who served in the French army in World War II and joined the Algerian nationalist movement in 1954, became the theoretical inspiration for Algeria's independence struggle. Fanon's two major books *Black Skin, White Masks* (1952) and *The Wretched of the Earth* (1961) were analyses of the psychological consequences of racism on both colonialists and colonized. Fanon argued that language plays a key role in colonialism. By speaking the language of the colonizers, the colonized are forced to accept the latter's cultural values and their own inferiority. Seeking to become "white," they come to see their own "blackness" as evil and are thereby alienated from themselves. Such psychological oppression, Fanon argued, can be overcome only through "collective **catharsis**" that severs all links with the past produced by violent revolution on the part of the peasantry, a strategy that Algeria's revolutionaries actually adopted from Fanon and used with great success. "The naked truth of decolonization," he declared, "evokes for us the searing bullets and bloodstained knives which emanate from it."[25]

catharsis a relief of emotional tension.

Following the massacre of civilians by the FLN in Philippeville in August 1955, all-out war involving a continuing cycle of atrocities and counter-atrocities began. Villages were destroyed, and millions of Algerians were forcibly removed from their homes and resettled in areas under military control. As successive French governments proved incapable of dealing with the Algerian problem, dissatisfied army commanders plotted to bring to power Charles de Gaulle (1890–1970), the leader of the Free French during World War II, first postwar French premier, and the symbol of French grandeur, whom they believed could rally the nation and end the rebellion in Algeria. A military coup overthrew the government in Paris and returned de Gaulle to power in June 1958. Within a year, de Gaulle, recognizing his country's international isolation over the Algerian question and the mounting dissatisfaction of French public opinion, had begun the process of granting Algeria its independence.

Believing that de Gaulle was selling them out, Algeria's white settlers, aided by dissident French generals, rose in revolt in January 1960 and began a terrorist campaign in France itself. A terrorist group called the *Organisation de l'Armée Secrète* (Secret Army Organization) sought to assassinate de Gaulle on several occasions, one of which was the basis for the plot of Frederick Forsyth's thriller, *The Day of the Jackal*. The insurrection was quashed, and negotiations began in May 1961, climaxing with the Evian Accords of 1962 that finally ended hostilities and granted Algeria its independence. In a subsequent referendum, the agreement was approved by over 90 percent of French voters.

Portuguese Africa

The Portuguese were both the first Europeans to colonize Africa and the last to leave, and their departure proved difficult and violent. The two most important Portuguese colonies in Africa were Angola and Mozambique, and both had to fight for their independence and then were engulfed by bloody civil wars.[26]

Portugal first entered Angola in the late fifteenth century, and the colony became central to the slave trade. As decolonization spread in the 1960s, Portugal, governed by the dictator António de Oliveira Salazar (1889–1970) since 1932, refused to budge. The Portuguese effort to retain their colonial empire dragged on for 14 years, sapping the country's economy, until the dictatorship, headed by Marcello Caetano (1906–80) following Salazar's 1968 illness, was overthrown by the Portuguese army.

Tribal politics and the Cold War played key roles in subsequent events. Three Angolan independence movements emerged, each with a different tribal base and political ideology. One, the Popular Movement for the Liberation of Angola (MPLA), enjoyed support among the Kimbundu people in the provinces surrounding the capital, Luanda, and received aid from the USSR and its allies. A second, the National Front of Angola (FNLA), attracted support from among the Bakongo people of northern Angola and was aided by the United States. A third movement, the National Union for Total Independence of Angola (UNITA), led by Jonas Savimbi (1934–2002), was popular among the Ovimbundu people of central and western Angola and was aided by communist China.

Following Angola's independence in November 1975, the new country descended into civil war among the three movements. Troops from white-dominated South Africa entered the country to aid Savimbi's UNITA faction, which by then also enjoyed US backing, and prevented the new Angolan government (the former pro-communist MPLA) from aiding the African independence movement in neighboring South African-controlled Southwest Africa (today, Namibia).[27] Coming at the height of the Cold War, South Africa's intervention triggered the entry of Cuban troops on the side of the Angolan government and its president, Agostinho Neto (1922–79). In addition to its ideological aspect, the civil war also involved conflict for control of Angola's rich resources, including diamonds and offshore oil.

Angola's civil war continued even after the Cold War's end. A peace agreement was reached in 1994 providing for the merger of government and UNITA forces, and a government of national unity took office in 1997. However, violence erupted again the following year and did not end until Savimbi's death in 2002. By this time, it was among the longest running conflicts in the world.

Mozambique, first penetrated by the Portuguese at the beginning of the sixteenth century, had a similar experience. In 1962, an independence movement called the Front for the Liberation of Mozambique (FRELIMO) launched a guerrilla war against the Portuguese. The conflict continued for more than a decade until the overthrow of Portugal's dictatorship led to Mozambique's independence in 1975. Thereafter, FRELIMO established single-party rule and close relations with the Soviet Union and began to aid the movements opposed to white rule in South Africa and Southern Rhodesia. These governments, in turn, armed and aided an anti-FRELIMO insurrection by the Mozambican National Resistance (RENAMO). As many as one million died in the violence and the country's economy was virtually destroyed before FRELIMO abandoned its socialist policies and established a multiparty system in 1990. Negotiations ended the civil war in 1992 and saw the return of the more than 1.5 million Mozambique refugees who had fled the country. Since then, economic development has quickened, and the country has enjoyed amicable relations with its neighbors, including the post-apartheid government in South Africa.

In retrospect, colonialism was a meeting of two vastly different cultures in which that of the colonizers began to alter the values of the colonized. Nevertheless, under colonialism, while the colonized might gain certain benefits such as improved medical treatment, very few "natives" could cross the line into the other culture and few key political, social, or economic positions were open to them. The first generation of postcolonial leaders sought to bridge the gap between these two cultures and acquire the trappings of their former colonial masters. This effort involved anchoring popular loyalties in the new states and creating conditions for rapid economic development.

The politics of nation building and economic development

Following independence, many of the first generation of African and Asian leaders like Kenya's Kenyatta and Indonesia's Sukarno followed a nation-building policy that tried to replicate the European experience by creating a unifying sense of nationalism among their countries' disparate peoples, building state institutions and bureaucracies, and fostering rapid economic growth. However, many of these leaders were attracted to leftist variants of national development, and the issue of how the global South could advance its interests proved controversial and became highly politicized.

Modernization theory

The efforts of African and Asian leaders to make their countries more like Western states were influenced by modernization theory, which was popular in the 1950s and 1960s. Modernization theorists assumed that there was a linear progression from "primitive" or traditional societies to modern ones through the process of industrialization. Unlike Marxist theorists who believed that the main impediments to national development were external, modernization theorists, emphasizing the state level of analysis, thought that internal factors such as traditional values and the absence of capital investment prevented development. As such, they were state-level theorists.

Sociologist Neal J. Smelser, for example, conceptualized modernization as consisting of four processes that occurred at different stages in different societies: a movement from simple to complex technology, urbanization, a shift from animal and human power to machines, and a shift from subsistence agriculture to cash crops.[28] And, in a 1960 book that influenced President John F. Kennedy,[29] economist Walt Rostow conceived of modernization proceeding through five stages: (1) "the traditional society" lacking science and technology and with a value system "geared to what might be called a long-run fatalism; that is, the assumption that the range of possibilities open to one's grandchildren would be just about what it had been for one's grandparents"[30]; (2) "the preconditions for take-off" featuring higher education, ideas favorable to economic growth, enterprising individuals, institutions able to amass capital, growing investment in transportation and communication and "the building of an effective centralized national state" but with traditional society persisting "side by side with modern economic activities"[31]; (3) "the take-off" "when the old blocks and resistances to steady growth are finally overcome,"[32] featuring growing productivity, commercialized agriculture, rising savings and investment rates, and growing numbers of entrepreneurs; (4) "the drive to maturity" in which "10–20% of the national income is steadily invested, permitting output regularly to outstrip the increase in population," technology grows more complex, heavy industry becomes less important, the "economy finds its place in the international economy: goods formerly imported are produced at home; new import requirements develop, and new export commodities to match them," and the "economy demonstrates that it has the technological and entrepreneurial skills to produce not everything, but anything that it chooses to produce"[33]; and, finally, (5) "the age of mass consumption" in which basic needs are satisfied and social welfare and social security become more important.

Modernization was not seen simply as a shift in technology and economics. Many observers, forerunners of contemporary constructivists, also focused on the shift from traditional to modern societies that involved changes in people's expectations, values, and beliefs. This involved examining **political culture**: the pattern of beliefs, identities, and values held by members of a society. History, myth, education, language, experience, and ideology are all reflections of a people's basic values and beliefs. Like today's constructivists, those who studied political culture argued that a people's behavior was more a product of **socialization** than of rational choice. The pioneers of this approach, political scientists Gabriel Almond and Sidney Verba, focused on a people's belief structure, differentiating among those they labeled "parochials," with little interest in or awareness of politics, "subjects," aware of politics but not participants, and "participants," making demands upon the government and taking part in its decisions.[34] When parochials and subjects predominate, a society will have little impact on foreign policy. By contrast, the greater the number of participants in a society, the larger the number of political and pressure groups that many believe are vital to a healthy democracy.

Political-culture theorists also tried to characterize the culture of societies and predict the impact that its core values would have on policy. These values can be predominantly instrumental (pragmatic) or consummatory (ideological). Only in societies in which instrumental values are dominant would we expect to find organized social groups involved in the policy process with any regularity. Such groups will be organized around common causes and interests. The social capital produced in such groups – good will, fellowship, sympathy, and social intercourse – is a critical factor in making democratic societies work well.[35] By contrast, in societies dominated by single ideologies, groups are largely manipulated by those who shape the ideologies, and those societies are likely to feature a single dominant political party that defines and upholds the ideology.

Modernization theorists like Smelser and Rostow, as well as students of political culture, were criticized for several reasons. First, they assumed that "modern" (e.g., Western) was progressive and superior and that "traditional" was inferior. Second, they seemed to suggest that the process

political culture a country's political psychology based on deep-seated, long-held values.

socialization the general process of acquiring culture through family, education, and interaction with others.

would make countries more alike and that this was a virtue. In other words, modernization theorists saw the United States and Western Europe as models that countries emerging from colonial tutelage should emulate and whose values they should adopt and whose policies they should follow. Third, they saw the process as irreversible, a claim that seems naive today in light of widespread state failure.

If early modernization theorists were unabashed admirers of Western practices and institutions and postcolonial theorists (see p. 580) were acerbic critics of the West, recent scholarship such as the work of British sociologist Anthony Giddens is more dispassionate in dealing with modernization.[36] In traditional cultures, Giddens argues, powerful customs and norms determine the roles individuals can play and make it difficult for them to make choices for themselves. Such societies are based on direct interaction among those who live near to one another, and people tend to defer to elders, thereby reinforcing existing ways of doing things. Modernization is not possible as long as such societies retain traditional norms such as the inferiority of women or the authority of elders.

In modern societies, by contrast, according to Giddens, individuals can define their identities and have great scope for making choices for themselves. Their capacity for defining and redefining who they are and, therefore, for producing social, political, and economic change is enhanced by global communications technologies like the Internet and by their participation in global markets. Thus, they can virtually lift themselves out of their own societies and in doing so continue to change those societies.

The leftist orientation of many early postcolonial leaders such as Ghana's Kwame Nkrumah (1909–72), Tanzania's Julius Nyerere (1922–99), and Guinea's Ahmed Sékou Touré (1922–84) led them to eschew Western democratic principles, preferring to rule through a single mass party that they hoped could integrate their countries' tribal groups, bring an end to traditional customs, and centrally manage the development effort. They were impressed by the centrally controlled Soviet and Chinese political and economic systems, and they tried to apply socialist principles to the problems they faced. They emphasized rapid industrialization and tended to spend their limited resources on large, showy projects such as dams, sports stadiums, and factories that served as symbols of their countries. In doing so, they ignored the real needs of citizens, most of whom remained agrarian.

The results were disappointing. Many African governments became increasingly dictatorial, and corruption became endemic. Leaders favored their own tribal groups, thereby intensifying political and tribal tensions. Socialist practices discouraged foreign investment, and ignoring agriculture contributed to periodic famine and environmental disasters like deforestation.

The intellectual side of this Marxist orientation took the form of postcolonial theorists who were more critical of Western practices in the developing world than the early modernization theorists. Theorists like Immanuel Wallerstein argued that, although formal colonialism had ended, rich countries retained the ability to control the economies of less-developed countries (LDCs) through practices dubbed as **neocolonialism**. Theorists like Wallerstein focused on the system level of analysis, arguing that the immense gap between rich and poor provided the rich with **structural power** over the poor so that economic exploitation of the LDCs by Western countries and transnational corporations continued despite the end of formal colonial rule. The wealth and technology available to rich countries enabled them to prevent LDCs from pursuing the policies they wished without resorting to overt threats or promises. In other words, the structure of global politics, reflected in such factors as trade relations and control over mass media, perpetuated the inferior position of the global South and its **subaltern**[37] or subordinate peoples, condemning them to permanent weakness and poverty.

Thus, echoing Frantz Fanon (see Theory in the real world, p. 574), Edward Said argued that Western culture and knowledge were among the most important elements of Western power over the Islamic world.[38] Those who suffer physical or psychological harm from global injustice and inequality in the form of hunger or poverty, for instance, or who cannot achieve their full potential owing to social and economic constraints are said to be victims of **structural violence**.[39]

Let us now examine two examples of Marxist approaches to the issue of development: world system theory and *dépendencia* theory.

World system theory

Influenced by Marxism, political scientist Immanuel Wallerstein developed world system theory to explain the gap between rich and poor. According to Wallerstein, the modern "capitalist world system" emerged from a feudal world and led to the rise of Western Europe between 1450 and 1670. After a period of stagnation that began about 1300, capitalism grew, accompanied by the formation of strong states in Europe. Capitalism then expanded beyond Europe, creating a world economic system that transcended national boundaries.[40]

According to Wallerstein, the capitalist world system involved a global division of labor in which some regions prospered and others languished.

neocolonialism assertion that, despite decolonization, relations between wealthy countries and the LDCs remain unequal with the rich still able to exploit the poor.

structural power power derived from control over resources, location in information networks, interpersonal connections with influential others, and reputation for being powerful.

subaltern a subordinate; someone who is lower in rank.

structural violence physical or psychological violence which is carried out, not by individuals, but by structures, for example the injustices of the worldwide trading system.

He identified four regional types, each with distinctive features: core, semi-periphery, periphery, and external. Core states in Europe and North America, he argued, were the main beneficiaries of the world economic system at the expense of countries on the periphery.

The periphery included regions that exported raw materials and were linked to the core by unequal trade relations. Initially, much of Latin America and Eastern Europe constituted the periphery, and these were later joined by the colonized areas in Africa and Asia. Eastern Europe, governed by aristocratic landowners, exported grain to the core, using poorly paid rural laborers to do the work. Latin America exported precious metals and raw materials to Europe, and the Spanish and Portuguese elites exploited the peoples they conquered, as well as African slaves, as cheap labor.

Wallerstein examined the evolution of the world economy, during which some countries moved from core to periphery and vice versa. From the eighteenth century, industrialization fostered imperialism in a search for new markets and raw materials, and Asia and Africa joined the world economy as part of the periphery, while Germany and the United States became core countries. In this way, world system theory, like classical Marxism, theorizes that economic change underlies historical evolution.

Dépendencia theory

The influence of Marxism was also apparent in the popularity of *dépendencia* (dependency) theory, especially in Latin America, between the 1960s and the 1980s. Like Wallerstein, *dépendencia* theorists such as Argentine economist Raúl Prebisch (1901–86), Brazilian economist Theotonio dos Santos (1936–), and German sociologist André Gunder Frank (1929–2005) argued that underdevelopment was due to the LDCs' inferior position in a world capitalist system.[41]

The world trading system, they contended, benefited only advanced capitalist counties. **Terms of trade** – the ratio of export prices to import prices – were stacked against the LDCs, especially those that exported raw materials and agricultural commodities, because the prices of imported manufactured goods rise faster than the price of commodity exports. Terms of trade for LDCs would improve only if prices of their exports rose faster than prices of imports. Worse, since much of world trade is among corporate subsidiaries and is not exposed to the market conditions, corporations can use accounting devices to avoid paying taxes. For example, by overpricing products sent to subsidiaries in high-tax countries and underpricing products sent to low-tax countries, TNCs can

terms of trade an index of the price of a country's exports in terms of its imports.

artificially reduce profits where tax rates are high, thereby lowering their tax burden.

According to *dépendencia* theorists, the key to breaking the cycle in which the rich got richer and the poor got poorer lay in reducing imports (import substitution), becoming as self-sufficient as possible, and establishing state control of the economy. Many of these countries depended on exports of a single primary commodity like cocoa from the Ivory Coast and so were vulnerable to fluctuations in price owing to rising or falling demand for their product. A rapid decline in commodity price, for example, would leave them awash in debt and unable to develop industries for economic development. The LDCs, argued the *dépendencia* theorists, should cease importing goods from the developed world, thereby ending their dependence on the capitalist core and, instead, adopt protectionist policies to reduce imports. Only by encouraging infant industries, nationalizing foreign enterprises, and regulating domestic prices, the argument went, could LDCs achieve economic independence.

Initially, the policies advocated by *dépendencia* theorists enjoyed some success, but by the 1980s the limits of these policies were apparent. Industries fostered by their policies remained inefficient, and the failure to invest in agriculture harmed the LDCs' most important economic sector. Government budget deficits had ballooned, and hyperinflation had become a staple of economic life owing to deficit spending and artificially low interest rates. Moreover, subsidizing domestic industry required large-scale capital that was only available through foreign loans. Thus, Latin American debt almost quadrupled between 1975 and 1982, until an acute debt crisis confronted the region. The effort to come to grips with the debt crisis produced a "lost decade" in Latin America, reducing per capita income and failing to reduce economic inequality.

The failure of policies fostered by *dépendencia* theory and the growing pressure on LDCs from the developed world to abandon import-substitution policies and adopt free-market export-led policies to attract foreign investment for industrialization largely discredited Marxian economic analysis. Nevertheless, Marxist analysis has not entirely disappeared. The persistence of economic inequality within and between countries and the cycles of recession and prosperity that still characterize global economics help Marxism to survive as an analytic tool and a critique of capitalism.

As we have seen, the process of decolonization took place during the Cold War, a struggle that pitted East against West. Although the global South became an arena for East–West competition, it did not belong to either Cold War bloc. The capitalist West became known as the First World and the socialist East, the Second World. The poor LDCs in Asia,

Africa, and Latin America with economies based on agriculture and raw materials whose prices were determined by wealthy countries became known as the Third World. This term was first used in 1952 by French demographer Alfred Sauvy, who saw the LDCs as analogous to the Third Estate in France before the French Revolution. The Third Estate included the exploited common people who were neither nobles nor clergy who were the members of the First and Second Estates.[42] We now examine the policy of nonalignment that many in the Third World pursued during the Cold War.

Nonalignment

In April 1955, the representatives of 29 African and Asian countries met in the Indonesian city of Bandung. In his opening speech to the gathering, Indonesia's President Sukarno declared: "We are united . . . by a common detestation of colonialism in whatever form it appears. We are united by a common detestation of racialism. And we are united by a common determination to preserve and stabilize peace in the world." Colonialism, he continued, was still alive though it had changed from direct control to "economic control, intellectual control, actual physical control by a small but alien community within a nation." Moreover, nuclear war, Sukarno warned, threatened everyone, but the Third World could "inject the voice of reason into world affairs."[43] Thus, the nonaligned movement was born.

Nonalignment, which Indian Prime Minister Nehru labeled "positive neutralism," was a typical response of many LDCs during the Cold War. Although the LDCs were a diverse group, most rejected permanent involvement in Cold War conflicts on either side. **Isolationism** was not an option because the LDCs needed trade and aid for economic development. Traditional **neutralism** as practiced by countries like Switzerland required abstaining from global politics and would have placed the Third World in a passive foreign posture. In contrast to traditional neutralism, nonalignment involved maximizing trade and aid while maintaining political independence through active involvement with a variety of states and international organizations. Far from remaining passive, the nonaligned regularly tried to play off East and West in order to get assistance from both. Nearly all carried on trade with and, in many cases, were provided arms by the superpowers.

Nonalignment did not prevent nonaligned countries from taking positions on specific issues. Many, for instance, condemned US involvement in Vietnam in the 1960s and 1970s; virtually all opposed South Africa's system of apartheid, denounced nuclear testing and

isolationism a policy aimed at avoiding overseas political and military involvement.

neutralism (traditional) neutrality, or a policy of abstaining from conflicts in global politics.

demanded nuclear disarmament; and most favored the Arab states in their conflict with Israel. The LDCs regularly pointed to US military aid to repressive governments as evidence of America's neocolonialism.

Nonalignment was justified as a strategy to prevent the Cold War from spreading to the Third World. It sought to base relations with one another on the five principles to which Nehru and China's Premier Zhou Enlai (1898–1976) had agreed in 1954 at a meeting in Colombo, Sri Lanka. These were: (1) mutual respect for one other's territorial integrity and sovereignty, (2) mutual nonaggression, (3) noninterference in one other's internal affairs, (4) equality and mutual benefit, and (5) peaceful coexistence.

The nonaligned states regarded the UN and related international organizations as very important and vigorously supported them, pressing for increases in their budgets, because the LDCs enjoyed a voting majority in the UN General Assembly and because these institutions provided forums for LDCs to express their views and were sources of economic aid. The LDCs also believed that the UN could help them avoid direct involvement in the Cold War and assist in solving divisive regional and local disputes. Nevertheless, most LDCs, rather than supporting **supranationalism**, remained highly nationalistic and opposed any dilution of their sovereign prerogatives.

supranational superior to states.

In practice, nonalignment did not mean impartiality between East and West in the Cold War. Communist countries like China and Cuba enjoyed key roles in the movement, and many LDCs adopted positions in opposition to the United States and its allies. Few LDCs had sympathy for democratic norms and practices, and many were attracted to central economic planning and socialist economic policies. Some backed Soviet and Chinese aid to "national liberation movements" that they equated with opposing neocolonialism.

Central to the nonaligned movement was the effort to reduce economic inequality in the global system. Demands to reform the global economic system dated from the 1961 meeting of nonaligned countries in Belgrade, Yugoslavia, and the establishment of the UN Conference on Trade and Development (UNCTAD) and the LDCs' "Group of 77" in 1964. UNCTAD sought to deal with economic issues from the poor countries' perspective and to challenge the global trading system, which favored rich states.

Passage of UN Resolutions 3201 and 3202 at the Sixth Special Session of the United Nations on May 1, 1974 marked the formal call for a New International Economic Order (NIEO). The resolutions set out principles to improve the economies of poor states, outlining six areas that needed attention to prevent conflict between rich and poor:

1 Regulating transnational corporations.
2 Transferring technology from rich to poor.
3 Reforming global trade to assist LDC development.
4 Canceling or renegotiating LDCs' debts.
5 Increasing economic aid to LDCs.
6 Changing voting procedures in international economic institutions to give LDCs more influence.

However, the NIEO had little lasting impact on global politics because of the negative reaction of rich states. American leaders denounced it as a "screwball effort" and as a way to "beat the West and the North over the head."[44]

The end of the Cold War removed the rationale for nonalignment. By that time, it was apparent that the policies of nation building, industrialization, and nonalignment were having uneven results. However, the growing acceptance of free-market policies in the developing world and the inflow of foreign investment began to bear fruit, especially in the 1990s, and, despite widespread poverty, the global South is becoming a major factor in the global economic system.

An economic giant awakens

Despite the difficulties confronted by the global South since independence, recent years have witnessed a dramatic surge in the economies of many of these countries, most importantly China and India, which prior to industrialization in Europe had been the world's largest economies. India, until 1980, was, in the words of one observer, "shackled" by "a mixed economy that combined the worst features of capitalism and socialism" based on a model that was "inward-looking and import-substituting rather than outward-looking and export-promoting."[45] However, since 1991, the Indian state has gradually reduced its role in the country's economy and encouraged greater entrepreneurship. As a result, India's economy grew at the rate of 7.5 percent a year between 2002 and 2006, in the process reducing population growth, enlarging its middle class, raising per capita income from $1,178 to $3,051, and becoming the world's fourth largest economy.[46] Other developing states, especially Brazil and Russia, are also rapidly emerging as economic powerhouses. Even Africa, historically the economic laggard, has shown signs of quickening economic growth in recent years.

This surge owes much to the shift in much of the global South from state-controlled and neo-Marxist to market-based policies. Finally, in 2005, the developing world of emerging markets accounted for more than half of world **gross domestic product** (measured in **purchasing-power**

gross domestic product (GDP) the total market value of all final goods and services produced in a country in a given year, equal to total consumer, investment, and government spending, plus the value of exports, minus the value of imports.

purchasing-power parity measurement of purchasing power in different countries that takes account of lower prices in developing countries compared to rich countries for a given basket of goods.

foreign-exchange reserves
deposits of hard currencies such as dollars, pounds, euros, and yen held by national banks of different countries.

parity). In addition, their share of global exports has risen from 20 percent in 1970 to 43 percent today, and they have about 70 percent of **foreign-exchange reserves**, making them less and less dependent on foreign investment.[47] During the past five years, LDCs' annual growth has been close to 7 percent per year, compared to 2.3 percent in the developed countries, and the International Monetary Fund predicts a similar difference during the next five years.[48]

In addition, the developing world has been caught up in economic globalization, and developed and developing countries have become increasingly interdependent. This is partly due to the transnational organization of production and distribution made possible by the Internet. China alone, on which we will focus attention next, will shortly be responsible for 10 percent of global trade, and China and India are increasingly competing with the developed countries in a range of high-tech as well as labor-intensive products and services.[49] While creating pockets of unemployment in the developing world as jobs are outsourced, greater economic inequality within both developed and undeveloped countries, and new sources of global pollution, rapid economic growth in the global South will benefit the developed countries in two ways. (1) The large numbers of newly enriched citizens in the global South will increase the demand for products from developed countries, and (2) the lower cost of production in the global South will limit inflation globally.

The rapid economic development of China and its transition from a centrally controlled Marxist economy to a market-based economy is the single most important factor in the shifting economic balance between developed and developing countries. We now examine that transition in greater detail.

China joins the global economy

After 15 years of often arduous negotiation, China's formal admission to the World Trade Organization on December 11, 2001 marked the country's full-scale entry into the global economy and its recognition as an economic superpower. For decades, observers had predicted that China would emerge as a superpower, but after China's civil war and the communist takeover of the country, it failed to fulfill its economic potential. In the following sections, we examine the dramatic evolution in China's economic policies from Maoist communism to capitalist competitor and the growing economic interdependence of the United States and China.

China from Mao to Deng

Mao was a dedicated Marxist who sought to follow a uniquely Chinese path to socialism. In November 1957, he announced a plan for China's rapid industrialization and self-sufficiency called the Great Leap Forward. His idea was to move millions of peasants into enormous communes where they could be mobilized to carry out large-scale industrial projects. In towns and villages throughout China, factories, schools, and other institutions were ordered to build furnaces to increase steel production. This effort proved disastrous for China's agricultural economy, but Mao crushed any criticism. Between 1959 and 1962, industrial production dropped precipitously, and famine swept the country. Economic conditions further deteriorated when the Soviet Union ceased providing China with economic aid in 1960.

Economic turmoil again struck China after Mao started the Great Proletarian Cultural Revolution in 1966, the purpose of which was to rid the country of lingering capitalist values and reawaken revolutionary fervor among China's citizens. Mao's other objectives were to weaken China's government bureaucracy, which he viewed as insufficiently radical, and to purge his opponents in the Communist Party.

The Chinese economy ground to a halt as the country descended into chaos. Radical pro-Mao students organized into groups of Red Guards attacked government and Communist Party officials, denouncing them as counterrevolutionaries and class enemies. Those with education became special targets of radicals, and many were killed or imprisoned. The country's schools and universities were closed; officials were purged from their jobs; and large-scale violence erupted in 1967 and 1968, ending only after China's People's Liberation Army intervened to restore order. The Cultural Revolution continued at a more muted level until 1976.

Following Mao's death in 1976, a power struggle ensued, and in 1977 Deng Xiaoping (1904–97), a victim of two of Mao's purges, won political power. Deng broke decisively with his predecessor, promoting China's economic growth by introducing material incentives and private property. Encouraging China's citizens to pursue the "Four Modernizations" – agriculture, industry, technology, and defense – Deng urged families to grow food for their own use on their own plots of land, set up businesses, and sell what they did not need for a profit. Rural communes were broken up, and peasants were allowed to lease land.

To encourage foreign investment, the government established special economic zones where foreign-financed enterprises could be built. Deng also abandoned Mao's radical social leveling, restoring education, sending students overseas to study science and technology, and permitting gaps in wealth between rich and poor to reappear. Individual initiative and

Figure 12.5 Deng Xiaoping

International Institute of Social History, Stefan R. Landsberger Collection, http://www.iisg.nl/~landsberger

entrepreneurship became the watchwords for Deng's new China. "We should," Deng declared, "let some people get rich first, both in the countryside and in the urban areas. To get rich by hard work is glorious."[50]

Under the slogan "Socialism with Chinese characteristics," China's economic growth quickened. Deng abandoned Mao's pursuit of self-sufficiency and sought foreign technology and investment to modernize the country. With this in mind, China improved its relations with the United States and Japan and negotiated the return of the bustling cities of Hong Kong from Britain in 1997 and Macao from Portugal in 1999. And in an effort to reduce China's wasteful and unprofitable public sector, Deng privatized ever more of China's enterprises, forcing them to become profitable or fail and allowing resources to be allocated by market prices.

Deng's market reforms unleashed China's immense economic potential. Growing at an annual rate of 9 percent, by 2003 China ranked fifth in the world in total gross domestic product (total value of all goods and services) and fourth in exports.[51] These figures do not include Hong Kong, which is a Special Administrative Region of China with exports equivalent to 50 percent of China's. During the same period the average income of China's 1.3 billion people tripled. According to some projections, by 2020, China will surpass Japan to become the second largest economy in the world.

China's admission to the WTO reflected its acceptance of global trade rules, its growing interdependence with other countries in the world economy, and its opening to the forces of globalization. Its entry bound it to make substantial tariff reductions, remove other trade barriers, and open up formerly closed sectors of its economy to foreign competition. US Trade Representative Charlene Barshefsky noted the contrast of the new China under Deng with the old Maoist China, which she described as "a nation with neither lawyers, nor law enforcement, nor laws" in which policy was based on "fiat and the interpretations of edicts and slogans" by officials constantly fearful of being arrested. China's entry was a "defining moment" because it had accepted "an entire body of agreements, rules and enforcement procedures developed over decades under western-based legal norms."[52]

Deng, however, was not prepared to let Western-style democracy emerge in China or to surrender the Communist Party's monopoly of power. He and his successors were painfully aware that Mikhail Gorbachev's policies of *perestroika* (economic modernization and restructuring) and *glasnost* (openness) had led to the collapse of the Soviet Union and the end of communism there. Thus, the regime brutally suppressed the country's budding democracy movement, which first appeared in 1978 and 1979 with posters on the "Democracy Wall" in

Beijing protesting corruption and the absence of democracy. The movement became popular among Chinese university students in the 1980s, especially as Soviet leader Gorbachev began to institute political and social reforms in his country. In April 1989, student protests erupted in Beijing and continued during a visit by Gorbachev. Students occupied Tiananmen Square in the city's center, but on June 4, 1989, Chinese military units, using tanks, brutally attacked the demonstrators and killed hundreds. Deng then ordered the ouster of the Communist Party's general secretary, Zhao Ziyang (1919–2003), who had opposed the use of force against the students, replacing him with Jiang Zemin (1926–).[53] After the Tiananmen Square massacre, China's democracy movement went into decline, and President George H. W. Bush suspended all government-to-government sales and commercial export of weapons as well as all visits by American and Chinese leaders.

China's economy today

China stands at the threshold of becoming an economic superpower and is "revolutionizing the relative prices of labor, capital goods, and assets in a way that has never happened so quickly before."[54] However, the country's rapid economic growth poses political and economic dilemmas for its leaders. For example, despite the privatization of many enterprises, many others, especially heavy industries established in the 1950s and 1960s, are unprofitable and remain state owned.[55] Indeed, China's People's Liberation Army continues to run a variety of businesses, many of which lose money. Efforts to privatize these enterprises and force them to become efficient and profitable will alienate the bureaucrats who manage them and, even worse, produce massive unemployment.

Already, as many as 100 million migrant workers, many peasants from China's interior, move from city to city in search of jobs. These migrants, called the "blind flow," pose huge social problems. Greater unemployment would create political discontent, especially since the country's social safety net, which provided free health care, housing, and education in earlier decades, has largely vanished. Another knotty problem is posed by widespread corruption of communist officials. Continued economic success requires ousting such officials but might imperil party control.

Another danger involves China's uneven economic development. Most of the country's growth has taken place in its coastal provinces, while much of the interior remains impoverished and agricultural. And regional disparities continue to grow. The coastal regions chafe under party control, as capitalist entrepreneurs, foreign investors, and local officials develop policy based on economic logic rather than communist ideology. These coastal regions also value warm relations between China and its leading trade partners and sources of investment, preferring to set aside foreign policy differences with the United States and Japan.

Communist Party control of the interior, however, remains strong, and the party is prepared to rouse Chinese nationalism against foreigners, especially Japan and America, to solidify its hold on power, despite the risk of frightening foreign investors. In effect, there are two Chinas – one an economically developed sector that encourages individual initiative and the other backward and traditional. An unanswered question is whether these two Chinas can coexist or whether they will grow apart and even separate.

Perhaps, the most significant unanswered question about China is whether economic liberalization based on individual initiative and a free market can succeed without political democracy. Many Western observers believe that a free market requires individual freedom and democratic institutions and that government intervention stifles economic growth. China's communists are betting that China's economic growth will continue, even while they retain central control of the country. Only time will tell who is correct.

China's integration in the world economy has made it a major recipient of US, Japanese, and European investment, roughly $1 billion every week, and a growing factor in world trade. Between 1994 and 2004, the value of China's exports soared from $121 billion to over $593 billion, and the value of its imports rose from $115 billion to over $561 billion.[56] In 2005 its trade surplus with the rest of the world tripled, reaching $105 billion.[57] With a vast pool of cheap labor, China has become a leading destination for American and Japanese transnational corporations wishing to reduce production costs and increase global competitiveness. This has meant a loss of jobs in the United States and elsewhere as companies shift operations to China. In addition, a persistent and growing US trade deficit with China (see next section) has created alarm among Americans who fear a further loss of jobs to China.

Chinese–American trade relations

In recent decades, Sino-American trade has increased dramatically. The value of US exports to China between 1994 and 2004 almost quadrupled from $9.3 billion to $34.7 billion. At the same time, the value of US imports from China rose from $41.4 to $210.5 billion, increasing America's trade deficit with China in a single decade by over $140 billion.[58] In 2004, the United States passed Japan to become China's leading trading partner.

In October 2005, the monthly US trade deficit hit $68 billion, the highest in history, hastening the loss of jobs overseas and running up the US debt to its trading partners. The trade deficit with China alone reached $20.5 billion, provoking calls from American politicians to protect US producers against Chinese imports. The deficit also intensified American demands that China allow its currency, the yuan, to appreciate in value relative to the dollar, thereby making US exports to China less expensive and raising the price of China's exports to the United States. American politicians threatened to impose across-the-board tariffs on Chinese imports unless China revalued its currency, and China began to do so in July 2005 and quickened the process the following year.

US officials also complain that intellectual piracy (the theft of inventions, trademarks, and designs and copyrighted materials) in China costs American manufacturers as much as $24 billion each year and that Chinese authorities have failed to crack down on this illegal industry. Thus, the US software industry reported that up to 98 percent of the copies of US software products sold in China in 1999 were "pirated."[59]

Did you know?

Wal-Mart imports over $15 billion worth of Chinese goods to sell in the United States.[60] In 2003, China produced three-quarters of the world's toys.[61]

US–Chinese economic interdependence has thickened as trade between the two countries has increased. Low-cost imported Chinese goods, such as McDonald's toys, provide US consumers with inexpensive products and help keep America's inflation rate low. US trade deficits have meant a huge outflow of dollars to China and other Asian countries. China and Japan have used these funds to purchase large amounts of US securities (**bonds** and **treasury notes** that are equivalent to dollars), and these purchases have kept US interest rates low, enabling Americans to borrow money cheaply and stabilizing the value of the dollar. With $250 billion in US treasury notes, as of November 2005, China's holdings are second only to Japan's.[62] In effect, China and Japan lend the United States almost $2 billion *a day* to buy their exports. Washington can pay its **current account** deficit at relatively low interest rates by borrowing money through the sale of government bonds. This situation is precarious, and some observers regard China's vast holdings of US and corporate securities as dangerous. China, they contend, can exert political pressure on the United States by threatening to sell those securities and buy European

bond a certificate promising to pay back borrowed money at a fixed-rate of interest on a specified date.

treasury note an interest-paying debt instrument issued by the US government, with an initial life of between one and ten years.

current account a statistic that registers all payments between a country and the rest of the world in goods and services, investment income and payments, and unilateral transfers.

and Japanese securities instead. The effect would be explosive: US stock prices would plummet; the price of imported products would soar; interest rates on everything from home mortgages to credit cards would balloon; and the value of the dollar would collapse.

Others argue that fear of Chinese influence is exaggerated because, as expected in an interdependent relationship, China would also suffer economically: The value of the securities China owned, as well as US dollars it has amassed, would drop precipitously. Moreover, a sudden drop in the dollar's value would end US imports of Chinese goods, and unemployment and bankruptcies would spread across China. In this view, what exists is a kind of economic mutually assured destruction in which US–Chinese fates are so entwined that neither country is likely to do anything drastic. The only way both countries can continue to prosper is for market forces to force the United States to reduce its trade deficit gradually, for Americans to save more of what they earn.

Conclusion

This chapter has traced the evolution of the developing world from its colonial past to the present. Nevertheless, the effects of colonialism can still be seen around the world, from India's railway system and bureaucratic organization that were established by the British to the widespread use of French and English in Africa and Southeast Asia. The experience affected both the colonizers, leaving many with a sense of guilt, and the colonized who, as we saw, have found it difficult to build their nations and develop economically and politically. In addition, Europe is home to large communities of former colonial subjects. And these communities – Pakistanis, Indians, and Jamaicans in Britain; Indonesians in the Netherlands; and North African Muslims in France – have become topics of heated debate, especially with the spread of militant Islam and the implication of some disaffected Muslims in terrorist activities in these countries.

Although the pace of economic development has quickened in many developing countries, poverty remains a common feature in much of the global South, along with associated woes such as disease and corruption. The next chapter turns to poverty and other threats to human security, including transnational crime, migration, and disease, with a focus on the less-developed countries.

Student activities

Discussion and essay questions

Comprehension questions

1 Describe the surge of imperialism in Asia and Africa in the nineteenth century. How was it different from the old imperialism?
2 Describe the different perspectives to nation building and modernization.
3 What is structural power, and how does it affect LDCs?

Analysis questions

4 Do persistent underdevelopment and conflict in the global South have their roots in colonialism? Why or why not?
5 Do Marxist theories offer any insights into the problems facing the global South?
6 Is Gandhi's theory of nonviolence suitable for current problems of global politics?
7 What consequences are likely to ensue in coming decades from the dramatic growth in the economies of the developing world? How should the United States and Europe respond to this growth?

Map exercise

Discuss the trends depicted in the maps of Africa in Map 12.5.

Year of independence

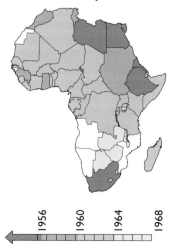

1956   1960   1964   1968

Years at war, 1956–95

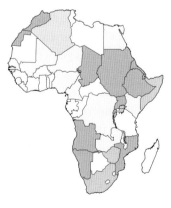

5   10   15   20

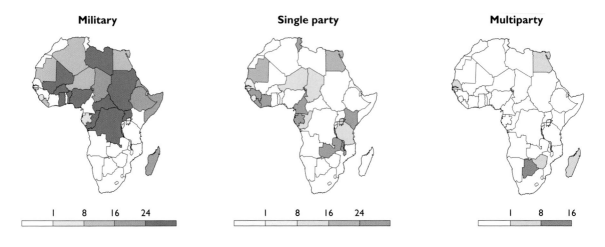

Military   Single party   Multiparty

Cultural materials

Joseph Conrad's (1857–1924), *Heart of Darkness*, published in 1899, is regarded as a literary classic. It is also an indictment of Belgian brutality in the Congo during King Léopold's ownership of that territory. Read the passage from the novel in the text (pp. 557–8). What does it tell you about Belgian imperialism? The 1979 film *Apocalypse Now*, starring Marlon Brando, involved a retelling of Conrad's novel moved to Vietnam. The film's hero is on a mission into Cambodia to assassinate a renegade Green Beret, Colonel Walter E. Kurtz (the parallel to Conrad's mysterious dying trader Georges-Antoine Kurtz) who has come to be regarded as a god among a local tribe. Why do you think director Francis Ford Coppola drew the analogy between the Belgian Congo and Vietnam?

Further reading

Cline, William R., *Trade Policy and Global Poverty* (Washington, DC: Center for International Development, 2004). Incisive account of how trade policies perpetuate poverty in the LDCs.

Fanon, Frantz, *The Wretched of the Earth* (New York: Grove Press, 1963). A classic radical analysis of the psychological impact of colonization upon the colonizers.

Gurr, Ted Robert and Barbara Harff, *Ethnic Conflict in World Politics*, 2nd ed. (Boulder, CO: Westview Press, 2004). A well-chosen set of cases of ethnic conflict.

Handelman, Howard, *The Challenge of Third World Development*, 4th ed. (Upper Saddle River, NJ: Prentice-Hall, 2005). Issues confronting the developing world such as democracy, religion, ethnic conflict, urbanization, and agrarian reform.

Harkavy, Robert E. and Stephanie G. Neuman, *Warfare and the Third World* (New York: Palgrave, 2001). Analysis of theories and key factors in wars in the Third World.

Harrison, David, *The Sociology of Modernization and Development* (New York: Routledge, 1988). Thorough review of the variants of modernization theory.

Rotberg, Robert I., ed., *When States Fail: Causes and Consequences* (Princeton, NJ: Princeton University Press, 2004). Excellent collection of essays on the various sources of state failure.

Sachs, Jeffrey D., *The End of Poverty: Economic Possibilities for Our Time* (New York: Penguin, 2005). Accessible and compelling analysis of what works and what does not in economic development, featuring excellent case studies.

13 Human security

In July 2005, the leaders of the world's seven major industrial economies (called the G7) plus Russia (the G8) met at a resort in Scotland for their annual conference. On July 2, with hundreds of millions of people around the world watching on television, a series of rock concerts called "Live 8" took place in Philadelphia, Paris, Johannesburg, Rome, Berlin, Moscow, and Barrie, Canada to pressure world leaders to fight poverty in Africa. The largest concert, bringing together about 200,000 people, took place in London's Hyde Park, and featured Paul McCartney, Madonna, Elton John, and others. Speaking at the Johannesburg concert, former South African president Nelson Mandela told his audience that the world's G8 leaders had a "historic opportunity to open the door to hope and the possibility of a better future for all." In Philadelphia, crowds gathered around the Museum of Art to hear Stevie Wonder and others. At Berlin's Brandenburg Gate, Rome's Circus Maximus, the Palais de Versailles outside Paris, and Moscow's Red Square, crowds also gathered for concerts.[1]

As we saw in chapter 12, the less-developed countries (LDCs), though beset by a host of challenges, are emerging as key actors in the global economy. Only now are serious efforts underway to address poverty, environmental degradation, and other woes in the LDCs, but progress is slowly being made. Although the economic output of the developing world as a whole (including China, India, and the rapidly growing countries of Southeast Asia) accounted for over half the global total in 2005,[2] these countries still account for most of the global poor. And looming above efforts to overcome global poverty is the need for honest and energetic leadership in many LDCs. As long as these countries are governed by corrupt leaders and lack good governance, they will be unable to overcome the poverty and the other threats to human security that afflict them.

human security protection against threats to human life and well being.

Poverty represents an enduring challenge to **human security**, especially in the global South. However, until recently, most scholars, especially realists, thought of security as involving only military protection of state interests; and, from the beginning of the Westphalian era until the end of the Cold War, the problem of security in global politics was limited to the threat of foreign invasion or attack. Although this problem still looms large, the security agenda has grown dramatically in recent years. Survival and well-being require more than military protection, and the concept of human security, developed mainly by liberals, takes account of this. People's lives and welfare are also threatened by crime, disease, civil strife, hunger, poverty, and, as we saw in chapter 10, human rights abuses that may trigger massive refugee flows. According to Canadian diplomat Rob McRae, the idea of human security "takes the individual as the nexus of its concern, the life *as lived*, as the true lens through which we should view the political, economic, and social environment. At its most basic level, human security means freedom from fear."[3]

Figure 13.1 London's Hyde Park Live 8 concert, held to bring attention to the demand to reduce Third World Debt

© PA Photos

This chapter examines the major challenges to human security. It begins by exploring the concept and then turns to the challenge of poverty that many observers regard as the most pervasive and enduring threat to human security, and examines efforts to achieve economic development. Among the poverty-related issues we survey are foreign investment and foreign aid, access to global markets, and global debt. Impoverished countries are especially vulnerable to a variety of other ills, including the problem of transnational crime that threatens personal safety and economic well-being, the global arms trade that fosters violence, and the complex issue of refugees and migrants. As you read this chapter, keep in mind that the several dimensions of human security are closely related. For example, the spread of diseases like HIV/AIDS is both a cause and consequence of poverty; poverty creates incentives for crime and corruption, while perpetuating the very poverty that contributed to them in the first place.

The idea of human security

In contrast to realists who remain focused on the traditional military dimension of security, liberal theorists have long recognized that famine, disease, crime, and natural disasters cost far more lives than do wars but, until recently, few countries were concerned about the welfare of individuals other than their own citizens. For their part, constructivists view human security as an evolving idea that is now taking root in global politics.

Yet, even now, while securing human security has become a central pillar of the foreign policies of a few countries like Canada, it attracts less attention and funding than does military security. The UN Economic and Social Council and the specialized agencies (chapter 9, p. 413) are responsible for improving human security. The UN has sponsored a variety of conferences dealing with human security issues, and some have been controversial. The 1992 UN Conference on Environment and Development, or "Earth Summit," in Rio de Janeiro, set out environmental goals that highlighted the trade-off between environmental degradation and economic development. As we saw in chapter 10, two other conferences, the 1994 UN Conference on Population and Development in Cairo and the 1995 UN World Conference on Women in Beijing, produced heated debates on women's rights.

The UN also sponsors a variety of programs through the General Assembly that deal with human security issues. The UN Children's Fund (UNICEF), for example, is responsible for improving the welfare of children worldwide. The World Food Program seeks to alleviate the threat of famine. The UN Relief and Works Agency for Palestine Refugees in the Near East (UNRWA) has become a giant welfare agency for Palestinians housed in refugee camps in Gaza, the West Bank, and Lebanon.

The idea of human security owes much to the economist Jeffrey Sachs. Recently, Sachs elaborated a detailed nine-step plan to eliminate global poverty, that he argues kills thousands daily, by 2025. His plan requires relatively little additional foreign aid from wealthy countries, but the very poor, he argued, do need help in reaching the first rung on the "ladder of economic development" to start the process of development, an achievement that he sees as not simply morally right but critical to global stability and security more generally.[4] Sachs emphasized how poor countries can help themselves, especially with assistance from international economic agencies like the World Bank and IMF, and why they should seek to integrate themselves in the globalizing market economy. The problem of poverty, in his view, is multifaceted, involving several dimensions, including the absence of capital investment, crippling debt, disease and ill-health, political instability, lack of education, ecological degradation, and inappropriate technology. Persuaded that Sachs's ideas would bear fruit, the philanthropist George Soros (1930–) contributed $50 million to support the efforts.[5]

Sachs has been an advisor to UN Secretary-General Kofi Annan, and his ideas strongly influenced the formulation of the UN's Millennium Goals as well as the effort to reduce the debt burden of the poorest countries. Many of the major issues that constitute human security can be found in the eight Millennium Goals that were endorsed at a UN-sponsored conference in 2000. These goals, to be met by 2015, are:[6]

- Reduce by half both the proportion of people living on less than a dollar a day and who suffer from hunger.
- Achieve universal primary education.
- Promote gender equality by reducing gender disparity in education.
- Reduce mortality by two-thirds among children under 5.
- Improve maternal health.
- Combat HIV/AIDS, malaria, and other diseases.
- Reduce by half those without access to safe drinking water and improving the lives of at least 100 million slum dwellers.
- Develop an open and non-discriminatory trading and financial system to provide developing states with access to markets of developed states, and reduction or cancellation of debts owed by poor states.

Realistically, it is unlikely that these goals will be met because major states are reluctant to provide sufficient resources.

Figure 13.2 The heads of the water committee of the Millennium Village Project in Sauri, Kenya pause for a photo on a community initiated work day to project local springs, the primary source of water for the community

Courtesy of Fabrice De Clerk, Millennium Villages Project

In January 2006, Sachs visited the model Millennium Village in Bar-Sauri in Kenya.[7] Sauri had suffered high rates of malaria, AIDS, malnutrition, and child mortality, and extremely low crop yields. On his visit, Sachs showed how a multidimensional attack on poverty had succeeded. Specifically, he used the village as a case to show that improvements in health, safe drinking water and sanitation, education, agricultural fertilizer, and infrastructure could eliminate poverty at a per capita cost of about $75 a year for the village's 5,000 residents. For that sum, villagers were able to acquire hybrid corn seeds, fertilizer, bed nets to prevent mosquito bites, school meals, and a truck.

Many of the human security issues are not new. One of the sources for the concept of human security was a speech given on January 6, 1941 in the depths of World War II by President Franklin D. Roosevelt before Congress in which he spoke of "four freedoms" (see Key document). What has changed is that the threats that they pose are transnational, even global, rather than local or national, and they have expanded the meaning of security. Echoing Roosevelt, UN Secretary-General Kofi Annan declared: "Freedom from want, freedom from fear and the freedom of future generations to inherit a healthy natural environment – these are the interrelated building blocks of human, and therefore national security."[8] Figure 13.3 illustrates how such factors are connected.

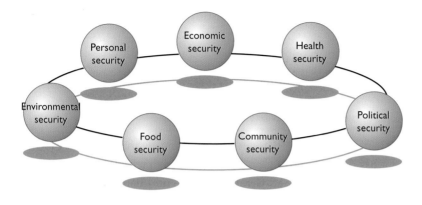

Figure 13.3 Realms of Human Security

United Nations Office on Drugs and Crime (UNODC)

Key document   Franklin D. Roosevelt, Annual Message to Congress, January 6, 1941[9]

In the future days, which we seek to make secure, we look forward to a world founded upon four essential human freedoms.

The first is freedom of speech and expression – everywhere in the world.

The second is freedom of every person to worship God in his own way – everywhere in the world.

The third is freedom from want – which, translated into world terms, means economic understandings which will secure to every nation a healthy peacetime life for its inhabitants – everywhere in the world.

The fourth is freedom from fear – which, translated into world terms, means a world-wide reduction of armaments to such a point and in such a thorough fashion that no nation will be in a position to commit an act of physical aggression against any neighbor – anywhere in the world.

Issues that individual states once confronted by themselves increasingly demand a global response, and growing interdependence complicates relations among different societies. On the one hand, common problems create common interests. On the other, they produce disputes about how to confront them and pay for their solution. The problem of global poverty to which we now turn our attention illustrates these disagreements.

Poverty and economic development

Poverty is among the greatest threats to human security. Although the total global economic pie is growing, now exceeding $31 trillion a year, its distribution is growing more unequal, with 2.8 billion of the world's 6.5 billion people subsisting on less than $700 a year.[10] In much of the global South, rapidly growing populations erase economic gains. By the late 1990s, a fifth of the world's population in wealthy countries enjoyed

86 percent of the world's gross domestic product and 82 percent of the world's export markets, while the poorest fifth had only 1 percent of each.[11] The next sections examine some of the efforts to alleviate poverty and describe key issues of concern to the world's poor.

Global dimensions of poverty

How many people remain impoverished; where do they live; and to what extent has the problem of global poverty eased in recent decades? These are *not* easy questions to answer. Using the World Bank's definition of *impoverished* as those who earn about $1 per day, the world's poor declined from 28 to 19 percent of the population of the developing world between 1990 and 2002 even as their total population grew some 20 percent to over 5 billion. Thus, about one billion people remain in extreme poverty.[12] Much of the reduction in poverty has taken place in one country – China – where some 400 million people emerged from poverty during this period. By contrast, in some regions, notably sub-Saharan Africa and Eastern Europe, the number of poor has actually grown. The World Bank predicts that about 600 million people will remain impoverished by 2015, still afflicted by poor health, widespread corruption, a lack of education, environmental degradation, and incompetent governments. Malnutrition rates are also declining globally except in sub-Saharan Africa.

Income measures do not paint a complete picture of poverty. They ignore other dimensions (some would say causes; others, consequences) of poverty. For instance, 33,000 children die in LDCs every day, and a woman dies every minute during childbirth.[13] Thus, in addition to income, some poverty measures also consider indicators of longevity (such as birth rates, infant mortality, life expectancy), standard of living (unemployment, sanitation, access to potable water), and knowledge (schooling and literacy).[14] LDCs are also victims of a "brain drain" in which over 80 percent of the college-educated citizens of Haiti and Jamaica live in rich countries, as do over a quarter of college-educated citizens from Ghana, Mozambique, Kenya, Uganda, and El Salvador.[15]

Corruption is pervasive in the developing world and greatly impedes economic development because it siphons funds from productive uses, discourages investors, and adds costs for consumers and producers. The NGO Transparency International (TI), a nongovernmental organization with chapters in 85 countries, has constructed a Corruption Perceptions Index (CPI) to rank countries' level of corruption. By that measure, the world's most corrupt countries in 2006 were Haiti and Myanmar (Burma), also two of the world's poorest countries. Other countries that were ranked among the most corrupt were Belarus, Cambodia,

Uzbekistan, Bangladesh, and Iraq and several impoverished sub-Saharan African countries including Ivory Coast, Equatorial Guinea, Chad, the Democratic Republic of the Congo, Sudan, and Guinea.[16] Not surprisingly, several of these, as we saw in chapter 12, are failed or failing states. As Transparency International's chairman, Peter Eigen, declared: "The world's people continue to suffer under the double yoke of extreme poverty and corrupt, unjust systems. But there will be no poverty alleviation, no political stability without the fight against corruption."[17]

The CPI was later augmented by a Bribe Payers Index to measure the extent to which exporting countries use bribes to get overseas business.[18] According to TI, of the 30 biggest exporting states that account for over 80 percent of all exports in 2006, the countries whose officials were most willing to accept bribes were India, China, Russia, Turkey, and Taiwan. By contrast, bribes were not accepted in Switzerland, Sweden, Australia, Austria, and Canada.[19]

Did you know?

As part of its effort to reduce corruption in countries that it helps, the World Bank has a Department of Institutional Integrity with a 24-hour Fraud and Corruption Hotline: 1-800-831-0463.[20]

The major international economic organizations that we discussed in chapter 11 are involved in efforts to alleviate global poverty. Let us now examine some of these efforts.

International institutions and global poverty

The question of how to measure poverty is not merely academic. How we answer it influences our efforts to combat poverty. The more complex our poverty measure, the more complex must be our strategies to overcome it. Thus, coordinated efforts are underway to attack global poverty with an eye to eradicating it by 2015. Article 55 of the UN Charter committed its members to advancing the economic and social well-being of peoples everywhere.

International institutions like the World Bank (IBRD) and IMF have taken the lead in trying to reach the UN's Millennium Goals, and they have become active in providing development assistance to poor states. The instrument the IMF uses in this regard is the Poverty Reduction and Growth Facility established in 1999 to provide poor countries with

> **Key document Article 55 of the UN Charter[21]**
>
> With a view to the creation of conditions of stability and well-being which are necessary for peaceful and friendly relations among nations based on respect for the principle of equal rights and self-determination of peoples, the United Nations shall promote:
>
> a higher standards of living, full employment, and conditions of economic and social progress and development;
>
> b solutions of international economic, social, health, and related problems; and international cultural and educational co-operation; and
>
> c universal respect for, and observance of, human rights and fundamental freedoms for all without distinction as to race, sex, language, or religion.

low-interest loans at a nominal interest rate of 0.5 percent a year.[22] The program works as follows: After consulting with domestic groups and foreign experts, governments prepare detailed Poverty Reduction Strategy Papers that describe economic and social programs designed to reduce poverty and stimulate growth. These plans become the bases for IMF and World Bank decisions about whether to provide loans and debt relief to countries in question. Governments are encouraged to present plans that (1) engage civil society, (2) assist their poorest citizens, (3) recognize that poverty has many causes, (4) involve cooperation among government, civil society, and external donors, and (5) have a long-term perspective. As of September 2004, 78 poor countries were eligible for low-interest IMF development loans.[23]

In 2004, the World Bank (IBRD) provided over $20 billion in loans to LDCs for 245 projects to provide education, health, electricity, environmental protection, and clean water. Almost half this funding was provided as grants, interest-free loans, and technical assistance to the world's poorest countries. Other IBRD clients – countries at higher levels of economic development – receive long-term loans for specific projects, usually with an extended time period before they begin to repay the loans' principal. In 2004, 33 countries were in this category, receiving $11 billion in loans for 87 projects. Overall, the World Bank is financing over 1,800 projects around the world, such as providing **microcredit** in Bosnia, improving health care in Mexico, educating girls in Bangladesh, and encouraging paper making in Brazil.[24]

As the results of providing microcredit show, small investments can have large effects. For example of all the technology available to relieve poverty, mobile phones appear to have the greatest impact. "Phones,"

microcredit small loans available to the poor to start small businesses.

declares *The Economist*, "let fishermen and farmers check prices in different markets before selling produce, make it easier for people to find work, allow quick and easy transfers of funds and boost entrepreneurship. The number of cell phones in Africa is growing faster than in any other region, more than doubling from 63 million users in 2004 to 152 million in 2006.[25] Phones can be shared by a village," and, according to a recent study, "in a typical developing country, a rise of ten mobile phones per 100 people boosts GDP growth by 0.6 percentage points."[26]

Along with the IMF, the IBRD is responsible for leading the effort to achieve the UN Millennium Development Goals and is deeply involved in overcoming the HIV/AIDS epidemic. Furthermore, the World Bank is increasing its commitment to fighting corruption, which deters foreign investors and squanders scarce resources, and encouraging good government, which is vital for a country to achieve economic development.

The IBRD is only one of several institutions that collectively constitute the "World Bank Group." In addition to the IBRD, this group includes the International Development Agency (IDA), the International Finance Corporation (IFC), the Multilateral Investment Guarantee Agency (MIGA), and the International Center for Settlement of Investment Disputes (ICSID). As the world's largest source of **concessional assistance** to poor countries, the IDA is the most important of these. In 2004, it funded 158 projects in 62 poor countries at a cost of $9 billion.[27]

concessional assistance economic assistance of which at least 35 percent consists of grants that do not need to be repaid.

The other members of the World Bank Group also aid poor countries. The IFC encourages private investment in poor countries. The MIGA encourages investment in poor countries by providing insurance to protect potential investors from loss in case their investments fail or LDCs default on their loans. Finally, the ICSID mediates disputes that arise between poor countries and foreign investors.

Currently, international organizations are deeply involved in helping poor states cope with the mountains of debt that impede their development efforts. Recognition of this problem has grown, and steps have been taken to ease the debt burden of the poor.

Debt relief

In recent years, the World Bank and IMF have begun to help deeply indebted poor countries that spend their export earnings and hard currency repaying interest on their debts. The debt crisis dates back to several trends in the 1970s and 1980s. First, a spike in oil prices in the late 1970s, a global recession in the mid-1970s, and a decline in commodity prices buried poor countries under mountainous debt. Second, some LDCs, like Mexico and Nigeria, counting on higher earnings from oil sales, borrowed heavily for domestic projects. When oil prices plummeted in the 1980s and 1990s, they, too, were left with huge debt burdens. Between 1955 and 1990, poor countries' debt rose from $9.69 billion to more than $1.3 trillion.[28] By 1985, debt-service ratios – the ratios of principal and interest due on debts to export earnings – were estimated at between 20 and 50 percent for non-oil-producing LDCs.[29]

With export earnings unavailable for new projects, LDCs faced declining standards of living, and the prospect that indebted countries might default threatened Western banks. As the debt issue festered, the United States took several steps to foster debt rescheduling, notably the Baker (named after Treasury Secretary James Baker) and Brady (named after Treasury Secretary Nicholas Brady) plans. Between 1978 and 1984, 29 countries negotiated debt rescheduling agreements that allowed them to postpone about $27 billion in debt.[30] Matters improved temporarily, but by 2001 total LDC debt reached $2.5 trillion.[31] Despite several efforts at debt restructuring, it was clear that a more coherent global policy was needed.

In 1996 the World Bank, the IMF, and the Paris Club (an informal group of creditor countries formed in 1956) jointly put forward a plan to provide debt relief for the world's poorest countries called the Debt Initiative for Heavily Indebted Poor Countries (HIPC). Their aim was to reward LDCs that pursued sound economic policies by reducing their debt burden. Only by easing the debt burden, it was argued, could LDCs free up resources to alleviate poverty at home and attract foreign investment.

The HIPC was revised in 1999 to provide assistance more quickly and assure that the resources made available would be used to reduce poverty.[32] LDCs confronting an "unsustainable debt situation" but with a good record of economic, political, and social reform, and a workable "poverty reduction strategy" were eligible for HIPC debt relief. Reforms had to include improving the quality of government and reducing official corruption. Such a country could obtain loans and grants to reduce debt for an interim period during which it would carry out its poverty reduction strategy and implement reforms. If it did so, it would receive further debt relief that it would not have to repay.

By late 2007, 40 countries, mainly in sub-Saharan Africa, were receiving HIPC debt relief. Of these, ten were receiving pre-decision assistance, nine had reached the decision point (at which lenders commit to debt relief) and were receiving interim aid, and 21 had reached the completion point and were receiving irrevocable aid, as pledged at the decision point. To date, some $54 billion in debt relief, entailing a two-thirds reduction in the debt of these countries, has been committed

under the HIPC initiative. By 2005, the costs of debt service had dropped
from $5 billion to $2.3 billion in countries receiving HIPC assistance.
This has freed up funds to reduce poverty, and in countries receiving
HIPC assistance such expenditures have risen from 6.4 percent of gross
domestic product (GDP) in 1999 to 7.9 percent of GDP in 2003.

Although the HIPC has been very valuable for some countries, overall
progress is slower than hoped. When the HIPC was begun in 1999, it was
hoped that many poor countries would quickly qualify for relief, but the
process proved complex, and some targeted countries still have difficulty
qualifying for aid, especially those afflicted by civil war. Thus, it has
proved necessary to bend the rules somewhat to enable countries like
Zambia to qualify.[33] Owing to the slow pace of debt relief, the G8
members led by British Prime Minister Tony Blair (1953–) agreed at
their 2005 meeting in Gleneagles, Scotland, to forgive some $40 billion
in debt owed them by 18 of the world's poorest countries. Among those
campaigning for such action was rock star Bob Geldof (1951–), who
declared, "Tomorrow 280 million Africans will wake up for the first time
in their lives without owing you or me a penny from the burden of debt
that has crippled them and their countries for so long."[34] Unfortunately, a
year after the Gleneagles meeting, the commitments of several of the
participating states, including the United States, remained unfulfilled.[35]
However, as a result of the G8 agreement, on July, 2006, the World Bank
cancelled about $37 billion in debt owed by 19 developing countries in
Africa and Latin America that had met the HIPC criteria, freeing up funds
for improving education and health services.[36] And economic
development is even beginning to accelerate in sub-Saharan Africa owing
to a combination of high demand for commodities, improving
governance, and lower inflation.[37]

Countries with large debt burdens are regarded as bad credit risks
and find it difficult to borrow the additional sums from private banks
or public institutions necessary to pay off existing debts or promote
economic development. At best, they only can borrow at high interest
rates that further mortgage their future. At worst, if they default, they
will get no additional loans at all. However, if they gain control of their
debt burdens, they become eligible for new loans at lower rates of interest.

Like IGOs, NGOs are also involved with the debt issue. For example,
private credit-rating institutions play a quiet but critical role by
determining the interest rates countries must pay on the bonds they issue
or the loans they make. Firms such as Moody's Investors Service, Standard
& Poor's, Fitch Ratings, and Dominion Bond Rating Service evaluate the
likelihood that LDCs will repay the interest and principal on their loans.
When these agencies conclude that the probability of repayment is low,

Figure 13.4   World leaders at the end of the 2005 G8 Summit in Gleneagles, Scotland

© PA Photos

the interest rates a debtor must pay will increase, thereby worsening its debt burden. If these firms conclude that a country is more able than before to pay its debts, interest rates go down, thereby reducing its debt burden. In addition, investors will be more likely to purchase the country's securities, providing additional funding to fuel economic growth.[38]

For many years, rich states have provided poor countries with foreign aid. However, developed countries, especially the United States, have increasingly emphasized the role of private investment as the way to stimulate economic growth. Developed countries also have a significant role to play in debt relief. For many years, rich states have provided poor countries with foreign aid. Such assistance from rich countries faces its own challenges. Domestic audiences may criticize these governments for the amount of aid they provide or the conditions on which it is distributed. In recent years developed countries, especially the United States, have increasingly emphasized the role of private investment as the way to stimulate economic growth.[39]

Foreign aid and foreign investment

Many Americans believe that the United States is the world's leading source of foreign aid and that such aid eats up a substantial proportion of America's annual budget. Both beliefs are wrong. In fact, American foreign aid amounts to only 0.13 percent of GDP, far short of the 1992 target of 0.7 percent. However, in response to President George W. Bush's proposal to increase US foreign aid and establish a Millennium Challenge Account to provide foreign aid to countries that encourage democracy, fight corruption, and adopt liberal economic policies, Congress established the Millennium Challenge Corporation in 2004. It provided $1 billion in funding in 2004 and $1.5 billion in 2005.

Theory in the real world

Do democratic systems and human freedom foster economic development? Does economic development foster democracy? Westerners, since Aristotle (384–22 BC), have believed that a relationship exists between these factors, while some Asian and African leaders have denied such a link. However, recent empirical research by a team of political scientists suggests that, though greater wealth does not produce democracy, the transformation to democracy accelerates economic growth, and such growth reinforces democratic institutions.[40] In addition, the Index of Economic Freedom compiled by the Heritage Foundation suggests that countries that provide the greatest economic freedom (as measured by factors like property rights and trade policy) are the most prosperous, while those that provide the least are the poorest.[41]

Overall, the United States ranks thirteenth among the 21 major developed countries in its "commitment to development" as measured by the Commitment to Development Index developed by the Center for Global Development.[42] The index is based on an average of scores in seven categories: (1) trade: access to a country's markets; (2) technology: government support for research as a percentage of GDP); (3) security: participation in peacekeeping operations; (4) environment: harm done to the global environment measured by low gas taxes, emission of greenhouse gases, use of ozone-depleting chemicals, and fishing subsidies; (5) migration: aid to refugees and asylum seekers and percentage of students from LDCs among total foreign students; (6) investment: policies aimed at promoting foreign investment in LDCs; and (7) aid: grants and low-interest loans to LDCs as a percentage of GDP.[43] By this index, the Netherlands is the most committed to poor states' development, and Japan the least.

The 2002 UN International Conference on Financing for Development in Monterrey, Mexico, discussed measures to spur economic growth in the developing world. It reviewed trade, aid, debt, and investment issues and concluded by issuing the "Monterrey Consensus," which identified key steps to promote economic development: good government, less corruption, investment in economic and social infrastructure, prudent monetary policies, development of capital markets, microcredit, and more foreign investment.

Much of the needed investment must come from private sources, especially the transnational corporations discussed chapter 11. TNCs bring capital investment, train local managers, provide jobs, develop new products (which can be substituted for imports), introduce new technology, foster exports, and are sources of hard currency for purchasing foreign goods. TNCs also link relatively isolated societies to the global economy through worldwide networks of production and distribution. As such, they are capitalism's engines of modernity. TNCs and the vast amounts of direct investment they control are vital to economic growth in the developing world. Thus, LDCs compete for their investment and the jobs they bring, but problems of poverty and economic development are complex.

A major barrier to ending global poverty remains the difficulties faced by poor countries in exporting their product to countries in the developed world. Despite rhetoric extolling free trade, rich countries have been reluctant to eliminate barriers to imports from the LDCs.

Access to markets

One of the most promising paths to economic development is through export growth. Currently, the United States and the European Union (EU) account for over one-third of the world's exports, while the poorest 49 countries with 10 percent of the world's population account for only 0.4 percent of global trade.[44] Moreover, as noted earlier, for several decades many poor countries tried to develop their economies by protecting home industries and limiting imports. In the main, these efforts failed, and in the 1990s the LDCs increasingly turned to economic neoliberalism to attract foreign investment.

Export industries provide employment and hard currency for investment in industry and infrastructure at home. This is the route to prosperity that Japan pioneered after World War II, and the "Asian Tigers" – Singapore, South Korea, Taiwan, Malaysia, Thailand, and, most recently, China – copied with great success. LDCs, however, have difficulty gaining access to rich states' markets. Enjoying plentiful cheap labor, their industries can undersell similar industries in developed countries, thereby generating unemployment in rich countries and political pressures for protection from LDCs' imports.

In some industries in which LDCs can compete with rich countries, for example, textile production, their exports have been limited by "voluntary" quotas. Thus, the 1974 Multi-Fiber Arrangement limited exports of cotton, wool, and textiles to rich countries in order to protect their home industries. In 1995, the WTO Agreement on Textiles and Clothing began to phase out these limits. The agreement was to be a boon for small textile exporters, but China's huge reservoir of low-cost labor and its access to Hong Kong's expertise and financial resources helped it reap most of the benefit as the Multi-Fiber Arrangement ended, while poor countries like Bangladesh gained little. In February 2005 alone, Chinese apparel exports to the West were well over 100 percent higher than the year before. Resulting complaints of US and European manufacturers, combined with the damage done to apparel exporters in poor countries, may lead to new protectionist measures to limit Chinese textiles exports.[45]

In addition, many poor countries still depend on agriculture, and their ability to export agricultural commodities to rich countries has been severely limited, thereby posing a major impediment to their economic development. In a free market, LDCs would enjoy a comparative advantage in agriculture over rich countries, but there is no free market in agriculture. Thus, Japan, which depends on exporting manufactured products, imposes a 500 percent tariff on imported rice.[46] Overall, rich countries provide $84 billion a year in subsidies to their farmers, thereby making it possible for farmers in rich countries to undersell farmers in poor countries. The EU is the worst offender. European farmers receive about $30 for every sheep they raise, and Swiss farmers get almost $1,000 in subsidies per cow.[47]

Historically, agriculture has been a thorny trade issue because of American and European powerful farm lobbies, as well as large agricultural exporters like Canada and Australia. No issue divides the United States and the EU more than competition for agricultural markets, and their disagreement makes it difficult for them to cooperate in reaching a joint agreement with the LDCs. In the United States, congressional representatives from the South and Midwest annually push for big subsidies that go mainly to large farmers, while the EU keeps its farm sector afloat with the Common Agricultural Policy (CAP).

The CAP provides subsidies to farmers that absorb most of the EU's annual budget. Farmers are assured of a minimum price for their produce, thereby providing them with predictable earnings. At the time the CAP was established in 1958, Europe suffered from food shortages, but since then, the CAP, like US subsidies, has led to agricultural overproduction[48] and the dumping of agricultural commodities on global markets at prices so low that farmers in LDCs cannot compete. As a result of these subsidies and US and European trade barriers, LDCs cannot export their produce and their farmers cannot even compete at home with agricultural exports from rich countries. This has perpetuated poverty among peasants in poor countries and, sometimes, famine amidst global plenty.

Both Europe and the United States have incentives to reduce agricultural subsidies. The US budget deficit requires big cuts in programs like agriculture, and the CAP, despite reform in 1992, costs Europeans $47 billion a year (40 percent of the EU budget). Moreover, EU enlargement doubled its number of farmers and included several countries like Poland with large and inefficient agricultural sectors that, without reform of the subsidy program, will send EU costs skyrocketing. Thus, direct subsidy payments to new members will be phased out by 2014. Some reform took place in 2003 when the EU decided to place a budget ceiling on the CAP and provide farmers with a single payment that does *not* increase with higher production. Farmers can produce what they want, but the market rather than the EU will determine the price they get for their products.[49] Nevertheless, a few EU countries, notably France, have made it clear that they will go no further.

Did you know?

In Europe, cows received more aid than people in 2000. The EU's annual dairy subsidy was $913 per cow, while its annual aid to sub-Saharan Africa was $8 per person. In Japan the corresponding figures were $2,700 and $1.47.[50]

---

preferential access more favorable than usual tariff treatment granted to another state or group of states.

Notwithstanding special arrangements that granted some LDCs **preferential access** for their products to rich countries' markets, protectionist walls still exclude most LDC exports of agricultural commodities from rich countries' markets. Declared Javier González Fraga, formerly head of Argentina's central bank: "The virtuous circle – we were to import capital goods from the industrialized nations and they were to buy our agricultural produce – never happened."[51]

The September 2003 and December 2005 WTO meetings in Cancún, Mexico and Hong Kong, which were held to reach agreement on trade issues in the Doha Round, failed dismally, largely owing to disagreement over trade in agriculture. This failure created doubt about further progress in reducing trade barriers. At Cancún, the United States, Europe, and Japan offered far less than the LDCs had hoped in the way of opening markets to agricultural exports. Thus, a group of LDC commodity exporters led by Brazil and India, representing almost 60 percent of the

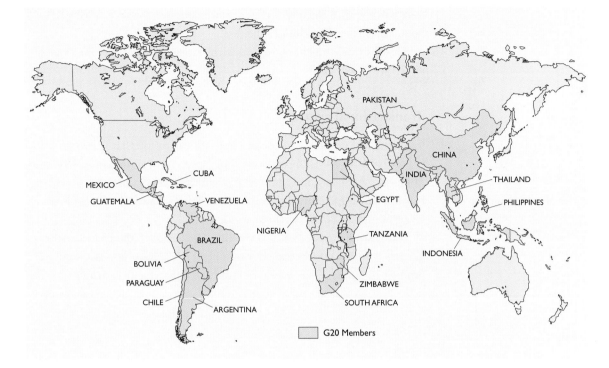

Map 13.1 G20 members

world's population, 70 percent of the world's rural population, and 26 percent of global agricultural exports, joined ranks as the G20 (Group of 20).[52] The G20 adamantly rejected the US–European offer, threatening to torpedo the entire Doha Round unless the United States, Europe, and Japan reduced subsidies and tariffs that protect such crops as US and European cotton and Japanese rice. In the end, amid mutual recriminations, negotiations collapsed in July 2006.[53]

Not all is bleak, and the logjam may break in the future. In a March 2005 decision, the WTO upheld a Brazilian complaint – the first of its kind – that annual US subsidies and **export credits** to its cotton farmers are illegal because they help US farmers sell their product at below production costs. The decision, along with America's offer in December 2005 to give West African countries free access to its cotton market, will aid Africa's cotton farmers. The WTO decision will increase pressure on rich countries to reduce agricultural subsidies and help American and European politicians who want to resolve the problem but fear a domestic political backlash.

As you can see, economic development involves a complex interaction between states and economic markets. In the past, most economic activity

export credits financing arrangements that permit a foreign buyer of exported goods to defer payment over a period of time.

took place within the boundaries of states and was congruent with those boundaries. This is no longer the case.

This is evident in efforts to deal with transnational crime, the topic to which we now turn.

Transnational crime[54]

Transnational crime has so thrived with globalization that it is estimated to cost wealthy states the equivalent of 2 percent of annual gross national product.[55] As shown in Figure 13.5, crime also poses a major obstacle to **human development**; thus, high crime rates are associated with low levels of human development and vice versa.

Transnational gangs with names like Mara 18 and Mara Salvatrucha in Central America cost El Salvador roughly 11.5 percent of gross domestic product in 2003.[56] The same processes that drive the growth and spread

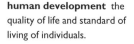
human development the quality of life and standard of living of individuals.

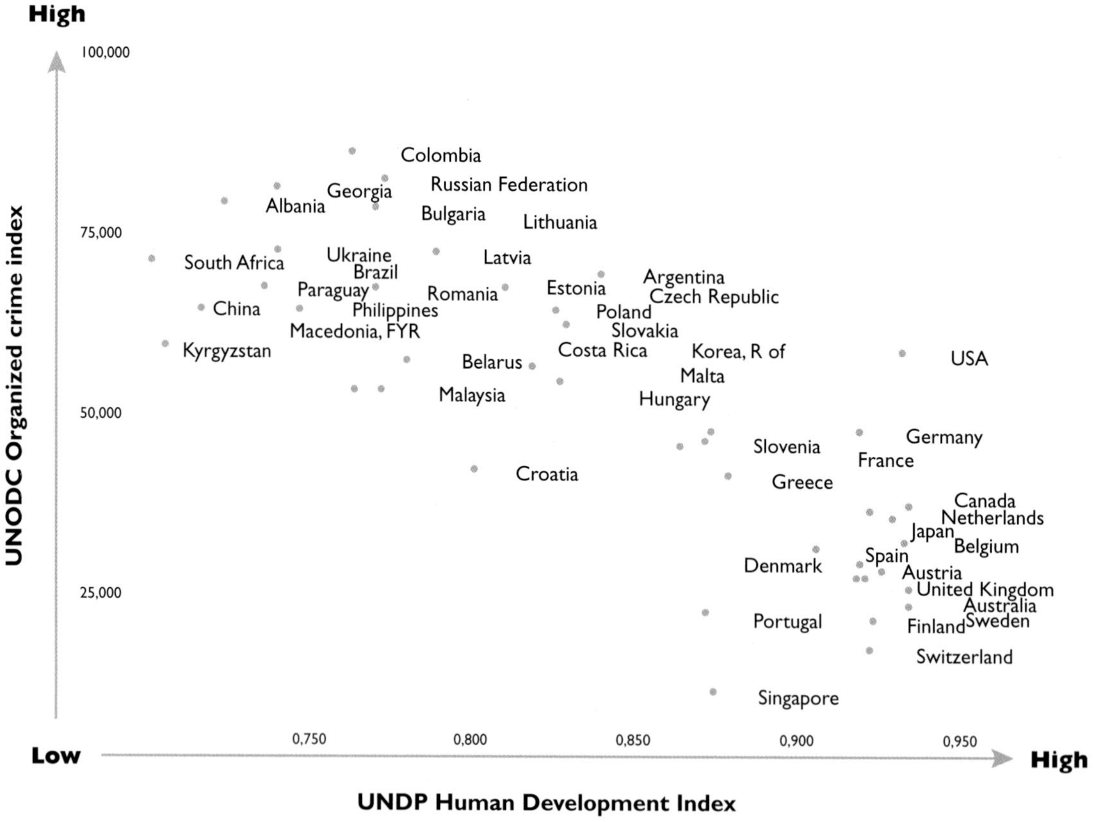

Figure 13.5 The impact of organized crime on human development

United Nations Office on Drugs and Crime (UNODC)

of TNCs fuel transnational crime. Like TNCs, crime also has profited from the technological advances accompanying globalization. Colombian kidnappers, for instance, use computers to check bank accounts of drivers they stop at roadblocks. Today's transnational criminals are also involved in a range of interconnected activities from drugs, bank and credit-card fraud, and trafficking in human beings to arms smuggling, counterfeiting of money and goods, intellectual piracy, and illegal smuggling of scarce natural resources like rare hardwoods. Finally, new technologies also allow criminal groups such as Russian and American mafias, Chinese triads, and Japanese *yakuzas* to enter alliances as the Sicilian and Colombian drug cartels did in the 1980s to bring cocaine to Europe.

Did you know?

The global drug trade accounts for about 7 percent of world commerce.[57]

Drug trafficking

One of the world's largest transnational economic enterprises is the illegal global drug trade that by UN estimates is worth about $400 billion with some 200 million "customers."[58] The global trade in drugs is especially hard to control because eliminating one source usually leads to greater production elsewhere. Thus, curbing cocaine production in Peru and Bolivia led to its spread in Colombia, and efforts to fight the Colombian cocaine trade caused the transfer of various cocaine operations to Brazil and Ecuador, as well as an explosion in the manufacture and smuggling of illicit drugs in Mexico, where the Arellano-Félix Organization has become the most violent drug trafficking cartel in North America. And, when Iran and Turkey cracked down on opium production (the basis of heroin) in the 1950s and 1970s respectively, Afghanistan and Pakistan took over the business. Along with Iran, these two countries form the "Golden Crescent," which, after 1991, surpassed the "Golden Triangle" (Burma, Laos, and Thailand) as the world's main source of opium.[59]

Furthermore, the potential rewards from the drug trade are so high that drug barons are prepared to take great risks. So much money is involved that it is easy for them to corrupt poorly paid police, judicial officials, and politicians in the developing world. Additionally, in countries such as Afghanistan, Colombia, and Peru, there are few crops as profitable for impoverished farmers as poppies and coca. Finally, drug cartels are able to integrate themselves in local communities, making themselves

Figure 13.6 Offer of reward for information about Mexico's Arellano-Félix Organization

Courtesy of the U.S. State Department

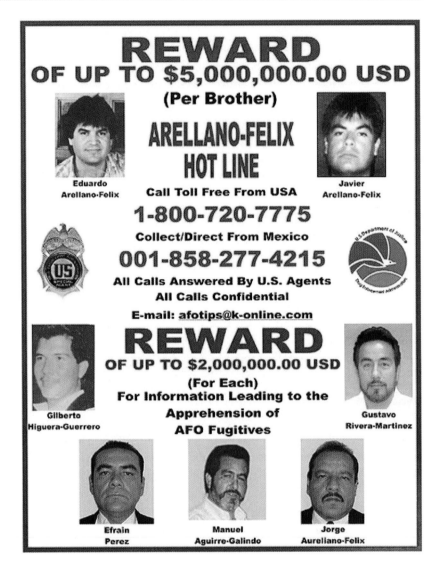

indispensable to residents. One observer explains how drug dealers, pretending to be businessmen, integrated themselves in a Peruvian community before beginning illegal operations:

> They enlisted local labor and revitalized the local airport that had been closed for lack of government repairs. They also brought in satellite television, and provided monies to repair local roads, docking facilities, the school and medical clinic. They also supplied supplemental income payments to police, politicians and other notables. Only after being in the community for close to a year, did they reveal their true identity and purposes. They then asked for and received a public community

vote of support to use the town as a major drug collection and transshipment site.[60]

So pervasive is the drug trade in some countries that they are called narco-states. One is Afghanistan, and another is Colombia. In Colombia, the Medellín and Cali drug cartels led by the Ochoa brothers and Pablo Escobar and the Rodriguez Orejuela brothers respectively used violence and bribery to subvert the government and to acquire enormous political influence in the 1970s and 1980s, until they were defeated in the 1990s by feuding between the cartels and close cooperation between US and Colombian officials. However, this did not solve the problem, as smaller, more agile gangs succeeded the cartels, and it is estimated that there are over 300 drug-smuggling gangs in Colombia today.[61]

One of the most dangerous aspects of the drug trade is its linkage to terrorism.[62] Terrorists turn to crime to fund their operations. In Peru, the Maoist guerrilla group Sendero Luminoso (Shining Path) and the Marxist Leninist Túpac Amaru Revolutionary Movement protected drug traffickers who in return helped fund these groups until their defeat in the 1990s. More recently, prior to outlawing opium production, Afghanistan's Taliban actually made $40 million a year from the country's heroin trade,[63] and it used drug revenues to fund Al Qaeda terrorists training in Afghanistan. Colombia's Revolutionary Armed Forces (FARC), a leftist guerrilla group, is also involved in the drug trade. It provides security for cocaine growers, refiners, and smugglers, who in return fund the insurgents who buy arms on the global market. According to a former Colombian finance minister, the country's guerrilla groups "doubled their funding between 1991 and 1994, with the drug business contributing 34 percent of income, extortion and robbery 26 percent and kidnaps 23 percent."[64]

Responses to drug trafficking

The drug trade is transnational as drug producers and traffickers in different countries cooperate. To meet this challenge, the UN General Assembly held a Special Session on the World Drug Problem in New York in June 1998 at which they agreed that:

> Effective international cooperation on judicial matters, such as the extradition of fugitives, mutual legal assistance, transfer of proceedings and controlled delivery, is essential for success in the global fight against illicit drugs. Without inter-State cooperation in these areas, few of the international treaty provisions against illicit drug trafficking,

such as those contained in the 1998 United Nations Convention against Illicit Traffic in Narcotic Drugs and Psychotropic Substances, can be implemented.[65]

Moreover, greater cooperation is needed to provide enhanced trade opportunities to developing countries that produce drugs and to finance crop-substitution programs.

For its part, the United States places agents from the Drug Enforcement Agency (DEA) in many of its embassies and provides assistance to governments that are struggling against drug trafficking. For example, the Clinton and Bush administrations have provided large-scale funding for the anti-narcotics campaign of Colombian presidents Andrés Pastrana (1954–) and Álvaro Uribe (1952–) known as "Plan Colombia" that was initiated in 1999.[66] US funding has been used to provide military equipment and training, encourage Colombian farmers to plant cash crops other than coca, interdict drug smuggling, and for fumigating the country's coca fields.[67] Despite this six-year effort at a cost of $4.7 billion, the availability and price of cocaine in the United States remains unchanged.[68]

The US war on drugs has been repeatedly compromised because some US allies have been involved – willingly or unwillingly – with illicit drugs. During the Vietnam War, the Hmong in Laos and the Nationalist Chinese in Burma that assisted the CIA were also opium producers, and the CIA may have used drug profits to finance covert operations in Southeast Asia.[69] In 1989, US forces even invaded Panama, seized Panamanian leader Manuel Noriega (1938–), and imprisoned him for drug trafficking. Nowhere is the issue more complex than in Afghanistan. Previously a leading source of opium, Afghan opium production was halted by the Islamic militants of the Taliban in 2000, but with America's overthrow of the Taliban in 2001, opium production resumed, and by 2005 Afghanistan had become the world largest heroin producer and exporter.[70]

Controversy

American policies aimed at curbing the global drug trade have focused on cutting supplies to the United States, and less effort has gone into reducing the demand for drugs either by decriminalizing drug use or rehabilitating drug users. Critics of US policy argue that, as long as demand for drugs is high and profits from their sale great, there will be criminals willing to provide them. Since drug demand is greater in the United States than in any other country, potential profits for drug traffickers are very great. According to the Drug Enforcement Agency, wholesale cocaine prices in the United States ranged from $12,000 to $35,000 per kilogram (2001), and heroin from South America cost from $50,000 to $200,000 per kilogram.[71] "The most effective approach towards the drug problem," declared the 1998 UN Declaration on the Guiding Principles of Drug Demand Reduction, "consists of a comprehensive, balanced and coordinated approach, encompassing supply control and demand reduction reinforcing each other . . . . There is now a need to intensify our efforts in demand reduction and to provide adequate resources towards that end."[72]

Money laundering

Globalization has facilitated **money laundering**, an essential component of transnational criminal activity. Utilizing advanced technologies to transfer funds among countries, as well as encryption of e-mail and cell and satellite phones, money laundering, involving between $300 and $500 billion a year, enables criminals and terrorists to hide evidence of their illegal profits. According to the UN's International Money Laundering Information Network (IMOLIN), "'Megabyte money' (in the form of symbols on a computer screen) operates 24 hours a day, seven days a week, and may be shifted dozens of times to prevent law enforcement officials from tracking it down."[73]

There are three steps to the "laundry cycle". First, criminals disassociate funds from criminal activity. Restaurants, hotels, and casinos are used as fronts to convert the small-denomination bills into larger denominations or cashier's checks. In the second stage, criminals mask the movement of those funds from law enforcement officials, often by sending funds electronically to other countries with strong bank secrecy laws or lax enforcement of money laundering laws. Favorite destinations include the Bahamas and the Cayman Islands. Finally, once the criminals are sufficiently distanced from the funds, they put them where they are again readily available, often by investing in legitimate businesses.[74]

Where successful, programs to eliminate money laundering can prevent terrorists from buying arms and reduce the profitability of transnational crime in general. IGOs like the UN Office of Drug Control and Crime Prevention have programs to promote national laws to combat the problem, and the US State Department's Bureau of International Narcotics and Law Enforcement develops programs to fight transnational crime and terrorism, including training police in Iraq, Afghanistan, and Kosovo. With US assistance, International Law Enforcement Training Academies have been established in the United States, Botswana, Hungary, and Thailand, which in 2001 trained over 1,500 law enforcement officers from 55 countries.[75]

money laundering disguising criminal profits to prevent their detection by law enforcement agencies.

Another aspect of globalization is the global arms trade that fuels arms races and conflicts around the world, arms rebels and terrorists, and creates dependence of arms purchasers on those that are the sources of arms sales.

The arms trade

Spending on armaments entails a vast diversion of resources from more productive uses and an enormous burden on taxpayers everywhere. In 2005, global spending on armaments soared to $1.12 trillion or roughly $173 per capita of which the United States accounted for 48 percent. Overall arms expenditures jumped 34 percent between 1996 and 2004.[76] Russia, however, surpassed the United States in terms of arms sales to the developing world, especially to China, India, and Iran.[77]

The global arms trade

A significant proportion of spending on arms involves the sale and purchase of weapons, and the global arms trade has long been a source of controversy. Some have argued that those who sell weapons try to encourage war and are "merchants of death." After World War I, it was widely suspected that a small group of profit-minded industrialists associated with giant munitions firms like Germany's Krupp, France's Schneider-Creusot and Britain's Vickers had encouraged the outbreak of war in 1914. In 1936, a special committee of the US Congress concluded that war profiteering had indeed been a factor. "The committee finds," declared its report "that some of the munitions companies have occasionally had opportunities to intensify the fears of people for their neighbors and have used them to their own profit" and that it is "against the peace of the world for selfishly interested organizations to be left free to goad and frighten nations into military activity."[78]

The growth of American defense budgets and the proliferation of interest groups profiting from defense spending during the Cold War fueled suspicions that defense industries enjoyed a chummy relationship with the Pentagon and members of Congress whose districts benefited from defense spending and military bases by getting defense-related jobs and federal grants for local school districts with large numbers of soldiers' children. This relationship was dubbed the **military-industrial complex** by President Eisenhower in 1961. "This conjunction of an immense military establishment," he declared, "and a large arms industry is new in the American experience. The total influence – economic, political, even spiritual – is felt in every city, every state house, every office of the Federal Government. . . . In the councils of Government, we must guard against

military-industrial complex
the idea that defense corporations, Congress, and the Pentagon cooperate to encourage higher US defense spending.

the acquisition of unwarranted influence . . . by the military-industrial complex."[79]

To impede the spread of WMD the Proliferation Security Initiative was announced by President George W. Bush on May 31, 2003 and in September 2003 endorsed by 11 countries (Australia, France, Germany, Italy, Japan, the Netherlands, Poland, Portugal, Spain, the United Kingdom, and the United States). The centerpiece of the initiative is agreement to cooperate in interdicting illegal shipments of material that can be used to produce WMD and to prevent such material from falling into the hands of terrorists or rogue states. The participants have agreed "to take action to board and search any vessel flying their flag in their internal waters or territorial seas, or areas beyond the territorial sea of any other state, that is reasonably suspected of transporting such cargoes to or from states or nonstate actors of proliferation concern, and to seize such cargoes that are identified" and to "require aircraft that are reasonably suspected of carrying such cargoes to or from states or nonstate actors of proliferation concern and that are transiting their airspace to land for inspection and seize any such cargoes that are identified."[80]

Sales of conventional armaments contribute to countries' exports and help sustain defense industries at home but also fuel violence around the world. Initial sales not only provide funding at the time arms are delivered but lock in purchasers to future sales of replacements and spare parts. Arms purchases reduce funding for social and economic development, and some countries, including Oman, Syria, Burma, Pakistan, Eritrea, and Burundi, spend more on arms than on health and education combined. According to the humanitarian NGO Oxfam, the amount spent on arms by the developing world would enable such countries to educate every child and reduce child mortality by two-thirds by 2015.[81]

Interstate arms sales have declined from a high of almost $58 billion in 1998. However, in 2004 they surged to the highest level since 2000 owing to purchases by developing countries, notably India, Saudi Arabia, and China.[82] The United States, the world's leading arms exporter, increased its new arms sales in 2003 to $14.5 billion, accounting for over half of all sales and in 2004 was the leading source of arms exports to the developing world. Between 1996 and 2003, the United States concluded about $105 billion in arms sales, while Russia, the second leading arms source, contracted $40 billion in new sales. America's main customers were Taiwan, Egypt, Britain, Greece, Turkey, and Japan; and Russia's were China and India.[83] Although not a leading source of arms sales, China has been especially irresponsible in this regard, by providing weapons to combatants in Sudan and Nepal. Between 1996 and 2003, the leading customers for arms were concentrated in conflict-prone regions in Asia and the Middle East – the United Arab Emirates ($15.7 billion), China ($13.7 billion), Egypt ($13.6 billion), India ($12.6 billion), and Israel ($9.9 billion).[84]

The black market in weapons of mass destruction

Some countries, including North Korea, have earned much-needed hard currency by illicitly selling WMD and missile technology. And one of the ways in which countries like North Korea and Iran managed to violate the Nuclear Nonproliferation Treaty and evade scrutiny of the IAEA and the Nuclear Suppliers Group (NSG),[85] a group of 44 nuclear-supplier countries that tries to prevent the illegal diversion of nuclear exports, was by dealing with a black market in nuclear technology. Such a market heightens the dangerous prospect of terrorists acquiring WMD. The most blatant evidence of this black market involved Dr. Abdul Qadeer Khan (1935–), the father of Pakistan's clandestine nuclear program, who admitted in February 2004 that he had sold nuclear technology, components, and equipment to Iran, Libya, and North Korea.[86] Although some Pakistani officials probably knew what was taking place, Dr. Khan was essentially running a private enterprise.[87]

The black market was discovered when IAEA inspectors in Iran in 2003 learned that Pakistani scientists had provided nuclear information and technology that enabled the Iranian government to embark on a secret program to build a gas centrifuge plant that could produce enriched uranium for making nuclear weapons. In addition, US intelligence operatives were able to seize equipment for making centrifuges[88] from a German ship heading to Libya in October 2003. Additional information became available after Libyan leader Muammar Qaddafi announced that his country had secretly sought to build a gas centrifuge plant in the 1990s, and he provided the West with information about Libya's WMD program in December 2003, as well as surrendering the plans and equipment that his country had acquired from Khan's black market. Khan had planned to provide Libya with some 10,000 centrifuges as well as the information and equipment for a large gas centrifuge plant. The plant could have been completed in a few years at which time Libya would have been able to manufacture nuclear weapons.

The discovery of Dr. Khan's activities provided significant information to the IAEA and others about how the black market operated and what companies and individuals were involved in it. As part of Pakistan's clandestine effort to build nuclear weapons, Khan's network had obtained nuclear secrets from China in the early 1980s, including the design for a small missile warhead. Although the network was managed by Dr. Khan from Pakistan, it involved others in Europe, the Middle East, South Africa, and Southeast Asia. For example, the Libyan project had been organized by a Sri Lankan based in Malaysia and the United Arab Emirates.

Thus, Dr. Khan had established a genuinely transnational enterprise to manufacture and distribute the huge number of sophisticated components needed to make the gas centrifuges. This work was subcontracted to manufacturers in several countries including Malaysia, Turkey, Spain, and Italy. According to Mohamed ElBaradei (1942–), the IAEA Director General:[89] "Nuclear components designed in one country could be manufactured in another, shipped through a third (which may have appeared to be a legitimate user), assembled in a fourth, and designated for eventual turn-key use in a fifth."[90] "What we are seeing," he declared, "is a very sophisticated and complex underground network of black market operators not that much different from organized crime cartels."[91]

Responses to the global arms trade

As a result of the revelations about the Khan network the UN Security Council in April 2004 passed Resolution 1540 which declared that the "proliferation of nuclear, chemical and biological weapons, as well as their means of delivery, constitutes a threat to peace and security."[92] The resolution expressed the Security Council's concern about the threat of terrorists acquiring WMD, a contingency not covered in the NPT, and declared that "all States shall refrain from providing any form of support to non-State actors that attempt to develop, acquire, manufacture, possess, transport, transfer or use nuclear, chemical or biological weapons and their means of delivery."[93]

Although much has been written about WMD exports, less attention has been paid to the illicit movement of small arms – rifles, machine guns, grenade launchers, and mortars – which play a key role in contemporary violence. Such weapons fuel much of the violence in the developing world and in the civil wars that cost the lives of countless civilians in countries like Sudan and Congo. And when such violence subsides, former combatants often sell their weapons to others who reuse them in new bloody arenas. Thus, the Pentagon cannot account for large numbers of Stinger shoulder-fired anti-aircraft missiles it sold overseas, and US commercial and military aircraft are threatened by terrorists using Stingers that were originally provided to Islamic militants fighting the USSR in Afghanistan after 1979.[94] The danger posed by such missiles was revealed in November 2002, when terrorists launched a missile that

Figure 13.7 Afghan Mujahidin with Stinger missile in the 1980s

© PA Photos

black market a system of illegal buying and selling of goods in violation of price controls or rationing.

almost brought down an Israeli plane filled with holiday travelers leaving Mombasa, Kenya.

Many small arms become available through **black market** sales or government-approved covert arms transfers to insurgents, terrorists, and criminals, often in violation of UN arms embargoes of which there were 15 between 1965 and 2001.[95] Few governments have strong laws regulating the production of and trade in small arms, and arms that were initially sold legally are often diverted to the black market. With the best will in the world, it would be difficult for governments to track the sales of the 385 arms manufacturers in 64 countries that were making guns in the 1990s, many of which were doing so under license, and which oppose any regulation of their business.[96] The situation is made worse by the porosity of many national borders and the vast number of surplus weapons left over from the Cold War. By UN estimates, there are about 500 million small arms in circulation worldwide. According to Oxfam:

- "In north-eastern Kenya, the barter rate for an AK-47 has dropped from ten cows in 1986 to its present level of two cows.
- In Sudan, an AK-47 can be purchased for the same price as a chicken.
- In Central America, automatic weapons sell for around $400.

- In the Philippines, local manufacturers sell machine-guns on the black market for around $375 and revolvers for as little as $15."[97]

Efforts to regulate the global small-arms trade are just beginning. A coalition of humanitarian NGOs, buoyed by their success in lobbying for a ban on the use, production, and trade of anti-personnel mines that became law in 1999,[98] is lobbying to regulate the small-arms trade. Following a convention adopted by the countries of the Americas against illicit trading in small arms, the UN held a world conference on the subject in 2001 from which emerged a proposed action program. Although significant limits on the arms trade are unlikely to be enacted in the near future, the issue is on the global agenda, and, if constructivists are right, it may only be a matter of time until global norms grow strong enough – as they did in the case of anti-personnel mines – to end the deadly traffic in small arms.

The arms trade is an example of the "movement of things." Now, let us turn to another aspect of globalization – the "movement of persons." The status of refugees and immigrants has become increasingly salient in global politics, whether in the massive flight of refugees in the face of violence in Congo or the growing number of Mexicans flowing across the Rio Grande into the United States.

Refugees and migrants

In December 1950, the UN created the office of High Commissioner for Refugees (UNHCR), responsible for implementing the 1951 Convention Relating to the Status of Refugees, reaffirmed in 2001. Since its establishment, UNHCR has aided over 50 million refugees by providing humanitarian assistance, including food, shelter, and medical assistance, and it was awarded Nobel Peace prizes in 1954 and 1981. Today, UNHCR has offices in 115 countries and a budget of about $1 billion, almost doubling since 1994, based largely on voluntary contributions. In recent years, its resources have been stretched to cope with refugee populations around the world.

Refugees

By the 1951 convention, countries are obliged to give asylum to refugees, defined as those who are outside the country of their nationality and are unable or unwilling to return home "owing to well-founded fear of being persecuted for reasons of race, religion, nationality, membership of a particular social group or political opinion."[99] According to the principle of **non-refoulement**, a country cannot expel or return a refugee. When the convention was enacted, it applied mainly to World War II refugees

non-refoulement the legal principle that a state cannot deport an alien to a territory where his or her life or freedom would be threatened on account of race, religion, nationality, or political opinion.

and those escaping communism. In recent decades, however, the refugee issue has come to encompass millions of people fleeing from violence in their homelands. Additional legal instruments dealing with refugees and migrants include the 1990 International Convention on the Protection of the Rights of all Migrant Workers and Members of their Families, the 2000 Protocol to Prevent, Suppress and Punish Trafficking in Persons, Especially Women and Children, and the 2000 Protocol against the Smuggling of Migrants by Land, Sea and Air. However, according to the UN High Commissioner for Refugees António Guterres (1949–), refugees are becoming victims of "asylum fatigue," being denied their rights by countries that were confusing them with illegal economic immigrants.[100]

Between 1984 and 2004, the number of refugees almost doubled, peaking in 1994 following the Rwanda genocide (chapter 7, p. 319). According to the UNHCR, the total "population of concern" consisting of refugees, asylum seekers, stateless persons, and internally displaced persons (IDPs) grew from 19.5 million at the beginning of 2005 to 20.8 million by the end of the year, of whom 40 percent were refugees and 32 percent were IDPs.[101] IDPs, like the hundreds of thousands of Chechens living in Russia, do not enjoy the legal status or protection of international refugees.[102] Although the number of refugees worldwide had declined to 8.4 million by the end of 2005,[103] the lowest number since 1980, the total population of concern to the UNHCR remained stubbornly high, the largest groups of which were Afghans (2.9 million), Colombians (2.5 million),[104] Iraqis (1.8 million), and Sudanese (1.6 million). Since then there have been increasing numbers of IDPs in Sudan owing to the Darfur conflict and in Lebanon owing to the 2006 war between Israel and Hezbollah. Major host countries for refugees were Pakistan, Iran, Germany, Tanzania, and the United States.

In Europe, there remain over two million refugees, many from Bosnia living in Serbia and Germany.[105] Although the number of refugees in Africa has decreased since the end of Angola's civil war in 2002, there are still over three million including 650,000 in Tanzania alone and over a quarter of a million in Kenya, Uganda, and Chad.[106] Somali and Sudanese refugees remain in camps throughout East Africa; many refugees from Burundi live in Tanzania; numerous Rwandans remain in Congo; and refugees flow from conflicts in Liberia and the Ivory Coast. In Asia, many Afghan refugees returned to their country after the 2001 overthrow of the Taliban, but millions remain in Pakistan and Iran. Perhaps the most controversial refugee issue, as we saw in chapter 5, is the roughly four million Palestinians living in camps throughout the Middle East who are aided by the UN Relief and Works Agency (UNRWA). Conflict

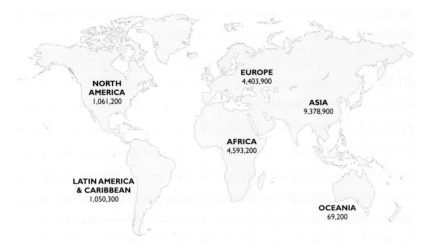

Map 13.2 People of concern to UNHCR, by region, January 2003

between UNRWA officials and Israel is frequent, and Israelis accuse UNRWA of siding with the Palestinians against them. Map 13.2 shows the concentration of refugees in different continents.

At first, UNHCR tried to settle refugees in new countries but, in recent years, as the refugee burden has grown, countries have become less willing to accept refugees on a permanent basis, and in some countries there have been backlashes against immigrants, sometimes with racial overtones. The sagas of Vietnamese boat people victimized by pirates and then refused entry into other Asian countries or of Albanians and Haitians fleeing hardship and tyranny turned away by Italy and the United States respectively are well known. Having lost special refugee status in 1994, many of the hundreds of thousands of Vietnamese refugees who fled their country after 1975 languished in crowded Asian detention camps. Because of demands from host countries, the UN High Commission agreed to repatriate these refugees to Vietnam, forcibly if necessary, and close the camps. Today, as many as 40 percent of the world's countries have implemented policies to reduce the level of immigration.[107]

National policies toward refugees are often dictated more by political than humanitarian motives. For example, during the Cold War the United States readily accepted Jewish refugees from the Soviet Union, as well as Eastern Europeans, Cubans, and Vietnamese fleeing communism. By contrast, in 1992 the United States detained the flood of Haitian refugees trying to escape poverty and violence at home at the US base at Guantánamo Bay in Cuba.

UNHCR now encourages the voluntary return of refugees to their home countries and provides them with the basic requirements to restart

their lives. In assisting refugees UNHCR draws assistance from other
international agencies such as the World Food Program, the UN
Children's Fund, the World Health Organization, the UN Development
Program, and the UN Commissioner for Human Rights, as well as NGOs
like the International Committee of the Red Cross.

Illegal migration

Illegal immigration is different than the refugee issue. Most migrants
leave poor countries for rich ones in search of a better life, and countries
are under no legal obligation to grant asylum to such "economic refugees."
Between 1990 and 2005, the number of migrants globally jumped from
155 to 191 million.[108] The United Nations projects that between 2000
and 2050, the countries that will receive the most migrants are the United
States (1.1 million annually), Germany (211,000), Canada (173,000), and
Britain (136,000). By contrast, most immigrants are expected to come
from China (303,000 annually), Mexico (267,000), India (222,000), the
Philippines (184,000), and Indonesia (180,000).[109]

   Those who migrate often take low paid jobs and remit part of their
earnings to relatives back home, estimated at $232 billion in 2005 of
which $167 billion went to developing countries.[110] This exceeded the
total official aid from rich to poor states. In 2004 alone, Mexican migrants
in the United States remitted about $16.6 billion back home, accounting
for more than 2 percent of Mexico's gross domestic product.[111] Host states
benefit from the influx of low-wage labor. Mexican workers, for example,
earn about one-tenth of what Americans earn in similar jobs. For these
reasons, UN Secretary General Kofi Annan declared that "migration is
not a zero-sum game" and that in "the best cases it benefits the receiving
country, the country of origin and migrants themselves."[112]

   As of 2002, about 175 million people were living outside the countries
in which they were born (roughly twice as many as in 1975), with most
living in Europe (56 million), Asia (50 million), and North America
(41 million).[113] The money that such migrants send home are a vital
financial resource for many poor countries, in 2000 adding more than
10 percent to the gross domestic product of such countries as El Salvador,
Eritrea, Jamaica, Jordan, Nicaragua, and Yemen.[114] Alien smuggling,
especially to Europe and the United States, has become a $7-billion-a-year
racket;[115] and, as the United States tightens its borders, illegal
immigration from Mexico has become extremely dangerous, involving
almost 1,000 deaths between October 2001 and July 2006.[116] And, as
of 2003, there were about eight million illegal aliens in the United
States.[117] According to estimates, Mexicans constitute by far the largest

illegal immigrant population in the United States with El Salvadorans a
distant second. However, as Table 13.1 shows, illegal immigrants in the
United States come from all over the world and are concentrated in
California, Texas, New York, Illinois, and Florida where they constitute
growing proportions of their states' populations.

The United States is a nation of immigrants, and successive immigrant
waves have enriched America's culture. However, some observers are
uneasy about the high level of Mexican immigration. They are concerned
about the pressures that immigrants place on local services like schools
and welfare. Labor unions fear that illegal immigrants will work for low
wages and compete with American workers for jobs.

The roughly 500,000 illegal immigrants entering Europe each
year come from a variety of locations – North Africa, Central Europe,
and South Asia. Their presence has created resentment and political
support for right-wing political parties. Owing to the end of border
controls in much of the EU, once illegal aliens enter Europe, they
enjoy considerable freedom of movement. And, despite efforts to
harmonize policies, EU members still pursue different policies toward
asylum seekers and illegal immigrants.[118] Problems of assimilating
culturally exotic groups are greater in Europe than the United States

Table 13.1 Estimates of illegal aliens in the United States by country of origin and states
of residence (2000)

Country of origin	Population	State of residence	Population
All countries	**7,000,000**	**All states**	**7,000,000**
Mexico	4,808,000	California	2,209,000
El Salvador	189,000	Texas	1,041,000
Guatemala	144,000	New York	489,000
Colombia	141,000	Illinois	432,000
Honduras	138,000	Florida	337,000
China	115,000	Arizona	283,000
Ecuador	108,000	Georgia	228,000
Dominican Republic	91,000	New Jersey	221,000
Philippines	85,000	North Carolina	206,000
Brazil	77,000	Colorado	144,000
Haiti	76,000	Washington	136,000
India	70,000	Virginia	103,000
Peru	61,000	Nevada	101,000
Korea	55,000	Oregon	90,000
Canada	47,000	Massachusetts	87,000
Other	795,000	Other	892,000

US Immigration and Naturalization Service

because European societies are more homogeneous and have less experience with large-scale immigration.

Whatever one's view of immigration, it must take account of significant demographic and economic trends. Although much attention has been paid to the threat that population growth poses to the global environment (see chapter 14, p. 650), only in recent decades have observers thought seriously about the *absence* of population growth in rich countries and the growing burden posed by aging populations. The growing number of elderly relative to younger people means that fewer people are available to pay the taxes needed to provide social security and medical services for growing populations of senior citizens. In addition, the dearth of younger people threatens future labor shortages, especially in lower paid jobs.

Immigration and demography

demography the study of the characteristics of human populations.

Although the proportion of elderly relative to the rest of the population is increasing globally, these trends are sharpest in the world's economically advanced regions. In Europe, the percentage of those over 60 years of age is expected to rise from 20 percent in 2000 to 37 percent in 2050. In countries such as Austria, the Czech Republic, Greece, Italy, Japan, Slovenia, and Spain, the percentage of those over 60 is expected to exceed 40 percent by 2050. By 2000, the median age of Europeans was 38 years, over twice that of Africans, and was projected to rise to 49 by 2050 (when most Africans will still be under 25 years of age).[119] These data translate into increasing numbers of dependents and a growing financial burden on a progressively smaller proportion of working adults. Thus, between 2000 and 2050, the ratio of people over 65 to those of working age is likely to jump from 22 to 51 in Europe and 19 to 35 in North America with Spanish, Japanese, and Italian workers bearing the largest burdens.[120]

birth rate annual number of births per thousand.

Other than higher **birth rates** and larger percentages of women and elderly in the workforce, immigration is the only solution to easing the negative consequences of aging populations. High rates of immigration – legal and illegal – mean that the United States is better prepared to deal with the social and economic burdens of aging populations than Japan or Europe where resistance to absorbing culturally different aliens is greater. The other side of the coin is that immigration from poor to wealthy regions is a safety valve for poor countries that affords opportunities for young people who would at best earn less and at worst be unemployed if they stayed at home where they would contribute to political and social unrest.

Having examined some of the problems posed by refugees and immigrants, we turn to the problem of disease, often associated with the increasing mobility of populations. Health and disease are entwined with economic underdevelopment. Underdevelopment contributes to poverty, weakened populations, refugee flows, famine, and disease. AIDS is one of the most high-profile diseases to engulf parts of the Third World and, in doing so, to decimate labor forces and strain already impoverished governments and societies.

Globalized diseases

Globalized diseases are not new. Bubonic and pneumonic plague, carried by fleas that live on rodents, especially rats that hitched rides aboard ships, repeatedly ravaged Europe. Plague epidemics, probably originating in China and Mongolia, followed the trade routes westward and reached Europe in the fourteenth century. By 1345 plague reached the lower Volga River and from there continued to the Caucasus, the Crimea, and Constantinople. In 1347, Genoese merchants carried the disease to Sicily from the Black Sea port of Kaffa. Within two months, half Messina's population was dead. The Black Death, as it was known, spread through Italy reaching France the following year, and then Germany and England. In less than three years, Europe's population declined by one-third, and about 25 million people perished. Western Europe's population did not again reach its pre-1348 level until the sixteenth century. Whole areas were depopulated and abandoned, and agriculture declined.[121]

Contemporary epidemics and pandemics

The large-scale movement of people associated with globalization has produced conditions for similar epidemics and pandemics (an epidemic that affects people in many countries). In 2004 and early 2005, the World Health Organization (WHO) dealt with a variety of potential epidemics, most importantly, avian influenza, cholera in Africa, yellow fever in Africa and Latin America, and Ebola hemorrhagic fever in Africa which causes death in 50 to 90 percent of all cases.[122] According to WHO, there are some 300 million serious cases of malaria annually, and more than a million people die from the disease each year, mainly children in sub-Saharan Africa.[123] In addition, 1.7 million die from tuberculosis, with the fastest increases in sub-Saharan Africa among populations weakened by HIV/AIDS.[124] Malaria alone is estimated to cost Africa over $12 billion annually. Other killing diseases that could be prevented if vaccines were available include diphtheria, measles, and polio.

High birth rates in poor countries among people living in crowded conditions with inadequate sanitary and medical facilities provide fertile soil for spreading diseases such as AIDS (acquired immune deficiency), malaria, and cholera, a disease arising from contaminated food and water. African sleeping sickness, river blindness, and the parasitic disease schistosomiasis also afflict many people in tropical regions.

Today's deadliest pandemic is HIV/AIDS and, along with cardiovascular disease, malaria, and tuberculosis, is one of the four major global killers and causes of disability in survivors.[125] By destroying lymphocytes necessary for the immune system to function, HIV causes AIDS which leaves victims vulnerable to a variety of deadly infections. The virus is transmitted through exposure to body fluids in the course of sexual relations, sharing hypodermic needles, and breast-feeding infants.

AIDS infected almost nine million people between 1980 and 1994, of whom 90 percent died. By the end of 2004, HIV/AIDS had cost over 20 million lives worldwide, and by 2006 about 39.5 million people were estimated to have contracted the HIV virus with two-thirds of the estimated 4.3 million new cases in sub-Saharan Africa, Eastern Europe, and Central Asia. In China, too, the disease is spreading rapidly, largely owing to growing drug use. In 2006, almost three million people died from AIDS or AIDS-related diseases.[126] The UN projects that between now and 2050 some 278 million people will die from AIDS. In some regions, the death toll is revising future population estimates downward.

As shown in Map 13.3 HIV/AIDS has become a disease of the global South, and deaths in high-income countries are dramatically down owing to the availability of antiretroviral drugs. Moreover, less-developed countries account for over 90 percent of HIV infections since 1980, and the disease is spreading rapidly in densely populated areas of Asia which had 1.1 million new cases of HIV in 2005. China, where the disease has spread to all that country's provinces, is especially at risk, and Russia and Ukraine, where social and political transformations have led to the opening of borders and widespread drug trafficking since the Cold War ended, have witnessed dramatic increases in HIV/AIDS. Nevertheless, with 5.7 million HIV cases, India overtook South Africa in 2005 as the country with the largest infected population.[127]

Overall, sub-Saharan Africa has been hardest hit, with just over 10 percent of the world's population, some 25.8 million people suffer from HIV (nearly two-thirds of all cases).[128] Among those in sub-Saharan Africa between the ages of 15 and 49 who should be the most productive in a population, 7.7 percent have HIV, including 39 percent in Swaziland, 37 percent in Botswana, 29 percent in Lesotho, and 25 percent in Zimbabwe.[129] And throughout Southern Africa about 20 percent of all

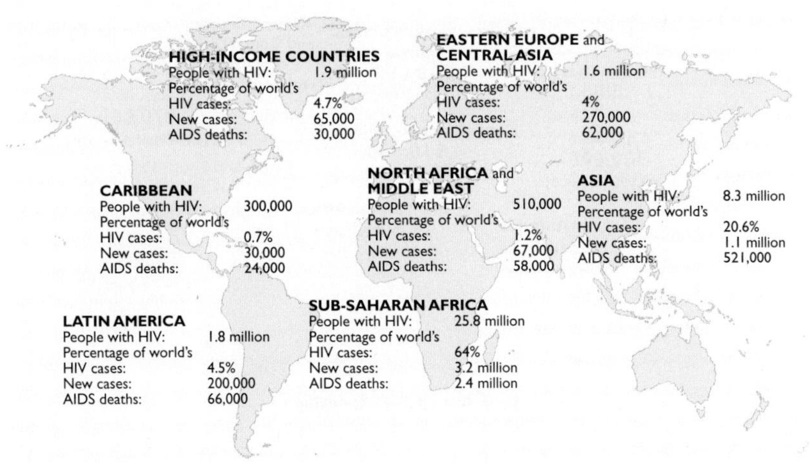

HIGH-INCOME COUNTRIES
People with HIV: 1.9 million
Percentage of world's
HIV cases: 4.7%
New cases: 65,000
AIDS deaths: 30,000

EASTERN EUROPE and CENTRAL ASIA
People with HIV: 1.6 million
Percentage of world's
HIV cases: 4%
New cases: 270,000
AIDS deaths: 62,000

CARIBBEAN
People with HIV: 300,000
Percentage of world's
HIV cases: 0.7%
New cases: 30,000
AIDS deaths: 24,000

NORTH AFRICA and MIDDLE EAST
People with HIV: 510,000
Percentage of world's
HIV cases: 1.2%
New cases: 67,000
AIDS deaths: 58,000

ASIA
People with HIV: 8.3 million
Percentage of world's
HIV cases: 20.6%
New cases: 1.1 million
AIDS deaths: 521,000

LATIN AMERICA
People with HIV: 1.8 million
Percentage of world's
HIV cases: 4.5%
New cases: 200,000
AIDS deaths: 66,000

SUB-SAHARAN AFRICA
People with HIV: 25.8 million
Percentage of world's
HIV cases: 64%
New cases: 3.2 million
AIDS deaths: 2.4 million

Map 13.3 HIV by region, 2005

adults are infected. In fact, among urban high-risk groups in Malawi and Zimbabwe, over 86 percent were infected with HIV,[130] and, owing to AIDS, life expectancy in South Africa plummeted from 63 in 1991 to under 50 today.[131] While life expectancy in developed countries like Japan is approaching 80, in the most afflicted African countries it has declined to nearly 40 or below, dropping to 34 for women and 37 for men in Zimbabwe.[132] By 2002, a combination of violence and disease had reduced life expectancy in Sierra Leone to 28.6 years.[133]

Poverty, poor health care, male dominance, and migrant workers living apart from families are among the causes of Africa's catastrophe. This portends economic and social disaster. As in Europe during the Black Death, whole villages and even regions have been depopulated. The consequences of HIV/AIDS illustrate how the various aspects of human security are tied together. The disease takes a heavy toll among teachers, doctors, and other professionals, thereby blighting the education, health, and economic progress of the afflicted communities. Among its consequences are vast numbers of orphans, industries without workers, and fields that are left untended.

AIDS has been attacked globally by research, treatment, publicity, and education, but little of this has taken place in the most severely affected regions. Global spending on HIV/AIDS reached $6.1 billion in 2004, and the UN estimates that as much as $20 billion will be needed by 2007. Increasingly, efforts are being made to provide antiretroviral drugs, which have prolonged life dramatically among HIV/AIDS patients in the developed world, to the LDCs at affordable cost. Cooperation among major US pharmaceutical companies, the United Nations, and the LDCs

Figure 13.8 Adults and children estimated to be living with HIV as of the end of 2005

Courtesy of Planet 21 (www.peopleandplanet.net)

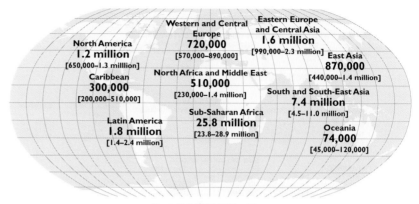

Total: 40.3 (36.7–45.3) million

made it possible for 700,000 AIDS patients in the developing world to receive these drugs by the end of 2004. Nevertheless, too few countries recognize how massive the problem is, and national efforts have been poorly coordinated. Indeed, as recently as 2001, South Africa's President Thabo Mbeki refused to declare AIDS a national emergency[134] even though an estimated 290,000 South Africans died of AIDS in 2003, 5.3 million aged 15 and above suffered from HIV in 2005 (18.8 percent of adults), and about 1.2 million children had been orphaned as a result of the epidemic.[135] Figure 13.8 shows the global distribution of HIV/AIDS. Nevertheless, global efforts to curb the AIDS epidemic seem to be working as reflected in the decline in 2005 in new HIV infections in ten key countries.[136]

Did you know?

In 2002 the Bill & Melinda Gates Foundation committed $100 million to slow the spread of HIV/AIDS in India. In 2005 it committed $750 million to underwrite vaccinations for children around the world[137] and $258 million to research on malaria.[138]

SARS, polio, and avian influenza

One disease that has taken advantage of globalization is severe acute respiratory syndrome or SARS. Between November 2002 and July 2003, over 8,000 people contracted SARS of whom 774 died. The disease involves a high fever, sometimes accompanied by chills, headache, coughing, and body aches as well as difficulties breathing. SARS was a challenge to WHO's Department of Communicable Disease Surveillance and Response that seeks to limit epidemics by using early warning systems, coordinating international responses, and sharing information. To this end, WHO has developed an Epidemic and Pandemic Alert and Response (EPR).[139] In the case of SARS, WHO, like good detectives, traced the outbreak of the epidemic from its first appearance in November 2002 and coordinated the international response.[140]

The story began with the appearance of a case of atypical pneumonia in Foshan City in Guangdong Province in southern China on November 16, 2002. Then, on February 10, 2003, the WHO office in Beijing received an e-mail that described a "strange contagious disease" that in a week had "already left more than 100 people dead" in Guangdong Province. Two days later, China's health officials admitted that there had been hundreds of cases including five deaths in Guangdong between November and February but claimed that it had brought the epidemic under control.

On February 21, a doctor from Guangdong Province, who had experienced respiratory problems some days earlier, arrived in Hong Kong for a wedding. After checking in to the Metropole Hotel, he went sightseeing. The next day he was admitted to hospital suffering from respiratory failure, where he died. A day later an elderly woman who had also stayed at the Metropole returned home to Toronto, Canada. On February 24, a Hong Kong resident, who had spent time in the Metropole, developed a respiratory infection but did not seek help. On the same day, the Global Public Health Intelligence Network learned of a "mysterious pneumonia" in the city of Guangzhou, Guangdong Province that had infected 50 hospital workers there.

The epidemic soon spread beyond China. On February 26, a businessman who had stayed at the Metropole across the hall from the Guangdong doctor was admitted to a hospital in Hanoi, Vietnam with respiratory distress. A few days later, seven Vietnamese health workers in Hanoi showed similar symptoms. On March 1, another former guest of the Metropole was hospitalized in Singapore with respiratory symptoms, and there followed other cases in Singapore involving young women who had traveled to Hong Kong and had stayed at the Metropole. The following week, the elderly woman in Toronto died, and five members of her family were admitted to hospital with the infection. In addition, health workers in Hong Kong's Prince of Wales Hospital who had been in Ward A where the doctor from Guangdong had been treated began to show respiratory symptoms. Within days, the infection appeared in Taiwan.

Only on March 10 did China officially ask WHO for assistance in determining the disease's cause, and WHO issued a global alert about the disease following its spread among health workers in Hong Kong and Hanoi. On March 14, Canadian authorities alerted doctors and hospitals in Ontario of the outbreak of atypical pneumonia in Toronto. Early the next morning, Singaporean authorities sent an urgent warning to WHO that a doctor who had treated the country's first two cases of atypical pneumonia and who had himself complained of symptoms had embarked on a flight from New York to Singapore. On landing in Frankfurt, Germany, the doctor and his family were taken off the plane and quarantined. At this point, WHO issued a warning that the infection was spreading by air travel and gave the infection its name – severe acute respiratory syndrome.

New cases appeared in Canada, Singapore, Germany, Hong Kong, Vietnam, Taiwan, Thailand, Britain, and, on March 20, the United States. Only on March 17 did China finally provide WHO with a report of the original SARS outbreak in Guangdong. Working rapidly, WHO set up a network of laboratories in nine countries to identify SARS's cause and develop a test for the infection. Within a month WHO identified a new coronavirus as the cause.

On April 11, South Africa became the fourteenth country to report the appearance of SARS. As the epidemic spread, China, Hong Kong, and Canada quarantined SARS victims, and on April 2 WHO issued a travel advisory, recommending that travelers avoid Hong Kong and Guangdong Province, later adding Beijing and Shanxi Province, Tianjin, Hebei, Inner Mongolia, and Taiwan to the list.

Not until late June were travel restrictions to Beijing lifted, and only in July were Toronto and Taiwan described as free of new infection. Initial Chinese efforts to hide the epidemic's seriousness had delayed an effective global response. Only on March 26 did Chinese officials admit the seriousness of the epidemic that had swept Guangdong Province, and only on April 19 did the country's leaders order officials to tell the truth about SARS. In addition to lives lost, the economic consequences of the epidemic were steep. Tourism in Hong Kong came to a standstill for months, and decline in travel was reported by all major airlines. SARS has not disappeared, and in April 2004, new cases appeared in Beijing and in east-central China.

Another disease that has been aided by globalization is polio. The disease, endemic to 125 countries in 1988, had been virtually wiped out by 2003 as a result of widespread immunization. However, in that year, the vaccination campaign was halted in northern Nigeria where local Islamic leaders alleged that the vaccine could make women sterile, transmit AIDS, and even that it was manufactured from pork. Travelers then spread the disease westward as far as Mali and southward as far as

Botswana. Prospects for controlling the disease worsened when it arrived in Saudi Arabia (which had been polio free since 1995) with a Sudanese girl and a Nigerian boy who were among the vast crowds of Muslim pilgrims crowding into Mecca on the annual *hadj* or pilgrimage in January 2005 and who returned to their homelands afterwards.[141] Some months later, it appeared in Indonesia, Yemen, Somalia, and then Angola. In the end, some 22 polio-free countries in Africa and Asia were reinfected after 2003.[142] Immunization was begun again in 2004, and more than 80 million children were vaccinated. Nevertheless, roughly seven million Nigerian children under the age of 5 have not been immunized, and polio cases appeared in 13 countries in 2006.[143]

Finally, the prospect of avian influenza mutating into an epidemic in which people can directly transmit the disease to one another is a frightening one that evokes memories of the 1918–19 Spanish influenza pandemic that infected a fifth of the world's population, killed between 20 and 40 million worldwide, and was the most virulent plague of the twentieth century. The Spanish influenza first appeared at Camp Funston (now Fort Riley) in Kansas in March 1918, and it was carried by American troops going to fight in Europe. Thereafter, it spread like wildfire to China and Japan and then to Africa and South America. In September 1918, the pandemic reappeared in the United States, via war shipments to Boston, where it took a deadly toll. Some 200,000 Americans died of influenza in October alone, and military conscription was suspended.[144] By the time the influenza had run its course, some 650,000 Americans had died as well as 450,000 Russians, 375,000 Italians, 228,000 Britons, 500,000 Mexicans, and millions of Asians. Americans' lifespan dropped by ten years, and children skipped rope to the rhyme:

> I had a little bird,
> Its name was Enza.
> I opened the window,
> And in-flu-enza.[145]

Medical experts believe that the world is closer to another influenza pandemic than at any time since 1968. In 2005 WHO, which uses a series of six levels of pandemic alert to inform the world of the seriousness of the threat, raised its alert to level 3 ("a new influenza virus subtype is causing disease in humans, but is not yet spreading efficiently and sustainably among humans") in the case of avian influenza (H5N1 virus).[146] In May 2006 WHO, the US Centers for Disease Control and Prevention, the giant transnational computer firm IBM, and a variety of other groups formed the Global Pandemic Initiative in order to develop "the use of advanced

Figure 13.9 An emergency hospital for influenza patients, 1918

Courtesy of the National Museum of Health and Medicine, Armed Forces Institute of Pathology, Washington, DC (NCP 1603)

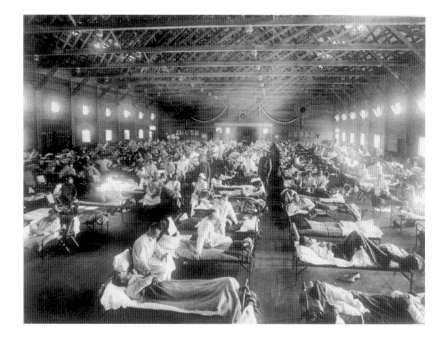

analytical and computer technology as part of a global preparedness program for responding to potential disease outbreaks,"[147] especially predicting the spread of such diseases.

The avian influenza has been spreading rapidly, and global response has been hampered by the failure of some countries to provide accurate and timely information about cases within their borders. A lethal strain of the virus struck Hong Kong in 1997, and the city responded by destroying large numbers of chickens and ducks. Additional outbreaks in Hong Kong were accompanied by outbreaks elsewhere, especially in Vietnam, Laos, and Cambodia. Failure to eradicate the virus, and the death of 44 victims in Thailand and Vietnam between December 2004 and January 2005 intensified fears that avian influenza might become a new pandemic. Migratory birds have been responsible for spreading the disease to China, Russia, Central Europe, and Turkey where several victims died in early 2006.

Doctors Without Borders

Although globalization has created the conditions for the spread of pathogens and previously exotic diseases, it has also fostered innovative responses to health issues. In addition to international organizations like WHO, a number of humanitarian NGOs that specialize in alleviating illness in the developing world have emerged. The best known is Doctors Without Borders (*Médecins Sans Frontières* or MSF) that originated in

NEWS
AVIAN FLU
WORLDWIDE
PANDEMIC?

"YA WANNA SEE HIM COMPLETELY FREAK?... SNEEZE!"

Figure 13.10 Gesundheit!

David Cartlow (US news), Courtesy of Springfield News Sun/Copley News Service

France and has gained global admiration for its activities, including the 1999 Nobel Peace Prize.

Doctors Without Borders[148] was founded in 1971 by a group of French doctors who sought to provide medical assistance to victims of armed conflict, epidemics, and natural and man-made disasters. MSF was the first group of its kind. In emergencies, MSF sends medical teams, armed with prepackaged medical kits. In addition to its humanitarian activities, Doctors Without Borders is politically active in trying to eliminate the causes of the medical problems it treats, and its members publicize the actions of governments and other groups that imperil the health and well-being of people in countries in which it operates.

Doctors Without Borders has become a transnational group with over 2,500 doctors, nurses, and other medical professionals, and 15,000 local staff in over 80 countries in some of the most remote and impoverished regions of the world. Its medical volunteers provide services ranging from primary health care and sanitation programs to surgery and the training of local doctors and nurses. It also runs programs to treat and eliminate diseases such as tuberculosis, AIDS, sleeping sickness, and malaria that take a heavy toll in poor countries, especially in Africa where MSF spent almost two-thirds of its funding in 2003. One of MSF's most spectacular successes was in Nigeria where its teams vaccinated some 4.5 million people during a 1996 outbreak of meningitis.

MSF has gained considerable publicity for its activities on behalf of civilians caught in war zones, especially the floods of refugees fleeing civil wars in Africa in recent decades. The group's first wartime mission took place during Lebanon's 1976 civil war where its doctors and nurses

Figure 13.11 Physicians, including a Doctors Without Borders member, attend a victim in Freetown

Courtesy of Robert Grossman, Africa Photos.com

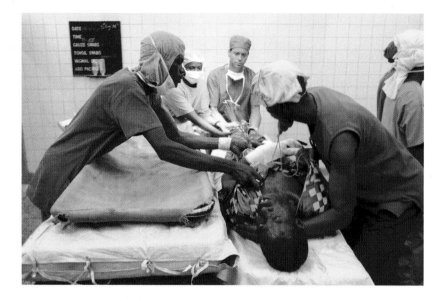

aided Muslim casualties of Christian militias. Among its most dangerous missions were those sent to help Afghans fighting Soviet occupation of their country in 1979, relieve famine during Somalia's 1992 civil war, aid Kurdish refugees fleeing Saddam Hussein's forces in 1991, and provide medical assistance to Bosnian Muslim casualties during the 1992–96 siege of Sarajevo and the 1995 atrocities at Srebrenica.

MSF's largest, most controversial, and complex mission was its effort to aid Hutu refugees fleeing Rwanda to refugee camps in Congo after the 1994 genocide against Rwanda's Tutsis. On that occasion, the group was accused of unwittingly aiding members of Hutu militias who had been involved in the genocidal killings and who had accompanied the refugees. At present, Doctors Without Borders is involved in meeting the humanitarian crises posed by civil war in the Ivory Coast and the genocide in Darfur.

Medical tourism

One of the consequences of the globalization of medical problems has been a growing global private market in medical treatment. As in global trade, countries have begun to specialize in treating and thereby profiting from particular illnesses. This has produced the phenomenon of "medical tourism." Countries like India have established high-quality medical centers to serve citizens from wealthy countries like the United States who seek medical treatment at lower cost than at home or from countries like Canada and Britain where socialized medical systems sometimes force people to wait long periods of time before receiving treatment.

Bumrungrad hospital in Thailand advertises a coronary angiogram for $3,000, including two nights in a single room, a Caesarean section for $1,000, including four nights in a single room, and breast augmentation for about $2,000.[149]

Using the Internet to advertise and send prescriptions and medical records anywhere on earth, some countries offers "package deals" in which patients are flown to a medical center, treated, and then enjoy a holiday at a local resort. For example, Sunway Medical Center located in Selangor Darul Ehsan in Malaysia promotes itself as "a private hospital offering specialized tertiary healthcare services." Prospective foreign clients are encouraged to come for a "vitality health package":

> Jumpstart your health with a "medical holiday" that's packed with relaxation and fun! Re-charge, with a medical check-up, while being pampered with 5-star luxury at Sunway Lagoon Resort Hotel. With shopping and dining privileges, it's all the convenience needed for a rejuvenating affair.
>
> *RM930.00++* per room per package (single occupancy) package includes:

- 3 days / 2 nights accommodation in a Deluxe Room at Sunway Lagoon Resort Hotel.
- One buffet lunch at Sun & Surf Café (consumed on the 2nd day).
- Welcome drink upon arrival.
- General medical health check-up/screening at Sunway Medical Center by Resident Medical Officer.
- Complimentary shuttle service to & from the hotel to Sunway Medical Center.
- Complimentary use of Fitness Center & Swimming Pool.
- Privilege shopping card for great discounts at Sunway Pyramid Shopping Mall.[150]

In this chapter, we have reviewed several issues associated with human security, including poverty, transnational crime, the global arms trade, refugees and migrants, and disease.

Conclusion

This chapter has introduced another major feature of the transformation of global politics now underway: the changing meaning of "security" and the emergence of new issues on the global security agenda. Today's security agenda reflects the widening range of border-spanning threats to human life and well-being and the growing difficulties that states face in dealing with them.

Thus, we have examined poverty, transnational crime, the global arms trade, and refugees and migrants. What these issues have in common is that they reflect the increasing interconnectedness of peoples around the world and the proliferation of problems that threaten everyone but that no single state or group of states can resolve by itself. All of these issues defy easy resolution in a politically fragmented world, and all encourage (but do not ensure) new forms of interstate and transnational cooperation. Resolving these problems will not only mean an expanding role for international and nongovernmental organizations but will also demand an increased and increasingly complex network of cooperation among states.

In the next chapter, we focus on what many observers regard as the single greatest threat to human security, our deteriorating global environment. Rapidly growing populations in poor countries represent a major obstacle to economic development and contribute to deteriorating environmental conditions in the LDCs. Environmental issues ranging from vanishing forests and declining water resources to global climate change threaten our very existence as a species and pose collective-goods dilemmas as to who should pay for their solution.

Student activities

Discussion and essay questions

Comprehension questions

1 What is meant by "human security," and how does it differ from security as traditionally defined in global politics?
2 List five of the poorest countries in the world. Then, consult the World Health Organization website (http://www.who.int/countries/en/) and describe the diseases common in those countries.
3 Find Moody's Investors Service website, and describe its role in determining poor countries' debt burden.
4 Find the World Health Organization website, and list the most dangerous diseases confronting global society today.

Analysis questions

5 How do Western agricultural policies affect the LDCs, and what should be done about these policies?
6 Select a poor country for research and show how the challenges to human security in that country are related to one another.

7 Should the United States focus on the "demand" side of the global drug issue? If it did so, what policies would it pursue?

8 Should the World Health Organization have the authority to quarantine countries in which infectious diseases appear? What would be the consequences of such a policy?

9 Why should the world care about the LDCs' debt problem, and what should rich countries' policies be concerning the issue?

Map exercise

Using Map 13.3, identify five countries that are significantly afflicted with HIV/AIDs. To what extent are these countries also afflicted with other challenges to human security such as poverty, drugs, and refugees?

Cultural materials

The great nineteenth-century British novelist Charles Dickens (1812–70) was personally acquainted with poverty, and several of his novels including *Oliver Twist*, *Bleak House*, and *Hard Times* depict poverty in England during the industrial revolution. Read one of these novels and report on the challenges to human security faced by Dickens's characters.

Further reading

Chepesiuk, Ron, *Drug Lords: The Rise and Fall of the Cali Cartel* (Preston, UK: Milo Books, 2005). How the world's most powerful drug mafia was finally defeated by anti-drug forces.

Clawson, Patrick and Rensselaer W. Lee III., *The Andean Cocaine Industry* (New York: St. Martin's, 1998). Analysis of the cocaine industry in Colombia, Peru, and Bolivia and of how American efforts to curb drug trafficking are hostage to local politics.

Garrett, Laurie, *The Coming Plague: Newly Emerging Diseases in a World Out of Balance* (London: Penguin Books, 1994). How diseases such as Lassa Fever, Ebola Fever, and tuberculosis thrive among growing populations and deteriorating environmental conditions in an era of globalization.

Hampson, Fen Olser, Jean Daudelin, John B. Hay, Holly Reid, and Todd Marting, *Madness in the Multitude: Human Security and World Disorder* (Oxford: Oxford University Press, 2002). How ideas about human security have evolved in recent decades with chapters on a variety of topics such as the global arms trade and economic development.

MacFarlane, S. Neil and Yuen Foong, *Human Security and the UN: A Critical History* (Bloomington, IN: Indiana University Press, 2006).

Evolution of the idea of security for individuals, focusing on UN efforts to promote human security in the 1990s in regard to issues such as economic development and environmental deterioration.

McRae, Robert Grant and Don Hubert, *Human Security and the New Diplomacy: Protecting People, Promoting Peace* (Montreal: McGill-Queen's University Press, 2001). Why human security matters, and how Canada's campaign to ban landmines led to a concern focused on foreign-based civilians caught in armed conflicts.

Newman, Edward and Joanne Van Selm, eds., *Refugees and Forced Displacement: International Security, Human Vulnerability, and the State* (Tokyo: United Nations University Press, 2003). How refugee movements are both a cause and a consequence of conflict within and among states, and why the issue should be treated as a problem of security.

Sachs, Jeffrey, *The End of Poverty: Economic Possibilities for Our Time* (New York: Penguin Press, 2005). A brilliant economist's plan to eliminate extreme poverty around the world by 2025.

Sen, Amartya, *Development as Freedom* (New York: Random House, 1999). A systematic argument that freedoms and political liberty are necessary for sustainable economic development.

Walters, Mark Jerome, *Six Modern Plagues and How We Are Causing Them* (Washington, DC: Island Press, 2003). Everything you wanted to know about six diseases from salmonella to SARS.

14 The environment

A global collective good

There have always existed environmental threats to human survival. For example, a popular explanation for the Roman Empire's fall was the declining birth rates caused by the use of lead in water pipes; the absence of sanitation in medieval Europe contributed to the incidence of diseases like cholera; in the nineteenth century, entire species of animals including the passenger pigeon – once the most numerous bird on earth – were wiped out, and the mercury used to turn fur into the felt in making hats was inhaled by hat makers, causing "mad hatters' disease" with symptoms such as trembling, slurring of speech, and anxiety.[1] The "mad hatter" was made famous in Lewis Carroll's *Alice in Wonderland*.

The chapter begins by examining the concept of collective goods originally elaborated by the economist Mancur Olson. This helps explain why it is so difficult to get countries to cooperate in meeting environmental threats.[2] The chapter then turns to the taproot of environmental concerns, growing populations in the developing world. The question of energy, which follows, like other environmental concerns, reflects the trade-off between ecology and economics. How do we provide sufficient energy to power economic development in less developed countries and maintain our standard of living while coping with challenges like **global warming**? Thereafter, we examine additional environmental challenges – food shortages, disappearing forests and spreading deserts, polluted seas and inadequate fresh water, and efforts to cope with them.

global warming warming of the earth's climate caused by the release of "greenhouse" gases trapping heat from the earth (also known as the greenhouse effect).

The challenge to survival and well-being is more global today than ever before. To date, the global record in dealing with environmental challenges has been dismal. According to an index developed by Yale University's Center for Environmental Law and Policy and Columbia University's Center for International Earth Science Information Network, only six countries (New Zealand, Sweden, Finland, the Czech Republic, Britain, and Austria) have exceeded 85 percent in meeting environmental

Figure 14.1 Overpopulation

© Original artist,
www.cartoonstock.com

*The number of bacteria living in your mouth can easily
exceed the number of people who live on the Earth.*

goals including environmental health, air quality, water resources,
biodiversity and habitat, productive natural resources, and sustainable
energy (see Map 14.1).[3] The United States ranked 28th. However,
the most worrisome were heavily populated China (94th) and India
(118th) which are in the midst of rapid economic development. Indeed,
China, which uses coal, the dirtiest of the fossil fuels, for much of its
electric power and is *annually* adding almost as much power as Britain's
entire capacity, will become the world's leading source of carbon gases by
2015.[4] Environmental threats do not respect national boundaries, and no
single state or group of states can successfully cope with environmental
threats. Cooperation, however, is elusive, partly because of the problem
of **collective goods**, the topic to which we now turn.

collective goods benefits such
as military security or clean air
from which individuals cannot
be excluded and, as a result, for
which beneficiaries have no
incentive to pay.

Collective goods and collective fates

Global actors are increasingly challenged by the emergence of issues
that affect peoples around the world and with which no single country or
group of countries can cope on their own. In the era of globalization, *issues
increasingly place actors in situations in which they win or lose jointly.* As noted

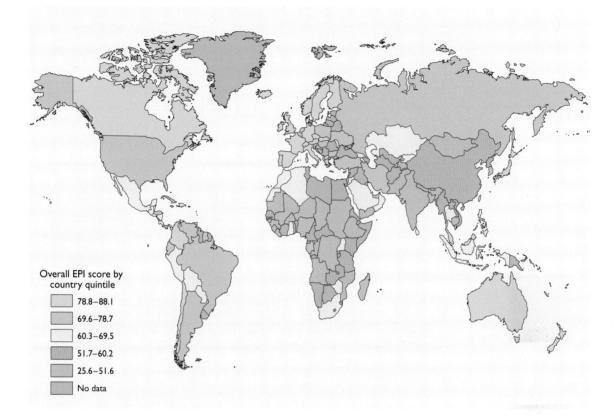

Map 14.1   Pilot 2006 environmental performance index

above, the deterioration of the global environment is a major challenge to global well-being; a cleaner environment is universally beneficial, whereas environmental degradation is harmful to everyone to a greater or lesser extent. Similarly, growing volumes of trade benefit all actors, though not equally, while declining trade harms all of them.

Issues such as the global environment and global trade challenge humanity as a whole and cannot be managed by individual actors on their own. For example, however much Europe reduces its emissions of the gases that cause global warming, that phenomenon will not be curbed unless the United States cooperates. Even then, the effort would probably be doomed unless rapidly industrializing countries like China, India, and Brazil also curb their growing appetite for fossil fuels.

Unlike traditional interstate disputes over objectives like territory, it is difficult for actors to profit at one another's expense in the case of such issues. There are winners and losers in territorial contests. The territory seized by one actor is lost to its opponent and vice versa. By contrast, when environmental conditions worsen or trade protectionism spreads, humanity *as a whole* suffers, though not equally, and when environmental conditions improve or impediments to trade are reduced everyone benefits, though not equally. Such issues defy conventional definitions of national security and national interest.

A healthy environment is one of many collective goods in global politics, so called because they *offer benefits that must be shared and made available to everyone if they are to be enjoyed by anyone.* Challenges such as global warming and water depletion threaten everyone's well-being. Their solution promises benefits that must be shared and made available to everyone if they are to be enjoyed by anyone. Paradoxically, because so many actors benefit from goods like clean air, none has an incentive to pay for them voluntarily because it would be difficult to deprive particular actors of such benefits even if they refuse to pay for them. Each, wishing the benefit, prefers that someone else pays and reasons that because the group is so large, one contribution more or less will not matter and will not be missed. Thus, as regards global warming, a country's leaders may reason that reducing the number of automobiles on its roads or buying expensive scrubbers for power plants will only affect the total amount of global emissions marginally and that their country can still benefit from ending global warming at no cost to itself.

In other words, in the face of collective challenges, it is in the interests of *each* actor to pay as little as possible to overcome the problem, instead letting others pay while they reap the benefits. To the extent that actors can get others to pay the costs, they can be **free riders**, enjoying benefits without having to pay for them. However immoral such behavior may be, it is also rational. Actors, though wishing the collective goods that would flow from a clean environment and unfettered trade, may be reluctant to pay the price for them. Such reluctance is strongest among those that do not expect to receive a share of the benefits commensurate with the costs they would have to pay. Since the United States as the leading source of carbon emissions would have to foot much of the economic bill to curb global warming, the country has dragged its feet on the issue.

free riders those who receive the benefits of a collective good without paying their fair share of the costs of producing that good.

Key document   Garrett Hardin, "The Tragedy of the Commons" (1968)[5]

The biologist and ecologist Garrett Hardin illustrated the problem posed by collective goods in a 1968 article entitled "The Tragedy of the Commons" in which he illustrated how the interests of individuals and the interests of the group can collide. The following is an excerpt from that classic statement of the problem:

The tragedy of the commons develops in this way. Picture a pasture open to all. It is to be expected that each herdsman will try to keep as many cattle as possible on the commons. Such an arrangement may work reasonably satisfactorily for centuries because tribal wars, poaching, and disease keep the numbers of both man and beast well below the carrying capacity of the land. Finally, however, comes the day of reckoning, that is, the day when the long-desired goal of social stability becomes a reality. At this point, the inherent logic of the commons remorselessly generates tragedy.

As a rational being, each herdsman seeks to maximize his gain. Explicitly or implicitly, more or less consciously, he asks, "What is the utility *to me* of adding one more animal to my herd?" This utility has one negative and one positive component.

1 The positive component is a function of the increment of one animal. Since the herdsman receives all the proceeds from the sale of the additional animal, the positive utility is nearly +1.

2 The negative component is a function of the additional overgrazing created by one more animal. Since, however, the effects of overgrazing are shared by all the herdsmen, the negative utility for any particular decision-making herdsman is only a fraction of −1.

Adding together the component partial utilities, the rational herdsman concludes that the only sensible course for him to pursue is to add another animal to his herd. And another; and another. . . . But this is the conclusion reached by each and every rational herdsman sharing a commons. Therein is the tragedy. Each man is locked into a system that compels him to increase his herd without limit – in a world that is limited. Ruin is the destination toward which all men rush, each pursuing his own best interest in a society that believes in the freedom of the commons. Freedom in a commons brings ruin to all.

There are two ways to prevent free-riding – by coercion or by providing **private goods** (sometimes called "side payments"). The imposition of penalties by the World Trade Organization on states that violate trade regulations is an example of using coercion to prevent free-riding. Private goods are benefits that are available only to those who pay for them, and actors that do not contribute can be excluded from such benefits. For example, allowing countries to get credit for reducing carbon emissions by planting trees that absorb carbon dioxide ("carbon sinks") or providing advanced technology and low-cost loans to countries that reduce emissions constitute private goods available only to actors that cooperate in reducing pollution.

private goods benefits that are enjoyed only by some and need not be shared.

There is, therefore, a tension between the general interests of any community and the particular interests of individual actors. This is why polls repeatedly show that citizens want *both* a stronger military establishment *and* lower taxes. All citizens benefit from a strong common defense, yet many prefer to let others pay for it. It is necessary to enforce tax laws (coercion) to fund national defense and to provide side payments like defense contracts for local industries to selected areas of the country in order to garner political support for defense spending. However, in a world populated by sovereign states, where there is no higher authority to coerce actors to contribute to the provision of collective goods, such dilemmas are difficult to resolve. Nowhere is this clearer than with the issue of population growth.

Theory in the real world

Environmental issues reflect the dilemma posed by the theory of collective goods in several ways. First, environmental improvements such as cleaner air and water and an end to climate change benefit everyone and every country. Second, it is difficult, if not impossible, to deprive individuals of such benefits. Third, individuals and countries, especially small countries, have an incentive to be free riders and avoid paying for such improvements because they believe they cannot be deprived of the benefits and their contribution makes little difference. And fourth, individuals and countries can be cajoled into contributing by being given side payments such as UN or US aid to fund environmental projects or the provision of emissions credits. Companies or countries that pollute are given credits which allow them to emit a specific amount of a pollutant. Those that emit more than they are allowed must purchase credits from other companies or countries that pollute less than their allowance. In other words, purchasers are being fined for exceeding their pollution allowance, and sellers are being rewarded for polluting less than allowed. There are even financial firms that specialize in "energy and emissions trading and environmental asset trading opportunities."[6]

For decades, a debate has raged about the earth's capacity to sustain continued growth. Central to this debate is population growth. In the next section, we will see how population growth can outstrip economic development, reduce standards of living, and place great strain on natural resources and the environment.

Population and environment

Growing populations present an unusually intractable collective-goods problem, especially in traditional agricultural societies. In such societies, it makes sense for families to have many children who can help work the land and who can care for parents as they grow old. However, what is rational for individual families is irrational for society as a whole because rapid population growth may outstrip economic development and place intolerable strains on a country's resources.

Historically, a large population was regarded as a key element of power that made it possible to field large armies and support labor-intensive industries at low wages. Countries tried to encourage higher rates of population than rivals. Italian dictator Benito Mussolini (1883–1945), for example, tried to encourage Italy's population growth in the 1930s to settle overseas colonies, recruit larger armies, and increase the labor pool. With this in mind he banned abortion and information on contraception in Italy and provided incentives such as family allowances, tax breaks, and loans to encourage large families of five children or more. On one occasion, he met with a group of 93 mothers who had collectively given birth to more than 1,300 children.

For some countries, a large population provided emigrants for overseas colonization that added to the power of the mother country. Overpopulation in the city-states of ancient Greece allowed for settlements in Asia Minor, North Africa, and elsewhere that spread Greek culture to the corners of the known world. The poor from Great Britain settled in North America and Australia, and excess population from many countries emigrated to the United States.

Despite the desire of great powers for growing populations to wage war, there were those who recognized that overpopulation could prove a serious problem. The most important of these observers was English political economist and clergyman Thomas Malthus (1766–1834) who two centuries ago predicted a growing imbalance between population and food supply, arguing that world population would be kept in balance with resources only by natural disasters like famine, disease, and war (see Key document: Thomas Malthus). Although Malthus's dire predictions have been averted by agricultural innovation, notably the "green revolution" of the 1960s and 1970s in which new strains of wheat dramatically increased yields,[7] it remains to be seen whether a "neo-Malthusian" future lies ahead.

Did you know?

Australia was originally colonized with British convicts. In 1788, British ships deposited 780 British convicts at Botany Bay in New South Wales, and two more convict fleets arrived in 1790 and 1791.

Key document   Thomas Malthus, *An Essay on the Principle of Population* (1798)[8]

Population, when unchecked, increases in a geometrical ratio. Subsistence increases only in an arithmetical ratio. A slight acquaintance with numbers will shew the immensity of the first power in comparison of the second.

By that law of our nature which makes food necessary to the life of man, the effects of these two unequal powers must be kept equal.

The power of population is so superior to the power in the earth to produce subsistence for man, that premature death must in some shape or other visit the human race. The vices of mankind are active and able ministers of depopulation. They are the precursors in the great army of destruction; and often finish the dreadful work themselves. But should they fail in this war of extermination, sickly seasons, epidemics, pestilence, and plague, advance in terrific array, and sweep off their thousands and ten thousands. Should success be still incomplete, gigantic inevitable famine stalks in the rear, and with one mighty blow levels the population with the food of the world.

Population trends

World population reached one billion in 1804. It took another 123 years for it to reach two billion, and 33 more years to reach three billion. According to UN estimates, world population – increasing by 77 million annually or about 146 every minute – reached the six billion mark in October 1999, only 12 years after reaching five billion.[9] And, according to the UN, by 2050, population may approach nine billion.[10] This increase is unequally distributed globally, and six countries account for half the annual population growth (India, China, Pakistan, Bangladesh, Nigeria, and the United States). In 1960, 70 percent or 2.1 billion of the world's three billion people lived in less-developed countries (LDCs); by late 1999, the LDCs were home to 80 percent of the world's population, and 98 percent of the projected growth of the world population by 2025 will take place in these countries.[11] Thus, most population growth will occur in the world's poor regions with the least capacity to sustain more people.

Population growth in these regions threatens to overwhelm economic development, reducing standards of living and fostering discontent especially among young people who constitute nearly half the world's population and who are concentrated in poor countries such as Rwanda, Pakistan, and Bangladesh. Rapid population growth increases the proportion of young people in a society, and declining or stabilizing growth rates produce an aging or graying society. Each trend entails different problems with consequences for global politics.

There are now more people between ages 15 and 24 who are entering their peak childbearing years, and almost nine out of ten live in the developing world.[12] Between 1995 and 2050, the number of young people will decline from 19 to 14 per cent of the world's population, but their numbers will increase from 859 million to 1.06 billion.[13] Young people place special burdens on a society's economic and social infrastructure. The very young need medical care and day care so that parents can work. They place heavy demands on education systems. Above all, they need land or jobs, and in much of the developing world these are scarce. If the educated have no opportunity to realize their aspirations, they become disillusioned, often rejecting the political system that has failed them. Large numbers of young people, especially males, without employment become available to political extremism, revolutionary or criminal groups, religious fundamentalism, and ethnic and national causes. The young were the backbone of Europe's fascist and communist movements in the 1930s, just as they are found in militant Islamic groups today. As was the case in the 1930s, so today they are sources of potential political and social instability and upheaval.

Fortunately, **birth rates** and **fertility rates** around the world have dropped significantly in recent decades, forecasting an end to exponential population growth. Even in the LDCs, where fertility levels had been highest, they have been halved from six to three children born per woman so that the rate of increase will slow. Elsewhere, the populations of Russia and Ukraine are expected to drop precipitously by mid-century, and China's population will start declining by the 2030s. Fertility levels in much of the developed world have fallen below replacement level and immigration is a key source of labor to support aging populations. Populations in a number of the developed countries, including Japan, Germany, and Italy, have begun or will begin to drop soon,[14] and birth rates are also dramatically dropping in the new EU members in Eastern Europe like the Czech Republic. As a result, the EU fears it may have a shortfall of 20 million workers by 2030.[15]

Large and growing populations produce environmental strains, especially in the developing world where many countries feature slowly declining birth rates and rapidly declining death rates (from 20 to fewer than ten deaths per thousand since 1950),[16] resulting in population growth that threatens to outstrip economic development. For example, the populations of Burkina Faso, Mali, Niger, Somalia, Uganda, and Yemen – all except the last in sub-Saharan Africa – are projected to quadruple by 2050. These data suggest a rapidly changing world with fewer Europeans and larger numbers of Asians and Africans. Thus, in 1950, of the 20 most populous countries, six were European. By 1999, only two were European, and by 2050 only one – Russia – is expected to remain among the top 20.

High birth rates in poor countries among people who live in crowded conditions with inadequate sanitary and medical facilities provide fertile soil for the spread of diseases such as AIDS and cholera. Economic development is itself a source of **urbanization**, and the flight of peasants into urban areas is part of the demographic transition from high to low birth rates that accompanies economic growth and development. As land-hungry peasants or those who can no longer make a living from agriculture abandon the countryside and flood cities in search of jobs, they create urban nightmares, overtaxing existing facilities and creating dense concentrations of poverty.

The proportion of people in LDCs living in cities has almost doubled since 1960 from less than 22 percent to over than 40 percent.[17] In fact, including the developed world, over half the world's population already live in cities, and this percentage is expected to grow to 60 percent by 2025.[18] In 1975, only five cities had populations of over ten million. By 2001, there were 17 cities of more than ten million, and by 2015, it is expected that there will be 21 cities of more than ten million, including

birth rate annual number of births per thousand.

fertility rate the number of children born to an average woman during her lifetime.

urbanization the social process during which cities grow and population becomes more concentrated in urban areas.

six (Tokyo, Dhaka, Bombay, São Paulo, New Delhi, and Mexico City) with more than 20 million.[19] The poor often live in illegal shanty towns that lack safe water or indoor plumbing. Many homes lack electricity; garbage is burned in the open; and sewerage flows through open ditches, creating the conditions for disease. The infrastructure of these cities is inadequate; crime is endemic, and police are often corrupt and incompetent.

Increasing conflict?

Rapid population growth breeds violence in crowded cities like Bogotá, Karachi, and Rio de Janeiro, and growing populations translate into demands for resources, which, if unmet, may generate conflict as countries try to satisfy the need for space and resources at one another's expense. Some analysts believe that crowding, which is a result of population density, triggers violence. Anthropologist Desmond Morris describes crowded urban conditions as a "human zoo":

> Only in the cramped quarters of zoo cages do we find anything approaching the human state. . . . But even the least experienced zoo director would never contemplate crowding and cramping a group of animals to the extent that man has crowded and cramped himself in his modern cities and towns. *That* level of abnormal grouping, the director would predict with confidence, would cause a complete fragmentation and collapse of the normal social pattern of the animal species concerned.[20]

From this perspective, urban crime and war have common roots. We would expect violence and crime to be greater in densely populated cities with few amenities and high poverty rates such as Calcutta or São Paulo than elsewhere. In Karachi, Pakistan, a city with a population of some 11 million that is growing at 5 percent annually,[21] "middle-class suburbs are virtually under siege from urban guerrillas, armed with automatic rifles, bombs and rocket-launchers."[22]

Japanese leaders in the 1930s claimed that the need for resources justified the country's aggressive imperialism, and Hitler invaded Russia in 1941 in search of *Lebensraum* (living space) for the German people. Today, there is growing concern over the possibility of resource wars, for example in the Middle East where the demand for water is outstripping its supply (see chapter 14, p. 675).

Population density, which as shown in Map 14.2 on average is greatest in the less-developed regions, and economic inequality also produce land hunger. Small elites own disproportionate amounts of arable

population density the number of individuals of a population per unit of living space.

land, leaving poor peasants with insufficient land to support themselves. Such conditions promote revolutionary violence and civil war as they did in El Salvador in the 1980s. More than half of El Salvador's population and three-quarters of those in rural areas lived in absolute poverty at that time, and the country's population was growing rapidly. The US-supported Salvadoran government resisted significant land reform, and Marxist guerrillas seized large estates and distributed them to landless peasants. Although a 1992 agreement ended the war in El Salvador, continuing population pressures and land hunger may rekindle social tension in the future and trigger massive waves of migrants northward toward the United States. Similar conditions exist in much of Central America.

A more complex view is that population growth produces environmental degradation that in turn leads to declining agricultural production, population movements, and disrupted institutions. According to political scientist Thomas F. Homer-Dixon, these conditions are associated with three types of war: scarcity conflicts that arise over

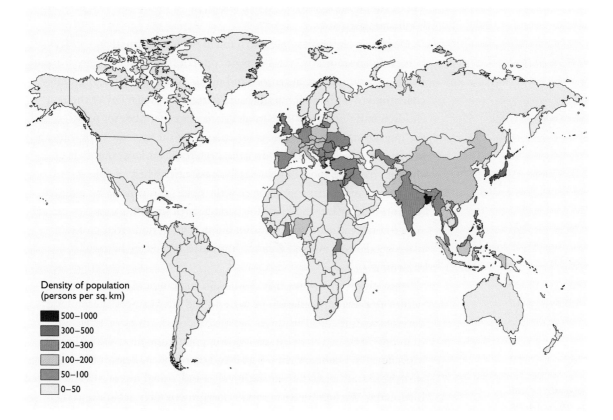

Map 14.2 Global population density

limited resources like fresh water, group-identity conflicts between ethnic and cultural communities, and relative-deprivation conflicts connected to inequalities within societies.[23] Journalist Robert Kaplan concludes that:

> It is time to understand "the environment" for what it is: *the* national-security issue of the early twenty-first century. The political and strategic impact of surging populations, spreading disease, **deforestation** and soil erosion, water depletion, air pollution, and, possibly, rising sea levels in critical, overcrowded regions like the Nile delta and Bangladesh – developments that will prompt mass migrations and, in turn, incite group conflicts – will be the core foreign-policy challenge from which most others will ultimately emanate.[24]

deforestation massive loss of forests with environmental consequences such as reduced oxygen production and soil erosion.

Defusing the population bomb

Economic and social development is the key to slowing population growth. Poor countries with traditional societies tend to have high birth and death rates, in contrast to rich and modern societies which have low birth and death rates.

Questions of population growth touch people's cultural and ethical beliefs. Infant mortality rates in poor countries are high owing to inadequate sanitation, nutrition, and medical care, and these high rates contribute to high birth rates because parents assume many of their children will die. In addition, males desire large families for prestige, and the inferior status of women is perpetuated by the imperative of constantly bearing and raising children. In sum, preference for large numbers of children has deep roots in poor agrarian societies where people want large numbers of male offspring to help in the fields, compensate for a high infant mortality rate, and provide parents with social insurance in old age. As we noted earlier, from a family's point of view, numerous children make good sense, even though more mouths to feed are harmful to society as a whole.

Most observers believe that changes in customs and values are needed to control population growth. In the initial stages of economic development, medical advances cause a drop in death rates, especially in infant mortality, thereby accelerating population growth and life expectancy in poor countries. Social and economic upheavals that increase wealth, education, and urbanization alter individual incentives and reduce birth rates. With prosperity, population growth rates decline and then stabilize. Economic development increases the demand for women in the workforce and provides new opportunities for educating both men and women. Wealth and education, especially of women, create new interests outside the home and provide knowledge about opportunities for personal growth that encourage later marriages and that only exist with a small family. In urban settings, women marry later; divorce is more common; and more women remain single. In a word, empowering women is probably the most effective way of slowing population growth in LDCs. Finally, urbanization and government social security reduce economic incentives to have large families and create practical constraints like insufficient housing.

Poor countries that emphasize the education of women as agents of change and offer family planning in community settings have done best in reducing birth and fertility rates, yet as many as 350 million families still have no access to family-planning services. And it is estimated that only 8 percent of married women in West Africa use contraception, even though population growth is explosive.[25] Combining economic development and coercion can make a big difference as shown by China's experience. By combining a coercive policy limiting families to one child since 1979, with free contraceptives and birth-control information and legalized abortion, China almost halved its birth rate and reduced its fertility rate from 5.7 to 1.4 between 1970 and 1999.[26] However, imposing birth control may entail running roughshod over traditional beliefs or, as in China, creating social tensions as families abort female fetuses because of the traditional preference for boys and so produce a surplus of males for whom there are no brides. Political scientists Valerie Hudson and Andrea Den Boer argue that this surplus of young males is a likely source of internal and international conflict.[27]

As we saw in chapter 10 (p. 490), China's coercive family-planning policies and especially its use of abortion and sterilization to control births became linked to the abortion debate in the United States. In announcing a cut-off of US funds to the UN Population Fund, a State Department spokesman declared that China's birth-control programs "have penalties that amount to coercion. Therefore we feel, by funding these programs, we would be indirectly helping the Chinese to improve their management of programs that result in coercive abortion, and that's prohibited by our law."[28]

In time, however, as birth rates decline, countries discover that they have an insufficient number of young people as workers and taxpayers, and the burden on societies of providing health care and retirement benefits for growing populations of elderly people may become onerous. These problems are sharpened by the disappearance of the extended families typical of traditional societies that provided care to the elderly and the inability and/or unwillingness of families, especially in urban settings, to care for elderly relatives who live ever longer. Increasingly, rich countries in North America, East Asia, and Western Europe are experiencing "graying" populations, with ever smaller numbers of young people having to provide for and finance growing numbers of retired citizens. Even China has begun to experience "graying" and, despite its enormous population, will begin to experience a shortage of cheap labor.[29] In the United States, Europe, and Japan, the prospect that government social security and medical insurance programs may go bankrupt has become a major political issue.

One solution for "graying" societies is encouraging more births, but, as we shall see, this threatens to exacerbate environmental problems and touches upon social issues such as women's independence. Another possibility is utilizing more and more women in the workforce, a route already largely exploited in Europe and North America but still available in Japan where the status of women has advanced only very slowly. As we saw in chapter 13 (pp. 628–9), migration is another partial solution that has postponed the demographic crisis in the United States. Indeed, labor shortages in countries like Italy, the first country with more people over the age of 65 than under the age of 15,[30] may help poor countries because they provide opportunities for them to "export" workers who then send money home. However, migration can produce severe social tension in relatively homogenous societies, and in some cases such as that of Japan violates a basic social consensus and is stubbornly resisted.

Nevertheless, continuing population growth in poor countries remains a major source of environmental degradation. Concern about global population and the environment surfaced in the 1960s and led to the 1972 UN Conference on the Human Environment in Stockholm, Sweden, and, then, two years later, to the UN World Population Conference in Bucharest, Rumania. The link between population and environment received much attention at the 1984 International Conference on Population in Mexico City, which urged countries to bring population and resources into balance. At the 1992 UN Conference on Environment and Development or "Earth Summit" held in Rio de Janeiro, representatives of 172 countries and 2,400 NGOs gathered to discuss ways to reduce strains on the global environment while fostering **sustainable development** to lower the tension between the desire of poor countries to develop their economies quickly and the preference of wealthy countries to impose environmental limits on development. The conference produced an ambitious set of objectives called Agenda 21 in which participants committed themselves to a program of environmental preservation, with emphasis on global warming, biodiversity and the linked problems of poverty, health, and population. These commitments proved

sustainable development development that meets the needs of the present without compromising the ability of future generations to develop.

ephemeral, and the US has dragged its feet regarding its obligations under Agenda 21.

The Rio conference was followed by the 1994 International Conference on Population and Development in Cairo, where efforts were made to find a balance between economic growth and population, while endorsing slower population growth and pointing out the link among production, consumption, and environmental health. There followed the 1996 UN Conference on Human Settlements, called Habitat II, in Istanbul, which focused on problems of rapid urbanization and population growth.

Population growth is a key cause of environmental stress and ecological deterioration. The following section examines a number of growing environmental challenges that we face and depicts the relationship among them.

Deteriorating global ecology

Population growth and rapid economic development diminish our physical space and strain the earth's physical, social, and political environments. Already, wealthy countries are running out of space in which to dump solid waste – some of it violently toxic or radioactive – and, in some cases, have exported it to poor countries in need of hard currency.[31]

The links among environmental problems, as well as their relationship to economic growth, are characteristic of globalization. One dilemma involves the trade-off between economic and environmental interests. Rapid industrialization and economic development are not unmitigated blessings. They bring with them mountains of waste and pollution.

Consider China: Despite the slowing of population growth, the country has such a large population (1.3 billion) that a growth rate of only 1 percent means an additional 12 million people annually, roughly the population of Tokyo. In China, which is modernizing at breakneck speed, "**acid rain** nibbles at the Great Wall; the Grand Canal . . . resembles an open sewer; part of Shanghai is slowly sinking as its water table is depleted; and Benxi, in Manchuria, is so thick with air pollution the city doesn't appear in satellite pictures."[32] Ozone pollution in China is so great that it is harming agriculture to the point that the country may not be able to feed itself in the future,[33] and 70 percent of Beijing's children are affected by lead poisoning.[34] Moreover, a great deal of arable land is taken out of production each year to provide industrial sites and housing. Also, China's reliance on coal to industrialize and its growing number of automobiles are making it a leading producer of climate-warming carbon dioxide, and global warming may inundate China's coastal plain,

acid rain precipitation made acidic by sulfur dioxide and nitrogen oxides that are produced by industry, automobiles, and power plants.

displacing millions around Shanghai and Guangzhou. China's Three Gorges Dam, the country's largest project since the Great Wall and the world's largest dam, that will end flooding along the Yangtze River, has created a vast reservoir 412 miles long and has inundated numerous cities and villages, many industrial sites with toxic materials, factories, and fertile farm land, forcing the resettlement of some 1.2 million people.[35] The toxic materials could leach into the reservoir and the Yangtze. Finally, the sources of the majestic Yellow River are drying up, and the river is almost entirely contaminated.[36] In addition, China's rapid development, more than any other factor, accounted for the dramatic rise in global oil prices in 2004–06.

The next section illustrates this trade-off between economic and environmental objectives in the context of growing energy demands for economic development and dangerous environmental side effects like global warming.

Global energy politics

Energy politics illustrate how environmental and economic imperatives collide and how actors have divergent views of trade-offs between the two. Energy consumption is essential for economic growth, and, although energy use has grown more efficient in recent decades, energy usage has risen significantly.

Fossil fuels and economic development

Harnessing new energy sources tells much about how human society has modernized. The industrial revolution was made possible by machinery that replaced human and animal labor and was built on mountains of cheap, plentiful fossil fuels like coal and coke. Transportation and distribution networks were based on the internal combustion engine – ships, trains, planes, and cars. However, the environmental and health toll of industrialization was enormous. Smog and toxic compounds inflicted disease and premature death. Air and water were poisoned; coal miners contracted tuberculosis and black lung; and the burning of coal in London made that city notorious for its pea-soup fogs. Although significant progress has been made in limiting certain dangerous pollutants like heavy metals such as mercury, cadmium, and nickel, societies continue to wrestle with the trade-offs between economic development and pollution, the depletion of nonrenewable resources, the storage of dangerous materials like nuclear waste, air pollution and acid rain, and global warming.

One of the most vexing problems in global politics is how to generate sufficient energy for growth while coping with associated environmental effects. This is complicated by the fact that the richest 20 percent of the world's population accounts for 86 per cent of total private consumption expenditure, including 58 percent of the world's energy and 87 percent of its automobiles.[37] With less than 5 percent of the world's population, the US uses more of the world's fossil fuels than any other country.[38] Poor countries are willing to sacrifice the environment for economic growth, while rich countries demand more stringent environmental standards.

The global community today is more sensitive to the relationship between energy and environment and better understands how both are needed for prosperity and health. The economic and political sides of the equation have received ever more attention since the formation of the Organization of Petroleum Exporting Countries (OPEC) at a conference in September 1960, attended by Iran, Iraq, Kuwait, Saudi Arabia, and Venezuela. These five were later joined by eight other oil-exporting countries: Qatar (1961), Indonesia (1962), Libya (1962), United Arab Emirates (1967), Algeria (1969), Nigeria (1971), Ecuador (1973–92), and Gabon (1975–94). Although OPEC is not strictly a regional organization, seven of its members are located in the oil-rich Middle East (see Map 14.3). OPEC is an important institution because of its role in the production and distribution of oil.[39] OPEC is a commodity cartel whose members aim to reduce competition and maintain higher prices for their product by controlling production. Together, they account for about 40 percent of the world's oil output and over three-quarters of the world's proven oil reserves. Inevitably there is global concern about OPEC's "oil power."

In the 1970s, the OPEC cartel, which had been established a decade earlier, emerged as an oligopoly able to determine oil price, an ability that gave it great political clout. Twice a year OPEC oil ministers meet at their Vienna headquarters to decide production levels and set production quotas for members. Oil-producing states seek to control their commodity and earn as much as possible while it lasts, and oil-consuming states want plentiful oil at stable prices.

Libya was the first oil producer to force foreign oil corporations to renegotiate earlier agreements. Threatening to seize their assets, in 1970 Libyan leader Muammar Qaddafi demanded that oil companies increase the price of Libyan crude. Companies' efforts to stand up to Libya collapsed when Occidental Petroleum broke ranks and raised prices. Libyan success led other oil-producing states to demand similar increases and, in an effort to stabilize prices, the oil companies tried to involve oil-producing states in multilateral negotiations to set a common price.

Map 14.3 OPEC countries

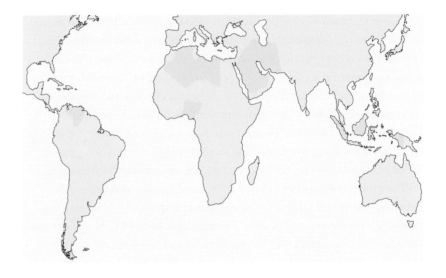

Several events triggered a new price spiral: growing global demand, devaluation of the US dollar, and the 1973 Yom Kippur War in the Middle East and subsequent Arab oil embargo. During the same period, oil-producing states seized control of price and production levels from companies and assumed ownership of company concessions on their territory, while continuing to rely on the companies for technology, capital, and markets.

Declining domestic oil production and growing consumption made the United States increasingly dependent on foreign oil. Between 1970 and 1973, crude oil prices jumped, but dollar devaluations in 1971 and 1973 diluted OPEC profits because consumers paid for oil in dollars. Although OPEC countries had more dollars, those dollars were worth less. After the 1973 war, Arab oil producers tried to use the oil weapon to make Israel's supporters change their policies while showing solidarity with fellow Arab states and the Palestinians in their conflict with Israel. A selective oil embargo was imposed on the US, the Netherlands, and Portugal, but failed to have the desired effect because of the availability of non-Arab oil supplies. Nevertheless, between 1972 and 1980, supplies remained tight; OPEC discipline held; and prices soared, especially in the last two years of the decade.

In response to increasing prices, the United States and other developed countries established the International Energy Agency in 1974.[40] The agency was intended to coordinate the policies of major oil-consuming countries in the event of another crisis, help reduce the overall demand for oil, monitor the oil market, and develop a system to facilitate sharing oil supplies among consumers if that became necessary. Unfortunately, the agency has been largely ineffective, a fact that became evident when it failed either to curb rising prices or facilitate sharing scarce oil supplies when the Iranian revolution brought a halt to Iranian oil exports in 1979.

Oil prices jumped following the beginning of the Iran–Iraq war in September 1980, peaking in 1981 and then beginning to fall because of global recession; Western efforts to conserve energy; and the violation of quotas by some OPEC members and resulting overproduction. Non-OPEC countries – Norway, Mexico, Britain, Oman, and Russia – also began to account for a greater share of oil production. By 1998, oil prices had dropped to $12 a barrel. Several factors in recent years, however, have produced a dramatic reversal in this trend. Flagging US conservation, reduced production in old oil fields, increased demand for energy in China and India, the end of global economic recession in 2003, and a variety of specific events in oil-producing countries – for example, the Iraq war, anti-American rhetoric by Venezuela's President Hugo Chavez and Iran's President Mahmoud Ahmadinejad, and civil strife in Nigeria – conspired to raise oil prices to over $70 a barrel in 2007.

Despite high prices, OPEC's influence has waned for several reasons. First, OPEC no longer has the excess pumping capacity needed to control prices. Second, non-OPEC oil producers, notably Russia and the countries of Central Asia like Azerbaijan and Kazakhstan, are increasing their role in the oil market. Third, leading OPEC members repeatedly ignore their production quotas. Finally, there is widespread recognition that efforts to use oil prices as a political weapon can backfire because the resulting decline in the value of the US dollar and inflation in the West harm oil producers themselves because they must pay higher prices for the goods they import with dollars that are worth less than before.

Fossil fuels and the environment

The environmental side of the oil equation became evident on March 24, 1989, when the tanker *Exxon Valdez* broke up on Bligh Reef, spilling nearly 11 million gallons of crude oil that poisoned Alaska's Prince William Sound. In January 1993, the tanker *Braer* spilled hundreds of thousands of gallons of oil on the Shetland Islands coastline, devastating its fragile ecology. In 1991, Saddam Hussein used environmental terrorism during his retreat from Kuwait by blowing up hundreds of Kuwaiti oil wells. During the months that followed over a billion barrels of oil were burned, creating a poisonous smoke throughout the region, causing black rain, leaving deep lakes of oil, and producing an increase in cancer in the area.[41] Elsewhere, insurgents in Colombia, Nigeria, and Iraq regularly blow up oil pipelines that produce oil spills.

Figure 14.2 Kuwaiti oil wells burn out of control, darkening the sky with smoke, after being set ablaze by retreating Iraqi forces during Operation Desert Storm, 1991

Courtesy of the US Department of Defence/Master Sgt. Kit Thompson

An environmental threat to the earth as a whole is posed by the gases released in burning fossil fuels that are responsible for heating the earth's atmosphere. Although sunlight can pass through these gases, they also reflect it back to the earth's surface as infrared radiation. According to the UN World Meteorological Organization, 1998 was the warmest year on record, closely followed by 2002, 2003, 2004, and 2005,[42] and it is estimated that global temperature has risen about 1 degree Fahrenheit in the past century.[43] Figure 14.3 illustrates how global warming works. Among fossil fuels, oil is not the only villain. The demand for coal, a dirty fuel that produces almost a third of global carbon emissions, has grown, especially in China and the United States, because oil prices have risen and oil supplies have grown tighter. Indeed, 80 percent of China's electricity comes from coal, and China plans to build over 500 coal-based power plants.[44]

In 2005, the atmospheric amounts of carbon dioxide and nitrous oxide – the two leading greenhouse gases – reached an all-time high.[45] Among

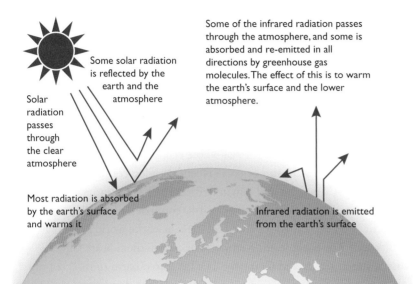

Some solar radiation is reflected by the earth and the atmosphere

Solar radiation passes through the clear atmosphere

Some of the infrared radiation passes through the atmosphere, and some is absorbed and re-emitted in all directions by greenhouse gas molecules. The effect of this is to warm the earth's surface and the lower atmosphere.

Most radiation is absorbed by the earth's surface and warms it

Infrared radiation is emitted from the earth's surface

Figure 14.3 The greenhouse effect

US Environmental Protection Agency

the signs of climate change are melting glaciers, shrinking Arctic ice, warming of Canadian and Alaskan permafrost, and changes in rainfall patterns. Even small temperature changes may have big effects. The earth 130,000 years ago was between 3.6 and 5.4 degrees Fahrenheit (2 and 3 degrees centigrade) warmer than today, and tropical swamps thrived where London now stands. As global warming increases, the polar ice caps may melt and flood populated coasts and islands. Island nations like Tuvalu, Kiribati, and Nauru may disappear beneath the waves, and heavily populated low areas in countries like Egypt and Bangladesh may be inundated. Thus, in 2003, Tuvalu's prime minister declared in a speech to the UN: "We live in constant fear of the adverse impacts of climate change. For a coral atoll nation, sea level rise and more severe weather events loom as a growing threat to our entire population. The threat is real and serious, and is of no difference to a slow and insidious form of terrorism against us."[46]

Among those hard hit by global warming will be the Eskimos, or Inuits, who follow a traditional life hunting seals and polar bears near the Arctic Circle. In December 2004, their leaders announced that they would seek a ruling from the Inter-American Commission on Human Rights against the US for contributing to global warming that threatens their existence and violates their human rights. Their case was strengthened when 300 scientists from the eight countries with territory in the Arctic, including the US, concluded that "human influences" are the major source of environmental change in the region.

In 1997 in Kyoto, Japan, a protocol to the 1992 UN treaty on climate change was negotiated under which 35 industrialized countries were

Did you know?

New Zealand has agreed to admit all 11,000 citizens of Tuvalu as global warming threatens to inundate that island country.

to cut back emissions of greenhouse gases[47] by 2012 to 5 percent below 1990 levels. The US Environmental Protection Agency estimates that concentrations of these gases – nitrous oxide, carbon dioxide, and methane – in the atmosphere have increased 15, 30, and 100 percent respectively since the beginning of the industrial revolution.[48] The cutbacks mandated at Kyoto translated into a reduction in US emissions by 24.3 percent, Japanese emissions by 21.4 percent, Canadian by 20.4 percent, and British by 6.6–7.3 percent. Russia, whose economic decline has reduced the country's energy consumption in recent decades, could increase its emissions by 4.4 percent and remain within the Kyoto limits.[49]

The Kyoto Protocol was ratified by 140 countries, excluding the US, which in 2003 accounted for about 24 percent of the world's carbon emissions.[50] The other leading emitters of carbon dioxide are China, Russia, India, Japan, and Germany. The US feared harm to its economy and demanded the application of emission limits to developing countries like China and India that were excused from the protocol, especially since China's emissions may exceed those of the US within a decade. The Kyoto Protocol could only come into force once countries that account for 55 percent of emissions had ratified it. With America's refusal to do so, Russia's ratification in late 2004 proved the necessary last step, and, in February 2005, the treaty came into force.

Controversy

The question of whether the earth's climate is growing warmer is controversial. Increasingly, scientists agree that global warming is taking place. However, some officials in the George W. Bush administration question the validity of the evidence. In March 2001, President Bush spoke of the "incomplete state of scientific knowledge," and a State Department spokesman declared: "We believe that it is premature to establish new mechanisms for negotiating future commitments," even though the US National Academy of Sciences later admitted that the warming trend was genuine[51] and leadings scientists from the world's developed countries agree that: "It is likely that most of the warming in recent decades can be attributed to human activities."[52] Thus, the US, which is the world's largest source of greenhouse gases, has refused to accept mandatory reductions. Although much evidence points to global warming, satellite measurements of the earth's temperature have failed to confirm the phenomenon. The issue is further complicated by the fact that even some scientists who agree that global warming is occurring disagree over the cause: is it a consequence of human activity or is it simply part of a natural cycle?

Further meetings including one in Montreal in 2005 and the G8 conference in 2007 in Germany produced modest progress towards curbing carbon emissions. There was unanimous agreement to begin negotiations toward a UN climate treaty that would include the US and

China, though the US declared it would still not accept binding emissions limits. In addition, agreement was reached to foster technologies to capture and store carbon as do forests. In sum, though a long road remains before agreement is possible on dealing with global warming, the US and China have at least been brought into negotiations.[53]

Although the US is not a party to the Kyoto Protocol, Europe has adopted an American idea that may produce global progress on the issue. The idea is an emissions trading system, under which governments allocate emissions quotas to industrial facilities. Those facilities that emit less gas than they are allowed can sell "carbon credits" to others that cannot meet their emissions quotas.

Fossil fuels are not renewable and produce pollution that exacerbates climate change and acid rain. As a result of tighter oil supplies, higher prices, and growing awareness of environmental costs, interest has picked up in energy conservation and in clean and renewable energy sources such as solar, geothermal, wind, hydrogen, biomass, and nuclear power.[54] For the most part, however, these alternatives remain expensive, technologically complex, or, in the case of nuclear energy, are seen by many people as dangerous.

By 1996, 476 nuclear plants were operating or under construction worldwide, but the nuclear alternative grew less attractive after two events made it appear that the cure might be worse than the disease. On March 28, 1979, a malfunctioning valve set in motion events at the Three Mile Island nuclear power plant near Harrisburg, Pennsylvania, that uncovered the nuclear reactor core. Although little nuclear material escaped, fear of nuclear meltdown gripped many Americans. Then, on April 26, 1986, Reactor No. 4 of the Chernobyl nuclear power plant, near Kiev in the USSR, blew up, sending toxic nuclear debris across much of Western and Central Europe and forcing the evacuation of 134,000 people living near the plant. Memories of Chernobyl and other incidents such as a 1995 accident at Japan's prototype fast-breeder reactor have fueled public fears about nuclear power.

Another problem involves storing nuclear wastes, some of which, like Plutonium-239, remain poisonous practically forever. Between 1947 and 1967, radioactive waste from uranium mining in Soviet Kyrgyzstan was dumped in 23 open sites; and, to avoid surface leaks of nuclear waste, the USSR secretly injected liquid nuclear material directly into the earth, a process described by a Nobel laureate in physics as the "most careless nuclear practice that the human race has ever suffered."[55] In the US, the problem of nuclear waste is complicated by rusting tanks of toxic by-products from nuclear weapons' manufacture and from the dismantling of Russian and US weapons after the Cold War. America's nuclear production facilities are responsible for widespread contamination of soil and water, and no solution has yet been found for disposing of nuclear wastes. Since 1981, the US has been moving toward disposing of nuclear-weapons waste in salt caverns at Yucca Mountain, Nevada. However, Nevada opposes this, and the issue remains unresolved. In sum, as a result of public concern about nuclear power, fewer nuclear power plants were operating in 2003 than in 1996.[56]

Without alternatives, the world will continue to rely on fossil fuels for energy. We will see more killer smogs in cities like Mexico City and Athens, where pollution is equivalent to smoking several packs of cigarettes a day. In rural societies, smog from wood and dung fires in poorly ventilated huts accounts for the death of countless children from respiratory distress. Another consequence of air pollution is acid rain and snow caused by sulfur dioxide and nitrogen oxide, much of which is spewed from energy plants in America's Midwest, which have denuded forests in eastern Canada, New England, Germany, and Central Europe and killed off fish in innumerable lakes.

Growing populations require more food, and energy is required to grow food. In the following section, we examine the problems of famine and malnutrition.

Too little food

The mass famine that Malthus feared has been averted by technology, including genetic engineering, new plant strains, improved fertilizers, and mechanized agriculture. Nevertheless, in some regions per capita food consumption is outstripping food production, while in some rapidly developing countries the problem of obesity exists alongside of widespread malnutrition.[57] According to the UN Food and Agriculture Organization (FAO) the most common forms of malnutrition are:

- Iron deficiency anemia that affects approximately 1.5 billion people, mostly women and children.
- Iodine deficiency disorders that affect about 740 million people.
- Vitamin A deficiency blindness that affects about 2.8 million children under 5 years of age.
- Calcium deficiency in pregnant and lactating women that can harm the development of their children, and appears as osteoporosis later in life.
- Vitamin C deficiency – scurvy – that is widespread among the poor and refugee populations.[58]

Although food output has tripled in the past 50 years and hunger has been reduced globally, some 800 million people in the developing world are victims of chronic malnutrition.[59] In Africa, food production in the early 1990s was actually 20 percent lower than two decades earlier.[60] In China, with its population growing by 15 million a year,[61] loss of 20 percent of cropland since the late 1950s to industrialization and urbanization, along with soil erosion, salting of irrigation systems, and global warming, ecologist Lester Brown, founder of the Earth Policy Institute, foresees a decline of 20 percent in grain production between 1990 and 2030, leaving a shortfall of 216 million tones – *a level that exceeds the world's entire 1993 grain exports of 200 million tons.*[62]

Despite problems posed by drought, flooding, soil exhaustion, **desertification**, and other natural disasters, sufficient food is still available, but distributing it to those in need is difficult. Moreover, poverty, the inevitable companion of famine and malnutrition, makes it impossible for those in need to purchase food when it is available. Both local and global political problems, including warfare and inadequate investment in agriculture, have shaped efforts to address that imperative demand. Somalia is a frightening illustration. After the global community's response to famine in Somalia had been an "abject failure,"[63] a UN-authorized and US-led humanitarian intervention in late 1992 tried to arrest famine in that country until continued violence climaxed in the withdrawal of US forces in March 1994. As in prior famines in Ethiopia and Sudan, the world community reacted too late, only after starvation was widespread. Part of the reason is that, in dealing with such hunger, knotty local political issues have to be addressed. Ethiopia, Sudan, and Somalia all suffered intractable political problems – petty warlords, weak central government, and ethnic rivalry – which make foreign assistance ineffective. Even if the global community wants to help, food assistance often fails to reach those who need it most and may create local dependency, preventing the agricultural reforms needed to make a country self-sufficient in food.

Sadly, food is used as a weapon in global politics, as it was by Somalia's rival warring clans. As more countries depend on a few food exporters, the latter may provide or withhold food exports to coerce political concessions, as did the Carter administration in the US when it halted grain shipments to the Soviet Union after that country's 1979 invasion of Afghanistan. For their part, the Soviets simply purchased the grain they needed from other countries. The United States also contributes to UN relief agencies and provides inexpensive credits to countries it wishes to reward so that they can purchase surplus US grain. However, domestic pressures from US farmers prevent the US government from providing funds for countries to purchase grain locally which would be far more cost-effective. In 2007, the Bush administration proposed a change to allow food purchases closer to where food aid is needed.

desertification the spread of deserts as a result of soil erosion, overfarming, and deforestation.

Various international efforts have been made to address problems of hunger and malnutrition and realize US Secretary of State Henry Kissinger's commitment to the 1974 World Food Conference in Rome that "within a decade, no child should go to bed hungry."[64] These include the UN World Summit for Children (1990) in which states promised to halve child malnutrition by 2000, the International Conference on Nutrition (1992) that reaffirmed that goal, the World Food Summit (1996) which set a goal of halving the number of the world's hungry by 2015, a pledge reaffirmed in the UN's 2000 Millennium Development Goals.[65] In 2006, the UN established a Central Emergency Response Fund (CERF) in its Office for the Coordination of Humanitarian Affairs to speed up its response in the event of famine.[66] In addition, a variety of humanitarian NGOs such as Oxfam actively seek to alleviate famine and malnutrition. However, if a country receives foreign food aid for prolonged periods, it may become dependent on that aid, as did Egypt, and fail to make suitable policy reforms or invest what is needed in local agriculture.

The need for additional farmland, the growth of cities, and the need for wood for construction, heating, and cooking are among the reasons that forests are vanishing, the issue to which we turn next.

Vanishing forests and encroaching deserts

salinization causing infertile soil by adding excessive salt.

The growing global need for food has important environmental consequences. Intensive farming contributes to soil erosion, **salinization**, desforestation, and desertification. According to the Food and Agriculture Organization, some 53,000 square miles of tropical forests were destroyed annually in the 1980s,[67] and between 2000 and 2005 an area about the size of Sierra Leone has been deforested each year.[68] This is equivalent to a net loss of 0.18 percent of the world's forests annually. Among the most visible effects of deforestation is southward expansion of the Sahara in Africa and sandbars created in the Bay of Bengal by silt runoff from the Himalayas. Many Bengalis who try to live on these islands perish during annual cyclones. Another effect of deforestation in the developing world where "**slash and burn**" techniques are used to provide additional farmland is the emission into the atmosphere of carbon dioxide, methane, and nitrous oxide in the burning of trees.[69] These gases contribute to the greenhouse effect, and nitrous oxide also helps destroy the **ozone layer**, which protects us from the sun's dangerous ultraviolet rays. Still another effect of deforestation is the loss of biodiversity. Tropical rain forests, for example, are home to between 50 and 90 percent of all living creatures, including most primates, and

slash and burn a technique to create additional farmland in which an area of forest is cleared by cutting and burning and is then planted, usually for several seasons, before being left to return to forest.

ozone layer a region in the upper atmosphere where most atmospheric ozone is concentrated and that protects us from dangerous solar radiation.

deforestation results in the loss of between 50 and 100 animal and plant species every day.[70]

At the 1992 UN Conference on Environment and Development, or Earth Summit, in Rio de Janeiro, a plan was adopted to halt desertification. The Convention on Desertification established a "Global Mechanism" to seek money for and coordinate projects to slow the spread of deserts. However, little money has been pledged for this task. An effort to limit logging was blocked by the United States, and international efforts to realize the promise of Rio have been unsuccessful.[71]

A special problem is posed by disappearing jungles. Already vast jungle tracts in the developing world have been denuded to slake the world's thirst for Southeast Asian, South Pacific, African, and Latin American hardwood and local demand for farmland, living space, and fuel. Every year an area the size of Belgium is cleared of jungles under pressure of local populations. Such loss reduces the earth's ability to produce oxygen, alters rainfall patterns and gives rise to droughts, and creates new deserts and enlarges old ones.

In Brazil's Amazon basin, home to 30 percent of the world's plant and animal species and source of as much as 20 percent of all fresh water flowing into oceans, economic pressures are colliding head-on with the imperatives of global survival. That region, drained by the Amazon River, covers 800 million acres, an area almost as large as Australia. Although rain forests absorb huge amounts of carbon dioxide, more than a fifth of the Amazon jungle has been burned away[72] at an annual rate (7,500 square miles) equivalent to an area the size of California by loggers and ranchers. These fires contribute more to global air pollution than did burning Kuwait's oil fields by retreating Iraqi troops in 1991,[73] and as a result Brazil, home to much of the basin, has become a major source of carbon greenhouse gases (some 200 million tons of carbon each year).[74] Although the Amazon basin was once known as the "lungs of the world," an American ecologist declared: "It's not the lungs of the world. It's probably burning up more oxygen now than it's producing."[75]

In September 1993, the space shuttle *Discovery* reported clouds of smoke over the Amazon. Air pollution from slash-and-burn fires in Indonesia in 1994 was so dense that two ships, unable to see each other, collided off Singapore, and in 1997 much of Southeast Asia was blanketed with smoke from Indonesia's burning forests.[76] And in 2006 illegal fires in Indonesia caused the worst pollution in Singapore since 1997.[77] As jungle is destroyed, animal and plant life is lost. Among the plants pushed to extinction are those with high medicinal potential. Plants that might help cure or prevent cancer or AIDS tomorrow are being destroyed today.

Several factors combined to induce land hunger among Brazilian peasants. After World War II, rapid population growth was accompanied by agricultural unemployment caused by drought, mechanization,[78] and shifts to less labor intensive crops (from rubber and coffee to soybeans). Today, about 47 percent of Brazil's farmland is owned by 1 percent of its population.[79] Brazil's cities attracted many rural poor and were unable to absorb such numbers, thus pushing the country's political and social fabric toward collapse. To hard-pressed Brazilians, the immense Amazon region seemed an answer, and Brazil's military leaders supported the idea of opening the Amazon as part of a campaign to suppress guerrilla and drug-related violence. Brazilian entrepreneurs too were excited about potential riches from lumber, oil, bauxite, gold, and hydroelectric power. In 1970, the government launched a vast program to colonize the basin. Any farmer could have 100 acres free. But the land is poor; the rainforest trees gather their own nutrients but store little in the soil, which, once cleared of jungle, can produce crops for only one or two seasons. Thereafter nothing grows; the remaining soil blows away, and the farmer must move elsewhere.

The fight to reduce slashing and burning of the Amazon has been led by foreign and local ecologists and by those who harvest the jungle to tap rubber (a harvest that does not destroy trees).[80] Resulting violence included the 1988 murder of Chico Mendes (1944–88), a leader in protecting the rain forest and helping the rubber workers, and the murder of indigenous Yanomami Indians by gold prospectors in 1993. Mendes's martyrdom turned Brazilian public opinion against the business interests that were exploiting the basin. In June 1991, Brazilian President Fernando Collor de Mello (1949–) took steps to save the Amazon: abolishing tax subsidies for farmers and ranchers, firing the head of Brazil's Indian Protection Agency, establishing the Chico Mendes Extraction Reserve, and, most important, embarking on a new policy of debts-for-nature swaps. These actions plus an economic recession slowed but did not halt deforestation of the Amazon rain forest.

The debts-for-nature swap is an imaginative approach suggested by tropical biologist Thomas Lovejoy in 1984 to reduce friction with indebted developing countries that are asked to bear a large share of the costs of global environmental reform. Lovejoy's idea was that a government or an environmental group pay off part of a debtor's obligation at reduced interest. In return, the debtor country would use the funds it would have paid in interest for environmental ends. The proposal attracted attention when it became apparent that some loans would never be repaid and banks became willing to accept partial repayment rather than confront a loan default.[81] The debts-for-nature tactic was used for the first time in 1987 in Ecuador. In 1998, the United States enacted the Tropical Forest Conservation Act to implement debt-for-nature swaps, and in the following years concluded agreements with ten countries. Most recently, in 2006, the United States along with two environmental groups forgave 20 percent of Guatemala's foreign debt in return for Guatemalan investment in conserving tropical forests.[82]

Another innovation involves the purchase by rich countries from poor ones of "carbon bonds" that allow the purchaser to continue emitting current levels of carbon while providing funds to poor countries to save forests and jungles.[83] Although deforestation in Brazil slowed until the mid-1990s, it has again accelerated, with over 10,000 square miles of rain forest destroyed in the year ending August 2004, the second most destructive year on record. Figure 14.4 shows the deforestation of the Amazon since 1985. However, even as forests disappear in countries such as Brazil and Indonesia, other countries such as China, India, Vietnam, and Turkey have undertaken reforestation campaigns and are limiting tree-cutting for agriculture. In fact, most of the world's wealthy countries like the United States have denser forests today than in 1990, and the introduction of efficient agricultural techniques combined with the movement of peasants into cities is helping to remedy the problem.[84]

Water is necessary for human survival, yet about 1.1 billion people had no access to clean drinking water as of 1996.[85] Vanishing forests and desertification, growing populations, intensive agriculture that uses

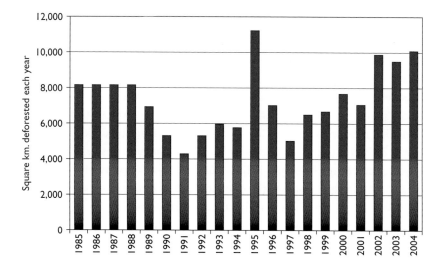

Figure 14.4   Deforestation in the Amazon

© Rhett A. Butler /mongabay.com

artificial fertilizers, and growing populations all strain existing water sources, the final environmental challenge we will discuss.

Water: dying seas and drying wells

Environmental stress is evident in the world's oceans, seas, lakes, and rivers, many of which are used as open sewers, and the world's water resources face mounting pressure. For example, for 30 years the Soviet Navy dumped its radioactive waste in the Barents and Kara seas in the Arctic.[86] Coral reefs, which support rich concentrations of life, have begun to die.[87] Plastic debris and oil slicks have killed countless seabirds, and whales, seals, turtles, and fish are victims of deadly toxins and viruses caused by chemical discharges. And these problems will worsen as we acquire the technology to exploit the wealth stored in ocean seabeds and rock chimneys – new microbes and metals such as zinc, copper, silver, and gold as well as potential oil reserves. China, Japan, and South Korea are already quarreling over a few uninhabited islets (the Senkakus) in the East China Sea because of the resource potential of the area.

Fishing

According to one estimate of the UN Food and Agriculture Organization (FAO), more than 70 percent of the world's fish species have been either "fully exploited or depleted," while in the north Atlantic "commercial fish populations of cod, hake, haddock and flounder have fallen by as much as 95 percent."[88] Indeed, nine of the world's 17 major fishing areas are presently overharvested,[89] and by mid-century there may be a global collapse of *all* species currently fished.[90] And, as fish prices rise, incentives for fishing using destructive high technology that destroys marine ecosystems increase, leading to efforts to impose drastic fishing quotas. Scarcity intensifies competition for what remains and deepens tension between the collective good of conservation and the individual incentive to catch as many as possible while they remain. Thus, American and Canadian fishermen heatedly argue about the distribution of declining stocks of Pacific salmon,[91] and Canadians and Spaniards quarrel about depleted stocks of Greenland halibut. And the issue of commercial whaling is highly divisive with countries such as Japan, Norway, and Iceland seeking to regain the right to hunt certain species of whales against the resistance of the United States, many Europeans, and most environmental NGOs.[92]

"The depletion of fisheries," declared the Secretary General of the 2002 UN World Summit on Sustainable Development, "poses a major threat to the food supply of millions of people."[93] The conference proposed a plan

Table 14.1 The Ocean Conservancy, overfishing scorecard

Council	Score (%)	% change since 1997
North Pacific	82	−2
Western Pacific	77	−8
Pacific	75	+24
Mid-Atlantic	70	+15
New England	58	+18
Gulf of Mexico	58	+7
South Atlantic	57	+12
Caribbean	50	+1

Note: The scores measure success at avoiding or ending overfishing and rebuilding depleted stocks.

to establish Marine Protected Areas to restore fish stocks. Currently, less than 1 percent of the world's oceans are protected in this way. And, although many governments have agreed to the UN's Global Program of Action for the Protection of the Marine Environment from Land-based Activities, very few are implementing the International Plan of Action to Prevent, Deter and Eliminate Unreported and Unregulated Fishing. Nevertheless, as the extent of **overfishing** has become clear, progress has been made. According to the Ocean Conservancy, except in the North and Western Pacific, there has been significant progress toward rebuilding overfished stocks as mandated by the Clinton administration's 1996 Sustainable Fisheries Act.

overfishing the rate of fishing that exceeds a maximum fishing mortality rate.

Fresh water

Supplies of fresh water are diminishing. Only 3 percent of the earth's water is fresh, and current demand is roughly 35 times as great as it was 300 years ago, tripling within the last half of the twentieth century. Agriculture accounts for about 70 percent of the fresh water that is used, industry 20 percent, and human consumption only about 10 percent.[94] Between 1950 and 2003, the area under irrigation almost tripled despite much greater efficiency in use as measured by irrigated area per person.[95] Growing demand threatens rivers, lakes, and underground aquifers.

Arid areas such as the Middle East, Central Asia, North Africa, South Asia, China, Australia, the western United States, and Mexico where population continues to grow rapidly, urbanization is producing "megacities" of more than ten million inhabitants, agricultural production is expanding, and demand for hydroelectric power is growing are experiencing ever tighter supplies of fresh water. Demand for fresh water is outstripping supply, and a "tragedy of the commons" (see Key document: Garrett Hardin at the beginning of this chapter) is overtaking the world's fresh water resources. In India alone, some 700 million people lack adequate sanitation owing mainly to a lack of clean water, and about 2.1 million children under the age of 5 die each year for the same reason. "If we become rich or poor as a nation," declared one Indian official bluntly, "it's because of water."[96] Table 14.2 shows how many of the world's great rivers ranging from the Colorado in the United States

Table 14.2 Major rivers running dry

River	Situation
Amu Darya	The Amu Darya is one of the two rivers that feed into the Aral Sea. Soaring demands on this river, largely to support irrigated agriculture, sometimes drain it dry before it reaches the sea. This, in combination with a reduced flow of the Syr Darya – the other river feeding into the sea – helps explain why the Aral Sea has shrunk by roughly 75 percent over the last 40 years and has split into two sections.
Colorado	All the water in the Colorado, the major river in southwestern United States, is allocated. As a result, this river, fed by the rainfall and snowmelt from the mountains of Colorado, now rarely makes it to the Gulf of California.
Fen	This river, which flows from the northern part of China's Shanxi Province and empties into the Yellow river at the province's southern end, has essentially disappeared as water withdrawals upstream in the watershed have lowered the water table, drying up springs that once fed the river.
Ganges	The Gangetic basin is home to some 450 million people. Flowing through Bangladesh en route to the Bay of Bengal, the Ganges has little water left when it reaches the bay.
Indus	The Indus, originating in the Himalayas and flowing southwest to the Arabian Sea, feeds Pakistan's irrigated agriculture. It now barely reaches the ocean during much of the year. Pakistan, with a population of 161 million projected to reach 305 million by 2050, is facing trouble.
Nile	In Egypt, a country where it rarely ever rains, the Nile is vitally important. Already drastically reduced by the time it reaches the Mediterranean, it may go dry further upstream in the decades ahead if the populations of Sudan and Ethiopia double by 2050, as projected.
Yellow	The cradle of Chinese civilization, the Yellow River has frequently run dry before reaching the sea over the past three decades. In 1997, the lower reaches saw no flow for 226 days. While better management practices have enabled the river to reach its mouth year-round during the past several years, flow levels are still extremely low during the dry season.

http://www.earth-policy.org/Updates/2005/Update47_data.htm

and the Ganges and Indus in India to the Nile in Egypt are on the verge of drying up. The Colorado, for example, is increasingly stressed by the booming demand of California's expanding population.

As reflected in Table 14.3, the same tragedy is afflicting many of the world's great lakes and seas. For example, in Central Asia so much water

Table 14.3 Disappearing lakes and shrinking seas

Lake	Situation
Aral Sea (Kazakhstan and Uzbekistan)	Excessive diversion of the Amu Darya and Syr Darya, largely for irrigation, has shrunk the 5-million-year-old lake to about 25 percent of its 1960s size of 66,000 square kilometers. It now holds less than one-fifth of its previous volume and has split into two sections. The larger South Aral Sea is unlikely to be restored, but the construction of a dam between the two sections, completed in September 2006, has already led to a rise in water level in the smaller North Aral Sea.
Lake Baikal (Russia)	Lake Baikal, the world's oldest and deepest lake, contains nearly one-fifth of the world's unfrozen fresh water. Over the past century the amount of soil flushed into the lake increased by two and half times due to regional agricultural and industrial development.
Lake Chad (Chad, Niger, Nigeria, and Cameroon)	Lake Chad has shrunk from 23,000 to 900 square kilometers over the past 40 years, a result of increased irrigation and decades of depressed rainfall. The lake, which once covered part of Chad, Niger, Nigeria, and Cameroon, is now contained entirely within Chad's borders.
Lake Chapala (Mexico)	Mexico's largest lake is the main water source for Guadalajara's five million people. Its long-term decline began in the late 1970s corresponding with expanded agricultural development in the Rio Lerma watershed. Since then, the lake has lost more than 80 percent of its water. Between 1986 and 2001, Chapala shrank from 1,048 to 812 square kilometers and its level dropped by up to four meters.
Dal Lake (India)	The Dal Lake has shrunk from 75 square kilometers in AD 1200 to 25 square kilometers in the 1980s, to smaller than 12 square kilometers today. Over the last decade the lake has dropped 2.4 meters in height. All the untreated sewage of Srinagar city and some 1,400 houseboats is deposited directly into the lake. Other lakes in the Kashmir Valley are facing similar problems.
Dead Sea (Jordan, Israel, and Palestine)	At 417 meters below sea level, the Dead Sea is the lowest place on earth, and is falling by up to one meter per year. The sea has shrunk in length since the early 1900s, from over 75 to 55 kilometers long, and has split in two, with the southern basin turned into evaporation ponds for potash extraction. The salty lake could disappear entirely by 2050, along with the 90 species of birds, 25 species of reptiles and amphibians, 24 species of mammals, and 400 plant species that live on its shores.
Dojran Lake (Macedonia and Greece)	More than 50 islands have appeared in the middle of the lake as overuse has dropped the water level by up to 3.48 meters below the minimal water level established in a 1956 bilateral agreement between Greece and Macedonia. Now with an average depth of 1.5 meters, the lake is turning into a swamp to the detriment of local plants and animals, especially fish.
Sea of Galilee (Lake Tiberias) (Israel)	The Sea of Galilee is Israel's largest freshwater lake, with a total area of 170 square kilometers and a maximum depth of approximately 43 meters. At 209 meters below sea level, it is the lowest freshwater lake on Earth and is expected to drop even lower as the lake shrinks and becomes saltier due to excessive water withdrawals, drought, and evaporation.

Table 14.3 continued

Lake	Situation
Lake Manchar (Pakistan)	Diversion of the Indus River, largely for irrigation schemes, has deprived Manchar, Pakistan's largest lake, of fresh water. Salt content has increased dramatically in recent years and the polluted water fosters diseases previously absent from the region. The lake had been a source of fish for at least 1,000 years, but due to its deterioration some 60,000 fishers have left the area.
Lake Nakuru (Kenya)	The lake has shrunk in area since the 1970s from 48 to less than 37 square kilometers today. Nearby forests are being cleared for farmland to feed a fast growing population, causing soils to erode and wash into the lake. Failed urban sewage systems and unregulated industrial effluent have polluted the lake.
Owens Lake (United States, California)	This perennial lake in southeastern California held water continuously for at least 800,000 years, spanning 518 square kilometers at its peak, but since the mid-1920s, after a decade of diverting water from the Owens River to Los Angeles, the lake has been completely drained. The dry lake bed, which contains carcinogens including nickel, cadmium, and arsenic, became the single largest source of particulate matter pollution in the United States, elevating air pollution in surrounding areas up to 25 times the acceptable level under national clean air standards. Since 1998, Los Angeles has tried to abate these toxic dust storms by shallowly flooding a portion of the lake, reclaiming saline soils, and cultivating fields of salt tolerant grass.
Tonle Sap (Cambodia)	Tonle Sap performs the important function of holding excess water during flood season, yet siltation from eroding farmland and deforested areas has reduced the lake's capacity and has destroyed aquatic habitat.

http://www.earth-policy.org/Updates/2005/Update47_data.htm

has been diverted from the Amu Darya and Syr Darya rivers that feed the Aral Sea to irrigate the region's cotton crop that the Aral is drying up, and its salinity has tripled. In addition, in Russia and Kazakhstan, the Aral, Caspian, and Black Seas are becoming irretrievably polluted, mainly by chemical fertilizers. Lake Chad, which once covered an area of 23,000 square kilometers in Nigeria, Niger, Cameroon, and Chad, has been reduced to 900 square kilometers, all in Chad, and in China, Hebei Province has only 83 of the more than 1,000 lakes it once had.[97]

Underground aquifers are also being depleted owing to agricultural irrigation and industrial demand in a variety of areas, including the United States (from South Dakota to Texas), Mexico, China, Iran, Spain, and India.[98] Such aquifers, many vital for areas that produce food, cannot be refilled, and they are becoming polluted by toxic chemicals that have leeched into groundwater.

As concern for the global environment has grown, international organizations and NGOs have dedicated ever more resources to turning the tide. Among the major transnational NGOs dedicated to ending environmental degradation and fostering sustainable growth are Greenpeace, Friends of the Earth, Nature Conservancy, Consultative

Group on International Agricultural Research, International Centre for Research in Agroforestry, National Councils for Sustainable Development, Public Services International, Taiga Rescue Network, World Conservation Union, and World Wide Fund for Nature. In addition, there are many other regional and national environmental NGOs.[99] The next section examines Greenpeace, one of the most controversial of environmental NGOs.

Greenpeace

"Greenpeace," according to its mission statement, "is an independent, campaigning organization that uses nonviolent, creative confrontation to expose global environmental problems, and force solutions for a green and peaceful future." Greenpeace International[100] is headquartered in Amsterdam, the Netherlands, from where it oversees 41 national offices and 2.8 million members.

Greenpeace was born in 1971 in Vancouver, Canada, when a group of activists sailed their ship to an island off Alaska's west coast to protest a US underground nuclear test.[101] Their protest stirred sufficient interest to help end testing on the island, which was later made into a bird sanctuary. The success of this venture led to the 1972 voyage of the Greenpeace ship *Vega* captained by David McTaggert (1932–2001) to protest French nuclear testing at the Moruroa Atoll in the Cook Islands of the South Pacific. France had cordoned off much of the surrounding ocean in preparation for testing, but McTaggert sailed into the test area and delayed the test. The next year McTaggert returned, and he and his crew were assaulted by French commandos who boarded his vessel.[102] McTaggert brought charges in a French court, and the publicity surrounding the case helped persuade France to end its above-ground nuclear testing program.

In 1976, Greenpeace launched another highly visible campaign, this time to protest the annual hunt of baby seals in Canada's Newfoundland. Greenpeace activists used their bodies to protect seal pups, and resulting publicity produced widespread revulsion against the hunt and resistance against purchasing products made from seal fur. Greenpeace opposition to seal hunting expanded to include the hunting of whales, and, in 1981, partly as a result of the group's highly public protests, the International Whaling Commission banned the hunting of sperm whales.

The following years saw additional Greenpeace environmental campaigns about issues as diverse as toxic dumping at sea (1982), offshore oil drilling (1983), acid rain (1984), chlorine bleaching in the wood pulp industry (1989), location of environmental hazards in poor communities (1990), prevention of mining in Antarctica (1991), global warming and

Figure 14.5 French commandos assaulting Greenpeace activist David McTaggert

© Greenpeace/Anne-Marie Horne

the export of hazardous wastes to poor countries (1994), nuclear testing (1996), trawler fishing (1997), and genetically engineered foods (1998).[103] One memorable incident in Greenpeace history was the bombing of its ship *Rainbow Warrior* (see Figure 14.6) in the harbor of Auckland, New Zealand, by French secret service agents in which a Greenpeace photographer was killed. Another took place in 1989 when the *M/V Greenpeace* successfully halted a US test of a Trident II ICBM off Florida. Four years later the same Greenpeace ship exposed Russia's practice of dumping radioactive materials into the Sea of Japan, an event that accelerated the permanent end of such practices in 1996. Greenpeace activists have also plugged toxic waste pipes in Spain (1986), sponsored a protest march along "Cancer Alley" from Baton Rouge to New Orleans to protest the presence of factories producing hazardous wastes in poor communities (1988), occupied a Shell oil platform in the North Sea (1995) to prevent toxic waste dumping, and organized successful protests against a proposed chemical plant in Convent, Louisiana, during which activists unfurled a 16 by 120-foot banner that read "No More Dioxin

Figure 14.6 The sinking of the Greenpeace ship, *Rainbow Warrior*

© Greenpeace/John Miller

Factories – Stop PVC the Poison Plastic – Environmental Justice Now – Greenpeace" (1997).[104] Recently, Greenpeace has successfully pressured corporations such as Home Depot, Kinko's, IBM, Nike, and Xerox not to sell products made from old-growth forests (1999).

Greenpeace's strategy of highly visible publicity stunts to embarrass governments and corporations has irritated and enraged its victims. One such stunt took place in April 2002 when two Greenpeace activists boarded a ship off the Florida coast that was carrying mahogany wood that was being illegally exported from Brazil. The activists unfurled a banner that read, "President Bush, Stop Illegal Logging." In July 2003, the US Justice Department charged Greenpeace with having violated an obscure 1872 statute against "sailor-mongering," a term that refers to waylaying ships coming into port and seducing sailors with prostitutes by the owners of inns and brothels.

The judge at the trial, which began in May 2004, admitted that "the indictment is a rare – and maybe unprecedented – prosecution of an advocacy group." "The prosecution has generated charges," he continued, "that the indictment of Greenpeace is politically motivated due to the organization's criticism of President Bush's environmental policies,"[105] and numerous observers denounced the government for trying to stifle free speech. After only two days, the judge dismissed all charges against Greenpeace. In sum, Greenpeace reflects the ways in which an activist NGO can forward its agenda by using imaginative forms of protest.

Conclusion

Environmental issues pose collective goods dilemmas and touch everyone, though not in the same way. These issues are interrelated, and they reveal an interdependent world. They have political, economic, health, ecological, and even military dimensions that frequently are at cross purposes. Global warming reveals the tension between global needs and actors' interests. Island states appeal for quick action, while oil producers fear a decline in demand for their chief export. Poor countries argue that the burden of reducing greenhouse gases should be borne by the rich that emit most of these gases. The rich argue that rapid economic growth in poor countries will worsen the problem and that such growth must be limited to avoid ecological catastrophe. No single actor or group of actors can solve major environmental challenges alone, yet individual actors are tempted to behave as "free riders" and let others pay for solutions.

Such questions have no simple answers. Even prosperous societies meet resistance at home to trade-offs between the environment and the economy. Passionate conflicts pit Americans who exploit forests and wetlands for jobs and profit and those who wish to preserve them, those who want to drill for oil in pristine regions of Alaska and those who fear environmental disaster, and those who advocate nuclear power and those who fear new Chernobyls. Nevertheless, no country can wall itself off from threats to the environment. The problem, however, as with collective goods in general, is to find a formula that encourages countries at different levels of economic development to cooperate in meeting environmental challenges.

In the next chapter, we examine an increasingly important aspect of global politics, the role of culture. Since the end of the Cold War and the virtual disappearance of ideological conflicts between capitalists and communists, identities associated with nation, religion, ethnicity, and tribe have come to occupy center stage. As we shall see, these are having a growing impact on global politics.

Student activities

Discussion and essay questions

Comprehension questions

1 What are the major trends in population growth, and what consequences do they portend?
2 What are the origins and consequences of populations with large numbers of young people or elderly people? How are these conditions related to each other?
3 Describe the trade-off between economic and environmental objectives in developing countries. Which is more important and why?
4 What is meant by "collective goods," and how can problems of collective goods be overcome?

Analysis questions

5 Should the United States approve the Kyoto Protocol? Why or why not?
6 Design a global energy policy to balance the competing needs for economic development and environmental safety.
7 Why does Brazil allow the destruction of its Amazon forests? How might Brazil be persuaded to save those forests?
8 What do you suppose is meant by "ecological interdependence"? Illustrate how environmental issues are connected to one another.

Map exercise

Using Maps 14.1 and 14.2, in what regions and countries do you think environmental pressures are greatest?

Cultural materials

Film and literature have been useful tools to portray the political and economic controversies surrounding global warming. The 2004 film, *The Day After Tomorrow*, concerns the effects that global warming may have in creating climatic changes such as super hurricanes, tidal waves, coastal flooding, and, most important, a new killing Ice Age. Some Republicans believed that the film was intended as a criticism of President George W. Bush's reluctance to accept the views of a majority of scientists regarding global warming or to support the Kyoto Protocol.

In his 2004 novel *State of Fear*, Michael Crichton tells the story of a group of eco-terrorists who keep the world in a state of anxiety by exaggerated claims about global warming. The plot involves an island nation in the Pacific that sues the United States for contributing to the greenhouse effect and how the eco-terrorists manufacture earthquakes and tidal waves to prove their claims about global warming. At the end of the novel, Crichton explains his personal skepticism about global warming.

Global warming does threaten the island nation of Tuvalu, motivating a poet from the island to write the following:

Tuvalu and global warming
Jane Resture

I hear the waves on our island shore
They sound much louder than they did before
A rising swell flecked with foam
Threatens the existence of our island home.
A strong wind blows in from a distant place
The palm trees bend like never before
Our crops are lost to the rising sea
And water covers our humble floor.

Our people are leaving for a distant shore
And soon Tuvalu may be no more
Holding on to the things they know are true
Tuvalu my Tuvalu, I cry for you.

And as our people are forced to roam
To another land to call their home
And as you go to that place so new
Take a little piece of Tuvalu with you.

Tuvalu culture is rare and unique
And holds a message we all should seek
Hold our culture way up high
And our beloved Tuvalu will never die.[106]

Find a film or novel that deals with global warming or another aspect of the environment. What message does the work try to convey? Using what methods and plot devices? How successfully does it accomplish its apparent goal?

Further reading

Axelrod, Regina S., David Leonard Downie, and Normand J. Vig, eds., *The Global Environment: Institutions, Law, and Policy*, 2nd ed. (Washington, DC: Congressional Quarterly, Inc., 2004). Essays on the development of environmental organizations and treaties with analyses of laws and policies governing environmental protection.

Dessler, Andrew E. and Edward A. Parson, *The Science and Politics of Global Climate Change: A Guide to the Debate* (Cambridge: Cambridge University Press, 2006). A comprehensive overview of the debate over global warming.

Klare, Michael T., *Resource Wars: The New Landscape of Global Conflict* (New York: Henry Holt, 2003). Argument that future wars will be fought over scarce natural resources.

Nadakavukaren, Anne, *Our Global Environment: A Health Perspective*, 6th ed. (Long Grove, IL: Waveland Press, 2006). Survey of major global environmental issues and their impact on issues of individual and community health.

Olson, Mancur Jr., *The Logic of Collective Action: Public Goods and Theory of Groups* (New York: Schocken Books, 1968). The theory of collective goods.

Roberts, Paul, *The End of Oil: On the Edge of a Perilous New World* (Boston, MA: Houghton Mifflin, 2004). The rapid depletion of oil and its consequences.

Williams, Michael, *Deforesting the Earth: From Prehistory to Global Crisis* (Chicago, IL: University of Chicago Press, 2003). The history and consequences of deforestation.

Part V
Peoples and Cultures in Global Politics

15 Identity politics

Nationalism and ethnicity

In 1976, a young Turk named Mihdat Guler moved to France, where he lived quietly as a legal immigrant with a wife and five children. Guler became one of France's 1,500 imams – Islamic scholars and prayer leaders – and, according to French authorities, began to incite hatred of the West in his sermons, allowing the distribution of newsletters in his prayer room that encouraged violence against non-Muslims. In May 2004, French authorities arrested Guler and sent him back to Turkey in accordance with a 1945 law that permits the government to deport any foreigner believed to be a threat "to the security of the state or public safety."[1] The French decision, authorities declared, was in the country's national interest.

The story of Mihdat Guler highlights the importance of people's **identities** in global politics. Identities reflect who people think they are and with whom they associate. Changing identities have always been a feature of global politics. For example, from Europe's Middle Ages to the twentieth century, a reshuffling of identities took place, so that citizenship and nationality, anchored in territory, took precedence over identities arising from religion, class, **ethnicity**, and locality. States have used various methods to alter citizens' identities. One is through colonization (for example, China's settlement of Han Chinese in Tibet in order to outnumber ethnic Tibetans); a second is forced assimilation (for example, Syria's repression of Kurdish language and customs); and a third is "ethnic cleansing" (for example, Serbia's effort to expel Croatians and Bosnian Muslims from Bosnia). For generations, the state provided the psychological satisfaction of a broad group identity and a heightened measure of physical security and material satisfaction. As we shall see, identities are today again undergoing significant reshuffling, and, as constructivists argue, identities give rise to interests that shape political behavior.

This chapter highlights the role of **culture**, by which we mean the shared beliefs and values of a group as reflected in people's customs,

identities a set of characteristics that individuals recognize as defining themselves and that, when shared, defines the group as a whole and its interests.

ethnicity affiliation based on racial and/or cultural ties.

culture the norms, customs and ways of living of a group of human beings that are transmitted from one generation to another.

Figure 15.1 Muslim women in France protesting a ban on wearing head scarves in schools

© PA Photos

practices, and social behavior. Constructivism is especially useful here in shedding light on how identities are critical for understanding interests. As political scientist Alexander Wendt explains it: "To have an identity is simply to have certain ideas about who one is in a given situation," and such ideas shape what we regard as in our interest. "Politicians," Wendt continues, "have an interest in getting re-elected because they see themselves as 'politicians'; professors have an interest in getting tenure because they see themselves as 'professors'."[2]

The chapter opens by defining identities and how they shape political behavior. While identities have always helped shape global politics, nonstate identities have become more important in recent decades. Moreover, individuals have many identities, and from time to time, these identities come into conflict. The chapter illustrates the suspicions that arise from the presence of multiple identities, as in the cases of Muslim residents in Europe today, as well as the dilemma posed when individuals must choose among identities, as many Americans were forced to do during the American Civil War.

The chapter continues with a discussion of how politicians can manipulate people's identities to increase their political power and achieve political objectives. Often they do so by promoting political myths and symbols that intensify in-group feelings and that demonize "others."

Nationalism, to which we then turn, is the best known political identity and has frequently been manipulated by leaders for political ends. We review the origins and bases of nationalism, including the role of common history and national myths, and contrast liberal with malignant nationalism. Thereafter, we discuss the relationship between nation and state, how the two ideas were merged, and how in recent years they are splitting apart.

The chapter then examines other identities that today are becoming more powerful. Among the most important are religious identities, many of which have a long history, but which are of renewed importance because of the spread of **religious fundamentalism**. Almost as important are ethnic and tribal identities that have triggered repeated spasms of violence in recent decades. Among the most deadly were the series of ethnic conflicts in Yugoslavia in the 1990s that led to the break-up of that country. Such conflicts, especially the Bosnian and Kosovo wars, influenced political scientist Samuel P. Huntington's belief that global politics is entering an era in which civilizations will collide and clash, the topic with which the chapter comes to a close.

religious fundamentalism the belief that law and politics derive solely from the word of God as stated in the holy book(s) of the religion in question.

Identities

Identities are those features that somebody recognizes as defining his- or herself and that, when shared with others, define a group. Every individual has multiple identities. A person may be a US citizen, an Asian-American, a Protestant, a student, a woman, a Democrat, and an investor all at the same time. Each identity implies a set of political interests. For example, those who identify themselves as "working people" may support such goals as increasing the minimum wage and enforcing safety in manufacturing enterprises. Women, for their part, may lobby to assure equal pay for men and women, and women's groups may sue companies that fail to do so.

In this section, we examine how multiple identities can produce conflict and how, both in the past and present, class, religious, and other nonstate identities may come into conflict with citizens' identities and loyalties to their countries. Especially in wartime, people's fears and prejudices may lead them to conclude falsely that ethnic or religious minorities are disloyal. As we shall shortly see, the growing population of Muslims in Europe in recent years has produced concern and unease in several European countries. This unease has intensified with Turkey's application to join the European Union (EU).

Conflicting identities and the threat to national unity

collective identity a shared set of characteristics that defines the boundaries of a group and distinguishes it from other groups.

Individuals who share identities have a **collective identity**. This means that they have some interests in common and, sometimes, have common enemies as well. American citizens, for example, have a common national identity that produces a common interest in ensuring the survival and security of the United States; during the Cold War, they perceived the USSR as a common foe. As a group, African-Americans have an interest in affirmative action and vote against those who oppose such policies. Whatever the common interest, it provides a psychological bond among people that is essential for political groups, including sovereign states, to endure for any length of time. Where it is absent, the group may fall apart, as did Somalia and Sierra Leone.

fifth columnists subversives working on behalf of a foreign power.

Although people have always had multiple identities, for much of the past three centuries people viewed citizenship as their principal political identity, and their strongest loyalties were reserved for their state. Those who identified strongly and publicly with other groups, for example their church or ethnic community, might be branded as traitors or **fifth columnists** and, if they openly opposed the state or rose up against it, could be brutally repressed. In the past, the question "what is your principal identity?" would in all likelihood have elicited the answer "American," "French," "Russian" or the name of some other country. It was not that people lacked other identities, but the dominance of the state in political life tended to marginalize those identities. Furthermore, by socializing citizens through education, indoctrinating the young by using symbols like a pledge of allegiance, and applying coercion if necessary, governments have tried, with differing degrees of success, to assure that their population identifies with and is loyal to the state first and foremost.

Enjoying legally recognized boundaries and sovereignty and having the military resources to control their borders, states provided a reliable territorial basis within which they could fix and enforce boundaries of identity.

From time to time the dominance of national identities in global politics has been challenged. In the decades before World War I, when industrialization and urbanization in Europe dramatically increased the size of the working class, or proletariat, **socialism**, an ideology that emphasized **class** rather than national or religious identities, grew in importance. In this case, being a worker was the primary identity, and thus the socialist ideology typically demanded an end to private property and to the exploitation of workers. Socialism trumped religious identity, and Karl Marx referred to religion "as the opiate of the masses." In their most famous political slogan, Marx and Friedrich Engels closed their *Communist Manifesto* (1848) by urging all those with proletarian identities to unite against the capitalists: "Let the ruling classes tremble at a communist revolution. The proletarians have nothing to lose but their chains. They have a world to win. Working men of all countries, unite!"

As World War I approached, some socialists argued that workers should refuse to fight for their countries because the coming conflict was really among capitalists seeking colonies and larger market shares for their products. Some like Russian Bolshevik leader Vladimir Lenin urged workers to remain loyal to their more fundamental identity, their class, "propagating the socialist revolution, and the necessity of using weapons *not against one's own brothers*, the hired slaves of other countries, *but against the reactionary and bourgeois governments and parties of all nations*."[3] However, when the war finally erupted, workers across Europe forgot their class identity, put down their shovels, picked up their rifles, and eagerly marched off to the war, arm in arm with their fellow citizens.

In recent decades, as states' dominance of global politics ebbs, other identities – old and new – are coming to the fore. Among the factors that account for the current upsurge in nonstate identities are the declining importance of territory as a source of power and prosperity and the proliferation of globalized communication networks that allow people however remote geographically to communicate almost instantaneously. Today, global politics is witnessing a revival of ancient ethnic, tribal, and religious identities as well as the invention of powerful new identities based on race, gender, and profession. Today, some of the answers one might get to the question "what is your principal identity?" are "I am a woman," "an African-American," "a Christian," "a Palestinian," "a Tutsi," "a poor person," and so forth. And, as in the past, the question of conflicting identities can produce intense passions.

socialism a political system in which the means of production and distribution are owned by the people as a whole, and in which people's needs are provided for by the government.

class a social stratum sharing economic and political characteristics.

Did you know?

The term "fifth column" was coined during the Spanish Civil War (1936–39) by fascist General Emilio Mola (1887–1937), who claimed in a radio broadcast that the city of Madrid, then under attack by his four advancing army columns, would fall into his hands because of a "fifth column" of sympathizers who were already in the city ready to rise up against the defenders. The term was popularized by Ernest Hemingway in a one-act play entitled *Fifth Column* and later extended to any unknown subversives.

The question of potentially conflicting identities and loyalties is a growing problem for Europe. For much of its history, Europe was overwhelmingly Christian, but large numbers of Muslims arrived after World War II as a result of guest-worker programs, filling poorly paid jobs that Europeans would not accept. Although initially they were only supposed to be temporary residents, many remained. Europe's Muslim population was enlarged by family reunification programs and additional immigrants, reaching an estimated 15 to 20 million today or between 4 and 5 percent of total population (and will double by 2025 at current growth rates), far more than the estimated three million or less than 2 percent in the United States.[4] Today, many of the children and grandchildren of the first generation of Muslim migrants to Europe are alienated from Western culture seeking their religious roots. Indeed, as shown in Figure 15.2, large majorities of Muslims think of themselves as Muslims first and only secondarily as citizens of their country.

Since the terrorist attacks of September 11, 2001, Europeans have grown uneasy about the increasing numbers of Muslims in their midst, although majorities of Europeans still regard immigration from the Middle East and North Africa as positive.[5] Large numbers of Muslims

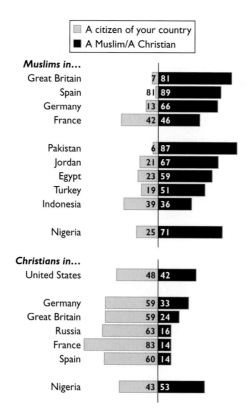

Figure 15.2 What do you consider yourself first?

Pew Global Attitudes Project – Muslims in Europe: Economic Worries Top Concerns about religions and Cultural attitudes – July 6 2006

from Pakistan, Turkey, and North Africa live in British, German, and French cities, and many consider Europeans to be hostile toward them.[6] France has the largest proportion of Muslims (8 to 10 percent of its total population), followed by the Netherlands, Germany, Denmark, Britain, and Spain. Europe's Muslim population has doubled in the past decade and is enlarged by some 500,000 new Muslim immigrants every year.[7] As a result, Islam is now the second largest religion in Europe, and growing European concern has been translated into increased votes for right-wing political parties.

This concern is reflected in the controversial issue facing the EU as to whether or not to admit Turkey as a member. Turkey is governed as a secular state and seeks to be a bridge between Europe and Asia, but is overwhelmingly Muslim. Those opposed to admitting Turkey cite historical clashes between the Ottoman Turks and Christianity, viewing Turkey as incompatible with other EU countries. Europe's unease with Turkey was reflected in comments by former French Prime Minister Jean-Pierre Raffarin (1948–) who posed the question: "Do we want the river of Islam to enter the riverbed of secularism?"[8] Other European leaders have made similar remarks: One EU commissioner commented that Turkey is more oriental than European, and former French President Valéry Giscard d'Estaing (1926–) declared that Turkey's admission to the EU "would mean the end of Europe."[9] Inasmuch as 56 percent of the French public and 57 percent of the German public oppose Turkey's admission to the EU, the admissions process, for which formal negotiations began in October 2005, is likely to be a thorny one.[10]

France, long regarded as the epitome of a nation-state with a single, distinctive secular and national culture, is confronting challenges to its homogeneity.[11] More than Americans or British, French citizens believe that "outsiders" in their country should assimilate, speaking French and adopting French customs. This belief has been challenged in recent years by growing numbers of Muslims, the largest number in Europe, who have heretofore kept to themselves and lived together mainly in urban slums. Today, France is home to about five million Muslims, largely North Africans who emigrated over the years from France's former colonial possessions of Algeria, Morocco, and Tunisia. In recent years, controversy has grown over French efforts to foster their secular national culture by banning the wearing of "conspicuous" religious symbols such as Muslim headscarves (hajibs) in French schools. With public opinion indicating that some 70 percent of its population favors such a ban, the French passed a law to that effect in February 2004.[12] Then, in November 2005, French cities were swept by violent unrest in their predominantly Muslim neighborhoods.

Unlike French Muslims who are mainly North African in origin, British Muslims or their parents are largely from Pakistan and India, former British colonies. On July 7, 2005, a series of suicide bombings carried out in London's transport system by Muslims with British citizenship resulted in 52 deaths and hundreds injured and created growing concern about public safety in the country. As a result, the British government passed a Terrorism Act in March 2006 that made it illegal to plan terrorism, "directly or indirectly incite or encourage others to commit acts of terrorism," including "the glorification of terrorism," disseminate terrorist publications, or provide training in terrorist techniques.[13] A little over a year later British authorities disrupted a plot to blow up ten US-bound passenger jets in flight with liquid explosives that would have caused what British authorities called "mass murder on an unimaginable scale."[14]

As a consequence of such incidents, some observers argue that London has become a dangerous locus for Islamist terrorists and their sympathizers. Referring to the city as "Londonistan," they argue that its mosques have become centers of recruitment for Islamic causes and a source of danger to US security.[15] In a 2006 poll, 81 percent of Muslims in Britain declared that they considered themselves as Muslims first and as British second. Majorities of 69 percent of Muslims in Spain and 66 percent of Muslims in Germany gave similar answers.[16] Many feel like outsiders in Europe's secular communities, especially while British and American troops are fighting Muslims in Iraq and Afghanistan.

The ambiguous position of Muslims in countries like Britain and France highlights the fact that multiple identities may produce divided loyalties. Sometimes such concerns are well founded, but often, as in the case of Japanese-Americans during World War II, they may lead to grave injustices.

Divided loyalties?

America's multicultural tradition permits students greater latitude in expressing their identities than in France, but even in the United States there have been incidents in which Muslim girls who wore headscarves have been sent home. One such incident occurred at the Benjamin Franklin Academy in Muskogee, Oklahoma in October 2003.

Opponents of such bans argue that they discriminate against observant Muslims who believe that women should dress modestly. Other observers contend that headscarves reflect the unwillingness of those who wear them to integrate into non-Muslim societies and symbolize women's subservience to men in Islam. In some Muslim societies, the failure

Figure 15.3 Muslim women in Afghanistan wearing *burqas*

© PA Photos

of women to dress as militant Muslim men believe they should has had fatal consequences. For example, in December 2002, three young women were killed in Kashmir for not wearing a *burqa*,[17] the head-to-toe covering worn by Muslim women in strict Muslim countries like Saudi Arabia.[18]

Although most people, including Europe's Muslims, have numerous identities, few of these are politically salient at any moment. It is only when a political issue affects the welfare of those in a particular group that identity assumes importance. For instance, when issues arise that touch on women's rights, women start to think of gender as their principal identity. Whether such women are American or Iranian or whether they are Catholic or Protestant matters less than the fact that they are women. Similarly, when famine and civil war threaten people in sub-Saharan Africa, many African-Americans are reminded of their kinship with the continent in which their ancestors originated centuries earlier, and they lobby their leaders to provide humanitarian relief. In other words, each issue calls forth somewhat different identities that help explain the political preferences people have regarding those issues.

Sometimes, issues arise that force individuals to choose between competing identities. When America's Civil War erupted, many people had to choose whether to fight for the United States (the Union) or

Figure 15.4 General Robert E. Lee in the uniform of a Confederate general

Library of Congress, Prints and Photographs Division, Photograph by Matthew Brady, 1865, LC-DIG-cwpb-04402

whether to join the Confederacy. Among those who confronted this fateful choice was General Robert E. Lee (1807–70), who had to decide between his identities as a Virginian and as an American. When the war loomed, Lee was regarded as perhaps the most talented general in the US Army. Although Lee was opposed to slavery, he felt a deeper tie to his native Virginia than to the United States. He explained his decision in a letter to his sister:

> With all my devotion to the Union and the feeling of loyalty and duty of an American citizen, I have not been able to make up my mind to raise my hand against my relatives, my children, my home. I have therefore resigned my commission in the Army, and save in defense of my native State, with the sincere hope that my poor services may never be needed, I hope I may never be called on to draw my sword.[19]

Since the September 11 attacks by Al Qaeda terrorists and the subsequent War on Terrorism, many American Muslims and Americans of Arabic origin have been torn between their identity as Americans and their identity as Muslims or Arabs. And many Americans have come to view Muslims living in the United States with suspicion even though virtually all American Muslims are loyal citizens.

The fear that US Muslims might put their religious identity before their national identity recalls a similar fear that swept the United States after the 1941 Japanese attack on Pearl Harbor. At that time, the US government feared that American-Japanese citizens might be fifth columnists who would place their Japanese identity ahead of their loyalty to the United States (see Key document: Letter to Miss Clara Estelle Breed). Thus, in February 1942, President Franklin D. Roosevelt ordered the internment of about 120,000 Japanese-Americans (two-thirds of whom were native-born citizens) living on the West Coast. In the 1944 case of *Korematsu* v. *United States*, the US Supreme Court ruled that the internments were constitutional even though those interned had been forced to sell their homes and had committed no crime. This episode in American history was finally closed in 1988 when the Congress apologized for the internments and agreed to pay compensation to the 60,000 surviving internees.

Key document **Letter to Miss Clara Estelle Breed, the Children's Librarian at the San Diego Public Library from 1929 to 1945, from a Japanese-American interned in Poston, Arizona[20]**

November 30, 1942

Dear Miss Breed,

Since I did not do any house moving in Santa Anita, I'm doing double duty here. . . .

Since 6 weeks of school life in camp has become similar to the life in San Diego. We now have a school paper. At the present there is a contest going on in submitting names for the school. . . .

A friend who returned from Colorado related the following incident to me. He said, while in town a few boys entered a restaurant to have a bite to eat. The first thing the waitress asked was "Are you Japs?" When they replied "yes" she turned her back on them and said they don't serve Japs. So they had to go to another restaurant to eat. Here is another incident which disgusted the boys. When the boys asked a policeman where a certain store was he replied – "I don't serve Japs." One of the boys became angry and remarked – "Alright be that way – what do you think we came out here for? We didn't come to be made fun of – we came to help out in this labor shortage." Then the policeman apologized and showed them to the store. This boy said he certainly was glad to return to camp where there is no unfriendliness. Of course, he knows and we all know that there are people all over the world who hate certain races and they just can't help it. But I am sure when this war is over there will be no radical discrimination and we won't have to doubt for a minute the great principles of democracy.

One discouraging thing which occurred here is the building of the fence. Now there is a fence all around this camp. I hope very soon this fence will be torn down. I always seem to rattle on and on about myself. . . .

Most sincerely,

Louise Ogawa

Please do write during your leisure time.

In sum, people with similar identities have something in common that distinguishes them from others, and as we shall see in the next section, they create boundaries that separate them from "others" outside their group. The process in which identities create in-groups and out-groups is a key feature of human behavior and a fundamental source of violence and war. Such groups, as we shall see, are separated by psychological distance even though they reside in close proximity. By contrast, modern technology makes it possible for people living even at great distances to feel a close kinship to one another.

"We" versus "them" in global politics

Common identities bring people together in groups (in-groups), while those with other identities remain "outsiders" or "aliens" (out-groups). As a result, one of the most basic facts in global politics is that the world is divided into groups that often mistrust one another. Hostility among territorial states reflect such inter-group mistrust, but so do conflicts among such diverse actors as the Hutu and Tutsi **tribes** in Rwanda and Burundi, and Sunni and Shia Muslims in Iraq. Such conflicts reflect age-old divisions between peoples with different and sometimes conflicting identities. Members of each group believe they have something in common with one another that distinguishes "them" from "others" who are different. People tend to like others who are like themselves and are members of the same identity group, and they come to depend on one another. As a result, people's loyalties follow their identities.

By contrast, people feel little loyalty to members of groups in which they are not members or from which they are excluded. "We" may dislike "them" or even regard "them" as inferior. Such identity-based feelings may strengthen the bonds within groups but also cause or exacerbate conflicts and violence in global politics. Sometimes, one group blames another unjustly – a **scapegoat** – for its own failings, thereby avoiding the need to acknowledge its own responsibilities.

When those in one group feel superior to those in another, they may try to persecute their "inferiors." In extreme cases, such as the Nazi belief that Jews were the cause of Germany's woes after 1919 and also inferior to German "Aryans," the result may be a **genocide**, in which one side seeks to exterminate the other. Thus, during World War II the Nazis murdered over six million Jews.

Many of today's most intractable conflicts pit identity groups against one another, as in the violence between Africans and Arabs in Sudan. For over 20 years, violence raged between the largely Christian black Africans in Sudan's south and the forces of Sudan's Islamic Arabs in the north. No sooner was this conflict settled in 2003 than Islamic black Africans living in the Darfur region of western Sudan arose in revolt against the country's Arab-dominated government. Both of these conflicts were wars of identity. The first involved conflicting religious and racial identities, while the second was mainly racial. When asked about the possibility of coexistence between Africans and Arabs in Darfur, a leader of the African rebels answered: "Impossible! Arabs and Africans living in one village? Impossible!"[21] In his view, too vast a psychological gulf separated Arabs and Africans in Sudan for them to live in peace.

tribe a social group comprising numerous families, clans, or generations together.

scapegoat someone selected to take the blame for someone else's problems.

genocide the extermination of an ethnic, racial, or cultural group.

Did you know?

The real Aryans were not Germans, but a nomadic people from Central Asia who settled in northern India in about 1500 BC.

We call the degree to which groups see the world differently **psychological distance**, and the greater that distance, the more that people will have different values and interests. When groups are separated by great psychological distance, they see the world through different lenses. Under those conditions, the probability is high that they will misperceive or misunderstand each other and, therefore, come into conflict. Today, psychological distance is largely unrelated to geographic distance. Technological advances and the advent of globalized economic and cultural systems make it possible to maintain relative intimacy even at great physical distance. By contrast, even people who live near one another, as in Darfur, may psychologically be worlds apart.

psychological distance the degree of dissimilarity between cognitive frameworks or ways of looking at, assigning meaning to, and coping with the world.

Today, in the world's urban centers, such as New York, Tokyo, London, and Rio de Janeiro, the very rich and very poor live next to one another even while they exist in different worlds. Despite physical proximity, they have little in common. Many of the rich are members of a growing globalized business elite that is psychologically distant from the poor whom they pass on the street every day. Members of this elite often work for giant transnational corporations like IBM or Sony. Regardless of nationality, most speak English as their common language, dress the same, have the same customs, take holidays together, share the same views on economics and politics, and send their children to the same universities. They travel widely and stay in touch with one another constantly by means of e-mail, fax machines, BlackBerries, and telephone. Overall, they have more in common with and feel a greater kinship toward one another than to their impoverished countrymen.

This new commercial elite resembles Europe's aristocracy in the eighteenth century, whose members had more in common with one another than with commoners in their own country. Most spoke French rather than their local language and were linked by bonds of marriage, personal friendship, and common interests in maintaining their status and privileges. Like those who constitute today's globalized elite, eighteenth-century aristocrats wore the same clothes, dressed the same way, and in general, enjoyed a shared culture that helped them empathize with and understand one another.

Identity groups tend to become **moral communities**, in which members feel that they are obliged to treat one another according to shared norms, rules, and standards that do *not* apply to "outsiders." Sameness provides the legitimacy for such communities and is one reason why members respect their laws and customs. By contrast, those outside the moral community may be viewed as *not* meriting equal treatment simply by virtue of being outsiders.

moral communities groups in which members are obliged to treat one another according to shared norms, rules, and standards that need not be applied to "outsiders."

Thus, Europeans in the seventeenth century saw themselves as united in a community of Christians who should treat one another as brothers and who were subject to the limitations of international law. Thus, when the Spaniards and Portuguese collided with indigenous "pagan" Indians during their conquest of South and Central America, they regarded them as beyond such legal protection. European lawyers and theologians argued that a war conducted in order to Christianize a pagan people constituted a "just war." Only when Spanish missionaries and theologians like the Dominican Francisco de Vitoria (c.1486–1546), backed eventually by the Spanish monarchy, declared that the indigenous people of the Americas had rights, did their situation improve. Vitoria argued that under natural law the Indians were free people who had owned their land before the Spaniards arrived.[22] He denied that the Indians lacked the power of reason and were, therefore, naturally slaves: "There is a certain method in their affairs," he wrote, "for they have polities which are orderly arranged and they have definite marriage and magistrates, overlords, laws, and workshops, and a system of exchange, all of which call for the use of reason: they also have a kind of religion. Further, they make no error in matters which are self-evident to others; this is witness to their use of reason."[23]

Today, identities are rapidly changing, and many states are hard pressed to maintain national identity as primary. As we shall see, one reason that state identities are weakening is the development of new globalized communications technologies that governments have difficulty controlling.

State erosion and technological change

In past centuries, governments fostered nation-state identities by controlling the main channels of social communication, making it difficult for "alien" identities to compete effectively. For centuries, governments had the ability to influence citizens' perceptions and beliefs by filtering the information available to them. The state's capacity to influence the printed word, radio, film, and television allowed it to define patriotism, promote domestic unity, and encourage amity or enmity toward "others."

But technological change is relentless. Iranians were urged to overthrow their Shah in 1979 on tapes with speeches by the Ayatollah Ruhollah Khomeini. In 1989 Chinese democracy protesters used fax machines to spread the news about what was happening in Beijing's Tiananmen Square. Today, microelectronic technologies further decentralize information production, and networking dramatically empowers social groups like Mexico's Zapatistas and China's Falun Gong. In short, technology fosters new identities, and weakens old ones.

The sheer pace of technological change in recent decades has dramatically complicated states' ability to control the flow of information and ideas to their citizens. Nowhere is this more evident than in China, which simultaneously wants to retain central Communist Party control over ideology and use new communications technologies for economic development. As long as television, radio, and the press were the sole sources of news, it was relatively easy for the regime to control information dissemination. Today, however, the Internet poses special problems in China – where there were 26 million users as of summer 2001, 17 million more than in 1999[24] – and the Chinese government has tried hard to regulate this technology.

Beijing tries to censor the Net by using filtering technologies in which users have unlimited access to one another but only screened links to the world beyond. Moreover, the Chinese government issued regulations that sought to limit the release of information on the Internet, including a prohibition against disseminating so-called "state secrets." The regulations cover chat rooms, e-mail, and Internet sites, and whoever puts an item on the Internet, whether they are the original source or not, is responsible for it. China's government showed its teeth when it charged a computer engineer with "inciting subversion of state power"[25] for sending 30,000 Chinese e-mail addresses to an electronic publication in the United States compiled by Chinese democracy advocates in Washington, DC. The case reflected how seriously Chinese officials regard the potential for disruptive electronic protest. However, government regulation of the Internet is not easy. For example, many Chinese users know how to use proxy servers that hide the site being served.

Nonstate groups not only use the Internet to express political and ideological positions but also to mobilize and coordinate activities, often against existing regimes. The Web is invaluable for mobilizing those with common aims who are geographically dispersed such as anti-globalization protesters against the World Trade Organization or activists lobbying for the Land Mines Treaty. The Internet makes it possible for such groups to exist in cyberspace rather than on any particular national territory. Without the Internet, they could not exist at all. Thus, the Internet has facilitated new forms of expression and connection among groups and the growth of new public spaces that are not easily controlled by states.[26]

China again reflects the problem states face. In April 1999, a previously little known quasi-religious meditation and exercise group called Falun Gong staged a massive silent protest around the Beijing compound housing China's communist leaders. What frightened China's leaders was that the group had organized and coordinated its activities by means of e-mail without alerting the country's extensive surveillance system. In effect, China's leaders were under siege by a movement that came together not on the streets but in cyberspace. It was not the number of people involved in the protest that disturbed China's leaders so much as the fact that they had come from all over China.

The same technologies threaten the state's ability to promote a unifying national cultural tradition that differentiates "us" from "them" and anchors people's loyalties. Such traditions – built on religion, language, mythology, literature and poetry, historical events, and ways of dress – provide political **legitimacy** and define the moral community. People can learn from satellite television, the Internet, and films that there are others not only "unlike themselves" but (more important) also "like themselves," about whom they had known little before and with whom they can communicate. New categories of "us" and "them" are made available for political mobilization and action. Local Islamic leaders, for example, fear that women and young people are susceptible to the attractions of Western materialism and individualism and that the conservative and stabilizing doctrines of piety and party may be swept aside. In this sense, Islamic fundamentalism is a backlash against Western materialism.

In sum, multiple identities produce conflict and can threaten the integrity and unity of sovereign states. Divided loyalties – real or imagined – produce fissures in society. Common identities are the bases of group loyalties, just as different identities separate groups, and new technologies make it easier for transnational identities and loyalties to arise and threaten state unity.

The next section examines how political leaders can manipulate identities for their own purposes. The cases of Yugoslavia and Chechnya in Russia illustrate how charismatic politicians can cleverly manage the national identities of followers to foster their personal power and pursue their own interests. Finally, myths and symbols are critical to sustaining identities as we shall see in the case of Northern Ireland.

Manipulating identities

When violence erupts between identity groups, newspapers often report the "appearance of ancient national rivalries" or "the resurgence of old hatreds." Such reports are deceptive. What often happens is that an event takes place that either sharpens an existing identity or reawakens a group's consciousness of old rivalries. Thus, British mistreatment of the 13 American colonies in the decades prior to the Revolutionary War

legitimacy the characteristic of a political or social institution that is perceived to have a right to make binding decisions for its members.

helped forge a common American identity where previously there had been 13 quite separate identities. Political leaders can take advantage of such events to increase their own power and achieve their own goals. They may manipulate identities for their own benefit and intensify the passions of their followers by the adroit use of symbols and historical myths, which they may tailor to reinforce their political power. Mythmaking, then, entails a struggle over how history is written and the memories it evokes.

A number of recent cases help illustrate how events can reawaken and reshape identities and how political leaders can manipulate symbols of identity for their own ends. In Bosnia, for example, people had adopted Islam following the area's conquest by the Ottoman Turks in 1463. However, Bosnian Muslims were laid-back about their religion. Far more important to them was their ethnic identity as Slavs. The most important political cause animating Bosnians in the decades prior to World War I was their desire for independence of the Slavic peoples like themselves who had been absorbed by the Austro-Hungarian Empire in 1878. Until civil war erupted in the former Yugoslavia in 1992, Bosnian Muslims had rarely identified themselves in terms of religion. "We never, until the war, thought of ourselves as Muslims," declared a school teacher. "We were

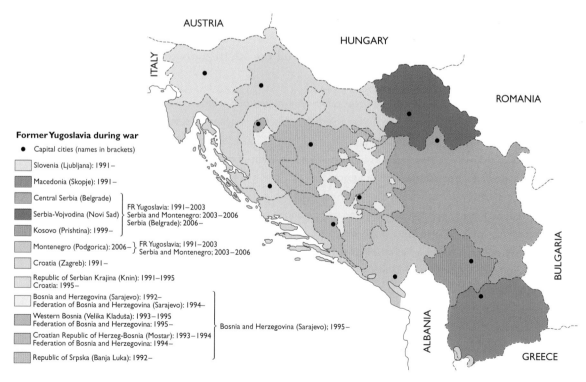

Map 15.1 The Former Yugoslavia

Yugoslavs. But when we began to be murdered, because we were Muslims, things changed. The definition of who we are today has been determined by our killers."[27]

Conflicting identities in Yugoslavia were encouraged and manipulated by the ambitious leader of Serbia, Slobodan Milošević. Milošević, who had been a communist all of his political career, rapidly transformed himself into a popular Serb nationalist as Yugoslavia began to disintegrate. Increasingly, he spoke of old wrongs done to Serbians by Croatians and other national groups in Yugoslavia, and so frightened these other groups that they, too, selected rabid nationalists to lead them. In his effort to foster his own nationalist credentials and rouse nationalist fervor among Serbs, Milošević focused especially on an ancient battle, the Battle of Kosovo on June 15, 1389, in which a Muslim Ottoman army had crushed a Christian Serbian army under King Lazar (see Key document: Speech by Slobodan Milošević). Over and over again, Milošević posed as the successor to King Lazar, defending Christian Serbs against Muslim "Turks," thereby intensifying Serbian hatred of Muslims in Yugoslavia, especially Bosnian Muslims and Muslim Albanians living in Kosovo. In this way, Milošević increased his popularity among Serbs, deepened Serbian nationalism, and unleashed the bloodiest wars that Europe had seen since 1945.

Key document   Speech by Slobodan Milošević on the 600th anniversary of the Battle of Kosovo, June 28, 1989[28]

By the force of social circumstances this great 600th anniversary of the Battle of Kosovo is taking place in a year in which Serbia, after many years, after many decades, has regained its state, national, and spiritual integrity. . . . Through the play of history and life, it seems as if Serbia has, precisely in this year, in 1989, regained its state and its dignity and thus has celebrated an event of the distant past which has a great historical and symbolic significance for its future. . . .

Today, it is difficult to say what is the historical truth about the Battle of Kosovo and what is legend. Today this is no longer important. Oppressed by pain and filled with hope, the people used to remember and to forget, as, after all, all people in the world do, and it was ashamed of treachery and glorified heroism. Therefore it is difficult to say today whether the Battle of Kosovo was a defeat or a victory for the Serbian people, whether thanks to it we fell into slavery or we survived in this slavery. . . . What has been certain through all the centuries until our time today is that disharmony struck Kosovo 600 years ago. If we lost the battle, then this was not only the result of social superiority and the armed advantage of the Ottoman Empire but also of the tragic disunity in the leadership of the Serbian state at that time. In that distant 1389, the Ottoman Empire was not only stronger than that of the Serbs but it was also more fortunate than the Serbian kingdom.

The lack of unity and betrayal in Kosovo will continue to follow the Serbian people like an evil fate through the whole of its history. Even in the last war, this lack of unity and betrayal led the Serbian people and Serbia into agony, the consequences of which in the historical and moral sense exceeded fascist aggression.

Even later, when a socialist Yugoslavia was set up, in this new state the Serbian leadership remained divided, prone to compromise to the detriment of its own people. The concessions that many Serbian leaders made at the expense of their people could not be accepted historically and ethically by any nation in the world, especially because the Serbs have never in the whole of their history conquered and exploited others. . . .

Six centuries ago, Serbia heroically defended itself in the field of Kosovo, but it also defended Europe. Serbia was at that time the bastion that defended the European culture, religion, and European society in general. Therefore today it appears not only unjust but even unhistorical and completely absurd to talk about Serbia's belonging to Europe. Serbia has been a part of Europe incessantly, now just as much as it was in the past, of course, in its own way, but in a way that in the historical sense never deprived it of dignity. In this spirit we now endeavor to build a society, rich and democratic, and thus to contribute to the prosperity of this beautiful country, this unjustly suffering country, but also to contribute to the efforts of all the progressive people of our age that they make for a better and happier world.

Let the memory of Kosovo heroism live forever!
Long live Serbia!
Long live Yugoslavia!
Long live peace and brotherhood among peoples!

Chechnya provides another example of a contemporary identity war. The Chechen republic is located in a rugged and inaccessible mountainous area of the Caucasus. In addition to Chechnya, this area includes another six republics, all of which are ethnically diverse. Indeed, among them, Dagestan alone is inhabited by about 30 nationalities, each with its own language and customs. Like Bosnia, much of the Caucasus adopted Islam while ruled by the Ottoman Empire, which retreated from the region in the face of Russian pressure in 1785. However, despite repeated Russian efforts to force them to assimilate, the mountain peoples of the Caucasus maintained their identity, and Chechnya did not become part of the Russian Empire until 1859. In 1943, Soviet dictator Josef Stalin deported some half-million Chechens to Kazakhstan and Siberia, turning over their lands to non-Chechens. Only in 1957 were the Chechens allowed to return.

Taking advantage of the turmoil that engulfed Russia during the final days of the Soviet Union, Dzhokhar Dudayev (1944–96) seized power in Chechnya in 1991 and declared Chechnya's independence. After three years of nominal independence, Russia launched military operations in

August 1994 to put an end to Chechnya's secession. After another two years of bloody but inconclusive warfare, the Russians withdrew, but following a series of terrorist explosions in Moscow and other Russian cities in 1999 and a Chechen incursion into neighboring Dagestan, President Vladimir Putin sent Russian troops back into Chechnya. Despite frequent Russian claims that Chechen resistance had ended,

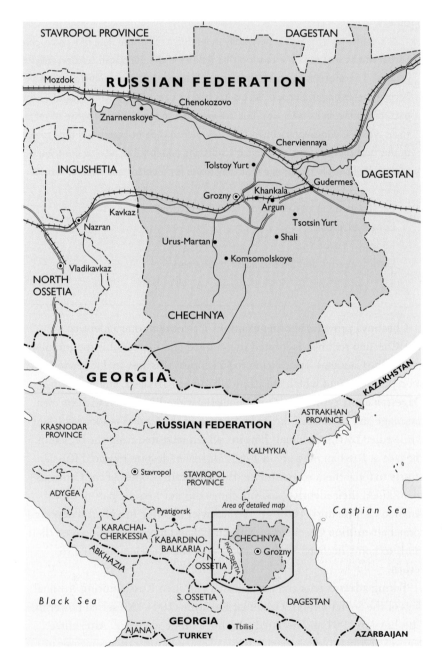

Map 15.2 The Chechen Republic in Russia and the neighboring Republics of Ingushetia, North Ossetia, and Dagestan

violence continued, climaxing in a series of terrorist incidents in Russia in 2004 that included the destruction of two Russian civilian airliners and the deaths of more than 350 hostages, mainly children, after the seizure of a Russian school in Northern Ossetia in September. So complex is the ethnic mix in the Caucasus that Ossetian anger was not only directed towards Chechnya but also toward the ethnic Ingush, some of whom may have been involved in the hostage crisis, are closely related to the Chechens, and live in neighboring Ingushetia.[29]

Like Bosnians, Chechens, though Muslim, rarely identified themselves in terms of their religion until after the Russian invasion. Prior to that event, according to one Chechen, "Nobody talked about religion. But these days it seems that nobody can stop talking about it. Nearly every Chechen soldier swears allegiance to Allah, taking *gazavat*, the holy oath to die fighting the invaders."[30]

Again, like Bosnia, the Chechen case has a contemporary figure who manipulated the identities of his people and tailored his own identity to mobilize political support. Shamil Basayev (1965–2006) was the leader of Chechnya's effort to gain independence from Russia. Basayev, who was responsible for the terrorist atrocities that shook Russia in the autumn of 2004 and who was finally killed by Russian authorities in July 2006, began his armed struggle against Russia as a Chechen nationalist and revolutionary romantic who idolized Ché Guevara but later adopted the new identity of fervent Islamic militant. Basayev, who took the name

Figure 15.5 Shamil Basayev, Chechen warlord and terrorist

© PA Photos

Did you know?

The Emperor Augustus of Rome commissioned Virgil to write the epic poem *The Aeneid* in order to legitimize imperial Rome (and Augustus as emperor) and to proclaim Rome's descent from Troy. After fleeing from the burning city of Troy, the hero Aeneas arrives in Italy, where he marries Lavinia, the daughter of the king of Latium, and becomes the ancestor of Romulus and the Romans.

Abdullah Shamil Abu Idris, and others like him who adopt the ideology of Radical Islam, whether from true conversion or not, can secure funding from wealthy Arab governments and can rally zealous Muslims from around the world to their cause.

Both Milošević and Basayev were able to provide their followers with victories, Milošević in seizing the city of Vukovar from Croatia in 1991 and Basayev in successful raids into Russia, including Moscow. They are only a few of the many leaders throughout history who have understood the power of myths and symbols, especially those that include some type of divine sanction, in manipulating people's identities and attracting their loyalties. Chinese dynasties routinely depicted themselves as heirs to China's mythical sage kings who were divinely mandated to rule the empire. Shinto, which also proclaimed Japanese emperors to be divine, depicted an unbroken line of over two millennia from the founding sun goddess.

Leaders realize that if they can rewrite history to show that they symbolize and represent an age-old struggle by an identity group to gain independence and respect, they can rally members of that group behind them. And in rewriting history to highlight ancient grievances and triumphs, these leaders create "memories" for their followers. To anchor those memories, such leaders encourage parades, tribal ceremonies and rituals, monuments, and pageants that remind people of who they are and what their ancestors did. Such symbols are highly valued in Ireland, which has for centuries witnessed conflict between Catholics and Protestants. This is a process that, as constructivists realize, allows political actors to construct reality, and it complicates efforts to ascertain objective historical "truth" since each generation writes history for its own purposes.

Thus, every year on July 12th, the city of Belfast in Northern Ireland, which for many years has witnessed violence between Catholics and Protestants, is the scene of rival parades in which Catholics wear green and Protestants orange. The most provocative of these parades is the "Orange Walk," in which militant Irish Protestants memorialize a battle in 1690 in which England's Protestant King William III defeated the former King James II, a Catholic who had lost his throne in England's "Glorious Revolution" of 1688. The color orange became a Protestant symbol because the Dutch-born William had been Prince of the House of Orange. The night before the parade, at the stroke of midnight, Protestants light huge bonfires throughout Northern Ireland to the singing of patriotic songs.

The whole affair, however, is a distortion of historical reality intended to deepen the sense of identity among Irish Protestants. The battle itself was actually relatively minor. It consisted largely of mercenaries of diverse religions from all over Europe. And William's victory, far from being regarded as a Catholic defeat, was actually celebrated by the pope in Rome as a victory of the "European Alliance" over the pope's enemies in France and Britain. "It is," declares one historian,

> unfortunately beyond all question that the Irish Catholics shed their blood like water and wasted their wealth like dirt in an effort to retain King James upon the throne. But it is equally beyond all question that the whole struggle was no earthly concern of theirs; that King James was one of the most worthless representatives of a race that ever sat upon the throne; that . . . William was a mere adventurer fighting for his own hand . . . ; and that neither army had the slightest claim to be considered as a patriot army combating for the freedom of the Irish race.[31]

As you can see, historical memories and myths sustain old identities and loyalties so that they may flicker for generations, even centuries. Religion, literature, dialect, poetry, painting, music, and ritual are only a few of the ways in which such identities are nourished and sustained. "[W]hat better way," asks the historian Anthony Smith, "of suggesting and inducing that sense of belonging than by 'rediscovering' submerged or lost ethnic roots in the mists of immemorial time?"[32] Such rediscovered roots also play an important role in creating and sustaining political communities and in providing such communities with legitimacy in the eyes of their members. However, the best known, most widely discussed, and probably the least understood of identities in global politics is nationalism.

Figure 15.6 An Irish approach to peace

Courtesy of Martyn Turner

Nationalism

nationalism the belief that a nation should be recognized as such, should enjoy equal rights with other nations, and should have political autonomy or independence.

Nationalism is based on the belief that the world is divided into distinctive "peoples." These peoples, it is believed, form nations whose members are loyal to one another and are united in their desire to protect the nation itself and maintain its distinctiveness. Nationalism has been at once hailed as a source of liberty and cultural flowering and denounced as a cause of war and hatred. In the following section, we shall discuss these differing views of nationalism and compare competing definitions of "nation" and "nationalism." Then, we shall look at how ambitious leaders manipulate nationalism to gain power and achieve their political aims. Finally, we shall look at how the ideas of nation and state merged following the French Revolution, thereby creating a powerful type of political community, and how in recent decades the two ideas have begun to separate and compete with each other for people's loyalties. Let us first consider what a nation is.

The bases of nationalism

Despite what you may think, recognizing a nation is not easy. When asked what the features of a nation are, some point to a common language; others see common ethnicity or religion as the basis of nations; still others believe that nations consist of people who have a common history.[33] More often than not, particular nations are defined by some mix of these characteristics. As a result, there is no single or common meaning of nation or of national origin. The only thing that everyone can agree on is that "nationals" share a sense of ownership in the "nation" as a whole and a sense of common destiny that excludes others. As Walker Connor observes, "the essence of a nation is intangible. The essence is a psychological bond that joins a people and differentiates it."[34] The "psychological bond" to which Connor refers is critical to understanding nations and nationalism. Nations are born and exist in people's minds and become objective features of global politics only after people believe in their existence. Unlike mountains or oceans, nations are invented by people who *believe* that they share a common destiny with others "like themselves." Nations, then, are "imagined communities" that reflect the reality of shared features such as language, race, religion, or kinship.

Frequently, those shared features assume special importance because an enemy points to them as the reason for persecuting or attacking those who have them. In this way, what begins in people's minds becomes real: Over time, people act in ways that deepen and anchor the bonds of nationhood, develop cooperative habits among themselves, and are threatened or persecuted by others as a group. Thus, when dominant nationalities try to force minority groups to give up their own language, as Turks did to Kurds living in Turkey or as Russians did to Latvians in the Soviet Union, those efforts are likely to deepen national feelings. In response, the victimized minorities resist as best they can the efforts to destroy their cultural inheritance. And such experiences then provide heroic myths and tales of resistance that deepen national feelings and national pride and that provide the members of a nation with a common history that "proves" their national identity.

As we observed in chapter 2 (p. 66), after the French Revolution, nationalism in Europe provided states and their rulers with greater political and military power than ever before, while making the borders between states more and more rigid. The creation of the nation-state convinced citizens that putting their lives on the line for "the fatherland" was somehow a noble expression of self and a means of defending home and loved ones as well. Popular sovereignty – the idea that the people, now citizens, were the owners of the states in which they lived – replaced dynastic sovereignty – the idea that kings owned both the territory of states and the people, subjects, who lived in that territory. In these nation-states, the identity of rulers and ruled was fused, and states acquired national interests.

Was the spread of nationalism a positive or negative development in global politics? During the first half of the nineteenth century, many Europeans regarded nationalism as a benevolent ideology that went hand in glove with liberalism and democracy. Among the leading advocates of **liberal nationalism** was the Italian patriot Giuseppe Mazzini (1805–1872). From an early age, Mazzini was a leading advocate of Italian unification and independence and fought Austrian domination of his countrymen. Mazzini believed that nationalism meant the liberation of people from foreign rule and that, when people were liberated and assumed control of their own affairs, they would naturally adopt democratic political institutions. Europe in 1848 seemed on the verge of realizing Mazzini's aspirations as revolutionary currents swept the continent, including Italy. In the end, however, liberal nationalism was crushed in Italy by conservative rulers, just as it was crushed elsewhere in Europe. Over a half a century later, another great liberal, President Woodrow Wilson, followed in Mazzini's footsteps in advocating **national self-determination** (see chapter 3, p. 124) as the way to bring about peace and democracy in global politics.

But even as Mazzini was advocating the liberal virtues of nationalism, others were exploring its darker side. Conservative politicians soon recognized that they could exploit nationalist passions for their own ends.

liberal nationalism a variant of nationalism that links the independence of national groups with human rights and democratic ideals.

national self-determination the doctrine that any people who consider themselves a nation should enjoy their own territorial state.

malignant nationalism a strain of nationalism based on the superiority of some nations over others and that admires the use of violence in politics.

By manipulating such passions, they could reinforce both their own personal power and the power of the states they controlled. Making use of crude analogies with Charles Darwin's theory of evolution, they argued that some nations were superior to others and that such superiority became apparent by "the survival of the fittest" in fighting and winning wars. Such **malignant nationalism** contrasted vividly with the liberal variant associated with Mazzini.

As Mazzini had been an eloquent spokesperson for liberal nationalism, so the Prussian historian Heinrich von Trietschke (1834–96) became the leading advocate of this darker interpretation of nationalism. As a young man, Treitschke had been disappointed by the failure of the liberal 1848 Revolution and became a supporter of German Chancellor Otto von Bismarck's realist policies of "blood and iron." Influenced by the philosopher Georg Hegel (1770–1831) and the jurist Friedrich Karl von Savigny (1779–1861), Treitschke, along with other Germans of his generation, regarded the nation (*Volk*) as a unique living and evolving cultural and historical institution with a collective will whose survival was guaranteed only by its military strength. States, he argued, exist to foster nations, not individuals, from generation to generation. War, in his view, created nations and showed whether or not they were worthy of survival. "Brave peoples alone," he declared, "have an existence, an evolution or a future; the weak and cowardly perish, and perish justly. The grandeur of history lies in the perpetual conflict of nations."[35]

Influenced by Treitschke's view of nations, German General Friedrich von Bernhardi (1849–1930), an ultranationalist military thinker, advocated German expansionism and contributed to the belligerent atmosphere in Germany in the years before World War I. In a widely read book entitled *Germany and the Next War* (1912), Bernhardi argued for the virtues of war, contending that the desire for peace "has rendered most civilized nations anemic" (see excerpts from this in Key document).

Key document Excerpts from Von Bernhardi's *Germany and the Next War*[36]

War is a biological necessity of the first importance, a regulative element in the life of mankind which cannot be dispensed with, since without it an unhealthy development will follow, which excludes every advancement of the race, and therefore all real civilization.

The struggle for existence is, in the life of Nature, the basis of all healthy development. All existing things show themselves to be the result of contesting forces. . . . The law of the stronger holds good everywhere. Those forms survive which are able to procure themselves the most favorable conditions of life, and to assert themselves in the universal economy of Nature. The weaker succumb. . . .

[I]n war, the nation will conquer which can throw into the scale the greatest physical, mental, moral, material, and political power, and is therefore the best able to defend itself. War will furnish such a nation with favorable vital conditions, enlarged possibilities of expansion and widened influence, and thus promote the progress of mankind; for it is clear that those intellectual and moral factors which insure superiority in war are also those which render possible a general progressive development. They confer victory because the elements of progress are latent in them. Without war, inferior or decaying races would easily choke the growth of healthy budding elements, and a universal decadence would follow. . . .

We have fought in the last great wars for our national union and our position among the Powers of *Europe*; we now must decide whether we wish to develop into and maintain a *World Empire*, and procure for German spirit and German ideas that fit recognition which has been hitherto withheld from them. . . .

We must rouse in our people the unanimous wish for power in this sense, together with the determination to sacrifice on the altar of patriotism, not only life and property, but also private views and preferences in the interests of the common welfare. Then alone shall we discharge our great duties of the future, grow into a World Power, and stamp a great part of humanity with the impress of the German spirit. If, on the contrary, we persist in that dissipation of energy which now marks our political life, there is imminent fear that in the great contest of the nations, which we must inevitably face, we shall be dishonorably beaten; that days of disaster await us in the future.

The virulent and malignant nationalism of Treitschke, Bernhardi, and other ultranationalists in the late nineteenth century not only produced the militarist and racist atmosphere that fed the fires of war in the years before 1914 but also had more lasting effects. Fascism, with its emphasis on national myths and renewal, drew on their ideas and became the ideology of ultranationalists throughout Europe in the 1920s and 1930s. Fascist dictators seized power in Italy (1923) and Spain (1939), and Hitler and his Nazis assumed power in Germany (1933). But fascism prospered elsewhere as well before World War II. In each case, historical memories of national greatness (for example, the Roman Empire in Italy) that was undermined by factors such as racial mixing were combined with promises of national revival and conquest. According to the Italian dictator Benito Mussolini (1883–1945), who coined the term, fascism "conceives of the State as an absolute, in comparison with which all individuals or groups are relative, only to be conceived of in their relation to the State," and "the growth of empire, that is to say the expansion of the nation, is an essential manifestation of vitality, and its opposite a sign of decadence."[37] Fascists viewed the relationship between state and nation as necessarily very close. But nations and states are not the same and, as we shall see in the next section, their relationship has evolved over time.

Nations, states, and nation-states

Following the French Revolution, nationalism reinforced the power of states by providing an emotional and psychological element that made people feel as though they genuinely belonged. What was then called the nation-state was a more cohesive and stronger political unit than any before it or since. At the same time, however, nationalism made the boundaries between states increasingly rigid, promoted interstate rivalry and conflict, and increased the size and intensity of wars. In sum, nationalism promoted unity within states and disunity among them.

In Western Europe, the boundaries of states and nations became largely compatible over time, and states' populations became increasingly homogeneous. But these processes were often bloody and lengthy. Both Greece and Turkey became homogeneous nation-states by the forcible exchange of populations in 1923 – over one million Greeks from Asia Minor and 400,000 Muslim Turks from Greece, and the expulsion from and massacre of some 800,000 Armenians by the Turks during World War I. The French, English, Dutch, and German nations also are largely located within the boundaries of a single sovereign state, but here too, in each case the process was lengthy and often violent.

However, the nation-state was and remains only one of many forms of political community. It was the product of a particular time and place. Moreover, its triumph over rival identities in Europe and, later, elsewhere was always partial and contingent. So, for example, today, many perceive the sense of nationhood and national homogeneity of Europe's states to be threatened by the influx of outsiders who are "different" because they worship different gods or have different tastes. The fear that national cohesion is endangered is reflected in the story of Mihdat Guler with which we began this chapter. In addition, nationality in Europe is also challenged by another, broader identity, the identity reflected by the European Union of being "European" rather than British, French, or German.

The incompatibility of national and state boundaries is even greater outside Western Europe. For example, the boundaries of some states enclose several nations and divide others, as did the ramshackle Austro-Hungarian, Russian, and Ottoman empires before their demise at the end of World War I and as do many of postcolonial states in Africa and the Middle East today. Among the most prominent nations that have no state of their own are the Kurds and the Palestinians.

The Kurds are an Indo-European people who number between 25 and 30 million and live mainly in mountainous areas of Turkey (15 million), Syria (1.5 million), Iraq (3.5–4 million), and Iran (six million), which they call "Kurdistan," as well as in communities in Europe and the United States. The Kurds are a mainly Sunni Muslim tribal people with their own language and customs who trace their history back thousands of years. There are as many as 800 separate Kurdish tribes in Kurdistan that are reflected in an individual's last name.

Kurdish history is a story of failed efforts to achieve independence. In the seventh century, the Kurds were conquered by the Arabs, in the eleventh century by the Seljuk Turks, and 200 years later, by the Mongols. Prior to World War I, the area they inhabited was part of the Ottoman Empire. After that war, they rose against the Turks and were crushed; but, attracted by President Woodrow Wilson's advocacy of national self-determination, they sent representatives to the 1919 Paris Peace Conference. The Treaty of Sèvres (1920), which carved up the Ottoman Empire, provided for the creation of an autonomous Kurdish state, but Kurdish aspirations were again thwarted when the Ottomans were overthrown by Kemal Atatürk (1881–1938), Turkey's modernizing national hero. Further Kurdish rebellions in Turkey in 1925, 1930, and 1937 only resulted in additional misery and death.

Without a state of their own, the Kurds have had a difficult time, especially in recent decades. Since 1984, the Kurds in Turkey have sought greater autonomy, including the right to use their own language, and their efforts have repeatedly been met by Turkish military repression. Again and again, the Kurds have been used as pawns by the states in which they live to destabilize neighboring states. Throughout the 1960s

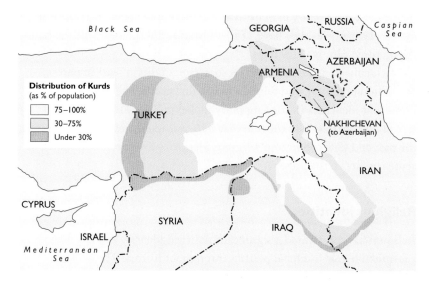

Map 15.3 Kurdistan

and 1970s, for example, Iran funded Kurdish resistance against Iraq, only to leave Iraqi Kurds in the lurch when relations between Iraq and Iran improved in 1975. Renewed resistance in Iraq during the Iran–Iraq War (1980–88) brought about terrible vengeance from Saddam Hussein who, in 1988, launched poison gas attacks on Kurdish villages and rounded up and executed as many as 200,000 Kurdish men.

In the 1991 Persian Gulf War, Iraq's Kurds again rose up against Saddam Hussein but were crushed by the Iraqi army, forcing hundreds of thousands of them to flee to Turkey. Between 1992 and the 2003 invasion of Iraq, the Kurds in Iraq enjoyed American military protection and exercised considerable autonomy. For the most part, Iraqi Kurds supported the overthrow of Saddam, but whether or not they achieve an independent Kurdistan remains to be seen. One important obstacle they face is the strong resistance of Turkey, Syria, and Iran, which fear that "their" Kurds may also try to secede, thereby threatening the territorial integrity of their countries.

Today, as the Kurdish case shows, nationalism no longer cements the unity of states as it did in France after 1789. Instead, in some cases, it subverts the unity of sovereign states, especially in regions of the world where states were artificially imposed by colonial conquerors. In those regions, nations and states have diverged, and states have remained weak and subject to civil strife. And where civil strife is endemic, state institutions have collapsed, threatening the spread of violence and larger regional wars as in the Democratic Republic of the Congo. Everywhere, it seems, national movements have proliferated, with leaders demanding their own independent state, often accompanied by large-scale violence. As former US Secretary of State Warren Christopher (1925–) put it, if matters continue as they have, "[w]e'll have 5,000 countries rather than the hundred plus we now have."[38]

Nationalism, as we have seen, is sometimes built at least in part on common religion, and religion has again become one of the most important identities in contemporary global politics. In the following section, we shall look at the role that religious identities have played in the past and how conflicting religious identities have become a source of acute conflict in the present.

Religious identities

Religion has constituted a significant political identity and has played a formidable role in global politics throughout history. The ancient Romans, like many other ancient peoples, recognized that religion, when harnessed to secular authority, was a powerful asset. In Chapter XI of

The Prince, Machiavelli declared that "ecclesiastical principalities" can survive without ability or fortune because "they are sustained by ancient religious customs, which are so powerful and are of such quality, that they keep their princes in power in whatever manner they proceed and live."[39] And, in *The Discourses*, he praised Rome's official religion and described religion as "the most necessary and assured support of any civil society . . . for where religion exists it is easy to introduce armies and discipline."[40]

Contemporary states, too, routinely seek to harness religion to promote legitimacy or at least to co-opt religious identities that might undermine the loyalty of citizens. Russia's post-communist leaders are reinventing themselves as defenders of Eastern Orthodoxy like the tsars of old. And Muslim leaders in Saudi Arabia and elsewhere have made Islamic law, called *sharia*, the law of their countries. Judaism is the basis for the founding of Israel; India, though a secular society, is the home of Hinduism; and Buddhist identities keep alive memories of independent statehood in Mongolia and Tibet. During the Cold War, Catholicism fostered nationalism and anti-communism in Poland, Czechoslovakia, and the Baltic republics.

Increasingly, however, religious identity competes with state citizenship for people's loyalties. Identity conflicts, especially those that involve religion, are especially sharp in today's Middle East. Nationalism associated with territorial states, as in Europe, did not take root in Arab lands, due in part to their traditional nomadic tribal culture, so the idea of sovereignty means little to many Arabs. The territorial states in the region – Iraq, Syria, Lebanon, Saudi Arabia, Kuwait, and Jordan – were imposed by Europe's colonial powers after World War I, and nationality has had a hard time competing with local clan-based identities and the transnational attractions of pan-Arabism and Islam that ignore state boundaries. These ideologies constantly threaten the stability of Arab states. And, in today's Middle East, it appears that Islamic identity is becoming more salient than Arab identity.[41]

History shows us that religious sentiment and identity can challenge a citizen's state identity for primacy. Prior to the 1648 Peace of Westphalia, for example, European princes competed with the Church for popular support. To achieve sovereign independence, many of them had to throw off papal claims to have the right to govern them, gain the loyalties of national clergy, and take over church resources within their realm, as did Henry VIII (1491–1547) in England in 1530. For its part, the Catholic Church provided legitimacy for monarchs – variously titled "Catholic Sovereigns," "Most Catholic," and "Most Christian" – who were prepared to accept the authority of the cross over the scepter.

In the eleventh and twelfth centuries, a bitter contest raged in Europe – the investiture controversy – over whether secular princes, especially the Holy Roman Emperor, could install bishops in offices without Church approval. The conflict climaxed in a trial of strength between Pope Gregory VII (c. 1020/25–1085) and Emperor Henry IV (1050–1106). When the emperor appointed the bishop of Milan despite papal prohibition, Gregory excommunicated Henry. In 1077, Henry journeyed to Canossa, in the Italian Alps, where he knelt in the snow to beg forgiveness from the Pope.

The struggle between church and state in Europe continued for centuries and included the Protestant Reformation, the Thirty Years' War, and the Counterreformation. Just as Islamic zealots seek to establish **theocracies**, that is, states governed by religious leaders, so Protestant zealots in sixteenth-century Europe established several theocracies. Europe's Reformation brought with it various forms of Christian fundamentalism, efforts to establish theocratic rule, and a host of willing martyrs – also features of contemporary Islamic movements. The Reformation also featured terrorism and counterterrorism, warfare unrestrained by legal conventions, and transnational proselytizing of fundamentalist principles. Thus, historical theocracies predated by centuries contemporary theocracies such as those in Afghanistan under the Taliban and Iran under its Shia ayatollahs.

The leading Reformation fundamentalists were Ulrich Zwingli (1484–1531) and John Calvin (1509–64), both of whom were active in Switzerland. In Zurich, Zwingli was among the most consistent fundamentalists of Protestant leaders, requiring that law and policy be based solely on a literal rendition of scripture and arguing that scripture could only have a single meaning. Biblical rules demanded absolute obedience; other laws could demand none. Calvin was the most influential of the Protestant reformers who advocated religious government, insisting that, since God was sovereign, bishops, kings, and other political leaders could not demand obedience. As virtual ruler of Geneva, he imposed his theocratic views, integrating the church with the civic government, assuring that the clergy would play a key role in political decisions, and incorporating into the law an austere morality on the city's citizens. Calvinism also deeply influenced early American settlers. God and the state were enshrined together in Puritan Plymouth and its Congregational Church.

Today, religious fundamentalism – belief in governance in accordance with religious dogma – informs Islam, some Christian movements in the United States, Orthodox Judaism in Israel, and Hindu nationalism in India. Religious fundamentalists of all stripes demand that government reflect a literal reading of God's word as revealed in holy texts. Some of

theocracy a form of government in which a deity is or a group of priests claiming to represent a deity are the supreme ruler(s).

these fundamentalists enjoy considerable political influence in their countries. For example, extreme Hindu nationalists have for some time enjoyed great influence in various heavily populated Indian states. Hindu extremists were instrumental in the 1992 destruction of an ancient mosque in the city of Ayodhya in the province of Uttar Pradesh and the ensuing violence that swept Bombay, and the nationalist party's Bharatiya Janata became the leader in a coalition government in New Delhi after elections in spring 1996.

However, today, it is in the spread of Islamic fundamentalism that the transnational challenge posed by religious identities is most evident. Events in Islamic history, some dating back 14 centuries, have been revived to undermine existing state practices. Islam is in the throes of a contest between militant and mainstream elements, and one of the key issues that defines the contestants is the relationship between religion and state, with militants seeking the revival of the medieval Islamic Caliphate (see chapter 2, pp. 88–90) and the establishment of theocratic authority over the global Islamic community.

One of the earliest political movements that emerged to promote transnational Islamic identities was the Muslim Brotherhood, which was founded in Egypt in 1928. More recently, militant Islamists from Indonesia to Nigeria have emerged and become active on behalf of a universal Islamic community. Their cause gained global attention with the 1979 overthrow of Iran's monarchy by Shia supporters of Ayatollah Khomeini (1900–89). Khomeini claimed to act not as an official of the Iranian state but as a spiritual leader of Shia Muslims everywhere. Today, as we saw in chapter 5, Western–Muslim conflicts threaten the stability of societies around the world.

Although religious identities have received most of the headlines in recent global politics, there has also been a resurgence of ethnic and tribal identities. Like religion, ethnicity has historically been a major factor in shaping nationalism but was largely repressed or ignored by governments that sought to foster patriotism and national unity. In addition, during the Cold War, the superpowers made a special effort to dampen ethnic consciousness both at home and abroad in order to focus attention on the ideological divide between East and West. With the end of the Cold War, almost every continent has been gripped by examples of impassioned ethnic conflict and separatist yearnings, the topic we will turn to next.

Ethnic and tribal identities

Both ethnic and tribal identities are based on the belief that members are linked by blood ties related to family and kinship, some of which are real and some invented. Ethnic and tribal consciousness is especially strong in areas of the world that were formerly ruled by European colonizers who imposed state boundaries with little consideration of whether these made sense in ethnic or tribal terms.

In Africa, following decolonization in the 1950s and 1960s, governments sought to build national loyalties and create states like those of the Europeans. For the most part, they failed because their governments rarely represented all the tribal and ethnic elements in their society. Instead, governments became extensions of *particular* tribal and ethnic groups that were then able to give public jobs and contracts to members of their immediate families and kinship group. In turn, their armies and police were not impartial protectors of public order and national defense but rather became the armed representatives of the groups and individuals in power. These conditions, along with the failure of authorities to cope with socioeconomic problems, impaired nation building and weakened loyalties to the state. At the same time, they intensified and deepened older ethnic and tribal identities that colonial and postcolonial leaders had sought to dampen.

Thus, in the years immediately following Nigerian independence in 1960, the country was the scene of coups and persistent unrest owing to tension between the Hausas of the northern region and the Yorubas and Ibos in the south and west. In Kenya, the period just before independence in 1963 featured intense jockeying for power between the country's leading political party, the Kenya African National Union (KANU), which enjoyed the support of the country's two largest ethnic groups, the Kikuyu and Luo, and the Kenya African Democratic Union (KADU), which was supported by several smaller ethnic groups. The late 1960s and 1970s saw a split in the KANU owing to increasing animosity between the Luo and Kikuyu.

In a few cases, such as those of the Kurds or the Druse, religious and tribal identities reinforce one another and foster transnational communities. The Druse, for example, are a fiercely independent tribal people of some 200–300,000 adherents who live mainly in Lebanon near Mount Hermon and in the mountains behind Beirut and Sidon. A few villages are also located on the Golan Heights, in Syria, and just inside Israel's northern border. The Druse sense of uniqueness and their tribal identity is fostered by the form of Islam that they practice. Their variant of Islam emerged in the tenth century, and believes that God had appeared in the form of a Muslim leader in Egypt whom most Muslims regard as a blasphemer. The Druse keep their religion secret, and do not accept converts or marry outsiders. As a result, their identity as a distinct people is deeply anchored and clearly bounded.

Ethnic identities threaten the integrity of countries in the developed as well as in the developing world. Across Europe and North America, for example, "ethno-national" groups claim that their culture has been submerged or swallowed up by majorities within nation-states – Spanish Basques and Catalans, Canadian Québécois, native Canadians and native Americans, and many others. Increasingly in recent years, the familiar ideas of "nation" and "nationalism" have taken on a distinctly subversive, anti-state connotation, even in the West.

Québec is an instructive case of just how complex such issues can be. When the secession movement of former Parti Québécois premier, Jacques Parizeau (1930–), lost its 1995 referendum, he blamed it on "money and the ethnic vote," highlighting the presence of a large number of non-French-speaking English and other minorities. To complicate matters further, Cree and other indigenous Indian groups who claim half the territory of Québec were so alarmed by the referendum that might subject them to Québécois control rather than the more generous federal government in Ottawa that they, in turn, threatened to secede from Québec, claiming the same right to national self-determination as the Québécois. And, were Québec ultimately to secede, others might follow, as the country is made up of numerous regional/provincial identities as well as ethnic ones: the Maritime Provinces, British Columbia, and so on.

The unraveling of Yugoslavia was an extreme example of ethnic passions and violence that for a time attracted global attention. There, as you will see in the next section, violence raged for much of the 1990s, and unspeakable atrocities were carried out by ethnic groups against one another.

The brutal break-up of Yugoslavia

As we saw in chapter 3, Serbia, which became the heartland of the new Yugoslav state, played a key role in bringing about World War I; and Bosnia, also a part of the future Yugoslavia, was the site of the assassination of Archduke Franz Ferdinand in June 1914. Yugoslavia (meaning Union of the South Slavs) emerged from the ruins of the Austro-Hungarian Empire in December 1918. Serbia united with Croatia, Slovenia, Montenegro, Bosnia, and Herzegovina into the new nation-state. However, both the birth and early years of the country were difficult, as non-Serbs eyed with suspicion Serbian efforts to predominate. In the 1920s, the Croatians demanded autonomy, but the king repressed their efforts to achieve it.

In 1941, Yugoslavia was invaded and conquered by Nazi Germany. Two Yugoslav resistance movements coalesced to fight the occupation.

One led by Draža Mihailović (1893–1946) consisted largely of Serb officers and soldiers of the Royal Army who were called Četniks. The second consisted of communists, called Partisans, and was led by Josip Broz Tito (1892–1980). By 1943, the two movements were fighting each other as much as they were fighting their common enemy. Further complicating matters, the Nazis set up a fascist puppet regime in Croatia, led by Ante Pavelić (1889–1959), known as the "butcher of the Balkans," and his followers called *Ustase* (Insurrection), who carried out brutal atrocities against the Serbs in which as many as 750,000 died. In the end, Tito and the communists triumphed and governed Yugoslavia with an iron hand for over four decades.

Tito became a popular figure in the country after he declared his country's independence of Stalin and the Soviet Union in 1948 and pioneered an ideology of **national communism**. He managed to repress conflicting ethnic identities in the country by maintaining strict political control. However, with Tito's death in 1980, ethnic groups in Yugoslavia began to resurface.

national communism the ideology of certain communists based on the claim that each communist party should follow its own distinctive national road and need not follow the same path as the Soviet Communist Party.

In 1987, Slobodan Milošević succeeded Tito as head of the Communist Party, and two years later he was also elected president of Serbia. Milošević concluded that communism was obsolete and decided that his political future depended on his becoming an extreme Serb nationalist. As a result, he began to advocate a greater Serbia that would include parts of Croatia, Bosnia and Herzegovina, and Macedonia.

Frightened by Serbian ambitions, Croatia and Slovenia declared their independence on June 25, 1991. In September, Macedonia declared its independence, and in February 1992 the predominantly Muslim republic of Bosnia and Herzegovina followed suit. The Serbs used force to try and prevent the break-up of the country or, if that failed, to gain as much territory as possible for themselves. Initially, this led to warfare in the Krajina region of Croatia along the Serb border, which was home to many ethnic Serbs. When Croatia finally regained the region in the summer of 1995, its forces drove some 200,000 ethnic Serbs from their homes and across the border.

However, the fighting spread as the struggle shifted to Bosnia, the most ethnically mixed of Yugoslavia's regions. Bosnia's Muslim and Croatian populations both feared Serbian ambition and demanded independence for their republic. In the autumn of 1990, Bosnia held elections in which the major political parties, each representing one of the region's ethnic groups, fielded candidates. Although the Muslim Slavs' Party of Democratic Action won a plurality of seats (34 percent), Bosnia's parliament was almost equally divided: The Serb Democratic Party led by Radovan Karadžić (1945–) and linked to Milošević's ruling party in

Serbia won 30 percent of the seats, and the Croatian Democratic Union of Bosnia-Herzegovina, the Bosnian branch of the ruling party in Croatia, won 18 percent. A Bosnian Muslim was named president of the country, heading a fragile coalition government. By the following year, the Serb deputies walked out of parliament because of Muslim and Croatian support for Bosnian independence, and Bosnian Serbs and Croats began to partition the country into ethnic subunits. Bosnian Serbs set up a separate parliament, trained their own armed militias, and in November 1991 held a referendum in which they voted to remain part of Yugoslavia. In another referendum held in February 1992 at the behest of the European Union (EU), Bosnia's Muslims and Croats voted overwhelmingly for independence, which was recognized by the United States and the European Union in April. Bosnia's Serbs boycotted the second referendum and proclaimed their own state.

War erupted almost immediately among the three groups, with Serbs and Croats getting aid and support from Serbia and Croatia. Initially, the Croatians fought with Bosnia's Muslims against their common foe, the Serbs. And with help from Serbia, Bosnia's Serbs engaged in "ethnic cleansing" – killing and terrorizing Muslims and Croatians, forcing them from their homes, and placing many in concentration camps. In addition, the Serbs systematically raped Muslim women to produce fear and destroy families. By mid-1992, most of Bosnia was in the hands of the Serbs, and Sarajevo, its capital, was surrounded and under continuous artillery shelling. In spring 1993, the Croats, too, turned on Bosnia's Muslims, seizing large areas in the country's center around the city of Mostar, which endured months of artillery bombardment.

ethnic cleansing the murder or expulsion from a territory of people from a particular ethnic background.

Theory in the real world

Nationalism, as we saw in chapter 8 (p. 353), especially when combined with feelings of national superiority, is believed to be a cause of war. Indeed, the role of nationalism in triggering violence and human-rights abuses is one reason why theorists believe it is necessary to include the state level of analysis in explaining war. The belief that nationalism can produce intense conflict was evident as Yugoslavia disintegrated in the 1990s. The wars in Bosnia and Kosovo featured extensive **ethnic cleansing** against civilians. As described in the *New York Times* on January 24, 2001, "Zeljko Raznatovic, the gangster turned paramilitary leader known as Arkan, stormed into the largely Muslim town with his Tigers militia, and the carnage began. 'They were going house to house, looking for fighters and things to take,' Mr. Haviv [a photographer] remembered. 'Inside a mosque, they had taken down the Islamic flag and were holding it like a trophy. They had a guy, they said he was a fundamentalist from Kosovo. He was begging for his life. There was shouting outside. They had taken the town butcher and his wife, and they were screaming. They shot him, and he was lying there. There was a truck that had crashed nearby. I got between the cab and the body and turned my back so the soldiers couldn't see me. They shot the woman, then they brought out her sister and shot her. There were the two soldiers. Another came from my left, he had a cigarette in one hand and sunglasses on top of his head. When he kicked her, it was like the ultimate disrespect for everything."'

As discussed in chapter 9 (pp. 423–4), the United Nations became involved in the Croatian and Bosnian conflicts in February 1992 with the establishment of the United Nations Protection Force (UNPROFOR). UNPROFOR was given the virtually impossible task of separating the protagonists and, in the spring of 1993, shielding civilians in six so-called "protection zones" in Muslim areas: Sarajevo, Tuzla, Bihać, Goražde, Srebrenica, and Zepa. At a conference in London in 1992, former US Secretary of State Cyrus Vance (1917–2002) and former British Foreign Secretary David Owen (1938) proposed ambitious terms to end the conflict:

- The withdrawal of Serbian forces from Croatia.
- Demilitarization of UN Protected Areas and enforcement of no-fly zones over Bosnia.
- UNPROFOR supervision of local authorities and police until the achievement of an overall political solution.
- Support for humanitarian organizations and the safe return of displaced persons to their homes in UN Protected Areas.

Finding itself in the midst of civil war, UNPROFOR was unable to maintain the security of the protected areas or to enforce the no-fly zones over Bosnia. Thus, NATO was empowered to carry out the job despite objections from Russia which had close ties with the Serbian government.

Finally, in May 1995 continued Serbian artillery attacks on civilians in Sarajevo triggered NATO air strikes on Serb military targets. Following Serb hostage taking of UNPROFOR soldiers and massacres of Muslim civilians in Zepa and Srebrenica in the summer of 1995, NATO began a sustained air and artillery campaign, called Operation Deliberate Force, against the offending Bosnian Serb forces. Simultaneously, Croatia launched a major offensive to drive the Serbs out of the Krajina region, and then, with Bosnian Muslim forces (with whom they allied after a February 2004 truce), seized control of large Serbian-inhabited areas in western Bosnia.

In October 1995 a ceasefire agreement was reached, and the enemy leaders agreed to attend a peace conference in Dayton, Ohio, the following month. The Dayton Peace Accord was reached three weeks later. By its terms, Bosnia was given a constitution that established a Serb Republic and a largely fictitious Muslim–Croat federation in the country. Bosnia would be run by an official selected by the EU and the UN. In addition, a NATO force of some 60,000 would replace UNPROFOR. The agreement also authorized elections and the return of the roughly 2.3 million Bosnian refugees (of a total population of 4.4 million) to their homes.[42]

The Dayton Accord did not, however, bring peace to the Balkans. In 1999, another deadly war exploded that, like the Bosnian war, was ignited by Serb leader Slobodan Milošević. In this instance, the site was the Serb province of Kosovo, an icon for Serb nationalists because of its historical association with Serb culture and religion and their age-old conflict with the Ottoman Turks (see p. 706). Serb nationalism in Kosovo was challenged, however, by Albanian nationalism. The majority Muslim Albanian population had agitated for independence or union with their Albanian homeland across the border ever since Serbia had annexed the province during the Balkan Wars of 1912–13. Following mass demonstrations by Albanian Kosovars for better living conditions and greater political freedom during the 1980s, Milošević sent the Serbian Army into Kosovo in 1989, cancelled the autonomy that the province had been granted two decades earlier under Tito, and forbade the use of the Albanian language in schools. In taking this action, Milošević burnished his credentials as a Serb nationalist but triggered a growing underground independence movement among Albania's Muslims. That movement elected its own president in 1992, set up its own schools and parliament, and began to pursue a policy of passive resistance which produced few results.

Under these repressive conditions, militant Albanian Kosovars took to the hills in the early 1990s to form the Kosovo Liberation Army (KLA) and began to attack Serb policemen. Assaults against Serb authorities escalated through the 1990s. In March 1998, Serb military units and security police began a major campaign against the KLA, in which many Albanian Muslims were killed, and hundreds of thousands were driven from their homes. This served only to increase the popularity of the KLA and provided it with additional recruits.

As the international community became increasingly concerned about events in Kosovo, diplomatic pressure on Milošević intensified, and threats were uttered of renewed NATO air attacks against the Serbs. Nevertheless, both sides continued the violence, and efforts to negotiate its end proved fruitless. In early 1999, Milošević initiated a major military offensive against Albanian villages in Kosovo, which to many observers augured a new campaign of ethnic cleansing. Under international pressure, new peace talks were held in France in February and March 1999, but neither side showed any flexibility or willingness to compromise. For example, Milošević refused a plan to insert a NATO force in Kosovo and permit NATO troops to enter Serbia.

War exploded in March as NATO forces began aircraft and cruise missile attacks against targets throughout Serbia, including the capital city of Belgrade. American expectations that the air campaign would lead to a rapid Serb capitulation were disappointed, as Serb army units poured into Kosovo and began systematic ethnic cleansing in an effort to drive the Albanian population from the province. Two wars appeared to be taking place at the same time – one involving NATO air attacks on Serbian targets outside of Kosovo and the second, a Serbian ground assault in Kosovo during which about 640,000 people fled Kosovo.

In June 1999, Milošević was compelled to turn over Kosovo to NATO control, although the province legally remained a part of Serbia. The UN Security Council, which had *not* authorized NATO's bombing campaign, authorized an international occupation by military units from NATO and Russia. This force, called the Kosovo Force or KFOR, was to maintain security, monitor the withdrawal of Serb forces, and ensure the safe return of the almost one million refugees who had fled the province during the violence. KFOR, whose mission continues to the present day, has resettled as many as 800,000 refugees (though relatively few Serbs), prevented acts of revenge (Albanian violence against Serbs), demilitarized the KLA, collected thousands of weapons from former combatants, removed most of the estimated 40,000 mines that had been laid, and reconstructed roads, bridges, and other elements of the province's infrastructure.[43]

Although the fighting has ceased in the former Yugoslavia, and six new states have emerged – Serbia, Montenegro, Croatia, Slovenia, the Republic of Macedonia, and Bosnia and Herzegovina – scars have not healed. The trials of alleged war criminals by the International Criminal Tribunal for the Former Yugoslavia (ICTY) in The Hague, that had been authorized in 1993 by the UN Security Council, were still underway over 14 years later. And many fear that when UN forces leave Bosnia, ethnic strife will recommence. In addition, the future of Kosovo remains unclear. Although it is still regarded as an integral part of Serbia, the Albanian population of the region is largely autonomous and is seeking independence, which could well provoke renewed violence and regional instability.

In sum, the ethnic hatreds that led to the destruction of Yugoslavia reflect the consequences of multiple and conflicting identities in the contemporary world. Far from seeing a universal triumph of liberal democracy and what political scientist Francis Fukuyama called "the end of history,"[44] observers of global politics in recent decades have seen an ugly upsurge in ethnic and religious violence. A variety of forces,

Table 15.1 Key events in the history of Yugoslavia

Year	Event
1389	Serbian defeat at the hands of the Ottoman Turks in their "ancestral home" of Kosovo.
1918	With the collapse of the Austro-Hungarian and Ottoman empires at the end of World War I, the Kingdom of Serbs, Croats, and Slovenes is established.
1929	The country becomes an absolute and centralized monarchy under King Alexander, its regions divided without regard to ethnic composition and its name is changed to Yugoslavia (Kingdom of the South Slavs).
1941	Yugoslavia is invaded by the Nazis. Germans occupy Serbia; Germany and Italy divide Slovenia; Italy controls Kosovo and Montenegro. A pro-German puppet state is set up in Croatia and Bosnia under Ante Pavelić sets out to exterminate the Serbs. Two resistance movements are formed. One, led by Colonel (later General) Draža Mihailović and other Serb officers and soldiers of the Royal Army called Četniks, and the second communists led by Josip Broz Tito, called the Partisans. Between 1941 and 1945 Yugoslavia is the scene of three armed conflicts: (1) Between the anti-Nazi resistance movements and the Axis occupiers and their allies; (2) between the Partisans and the Četniks; (3) among Serbs, Croats, and Muslim Slavs on both sides of the other two conflicts.
1945	At the end of World War II, Yugoslavia becomes a federated pro-Soviet communist republic under Tito.
1948	Tito breaks with the Soviet Union and institutes "national communism" in Yugoslavia.
1974	A new Yugoslav constitution grants autonomy to Kosovo, a Serbian province largely occupied by ethnic Muslim Albanians. Yugoslavia became a confederation with the central government retaining only limited powers.
1980	Death of Tito.
1987	Aided by Serbian President Ivan Stambolić, Milošević becomes leader of the Serbian Communist Party, then turns against Stambolić, denouncing his allies as being "soft" on Albanian nationalists in Kosovo.
1988	Slobodan Milošević, the president of the Serbian Communist Party and president of Serbia (after 1989) begins a campaign to reassert Serb and communist control over Yugoslavia.
1988	Mass pro-Serbian demonstrations orchestrated by Milošević in Vojvodina forces resignation of the Vojvodina provincial party presidium.
1989	Milošević ends Kosovo's autonomy.
1990	Disintegration of the Yugoslav Communist Party.
1991	Croatia, Slovenia, and Bosnia-Herzegovina declare independence, triggering ethnic fighting among Croats, Muslims, and Serbs.
1992	Serb forces massacre thousands of Bosnian Muslims and carry out "ethnic cleansing" by expelling Muslims from areas under Bosnian Serb control. Kosovo's Albanian majority votes to secede from Serbia. Serbia and Montenegro declare themselves the Federal Republic of Yugoslavia.
1995	Leaders of Bosnia, Croatia, and Serbia reach the Dayton Peace Accord to end the Bosnian War.
1997	Kosovo Liberation Army (KLA) begins killing Serb policemen and establishing areas from which the Serbs are driven entirely.
1998–99	Kosovo War between Serbia and NATO forces. Agreement to end NATO bombing of Serbia and withdrawal of Serb troops from Kosovo reached in June.
2000	Resignation of Milošević as Serbia's president.
2001	Trial of Milošević by the International Criminal Tribunal for the Former Yugoslavia (ICTY) in The Hague, the Netherlands, for alleged atrocities in Kosovo in 1999 and in Croatia between 1991 and 1992 and for genocide in Bosnia between 1992 and 1995 begins.
2006	Sudden death of Milošević in March before the conclusion of his trial.
2006	In June following a referendum, Montenegro declares its independence, bringing an end to the rump Yugoslav Federation.

including growing divorce of "nation" and "state" and the proliferation of nonstate identities have conspired to erode the capacity of most states, threatening their autonomy and their ability to satisfy citizens and thereby to retain legitimacy. This does *not* mean that a "global citizenship" or "a global identity" has emerged with a set of universal norms. Instead, in the words of one observer, "our psychic and even our material rewards seem to rest on fragmented and compounded self-identification."[45]

The Yugoslav case also is a reminder of the problem posed by human rights abuses. "Ethnic cleansing," for example, a euphemism for genocide, was first heard during the Bosnian conflict. In addition, the Kosovo conflict involved external intervention in the "domestic" affairs of a sovereign country in violation of traditional international law. However, as we shall see in the next chapter, traditional state sovereignty is gradually yielding to individual rights.

In sum, ethnic and tribal identities continue to have important consequences for global politics. The United States itself, once thought of as a "melting pot" in which different ethnic groups lost their older identities to become American, has become a country of numerous hyphenated Americans who are conscious of and take pride in their ethnic origins. The growing role of identities in global politics combined with the perceived erosion of states have produced the startling idea on the part of some observers that we may be entering an era of conflict among whole **civilizations**.

civilization the type of culture of a specific place, time, or group.

The collapse of Yugoslavia piqued an interest in clashing civilizations and the idea that Yugoslavia was at the "fault line" of three great civilizations – the Serb, the Croation, and the Bosnian Muslim. The Serbs, the largest single group in Yugoslavia, are a Slavic people, with close cultural ties to other Slavic peoples like the Russians. With the Slavs, the Serbs share a common religion,[46] Eastern Orthodoxy that evolved in Byzantium (Constantinople) after the split of Rome into Eastern and Western empires. The Serbs also share an alphabet with other Slavs, derived from Greek letters, known as Cyrillic that was developed in the ninth century for the use of Eastern Orthodox Slavs. The Cyrillic alphabet is also used in the Russian, Ukrainian, Belarusian, Macedonian, and Bulgarian languages.

By contrast, the Croatian people, though speaking a language virtually the same as Serbian, use the Latin alphabet, and most are Roman Catholics. Whereas Serbia historically enjoyed close ties with Russia, Croatia was part of the Catholic Austro-Hungarian Empire, and Croatians regard themselves as Western, rather than Eastern, European. Finally, Bosnia's Muslim population, though also Slavic, worships Allah and for centuries was governed by the Ottoman Turks. In short, Bosnia's Muslims are Slavs who converted to Islam in the fourteenth and fifteenth centuries after the Ottoman Empire conquered the region. Overall, however, Bosnia has a complex mix of religious traditions, which helps explain why it became a battleground in 1992. Of its 4.4 million people, 44 percent are Muslim, 31 percent are Eastern Orthodox, and 17 percent are Roman Catholics.[47]

The idea that the fault lines between clashing civilizations, such as those within the former Yugoslavia, might be "the battle lines of the future" has both passionate advocates and equally passionate detractors, and it forces us to think seriously about some of the identities we have been discussing to this point. In the following section, we examine the provocative claim that a looming clash of cultures will bring the world's great civilizations into conflict with one another.

The clash of civilizations?

In 1993, Harvard political scientist Samuel P. Huntington published an article in the journal *Foreign Affairs* entitled "The Clash of Civilizations?"[48] The article began with a provocative claim that the European epoch of global politics was coming to an end and, with it, interstate conflicts such as World Wars I and II and the Cold War. With the end of the Cold War, Huntington asserted, the world was changing. "World politics," he declared, "is entering a new phase" in which "the fundamental source of conflict" will "occur between nations and groups of different civilizations."

A civilization, Huntington argued, is "a cultural entity,"[49] and he proceeded to identify eight such civilizations – Western, Confucian, Japanese, Islamic, Hindu, Slavic-Orthodox, Latin American, and African. Civilizations differed in terms of "history, language, culture, tradition, and, *most important, religion*."[50] Each civilization, Huntington argued, had a core state – for example, India in Hindu civilization, Russia in Slavic-Orthodox, and China in Confucian – but nation-states were becoming less important sources of identity for people. The future, then, would be one of ever-widening collisions among groups and countries from different civilizations, such as the war in Chechnya that pit "Slavic-Orthodox" Russians against "Islamic" Chechens, or the "Hindu"–"Islamic" (India–Pakistan) clash over Kashmir. Empirical analysis to discover whether Huntington's different civilizations were "real" led political scientists Ronald Inglehart and Wayne E. Baker to the cautious conclusion that "societies with a common cultural heritage generally *do* fall into common clusters" but that their positions also reflect other facts like economic development.[51]

Osama bin Laden's declaration of war "between the Islamic world and the Americans and their allies" to combat a "new crusade led by America against the Islamic nations" seems to reflect Huntington's argument regarding the clash of civilizations.[52] The United States, bin Laden argued, had made "a clear declaration of war on God, his messenger, and Muslims," and he urged Muslims everywhere to take up arms against America.[53]

Civilizational conflicts, Huntington argued, would feature a "kin-country syndrome" in which members of a civilization would try to help others from the same civilization against their common foe. Thus, Muslim militants from many countries who joined the Afghan resistance to Soviet occupation after Moscow's 1979 invasion have reappeared in a variety of settings pitting Muslims against non-Muslims including Chechnya, Kosovo, and Iraq. In Iraq, for example, the militant Jordanian Abu Musab al-Zarqawi (1966–2006), deceased leader of the group Al Qaeda in Mesopotamia, frequently used non-Iraqi volunteers, "holy warriors" he called them, as suicide bombers against US forces and Shia civilians. "O Muslim youths . . . especially in neighboring countries and Yemen," Zarqawi declared, "jihad is your duty."[54] Most of these volunteers were non-Iraqi Arabs, many of whom came from Saudi Arabia; others came from Syria, Kuwait, Jordan, Lebanon, Libya, Algeria, Morocco, Yemen, and elsewhere, including Europe.[55]

To buttress his case Huntington pointed to a number of events in global politics in 1993 that reflected growing tensions between countries in different civilizations, assistance among people within the same civilization, or potential alliances between certain civilizations against others, especially the West. They included:[56]

- Fighting among Croats, Muslims, and Serbs in Bosnia, Western failure to help Bosnia's Muslims in an appreciable way, and Russia's support for Slavic Serbia in the Bosnian conflict.
- Muslim and Chinese rejection of the West's version of universal human rights, suggesting a Confucian–Islamic alliance against the West.
- The voting along civilization lines to hold the 2000 Olympics in Australia rather than China.
- China's sale of missile components to Pakistan; China's testing a nuclear weapon; and North Korea's effort to obtain nuclear weapons, suggesting a growing Confucian threat to the West.
- America's "dual containment" policy toward Iran and Iraq, and America's military preparations for two major regional conflicts against North Korea and Iran or Iraq.
- German limitations on admission of refugees.
- US bombing of Baghdad.

Huntington argued that the West's influence had begun to decline and that it increasingly had to face challenger civilizations that "have the desire, the will and the resources to shape the world in non-Western ways."[57] Asian civilizations were enlarging their economic, military, and political power, and Islamic countries had rapidly growing populations and an expansive religious ideology. Western primacy, Huntington feared, was threatened by the rapidly growing power of China and the possibility of an emerging "Confucian–Islamic military connection."[58] Under these conditions, global politics would become "the West versus the rest."

Despite the emphasis Huntington placed on the threat from China, the best remembered phrase from his article was his assertion that the "crescent-shaped Islamic bloc, from the bulge of Africa to central Asia, has bloody borders."[59] This phrase was widely recalled after the terrorist attacks of September 11, 2001 by Islamic terrorists. Observers invoked Huntington's clash-of-civilizations thesis as they asserted that the attacks marked the beginning of a war between the Western and Islamic worlds, not a conflict with a relatively small minority of militant and fanatic Muslim fundamentalists.

Huntington's concern that Muslim and Western values were in conflict seemed to be reinforced by the storm of anger that swept Muslim communities around the world after a Danish newspaper in September 2005 published 12 cartoons satirizing Muhammad and ridiculing the activities of Muslim militants. The cartoons were then reproduced in other newspapers across Europe.[60] Their publication aroused Muslims because Islam bans depictions of the Prophet and because many Muslims regarded the cartoons as highly provocative. By contrast, many Westerners regarded the issue as one of freedom of speech and thought that Muslim protests and intimidation threatened individual freedom and secular values. Twelve writers, most of whom were Muslims living in the West, declared that the furor showed that: "After overcoming fascism, Nazism, and Stalinism, the world now faces a new global totalitarian threat: Islamism."[61] The growing gap between Muslim and non-Muslim perceptions of the world were reflected in a recent poll in which majorities or near majorities of non-Muslims in the West viewed Muslims as "fanatical" and not respectful of women, while Muslims viewed Westerners as "immoral" and "selfish."[62]

More recently, Huntington produced heated reactions when he expressed concern at the large-scale immigration of Hispanics to the United States who, he argued, were not assimilating into American society. Americans, he argued, define their national identity and culture to include "the English language; Christianity; religious commitment; English concepts of the rule of law, including the responsibility of rulers and the rights of individuals; and dissenting Protestant values of individualism, the work ethic, and the belief that humans have the ability and the duty to create a heaven on earth, a 'city on a hill.'"[63] In his view, Hispanics, more than other minorities, were establishing insulated cultural islands in areas such as Southern California and South Florida, and the sheer number of Hispanics in the United States – up from almost 9 percent of the population in 1990 to 13.7 percent in 2003 or close to 40 million (not counting 3.9 million citizens of Puerto Rico), of whom as many as a quarter are illegal – threaten to undermine America's culture.

According to Huntington, the "Mexican/Hispanic Challenge" posed by Mexican immigration is unlike previous waves of immigration into the United States. Mexican immigrants, he argues, unlike their predecessors, do not assimilate. The result, he fears, will be "a culturally bifurcated Anglo-Hispanic society with two national languages."[64] A number of factors, he believes, make Mexican immigration to the United States unique, including the fact that Mexico is America's neighbor, thereby permitting continuous movement back and forth across the border, the high concentration of Mexicans in particular localities like Los Angeles, the high proportion who enter the United States illegally, the persistence of the immigration northward, and Mexico's historical claim to American territory. In addition, the Mexican government supports the flow northward as an economic and political safety valve, advocates an open border, and is prepared to let Mexicans living in the United States vote in Mexico's elections. Mexico even published a pamphlet entitled "Guide to the Mexican Migrant" that is filled with practical hints to help migrants enter the United States illegally and safely. The publication infuriated US opponents of illegal immigration.[65]

Huntington argues that factors limiting the assimilation of Mexican migrants are failure to learn English, poor education levels, low income, low naturalization and intermarriage rates, and, most importantly, failure to acquire American identity. The density of links across the US–Mexican border and the mixing of cultures has produced a unique region in southwestern US and northern Mexico "variously called 'MexAmerica,' 'Amexica,' and 'Mexifornia'" which, Huntington believes, "could produce a consolidation of the Mexican-dominant areas into an autonomous, culturally and linguistically distinct, economically self-reliant bloc within the United States."[66]

Huntington's analysis is an extension of his view that we are entering an era of clashing civilizations. He is a nationalist whose views are those of one who fears that relentless globalization will undermine existing national cultures and perhaps even national independence. To his critics, Huntington is a **xenophobe**, even a racist, whose belief that American

xenophobe one who fears or dislikes foreigners.

culture is rooted in Anglo-Protestant tradition is false and whose fears are overheated. To his supporters, he summarizes the resentment against a global tidal wave that threatens national identities, boundaries, and traditional values. Some of his critics contend that Hispanics do, in fact, assimilate in the same way that their predecessors did. Others argue that his version of American culture, while suitable for the Pilgrim Fathers, had already been made obsolete by previous generations of immigrants. Finally, many of his critics argue that Huntington simply does not understand how the United States has repeatedly integrated waves of immigrants into a culture that reflects them all.

Huntington's overall clash-of-civilizations thesis is flawed in a number of respects. First, the concept of the state is central to his framework; indeed one of his civilizations consists of a single country, Japan, and three others are virtually coterminous with a single state: Confucian and China, Hindu and India, and Slavic-Orthodox and Russia. Second, it remains unclear precisely what a civilization is. In some cases, the definition seems to rest on a common religion, whereas in others ethnicity or other factors play a major role. Third, even in recent years, major conflicts have arisen between countries from within the same civilizations that Huntington identifies, for example, the war between Islamic Iran and Iraq between 1980 and 1988. Fourth, each of the civilizations Huntington identifies has any number of internal fault lines. Muslims, for example, are engaged in conflict among themselves in a number of countries, such as Pakistan, Afghanistan, and Iraq. China and North Korea eye one another with suspicion, as do China and Vietnam. Moreover, strong alliances exist between countries from different civilizations, like that between the United States and Japan. Finally, to some extent, Western culture is less about religion and language and more about modernization, and modernization is spreading globally, toppling traditional institutions and ways of life that stand in its way. Nevertheless, Huntington's argument highlights the growing importance of identity in global politics and the growing resentment of non-Western societies toward cultural and economic globalization, which non-Westerners view as a kind of Western cultural and economic hegemony over them.

Civilizations have, of course, come in contact on many occasions in the past. As we saw in chapter 2, Christian–Islamic conflict dates back over a millennium. Other cultural collisions include the arrival of Europeans in the New World and their meeting with indigenous peoples ranging from the Aztecs in Mexico, the Incas in Peru, and the Native Americans in Virginia. Today, we still debate the meaning of these cultural encounters. For example, did Christopher Columbus's "discovery" of the New World mark the first step in Europe's "civilizing" mission? Was it the beginning of Europe's extermination of vibrant indigenous cultures? Or was it a morally neutral "clash" or "encounter" of "civilizations"?

Perhaps the most controversial of Huntington's claims about civilization is that when they come into contact, they "clash." In fact, encounters among those from different civilizations rarely result in conflict. Instead, they often bring cultural enrichment for the civilizations involved, especially for those who encounter a more advanced civilization, like the nomadic Mongols and Jurchens (Manchus) who conquered China in the thirteenth and seventeenth centuries.[67] Empirical analysis tends to refute Huntington's conclusion. For example, political scientists Bruce Russett, John Oneal, and Michaelene Cox argue that "traditional realist influences as contiguity, alliances, and relative power, and liberal influences of joint democracy and interdependence, provide a much better account of interstate conflict" and that pairs of countries "split across civilizational boundaries are no more likely to become engaged in disputes than are other states."[68] Even disputes between the West and the rest of the world, or with Islam, were no more common than those between or within most other groups.

In conclusion, according to data collected by the World Values Survey,[69] Huntington is correct in identifying a clash of civilizations but is wrong in concluding that the clash between the West and Islam concerns political values, particularly over the desirability of democracy. Democracy is, in fact, popular in both civilizations. "Instead," declare Inglehart and Pippa Norris, "the real fault line between the West and Islam, which Huntington's theory completely overlooks, concerns gender equality and sexual liberalization."[70]

Conclusion

In sum, identity is a critical factor in global politics. As constructivists suggest, the answer to the question "who are we?" informs us of our interests and shapes our political behavior. Historically, nationalism was the most important identity in global politics, but always had to share pride of place with other identities such as class and religion. Today, a host of identities based on religion, ethnicity, race, and gender, to name a few, challenge nationality; and, where there are conflicting identities as in contemporary Europe, the unity of states may be profoundly challenged by divided loyalties.

Identity groups that form the basis of "we"–"they" divisions may violently collide, as is the case in a host of wrenching ethnic, tribal, and national conflicts that have taken place mainly in the global South since the end of the Cold War, though also in Europe in the violent break-up of

Yugoslavia. Extreme cases may lead to "ethnic cleansing," even genocide. The declining capacity of states to control activities within their frontiers, partly a result of technological change and the willingness of unscrupulous leaders to manipulate identities for their own ends, complicates the problem of identity divisions. Identity groups such as Chechens and Kurds clamor for independence and pose mortal danger to the countries in which they reside. Even more pessimistic is the controversial claim that the world is entering a period of clashes among civilizations. Whether or not this is the case, there is a backlash among traditional cultures and their elites against the modernizing and secularizing consequences of globalization, the topic addressed in our final chapter.

Student activities

Discussion and essay questions

Comprehension questions

1 What is the importance of "identity" in global politics?
2 What is nationalism, and how does it develop?
3 What does the break-up of Yugoslavia tell you about the role of ethnicity in global politics?
4 What are the most important identities in today's global politics, and how do they challenge loyalty to the state?

Analysis questions

5 Describe your own identities and explain how they have an impact on your views of global politics.
6 Do you think that the West is engaged in a "clash of civilizations" with Islam? Why or why not? If you believe the West is in such a clash, how should it wage the conflict?
7 Is nationalism a positive or negative phenomenon? Explain your position.
8 Should religious fundamentalism be outlawed as a threat to political stability?

Map exercise

Using a blank world map, locate and label the eight civilizations that Samuel P. Huntington identifies in his article "The Clash of Civilizations?" Is each truly a distinct civilization?

Cultural materials

Few works of literature reveal the profound impact of identity better than the novel *Roots* by Alex Haley. The 1977 mini-series based on the novel was among the most widely viewed and celebrated television events of the decade. The plot was based on the author's family history. It tells of how Kunta Kinte was kidnapped from his village in Africa and sold into slavery in America. It also tells of his marriage and the birth of his daughter, Kizzy, who was sold to another plantation owner, where she had a son. Great events such as the American Revolutionary War and the Civil War form the backdrop before which the epic unfolds. Read the book and describe the key elements in Kunta Kinte's identity.

Further reading

Anderson, Benedict, *Imagined Communities: Reflections on the Origin and Spread of Nationalism* (London: Verso, 1983). Insightful analysis of nationalism as an imagined construction.

Christie, Kenneth, ed., *Ethnic Conflict, Tribal Politics: A Global Perspective* (Richmond, UK: Curzon Press, 1999). Collection of essays on ethnic conflicts around the world.

Esposito, John L., *Unholy War: Terror in the Name of Islam* (New York: Oxford University Press, 2003). Balanced, informed, and thoughtful analysis of militant Islam.

Gellner, Ernest, *Nationalism* (New York: NYU Press, 1998). Short and accessible analysis of how nationalism is linked to modernity.

Hobsbawm, E. J., *Nations and Nationalism Since 1780* (New York: Cambridge University Press, 1990). Insightful examination of the changing role of nations and nationalism in modern history.

Huntington, Samuel P., *The Clash of Civilizations and the Remaking of World Order* (New York: Simon & Schuster, 1998). Provocative argument that we should view the world as a set of seven or eight cultural "civilizations" in which conflict will pit civilizations against one another.

Huntington, Samuel P., *Who Are We? The Challenges to America's National Identity* (New York: Simon & Schuster, 2004). Provocative claim that Hispanics are diluting America's identity through a failure to assimilate.

Hutchinson, John and Anthony D. Smith, eds., *Nationalism* (New York: Oxford University Press, 1994). Superb collection of essays on all aspects of nationalism.

Mayall, James, *Nationalism and International Society* (Cambridge: Cambridge University Press, 1990). Wide-ranging analysis of different types of nationalism in different historical and political settings.

Moynihan, Daniel Patrick, *Pandaemonium: Ethnicity in International Politics* (New York: Oxford University Press, 1993). Passionate analysis of the destructive consequences of national and ethnic conflicts.

Part VI
And
Tomorrow?

16 Globalization

The new frontier

On the morning of November 30, 1999, 50,000 people packed downtown Seattle, as leaders of 135 governments gathered for the third Ministerial Meeting of the World Trade Organization (WTO). It was a diverse group, including environmentalists, proponents of social justice, students, teachers, and workers. All were there to protest the WTO's free trade policies. Some demanded fair trade that does not exploit the world's poorest populations or its nonrenewable environmental resources. Others protested the loss of American jobs that they attributed to free trade. Hoping to halt the meeting, some engaged in civil disobedience, trying to block delegates from reaching the convention center. A few smashed store windows and started fires. Officials ordered the streets cleared and established a no-protest zone in the downtown area. Thousands of riot police moved in with tear gas, rubber bullets, and concussion grenades. They were followed by the National Guard. Armored vehicles and police helicopters patrolled the city streets around the Seattle convention center. In the end, over 500 people were arrested, though most were soon released, and downtown Seattle sustained over $2.5 million in property damage. The WTO meeting lasted the week, but delegates left without reaching agreement. Many attributed this failure, in large part, to the anti-globalization protestors.[1]

Implicit throughout this text is a recognition that global politics is in the midst of a process called **globalization**, and so it is appropriate that, as we near its conclusion, we examine that process more fully. In what follows, we shall first define globalization and then observe its major features. You will see that globalization is a complex phenomenon with many dimensions. To illustrate this complexity, the chapter then examines several perspectives on globalization and the heated debate over whether or not globalization is a positive or negative phenomenon. Finally, we will recapitulate some of the key trends in today's global politics and evaluate several possible futures.

globalization those processes that knit people everywhere together, thereby producing worldwide interdependence and featuring the rapid and large-scale movement of persons, things, and ideas across sovereign borders.

What is globalization?

Globalization consists of those processes that knit people everywhere together, thereby producing worldwide interdependence and featuring the rapid and large-scale movement of persons, things, and ideas across sovereign borders. Political scientist David Held and his colleagues define it as "the widening, deepening and speeding up of worldwide interconnectedness in all aspects of contemporary social life, from the cultural to the criminal, the financial to the spiritual."[2] In a globalized world, contacts among people and their ideas are growing as a result of advances in communication, travel, and commerce that produce mutual awareness among individuals. Under these conditions, many observers believe, states enjoy less and less control of their destinies and are buffeted by forces outside their borders and beyond their control. We will briefly recapitulate some of globalization's key features: (1) the spread of global communication, (2) the growing competence of ordinary people and their participation in global politics, (3) the emergence of a global market, (4) the worldwide diffusion of a secular and consumerist culture, (5) the emergence of English as the language of globalization, (6) the widening demand for democratic institutions and norms, and (7) the networking of groups to form a nascent global civil society.

Features of globalization

The spread of communications technologies that shrink the role of geographic distance Globalization is built on the proliferation of powerful computers and microelectronic technologies that help individuals and groups to communicate virtually instantaneously by e-mail, cellular and satellite telephones, and fax machine and to move vast amounts of money and information via these technologies. It also involves the spread of satellite technology for television and radio, as well as the global marketing of films and television programs. Overall, these technological revolutions overcome physical distance in politics, economics, and war. Could Alexander Graham Bell (1847–1922), who invented the telephone, have imagined that some day people could acquire an MSAT Mobile System to allow them to make or receive calls and e-mail from vehicles, planes, or ships, or an Immarsat satellite service that provides telephone and fax access to over 98 percent of the world, including areas beyond the reach of any other communications?[3]

The spread of knowledge and skills and an explosion in political participation The spread of mass media and the communications and transportation revolutions enable ever more people, even in remote corners of the world, to be informed about the world around them, form opinions about events, and get involved in politics in ways that were unimaginable until now. Even the poorest peasant has access to radio broadcasts that provide information and that give both governments and anti-government groups new ways to cajole and persuade populations. Cable and satellite television provide exposure to a vast variety of opinion and information. And the Internet may become the most important tool of all in facilitating the exchange of views, the dissemination of information and propaganda, and the coordination of activities because it is relatively inexpensive and accessible. **Blogs** (short for weblogs) and bloggers are beginning to influence people around the world by transmitting information and opinion on the Internet.[4]

blog a personal online journal that is updated and intended for general public consumption.

The global triumph of capitalism and, as noted in chapter 11, the emergence of a global market that transcends state boundaries and limits states' control of their economies With the end of the Cold War, free-market capitalism as an economic ideology triumphed in much of the world, including China, Russia, and the less-developed regions. Its triumph has been accompanied by an expansion of TNCs, the rapid movement of investments, the shifting of jobs and industries "off shore," the proliferation of global networks of production and distribution, the emergence of "world cities" such as New York, Tokyo, Frankfurt, and Shanghai, and the emergence of an urbanized economic elite.

The spread of a global culture Globalization has been accompanied by the spread of culture, originally Western, featuring shared norms based on mass **consumerism**. Increasingly, societies are adopting the West's secular norms and are acting according to the norms of global capitalism. The homogenization of mass culture can be seen in everything from dress, diet, and education to advertising and the spreading belief in human rights. Globalization ranges from Big Macs and designer jeans to abhorrence of torture and racism. "McDonald's," writes political scientist Benjamin Barber, "serves 20 million customers around the world every day, drawing more customers daily than there are people in Greece, Ireland, and Switzerland together."[5] This process, however, undermines older local cultures and religious beliefs and has caused a backlash among some local political elites. "Modernization, economic development, urbanization, and globalization," argues Samuel Huntington, "have led people to rethink their identities and to redefine them in narrower, more intimate, communal terms."[6] The popularity of religious fundamentalism reflects this backlash.

consumerism a norm that values the acquisition of material goods.

The spread of English as a global language English links elites across the globe much as Latin and French did in earlier epochs and enjoys a special status in 75 countries. It is spoken as a native language by between

300- and 400-million people and as a second language by about 375 million more. Everywhere, the demand to learn English is intense because it is the language of commerce, science, and technology.[7] Although many more people are native speakers of Mandarin Chinese and Hindi, what makes English dominant is that it is spoken so widely compared to other languages – in 104 countries. "It's no longer just top execs who need to speak English," declares one commentary. "Everyone in the corporate food chain is feeling the pressure to learn a common tongue as companies globalize and democratize. These days in formerly national companies such as Renault and BMW, managers, engineers, even leading blue-collar workers are constantly calling and e-mailing colleagues and customers in Europe, the United States, and Japan."[8]

The spread of democracy Globalization has been accompanied by the spread of democratic norms from the core areas of North America, Western Europe, and Japan to Latin America, Asia, the countries of the former Soviet bloc, and even to Africa. Although it is premature to declare the global triumph of **liberal democracy**, as did political scientist Francis Fukuyama when he wrote of an "end to history" in 1989,[9] globalization is witnessing a growing acceptance of individual rights, including that of choosing one's own leaders. Democracy remains fragile at best in some regions, non-existent in others, and is violently contested by those whose authority would vanish in the face of free elections. Thus, the terrorist Abu Musab al-Zarqawi, who was killed in 2006, denounced Iraq's 2005 elections by announcing: "We have declared an all-out war on this evil principle of democracy and those who follow this wrong ideology."[10]

The spread of global civil society As described in chapter 9, the proliferation of NGOs has led some to suggest that a global civil society is beginning to coalesce. Such a society, according to its advocates, "champions the political vision of a world founded on nonviolent, legally sanctioned power-sharing arrangements among many different and interconnected forms of socio-economic life that are distinct from governmental institutions."[11] Although these organizations and movements have different aims, many collaborate in confronting global challenges. Today, there exist global networks of individuals and NGOs – made possible by the communications revolution – concerned with many issues such as human rights, women's rights, and the environment, and leaders in some countries like Russia fear the democratizing effects of these networks and have taken steps to suppress them.

liberal democracy a political system in which the authority of elected representatives to make decisions is governed by the rule of law under a constitution that protects individual and minority rights.

Figure 16.1 Islamic terrorist Abu Musab al-Zarqawi

© PA Photos

Competing perspectives on globalization

Held and his colleagues identify three distinct perspectives toward globalization that they label *hyperglobalist*, *skeptical*, and *transformationalist*.

Hyperglobalists, who consist of both neoliberals and Marxists, focus on the economic dimension of globalization. They believe that changes in the global economy are ushering in "a new epoch of human history"[12] in which territorial states have become obsolete economic units. Globalization, in their view, has produced a single global market in

Table 16.1 Conceptualizing globalization: three tendencies

	Hyperglobalization	*Skeptics*	*Transformationalists*
What's new	A global age	Trading blocs, weaker geogovernance than in earlier periods	Historically unprecedented levels of global interconnectedness
Dominant features	Global capitalism, global governance, global civil society	World less interdependent than in the 1890s	"Thick" (intensive and extensive) globalization
Power of national governments	Declining or eroding	Reinforced or enhanced	Reconstituted, restructured
Driving force of globalization	Capitalism and technology	States and markets	Combined forces of modernity
Pattern of stratification	Erosion of old hierarchies	Increased marginalization of South	New architecture of world order
Dominant motif	McDonald's, Madonna, etc.	National interest	Transformation of political community
Conceptualization of globalization	As a reordering of the framework of human action	As internationalization and regionalization	As the reordering of interregional relations and action at a distance
Historical trajectory	Global civilization	Regional blocs/clash of civilizations	Indeterminate: global integration and fragmentation
Summary argument	The end of the nation-state	Internationalization depends on state acquiescence and support	Globalization transforming state power and world politics

which transnational corporations (TNCs) from many countries vigorously compete with one another. "Hyperglobalizers," they write, "argue that economic globalization is bringing about a 'denationalization' of economies through the establishment of transnational networks of production, trade, and finance," "a 'borderless' economy" in which "national governments are relegated to little more than transmission belts for global capital."[13] Neoliberal hyperglobalizers applaud the growth in overall wealth and minimize the fact of growing inequality within and between states, whereas Marxist hyperglobalizers focus on the growth of inequality.

Skeptics[14] argue that contemporary globalization is not really new or revolutionary. Interdependence, in their view, is no higher today than it was in the late nineteenth century. Like hyperglobalizers, skeptics focus on the economic dimension of globalization, arguing that it features high levels of interstate trade and the expansion of regional common markets such as the European Union (EU) and the North American Free Trade Agreement (NAFTA) that, they claim, actually reduce global economic integration. In their view, however, states retain a dominant role in these activities, including an ability to regulate and even unravel economic processes. The power of governments, in other words, has not ebbed; state sovereignty has not eroded; and transnational corporations, they contend, remain under national control and retain national attitudes. States, especially the United States, are responsible for higher levels of economic intercourse and the existence of global institutions like the World Trade Organization.

Transformationalists, according to Held, are convinced that "globalization is a central driving force behind the rapid social, political and economic changes that are reshaping modern societies and world order."[15] In this sense, globalization has no historical parallel. According to transformationalists, one consequence of growing interconnectedness is a merging of the foreign and domestic policy arenas. In addition, microelectronic technologies like the Web are erasing physical distance and reducing the traditional role of territory as **cyberspace** becomes more important, especially in the economic realm. Thus, Held *et al.* describe "the growing deterritorialization of economic activity as production and finance increasingly acquire a global and transnational dimension."[16] In addition, states are weakening as they are pulled in different directions in a process that political scientist James N. Rosenau labels "fragmegration" (a combination of integration and fragmentation) that involves the simultaneous impact of globalization and localization.[17] According to transformationalists, international, subnational, and transnational groups are growing more important as state power wanes. And, with the

cyberspace the electronic medium of computer networks in which online communication takes place.

declining capacity of sovereign states and the reduced importance of territory, the role of identity based on features such as religion and ethnicity has grown in global politics. The differences between the three perspectives on globalization are summarized in Table 16.1.

As you can see, globalization has produced considerable disagreement. The following section examines additional sources of disagreement, notably whether globalization can be reversed and whether it is a positive or negative development in global politics.

The globalization debate

Globalization is controversial in several ways. One unresolved question concerns whether the process is inexorable or whether it can be reversed. A second question that is heatedly debated is whether the process is, on balance, beneficial or harmful. As you have read, some fear that an emerging global identity will inundate local and national identities and customs and erode state sovereignty. However, as we shall see, globalization has "losers" as well as "winners," and individuals everywhere are increasingly discovering that their welfare is determined by remote forces beyond their control and beyond the control of their governments, including governments that were democratically elected.

It is difficult to say whether the movement toward globalization is irreversible. The process owes much to American hegemony following World War II and, even more, since the end of the Cold War. It also flows from the desire of US leaders to encourage and sustain an open trading system, global economic growth, and the spread of American values such as individualism, democracy, free enterprise, and open borders. Some argue that globalization could not survive if the United States and major countries such as Japan, Germany, France, and Great Britain no longer supported it. They believe that if today's major powers became disillusioned with globalization, their withdrawal could bring about the collapse of key public and private institutions that sustain it. Others argue that the process is so far along that it can no longer be reversed, that it is no longer controlled by any country or countries, and that the costs for a country to cut the web of interdependence in which it is enmeshed are too high to consider.

Certainly, recent years have been testing ones from the point of view of globalization. For example, a number of events have challenged the globalization process, including the collapse of WTO negotiations (chapter 13, pp. 610–13); the proliferation of US–European trade disputes; the rejection of the EU constitution by French and Dutch voters; America's unilateralist foreign policies, including its refusal to join the

International Criminal Court or accept the Kyoto Protocol on global warming; the growing complaints about the outsourcing of jobs from the developed to the less developed world and resulting unemployment in the developed world; and growing resistance in the developed world to the flow of migrants and asylum seekers from poor countries. Probably the most important threats to globalization were the 9/11 terrorist attacks and America's subsequent "War on Terror." These events, which were followed by growing impediments to the free movement of persons, ideas, and things, suggested that state frontiers were again of critical importance and that the world was breaking up into hostile "tribes" and cultures rather than uniting within a single, homogenized culture of modernity based on Western democracy, **secularism**, and consumerism.

secularism the attitude that religious considerations should be excluded from public affairs.

However, there is little evidence that these challenges have curbed globalization. In fact, the year 2002 did not show any marked reduction in globalization. How do we know this? A measure developed jointly by A. T. Kearney, Inc. and the Carnegie Endowment for International Peace scores countries in four categories, each of which consists of several factors that reflect the degree to which countries and their societies are embedded in the global system and interact with one another. These categories and the factors that constitute them are as follows:[18]

- Economic integration
  - trade
  - portfolio capital flows (investment in foreign securities)
  - foreign direct investment that a country receives
  - investment income from all sources
- Personal contact
  - international travel and tourism
  - international telephone traffic
  - remittances and personal transfers (including remittances, compensation to employees, and other person-to-person and nongovernmental transfers from overseas)
- Technology
  - Internet users
  - Internet hosts
  - secure servers
- Political engagement
  - memberships in international organizations
  - personnel and financial contributions to UN Security Council missions
  - international treaties ratified
  - amount of governmental transfer payments and receipts to and from overseas.

Of the 62 countries that were ranked, the ten most globalized were mainly small, highly developed democratic countries: (1) Singapore, (2) Switzerland, (3) United States, (4) Ireland, (5) Denmark, (6) Canada, (7) the Netherlands, (8) Australia, (9) Austria, and (10) Sweden. By contrast, the least globalized – (62) Iran, (61) India, (60) Indonesia, (59) Venezuela, (58) Bangladesh, (57) Turkey, (56) Pakistan, (55) Egypt, (54) Colombia, and (53) Kenya – were large, for the most part relatively poor, and, with some exceptions, subject to authoritarian governments.[19] In addition, a country's overall rank may hide the fact that it scores well on one or another measure but not on others. The United States, for example, ranks first in regard to technology but is far lower in terms of economic integration and personal contact. Singapore ranked first in economic integration but is lower in terms of political engagement.[20]

Globalization, then, continues to flourish, though it has passionate detractors as well as supporters. Let us look first at the thinking of those who oppose it.

The anti-globalizers

Globalization incites passionate critics and diverse groups, including some violent extremists, have demonstrated against its principles and process at, for example, the 1999 Seattle WTO Ministerial Conference, the 2001 G8 meeting in Genoa, and the 2001 and 2003 EU summits in Gothenburg, Sweden, and Athens, Greece. Using cell phones, encrypted Internet messages, and e-mail to mobilize, the groups represented at these demonstrations included union members from the American Federation of Labour and Congress of Industrial Organizations (AFL-CIO); animal-rights defenders from People for Ethical Treatment of Animals; environmental activists from Rainforest Action Network, Earth First!, and the Sierra Club; and human-rights activists from Global Exchange and Direct Action Network. Militant demonstrators have used vinegar-soaked rags to counteract tear gas, and chicken wire, PVC pipe, and linked arms to barricade streets, as well as ball bearings and marbles to hamper police horses.[21] Finally, some extremists have used more violent tactics such as South Korean farmers who rioted in Hong Kong in December 2005 and claim to have lost farmland to expanding corporations, and anarchists who have assaulted police officers and committed vandalism at WTO meetings in Seattle, Geneva, Hong Kong, and elsewhere.

Despite the diversity of opinion, many of those opposed to globalization accord their highest loyalties to the sovereign state, which they believe exists to protect their interests. In particular, anti-globalizers argue that in democratic states, such as those in Europe and North America, the people have a voice in determining their own fates. By contrast, citizens have little or no voice in the boardrooms of giant transnational corporations, remote international bureaucracies like the EU or the WTO, or economic markets, and such institutions are not accountable to citizens. Thus, the anti-globalizers argue, globalization has created a democratic deficit by empowering institutions in which people have no voice and unleashing economic and cultural forces over which people have no control. Globalization, they say, is gradually eroding the rights and capacity of people to determine their own future. The result is growing alienation and anxiety, as people's lives are buffeted by remote forces beyond their control or understanding.

Anti-globalizers ask hard questions about an era in which the rigors of the global marketplace force countries and industries to shed jobs, reduce welfare and health programs, and become more efficient to survive in the cut-throat world of global capitalism. If states lose authority, who will assume responsibility for the general welfare, and who will uphold citizens' rights? Who will tend to their economic needs, and who will deliver justice? Who will see to the national interest? "No one," answer the anti-globalizers; certainly not the emerging global elite of corporate executives and shareholders who are the main beneficiaries of globalization. Overall, then, according to this view, globalization reduces the rights and responsibilities of citizenship, ranging from state contributions to public welfare to democratic participation.

According to the anti-globalizers, the operations of giant multinational conglomerates and financial institutions undermine national economic and social policies and, consequently, constitute a form of structural violence against the poor (see chapter 12, p. 580). Moreover, the movement of investment capital to countries with low environmental and labor standards threatens reductions in living, working, and environmental standards achieved over years of struggle. In the globalized world, argue the anti-globalizers, oligarchic corporations and banks scour the world for cheap labor, moving jobs from country to country, forcing workers into sweatshop conditions, using child labor, and destroying the environment in an effort to remain competitive and increase profits. In short, anti-globalizers sometimes refer to the search for cheap labor, minimal protection for workers, and minimal environmental standards to maximize global competitiveness as "the race to the bottom."

International institutions like the IMF and the WTO, the argument continues, serve corporate interests, force countries to adopt policies that are not in citizens' interests, and place harsh conditions on loans against which populations can only feebly protest. In sum, globalization threatens a reduction in the rights and responsibilities of citizenship, in the state's capacity to ensure public welfare, and in the possibilities for serious democratic participation.

In addition to eroding the democratic rights and liberties of citizens, some anti-globalizers denounce the way in which the global economy and global culture have homogenized distinctive local tastes, traditions, and even languages. Ancient cultures are giving way before the onslaught of a superficial "Coca-Cola/McDonald's/Levi's Jeans" culture. Traditional values, argue anti-globalizers, are eroded, by made-in-the-US television programs, movies, radio, and pop music. In turn, this consumerist culture promotes individualism, narcissism, and greed; spreads pornographic and violent images; and eats away at moral standards and religious beliefs. Thus, ethnic, national, and religious groups bridle at the threat they perceive to their uniqueness, dignity, and values. Then, this perception may fuel a backlash against globalization and the United States, which is seen as its leading advocate. Furthermore, the argument

"Sorry lads. I'm closing this workshop down, and relocating in the far east."

Figure 16.2 A Christmas gift!

© Original artist,
www.cartoonstock.com

goes, nation-states provided a measure of physical and psychological security to citizens, a clear identity and a sense of belonging to something larger than themselves. As culture is homogenized in the process of globalization, it leaves a psychological void that had formerly been filled by other identities – religious and tribal, for example.

Other baneful consequences of globalization, according to its opponents, are that it prompts massive migrations of people, who leave in search of jobs or to flee violence. In turn, these mass migrations disrupt communities, create cultural ghettos, and foster transnational criminal industries in drug smuggling and human trafficking, as desperate people seek work, and women become trapped in domestic or sexual slavery. In addition, the acclaimed technologies of globalization such as the Internet facilitate **money laundering** and financial speculation, and they aid political fanatics and terrorists.

money laundering disguising criminal profits to prevent their detection by law enforcement agencies.

The pro-globalizers

Turning to the pro-globalizers, one is struck by the fact that they seem to be looking at a totally different world than globalization's opponents. Pro-globalizers' view of states, for example, is profoundly negative. For them, these territorial leviathans were created to wage wars that benefit rulers but not citizens. Despite the spread of popular sovereignty, decisions about war and peace and the distribution of wealth, they believe, remain largely in the hands of ruling elites who cultivate and manipulate nationalism, patriotism, and imperialism to rally the masses and to paper over domestic woes.

Pro-globalizers claim that nationalism in particular, far from being a virtue, has erected barriers between peoples, stymied efforts to deal with global problems, produced ever larger and bloodier wars, climaxing in World Wars I and II, the use of nuclear weapons against Japan, and vast expenditures on arms in the Cold War. Finally, argue the pro-globalizers, after a century of slaughter and potential nuclear annihilation, processes are at work that are eroding the state, dissolving the barriers of nationalism, and making people more prosperous and interdependent. As a result, the number of wars between states is declining, and the human rights abuses committed by governments are losing the protection of state sovereignty.

Although states continue to exist, the forces of globalization are replacing the ideologies that divided the world in the twentieth century with a single ideology based on liberal democracy. And the spread of liberal democracy will assure the "democratic peace." As publics come to recognize that states cannot deal with collective dilemmas like environmental degradation, they are placing their faith in NGOs and international institutions that can coordinate their activities and enhance cooperation globally, thereby enabling the world to cope with global challenges. Thus, in recent decades, international law has expanded to protect people rather than states (chapter 9) and the number of actors has proliferated (chapters 9 and 11) ranging from corporations and NGO networks to international organizations that oppose war, enhance global prosperity, and confront collective dilemmas.

Although globalization has widened the gap between rich and poor, the pro-globalizers assert, it has reduced overall poverty and stimulated rapid economic growth in formerly impoverished regions such as Southeast Asia, China, and India. A global market with ever fewer barriers to trade provides consumers an unprecedented choice of increasingly inexpensive goods. Overall, then, globalization has been accompanied by sustained growth and has brought countless workers around the world new jobs and higher living standards. Growing world trade benefits everyone, and vast increases in foreign investment are increasing incomes in *both* rich and poor countries. Losers are associated with obsolete or uncompetitive enterprises, but without losers, there could be no winners. And, despite growing inequality, the economic pie as a whole is growing, and global poverty is declining.

The pro-globalizers dismiss opponents as an odd mixture of old Marxists who still hope to destroy capitalism; militant anarchists like the members of the Black Bloc,[22] a collection of anarchist groups that cooperate in protests and that are responsible for much of the violence at anti-globalization demonstrations; animal-rights activists and environmentalists who value snail darters more than jobs; labor unionists trying to keep alive industries that should peacefully die; and xenophobic nationalists whose opposition to globalization is based on sentiment rather than facts or logic.

In addition, according to globalization's proponents, the threat of cultural homogenization is vastly overstated, and local cultures can thrive alongside the global culture of modernity. "[C]ontrary to the warnings of those who fear globalization," argues Latin American novelist Mario Vargas Llosa,

> it is not easy to completely erase cultures – however small they may be – if behind them is a rich tradition and people who practice them, even in secret. And, today, thanks to the weakening of the nation-state, we are seeing forgotten, marginalized, and silenced local cultures reemerging and displaying dynamic signs of life in the great concert of this globalized planet.[23]

More important, perhaps, the defense of local cultures often means the defense of reprehensible practices and conditions that *should* disappear, such as genital mutilation of women in Africa, the Muslim practice of polygamy, or the Indian caste system.

Pro-globalizers similarly reject criticism of modern technology such as the Internet, arguing that anti-globalizers reject modernity and ignore the key role these new technologies play in expanding the global economy and the participation of vast numbers of people who formerly were excluded from politics. More information creates an informed citizenry, makes it harder for politicians to mislead citizens, enhances democracy, facilitates the networking of NGOs for civil society, and enables the mobilization of people for political ends. And, although a **digital divide** still exists between rich and poor, the new communications and transportation technologies are already speeding up economic development in the LDCs.

Finally, concern that globalization erodes democracy is exaggerated. Historically, few states were democratic, and most states today are either authoritarian or very imperfect democracies at best. In much of the developing world, particular ethnic, racial, religious, or regional groups control governments at the expense of other groups. If anything, the enormous information accessible to more and more people and their growing ability to mobilize in cyberspace contribute to the diversity of views and enhance the quality of democracy.

digital divide the gap between those who have access to new information and communication technologies like the Internet, and those who do not have such access.

The state in decline?

How has the nation-state changed, and why have other political associations assumed greater significance in global politics? The field of international relations, at least in the West, emerged as a state-centric discipline, and some scholars have been reluctant to admit that the state may not be the only game in town because, without it, the unique element of *international* or *interstate* politics seems to disappear. Until recently, international relations scholars viewed states and their relations as all that mattered. Realists, in particular, still conceive of sovereign states as unitary actors pursuing their national interests in an anarchic world dominated by the security dilemma. The dominance of realism, especially among American scholars, kept the focus on unitary states competing for power and the only (unlikely) alternatives to unitary states that most students were offered were world government or world empire.

Political scientists are not alone. Social scientists more generally are still deeply influenced by a vision of the world as it existed about a century ago, a world in which states dominated war-making, economic policy-making, and even cultural and social policy. Historians also have tended to organize scholarship around interstate relations. Thus, historian William H. McNeill insists that: "So far, no promising alternative to the territorial organization of armed force has even begun to emerge."[24] Economists, too, developed their discipline with a focus on states as complete economic units, writing about "the American economy" or "China's economic system." Yet today's trade is largely among transnational corporations (TNCs) or the subsidiaries of such corporations, and national economic units are no longer compatible with markets in a globalized world. At present, the resources controlled by large TNCs and banks, and of certain super-rich individuals, dwarf the resources of the governments of most states, and the wealth of large TNCs like Microsoft (as measured by sales or stock value) exceeds the gross domestic product of most sovereign states. Indeed, most states are losing or have lost control over their own economies. Thus, even major countries like Russia and Argentina, buffeted by private market forces, have found themselves in a condition of economic and political near-collapse that makes a mockery of their sovereign status. Nevertheless, to a large extent, the discipline of economics still thinks of global economics as a world of trading nations that has changed little since Adam Smith.

Although state sovereignty, as we shall see in the next section, was never absolute and has been routinely violated for centuries, it should assure a state's right to exist and its freedom from external intervention. In fact, it often does not do so, and today it provides fewer and fewer privileges to states than it did in the past.

The limits of sovereignty

Many international relations scholars still regard state sovereignty as the basis of their field. Much of Western political philosophy focused on the state itself and its relationship to citizens, and the field of international relations was a logical extension that dealt with the relations among states. In reality, from the outset sovereignty has always been more of an aspiration than a reality. For many rulers, sovereignty was a useful legal device that, as argued by realist Stephen Krasner, "was used to legitimate the right of the sovereign to collect taxes, and thereby strengthen the position of the state, and to deny such rights to the church, and thereby weaken the position of the papacy."[25]

Sovereignty is treated as a given by realists, the organizing principle of global politics that gives rise to anarchy. Liberals regard sovereignty as something to be overcome in the effort to achieve desirable goals such as safeguarding human rights, intervening in despotic states to spread democracy and end violence, spreading free trade, and enforcing global rules to end undesirable national environmental and labor practices. For constructivists, sovereignty is an institution that was invented by European political leaders as the necessary prerequisite for creating the territorial state and that today serves as the chief norm that provides legitimacy for states. Sovereignty is as Tim Dunne observes, "the founding moment of politics" that "represents the fault-line between community and anarchy."[26]

Today, sovereignty tells us little about real states. The world's nearly 200 states includes one superpower and a host of "mini-states," including tiny islands of the Caribbean and South Pacific that are scarcely viable. Some 87 states have fewer than five million inhabitants, 58 have less than 2.5 million, and 35 fewer than 500,000. Consider the sovereign state of Tuvalu – a group of Pacific reef islands and atolls, with a population of 10,000, and an area of 9.5 square miles. In 2000 Tuvalu sold the rights to the web domain ".tv" for $50 million in royalties for the next 12 years in a deal worth more than half its annual gross domestic product (earned from subsistence agriculture and fishing). By contrast, California with over 31 million inhabitants and the world's fifth largest economy is not sovereign and, despite having a budget deficit in 2003 that is greater than the deficits of all other US states combined (excluding New York's), is not entitled to aid from the International Monetary Fund or the World Bank.

Did you know?

Tuvalu will probably be the first sovereign state to be destroyed by the consequences of global warming. Rising sea levels have caused coastal erosion and the contamination of the island's drinking water by salt, and New Zealand has agreed to allow all of Tuvalu's residents to resettle there. Should this occur, Tuvalu could become the first virtual nation – its sovereignty would remain intact under international law, but it would only continue to exist in the Internet domain ".tv."[27]

Or, consider the dramatic contrast between the prosperous and well-ordered city-state of Singapore and the state-like remains of Sierra Leone, which features more than a dozen hostile ethnic groups, and has been victimized by repeated coups, brigands, and "sobels" ("soldier by day, rebel by night"), along with the misnamed Revolutionary United Front that engaged in looting, diamond smuggling, and the terrorizing of citizens by amputation of limbs. In countries like Sierra Leone, the idea of sovereignty is turned on its head; instead of providing citizens with security from foreign aggression by guarding the country's borders, the army *is the source of insecurity* for citizens who are desperate to flee the army by crossing those very borders. Private mercenaries are frequently employed to substitute for a national army or to protect a government from its own army.

Often, sovereignty, which provides *legal* independence, is confused with genuine authority and autonomy. Sovereignty *asserts* that outsiders *should not* intervene in a state's internal affairs and that citizens *should* respect its legitimacy and obey its laws, but there is no guarantee that they will follow these norms. All in all, in recent decades sovereign independence has offered only modest protection against military predation and boundary changes. In some cases, this amounts to what political scientist Robert Jackson calls "negative sovereignty," that is, little more than protection for corrupt regimes in what he calls "quasi-states."[28]

Nevertheless, realists and neorealists argue that little has changed and that state sovereignty remains almost as important today as it was during the previous three centuries. Krasner identifies four aspects of state sovereignty: *domestic sovereignty*, *interdependence sovereignty*, *international legal sovereignty*, and *Westphalian sovereignty*.[29] Domestic sovereignty refers to the exercise of authority within a state; interdependence sovereignty involves control of movements across state boundaries; international legal sovereignty refers to a state's recognition by other states as their legal equal; and Westphalian sovereignty denotes the exclusion of unwanted external interference within a state. Of these four dimension, Krasner argues, only the second, interdependence sovereignty, has significantly eroded. All four dimensions have been violated from time to time in the past and remain largely intact today.

Notwithstanding sovereignty, states have, in fact, rarely enjoyed anything like complete control over subjects or their resources. Sovereignty has never prevented states from intervening in one another's affairs. Neither France's King Louis XIV nor Napoléon Bonaparte respected neighbors' sovereign boundaries. In fact, the only European country that did not have its boundaries altered after the 1648 Peace of Westphalia was Portugal. Indeed, states' use of violence in relations with one another has been the main subject of founding documents for the League of Nations and the United Nations, as well as both customary and positive laws of warfare like the Kellogg-Briand Pact (1928) that outlawed war. As we have seen, in regulating state violence, a distinction is made between aggression and self-defense. Article 51 of the UN Charter recognizes the inherent right to individual or collective self-defense *only* in the event of armed attack and then *only* until the UN has taken "appropriate action." And, countries routinely defend even acts of flagrant aggression as "self-defense."

The limits of sovereignty in providing protection from external interference even in earlier centuries was reflected by the popularity of balance of power which, in effect, substituted power for sovereignty in providing such protection. Balance-of-power rhetoric expressed the obligations that states were believed to owe one another when sovereignty alone provided inadequate protection. The Prussian civil servant Friedrich von Gentz (1764–1832) spoke of balance of power as "that constitution subsisting among neighboring states more or less connected with one another,"[30] and Jean-Jacques Rousseau saw the balance as the result of Europeans' "identity of religion, of moral standard, of international law."[31]

The sovereign state: sharing center stage

Although sovereignty never provided states with the protection it promised, recent decades have witnessed a growing gap between the capacity of states to manage violence at home and act independently in global politics – the promise of sovereignty and the reality of global politics. In many states, citizens flout the authority of their governments and actively participate in global politics *directly* through groups ranging from terrorist bands, giant corporations, and humanitarian organizations to street mobs and protest groups. Such activity is a far cry from the idea that citizens only participate in global politics *indirectly* by lobbying their governments and voting. "Today," argues British political scientist Susan Strange, "it is much more doubtful that the state – or at least the majority of states – can still claim a degree of loyalty from the citizen greater than the loyalty given to family, to the firm, to the political party or even in some cases to the local football team."[32]

With few exceptions, today's states are less autonomous and less able to protect or inspire citizens than at any time in recent centuries. The erosion of state institutions and frontiers is least evident in the richer and older states, especially in Europe, East Asia, and North America. By contrast, the capacity of states in postcolonial countries of the developing world to protect citizens and provide for their well-being has declined precipitously.

In Africa, the existence of governments that are extensions of tribal or clan power, along with the failure of authorities to cope with explosive socioeconomic problems of poverty, population density, disease, and environmental catastrophe, weakens loyalties to the state, while intensifying older tribal loyalties that colonial and postcolonial leaders had sought to dampen. A number of African countries like the Ivory Coast currently express their sovereignty chiefly through the diplomatic protocols of the United Nations. Rwanda and Burundi exist largely in atlases; in reality, the organizing labels are tribal: Hutu and Tutsi, Bakongo and Ovimbundu, and so forth. The Liberian state is dead; the country is little more than an arena for conflict among the Krahn, Mende, and Gbandi tribal groups. Some states, like Sierra Leone and Somalia, have been sustained (barely) by humanitarian organizations and international institutions.

Nevertheless, the sovereign state is *not* vanishing, and the habit of patriotism is slow to die in many countries. But patriotism should not be confused with faith in government or politicians and, except for the burden of paying national taxes (if one does not evade them), patriotism tends to be a cheap sentiment, limited to flag waving and road signs demanding that we "support our troops."

One response to claims of state erosion might be that citizens are prepared to die for their country but not for international or nongovernmental organizations. Yet, it is hard to imagine citizens of modern states lining up as they did between 1914 and 1918 to join armies in battles that will cost thousands of lives. In fact, readiness to die for a cause is found more frequently among ethnic or religious minorities than among the ordinary citizens in an average state.

State erosion is not universally recognized in part because of three paradoxes that Susan Strange describes.[33] The first is that, while overall state power and capacity have declined, some governments retain a key role in public education, policing, and health and welfare. Moreover, the intervention of government agencies in certain aspects of citizens' lives has continued to increase. Government regulations create affirmative action quotas, establish high-occupancy traffic lanes, force automobile passengers to wear seat belts, and so on. Nevertheless, states are unable to protect citizens from globalization shocks, environmental catastrophes, energy shortages, and economic cycles; and ordinary citizens today are becoming harder to persuade and satisfy.

Strange's second paradox is that, notwithstanding the state's "retreat," there is a growing "queue" of groups that want to have their own state. Die-hard realists like to seize on this apparent paradox to insist that, appearances to the contrary, nothing has really changed – the state is doing fine, thank you, since everyone seems to want one. However, the major reason more states exist today than during the Cold War is that some states such as the Soviet Union, Czechoslovakia, and Yugoslavia have disintegrated and have spawned weak successors such as Bosnia or Georgia.

The third paradox that Strange cites is the apparent success of the Asian state model as reflected in strong states like Japan and South Korea. The success of these states is due largely to special conditions that are ending and will not be repeated, mainly post-World War II and Cold War development aid and technology from the United States. Economically, these states thrived because a strategic alliance existed between governments and private corporations and banks and because the West permitted them to pursue protectionist economic policies that shielded them from the worst effects of globalization. However, Asian governments now face greater pressures to adopt non-discriminatory trade and investment policies that may threaten their economic and political stability. Even China, where the communist regime succeeded in maintaining a strong central state partly by allowing the private sector and prosperous coastal regions great autonomy, is likely to face crisis in the near future. There, it remains to be seen whether strong central control can survive privatization of state-owned enterprises and resulting unemployment, the growing pluralization of society that is accompanying market reforms, and the growing economic inequality between prosperous urban centers like Shanghai and impoverished rural regions.

Yet, the erosion of state capacity does *not* necessarily portend great disorder and violence in the future (though in some countries those are serious possibilities). New sources of authority and new forms of cooperation and global management are evolving that, at least in part, foster order in global politics. As argued by neoliberals, these new institutional forms are displacing states in some respects even while assisting states to carry out their responsibilities.

In sum, globalization is revolutionizing international relations. It will certainly have its ups and downs in the coming years, but it is unlikely to be reversed barring a major global war or other catastrophe. In the next and final section of this book, we will recapitulate some of the key trends in today's global politics and ponder several alternative futures that may await us.

A future dimly seen

By now, it is evident that global politics features both change and continuity. One of the great changes of a globalizing world is the spread of Internet technology and, in consequence, the linking of peoples around the world. However, as we turn our attention to the future of global politics, it is helpful to recall predictions that have been made in the past.

- "I think there is a world market for maybe five computers." – Thomas Watson, chairman of IBM, 1943.

- "The idea that cavalry will be replaced by these iron coaches is absurd. It is little short of treasonous." – Aide-de-camp to Field Marshal Douglas Haig, at tank demonstration, 1916
- "We will bury you." – Soviet Premier Nikita S. Khrushchev, 1958
- "There is not the slightest indication that nuclear energy will ever be obtainable. It would mean that the atom would have to be shattered at will." – Albert Einstein, 1932
- "No matter what happens, the US Navy is not going to be caught napping." – US Secretary of the Navy Frank Knox, December 4, 1941
- "It will be years – not in my time – before a woman will become Prime Minister." – Margaret Thatcher, 1974
- "With over 50 foreign cars already on sale here, the Japanese auto industry isn't likely to carve out a big slice of the US market." – *Business Week*, August 2, 1968
- "Stocks have reached what looks like a permanently high plateau." – Irving Fisher, Professor of Economics, Yale University, 1929
- "The bomb will never go off. I speak as an expert in explosives." – Admiral William Leahy, US Atomic Bomb Project, 1944
- "Airplanes are interesting toys but of no military value." – French Field Marshal Ferdinand Foch, 1912.

Can we see the future any better today? In what follows, we will address two central questions in global politics: What key trends are likely to have a significant impact on the future of global politics, and what alternative futures lie before us? Is globalization inevitable and desirable? Unfortunately, such questions defy clear answers for two reasons. The first is that an observer's view of change depends on how it affects her interests. Thus, we have seen how the world's poor are prepared to endure greater environmental pollution in favor of rapid economic growth and how traditional religious and cultural leaders react passionately against globalizing trends that undermine their authority. The second is that we do not know which trends will be dominant. For example, will population rates continue to decline? Will we run out of oil before other energy sources become widely available? Will globalization cease and be reversed, or is globalization irreversible? Hence, several futures are possible, some of which we may prefer to others. And, as the predictions above suggest, even the best informed observers often get it wrong.

Throughout this book, we have seen how contemporary global politics combines both the old and the new, and the result is a complex world that challenges our capacity to make sense of what is happening around us. At any moment, we cannot be certain whether change or continuity will dominate. Realists tell us that little has changed over the millennia and that military threats continue to overshadow all other problems. Since, in their view, we can do little to improve our condition, we must remain vigilant and prudent, always trying to contain threats to our survival and security. Liberals, by contrast, see ceaseless change all around us. Democracy is on the march, they say, and with its triumph, war will end. Globalization, too, some believe, is unstoppable and promises to end poverty and ignorance. In contrast, constructivists see change as possible, though not necessary, depending on the evolution of norms and beliefs. However, to the constructivist, change is not unidirectional. Despite liberal optimism, the constructivist says, history suggests that change is as likely to reproduce past conditions as it is to introduce genuinely novel circumstances. Thus, interest may grow in new concepts such as human security, global civic society, and human rights at the expense of state sovereignty. Nevertheless, despite the brief interlude since the end of the Cold War, we may soon return to security-business-as-usual, meaning an intense and dangerous rivalry among major states.

Controversy

Liberals and neoliberals believe that globalization is inevitable, involving a fundamental transformation of global politics away from state control and toward market control of global economic life, due in part to technological change. Others, especially realists and neorealists argue that globalization is the consequence of power arrangements, political and ideological preferences, and policy choices and that it is reversible if those arrangements, preferences, and choices are altered, just as global interdependence before 1914 ended in World War I and free trade ceased in the Great Depression. Globalization, they believe, will persist only so long as major states find it in their interest to promote the free movement of persons, things, and ideas across borders and to maintain the liberal economic system that has prevailed since World War II.

Although we can identify certain key trends in global politics, the future remains contingent. Trends can accelerate, slow down, or even be reversed. The future is not determined. Thus, we should remain skeptical when told that such-and-such an event "made war (or anything else) inevitable." Leaders' choices and the actions of individuals, while conditioned by factors beyond their control, do matter. Thus, in October 1962 American President John F. Kennedy (1917–63) or Soviet leader Nikita S. Khrushchev (1894–1971) *might* well have made a fatal misstep in the midst of the Cuban missile crisis, and this misstep could have sparked a nuclear exchange between the United States and the USSR. Historians would, then, not have been able to claim, as they often do today, that the superpowers avoided hot war during the Cold War because both possessed nuclear weapons.

Let us now recapitulate some of the major trends in global politics that we have identified in this book

Key trends

One way of trying to think about the future of global politics is to identify important trends. We must keep in mind that these are *only* trends, and they may not persist indefinitely. However, they provide helpful clues about the world we will have to confront tomorrow and the threats to our welfare and survival. A number of trends that we have discussed in this and earlier chapters merit special attention.

1 *Intensified globalization* The growing movement of persons, things, and ideas is likely to continue and intensify despite the opposition of diverse groups who fear the process. Although individual countries may be able to opt out of globalization, the economic costs to do so will be high. As a result, some problems associated with globalization – for example, the rapid spread of disease and economic crises, transnational crime, higher energy costs, a deteriorating environment, and migration from poor to wealthy societies – are likely to become more pressing. Whether or not these problems will defy collective attempts to find solutions remains to be seen. Recent history involving issues like global warming does not provide grounds for optimism.

2 *Spread of free market capitalism* The global triumph of free-market capitalism is partly responsible for driving and sustaining economic globalization. Although most countries – rich and poor – have come to applaud free trade and investment, this enthusiasm is unlikely to continue if global prosperity diminishes. Support for the global economic system by developing societies depends in part on the system's ability to reduce the gaps between rich and poor and bring ever larger numbers of people out of poverty.

3 *Diffusion of global power* With the end of the Cold War, many observers concluded that the world had entered a period of unipolarity, with the United States as undisputed top dog. Today, the United States remains the world's leading military power. However, its military superiority, especially in high-tech weapons, is no guarantee that it can realize its objectives, as demonstrated in the limited success of American efforts to spread democracy, win the war in Iraq, and prevent proliferation of weapons of mass destruction. The United States also remains the world's leading economic power, but its superiority in this realm is eroding as other centers of economic power, especially the European Union, Japan, India, and China, prove

able competitors in global trade and as American dependence on foreign energy remains high. Although the West will remain significant, China and the Islamic Middle East will increasingly become focuses of world attention.

4 *Environmental degradation* Depletion of fossil fuels, fish, fresh water, and arable land continues. Human wealth and welfare are challenged by global warming, deforestation, desertification, the loss of biodiversity, and other negative environmental trends. To date, global responses have been spotty, and vested economic interests have resisted concerted global responses. It is difficult for people to focus on these trends because many of them pose long-term rather than imminent hazards. However, as such threats pose greater economic burdens, markets may begin to facilitate investments in solutions such as wind and solar energy. In addition, science may provide partial answers to some of these problems. Finally, concerned individuals have mobilized their skills and influence transnationally to find answers, formed national and transnational NGOs, and created global networks to lobby and work for cooperative responses to environmental challenges.

Did you know?

The spread of deserts owing to human activities directly affects the lives of more than 250 million people and one third of the earth's surface. Between 1997 and 2020, some 60 million people are expected to move from desertified regions in sub-Saharan Africa to northern Africa and Europe.[34]

5 *Widening democracy and mass participation* Although globalization may weaken conventional forms of democracy, the desire of people to control their destinies is likely to intensify. As people acquire access to more information than ever before by means of technologies ranging from the Internet to satellite television, they are likely to act in ways that defend their interests and improve their well-being. Thus, political participation will continue to grow and manifest itself in a variety of unconventional ways ranging from street demonstrations and formation of new political groups to political agitation and even terrorism.

6 *Declining importance of territory* Some territories will remain important, especially if they are sources of critical raw materials like oil, but on the whole, geography is growing less relevant. Distance no longer

poses a significant obstacle to many important global economic, political, and military activities. Vast amounts of money can be moved around the world almost instantaneously, 24 hours a day, by electronic means. Individuals can conduct business globally from their own homes and can send ideas and information back and forth by e-mail and mobile telephone regardless of distance. People living thousands of miles apart can be mobilized in cyberspace for political ends. Intercontinental missiles can deliver nuclear warheads in minutes, and terrorists can move across national borders with relative ease.

7 *Erosion of state autonomy* The sovereign boundaries of states are becoming more porous every day. Even a powerful country like the United States is virtually helpless in the face of streams of migrants moving northward from Mexico or in slowing down the veritable flood of drugs coming to American cities and towns from around the world. Moreover, the existence of global communications technologies makes it virtually impossible to prevent subversive ideas and ideologies from crossing a state's boundaries. Nor can countries control their own economy or protect themselves from the vagaries of global markets. Finally, the probability that a number of countries will collapse in the face of mounting economic, environmental, and political pressures from within and without means that there will be new failed states.

8 *From conventional to irregular warfare* Although interstate warfare between uniformed and organized armies will continue to erupt from time to time, a combination of factors will minimize its occurrence. These factors include the declining importance of territory described above and the growing difficulty in occupying territory, the role of economic interdependence, the proliferation of weapons of mass destruction, and the spread of civil war. Thus, the difference between legitimate war and crime will grow increasingly blurred, and violence among groups competing for power over the carcasses of failed or failing states or over sources of wealth like diamonds, oil, and cocaine will increase. Terrorism, a weapon of the weak, will persist, as dissatisfied individuals and fanatical non-territorial groups seek vengeance for real or imagined wrongs, endeavor to prevent the erosion of local cultures and traditional beliefs via globalization, or try to spread messianic **ideologies**.

ideology a doctrinaire system of ideas that guides behavior.

9 *Proliferation of weapons of mass destruction* One major challenge of the near future involves the continuing spread of weapons of mass destruction (WMD). American anti-proliferation policy is in tatters. Moreover, the use of force against countries such as Serbia and Iraq may actually provoke other countries to acquire WMD to deter the

United States. North Korea has acquired nuclear weapons, and Iran is nearing that goal as well. And as these countries acquire WMD, those who fear them, for example, South Korea and Japan, may be tempted to acquire their own. Although deterrence threats may prevent countries from using WMD, they are unlikely to stop terrorist groups.

10 *Intensification of religious, ethnic, and civilizational identities* The weakening of territorial states, the growing separation of nationalism from citizenship, the degree to which new technologies have made it easier for ideas to be communicated and people mobilized at vast distances, and the dehumanizing and homogenizing impact of the global economy and culture suggest the continuing importance of traditional identities associated with religion, ethnicity, and civilization. Groups based on these identities are likely to proliferate and to lead a backlash against globalization. As a result, ethnic, tribal, and religious groups will increasingly demand self-determination, and their aspiration for autonomy within existing states or for secession from existing states will threaten the integrity of heterogeneous societies such as Nigeria, Russia, Indonesia, and Pakistan. Chinese and Muslim civilizations will increasingly compete with Western culture.

11 *Proliferation of IGOs and NGOs and formation of global civil society* The proliferation of intergovernmental organizations (IGOs) and nongovernmental organizations (NGOs) continues. The UN remains the most important international organization. Its future is cloudy, however, as it enters a period of reform, and it especially needs to win the support of Americans who are unconvinced that it serves their interests. For their part, the growing number of NGOs in fields as disparate as human rights, the environment, and women's rights may give rise to a global civic society of individuals and groups committed to finding cooperative solutions to collective dilemmas. These NGOs are sources of activism and expertise and are increasingly welcomed by countries seeking to manage change in nonviolent ways.

12 *Spreading acceptance of human rights* Human rights norms, like democratic norms, have spread globally. However, human rights abuses including genocide and ethnic cleansing by governments and other groups remain widespread as well. Nevertheless, despite setbacks in countries like Russia and Uzbekistan and the continued reluctance of countries like China to accept human rights, human rights norms are deepening and will continue to elicit widespread support, especially as more people become prosperous and as states and international organizations adopt new human rights conventions

and set legal precedents that, as constructivists claim, will gradually earn broad acceptance.

13 *Changing definition of security* A host of global problems, including poverty, environmental deterioration, drugs, famine, crime, and disease, imperil human survival and well-being. As awareness of these problems has grown, so has the recognition that security encompasses more than guarding against military threats. Recognition of these additional threats to human security is likely to widen in coming decades as more information becomes available to more people, as networks of IGOs and NGOs continue to form, and as potential solutions emerge to problems that for most of history have been regarded as insoluble.

14 *The privatization of public functions* Many functions once performed by states are increasingly outsourced to private actors and firms. Although states have long relied on mercenaries to fight their wars, in contemporary conflicts such as those in Iraq and Afghanistan, for example, they now turn to private military firms (PMFs) to provide logistical support, training, security, and intelligence. At home, they are slashing expensive social-welfare programs and selling off inefficient state-owned companies and are sending their citizens to the marketplace to find new suppliers for healthcare, pensions, and utilities. Privatization of costly state functions is likely to continue as free-market capitalism spreads and globalization intensifies.

Alternative futures

Given the trends outlined above, some of which seem contradictory, what does the future portend? Four possibilities suggest themselves, depending on which trends prove more potent. Three of these possible worlds assume weaker territorial states; the fourth allows for the reinvigoration of states. The first involves the triumph of globalization and the dominance of economic forces and economic logic. The second involves a restructuring of the global system to provide a greater role for NGOs and IGOs. The third envisions a world of escalating chaos brought on by the collapse of existing state and interstate institutions and the incapacity of the present system to manage widespread violence. The fourth possibility allows for the return to a realist world of states. *In actuality, the world will probably feature elements of some or all of these patterns, with different regions reflecting more of one or another of them.*

A globalized world

In the first scenario, major global outcomes are the result of market forces that governments may try to soften but cannot resist. States remain, but they have been thoroughly penetrated by global economic forces over which they have little control. In this world, governments have grown less significant than the global market. Thus, the global market, along with giant transnational corporations, distributes and redistributes global resources and determines the well-being of individuals everywhere, sometimes for better and sometimes for worse.

This is the world foreseen and avidly desired by liberals of the late nineteenth and early twentieth centuries and, more recently, political scientist Richard Rosecrance. In this world, economic interdependence has produced peace and prosperity. Thus, Rosecrance confidently asserts that, "despite retrogressions that capture our attention, the world is making steady progress toward peace and economic security" and "as factors of labor, capital, and information triumph over the old factor of land, nations no longer need and in time will not covet additional territory."[35]

The world envisioned by Rosecrance has "virtual" rather than power-maximizing states. Virtual states, built on information processing and service production, have little in common with the territorial leviathans celebrated by realists. In addition, Rosecrance argues, a global division of labor exists "between 'head' countries like Singapore" that specialize in "research and development, product design, financing, marketing, transport, insurance, and legal services,"[36] and "'body' nations like China that manufacture physical products."[37] Head and body states, therefore, enjoy a symbiotic relationship, helping to create a secure world based on open trade, uninterrupted production, and instantaneous communication.

In this world, sectarian identities based on tribe, ethnicity, religion, and nationality have softened. What it "means" to be American, Canadian, French, or Chinese becomes less important than the opportunities an individual is entitled to. The role of the state in this world (aided by the market) is to establish and protect these opportunities, as well as to maintain majoritarian democracy and minority rights. In a globalized world such as this, sovereign states will evolve in a direction akin to that followed by the states within the United States: giving up their once-important local authority and identity and, due to increased economic integration and mobility across state lines, eventually taking on more mundane tasks such as fostering education and citizens' welfare.

Governments in this world are mainly democracies whose ability to manage external violence lies in (1) the Kantian hope that all states can be simultaneously restructured along liberal lines and (2) the research noted earlier that suggests that democracies do not fight one another (chapter 8, p. 350). In sum, the liberal solution is, at best, a very long-term one and makes the dubious assumption that individuals will abandon subnational and transnational identities in favor of democratic citizenship. The model also makes the unlikely assumption that the liberal state can or will accommodate identity groups despite their irreconcilable differences regarding the values that underlie resource allocation.

This, then, is a world that rejects violence as destructive to economic well-being. In other words, war is viewed as a waste of resources that disrupts markets. The growing importance of knowledge industries, Rosecrance believes, makes war obsolete because of the decreasing importance of territory.[38] "The rise of the virtual state," he concludes, "inaugurates a new epoch of peaceful competition among nations."[39] Where the threat of violence remains high, for example in Palestine, the causes can be traced to the fact that societies have failed to satisfy the requirements of the liberal model, notably providing equal life chances for all.

How likely is such a benign future? The European Union suggests that such a world is possible, and communications and transportation technologies make it feasible. However, although some countries in the developing world are being integrated into the global market, the growing gap between rich and poor countries, the proliferation of failed states, and the spreading impact of ethnic intolerance and religious fundamentalism suggest that, at best, such a world would be limited to the developed world. Furthermore, the survival of that world would depend on its ability to ward off threats from outside like transnational terrorism and its capacity to assimilate the ever growing number of migrants from poor countries and persuade them to accept the values of their new countries. This is, in sum, the world foreseen by Robert Wright who argues that "globalization makes relations among nations more and more non-zero-sum" in a process that is moving so rapidly that "we're going to reach a system of institutionalized cooperation among nations that is so thorough it qualifies as world governance."[40] This argument, then, overlaps with a second possible future that features a growing role for international institutions.

A world of liberal institutions

A second possibility, also desired and predicted by many liberals, is a world in which international organizations like the UN, the EU, the IMF, and NATO, aided by a variety of nongovernmental organizations and wealthy states, actively intervene to restore peace or provide for the welfare of citizens living in states that have failed or are in imminent danger of doing so. States play a more significant role in this model than in the first, but the impetus for restructuring global politics arises from the interstate system, from the norms and institutions of interstate and transnational collaboration that have been evolving much as constructivists predict.

This is a world in which sovereignty has come to mean less and less and no longer poses a serious obstacle to humanitarian intervention or regime change. In this scenario – reminiscent of the League of Nations Mandate system and its successor, the UN Trusteeship system – international organizations, along with regional regimes or even former colonial powers try to restore order, promote reconciliation in post-conflict environments, and reconstruct state institutions in failed states. International and NGO efforts to help East Timor prepare for self-rule (see chapter 7, p. 325) illustrate how humanitarian intervention works.

In a world dominated by liberal institutions, intervention like that in East Timor is legitimated by norms compelling states to cooperate with

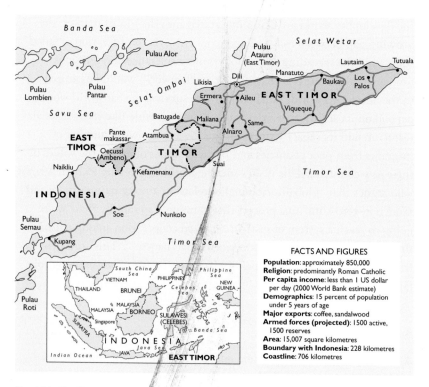

FACTS AND FIGURES

Population: approximately 850,000
Religion: predominantly Roman Catholic
Per capita income: less than 1 US dollar per day (2000 World Bank estimate)
Demographics: 15 percent of population under 5 years of age
Major exports: coffee, sandalwood
Armed forces (projected): 1500 active, 1500 reserves
Area: 15,007 square kilometres
Boundary with Indonesia: 228 kilometres
Coastline: 706 kilometres

Map 16.1   East Timor

IGOs, construct democratic institutions, protect minority and human rights, and take responsibility for those unable to help themselves. However, because sovereignty still legally forbids interference in domestic politics, the norms regarding global responses to civil strife still remain much less developed than those pertaining to interstate war. However, beginning with UN and NATO intervention in Yugoslavia in the 1990s (chapter 9, pp. 423–4), norms and precedents have begun to evolve that may in this hypothetical future world be translated into practical guidelines for actions by outsiders in civil wars.

How likely is this scenario? First, the absence of institutional authority and enforcement capacity would make it difficult to realize this model. More serious obstacles, however, are the absence of political will among major states to allow international institutions to manage the use of force during transnational or civil strife. To date, human rights norms and the laws of war have not been consistently enforced. As a result, international responses to tragedies like the 1994 Rwanda genocide or the 2004–07 Darfur genocide in Sudan have been woefully inadequate. Indeed, to date, humanitarian intervention has been haphazard, depending on the attitude of major powers like the United States (which opposed declaring Rwanda the victim of Hutu genocide against Tutsis) and China (which opposed

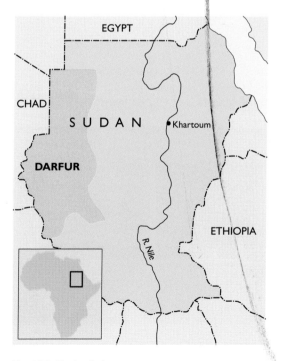

Map 16.2 Darfur, Sudan

large-scale intervention in Darfur, Sudan, where Muslim Arab militias have carried out genocidal attacks against Muslim Africans).

In a world dominated by liberal institutions, nongovernmental organizations would play a major role in managing violence and relieving human suffering. Already a variety of NGOs like Oxfam and CARE provide humanitarian relief and protection for civilian victims of global violence. In one proposal, the UN Trusteeship Council would be reformed as a Forum for Indigenous Peoples. In this forum nongovernmental representatives of indigenous peoples could discuss their status and seek redress for their grievances against states without violence. Proposals such as this aim to increase NGO participation as a way to prevent conflict or reduce its consequences. NGOs might also utilize strategies of conflict management and resolution, which are being developed in academic settings such as the Carter Center, established in 1982 by former President Jimmy Carter at Emory University in Atlanta, Georgia. According to the Center, its staff "wage peace, fight disease, and build hope by both engaging with those at the highest levels of government and working side by side with poor and often forgotten people." It cites as its accomplishments strengthening democracies in Asia, Latin America, and Africa; helping farmers increase grain production in 15 African countries;

Figure 16.3 The Carter Presidential Center in Atlanta, Georgia

Courtesy of the Jimmy Carter Library

working to prevent civil and international conflicts; and intervention to prevent unnecessary diseases, such as Guinea worm disease, in Latin America and Africa.[41] Thus, a liberal world such as this would feature democratic institutions, international and nongovernmental organizations dedicated to improving human welfare and assuring human security, and a widespread sense that the important human community is humanity as a whole.

A world in chaos

The first two prospective futures owe much to liberal and constructivist optimism. The third, however, is of a very different stripe, an apocalyptic vision of a world run amok. This is a world described in sensational fashion by the journalist Robert Kaplan as dominated by "poverty, the collapse of cities, porous borders, cultural and racial strife, growing economic disparities, weakening nation states," a world of "disease pandemics like AIDS, environmental catastrophes, organized crime."[42] "I believe," argues Kaplan, "that, for a number of reasons, we're going to see the weakening, dilution, and perhaps even crackup of larger, more complex, modern societies in the next 10 or 15 years in such places as Nigeria, Ivory Coast and Pakistan"[43] and that a combination of political upheavals, demographic factors, resource scarcity, and climate change will produce global chaos.

In this world of failed states and failed institutions, political authority has broken down, and local militias, criminal gangs, and religious fanatics and terrorists roam freely. It is a world of terrorists with nuclear weapons in suitcases, snipers on street corners, bioterror outbreaks, and resource scarcity. This despairing vision owes much to events like the apocalyptic terror attacks of Al Qaeda, waves of suicide bombers in Israel and Iraq, the Washington DC Beltway sniper, the Bali nightclub bombing, and the acquisition of weapons of mass destruction by rogue states and possibly even terrorist groups. Kaplan summarizes his fears in a non-territorial "last map" drawn from travel amid the ruins of "failed states" and "postmodern wars."

> Imagine cartography in three dimensions, as if in a hologram. In this hologram would be the overlapping sediments of various group identities such as those of language and economic class, atop the two-dimensional color distinctions among city-states and the remaining nations, themselves confused in places by shadows overhead, indicating the power of drug cartels, mafias, and private security agencies that guard the wealthy in failing states and hunt

down terrorists. Instead of borders, there would be moving "centers" of power, as in the Middle Ages. . . . To this protean cartographic hologram one must add other factors, such as growing populations, refugee migrations, soil and water scarcities and . . . vectors of disease. . . . On this map, the rules by which diplomats and other policymaking élites have ordered the world these past few hundred years will apply less and less.[44]

Should a genuine and widespread political smash-up occur, it might usher in an extended period of almost unimaginable chaos and would drastically raise popular anxiety and encourage authoritarian solutions that seem to offer some form of protection. This, of course, is the path that publics in Germany, Italy, and Japan chose to follow after the Great Depression in their "escape from freedom."[45] It is the path that produced fascism, Nazism, and militarism. More recently, it is the path followed by Chile, Uruguay, and Argentina in the 1970s, where military dictatorships took power as fear of leftist terrorism spread among the country's middle classes.

How likely is this world? The kind of chaos described in this model is likely to afflict parts of the developing world where a toxic combination of poverty, population growth, ecological disaster, and corruption foster state failure. However, it will be possible, though difficult, to limit the spread of disorder and turmoil, preventing it from infecting more developed regions. Contemporary Russia illustrates how creeping authoritarianism can take place as a way of trying to prevent disorder. Other countries are likely to emulate this "solution," possibly even Iraq as civil war engulfs the country, and this brings us to a fourth possible future.

A realist world

A fourth possibility, then, is a revival of the state system resulting either from the breakdown of global authority as depicted above or a new era of old tensions among major powers such the United States, China, and Russia. Such tension could arise from a variety of sources. One would be the proliferation of nuclear weapons in countries like North Korea and Iran, followed by an arms race involving additional countries like Turkey and Japan that felt threatened. Another would be the continued expansion of Chinese military capabilities, and the concern that expansion may produce in China's neighbors and in the United States (see chapter 5, p. 205). Regional conflicts that are most likely to bring about a renewal of tensions include those between India and Pakistan over Kashmir; China, the United States, and Japan over Taiwan; and Israel and Iran over

Palestine. Or Lebanon. Were a new era of old tensions to begin, it would strengthen the governments of some states vis-à-vis their own peoples, again highlight military preparation and alliances, and encourage us to dust off all the old realist and neorealist literature.

The world would most likely retreat to a realist path, however, if other major states increasingly view US policies as dangerous. Recent years have witnessed a variety of American actions that other countries regard as superpower unilateralism and even disregard for the sovereign rights of other states. This propensity became stronger after the terrorist attacks on New York and Washington on September 11, 2001. The most important of these unilateral actions was America's 2003 invasion of Iraq in defiance of a majority of UN members, including Russia and NATO allies France and Germany. Other widely criticized American foreign policy actions include its 2001 decision to withdraw from the 1972 Antiballistic Missile (ABM) Treaty and its planned deployment of a "light" ABM system, ostensibly to guard the United States from a nuclear attack by a rogue state. Still others include US refusal to ratify the Kyoto Protocol on global warming, its continued criticism of the UN, its unwillingness to join the International Criminal Court or the ban on landmines, and its refusal to ratify the Comprehensive Test Ban Treaty.

Theory in the real world

Shortly before the Bush administration took office in 2001, Condoleezza Rice, who was to become the president's National Security Advisor and, later, Secretary of State, outlined the administration's foreign policy. She argued for a policy based on realism and the pursuit of **national interest** over the pursuit of values. For this reason, she argued, relations with "the big powers, particularly Russia and China" would occupy most of the administration's time and energy, and a special effort would be made "to renew strong and intimate relationships with allies." She also noted that US military forces were "certainly not designed to build a civilian society."[46] Events in the real world, notably the terrorist attacks on New York's World Trade Center and the Pentagon in Washington, DC, dramatically altered this realist agenda. The priorities outlined by Rice were largely abandoned in favor of America's War on Terrorism. Instead of renewing "strong and intimate relationships with allies," the United States found itself in a bitter quarrel with France and Germany over America's 2003 intervention in Iraq, where American soldiers remained "to build a civilian society" after the removal of Saddam Hussein.

American leaders have justified all these unilateral actions on the basis of their reluctance to consent to any arrangement they believe could undermine American sovereignty and freedom of action. However, this assertion of realist principles might produce a realist reaction in the form of efforts to balance American power. American military power is so great

Figure 16.4 Condoleezza Rice

Courtesy of the US State
Department

that it is difficult to imagine any effective countervailing alliance or any
country with the resources to match American military strength.
Nevertheless, global nervousness about American unilateralism is
widespread. One result has been closer Chinese–Russian relations and
their joint efforts to dissuade the United States from deploying an ABM
system. Another was the combined diplomatic effort of Germany, France,
and Russia to prevent the United States and Britain from attacking
Iraq in 2003.

> **Did you know?**
>
> By mid-November 2006, American intervention in Iraq ("Operation Enduring
> Freedom") had lasted over three years resulting in 2,863 US fatalities and 125
> British deaths and 21,572 additional wounded, with most casualties occurring
> after the fall of Baghdad.[47]

How likely is this world? As long as states remain central players in
global politics and as long as globalization does not rob them of their
autonomy and independence, many governments and leaders will view
events through the prism of the national interest, especially as long as
territorial issues like those that divide India and Pakistan and Israel and
Palestinians persist. An even more dangerous source of realist behavior
would be a serious challenge to US hegemony in global politics posed
by an ambitious, rising state like China. Such an event would challenge
the global status quo and would probably trigger an American effort
to increase its power or even a war between the United States and its
challenger. According to what is called power transition theory, a
condition of rough military equality between hegemon and challenger
is likely to produce such a war.

Although the changing nature of security, deepening interdependence,
and resulting shared fates all induce leaders to think beyond the national
interest, defined narrowly, there is no certainty that they will do so. After
all, governments of states are responsible to their own citizens, and the
actions of those citizens, either at the ballot box or in the streets, are more
likely to determine whether leaders remain in office than the actions
of those outside the country. If that begins to change, the prospects for
a realist future will diminish. Which of these possible futures is most
likely? Evidence already exists for all of them, and they by no means
exhaust all possibilities. Furthermore, no one vision is necessarily
incompatible with any other. Thus, the state of current relations among

Europe, the United States, Japan, Canada, and other highly developed countries resemble the globalized world depicted in the first model. By contrast, much of Africa resembles Robert Kaplan's chaotic world. And certainly the realist world vision appears in a variety of relationships, including those between India and Pakistan and between the United States and China.

Conclusion: an uncertain future

The transformation of global politics and changing patterns of authority, identities, and resource distribution in *any* era are likely to be accompanied by anxiety and instability. Whatever the precise form it assumes, tomorrow's world is likely to be more complex and probably more unpredictable than today's. All of this leads Kaplan to conclude that *"We are not in control.* As societies grow more populous and complex, the idea that a global elite like the UN can engineer reality from above is just as absurd as the idea that political 'scientists' can reduce any of this to a science."[48] *Complexity produces misunderstanding; misunderstanding creates unpredictability; unpredictability breeds instability; and instability threatens conflict.*

Global politics is a system of organized complexity in which the fate of millions of people often depends on decisions of relatively few fallible leaders. History with its record of wars and mistaken decisions suggests how dangerous it is to place our faith in leaders whose understanding of their own behavior and of the consequences of that behavior is imperfect. As political scientist Karl Deutsch once observed: "If one looks over the major decisions about initiating war . . . the probability of a major decision being realistic may well have been less than one-half, on the average. That is to say, *if in the last half-century statesmen made major decisions on matters of war and peace, the chances were better than even that the particular decision would be wrong."*[49]

Yet what choice do we have? "There remains," as sociologist Peter Berger argues, "something in all of us of the childish belief that there is a world of grownups *who know."* As a result, it "is very shocking then to suspect that the knowers do not exist at all. Everyone is groping around in the dark, just as we are."[50] Thus, if we let others tell us what we ought to believe and allow them to formulate our ideas, we may find ourselves like passengers in a defective airplane, unable to bail out, even though a safe landing is highly improbable. Despite the dramatic changes in global politics in recent decades described in this book, decisions in global politics are made in much the same way as they were 50 or 100 years ago. The governments of major states acting in what they call the national interest make decisions on our behalf. At the same time, the changes that generate the need for decisions are outpacing leaders' capacity to anticipate them. In addition, the rapidity of change, especially in technology, gives them less time to prepare for its consequences, even while interdependence makes it inevitable that the results of mistakes will affect more and more people.

Towards the end of *The Prince*, Machiavelli exclaims that "fortune is the ruler of half our actions," like an "impetuous river that, when turbulent, inundates the plains, casts down trees and buildings, removes earth from this side and places it on the other; everyone flees before it, and everything yields to its fury without being able to oppose it." Our task is, in Machiavelli's words, to "make provisions against it by dikes and banks, so that when it rises it will either go into a canal or its rush will not be so wild and dangerous."[51] By now, you are in a position as future citizens and leaders to understand the complexities of global politics and to help "make provisions" against "fortune."

Student activities

Discussion and essay questions

Comprehension questions

1 What are the key differences among the four possible futures outlined in this chapter?
2 What are the key features of globalization, and how are they related?
3 What issues reflect globalization and what challenges do they pose for the global community?
4 Describe the key features of five important trends in global politics.
5 Have any of the major trends in global politics identified in this chapter had an impact on you personally? Which? How have they affected you?

Analysis questions

6 What do you regard as the most dangerous trend in global politics? Explain how you reached this conclusion.
7 Which of the alternative futures do you regard as most likely? Why?
8 Identify elements from all four futures that can be found in contemporary global politics.
9 Can you think of any ways of measuring the extent of globalizing? Which are most useful and why?
10 Is globalization desirable or not? Can it be stopped? If so, how?

Map exercise

Using a blank map, identify places and regions that exhibit the following features from the four futures described in this chapter:

1   Use lines to connect the world's leading trading partners (Model 1).
2   Place an "X" in countries in which major UN operations are taking place (Model 2).
3   Color red those countries that are currently in the midst of major civil wars (Model 3).
4   Draw arrows connecting countries that have major war-threatening disputes (Model 4).

Cultural materials

One of the best known works in fiction that seeks to describe the global future is George Orwell's *1984*, written in 1949. The story takes place in England, known as Airstrip One, in the year 1984. England is part of Oceania, one of three great states in the world along with Eastasia and Eurasia. The country, which resembles the Soviet Union under Stalin, is governed by the Party led by "Big Brother." The protagonist Winston Smith works for the Ministry of Truth rewriting history. The plot follows Smith's disenchantment with the Party, his effort to write a diary which is illegal, his love affair with Julia, and his friendship with his boss O'Brien, who claims to be working against the Party. Smith is betrayed by O'Brien, who tortures him until he comes to believe all the lies he is told. Finally, Smith even betrays Julia when he is threatened with his worst nightmare, rats gnawing his face. And, in the end, he realizes that he loves Big Brother.

1   Can you identify any elements from *1984* in contemporary global politics?
2   If Orwell were writing today, what might *2084* look like? What aspects of global politics might be critiqued in this future world?

Further reading

Aaronson, Susan A., *Taking Trade to the Streets: The Lost History of Public Efforts to Shape Globalization* (Ann Arbor: University of Michigan Press, 2001). Examination of the rise of the anti-globalization movement.

Aguilar, Delia D. and Anne E. Lacsamana, eds., *Women and Globalization* (Amherst, NY: Humanity Books, 2004). Critique of the effects of globalization on women in the developing world.

Berger, Peter L. and Samuel P. Huntington, eds., *Many Globalizations: Cultural Diversity in the Contemporary World* (Oxford: Oxford University

Press, 2003). Comparative analysis of globalization in different countries and different regions.

Bhagwati, Jagdish, *In Defense of Globalization* (New York: Oxford University Press, 2005). Why the anti-globalization critique is exaggerated.

Friedman, Thomas L., *The World Is Flat: A Brief History of the Twenty-first Century* (New York: Farrar, Straus & Giroux, 2005). The meaning and consequences of a "connected" world.

Held, David and Anthony McGrew, *Globalization/Anti-Globalization* (Malden, MA: Blackwell, 2002). Analysis of issues of governance, culture, and economics in the globalization debate.

Lechner, Frank and John Boli, eds., *The Globalization Reader*, 2nd ed. (Malden, MA: Blackwell, 2003). Collection of classic articles analyzes the political, economic, and cultural dimensions of globalization.

Scholte, Jan Aart, *Globalization: A Critical Introduction* (New York: St. Martin's Press, 2000). Comprehensive analysis of the causes and consequences of globalization.

Steger, Manfred, *Globalization: A Very Short Introduction* (New York: Oxford University Press, 2003). A very accessible and balanced examination of the key aspects of globalization and on their positive and negative consequences.

Stiglitz, Joseph E., *Making Globalization Work* (New York: Norton, 2006). A series of pointed analyses of key problems posed by globalization and the way to confront them.

Glossary of key terms

absolute gains efforts to ensure everyone gains something from cooperation.

absolute war war in which adversaries use every available means to defeat one another.

acid rain precipitation made acidic by sulfur dioxide and nitrogen oxides that are produced by industry, automobiles, and power plants.

actual power the power an actor is able to realize in practice; actual power can only be measured by observing the changed behavior of others.

agent-structure problem a controversy about whether individuals and groups play the major role in explaining global politics or whether features of global structure determine the behavior of actors.

aggression the initiation of actions that violate the rights and interests of other actors.

alliance a formal agreement to cooperate to achieve joint security.

anarchist one who seeks to overturn all constituted forms and institutions of government.

anarchy the absence of a higher authority above sovereign states.

antiballistic missile (ABM) missile designed to destroy incoming enemy missiles.

anti-foundationalists those who claim that there are no neutral, value-free tests to determine the truth of a proposition.

anti-Semitism irrational dislike, prejudic, or hatred of Jews.

appeasement a policy of concessions that aims to satisfy another actor's grievances and thereby keep the peace.

arbitration the process of resolving disputes by referring them to a third party, either agreed on by them or provided by law, that is empowered to make a judgment.

arms control any approach designed to regulate levels and types of arms in a manner that enhances strategic stability.

arms race an action–reaction process in which increases in armaments by one state is reciprocated by an increase in armaments by the other.

assimilate to absorb a culturally distinct group into the dominant culture.

attrition the gradual erosion of an enemy's army by constant attack.

austerity policies aimed at balancing the budget by reducing expenditures.

authority the idea of legitimate power or the right to exercise influence over others.

autonomy the capacity to behave independently.

balance of payments a tabulation of a country's debt and credit transactions with other countries.

balance of power policy of states aimed to prevent any other state(s) from gaining a preponderance of power in relation to its rivals.

Balkans a peninsula in southeastern Europe that includes Slovenia, Croatia, Bosnia and Herzegovina, Macedonia, Serbia and Montenegro, Albania, Greece, Romania, Bulgaria, and European Turkey.

bargaining an interactive process involving threats and promises between two or more parties with common and conflicting interests seeking to reach an agreement.

behavioral revolution a shift in political science from the study of institutions, laws, history, and single case studies and toward the observation of human behavior or its artifacts with an eye toward uncovering general propositions.

bipartisanship the effort to include and gain the approval of members of both political parties in the formation of foreign policy.

bipolarity a political system with two centers of power.

birth rate annual number of births per thousand.

black market a system of illegal buying and selling of goods in violation of price controls or rationing.

blog a personal online journal that is updated and intended for general public consumption.

bond a certificate promising to pay back borrowed money at a fixed-rate interest on a specified date.

bourgeoisie the middle class in society that supports the capitalist economic system.

Caliphate Muslim empire from 661 to 1258.

capabilities resources available to actors that can be used to influence other actors.

capitalism an economic system based on the private ownership of property and the means of production and a free market for exchanging goods and services that allows competition.

caste a hereditary social class system of traditional Hindu society.

catharsis a relief of emotional tension.

city-state the independent political entity consisting of a city and its outskirts that dominated global politics in ancient Greece and Renaissance Italy.

civil disobedience illegal acts designed to bring public attention to laws regarded as unjust.

civil society a complex global network of institutions that link individuals with common values from many countries who regularly communicate ideas and coordinate activities.

civilization the type of culture of a specific place, time, or group.

class a social stratum sharing economic and political characteristics.

Cold War the period of hostility short of open warfare between the United States and its allies and the USSR and its allies that erupted after World War II and lasted until 1989.

collective dilemmas problems that require the cooperation of actors for solution and that no one actor can resolve on its own.

collective goods benefits such as military security or clean air from which individuals cannot be excluded and, as a result, for which beneficiaries have no incentive to pay.

collective identity a shared set of characteristics that defines the boundaries of a group and distinguishes it from other groups.

collective security the principle under which the invasion of *any* country would automatically bring forward the combined might of *all* countries.

colonialism the political control of a dependent territory and its people by a foreign military power.

communism a social system without states or classes featuring common ownership of property in which each member contributes according to capabilities and gains according to need.

comparative advantage the ability to produce a good at lower cost, relative to other goods, compared to other countries.

compellence the threat or use of force to make an adversary alter its behavior.

complex interdependence an interdependent relationship among actors characterized by multiple channels of interaction, multiple issues, and the absence of military force.

concessional assistance economic assistance of which at least 35 percent consists of grants that do not need to be repaid.

concessional loans loans at interest rates below market rates.

consociationalism a political system in which there is an explicit bargain that power be shared among distinct ethnic, religious, or linguistic groups.

constructivism an approach to global politics that assumes that political structures and behavior are shaped by shared ideas and that actors' identities and interests are the result of those ideas.

consumerism a norm that values the acquisition of material goods.

containment a US foreign policy that sought to prevent the spread of communism by applying diplomatic and economic pressure on the USSR.

crimes against humanity ill-treatment of civilians in wartime defined at the Nuremberg trials to include "murder, extermination, enslavement, deportation and other inhumane acts against any civilian population."

crimes against peace planning, provoking, and waging an aggressive war.

cultural relativism the belief that ethical beliefs vary by culture and that there are few, if any, universal principles of human rights.

culture the norms, customs, and ways of living of a group of human beings that is transmitted from one generation to another.

current account a statistic that registers all payments between a country and the rest of the world in goods and services, investment income and payments, and unilateral transfers.

cyberspace the electronic medium of computer networks in which online communication takes place.

data factual information.

decapitation attack an attack that aims to kill an enemy's leaders.

decolonization the process by which the major colonial powers granted independence to the majority of states in the Third World.

defense the use of power to prevent an attack or minimize damage from an attack.

deflation persistent decrease in consumer prices.

deforestation massive loss of forests with environmental consequences such as reduced oxygen production and soil erosion.

democracy a political system based on the right of all persons to participate in government, often by electing representatives of the people.

democratic peace theory the theory that democracies do not fight wars with one another.

demography the study of the characteristics of human populations.

desertification the spread of deserts as a result of soil erosion, overfarming, and deforestation.

détente periods of lessened tension between the United States and Soviet Union during the Cold War.

deterrence a strategy aimed at preventing an adversary from acting in a certain way by threatening to retaliate with military force.

dialectical materialism the Marxist belief that material factors constantly change owing to the tension between conflicting economic forces.

diaspora a community of people living outside their original homeland.

digital divide the gap between those who have access to new information and technologies like the Internet, and those who do not have such access.

diplomacy the art of conducting negotiations and managing relations among actors.

disarmament any effort to reduce the number of weapons in actors' arsenals.

discrimination in warfare, distinguishing between legitimate and improper military targets.

distribution of power the distribution among actors in global politics of the capacity to compel one another to carry out their preferences.

divide and rule retaining control by keeping the opposition divided.

due process in law, the administration of justice according to established rules based on the principle that no one can be deprived of life, liberty or property without suitable legal procedures and safeguards.

dynastic sovereignty sovereignty that is vested in a monarch and the monarch's heirs.

economic liberalism belief in free trade and the dominance of a free market.

economies of scale reductions in unit cost owing to increased production.

emergent properties characteristics of a group that are the unforeseen consequence of interaction among its members.

emerging market a financial market of a developing country.

empire a political unit having an extensive territory or comprising a number of territories or nations and ruled by a single supreme authority.

empirical theory (positivism) theories built on knowledge derived from experiment and experience.

epistemic communities communities of experts and advocates who share information about an issue and maintain contact with one other.

escalation an upward spiral in the level of conflict or violence.

ethnic cleansing the murder or expulsion from a territory of people from a particular ethnic background.

ethnicity affiliation based on racial and/or cultural ties.

expected utility theory an approach to decision-making predicated on the belief that leaders are rational and seek to maximize gains.

explanatory theory theory that explains why things happen as they do.

export controls rules limiting the export of goods, technology, and data, particularly that which is considered to have a dual-use or a military purpose.

export credits financing arrangements that permit a foreign buyer of exported goods to defer payment over a period of time.

external face of sovereignty the legal equality of sovereign states.

extraterritorial relating to persons exempt from the legal jurisdiction of the country in which they reside.

failed state a state that has collapsed and cannot provide for its citizens' basic needs.

fascism an anti-democratic political philosophy that advocates rule by a nationalist dictator aided by a mass party enforcing obedience by using violence.

federalism a political system in which authority is divided between a central authority and constituent political units.

fertility rate the number of children born to an average woman during her lifetime.

feudal system the legal, political, and social system of medieval Europe, in which vassals held land from lords in exchange for military service.

fifth columnists subversives working on behalf of a foreign power.

first-strike capability the ability to launch an attack and successfully destroy an enemy's capability to retaliate.

fixed exchange rate a system in which the value of one currency against other currencies is not permitted to vary.

floating exchange rate a system in which the value of a currency against other currencies is determined by supply and demand.

foreign direct investment (FDI) overseas investment in buildings, machinery, and equipment.

foreign-exchange reserves deposits of hard currencies such as dollars, pounds, euros, and yen held by national banks of different countries.

foreign policy the sum of an actor's goals and purposive actions in global politics.

foundationalists those who believe truth can be determined through empirical testing.

fragging the practice of some US soldiers in Vietnam who threw grenades into the tents of gung-ho officers.

free riders those who receive the benefits of a collective good without paying their fair share of the costs of producing that good.

freebooting pirating or looting.

functionalism a theory that conflict can be reduced if actors cooperate in technical and nonpolitical areas and that such cooperation will then become habitual and spread to other areas.

game an interaction among actors characterized by rules and strategies in which each actor's outcome depends partly on what other actors do and in which actors try to outwit one another.

genocide the extermination of an ethnic, racial or cultural group.

glasnost policy of openness initiated by Soviet leader Mikhail Gorbachev.

global governance the existence of order and authoritative decision-making in the absence of formal government.

global politics the political interactions among sovereign states as well as nonstate actors.

global system the sum of the interactions of the actors in global politics and the consequences of that interaction.

global warming warming of the earth's climate caused by the release of "greenhouse" gases trapping heat from the earth that would otherwise escape into space (also known as the greenhouse effect).

globalization those processes that knit people everywhere together, thereby producing worldwide interdependence and featuring the rapid and large-scale movement of persons, things, and ideas across sovereign borders.

gold standard a monetary system in which the basic unit of currency is equal in value to and exchangeable for a specified amount of gold.

governance authoritative demands, goals, directives, and policies of any actor, whether a government or not.

great power in the eighteenth century, the name for a European state that could not be conquered even by the combined might of other European states. Today, the term is applied to a country that is regarded as among the most powerful in the global system.

greenhouse effect the process in which the earth's atmosphere traps solar radiation, caused by the presence in the atmosphere of gases such as carbon dioxide and methane that allow incoming sunlight to pass through but absorb heat radiated back from the earth's surface.

gross domestic product (GDP) the total market value of all final goods and services produced in a country in a given year, equal to total consumer, investment, and government spending, plus the value of exports, minus the value of imports.

gross national product (GNP) the total value of all goods and services produced by a country in one year.

guerrilla warfare use of hit-and-run tactics including ambush and surprise raids.

hard currency a currency that is generally accepted for payment of obligations.

hard power power based on the use of coercion and rewards.

hard shell of impermeability the capacity, now largely gone, of states to defend their frontiers by military means.

hegemon an actor that is able to dominate the global political system.

hegemonic stability theory the theory that global order results from the domination of a single great power and that for the order to be maintained this dominance must continue.

honor killings the murder of women for dishonoring the family or clan.

human development the quality of life and standard of living of individuals.

human rights the rights that individuals enjoy by virtue of their humanness.

human security protection against threats to human life and well being.

humanitarian intervention intervention by states or by an IGO into the domestic politics of another state to protect people from human rights abuses or other threats to their survival.

hyperglobalist an analyst who believes that the essence of globalization is the creation of a single global economic market.

hypothesis a tentative prediction or explanation that a theorist intends to test.

idealism/utopianism a term coined by realists to deride other scholars of global politics who believe in the importance of international law, treaties, morality, and international institutions.

identities a set of characteristics that individuals recognize as defining themselves and that, when shared, defines the group as a whole and its interests.

ideology a doctrinaire system of ideas that guides behavior.

imam an Islamic religious leader.

imperialism the political control of one state by another.

industrialization a process in which production and manufacturing are mechanized, bringing with it a complex of political, social, and economic changes.

infant industries industries that have recently been

established and are thought to have the potential to achieve comparative advantage if protected until they mature.

influence an actor's ability to cause another actor to behave differently than it would otherwise have.

intellectual property property like books or computer software that reflects intellectual achievement and is protected by patents, copyrights, and trademarks.

intercontinental ballistic missile (ICBM) ballistic missile with a range of 3,000 to 8,000 nautical miles.

interdependence a relationship in which two or more actors are sensitive and vulnerable to each other's behavior and in which actions taken by one affect the other.

internal face of sovereignty the complete legal authority that states enjoy over the subjects within their territorial boundaries.

international law the body of legally binding rules that governs relations among states and other groups and that also increasingly provides rights for individuals in relation to states.

international organization (IGO) an organization established by and whose members are sovereign states.

international political economy (IPE) analysis of the relationship between international economics and politics.

international politics political interaction among sovereign states.

international regime a set of rules, norms, and decision-making procedures that govern actors' behavior in an international issue-area.

interventionist liberalism a version of classical liberalism that sees it as a duty to intervene overseas to bring freedom, democracy, and other liberal virtues to people everywhere.

Iron Curtain a metaphor Winston Churchill coined in 1946 to describe the line separating the area in Europe under Soviet control from the free countries in Western Europe.

irredentism a claim to territory based on historical ties to the land or an ethnic or cultural affinity with its population.

isolationism a policy aimed at avoiding overseas political and military involvement.

issue linkage a bargaining strategy in which an actor gains favorable concessions in one issue area, by making concessions in another.

jihad a holy war undertaken as a sacred duty by Muslims.

justice fairness, honesty, and impartiality in dealing with individual citizens including according them equal treatment, upholding their rights, affording them what is legally theirs or theirs on the basis of merit.

Koran the book composed of sacred writings accepted by Muslims as revelations made to Muhammad by Allah through the angel Gabriel.

legal positivism a theory that international law is derived from voluntary agreements among states and that contends that states are bound only by the rules that they freely accept.

legitimacy the characteristic of a political or social institution that is perceived to have a right to make binding decisions for its members.

levels of analysis an analytical tool that simplifies theorizing by categorizing key factors in global politics at the level of the whole global system or of some of its constituent parts (individual, state).

liberal democracy a political system in which the authority of elected representatives to make decisions is governed by the rule of law under a constitution that protects individual and minority rights.

liberal nationalism a variant of nationalism that links the independence of national groups with human rights and democratic ideals.

liberalism an optimistic approach to global politics based on the perfectibility of humankind, free trade, and democracy; focuses on individuals rather than states.

liquidity crisis a situation in which there is inadequate cash for the needs of consumers and businesses.

madrasas Muslim religious schools.

malignant nationalism a strain of nationalism based on the superiority of some nations over others and that admires the use of violence in politics.

Mandates of the League of Nations colonial territories taken from the defeated states of World War I and entrusted by the League of Nations to the victors that were to prepare them for independence.

GLOSSARY OF KEY TERMS

Marxism a revolutionary doctrine based on the belief that history proceeds through class struggle.

mediation intervention by a third party in a dispute in order to help adversaries reach an agreement.

mercantilism belief that economic policy should increase state power by protecting infant industries, increasing imports, and restricting exports.

methodology the rules and procedures by which research is conducted.

microcredit small loans available to the poor to start small businesses.

migrant a person who moves from one country to another in search of work or other economic opportunities.

military-industrial complex the idea that defense corporations, Congress, and the Pentagon cooperate to encourage higher US defense spending.

mirror image the propensity of groups and individuals to hold similar views of each other; we see in others what they see in us.

modernization economic and political development in the Third World.

money laundering disguising criminal profits to prevent their detection by law enforcement agencies.

monotheism belief in a single god.

moral communities groups in which members are obliged to treat one another according to shared norms, rules, and standards that need not be applied to "outsiders."

most-favored nation (MFN) rule requirement for countries to treat one another equally in trade relations.

multilateralism a policy of working with other states to achieve policy goals.

multipolarity a political system having three or more dominant centers of power.

mutual assured destruction (MAD) a condition of nuclear deterrence in which each state has the capacity to survive the attack of another state and retaliate with its own devastating second strike.

nation a group of people united on the basis of some combination of shared history, religion, language, or ethnicity.

nation building efforts to create a sense of belonging and cohesion among a disparate group of people in a common state.

national communism the ideology of certain communists based on the claim that each communist party should follow its own distinctive national road and need not follow the same path as the Soviet Communist Party.

national interest the idea that a state has a set of goals that will collectively benefit its citizens.

national self-determination the doctrine that any people who consider themselves a nation should enjoy their own territorial state; the right of a nation to govern itself.

national wars wars fought with enthusiasm by citizens with a strong national attachment to their state.

nationalism the belief that a nation should be recognized as such, should enjoy equal rights with other nations, and should have political autonomy or independence; fervent attachment to a national or ethnic group.

nationalize to convert from private to government ownership and control.

natural law principles of law derived from nature, right reason, or God.

necessary cause a factor that must be present for a particular result to follow but whose presence does not necessitate that result.

negative rights the rights of individuals not to suffer from undue government interference in political, economic, and social independence and autonomy.

neocolonialism assertion that, despite decolonization, relations between wealthy countries and the LDCs remain unequal with the rich still able to exploit the poor.

neoconservative sometimes shortened to "neocon," neoconservative refers to those who advocate US intervention overseas to further democracy and individual freedom.

neofunctionalism a changed version of functionalist theory claiming that organizations established by interstate agreements create political pressures for additional agreements and greater authority for existing IGOs.

neoliberalism the school of liberals that believes in the critical role of international organizations in improving the prospects for order and peace.

neorealism (structural realism) the school of realism that holds that the structural properties of global politics, especially anarchy and the distribution of power among states, cause conflict and war.

neutralism (traditional) neutrality, or a policy of abstaining from conflicts in global politics.

nonalignment policy of not entering into military alliances with members of the two blocs during the Cold War.

nongovernmental organization (NGO) an organization whose members are individuals who do not represent the government of any state.

noninterventionist liberalism the school of liberalism that holds that history will bring improvement in society without help from external actors.

non-refoulement the legal principle that a state cannot deport an alien to a territory where his or her life or freedom would be threatened on account of race, religion, nationality, or political opinion.

nonstate actors actors whose members are individuals or groups other than sovereign states.

nontariff barrier any policy that intentionally makes it more difficult or expensive for foreign competitors to do business in a country.

normative theory theory concerning what is right and wrong.

nuclear winter a period of cold and darkness following a nuclear war, caused by the blocking of the sun's rays by high-altitude dust clouds.

oligopoly the market condition that exists when there are so few sellers that each can affect the price of a product being sold.

one China policy the policy of the Chinese government that there is only one China and Taiwan is part of it.

opportunity cost the cost of something in terms of opportunity forgone.

outsourcing subcontracting the purchase of labor or parts by a company with a source outside the company's home country.

overfishing the rate of fishing that exceeds a maximum fishing mortality rate.

ozone layer a region in the upper atmosphere where most atmospheric ozone is concentrated and that protects us from dangerous solar radiation.

pacifist one who refuses to support violence or war for any purpose.

paradigm an example that serves as a pattern or model for something, especially one that forms the basis of research and theory.

patterned behavior behavior that is repeated over and over again and seen to be orderly and predictable.

peace enforcement authorization under the provisions of Chapter 7 of the UN Charter for member states to use military force to end aggression.

peacekeeping the use of lightly armed military forces to separate warring parties, contain violence, and impose calm in situations of potential violence.

people's war Mao Zedong's theory of peasant guerrilla warfare.

perestroika policy of economic restructuring initiated by Soviet leader Mikhail Gorbachev.

pogrom an organized campaign of persecution sanctioned by a government and directed against an ethnic group, especially against the Jewish population of tsarist Russia.

polarity the number of power centers in a global system.

political culture a country's political psychology based on deep-seated, long-held values.

political integration a voluntary process of joining together to create a new political community.

politicide mass killings in order to eradicate a group of people owing to their political or ideological beliefs.

polytheism worship of or belief in several gods.

popular sovereignty sovereignty invested in the entire people of a state.

population density the number of individuals of a population per unit of living space.

portfolio (indirect) investment foreign investment in a country's stocks and bonds.

positive rights the rights of individuals to have their essential needs such as food and health seen to by government.

postpositivists those who reject empiricism on the grounds that there are no objective facts and that reality is subject to interpretation.

potential power the capabilities that an actor might use to create a power relationship.

power a psychological relationship between actors in which one influences another to behave differently than it would have if left to its own devices.

power vacuum an area not under the control of any strong country and that strong states may wish to control to prevent others from doing so.

predictive theory theory based on induction that predicts what will happen under specified conditions.

preemptive war a war initiated to gain the advantage over an adversary that it is thought is itself about to strike.

preferential access more favorable than usual tariff treatment granted to another state or group of states.

prescriptive theory theory about correct policies to use to reach a desired objective.

preventive war a war launched by one actor in order to prevent another actor from growing strong enough in the future to pose a threat.

private goods benefits that are enjoyed only by some and need not be shared.

proletariat the class of industrial workers who lack their own means of production and hence sell their labor to live.

proportionality in international law, the norm that a response to a wrong should not exceed the harm caused by the wrong.

protectionism the practice of shielding a country's domestic industries from foreign competition by taxing imports or otherwise impeding.

protectorate a state or territory that is under the protection of a more powerful state.

psychological distance the degree of dissimilarity between cognitive frameworks or ways of looking at, assigning meaning to, and coping with the world.

purchasing-power parity measurement of purchasing power in different countries that takes account of lower prices in developing countries compared to rich countries for a given basket of goods.

quantification the use of numbers and statistics to describe and explain political behavior.

rationality acting to promote one's interests by adopting means that are conducive to achieving desired and feasible ends.

realism an approach to global politics derived from the tradition of power politics and belief that behavior is determined by the search for and distribution of power.

realpolitik a policy premised on material factors, especially power, rather than on theoretical or ethical considerations.

reciprocity strategy by which one actor behaves toward others as they have behaved toward it.

reflexivism contemplation of global politics based on one's own subjective ideas and reason.

regime change the overthrow or ousting of a government.

relative gains efforts to gain more relative to others so as not to be exploited by others at some future point.

relativists those who believe that there are no clear truths and that what is right or wrong varies from person to person or from society to society.

religious fundamentalism the belief that law and politics derive solely from the word of God as stated in the holy book(s) of the religion in question.

resolve the willingness to use force.

Riga Axioms the belief that Soviet policy was driven by ideology rather than power.

rights privileges and prerogatives to which one has an established claim.

rogue states countries that are said to flout the norms, rules, and practices followed by most other states.

safeguards measures intended to ensure the security of nuclear materials and technologies.

salinization causing infertile soil by adding excessive salt.

scapegoat someone selected to take the blame for someone else's problems.

second-strike capability the capability to absorb an enemy first strike and deliver a counterblow to the enemy.

secularism the attitude that religious considerations should be excluded from public affairs.

security dilemma the inability of actors under conditions of anarchy to trust each other; the fear of aggression created in one actor by the growth of military power in another; a situation in which one actor's effort to increase its security makes other actors less secure with the unintended consequence of greater insecurity for all.

self-determination the right of groups in global politics to choose their own fate and to govern themselves.

Sino-Soviet split the 1960s ideological split between China and the USSR that resulted in closer Sino-American ties.

skeptic an analyst who believes that, despite growing international interactions, interdependence was greater in the nineteenth century, and that globalization is no more than intensified interstate interdependence.

slash and burn a technique to create additional farmland in which an area of forest is cleared by cutting and burning and is then planted, usually for several seasons, before being left to return to forest.

Social Darwinism the theory that nations and races are subject to the same laws of natural selection as Charles Darwin had perceived in plants and animals in nature.

socialism a political system in which the state controls the means of production and provides for citizens' basic needs.

socialization the general process of acquiring culture through family, education, and interaction with others.

soft power power based on culture and reputation and that is used to set the global agenda and shape the preferences of others.

sovereignty the status of states as legal equals under international law, according to which they are supreme internally and subject to no higher external authority.

specialized agencies IGOs with responsibility limited to a single, often narrow, area of human behavior.

speculation engaging in risky business transactions on the chance of a quick profit.

sphere of influence a geographic region dominated by a major power.

standard operating procedures (SOPs) established routines that bureaucracies follow to carry out recurring tasks.

state a political entity that is sovereign and has a government that is said to enjoy exclusive control over a defined territory and population.

state-centric a perspective or model of global politics in which states are the source of all important activities.

strategic stability a condition in which leaders have few incentives to launch a military first strike.

structural power power derived from control over resources, location in information networks, interpersonal connections with influential others, and reputation for being powerful; the power to determine how things will be done.

structural violence physical or psychological violence which is carried out, not by individuals, but by structures, for example the injustices of the worldwide trading system.

structure any set of relatively fixed constraints on global actors.

subaltern a subordinate; someone who is lower in rank.

subnational taking place within the boundaries of a single state.

subsidy any government financial contribution that benefits home industries by reducing production costs.

sufficient cause a factor that when present always assures that a particular result will follow.

supranational above the authority of national governments.

sustainable development development that meets the needs of the present without compromising the ability of future generations to develop.

tariff a duty levied by a government on imported goods.

terms of trade an index of the price of a country's exports in terms of its imports.

terrorism calculated use of violence against innocent civilians for political ends, especially to gain public attention.

theocracy a system of government by religious leaders and based on religious dogma.

theory an abstract, simplified, and general proposition that answers "why" and "how" questions.

totalitarianism a political system in which rulers control all aspects of society.

transaction costs the costs involved in any transaction

other than the price paid such as time spent or information about others involved in the transaction.

transformationalist an analyst who believes that globalization or human interconnectedness has no historical parallel and that it is producing a merger of the foreign and domestic policy arenas and is weakening states and the role of territory in global politics.

transnational crossing national frontiers and involving social groups and nongovernmental actors.

transnational corporations (TNCs) economic enterprises with operations in two or more countries.

transnational relations direct interactions or transactions between separate societies across national frontiers, involving nongovernmental groups.

transnational war war involving unofficial militias and violent groups that flows across state frontiers.

treasury note an interest-paying debt instrument issued by the US government, with an initial life of between one and ten years.

tribe a sociopolitical community consisting of a number of families, clans, or other groups who share a common ancestry.

Triple Alliance the alliance between Germany, Austria-Hungary, and Italy (which declined to honor its commitment) that entered World War I.

Triple Entente the alliance between France, Great Britain, and Russia that entered the war against Germany and Austria-Hungary in 1914.

ulema the community of Islamic legal scholars and the Sharia, the body of traditional Islamic law.

unilateralism the practice of acting alone, without consulting friends and allies.

unipolarity an international political system dominated by one center of power.

unitary-actor approach the assumption that actors' internal attributes or differences among such attributes have little impact on foreign-policy behavior.

urbanization the social process during which cities grow and population becomes more concentrated in urban areas.

utopianism see idealism.

variable-sum (non-zero-sum) game a situation in which the total gain for one party is *not* identical to the losses of the other; both can gain, both can lose, or one can gain or lose more or less than the other.

veto the legal power of any of the permanent members of the UN Security Council to reject a Council resolution.

virtual state a state that has outsourced much of its territorially based production capability.

vulnerability the degree to which an actor's nuclear retaliatory force can be destroyed by an enemy attack.

war crimes abuse of enemy soldiers or prisoners of war during wartime.

weapons of mass destruction (WMD) nuclear, biological, or chemical weapons that can kill large numbers of people indiscriminately.

xenophobe one who fears or dislikes foreigners.

Yalta Axioms the belief of US leaders before the Cold War that it was possible to bargain with the Soviet Union and that the USSR was much like other states that designed foreign policies based on power.

zero-sum a relationship of pure conflict in which a gain for one actor is equal to the loss for another.

zero-sum game a situation of pure conflict in which the gain of one side is equal to the loss of the other.

Notes

1 An introduction to global politics: change and continuity

1 George Modelski and William R. Thompson, *Leading Sectors and Global Power: The Coevolution of Global Politics and Economics* (Columbia, SC: University of South Carolina Press, 1996).

2 The transition from British to American leadership was peaceful owing to Britain's willingness to accommodate growing US power.

3 See A. F. K. Organski and Jacek Kugler, *The War Ledger* (Chicago, IL: University of Chicago Press, 1980).

4 Zechariah 7:14.

5 As we shall see, "states" and "nations" are not the same. Thus, "interstate politics" would have been a more accurate title for the field.

6 Charles E. Lindblom, "The Science of Muddling Through," *Public Administration Review* 19:2 (1959), 79–88.

7 Robert Jervis, "Rational Deterrence: Theory and Evidence," *World Politics* 41:2 (1989), 204–5.

8 Peter Gourevitch, "The Second Image Reversed: The International Sources of Domestic Politics," *International Organization* 32:4 (Autumn 1978), 882, 883.

9 Robert D. Putnam, "Diplomacy and Domestic Politics: The Logic of Two-Level Games," *International Organization* 42:3 (Summer 1988), 460.

10 James N. Rosenau and Mary Durfee, *Thinking Theory Thoroughly*, 2nd ed. (Boulder, CO: Westview Press, 2000), 3.

11 Stephen Walt, *The Origins of Alliances* (Ithaca, NY: Cornell University Press, 1987).

12 Niccolò Machiavelli, *The Prince* (Cambridge: Cambridge University Press, 1988), 52.

13 Thomas Hobbes, *Leviathan Parts I and II* (Indianapolis, IN: Bobbs-Merrill, 1958), Part I. 1, ch. 11, 86.

14 For a succinct and influential definition of realism, see John A. Vasquez, *The Power of Power Politics: From Classical Realism to Neotraditionalism* (Cambridge: Cambridge University Press, 1998), 47–52.

15 Hans J. Morgenthau, *Politics Among Nations: The Struggle for Power and Peace*, 7th ed., rev. by Kenneth W. Thompson and W. David Clinton (New York: McGraw-Hill, 2006), 4.

16 Cited in Kenneth N. Waltz, *Man, the State and War* (New York: Columbia University Press, 1959), 237.

17 Jack Donnelly, "Realism," in Scott Burchill, *et al.*, *Theories of International Relations*, 3rd ed. (New York: Palgrave Macmillan, 2005), 32.

18 Hobbes, *Leviathan*, Part I, ch. 13, 108.

19 E. H. Carr, *The Twenty Years' Crisis, 1919–1939* (New York: Harper & Row, 1964), vii.

20 Ibid., 11.

21 Ibid., 41.

22 http://www.yale.edu/lawweb/avalon/imt/kbpact.htm

23 Condoleezza Rice, "Promoting the National Interest," *Foreign Affairs* 79:1 (January/February 2000), 48.

24 Ibid., 47, 62.

25 Kenneth N. Waltz, *Theory of International Politics* (New York: McGraw-Hill, 1979).

26 See Edward Rhodes, "The Good, the Bad, and the Righteous: Understanding the Bush Vision of a New NATO Partnership," *Millennium Journal of International Studies* 33:1 (2004), 123–43.

27 The concept is closely associated with the philosopher of science, Thomas Kuhn. See *The Structure of Scientific Revolutions* (Chicago, IL: University of Chicago Press, 1970).

28 The best source for this debate remains Klaus Knorr and James N. Rosenau, eds., *Contending Approaches to International Politics* (Princeton, NJ: Princeton University Press, 1969).

29 Yosef Lapid, "The Third Debate: On the Prospects for International Theory in a Post-Positivist Era," *International Studies Quarterly* 33:3 (September 1989), 235–54.

30 Richard K. Ashley and R. B. J. Walker, "Speaking the Language of Exile: Dissident Thought in International Studies," *International Studies Quarterly* 34:3 (September 1990), 263.

31 Martha Finnemore and Kathryn Sikkink, "International Norm Dynamics and Political Change," *International Organization* 52:4 (Autumn 1998), 889.

32 Robert Cox, "Social Forces, States, and World Orders: Beyond International Relations Theory," *Millennium Journal of International Studies* 10:2 (1981), 128.

33 Peter J. Katzenstein, Robert O. Keohane, and Stephen D. Krasner, "International Organization and the Study of World Politics," *International Organization* 52:4 (Autumn 1998), 678.

34 See John Gerard Ruggie, *Constructing the World Polity* (New York: Routledge, 1998).

35 See Thomas Risse-Kappen, "Collective Identity in a Democratic Community: The Case of NATO," in Peter J. Katzenstein, ed., *The Culture of National Security: Norms and Identity in World Politics* (New York: Columbia University Press, 1996).

36 See Alexander E. Wendt, "The Agent–Structure Problem in International Relations Theory," *International Organization* 41:3 (Summer 1987), 335–70.

37 Alexander E. Wendt, *Social Theory of International Politics* (Cambridge: Cambridge University Press, 1999), 87–8.

38 J. Ann Tickner, "You Just Do not Understand: Troubled Engagements Between Feminists and IR Theorists," *International Studies Quarterly* 41:4 (December 1997), 614–15.

39 Ibid., 629.

40 J. Ann Tickner, *Gender in International Relations* (New York: Columbia University Press, 1992), 4.

41 Cynthia Enloe, *Bananas, Beaches and Bases* (Berkeley, CA: University of California Press, 1990), 3.

42 Christine Sylvester, *Feminist Theory and International Relations in a Postmodern Era* (New York: Cambridge University Press, 1994), 4–5.

43 Tickner, *Gender in International Relations*, 19, 22–3.

44 Sylvester, *Feminist Theory and International Relations in a Postmodern Era*, 31.

45 Karl Marx and Friedrich Engels, *The Communist Manifesto* (1848), http://www.wsu.edu:8080/~wldciv/world_civ_ reader/world_civ_reader_2/marx.html

46 Brainy Quote, http://www.brainyquote.com/quotes/quotes/f/friedriche201832.html

47 Friedrich Engels, *The Origin of the Family, Private Property and the State* (1884), chapter 9, http://www.marxists.org/archive/marx/works/1884/origin-family/ch09.htm

48 See, for example, Jutta Weldes, ed. *To Seek Out New Worlds: Exploring Links between Science Fiction and World Politics* (London: Palgrave, 2003).

2 The evolution of the interstate system and alternative political systems

1 Articles of Confederation, http://www.yale.edu/lawweb/avalon/artconf.htm#art1

2 *The Federalist Papers No. 9*, http://www.yale.edu/lawweb/avalon/federal/fed09.htm. *The Federalist Papers* were a series of essays written by Alexander Hamilton, James Madison, and John Jay to persuade the citizens of New York State to support the new constitution. They are regarded as a masterpiece of political philosophy.

3 For an accessible analysis of how the flourishing Islamic civilization became a "poor, weak, and ignorant" backwater of petty authoritarian regimes, see Bernard Lewis, *What Went Wrong?: The Clash between Islam and Modernity in the Middle East* (London: Orion Publishing, 2004).

4 George Shultz, "A Changed World," Foreign Policy Research Institute, March 22, 2004, http://www. fpri.org/enotes/20040322.americawar.shultz.changedworld.html. For an analysis of why "predator" groups that challenge basic system norms trigger a strong reaction on the part of major states, see Oded Löwenheim, *Predators and Parasites: Persistent Agents of Transnational Harm and Great Power Authority* (Ann Arbor, MI: University of Michigan Press, 2007).

5 See Stephen D. Krasner, *Sovereignty: Organized Hypocrisy* (Princeton, NJ: Princeton University Press, 1999.)

6 Saskia Sassen, *Cities in a Global Economy* (Thousand Oaks, CA: Pine Forge Press, 1994), 42–57.

7 See Douglass C. North and Robert Thomas, *The Rise of the Western World: A New Economic History* (Cambridge: Cambridge University Press, 1972).

8 Charles Tilly, *The Formation of National States in Western Europe* (Princeton, NJ: Princeton University Press, 1975), 7.

9 Hendrik Spruyt, *The Sovereign State and Its Competitors* (Princeton, NJ: Princeton University Press, 1994), 18–19.

10 Ibid., 28.

11 Francesco Guicciardini, *The History of Italy*, trans. Sidney Alexander (London: Collier-Macmillan, 1969), 48.

12 *The Religious Peace of Augsburg, 1555*, http://www.uoregon.edu/~sshoemak/323/texts/augsburg.htm

13 J. H. Robinson, ed., *The Destruction of Magdeburg, Readings in European History*, 2 vols. (Boston, MA: Ginn, 1906), 211–12, in *Hanover Historical Texts Project*, scanned by Brian Cheek, Hanover College. November 12, 1995, http://history.hanover.edu/texts/magde.html

14 Marxist theorists who emphasize the economic basis of the modern state argue that there is a propensity to

exaggerate the importance of the Peace of Westphalia. The modern state, in their view, only emerges with nineteenth-century industrialization. See Benno Teschke, *The Myth of 1648: Class, Geopolitics and the Making of Modern International Relations* (London: Verso, 2003).

15 *Montevideo Convention on the Rights and Duties of States*, http://www.yale.edu/lawweb/avalon/intdip/interam/intam02.htm#art1

16 During this period, the concept "great power" was well understood by statesmen as that small group of states with the responsibility to manage global politics and, in this sense, has a formal meaning. Thus, one historian described the 1815 Quadruple Alliance as marking "the ascendance of the Great Powers" in managing the European system after Napoléon's defeat. C. K. Webster as cited in Edward Vose Gulick, *Europe's Classic Balance of Power* (New York: W.W. Norton, 1955), 290. Today, the concept is used more loosely to denote powerful states.

17 R. R. Palmer, "Frederick the Great, Guibert, Bülow: From Dynastic to National War," in Peter Paret, ed., *Makers of Modern Strategy* (Princeton, NJ: Princeton University Press, 1986), 99, 103, 105.

18 See Hedley Bull, *The Anarchical Society: A Study of Order in World Politics* (Irvington, NY: Columbia University Press, 1995).

19 Cited in Adam Watson, *The Evolution of International Society* (New York: Routledge, 1992), 199.

20 Ernst B. Haas, "The Balance of Power: Prescription, Concept or Propaganda?" *World Politics* 10 (July 1953), 442–77.

21 Emmerich de Vattel, "The Law of Nations," in M. G. Forsyth, H. M. A. Keens-Soper, and P. Savigear, eds., *The Theory of International Relations* (New York: Atherton Press, 1970), 118.

22 Jean-Jacques Rousseau, "Abstract of the Abbé de Saint Pierre's Project for Perpetual Peace," in ibid., 136.

23 Henry Brougham, "Balance of Power," in ibid., 269.

24 George Canning's Address on the King's Message Respecting Portugal, Hansard, XVI [N.S.], 390–8, http://dspace.dial.pipex.com/town/terrace/adw03/polspeech/portugal.htm. Emphasis added.

25 It is difficult to sustain this claim. See the majority of essays in T.V. Paul, James J. Wirtz, and Michael Fortmann, *Balance of Power: Theory and Practice in the 21st Century* (Stanford, CA: Stanford University Press, 2004).

26 Gulick, *Europe's Classical Balance of Power*, 4.

27 Ibid., 19.

28 *Levée en Masse, The*, August 23, 1793, *Modern History Sourcebook*, http://www.fordham.edu/halsall/mod/1793levee.html

29 Baroness Emmuska Orczy, *The Elusive Pimpernel* (New York: Buccaneer Books, 1984), 245. The book was made into a classic Hollywood epic in 1934 called *The Scarlet Pimpernel* that was remade as a musical in 1999.

30 A great column was erected in Nelson's memory and still stands in London's Trafalgar Square. Nelson's fictional counterpart is Captain Horatio Hornblower who is the hero in a series of novels by C. S. Forester.

31 Henry Kissinger, a realist scholar and practitioner, published his doctoral dissertation on the Congress. See Kissinger, *A World Restored: Metternich, Castlereagh and the Problems of Peace, 1812–22* (New York: Houghton Mifflin, 1973).

32 Declaration of February 5, 1814, cited in Hans J. Morgenthau, *Politics Among Nations*, 7th ed., rev. by Kenneth W. Thompson and W. David Clinton (New York: McGraw-Hill, 2006), 228.

33 Watson, *The Evolution of International Society*, 245.

34 The First Empire had lasted only ten years, from 1804 until Napoléon's defeat and abdication in 1814 and the restoration of the monarchy.

35 Otto von Bismarck, *Life and Works*, vol. 4 (1878), cited in http://www.bartleby.com/66/30/7330.html

36 James N. Rosenau, *Distant Proximities, Dynamics beyond Globalization* (Princeton, NJ: Princeton University Press, 2003), 62–3, and Rosenau, *Turbulence in World Politics: A Theory of Change and Continuity* (Princeton, NJ: Princeton University Press, 1990), 36.

37 Watson, *The Evolution of International Society*, 85.

38 John King Fairbank, *China: A New History* (Cambridge, MA: Harvard University Press, 1992), 112.

39 *Internet Modern History Source Book* http://www.fordham.edu/halsall/mod/1793qianlong.html

40 Adda Bozeman, *Politics and Culture in International History* (Princeton, NJ: Princeton University Press, 1960), 134.

41 Dennis and Ching Ping Bloodworth, *The Chinese Machiavelli* (New York: Farrar, Straus and Giroux, 1976), 4.

42 John K. Fairbank, "A Preliminary Framework," in Fairbank, ed., *The Chinese World Order* (Cambridge, MA: Harvard University Press, 1968), 5.

43 Ibid., 6.

44 Milton Friedman and Rose Friedman, *Free To Choose* (New York: Avon Books, 1979), 120.

45 Samuel P. Huntington, "The West: Unique, Not Universal," *Foreign Affairs* 75:6 (November/December 1996), 28.

46 For a balanced analysis of this issue, see Takashi Inoguchi and Edward Newman, "Introduction: 'Asian Values' and Democracy in Asia," *Proceedings of 1997 First Shizuoka Asia–Pacific Forum: The Future of the*

Asia–Pacific Region, http://www.unu.edu/unupress/asian-values.html

47 See, for example, Samuel P. Huntington, *The Third Wave: Democratization in the Late Twentieth Century* (Norman: University of Oklahoma Press, 1991), 301.

48 Cited in "Asia's Different Drum," *Time*, June 14, 1993, 18.

49 C.O. Khong, "Asian Values: The Debate Revisited," *Proceedings of 1997 First Shizuoka Asia-Pacific Forum: The Future of the Asia-Pacific Region.* http://www.unu.edu/unupress/asian-values.html.

50 Charles Wolf, Jr. "Are 'Asian Values' Really Unique?" Hoover Institution, *Hoover Digest* (2000), No. 2, http://www.hooverdigest.org/002/wolf.html

51 Ibid.

52 See Susan Strange, *Casino Capitalism* (Manchester: Manchester University Press, 1997).

53 Bozeman, *Politics and Culture in International History*, 366.

54 For an excellent source of Islam from its birth to 1600, see "The Islamic World to 1600," The Applied History Research Group, The University of Calgary, http://www.ucalgary.ca/applied_history/tutor/islam/index.html. Other excellent web sources on Islam include Hsiao-pei Yen, "The Middle East," Department of History SUNY-Albany, http://www.albany.edu/history/middle-east/index.html, "Exploring Ancient World Cultures: Early Islam," University of Evansville, http://eawc.evansville.edu/ispage.htm, and Paul Halsall, "Internet Islamic History Sourcebook," http://www.fordham.edu/halsall/islam/islamsbook.html

55 Philip K. Hitti, *The Arabs: A Short History* (Cambridge, MA: Harvard University Press, 1956), 5.

56 Paul Halsell, ed., *Internet Medieval Sourcebook*: Urban II: Speech at Clermont 1095, http://www.fordham.edu/halsall/source/urban2a.html

57 Michael N. Barnett, "Sovereignty, Nationalism, and Regional Order in the Arab States System," *International Organization* 49:3 (Summer 1995), 492.

58 Useful sources on the Islamic chronology include WebChron, *Islamic Chronology*, http://www.thenagain.info/WebChron Islam/Islam.html, and *Internet Islamic Sourcebook*, http://www.fordham.edu/halsall/islam/islamsbook.html

59 To read more on Islamic architecture, see for example Robert Hillenbrand, *Islamic Architecture: Form, Function, and Meaning* (New York: Columbia University Press, 2004); Attilio Petruccioli and Hkalil K. Pirani, *Understanding Islamic Architecture* (New York: RoutledgeCurzon, 2002); and Richard Yeomans, *The Story of Islamic Architecture* (New York: New York University Press, 2000).

3 The world wars

1 Cited in Laurence Lafore, *The Long Fuse*, 2nd ed. (New York: J. P. Lippincott Co., 1971), 256.

2 Cited in ibid., 256, 257.

3 Cited in ibid., 257.

4 There are many useful websites concerning World War I. Some are general, and some focus on particular aspects of the conflict. Some of the good ones are Public Broadcasting Service, "The Great War and the Shaping of the Twentieth Century," www.pbs.org/greatwar, World War I Document Archive, Brigham Young University, www.lib.byu.edu/~rdh/wwi, The Great War Society, "World War I Trenches on the Web," www.worldwar1.com, "WW I A British Focus," www.warlinks.com

5 E. H. Carr, *The Twenty Years' Crisis* (New York: Palgrave, 2001).

6 Stephen D. Krasner, "State Power and International Trade," *World Politics* 28:3 (April 1976), tables 1.1 and 1.2, 144–5.

7 "The Franco-Russian Alliance Military Convention," The World War I Document Archive, http://www.lib.byu.edu/~rdh/wwi/1914m/franruss.html. Italics added.

8 Jonathan Steinberg, *Yesterday's Deterrent: Tirpitz and the Birth of Germany's Battle Fleet* (New York: Macmillan, 1965), 20.

9 British *Parliamentary Debates*, March 29, 1909, cols. 52ff. also available from "Britain's Policy as Outlined in the Speech in Parliament of the Foreign Secretary, Sir Edward Grey: March 29, 1909," http://web.jjay.cuny.edu/~jobrien/reference/ob71.html

10 This was realized after the war in the formation of Yugoslavia which means "Union of the Southern Slavs."

11 David Fromkin, *Europe's Last Summer: Who Started the Great War in 1914?* (New York: Vintage, 2004), 289–91.

12 The World War I Document Archive, http://www.lib.byu.edu/~rdh/wwi/1914/blankche.html

13 "Primary Documents: Austrian Ultimatum to Serbia, 23 July 1914," *First World War.Com*, http://www.firstworldwar.com/source/austrianultimatum.htm

14 Cited at http://www.bridgewater.edu/~slongene/summit/russia.html

15 Fromkin, *Europe's Last Summer*, 273.

16 Cited in Imanuael Geiss, "The Outbreak of the First World War and German War Aims," in Walter Laqueur and George L. Mosse, eds., *1914: The Coming of the First World War* (New York: Harper & Row, 1966), 78.

17 John Strachey, *The End of Empire* (New York: Praeger, 1964), 103.

18 See Margaret Macmillan, *Paris 1919: Six Months That Changed the World* (London: Macmillan, 2002).

19 "Fourteen Points Speech by President Woodrow Wilson," http://www.age-of-the-sage.org/history/wilson_fourteen_points.html

20 Japan was angered by Wilson's refusal to include a clause in the treaty recognizing racial equality even though the treaty called for religious equality.

21 Cited in Winston S. Churchill, *The Gathering Storm* (Boston, MA: Houghton Mifflin, 1948), 7.

22 Cited in F. P. Walters, *A History of the League of Nations*, vol. 2 (London: Oxford University Press, 1952), 653.

23 "The Covenant of the League of Nations," The Multilaterals Project, the Fletcher School, Tufts University, http://fletcher.tufts.edu/multi/www/league-covenant.html

24 A reservation as defined by the Vienna Convention on the Law of Treaties, May 23, 1969, art. 2(1)(d), 1155 UN Treaty Series 331 is "a unilateral statement, however phrased or named, made by a State, when signing, ratifying, accepting, approving or acceding to a treaty, whereby it purports to exclude or to modify the legal effect of certain provisions of the treaty in their application to that State."

25 Ray S. Baker and William E. Dodd, eds., *The Public Papers of Woodrow Wilson*, vol. 1 (New York: Doubleday, Page, & Co., 1924), 30–44.

26 F. S. Northedge, *The League of Nations: Its Life and Times, 1920–1946* (Leicester: Leicester University Press, 1986), 159.

27 Cited in David F. Schmitz, *Henry L. Stimson: The First Wise Man* (Wilmington, DE: Scholarly Resources, 2001), 111.

28 Piers Brendon, *The Dark Valley: A Panorama of the 1930s* (New York: Random House, 2000), p. 324.

29 Winston S. Churchill, *The Gathering Storm* (Boston, MA: Houghton Mifflin, 1948), 175.

30 Ernst B. Haas, *Collective Security and the Future International System*, University of Denver Monograph Series in World Affairs, 5:1 (Denver: 1967–68), 34.

31 John W. Wheeler-Bennett, *Munich: Prologue to Tragedy* (New York: Viking Press, 1964), 55.

32 William L. Shirer, *The Rise and Fall of the Third Reich*, vol. 1 (New York: Simon and Schuster, 1966), 138, 166, 195–6).

33 Cited in Frank McDonough, *The Origins of the First and Second World Wars* (Cambridge: Cambridge University Press, 1997), 85.

34 There were few Germans in the ancient Czech provinces of Bohemia and Moravia, making German claims of fighting for self-determination very hollow indeed.

35 WorldofQuotes.com, http://www.worldofquotes.com/docs/53

36 Cited in Daniel L. Byman and Kenneth M. Pollack, "Let Us Now Praise Great Men: Bringing the Statesman Back In," *International Security* 25:4 (Spring 2001), 115–16.

37 Randall L. Schweller, "Unanswered Threats: A Neoclassical Realist Theory of Underbalancing," *International Security* 29:2 (Fall 2004), 189–96.

4 The Cold War

1 The term Cold War was first popularized by the American journalist Walter Lippmann (1889–1974) in 1947. For materials on the Cold War, see http://www.cnn.com/SPECIALS/cold.war/. On dating the origins of the Cold War, see John Lewis Gaddis, "Was the Truman Doctrine a Real Turning Point?" *Foreign Affairs* 52:2 (January 1974), 386–402.

2 John Lewis Gaddis, *The Long Peace: Inquiries into the History of the Cold War*, new ed. (New York: Oxford University Press, 1989).

3 John Lewis Gaddis, *Russia, the Soviet Union, and the United States* (New York: Wiley, 1978), 76.

4 Modern History Sourcebook, http://www.fordham.edu/halsall/mod/churchill-iron.html

5 Stephen E. Ambrose, *Rise to Globalism: American Foreign Policy 1938–1976* (New York: Penguin Books, 1976), 16.

6 Geir Lundestad, *The United States and Western Europe Since 1945: From "Empire" by Invitation to Transatlantic Drift* (New York: Oxford University Press, 2003).

7 Gary B. Ostrower, "Origins of the United Nations," US Department of State (2005), http://usinfo.state.gov/is/Archive/2005/Sep/06-534246.html

8 Winston S. Churchill, *Triumph and Tragedy*, Vol. 6, *The Second World War* (Boston, MA: Houghton Mifflin, 1953), 194–5.

9 Cited in John Lewis Gaddis, *The Long Peace* (New York: Oxford University Press, 1987), 48.

10 The Avalon Project at Yale Law School, "The Yalta Conference," http://www.yale.edu/lawweb/avalon/wwii/yalta.htm

11 "Extracts from the Yalta Conference," 3rd Plenary Meeting, February 6, 1945, as cited in John W. Young and John Kent, *International Relations Since 1945: A Global History* (Oxford: Oxford University Press, 2004), 57.

12 Cited in Daniel Yergin, *Shattered Peace* (Boston, MA: Houghton Mifflin, 1977), 58, 66.

13 Cited in Robert H. Ferrell, *American Diplomacy: A History* (New York: Norton, 1975), 623.

14 Yergin, *Shattered Peace*, 42–68.

15 Ibid., 17–41. "Riga" refers to the Latvian city where the first American Soviet observers were posted after the USSR was established.

16 Ibid., 35.

17 George F. Kennan, *Memoirs 1925–1950* (Boston, MA: Little Brown, 1967), 557.

18 Ibid., 555–6.

19 Nikolai Novikov, Soviet Ambassador in Washington, Telegram, September 1946, http://www.mtholyoke.edu/acad/intrel/novikov.htm

20 Ibid.

21 Alexis de Tocqueville, *Democracy in America*, vol.1, ch. 18, http://xroads.virginia.edu/~HYPER/DETOC/1_ch18.htm

22 George F. Kennan [X], "The Sources of Soviet Conduct," *Foreign Affairs* 25 (July 1947), 582.

23 The Avalon Project at Yale Law School, "Truman Doctrine," http://www.yale.edu/lawweb/avalon/trudoc.htm

24 Instead, in 1949, the members of the East bloc formed the Council for Mutual Economic Assistance (Comecon) to reinforce Soviet control over allies' economies, create a socialist trade bloc, and force members to specialize in producing items desired by others. The West sought to deny the USSR access to technology that might contribute to Soviet power, and in 1949 established a Coordinating Committee (Cocom) to coordinate the allied embargo of strategic goods to the East. The 1949 US Export Control Act, not revoked until 1969, gave the president authority to prevent exports to the USSR. Thus, the economies of the East bloc were isolated from the West, subordinated to Soviet interests, and made to depend on the USSR.

25 The city of Bonn, located further west on the Rhine River had been the capital of West Germany.

26 Peter Calvocoressi, *World Politics Since 1945*, 6th ed. (New York: Longman, 1991), 19.

27 See Paul Nitze "The Development of NSC-68," *International Security* 4:4 (Spring 1980), 170–6.

28 The National Security Council was established by the National Security Act of 1947 to advise the President on foreign policy and national security issues. Chaired by the President, Council members include the Vice President, the Secretary of State, the Secretary of the Treasury, the Secretary of Defense, and the Assistant to the President for National Security Affairs. The Chairman of the Joint Chiefs of Staff is the Council's military advisor, and the Director of Central Intelligence is its intelligence advisor.

29 NSC-68: United States Objectives and Programs for National Security, http://www.fas.org/irp/offdocs/nsc-hst/nsc-68-1.htm

30 Cited in John Lewis Gaddis, *Strategies of Containment. A Critical Appraisal of Postwar American National Security Policy* (New York: Oxford University Press, 1982), 340.

31 John Lewis Gaddis, *The United States and the Origins of the Cold War, 1941–1947* (New York: Columbia University Press, 1972), 303.

32 NSC-68: United States Objectives and Programs for National Security, http://www.fas.org/irp/offdocs/nsc-hst/nsc-68-1.htm

33 Ibid.

34 NSC-68: United States Objectives and Programs for National Security, http://www.fas.org/irp/offdocs/nsc-hst/nsc-68-1.htm

35 On March 29, 1951 husband and wife Julius and Ethel Rosenberg were convicted of conspiracy to commit espionage in turning over atomic secrets to the Soviet Union, and on June 19, 1953 they were executed. In 1995, the US National Security Agency released translations of Soviet cables decrypted back in the 1940s by the Venona Project, a highly secret US effort to gather and decrypt messages sent by Soviet agents in the 1940s. The cables revealed that Julius Rosenberg – but not Ethel Rosenberg – had spied on behalf of the USSR. According to former KGB agent Alexander Feklisov, Julius Rosenberg had provided him with military secrets but nothing of value about the atomic bomb. As for Ethel Rosenberg: "She had nothing to do with this – she was completely innocent. I think she knew, but for that you don't kill people," CNN, "KGB agent says Rosenbergs were executed unjustly," March 16, 1997, http://www.cnn.com/US/9703/16/rosenbergs/

36 *"Enemies from Within": Senator Joseph R. McCarthy and President Harry S Truman Trade Accusations of Disloyalty*, http://historymatters.gmu.edu/d/6456/. A special Senate committee found McCarthy's charges to be groundless.

37 Gulag is a Russian acronym for the Soviet agency that ran the camps. See Aleksandr I. Solzhenitsyn's brilliant three-volume semi-autobiographical novel, *The Gulag Archipelago: 1918–1956* (New York: Harper & Row, 1973, 1975, 1976).

38 See, for example, Robert P. Newman, *Owen Lattimore and the "Loss" of China* (Berkeley, CA: University of California Press, 1992).

39 Ibid., 124.

40 Ibid., 227.

41 Harry S Truman, *Memoirs*, Vol. 2, *Years of Trial and Hope* (Garden City, NY: Doubleday, 1956), 332–3.

42 Paul Lashmar, "Stalin's 'Hot' War," *New Statesman & Society* 9:388 (February 2, 1996). http://www.mtholyoke.edu/acad/intrel/lashmar.htm. See also S. N. Goncharov, John W. Lewis, Xue Litai, Sergei N. Goncharov, John Wilson Lewis, and Litai Xue, *Uncertain Partners: Stalin, Mao, and the Korean War* (Stanford, CA: Stanford University Press, 1993) for documentary evidence that Stalin had pressed North Korea to initiate the war.

43 William Keylor, *The Twentieth Century World*, 3rd ed. (Oxford: Oxford University Press, 2001), 357; Shen Zhihua, "The Sino-North Korean Conflict and its Resolution During the Korean War," trans. Doug Gil Kim and Jeffrey Becker, *Cold War International History Project Bulletin* 14/15 (Winter 2003/Spring 2004), 9–12.

44 Robert Jervis, "The Impact of the Korean War on the Cold War," *Journal of Conflict Resolution* 24:4 (December 1980), 563.

45 Alice C. Moroni, *The Fiscal Year 1984 Defense Budget Request: Data Summary* (Washington, DC: Congressional Reference Service, 1983), 13.

46 "Vietnam Veterans Against the War," http://encarta. msn.com/sidebar_762504451/Vietnam_Veterans_ Against_the_War.html

47 For declassified CIA documents on Soviet efforts to develop ICBMs, see http://www.cia.gov/csi/books/ nieuncls/1957.htm. For declassified Soviet descriptions and photographs of efforts to develop nuclear weapons and delivery systems, see http://nuclearweaponarchive. org/Russia/Sovwarhead.html

48 See the eyewitness account by the president's brother, Robert F. Kennedy, *Thirteen Days* (New York: W.W. Norton, 1969). The book gave its title to a 2000 film about the crisis starring Kevin Costner.

49 For the classic explanation of the missile crisis, see Graham T. Allison and Philip Zelikow, *Essence of Decision: Explaining the Cuban Missile Crisis*, 2nd ed. (New York: Longman, 1999).

50 See Joseph S. Nye, Jr., "Nuclear Learning and the US–Soviet Security Regime," *International Organization* 41:3 (September 1987), 394.

51 See Andrew M. Scott, *The Revolution in Statecraft: Informal Penetration* (New York: Random House, 1965).

52 "Interview with Zbigniew Brzezinski US President Carter's National Security Adviser," *Le Nouvel Observateur* (France) (Jan 15–21, 1998), http://www.globalresearch.ca/articles/BRZ110A.html

53 Alexander Haig, ""Opening Statement at Confirmation Hearings," Washington, DC: Bureau of Public Affairs, Department of State (January 9, 1981), 2.

54 Modern History Sourcebook: Ronald Reagan: Evil Empire Speech, June 8, 1982, http://www.fordham.edu/ halsall/mod/1982reagan1.html

55 "Excerpts from President's Speech to National Association of Evangelicals", *New York Times*, March 9, 1983, A18.

56 EIA Country Analysis Briefs, http://www.eia.doe.gov/ emeu/cabs/russia.html

57 Cited in Serge Schmemann, "Russia Lurches into Reform but Old Ways are Tenacious," *New York Times*, February 20, 1994, p. 6.

58 Andrei Shleifer and Daniel Treisman, "A Normal Country," *Foreign Affairs* 83:2 (March/April 2004), 27.

59 Ibid., 38.

60 Ibid., 20, 21.

61 David E. Sanger, "Bush Backs Plan to Move Iran's Uranium Enrichment to Russia," *New York Times Online*, November 18, 2005, http://nytimes.com/2005/11/18/ international/asia/18cnd-prexy.html?ei=5094&en=eefa1 66c8aee73cf&hp=&ex=1132376400&adxnnl=1&partn er=homepage&adxnnlx=1132344040-VyP9y/PToHTe 2kWacWfzlA

5 Great issues in contemporary global politics

1 Dennis Smith, "A Firefighter's Story," *New York Times*, September 14, 2001, 27.

2 Thomas L. Friedman argues that China and India will be the major powers of the twenty-first century. *The World Is Flat: A Brief History of the Twenty-First Century* (New York: Farrar, Strauss & Giroux, 2005).

3 Zbigniew Brzezinski and John Mearsheimer, "Clash of the Titans," *Foreign Policy* 146 (January/February 2005), 46–50.

4 Nixon's China Game, *The American Experience*, Public Broadcasting Service, http://www.pbs.org/wgbh/amex/ china/peopleevents/pande06.html

5 Cited in Greg Jaffe and Neil King Jr., "US Sees Broad China Threat in Asia," *Wall Street Journal*, July 20, 2005, A6.

6 "Clinton Defends 'Constructive Engagement' Of China," CNN/Time Online, http://www.cnn.com/ ALLPOLITICS/1997/10/24/clinton.china/

7 Chris Buckley, "Beijing Leaders Speak of Force to Keep Taiwan 'Chinese'," *New York Times*, March 8, 2005, A10.

8 Jim Yardley and Thom Shanker, "Chinese Navy Buildup Gives Pentagon New Worries," *New York Times*, April 8, 2005, A3.

9 Department of Defense, *The Military Power of the People's Republic of China 2005*, p. 13, http://www. defenselink.mil/news/Jul2005/d20050719china.pdf

10 *The Military Power of the People's Republic of China 2005*, 4–5.

11 Yardley and Shanker, "Chinese Navy Buildup."

12 Neil King Jr., "As China Boosts Defense Budget, US Military Hedges Its Bets," *Wall Street Journal*, April 20, 2006, A1, A8.

13 Joseph Kahn, "China's Costly Quest for Energy Control," *New York Times*, June 27, 2005, C1.

14 Andrew Ross Sorkin and Jad Mouawad, "Bid by Chevron in Big Oil Deal Thwarts China," *New York*

Times Online, July 20, 2005, A1, http://nytimes.com/2005/07/20/international/asia/20unocal.html?hp&ex=1121918400&en=8b3a5c2171ee08a4&ei=5094&partner=homepage

15 "The Balfour Declaration," The Avalon Project at Yale Law School, http://www.yale.edu/lawweb/avalon/mideast/balfour.htm

16 The PLO was actually an umbrella organization consisting of other Palestinian organizations, some terrorist, some not, and with different ideologies. These included Al Fatah and the Popular Front for the Liberation of Palestine (PFLP).

17 "Ending will be harder," *The Economist*, July 22, 2006, 29–32; Michael Young, "Hezbollah's Other War," *New York Times Magazine*, August 4, 2006, http://www.nytimes.com/2006/08/04/magazine/04lebanon.html?ex=1159329600&en=062648aa26b5b59b&ei=5070

18 "Intifada toll Sept 2000–Sept 2005," *BBC News*, September 30, 2005, http://newsvote.bbc.co.uk/2/hi/middle_east/4294502.stm

19 "Text UN Lebanon resolution", *BBC News*, August 12, 2006, http://news.bbc.co.uk/2/hi/middle_east/4785963.stm

20 "The extraordinary revival of the Islamic Republic," *The Economist*, August 26, 2006, 35–6.

21 World Bank, Middle East and North Africa Sector, "Overview and Development Context: Water Scarcity is a Serious Development Challenge Facing the Region," Water Resource Management, 2004. http://lnweb18.worldbank.org/mna/mena.nsf/0/27f2effc455749ce8525694a0072d3c3?OpenDocument. See also Applied Research Institute, Jerusalem, "The Water Conflicts in the Middle East from a Palestinian Perspective," http://www.arij.org/pub/wconflct

22 Ian J. Bickerton, *A Concise History of the Arab–Israeli Conflict* (Upper Saddle River, NJ: Prentice-Hall, 1998), 100.

23 Palestinians came to form a major proportion of the working population in neighboring Arab states, including Kuwait. After Kuwait was liberated in 1991, most Palestinians, who had supported Iraq, were expelled from Kuwait.

24 Al Qaeda has used the Internet effectively to coordinate its supporters' activities around the world. See Scott Shane, "Zarqawi Build Global Jihadist Network on Internet," *New York Times*, June 9, 2006, A9.

25 Judith Miller, "Faces of Fundamentalism," *Foreign Affairs* 73:6 (November/December 1994), 137.

26 Ibid., 126.

27 "Bin Laden's Fatwa," *Online NewsHour*, http://www.pbs.org/newshour/terrorism/international/fatwa_1996.html

28 There was a struggle between terrorists and passengers on another aircraft that ended with its crashing into a field near Pittsburgh, PA.

29 See Cofer Black, "How US Diplomacy Supports the Campaign Against International Terrorism," October 30, 2003, US Department of State, http://www.state.gov/s/ ct/rls/rm/2003/26961.htm

30 US Department of State, "Background Note: Iraq," August 2004, http://www.state.gov/r/pa/ei/bgn/6804.htm

31 Margaret MacMillan, *Paris 1919: Six Months That Changed the World* (London: Macmillan, 2001), 387–8. Emphasis added.

32 Cited in Lawrence Freedman and Efraim Karsh, *The Gulf Conflict, 1990–91: Diplomacy and War in the New World Order* (London: Faber, 1993), 53. Another excellent source is Alastair Finlan, *Essential Histories: The Gulf War 1991* (New York: Routledge, 2003).

33 Speech to the Aspen Institute on Sunday August 5, 1990. Cited in Freedman and Efraim Karsh, *The Gulf Conflict*, 111.

34 President Bush, October 9, 1990. Cited in ibid., 204.

35 Excellent web sources for the war are "The Gulf War," *Frontline* http://www.pbs.org/wgbh/pages/frontline/gulf and Richelson, Jeffrey T. ed., "Operation Desert Storm: Ten Years After," A National Security Archive Briefing Book, January 17, 2001, http://www.gwu.edu/~nsarchiv/NSAEBB/NSAEBB39

36 See "Iraq Conflict: The Historical Background," Global Policy Forum, http://www.globalpolicy.org/security/issues/iraq/histindex.htm. The US and Britain claimed that the action was authorized under Security Council Resolution 688 of April 5, 1991 which condemned Iraqi repression of its Kurds. Their claim, however, was something of a stretch.

37 Kenneth Janda and Stefano Mula, "Dubya, Meet Il Duce: Who Said 'Axis' First?" *Chicago Tribune*, April 21, 2002, http://wwwjanda.org/politxts/State%20of%20Addresses/2001-2004%20Bush/AxisofEvil.htm

38 "US–British Draft Resolution Stating Position on Iraq," *New York Times*, February 25, 2003, A14.

39 "Memorandum Opposing US Iraq Policy," *New York Times*, February 25, 2003, http://www.nytimes.com/2003/02/25/international/europe/25FTEX.html?ex=1159416000&en=9ada86a23a443e15&ei=5070

40 Security Council Resolution 1441 (2002), http://daccessdds.un.org/doc/UNDOC/GEN/N02/682/26/PDF/N0268226.pdf?OpenElement

41 See Iraq Coalition Casualty Count, http://icasualties.org/oif

42 See, for example, Mark Mazzetti, "Insurgent Attacks on Iraqis Soared, Report Says," *New York Times*, April 29, 2006, http://www.nytimes.com/2006/04/29/world/

middleeast/29terror.html?ex=1303963200&en=28451
b86bb9bbc44&ei=5088&partner=rssnyt&emc=rss

43 Robin Toner and Jim Rutenberg, "Partisan Divide on
Iraq Exceeds Split on Vietnam," *New York Times*, July 30,
2006, http://www.nytimes.com/2006/07/30/
washington/ 30war.html?ex=1311912000&en=
c6a6066ff004210e&ei=5088&partner=rssnyt&emc=rss

44 Edward Wong, "For an Iraq Cut in 3, Cast a Wary
Glance at Kurdistan," *New York Times*, August 27, 2006,
sec. 4, 12.

45 Mark Mazzetti, "Spy Agencies Say Iraq War Worsens
Terrorism Threat," *New York Times*, September 24,
2006, http://www.nytimes.com/2006/09/24/world/
middleeast/24terror.html

46 See "Changing Minds, Winning Peace," http://www.
state. gov/documents/organization/24882.pdf, pp. 16,
19.

47 Joseph Kahn, "Where's Mao? Chinese Revise History
Books," *New York Times*, September 1, 2006, A1.

6 Anarchy, power, and war

1 John McPhee, "Forensic Geology: Balloons of War," *The
New Yorker* 71:46 (January 29, 1996), 52–60.

2 Hans J. Morgenthau, *Politics Among Nations*, 7th ed., rev.
by Kenneth T. Thompson and W. David Clinton (New
York: McGraw-Hill, 2006), 5.

3 Ibid.

4 Hedley Bull, *The Anarchical Society: A Study of Order in
World Politics* (New York: Columbia University Press,
1977), 13.

5 Ibid., 24.

6 Joseph Grieco, "Anarchy and the Limits of
Cooperation," in David A. Baldwin, ed., *Neo-realism and
Neo-liberalism* (New York: Columbia University Press,
1993), 126. Emphasis in original.

7 Kenneth N. Waltz, *Man, the State, and War* (New York:
Columbia University Press, 1959), 159.

8 Thomas Hobbes, *Leviathan* (Oxford: Clarendon Press,
1909).

9 Joseph Grieco, "Understanding the Problem of
International Cooperation," in Baldwin, ed., *Neo-realism
and Neo-liberalism* (New York: Columbia University
Press, 1993), 303.

10 John J. Mearsheimer, *The Tragedy of Great Power Politics*
(New York: W.W. Norton, 2001), 35.

11 Robert Keohane, *After Hegemony: Cooperation and
Discord in the World Political Economy* (Princeton, NJ:
Princeton University Press, 1984), 27.

12 Grieco, "Anarchy and the Limits of Cooperation,"
126.

13 See Robert O. Keohane and Joseph S. Nye, *Power and
Interdependence: World Politics in Transition*, 3rd ed.
(New York: Addison-Wesley Longman, 2001), 275.

14 Robert O. Keohane, *International Institutions and State
Power* (Boulder, CO: Westview Press, 1989).

15 Stephen D. Krasner, "Structural Causes and Regime
Consequences: Regimes as Intervening Variables," in
Krasner, ed., *International Regimes* (Ithaca, NY: Cornell
University Press, 1983), 2.

16 Oran R. Young, *International Cooperation: Building
Regimes for Natural Resources and the Environment*
(Ithaca, NY: Cornell University Press, 1989).

17 Keohane, *International Institutions and State Power*,
see also Stephen Krasner, ed., *International Regimes*
(Ithaca, NY: Cornell University Press, 1982); and
Robert Keohane and Lisa Martin, "The Promise of
Institutionalist Theory," *International Security* 20 (1995),
39–51.

18 In a controversial deal, the Bush administration reached
an agreement with India to send that country nuclear
fuel and technology although India still refuses to sign
the Nuclear Nonproliferation Treaty. For its part, India
agreed to open some of its nuclear facilities to
international inspection. Foes of the agreement argue
that the deal legitimizes India's acquisition of nuclear
weapons and will encourage others to do the same.
See Thom Shanker, "Nuclear Deal With India Wins
Senate Backing," *New York Times*, November 17, 2006,
A10.

19 See "The Long, Long Half-life," *The Economist*, June 10,
2006.

20 Press Conference, 21 March 1963, *Public Papers of the
President of the United States: John F. Kennedy, 1963*
(Washington, DC: US Government Printing Office
[GPO], 1964), 280.

21 International Atomic Energy Agency, "IAEA Safeguards:
Stemming the Spread of Nuclear Weapons," *IAEA
Bulletin* 43:4 (2001), available from http://www.iaea.
org/programmes/safeguards/index.sthml

22 Proliferation Security Initiative, http://www.
proliferationsecurity.info; "The Proliferation Security
Initiative (PSI) At a Glance," *Fact Sheet*, September
2005, Arms Control Association, http://www.
armscontrol.org/ factsheets/PSI.asp

23 Nuclear Threat Initiative, http://www.nti.org/h_
learnmore/nwfztutorial/chapter02_01.html

24 Scott D. Sagan and Kenneth N. Waltz, *The Spread of
Nuclear Weapons: A Debate* (New York: Norton, 1995),
44.

25 Iran's president is not the country's leader. That
position is held by Grand Ayatollah Sayyid Ali
Khamenei. His official website is www.khamenei.ir/

26 *BBC News*, October 27, 2005, http://news.bbc.co.uk/
2/hi/middle_east/4107270.stm

27 For an excellent source of information on WMD proliferation, see John E. Pike, GlobalSecurity.org http://www.globalsecurity.org/wmd/index.html

28 The official IAEA website is http://www.iaea.org/

29 The US refused to participate in bilateral negotiations in order to avoid extending diplomatic recognition to North Korea as well as to involve other major players, especially China, to exert additional pressure on the North Koreans.

30 GlobalSecurity.org, http://www.globalsecurity.org/wmd/world/dprk/nuke.htm. Uranium enrichment is permitted under the NPT for use in generating energy but not to the level of weapons-grade uranium. Weapons-grade uranium is pure uranium at high enrichment levels of over 90 percent uranium 235. Weapons-grade plutonium is pure plutonium that is produced in heavy water- or graphite-moderated production reactors and separated from spent fuel in reprocessing plants. See "Key Nuclear Explosives Material," http://www.isis-online.org/publications/fmct/primer/Section_I.html

31 UN Security Council Resolution 1718, October 14, 2006, http://daccessdds.un.org/doc/UNDOC/GEN/N06/572/07/PDF/N0657207.pdf?OpenElement

32 "When the Soft Talk has to Stop," *The Economist*, January 14, 2006, 30.

33 See Nicholas G. Onuf, *World of Our Making: Rules and Rule in Social Theory and International Relations* (Columbia, SC: University of South Carolina Press, 1989).

34 Alexander Wendt, "Anarchy Is What States Make of It: The Social Construction of Power Politics," *International Organization* 46:2 (Spring 1992), 406.

35 Wendt, "Anarchy Is What States Make of It."

36 Wendt, "Anarchy Is What States Make of It," 405. Emphasis added.

37 Arnold Wolfers, *Discord and Collaboration* (Baltimore, MD: Johns Hopkins University Press, 1962), 106.

38 Joseph S. Nye, Jr., "The Changing Nature of World Power," *Political Science Quarterly* 105:2 (Summer 1990), 177.

39 Inis Claude, *Power and International Relations* (New York: Random House, 1962), 6.

40 Waltz, *Man, the State, and War*, 205.

41 Joseph S. Nye, Jr., *Soft Power: The Means to Success in World Politics* (New York: Public Affairs, 2004), 5.

42 Susan Strange, *States and Markets: An Introduction to Political Economy*, 2nd ed. (London: Pinter, 1994), 25.

43 Immanuel Wallerstein, *The Politics of the World Economy: The States, the Movements and the Civilizations* (Cambridge: Cambridge University Press, 1984), 37.

44 Susan Strange, "The Persistent Myth of Lost Hegemony," *International Organization* 41:4 (Autumn 1987), 565.

45 Jennifer Sterling-Folker, "Postmodern and Critical Theory Approaches," in Sterling-Folker, ed., *Making Sense of International Relations Theory* (Boulder, CO: Lynne Rienner, 2006), 159.

46 Wolfers, *Discord and Collaboration*, 103.

47 J. David Singer, Stuart Bremer, and John Stuckey, "Capability Distribution, Uncertainty, and Major Power War, 1820–1965," in Bruce M. Russett, ed., *Peace, War, and Numbers* (Beverly Hills, CA: Sage, 1972), 19–48.

48 Ray S. Cline, *World Power Assessment: A Calculus of Strategic Drift* (Boulder, CO: Westview Press, 1975).

49 The exception is a situation in which a target behaves as it does because it *anticipates* that the actor will otherwise exert power against it.

50 Bruce Bueno de Mesquita, *The War Trap* (New Haven, CT: Yale University Press, 1983), 1.

51 J. David Singer and Melvin Small, *The Wages of War, 1816–1965: A Statistical Handbook* (New York: Wiley, 1972), 37.

52 Meredith R. Sarkees, Frank W. Wayman, and J. David Singer, "Inter-State, Intra-State, and Extra-State Wars: A Comprehensive Look at Their Distribution over Time, 1816–1997," *International Studies Quarterly* 47:1 (March 2003), 58–9.

53 Kenneth N. Waltz, *Theory of International Politics* (Reading, MA: Addison-Wesley, 1979), 40.

54 Ibid., 88.

55 Ibid., 93.

56 Kenneth N. Waltz, "The Stability of a Bipolar World," in David Edwards, ed., *International Political Analysis* (New York: Holt, Rinehart & Winston, 1970), 340.

57 Kenneth N. Waltz, "International Structure, National Force, and the Balance of World Power," *Journal of International Affairs* 21:2 (1967), 220, 223.

58 Karl W. Deutsch and J. David Singer, "Multipolar Power Systems and International Stability," in James N. Rosenau, ed., *International Politics and Foreign Policy*, rev. ed. (New York: Free Press, 1969), 315–24. Richard N. Rosecrance took issue with both Waltz and Deutsch/Singer, reasoning that a system with features from both ("bimultipolarity") would be the safest. Rosecrance, "Bipolarity, Multipolarity, and the Future," in ibid., 325–35.

59 Waltz, *Man, the State, and War*, 232.

60 Thomas Hobbes, *Leviathan: Parts I and II* (Indianapolis: Bobbs-Merrill, 1958), 106.

61 See Waltz, *Man, the State, and War*, 167–9.

62 Mearsheimer, *The Tragedy of Great Power Politics*, 21.

63 See Robert Axelrod and Robert O. Keohane, "Achieving Cooperation Under Anarchy: Strategies and Institutions," *World Politics* 38:1 (October 1985), 226–54, and Robert O. Keohane, "Reciprocity in

International Relations," *International Organization* 40:1 (Winter 1986), 1–27.

64 The reference is to the liberal English political philosopher John Locke (1632–1704) whose view of human nature was far more optimistic than that of Hobbes. Unlike Hobbes, Locke argued that the state should be limited and that it did not have to exert significant power to maintain domestic tranquility.

65 Alexander E. Wendt, *Social Theory of International Politics* (Cambridge: Cambridge University Press, 1999), 279, 280.

66 Thucydides, *The Pelonnesian War*, trans. Rex Warner (Harmondsworth: Penguin Books, 1954), Book I, ch. 1, 25.

67 Hans Morgenthau, *Politics Among Nations: The Struggle for Power and Peace* (New York: Knopf, 1948), 155; Michael Doyle, *Ways of War and Peace: Realism, Liberalism and Socialism* (New York: Norton, 1997), 168.

68 Thomas J. Christensen and Jack Snyder, "Chain Gangs and Passed Bucks: Predicting Alliance Patterns in Multipolarity," *International Organization* 44:2 (Spring 1990), 137–68.

69 T. V. Paul, "Soft Balancing in the Age of U.S. Primacy," *International Security* 30:1 (Summer 2005), 46–71.

70 Cited in ibid., 66.

71 A. F. K. Organski, *World Politics*, 2nd ed. (New York: Random House, 1968), 338–76.

72 Keir Lieber and Daryl Press, "The Rise of US Nuclear Primacy," *Foreign Affairs* (March/April 2006), 45–9.

73 Peter C. W. Flory, Keith Payne, Pavel Podvig, Alexei Arbatov, Keir A. Lieber, and Daryl G. Press, "Nuclear Exchange: Does Washington Really Have (or Want) Nuclear Primacy?" *Foreign Affairs* 85:5 (September/October 2006), 149–57.

74 Lieber and Press, "The Rise of US Nuclear Primacy," 43.

75 George Modelski, *Long Cycles in World Politics* (Seattle: University of Washington Press, 1987); see also George Modelski and William R. Thompson, "Long Cycles and Global War," in Manus I. Midlarsky, ed., *Handbook of War Studies* (Boston, MA: Unwin Hyman, 1989), 23–54.

76 Steven Van Evera, "Offense, Defense, and the Causes of War," *International Security* 22:4 (Spring 1998), 5–43.

77 Robert Jervis, "Cooperation under the Security Dilemma," *World Politics* 30:2 (January 1978), 167–214.

7 The changing nature of war

1 John Hershey, *Hiroshima*, new ed. (New York: Alfred A. Knopf, 1985), 8.

2 "On This Day 1945: US Drops Atomic Bomb on Hiroshima," *BBC News*, August 6, 2004, http://news.bbc.co.uk/onthisday/hi/dates/stories/august/6/newsid_3602000/3602189.stm

3 Karl Maria von Clausewitz, *On War*, edited by Anatol Rapoport (Baltimore, MD: Penguin Books, 1968), Bk. I, ch. 1, 119.

4 Ibid., 110.

5 Robert F. Kennedy, *Thirteen Days* (New York: Norton, 1969), 48.

6 Roger A. Leonard, ed., *Clausewitz on War* (New York: Capricorn, 1967), 57.

7 Cited in J. F. C. Fuller, *War and Western Civilization 1832–1932: A Study of War as a Political Instrument and the Expression of Mass Democracy* (London: Duckworth, 1932), 99.

8 Barbara W. Tuchman, *The Guns of August* (New York: Bantam Books, 1962), 488.

9 "Notes from a suicide manual," http://www.ussyorktown.com/yorktown/kamikaze.htm

10 The USSR remained neutral as regards Japan until August 8, 1945 when it fulfilled the promise made to its allies at the February 1945 Yalta Conference to enter the Pacific war three months after Germany's surrender.

11 Robert Jervis, "Cooperation Under the Security Dilemma," *World Politics* 30:2 (January 1978), 167–214.

12 In 1862, Richard Jordan Gatling took out a patent for a *mechanical* gun that is remembered as the Gatling Gun. It consisted of a number of gun barrels mounted in a revolving frame.

13 Stefan T. Possony and Etienne Mantoux, "Du Picq and Foch: The French School," in Edward Mead Earle, ed., *Makers of Modern Strategy* (New York: Atheneum, 1967), 206–33.

14 See Barbara W. Tuchman, *The Zimmermann Telegram* (New York: Random House, 1966).

15 In fairness to Germany, the question can be raised as to why American vessels that were providing supplies to Britain and France should not be regarded as legitimate military targets.

16 De Gaulle led the Free French resistance movement in World War II, founded the French Fifth Republic, and was President of France between 1959 and 1969.

17 Cited in Thomas Gordan and Max Morgan, *Guernica: The Crucible of WWII* (New York: Witts, Stein, and Day, 1975), 258.

18 *Official Bombing Order, July 25, 1945*, http://www.dannen.com/decision/handy.html

19 John H. Herz, *International Politics in the Atomic Age* (New York: Columbia University Press, 1959).

20 Carl Sagan, "Nuclear War and Climatic Catastrophe: Some Policy Implications," *Foreign Affairs* 62:2 (Winter 1983/84), 257–92.

21 For a discussion of America's Quadrennial Defense Review, a compendium of future military threats and efforts to meet them, see "Rummy's wish list," *The Economist*, February 11, 2006, 29, 31.

22 Tom Weiner, "Pentagon Envisioning a Costly Internet for War," *New York Times*, November 13, 2004, A1.

23 Steven Metz, "Racing Toward the Future: The Revolution in Military Affairs," *Current History* (April 1997), 185.

24 Tim Weiner, "Air Force Seeks Bush's Approval for Space Arms," *New York Times*, May 18, 2005, A1.

25 "The March of Technology," in "Technology Quarterly," *The Economist*, June 10, 2006, 27. See Steven Metz, *Armed Conflict in the 21st Century: The Information Revolution and Post-Modern Warfare* (Carlisle, PA: Strategic Studies Institute, April 2000), 66–8.

26 "President Bush Announces Major Combat Operations in Iraq Have Ended," Remarks by the President from the USS *Abraham Lincoln*, at sea off the coast of San Diego, California. Office of the Press Secretary, May 1, 2003.

27 "'Cyber Storm' tests US defences," *BBC News*, February 12, 2006, http://news.bbc.co.uk/2/hi/americas/4706316.stm

28 Metz, *Armed Conflict in the 21st Century*, 185, 187.

29 Ibid., xiii.

30 *Sun Tzu on the Art of War: The Oldest Military Treatise in the World*, trans. Lionel Giles, 1910, http://www.chinapage.com/sunzi-e.html#02

31 Yochi J. Dreazen and Philip Shishkin, "Growing Concern: Terrorist Havens In 'Failed States'," *Wall Street Journal*, September 13, 2006, A1, A16.

32 The Fund for Peace, http://www.fundforpeace.org/publications/reports/iraq-report03-xsum.pdf

33 "The Failed States Index," *Foreign Policy* 154 (May/June 2006), 53.

34 "Guess Who's Running it Now," *The Economist*, June 10, 2006, 44–5.

35 "The Path to Ruin," *The Economist*, August 12, 2006, 18–20.

36 Cited in International Rescue Committee, "Rwanda – 10 Years Later," http://www.theirc.org/index.cfm/wwwID/1975

37 Cited in Christiane Amanpour, "Amanpour: Looking Back at Rwanda Genocide," *CNN.com*, April 6, 2004, http://www.cnn.com/2004/WORLD/africa/04/06/rwanda.amanpour/

38 Lydia Polgreen, "In Congo, Hunger and Disease Erode Democracy," *New York Times*, June 23, 2006, http://www.nytimes.com/2006/06/23/world/africa/23congo.html?ex=1308715200&en=7f73c59882c02be8&ei=50

88&partner=rssnyt&emc=rss, and Lydia Polgreen, "War's Chaos Steals Congo's Young by the Millions," *New York Times*, July 30, 2006, http://www.nytimes.com/2006/07/30/world/africa/30congo.html?ex=1156910400&en=b379ab8a3400b8be&ei=5070

39 "After the Poll," *The Economist*, August 5, 2006.

40 The United States occupied Haiti between 1915 and 1934 during which time it unsuccessfully sought to build a functioning state.

41 "Wars 'Less Frequent, Less Deadly'," *BBC News*, October 17, 2005. These figures do not take into account ongoing conflicts in Iraq and Darfur.

42 J. David Singer and Melvin Small, *The Wages of War, 1816–1965: A Statistical Handbook* (New York: Wiley, 1972), 31.

43 Paul Collier and Anke Hoeffler, "Greed and Grievance in Civil War," 3, http://www.worldbank.org/research/conflict/papers/greedandgrievance.htm

44 Raymond Taras and Rajat Ganguly, *Understanding Ethnic Conflict: The International Dimension* (New York: Addison-Wesley, 2002), 27.

45 Paul Collier, "The Market for Civil War," *Foreign Policy* 136 (May 2003), 40.

46 Ibid., and Ibrahim Elbadawi and Nicholas Sambanis, "How Much War Will We See? Estimating the Incidence of Civil War in 161 Countries," World Bank, http://www.worldbank.org/research/conflict/papers/incidencev2.htm

47 See Ted Robert Gurr, *Minorities at Risk: A Global View of Ethnopolitical Conflicts* (Washington, DC: United States Institute of Peace Press, 1993).

48 Eghosa E. Osaghae, "Explaining the Changing Patterns of Ethnic Politics in Nigeria," *Nationalism and Ethnic Politics* 9:3 (2003), 57.

49 Nancy Birdsall, "Chad and the Oil Curse," Center for Global Development, January 2, 2006, http://www.cgdev.org/content/article/detail/5549/

50 See Barbara F. Walter and Jack Snyder, eds., *Civil Wars, Insecurity, and Intervention* (New York: Columbia University Press, 1999); Barry Posen, "The Security Dilemma in Ethnic Conflict," *Survival* 35:1 (1993), 27–47; and Chaim Kaufmann, "Possible and Impossible Solutions to Ethnic Civil Wars," *International Security* 20:4 (1996), 136–75.

51 Donald M. Taylor and Fathali M. Moghaddam, *Theories of Intergroup Relations: International Social Psychological Perspectives* (Westport, CT: Praeger, 1994), 78–84.

52 Barbara F. Walter, "The Critical Barrier to Civil War Settlement," *International Organization* 51:3 (Summer 1997), 335.

53 Ibid., 340–1.

54 Chaim Kaufmann, "Intervention in Ethnic and Ideological Civil Wars: Why One Can Be Done and the Other Can't," *Security Studies* 6:2 (1996), 62–100.

55 Cited in Center for Defense Information, "A Brief History of Terrorism" (2003), http://www.cdi.org/friendlyversion/printversion.cfm?documentID=1502#_edn8

56 See Walter Laqueur, "Postmodern Terrorism", *Foreign Affairs* 75:5 (September/October 1996), 24–36.

57 The Liberation Tigers seek independence for the Tamils in a country dominated by a Sinhalese majority.

58 US Department of State, Office of the Coordinator for Counterterrorism, *Country Reports on Terrorism, 2005* (April 2006),12, http://stockholm.usembassy.gov/terror/2005.pdf

59 Ibid., Statistical Annex, v, vi.

60 See ibid., 178–82. The Pentagon has nuclear experts who can assess fallout in the event of a terrorist attack and identify the perpetrators. William J. Broad, "New Team Plans to Identify Nuclear Attackers," *New York Times*, February 2, 2006, A17.

61 Henry Clay Work, *Marching Through Georgia*, http://freepages.music.rootsweb.com/~edgmon/cwmarching.htm

62 James Brandon, "In Poetry-Loving Yemen, Tribal Bard Takes on Al Qaeda – With His Verse," *Christian Science Monitor*, May 12, 2006, http://www.csmonitor.com/2006/0512/p01s02-wome.html

8 Foreign policy and war

1 "NATO's Blunder Ignites Rage in Belgrade," *Washington Post*, May 9, 1999.

2 Robert L. Suettinger, *Beyond Tiananmen: The Politics of US–China Relations, 1989–2000* (Washington, DC: Brookings Institution Press, 2003), 370.

3 "Chinese Embassy Bombings: A Wide Net of Blame," *New York Times*, April 17, 2000.

4 Suettinger, *Beyond Tiananmen*, 371.

5 David M. Lampton, *Same Bed, Different Dreams: Managing US–China Relations, 1989–2000* (Berkeley, CA: University of California Press, 2001), 61.

6 Charles F. Hermann, "Policy Classification: A Key to the Comparative Study of Foreign Policy," in James J. Rosenau, Vincent Davis, and Maurice A. East, eds., *The Analysis of International Politics* (New York: Free Press, 1972), 72.

7 Hans J. Morgenthau, *Politics in the Twentieth Century*, abridged ed. (Chicago, IL: University of Chicago Press, 1962), 95, 97.

8 K. J. Holsti, *The Dividing Discipline: Hegemony and Diversity in International Theory* (Boston, MA: Allyn & Unwin, 1985), 9.

9 Oxfam, "Free Trade Agreements," http://www.oxfamamerica.org/whatwedo/campaigns/ft_agreements

10 Revelation 7 declares: "And I heard the number of them which were sealed: and there were sealed an hundred and forty and four thousand of all the tribes of the children of Israel." See also David D. Kirkpatrick, "For Evangelicals, Supporting Israel Is 'God's Foreign Policy'," November 14, 2006, http://www.nytimes.com/2006/11/14/washington/14israel.html?ei=5088&en=60ed9b6dc9e3816e&ex=1321160400&adxnnl=1&partner=rssnyt&emc=rss&adxnnlx=1163700443-I4LvdE3exdD76F6i0LXTPA. For a highly controversial description of the influence of the Israeli lobby in the United States, see John Mearsheimer and Stephen Walt, "The Israel Lobby," *London Review of Books* 28:6 (March 2006), http://www.lrb.co.uk/v28/n06/mear01_.html. A passionate video debate on the issue held on October 11, 2006 can be found online on ScribeMedia.Org, http://www.scribemedia.org/2006/10/11/israel-lobby/

11 John A. Vasquez, *The Power of Power Politics: From Classical Realism to Neotraditionalism* (Cambridge: Cambridge University Press, 1998), 48.

12 Kenneth N. Waltz, "Kant, Liberalism, and War," *American Political Science Review* 56:2 (June 1962), 332.

13 See Michael W. Doyle, "Kant, Liberal Legacies, and Foreign Affairs," *Philosophy and Public Affairs* 12:3 (Summer 1983), 205–35; Doyle, "Kant, Liberal Legacies, and Foreign Affairs, Part 2," ibid., 12:4 (Autumn 1983), 323–53; and Doyle, *Ways of War and Peace* (New York: Norton, 1997).

14 This triumph was celebrated by Francis Fukuyama as the "end of history." See Fukuyama, *The End of History and the Last Man* (New York: Free Press, 1992).

15 Bruce M. Russett, *Grasping the Democratic Peace: Principles for a Post-Cold War World* (Princeton, NJ: Princeton University Press, 1993). For a review of the vast literature on the "democratic peace," see James Lee Ray, *Democracy and International Conflict: An Evaluation of the Democratic Peace Proposition* (Columbia, SC: University of South Carolina Press, 1995).

16 Paul R. Hensel, Gary Goertz, and Paul F. Diehl, "The Democratic Peace and Rivalries," *Journal of Politics* 62:4 (November 2000), 1174.

17 See, for example, Edward S. Mansfield and Jack Snyder, "Democratic Transitions, Institutional Strength, and War," *International Organization* 56:2 (Spring 2002), 297–337.

18 Edward S. Mansfield and Jack Snyder, "Democratization and War," *Foreign Affairs* 74:3 (May/June 1995), 351.

19 See, for example, Michael E. Brown, Sean M. Lynn-Jones, and Steven E. Miller, eds. *Debating the Democratic Peace* (Cambridge, MA: The MIT Press, 1996).

20 Speech by George W. Bush to the United Nations General Assembly, September 21, 2004, http://www. whitehouse. gov/news/releases/2004/09/20040921-3.html

21 Norman Angell, *The Great Illusion* (1913), 381–2, http://www.lib.byu.edu/~rdh/wwi/1914m/illusion.html

22 Susan M. McMillan, "Interdependence and Conflict," *Mershon International Studies Review* 41:1 (1997), 33–58; David H. Bearce, "Grasping the Commercial Institutional Peace," *International Studies Quarterly* 47:3 (September 2003), 347–70.

23 John A. Hobson, *Imperialism* (London: George Allen & Unwin, 1954).

24 V. I. Lenin, *Imperialism, the Highest Stage of Capitalism*, http://www.marxists.org/archive/lenin/works/1916/imp-hsc/

25 Stephen Van Evera, "Hypotheses on Nationalism and War," *International Security* 18:4 (Spring 1994), 5–39.

26 T. Knecht and M. S. Weatherford, "Public Opinion and Foreign Policy: The Stages of Presidential Decision Making," *International Studies Quarterly* 50:3 (September 2006), 705–27.

27 James Lindsay, "Rally Round the Flag," *Brookings Daily War Report*, March 25, 2003, http://www.brookings.edu/views/op-ed/lindsay/20030325.htm

28 John R. Oneal and Jaroslav Tir, "Does the Diversionary Use of Force Threaten the Democratic Peace? Assessing the Effect of Economic Growth on Interstate Conflict, 1921–2001," *International Studies Quarterly* 50:4 (December 2006), 755–79.

29 Ahmer Tarar, "Diversionary Incentives and the Bargaining Approach to War," *International Studies Quartery* 50:1 (March 2006), 169–88.

30 Randall L. Schweller, "Unanswered Threats: A Neoclassical Realist Theory of Underbalancing," *International Security* 29:2 (Fall 2004), 168–9.

31 See John G. Stoessinger, *Crusaders and Pragmatists* (New York: W.W. Norton, 1979).

32 See James David Barber, *Presidential Character: Predicting Performance in the White House*, 4th ed. (Upper Saddle River, NJ: Prentice-Hall, 1992).

33 Hans J. Morgenthau, *Politics Among Nations: The Struggle for Power and Peace*, revised by Kenneth W. Thompson and W. David Clinton (New York: McGaw-Hill, 2006), 5.

34 Cited in Frank C. Zagare, "Rationality and Deterrence," *World Politics* 42:2 (1990), 240.

35 See, for instance, James D. Fearon, "Rationalist Explanations for War," *International Organization* 49:3 (Summer 1995), 379–414; Andrew Kydd, "Game Theory and the Spiral Model," *World Politics* 49 (April 1997), 371–400; Bruce Bueno de Mesquita, James D.

Morrow, and Ethan R. Zorik, "Capabilities, Perception, and Escalation," *American Political Science Review* 91:1 (March 1997), 15–27.

36 Ole R. Holsti, "The Belief System and National Images: A Case Study," *Journal of Conflict Resolution* 6:3 (September 1962), 244–52. See also Leon Festinger, *A Theory of Cognitive Dissonance* (Stanford, CA: Stanford University Press, 1957).

37 Robert Jervis, "Hypotheses on Misperception," *World Politics* 20:3 (April 1968), 454–79.

38 See Ernest R. May, *"Lessons" of the Past: The Use and Misuse of History in American Foreign Policy* (New York: Oxford University Press, 1973) and Richard E. Neustadt and Ernest R. May, *Thinking in Time: The Uses of History for Decision-Makers* (New York: Free Press, 1986).

39 Irving L. Janis and Leon Mann, *Decision Making: A Psychological Analysis of Conflict, Choice and Commitment* (New York: Free Press, 1977).

40 Irving L. Janis, *Victims of Groupthink* (Boston, MA: Houghton Mifflin, 1972), 35–6, and William A. Boettcher III, "The Prospects for Prospect Theory: An Empirical Evaluation of International Relations Applications of Framing and Loss Aversion," *Journal of Psychology* 25:3 (2004), 333.

41 Jeffrey Berejekian, "The Gains Debate: Framing State Choice," *American Political Science Review* 94:4 (December 1997), 790. See also, Daniel Kahneman and Amos Tversky, "Prospect Theory: An Analysis of Decision under Risk," *Econometrica* 47 (1979), 263–91 and Jack Levy, "Prospect Theory and International Relations: Theoretical Applications and Analytical Problems," *Political Psychology* 13:2 (June 1992), 283–310.

42 Janis, *Victims of Groupthink*.

43 Janis, *Victims of Groupthink*, 91; see also 82–90.

44 Bob Woodward, *Plan of Attack* (New York: Simon and Schuster, 2004).

45 Adda B. Bozeman, *Politics and Culture in International History* (Princeton, NJ: Princeton University Press, 1960), 464–77.

46 Morgenthau, *Politics Among Nations*, 558–66.

47 A game in this sense refers to "a struggle in which complete 'rationality' of the opponent is assumed and in which the object is to outwit the opponent." Anatol Rapoport, *Fights, Games, and Debates* (Ann Arbor, MI: University of Michigan Press, 1960), 10.

48 See Thomas C. Schelling, *The Strategy of Conflict* (Cambridge, MA: Harvard University Press, 1966), 5.

49 Robert J. Art, "To What Ends Military Power," *International Security* 4:4 (Spring 1980), 5.

50 On this distinction, see ibid., and Lawrence Freedman, "Prevention, Not Preemption," *The Washington Quarterly* 26:2 (2003), 105–14.

51 Cited in Neil Sheehan, ed., *The Pentagon Papers* (New York: Bantam, 1971), 432.

52 Schelling, *Strategy of Conflict*, 186–203.

53 Ibid., 188. Emphasis in original.

54 See Thomas C. Schelling, *Arms and Influence* (New Haven, CT: Yale University Press, 1966), 36 ff.

55 Edward Rhodes, *Power and MADness: The Logic of Nuclear Coercion* (New York: Columbia University Press, 1989), 45–6.

56 Robert F. Kennedy, *Thirteen Days: A Memoir of the Cuban Missile Crisis* (New York: Norton, 1971), 4, 156.

57 Gregory W. Pedlow, ed., *NATO Strategy Documents, 1949–1969*, www.nato.int/docu/stratdoc/eng/a570523a.pdf

58 Cited in Lawrence Freedman, *The Evolution of Nuclear Strategy*, 2nd ed. (New York: St. Martins, 1989), 86.

59 Cited in Anthony Read, *The Devil's Disciples: Hitler's Inner Circle* (New York: Norton, 2003), 392.

60 Schelling, *Arms and Influence*, 66–7.

61 Albert Wohlstetter, "The Delicate Balance of Terror," *Foreign Affairs* 37: 2 (January 1959), 211–34 and P-1472, RAND Corporation (November 6, 1958).

62 Ibid., http://www.polisci.ucsd.edu/~bslantch/courses/nss/documents/wohlstetter-balance-of-terror.html

63 Center for Defense Information, "Nuclear Facts at a Glance," February 4, 2003, http://www.cdi.org/friendlyversion/printversion.cfm?documentID=173&from_page=../program/document

64 "The National Security Strategy of the United States of America," The White House, September 2002,15, http://www.whitehouse.gov/nsc/nss.html

65 Gordon A. Craig and Alexander L. George, *Force and Statecraft: Diplomatic Problems of our Time*, 3rd ed. (New York: Oxford University Press, 1995), 197.

66 Schelling, *Arms and Influence*, 44–5.

67 Howard W. French, "Shanghai Club, Once Obscure, Now Attracts Wide Interest," *New York Times*, June 16, 2006, http://www.nytimes.com/2006/06/16/world/asia/16shanghai.html?ex=1308110400&en=017520b0528f29ba&ei=5088&partner=rssnyt&emc=rss, and "The Shanghai Six at Five," *The Economist*, June 10, 2006.

68 Stephen Walt, *The Origins of Alliances* (Ithaca, NY: Cornell University Press, 1987).

69 John Vasquez, *The War Puzzle* (Cambridge: Cambridge University Press, 1993), 166–7.

70 Amy F. Woolf, "Arms Control and Strategic Nuclear Weapons: Unilateral vs. Bilateral Reductions," *CRS Report for Congress*, December 17, 2001; fpc.state.gov/documents/organization/7946.pdf

71 Cited in Scott Peterson, "Can Hussein Be Deterred?" *Christian Science Monitor*, September 10, 2002, http://www.csmonitor.com/2002/0910/p01s03-wosc.html

72 Kenneth M. Pollack, "Why Iraq Can't Be Deterred," *New York Times*, September 26, 2002, http://www.brook.edu/views/op-ed/pollack/20020926.htm

73 Ibid.

74 Richard Ned Lebow, *Nuclear Crisis Management: A Dangerous Illusion* (Ithaca, NY: Cornell University Press, 1987), 121.

75 "Peace and Security," President Reagan's televised address to the nation, March 23, 1983, reprinted in *Realism, Strength, Negotiation: Key Foreign Policy Statements of the Reagan Administration* (Washington, DC: Department of State, May 1984).

76 "Dr. Condoleezza Rice Discusses President's National Security Strategy," (October 1, 2002), The White House, http://www.whitehouse.gov/news/releases/2002/10/20021001-6.html

77 Commission of Presidential Debates, "Debate Transcript" (September 30, 2004), http://www.debates.org/pages/trans2004a.html

78 "President Bush Delivers Graduation Speech at West Point," (June 2002), The White House, http://www.whitehouse.gov/news/releases/2002/06/print/20020601-3.html. Emphasis added.

9 International law and organization and the quest for peace

1 Cited in Julian Borger, "Was it an Adlai Stevenson Moment? Powell Did Not Even Come Close, Says UN Veteran," *The Guardian*, February 6, 2003.

2 Union of International Associations, *Yearbook of International Organizations 2003–04*, 40th ed. (Munich: K.G. Saur Verlag, 2005), vol. 2, appendix 3, 2914.

3 *The Cuban Missile Crisis: Letter from Chairman Khrushchev to President Kennedy*, October 24, 1962, The Avalon Project at Yale Law School, http://www.yale.edu/lawweb/avalon/diplomacy/forrel/cuba/cuba061.htm

4 Abram Chayes, *The Cuban Missile Crisis: International Crisis and the Role of Law* (New York: Oxford University Press, 1974), 15.

5 Customary international law should be distinguished from mere comity, which involves the informal and voluntary recognition by courts of one jurisdiction of the laws and judicial decisions of another.

6 International Criminal Court, "Statute of the International Court of Justice," chap. II art. 36, http://www.icj-cij.org/icjwww/ibasicdocuments/ibasictext/ibasicstatute.htm

7 "Military and Paramilitary Activities in and Against Nicaragua," in Mary Ellen O'Connell, *International Law and the Use of Force: Cases and Materials* (New York: Foundation Press, 2005), 96.

8 Jean-Marie Henkaerts, "Study on Customary International Humanitarian Law: A Contribution to the Understanding and Respect for the Rule of Law in Armed Conflict," *International Review of the Red Cross* 87:857 (March 2005), 187,188, http://www.icrc.org/Web/eng/siteeng0.nsf/htmlall/review-857-p175/$File/irrc_857_Henckaerts.pdf

9 UN Division for Oceans and Law of the Sea, *Oceans and Law of the Sea*, http://www.un.org/Depts/los/index.htm

10 Before 1982, territorial waters extended only three miles because this was the range of most shore batteries.

11 UN Convention on the Law of the Sea, http://www.globelaw.com/LawSea/ls82_1.htm#section_1_general_provisions

12 International Seabed Authority, *The International Seabed Authority: Structure and Functioning*, http://www.isa.org.jm/ en/seabedarea/TechBrochures/ENG2.pdf

13 Legal positivism should not be confused with empirical or logical positivism which refers to the belief that the only reliable knowledge is that which is based on observation of facts that can be verified.

14 Hugo Grotius, *Prolegomena to the Law of War and Peace* (New York: Bobbs-Merrill, 1957), 21.

15 Cited in "The Ethics of War," bbc.co.uk, http://www.bbc.co.uk/print//religion/ethics/war/jwhistory.shtml

16 St. Thomas Aquinas, *Summa Theologica*, II-II, http://www.newadvent.org/summa/304001.htm

17 Grotius, *Prolegomena to the Law of War and Peace*, 18.

18 For an excellent analysis of just war theory, see Mark Amstutz, *International Ethics: Concepts, Theories, and Cases in Global Politics* (Lanham, MD: Rowman & Littlefield, 1999), 93–118.

19 John Lothrop Motley, *The Life and Death of John of Barneveld* (New York: Harper and Brothers Publishers, 1880), vol. 2, chapter 22.

20 Cited in Colum Lynch, "US, Allies Dispute Annan on Iraq War," *Washington Post*, September 17, 2004, A18.

21 *Frontline*, "The Gulf War: An Oral History," http://www.pbs.org/wgbh/pages/frontline/gulf/oral/powell/4.html

22 Joseph S. Nye, Jr., *Nuclear Ethics* (New York: Free Press, 1986), 98–9.

23 Bruce Russett and John Oneal, *Triangulating Peace: Democracy, Interdependence, and International Organizations* (New York: Norton, 2001), 17.

24 Cited in Kenneth N. Waltz, *Man, the State, and War* (New York: Columbia University Press, 1959), 185.

25 Barbara W. Tuchman, *The Proud Tower: A Portrait of the World Before the War: 1890–1914* (New York: Macmillan, 1962), 236–7.

26 "Pope Kofi's Unruly Flock," *The Economist*, August 8, 1998, 19.

27 "Charter of the United Nations," The Avalon Project at Yale Law School, http://www.yale.edu/lawweb/avalon/un/unchart.htm

28 A sixth organ, the Trusteeship Council, essentially closed after all the non-self-governing territories for which it was responsible gained independence.

29 Tarik Kafala, "The Veto and How to Use It," *BBC News Online*, September 17, 2003, http://www.bbc.co.uk/1/hi/world/middle_east/2828985.stm

30 International Court of Justice, "Legal Consequences of the Construction of a Wall in the Occupied Palestinian Territory: Summary of the Advisory Opinion of 9 July 2004," http://www.icj-cij.org/icjwww/idocket/imwp/imwpframe.htm

31 For more on UN agencies, see "Official Website Locator for the United Nations System of Organizations," http://www.unsystem.org

32 International Labour Organization, "About the ILO," http://www.ilo.org/public/english/about/index.htm

33 See Ernst B. Haas, *The Uniting of Europe* (Stanford, CA: Stanford University Press, 1958), 16.

34 For a comprehensive survey of UN peacekeeping missions, see United Nations, "United Nations Peacekeeping," http://www.un.org/Depts/dpko/dpko/ops.htm

35 "United Nations Peacekeeping Operations," http://www.un.org/peace/bnote010101.pdf

36 The Uniting for Peace Resolution has been used rarely because it entails directly challenging a major state. Thus, though some opponents of America's 2003 invasion of Iraq wanted to invoke it to circumvent the US veto in the Security Council, the Assembly did not do so.

37 *Introduction to the Annual Report of the Secretary-General on the Work of the Organization*, June 16, 1959 to June 15, 1960, General Assembly, Official Records, 15th sess., supp. No. 1A, 4.

38 Cited in Warren Hoge, "Official of UN Says Americans Undermine It With Criticism," *New York Times*, June 7, 2006, http://www.nytimes.com/2006/06/07/ world/americas/07nations.html?ex=1307332800&en=271a43f723d2841b&ei=5088&partner=rssnyt&emc=rss

39 United Nations, "Is The United Nations Good Value for the Money?" http://www.un.org/geninfo/ir/ch5/ch5_txt.htm

40 United Nations, "UN Peacekeeping Operations," November 30, 2005, http://www.un.org/Depts/dpko/dpko/bnote.htm

41 Global Policy Forum, "Background and History of the Financial Crisis," http://www.globalpolicy.org/finance/chronol/hist.htm

42 Global Policy Forum, " Financial Crisis," http://globalpolicy.igc.org/finance/index.htm

43 Warren Hoge, "General Assembly Committee Lifts a Cap on UN Spending," *New York Times*, June 29, 2006, A8.

44 "Ted Turner Donates $1 Billion to 'UN Causes,'" *CNN Interactive*, September 19, 1997, http://www.cnn.com/US/9709/18/turner.gift

45 Alexandra MacRaw, "More Firms Join UN Push to be Good Corporate Citizens," *Christian Science Monitor* July 19, 2004.

46 United Nations, "Security Council Resolutions-2002," http://www.un.org/Docs/scres/2002/sc2002.htm

47 This is a controversial claim. In fact, the claim was previously made, when US and European military forces intervened in Kosovo in 1999 without UN approval. See Robert Kagan, "America's Crisis of Legitimacy," *Foreign Affairs* 83:2 (March/April 2004), 73–7.

48 Robert F. Worth, "Sudan Says It Will Accept UN–African Peace Force in Darfur," *New York Times*, November 17, 2006, A3.

49 This concern was borne out in a US National Intelligence Estimate that was leaked and then made public in September 2006. Mark Mazzetti, "Spy Agencies Say Iraq War Worsens Terror Threat," *New York Times*, September 24, 2006, sec. 1, 1.

50 Cited in Alan Cowell, "A New Survey Suggests That Britons Take a Dim View of the US," *New York Times*, July 3, 2006, A5.

51 "A Winning Recipe for Reform?" *The Economist*, July 24, 2004, 45.

52 The US contribution is about 0.15 percent.

53 Warren Hoge, "Annan Offers Plans for Changes in UN Structure," *New York Times*, March 21, 2005, http://www.nytimes.com/2005/03/21/international/21cnd-nations.html?ei=5088&en=f0a40d3e870b47e5&ex=1269061200&adxnnl=1&partner=rssnyt&adxnnlx=1137434404-2n9C4tJqeQW1emgVOg42+g

54 See, for example, Eric Jansson, "Serbia Hits at UN for Giving Kosovo More Power," *New York Times*, January 3, 2004, and "Gunning for Local Power," *The Economist*, August 7, 2004, 43–4.

55 Tom Regan, "Bolton Wants '11th Hour' Change to UN Reform Plan," *Christian Science Monitor*, August 29, 2005, http://www.csmonitor.com/2005/0829/dailyUpdate.html

56 Warren Hoge, "UN and US Again Display Testiness of Their Relations," *New York Times*, June 8, 2006, A10.

57 Stephen D. Krasner, *Sovereignty: Organized Hypocrisy* (Princeton, NJ: Princeton University Press, 1999), 235.

58 Christer Jönsson, Sven Tägil, and Gunnar Törnquist, *Organizing European Space* (London: Sage, 2000), 173.

59 In 1961, the OEEC became the Organization for Economic Cooperation and Development (OECD) with the task of coordinating the economic policies of the world's major industrialized countries.

60 Cited in Jean Monnet, *Memoirs* (Garden City, NY: Doubleday, 1978), 222.

61 Karl W. Deutsch et al., *Political Community and the North Atlantic Area: International Organization in the Light of Historical Experience* (Princeton, NJ: Princeton University Press, 1957).

62 Karl W. Deutsch, *The Analysis of International Relations*, 3rd ed. (Englewood Cliffs, NJ: Prentice-Hall, 1988), 281.

63 Cited in "An Affair to Remember," *The Economist*, July 29, 2006, 24.

64 Data from Delegation of the European Commission to the United States, "European Union in the US: Facts and Figures," http://www.eurunion.org/profile/EUUSStats. htm

65 Cited in "Chirac Lashes Out at 'New Europe'," CNN.com, February 18, 2003, http://www.cnn.com/2003/WORLD/europe/02/18/sprj.irq.chirac

66 "Abroad be Dangers," *The Economist*, August 26, 2006.

67 The African Union website is http://www.africa-union.org

68 The ECOWAS website is http://www.ecowas.int

69 The OAS website is http://www.oas.org

70 The NAFTA website is http://www.nafta-sec-alena.org

71 For a systematic critique of NAFTA, see Public Citizen, "North American Free Trade Agreement (NAFTA)," http://www.citizen.org/trade/nafta

72 International Trade Canada, "Overview of the NAFTA: A Foundation for Canada's Future Prosperity," http://www.dfait-maeci.gc.ca/nafta-alena/over-en.asp

73 The FTAA website is http://www.ftaa-alca.org/View_e.asp

74 APEC's website is http://www.apec.org/apec.html

75 Alex Keto, Geraldo Samor, and Carla Anne Robbins, "Bush Pushes His Top Priorities At APEC Meeting," *Wall Street Journal*, November 22, 2004, A12, A13.

76 NATO's website is http://www.nato.int

77 In part, this action was taken in order to provide Europe additional influence over subsequent US actions.

78 See "NATO in Afghanistan," http://www.nato.int/issues/afghanistan

79 See the OSCE website at http://www.osce.org

80 Russett and Oneal, *Triangulating Peace*, 166.

81 Ibid., 194.

82 Peter Willetts, "Transnational Actors and International Organizations in Global Politics," in John Baylis and Steve Smith, eds., *The Globalization of World Politics: An Introduction to International Relations* (New York: Oxford University Press, 1997), 290.

83 Visit the ICRC website at http://www.icrc.org/eng, for more about Henry Dunant and the ICRC's founding

at "From the Battle of Solferino to the Eve of the First World War," http://www.icrc.org/web/eng/siteeng0.nsf/html/57JNVP

84 A listing and description of major NGOs can be found at Duke University, Public Documents & Map Department, "Non-governmental Organizations, Research Guide," http://docs.lib.duke.edu/igo/guides/ngo/db/a-e.asp

85 UN Department of Public Information, "NGOs and the United Nations Department of Public Information: Some Questions and Answers," http://www.un.org/dpi/ngosection/brochure.htm

86 See Margaret E. Keck and Kathryn Sikkink, *Activists Beyond Borders: Advocacy Networks in International Politics* (Ithaca, NY: Cornell University Press, 1998).

87 Paul Wapner, *Environmental Activism and World Civic Politics* (Albany, NY: State University of New York Press, 1996).

10 Human rights: the individual in global politics

1   "Sudan: The Rape of an 11-Year Old Girl in Police Custody," Amnesty International's Work on Women, http://www.amnesty.org/ailib/intcam/women/2000/appeal_sudan.html#update

2   Cited in Carrie Chapman Catt and Nettie Rogers Shuler, "Woman Suffrage and Politics," http://www.infoplease.com/t/hist/suffrage-inner-story/chapter3.html

3   Amnesty International, "United States of America Human Dignity Denied: Torture and Accountability in the 'War on Terror'," October 27, 2004, http://web.amnesty.org/library/Index/ENGAMR511452004

4   "US Troops Face 'War Crimes' Claim," *BBC News*, August 5, 2006, http://newsvote.bbc.co.uk/go/pr/fr/-/2/hi/middle_east/5246424.stm

5   The term was invented by the Jewish Polish lawyer Raphael Lemkin (1900–59) in 1943 who combined the Greek word for race (*genos*) with the Latin word for kill (*cide*). See Raphael Lemkin, *Axis Rule in Occupied Europe: Laws of Occupation – Analysis of Government – Proposals for Redress* (Washington, DC: Carnegie Endowment for International Peace, 1944), 79–95, http://www.preventgenocide.org/lemkin/AxisRule1944-1.htm

6   Tony Trainor, "Education Would Have Benefited Idi Amin," *Western Mail*, August 22, 2003, http://icwales.icnetwork.co.uk/0100news/0200wales/tm_objectid=13324008%26method=full%26siteid=50082-name_page.html

7   M. J. Lerner. "Integrating Societal and Psychological

Rules: The Basic Task of Each Social Actor and Fundamental Problem for the Social Sciences," in R. Vermunt and H. Steensma, eds., *Social Justice in Human Relations: Societal and Social Origins*, vol. 1 (New York: Plenum Press, 1991), 13.

8   David Rodin, *War and Self-Defense* (Oxford: Oxford University Press, 2002), 17–23.

9   Cited in Judith Miller, "Sovereignty Isn't So Sacred Anymore," *New York Times*, April 18, 1999, sec. 4, 4.

10 "The Nuremberg Race Laws," United States Holocaust Memorial Museum, http://www.ushmm.org/outreach/nlaw.htm

11 http://www.remember.org/witness/babiyar.html

12 Text can be found at the Office of the United Nations High Commissioner for Human Rights (OHCHR), http://www.unhchr.ch/html/menu3/b/p_genoci.htm

13 The Avalon Project at Yale Law School, *Nuremberg Trial Proceedings Vol. 1,Charter of the International Military Tribunal*, http://www.yale.edu/lawweb/avalon/imt/proc/imtconst.htm

14 Kellogg-Briand Pact of 1928, http://www.yale.edu/lawweb/avalon/imt/kbpact.htm

15 Cited in Indictment from the International Military Tribunal for the Far East, World War II File, Bontecou Papers, Harry S Truman Presidential Museum & Library, http://www.trumanlibrary.org/whistlestop/study_collections/nuremberg/tokyo.htm

16 The official website of the ICTY is http://www.un.org/icty/glance/index.htm

17 Ibid.

18 The tribunal's official website is http://www.ictr.org/default.htm

19 Seth Mydans, "27 Years Later, a Formal Inquiry Begins Into Khmer Rouge Atrocities," *New York Times*, August 6, 2006, A6.

20 Beth K. Dougherty, "Right-Sizing International Criminal Justice: The Hybrid Experiment at the Special Court for Sierra Leone," *International Affairs* 80:2 (2004), 311–28; "Eleventh Annual Report of the International Tribunal for the Prosecution of Persons Responsible for Serious Violations of International Humanitarian Law Committed in the Territory of the Former Yugoslavia since 1991," August 13, 2004, 68, http://www.un.org/icty/rappannu-e/2004/AR04.pdf; Human Rights Watch, "Essential Background: Overview of Human Rights Issues in Rwanda," http://hrw.org/english/docs/2005/01/13/ rwanda9860.htm

21 No one will be indicted on this charge until agreement is reached in defining aggression, an unlikely prospect in the foreseeable future.

22 The official website of the ICC is http://www.icc-cpi.int

23 International Criminal Court, "Jurisdiction," http://www.un.org/icty/rappannu-e/2004/AR04.pdf

24 Marlise Simons, "Sudan Poses First Big Trial For World Criminal Court," *New York Times*, April 29, 2005, A12.

25 US Department of State, "Explanation of Vote on the Sudan Accountability Resolution," March 31, 2005, http://www.state.gov/p/io/44388.htm

26 "Hunting Uganda's Child-killers," *The Economist*, May 7, 2005, 41–2.

27 See Elizabeth Rubin, "If Not Peace, Then Justice," *New York Times Magazine*, April 2, 2006, http://www.nytimes.com/2006/04/02/magazine/02darfur.html?ex=1301634000&en=dc61bea13467209a&ei=5088&partner=rssnyt&emc=rss

28 Owen C. Pell, "Tort Claims Under International Law," *New York Law Journal* 24 (August 4, 2004), 4.

29 United Nations International Law Commission, "Vienna Convention on the Law of Treaties," http://www.un.org/law/ilc/texts/treatfra.htm

30 Over 500 years later, Thomas Jefferson declared that one reason why America's colonists were declaring independence was that England's King George III had imposed "taxes on us without our consent."

31 King John quickly tried to escape his obligations, claiming that the Magna Carta had been obtained by force. After the pope agreed, the barons again rose up against King John and after his death, his son, Henry III, forced the Crown to accept the Magna Carta in perpetuity.

32 Cited in Michael J. Glennon, "Why the Security Council Failed," in James F. Hoge Jr. and Gideon Rose, *American Foreign Policy: Cases and Choices* (New York: Council on Foreign Relations, 2003), 263.

33 Terence Neilan, "US Returns 'Enemy Combatant' After 3 Years," *nytimes.com*, October 11, 2004, http://www.nytimes.com/2004/10/11/international/middleeast/11CND-HAMD.html?ex=1138942800&en=38a17abf74034498&ei=5070

34 Supreme Court of the United States, Hamdi *et al.* v. Rumsfeld, Secretary of Defense, *et al.* http://www.supremecourtus.gov/opinions/03pdf/03-6696.pdf

35 The website for the Office of the High Commissioner for Human Rights is http://www.ohchr.org/english/about/index.htm

36 The Council's website is http://www.ohchr.org/english/bodies/hrcouncil/

37 Tom Wright, "Annan Cautions Rights Council to Avoid Rifts," *New York Times*, June 20, 2006, A7.

38 For the text, see United Nations, "Universal Declaration of Human Rights," http://www.un.org/Overview/rights.html

39 Data can be found at Freedom House, *Freedom in the World 2005*, http://www.freedomhouse.org/research/freeworld/2005/table2005.pdf

40 Ronald Inglehart, "Globalization and Postmodern Values," *The Washington* Quarterly 23:1 (Winter 2000), 228.

41 See the Human-Rights.net for links to human rights NGOs, http://www.human-rights.net/

42 For Amnesty International's official website, see http://www.amnesty.org. Another effective and similar group, Human Rights Watch, was founded in 1978. Its website is http://www.hrw.org

43 Amnesty International UK, "Peter Benenson's Biography," http://www.amnesty.org.uk/amnesty/history/biography.shtml

44 See Amnesty International, Online documentation archive, http://web.amnesty.org/library/Index/ENGACT300112001?open&of=ENG-FJI

45 Amnesty International, "Previous Campaigns," http://www.amnesty.org/campaign/index2.html

46 Amnesty International, "Current Campaigns," http:// www.amnesty.org/campaign

47 Cited in Patrick E. Tyler, "Hillary Clinton In China, Details Abuse Of Women," *New York Times*, September 6, 1995, A1.

48 United Nations, Division on the Advancement of Women, "Convention on the Elimination of All Forms of Discrimination against Women," http://www. un.org/womenwatch/daw/cedaw/text/econvention.htm

49 *Human Development Report, 1995* (New York: Oxford University Press, 1994), 78–80. This is the last HDI dedicated to the status of women.

50 "No Place for Your Daughters," *The Economist*, November 26, 2005, 58.

51 Unless otherwise noted, the data bullets in this section are compiled in Amnesty International, "Making Violence against Women Count: Facts and Figures – a Summary," March 5, 2004, http://news.amnesty.org/index/ENGACT770342004

52 World Health Organization, *WHO Multi-country Study on Women's Health and Domestic Violence against Women* (2006), http://www.who.int/gender/violence/who_ multicountry_study/en/

53 It is estimated that such practices, along with other forms of violence against women, cost the lives of between 1.5 and 3 million women every year. "No Place for Your Daughters."

54 Cited in John F. Burns, "India Fights Abortion of Female Fetuses," *New York Times*, August 27, 1994, 5.

55 Valerie M. Hudson and Andrea Den Boer, "A Surplus of Men, A Deficit of Peace," *International Security* 26:4 (Spring 2002), 5.

56 http://www.amnestyusa.org/amnestynow/legalizedmurder.html

57 http://archives.cnn.com/2002/WORLD/asiapcf/south/12/11/pakistan.women/

58 United Nations Population Fund, "Taking a Stand against Practices That Harm Women," http://www.unfpa. org/gender/traditions.htm

59 National Organization for Women, "Fact Sheet: Women's Rights Under Sharia in Northern Nigeria," August 22, 2002, http://www.now.org/issues/global/082202sharia.html

60 These data are from "Womens, Girls and War: Sexual Violence as a Weapon of War," http://www.wibfrederick.org/pdfs/Comfort%20Women%20flyer.2.pdf

61 Cited in Barbara Crossette, "Population Meeting Opens with Challenge to the Right," *New York Times*, September 6, 1994, A1, A6.

62 Cited in Alan Cowell, "Vatican Attacks Population Stand Supported by US," *New York Times*, August 9, 1994, A4.

63 United Nations, Fourth World Conference on Women, "Beijing Declaration," http://www.un.org/womenwatch/daw/beijing/platform/declar.htm

64 International Women's Health Coalition, "Bush's Other War," http://www.iwhc.org/resources/bushsotherwar/intl.cfm

65 Helena Andrews, "Muslim Women Don't See Themselves as Oppressed, Survey Finds," *New York Times*, June 8, 2006, http://www.nytimes.com/2006/06/08/world/middleeast/08women.html?ex=1307419200&en=e2d514a70cc63246&ei=5088&partner=rssnyt&emc=rss

66 UN, Fourth World Conference on Women, Beijing Declaration, http://www.un.org/womenwatch/daw/beijing/platform/declar.htm. Emphasis added.

67 Michael Ignatieff, "The Attack on Human Rights," *Foreign Affairs* 80:6 (Nov./Dec. 2001), 1.

68 Mary Ann Glendon, *A World Made New* (New York: Random House, 2001), 39.

69 Robert F. Worth, "In Jeans or Veils, Iraqi Women are Split on New Political Power," *New York Times*, April 12, 2005, A1.

70 Cited in "Clinton's Call: Avoid Isolating China on Trade and Rights," *New York Times*, May 27, 1994, A4.

11 International political economy

1 See George Draffan, "Directory of Transnational Corporations," http://www.endgame.org/dtc/directory.html

2 "Mine Giant Settles Pollution Case," *BBC News*, February 16, 2006, http://news.bbc.co.uk/2/hi/asia-pacific/4718672.stm

3 OECD, *International Investment Perspectives* (2005), 11, http://www.oecd.org/dataoecd/13/62/35032229.pdf#search=%22trends%20in%20Foreign%20Direct%20Investment%22

4 A. T. Kearney, *FDI Confidence Index* (2005), http://www.atkearney.com/shared_res/pdf/FDICI_2005.pdf

5 Bank for International Settlements, "Triennial Central Bank Survey" (March 2005), http://www.bis.org/publ/rpfx05t.pdf, and Joseph M. Grieco and G. John Ikenberry, *State Power and World Markets* (New York: Norton, 2003), 214.

6 Adam Smith, *The Wealth of Nations*, Bk 4, Ch. 8, http://bartleby.school.aol.com/10/408.html

7 Gerhard Rempel, "Mercantilism," http://mars.acnet.wnec.edu/~grempel/courses/wc2/lectures/mercantilism.html

8 Alexander Hamilton, Report on Manufactures (December 5, 1791), The Gilder Lehrman Institute of American History, http://www.gilderlehrman.org/collection/document.php?id=326

9 Japan inspects every one of its cows as well.

10 Frédéric Bastiat "A Petition From the Manufacturers of Candles, Tapers, Lanterns, Sticks, Street Lamps, Snuffers, and Extinguishers, and from Producers of Tallow, Oil, Resin, Alcohol, and Generally of Everything Connected with Lighting," http://bastiat.org/en/petition.html. Emphasis in original.

11 Adam Smith, *An Inquiry into the Nature and Causes of the Wealth of Nations*, The Library of Economics and Liberty, http://www.econlib.org/library/Smith/smWN.html

12 See Grieco and Ikenberry, *State Power and World Markets*, 30–6.

13 David Ricardo, *On the Principles of Political Economy and Taxation*, The Library of Economics and Liberty, http://www.econlib.org/library/Ricardo/ricP2a.html

14 World Trade Organization, "Trade Liberalization Statistics," http://www.gatt.org/

15 Marxists.org Internet Archive, http://www.marxists.org/archive/marx/works/1845/condition-working-class/ch08.htm

16 Karl Marx, "The Working Day," *Capital*, Vol. 1, Ch. 10, http://www.marxists.org/archive/marx/works/1867-c1/ch10.htm

17 Karl Marx, *Critique of the Gotha Programme*, Part I (1875), http://www.marxists.org/archive/marx/works/1875/gotha/

18 Vladimir Lenin, *On Democratic Centralism*, http://www.plp.org/pl_magazine/democent.html

19 Cited in Stanley K. Schultz, "The Crash and the Great Depression," http://us.history.wisc.edu/hist102/lectures/textonly/lecture18.html

20 Cited in Dustin Woodard, "Black Thursday 1929,"

http://mutualfunds.about.com/cs/history/a/black_thursday.htm

21 Cited in ibid.

22 Richard Lancaster, "Black Tuesday October 29th 1929 Revisited?" http://www.gold-eagle.com/editorials_02/lancaster102102.html

23 "Descent Into the Depths (END 1931): The Collapse of International Finance," FUTURECASTS online magazine, 3:6 (June 1, 2001), www.futurecasts.com

24 Ibid.

25 Anthony O'Brien, "Smoot-Hawley Tariff," *EH.Net Encyclopedia*, ed. Robert Whaples. August 15, 2001. http://eh.net/encyclopedia/?article=obrien.hawley-smoot.tariff

26 US Department of State, "Smoot-Hawley Tariff," http://www.state.gov/r/pa/ho/time/id/17606.htm

27 "The Great Depression," http://mars.acnet.wnec.edu/~grempel/courses/wc2/lectures/depression.html

28 The US has been pressuring China to increase the value of its currency relative to the US dollar in order to reduce America's yawning trade deficit by increasing US exports to China and reducing imports from China.

29 See the IMF's official website, http://www.imf.org/

30 International Monetary Fund, "IMF's Financial Resources and Liquidity Position, 2004–June 2006," http://www.imf.org/external/np/tre/liquid/2006/0606.htm

31 The term was coined by economist John Williamson "to refer to the lowest common denominator of policy advice being addressed by the Washington-based institutions to Latin American countries as of 1989." Cited in Center for International Development at Harvard University, "Global Trade Negotiations Home Page," http://www.cid.harvard.edu/cidtrade/issues/washington.html. See also John Williamson, "What Should the World Bank Think About the Washington Consensus?" *World Bank Research Observer*, Washington, DC: The International Bank for Reconstruction and Development 15:2 (August 2000), 251–64.

32 Ibid.

33 IMF, "Total IMF Credit Outstanding for All Members from 1984–2006," http://www.imf.org/external/np/tre/tad/extcred1.cfm. For data on IMF loans over time, see IMF, "Total IMF Credit Outstanding for All Members from 1984–2006," http://www.imf.org/external/np/tre/tad/extcred1.cfm

34 Republic of Korea–IMF Arrangement, December 5, 1997, http://www.imf.org/external/np/oth/korea.htm

35 Ricardo Hausmann, "Will Volatility Kill Market Democracy?" *Foreign Policy* 108 (Fall 1997), 54.

36 Jessica Einhorn, "The World Bank's Mission Creep," *Foreign Affairs* 80:5 (2001), 22–35.

37 Regional trade agreements like NAFTA are exceptions to this principle.

38 See George Washington University, Elliott School of International Affairs, "The WTO: An Historical, Legal, and Organizational Overview" (1998), http://internationalecon.com/wto/ch1.html

39 Ibid.

40 World Trade Organization, "Disputes, Chronologically," http://www.wto.org/english/tratop_e/dispu_e/dispu_status_e.htm#yr2006

41 World Trade Organization, "Panel Reports Out on US Safeguard Measures on Steel Products," July 11, 2003, http://www.wto.org/english/news_e/news03_e/panel_report_11july03_e.htm

42 "WTO Rebuffs US on Steel Duties," CNN.com, November 10, 2003, http://edition.cnn.com/2003/BUSINESS/11/10/wto.steel.reut

43 World Trade Organization, "GATT 1994 – Article XX on General Exceptions," http://www.wto.org/english/tratop_e/envir_e/envir_backgrnd_e/c7s3_e.htm

44 Elizabeth Becker, "US Takes Food Dispute to the WTO," *International Herald-Tribune Online*, May 14, 2003, http://www.iht.com/articles/96262.html; Guy de Jonquières, Edward Alden, and Tobias Buck, "Showdown Over Genetically Modified Crops," May 13, 2003, http://www.ifg.org/analysis/wto/cancun/usmoratorium/showdown.htm; and *USA Today*, September 20, 2003, http://www.usatoday.com/tech/news/techpolicy/2003-09-20-wto-gen-mod_x.htm

45 "EU Loses a Round on Biotech Crops," *Wall Street Journal*, February 8, 2006, A5.

46 Janice E. Thomson, *Mercenaries, Pirates, and Sovereigns* (Princeton, NJ: Princeton University Press, 1994), 32.

47 David Shearer, "Outsourcing War," *Foreign Policy* 112 (Fall 1998), 70.

48 UNTAD, *World Investment Report 2004*, http://www.unctad.org/en/docs/wir2004annexes_en.pdf, 279, 280.

49 One corporation, the Royal Dutch/Shell Group is jointly British and Dutch. *Forbes*, http://forbes.com/lists/results.jhtml?passListId.

50 Jathon Sapsford and Norihiko Shirouzo, "Mom, Apple Pie and . . . Toyota?" *Wall Street Journal*, May 11, 2006, B1.

51 Sarah Anderson and John Cavanagh, "Top 200: The Rise of Global Corporate Power" (2000), http://www.globalpolicy.org/socecon/tncs/top200.htm

52 "The Forbes Global 2000: Where the Money Is," April 17, 2006, http://www.forbes.com/free_forbes/2006/0417/159.html

53 World Trade Organization, "Trade Liberalization Statistics," http://www.gatt.org/

54 UNCTAD, *World Investment Report 2004*, http://www.unctad.org/en/docs/wir2004annexes_en.pdf, 276, 277.

55 UNCTAD, "Inward FDI Indices," http://www.unctad.org/ Templates/Page.asp?intItemID=2468&lang=1

56 E-Week Enterprise News & Reviews, "Report: Why EU Socked It to Microsoft," http://www.eweek.com/article2/ 0,1759,1572110,00.asp

57 Steven Greenhouse, "Opponents of Wal-Mart To Coordinate Efforts," *New York Times*, April 3, 2005, http://www.nytimes.com/2005/04/03/business/03 walmart.html

58 Sarah Anderson and John Cavanagh, "Top 200: The Rise of Global Corporate Power," http://www.globalpolicy.org/socecon/tncs/top200.htm

59 Dulue Mbachu, "Shell Shuts Down More Nigerian Oil Output," January 13, 2005, http://seattlepi.nwsource.com/business/apbiz_story.asp?category=1310&slug=Nigeria%20Oil%20Protest

60 See "Nigeria Troops 'Burn Delta Slums'," *BBC News*, August 25, 2006, http://news.bbc.co.uk/2/hi/africa/5285556.stm

61 Amnesty International, "Nigeria: Are Human Rights In the Pipeline?" November 9, 2004, http://web.amnesty.org/pages/ec-nigeria2004-eng

62 Glenn R. Simpson, "Multinational Companies Unite to Fight Bribery," *Wall Street Journal*, January 27, 2005, A2, A8.

63 Cited in Clayton E. Cramer, "An American Coup d'Etat?" *History Today* (November 1995), http://home.iprimus.com.au/korob/fdtcards/Butler.htm and in Stanley Kutler, "Review of Chalmers Johnson's *The Sorrows of Empire*," *History News Network* (January 12, 2004), http://hnn.us/articles/3015.html. Originally published in *Common Sense* (November, 1935).

64 James Risen, "Secrets of History: The C.I.A in Iran," *New York Times*, http://www.nytimes.com/library/world/mideast/041600iran-cia-index.html

65 Risen, "Secrets of History."

66 UN Economic and Social Council, "Economic, Social, and Cultural Rights," http://www.unhchr.ch/huridocda/huridoca.nsf/(Symbol)/E.CN.4.Sub.2.2003.12.Rev.2.En?Opendocument

67 http://www.un.org/Depts/ptd/global.htm

68 http://www.iccwbo.org/home/menu_global_compact.asp

69 *Forbes*, http://forbes.com/lists/results.jhtml?passListId

70 See Hendrik Spruyt, *The Sovereign State and Its Competitors* (Princeton, NJ: Princeton University Press, 1994), 105–6.

71 Robert Gilpin, *The Political Economy of International Relations* (Princeton, NJ: Princeton University Press, 1987), 10–11.

72 Robert O. Keohane and Helen V. Milner, eds., *Internationalization and Domestic Politics* (Cambridge: Cambridge University Press, 1996), 257.

73 Desmond Supple, "Asia's Financial Crisis," Statement to the House Banking and Financial Services Committee, September 14, 1998, http://financialservices.house.gov/banking/91498sup.htm

74 PBS Commanding Heights, "Up for Debate: Contagion," http://www.pbs.org/wgbh/commandingheights/shared/minitextlo/ufd_contagion_full.html

75 Ricardo Hausmann, "Will Volatility Kill Market Democracy?" *Foreign Policy* (Fall 1997), 54.

76 Moises Naim, "Mexico's Larger Story," *Foreign Policy* 99 (Summer 1995), 125.

12 The global South

1 Jill McGivering, "China's Growing Focus on Africa," *BBC News*, January 17, 2006, http://news.bbc.co.uk/2/hi/africa/ 4619956.stm; Peter Ford, "China Woos African Trade," *Christian Science Monitor*, November 3, 2006, 1, 4; Craig Timberg, "From Competitors to Trading Partners; Africans Adjust as Business Ties with China Grow," *Washington Post*, December 3, 2006, A23.

2 "From Competitors to Trading Partners."

3 We use the designation global South because many of the world's less-developed countries are located in the southern hemisphere.

4 Columbus referred to the indigenous people he encountered as "Indians" because he believed that he had reached India.

5 Racism was evident in immigration laws of the time. The US, for example, excluded Chinese immigrants after 1882, Japanese after 1907, and other non-Europeans after 1917.

6 Cited in Lawrence A. Clayton and Michael L. Conniff, *A History of Modern Latin America*, 2nd ed. (Belmont, CA: Wadsworth, 2005), 3.

7 Previously, Japanese ports had been closed to all but a few Dutch and Chinese merchants.

8 Joseph Conrad, *Heart of Darkness*, 78–82, http://etext.lib. virginia.edu/etcbin/toccer-new2?id=ConDark.sgm& images=images/modeng&data=/texts/english/modeng/parsed&tag=public&part=1&division=div1

9 Italy, Portugal, and Spain also had relatively small imperial possessions in Africa.

10 Mussolini's 1935 invasion of Ethiopia stemmed in part from his desire to revenge the defeat at Adowa.

11 Article 6, The General Act of The Berlin Conference, February 26, 1885, http://web.jjay.cuny.edu/~jobrien/reference/ob45.html

12 See Brooke Larson, *Trials of Nation Making: Liberalism, Race, and Ethnicity in the Andes, 1810–1910* (New York: Cambridge University Press, 2004).

13 West Bengal (less Bihar and Orissa), part of present-day India, is largely Hindu, and has its capital at Calcutta. East Bengal is the present-day country of Bangladesh, with its capital at Dhaka.

14 Dennis Dalton, *Mahatma Gandhi: Nonviolent Power in Action*, rev. ed. (New York: Columbia University Press, 1993), 10–11.

15 Judith Brown, *Gandhi: Prisoner of Hope* (New Haven, CT: Yale University Press, 1989), 55–7.

16 Cited in Dalton, *Nonviolent Power in Action*, 9.

17 Resolution 91 (1951) Concerning the India–Pakistan question submitted by the Representatives of United Kingdom and United States and adopted by the Security Council on March 30, 1951 (Document No. S/2017/ Rev. 1, dated the 30th March, 1951, http://www. mtholyoke.edu/acad/intrel/kashun91. htm.Resolution 91), and reaffirmed by the UN Security Council in 1957.

18 http://www.jammu-kashmir.com/documents/harisingh47.html

19 "Peace Quotations," http://www.infoaction.org.uk/misc-html/peace-quotations.html

20 Quotesplace.com, http://quotesplace.com/i/b/Mahatma_ Gandhi

21 *BBC News*, "Suharto Tops Corruption Rankings," March 25, 2004, http://news.bbc.co.uk/2/hi/business/3567745.stm

22 Harold Macmillan's "Wind of Change" Speech: Extract, February 3, 1960, http://africanhistory.about.com/od/eraindependence/p/wind_of_change2.htm

23 Office of the High Commissioner for Human Rights, *Declaration on Granting Independence to Colonial Countries and Peoples*, General Assembly Resolution 1514, December 14, 1960, http://www.unhchr.ch/html/menu3/b/c_coloni.htm

24 "Emily Hobhouse," The Anglo-Boer War Museum, http://www.anglo-boer.co.za/emily.html

25 Franz Fanon, *The Wretched of the Earth* (New York: Grove Press, 1963), 37.

26 A third colony, Portuguese Guinea, also was the scene of anti-Portuguese violence and emerged as the independent country of Guinea-Bissau in 1974.

27 The third group, the FNLA, was decisively defeated in 1976.

28 See, for example, Neal J. Smelser, "Toward a Theory of Modernization" in Amitai and Eva Etzioni, eds., *Social Change: Sources, Patterns and Consequences* (New York: Basic Books, 1964), 258–74 and Smelser, "The Modernization of Social Relations," in Myron Weiner,

ed., *Modernization* (New York: Basic Books, 1966), 110–21.

29 In 1961 Kennedy appointed Rostow deputy to his national security assistant and then chairman of the State Department's Policy Planning Council.

30 Walt W. Rostow, *The Stages of Economic Growth: A Non-Communist Manifesto* (Cambridge: Cambridge University Press, 1960), ch. 2, http://www.mtholyoke.edu/acad/intrel/ipe/rostow.htm

31 Ibid.

32 Ibid.

33 Ibid.

34 Gabriel Almond and Sidney Verba, *The Civic Culture: Political Attitudes and Democracy in Five Nations* (Boston, MA: Little Brown, 1963).

35 See, for example, Robert Putnam, ed., *Democracies in Flux: The Evolution of Social Capital in Contemporary Society* (New York: Oxford University Press, 2004).

36 Anthony Giddens, *The Consequences of Modernity: Self and Society in the Late Modern Age* (Stanford, CA: Stanford University Press, 1990) and *Modernity and Self-Identity. Self and Society in the Late Modern Age* (Cambridge: Polity Press, 1991).

37 This term was popularized by the Italian Marxist theorist Antonio Gramsci in Gramsci, *Selections from the Prison Notebooks*, Q. Hoare and G. Nowell Smith, eds. and trans. (London: Lawrence & Wishart, 1971).

38 Edward Said, *Culture and Imperialism* (New York: Vintage Books, 1993) and *Orientalism: Western Conceptions of the Orient* (London: Penguin, 1995).

39 See Johan Galtung, *Peace by Peaceful Means: Peace and Conflict, Development and Civilization* (London: Sage, 1996), 197–9.

40 Immanuel Wallerstein, *The Modern World System: Capitalist Agriculture and the Origins of the European World Economy in the Sixteenth Century* (New York: Academic Press, 1974).

41 See, for example, Raúl Prebisch, *Change and Development – Latin America's Great Task: Report Submitted to the Inter-American Development Bank* (New York: Praeger, 1971), and André Gunder Frank, *The World System* (London: Routledge, 1993).

42 Alfred Sauvy, "Three Worlds, A Planet," *The Observer*, August 14, 1952, 14. In later decades, observers began to speak of the poorest of the poor countries as the Fourth World.

43 Modern History SourceBook, http://www.fordham.edu/halsall/mod/1955sukarno-bandong.html

44 The quotations are from interviews with members and staff of the House Foreign Affairs Committee and officials at the US Agency for International Development during the early 1980s, as reported in James M. McCormick, "Congressional-Executive

Attitudes Toward the NIEO," *International Studies Notes* 10 (Spring 1983), 12–17.

45 Gurcharan Das, "The India Model," *Foreign Affairs* 85:4 (July/August 2006), 4.

46 Ibid., 2.

47 "Surprise!" *The Economist*, September 16, 2006, 13, and "The New Titans: A Survey of the World Economy," special section, *The Economist*, September 16, 2006, 3–4. If one uses current exchange rates, the LDCs' proportion of the world economy is much lower.

48 "The New Titans," 4.

49 Ibid.

50 Cited in Ahmed Shawki, "China: From Mao to Deng," *International Socialist Review* (Summer 1997), online edition, http://www.isreview.org/issues/01/mao_to_deng_1.shtml

51 *World Development Report 2005: A Better Investment Climate for Everyone* (New York: Oxford University Press, 2004), Table 1, 256–7; Table 3, 260–1; Table 4, 262–3.

52 USIS *Washington File*, May 16, 2000, http://www.globalsecurity.org/wmd/library/news/china/2000/00051 3-prc-usia1.htm

53 Jiang was replaced by Hu Jintao in 2003.

54 "How China Runs the World Economy," *The Economist*, July 30, 2005, 11.

55 See Parliament of Australia, Stephen Sherlock, "China's Admission to the World Trade Organization (WTO): What Does it Mean? Who Will/Won't Benefit?" (Research Note 24 2001–02, February 12, 2002), http:// www.aph.gov.au/library/pubs/rn/2001-02/02m24.htm

56 The US–China Business Council, Table 4, http://www.uschina.org/statistics/tradetable.html

57 David Barboza, "China's Trade Surplus Tripled in 2005," *New York Times*, January 11, 2006, http://www.nytimes. com/2006/01/11/business/11cnd-yuan.html?ex=12946

58 The US–China Business Council, "Understanding the US–China Balance of Trade," http://www.uschina.org/statistics/2004balanceoftrade.html

59 Jonathan Spierer, "Intellectual Property in China: Prospectus for New Market Entrants," *Harvard Asia Quarterly* 3:3 (Summer 1999), http://www.fas.harvard.edu/~asiactr/haq/199903/9903a010.htm

60 Frontline, "Wal-Mart at a Glance," November 16, 2004, http://www.pbs.org/wgbh/pages/frontline/shows/walmart/secrets/stats.html

61 Darek Johnson, "World Trade," http://www.signweb.com/digital/cont/worldtrade.html

62 "Major Foreign Holders of Treasury Securities," http://www.treas.gov/tic/mfh.txt

13 Human security

1 "Live 8 Concerts Bridge the World," *BBC News*, July 2, 2005, http://news.bbc.co.uk/2/hi/entertainment/4641999.stm

2 "Climbing Back," *The Economist*, January 21, 2006, 69–70.

3 Rob McCrae, "Human Security in a Globalized World," in Richard W. Mansbach and Edward Rhodes, eds., *Global Politics in a Changing World*, 3rd. ed. (Boston: Houghton Mifflin, 2006), 260.

4 Jeffrey Sachs, *The End of Poverty: Economic Possibilities for Our Time* (New York: Penguin Press, 2005).

5 Celia W. Dugger, "Philanthropist Gives $50 Million to Help Aid Poor in Africa," *New York Times*, September 13, 2006, http://www.nytimes.com/2006/09/13/us/13soros.html?ref=business

6 United Nations, "Millennium Development Goals," http://www.un.org/millenniumgoals

7 UN Development Programme, "Millennium Project Update," http://www.ke.undp.org/UNDP%20Millenium%20Project%20Update.htm. See also The Earth Institute at Columbia University, "The Millennium Villages Project," http://www.earthinstitute.columbia.edu/mvp/locations/sauri/index.html

8 Cited in Jan Van Dijk, "Human Security: A New Agenda for Integrated, Global Action," keynote lecture at the International Conference on Space and Water: Towards Sustainable Development and Human Security, Santiago de Chile, Chile, 1–2 April, 2004, http://www.unodc.org/ unodc/speech_2004-04-01_1.html

9 Franklin D. Roosevelt Presidential Library and Museum, "The 'Four Freedoms' Speech," http://www.fdrlibrary.marist.edu/4free.html

10 World Bank, "What Is the World Bank?" http://web.worldbank.org/WBSITE/EXTERNAL/EXTABOUTUS/0,,contentMDK:20040558~menuPK:34559~pagePK:34542~piPK:36600,00.html

11 UN Development Programme, *Human Development Report 1999* (New York: Oxford University Press), 3.

12 *World Development Indicators, 2006*, http://devdata.worldbank.org/wdi2006/contents/Section1_1_1.htm. See also Shaohua Chen and Martin Ravaillon, "How Have the World's Poorest Fared Since the 1980s?" *Development Research Group, World Bank*, 14, 17, http://www.worldbank.org/research/povmonitor/MartinPapers/How_have_the_poorest_fared_since_the_early_1980s.pdf

13 World Bank, "What Is the World Bank?"

14 See United Nations Development Program, http://www. undp.org

15 Celia W. Dugger, "Developing Lands Hit Hardest by

'Brain Drain'," *New York Times*, October 25, 2005, A9.

16 Transparency International, "Corruption Perceptions Index 2006," http://www.transparency.org/news_room/in_focus/cpi_2006/cpi_table

17 Peter Eigen, "Opening Statement," Transparency International Corruption Perceptions Index Press Conference, 18 October 2005, http://ww1.transparency.org/cpi/2005/dnld/cpi2005.pe_statement.pdf

18 See TI's official website at http://www.transparency.org/about_ti/index.html

19 Transparency International, *Bribe Payers Index (BPI) 2006: Analysis Report*, October 4, 2006, http://www.transparency.org/policy_research/surveys_indices/bpi/bpi_2006

20 World Bank, *Department of Institutional Integrity* (2006), http://web.worldbank.org/WBSITE/EXTERNAL/EXTABOUTUS/ORGANIZATION/ORGUNITS/EXTDOII/0,,contentMDK:20542001~pagePK:64168427~piPK:64168435~theSitePK:588921,00.html

21 Charter of the United Nations, The Avalon Project at Yale Law School, http://www.yale.edu/lawweb/avalon/un/unchart.htm

22 IMF, "The Poverty Reduction and Growth Facility (PRGF)" (September 2004), http://www.imf.org/external/np/exr/facts/prgf.htm

23 IMF, "Poverty Reduction Strategy Papers (PRSP)" (September 2004), http://www.imf.org/external/np/exr/facts/prsp.htm

24 World Bank, "What Is the World Bank?" http://web.worldbank.org/WBSITE/EXTERNAL/EXTABOUTUS/0,,contentMDK:20040558~menuPK:34559~pagePK:34542~piPK:36600~theSitePK:29708,00.html

25 Kevin Sullivan, "Bridging the Digital Divide," *Washington Post National Weekly Edition*, July 17–23, 2006, 10.

26 "Calling an End to Poverty," *The Economist*, July 9, 2005, 51.

27 Ibid.

28 Pushpa Kumari, "External Debt, Foreign Exchange Constraint and Economic Growth in Developing Countries," *Finance India* 10:2 (June 1996), http://www.iif.edu/data/fi/journal/FiI02/FII02Abs3.pdf

29 Table B-3 in John W. Sewell, Richard E. Feinberg, and Valleriana Kallab, eds., *US Foreign Policy and the Third World: Agenda 1985–86* (Washington, DC: Overseas Development Council, 1985), 174.

30 UNITAR, "Official Debt. The Paris Club: Creditor's and Debtor's Perspectives," http://www.unitar.org/dfm/Resource_Center/TrainingPackage/Tp9/ChIX2/4section1.htm

31 Paris Club, "The Debt of Developing Countries,"

http://www.clubdeparis.org/en/presentation/presentation.php?BATCH=B05WP01

32 See World Bank, Debt Department, "The Enhanced HIPC Initiative," http://web.worldbank.org/WBSITE/EXTERNAL/TOPICS/EXTDEBTDEPT/0,,contentMDK:20260411~menuPK:528655~pagePK:64166689~piPK:64166646~theSitePK:469043,00.html; http://siteresources.worldbank.org/INTDEBTDEPT/DataAndStatistics/20263217/hipc-pages.pdf; and IMF, "Debt Relief Under the Heavily Indebted Poor Countries (HIPC) Initiative" (September 2004), http://www.imf.org/external/np/exr/facts/hipc.htm

33 Christina Katsouris, "A Year-end Sprint for Debt Relief," *Africa Recovery* 14:4, http://www.un.org/ecosocdev/geninfo/afrec/subjindx/144debt.htm

34 Sumeet Desai and Brian Love, "G8 Hammers Out Debt Relief Deal for Poor Nations," *Yahoo news*, June 11, 2005, http://p71.news.scd.yahoo.com/s/nm/group1_dc

35 "Has the G8 Met its Promises to Africa?" *BBC News*, June 26, 2006, http://news.bbc.co.uk/2/hi/business/5086526.stm

36 "$37bn Debt Cut for Poor Nations," *BBC News*, June 30, 2006, http://news.bbc.co.uk/2/hi/business/5130450.stm

37 "A Glimmer of Light at Last?" *The Economist*, June 24, 2006, 51–2.

38 See Dale Jackson, "At Debt's Door" (2005), http://magazine.globeinvestor.com/servlet/ArticleNews/commentarystory

39 Center for Global Development, "Commitment to Development Index 2006," http://www.cgdev.org/section/initiatives/_active/cdi/. The records of individual countries can be found here.

40 Adam Przeworski, Michael E. Alvarez, José Antonio Cheibub, and Fernando Limongi, *Democracy and Development: Political Institutions and Well-being in the World 1950–1990* (New York: Cambridge University Press, 2000).

41 Mary Anastasia O'Grady, "Wish They All Could Be Like Estonia," *Wall Street Journal*, January 4, 2006, A10.

42 "The FP Index: Ranking the Rich," *Foreign Policy* 156 (September/October 2006), 68.

43 Ibid., 48–9.

44 World Trade Organization, "Trade Liberalization Statistics," http://www.gatt.org/

45 Mei Fong and Dan Morse, "Backlash Is Likely As Chinese Exports of Apparel Surge," *Wall Street Journal*, March 28, 2005, A3, A9.

46 "Harvesting Poverty: The Unkept Promise," *New York Times*, December 30, 2003, http://www.mtholyoke.edu/acad/intrel/ipe/food.htm

47 "The Government Trough," *Foreign Policy* 156 (September/October 2006), 73.

48 See European Parliament Fact Sheets, "The Treaty of Rome and the Foundations of the CAP," April 7, 2003, http://www.europarl.eu.int/facts/4_1_1_en.htm

49 European Commission, "CAP Reform-A Long-Term Perspective for Sustainable Agriculture," http://europa.eu.int/comm/agriculture/capreform/index_en.htm

50 United Nations Development Program, *Human Development Report 2003* (New York: UNDP, 2003), 155, http://hdr.undp.org/reports/global/2003

51 Cited in David Leonhardt, "Globalization Hits a Political Speed Bump," *New York Times*, June 1, 2003, http://www.lexisnexis.com/universe

52 G20, "History," http://www.g-20.mre.gov.br/history.asp

53 Tom Wright and Steven R. Weisman, "Trade Talks Fail Over an Impasse on Farm Tariffs," *New York Times*, July 25, 2006, http://www.nytimes.com/2006/07/25/business/ worldbusiness/25trade.html?ei=5090&en=5cad858db5a81595&ex=1311480000&partner=rssuserland&emc=rss&pagewanted=all, and "Europe blames US for WTO failure," *BBC News*, July 25, 2006, http://news.bbc.co.uk/ 2/hi/business/5209010.stm

54 For a concise summary of the implications of transnational crime, see Susan Strange, *The Retreat of the State* (Cambridge: Cambridge University Press, 1996), 110–21.

55 Canadian Security Intelligence Service, "Transnational Criminal Activity," March 2003, http://www.csis-scrs.gc.ca/eng/backgrnd/back10_e.html

56 "Out of the Underworld," *The Economist*, January 7, 2006, 23.

57 UN International Drug Control Programme, *World Drug Report* (Oxford: Oxford University Press, 1997), 124.

58 *Human Development Report 1999: Globalization with a Human Face*, 41, http://hdr.undp.org/reports/global/1999/en/. See US Drug Enforcement Administration, http://www.dea.gov/concern/concern.htm

59 Pierre-Arnaud Chouvy, "Geography and Opium," *Encyclopedia of Modern Asia*, http://www.pa-chouvy.org/drugtradeinasia.html

60 Cited in Samuel D. Porteus, "The Threat from Transnational Crime: An Intelligence Perspective" (Winter 1996), Canadian Security Intelligence Service, http://www.csus-scrs.gc.ca/eng/comment/com70_e.html

61 Frontline, *Drug Wars*, "The Colombian Cartels," http://www.pbs.org/wgbh/pages/frontline/shows/drugs/business/inside/colombian.html

62 See, for example, Louise I. Shelley, "The Nexus of Organized International Criminals and Terrorism," US Department of State, http://usinfo.state.gov/eap/Archive_Index/The_Nexus_of_Organized_International_Criminals_and_Terrorism.html

63 Jerry Seper, "Afghanistan Leads Again in Heroin Production," *Washington Times*, August 11, 2003, http://www.washingtontimes.com/national/20030811-100220-8928r.htm

64 Cited in Porteus, "The Threat from Transnational Crime."

65 UN Drug Control Programme (UNDCP), "Joint Cooperation to Promote Drug Control," Fact Sheet #1 (June 1998), http://www.un.org/ga/20special/presskit/themes/judcoo-1.htm

66 US Department of State, "Support for Plan Colombia," http://www.state.gov/p/wha/rt/plncol/. See also CNN.com, "Bush Hails Colombia's Efforts against Drug Trade," November 22, 2004, http://www.cnn.com/2004/WORLD/americas/11/22/colombia.bush.index.html

67 See US Department of State, "A Report to Congress on United States Policy Towards Colombia and Other Related Issues," February 3, 2003, http://www.state.gov/p/wha/rls/rpt/17140.htm

68 Juan Forero, "Colombia's Coca Survives US Plan to Uproot It," *New York Times*, August 19, 2006, http://www.nytimes.com/2006/08/19/world/americas/19coca.html?ex=1156651200&en=46f7ce41fe6b6597&ei=5070&emc=eta1

69 Chouvy, "Geography and Opium."

70 Philip Shishkin and David Crawford, "In Afghanistan, Heroin Trade Soars Despite US Aid," *Wall Street Journal*, January 18, 2006, A1, A8.

71 DEA, "Drug Trafficking in the United States," http://www.dea.gov/concern/drug_trafficking.html

72 UN General Assembly Declaration on the Guiding Principles of Drug Demand Reduction, http://www.unodc.org/pdf/resolution_1998-09-08_1.pdf

73 IMOLIN, "United Nations Global Programme against Money Laundering," http://www.imolin.org/imolin/gpml.html

74 Paul Bauer and Rhoda Ullman, "Understanding the Wash Cycle," *Economic Perspectives*, May 2001, http://usinfo.state.gov/journals/ites/0501/ijee/clevelandfed.htm; Mike Brunker, "Money Laundering Finishes the Cycle," MSNBC, August 31, 2004, http://msnbc.msn.com/id/3071666

75 Steven Schrage, "Transnational Crime," (US Department of State, September 30, 2002), http://www.state.gov/p/io/rls/rm/2002/14065.htm

76 SIPRI, "Recent Trends in Military Expenditure," http://www.sipri.org/contents/milap/milex/mex_trends.html

77 Thom Shanker, "Russia Led Arms Sales to Developing World in '05," *New York Times*, October 29, 2006, http://www.nytimes.com/2006/10/29/world/europe/29weapons.html?bl&ex=1162443600&en=b48583bef0d95963&ei=5087%0A

78 Report of the Special Committee on Investigation of the Munitions Industry (The Nye Report), US Congress, Senate, 74th Congress, 2nd sess., February 24, 1936, http://www.mtholyoke.edu/acad/intrel/nye.htm

79 Dwight D. Eisenhower, "The Military-Industrial Complex," in Richard Gillam, ed., *Power in Postwar America* (Boston, MA: Little Brown, 1971), 258.

80 See US Department of State, "Proliferation Security Initiative," http://www.state.gov/t/np/c10390.htm

81 Stefania Bianchi, "Arms Sales Killing Development Goals," *Global Policy Forum*, June 22, 2004, http://www.globalpolicy.org/socecon/ffd/2004/0622 arms.htm

82 Thom Shanker, "Weapons Sales Worldwide Rise to Highest Level Since 2000," *New York Times*, August 30, 2005, A8.

83 See Wade Boese, "Global Arms Market Still US Domain," *Arms Control Association* (October 2004), http://www.armscontrol.org/act/2004_10/Grimmett.asp

84 Merle D. Kellerhals, Jr., "Global Arms Sales Fell 12 Percent in 2003," *USINFO*, August 31, 2004, http://usinfo.state.gov/is/Archive/2004/Aug/31-491642.html

85 The official NSG website is http://www.nuclearsuppliersgroup.org/

86 The following paragraphs are based on David Albright and Corey Hinderstein, "Uncovering the Nuclear Black Market: Working Toward Closing Gaps in the International Nonproliferation Regime," paper prepared for the Institute for Nuclear Materials Management (July 2, 2004), http://www.isis-online.org/publications/southasia/nuclear_black_market.html

87 Dr. Khan was so popular in Pakistan that, even after he admitted his crimes, the country's president decided to grant him a pardon.

88 Centrifuges are metal tubes that spin uranium hexafluoride gas to separate out the uranium 235 that is necessary for a nuclear reaction.

89 ElBaradei and the IAEA were jointly awarded the 2005 Nobel Peace Prize.

90 Cited in Albright and Hinderstein, "Uncovering the Nuclear Black Market."

91 IAEA.Org, "IAEA Probing Nuclear 'Black Market' Director General Urges Stronger Security Framework" (February 3, 2004), http://www.iaea.org/NewsCenter/News/2004/trafficking20040203.html

92 US Department of State, "UN Security Council Resolution 1540 (2004)," http://www.state.gov/t/np/rls/other/31990.htm

93 Ibid.

94 Paul J. Caffera, "Pentagon Has Lost Yrack of Exported Missiles. Terrorists Could Use Anti-aircraft Stinger Missiles, Critics Say," *San Francisco Chronicle*, June 2, 2004, http://www.sfgate.com/cgi-bin/article.cgi?file=/chronicle/archive/2004/06/02/MNGT26VCPB1.DTL

95 Few countries have effective laws to prevent firms and citizens from violating such embargoes. The US does better than most in this respect, requiring arms dealers to register and requiring State Department approval for arms sales by its citizens whether living at home or abroad.

96 Lora Lumpe, "A 'New' Approach to the Small Arms Trade," *Arms Control Association* (January/February 2001), http://www.armscontrol.org/act/2001_01-02/lumpejanfeb01.asp

97 Global Policy Forum, "Small Arms and Light Weapons," http://www.globalpolicy.org/security/smallarms/salwindx.htm#conf

98 As of December 2004, 42 countries, including the United States, China, North Korea, and Russia, had not ratified the treaty.

99 UNHCR, "Convention and Protocol Relating to the Status of Refugees," 16, http://www.unhcr.ch/cgi-bin/texis/vtx/basics/+SwwBmeJAIS_wwww3wwwwwwwhFqA72ZR0gRfZNtFqtxw5oq5zFqtFEIfglAFqA72ZR0gRfZNDzmxwwwwwww1FqtFEIfgl/opendoc.pdf

100 "UN Alarmed Over 'Asylum Fatigue'," *BBC News*, April 19, 2006, http://news.bbc.co.uk/2/hi/in_depth/4919746.stm

101 UNHCR, 2005 *Global Refugee Trends*, June 9, 2006, http://www.unhcr.org/cgi-bin/texis/vtx/statistics/opendoc.pdf?tbl=STATISTICS&id=4486ceb12

102 "World 'Forgets' Internal Refugees," *BBC News*, World Edition, November 5, 2004, http://news.bbc.co.uk/2/hi/europe/3985159.stm

103 "Global Refugees 'At 26-year Low'," *BBC News*, June 9, 2006, http://news.bbc.co.uk/2/hi/in_depth/5061322.stm

104 See "No Direction Home," *The Economist*, February 11, 2006, 37–8.

105 UNHCR, *The State of the World's Refugees 2006: Human Displacement in the New Millennium*, Annex 2, 211, http://www.unhcr.org/cgi-bin/texis/vtx/publ/opendoc.pdf?id=4444afc42&tbl=PUBL

106 Ibid., 209.

107 UN Population Division, "Number of World's Migrants Reaches 175 Million Mark," UN Press Release POP/844 (2002), un.org/esa/population/publications/ittmig2002/press-release-eng.htm

108 Warren Hoge, "UN Chief Backs Growth of Global Migration," *New York Times*, June 6, 2006, http://www.nytimes.com/2006/06/06/world/06cnd-nations.html?ex=1155441600&en=d2d201b001f30f0a&ei=5070

109 United Nations Population Network, *World Population Prospects: The 2002 Revision*, http://www.un.org/popin/data.html

110 Hoge, "UN Chief Backs Growth of Global Migration."

111 FT.COM, "Mexican Migrants Send $16bn in Remittances," *New York Times Online*, February 1, 2005, http://www.nytimes.com/financialtimes/international/FT20050201_

112 Cited in Hoge, "U.N. Chief Backs Growth of Global Migration."

113 UN Population Division, "Number of World's Migrants Reaches 175 Million Mark."

114 Ibid.

115 "On the Fence," *Foreign Policy* 129 (March/April 2002), 23. See Yvonne Ndege, "African Migrants' Desperate Journey," *BBC News*, July 6, 2006, http://news.bbc.co.uk/2/hi/africa/5151740.stm, and N. C. Aizenman, "South of the Border," *Washington Post National Weekly Edition*, July 17–23, 2006, 6–7.

116 John Pomfret, "A Deadly Passage," *Washington Post National Weekly Edition*, June 26–July 9, 2006, 9.

117 "Illegal Immigration," Center for Immigration Studies, http://www.cis.org/topics/illegalimmigration.html

118 See "Huddled Masses: Stay Out," *The Economist*, June 21, 2002, http://www.economist.com/agenda/displayStory.cfm?story_id=1198910

119 UN Department of Economic and Social Affairs, Population Division, "World Population Ageing: 1950–2050," http://www.un.org/esa/population/publications/worldageing19502050/, 12, 17.

120 Ibid., 19.

121 "History of Epidemics and Plagues," October 2001, http://uhavax.hartford.edu/bugl/histepi.htm, and "Black Death," *Encyclopædia Britannica* from Encyclopædia Britannica Premium Service, http://www.britannica.com/eb/article?tocId=9015473

122 World Health Organization, *Communicable Disease Surveillance & Response*, http://www.who.int/csr/don/archive/year/2004/en/, http://www.who.int/csr/don/archive/year/2005/en/

123 World Health Organization, RBM Infosheet, "Malaria in Africa," http://www.rbm.who.int/cmc_upload/0/000/015/370/RBMInfosheet_3.htm

124 WHO, "WHO and the Millennium Development Goals," http://www.who.int/mdg/en/

125 Malaria R&D Alliance, "Assessment of Global Development," Table 7, 34. http://www.malariaalliance.org/PDFs/RD_Report_complete.pdf

126 HIV/AIDS data from UN Programme on HIV/AIDS, "AIDS Epidemic Update 2004," http://www.unaids.org/wad2004/report.html; UNAIDS, "World AIDS Day 2004," http://www.unaids.org/wad2004/factsheets.html; and World Health Organization, "Global AIDS Epidemic Continues to Grow," November 21, 2006, http://www.who.int/hiv/mediacentre/news62/en/index.html

127 "India 'Has the Most People with HIV'," *BBC News*, May 30, 2006, http://newsvote.bbc.co.uk/mpapps/pagetools/print/news.bbc.co.uk/2/. India denies this claim, "India Rejects Claims It Has the Most People with HIV," *ABC Radio Australia* (2006), http://www.abc.net.au/ra/news/stories/s1350010.htm

128 "HIV Impact: Region-by-region," *BBC News*, November 20, 2005, http://news.bbc.co.uk/2/hi/health/4456900.stm

129 *Human Development Report 2004* (New York: Human Development Programme, 2004), Table 8, 166.

130 *World Development Indicators* (Washington, DC: The World Bank, 1999), Table 2.17, 102.

131 "Beetroot but No Blushes," *The Economist*, August 26, 2006.

132 Stephanie Nebehay, "HIV Infections on Rise in All Regions – UN Report," *Reuters UK*, http://today.reuters.co.uk/news/CrisesArticle.aspx?storyId=L17181193&WTmodLoc=World-R5-Alertnet-2

133 World Health Organization, "Sierra Leone," http://www.who.int/whr/2004/annex/country/sle/en/

134 Greg Barrow, "Mbeki Rejects Aids Emergency Measures," *BBC News*, March 14, 2001, http://news.bbc.co.uk/2/hi/africa/1220434.stm

135 *Annex 2: HIV and AIDS, estimates and data, 2005 and 2003*, 505, 508, 509, http://data.unaids.org/pub/GlobalReport/2006/2006_GR_ANN2_en.pdf

136 Lawrence K. Altman, "Report Shows AIDS Epidemic Slowdown in 2005," *New York Times*, May 31, 2006, http://www.nytimes.com/2006/05/31/world/31aids.html?ex=1155441600&en=7a527fc51114e4b0&ei=5070

137 Bill & Melinda Gates Foundation, *Global Health*, http://www.gatesfoundation.org/GlobalHealth/

138 "Gates Announces Anti-Malaria Donation," *New York Times*, October 31, 2005, http://query.nytimes.com/gst/fullpage.html?sec=health&res=9C0CE5DB1F3FF932A05753C1A9639C8B63

139 World Health Organization, "Epidemic and Pandemic Alert and Response (EPR)," http://www.who.int/csr/en/

140 The following paragraphs are largely based on World Health Organization, "Update 95-SARS: Chronology of a Serial Killer," *Communicable Disease Surveillance & Response*, http://www.who.int/csr/don/2003_07_04/en/

141 William G. McNeil, Jr., "Health Officials Fear New Spread of Polio," *New York Times*, February 10, 2005, http://www.nytimes.com/2005/02/10/health/10cnd-polio.html, and William G. McNeil, Jr., "New Concern on Polio Among Mecca Pilgrims," *New York Times*, February 11, 2005, http://www.nytimes.com/2005/02/11/health/11polio.html

142 Department of Health and Human Services, Centers for Disease Control and Prevention, "Progress Toward Interruption of Wild Poliovirus Transmission – Worldwide, January 2005–March 2006," *Morbidity and*

Mortality Weekly Report (MMWR), 55:16 April 28, 2006. http://www.cdc.gov/mmwr/preview/mmwrhtml/mm551 6a5.htm

143 Global Polio Eradication Initiative (August 2006), http://www.polioeradication.org/casecount.asp

144 Ibid.

145 See Molly Billings, "The Influenza Pandemic of 1918" (June, 1997), http://www.stanford.edu/group/virus/uda/

146 World Health Organization, Epidemic and Pandemic Alert and Response (EPR), November 2005, http://www.who.int/csr/disease/avian_influenza/phase/en/inde x.html. WHO has established a special website (http://www.who.int/csr/disease/avian_influenza/en/) to report developments in avian flu.

147 Cited in "A Shot of Transparency," *The Economist*, August 12, 2006, 65. See also IBM, "IBM, Public Health Groups Form Global Pandemic Initiative," http://www-03.ibm.com/press/us/en/pressrelease/19640.wss

148 The website for Doctors Without Borders is http://www.doctorswithoutborders.org

149 Michael Tan, "Medical Tourism?" *Inq7.net*, http://news.inq7.net/opinion/index.php?index=2&story _id=14917&col=81

150 Sunmed Medical Center, "Medical Tourism," http://www.sunway.com.my/sunmed/medical_tourism/ medical_tourism.asp

14 The environment: a global collective good

1 Complementary Medical Association, "Mad Hatter Syndrome," http://www.the-cma.org.uk/HTML/ hatter.htm

2 Mancur Olson, Jr., *The Logic of Collective Action: Public Goods and the Theory of Groups* (New York: Schocken Books, 1968).

3 *Pilot 2006 Environmental Performance Index*, http://www.yale.edu/epi/2006EPI_MainReport.pdf

4 "Anti-hero," *The Economist*, special section "A Survey of Climate Change," September 9, 2006, 18.

5 Garrett Hardin, "The Tragedy of the Commons," *Science* 162 (1968), 1243–8, http://dieoff.org/ page95.htm

6 Cantor Energy & Environment, http://www. emissionstrading.com/

7 Geneticist Norman Borlaug was awarded the 1970 Nobel Peace Prize for developing the high-yielding disease-resistant wheat that started the "green revolution."

8 Thomas Malthus, *An Essay on the Principle of Population*, http://socserv2.socsci.mcmaster.ca/~econ/ugcm/3ll3/ma lthus/popu.txt

9 United Nations Population Network, *World Population Prospects: The 2002 Revision*, http://www.un.org/popin/ data.html

10 UNFPA, *State of the World Population 2004*, 8, http://www.unfpa.org/swp/2004/pdf/en_swp04.pdf

11 United Nations Population Fund, "The Day of 6 Billion – Fast Facts," October 12, 1999, http://www.unfpa. org/6billion/facts.htm

12 UNFPA, *State of the World Population 2004*, 76.

13 United Nations Population Fund, "The Day of 6 Billion – Fast Facts."

14 "Incredible Shrinking Countries," *The Economist*, January 7, 2006, 12.

15 Elisabeth Rosenthal, "European Union's Plunging Birthrates Spread Eastward," *New York Times*, September 4, 2006, A3.

16 United Nations Population Fund, "The Day of 6 Billion – Fast Facts."

17 Ibid.

18 "Urbanization and Global Change," University of Michigan, 2005, www.globalchange.umich.edu/ globalchange2/current/lectures/urban_gc/

19 United Nations Population Network, *World Population Prospects: The 2002 Revision*.

20 Desmond Morris, *The Human Zoo* (New York: Dell, 1969), 77–8. Emphasis in original.

21 "Karachi," http://www.geospace.co.at/atlas_megacities/ pdf/karachi.pdf

22 "Asia's Answer to Beirut," *The Economist*, July 1, 1995, 30.

23 Thomas F. Homer-Dixon, "On the Threshold: Environmental Changes as Causes of Acute Conflict," *International Security* 16:2 (Fall 1991), 76–116.

24 Robert D. Kaplan, "The Coming Anarchy," in Phil Williams, Donald M. Goldstein, and Jay M. Shafritz, eds., *Classical Readings and Contemporary Debates in International Relations*, 3rd ed. (Belmont, CA: Thomson Wadsworth, 2006), 606. Emphasis in original.

25 UN Department of Economic and Social Affairs, Population Division, "Levels and Trends of Contraceptive Use as Assessed in 1998," http://www. un.org/esa/population/pubsarchive/contraceptives1998/ contraceptives1998.htm

26 UN Department of Economic and Social Affairs, Population Division, *World Fertility Report 2003*, http:// www.un.org/esa/population/publications/worldfertility/ Country_Profiles.pdf

27 Valerie M. Hudson and Andrea Den Boer, "A Surplus of Men, A Deficit of Peace: Security and Sex Ratios in Asia's Largest States," *International Security* 26:4 (Spring 2002), 5–38.

28 Jim McGivering, "US Cuts UN Funds in Abortion Row," *BBC News*, July 17, 2004, http://news.bbc.co.uk/2/hi/ americas/3902311.stm

29 Howard W. French, "As China Ages, a Shortage of Cheap Labor Looms," *New York Times*, June 30, 2006, http://www.nytimes.com/2006/06/30/world/asia/30agin g.html?ex=1309320000&en=6bedd74df81e2384&ei=5 090&partner=rssuserland&emc=rss

30 Alan Cowell, "In an Affluent Europe, the Problem is Graying," *New York Times*, September 8, 1994, A4.

31 Steve Coll, "Dumping on the Third World," *Washington Post National Weekly Edition*, April 18–24, 1994, 9–10.

32 Marcus W. Brauchli, "China's Environment Is Severely Stressed as Its Industry Surges," *Wall Street Journal*, July 25, 1994, A1.

33 R. Monastersky, "China's Air Pollution Chokes Crop Growth," *Science News Online* 155:13 (March 27, 1999), http://www.sciencenews.org/pages/sn_arc99/ 3_27_99/fob4.htm

34 Duncan Hewitt, "Beijing," *BBC News*, February 12, 1998, http://news.bbc.co.uk/1/hi/despatches/55882.stm

35 Steven Mufson, "The Yangtze Dam: Feat or Folly?" *Washington Post*, November 9, 1997, A01.

36 Jim Yardley, "A Troubled River Mirrors China's Path to Modernity," *New York Times*, November 19, 2006, sec.1, 1.

37 GEO: Global Environment Outlook 3, "Past, Present and Future perspectives," http://www.grida.no/geo/ geo3/english/086.htm

38 Worldwatch Institute, *Vital Signs*, 2003, http://www. worldwatch.org/pubs/vs/2003

39 OPEC's official website is http://www.opec.org

40 The IEA's homepage can be found at http://www.iea. org/

41 Ryan Chilcote, "Kuwait Still Recovering from Gulf War Fires," January 3, 2003, CNN.com./world, http://www. cnn.com/2003/WORLD/meast/01/03/sproject.irq.kuwai t.oil.fires

42 Alister Doyle, "It's a Warmer World, But Does That Mean Armageddon?" February 11, 2005, *Reuters*, http://today.reuters.co.uk/news/newsArticle.aspx?type= scienceNews&storyID=2005-02-11T151507Z_01_ L01638957_RTRIDST_0_SCIENCE-ENVIRONMENT- WARMING-DC.XML

43 US Environmental Protection Agency, "Global Warming – Climate," http://yosemite.epa.gov/oar/ globalwarming.nsf/content/Climate.html

44 Susan Watts, "A Coal-dependent Future?" *BBC News*, March 9, 2005, http://news.bbc.co.uk/2/hi/programmes/ newsnight/4330469.stm

45 "Greenhouse Gases Hit Record Levels in 2005: UN," *New York Times*, November 3, 2006, http://www. nytimes.com/reuters/world/international-environment- un-gases.html

46 Cited in "Tuvalu and Global Warming," Tuvalulslands. com, http://www.tuvaluislands.com/ warming.htm

47 Greenhouse gases that produce global warming are carbon dioxide (CO_2), methane (CH_4), nitrous oxide (N_2O), hydrofluorocarbons (HFCs), perfluorocarbons (PFCs), and sulfur hexafluoride (SF_6).

48 US Environmental Protection Agency, "Global Warming – Climate."

49 UN Environmental Program, "Greenhouse Gas Emission Graphics" (2001), http://www.grida.no/db/ maps/collection/climate6/index.htm

50 Agence France-Presse, "US Greenhouse Toll," December 13, 2004, http://www.climateark.org/articles/ reader.asp?linkid=37280

51 Cited in Charles J. Hanley, "Global Warming Pact Takes Effect, Without United States but With Hopes for More Cuts Later," *New Mexican*, February 11, 2005, http://www.freenewmexican.com/news/10396.html

52 Cited in "World Scientists Urge CO_2 Action," *BBC News*, June 8, 2005, http://news.bbc.co.uk/2/hi/science/ nature/4616431.stm

53 See "Pricking the Global Conscience," *The Economist*, December 17, 2005, 77.

54 See US Department of Energy, "Energy Sources," http://www.energy.gov/energysources/bioenergy.htm

55 Cited in William J. Broad, "Nuclear Roulette for Russia: Burying Uncontained Waste," *New York Times*, November 21, 1994, A8.

56 Nuclear Energy Institute, "Reliable Electricity," http://www.nei.org/index.asp?catnum=2&catid=47

57 Lester R. Brown, "Facing the Prospect of Food Scarcity," in Brown *et al.*, *State of the World 1997* (New York: Norton, 1997), 22–41; Food and Agriculture Organization, *Agriculture 21*, "Fighting Hunger and Obesity" (2006), http://www.fao.org/ag/magazine/ 0602sp1.htm

58 FAO, "National Status and Vulnerability: The Spectrum of Malnutrition," http://www.fao.org/docrep/x8200e/ x8200e04.htm

59 FAO, "Special Feature: Globalization, Urbanization and Changing Food Systems in Developing Countries," *The State of Food Insecurity in the World 2004*, http://www. fao.org/docrep/007/y5650e/y5650e04.htm

60 Lester R. Brown, *State of the World 2001* (New York: Norton 2001), 44; Marguerite Michaels, "Retreat from Africa," *Foreign Affairs* 72:1 (1992/93), 95–6.

61 Don Hinrichson, "Putting the Bite on Planet Earth," http://dieoff.org/page120.htm

62 Lester R. Brown, "The Making of a Feeding Frenzy," *Washington Post National Weekly Edition*, September 5–11, 1994, 23. Emphasis in original. See also Lester R. Brown, "Struggling to Raise Cropland Productivity," in Brown *et al.*, *State of the World 1998* (New York: Norton, 1998), 79–95, and Megan Ryan and Christopher Flavin, "Facing China's Limits," in ibid., 113–31.

63 Jeffrey Clark, "Debacle in Somalia," *Foreign Affairs* 72:1 (1992/93), 109.

64 Cited in John B. Mason, "Keynote Paper: Measuring Hunger and Malnutrition," *FAO Corporate Document Repository*, http://www.fao.org/docrep/005/y4249e/y4249e0d.htm#fn23

65 Ibid.

66 "Help the Hungry More Efficiently," *The Economist*, March 11, 2006, 44.

67 Gerald Urquhart, Walter Chomentowski, David Skole, and Chris Barber, "Tropical Deforestation: The Rate of Deforestation," http://earthobservatory.nasa.gov/Library/Deforestation/deforestation_2.html

68 FAO NewsRoom, "Deforestation Continues at an Alarming Rate," November 14, 2005, http://www.fao.org/newsroom/en/news/2005/1000127/index.html

69 For a summary of the causes and effects of tropical deforestation, see Nicholas Guppy, "Tropical Deforestation: A Global View," *Foreign Affairs* 62:4 (Spring 1984), 928–65.

70 Jocelyn Stock and Andy Rochen, "The Choice: Doomsday or Arbor Day," http://www.umich.edu/~gs265/society/deforestation.htm

71 Janet N. Abramowitz, "Sustaining the World's Forests," in *State of the World 1998*, 21–40.

72 Steven Klingstone, "Amazon Destruction Accelerating," *BBC News*, May 19, 2005, http://news.bbc.co.uk/2/hi/americas/4561189.stm#map

73 Frederic Golden, "A Catbird's Seat on Amazon Destruction (Monitoring of Illegal Agricultural Burning by Remote Sensing Satellites)," *Science* 246, October 13, 1989, 201, and Reginald Newell, Henry Reichle, Jr., and Wolfgang Seiler, "Carbon Monoxide and the Burning Earth," *Scientific American*, October 1989, 82–8.

74 Even with the burning of the rain forest, Brazil's output of carbon pollutants is small compared with that of the US. However, under the international environmental treaty known as the Kyoto Protocol, developing countries like Brazil are not required to reduce their emissions of greenhouse gases.

75 Cited in Henry Chu, "Deforestation, Burning Turns Amazon Rain Forest into Major Pollution Source" *Los Angeles Times*, June 20, 2005, http://www.post-gazette.com/pg/05171/524318.stm

76 Don Podesta, "A Burning Issue in Brazil," *Washington Post National Weekly Edition*, October 18–24, 1993, 18, and "Some Vision," *The Economist*, October 8, 1994, 36.

77 "Indonesia Smoke Blankets Region," *BBC News*, October 7, 2006, http://news.bbc.co.uk/2/hi/asia-pacific/5415944.stm

78 A tractor replaces about 19 farm workers.

79 "Brazil," *Land Research Action Network*, http://www.landaction.org/category.php?section=19.The more equal the land distribution in a country, the more rapid its economic development.

80 The harvesting of rubber from wild trees in the Amazon can no longer compete with rubber plantations in southern Brazil. James Brooke, "Rubber Trees Grow Again in Brazil," *New York Times*, July 9, 1995, sec.1, 7.

81 Peter Passell, "Washington Offers Mountain of Debt to Save Forests," *New York Times*, January 22, 1991, C1.

82 Marc Lacey, "US to Cut Guatemala's Debt for Not Cutting Trees," *New York Times*, October 2, 2006, A4.

83 "Your Pollution, Our Forests," *The Economist*, June 27, 1998, 36, 38.

84 Elisabeth Rosenthal, "Many Nations' Forests Regrow, Study Finds," *New York Times*, November 14, 2006, http://www.nytimes.com/2006/11/14/world/14forest.html?ex=1321160400

85 United Nations Population Fund, "The Day of 6 Billion – Fast Facts."

86 Patrick E. Tyler, "Soviets' Secret Nuclear Dumping Raises Fears for Arctic Waters," *New York Times*, May 4, 1992, A1, A4.

87 See, for example, William J. Broad, "Coral Reefs Endangered in Jamaica," *New York Times*, September 9, 1994, A11.

88 United Nations, "Overfishing: A Threat to Marine Diversity" (2006), http://www.un.org/events/tenstories/story.asp?storyID=800

89 Greenpeace, "Frightening Facts about Overfishing and Pirate Fishing," August 26, 2003, http://www.greenpeace.org/raw/content/usa/press/reports/frightening-facts-about-overfi.html

90 Cornelia Dean, "Study Sees 'Global Collapse' of Fish Species," *New York Times*, November 3, 2006, A21.

91 "Salmon War on Two Fronts," *The Economist*, June 28, 1997, 36, and "Net Losses," *The Economist*, June 20, 1998, 38.

92 The International Whaling Commission was established in 1946 under the International Convention for the Regulation of Whaling to conserve whale stocks. See its homepage, http://www.iwcoffice.org/commission/iwcmain.htm

93 Cited in "Overfishing: A Threat to Marine Diversity."

94 Elizabeth Mygatt, "World's Water Resources Face Mounting Pressure," Earth Policy Institute, August 1, 2006, http://www.yubanet.com/artman/publish/article_39865.shtml

95 Ibid. Compiled by Earth Policy Institute using 1950–60 data from Worldwatch Institute, compiled for Lester R. Brown, "Eradicating Hunger: A Growing Challenge," in *State of the World 2001* (New York: Norton, 2001), 52–3; 1961–2003 data from UN FAO, "Irrigation" data

collection, FAOSTAT Statistics Database, apps.fao.org, updated 19 January 2006; population data from UN, *World Population Prospects: The 2004 Revision* (New York, February 2005).

96 Cited in Somini Sengupta, "In Teeming India, Water Crisis Means Dry Pipes and Foul Sludge," *New York Times*, September 29, 2006, http://www.nytimes.com/ 2006/09/29/world/asia/29water.html?ex=1317182400 &en=0059effdd12b7233&ei=5088&partner=rssnyt& emc=rss

97 Elizabeth Mygatt, Earth Policy Institute, Yubanet.com, Aug 1, 2006, http://www.yubanet.com/artman/publish/ article_39865.shtml

98 Ibid.

99 Duke University, Public Documents & Maps Department, "Non-governmental Organizations, Research Guide," http://docs.lib.duke.edu/igo/guides/ ngo/db/environment.asp

100 See Greenpeace website at http://www.greenpeace.org/international

101 The following paragraphs regarding the organization's history are based on Greenpeace, "The History of Greenpeace," http://www.greenpeace.org/international/ about/history and "How is Greenpeace Structured?" http://www.greenpeace.org/international/about/how-is- greenpeace-structured

102 See EuropaWorld, "David Fraser McTaggert: 1932–2001," http://www.europaworld.org/issue28/ davidfrasermctaggart.htm

103 More on Greenpeace campaigns can be found at http://www.greenpeaceusa.org/campaigns

104 Greenpeace.org Archive, "GP & Lake Charles Residents Protest PVC "Poison Plastic," http://archive.greenpeace. org/majordomo/index-press-releases/1997/msg00253. html

105 Cited in Greenpeace.org, "Jury Trial Awarded in Bush vs. Greenpeace," April 15, 2004, http://www. greenpeace.org/international/news/jury-for-bush-vs- greenpeace

106 "Aspects of Global Warming," http://www.janeresture. com/oceania_warming1/

15 Identity politics: nationalism and ethnicity

1 John Carreyrou, "France Moves Fast To Expel Muslims Preaching Hatred," *Wall Street Journal*, August 9, 2004, A1, A10.

2 Alexander E. Wendt, *Social Theory of International Politics* (Cambridge: Cambridge University Press, 1999), 170.

3 V. I. Lenin, "The Tasks of Revolutionary Social Democracy in the European War," *Lenin Collected Works* (Moscow: Progress Publishers, 1964), Vol. 21.

4 Robert S. Leiken, "Europe's Angry Muslims," *Foreign Affairs* 84:4 (July/August 2005), http://www. foreignaffairs.org/20050701faessay84409/robert-s- leiken/europe-s-angry-muslims.html

5 "Muslims in Europe: Economic Worries Top Concerns About Religious and Cultural Identity" (July 6, 2006), *Pew Global Attitudes Project*, http://pewglobal.org/ reports/display.php?ReportID=254

6 Ibid.

7 "An Islamic Journey Inside Europe," National Public Radio, February 24–28, 2003, http://www.npr.org/ programs/atc/features/2003/feb/europe_muslims

8 Cited in John Carreyrou and Dan Bilefsky, "Raffarin Demurs on Turkey's EU Bid," *Wall Street Journal*, September 23, 2004, A13.

9 "The Impossibility of Saying No," *The Economist*, September 18, 2004, 30.

10 Elaine Sciolino, "European Public Uneasy Over Turkey's Bid to Join Union," *New York Times*, October 2, 2004.

11 For an optimistic view of the prospects for Muslim assimilation in France, see Stéphanie Giry, "France and Its Muslims," *Foreign Affairs* 85:5 (September/October 2006), 87–104.

12 "France Backs Head Scarf Ban," CNN.com, February 10, 2004, http://www.cnn.com/2004/WORLD/europe/ 02/10/france.headscarves

13 Home Office, "Terrorism Act 2006," http://www. homeoffice.gov.uk/security/terrorism-and-the- law/terrorism-act-2006/

14 "'Airlines Terror Plot' disrupted," *BBC News*, August 10, 2006, http://news.bbc.co.uk/2/hi/uk_news/4778575.stm

15 Melanie Phillips, *Londonistan* (New York: Encounter Books, 2006).

16 Sarah Lyall and Ian Fisher, "Many Muslims in Britain Tell of Feeling Torn Between Competing Identities," *New York Times*, August 13, 2006, sec. 1, 6.

17 The *burqa* is more conservative than the *chador*, and is a full-body cloak worn by women in Iran which, unlike the *burqa*, need not cover the face.

18 "Kashmir Women 'Slain Over Islamic Dress'" NewsMax Wires, December 20, 2002, http://www.newsmax.com/ archives/articles/2002/12/20/65306.shtml

19 Cited in Robert E. Lee, *Recollections and Letters of General Robert E. Lee* (Garden City, NY: Doubleday, 1924), 26.

20 Japanese American National Museum, http://www. janm.org/exhibits/breed/11_30_42_t.htm

21 Cited in Somini Sengupta, "Sudan Government's Attacks Stoke Rebels' Fury," *New York Times*, September 11, 2004, A1.

22 Gerhard von Glahn, *Law among Nations*, 7th ed. (Boston, MA: Allyn & Bacon, 1996), 25–6.

23 Cited in Antonio Truyol Serra (ed.), *The Principles of Political and International Law in the Work of Francisco de Vitoria* (Madrid: Ediciones Cultura Hispanica, 1946), 58.

24 Jennifer Lee, "United States Backs Plan to Help Chinese Evade Government Censorship of the Web," *New York Times*, August 30, 2001, A10.

25 Cited in Erik Eckholm, "A Trial Will Test China's Grip on the Internet," *New York Times*, November 16, 1998, A1.

26 See Peter J. Smith and Elizabeth Smythe, "Sleepless in Seattle: Challenging the WTO in a Globalizing World," paper presented at the Annual Meeting of the International Science Association, Chicago, February 2001.

27 Cited in Chris Hedges, "War Turns Sarajevo Away From Europe," *New York Times*, July 28, 1995, A4. See also Roger Thurow, "Muslims from Bosnia Find Refuge in Islam While Adrift in Europe," *Wall Street Journal*, September 6, 1994, A1, A5.

28 Slobodan Milošević's 1989 St. Vitus Day Speech, http://www.slobodan-milosevic.org/spch-kosovo1989.htm

29 See Seth Mydans, "In Ethnic Tinderbox, Fear of Revenge for School Killings," *New York Times*, September 20, 2004, A1.

30 Cited in Michael Specter, "Faith Reinforces Hate in the Caucasus," *New York Times*, January 15, 1995, sec. 4, 5.

31 James Connolly, "Labour in Irish History," as cited in a talk by Gregor Kerr, July 7, 1997, http://flag.blackened.net/revolt/talks/king billy.html

32 Anthony D. Smith, *The Ethnic Origins of Nations* (New York: Basil Blackwell, 1986), 2.

33 See John Hutchinson and Anthony D. Smith, eds., *Nationalism* (New York: Oxford, 1994).

34 Walker Connor, "A Nation is a Nation, is an Ethnic Group, is a . . ." in ibid, 361.

35 Heinrich von Treitschke, "The State Idea," in M. G. Forsyth, H. M. A. Keens-Soper, and P. Savigear, eds., *The Theory of International Relations: Selected Texts from Gentili to Treitschke* (New York: Atherton Press, 1970), 327.

36 http://www.h-net.msu.edu/~german/gtext/kaiserreich/bernhardi.html

37 Benito Mussolini, "What is Fascism?" *Modern History Sourcebook*, http://www.fordham.edu/halsall/mod/mussolini-fascism.html

38 Cited in David Binder with Barbara Crossette, "As Ethnic Wars Multiply, US Strives for a Policy," *New York Times*, February 7, 1993, 1.

39 Niccolò Machiavelli, *The Prince and The Discourses*, Modern Library College Editions (New York: Random House, 1950), 41.

40 Ibid., 146, 147.

41 Michael Slackman, "And Now, Islamism Trumps Arabism," *New York Times*, August 20, 2006, http://www.nytimes.com/2006/08/20/weekinreview/20slackman.html?ex=1156737600&en=d335719afc4083c1&ei=5070&emc=eta1

42 Bosnia remained under the authority of NATO, the EU, the UN, and their (reduced) military forces until the EU formally took over NATO's Bosnian peacekeeping operations in December 2004.

43 See KFOR, "Background to the Conflict," http://www.nato.int/kfor/kfor/intro.htm

44 Francis Fukuyama, "The End of History?" *National Interest* (Summer 1989), 3–18.

45 Thomas M. Franck, "Tribe, Nation, World: Self-Identification in the Evolving International System," *Ethics and International Affairs* 11 (1997), 151.

46 About two-thirds of those in Serbia are Eastern Orthodox.

47 See "History of the War in Kosovo," Center for Balkan Development, http://www.friendsofbosnia.org/edu_kos.html

48 Samuel P. Huntington, "The Clash of Civilizations?" *Foreign Affairs* 72:3 (Summer 1993), 22–49. The title of the initial article ended with a question mark but by 1996, when Huntington published the book-length version, the question mark had disappeared. See Samuel P. Huntington, *The Clash of Civilizations: Remaking of World Order* (New York: Simon & Schuster, 1996).

49 Huntington, "The Clash of Civilizations?" 22, 23.

50 Ibid., 25. Emphasis added.

51 Ronald Inglehart and Wayne E. Baker, "Modernization, Cultural Change, and the Persistence of Traditional Values," *American Sociological Review* 65 (February 2000), 32.

52 Cited in Christopher M. Blanchard, "Statements and Evolving Ideology," *Congressional Research Service Report for Congress* (June 20, 2005), http://www.history.navy.mil/library/online/al-queda%20evolve.htm#intro

53 Ibid.

54 Cited in Firouz Sedarat, "Zarqawi Asks Sunnis to Shun Politics for Jihad: Web," *Yahoo! News*, January 8, 2006, http://news.yahoo.com/s/nm/20060109/ts_nm/iraq_zarqawi_dc

55 Reuven Paz, "Arab Volunteers Killed in Iraq: An Analysis," *The Project for the Research of Islamic Movements (PRISM)* 3:1 (March 2005), http://www.e-prism.org/images/PRISM_no_1_vol_3_-_Arabs_killed_in_Iraq.pdf

56 Samuel P. Huntington, "If Not Civilizations, What?"

Foreign Affairs 73:5 (November/December 1993), 188–9.

57 Huntington, "The Clash of Civilizations?" 26.

58 Ibid., 47.

59 Ibid., 34.

60 "Muhammad Cartoon Row Intensifies," *BBC News*, February 1, 2006, http://news.bbc.co.uk/2/hi/europe/670370.stm

61 "Full Text: Writers' Statement on Cartoons," *BBC News*, March 1, 2006, http://news.bbc.co.uk/2/hi/europe/4764730.stm

62 Meg Bortin, "Poll Finds Discord Between the Muslim and Western Worlds," *New York Times*, June 23, 2006, http://www.nytimes.com/2006/06/23/world/23pew.html?ex=1308715200&en=5b361ce4828f5847&ei=5090&partner=rssuserland&emc=rss

63 Samuel P. Huntington, "The Hispanic Challenge," *Foreign Policy* 141 (March/April 2004), 31–2.

64 Samuel P. Huntington, *Who Are We? The Challenges to America's National Identity* (New York: Simon & Schuster, 2004), 221. See also Victor Davis Hanson who writes that "the old assimilationist model . . . is working efficiently for only a minority of new immigrants given their enormous numbers and peculiar circumstances of immigration from Mexico in the last half-century." Hanson, *Mexifornia: A State of Becoming* (San Francisco, CA: Encounter Books, 2003), 20.

65 Charlie LeDuff and J. Emilio Flores, "The Everymigrant's Guide to Crossing the Border Illegally," *New York Times*, February 9, 2005, A16.

66 Ibid., 246, 247.

67 Donald J. Puchala, "International Encounters of Another Kind," in Puchala, *Theory and History in International Relations* (New York: Routledge, 2003), 119–42.

68 Bruce M. Russett, John R. Oneal, and Michaelene Cox, "Clash of Civilizations, or Realism and Liberalism Déjà Vu? Some Evidence," *Journal of Peace Research* 37:5 (2000), 583. See also Giacomo Chiozza, "Is There a Clash of Civilizations? Evidence from Patterns of International Conflict Involvement, 1946–97," *Journal of Peace Research* 39:6 (2002), 711–34; Errol A. Henderson, "Mistaken Identity: Testing the Clash of Civilizations Thesis in Light of Democratic Peace Claims," *British Journal of Political Science* 34 (2004), 539–54; and Erik Gartzke and Kristian Skrede Gleditsch, "Identity and Conflict: Ties that Bind and Differences that Divide," *European Journal of International Relations* 12:1 (2006), 53, 87.

69 The World Values Survey is a global investigation of sociocultural and political changes. See World Values Survey, http://www.worldvaluessurvey.com/

70 Robald Inglehart and Pippa Norris, "The True Clash of Civilizations," *Foreign Policy* 135 (March/April 2003), 68–9.

16 Globalization: the new frontier

1 Brian Hansen, "Globalization Backlash," *CQ Researcher*, September 28, 2001; "WTO Coverage: Battle in Seattle," Fairness and Accuracy in Reporting (FAIR), December 7, 1999, Global Policy Forum, http://www.globalpolicy.org/socecon/bwi-wto/media.htm

2 David Held, Anthony McGrew, David Goldblatt, and Jonathan Perraton, "The Globalization Debate," in Phil Williams, Donald M. Goldstein, and Jay M. Shafritz, eds., *Classic Readings and Contemporary Debates in International Relations*, 3rd ed. (Belmont, CA: Thomson/Wadsworth, 2006), 548.

3 See Inforsat, "Satellite Telephone Service," http://www.infosat.com/satellite-telephone.htm

4 See Daniel W. Drezner and Henry Farrell, "Web of Influence," *Foreign Policy* 145 (November/December 2004), 32–40.

5 Benjamin Barber, *Jihad vs. McWorld: How Globalism and Tribalism Are Reshaping the World* (New York: Ballantine Books, 1995), 23.

6 Samuel P. Huntington, *Who Are We? The Challenges to America's National Identity* (New York: Simon & Schuster, 2004), 13.

7 "Some Facts and Figures About the English Language," http://members.tripod.com/the_english_dept/esc.html

8 Stephen Baker and Inka Resch, with Kate Carlisle and Katharine A. Schmidt, "The Great English Divide," *Business Week Online*, August 13, 2001, http://www.businessweek.com/magazine/content/01_33/b3745009.htm

9 Francis Fukuyama, "The End of History?" *National Interest* (Summer 1989), 3–18.

10 Cited in John F. Burns, "Tape in Name of Leading Insurgent Declares 'All-Out War' on Iraq Elections and Democracy," *New York Times*, January 24, 2005, A8.

11 John Keane, *Global Civil Society* (Cambridge: Cambridge University Press, 2003), 62.

12 Held *et al.*, "The Globalization Debate," 549.

13 Ibid., 550.

14 See, for example, Paul Hirst and Grahame Thompson, *Globalization in Question: The International Economy and the Possibilities of Governance*, 2nd ed. (Cambridge: Polity Press, 1999).

15 Held *et al.*, "The Globalization Debate," 554.

16 Ibid., 555.

17 James N. Rosenau, *Along the Domestic–Foreign Frontier: Exploring Governance in a Turbulent World* (Cambridge: Cambridge University Press, 1997), 99–117.

18 "Measuring Globalization," *Foreign Policy* 141 (March/April 2004), 58–9.

19 "The Globalization Index," *Foreign Policy* 157 (November/December 2006), 77.

20 Ibid.

21 Canadian Security Intelligence Service, "Anti-Globalization – A Spreading Phenomenon," Report # 2000/08, *Perspectives*, August 22, 2000, http://www. csis-scrs.gc.ca/eng/miscdocs/200008_e.html

22 See Infoshop.org, "Black Blocs for Dummies," www. infoshop.org/blackbloc.html

23 Mario Vargas Llosa, "The Culture of Liberty," *Foreign Policy*, 112 (January/February 2001), 66–71.

24 William H. McNeill, "Territorial States Buried Too Soon," *Mershon International Studies Review* 41, Supplement 2 (November 1997), 273–4.

25 Stephen D. Krasner, "Westphalia and All That," in Judith Goldstein and Robert O. Keohane, *Ideas and Foreign Policy* (Ithaca, NY: Cornell University Press, 1993), 238.

26 Tim Dunne, "Sociological Investigations: Instrumental Legitimist and Coercive Interpretations of International Society," *Millennium* 30:1 86–7.

27 Kevin Maney, "Tuvalu's Sinking, but Its Domain is on Solid Ground," *USA Today*, April 27, 2004, http://www. usatoday.com/tech/columnist/kevinmaney/2004-04-27-tuvalu_x.htm

28 Robert H. Jackson, *Quasi-States: Sovereignty, International Relations and the Third World* (Cambridge: Cambridge University Press, 1990). Jackson goes on to argue that, even if there is an abyss between reality and aspiration, sovereignty *does* provide states with a degree of legitimacy denied other actors.

29 Stephen D. Krasner, *Sovereignty: Organized Hypocrisy* (Princeton, NJ: Princeton University Press, 1999), 2–4.

30 Cited in M. G. Forsyth, H. M. A. Keens-Soper, and P. Savigear, eds., *The Theory of International Relations: Selected Texts from Gentili to Treitschke* (New York: Atherton Press, 1970), 281.

31 Cited in ibid., 133.

32 Susan Strange, *The Retreat of the State* (Cambridge: Cambridge University Press, 1996), 72.

33 Ibid., 4–7.

34 UN Secretariat of the Convention to Combat Desertification, "Media Brief," http://www.unccd.int/ publicinfo/mediabrief/mediabrief-eng.pdf

35 Richard Rosecrance, *The Rise of the Virtual State: Wealth and Power in the Coming Century* (New York: Basic Books, 1999), xi.

36 Ibid., xii.

37 Ibid., xi–xii.

38 Ibid., 16–17. Rosecrance does *not* assume that the virtual state will enhance global democracy (18–19).

39 Ibid., xv.

40 Robert Wright and Robert Kaplan, "Mr. Order Meets Mr. Chaos," *Foreign Policy* 124 (May/June 2001), 52.

41 The Carter Center, "About Us," http://www. cartercenter.org/aboutus/aboutus.htm

42 Robert D. Kaplan, *The Ends of the Earth* (New York: Vintage, 1996), 436.

43 "Mr. Order Meets Mr. Chaos," 54.

44 Kaplan, *The Ends of the Earth*, 336–7.

45 Erich Fromm, *Escape from Freedom* (New York: Henry Holt, 1941).

46 Condoleezza Rice, "Promoting the National Interest," *Foreign Affairs* 79:1 (January/February 2000), 47, 53.

47 "Iraq Coalition Casualty Count," http://icasualties.org/ oif/

48 Kaplan, *The Ends of the Earth*, 436. Emphasis in original.

49 Karl W. Deutsch, "The Future of World Politics," *Political Quarterly* 37 (January/March 1966), 13. Emphasis added.

50 Peter Berger, *The Precarious Vision* (Garden City, NY: Doubleday, 1961), 83–4. Emphasis in original.

51 Niccolò Machiavelli, *The Prince and The Discourses* (New York: Modern Library, 1950), 91.

Index

Van Evera, Stephen 288, 354
Vance, Cyrus 726
Vasquez, John A. 349
Vattel, Emmerich de 399
Verba, Sydney 578
Versailles Treaty *see* Peace of Versailles)
Victor Emmanuel II, King of Italy 78
Victoria, Queen of Great Britain 104, 553–54
Vietnam War 179–84; partitioning of 179; US anti-war movement 183; *see also* warfare, guerrilla
Vincent, John Carter 175
Vitoria, Fancisco de 398, 702
Voltaire, François Marie Arouet 23

Wagner, Richard 458
Wal-Mart 533–34, 591
Walker, R. B. J. 32
Wallace, Henry 161
Wallerstein, Immanuel 271, 580–81
Walt, Stephen 15, 380
Walter, Barbara 331–33
Waltz, Kenneth N. 23, 255, 264, 270, 278, 282, 350
war; absolute war 294–95; defined 327; interstate war 313–14, 254; intrastate (civil) war 326–34; proliferation of intrastate wars 313; sources of 102, 118, 277; transnational war 317; *see also* neorealism; realism
warfare; conventional 314; eighteenth century 295–96; guerrilla 294; national 72–73; technology 299–313

Warsaw Pact 169, 184, 192
Watson, Adam 78–79
Watson, Thomas 762
wealth disparities 4, 330, 587
Weapons of Mass Destruction (WMD) 4, 259, 262, 294, 297, 309–10, 313, 338, 386–90, 621–23, 767–68; Iraq and 23, 240–46, 401, 408, 426–27, 429; *see also* biological weapons, chemical weapons, North Korea, nuclear weapons
Weizmann, Chaim 208–9
Wendt, Alexander E. 36, 268–69, 283, 690
Westmorland, William 180
Westphalia, Peace of 64, 314, 719, 759
White, Harry Dexter 519
Whitney, Eli 550
Whitney, Richard 515
Wilberforce, William 444, 550
Wilhelm II, Kaiser of Germany 104, 109, 111, 115, 365
Willetts, Peter 443
William III, King of England 71, 710
Winthrop, John 24
Wilson, Woodrow 119, 120–21, 127–28, 132–33, 153, 179, 246, 364, 381, 713; as an interventionist liberal 25; Fourteen Points 25, 120–24
Wohlstetter, Albert 374–75
Wolfowitz, Paul 189
women 37–38, 448–51, 482–93, 656–58, 696–97
Wonder, Stevie 596
Woolf, Leonard 413

World Bank 7, 501, 524–25, 603–7
World Chamber of Commerce 27
World Health Organization (WHO) 5, 393, 413, 631
world system theory 580–81
World Trade Organization (WTO) 5, 525–26, 649, 743
World War I 101–26, 296–98, 300–304; levels of analysis 115–19; sources of 102, 118; *see also* Peace of Versailles)
World War II 139–47, 296–98, 304–7; atom bombs 145, 292; battles 145, 298–99; levels of analysis 145–46; *see also* Japan
Wright, Robert 771

Yalta Conference 157–58
Yamashita, Tomoyuki 466
Yassin, Sheik Ahmed 221
Yeltsin, Boris 193, 196
Yergin, Daniel 161
Yevtushenko, Yevgeni 460
Young, Oran 259
Yuan Shikai 83
Yugoslavia 124–25, 468, 705–7, 723–31

Zarqawi, Abu Musab al 732, 746
Zhao Ziyang, 589
Zhou Enlai 83, 203, 584
Zhu De, General 83
Zionism 208–9
Zoellicker, Robert 524
Zwingli, Ulrich 720